CASES AND PROBLEMS

REMEDIES

FIFTH EDITION

by

ELAINE W. SHOBEN

Judge Jack and Lulu Lehman Professor
University of Nevada, Las Vegas Boyd School of Law

WILLIAM MURRAY TABB

Professor and Judge Fred A. Daugherty Chair in Law
and David Ross Boyd Professor
University of Oklahoma College of Law

RACHEL M. JANUTIS

Associate Professor of Law
Capital University Law School

FOUNDATION PRESS
2012

THOMSON REUTERS™

1 New York Plaza, 34th Floor
New York, NY 10004
Phone Toll Free 1–877–888–1330
Fax 646–424–5201
foundation–press.com
Printed in the United States of America

ISBN 978–1–60930–119–4

Mat #41248191

To our supportive families

PREFACE

Few casebooks are prepared to accommodate a well-established fact about law professors: They never teach a book from start to finish. Similarly, they do not always teach in the order and manner that the casebook authors intend. This practice in part reflects curricular differences among schools, such as the number of units assigned to the course and the degree of students' knowledge about remedies from other courses. It also reflects professors' independence of thought—the very quality that brought their entry into the teaching profession.

This casebook is designed to provide law teachers with a flexible book to accommodate that practice. Each chapter and section can be used selectively or rearranged without damaging the development of the central themes. A similar philosophy of flexibility is reflected in the internal design of each section. The most important coverage comes first so that any topic can be covered on a "once over lightly" basis by assigning only the material through the first case or two.

Several other features also define the character of this casebook: (1) The overall organization is by the major groups of remedies: Injunctions & Specific Performance, Damages, and Restitution. (2) The book seeks to achieve a balanced coverage of these areas as well as to provide introductory text and problems for discussion, and concluding materials on jury trials, attorneys' fees and declaratory relief. (3) There are complex problems for class discussion integrated with the case materials to provide a daily choice of teaching style. (4) The cases are a mix of recent ones to give a modern context to the material and classic cases to cover the traditional material. (5) The book provides broad coverage of the field, with more extended coverage in certain areas that are rarely mentioned in other courses, such as contempt.

Integration of Cases and Problems

This book features a thorough integration of problems with related cases. The problems are ones without solutions provided by existing case-law; instead they are constructed with elements of several cases or issues uniquely combined. Only future litigation of such a case would provide an "answer" to the problems, although the text provides some guidance on the relative strength of the parties' positions under existing law.

The problems can be used flexibly. An entire class session could be focused around one of them; on such days the class can accomplish case coverage indirectly by relating the cases to the problem. Alternatively, the professor can pass quickly over the problem and focus on the surrounding cases. Complex problems are a wonderful tool for teaching Remedies, but teaching from them constantly is difficult for everyone on both sides of the podium. Their frequent appearance throughout this book allows daily choice of teaching style.

Each section of the book begins with a textual introduction and a "model case" that gives a factual reference point for established principles. The model case offers a simple example to contrast with the cases and complex problems later in the section. It also encourages students to work with factual comparisons when dealing with abstract concepts. The overall purpose of this approach is to provide students with an early foundation of knowledge that allows quick progression to more difficult issues.

Structure

The structure of this book was designed to provide law teachers with maximum flexibility in arranging the course to meet individual needs and preferences. Each chapter and section is designed such that selective use or rearrangement would not damage the overall structure of the course. Although the remedial themes occur throughout the book, the sections and chapters are not interwoven so strongly that re-arrangement of the order would be confusing to the students. This book was designed for professors who want flexibility.

This book also adapts well to the necessity of last minute coverage changes as the semester progresses. The core material is presented in the earliest chapters of each major subject so that the professor can decide if there is enough time for the more extended coverage that comes at the end of each subject area. For example, if the budgeted class time for the chapters in the Part on Injunctions & Specific Performance is exceeded before the subject is completed, it is possible to omit the long chapter on "Special Issues in Equity" without doing serious damage to the coverage of the general subject area. The same organizational structure allows early termination of Damages to move easily on to Restitution.

The book achieves this flexibility with the use of the "Special Issues" chapters at the end of both the Part on Injunctions & Specific Performance and the one on Damages. These chapters contain interesting materials that are not essential to the course and that invite selective use.

A similar philosophy is reflected in the design of each section. The most important coverage comes first so that a topic could be covered quickly by assigning the earliest material. Conversely, if a professor wishes to dwell at greater length on a topic, there is more extended coverage at the end. Everyone has a favorite area in which greater depth of coverage can bring a greater depth of the students' understanding of the overriding principles. This approach allows maximum choice of that area.

Coverage

The book seeks to achieve a balanced coverage of injunctions, damages, and restitution. Within those broad areas, we further attempted to provide a balanced coverage of the topics as well. Professors who have a clear and strong preference for one area or another already have other excellent choices for their courses. This book is for a traditional survey course on Remedies.

In addition to the rule of balance that governed the structure of the book, there was a second guiding principle: Special attention was given to areas that are rarely covered even briefly elsewhere in the curriculum. For example, most students receive exposure to general damages issues in other courses, but contempt is rarely studied or even mentioned. Similarly, the equitable defenses such as unclean hands are unlikely to cross the consciousness of most law students except as a joke in the student newspaper.

There are several other Remedies topics that we identified as ones to which students typically lack any prior introduction. These are interlocutory injunctions, structural injunctions, inflation and prejudgment interest, punitive damages, attorneys' fees, and declaratory judgments. Whereas the goal in areas such as contract damages is to build upon the students' basic knowledge from other courses, the goal in these areas is to provide a broad exposure to the issues.

Case Selection

We have kept in mind two goals in our case selection. First, we have attempted to use recent cases whenever possible. In our experience students enjoy modern cases mixed with the old classic gems. Second, we have tried to limit the number of cases in which the holding states the minority position on a topic or in which the dissent takes the apparently better position. When such cases are best for the topic we use them, but excessive use deadens their provocative effect. Some cases include excerpts from dissenting opinions when the effect is to illustrate why the issue presented is more difficult than the majority opinion makes it appear.

The philosophy of this book is to teach the well-established principles quickly with the textual materials at the beginning of every section. The cases then function to present the troublesome issues in the area rather than to illustrate some basic point.

The authors would like to thank Professors Denis F. McLaughlin and Barbara Glesner Fines for their exceptionally helpful comments. We would also like to thank Annette "Nettie" Mann and Debbie Scott, in addition to Darin Fox, Jennifer Gerrish, and Erin Kessler for their collective help and outstanding assistance.

ELAINE W. SHOBEN
WILLIAM MURRAY TABB
RACHEL M. JANUTIS

May 2012

ACKNOWLEDGMENTS

Appreciative acknowledgment is made to the following for permission to reprint copyrighted materials:

The American Law Institute

The National Conference of Commissioners on Uniform State Laws

SUMMARY OF CONTENTS

TABLE OF CONTENTS

TABLE OF CASES

The principal cases are in bold type. Cases cited or discussed in the text are in roman type. References are to pages. Cases cited in principal cases and within other quoted materials are not included.

REMEDIES

PART I

INTRODUCTION

1

CHAPTER 1

BASIC REMEDIAL TOOLS

A. TYPES OF REMEDIES

The study of remedies is concerned principally with the nature and the measurement of relief to which a party may be entitled. An appreciation of the nature of each legal and equitable remedy includes an understanding of the prerequisites for entitlement to it. It is not sufficient to establish the violation of a substantive right; a plaintiff must also establish the basis for any desired remedy.

A remedies course is a unique combination of substance and procedure because the subject focuses upon declaration and enforcement of rights, compensation for past violations of rights, and prevention of future threatened harms. As the name suggests, Remedies is a multi-faceted field that draws principles from many legal disciplines. The study is simultaneously practical and theoretical because the subject examines unifying themes and problems with relief across many substantive areas of the law while always focusing upon the important "bottom line" for parties in litigation.

Multiple substantive claims may spring from a single core of facts and several choices of remedies may arise from a single claim. There are four basic types or classifications of remedies: (1) coercive remedies, (2) damages, (3) restitution, and (4) declaratory relief. The processes and principles by which the most effective remedies are selected, and the relationship of alternative remedies to each other, are the central themes of this casebook.

Coercive Remedies. A coercive remedy, such as an injunction or specific performance order, is available from a court sitting in equity. The judge determines whether the plaintiff is entitled to the "extraordinary relief" of an order commanding the defendant to do or refrain from doing specific acts. (Chapters 3 and 4) These remedies, like all equitable ones, are subject to the equitable defenses, including unclean hands, laches, estoppel, and unconscionability. (Chapter 5)

Upon a compelling showing, a plaintiff may receive injunctive relief even before full trial on the merits. A preliminary injunction gives the plaintiff temporary relief pending trial on the merits. Similarly, a temporary restraining order affords immediate relief pending the hearing on the preliminary injunction. The principle behind both of these types of interlocutory relief is to preserve the *status quo* to prevent irreparable harm. The plaintiff must make a strong showing of the necessity for such relief and it must be consistent with the demands of due process. (Chapter 6)

A coercive remedy is backed by the contempt power. A disobedient defendant can be jailed or fined or required to compensate the plaintiff for losses incurred by the disobedience of an order. Criminal contempt punishes a defendant for violation of a court order and must meet the constitutional standards for a criminal conviction. Civil contempt may take the form either of compensating the plaintiff for the losses caused by the defendant's contempt, or coercion of the defendant through jail or fines to force compliance of the order for the benefit of the plaintiff. (Chapter 7)

In modern law there are three types of injunctions in addition to preventive ones: restorative injunctions, prophylactic injunctions, and structural ones. A restorative injunction principally operates to correct the present by undoing the effects of a past wrong. The notion of "restoring" means that it focuses not only prospectively, as does the traditional preventive injunction, but also retroactively. A prophylactic injunction seeks to safeguard the plaintiff's rights by directing the defendant's behavior so as to minimize the chance that wrongs might recur in the future. A structural injunction, such as a school desegregation order, derives its name from the involvement of the courts in the institutional policies and practices of the defendant entities. (Chapter 8)

Special problems with fashioning injunctive relief arise in cases involving prior restraints of speech, abatement of nuisances orders, and injunctions of crimes. In addition to the common law limitations that have evolved in such areas, the legislature occasionally affects the process of judicial discretion in these areas and others. Statutes may prohibit some remedies in some contexts; or they may provide for some remedies but not others; or some rare statutes mandate particular relief, such as an injunction, in circumstances that would otherwise be left to the court's discretion. (Chapter 9)

Damages. The purpose of the damages remedy is to compensate plaintiffs for losses sustained in violation of their rights. Once a plaintiff has established both the claim in substantive law and the entitlement to a particular type of damages, the problem of measurement remains. When a defendant breaches a contract with the plaintiff, there is often more than one measure of recovery for compensatory damages, and there may be an alternative restitutionary claim. (Chapter 10)

In tort, if a car is severely damaged in an automobile accident, is the appropriate measure of damages the cost of repair or the diminution in fair market value of the car? Measurement issues arise also in cases of real property damage, personal injury, and wrongful death. These areas have often been affected by tort reform statutes as well. (Chapter 11) Similarly, certain adjustments may be made to the award, such as to account for the use and changing value of money in the awards for personal injury victims with permanent injuries. (Chapter 12)

The common law imposes certain limitations on damages. They cannot be too remote, speculative, or uncertain. Other forms of limitation come from rules such as the collateral source rule and the avoidable consequences rule. (Chapter 13)

There are limitations on the types of losses that a plaintiff can claim; not all losses are compensable ones. Substantive law imposes restrictions on certain types of losses, such as the restrictions on the recovery of mental distress damages in the absence of physical injury and the limitations on recovery of purely economic losses. (Chapter 14)

The only exception to the compensation goal of damage law is punitive damages. These damages, which are also called exemplary damages, are designed to punish and deter wrongdoers in cases involving egregious conduct. This discretionary remedy is never a matter of right, and is governed by both common law and constitutional restrictions. (Chapter 15)

Restitution. The goal of restitution is to restore property to its rightful owner by returning the plaintiff to a position held before a wrong, or to disgorge from a defendant any unjust enrichment occasioned by the wrong to the plaintiff. The recovery may or may not involve money, but its goal is not a compensatory one. The measurement of restitution is the defendant's gains rather than the plaintiff's losses. For example, an embezzler who purchases land with the misappropriated money is not allowed to keep any profit from the investment in the land. A plaintiff may receive the land itself by imposition of a constructive trust. If money profits can be traced, those profits can be received. The plaintiff thus may receive more than was lost in the original embezzlement, but the defendant wrongdoer is prevented from being enriched by his own intentional wrong. Other types of restitutionary remedies include equitable liens, rescission, and suits in assumpsit for quasi-contract. A distinction must be made between substantive restitution and remedial restitution. Substantive restitution concerns the entitlement to a restitutionary remedy: courts evaluate whether the defendant has acquired or holds a benefit which, if retained, would constitute unjust enrichment. Remedial restitution concerns the measurement of that remedy. (Chapters 16)

Restitutionary remedies are subject to limitations and defenses. Those topics include the tracing requirement for some remedies, and the defenses of bona fide purchaser, change in position, and volunteers. (Chapter 17)

Jury Trials and Attorney Fees. Other areas important to the study of remedies are jury trial rights and attorneys' fees. Under the Seventh Amendment there is a right to a jury trial in legal cases but not equitable ones. Although this amendment does not apply to the states, the states generally follow that same distinction. Differences between federal and state law occur in some areas, however, such as cases where there are mixed claims of law and equity. (Chapter 18)

The American Rule on attorney fees is that parties bear their own costs of litigation. There are a few common law exceptions to this rule, and several important statutory ones. The major area of statutory change is in the area of civil rights. Further statutory changes have been proposed, including a "loser pays" model. (Chapter 19)

Declaratory Remedies. The purpose of a declaratory remedy is to obtain a declaration of the rights or legal relations between the parties. This remedy is often used to determine the constitutionality of a statute or to construe a private instrument so that the interested parties may obtain a resolution of the dispute at an early stage. Federal and state statutes provide that declaratory relief is to be liberally administered, but the parties must demonstrate a justiciable controversy rather than one of a hypothetical or advisory nature.

Nominal damages also serve to declare the relative rights of the parties. They are awarded when a plaintiff establishes a substantive claim but cannot establish damages. Whether through a declaratory judgment or through a civil claim that results in nominal damages, plaintiffs can seek a vindication and declaration remedy. (Chapter 20)

B. REMEDIES AT LAW AND IN EQUITY

The term "to do equity" in everyday speech implies that a decision-maker has reached a fair and impartial result in a conflict. An "equitable result" usually means a resolution that does not come from established principles but simply derives from common sense and socially acceptable notions of fair play. In the judicial system this popular concept of "equity" is not the essence of equitable jurisprudence; equity refers to a system of jurisprudence distinguishable from the system "at law." Although the judge sitting in equity has discretion whether to allow a particular remedy, that process is guided by principles established by *stare decisis*.

Equity was originally a separate court system that afforded relief to petitioners who had no adequate remedy at law because of some harsh legal doctrine. Sometimes a remedy at law was unavailable because the cause of action was not one recognized at law, such as shareholders' derivative actions. Sometimes petitioners came to equity for protection from the legal enforcement of contracts. Equity was the original source of concepts such as promissory estoppel and unconscionability. Today those historically equitable doctrines have been incorporated into legal jurisprudence as well. Indeed, in most American jurisdictions there has been a merger of law and equity such that one no longer thinks of two separate systems of justice.

Despite the diminished importance of recognizing the substantive contributions of equity, the concept of equitable remedies distinct from legal ones remains important. Equitable remedies include flexible coercive orders such as injunctions and specific performance orders. Some restitutionary remedies are equitable, such as constructive trusts or rescission and restitution in contract.

The most prevalent legal remedy is damages. Some restitutionary remedies are also legal, such as quasi-contract. In a merged system of law and equity, a plaintiff may seek both legal and equitable remedies in the same claim. The importance of the distinction between legal and equitable remedies, however, lies with the availability of a jury trial.

The Seventh Amendment of the Constitution provides that there is a right to trial by jury for causes "at law." There is no similar right to trial by jury for actions in equity. In the federal system, this constitutional right has been interpreted to mean that causes of action seeking legal remedies as opposed to equitable ones must be afforded trial by jury. An action seeking only equitable remedies may be tried by the judge without a jury, although an advisory jury can be impaneled.

The United States Supreme Court has held that it is the type of remedy that controls jury trial rights rather than the historical origin of the substantive right. Moreover, if a plaintiff presents a mixed claim of law and equity, the legal issues must be tried first by the jury and any remaining equitable issues may be tried by the judge in a manner not inconsistent with the jury verdict. Both plaintiffs and defendants possess jury trial rights, which may be waived.

In the state court systems the right to trial by jury is often different. The Seventh Amendment has not been held to apply to the states. Some states have constitutional provisions of their own affecting the right, but others rely entirely upon historical precedent. Cases in which the plaintiff seeks only legal remedies usually entitle the parties to trial by jury; cases seeking only equitable remedies do not. In a merged state court system, a mixed claim of legal and equitable remedies may not entitle the parties to a jury trial if the primary character of the case is equitable. The doctrine of "equitable clean-up" may control whereby the judge as trier of fact in equity may decide also any incidental damages issues.

Declaratory Remedies. The purpose of a declaratory remedy is to obtain a declaration of the rights or legal relations between the parties. This remedy is often used to determine the constitutionality of a statute or to construe a private instrument so that the interested parties may obtain a resolution of the dispute at an early stage. Federal and state statutes provide that declaratory relief is to be liberally administered, but the parties must demonstrate a justiciable controversy rather than one of a hypothetical or advisory nature. (Chapter 20)

Nominal damages (Chapter 20) also serve to declare the relative rights of the parties. They are awarded when a plaintiff establishes a substantive claim but cannot establish damages.

C.   Introductory Remedies Problems

Consider the following problem concerning the injury or possible destruction of a farm's productivity. At the end of the problem there are a number of questions concerning appropriate remedies. The notes that follow give capsule summaries of how related problems have been resolved by the law in the past. The purpose of these problems is to illustrate recurring remedial problems; future chapters will provide greater depth on these issues.

PROBLEM: THE WASTE LAGOON

Jim and Joan Pollard own a farm on which they grow feed corn. A few years ago Krystal Refining Co. constructed wastewater lagoons on the land adjacent to the Pollards' farm land. Last year the Pollards began experiencing crop losses on the strip of land immediately adjacent to the Krystal Refining lagoons. Although the crops on other fields did very well that year, the corn in the field adjacent to the lagoons did very poorly. The Pollards hired a soil analyst who informed them that a new chemical recently introduced into Krystal's refining process has seeped from the wastewater lagoons into the soil on the Pollards' land. This chemical was responsible for the poor crop last year. Moreover, the expert informed the Pollards that the increased presence of this chemical may now have irreversibly precluded that strip for any farm cultivation. Only expensive additional testing could determine the permanency of the damage.

Legal Remedies. Assuming that the Pollards can establish a cause of action against Krystal Refining, what should be the available remedies? First consider that the damage to the land may be reversible, but only at enormous cost. Should the high cost of restoration be the measure of damages? What if that amount exceeds the fair market value of the land? Would it matter if the Pollards depended upon farming for their livelihood and there were no other acres for sale in the vicinity? If the court rejects the cost of restoration as the measure of damages, what are alternative measures?

Now consider the result if the chemical has caused irreversible injury. What should be the measure of damages? Is it appropriate to award the fair market value of the land when the land itself—as opposed to its productivity—has not been destroyed?

What measure of damage should be used for the injury to last year's crops? Consider both the appropriate measure of damages and the kind of evidence that the plaintiffs should have to produce to support their claim.

Who should have to pay for the expensive test in anticipation of litigation to determine the permanency of the damage to the soil? What if the Pollards do not pay for the test but simply plant again the next year to let the new crop itself be the "test" of the soil's productivity while litigation is pending? Should they recover damages for losses to this new crop as well?

Equitable Relief. Should a court issue an injunction against Krystal to prevent future use of the waste lagoons? Should there be an injunction limiting the use by prohibiting the injurious chemical? Should Krystal be required to drain the lagoons currently in existence? Would it matter if a state or federal environmental protection statute expressly prohibited the discharge of the chemicals into water bodies such as the lagoon? Conversely, what if a zoning ordinance permitted the operation of the chemical plant as it is presently being conducted? Consider, with respect to these questions, whether it would matter if the cost of draining the lagoon or seeking alternative disposal of the waste would exceed the value of the Pollards' land.

1. The Restatement (Second) of Torts § 929 concerns harm to land from past invasions. It summarizes the common law rule:

> (1) If one is entitled to a judgment for harm to land resulting from a past invasion and not amounting to a total destruction of value, the damages include compensation for
>
> > (a) the difference between the value of the land before the harm and the value after the harm, or at his election in an appropriate case, the cost of restoration that has been or may be reasonably incurred,
> >
> > (b) the loss of use of the land, and
> >
> > (c) discomfort and annoyance * * *

2. In the Comments to the Restatement § 929,* it is noted:

> * * * [T]he reasonable cost of replacing the land in its original position is ordinarily allowable as the measure of recovery. Thus if a ditch is wrongfully dug upon the land of another, the other normally is entitled to damages measured by the expense of filling the ditch, if he wishes it filled. If, however, the cost of replacing the land in its original position is disproportionate to the diminution in the value of the land caused by the trespass, unless there is a reason personal to the owner for restoring the original condition, damages are measured only by the difference between the value of the land before and after the harm. This would be true, for example, if in trying the effect of explosives, a person were to create large pits upon the comparatively worthless land of another.

3. The Restatement (Second) of Torts § 930 concerns damages for future invasions of land. It provides that if future invasions are not enjoined because of public interest in the defendant's enterprise, the court may allow the plaintiff to recover damages for both past and future invasions in the single action. Section (3) provides:

> (3) The damages for past and prospective invasions of land include compensation for
>
> > (a) the harm caused by invasions prior to the time when the injurious situation became complete and comparatively enduring, and
> >
> > (b) either the decrease in the value of the land caused by the prospect of the continuance of the invasion measured at the time when the injurious situation became complete and comparatively enduring, or the reasonable cost to the plaintiff of avoiding future invasions.

4. Comments to the Restatement (Second) of Torts § 930(3) say:

> Depreciation in the value of the damaged land is the usual standard of compensation when the injured person recovers full damages for the continuance of the invasions. * * * Manifestly, this element of depreci-

ation is distinct from the loss in value brought by the actual effects of past invasions such as damage by floods to the soil's fertility.

5. Comments on Restatement (Second) of Torts § 929(2) say:

For the destruction of or damage to houses, buildings, crops or mature timber trees that have a market value or a value distinguishable from the value of the land, the owner can, at his election, recover for the loss or diminution of the value of the thing injured or destroyed, in substitution for the diminution in value of the land as a whole. The value of a growing crop at the time of injury or destruction is the value of the yield that at that time would reasonably have been anticipated, less the prospective cost of further cultivation and marketing and a deduction for such hazards as hail and flood. * * *

6. Should Krystal be enjoined against future use of the waste lagoons? Consider the famous New York case *Boomer v. Atlantic Cement Co.,* reprinted *infra* in Chapter 3. The defendant in that case was a multi-million dollar cement plant sued by neighbors who were victimized by its air pollution. Although the usual remedy for nuisance in New York was an injunction, the court in this 1970 case declined to issue one. Rather than enjoining the operation of the plant, the court required the defendant to pay permanent damages to the plaintiff in exchange for a "servitude on the land" for the company. An injunction was denied because of the harsh result on the defendant compared with the relatively small loss in the plaintiffs' property value. The dissenting opinion complained that the majority view in effect was licensing a continuing wrong. The dissenting judges thought that the majority allowed the defendant to engage in inverse condemnation of the plaintiffs' land. Where does the public interest lie in such cases?

7. Should Krystal be required to return the Pollards' land to its pre-tort condition? A related issue was presented in the now famous environmental case *Puerto Rico v. SS Zoe Colocotroni,* 628 F.2d 652 (1st Cir.1980) reprinted *infra* in Chapter 11. This 1980 Fifth Circuit opinion concerned an oil spill from a tanker. The tanker was stuck on a reef off the coast of Puerto Rico and the captain ordered some 5,000 tons of crude oil to be dumped in the surrounding waters in order to refloat the vessel. The resulting oil slick damaged an isolated peninsula owned by the Commonwealth of Puerto Rico. Severe environmental harm resulted to plant and marine animal life on the peninsula. The injured land and marine life did not have a significant market value, however.

An environmental protection statute permitted recovery of the "total value" of the damages, which the court interpreted to mean that the Commonwealth was not restricted to common law damages. Nonetheless, the court refused to uphold the district court's award of damages based upon the replacement value of the marine creatures. There was no actual restoration plan to replace these lost animals, even though experts testified that they were available at an ascertainable market price. The $5.5 million judgment based upon this measure was reversed. The case was remanded to reopen the possibility of damages based on an alternative-site restoration plan or other appropriate measures of damages.

D. ADDITIONAL INTRODUCTORY PROBLEMS

Consider the following problems that present issues to be covered later in this course. Although you have not yet studied the manner in which the law to date has resolved these problems, consider the issues presented in these problems and the ways in which you think they ought to be resolved. These problems are intended to introduce future material, but they would also be useful for your review at the end of the course.

INTRODUCTORY PROBLEM: THE STUDENT PROTESTER

Assume that you have recently graduated from law school, passed the bar exam, and opened a law office with some friends in a small university town. You hear the following story on the six o'clock local news:

"Students at the University are protesting the quality of dormitory food. There was a noon rally on this subject today which became a rather rowdy demonstration." The camera then showed a taped interview with the student who organized the rally, Ken Maxwell, who announced that a second demonstration was planned for that evening. He said that a protest march would happen and that all students should assemble with tonight's dinner tray of dormitory food. Maxwell said that they would march on the home of the University president and leave their evidence (the trays of food) on the lawn.

Immediately after you see this story on the news, the telephone rings and the caller is Maxwell. He tells you that he was just served with an order signed by a state court judge which forbids him from holding the rally, encouraging others to demonstrate tonight, and from "contributing to or inciting any breaches of the peace" in the town in the future. His answers to your questions lead you to the conclusion that the city and University successfully sought an ex parte injunction against Maxwell.

Maxwell says that he has had an undergraduate course in constitutional law and knows perfectly well that "they" cannot keep him from speaking and petitioning the president of the University. Nonetheless, Maxwell says that a friend urged that he call a lawyer before running off to the rally. The rally is due to take place in a few minutes. What do you say? Who else may be bound by the court's order? What if Maxwell's friends demonstrated and he stayed at home?

INTRODUCTORY PROBLEM: THE LOTTERY WINNER

You are engaged in a law practice with an office that hires several part-time workers. One of the part-time workers was out of cash immediately before payday and wrongfully took some money from petty cash to buy lunch and to purchase a lottery ticket at the restaurant. As luck would have it, the lottery ticket was a big winner.

Assume that the theft is proven and that the use of the office money for the purchase of the lottery ticket is clearly traced. Should the law partnership be able to recover only the amount taken from petty cash or the full amount of the lottery winnings?

Would it make a difference if the money used to purchase the lottery ticket was an embezzlement by a partner from a client's account? Should the client be reimbursed the embezzled funds or the lottery winnings?

INTRODUCTORY PROBLEM: THE ANXIOUS CLIENT

The town council of the city of Brookfield recently decided to crack down on pornography. It passed an ordinance that prohibited the sale of obscene books within one mile of churches and schools. The ordinance defines obscenity, in part, as "anything which may contribute to the corruption or debauchery of the morals of youth." The ordinance carries stiff criminal and civil penalties for its violation.

You have a client, Pat Caruthers, who owns a popular full-line bookstore called The Bookplace. Caruthers telephones you after reading about the ordinance in the local newspaper, and is concerned that the ordinance may be applied to several of the books sold by The Bookplace. Caruthers is also not certain whether the store is located within one mile of any church or school.

What remedy, if any, might be available to Pat Caruthers to obtain a determination as to whether the ordinance is unconstitutionally vague and overbroad? Would it make any difference if the local prosecuting attorney had already mentioned the possibility that criminal proceedings might be instituted against Caruthers unless The Bookplace stopped selling several "art" books?

INTRODUCTORY PROBLEM: THE LEMON

Your client, Chris Engle, recently purchased a used car from an established used car dealer. The car has needed frequent repair and never has run completely satisfactorily. Engle wishes to force the dealer to take this "lemon" back, but there is no provision for such return in the sales contract. In your initial client meeting with Engle a few weeks ago you explored any possible claim for fraud or other basis under state law that would support rescission, but you find nothing wrong with the transaction.

Engle just called you with a new piece of information discovered when a garage was changing the car's oil. The mechanic discovered an old oil-change sticker on the inside of the front door, and that sticker indicated a mileage greater than the current mileage on the odometer. Apparently someone, either the dealer or a former owner, turned back the odometer after the date of that prior oil change.

A state statute provides that a used car dealer cannot sell a car in which the odometer has been turned back. The statute does not require scienter, but an affirmative defense is the lack of knowledge by the dealer that someone previously had rolled back the odometer. The remedies provided in this statute are "actual damages or other relief as the court deems appropriate."

If Engle successfully sues the dealer under this statute, should rescission be an available remedy? Note that Engle's desire for rescission was formed on grounds other than the incorrect representation of mileage.

Does the reference to "actual damages" in the statute suggest that only damage remedies are appropriate? If so, how should such damages be measured? If scienter is proven, should punitive damages also be allowed?

INTRODUCTORY PROBLEM: THE INVESTIGATIVE REPORTERS

A television station received a tip that a local grocery engaged in unsafe food handling practices. The station sent two reporters to obtain proof of the practices by having them apply for employment in the grocery with false resumes. They were hired and worked for several days, performing well the assigned work for the grocery but also secretly videotaping the unclean practices of other workers. This footage was later used in an investigative report on the television station.

The grocery sued the reporters and the station for the fraudulent way they obtained the inside information about the store. They did not have a substantive claim for defamation because the video was true, nor a claim for unfair trade practices because the station was not a competitor, nor a claim for return of the wages paid because useful work was performed. The successful claim was for breach of the duty of loyalty that employees owe employers and only nominal damages were recoverable.

Is there any point to suing in such a situation when only nominal damages result? Would it be appropriate to require the defendants to pay the attorneys' fees of the plaintiff in such a situation? Does the availability of nominal damages serve a useful function to society in such a case?

CHAPTER 2

SCOPE OF LEGAL AND EQUITABLE REMEDIES

A desired remedy does not automatically follow from the violation of any particular right. A plaintiff must first establish the substantive entitlement to relief and then must establish a legal basis for the desired remedy. For example, a winning case may show that the defendant violated specific statutory rights and that the remedy sought is provided expressly by the statute. The plaintiff then must establish factually the requirements for the desired remedy. Damages require proof of loss, for example, and an injunction requires a showing of irreparable harm. Future chapters examine such requirements. This chapter focuses upon the legal basis for particular remedies and the limitations imposed by the source of the remedy. It also examines briefly the significance of whether that basis is legal or equitable in nature.

A. LIMITATIONS ON REMEDIES

Section Coverage:

There are three sources of remedial rights: statutes, federal and state constitutions, and common law. One or all of these sources may establish a basis for one or more remedies in a particular case. The source of a plaintiff's desired remedies is important because (1) the plaintiff must establish that a particular remedy is permissible, and (2) the source may place some limitations upon the remedy. It is axiomatic that a right is only as great as the remedy that accompanies it. The materials in this section illustrate this principle and provide practical applications of it.

Model Case:

A state statute prohibits retailers from posting customer checks that have been returned as uncollectible from the bank. This "bad checks" bill was designed to curb the growing practice of stores to make a prominent public display of uncollected checks.

The statute provides that the State's Attorney may seek an injunction against any retailer in wilful violation of the act. It also provides a civil action for individuals whose checks have been posted in violation of the act. The civil remedy provision allows $500 damages per violation and attorney's fees.

Baxter is a consumer who was the victim of a wrongfully denied check. The bank erroneously returned for insufficient funds a check that Baxter had written to a store. The retailer did not contact Baxter, but simply posted the check with other "bad checks" on the front wall. A sign over the checks read: "Look Who Took Me Now!"

Baxter's boss saw the returned check on the retailer's wall and summarily discharged the luckless Baxter. Baxter's suit under the act seeks actual damages and a corrective notice of equal prominence to explain the true facts.

Courts are not in agreement whether it is permissible ever to expand the damage remedy beyond its statutory dollar limitation. Therefore Baxter's recovery of actual damages beyond $500 is uncertain.

There is also disagreement whether courts should interpret statutes to allow wholly different types of remedies. The statutory remedy here is damages, whereas Baxter seeks affirmative equitable relief as well. Equitable relief is provided specifically to the State's Attorney, but not to private claimants. Most courts are unlikely to grant plaintiff's request for a corrective statement under statutory authority, but some may do so if the order were consistent with the overall legislative purpose of the act.

Baxter may have separate claims for defamation and privacy. Remedies for these claims would come from common law. If Baxter brings an action with mixed statutory and common law claims in a court with proper jurisdiction, the court may grant separate remedies for violations of the different rights. Two limitations are noteworthy: (1) a plaintiff cannot get a double recovery of the same damages simply because there are two sources of remedies; and (2) the statute may address its relationship to any common law rights. If the statute eliminates an existing right at common law, it may not be constitutional under some state law. If the statute only limits the remedies available for the common law right and substitutes other remedies, it will probably pass muster under state and federal constitutional law.

Orloff v. Los Angeles Turf Club

30 Cal.2d 110, 180 P.2d 321 (1947).

■ CARTER, JUSTICE:

Plaintiff commenced this action for injunctive relief, alleging in his complaint that defendant Los Angeles Turf Club, a corporation, is engaged in operating a horse racing course and enterprise and a gambling establishment in connection therewith, and invites the public to attend. In January, 1946, plaintiff, an adult, purchased a ticket for admission to the defendant's place of business and was admitted thereto. Thereafter plaintiff was ejected from the establishment by defendant and its employees. In February he was again admitted thereto and was again ejected. The ousting of plaintiff was without cause, he being of good moral character and having conducted himself properly at all times. At the time of the ejections above mentioned "defendants and each of them unlawfully ordered plaintiff not to return to said race course thereafter, and unlawfully threatened to thereafter refuse to admit plaintiff thereto, or if admitted to forcibly remove and eject plaintiff therefrom." By reason of defendant's conduct, plaintiff was humiliated and embarrassed and sustained mental anguish.

* * *

* * * [T]here are specific statutory mandates which are here applicable. "It is unlawful for any corporation, person, or association, or the proprietor, lessee, or the agents of either, of any opera-house, theater, melodeon, museum, circus, caravan, *race-course*, fair or other place of public amusement or entertainment, to refuse admittance to any person over the age of twenty-one years, who presents a ticket of admission acquired by purchase, or who tenders the price thereof for such ticket, and who demands admission to such place. Any person under the influence of liquor, or who is guilty of boisterous conduct, or any person of lewd or immoral character, may be excluded from any such place of amusement." [Emphasis added.] Civil Code, sec. 53. The following section reads: "Any person who is refused admission to any place of amusement contrary to the provisions of the last preceding section, is entitled to recover from the proprietor, lessee, or their agents, or from any such person, corporation, or association, or the directors thereof, his actual damages, and one hundred dollars in addition thereto." Civil Code, sec. 54. And it is that section which is invoked by defendant as establishing the exclusive remedy for the violation of section 53. It is argued that the right established by section 53 was unknown at common law (a question we do not decide); that it is therefore in derogation of the common law, and thence must be strictly construed to the end that the remedy provided by section 54 is exclusive. Thus preventative or specific relief such as injunction or mandamus is not available in the instant case inasmuch as $100 and compensatory damages are the only remedies available.

Defendant relies upon the rule of statutory construction, that where a new right, one not existing at common law, is created by statute and a statutory remedy for the infringement thereof is provided, such remedy is exclusive of all others. * * * The rule of statutory interpretation here invoked is a corollary of, a consequence flowing from, or a specific application of, the general common-law rule of statutory construction that statutes in derogation of the common law will be strictly construed. [Citations.] But that rule does not prevail in this state, at least, as to the provisions of the four original codes. The statute in the instant case is in the Civil Code and it is provided therein: "The rule of the common law, that statutes in derogation thereof are to be strictly construed, has no application to this code. The code establishes the law of this state respecting the subjects to which it relates, and its provisions are to be liberally construed with a view to *effect its objects and to promote justice*." [Emphasis added.] Civil Code, sec. 4.

A factor of importance in interpreting the statute and in applying the above-mentioned rule of statutory construction is the adequacy of the remedy provided by the statute. It has been intimated in regard to the rule of statutory interpretation here discussed, that it should not apply when the remedy provided by statute is inadequate. [Citations.] A recovery of compensatory damages and $100 is plainly inadequate relief in a case of this character. [Citations.] Compensable damages would be extremely difficult if not impossible to measure and prove. The sum of $100 is a relatively insignificant recovery when we consider that a positive and unequivocal right has been established and violated. * * * If the objects of the Civil Code are to be effectuated, and justice promoted as required by section 4 thereof, certainly specific relief should be available where the object is to prevent the exclusion of persons from certain places and there are no valid reasons why such relief should be denied.

* * *

We conclude, therefore, that the statutes here involved do not purport to exclude all other remedies for the violation of the right conferred. * * *

The positive declaration of the personal right and the importance of its preservation together with the inadequacy of the remedy by way of damages and the $100 penalty furnish sufficient reason for injunctive relief.

The judgment is reversed.

---

1. The California legislature amended this statute subsequent to the *Orloff* decision. The amended statute raises the statutory recovery from $100 to $250, in addition to any actual damages. The legislature did not see fit to add equitable remedies to the act. Should future enforcements of the act include injunctions under appropriate circumstances, or should California courts now consider the *amended* statutory remedies exclusive? If there is no legislative history commenting on *Orloff*, is the legislative action approving or disapproving of the opinion? Is there any reason to believe that individual legislators were even aware of the opinion? Would it matter if this act were one among many with specific dollar damages that were all amended simultaneously upward? What if the legislature considered only this statute and discussed it specifically in relation to its remedies? Is this level of scrutiny into legislative intent desirable?

2. Some acts providing for civil remedies have criminal counterparts. A defendant thus may be subject to more than one proceeding for the same wrong. Should the availability of criminal sanctions affect a court's implementation of remedies under the civil statute? *See* Fletcher v. Coney Island, Inc., 165 Ohio St. 150, 134 N.E.2d 371 (1956) (rejecting *Orloff* and refusing to expand legislative remedies).

3. *Orloff* involved the creation of a new statutory right with a specific remedial provision which the court expanded in an effort to reflect the underlying legislative purpose. What if a legislature instead wishes to eliminate rights or remedies?

Legislative substitution of remedial schemes is common. For example, every state has a workers' compensation act, which is a no-fault compensation scheme for workers' injuries. The universal features are that an injured worker has an easier substantive claim in exchange for a reduced monetary recovery. The worker no longer needs to prove that the employer was negligent, and is no longer barred by any defense such as assumption of the risk. The price of this no-fault scheme is statutorily set damages that provide for lower recoveries than a successful personal injury tort claimant ordinarily would recover. Another area of legislature reform of tort is no-fault automobile legislation. About half of the states have passed some form of automobile no-fault act with great variation among them. Unlike workers' compensation acts, the no-fault plans for auto accidents replace only part of the existing system. These topics are covered in chapter 11.

Some legislatures have changed remedies in the area of medical malpractice. The California legislature, responding to the rise in malpractice insurance premiums, established a dollar limit on non-pecuniary losses such as pain and suffering. The California Supreme Court upheld the constitutionality of this change in the common law. Fein v. Permanente Medical Group, 38 Cal.3d 137, 211 Cal.Rptr. 368, 695 P.2d 665 (1985). The United States Supreme Court denied certiorari, with a dissenting opinion by Justice White who found serious constitutional questions when a legislature alters common law remedies without creating a reasonable alternative scheme. 474 U.S. 892, 106 S.Ct. 214, 88 L.Ed.2d 215 (1985).

The state courts have divided on the constitutionality of such damages limitations. *See* Judd v. Drezga, 103 P.3d 135 (Utah 2004), reprinted *infra* in Chapter 11, and accompanying notes in the section on tort reform of compensatory damages.

4. Distinguish the alteration or elimination of existing rights versus existing remedies. An interesting example of this distinction occurred in Illinois when the legislature decided to eliminate the old common law cause of action for alienation of affections. Like many other states, Illinois passed a "Heart Balm" statute eliminating several torts relating to domestic relations. Heck, a soldier returning from World War II, wished to sue the man who had an affair with Heck's wife Henrietta. The defendant cited the state statute that eliminated the cause of action, but did not prevail. Although courts in other jurisdictions have upheld Heart Balm Acts as an appropriate exercise of state police power, the Illinois Supreme Court found the act in violation of a state constitutional provision: "Every person ought to find a certain remedy in the laws for all injuries and wrongs which he may receive in his person, property or reputation * * *." Heck v. Schupp, 394 Ill. 296, 68 N.E.2d 464 (1946).

After the Illinois Supreme Court held that a state statute could not eliminate an existing common law right, the legislature tried a different approach. A new act preserves the existing right but restricts the remedy to allow only "actual damages." This term is defined as *excluding* mental anguish, shame, humiliation, sorrow, mortification, or loss in reputation. The excluded elements would usually be the major components of such claims, so the restriction on the remedy severely curtails the right. Nonetheless, the Illinois Supreme Court upheld the constitutionality of the new act as a mere alteration of the remedy rather than an elimination of a common law right. Siegall v. Solomon, 19 Ill.2d 145, 166 N.E.2d 5 (1960).

PROBLEM: THE FIRED NURSE

Susan Kaye is a nurse who was formerly employed by Southside Clinic. Nurse Kaye is a very religious person and she does not want to perform certain nursing tasks that conflict with her religious beliefs. She carefully inquired about the nature of the tasks she would have to perform before she accepted the job at the clinic.

The clinic reorganized after her employment and Nurse Kaye was reassigned. The new assignment put her in a position where she could be required occasionally to perform tasks that conflicted with her religious beliefs. She expressed her concern to her supervisor and the supervisor provided reassurance that other nurses would always do any procedure that Nurse Kaye could not do for religious reasons.

Despite this reassurance, Nurse Kaye was fired for insubordination one day when she refused a doctor's direct order to perform a task offensive to her religious principles. The incident was humiliating to Nurse Kaye. She told the doctor of her supervisor's promise and explained that other nurses were available, but the doctor was highly insulting about it and berated her loudly in front of co-workers and patients. Another nurse then volunteered to perform the task.

Nurse Kaye suffered great embarrassment. Moreover, the doctor secured her discharge later that day. Her distress resulting from this episode caused her to be unable to seek any employment for a short time. She then obtained a job with a private doctor who shares her religious views.

The state in which Southside Clinic is located has a Right of Conscience Act. That Act provides: "No person engaged in the delivery of medical services may be discriminated against by reason of refusal to act contrary to individual conscience." Conscience is defined to include sincerely held religious convictions such as those held by Nurse Kaye. The remedial portion of the Act contains only the following provision: "The court may enjoin discrimination prohibited by the Act, and may order such affirmative relief as may be appropriate, which may include, but is not limited to reinstatement or hiring of employees, with or without back pay, or any other equitable relief as the court deems appropriate."

Nurse Kaye does not want to be reinstated because she prefers her present job. She does not want any affirmative order or equitable relief for herself, but she would like an order that the Southside Clinic may not violate anyone else's rights under the Act in the future. Kaye wants damages for her humiliation and emotional distress. She also wants damages for the brief period of time she was out of work between jobs, and she would like attorney fees to cover the major cost of bringing the suit under the Right of Conscience Act. Should a court grant any of the relief sought by Nurse Kaye?

Cowin Equipment Co. v. General Motors Corp.

734 F.2d 1581 (11th Cir.1984).

■ RONEY, CIRCUIT JUDGE:

Plaintiff Cowin Equipment Co., Inc. sued General Motors Corporation (GMC) for damages on the ground that the terms of its dealer sales and service agreement were unconscionable under § 2–302 of the Uniform Commercial Code. The district court held the provision was unconscionable as a matter of law and denied defendant's motion for summary judgment. * * * We reverse on the ground that U.C.C. § 2–302, which concerns unconscionable contracts, does not create a cause of action for damages.

* * *

Briefly, the facts are as follows: In early 1978, GMC and its dealers anticipated an increase in demand for Terex heavy equipment, which GMC manufactured and Cowin sold. GMC responded * * * by requiring Cowin and other dealers handling Terex equipment to place non-cancellable orders in advance for equipment to be shipped between September 1, 1978 and August 1, 1979. Formerly GMC had permitted liberal cancellation. * * *

Cowin ordered forty-four machines in the months following. Due to a downturn in the economy, however, Cowin later attempted to cancel some of the orders. GMC refused to permit cancellation and delivered all of the machines as ordered, leaving Cowin with excess inventory. Cowin sued in December, 1980 seeking damages on grounds that the [contract terms] were unconscionable. Specifically, plaintiffs sought compensation for (1) interest incurred on loans necessary in order to buy equipment which defendant would not allow cancellation on; (2) insurance on the equipment; (3) storage and maintenance fees on the equipment; (4) loss incurred from sale of certain equipment sold for less than its purchase price.

The district court viewed the case as a "Uniform Commercial Code unconscionability action for damages" based upon what it found to be unconscionable terms in the sales and service agreement between the parties. Our review of the Code provisions and the relevant cases persuades us that U.C.C. § 2–302 was not intended to create a cause of action, and cannot be used as a basis for damages in the instant case.

The language of § 2–302 and the Official Comment which follows it make no mention of damages as an available remedy for an unconscionable contract. This is consistent with traditional common law unconscionability theory. When the equity courts found contracts to be unconscionable, they refused specific enforcement. [Citations.] The remedies available to modern courts under § 2–302 are of similar equitable nature:

(1) If the court as a matter of law finds the contract or any clause of the contract to have been unconscionable at the time it was made the court may refuse to enforce the contract, or it may enforce the remainder of the contract without the unconscionable clause, or it may so limit the application of any unconscionable clause to avoid any unconscionable result.

U.C.C. § 2–302 (1983).

* * *

Reversed and remanded.

———

1.   Was Cowin not injured or not injured in a manner that would give a remedy under U.C.C. § 2–302? Would you characterize the problem in this case as substantive or remedial? Is there a meaningful difference between right and remedy here?

2.   Title VII of the Civil Rights Act of 1964 is another example of a statute that limits remedies. That Act prohibits employment discrimination on the basis of race, sex, ethnicity, color or religion. The original remedial provision in the Act, before its amendment in 1991, provides: "The court may enjoin the respondent from engaging in such unlawful employment practice, and order such affirmative act as may be appropriate, which may include, but is not limited to, reinstatement or hiring of employees, with or without back pay (payable by the employer, employment agency, or labor organization, as the case may be, responsible for the unlawful employment practice), or any other equitable relief as the court deems appropriate." 42 U.S.C. § 2000e–5(g).

Courts have interpreted this remedial provision to preclude compensatory and punitive damages. Back pay is considered restitutionary, and the reference to "other equitable relief" has been held to preclude legal damages. *See, e.g.* Pearson v. Western Electric Co., 542 F.2d 1150 (10th Cir.1976) (no "compensatory damages" for humiliation and loss of credit rating).

Congress held hearings in 1989 to determine, among other things, the effect of the remedial limitation. The result was the Civil Rights Act of 1991 which amended Title VII in several respects. One provision of the new Act was to expand the remedies to include compensatory and punitive damages, but again with limitation. First, such damages are permissible only in cases proving intentional discrimination. Second, the Act provides for caps on damage recovery, scaled to the size of the defendant employer.

Jurisdictional Remedy Limitations: The Norris–LaGuardia Act

Statutes may limit the availability of remedies by the language used in the remedial provisions of acts, as illustrated by the acts involved in the two preceding cases and problem. Legislators have occasionally sought to control the remedies available to a court by imposing a jurisdictional limitation. The Norris–LaGuardia Act, passed by the U.S. Congress in 1932, provides a good example. The relevant portions of the Act are:

"No court of the United States shall have jurisdiction to issue any restraining order or temporary or permanent injunction in any case involving or growing out of any labor dispute to prohibit any person or persons participating or interested in such dispute (as these terms are herein defined) from doing, whether singly or in concert, any of the following acts:

"(a) Ceasing or refusing to perform any work or to remain in any relation of employment; * * *

"(e) Giving publicity to the existence of, or the facts involved in, any labor dispute, whether by advertising, speaking, patrolling, or by any other method not involving fraud or violence;

"(f) Assembling peaceably to act or to organize to act in promotion of their interests in a labor dispute;

"(i) Advising, urging, or otherwise causing or inducing without fraud or violence the acts heretofore specified * * *." § 4, 47 Stat. 70, 29 U.S.C. § 104.

---

1. The history and purpose of the Norris–LaGuardia Act are explained in the 1970 Supreme Court case Boys Markets, Inc. v. Retail Clerks Union, 398 U.S. 235, 250–252, 90 S.Ct. 1583, 1591–1593, 26 L.Ed.2d 199 (1970).

The issue in the case was whether a federal district court could enjoin a strike in breach of a no-strike obligation under a collective bargaining agreement. The contract required the parties to take their grievance to binding arbitration. An act of Congress passed after Norris–LaGuardia, but making no reference to it, allowed federal courts to enforce the arbitration agreement by injunction. The question before the Court was whether the Norris–LaGuardia Act still operated to deprive the district court of jurisdiction to issue an injunction against the strike in order to enforce the arbitration agreement under the subsequent act. Justice Brennan's opinion for the Court explores the Act's history and purpose.

"The Norris–LaGuardia Act was responsive to a situation totally different from that which exists today. In the early part of this century, the federal courts generally were regarded as allies of management in its attempt to prevent the organization and strengthening of labor unions; and in this industrial struggle the injunction became a potent weapon that was wielded against the activities of labor groups. The result was a large number of sweeping decrees, often issued *ex parte,* drawn on an *ad hoc* basis without regard to any systematic elaboration of national labor policy. [Citation.]

"In 1932 Congress attempted to bring some order out of the industrial chaos that had developed and to correct the abuses that had resulted from the interjection of the federal judiciary into union-management disputes on the behalf of management. See declaration of public policy, Norris–LaGuardia Act, § 2, 47 Stat. 70. Congress, therefore, determined initially to limit severely the power of the federal courts to issue injunctions 'in any case involving or growing out of any labor dispute * * *.' § 4, 47 Stat. 70. Even as initially enacted, however, the prohibition against federal injunctions was by no means absolute. *See* Norris–LaGuardia Act, §§ 7, 8, 9, 47 Stat. 71, 72. Shortly thereafter Congress passed the Wagner Act, designed to curb various management activities that tended to discourage employee participation in collective action.

"As labor organizations grew in strength and developed toward maturity, congressional emphasis shifted from protection of the nascent labor movement to the encouragement of collective bargaining and to administrative techniques for the peaceful resolution of industrial disputes. This shift in emphasis was accomplished, however, without extensive revision of many of the older enactments, including the anti-injunction section of the Norris–LaGuardia Act. Thus it became the task of the courts to accommodate, to reconcile the older statutes with the more recent ones.

"A leading example of this accommodation process is Brotherhood of Railroad Trainmen v. Chicago River & Ind. R. Co., 353 U.S. 30, 77 S.Ct. 635, 1 L.Ed.2d 622 (1957). There we were confronted with a peaceful strike which violated the statutory duty to arbitrate imposed by the Railway Labor Act. The Court concluded that a strike in violation of a statutory arbitration duty was not the type of situation to which the Norris–LaGuardia Act was responsive, that an important federal policy was involved in the peaceful settlement of disputes throughout the statutorily mandated arbitration procedure, that this important policy was imperiled if equitable remedies were not available to implement it, and hence that Norris–LaGuardia's policy of nonintervention by the federal courts should yield to the overriding interest in the successful implementation of the arbitration process."

398 U.S. 235, 250–252, 90 S.Ct. 1583, 1591–1593, 26 L.Ed.2d 199 (1970).

2. More recently, the Norris–LaGuardia Act became central to the litigation involving the National Football League when the owners locked out the players from team facilities and shut down league operations in the spring of 2011 due to a labor dispute. The players sued to enjoin the lockout and the federal district court granted a preliminary injunction. Because the players had voted to decertify the players' union, the district court judge did not find that the Norris–LaGuardia Act applied.

The Eighth Circuit reversed in *Brady v. National Football League*, 644 F.3d 661 (8th Cir. 2011). The majority found that it was not necessary to have the present existence of a union for the Norris–LaGuardia Act to apply. The court was thus deprived of jurisdiction to issue the injunction against the lockout.

A strong dissent noted that the legislative history of the Norris–LaGuardia Act made clear that the purpose of the Act was to protect employees rather than employers. Judge Bye noted that the Act was passed in 1914, when "after twenty years of judicial interference in labor conflicts on the side of the employers, Congress stepped in to protect organized labor." 644 F.3d 661, 682 (Bye, J. dissenting). He would have affirmed the district court.

Treister v. American Academy of Orthopaedic Surgeons

78 Ill.App.3d 746, 33 Ill.Dec. 501, 396 N.E.2d 1225 (1979).

■ McGILLICUDDY, JUSTICE:

On November 3, 1976, the plaintiff, Michael R. Treister, M.D., filed a three-count complaint against the defendant, American Academy of Orthopaedic Surgeons, challenging the academy's denial of his initial application for membership in the academy. The academy filed a motion to dismiss plaintiff's complaint on various grounds which included the failure to state a cause of action because the decision of a private professional association rejecting an application for membership is not subject to judicial review. The plaintiff filed a motion to strike the motion to dismiss. On January 24, 1977, the trial court denied the academy's motion to dismiss count I. * * *

Count I of the complaint states that the plaintiff is an orthopaedic surgeon licensed to practice medicine and surgery in the State of Illinois and has been certified by the American Board of Orthopaedic Surgery. The plaintiff is a member of numerous professional associations, holds several teaching positions, is the author of numerous papers relating to the field of medicine and is a member of the attending staff of seven Chicago hospitals.

The plaintiff asserts that the American Academy of Orthopaedic Surgeons, a not-for-profit corporation, admits board-certified orthopaedic surgeons to fellowship and membership in the academy on the basis of standards and rules adopted by the academy and published in their by-laws. The plaintiff claims that active fellowship in the academy is a factor relied upon by hospitals in the granting of orthopaedic surgical privileges, by insurance companies in the establishment of malpractice rates, by courts in determining the expertise of an orthopaedic surgeon whose testimony is offered as expert and by young physicians selecting a clinic in which to practice. The plaintiff characterizes membership in the academy as "a practical necessity for an orthopaedic surgeon who wishes to realize maximum potential achievement and recognition in his specialty."

In November 1974 the plaintiff applied for membership in the academy by submitting an application form. According to the plaintiff, the academy prepared a list of applicants for active fellowship and broadly distributed it to physicians throughout the United States together with a request for information concerning the reputation and qualifications of the persons named thereon.

In 1976 the plaintiff was interviewed by Dr. Louis Kolb, who informed him that there was adverse information in the plaintiff's file. Dr. Kolb predicted that this information would result in the rejection of his application. Although Dr. Kolb informed the plaintiff of the general nature of the charges, the plaintiff asserts that Dr. Kolb did not provide sufficient detail to enable him to rebut the charges. When the plaintiff requested that Dr. Kolb permit him to examine the file, the doctor replied that academy regulations forbade such an examination. Dr. Kolb also denied the plaintiff's request that he further specify the nature of the charges and that he identify the persons making the charges. In addition, Dr. Kolb refused to cite any authority for denying the plaintiff's request to see his file and to be informed of the charges and the identity of his accusers.

The plaintiff states that, at the suggestion of Dr. Kolb, he wrote a letter to the academy attempting to rebut the charges as well as possible under the circumstances and requesting all available appeal rights and the right to be represented by counsel. The plaintiff received no communication from the academy until October 1976 when he received a letter notifying him that his application had been rejected, that the matter was closed and that he could not reapply for admission for three years.

* * *

In his prayer for relief the plaintiff asks for a declaration that he is entitled to be informed of any charges against him; to be informed of the identity of his accusers; to have a fair hearing before an impartial adjudicator, and to have conclusions of fact fairly supported by evidence of record. In addition, the plaintiff asks for a declaration that the rejection of his application was void.

* * *

The academy argues that the trial court lacked jurisdiction of matters alleged in count I and maintains that the traditional rule is that judicial review is not available to examine a decision by a private professional association to reject an application for initial membership. [Citation.] The plaintiff contends that in recent years courts have decided that an applicant to professional associations has a right to a fair hearing on his application and to reasonable standards for admission. * * *

In determining whether we should permit judicial review of the denial of the plaintiff's membership application, we must weigh the importance of two values which are in conflict in this situation. On the one hand, we recognize the necessity of judicial restraint from interfering with or regulating the affairs and decisions of a private, voluntary association. However, we also find it unconscionable that a private association could deprive an individual of the right to pursue his or her profession because of a personality conflict, his or her race or religion, or, as the plaintiff suggests in his brief, testimony on behalf of plaintiffs in malpractice actions.

Balancing these two interests, we hold that our courts can review the application procedures of a private association when membership in the organization is an economic necessity. We approve of the opinions in *Falcone* [*v. Middlesex County Medical Society*, 34 N.J. 582, 170 A.2d 791 (1961)] and *Blende* [*v. Maricopa County Medical Society*, 96 Ariz. 240, 393 P.2d 926 (1964)] which hold that a medical society cannot arbitrarily deny membership to an applicant when the society controls access to local hospital facilities and thus can deprive the applicant of his ability to practice medicine.

We find, however, that the plaintiff has not alleged that membership in the American Academy of Orthopaedic Surgeons is an economic necessity. Membership is not a requisite to hospital staff privileges as evidenced by the fact that the plaintiff is a member of the attending staff at seven Chicago hospitals. In addition, the plaintiff was board-certified and licensed by the State without academy membership.

* * *

Although in this case we sympathize with the plaintiff's frustration with the academy's refusal to give him the courtesy of an explanation of the denial of his application, we believe the courts must refrain from interfering in the affairs of a private association absent a showing of economic necessity.

* * * [Reversed and action dismissed.]

■ SIMON, PRESIDING JUSTICE, dissenting: * * *

I believe the majority understates Dr. Treister's interest. At the same time, it overestimates the Academy's legitimate interests, and by focusing on the effects of exclusion on Dr. Treister personally, obscures an essential aspect of this case, the nature of the Academy. The public interest at stake is also slighted. * * *

Apart from any established law, I believe that logically the majority's strict economic necessity test is too stringent, and that Count I of the complaint should be sustained. The Academy is not simply a private body, accepting and rejecting applicants according to its private needs and desires. It would no doubt deny indignantly that it exists primarily to fatten its members' wallets and egos. Rather, it aspires to a more exalted function, as guardian of the profession and of the public generally. It purports to be judicious rather than exclusive. The Academy holds itself out as the sole legitimate organization of its kind in the profession, and is widely recognized as such. It is a monopoly; and it is affiliated with the A.M.A., itself a monopoly, and no doubt with many local groups. * * *

The majority underrates the Academy's capacity to harm Dr. Treister. It is true that he has so far done quite well without Academy membership; but that is because until recently his inexperience has made him obviously unripe for membership, so that his nonmembership has been perceived as routine, temporary, and insignificant. From now on, things will be different. Count I of the complaint alleges that hospitals and insurance companies rely on Academy membership. Some of these institutions require disclosure of membership status in professional organizations like the

Academy, and, in addition, specifically require disclosure of rejections from such organization. Hospitals, insurance companies, and others know that almost all Board-certified orthopaedic surgeons become members of the Academy 2 years after Board certification. A questionnaire or application form filled out by an orthopaedic surgeon who has not been admitted to Academy membership 2 years after this certification raises serious questions and can substantially impair the practitioner's career.

The revelation that Dr. Treister has been rejected by the Academy is going to "red-flag" every application for staff privileges or insurance that he will ever make, subjecting him to close scrutiny, and making every one of his applications a major event when it would otherwise be approved as a matter or routine. Particularly because Dr. Treister is known to meet every formal requirement for Academy membership, hospitals and insurers can logically conclude that he must have been excluded for incompetence or unethical conduct. It will be difficult for Dr. Treister to rebut this inference with the facts, since the Academy refuses to particularize any accusation.

Also, it is well-known that medical malpractice insurance rates have rocketed and are now a large part of the cost of practice. Although Dr. Treister is now considered a prime risk, paying the lowest rate, his premium is almost $20,000 per year. Even a modest percentage surcharge is substantial.

The more subtle effects of rejection could prove even more crippling. The emerging pattern of medical care distinguishes between internists, who have a stable patient pool, and other specialists, who rely on referrals. Because a single patient is likely to see an orthopaedic surgeon only rarely over the course of a lifetime, while he might see an internist many times, the surgeon is peculiarly dependent on referrals. Referring doctors often use Academy membership to verify their impression of specialists, and may even find a doctor for a referral by examining the Academy membership list. New associates, necessary for the growth of a medical practice, also rely on Academy membership in evaluating an orthopaedic surgeon who seeks to employ them. Finally, many attorneys prefer Academy members as expert witnesses.

* * *

On the other side of the balance, the Academy's legitimate interest is lighter than the majority supposes. It is important to note how modest is Dr. Treister's prayer for relief. He does not seek to compel the Academy to admit him to membership. He asks only that it consider his application fairly, in accordance with its own bylaws and the principles of ethics established by the Academy's affiliate the A.M.A.—a set of principles the Academy requires every member to adhere to. There should be nothing directly offensive to the Academy about doing in fact what it publicly professes to do.

* * *

The Academy's unjust rejection of applicants, resulting from unfair admissions standards and procedures, could have pernicious effects on society. The rejection of qualified applicants injures the public—whom, after all, physicians are licensed to serve—by disabling physicians who might otherwise have been able to perform great public service. Also, applicants who were accepted for membership according to unfair procedures based on arbitrary or biased standards might advance to positions of trust and importance they otherwise would not attain—and for which they were not qualified. Thus, the public has a strong and often-ignored stake in the membership practices of such societies. A professional society that uses its membership policies in the following ways does the public a grave disservice: (i) to enforce a "conspiracy of silence" by excluding doctors who truthfully testify against other members of their professions in instances of malpractice [citation]; (ii) to unreasonably exclude physicians who criticize sacred cows of the profession, thereby stifling creative thought and constructive criticism [citation]; (iii) to deny membership privileges to doctors because of their race, etc. In fact, a professional society using admission and rejection to produce such results betrays the trust of a public it exists to benefit. And it abuses the power it has acquired, advancing some to positions they do not merit, and retarding other, more worthy, orthopaedic surgeons. I find it unconscionable that an association might engage in such conduct, even if it does not thereby succeed in driving the victims entirely out of the profession.

* * *

I believe Dr. Treister is entitled to a fair hearing on the application, to be judged by standards reasonably related to the Academy's purposes, and to be informed of the reasons for his rejection. I would affirm the circuit court's order sustaining Count I of the complaint and permit Dr. Treister to have a trial on the merits of that count. * * *

1.   What if an influential medical organization that previously chose members on the basis of skill and ethics suddenly began to use secret criteria unrelated to medicine? Would judicial intervention be appropriate to prevent a fraud on the public? Does it matter if the organization concerns services other than medicine: lawyers, architects, plumbers, or real estate developers?

2.   Did the plaintiff in the principal case fail to state a cause of action, or fail to establish a basis for the relief he desired? If the complaint had asked also for damages, might the court have awarded at least nominal damages to declare the right?

3.   At one time courts said equitable relief was available only to preserve rights in "property." Is there any reason why equity should protect some rights more vigorously than others?

Pulliam v. Allen

466 U.S. 522, 104 S.Ct. 1970, 80 L.Ed.2d 565 (1984).

■ JUSTICE BLACKMUN delivered the opinion of the Court.

This case raises issues concerning the scope of judicial immunity from a civil suit that seeks injunctive and declaratory relief under § 1 of the Civil Rights Act of 1871, as amended, 42 U.S.C. § 1983. * * *

Petitioner Gladys Pulliam is a state Magistrate in Culpeper County, Va. Respondents Richmond R. Allen and Jesse W. Nicholson were plaintiffs in a § 1983 action against Pulliam brought in the United States District Court for the Eastern District of Virginia. They claimed that Magistrate Pulliam's practice of imposing bail on persons arrested for nonjailable offenses under Virginia law and of incarcerating those persons if they could not meet the bail was unconstitutional. The District Court agreed and enjoined the practice. * * *

Respondent Allen was arrested in January 1980 for allegedly using abusive and insulting language, a Class 3 misdemeanor under Va. Code § 18.2–416 (1982). The maximum penalty for a Class 3 misdemeanor is a $500 fine. Petitioner set a bond of $250. Respondent Allen was unable to post the bond, and petitioner committed Allen to the Culpeper County jail, where he remained for 14 days. He was then tried, found guilty, fined, and released. The trial judge subsequently reopened the judgment and reversed the conviction. Allen then filed his § 1983 claim, seeking declaratory and injunctive relief against petitioner's practice of incarcerating persons waiting trial for nonincarcerable offenses.

Respondent Nicholson was incarcerated four times within the 2–month period immediately before and after the filing of Allen's complaint. His arrests were for alleged violations of Va. Code § 18.2–388 (1982), being drunk in public. Section 18.2–388 is a Class 4 misdemeanor for which the maximum penalty is a $100 fine. Like Allen, respondent Nicholson was incarcerated for periods of two to six days for failure to post bond. He intervened in Allen's suit as a party plaintiff.

The District Court found it to be petitioner's practice to require bond for nonincarcerable offenses. The court declared the practice to be a violation of due process and equal protection and enjoined it. * * *

Although injunctive relief against a judge rarely is awarded, the United States Courts of Appeals that have faced the issue are in agreement that judicial immunity does not bar such relief. This Court, however, has never decided the question.

The starting point in our own analysis is the common law. Our cases have proceeded on the assumption that common-law principles of legislative and judicial immunity were incorporated into our judicial system and that they should not be abrogated absent clear legislative intent to do so. [Citations.] Accordingly, the first and crucial question is whether the common law recognized judicial immunity from prospective collateral relief.

At the common law itself, there was no such thing as an injunction against a judge. Injunctive relief was an equitable remedy that could be awarded by the Chancellor only against the parties in proceedings before other courts. *See* 2 J. Story, Equity Jurisprudence ¶ 875, p. 72 (11th ed. 1873). This limitation on the use of the injunction, however, says nothing about the scope of judicial immunity. And the limitation derived not from judicial immunity, but from the substantive confines of the Chancellor's authority.

Although there were no injunctions against common-law judges, there is a common-law parallel to the § 1983 injunction at issue here. That parallel is found in the collateral prospective relief available against judges through the use of the King's prerogative writs. A brief excursion into common-law history helps to explain the relevance of these writs to the question whether principles of common-law immunity bar injunctive relief against a judicial officer.

The doctrine of judicial immunity and the limitations on prospective collateral relief with which we are concerned have related histories. Both can be traced to the successful efforts of the King's Bench to ensure the supremacy of the common-law courts over their 17th—and 18th–century rivals. *See* 5 W. Holdsworth, A History of English Law 159–160 (3d ed. 1945).

A number of courts challenged the King's Bench for authority in those days. Among these were the Council, the Star Chamber, the Chancery, the Admiralty, and the ecclesiastical courts. In an effort to assert the supremacy of the common-law courts, Lord Coke forbade the interference by courts of equity with matters properly triable at common law. * * *

The King's Bench exercised significant collateral control over inferior and rival courts through the use of prerogative writs. The writs included habeas corpus, certiorari, prohibition, mandamus, quo warranto, and *ne exeat regno*. 1 Holdsworth, at 226–231 (7th ed. 1956). Most interesting for our current purposes are the writs of prohibition and mandamus.[9] The writs issued against a judge, in theory to prevent him from exceeding his jurisdiction or to require him to exercise it. In practice, controlling an inferior court in the proper exercise of its jurisdiction meant that the King's Bench used and continues to use the writs to prevent a judge from committing all manner of errors, including departing from the rules of natural justice, proceeding with a suit in which he has an interest, misconstruing substantive law, and rejecting legal evidence. [Citations.]

* * *

---

9. The writ of prohibition appears to have been used more than the writ of mandamus to control inferior courts. Mandamus could issue to any person in respect of anything that pertained to his office and was in the nature of a public duty. *See* 1 Halsbury's Laws of England ¶ 81 (4th ed. 1973). The other prerogative writs are also of some relevance here. The writ of certiorari, for instance, issued to remove proceedings from an inferior tribunal to ensure that the court was keeping within its jurisdiction and effectuating the rules of the common law. Once a writ of certiorari was delivered to a judge, he was forbidden to proceed further in the case. Failure to suspend proceedings amounted to a contempt. *See* R. Pound, Appellate Procedure in Civil Cases 61 (1941).

The relationship between the King's Bench and its collateral and inferior courts is not precisely paralleled in our system by the relationship between the state and federal courts. To the extent that we rely on the common-law practice in shaping our own doctrine of judicial immunity, however, the control exercised by the King's Bench through the prerogative writs is highly relevant. It indicates that, at least in the view of the common law, there was no inconsistency between a principle of immunity that protected judicial authority from "a wide, wasting, and harassing persecution," *Taaffe v. Downes,* 13 Eng.Rep., at 18, n. (a), and the availability of collateral injunctive relief in exceptional cases. * * *

Our own experience is fully consistent with the common law's rejection of a rule of judicial immunity from prospective relief. We never have had a rule of absolute judicial immunity from prospective relief, and there is no evidence that the absence of that immunity has had a chilling effect on judicial independence.

* * *

For the most part, injunctive relief against a judge raises concerns different from those addressed by the protection of judges from damages awards. The limitations already imposed by the requirements for obtaining equitable relief against any defendant—a showing of an inadequate remedy at law and of a serious risk of irreparable harm, [citation]—severely curtail the risk that judges will be harassed and their independence compromised by the threat of having to defend themselves against suits by disgruntled litigants. Similar limitations serve to prevent harassment of judges through use of the writ of mandamus. Because mandamus has "the unfortunate consequence of making the judge a litigant, obliged to obtain personal counsel or to leave his defense to one of the litigants before him," the Court has stressed that it should be "reserved for really extraordinary causes." [Citation.] Occasionally, however, there are "really extraordinary causes" and, in such cases, there has been no suggestion that judicial immunity prevents the supervising court from issuing the writ.[19]

* * *

We conclude that judicial immunity is not a bar to prospective injunctive relief against a judicial officer acting in her judicial capacity. In so concluding, we express no opinion as to the propriety of the injunctive relief awarded in this case. Petitioner did not appeal the award of injunctive relief against her. The Court of Appeals therefore had no opportunity to consider whether respondents had an adequate remedy at law, rendering

---

19. In *Hall v. West,* 335 F.2d 481 (C.A.5 1964), a petition for writ of mandamus was filed by Negro plaintiffs in a civil rights case that had been pending before the District Court more than 11 years. Although two other District Courts, affirmed by this Court, had declared unconstitutional the Louisiana segregated school system and the state statute passed to allow the school board to close public schools to avoid desegregation, the board had made clear that it intended to take no action to change the segregated system without a further order from the District Court. The court, however, refused to act. The Court of Appeals therefore issued a writ of mandamus, compelling the District Court to order the defendants to submit a plan for the commencement of desegregation of the schools under their control. * * *

equitable relief inappropriate,[22] or whether the order itself should have been more narrowly tailored. On the record before us and without the benefit of the Court of Appeals' assessment, we are unwilling to speculate about these possibilities. * * *

■ JUSTICE POWELL, with whom THE CHIEF JUSTICE, JUSTICE REHNQUIST, and JUSTICE O'CONNOR join, dissenting.

The Court today reaffirms the rule that judges are immune from suits for damages, but holds that they may be sued for injunctive and declaratory relief. * * *

* * * A review of the common law reveals nothing that suggests— much less requires—the distinction the Court draws today between suits for prospective relief (with the attendant liability for costs and attorney's fees) and suits for damages.

* * *

The prerogative writs of mandamus and prohibition are simply not analogous to suits for injunctive relief from the judgments of common-law courts, and the availability of these writs against judicial officials has nothing to do with judicial immunity. It has long been recognized at common law that judicial immunity protects only those acts committed within the proper scope of a judge's jurisdiction, but provides no protection for acts committed in excess of jurisdiction. Because writs of prohibition and mandamus were intended only to control the proper exercise of jurisdiction, they posed no threat to judicial independence and implicated none of the policies of judicial immunity. Thus, the judges of England's inferior courts were subject to suit for writs of mandamus and prohibition, but judicial immunity barred all suits attacking judicial decisions made within the proper scope of their jurisdiction. There is no allegation in this case that petitioner exceeded her jurisdiction. The suit for injunctive relief is based solely on an erroneous construction and application of law. It is precisely this kind of litigation that the common-law doctrine of judicial immunity was intended to prohibit.

B.   CONSEQUENCES OF REMEDY CHARACTERIZATIONS

Section Coverage:

As discussed in Chapter 1, remedies are broadly categorized as legal or equitable depending upon their historical origin. Remedies are further classified functionally into types, such as injunctive relief, damages, declaratory and restitutionary relief. This section explores the problems involved

---

22. Virginia provides, for instance, for appellate review of orders denying bail or requiring excessive bail, *see* Va.Code § 19.2–124 (1983), and for state habeas corpus relief from unlawful detention, *see* Va.Code § 8.01–654 (Supp.1983). On the other hand, the nature and short duration of the pretrial detention imposed by petitioner was such that it may have been impossible for respondents to avail themselves of these remedies. * * *

in the characterization of remedies and focuses on some of the consequences that can flow from those remedial labels.

The process of remedial characterization is often complex because no single test may be employed in all situations. For example, money can pass from a defendant to a plaintiff under several different types of remedies both at law and in equity; however, in one instance the payment may be classified as "damages" and yet in another it may be viewed as equitable relief. The significance of a given remedial label is that it can affect matters such as insurance coverage, right to jury trial, and method of judicial enforcement of the remedy.

Model Case:

Defendant company dumped large slabs of broken concrete pieces at the back of a neighboring homeowner's yard. The neighbor's suit for trespass seeks both an injunction to remove the slabs and damages for injury done to the land. The availability of a jury trial for these mixed claims of law and equity varies by state law. Under the federal system, also followed in some states, the legal issue must be tried first by a jury unless the parties waive this right. The court then decides the equitable issue in a manner consistent with the findings of fact for the legal claim. Therefore, the parties in this trespass case would have a jury trial right for the damages claim. The judge then would decide the equitable issue whether to issue an injunction.

In many states the jury trial right rests with the judge's determination of whether the claim is predominantly legal or equitable. If the claim is characterized as predominantly equitable, then there is no right to a jury trial for any of the issues. If it is considered predominantly legal, the parties have a right to a jury trial on the legal issues.

The defendant company in this trespass case has insurance to cover "damages" arising out of the business operation, so the policy will cover any money liability to the neighbor if no exceptions apply. The insurance policy may not cover all losses associated with the suit, however. If the court grants the injunction, the policy may not cover the cost of compliance with it because costs expended to comply with court orders are not legal damages and therefore may not be "damages" within the meaning of the contract.

Hanna v. WCI Communities, Inc.

348 F.Supp.2d 1332 (S.D.Fla.2004).

■ HURLEY, DISTRICT JUDGE.

This cause comes before the court upon a motion by the defendants to strike: 1) Plaintiff Robert Hanna's demands for punitive damages in Counts I and II of his complaint; 2) Mr. Hanna's demand for damages for injury to reputation in Count I and 3) Mr. Hanna's demand for a jury trial.

1. *Plaintiff's Demands for Punitive Damages*

Mr. Hanna's complaint seeks punitive damages for both his Sarbanes–Oxley Act whistle-blower claim (Count I) and for his Florida Whistleblower Act claim (Count II). Mr. Hanna's response concedes that punitive damages are unavailable under the Sarbanes–Oxley Act, Pl's Resp. at 2. Thus, Mr. Hanna's request for punitive damages is stricken as to Count I of his complaint.

Defendants also contend that punitive damages are unavailable under the Florida Whistleblower Act ("FWA"). Both sides concede that *Branche v. Airtran Airways, Inc.,* 314 F.Supp.2d 1194 (M.D.Fla.2004) is the only reported decision that directly addresses this question. In that case, the court explicitly held that "punitive damages are not available under the FWA." *Id.* at 1195. In *Branche,* the court reasoned that the FWA's plain language only lists "compensatory" damages and that the "use of the word 'compensatory' in Section 448.103(2)(e) clearly indicates that punitive damages and other forms of non-compensatory damages are unavailable to correct FWA violations." *Id.* at 1196.

The court agrees with the logic expressed in *Branche* and holds that punitive damages are not available under the Florida Whistleblower Act. The court, however, recognizes that this is an issue "the Florida Courts have yet to address" that is "entirely controlled by Florida law." * * * Mr. Hanna's request for punitive damages is stricken as to Count II of his complaint.

2. *Plaintiff's Demands for Damages for Injury to Reputation under the Sarbanes–Oxley Act*

The Sarbanes–Oxley Act does not specifically mention whether a plaintiff may demand damages for loss of reputation under the Act. *See* 18 U.S.C. § 1514A(c). The Act simply states that "an employee prevailing in any action under subsection (b)(1) shall be entitled to all relief necessary to make the employee whole." 18 U.S.C. § 1514A(c)(1). While the Act enumerates certain types of compensatory damages, (i.e. back pay, litigation costs, expert witness fees, and attorney fees) it is silent as to other types of compensatory damages. *See* 18 U.S.C. § 1514A(c). The parties concede that Mr. Hanna's entitlement to receive reputation damages under the Sarbanes–Oxley Act is an issue of first impression.

The text of the Sarbanes–Oxley Act provides for the following remedies:

(1) In general.—An employee prevailing in any action under subsection (b)(1) shall be entitled to all relief necessary to make the employee whole.

(2) Compensatory damages. Relief for any action under paragraph (1) shall include—

(A) reinstatement with the same seniority status that the employee would have had, but for the discrimination;

(B) the amount of back pay, with interest; and

(C) compensation for any special damages sustained as a result of the discrimination, including litigation costs, expert witness fees, and reasonable attorney fees.

18 U.S.C. § 1514A(c).

The remedies section of the Title VII statutory framework provides an analogous employment statute with which to analyze the remedies available under the Sarbanes–Oxley Act. In the Title VII context, prior to the 1991 amendments codified at 42 U.S.C. § 1981(a), courts had held that "nothing in this remedial scheme purports to recompense a Title VII plaintiff for any of the other traditional harms associated with personal injury, such as pain and suffering, emotional distress, *harm to reputation,* or other consequential damages . . ." *United States v. Burke,* 504 U.S. 229, 239, 112 S.Ct. 1867, 119 L.Ed.2d 34 (1992) (emphasis added). Prior to the passage of 42 U.S.C. § 1981(a), the remedies section of Title VII only provided for the same remedies listed in the Sarbanes–Oxley Act under 18 U.S.C. § 1514A(c)(2). *See Burke* 504 U.S. at 239, 112 S.Ct. 1867.

After the 1991 amendments, however, the Title VII statute specifically provided for "compensatory damages under this section for . . . other non-pecuniary losses." 42 U.S.C § 1981a(b)(3). Though 42 U.S.C. § 1981a(b)(3) never specifically mentions "reputation damages," courts have held that "injury to character and reputation . . . [are] non-pecuniary losses compensable under the 1991 Act." [Citation.]

Thus, the court must decide whether the Sarbanes–Oxley Act's language stating that "[a]n employee prevailing in any action under subsection (b)(1) shall be entitled *to all relief necessary to make the employee whole*" should be read to include damages for loss of reputation. 18 U.S.C. § 1514A(c)(1) (emphasis added). As the Seventh Circuit Court of Appeals has noted in the Title VII context, "[w]hen reputational injury caused by an employer's unlawful discrimination diminishes a plaintiff's future earnings capacity, *[he] cannot be made whole* without compensation for the lost future earnings [he] would have received absent the employer's unlawful activity." *Williams v. Pharmacia, Inc.,* 137 F.3d 944, 953 (7th Cir.1998) (emphasis added). Therefore, employing the logic expressed in *Williams* to Mr. Hanna's whistle-blower claim, the court holds that a successful Sarbanes–Oxley Act plaintiff cannot be made whole without being compensated for damages for reputational injury that diminished plaintiff's future earning capacity. Accordingly, the court denies the defendants' request to strike plaintiff's demand for damages to Mr. Hanna's reputation.

3. *Plaintiff's Demand for a Jury Trial*

Unlike Title VII, the Sarbanes–Oxley Act is silent as to whether a plaintiff may demand a jury trial. (*Compare* 42 U.S.C. § 1981a *with* 18 U.S.C. § 1514A). Again, both parties concede that this is also an issue of first impression. Rather than address the issue at this time, the court will deny the defendants' motion to strike a jury trial in this case without prejudice to bring this motion again if all of the parties' case-dispositive motions have been denied prior to trial. At that time, the court might have the benefit of guidance from other courts that have considered the availability of jury trials under the Sarbanes–Oxley Act.

* * *

Defendants' motion to strike plaintiff's demand for reputational damages is denied. Defendants' motion to strike plaintiff's demand for a jury trial is denied without prejudice for later re-filing if this case has not been resolved by the filing of dispositive motions.

----

1.   The sources of remedies as well as their classification dictate the types of remedies that are available. Both compensatory damages and punitive damages are available as legal remedies in circumstances where either common law or statutory legal remedies are appropriate. As the principal case reflects, entitlement to one legal remedy does not necessarily entitle a plaintiff to all legal remedies.

2.   The substantive issues of interpreting the Sarbanes–Oxley Act in the principal case remain open in federal law. Some other courts have reasoned that because reputational damages are not specifically provided in SOX, they are more like emotional distress damages and thus not recoverable under SOX. Walton v. Nova Information Systems, 514 F.Supp.2d 1031 (E.D.Tenn.2007); Murray v. TXU Corp., 2005 WL 1356444 (N.D.Tex.2005).

On the jury trial issue under the Sarbanes–Oxley Act, there are few decisions and they are split. *Compare* Jones v. Home Fed. Bank, 2010 WL 996476 (D.Idaho 2010) *with* Fraser v. Fiduciary Trust Co. Int'l, 417 F.Supp.2d 310 (S.D.N.Y.2006).

3.   If an act provides for equitable relief, a monetary recovery is not precluded. It is not the mere fact that money is recovered that makes a remedy legal. The key is the *function* of the remedy. In *United States v. Price*, 688 F.2d 204 (3d Cir.1982), for example, the plaintiffs sought the funding of a diagnostic study. The study would concern the threat to a public water supply posed by toxic chemicals emanating from a landfill and the provision of an alternate water supply. The court held these remedies were permissible forms of equitable relief at common law and under certain federal environmental statutes. The court reasoned that although the study would require the payment of money, it would be preventive rather than compensatory in character. It nonetheless failed on procedural grounds.

The *Price* opinion, *supra,* articulated the distinction that compensating for past harm is a "damages" remedy and protecting against further harm is an "equitable" one. This distinction also played a determining role in Penn Terra Ltd. v. Department of Environmental Resources, 733 F.2d 267 (3d Cir.1984). In this case the Commonwealth obtained a consent decree requiring Penn Terra to perform reclamation work of coal surface mines to correct violations of certain state environmental protection statutes. Penn

Terra, however, failed to take the mandated remedial measures and filed a bankruptcy petition. The government, before receiving notice of the bankruptcy filing, obtained a preliminary injunction in state court to enforce the terms of the consent decree.

The issue presented to the bankruptcy court involved an interpretation of several sections of the automatic stay provisions of the bankruptcy code. The sections operate to halt the commencement or continuation of legal proceedings against the debtor while the bankruptcy administration is pending. Specifically, the controversy involved whether the government's injunction to correct the environmental violations constituted an exception to the stay as a valid exercise of its police power or was merely a veiled attempt to enforce a "money judgment" which would be susceptible to the automatic stay. The court of appeals recognized that compliance with the injunction would necessitate the expenditure of the debtor's funds, but held that it was not a money judgment because (1) the compensation was not payable to the government, (2) the reclamation obligation was not reduced to a sum certain, and (3) it was aimed at the prevention of future harm.

Was the court correct? The reclamation of the soil certainly would result in prospective benefits, yet the order would also rectify the past injuries to the environment. Competing policies may be readily seen in the court's decision. If a governmental unit can, through the form of an injunction, require a bankruptcy debtor to expend money to correct past harms several effects will necessarily follow: (a) the total funds in the debtor's estate otherwise available to compensate general creditors will be reduced or perhaps exhausted, (b) the government's position vis-a-vis other creditors may be viewed as a "super-priority" above the statutory scheme of payment priorities, and (c) it depletes the pool of assets which the debtor might have utilized to effect a successful reorganization and have a "fresh start." Conversely, the public interest, as expressed in the environmental protection statutes, deserves to be recognized and fully enforced. Where should the line be drawn?

4. In *Jaffee v. United States*, 592 F.2d 712 (3d Cir.1979), the plaintiff alleged that he had developed cancer as a result of radiation exposure while in the army. The court affirmed the district court's denial of an injunction which would have required the government to pay medical expenses. The opinion characterized the plaintiff's request for such expenditures as traditional tort damages rather than a proper subject for equitable relief. Accordingly, the court viewed the plaintiff's claim as an attempt to collect money damages rather than a request for an injunction. This difference was relevant procedurally because an injunction would have been appealable under 28 U.S.C. § 1291(a)(1).

The court also considered the legal or equitable nature of the plaintiff's request that the government be required to warn members of plaintiff's class about medical risks from their radiation exposure. On that issue it held: "The payment of money cannot satisfy this claim. Although providing the warning will impose an expense on the Government, the creation of expense does not necessarily remove a form of relief from the category of equitable remedies." This aspect of the appeal was considered a petition for an injunction such that its denial would be properly appealable.

5. Consider the relationship of interlocutory equitable relief and damages after trial. For example, in *Crawford v. University of North Carolina*, 440 F.Supp. 1047 (M.D.N.C.1977), the district court issued a preliminary injunction ordering the university to procure and pay an interpreter for the benefit of a deaf student. What difference would it make to the student that the remedy take the form of an injunction as opposed to receiving a money judgment?

Brunecz v. Houdaille Industries, Inc.

13 Ohio App.3d 106, 468 N.E.2d 370 (1983).

■ BROGAN, JUDGE:

Plaintiff-appellant, Thomas Brunecz, on August 7, 1980 brought an action in the Court of Common Pleas of Cuyahoga County, against defendant-appellee, Houdaille Industries, Inc., for wrongful discharge under R.C. 4123.90.

Plaintiff alleged that he was injured at his place of employment, and that defendant wrongfully discharged him because he filed a claim for compensation with the Bureau of Workers' Compensation. Plaintiff demanded reinstatement, back pay and reasonable attorney fees. He also made a demand for a jury trial. After an answer was filed by defendant, plaintiff moved for leave to amend his complaint, which was granted. The amendment deleted from the prayer the request for reinstatement. Defendant again answered with a general denial.

After a motion for summary judgment filed by defendant was overruled, the trial court referred the claim of plaintiff to arbitration. The board of arbitrators found for plaintiff in the sum of $1838, plus attorney fees. Defendant appealed to the trial court for a hearing *de novo*. Defendant also moved to strike the plaintiff's jury demand, * * * [asserting that] no jury trial right exists where a claim pursuant to R.C. 4123.90 is made. Plaintiff opposed said motion on the basis that * * * since the complaint was for money damages only, a jury trial existed under R.C. 2311.04. The trial was conducted without a jury and the trial court found for defendant.

* * *

Appellant brought his action against appellee for wrongful discharge under R.C. 4123.90 which reads in pertinent part:

"No employer shall discharge, demote, reassign, or take any punitive action against any employee because such employee filed a claim or instituted, pursued or testified in any proceedings under the workers' compensation act for an injury or occupational disease which occurred in the course of and arising out of his employment with that employer. Any such employee may file an action in the common pleas court of the county of such employment in which the relief which may be granted *shall be* *limited to reinstatement with back pay, if the action is based upon discharge,* or an award for wages lost if based upon demotion, reassignment, or punitive action taken, offset by earnings subsequent to discharge, demotion, reassignment, or punitive action taken * * * '' (Emphasis added.)

* * *

There is a conspicuous absence of any reference to a jury trial in R.C. 4123.90 because the remedy provided is essentially equitable in nature, *i.e.,* reinstatement. The back pay is merely a matter of arithmetic computation and ancillary to restoration of the claimant's job.

While we can find no Ohio case wherein a court has addressed the issue of a right to a jury trial in an R.C. 4123.90 action, federal case law has clearly indicated that employer discrimination claims brought under Title VII of the Civil Rights Act of 1964, which like R.C. 4123.90 limits relief to reinstatement and back pay, are clearly equitable in nature and that no right to a jury trial exists. For example, the Sixth Circuit Court of Appeals noted:

"A key dividing line between law and equity has historically been that the former deals with money damages and the latter with injunctive relief. *This distinction has been blurred by court decisions indicating that not all money damages claims will be deemed 'legal.'* * * * A common example is an employment discrimination claim brought under Title VII of the Civil Rights Act of 1964, 42 U.S.C. § 2000e *et seq. which seeks injunctive relief (i.e.* reinstatement) *and back pay.* Although the Supreme Court has never directly addressed this question, the courts of appeals have uniformly held *that no jury trial right exists.* * * * '' [Citations.]

In *Great American Fed. S. & L. Assn. v. Novotny* (1979), 442 U.S. 366, at 374–375, 99 S.Ct. 2345, at 2350, 60 L.Ed.2d 957, the Supreme Court in dicta commented on the right to a jury trial in an action pursuant to Title VII of the Civil Rights Act of 1964:

"The Act provides for injunctive relief, specifically including back pay relief. * * * Because the Act expressly authorizes only equitable remedies, the courts have consistently held that neither party has a right to a jury trial."

* * * We find the federal cases interpreting the Title VII discrimination suits to be persuasive. Relief under R.C. 4123.90 is equitable in nature. The fact that appellant amended his complaint to give up his claim for reinstatement does not convert his claim under R.C. 4123.90 into a legal one triable to a jury. The assignment of error is overruled.

The judgment of the trial court is affirmed.

---

1. The entitlement to a jury is different under state and federal law. The Seventh Amendment of the federal Constitution provides a right to a

jury in all cases "at law," but the Supreme Court has applied the right only to federal courts; it does not apply to the states. States thus are free to interpret their own state constitutional and common law rights. The right to a trial by jury is covered more extensively in Chapter 18.

2. As the principal case reflects, the most common method used to determine the right to a trial by jury is whether the remedy sought is considered a legal or equitable remedy. Historically there was a right to a trial by jury at law, but not in equity. This historical approach, sometimes called the analogical approach, requires courts to analogize a cause of action to historical counterparts.

When statutes are involved, courts pay close attention to the remedial provisions to determine the essential nature of the remedy sought. If it is legal, there is a right to a jury trial. If it is equitable, there is no jury right. What if there are mixed legal and equitable remedies sought? This topic is covered in Chapter 18.

3. The court in the principal case analogizes to federal employment discrimination law where parties are not entitled to a jury trial when only equitable relief is sought. In cases claiming intentional discrimination, federal employment discrimination plaintiffs with a claim under Title VII may now recover compensatory and punitive damages. When such damages are claimed, either party may demand a jury trial. When the claim is not one for intentional discrimination, or when the plaintiff seeks only equitable relief for whatever reason, there is no right to a jury trial.

4. Reconsider the jury trial issue reserved in *Hanna v. WCI Communities*, reproduced earlier in this section. On the basis of this introduction to the issue of jury trial rights, what do you expect the parties to argue in *Hanna*?

Pollard v. E.I. du Pont de Nemours & Co.

532 U.S. 843, 121 S.Ct. 1946, 150 L.Ed.2d 62 (2001).

■ JUSTICE THOMAS delivered the opinion of the Court.

This case presents the question whether a front pay award is an element of compensatory damages under the Civil Rights Act of 1991. We conclude that it is not.

Petitioner Sharon Pollard sued her former employer, E.I. du Pont de Nemours and Company (DuPont), alleging that she had been subjected to a hostile work environment based on her sex, in violation of Title VII of the Civil Rights Act of 1964, 78 Stat. 253, 42 U.S.C. § 2000e *et seq.* After a trial, the District Court found that Pollard was subjected to co-worker sexual harassment of which her supervisors were aware. The District Court further found that the harassment resulted in a medical leave of absence from her job for psychological assistance and her eventual dismissal for refusing to return to the same hostile work environment. The court awarded Pollard $107,364 in backpay and benefits, $252,997 in attorney's fees, and, as relevant here, $300,000 in compensatory damages—the maximum permitted under the statutory cap for such damages in 42 U.S.C. § 1981a(b)(3). The Court of Appeals affirmed, concluding that the record demonstrated that DuPont employees engaged in flagrant discrimination based on sex and that DuPont managers and supervisors did not take adequate steps to stop it.

The issue presented for review here is whether front pay constitutes an element of "compensatory damages" under 42 U.S.C. § 1981a and thus is subject to the statutory damages cap imposed by that section. Although courts have defined "front pay" in numerous ways, front pay is simply money awarded for lost compensation during the period between judgment and reinstatement or in lieu of reinstatement. For instance, when an appropriate position for the plaintiff is not immediately available without displacing an incumbent employee, courts have ordered reinstatement upon the opening of such a position and have ordered front pay to be paid until reinstatement occurs. * * *

Under § 706(g) of the Civil Rights Act of 1964 as originally enacted, when a court found that an employer had intentionally engaged in an unlawful employment practice, the court was authorized to "enjoin the respondent from engaging in such unlawful employment practice, and order such affirmative action as may be appropriate, which may include, but is not limited to, reinstatement or hiring of employees, with or without back pay." 42 U.S.C. § 2000e–5(g)(1). * * *

In 1972, Congress expanded § 706(g) to specify that a court could, in addition to awarding those remedies previously listed in the provision, award "any other equitable relief as the court deems appropriate." After this amendment to § 706(g), courts endorsed a broad view of front pay. * * *

In 1991, without amending § 706(g), Congress further expanded the remedies available in cases of intentional employment discrimination to include compensatory and punitive damages. See 42 U.S.C. § 1981a(a)(1). * * *

In the abstract, front pay could be considered compensation for "future pecuniary losses," in which case it would be subject to the statutory cap, and, out of context, its ordinary meaning could include all payments for monetary losses after the date of judgment. However, we must not analyze one term of § 1981a in isolation. [Citation.] When § 1981a is read as a whole, the better interpretation is that front pay is not within the meaning of compensatory damages in § 1981a(b)(3), and thus front pay is excluded from the statutory cap.

In the Civil Rights Act of 1991, Congress determined that victims of employment discrimination were entitled to *additional* remedies. Congress expressly found that "additional remedies under Federal law are needed to deter unlawful harassment and intentional discrimination in the workplace," without giving any indication that it wished to curtail previously available remedies. See Civil Rights Act of 1991, 105 Stat. 1071, § 2. Congress therefore made clear through the plain language of the statute that the remedies newly authorized under § 1981a were *in addition to* the relief authorized by § 706(g). Section 1981a(a)(1) provides that, in intentional discrimination cases brought under Title VII, "the complaining party may recover compensatory and punitive damages as allowed in subsection (b) of [§ 1981a], *in addition to any relief authorized by section 706(g) of the Civil Rights Act of 1964*, from the respondent." (Emphasis added.) And § 1981a(b)(2) states that "[c]ompensatory damages awarded under [§ 1981a] shall not include backpay, interest on backpay, *or any other type of relief authorized under section 706(g) of the Civil Rights Act of 1964*." (Emphasis added.) According to these statutory provisions, if front pay was a type of relief authorized under § 706(g), it is excluded from the meaning of compensatory damages under § 1981a.

* * * [T]he original language of § 706(g) authorizing backpay awards was modeled after the same language in the NLRA. This provision in the NLRA had been construed to allow awards of backpay up to the date of reinstatement, even if reinstatement occurred after judgment. Accordingly, backpay awards made for the period between the date of judgment and the date of reinstatement, which today are called front pay awards under Title VII, were authorized under § 706(g).

As to front pay awards that are made in lieu of reinstatement, we construe § 706(g) as authorizing these awards as well. We see no logical difference between front pay awards made when there eventually is reinstatement and those made when there is not.[3] Moreover, to distinguish between the two cases would lead to the strange result that employees could receive front pay when reinstatement eventually is available but not when reinstatement is not an option—whether because of continuing hostility between the plaintiff and the employer or its workers, or because of psychological injuries that the discrimination has caused the plaintiff. Thus, the most egregious offenders could be subject to the least sanctions. Had Congress drawn such a line in the statute and foreclosed front pay awards in lieu of reinstatement, we certainly would honor that line. But, as written, the text of the statute does not lend itself to such a distinction, and we will not create one. The statute authorizes courts to "order such affirmative action as may be appropriate." 42 U.S.C. § 2000e–5(g)(1). We conclude that front pay awards in lieu of reinstatement fit within this statutory term.

Because front pay is a remedy authorized under § 706(g), Congress did not limit the availability of such awards in § 1981a. Instead, Congress sought to expand the available remedies by permitting the recovery of compensatory and punitive damages in addition to previously available remedies, such as front pay.

* * *

---

3. We note that the federal courts consistently have construed § 706(g) as authorizing front pay awards in lieu of reinstatement. See, *e.g., Blum v. Witco Chem. Corp., supra,* at 383 ("A front pay ... award is the monetary equivalent of the equitable remedy of reinstatement"); *Williams v. Pharmacia, Inc., supra,* at 952 (stating that "front pay is the functional equivalent of reinstatement").

The judgment of the Court of Appeals is reversed, and the case is remanded for further proceedings consistent with this opinion.

It is so ordered.

---

1.   The Supreme Court in *Pollard* resolved a split that had emerged among the circuit courts concerning the proper classification of front pay awards in light of the statutory provision that put a cap on compensatory and punitive damages. Most courts concluded that front pay was simply a substitute equitable remedy in the absence of the equitable remedy of reinstatement. See, *e.g., Pals v. Schepel Buick & GMC Truck, Inc.,* 220 F.3d 495 (7th Cir.2000); *Kramer v. Logan County School Dist. No. R–1,* 157 F.3d 620 (8th Cir.1998).

2.   The Sixth Circuit, which had been the first to consider the issue in *Hudson v. Reno,* 130 F.3d 1193 (6th Cir.1997), came to the conclusion that front pay was covered by the damages cap. That opinion focused on the statutory term "compensatory damages ... for future pecuniary losses" and, in the absence of a definition in the act, relied upon the dictionary definition for those term rather than upon the legal history of front pay as an equitable remedy. The *Pollard* case arose in the Sixth Circuit and thus provided a good opportunity for the Supreme Court to resolve the conflict in the circuits.

Does the Supreme Court opinion focus upon the equitable nature of front pay in its decision? Why is it relevant to this case that the historical roots of front pay are in equity rather than in law?

PART II

INJUNCTIONS AND SPECIFIC PERFORMANCE

CHAPTER 3

PREVENTIVE INJUNCTIONS

A preventive injunction is a court order designed to avoid future harm to a plaintiff by controlling a defendant's behavior. The injunction is "preventive" in the sense of avoiding harm; the term does not refer to the wording of the order. The wording may be either prohibitory ("Do not trespass") or mandatory ("Remove the obstruction"). A preventive injunction is traditional equitable relief in private law, such as an injunction against trespass. Chapter 8 covers other types of injunctions that are more recent developments of public law, such as structural injunctions for institutional reform. The present chapter begins the study of injunctive relief with traditional equity considerations: inadequacy of the remedy at law, irreparable harm, relative hardships, practicality, and public interest.

A.   INADEQUACY OF REMEDY AT LAW

Section Coverage:

Courts traditionally cite the maxim that equity will not grant relief when the remedy at law, usually damages, is adequate. History explains the rule better than logic, but the rule still has force to restrict the availability of equitable remedies. Although it is rare for opinions to contain lengthy considerations of the abstract proposition of "adequacy," courts frequently invoke the rule as a shorthand explanation for granting or denying equitable relief. In cases involving interests in real property, as one example, courts often say that the uniqueness of each parcel of land makes damages inadequate to compensate losses. If the threatened loss concerned a contract for the purchase of land a judge could grant specific performance, as studied in the next chapter.

The present chapter examines injunctions to protect non-contractual interests, such as invasions of land. A court may enjoin a trespass if damages would be too speculative, if multiple damage actions would be necessary, or if special circumstances warrant extraordinary relief. Other groups of interests typically covered by the inadequacy at law standard are intangible business interests, nuisances, and civil rights.

Model Case:

Plaintiff CompuGame is in the business of selling computer games. Defendant PC–Fun is a competitor that maliciously tries to hurt the plaintiff's reputation for quality games. A clever programmer at PC–Fun devised a devious method for doing so. The PC–Fun games contain a secret code that does its work whenever a consumer installs a new PC–Fun game on a personal computer. The code searches for other programs on the computer that are CompuGame programs. When one is found, the secret code scrambles just a little of the CompuGame program so that it will malfunction every fourth time it is played.

The defendant's purpose is to gain a competitive advantage. Because many of PC–Fun's customers also purchase CompuGame products, the effect is to make the PC–Fun games appear better than those of the rival. Consumers are annoyed to find that CompuGame products malfunction periodically. They conclude that CompuGame makes worse games than PC–Fun ones, which rarely malfunction.

This practice was discovered when a disgruntled PC–Fun employee quit and told CompuGame of the malicious practice. CompuGame sues PC–Fun. A court of equity would enjoin the defendant from engaging in the practice in the future because the plaintiff's remedy at law is inadequate. First, damages for lost customers and future sales would be very speculative. Second, even if damages were ascertainable, the plaintiff would have to return to court repeatedly to sue for future losses caused by Defendant's continuing conduct. Courts enjoin conduct if a multiplicity of suits would otherwise be necessary for redress.

Thurston Enterprises, Inc. v. Baldi

128 N.H. 760, 519 A.2d 297 (1986).

■ BATCHELDER, JUSTICE. * * *

Thurston operated a marina. On adjoining property, Baldi operated a drive-in movie theater. In 1978, Baldi sold part of his land to Thurston. The transferred land was rocky, steep, and covered with slash. Baldi knew Thurston planned to develop the land into parking and boat storage facilities for the marina. Although there is now an alternative access, the only way vehicles could reach it at the time Baldi sold the land was to travel over Baldi's drive-in theater. Consequently, Baldi deeded Thurston an easement across the theater.

The easement is a fifty foot wide specified course. It begins at the theater entrance on Route 3, passes under the theater marquee, continues past the ticket booth, which sits roughly in the center of the right-of-way, and crosses the theater lot to Thurston's parcel. * * *

In the spring of 1979, Thurston began using the easement to truck fill into his parcel. The light paving was not designed for heavy truck traffic. * * * The ten-wheel trucks were too high to pass under the marquee and too wide to stay on the right-of-way as it deflected around the ticket booth. Consequently, Thurston's trucks swung around the marquee and deviated from the right-of-way into speaker aisles 1–3. The trucks destroyed the pavement and caused deep ruts in the earth, both in the right-of-way and in the speaker aisles. * * *

The master concluded that, at the time of the conveyance, neither party contemplated such extensive use of heavy trucks. He found that Thurston had caused the destruction of the surface and sub-surface of the right-of-way by using the easement unreasonably and by enlarging upon the granted easement. Accordingly, he ordered Thurston to repave the right-of-way. * * * Thurston was ordered to repair the speaker aisles, limit his trucks to no more than five per day, and to rebuild the rutted right-of-way. * * *

* * * The grantee of the easement, who is the possessor of the dominant estate, must use the easement reasonably, [citation.], so as not to damage the possessory interest of the grantor, who is the possessor of the servient estate upon which the easement lies, [citation]. Injunctive actions, such as the present claim and counterclaim, look to prevent future conduct rather than to remedy past conduct. [Citation.] Thus, injunctions issue only to prevent imminent irreparable harm. [Citation.] Because the separation between law and equity is not sharp, courts in New Hampshire have broad discretion in exercising equity jurisdiction. [Citation.] Nonetheless, equitable jurisdiction lies only when there is no plain and complete remedy at law. Applying these jurisdictional rules to easements, in an equitable action to determine the scope of rights in an easement, the remedy will ordinarily be limited to future conduct affecting the reasonable use of the easement and possession of the servient estate.

Thus, because the orders to repair look to remedy the effects of past conduct, we vacate them. Those issues involve legal questions of damage. * * * We respectfully advise the superior court to allow the parties to litigate these damage issues in the severed action, with leave to amend their pleadings if necessary. We emphasize, however, that our decision to vacate these rulings does not mean Thurston has no prospective duty to maintain the right-of-way.

[Remanded.]

---

1. Whether at law or in equity, the defendant in the principal case will have to pay for the cost of repairing the drive-in. Does it matter whether the court makes an equitable order to repair or gives a legal damage remedy equal to the cost? One practical difference is the greater use of judicial resources in an equitable decree because the court retains jurisdiction of the case while the defendant complies with the order. Other differences between law and equity include the availability of a jury trial (*see* Chapter 18) and the method of enforcement (*see* Chapter 7). If the court issues an injunction and the defendant does not arrange for satisfactory repairs, the plaintiff returns to court with evidence that the defendant disobeyed the order. In contrast, a damages remedy gives the plaintiff money to undertake the necessary repairs as the plaintiff sees fit, without further interaction with the defendant or the court unless the plaintiff encounters difficulty with obtaining satisfaction of the judgment.

2. *Multiplicity of Lawsuits.* Damages for past losses is the province of law, but prevention of a multiplicity of future suits for damages is a ground for equitable relief. For example, in *Berin v. Olson*, 183 Conn. 337, 439 A.2d 357 (1981), the plaintiff sued for water damage caused by the discharge of surface water onto his land by the adjoining landowner. The plaintiff received damages for past losses plus an injunction prohibiting future diversions of water onto his land. The court rejected the defendant's argument that the damage recovery proves the adequacy at law because the basis for the injunctive relief was the probable multiplicity of future suits. *Id.* at 360. *See also* 4 Pomeroy, Equity Jurisprudence (5th ed. Symonds) § 1357.

3. *Inadequacy for Remedial Equity.* The inadequacy limitation applies only to remedial equity, not to substantive equity. Substantive equity, distinguished previously in Chapter 1, allows a cause of action for certain types of interests—like trusts, mortgages, and stockholders' derivative actions—without consideration of adequacy. The Supreme Court noted this distinction in the context of Seventh Amendment rights to jury trials. Ross v. Bernhard, 396 U.S. 531, 90 S.Ct. 733, 24 L.Ed.2d 729 (1970).

4. *Probability of Future Infringement.* As the principal case reflects, injunctive relief requires proof that the defendant is likely to repeat the wrongful behavior in the future. What kind of proof can a plaintiff present to make that proof? Consider a securities case where the defendants failed to follow securities laws by fraudulently violating the prospectus delivery requirement. What evidence should the plaintiff Securities and Exchange Commission use to convince the court that the defendants have a reasonable likelihood of repeating the wrong? See Securities and Exchange Commission v. Manor Nursing Centers, Inc., 458 F.2d 1082 (2d Cir. 1972).

PROBLEM: THE BORROWED LOT

A commercial trucking company named Wheelco does not have a big enough parking lot. Wheelco's owner has instructed employees to park trucks on the vacant lot next door when the Wheelco lot is full. That lot belongs to Landry, who is keeping the property for a long-term investment. Landry is not using the lot and has no immediate plans to use it.

Wheelco engaged in this practice for several months without Landry's knowledge. Landry eventually discovered the trespass and contacted Wheelco's owner to complain. The owner offered Landry a rental fee which Landry rejected as low. Since then Wheelco has continued to use Landry's lot when needed. Other calls from Landry to Wheelco have produced only insincere promises to stop and repetition of the offer to rent. Landry has countered with an offer to rent at a high rate. Wheelco rejects the high rate and simply ignores the request to stop trespassing.

Landry has contacted you to see if you could get a court order to keep Wheelco off the lot. Would an injunction be appropriate? Consider the case and notes that follow.

Wheelock v. Noonan

108 N.Y. 179, 15 N.E. 67 (1888).

■ FINCH, J.

The findings of the trial court establish that the defendant, who was a total stranger to the plaintiff, obtained from the latter a license to place upon his unoccupied lots, in the upper part of the city of New York, a few rocks for a short time, the indefiniteness of the period having been rendered definite by the defendant's assurance that he would remove them in the spring. Nothing was paid or asked for this permission, and it was not a contract in any just sense of the term, but merely a license which by its terms expired in the next spring. During the winter, and in the absence and without the knowledge of plaintiff, the defendant covered six of the lots of plaintiff with "huge quantities of rock," some of them 10 or fifteen feet long, and piled to the height of 14 to 18 feet. This conduct was a clear abuse of the license, and in excess of its terms, and so much so that if permission had been sought upon a truthful statement of the intention it would undoubtedly have been refused. In the spring the plaintiff, discovering the abuse of his permission, complained bitterly of defendant's conduct, and ordered him to remove the rocks to some other locality. The defendant promised to do so, but did not, and in the face of repeated demands has neglected and omitted to remove the rocks from the land. The court found as a matter of law from these facts that the original permission given did not justify what was done, either as it respected the quantity of rock or the time allowed; that after the withdrawal of the permission in the spring, and the demand for the removal of the rock, the defendant was a trespasser, and the trespass was a continuing one which entitled plaintiff to equitable relief; and awarded judgment requiring defendant to remove the rocks before March 15, 1886, unless for good cause shown the time for such removal should be extended by the court.

The sole question upon this appeal is whether the relief granted was within the power of the court, and the contention of the defendant is mainly based upon the proposition that the equitable relief was improper since there was an adequate remedy at law. * * * [P]arol license, founded upon no consideration, is revocable at pleasure, even though the licensee may have expended money on the faith of it. [Citation.] And this was a continuing trespass. So long as it lasted it encumbered the lots, prevented their use and occupation by the owner, and interfered with the possibility of a sale. It is now said that the remedy was at law, that the owner could have removed the stone and then recovered of the defendant for the expense incurred. But to what locality could the owner remove them? He could not put them in the street; the defendant presumably had no vacant lands of his own on which to throw the burden; and it would follow that the owner would be obliged to hire some vacant lot or place of deposit, become responsible for the rent, and advance the cost of men and machinery to effect the removal. * * *

But it is further said that he could sue at law for the trespass. That is undoubtedly true. * * * [But there is] abundant authority that in such action only the damages to its date could be recovered, and for the subsequent continuance of the trespass new actions following on in succession would have to be maintained. But in a case like the present, would that be an adequate remedy? In each action the damages could not easily be anything more than the fair rental of the lot. It is difficult to see what other damages could be allowed, not because they would not exist, but because they would be quite uncertain in amount and possibly somewhat speculative in their character. The defendant, therefore, might pay those damages, and continue his occupation, and if there were no other adequate remedy, defiantly continue such occupation, and in spite of his wrong make of himself in effect a tenant who could not be dispossessed. * * * [W]hile, ordinarily, courts of equity will not wield their power merely to redress a trespass, yet they will interfere under peculiar circumstances, and have often done so where the trespass was a continuing one, and a multiplicity of suits at law was involved in the legal remedy. * * *

[Affirmed.]

---

1.   Is the availability of damages a meaningful test for whether to issue an injunction? Would such an absolute test make all injunctions theoretically impossible?

What if the defendant were willing to pay the amount of damages in order to continue use of plaintiff's land? He would then become the forced tenant of an unwilling landlord with the "rent" being the damages imposed by the court. If the damages are measured as the "fair rental value" of the land, the defendant has no incentive to remove the rocks. Only a high damage award would create the incentive to move. Should a court choose a measure of damages to affect the defendant's future conduct or to measure the plaintiff's past loss?

2.   *Future Infringements*. The plaintiff must establish the probability that the defendant will make future infringements of the plaintiff's rights. A *continuing* trespass, such as the one in the main case, requires a showing that the defendant will not follow a demand to vacate. *See, e.g.,* Lucy Webb Hayes National Training School for Deaconesses and Missionaries v. Geoghegan, 281 F.Supp. 116 (D.D.C.1967) (patient at private hospital no longer needed medical care but husband refused hospital's repeated demands to arrange transfer of patient to nursing home).

A pattern of *repeated* trespasses requires a showing that the defendant is likely to continue to repeat the invasions in knowing violation of the plaintiff's rights. *See, e.g.,* Thomas v. Weller, 204 Neb. 298, 281 N.W.2d 790 (1979) (duck hunter enjoined from annual trespasses on neighboring land); Phillips v. Wertz, 546 S.W.2d 902 (Tex.Civ.App.1977) (hedge repeatedly knocked down by neighbor during construction).

3. *Trespass by Trash.* The remedy at law is considered adequate if the defendant simply littered the plaintiff's land with trash; the plaintiff can pay for someone to remove the trash and then sue the defendant for the cost incurred. *See* Connor v. Grosso, 41 Cal.2d 229, 259 P.2d 435 (1953) (liability is limited to costs to remove defendant's trash, not a general clean-up). What if the "trash" dumped is snow shoveled off the defendant's land onto plaintiff's neighboring property? *Compare* Marder v. Realty Construction Co., 43 N.J. 508, 205 A.2d 744 (1964) (damages for use of land by dumping snow, parking cars, and placing trash cans on neighbor's property).

4. *Waste.* Injunctive relief is appropriate to prevent ongoing waste, even though there are legal remedies available, if the injunction is necessary to halt immediate serious injury to the detriment of the inheritance. *See, e.g.,* Allegheny Development Corp. v. Barati, 166 W.Va. 218, 273 S.E.2d 384 (1980) (removing top soil, rock, and road building material).

5. The court in the principal case refers to the "old rule" that an oral license without consideration can be revoked even if the licensee has incurred expenses in good faith. Should every trespass resulting from such revocation support an injunction, or should the court consider the relative hardships of the parties? Should the good or bad faith of either party be relevant to the equity determination? These issues are addressed by the materials in sections C and D of this chapter, *infra.* The substantive law may affect the result by finding that the good faith reliance has created an easement. *See* Stoner v. Zucker, 148 Cal. 516, 83 P. 808 (1906) (oral license allowing defendant to construct ditch on plaintiff's land could not be revoked because defendant's expenditures in reasonable reliance created an easement).

Should good faith and relative hardship affect the substantive right, the available remedy, or both? Do you think that the apparent lack of good faith by the defendant in the principal case affected the court's determination of the inadequacy of the damage remedy at law for the cost of removing the stones?

B. IRREPARABLE HARM

Section Coverage:

Courts frequently say that equity will aid a suitor only if the threatened future harm would be "irreparable." This requirement is usually just an alternative phrasing of the inadequacy rule; the harm is irreparable because the damage remedy is inadequate. In some jurisdictions, however, irreparable harm is considered a separate requirement and the plaintiff must show not only that the remedy at law is inadequate but that the harm threatened is great. Arguably this test avoids burdening the courts with trivialities, although in practice the irreparable harm rule overlaps significantly with the inadequacy of the remedy at law requirement.

Model Case:

Plaintiff homeowner is annoyed that Defendant neighbor's dog Rover makes a practice of trotting across plaintiff's yard when going to and from defendant's house. Plaintiff's petition for an injunction should be denied because the harm done by the dog's repeated trespasses is not great and irreparable. The Plaintiff's use and enjoyment of the land is not substantially impaired, unless special circumstances are shown. The adequate remedy at law is nominal damages or sanctions provided by a leash law ordinance.

K–Mart Corp. v. Oriental Plaza, Inc.

875 F.2d 907 (1st Cir.1989).

■ SELYA, CIRCUIT JUDGE.

Concerned that its landlord's word was somewhat shy of its bond, plaintiff-appellee K–Mart Corporation (K–Mart), a tenant at the Oriental Plaza Shopping Center (the Center) in Humacao, Puerto Rico, brought suit in federal district court against the Center's owner, defendant-appellee Oriental Plaza, Inc. (OPI). K–Mart asserted that OPI had perpetrated a breach of the lease agreement (the Lease) between the two corporations. At the bottom line, the question presented on appeal is whether the court below erred in ordering mandatory injunctive relief in plaintiff's favor. Seeing nothing amiss, we affirm.

The parties entered into the Lease on September 21, 1983. During the negotiations, both sides were concerned with possible future construction of retail space in areas of the Center reserved for parking. The Lease resolved these concerns by the inclusion of two key covenants: OPI would build no more than 10,000 sq. ft. of retail space in the parking area north of K–Mart's store (*i.e.,* between its premises and the neighboring Pueblo Supermarket), and any such new construction would not deviate from an agreed site plan without K–Mart's express written consent.

* * *

[As promised in the lease, the defendant presented K–Mart with a site plan for the development of the rest of the shopping center. After considerable discussion and alteration of the plans, K–Mart eventually approved a plan. Construction began, however, according to an earlier version of the plan that K–Mart had rejected. It took eleven weeks for K–Mart to realize the deviation. At that point the construction was nearly complete.]

K–Mart's verified complaint and motion for preliminary injunction were docketed on June 22, 1988. The complaint asserted that the development violated the Lease and harmed plaintiff in that parking near its store would be reduced; traffic congestion would be increased; plaintiff's store and signage would be obstructed; and in the bargain, the chances of impulse shopping were lessened. * * *

A written decision was soon issued. The court held that defendant had breached the Lease. It concluded that injunctive relief was merited, emphasizing that "K–Mart cannot recoup, even through legal damages, the injury to its goodwill caused by the visual obstruction of its store." In settling upon remediation, the court ordered OPI to raze the southernmost structure under construction and to replace it with no fewer than 30 parking spaces within 60 days. The court allowed completion of the two restaurant buildings, but permanently enjoined further development in the parking area except in strict compliance with the Lease.

* * *

[The court affirmed the district court's finding that K–Mart was not at fault for failure to discover for eleven weeks that the construction was the plan that it had disapproved rather than the one that it had approved.]

Appellant's last line of defense is that, even if K–Mart was entitled to some relief, money damages would have been an adequate anodyne. Although the question may be arguable, we believe that the lower court acted within its proper province.

A district court may grant injunctive relief to a prevailing plaintiff to correct an injury which would, absent an injunction, be irreparable. The irreparability of the injury is of paramount concern. [Citation.] The necessary concomitant of irreparable harm is the inadequacy of traditional legal remedies. The two are flip sides of the same coin: if money damages will fully alleviate harm, then the harm cannot be said to be irreparable.

* * *

Here, the district court found OPI guilty of a breach of the Lease and found the harm to K–Mart from construction of the southernmost building irremediable. It stated that "K–Mart cannot recoup, even through legal damages, the injury to its goodwill caused by the visual obstruction of its store." The court went on to explain that the harm did not consist merely of lost sales (in themselves difficult to calculate and monetize), but also involved a detriment in "presentation of the store to the public," detracting from the desired uniformity in appearance among K–Mart's stores across the nation. These factual findings may not be inevitable, but they derive acceptable support from the record. The court below received photographic and testimonial evidence that the offending construction blocked public view of K–Mart's building from the highway, that it interfered with the store's "presence" (an item bargained for in the lease negotiations), that it lessened available parking, and that it interfered with both vehicular maneuverability and pedestrian safety.

* * * Real estate has long been thought unique, and thus, injuries to real estate interests frequently come within the ken of the chancellor. Then, too, harm to goodwill, like harm to reputation, is the type of harm not readily measurable or fully compensable in damages—and for that reason, more likely to be found "irreparable." * * *

1.   *Equity Jurisdiction.* Courts have often used the phrase "equity jurisdiction" to refer simply to the propriety of granting equitable relief. *See, e.g., Lashe v. Northern York County School Dist.,* 52 Pa.Cmwlth. 541, 417 A.2d 260 (1980) (equity jurisdiction describes remedies available whereas subject matter jurisdiction concerns the power of the court to act at all). The inadequacy rule was originally applied by the Chancellor in the sixteenth century to determine whether to take a case or to leave the petitioner to go to the law courts with a writ for relief. *See* W. Blackstone, *Commentaries* *46–*55; F. Maitland, *Equity* 7 (1930).

Although there was some historical justification for the term "jurisdiction," the use of the word in modern law is unduly confusing. The phrase "equity jurisdiction" does not refer to the power of the court in the sense that subject matter jurisdiction and personal jurisdiction concern the court's power. Instead the concept refers to the appropriateness of equitable relief in light of the adequacy of the remedy at law, the irreparability of future harm to the plaintiff, the relative hardships of the parties, and the public interest. If a court erroneously concludes that equitable relief should be granted, a defendant must appeal the case and cannot collaterally attack the order by disobedience on the ground that the court lacked "jurisdiction." *See* Z. Chafee, Jr., *Some Problems of Equity* 296–336 (1950).

2.   In *Compute–A–Call, Inc. v. Tolleson,* 285 Ark. 355, 687 S.W.2d 129 (1985), parties to a contract claim sought relief in the court of chancery for money due. The judge granted an injunction and ordered the defendants to pay several installments into the registry of the court. The order was reversed on appeal because chancery lacked equity jurisdiction. The appellate opinion explained:

> The prospect of irreparable harm or lack of an otherwise adequate remedy is at the foundation of the power to issue injunctive relief. Harm is normally only considered irreparable when it cannot be adequately compensated by money damages or redressed in a court of law. [Citation.] Money damages are the only damages asked in this case. The remedy at law is adequate. The chancellor erred in refusing to transfer the case to circuit court and erred in granting an injunction for money damages.

> The complaint does state that appellees suffered irreparable damage. However, such a conclusory allegation, with no statement of fact, is not sufficient to give equity jurisdiction.

3.   The trial judge has sole discretion in deciding whether a case is appropriate for equitable relief. The parties cannot by contract waive or confer "equity jurisdiction." *See* Sherrer v. Hale, 248 Ga. 793, 285 S.E.2d 714 (1982).

PROBLEM: THE WANDERING GOLF BALLS

The Williams family bought a home next to a country club golf course. The location of the ninth green is such that errant golf balls occasionally intrude onto their property. The Williams erected a fence, but the balls sail over it. The family's complaints to the country club have not abated the problem. The Williams seek an injunction against the club to require relocation of the ninth green. Is relief appropriate? Consider the case and notes that follow.

Muehlman v. Keilman

257 Ind. 100, 272 N.E.2d 591 (1971).

■ HUNTER, JUDGE.

* * * The action was brought by appellees, Paul A. Keilman and Lorraine Keilman, for an injunction and damages against appellants, Carl F. Muehlman, Jr. and Janice I. Muehlman. Appellees claimed appellants, over a period of four months, maliciously ran, started and raced the diesel engines of their two semi-trailer trucks at all times during the day and night immediately adjacent to the appellees' residence property and in close proximity to appellees' bedroom. It was further alleged that the noise and fumes were destructive to the health and comfort of appellees and their family in the use and occupation of their dwelling house and that it had rendered the use of said real estate unhealthy, undesirable, and annoying. It was asserted that such actions of the appellants constituted a nuisance, and appellees sought an injunction to have this nuisance permanently abated, claiming, in addition, damages in the amount of ten thousand dollars ($10,000.00). * * * The trial court found for appellees and granted a temporary injunction against appellants, enjoining and restraining them from starting, idling, and revving their trucks between the hours of 8:30 P.M. and 7:00 A.M. until a further hearing could be had on the permanent injunction. Appeal is taken from this injunction.

* * *

We cannot agree with appellants' contention that these actions cannot constitute a nuisance. Noise, in and of itself, has been held to sufficiently constitute a nuisance. * * *

Appellants next contend that there was a failure to show irreparable harm. * * * The general rule in Indiana is that if there is great injury and no adequate remedy at law then an injunction can be issued. [Citations.] Appellants cite the case of *Spurgeon v. Rhodes* (1906), 167 Ind. 1, 78 N.E. 228, which apparently requires that the harm be irreparable. However, this is essentially an exercise in semantics. Definitions of "irreparable injury" are somewhat sparse, but we agree with that found in Black's Law Dictionary 924 (4th ed. 1951):

"This phrase does not mean such an injury as is beyond the possibility of repair or beyond possible compensation in damages, or necessarily great damage, but includes an injury, whether great or small, which ought not to be submitted to, on the one hand, or inflicted, on the other; and which, because it is so large or so small, or is of such constant and frequent occurrence, or because no certain pecuniary standard exists for the measurement of damages, cannot receive reasonable redress in a court of law."

Thus, it can be seen that a standard of "irreparable injury" would be nearly synonymous with a standard of great harm coupled with no adequate remedy at law. In fact, the former might require a *less* stringent standard than the latter.

If plaintiff can show great damage and no adequate remedy at law, he is entitled to injunctive relief. A definition of "great damage" is difficult and will depend on the individual circumstances of each case. In the instant case, appellants' conduct has deprived appellees of their sleep which, if allowed to continue over an extended period could be extremely injurious to their health. Appellants' action clearly interfered with appellees' comfortable enjoyment of their property. We consider this sufficient to be considered great damage. Appellees too must show that they have no adequate remedy at law.

> "The power of a court of equity, in a proper case, to enjoin a nuisance is of long standing, and apparently has never been questioned since the earlier part of the eighteenth century. As in other cases of equity jurisdiction, it must appear that recovery of damages at law will not be an adequate remedy; but since equity regards every tract of land as unique, it considers that damages are not adequate where its usefulness is seriously impaired." William L. Prosser, Law of Torts 624 (3d ed. 1964).

In this instance, appellees' enjoyment has been substantially impaired. If their health is damaged it is difficult to perceive of a truly adequate remedy at law by which they could receive reparation for the injury done. Such conduct is of a continuing nature so that damages would then become a continuing occurrence and require repeated court actions for the complainant to receive reparation. It is extremely difficult to establish a fixed sum as damages for an injury of this sort; such matters as good health and enjoyment of one's property transcend material wealth and defy attempts to affix a price tag to them. * * * Clearly, in a case such as the one at bar, injunctive relief is a proper remedy.

* * * Evidence was presented by appellees that on numerous occasions they were awakened from their sleep by the noise from Muehlman's truck. Appellees testified as to the damaging effect this was having on their household. There was also testimony by other neighbors as to the interference with the enjoyment of their property caused by appellants' conduct and their annoyance with the manner in which Muehlman operated his trucks. Upon appellants' request, the trial judge himself viewed one of the trucks in front of the courthouse to discern the nature of the noise and fumes. This evidence is sufficient to uphold the trial court's judgment. * * *

Appellants' second contention is that the relative inconvenience, damage, and injury to them cannot be balanced by any benefit to the appellees under the circumstances. Appellants claim irreparable harm will result from the injunction if enforced; however, there is no evidence on the record to support this. Mr. Muehlman merely said he normally started work between 6:00 A.M. and 9:00 A.M. There was no testimony that he would be injured by precluding him from starting until 7:00 A.M., only that he sometimes started at 6:00 A.M. No showing was made that an occasional one hour delay would cause any harm at all. The time restrictions of the injunction seem a fairly reasonable compromise. * * *

Appellants rely on [Owen v. Phillips, 73 Ind. 284 (1881)]. * * * In the *Owen* case, appellants were trying to prevent a flour mill from rebuilding so that to allow the injunction would be to deny appellees' livelihood altogether. The court in that case recognized there must be a weighing of equities and interests when it said,

> "A lawful and useful business is not to be *destroyed* by injunction unless the necessity for doing so be strong, clear and urgent." (our emphasis) 73 Ind. at 290–291.

In the instant case, appellants have not shown that any extensive injury will result, much less a destruction of their livelihood. * * * [Affirmed.]

---

1. *Irreparability and Inadequacy.* The principal case suggests that irreparability may be a necessary component of inadequacy, but nonetheless accepts the historical characterization that there is a two-pronged test: inadequacy and great harm. Compare the observation of Judge Sobeloff: "In one sense, of course, the inadequate remedy requirement is indistinguishable from the irreparable injury requirement. The very thing which makes an injury 'irreparable' is the fact that no remedy exists to repair it." Bannercraft Clothing Co. v. Renegotiation Board, 466 F.2d 345, 356, n. 9 (D.C.Cir.1972), *rev'd on other grounds,* 415 U.S. 1, 94 S.Ct. 1028, 39 L.Ed.2d 123 (1974). He finds that there is a distinction, however, because "the irreparable injury rubric is intended to describe the quality or severity of the harm * * * [whereas] the inadequate remedy test looks to the possibilities of alternative modes of relief, however serious the initial injury." *Id.*

2. *Nuisance.* Courts frequently enjoin private nuisances, such as the one in the principal case, if the loss in the use or enjoyment of the property is great. If the interference is slight, equity will not intervene. For example, in *Nussbaum v. Lacopo*, 27 N.Y.2d 311, 317 N.Y.S.2d 347, 265 N.E.2d 762 (1970), the court denied relief to homeowners who sued a neighboring golf course. The proof showed that only "once or twice a week" errant golf balls were found in the bushes and fence area of the plaintiff's property. The court characterized these invasions as minimal intrusions not worthy of relief.

A number of cases have involved roots from trees or hedges protruding underground into neighboring property. Injunctive relief is available to abate the nuisance only if there is a "sensible injury," such as poisoning of other plants from roots of noxious trees. Otherwise equity will not grant relief even if there is a technical trespass cognizable at law. *See, e.g.,* Cannon v. Dunn, 145 Ariz. 115, 700 P.2d 502 (1985); Smith v. Holt, 174 Va. 213, 5 S.E.2d 492 (1939).

3.   There are problems in drafting an injunction when the nuisance arises from the conduct of third parties over whom the defendant has only indirect control. What if a line of customers waiting to see a movie completely block the sidewalk, thus interfering with access to a neighboring store? How should a court word an injunction against the theater owner? *See, e.g.,* Tushbant v. Greenfield's Inc., 308 Mich. 626, 14 N.W.2d 520 (1944) (restaurant ordered to have employees handle the lining up of customers outside).

4.   *Intangible Business Interests.* Irreparable harm sufficient to support an injunction is often found in cases involving intangible business interests, such as unauthorized use of customer lists. *See* Merrill Lynch, Pierce, Fenner & Smith, Inc. v. Stidham, 658 F.2d 1098 (5th Cir.1981).

C.   BALANCING INTERESTS AND PRACTICALITY CONSIDERATIONS

Section Coverage:

Injunctions are discretionary, not a matter of right. A judge may appropriately weigh the relative hardships of the parties in the matter and may consider any problems of practicality in enforcing an order. The factors of practicality and hardship can affect the case in two ways: the judge may consider them both in deciding whether to issue an injunction at all as well as in choosing the scope of the order.

Model Case:

Douglas, a former employee of Parker's health spa, quits work and establishes a rival spa in a near-by community that happens to be across the state line. The original employment contract contained a clause concerning post-employment conduct: Douglas could not compete against Parker in a wide geographic radius for a period of five years. The court could appropriately consider the relative hardships of the parties in deciding whether to enforce the noncompetition clause by injunction. Alternatively, the judge could narrow the scope of the order by changing the time period or radius of noncompetition. Another relevant consideration is the practical problem of enforcing an order that would operate out-of-state.

Triplett v. Beuckman

40 Ill.App.3d 379, 352 N.E.2d 458 (1976).

■ JONES, JUSTICE.

Plaintiffs appeal from a judgment for defendants rendered in a bench trial in plaintiffs' action for a mandatory injunction requiring defendants to remove a causeway access to an island and replace it with a bridge. * * *

On March 10, 1971, Susan Triplett, as executrix of the estate of Francis L. Wortman, and defendants entered into a written contract for the sale of certain real property from the Wortman estate to defendants. The property conveyed consisted of an island, with residential improvements, except for a riparian ten foot circumferential strip, which was retained by the grantor. Defendants were granted the right to use and cross that ten foot strip of land but not to improve it. The lake in which the island was located and all of the land surrounding the lake were also part of the estate of Francis L. Wortman. Defendants were granted "the right to recreational use" of the lake "jointly with the owners of said lake." They were also granted an easement "for roadway purposes" across a described portion of the land surrounding the lake to a bridge, "thence North across said bridge a distance of 60 feet more or less to the island."

The bridge referred to provided the only above-water access to the island. It was wooden; and at the time of the conveyance was in need of repair. According to his uncontradicted testimony, defendant Fred Beuckman attempted to obtain the assistance of plaintiffs in repairing the bridge not long after defendants began to occupy the island residence. However, in response to this request Susan Triplett had stated "that's not my baby, it's all yours." Thereafter defendants repaired the bridge by resurfacing it with concrete and iron reinforcing rods. These repairs proved unsuccessful when a portion of the bridge "gave way." Consequently, defendants removed the bridge, filled the same area with soil, rock, and concrete, paved the surface with asphalt, and covered the sides of the fill with stone.

According to the testimony of Susan Triplett and William Wortman, the removal of the bridge and construction of the causeway deprived the plaintiffs of the fastest or most convenient water access from some points along the lake to other points and cut off plaintiffs' ability to take advantage of the circular nature of the lake for boating and water-skiing activities. Plaintiffs introduced evidence that prior to the construction of the causeway they were able to boat and water-ski completely around the island by passing under the bridge. Accordingly the causeway constituted a severe restriction on the recreational use of their lake. In the opinion of Susan Triplett the property surrounding the lake would decrease in value as a consequence of the construction of the causeway.

Fred Beuckman, on the other hand, testified that at the time the bridge was removed "there was hardly any water underneath the bridge to start with. It was all dried up." In Beuckman's opinion it would not have been possible to water-ski under the bridge "unless you put wheels on the bottoms of the skis, cause there was no water there at all hardly."

Joan Beuckman testified that the causeway was "[m]uch more attractive" than the bridge. Additionally an engineer and two iron workers testified that they had advised defendants prior to the removal of the bridge that the bridge could not be sufficiently repaired and would have to be replaced.

Based upon the testimony and the trial court's personal viewing (by stipulation of the parties) of the causeway, the court found "[t]he entire result is a practical result to an unusual problem and presents a reasonably attractive access to the 'island' [now 'peninsula']." The court also found that any injury to plaintiffs because of the construction of the causeway "was occasioned by plaintiffs' joint and several acts of disinterest or refusal to cooperate," and refused to issue the requested injunction.

We are of the opinion that the trial court erred in refusing to issue a mandatory injunction requiring the removal of the causeway and reconstruction of the bridge. The easement in this case was determined by express grant. The grant fixed the passage over the water or lakebed as being "across" a bridge then in existence at a described location. * * * In light of the fact that the lake was and is used primarily for recreation, the limitation to access by bridge cannot be ignored. * * *

It is well settled that, in the absence of an agreement to the contrary, the owner of the easement has not only the right but the duty to keep the easement in repair, while the owner of the servient tenement has no duty to either put or keep the easement in repair. * * *

* * * Moreover, although the owner of the dominant estate has the duty to maintain and repair the easement, he cannot make a material alteration in the character of the easement, even though it be more to his convenience to do so, if the alteration places a greater burden upon the servient estate or interferes with the use and enjoyment of the servient estate by its owner. [Citations.]

In light of the above authorities, it is apparent that the duty to maintain and repair the bridge in the instant case was that of defendants, the Beuckmans. In destroying the bridge and constructing a causeway, defendants materially altered the character of the easement and increased the burden on the servient tenement. Plaintiffs are unable to use and enjoy that portion of the lake or lakebed which was previously accessible under the bridge, but which now is covered by the causeway. Plaintiffs had the right to have the bridge maintained and are entitled to injunctive relief; and the court below erred in refusing to grant that relief.

We expressly decline to conclude, however, that defendants should be required to reconstruct a bridge 60 feet in length. A court of chancery can balance the hardships involved and grant relief upon whatever terms it deems equitable when the owner of either the dominant or the servient estate interferes with the rights of the other, under a mistaken belief that he owns the area or structure in dispute. [Citation.] In the instant case both Susan Triplett and Fred Beuckman testified that they had thought that the Beuckmans owned the bridge as a result of the conveyance discussed above. It was under this mistaken belief that Fred Beuckman had the bridge removed.

* * *

We, of course, do not have, and cannot have, the benefit of a personal examination of the lake to determine what amount of water may have been in that part of the lake at the time the bridge was destroyed or at the time of the decision of the trial court. Nor do we know what amount of water may have been under the bridge at times prior to its removal or what amount might have been there in the future. The trial court had the opportunity of personal examination. Based upon that examination, the trial court should be able to determine the length of the bridge span necessary for the reasonable use of the water that can reasonably be expected to be in that portion of the lake. It may very well be that use can be made of some of the causeway and that a bridge of less than 60 feet is sufficient for recreational use of that portion of the lake. If so, the trial court, acting in equity, should frame the relief granted in such terms as will take those factors into account.

We, therefore, reverse the judgment of the trial court with respect to plaintiffs' complaint and remand for further proceedings consistent with this opinion.

Reversed and remanded with directions.

■ EBERSPACHER, JUSTICE (dissenting).

I agree, as the majority states, "A court of chancery can balance the hardships involved and grant relief upon whatever terms it deems equitable when the owner of either the dominant or the servient estate interferes with the rights of the other, under a mistaken belief that he owns the area or structure in dispute." That, however, is not the function of an intermediate reviewing court.

It appears that the trial court has applied that principle, after hearing the testimony and examining the premises. It has obviously balanced the hardships involved and granted relief upon terms it deemed equitable. The majority is saying, balance the hardships again and grant relief upon different terms which we consider equitable. If the principle is to be here applied, the uncontradicted testimony that there is and was at the point where the bridge existed, an inadequate amount of water to boat, ski or swim, has to be, and obviously was, taken into consideration.

---

1. *Balance of Hardships.* A plaintiff is not entitled to an injunction simply upon proof that an interest has been invaded and that the harm is great and irreparable. Proof of the wrong supports a damage recovery, but equitable relief is always at the discretion of the court. The relative hardship that the injunction would place on each party is an important consideration. The judge weighs how much the plaintiff would benefit by the injunction against the burden to the defendant. After the plaintiff shows irreparable harm from the defendant's conduct, the defendant may show the harm that would be caused by an order to change conduct. *See*

Muehlman v. Keilman, *supra* (curtailment of trucking business during certain hours).

2. The burden on the defendant is often economic, as in the principal case, but it need not be a dollar loss. In a 1926 opinion by Justice Cardozo, Yome v. Gorman, the petitioner sought an injunction to disinter the bodies of several relatives in order to move them to another cemetery with a different religious affiliation. The interests balanced in that case were the consciences of the deceased as expressed in their lifetimes, the motives and feelings of the survivors, and the sentiments and usages of the religious body which conferred the original right of burial. The opinion concluded that it is not possible to formulate a rule in such an opinion, but only "to exemplify a process." 242 N.Y. 395, 403, 152 N.E. 126, 129 (1926).

3. *Speech.* Another noneconomic burden that an injunction may impose is a restraint on speech. In the exceptional case where a court grants a restraint on speech, the injunction must be tailored to withstand Constitutional scrutiny and the value of what is protected by the injunction must be balanced against the important value of the First Amendment. The Supreme Court considered such an injunction against abortion protestors at a health clinic in Madsen v. Women's Health Center, Inc., 512 U.S. 753, 114 S.Ct. 2516, 129 L.Ed.2d 593 (1994). The Court held that a state court injunction restraining the protestors' speech is permissible if the rights of the parties are carefully balanced and the injunction narrowly tailored. States may issue injunctions that serve the governmental interest in protecting woman's freedom to seek lawful medical and counseling services, but such injunctions must also protect the protestors' right of speech because they could still be seen and heard from the clinic parking lots.

In *Madsen* the injunction established a 36–foot buffer zone around the clinic entrances, driveway and surrounding private property. It also imposed limited noise restrictions and provided for a 300–foot no-approach zone around the clinic and staff residences. The Court held that the provisions establishing a 36–foot buffer zone around the clinic entrances and driveway and imposing noise restrictions did not violate the First Amendment, but that the buffer zone on private property and the no-approach zone burdened more speech than necessary.

In another case involving abortion protestors, the Supreme Court considered the constitutionality of "fixed" and "floating" buffers in an injunction. In *Schenck v. Pro–Choice Network of Western N.Y.*, 519 U.S. 357, 117 S.Ct. 855, 137 L.Ed.2d 1 (1997), the injunction banned demonstrating within 15 feet of the clinic entrances, driveways, and parking lots (fixed buffer zones), and within 15 feet of any person or vehicle coming or going from the clinic (floating buffer zones) except that two individuals could go inside the buffer zones for sidewalk counseling. Those individuals within the buffer, however, were required to cease and desist their counseling if the patient so requested. This latter provision was upheld as an appropriate balance of rights, since the patient could terminate the right of the protestors to speak only within the buffer. The floating buffer zone concept was unconstitutional, however, because it created too much uncertainty about its parameters and thus would tend to burden speech. In contrast, the "fixed" buffers were permissible as necessary to ensure that people and vehicles trying to enter or exit the clinic could do so freely. *See also* Hill v. Colorado, 530 U.S. 703, 120 S.Ct. 2480, 147 L.Ed.2d 597 (2000) (state statute sufficiently narrow for balanced interests).

4. *Nuisance.* To obtain an injunction against a private nuisance, a plaintiff must establish more than the existence of an intentional nuisance. The unreasonableness of the activity must be established because it is an undue hardship to stifle a useful enterprise at a reasonable location by injunction. If there is sufficient social value to the activity, then it should continue to operate while it pays its way with damages to those privately harmed. *See* Prosser and Keeton on Torts, 5th edition, 1984, sec. 88A. The subjects of injunctions restraining speech and nuisances are treated more extensively as special issues in equity in Chapter 9.

PROBLEM: THE PERSISTENT SPOUSE

You are clerking for a state court appellate judge who is considering an appeal from an injunction entered against an ex-husband. The action was brought by the ex-wife who has successfully enjoined her former spouse from continuing to broadcast his belief that the couple is still married. The ex-wife formerly brought a successful action for divorce, but the ex-husband refuses to recognize it. He maintains that they are still married in the eyes of God, and he has repeatedly and belligerently told everyone who has any contact with the ex-wife that they are still married. The ex-wife has custody of their minor children and the ex-husband has weekend visitation rights with them.

This practice of insisting on the vitality of the marriage has caused considerable embarrassment for the ex-wife and has distressed their minor children. The ex-wife has attempted to develop relationships with other men, but the ex-husband has always contacted her dates to proclaim that they are interfering with his marriage and, as a result, they do not continue to date her. The children have found their father's insistence on this subject to be painful and confusing.

The district court issued an injunction prohibiting the ex-husband from further representation that the ex-wife remains married to him. The ex-husband appeals on the grounds that the injunction fails to give adequate consideration to his First Amendment rights of free speech and religion.

Your judge has concluded that an injunction against speech is a permissible restraint under the First Amendment in this circumstance, but that it should be tailored as narrowly as possible to preserve the ex-husband's First Amendment rights while still protecting the reputational interest of the ex-wife and the emotional interest of the minor children. Your judge asks you for ideas about how on remand the injunction could be more narrowly tailored.

Galella v. Onassis

353 F.Supp. 196 (S.D.N.Y.1972).

■ COOPER, DISTRICT JUDGE.

In the fall of 1970, plaintiff, a professional free-lance photographer, instituted an action against defendant Onassis and three agents of the United States Secret Service (Agents)—Walsh, Kalafatis and Connelly. The verified complaint seeks damages for alleged false arrest and malicious prosecution and damages for, and an injunction against, the interference with his business by the alleged acts of defendant Onassis in resisting his efforts to photograph her, and by the alleged acts of defendant Agents in obstructing these efforts at the contended behest and inducement of defendant Onassis. The damage claims aggregated $1.3 million.

The answer of defendant Onassis was filed March 8, 1971 with a counterclaim seeking compensatory and punitive damages of $1.5 million and injunctive relief, based on claimed violations of her common law, statutory and constitutional rights of privacy and intentional infliction of emotional distress, assault, harassment and malicious prosecution. * * *

On July 6, 1971 Judge McLean of this Court granted a motion by the United States Government (Government) to intervene. The complaint in intervention, filed October 20, 1971 sought injunctive relief (pursuant to 18 U.S.C. § 3056) against the plaintiff for alleged interference with the protective duties of the United States Secret Service (Secret Service) toward the minor children of defendant Onassis and her late husband John F. Kennedy, a former President of the United States. * * *

[The court examined the plaintiff photographer's evidence and found it baseless. The opinion states that Galella committed blatant perjury for publicity and that the purpose of filing suit was to induce by harassment the payment of money and to obtain publicity from the action.

The court then gives several examples of the photographer's "typical callous behavior" such as jumping out of hiding in front of Onassis and her children in his effort to obtain pictures showing expressions of surprise, fear or anger in the faces of the Presidential widow and the children.]

* * * In addition to these episodes, twenty further episodes are summarized in our supplemental findings of fact. These include instances where the children were caused to bang into glass doors, school parents were bumped, passage was blocked, flashbulbs affected vision, telephoto lenses were used to spy, the children were imperiled in the water, a funeral was disturbed, plaintiff pursued defendant into the lobby of a friend's apartment building, plaintiff trailed defendant through the City hour after hour, plaintiff chased defendant by automobile, plaintiff and his assistants surrounded defendant and orbited while shouting, plaintiff snooped into purchases of stockings and shoes, flashbulbs were suddenly fired on lonely black nights—all accompanied by Galella jumping, shouting and acting wildly. Many of the incidents were repeated time after time; all preceded our restraining orders.

He was like a shadow: everywhere she went he followed her and engaged in offensive conduct; nothing was sacred to him whether defendant went to church, funeral services, theater, school, restaurant, or board a yacht in a foreign land. * * *

Outside of movieland, reporters do not normally hide behind restaurant coat racks, sneak into beauty parlors, don "disguises", hide in bushes and theater boxes, intrude into school buildings and, when ejected, enlist the aid of schoolchildren, bribe doormen and romance maids. * * *

Galella's objective? To establish himself as the peerless photographer who could capture the comings and goings and doings of Mrs. Onassis and her children, and by frightening them, to obtain unusual photographs which bring him handsome returns—financial and otherwise. He made it a world venture. His renown would take him into other fields, other subjects. * * *

[The court found that Galella had committed several torts against Onassis, and that she had not committed any torts against him.] * * *

Intervenor complaint. The Government is entitled to an injunction against interference with the protective duties of the United States Secret Service. 18 U.S.C. § 3056.[53]

* * *

Injunctive relief appears appropriate either as implicit in the statute or on common law principles of equity. The manifold threats to which the minor children of a former president may be exposed requires the most flexible legal tools to protect them, a task for which equity has traditionally been well suited. * * *

Private injunctive relief. Permanent injunctive relief is available where there is no adequate remedy at law, where the balance of the equities favor the moving party, and where success on the merits (probability of success for a preliminary injunction) have been demonstrated. As we have already dealt with the merits, we confine the present analysis to the [following] points. [Citation.]

No adequate remedy at law. We conclude there is no adequate remedy at law because of: the recurrent nature of plaintiff's invasions of defendant's rights; the need for a multiplicity of damage actions to assert defendant's rights; the imminent threat of continued emotional and physical trauma; and the difficulty of evaluating the injuries in this case in monetary terms. * * *

---

53. 3056. Secret Service Powers

(a) * * * [T]he United States Secret Service, Treasury Department, is authorized to protect the person of the President of the United States, the members of his immediate family, * * * the person of a former President and his wife during his lifetime, the person of the widow of a former President until her death or remarriage, and minor children of a former President until they reach sixteen years of age, unless such protection is declined; * * *

In Clemons v. Board of Education, 228 F.2d 853 (6th Cir.), *cert. denied*, 350 U.S. 1006, 76 S.Ct. 651, 100 L.Ed. 868 (1956), the Sixth Circuit adopted Pomeroy's formulation:

"In determining whether an injunction will be issued to protect any right of property, to enforce any obligation, or to prevent any wrong, there is one fundamental principle of the utmost importance. * * * Wherever a right exists or is created, by contract, by the ownership of property or otherwise, cognizable by law, *a violation of that right will be prohibited,* unless there are other considerations of policy or expediency which forbid a resort to this prohibitive remedy. * * * This jurisdiction of equity to prevent the commission of wrong is, however, modified and restricted by considerations of expediency and of convenience which confine its application to those cases in which the legal remedy is not full and adequate. * * * The incompleteness and inadequacy of the legal remedy is the criterion which, under the settled doctrine, determines the right to the equitable remedy of injunction." 4 Pomeroy, Equity Jurisprudence § 1338, at 935–36 (5th ed.).

* * *

The record demonstrates that Galella's surveillance and harassment of Mrs. Onassis has already gone on for a number of years and will continue, by his own account, for "another four or five years." Hence, Mrs. Onassis' legal remedies are inadequate on this ground alone.

Balance of the equities. The equities clearly balance in favor of defendant, particularly in view of our order which is addressed to protecting Galella's ability to continue his livelihood. * * *

We regarded the portion of the proposed order which would have completely prevented Galella from photographing Mrs. Onassis or her children to be clearly overbroad, struck it, and will not include it in a final order. Galella's occupation is lawful and the objective of the order is to modify his conduct, not to prevent his photography.

For practical reasons, the injunction cannot be couched in terms of prohibitions upon Galella's leaping, blocking, taunting, grunting, hiding and the like. Nor have abstract concepts—harassing, endangering—proved workable. No effective relief seems possible without the fixing of proscribed distances.

We must moreover make certain plaintiff keeps sufficiently far enough away to avoid problems as to compliance with the injunction and injurious disobedience. Disputes concerning his compliance may be frequent, thereby necessitating repeated application to the Court. Hence, the restraint must be clear, simple and effective so that Galella's substantial compliance cannot seriously be disputed unless a violation occurs.

* * *

The permanent injunction * * * shall enjoin plaintiff, his agents, servants, employees and all persons in active concert and participation with him from, *inter alia,* approaching within 100 yards of the home of defendant and her children, 100 yards of the schools attended by the children; at all other places and times 75 yards from the children and 50 yards from defendant; from performing surveillance of defendant or her children; from commercially appropriating defendant's photograph for advertising or trade purposes without defendant's consent; from communicating or attempting to communicate with defendant or her children.

* * *

1.   This order was modified by the Circuit Court upon appeal. The court noted that injunctive relief was appropriate because of Galella's stated intention to continue his coverage of Onassis, but found the injunction broader than necessary to protect her rights. The order was modified to prohibit only (1) any approach within twenty-five feet or any touching of Jacqueline Onassis; (2) any blocking of her movement; (3) any act foreseeably or reasonably calculated to place her life or safety in jeopardy; and (4) any conduct which would reasonably be foreseen to harass, alarm or frighten her. 487 F.2d 986, 998 (2d Cir.1973). Why make these changes? Did the trial judge balance interests incorrectly? Are there other considerations, such as Constitutional protections, that could affect the availability of the injunction or at least its wording?

2.   Will Galella's wrongful conduct necessarily stop because the court orders him to stop? The materials on contempt in Chapter 7 consider the means available to punish a contemnor for disobedience or to compensate the victim for noncompliance with the order.

3.   Does the statute providing for Secret Service Powers, printed in footnote 53 of the case, contemplate judicial enforcement? Why does the opinion state that injunctive relief is appropriate "either as implicit in the statute or on common law principles of equity"? Is injunctive relief "implicit" in this statute? Compare Orloff v. Los Angeles Turf Club, 30 Cal.2d 110, 180 P.2d 321 (1947), *supra* in Chapter 2.

4.   Although the principal case involved the harassment of a public figure by a member of the press, the most common type of individual harassment arises among persons who have had intimate relationships. States have responded with domestic violence statutes that typically permit criminal and civil remedies, including protective orders. For example, the Maryland code provides that a protective order may include any or all of the following relief

(1) order the respondent to refrain from abusing or threatening to abuse any person eligible for relief;

(2) order the respondent to refrain from contacting, attempting to contact, or harassing any person eligible for relief;

(3) order the respondent to refrain from entering the residence of any person eligible for relief;

(4) where the person eligible for relief and the respondent are residing together at the time of the abuse, order the respondent to vacate the

home immediately and award temporary use and possession of the home to the person eligible for relief or, in the case of alleged abuse of a child or alleged abuse of a vulnerable adult, award temporary use and possession of the home to an adult living in the home, provided that the court may not grant an order to vacate and award temporary use and possession of the home to a nonspouse person eligible for relief unless the name of the person eligible for relief appears on the lease or deed to the home or the person eligible for relief has shared the home with the respondent for a period of at least 90 days within 1 year before the filing of the petition; the respondent shall not cut off or cause to be cut off any utilities or telephone lines, but may arrange to have said utilities transferred to the petitioner's name (emphasis added to indicate author's addition to the statute).

Md. Code Ann., Fam. Law § 4–506.

5. Does an order prohibiting the defendant from "harassing" someone provide enough notice to the defendant as to what conduct is prohibited? Chapter 7 explores the contempt remedy for wilful violations of orders, including criminal contempt sanctions. The constitutional protections for criminal prosecutions apply, including the due process requirement of notice. The constitutional sufficiency of an order prohibiting "harassment" was upheld in *People v. Reynolds*, 302 Ill.App.3d 722, 235 Ill.Dec. 789, 706 N.E.2d 49 (1999). The defendant was properly sanctioned for his wilful violation of an order not to harass his ex-wife under the state's Domestic Violence Act. The court reasoned:

> To withstand a challenge for vagueness, a statute must give a person of ordinary intelligence a reasonable opportunity to know what conduct is lawful and what conduct is unlawful. * * * The Act defines "harassment" as knowing conduct that is not necessary to accomplish a reasonable purpose, would cause a reasonable person emotional distress, and does cause the petitioner emotional distress. [Citations.] It results from intentional acts that cause someone to be worried, anxious, or uncomfortable. 706 N.E.2d at 55.

6. Compare the principal case with *Portland Feminist Women's Health Center v. Advocates for Life, Inc.*, 859 F.2d 681 (9th Cir.1988). A women's clinic obtained a preliminary injunction against right-to-life demonstrators. The order provided that the defendants were prohibited from "shouting, screaming, chanting, or yelling during on-site demonstrations." They were further enjoined from "producing noise by any other means which substantially interferes with the provision of medical services within the Center." The Court of Appeals found that the injunction was not impermissibly vague even though the order did not include a specific decibel level or other objective standard.

eBay Inc. v. MercExchange
547 U.S. 388, 126 S.Ct. 1837, 164 L.Ed.2d 641 (2006).

■ JUSTICE THOMAS delivered the opinion of the Court.

Ordinarily, a federal court considering whether to award permanent injunctive relief to a prevailing plaintiff applies the four-factor test historically employed by courts of equity. Petitioners eBay Inc. and Half.com, Inc., argue that this traditional test applies to disputes arising under the Patent Act. We agree and, accordingly, vacate the judgment of the Court of Appeals.

Petitioner eBay operates a popular Internet Web site that allows private sellers to list goods they wish to sell, either through an auction or at a fixed price. Petitioner Half.com, now a wholly owned subsidiary of eBay, operates a similar Web site. Respondent MercExchange, L.L.C., holds a number of patents, including a business method patent for an electronic market designed to facilitate the sale of goods between private individuals by establishing a central authority to promote trust among participants. See U.S. Patent No. 5,845,265. MercExchange sought to license its patent to eBay and Half.com, as it had previously done with other companies, but the parties failed to reach an agreement. MercExchange subsequently filed a patent infringement suit against eBay and Half.com in the United States District Court for the Eastern District of Virginia. A jury found that MercExchange's patent was valid, that eBay and Half.com had infringed that patent, and that an award of damages was appropriate.[Footnote concerning continued challenge of the patent omitted.]

Following the jury verdict, the District Court denied MercExchange's motion for permanent injunctive relief. [Citation.] The Court of Appeals for the Federal Circuit reversed, applying its "general rule that courts will issue permanent injunctions against patent infringement absent exceptional circumstances." [Citation.] We granted certiorari to determine the appropriateness of this general rule. [Citation.]

According to well-established principles of equity, a plaintiff seeking a permanent injunction must satisfy a four-factor test before a court may grant such relief. A plaintiff must demonstrate: (1) that it has suffered an irreparable injury; (2) that remedies available at law, such as monetary damages, are inadequate to compensate for that injury; (3) that, considering the balance of hardships between the plaintiff and defendant, a remedy in equity is warranted; and (4) that the public interest would not be disserved by a permanent injunction. [Citations.] The decision to grant or deny permanent injunctive relief is an act of equitable discretion by the district court, reviewable on appeal for abuse of discretion. [Citation.]

These familiar principles apply with equal force to disputes arising under the Patent Act. As this Court has long recognized, "a major departure from the long tradition of equity practice should not be lightly implied." [Citations.] Nothing in the Patent Act indicates that Congress intended such a departure. To the contrary, the Patent Act expressly provides that injunctions "may" issue "in accordance with the principles of equity." * * *

To be sure, the Patent Act also declares that "patents shall have the attributes of personal property," § 261, including "the right to exclude others from making, using, offering for sale, or selling the invention,"

§ 154(a)(1). According to the Court of Appeals, this statutory right to exclude alone justifies its general rule in favor of permanent injunctive relief. But the creation of a right is distinct from the provision of remedies for violations of that right. * * *

This approach is consistent with our treatment of injunctions under the Copyright Act. Like a patent owner, a copyright holder possesses "the right to exclude others from using his property." * * * Like the Patent Act, the Copyright Act provides that courts "may" grant injunctive relief "on such terms as it may deem reasonable to prevent or restrain infringement of a copyright." 17 U.S.C. § 502(a). And as in our decision today, this Court has consistently rejected invitations to replace traditional equitable considerations with a rule that an injunction automatically follows a determination that a copyright has been infringed. [Citations.]

Neither the District Court nor the Court of Appeals below fairly applied these traditional equitable principles in deciding respondent's motion for a permanent injunction. Although the District Court recited the traditional four-factor test, it appeared to adopt certain expansive principles suggesting that injunctive relief could not issue in a broad swath of cases. Most notably, it concluded that a "plaintiff's willingness to license its patents" and "its lack of commercial activity in practicing the patents" would be sufficient to establish that the patent holder would not suffer irreparable harm if an injunction did not issue. [Citation.] But traditional equitable principles do not permit such broad classifications. For example, some patent holders, such as university researchers or self-made inventors, might reasonably prefer to license their patents, rather than undertake efforts to secure the financing necessary to bring their works to market themselves. Such patent holders may be able to satisfy the traditional four-factor test, and we see no basis for categorically denying them the opportunity to do so. To the extent that the District Court adopted such a categorical rule, then, its analysis cannot be squared with the principles of equity adopted by Congress. * * *

In reversing the District Court, the Court of Appeals departed in the opposite direction from the four-factor test. The court articulated a "general rule," unique to patent disputes, "that a permanent injunction will issue once infringement and validity have been adjudged." The court further indicated that injunctions should be denied only in the "unusual" case, under "exceptional circumstances" and " 'in rare instances . . . to protect the public interest.' " [Citation.] Just as the District Court erred in its categorical denial of injunctive relief, the Court of Appeals erred in its categorical grant of such relief. [Citations.]

Because we conclude that neither court below correctly applied the traditional four-factor framework that governs the award of injunctive relief, we vacate the judgment of the Court of Appeals, so that the District Court may apply that framework in the first instance. In doing so, we take no position on whether permanent injunctive relief should or should not issue in this particular case, or indeed in any number of other disputes arising under the Patent Act. We hold only that the decision whether to grant or deny injunctive relief rests within the equitable discretion of the district courts, and that such discretion must be exercised consistent with traditional principles of equity, in patent disputes no less than in other cases governed by such standards.

Accordingly, we vacate the judgment of the Court of Appeals, and remand for further proceedings consistent with this opinion.

It is so ordered.

■ CHIEF JUSTICE ROBERTS, with whom JUSTICE SCALIA and JUSTICE GINSBURG join, concurring.

I agree with the Court's holding that "the decision whether to grant or deny injunctive relief rests within the equitable discretion of the district courts, and that such discretion must be exercised consistent with traditional principles of equity, in patent disputes no less than in other cases governed by such standards," and I join the opinion of the Court. That opinion rightly rests on the proposition that "a major departure from the long tradition of equity practice should not be lightly implied." *Weinberger v. Romero–Barcelo,* 456 U.S. 305, 320, 102 S.Ct. 1798, 72 L.Ed.2d 91 (1982).

From at least the early 19th century, courts have granted injunctive relief upon a finding of infringement in the vast majority of patent cases. This "long tradition of equity practice" is not surprising, given the difficulty of protecting a right to *exclude* through monetary remedies that allow an infringer to *use* an invention against the patentee's wishes—a difficulty that often implicates the first two factors of the traditional four-factor test. This historical practice, as the Court holds, does not *entitle* a patentee to a permanent injunction or justify a *general rule* that such injunctions should issue. * * * At the same time, there is a difference between exercising equitable discretion pursuant to the established four-factor test and writing on an entirely clean slate. * * * When it comes to discerning and applying those standards, in this area as others, "a page of history is worth a volume of logic." *New York Trust Co. v. Eisner,* 256 U.S. 345, 349, 41 S.Ct. 506, 65 L.Ed. 963 (1921) (opinion for the Court by Holmes, J.).

■ JUSTICE KENNEDY, with whom JUSTICE STEVENS, JUSTICE SOUTER, and JUSTICE BREYER join, concurring.

The Court is correct, in my view, to hold that courts should apply the well-established, four-factor test—without resort to categorical rules—in deciding whether to grant injunctive relief in patent cases. The Chief Justice is also correct that history may be instructive in applying this test. *Ante* (concurring opinion). The traditional practice of issuing injunctions against patent infringers, however, does not seem to rest on "the difficulty of protecting a right to *exclude* through monetary remedies that allow an infringer to *use* an invention against the patentee's wishes." *Ante* (Roberts, C.J., concurring). Both the terms of the Patent Act and the traditional view of injunctive relief accept that the existence of a right to exclude does not dictate the remedy for a violation of that right. *Ante* (opinion of the Court). To the extent earlier cases establish a pattern of granting an injunction against patent infringers almost as a matter of course, this pattern simply illustrates the result of the four-factor test in the contexts then prevalent. The lesson of the historical practice, therefore, is most helpful and instructive when the circumstances of a case bear substantial parallels to litigation the courts have confronted before.

In cases now arising trial courts should bear in mind that in many instances the nature of the patent being enforced and the economic function of the patent holder present considerations quite unlike earlier cases. An industry has developed in which firms use patents not as a basis for producing and selling goods but, instead, primarily for obtaining licensing fees. See FTC, To Promote Innovation: The Proper Balance of Competition and Patent Law and Policy, ch. 3, pp. 38–39 (Oct.2003), available at http://www.ftc.gov/os/2003/10/innovationrpt.pdf (as visited May 11, 2006, and available in Clerk of Court's case file). For these firms, an injunction, and the potentially serious sanctions arising from its violation, can be employed as a bargaining tool to charge exorbitant fees to companies that seek to buy licenses to practice the patent. See *ibid*. When the patented invention is but a small component of the product the companies seek to produce and the threat of an injunction is employed simply for undue leverage in negotiations, legal damages may well be sufficient to compensate for the infringement and an injunction may not serve the public interest. In addition injunctive relief may have different consequences for the burgeoning number of patents over business methods, which were not of much economic and legal significance in earlier times. The potential vagueness and suspect validity of some of these patents may affect the calculus under the four-factor test.

The equitable discretion over injunctions, granted by the Patent Act, is well suited to allow courts to adapt to the rapid technological and legal developments in the patent system. For these reasons it should be recognized that district courts must determine whether past practice fits the circumstances of the cases before them. With these observations, I join the opinion of the Court.

---

1. What is the practical difference in the approaches of the majority opinion and the two concurrences? Under which approach is a plaintiff most likely to get an injunction to prevent a defendant from future patent violations?

2. Would you expect *eBay* to result in more injunctions in patent cases, or fewer? A study of pre- and post-*eBay* patent injunctions concluded that after *eBay* significantly fewer injunctions are granted when the patent holder and alleged infringer do not compete in the marketplace. Lily Lim & Sarah E. Craven, Injunctions Enjoined; Remedies Restructured, 25 Santa Clara Computer & High Tech. L.J. 787 (2009). *See also* Stijepko Tokic, The Role of Consumers in Deterring Settlement Agreements Based on Invalid Patents, 2012 Stanford Tech. L. Rev. (2012).

3. Does *eBay* affect the federal law of equity beyond patents? The case comes from the Court of Appeals for the Federal Circuit, which hears patent appeals. It is the only circuit court whose jurisdiction is based on subject matter rather than geography. It develops its own precedent, reviewable only by the Supreme Court, and thus provides greater certainty and uniformity in patent law because it is not possible to have splits among the circuits on patent law issues. One view of *eBay* is that the Supreme Court was bringing the Federal Circuit into line with other federal law and declining to permit a separate line of equity jurisprudence just for patents. *See* S.J. Plager, *The Price of Popularity: The Court of Appeals for the Federal Circuit 2007,* 56 Am. U. L. Rev. 751 (2007).

D. PUBLIC INTEREST AND TRIBUNAL INTEGRITY

Section Coverage:

The public interest is another relevant consideration for the issuance of an injunction. A court does not ignore the overall public context of a lawsuit. Conversely, courts are resistant to prayers for comprehensive relief in the name of public interest in areas that more properly are within the province of the legislature. Nonetheless, courts often need to use broad equitable powers to resolve immediate threats of harm to important private rights or public interests.

The public interest affects the decision whether to grant an equitable remedy as well as the scope and nature of any relief granted. A related factor is whether the relief sought threatens the integrity of the court by being impossible to enforce or unlikely to be enforced. A judge can consider the practical problem of whether enforcement by contempt will be possible when, for example, an order requires performance out of the court's jurisdiction. Another appropriate consideration is the effect of an injunction on the relative bargaining position of the parties. Consider the plaintiff who really wants to make a favorable monetary arrangement with a defendant but asserts to the court that the damage remedy cannot adequately compensate for the threatened future harm. An injunction would afford the plaintiff an unfairly strong negotiating position for a settlement. Conversely, the court may also consider whether the defendant deliberately took liberty with the plaintiff's rights on the assumption that equity would not interfere later. The integrity of the court requires careful deliberation on these issues.

Model Case:

A major manufacturing company announces a new plant location in an economically depressed town. Construction of the plant begins. A neighboring landowner sues to enjoin construction because it interferes with a minor easement. In evaluating the merits of an injunction, a court may properly consider the public interest in the construction in addition to the factors of adequacy at law and relative hardships.

The landowner may have no intention of demanding enforcement of an injunction against construction even if it were granted. The purpose of the suit may be to delay construction and force the defendant to pay an unreasonably large price to eliminate the easement. The court may consider these factors, including the good faith of both parties with respect to the controversy.

Graham v. Cirocco

31 Kan.App.2d 563, 69 P.3d 194 (2003).

■ BEIER, J.:

Defendant William Cirocco, M.D., appeals the district court's permanent injunction enforcing a noncompetition covenant of his employment contract with plaintiff Bruce D. Graham, M.D., P.A. Bruce Graham, a colorectal surgeon, has practiced in the Kansas City area since 1987, doing business as Bruce D. Graham, M.D., P.A. In 1994, finding he had more work than he could do, Graham recruited Cirocco to join his practice. Cirocco moved from New York to do so. * * *.

The parties entered into an employment contract on July 1, 1994, and each year thereafter until Cirocco left Graham's practice. The last of these contracts, which is the one at issue here, read in pertinent part:

"XVII.   Noncompetition Agreement

"(B) . . . (ii) For a period of two (2) years after leaving the employment of [Graham] and within the geographic area measured by a radius of one hundred fifty (150) miles from each of the offices of [Graham], [Cirocco] agrees that he will not solicit business from the patients or referral sources of [Graham] with whom he came in contact as an employee of [Graham]. * * *

"(C) [Cirocco] further agrees that for a period of two (2) years after leaving the employment of [Graham], [Cirocco] will not open an office within twenty-five (25) miles of the hospitals listed in the recitals of this Agreement or provide services at said hospitals." * * *

Cirocco tendered his resignation on May 24, 2000, [and] opened his own new office for the practice of colorectal surgery next door to Graham[.] * * * The district court also heard evidence that Cirocco began soliciting patients and referral sources of Graham's shortly before he left their joint practice.

Despite Cirocco's tactics, Graham's schedule remained full. The record on appeal demonstrates that some patients had to wait three to four weeks for an appointment. Moreover, Graham had to remain on call 24 hours a day, 7 days a week, and he was again considering adding another surgeon to his practice to help with the workload.

Graham sued to enjoin Cirocco, alleging Cirocco had breached the noncompetition covenant by opening an office within 25 miles of the prohibited hospitals and by soliciting patients. In response, Cirocco argued that the covenant was unenforceable as against public policy because it suppressed ordinary competition by protecting interests in patient and referral contacts and would leave northeast Kansas with a shortage of colorectal surgeons.

At trial, Cirocco presented testimony of Dr. John Heryer, a former colorectal surgeon and current Vice–President and Medical Director of Blue Cross and Blue Shield of Kansas City. Heryer testified northeast Kansas would be underserved if it had only one colorectal surgeon. In his view, such a surgeon could not serve [the local hospitals] adequately. The district court also heard testimony that patients requiring colorectal surgery whose surgeries were performed by general surgeons rather than members of the colorectal subspecialty have higher death rates than patients treated by colorectal surgeons.

The district court concluded Graham had protectable interests in his patient base and contacts with referring physicians. * * * The court granted a permanent injunction for 2 years, beginning March 1, 2001, pursuant to the duration term of the agreement.

Our Supreme Court has evaluated noncompetition agreements between physicians only three times. See *Weber v. Tillman,* 259 Kan. 457, 913 P.2d 84 (1996) (involving dermatologist); *Ferraro v. Fink,* 191 Kan. 53, 379 P.2d 266 (1963) (involving pathologist); *Foltz v. Struxness,* 168 Kan. 714, 215 P.2d 133 (1950) (involving physician/surgeon). * * * In each, the Supreme Court upheld the covenant, although the geographic term of the *Foltz* covenant had been modified previously by the district court. * * *

In *Foltz,* the Supreme Court noted that the purpose and intent of such a covenant was to protect encroachment on the professional business the plaintiff employer had devoted a life to building. * * * The outcome of the *Foltz* case was influenced by the district court's findings that the city in which the parties practiced had an adequate number of physicians and that it was no more in need of additional physicians and surgeons than many similar communities. The district court also had found there was no attempt at a monopoly by the plaintiff employer. These findings left no room to disturb the district court's conclusion that no public policy or public interest was affected by the restriction on the former employee's practice. * * *

In this case, the district court judge concluded the noncompetition covenant was reasonable, enforceable, and not against public policy[.] * * * However, the ultimate question of whether a restrictive covenant is contrary to public policy is a question of law over which this court exercises unlimited review. * * *

Injury to Public Welfare

Cirocco addresses this factor on appeal by arguing that enforcement of the covenant threatens the health of northeast Kansans. He points to the testimony of Heryer that the covenant's restrictions leave the area with one colorectal surgeon for 700,000 potential patients, a ratio Heryer characterized as dangerous. Cirocco also emphasizes that Graham originally recruited him because there was a need for an additional colorectal surgeon to handle the workload. It is also persuasive on this point that, since Cirocco left Graham's employ, Graham is again overbusy and considering bringing on another physician. Seriously ill patients are faced with long waits for appointments.

* * *

The *Weber* decision summarizes several cases from other jurisdictions in which courts refused to enforce noncompetition covenants because they would result in shortages of physicians in medically necessary specialties. [Citation.] Unlike the dermatologists involved in *Weber*, colorectal surgeons such as Graham and Cirocco are engaged in a medically necessary subspecialty. Limitation of their number in populous areas threatens the public's welfare.

* * *

Considering the entire appellate record * * * we hold that the noncompetition covenant in this case should be modified to eliminate the 25–mile restriction on placement of Cirocco's office, as well as the prohibition on Cirocco's delivery of services at any listed hospital located in Kansas.

Mootness

One might argue that this case has become moot because of the passage of time. We disagree. Although this particular dispute may have outlived the 2–year period ordered by the district judge, the general situation qualifies as " 'capable of repetition, yet evading review.' " [Citation.] We have therefore examined the merits and made a ruling. * * *

---

1. Public interest can take a variety of forms. As the principal case reflects, consideration of the public interest is a requirement for the issuance of a permanent injunction even when the litigation is entirely between private parties.

When the plaintiff is the government, public interest is the centerpiece of the litigation in a much more direct manner. It is for the court, however, rather than the government to determine whether the position of the governmental plaintiff is necessarily consistent with the public interest. The government in such cases is simply a litigant arguing the nature of the public interest as reflected in the legislation empowering the government to bring the case.

2. The public interest concept does not necessarily refer to life and death issues, such as the potential deaths from an inadequate number of surgeons in a speciality as in the principal case. The public has an interest in small matters too. In some sense, every tree in a national forest is a matter of public interest because it is owned by the public.

An interesting case involving the public interest in regulating gatherings in national forests is *United States v. Rainbow Family*, 695 F.Supp. 314 (E.D.Tex.1988). In that case the United States sought to enjoin a loosely affiliated group called the Rainbow Family from holding its annual summer gathering in a national forest in Texas. The allegations were that the gathering would do irreparable harm to public health and safety.

The government's evidence went to the problems created by the gathering of the same group when it had its annual gathering in a national forest in North Carolina the preceding year. The argument was that the past conduct of the Rainbow Family at its annual gathering did irreparable harm to the forest. Further, the government argued that the gathering was a public nuisance because of disturbances, nudity, unsanitary health conditions, traffic congestion, and the use of illicit drugs.

Consideration of the public interest in this context does not raise issues of standing. This issue naturally calls to mind the famous dissent by Justice Douglas in *Sierra Club v. Morton*, 405 U.S. 727, 92 S.Ct. 1361, 31 L.Ed.2d 636 (1972), where he suggested that rivers, lakes and trees should have standing to assert environmental issues. In contrast, the governmental plaintiff in *Rainbow Family* already had standing; the issue was the weight to give the public interest when the court chose a remedy.

The court balanced the public interest as established by the government against the First Amendment right of the Rainbow Family to gather. The judge found that the government had not produced strong enough evidence concerning the problems with the previous year's gathering to forbid the future gathering. Although the district court refused to enjoin the gathering altogether, it did nonetheless issue a limited injunction that permitted the gathering under fairly severe restrictions in terms of the number of people at the site and sanitation requirements.

Why was the "public interest" involved so compelling? Are forests more important than First Amendment rights? Is the prevention of treatable illnesses from poor sanitation more compelling than First Amendment rights? Does it matter that this group contains people who are socially unconventional? What if the gathering was an historical society reliving the hardships of the first settlers? What really was at stake if no injunction restrained the group?

What would the government's remedy at law be against members of the gathering if the court does not issue the injunction and the feared conduct occurs? The government can prosecute for public nudity, disorderly conduct, use of illegal drugs, and destruction of Forest Service property. Why would prosecution not be an adequate remedy?

The government successfully argued that its regulations would not be enforceable against such a large crowd. Moreover, criminal sanctions occur only after the fact and cannot protect public health when problems have already developed. For example, the government demonstrated that several thousand people at the North Carolina contracted shigellosis. Problems associated with the spread of bacteria cannot be redressed with criminal sanctions.

3.   Under the Federal Rule of Civil Procedure 65(d), an injunction binds the parties enumerated in the order and those in "active concert or participation" with them when such persons receive actual notice of the decree "by personal service or otherwise." Although personal service on each member of a group, such as the Rainbow Family in note 2, is not practical, what steps might satisfy the "otherwise" language of the alternative notice requirement in Rule 65(d)?

Injunctions against crimes, studied in Chapter 9, pose special due process considerations. Nonetheless, courts do enjoin crimes when the conduct is a public nuisance if the balance of hardships favors the order. Contempt sanctions for disobedience of the order then can be greater than the maximum fine or jail term set for the criminal violation. Are these powerful means to compel conformity with the law justified in the name of public interest?

Some of the conduct enjoined in *Rainbow Family,* in note 2, was also subject to the First Amendment's protection of free speech. This topic is also covered in greater detail in Chapter 9. When speech is involved, an injunction must be narrowly tailored to protect the defendant's right of expression. Courts have found it challenging to balance the rights of the parties in fashioning relief in such cases. Many of the recent cases in the area have involved protesters at abortion clinics. *See, e.g., Madsen v. Women's Health Center, Inc.*, 512 U.S. 753, 114 S.Ct. 2516, 129 L.Ed.2d 593 (1994).

Boomer v. Atlantic Cement Company

26 N.Y.2d 219, 257 N.E.2d 870, 309 N.Y.S.2d 312 (1970).

■ BERGAN, JUDGE.

Defendant operates a large cement plant near Albany. These are actions for injunction and damages by neighboring land owners alleging injury to property from dirt, smoke and vibration emanating from the plant. A nuisance has been found after trial, temporary damages have been allowed; but an injunction has been denied.

* * * The threshold question raised by the division of view on this appeal is whether the court should resolve the litigation between the parties now before it as equitably as seems possible; or whether, seeking promotion of the general public welfare, it should channel private litigation into broad public objectives.

A court performs its essential function when it decides the rights of parties before it. Its decision of private controversies may sometimes greatly affect public issues. Large questions of law are often resolved by the manner in which private litigation is decided. But this is normally an incident to the court's main function to settle controversy. It is a rare exercise of judicial power to use a decision in private litigation as a purposeful mechanism to achieve direct public objectives greatly beyond the rights and interests before the court.

Effective control of air pollution is a problem presently far from solution even with the full public and financial powers of government. In large measure adequate technical procedures are yet to be developed and some that appear possible may be economically impracticable.

It seems apparent that the amelioration of air pollution will depend on technical research in great depth; on a carefully balanced consideration of the economic impact of close regulation; and of the actual effect on public health. It is likely to require massive public expenditure and to demand more than any local community can accomplish and to depend on regional and interstate controls.

A court should not try to do this on its own as a by-product of private litigation and it seems manifest that the judicial establishment is neither equipped in the limited nature of any judgment it can pronounce nor prepared to lay down and implement an effective policy for the elimination of air pollution. This is an area beyond the circumference of one private lawsuit. It is a direct responsibility for government and should not thus be undertaken as an incident to solving a dispute between property owners and a single cement plant—one of many—in the Hudson River valley.

* * *

The ground for the denial of injunction, notwithstanding the finding both that there is a nuisance and that plaintiffs have been damaged substantially, is the large disparity in economic consequences of the nuisance and of the injunction. This theory cannot, however, be sustained without overruling a doctrine which has been consistently reaffirmed in several leading cases in this court and which has never been disavowed here, namely that where a nuisance has been found and where there has been any substantial damage shown by the party complaining an injunction will be granted.

The rule in New York has been that such a nuisance will be enjoined although marked disparity be shown in economic consequence between the effect of the injunction and the effect of the nuisance.

* * *

Although the court at Special Term and the Appellate Division held that injunction should be denied, it was found that plaintiffs had been damaged in various specific amounts up to the time of the trial and damages to the respective plaintiffs were awarded for those amounts. The effect of this was, injunction having been denied, plaintiffs could maintain successive actions at law for damages thereafter as further damage was incurred.

The court at Special Term also found the amount of permanent damage attributable to each plaintiff, for the guidance of the parties in the event both sides stipulated to the payment and acceptance of such permanent damage as a settlement of all the controversies among the parties.

The total of permanent damages to all plaintiffs thus found was $185,000.
* * *

This result at Special Term and at the Appellate Division is a departure from a rule that has become settled; but to follow the rule literally in these cases would be to close down the plant at once. This court is fully agreed to avoid that immediately drastic remedy; the difference in view is how best to avoid it.[54]

One alternative is to grant the injunction but postpone its effect to a specified future date to give opportunity for technical advances to permit defendant to eliminate the nuisance; another is to grant the injunction conditioned on the payment of permanent damages to plaintiffs which would compensate them for the total economic loss to their property present and future caused by defendant's operations. For reasons which will be developed the court chooses the latter alternative.

If the injunction were to be granted unless within a short period—*e.g.*, 18 months—the nuisance be abated by improved methods, there would be no assurance that any significant technical improvement would occur.

The parties could settle this private litigation at any time if defendant paid enough money and the imminent threat of closing the plant would build up the pressure on defendant. If there were no improved techniques found, there would inevitably be applications to the court at Special Term for extensions of time to perform on showing of good faith efforts to find such techniques.

Moreover, techniques to eliminate dust and other annoying by-products of cement making are unlikely to be developed by any research the defendant can undertake within any short period, but will depend on the total resources of the cement industry nationwide and throughout the world. The problem is universal wherever cement is made.

For obvious reasons the rate of the research is beyond control of defendant. If at the end of 18 months the whole industry has not found a technical solution a court would be hard put to close down this one cement plant if due regard be given to equitable principles.

On the other hand, to grant the injunction unless defendant pays plaintiffs such permanent damages as may be fixed by the court seems to do justice between the contending parties. All of the attributions of economic loss to the properties on which plaintiffs' complaints are based will have been redressed.

The nuisance complained of by these plaintiffs may have other public or private consequences, but these particular parties are the only ones who have sought remedies and the judgment proposed will fully redress them. The limitation of relief granted is a limitation only within the four corners of these actions and does not foreclose public health or other public agencies from seeking proper relief in a proper court.

---

54. Respondent's investment in the plant is in excess of $45,000,000. There are over 300 people employed there.

It seems reasonable to think that the risk of being required to pay permanent damages to injured property owners by cement plant owners would itself be a reasonable effective spur to research for improved techniques to minimize nuisance.

The power of the court to condition on equitable grounds the continuance of an injunction on the payment of permanent damages seems undoubted. * * *

The orders should be reversed, without costs, and the cases remitted to Supreme Court, Albany County to grant an injunction which shall be vacated upon payment by defendant of such amounts of permanent damage to the respective plaintiffs as shall for this purpose be determined by the court.

■ JASEN, JUDGE (dissenting).

I agree with the majority that a reversal is required here, but I do not subscribe to the newly enunciated doctrine of assessment of permanent damages, in lieu of an injunction, where substantial property rights have been impaired by the creation of a nuisance.

It has long been the rule in this State, as the majority acknowledges, that a nuisance which results in substantial continuing damage to neighbors must be enjoined. [Citations.] To now change the rule to permit the cement company to continue polluting the air indefinitely upon the payment of permanent damages is, in my opinion, compounding the magnitude of a very serious problem in our State and Nation today.

* * *

I see grave dangers in overruling our long-established rule of granting an injunction where a nuisance results in substantial continuing damage. In permitting the injunction to become inoperative upon the payment of permanent damages, the majority is, in effect, licensing a continuing wrong. It is the same as saying to the cement company, you may continue to do harm to your neighbors so long as you pay a fee for it. Furthermore, once such permanent damages are assessed and paid, the incentive to alleviate the wrong would be eliminated, thereby continuing air pollution of an area without abatement.

* * *

This kind of inverse condemnation * * * may not be invoked by a private person or corporation for private gain or advantage. Inverse condemnation should only be permitted when the public is primarily served in the taking or impairment of property. [Citations.] The promotion of the interests of the polluting cement company has, in my opinion, no public use or benefit.

Nor is it constitutionally permissible to impose servitude on land, without consent of the owner, by payment of permanent damages where the continuing impairment of the land is for a private use. [Citations.] This is made clear by the State Constitution (art. I, § 7, subd. [a]) which provides that "[p]rivate property shall not be taken for *public use* without just compensation" (emphasis added). It is, of course, significant that the section makes no mention of taking for a *private* use.

* * *

I would enjoin the defendant cement company from continuing the discharge of dust particles upon its neighbors' properties unless, within 18 months, the cement company abated this nuisance.

It is not my intention to cause the removal of the cement plant from the Albany area, but to recognize the urgency of the problem stemming from this stationary source of air pollution, and to allow the company a specified period of time to develop a means to alleviate this nuisance.

* * *

In a day when there is a growing concern for clean air, highly developed industry should not expect acquiescence by the courts, but should, instead, plan its operations to eliminate contamination of our air and damage to its neighbors.

Accordingly, the orders of the Appellate Division, insofar as they denied the injunction, should be reversed, and the actions remitted to Supreme Court, Albany County to grant an injunction to take effect 18 months hence, unless the nuisance is abated by improved techniques prior to said date.

---

1.   Problems arise when the conduct that adversely affects the plaintiff simultaneously confers a societal benefit. To what extent should a court consider that the polluting factory employs hundreds of workers in the community, provides a sizable tax base, and cost millions of dollars to build? Should it make a difference that the factory is validly operating within the requirements of a local zoning ordinance, yet has the ancillary negative consequences on the surrounding property?

2.   Nuisance cases often require a court to exercise a quasi-legislative role. Judges are called upon to decide whether to allow a factory in one locale to discharge pollutants that adversely affect others, often in adjoining communities or even in other states. When, in the absence of state or federal legislative guidance, should courts act? Nuisance decisions have other political ramifications; if courts in state A historically allow factories to pollute and pay damages for their harm as a cost of doing business, while state B courts tend to enjoin such conduct, this difference could affect the location of new plants. Are such considerations properly weighed in a suit between two private parties?

3.   Did the court in the principal case effectively license a wrong simply because of the potentially disparate economic consequences? Has the court essentially granted a power of inverse condemnation? If damages are

awarded, should the court measure the harm based only on past conduct or should compensation be given also for future injury?

4.   It is noteworthy that *Boomer* was decided in 1970, at the beginning of what became an explosion of legislative action at both the state and federal level to address environmental concerns.

The Environmental Protection Agency [EPA] was created in 1970 and charged with the responsibility of establishing national ambient air quality standards for air pollutants which endanger public health or welfare. Congress further enacted a series of amendments in 1972 and 1977 to the forerunner of the Clean Water Act. In 1971 the EPA administrator, in response to a court order, cancelled and suspended certain pesticides, DDT 2, 4 5–T and aldrin-dieldrin, and in the so-called "18th of March Statement" declared that pesticides would no longer be given perfunctory review regarding registration and enforcement. Additional key federal legislation was passed to combat the serious risks posed by hazardous waste products. The Resource Conservation Recovery Act of 1976 (RCRA), 42 U.S.C. §§ 6901 et seq., and the "Superfund" statute, the Comprehensive Environmental Response, Compensation and Liability Act of 1980 (CERCLA), 42 U.S.C. §§ 9601 et seq., reflect a toughened approach to enforcement by adding more stringent liability provisions for violators. The effectiveness of these various statutory schemes is disputed; nonetheless, there is a clearly identifiable movement toward increased legislative intervention to solve pollution. *See generally* "Developments in the Law—Toxic Waste Litigation," 99 Harv.L.Rev. 1458 (1986).

5.   Can health concerns be accurately balanced against economic costs, particularly when those who bear the health risks are not necessarily the same persons as the ones who would enjoy the economic gains? The essence of nuisance law involves a balancing of costs and benefits in a private market system. That market functions well, however, only to the extent that prices reflect the costs and benefits to society. One problem when dealing with the sort of environmental issues involved in *Boomer* is that several factors distort the efficient operation of that private system of property rights.

The manufacturer who owns and operates the polluting factory has an economic interest in forcing the costs of production onto someone else, normally by passing along the costs of production to the consuming public. An economist's model postulates that resources should be allocated efficiently to maximize total production. Therefore, where costs exceed the benefits, production is considered inefficient. A manufacturer has no economic incentive to install costly pollution control equipment because it does not translate into higher productivity gains for the manufacturer. Rather, the persons who stand to benefit from pollution reduction—the general public—would not directly pay for that benefit. The notion that the public receives the collective goods in pollution abatement, yet does not pay the costs directly, further distorts the economist's model of an efficient private market system. *See generally* Coase, The Problem of Social Cost, 3 Journal of Law and Econ. 1 (1960); Farber, Contract Law and Modern Economic

Theory, 78 Nw.U.L.Rev. 303 (1983); Sagoff, Economic Theory and Environmental Law, 79 Mich.L.Rev. 1393 (1981).

6. *Boomer* reflects in part the tension between efficient economic-based decisions predicated upon a cost-benefit analysis and the public interest in enjoying a pollution-free environment. Part of the solution has been direct public intervention by legislation where the private market system fails to provide a sufficient incentive to manufacturers to clean up the waste that they generate.

Direct regulation has flaws as well. The regulatory schemes typically have gaps in coverage and normally carry high administrative costs to gather information, set standards, and monitor compliance. The information necessary to regulate effectively is largely in the hands of industry—those with the least incentive to disclose it. Furthermore, scientific evidence is often inconclusive regarding "safe" levels of human exposure to certain pollutants.

PROBLEM: THE ENCROACHMENT

Stone constructed his vacation home on a large wooded site. Stone owns the property under most of the house, but six inches extended onto the property of the adjoining landowner, Blanzy. Blanzy's property is also a large wooded lot, and Blanzy has not constructed anything on it.

Stone offers to pay Blanzy a reasonable price for the sale of enough land to move the boundary between the two large lots and thus to accommodate the house. Blanzy counteroffers at a price ten times higher. Stone refuses to pay it and Blanzy will not negotiate further. Blanzy sues Stone to enjoin the encroachment of the house.

Should the court grant the injunction? Would it matter if Stone had made an innocent mistake about the boundary when the house was constructed as opposed to making an intentional encroachment?

1. If Blanzy is willing to sell the property at some price, then would damages be the appropriate remedy? What would Blanzy do with an injunctive order if Blanzy is willing to sell to Stone at some price? Should a court take such factors into account in deciding whether to issue the injunction?

Reconsider *K–Mart Corp. v. Oriental Plaza, Inc.*, earlier in this chapter. Does it matter whether K–Mart would use the injunction to settle the case for more favorable terms in its lease rather than having the offending buildings moved?

2. In many jurisdictions, courts will order a conveyance of the land necessary to remove an encroachment if the encroacher has acted in good faith. Such orders permit a fair market value recovery for the landowner but the conveyance is through a mandatory injunction. *See* Restatement

(Second) of Torts § 941. Alternative remedies are to order a removal of the encroachment or to award compensatory damages for the permanent trespass, measured by the diminution in the value of the land.

Where the encroachment is significant in scope, a conveyance order is not appropriate because it amounts to granting the encroacher with the power of private eminent domain. In *Amkco, Ltd., Co. v. Welborn*, 127 N.M. 587, 985 P.2d 757 (App.1999), for example, the trial court found that a truck stop and travel center was mistakenly built to extend over the neighbor's land and encroached on nine percent of that neighboring parcel. The builders were innocent and had relied in good faith on an erroneous survey. Nonetheless, the court found that the trial court had abused its discretion to order a conveyance of the land when the encroachment was significant and the victims were themselves blameless. The court observed:

> Finally, we address Appellees' protest that ejectment and removal of their encroachment constitute impermissible economic waste. We readily acknowledge some harm will result to Appellees from dismantling and removal of the encroachment. But that fact alone cannot justify use of the courts to require a conveyance of this magnitude to Appellees. We note the absence here of any benefit to the public of the kind that traditionally justifies a forcible taking of private property. If Appellees do not wish to waste their investment, then as this Court has said in the past under somewhat analogous circumstances, nothing forbids [Appellees] from negotiating with [Appellant] to waive its right to compel removal of the building. [Citation.] The fact that a court "injunction provides [Appellant] with a very strong bargaining position," is no grounds for denying Appellant the sole use and possession of his own private property, particularly when that bargaining position is simply a natural consequence of Appellees' own mistake. 985 P.2d at 764.

3. Should the good or bad faith of the defendant matter to the court in deciding whether to issue an injunction? In *Welton v. 40 East Oak St. Bldg. Corp.*, 70 F.2d 377 (7th Cir.1934), the court ordered the reconstruction of a twenty story apartment building to meet zoning set back requirements. The defendants had obtained a variance which the plaintiffs were appealing. During the appeal the defendants continued to build the structure. In granting the injunction, the court observed:

> It is impossible for a court or jury to correctly say that a building erected in the face of a city ordinance and in spite of litigation which sought to prevent its erection was nevertheless undertaken in good faith and so carried through. * * * [T]he company and its officers * * * acted knowingly, defiantly, and in reckless disregard of the warnings which the pending litigation effectively proclaimed.

* * *

Pomeroy, in dealing with the subject of balancing conveniences where the wrongdoer deliberately erects the offending building with notice of the pendency of a suit or an appeal, puts it thus:

> They (the cases) all agree in one particular, however, viz., that the defendant who would claim its consideration in his favor must have committed the tort innocently; a willful wrong-doer is entitled to claim no favor. * * * It is hard to see how anyone can claim any immunity for a tort on the ground that it was innocently done, when at the time of doing it he knew his right to do it was disputed by the person affected. Pomeroy, Equity Jurisprudence § 1966.

70 F.2d at 381.

4. In *Jerome v. Ross*, 7 John.Ch.R. 315 (1823), a court of equity denied an injunction against a continuing trespass to land. The trespasses were made to lots near the Hudson River and the trespassers were building a dam on the river. The land consisted of an extensive ledge of stone and mass of rock, and the construction workers needed such rock for building the dam. The dam was needed for the construction of the Champlain canal. The rock was needed urgently for the completion of the canal at this point, and the public interest was at stake in the swift completion of the canal.

Ross was the owner of the rock and it appeared that the rock had no value except for its use in the construction of this dam. Ross sued at law for the trespass and conversion when the first load of rock was removed. He received very small damages. When the trespass and conversion of the rock was repeated, Ross sought an injunction.

The court denied the injunction. One of the grounds for the denial was that Ross was not suffering an irreparable injury. The trespass was not considered so grievous as to cause a loss that could not be remedied at law. The court also referred to the public interest in completing the canal.

Is this result correct? If the injunction had been granted, would Ross have been in a position to demand an unconscionable price for the rock? Should it matter to the dignity of the court if the injunction would have that effect? What is the economically efficient result in such a situation?

United States v. Oakland Cannabis Buyers' Cooperative

532 U.S. 483, 121 S.Ct. 1711, 149 L.Ed.2d 722 (2001).

■ JUSTICE THOMAS delivered the opinion of the Court.

The Controlled Substances Act, 84 Stat. 1242, 21 U.S.C. § 80 *et seq.*, prohibits the manufacture and distribution of various drugs, including marijuana. In this case, we must decide whether there is a medical necessity exception to these prohibitions. We hold that there is not.

In November 1996, California voters enacted an initiative measure entitled the Compassionate Use Act of 1996. Attempting "[t]o ensure that seriously ill Californians have the right to obtain and use marijuana for medical purposes," Cal. Health & Safety Code Ann. § 11362.5 (West Supp.2001), the statute creates an exception to California laws prohibiting the possession and cultivation of marijuana. These prohibitions no longer apply to a patient or his primary caregiver who possesses or cultivates marijuana for the patient's medical purposes upon the recommendation or approval of a physician. *Ibid.* In the wake of this voter initiative, several groups organized "medical cannabis dispensaries" to meet the needs of qualified patients. *United States v. Cannabis Cultivators Club,* 5 F.Supp.2d 1086, 1092 (N.D.Cal.1998). Respondent Oakland Cannabis Buyers' Cooperative is one of these groups.

The Cooperative is a not-for-profit organization that operates in downtown Oakland. A physician serves as medical director, and registered nurses staff the Cooperative during business hours. To become a member, a patient must provide a written statement from a treating physician assenting to marijuana therapy and must submit to a screening interview. If accepted as a member, the patient receives an identification card entitling him to obtain marijuana from the Cooperative.

In January 1998, the United States sued the Cooperative and its executive director, respondent Jeffrey Jones (together, the Cooperative), in the United States District Court for the Northern District of California. Seeking to enjoin the Cooperative from distributing and manufacturing marijuana, the United States argued that, whether or not the Cooperative's activities are legal under California law, they violate federal law. Specifically, the Government argued that the Cooperative violated the Controlled Substances Act's prohibitions on distributing, manufacturing, and possessing with the intent to distribute or manufacture a controlled substance. * * *

[The district court issued the injunction and the Cooperative at first contested it by violation. When the Government initiated contempt proceedings, the Cooperative complied and sought modification of the injunction to exempt distribution for medical necessity. The court denied the request and the Cooperative appealed.]

Reaching the merits of this issue, the Court of Appeals reversed and remanded. According to the Court of Appeals, the medical necessity defense was a "legally cognizable defense" that likely would apply in the circumstances. 190 F.3d, at 1114. Moreover, the Court of Appeals reasoned, the District Court erroneously "believed that it had no discretion to issue an injunction that was more limited in scope than the Controlled Substances Act itself." *Id.,* at 1114–1115. Because, according to the Court of Appeals, district courts retain "broad equitable discretion" to fashion injunctive relief, the District Court could have, and should have, weighed the "public interest" and considered factors such as the serious harm in depriving patients of marijuana. Remanding the case, the Court of Appeals instructed the District Court to consider "the criteria for a medical necessity exemption, and, should it modify the injunction, to set forth those criteria in the modification order." Id. Following these instructions, the District Court granted the Cooperative's motion to modify the injunction to incorporate a medical necessity defense.

The United States petitioned for certiorari to review the Court of Appeals' decision that medical necessity is a legally cognizable defense to violations of the Controlled Substances Act. Because the decision raises significant questions as to the ability of the United States to enforce the Nation's drug laws, we granted certiorari.

* * * [W]e hold that medical necessity is not a defense to manufacturing and distributing marijuana. The Court of Appeals erred when it held that medical necessity is a "legally cognizable defense." It further erred when it instructed the District Court on remand to consider "the criteria for a medical necessity exemption, and, should it modify the injunction, to set forth those criteria in the modification order."

The Cooperative contends that, even if the Controlled Substances Act forecloses the medical necessity defense, there is an alternative ground for affirming the Court of Appeals. This case, the Cooperative reminds us, arises from a motion to modify an injunction to permit distributions that are medically necessary. According to the Cooperative, the Court of Appeals was correct that the District Court had "broad equitable discretion" to tailor the injunctive relief to account for medical necessity, irrespective of whether there is a legal defense of necessity in the statute. To sustain the judgment below, the argument goes, we need only reaffirm that federal courts, in the exercise of their equity jurisdiction, have discretion to modify an injunction based upon a weighing of the public interest.

We disagree. Although district courts whose equity powers have been properly invoked indeed have discretion in fashioning injunctive relief (in the absence of a statutory restriction), the Court of Appeals erred concerning the factors that the district courts may consider in exercising such discretion.

As an initial matter, the Cooperative is correct that, when district courts are properly acting as courts of equity, they have discretion unless a statute clearly provides otherwise. For "several hundred years," courts of equity have enjoyed "sound discretion" to consider the "necessities of the public interest" when fashioning injunctive relief. *Hecht Co. v. Bowles,* 321 U.S. 321, 329–330, 64 S.Ct. 587, 88 L.Ed. 754 (1944). See also *id.,* at 329, 64 S.Ct. 587 ("The essence of equity jurisdiction has been the power of the Chancellor to do equity and to mould each decree to the necessities of the particular case. Flexibility rather than rigidity has distinguished it"); *Weinberger v. Romero–Barcelo,* 456 U.S. 305, 312, 102 S.Ct. 1798, 72 L.Ed.2d 91 (1982) ("In exercising their sound discretion, courts of equity should pay particular regard for the public consequences in employing the extraordinary remedy of injunction"). Such discretion is displaced only by a "clear and valid legislative command." Porter v. Warner Holding Co., 328 U.S. 395, 398, 66 S.Ct. 1086, 90 L.Ed. 1332 (1946). See also *Romero–Barcelo, supra,* at 313, 102 S.Ct. 1798 ("Of course, Congress may intervene and guide or control the exercise of the courts' discretion, but we do not lightly assume that Congress has intended to depart from established principles").

The Cooperative is also correct that the District Court in this case had discretion. * * * But the mere fact that the District Court had discretion does not suggest that the District Court, when evaluating the motion to modify the injunction, could consider any and all factors that might relate to the public interest or the conveniences of the parties, including the medical needs of the Cooperative's patients. On the contrary, a court sitting in equity cannot "ignore the judgment of Congress, deliberately expressed in legislation." [Citation.]. A district court cannot, for example, override Congress' policy choice, articulated in a statute, as to what behavior should be prohibited. "Once Congress, exercising its delegated powers, has decided the order of priorities in a given area, it is . . . for the courts to enforce them when enforcement is sought." [Citation.] Courts of equity cannot, in their discretion, reject the balance that Congress has struck in a statute. Their choice (unless there is statutory language to the contrary) is simply whether a particular means of enforcing the statute should be chosen over another permissible means; their choice is not whether enforcement is preferable to no enforcement at all. Consequently, when a court of equity exercises its discretion, it may not consider the advantages and disadvantages of nonenforcement of the statute, but only the advantages and disadvantages of "employing the extraordinary remedy of injunction," [citation] over the other available methods of enforcement. [Citation.] To the extent the district court considers the public interest and the conveniences of the parties, the court is limited to evaluating how such interest and conveniences are affected by the selection of an injunction over other enforcement mechanisms.

In this case, the Court of Appeals erred by considering relevant the evidence that some people have "serious medical conditions for whom the use of cannabis is necessary in order to treat or alleviate those conditions or their symptoms," that these people "will suffer serious harm if they are denied cannabis," and that "there is no legal alternative to cannabis for the effective treatment of their medical conditions." As explained above, in the Controlled Substances Act, the balance already has been struck against a medical necessity exception. Because the statutory prohibitions cover even those who have what could be termed a medical necessity, the Act precludes consideration of this evidence. It was thus error for the Court of Appeals to instruct the District Court on remand to consider "the criteria for a medical necessity exemption, and, should it modify the injunction, to set forth those criteria in the modification order."

* * * [Reversed and remanded.]

---

1. *Statutes Affecting Public Interest Determinations.* Are courts bound by a Congressional assessment of the public interest in cases of the general type covered by the statute? As the principal case reflects, the Supreme Court has held that if that expression has been clear and unambiguous, then courts are bound by it. It has reasoned that such legislative constraint on the equitable discretion of courts is not a violation of separation of powers because the source of the right is integrally tied to the constraint on the remedy.

Thus, in *TVA v. Hill*, 437 U.S. 153, 98 S.Ct. 2279, 57 L.Ed.2d 117 (1978), reprinted *infra* in Chapter 9, Supreme Court held that the Endangered Species Act of 1973 required the District Court to enjoin completion of a dam. The judge had no discretion to weigh the public interest in the dam against the public interest in the endangered species because Congress had already made that choice in the statute. It made no difference that the species was a little known organism called the snail darter. Once it was determined that the operation of the dam would either eradicate the known population of the snail darter or destroy its critical habitat, then an injunction against the dam was mandatory. The Court reasoned that Congress had intended the restraint on discretion because an injunction was the only means of ensuring compliance with the Act. This topic is covered more fully in Chapter 9.

2. *Good Faith.* Consider further the role of good faith in the context of the principal case. The Cooperative appears to have changed its status over time in terms of its good faith effort to comply with the law. The initial operation of the Cooperative appears to be a good faith application of the new California law, but its contemptuous violation of the court's injunction was a knowing violation. As covered in Chapter 7 on contempt, a good faith belief in the interpretation of the underlying law is not a defense to a wilful violation of a court order. Therefore, the Cooperative could have been held in criminal contempt even if it had been correct ultimately about its ability to distribute cannabis for medical necessity.

CHAPTER 4

SPECIFIC PERFORMANCE

The remedy of specific performance is a specialized form of injunctive relief that functions to ensure enforcement, as far as is practicable, of otherwise valid contractual obligations. A court of equity exercises its discretion in determining whether specific performance is an appropriate remedy by considering the following factors: the inadequacy of available legal remedies, the likelihood of future performance by the party seeking enforcement of the contract, the ability of the breaching party to render performance, the balance of interests and relative hardships of the contracting parties, and any potential difficulties in supervision or enforcement of the decree. These determinations affect both the availability of the order and its scope.

This equitable remedy is an *in personam* order that is punishable by contempt if disobeyed. The specific performance remedy is available both at common law and, in a liberalized form, under the Uniform Commercial Code with respect to transactions involving the sale of goods. The equitable defenses, like laches and unclean hands, may preclude specific performance (*see* Chapter 5). If specific performance is denied, the non-breaching party may still seek any available legal remedies.

A. ENTITLEMENT

Section Coverage:

Specific performance, as a discretionary equitable remedy, traditionally would not be ordered if the court determined that an award of damages at law would adequately protect the interests of the injured party. "Adequacy" in this equitable application has taken on a qualitative or relative meaning rather than being viewed purely in a quantitative sense. When the subject matter of the dispute has involved unique or non-fungible items, such as heirlooms or land, courts typically have considered substitutionary relief of money to be inadequate. Thus, a court's evaluation of legal remedies involves the difficulty of proving damages with reasonable certainty or the availability of an appropriate substitute in the market.

Courts traditionally have refused to decree specific performance of contracts that involve rendering personal services, such as contracts with professional athletes or artistic performers. Various reasons support this refusal including the difficulties of enforcement and supervision, the pragmatic need for loyalty and cooperation in the workplace, and the constitutional prohibition of involuntary servitude. Similarly, employers are rarely compelled to accept services tendered under contract unless there is a statutory basis for the order, such as in fair employment acts.

The common law refusal to compel acceptance of unwanted services is derived partly from public policy and partly on the basis of "lack of mutuality." The mutuality of remedy rule in pure form requires perfect symmetry of remedies for whichever party to a contract might breach. In the employment context this rule means that because an employer cannot have specific performance to compel a breaching employee to work, an employee should be denied that remedy against a breaching employer. The lack of mutuality defense, however, has been diminishing steadily in vitality; cases have created numerous exceptions and sometimes have rejected it outright. Under modern contract law there is no general requirement of perfect symmetry of remedies for contracting parties, particularly when the expectation of benefits differ.

Although specific performance may be denied, a court may still prohibit a person under contract with an employer from performing such services for anyone other than the plaintiff. The judge will issue such an injunction upon a showing that the services are unique or involve special skills. This inquiry is simply revisiting the role of equity to provide relief when the damages remedy is inadequate to protect an employer's interests.

Model Case:

On January 1, Owens contracted to sell Blackacre, a 160 acre tract of land, to Farmer Brown for a total purchase price of $100,000. In accordance with the contract Farmer Brown paid to Owens $10,000 as earnest money, with the balance to be paid on July 1, upon Owens' delivery of the deed. On February 1, however, Owens repudiated and refused to convey Blackacre.

Farmer Brown will be entitled to a decree for specific performance immediately, although Owens' delivery of the deed will not be required until July 1, conditioned upon Farmer Brown's payment of the remaining $90,000. The court will rely upon the rationale that each parcel of land is unique, thus making substitutionary relief of damages inadequate to compensate Farmer Brown.

Estate of Lucille Osborn v. Kemp

991 A.2d 1153 (Del. 2010).

■ STEELE, CHIEF JUSTICE:

I.   Facts and Procedure Posture

Osborn lived in Wilmington and had a beach house in Slaughter Beach, Sussex County. Lucille and her husband bought the beach house back in 1968. The beach house had two floors which were divided into two separate apartments. In 1984, Osborn decided to rent out the top floor, but wanted to keep the bottom floor for herself, so she could enjoy the beach from time to time. Osborn found a lessee in Kemp and on November 9, 1984, Kemp began leasing the upper apartment at a rate of $275 a month, plus utilities. Later that year, Kemp's friend, Roxanne Danburg also moved in and both took to living in the upper apartment and have lived there ever since.

From the start Kemp wanted to buy the beach house and on April 16, 1985, Osborn and Kemp entered into an agreement which is the subject of this litigation. That day Osborn allegedly agreed to sell the beach house to Kemp. Kemp drafted the holographic document which provided, in its entirety,

I, Michael Kemp agree to pay Lucille Menicucci $275.00 per month plus utilities for twenty years for the purchase of property at 292 S. Delaware and Bay Ave. Slaughter Beach for $50,000.

Kemp signed his name on the bottom right of the document and Osborn signed under Kemp's name. 1 Osborn and Kemp decided to get the document notarized that very same day and, eventually, arrived at Cedar Creek Bait and Tackle Shop.

At the bait shop, Joyce M. Macklin, a public notary, notarized the agreement and placed an embossed seal on the document. Macklin signed at the bottom, to the left of the signatures of both Osborn and Kemp. Macklin testified at trial that she remembered signing this document because she did not see many handwritten documents for the sale of real property. * * *

By the document's express terms, Kemp would pay $275 per month for twenty years. For those next twenty years, Kemp and Danburg lived together in the beach house. Kemp made $11,000 worth of improvements to the house. Kemp and Danburg made their scheduled payments lackadaisically, paying several months at once and frequently late, but, in the end, no dispute with Osborn arose over any missed payments. Kemp or Danburg would send payment to Osborn and she would send them a copy of the receipt. These receipts refer to the payments only as "rent." Also, Osborn listed on a 2004 tax return that the payments made by Kemp and Danburg were "rent" and did not indicate Kemp's ownership stake. * * *

As of May 2006, Osborn still owned the property of record when tragedy struck. Osborn's neighbors in Wilmington found her unconscious on the floor of her home. Osborn never recovered and began to suffer from dementia. Fortunately for Osborn, her adoring niece, Sharon Gillespie, took care of her needs and soon assumed all of Osborn's affairs under a previously executed power of attorney. While going over Osborn's records, Gillespie noticed that Kemp had stopped making payments on the beach house. Osborn never told Gillespie, nor did Gillespie have any reason to know, about the holographic contract. Gillespie assumed that Kemp merely leased the beach house. * * *

On August 17, 2007, Gillespie filed suit on behalf of Osborn seeking a permanent injunction, declaratory judgment, and restitution against Kemp. Kemp answered and on August 8, 2008, Kemp amended his complaint to include a counterclaim for specific performance. The parties went to trial in the Court of Chancery on October 29, 2008. Osborn could not testify at trial because her mental faculties declined. She died on December 15, 2008. At the conclusion of the trial, the Vice Chancellor ordered specific performance and dismissed Osborn's complaint with prejudice.

The Vice Chancellor issued a memorandum opinion in which, first, he found that the photocopy of the holographic installment contract is authentic and then held (1) the parties entered into a valid contract, (2) Kemp was ready, willing, and able to perform, and (3) the balance of the equities tipped in favor of specifically enforcing the contract. The Vice Chancellor also rejected Osborn's argument that the doctrine of laches barred Kemp's claim.

The Vice Chancellor set the terms of specific performance as (1) Kemp must pay the Estate of Osborn $50,000 within 90 days, (2) Kemp must pay interest, compounded quarterly, accruing from April 16, 2005, (2) Kemp must remit to the Estate payment for utilities up until the present time, (3) Kemp must pay for the deed preparation and closing costs, (4) and the Estate would pay the transfer tax pursuant to 30 *Del. C.* § 5412. Gillespie, as co-executrix of Osborn's estate, appeals the Vice Chancellor's decision. * * *

II. Analysis.

1. *Specific Performance*

Specific performance for the transfer of real property is an extraordinary remedy and we will not award it lightly. A party must prove by clear and convincing evidence that he or she is entitled to specific performance and that he or she has no adequate legal remedy. A party seeking specific performance must establish that (1) a valid contract exists, (2) he is ready, willing, and able to perform, and (3) that the balance of equities tips in favor of the party seeking performance. We will examine each element separately.

(A) *Validity of the Contract*

First, a valid contract exists when (1) the parties intended that the contract would bind them, (2) the terms of the contract are sufficiently definite, and (3) the parties exchange legal consideration. Gillespie does not seriously dispute that the parties intended to be bound nor does she dispute that consideration passed hands. We will only briefly examine these elements.

The face of this contract manifests the parties' intent to bind one another contractually. Both parties signed the contract and had the contract notarized. The parties also exchanged consideration for the beach house. The Vice Chancellor could not have more correctly held that we limit our inquiry into consideration to its existence and "not whether it is fair or adequate. Mere inadequacy of consideration, in the absence of any unfairness or overreaching, does not justify a denial of . . . specific performance where in other respects the contract conforms with the rules and principles of equity." Here, Kemp paid Osborn an uninterrupted stream of income for twenty years, plus, an additional $50,000 due at settlement. These payments indisputably constitute consideration.

Gillespie does argue that the contract fails for indefiniteness and, thus, the Vice Chancellor erred by granting specific performance. Gillespie contends that we may reasonably interpret the price term in ways, which create an indefinite ambiguity, and obviates specific performance. Gillespie points to the "$50,000" term and asserts that when the contract is read *in toto* the term could mean that Kemp has the option of paying $50,000 after making all monthly payments to fully consummate the transaction, or that Kemp would make installment payments of $275 per month for twenty years, on a $50,000 base price with the overage consisting of an amalgamation of interest, fees, and carrying costs for which the parties did not expressly provide.

The Vice Chancellor held that Kemp must pay $50,000 in order to obtain the property because (1) courts must read the contract in its entirety and give effect to all of its terms and provisions, and (2) the contract was ambiguous and applied the doctrine of *contra proferentem* to interpret the terms against the drafting party. The Vice Chancellor did not err when he held that he must read the contract in its entirety and give effect to all of its terms and provisions, however, the Vice Chancellor incorrectly found that the contract is ambiguous.

"Delaware adheres to the 'objective' theory of contracts, i.e. a contract's construction should be that which would be understood by an objective, reasonable third party." "We will read a contract as a whole and we will give each provision and term effect, so as not to render any part of the contract mere surplusage." We will not read a contract to render a provision or term "meaningless or illusory." "[A] contract must contain all material terms in order to be enforceable, and specific performance will only be granted when an agreement is clear and definite and a court does not need to supply essential contract terms."

When the contract is clear and unambiguous, we will give effect to the plain-meaning of the contract's terms and provisions. On the contrary, when we may reasonably ascribe multiple and different interpretations to a contract, we will find that the contract is ambiguous. An unreasonable interpretation produces an absurd result or one that no reasonable person would have accepted when entering the contract.

If a contract is ambiguous, we will apply the doctrine of *contra proferentem* against the drafting party and interpret the contract in favor of the non-drafting party. The parties' steadfast disagreement over interpretation will not, alone, render the contract ambiguous. The determination of ambiguity lies within the sole province of the court.

This contract's only reasonable interpretation creates an installment contract with an option to purchase at the end of the term. The parties do not dispute the import of the $275 per month for twenty years. Under these terms, Kemp agreed to pay Osborn $275 a month for twenty years.

CHAPTER 4 SPECIFIC PERFORMANCE   **95**

As for the language "purchase of property ... for $50,000", we let the plain-meaning of this term guide us. The contract includes a price term of $50,000 which clearly indicates that Kemp must remit $50,000 in additional proceeds to "purchase" the property. This prototypical condition commonly precedes the offeror's performance. Therefore, the ordinary, plain meaning of this term establishes installment payments with an option to purchase at the end of the term and obtain title. [The court held that the unambiguous contract stated a definite price term.] * * *

(B) *Ready, Willing and Able to Perform*

We will order specific performance only if a party is ready, willing, and able to perform under the terms of the agreement. Unless the contract provides that time is of the essence, we will permit the parties a reasonable time to obtain financing and conclude the transaction.

Gillespie argues that Kemp is not ready, willing, and able to perform because he did not have the necessary financing at the time of trial. The Vice Chancellor found that Kemp could put the property up as collateral to obtain the funding and he held that Kemp had 90 days to exercise the option. We find no fault in the Vice Chancellor's reasoning. Kemp may put the property up as collateral and obtain financing. We hold that 90 days is a reasonable time period when a contract does not include a "time is of the essence" clause to exercise an option to buy real property.

(C) *Balance of Equities Tips in Favor of Kemp*

Lastly, we will only order specific performance where the balance of equities tips in favor of specific performance. When balancing the equities "[we] must be convinced that 'specific enforcement of a validly formed contract would [not] cause even greater harm than it would prevent.'"[28]

Gillespie argues that, when looking at the "big picture," the balance of the equities tips against Kemp and specific performance. First, Gillespie introduced evidence that a one-story home in Slaughter Beach cost $106,000 in 1986 and that Kemp will only pay $116,000 for a far superior house, twenty years later.[29] Second, Osborn did not increase the rent over the course of twenty years and Kemp received ample benefit from this cheap rental rate. Third, Kemp and Danburg started out living only on the second floor, but eventually occupied the entire house and, even when they occupied both floors, they did not pay increased rent. Fourth, Osborn paid all, and Kemp did not pay any, of the property taxes for twenty years. Finally, the Vice Chancellor erred by not taking into account the appreciation value of the property and the interest that would have accumulated when he held that the balance of equities tipped in favor of awarding specific performance.

---

28. *See Morabito v. Harris*, 2002 WL 550117, at 2 ("The balance of equities issue 'reflect[s] the traditional concern of a court of equity that its special processes not be used in a way that unjustifiably increases human suffering.'") (quoting *Bernard Pers. Consultants, Inc. v. Mazarella*, 1990 WL 124969, at 3 (Del. Ch. Aug. 28, 1990)).

29. If you add the $50,000 payment ordered by the Vice Chancellor and the $66,000 which was the total payment of $275 a month for twenty years this equals the $116,000.

While Gillespie has made a robust argument, the balance of the equities tips in favor of Kemp and specific performance. We recognize that real property is unique and often the law cannot adequately remedy a party's refusal to honor a real property contract. We also take note of the improvements that Kemp made to the property that cost him approximately $11,000. If we add this to the Vice Chancellor's $116,000 purchase price, then the $127,000 total amount further tips the scales against Gillespie's proffered property that sold for $106,000 in 1986. Osborn not only received an income stream for twenty years, but she also used the first floor of the property for her personal use over the course of the contract. Osborn indisputably benefitted from this arrangement.

We do not discount that beach front property has appreciated over the span of twenty years, however, the "mere increase in land values, unaccompanied by other circumstances showing inequity, is not such hardship as justifies a court of equity in denying specific performance."

Finally, and most importantly, Kemp and Danburg lived in this property for twenty years. They made it their home. Equity would not be served by ousting Kemp and Danburg from their long-time residence.[32]

In sum, we affirm the order for specific performance because the parties validly executed a contract; the party seeking specific performance is ready, willing, and able to perform under the contract; and the balance of equities tips in favor of specific performance. * * *

---

1. *Performance.* An important requirement for specific performance is that the claimant demonstrates the readiness and ability to satisfy the contract conditions. In *Clark v. Route*, 951 A.2d 757 (D.C. App. 2008) during a routine inspection of a residential property, a dispute developed over whether the sellers should be required to waterproof the basement and produce a related warranty. The buyer simply left the house, said "see you in court" and had no further communication with the sellers. Also, the buyer indefinitely postponed the closing and failed to complete the necessary financing arrangements. The court found that the buyer's behavior demonstrated an unwillingness to be ready, willing and able to perform the contract. *See also* DiGiuseppe v. Lawler, 269 S.W.3d 588 (Tex. 2008) (even where pre-suit actual tender of performance is excused, plaintiff is still required to plead and prove readiness, willingness and ability to perform before specific performance will be granted).

2. *Balancing Equities.* The hallmark of equity is the discretion of courts to mold the decree to achieve fairness through balancing the potential hardships of the parties. Balancing occurs on two levels: the weighing of respective potential hardships if an equitable order is granted

---

32. *Morabito*, 2002 WL 550117, at 3 (holding that a family would experience significant hardship because an order of specific performance cast the family out of their home and render them homeless).

or denied, and then with fashioning the decree. The question is not whether a burden can be avoided entirely but rather which party should bear the hardship and the specific manner of assignment of that burden.

In *Norwich Community Dev. Corp. v. Arbucci*, 1993 WL 7242 (Conn.Super. 1993), the development board of a city, seeking to rehabilitate its downtown area, entered into a contract to transfer a railroad depot and adjacent land to a real estate developer. Years passed and the board sought specific performance to reconvey the property, claiming that the developer had not discharged its obligations. The court observed that the balance of equities presented the choice of either continuing the urban blight resulting from lack of rehabilitation of the building or depriving the defendant contractor of its substantial investment in time and money. The court ordered the reconveyance, making appropriate adjustments in the contract terms to avoid giving the claimant a windfall.

In *Sykes v. Payton*, 441 F.Supp.2d 1220, 1226 (M.D.Ala. 2006) a contestant in a university beauty pageant was crowned the winner until the results were questioned. An official investigation revealed a scoring error and the title was subsequently bestowed on another contestant. The losing contestant sought injunctive relief to specifically enforce the original results based on a theory of promissory estoppel. The court noted that specific performance generally awards the expectation interest to give the benefit of the bargain in a contract, rather than the reliance interest. In balancing the equities, the court observed, "Simply put, one person will be hurt, and one person will miss out on the opportunities and benefits attendant to the crown. Should it be the person that actually won, or should it be the person who was promised that, despite a scoring error, she would retain the crown?" The court concluded that resolution of the dispute was better left to university officials rather than a court of equity.

3. *Land Sale Contracts.* Courts traditionally have considered a contract for the sale of land to be a proper subject for specific performance. Land is incapable of duplication and therefore each parcel is regarded as unique. Also, valuation problems may exist for certain tracts of land. Damages, then, are viewed as inadequate for a contract to convey an interest in land. *But see* Ash Park, LLC v. Alexander & Bishop, Ltd., 324 Wis.2d 703, 783 N.W.2d 294 (2010) (Wisconsin statutory law does not require a seller to show an inadequate remedy at law as a prerequisite to an award of specific performance).

What if the purchaser in a land sales contract makes another contract to reconvey the land to a third party? Are damages still inadequate now that the purchaser's expected profit from the resale can be measured precisely? The traditional rule is that the purchaser should receive specific performance for the land even when there is a second contract for reconveyance. The rationale is that courts should routinely grant specific performance for land sales contracts to avoid litigation and damages. Restatement (Second) of Contracts § 360 comment e. Is this rationale satisfactory in terms of theoretical consistency? Does it comport with business reality?

4. Not all real estate contracts necessarily are proper subjects for specific performance, however. For instance, in *Van Wagner Advertising Corp. v. S & M Enterprises*, 67 N.Y.2d 186, 492 N.E.2d 756, 501 N.Y.S.2d 628 (1986), following the sale of a commercial building, the new owner sought to cancel a leasehold which involved certain advertising space on billboards. The lessee sought a declaratory judgment that the cancellation was ineffective and also requested specific performance and damages. The lessee asserted that because the billboards were visible to motorists entering Manhattan, they had a prime and unique location for the intended advertising purpose. The court disagreed, drawing a distinction between a leasehold and a sale of real property, and denied equitable relief, observing:

> The word "uniqueness" is not * * * a magic door to specific performance. A distinction must be drawn between physical difference and economic interchangeability. The trial court found that the leased property is physically unique, but so is every parcel of real property and so are many consumer goods. Putting aside contracts for the sale of real property, where specific performance has traditionally been the remedy for breach, uniqueness in the sense of physical differences does not itself dictate the propriety of equitable relief.
>
> By the same token, at some level all property may be interchangeable with money. Economic theory is concerned with the degree to which consumers are willing to substitute the use of one good for another the underlying assumption being that "every good has substitutes, even if only very poor ones", and that "all goods are ultimately commensurable". Such a view, however, could strip all meaning from uniqueness, for if all goods are ultimately exchangeable for a price, then all goods may be valued. Even a rare manuscript has an economic substitute in that there is a price for which any purchaser would likely agree to give up a right to buy it, but a court would in all probability order specific performance of such a contract on the ground that the subject matter of the contract is unique. The point at which breach of a contract will be redressable by specific performance thus must lie not in any inherent physical uniqueness of the property but instead in the uncertainty of valuing it [.]

5. *Certainty*. The choice and measure of available remedies for breach of contract are often shaped by issues of certainty. For example, if a party contracted to use their best efforts in building a bridge, legal damages for breach would be ascertainable but a court would decline specific performance because no appropriate decree could govern or enforce "best efforts." The need for certainty of terms, then, dovetails with the consideration of potential difficulties in supervision of the decree. The contract terms must be sufficiently definite and certain to achieve contract formation as well as to calculate damages for breach.

Although more certainty is required for equitable relief than for damages at law, courts may supply missing subordinate details upon which to predicate the equitable order. Thus, while an output contract inherently is uncertain as to the final quantity to be produced, an equity court will not hesitate to draft a decree. *See* U.C.C. § 2–716 comment 2. The absence of a time requirement will not necessarily defeat a request for specific performance. Laclede Gas Co. v. Amoco Oil Co., 522 F.2d 33 (8th Cir. 1975).

In *Patel v. Liebermensch*, 45 Cal.4th 344, 197 P.3d 177, 86 Cal.Rptr.3d 366, 369 (2008), a tenant sought specific performance of an option contract to purchase residential property. Although the contract did not specify the time and manner of payment, the court found that reasonable terms could be supplied by implication to avoid destruction of the contract because of uncertainty. *Also see* Tauber v. Quan, 938 A.2d 724, 730 (D.C. App. 2007) (omission of non-material terms of default, such as allocation of attorney's fees, did not render commercial real estate agreement unenforceable through specific performance); Laclede Gas Co. v. Amoco Oil Co., 522 F.2d 33, 39 (8th Cir.1975) (absence of a time requirement will not necessarily defeat a request for specific performance).

6.   In some instances, the contract terms may be definite yet damages are uncertain or speculative due to the nature of the subject matter of the agreement. See Restatement (Second) of Contracts § 360 comment b. If so, courts may find the damages remedy inadequate and order specific performance. Traditional illustrations where injunctive relief may be appropriate include the potential loss of customers or goodwill from a breach of a covenant not to compete, sale of an enterprise, and lost business opportunities. *See* Philip Morris Inc. v. Pittsburgh Penguins, Inc., 589 F.Supp. 912 (W.D.Pa. 1983) (the loss of prospective customers due to absence of plaintiff's advertising signs at sports arena venue could not be calculated in money damages)

7.   A higher threshold of certainty may be required to support specific performance because a court of equity must be able to fashion the decree with specificity such that the enjoined party will clearly understand the duties owed. In *Petrello v. White*, 533 F.3d 110 (2d Cir. 2008), the court found that the language in a specific performance order to convey real property was deficient because it failed to describe required conduct in detail and did not impose a deadline to complete the mandated actions. The court noted that an injunction must be drawn with specificity to provide fair notice to the enjoined party of all affirmative obligations which must be undertaken in order to avoid the sanction of contempt for noncompliance.

Houseman v. Dare

405 N.J.Super. 538, 966 A.2d 24 (2009).

■ GRALL, J.A.D.

Plaintiff Doreen Houseman appeals from a judgment of the Family Part awarding her $1500 for a dog she and defendant Eric Dare jointly owned when they separated and ended their engagement to be married. Alleging that she and Dare had an oral agreement giving her possession of the dog that Dare breached by wrongfully retaining the dog after a post-separation visit, Houseman sought specific performance of the agreement and a judgment declaring her ownership of the animal. Prior to trial, the court determined that pets are personal property that lack the unique value essential to an award of specific performance. On appeal Houseman claims that the pretrial ruling was erroneous as a matter of law. We agree and remand for further proceedings.

The following facts are not in dispute. Houseman and Dare had a relationship for thirteen years. In 1999 they purchased a residence, which they owned as joint tenants and made their home. In 2000 they engaged to marry, and in 2003 they purchased a pedigree dog for $1500, which they registered with the American Kennel Club reporting that they both owned the dog. In May 2006 Dare decided to end his relationship with Houseman. At that time, Dare wanted to stay in the house and purchase Houseman's interest in the property. In June 2006, Houseman signed a deed transferring her interest in the house to Dare. When she vacated the residence on July 4, 2006, Houseman took the dog and its paraphernalia with her. She left one of the dog's jerseys and some photographs behind as mementos for Dare.

The trial court limited presentation of evidence about the parties' dog in accordance with its pretrial ruling foreclosing Houseman's claim for specific performance and the parties' stipulation that $1500 was the intrinsic value of the dog. * * *

According to Houseman, "from the minute [Dare] told [her they] were breaking up, he told [her she] could have" the dog. She and Dare agreed that she would get the dog and one-half the value of the house. Although she admitted that she would not have wanted more than one-half the value of their house if she were not taking the dog, she asserted that her primary concern during her negotiations with Dare was possession of their dog and that she accepted his representations that her share of the equity was $45,000.

* * *

Dare and Houseman did not have a written agreement about the dog, but after Houseman left the residence she allowed him to take the dog for visits after which he returned the pet to her. According to Houseman, when she asked Dare to memorialize their agreement about the dog in a writing, he told her she could trust him and he would not keep the dog from her. Although Dare admitted to making that promise in his answer to Houseman's complaint, he offered no testimony on that point at trial.

In late February 2007, Houseman left the dog with Dare when she went on vacation. On March 4, 2007, she asked Dare for the dog, but the pet was not returned. Houseman filed the complaint that initiated this litigation on March 16, 2007, and when trial commenced in December 2007 Dare still had the dog.

Prior to trial, the parties stipulated that Dare sold the residence in December 2006 and received equity in an amount that exceeded $90,000. * * *

The court made the following findings relevant to the dog:

I'm more than satisfied, hearing Ms. Houseman testify, that the dog was in no way related to the sale of the house. They may have an understanding about the dog. She thought she was getting the dog. He picked the dog up later. He has the dog. We know what the value of the dog is. The dog is worth $1500. I believe it's now in Mr. Dare's possession. He'll pay Ms. Houseman $1500 [the full value stipulated by the parties] for the dog.

The foregoing passage suggests, although not with unmistakable clarity, that the court found that Houseman established an oral agreement under which she was to obtain possession and ownership of the dog. Despite that finding and solely on the ground that Dare had possession of the dog at that time, the court awarded Dare possession and Houseman the dog's stipulated value.

The court's conclusion that specific performance is not, as a matter of law, available to remedy a breach of an oral agreement about possession of a dog reached by its joint owners is not sustainable. The remedy of specific performance can be invoked to address a breach of an enforceable agreement when money damages are not adequate to protect the expectation interest of the injured party and an order requiring performance of the contract will not result in inequity to the offending party, reward the recipient for unfair dealing or conflict with public policy. *See Restatement (Second) of Contracts* §§ 357, 358, 360, 364, 365 (1981).

Specific performance is generally recognized as the appropriate remedy when an agreement concerns possession of property such as "heirlooms, family treasures and works of art that induce a strong sentimental attachment." *Id.* at § 360 comment b. That is so because money damages cannot compensate the injured party for the special subjective benefits he or she derives from possession.

On the same reasoning, when personal property has such special subjective value courts have determined that an award of possession of personalty is the only adequate remedy for tortious acquisition and wrongful detention of property. *See Burr v. Bloomsburg*, 101 N.J. Eq. 615, 621, 138 A. 876 (Ch.1927); *see also Restatement (Second) of Torts* § 946 (1979). And, consideration of special subjective value is equally appropriate when a court is called upon to exercise its equitable jurisdiction to resolve a dispute between joint owners of property that cannot be partitioned or sold without hardship or violation of public policy. *See Newman v. Chase*, 70 N.J. 254, 263, 359 A.2d 474 (1976) (recognizing partition as "an ancient head of equity jurisdiction [and] an inherent power of the court"); *Swartz v. Becker*, 246 N.J. Super. 406, 413, 587 A.2d 1295 (App.Div.1991) (recognizing the relevance of hardship to partition); *Michalski v. Michalski*, 50 N.J. Super. 454, 467, 142 A.2d 645 (App.Div.1958) (considering acrimonious and litigious nature of parties' relationship in ordering partition rather than enforcing an agreement barring partition); *Hotchkin v. Hotchkin*, 105 N.J. Super. 475, 480, 253 A.2d 184 (Ch.Div.1969) (addressing partition of personal property); *Woodruff v. Woodruff*, 44 N.J. Eq. 349, 358, 16 A. 4

(Ch.1888) (considering sentiments asserted in resolving a dispute about a farm that favored leaving undivided possession with the party who had remembrances and associations with the property owned by her father and grandfather).

The special subjective value of personal property worthy of recognition by a court of equity is sentiment explained by facts and circumstances—such as the party's relationship with the donor or prior associations with the property—that give rise to the special affection. *See* 876; Pomeroy, *Specific Performance of Contracts* §§ 12, 34 (3d ed. 1926). In a different context, this court has recognized that pets have special "subjective value" to their owners. *Hyland v. Borras*, 316 N.J. Super. 22, 25, 719 A.2d 662 (App.Div.1998) (concluding that the owner of an injured dog was entitled to recover costs of treatment that exceeded replacement cost); *see also Pitney v. Bugbee*, 98 N.J.L. 116, 120, 118 A. 780 (Sup.Ct.1922) (noting the importance of the "companionship" of animals to humans in concluding that a bequest to the Society for Prevention of Cruelty to Animals was exempt from tax as a transfer to a benevolent and charitable organization). Courts of other jurisdictions have considered the special subjective value of pets in resolving questions about possession. *See, e.g., Morgan v. Kroupa*, 167 Vt. 99, 702 A.2d 630, 633 (1997) (affirming a decision awarding possession of a dog to a person who found the lost pet, "diligently attempted to locate the dog's owner and responsibly sheltered and cared for the animal for over a year").

There is no reason for a court of equity to be more wary in resolving competing claims for possession of a pet based on one party's sincere affection for and attachment to it than in resolving competing claims based on one party's sincere sentiment for an inanimate object based upon a relationship with the donor. In both types of cases, a court of equity must consider the interests of the parties pressing competing claims for possession and public policies that may be implicated by an award of possession. *Cf. Juelfs v. Gough*, 41 P.3d 593, 597 (Alaska 2002) (approving modification of a property settlement agreement providing for shared possession of a dog because the arrangement assumed cooperation between the parties that did not exist); *Akers v. Sellers*, 114 Ind. App. 660, 54 N.E.2d 779, 779–80 (1944) (speculating that the interests of the pet might be different but finding the evidence adequate to support an award of possession to the wife, rather than husband, on the ground that the husband had given her the dog).

In those fortunately rare cases when a separating couple is unable to agree about who will keep jointly held property with special subjective value (either because an agreement is in dispute or there is none) and the trial court deems division by forced sale an inappropriate or inadequate remedy given the nature of the property, our courts are equipped to determine whether the assertion of a special interest in possession is sincere and grounded in "facts and circumstances which endow the chattel with a special ... value" or based upon a sentiment assumed for the purpose of litigation out of greed, or other sentiment or motive similarly unworthy of protection in a court of equity. We are less confident that there are judicially discoverable and manageable standards for resolving questions of possession from the perspective of a pet, at least apart from cases involving abuse or neglect contrary to public policies expressed in laws designed to protect animals, *e.g.*, *N.J.S.A.* 4:22–17 to– 26.; *see Morgan, supra*, 702 A.2d at 633 (noting that "[h]owever strong the emotional attachments between pets and humans, courts simply cannot evaluate the 'best interests' of an animal" and resolving a dispute about possession in light of the interests asserted by the parties).

We conclude that the trial court erred by declining to consider the relevance of the oral agreement alleged on the ground that a pet is property. Agreements about property jointly held by cohabitants are material in actions concerning its division. They may be specifically enforced when that remedy is appropriate.

Houseman's evidence was adequate to require the trial court to consider the oral agreement and the remedy of specific performance. The special subjective value of the dog to Houseman can be inferred from her testimony about its importance to her and her prompt effort to enforce her right of possession when Dare took action adverse to her enjoyment of that right. Her stipulation to the dog's intrinsic monetary value cannot be viewed as a concession that the stipulated value was adequate to compensate her for loss of the special value given her efforts to pursue her claim for specific performance at trial. *See Burr, supra*, 101 N.J. Eq. at 629, 138 A. 876 (concluding that a payment made on demand to avoid loss of an heirloom did not bar a claim for possession based on an assertion that money damages were inadequate). And, Dare did not establish that an order awarding specific performance would be harsh or oppressive to him, reward Houseman for unfair conduct or violate public policy. To the contrary, assuming an oral agreement that Dare breached by keeping the dog after a visit, an order awarding him possession because he had the dog at the time of trial would reward him for his breach.

Recognizing that the trial court is in the best position to evaluate the equities implicated by Houseman's request for possession of the dog, and that Dare had no reason to present relevant evidence because he had possession of the dog when the trial court made its improvident pretrial ruling on specific performance, we remand for further proceedings on the existence of an oral agreement about ownership and possession of the dog and the propriety of specific performance.

The trial court's conclusion that the parties' agreement about their dog and residence were independent of one another and the court's findings on the amount due Houseman for her interest in the residence and jointly held savings account are supported by substantial credible evidence in the record. Consequently, we affirm those determinations, *R.* 2:11–3(e)(1)(A), and reverse and remand to the trial court that part of the judgment awarding Dare possession of the dog and Houseman $1500 for her interest in the pet for further proceedings in conformity with this opinion.

1. *Personal Association*. As recognized in the principal case, the concept of uniqueness may range from intrinsically one-of-a-kind, irreplaceable items such as family heirlooms or may be defined in relationship to the particular needs and purposes of the parties to the contract. For instance, in *Sokoloff v. Harriman Estates Development Corp.*, 96 N.Y.2d 409, 754 N.E.2d 184, 729 N.Y.S.2d 425 (2001) the court found that architectural plans and drawings for a new home were considered unique and a proper subject for specific performance because they were based on a design conceived by plaintiffs and, absent equitable intervention, would require the claimant to change the requirements of the design. Also see Restatement (Second) of Contracts § 360 comment c (specific performance is an appropriate remedy for contract breach with respect to goods that are "unique in kind, quality or personal association").

In a case pre-dating adoption of the U.C.C., a court ordered specific performance of an agreement to deliver a horse to a cowboy who had specially trained it into a "first class roping horse" from a "green, unbroken pony". Therefore, the court reasoned, the horse had a peculiar and unique value to the cowboy and could not be replaced in the market. *See* Morris v. Sparrow, 225 Ark. 1019, 287 S.W.2d 583 (1956).

Cumbest v. Harris, 363 So.2d 294 (Miss. 1978), involved a suit for specific performance of a stereo system that had been acquired over a fifteen year period and was designed and partially constructed by the claimant. The court found that the assembled property had a unique value and was not readily obtainable due to scarcity of some of the components. Also, the court acknowledged the sentimental value of the equipment as the claimant testified that their "blood, sweat and tears" went into acquiring the various pieces of the system. Accordingly, the chancery court erred in not finding equity jurisdiction.

2. *Inadequate Remedy at Law*. Specific performance, as an equitable discretionary decree, is predicated on the determination that no adequate remedy at law exists to fulfill the expectations of the parties. The idea that equity is subordinated to law reflects the harshness of such orders which bind a party in personam and is backed by the contempt power of the court. The concept of "at law" includes damages, statutory and administrative remedies. Although courts vary somewhat in their formulation of what constitutes an inadequate remedy, some commonly recognized factors include problems in valuation, the difficulty in obtaining a substitute due to the uniqueness of the subject matter of the contract, and problems in collectability of damages. *See* Restatement (Second) of Contracts Section 360; JP Morgan Chase Bank v. Winget, 510 F.3d 577 (6th Cir. 2007) (specific performance order enforcing bank's inspection rights under guaranty agreement deemed essential as lender otherwise lacked adequate remedy at law to protect pledged collateral).

3. In *Niagara Mohawk Power Corp. v. Graver Tank & Mfg. Co.*, 470 F.Supp. 1308 (N.D.N.Y. 1979) a public utility, concerned about faulty performance by a contractor in the fabrication and erection of a primary containment steel liner plate for a nuclear power plant, sought an equitable

decree to exercise a termination clause in the agreement. The court granted the utility's request, observing that no adequate remedy at law existed due to the difficulty in computing the potential damages associated with the breach. Also, the court observed that an action in replevin to recover possession of the goods wrongfully detained would be an ineffectual legal remedy because of jurisdictional barriers to potentially recovering the subject goods. Even when there is no jurisdictional problem with the court's power to seize the goods, state law typically provides that a defendant may give a bond in place of surrendering the goods. *See* Chabert v. Robert & Co., 273 App.Div. 237, 76 N.Y.S.2d 400 (1st Dept.1948); Restatement (Second) of Contracts § 359 Comment e; Corbin, Contracts, 5A § 1157.

4. What if the breaching party creates a situation which makes a damages remedy unavailing? In *McCollam v. Cahill*, 766 N.W.2d 171 (S.D. 2009),a buyer brought an action seeking equitable rescission of an agreement to purchase a family home, alleging that the sellers failed to disclose the presence of snakes on the property. The trial court found, however, that the presence of one bull snake in the house on a single occasion over a thirty year period was not a material fact required by applicable state disclosure statutes. Nevertheless, the buyer's own conduct in allowing the property to deteriorate and creating a perception in the community that the house had a "snake problem" substantially affected its marketability. Consequently, damages would be difficult to quantify and the sellers lacked an adequate remedy at law. Specific performance of the purchase agreement was granted.

PROBLEM: THE FAMILY CARE CONTRACTS

Part (A)

Bill and Marge always planned on retiring early and moving south to Florida to enjoy golf, travel, and the sunshine in a more relaxed environment. Although their finances were fairly tight, when Bill reached age 62 he decided to take early retirement from his position as an accountant with ABC Corporation. Marge, age 57, sold her antique store in preparation for the long-awaited transition to their new lifestyle. They made a written contract with their only child, Jim, who was a successful realtor in the same city, to convey the family home in exchange for a promise of "lifetime support." Jim hired an attorney to draft the contract, which was signed by the parents without negotiation. The house, a beautiful restored Victorian mansion in the historical district of the city, was duly conveyed.

For several years Jim lived in the house and supported the parents. He paid the bills and took care of any needed repairs to the house. Their dreams of Florida remained intact while they saved their money in anticipation of their move. Eventually Jim married, sold the family house, and moved. The parents also moved to the new house and lived there for a time with the newly wedded couple. A serious dispute between the new spouse and the parents resulted in Jim asking the parents to move to Ocean Side

Manor, an assisted living facility located in Florida. This arrangement was agreeable to the parents.

After living at the facility for six months, Ocean Side raised the monthly costs by 12% to take into account inflation factors and individualized levels of care for its residents. Jim complained but continued to pay the bills for another year, when Bill suddenly experienced a stroke that caused some disability in speech and movement. As a result of Bill's change in condition, Bill and Marge moved to a different wing in the facility which provided expanded nursing care. With the increase in medical services, the monthly bills immediately jumped another 15%. Jim then stopped making payments, claiming that their original agreement never contemplated such exorbitant costs.

The parents seek to compel Jim to make the monthly payments to the nursing home as fulfillment of the contract. Should the order be granted?

Part (B)

Another couple in their eighties made a contract with their child, Lee, who was fifty. In this contract the parents agreed to convey the family home to Lee "within a reasonable time" in exchange for a promise that Lee would nurse the parents until their death. After three years, however, the parents had not conveyed, although Lee had personally provided nursing services. A family quarrel resulted in the parents throwing Lee out of the house and hiring another person to provide nursing care. Lee seeks specific performance of the promise to convey the house. What result? Are the ages of the parties in either case relevant to the legal analysis?

Henderson v. Fisher

236 Cal.App.2d 468, 46 Cal.Rptr. 173 (1965).

■ Molinari, Justice.

Plaintiffs appeal from a judgment entered after a trial by the court awarding them $381.85 on a *quantum meruit* basis but refusing to grant specific performance of a written contract entered into between plaintiffs and decedent, Marion D. Baker. The sole issue presented on appeal is whether plaintiffs are entitled to specific performance of the subject agreement. We have concluded that they are and that the trial court erred in refusing to grant plaintiffs relief in this form.

On August 11, 1959, plaintiffs and decedent entered into a written contract which provided as follows:

"Whereas, the first party, Marion D. Baker, is 86 years of age and blind and is in need of constant care, the parties of the second part agree to move into the home of Mr. Baker at 717 College Street in the city of Healdsburg, state of California, and to furnish all food necessary or reasonably required by Mr. Baker; and to do all laundry work required by him and to keep the house clean and in good repair and to water the trees and shrubbery and to keep the premises in good condition as long as Mr. Baker lives.

* * *

"It is further agreed that Mr. Baker shall execute and deliver a deed of his interest in the real property, including his home and furniture at 717 College Street in Healdsburg, California, to the second parties, reserving to himself a life estate[.] * * * "

The factual background surrounding the making of this contract was as follows: For about 7 years prior to 1959 plaintiffs had been friends of decedent and his wife. They often referred to the Bakers as Grandma and Grandpa, and they had on numerous occasions helped the Bakers by performing various household chores for them. On July 24, 1959 Mrs. Baker died. About a week after her death and because Mr. Baker, who was blind and 86 years old, could not be left alone, plaintiffs moved into the Baker home. On August 11, 1959, at Baker's request, his attorney, Mr. Sayre, drew up the subject agreement. At this time Baker was in good health. However, 18 days after the execution of this agreement, Baker died. During this 18–day period plaintiffs performed the services set forth in the agreement. Baker did not, however, during this period execute the deed called for in the contract.

Based on these facts, plaintiffs on May 13, 1960 filed a creditor's claim in decedent's estate, demanding specific performance of the agreement or in the alternative $5,000, the reasonable value of the real and personal property which was the subject matter of the contract. This claim was rejected by defendant, the administrator of decedent's estate. [The trial court denied the claim for specific performance but held that plaintiffs were entitled to $381.85 on a *quantum meruit* basis, this being the amount which it determined as the value of the services and supplies which plaintiffs furnished to decedent during his lifetime.] * * *

Beginning with some general principles concerning specific performance, we note that the type of action with which we are involved in the instant case is not truly one for specific performance since Baker, who is now deceased, cannot be compelled to execute the promised conveyance. However, if it is determined that plaintiffs are entitled to the property which Baker promised to convey to them, then the court may declare a constructive trust upon this property in the hands of those who have succeeded to the estate. This is, in effect, the equivalent of specific performance and is sometimes termed "quasi-specific performance." [Citations.]

Although the relief in a "quasi-specific performance" action differs from that in the traditional specific performance action the requisites for relief are identical. They are as follows: The plaintiff must show that his remedy at law is inadequate; the contract must be supported by adequate consideration; there must be a mutuality of remedies, that is, the contract must be subject to specific performance by both of the contracting parties; the terms of the contract must be sufficiently definite for the court to know what to enforce; and the performance which the court is asked to compel must be substantially identical to that promised in the contract.

Proceeding to discuss each of these basic requirements as they specifically apply to the contract before us, we note, first, as to the inadequacy of plaintiffs' remedy at law, it is the general rule that in the case of a contract for the transfer of an interest in land it is presumed that damages would not adequately compensate for the breach. This presumption is based on the historic treatment of land as unique. Therefore, in cases involving the breach of a contract to transfer an interest in land, specific performance will be granted as a matter of course unless some other equitable reason for denial is shown. Accordingly, the party seeking specific performance need not establish inadequacy of the legal remedy and may rely upon this presumption.

Where, as in the instant action, only part of the subject matter of the contract consists of land, specific performance of the whole of the contract may be decreed even though compensation in money would be an adequate remedy for the promisor's failure to perform that part of the contract calling for the transfer of ordinary chattels.

As applied to the instant case, therefore we conclude that the contract between plaintiffs and decedent being one involving the transfer of land, plaintiffs' remedy at law is inadequate. The trial court's statement in its opinion that this contract "is within the class of cases that afford an adequate remedy at law upon quantum meruit" is not a correct articulation of the principle involved. The question, in determining the adequacy of plaintiffs' remedy at law, is not whether they have some remedy at law apart from the contract, but whether their remedy at law upon the contract itself, that is, for damages, is sufficient. Accordingly, the fact that plaintiffs are entitled at law to reimbursement upon a *quantum meruit* theory for the services and supplies which they furnished decedent is not dispositive of the issue of whether their remedy at law upon the contract which they entered into with decedent is adequate.

The second requirement for the specific enforcement of a contract is that the consideration be adequate. The proper time for testing the adequacy of consideration is as of the formation of the contract. And the proper test to apply in determining adequacy of consideration in a contract involving the transfer of property is not whether the promisor received the highest price obtainable for his property, but whether the price he received is fair and reasonable under the circumstances. Moreover, in addition to the value of the property to be conveyed, the court may consider such factors as the relationship of the parties, their friendship, love, affection, and regard for each other, and the object to be obtained by the contract.

In the instant action, the trial court made no specific finding as to adequacy of consideration except insofar as it found that "the services and expenses laid out by plaintiffs for Marion D. Baker during his lifetime were not and are not worth the full value of the aforedescribed real property and personal property, nor any substantial part thereof." While the question of adequacy of consideration is generally considered as a question of fact, the determination of the trial court being final unless totally unsupported by the evidence, it appears in the instant case that the trial court erroneously determined this question as of the date of trial rather than as of the date of execution of the contract. Accordingly, we are not bound by such determination. We are satisfied, moreover, that the evidence adduced at the trial can support no other conclusion than that decedent's promise to convey his property to plaintiffs was amply supported by consideration. At the time the contract was entered into Baker was in good health and the duration of his life was uncertain. * * * The fact that Baker died within a short time after entering into the contract so that plaintiffs' services were of short duration cannot alter this conclusion. * * *

Adverting to the question of mutuality of remedies we first note the applicable rule as stated in [California Civil Code] section 3386 as follows: "Neither party to an obligation can be compelled specifically to perform it, unless the other party thereto has performed, or is compellable specifically to perform, everything to which the former is entitled under the same obligation, either completely or nearly so, together with full compensation for any want or entire performance." In contracts involving the performance of personal services by one of the contracting parties, it is clear that at the inception of the contract specific performance cannot be decreed against this party because of the rule of long standing that a person cannot be compelled to perform personal services. Accordingly, such a contract, at its inception, lacks mutuality of remedies and is, therefore, not specifically enforceable against the other party. The prevailing rule, and that adopted in California in section 3386, is, however, that such contracts which lack mutuality in their inception may be specifically enforced after the want of mutuality is removed by the performance by one party of his obligation under the contract. Thus, although the party who has contracted to perform personal services cannot maintain an action for specific performance while the contract remains executory as to him, if at the time he brings his action for specific performance he has fully carried out his promise to perform such services, then the defense of lack of mutuality can no longer be asserted and the court may properly grant the requested remedy and order the other party to specifically perform his promise.

* * * [I]n making its determination as to mutuality the [trial] court did so on the basis of obligations which existed between Baker and plaintiffs while the latter was still alive. As we have indicated, the trial court should, instead, have considered the problem of mutuality as of the date at which plaintiffs sought enforcement of the contract, that is, after Baker's death. Had the court done so, it is clear that the defense of lack of mutuality would not have been valid since plaintiffs had at this time fully performed their obligation to take care of Baker during his lifetime.

With respect to the requirement for specific performance that the subject contract be certain in its terms, defendant contends that the contract which plaintiffs seek to enforce is uncertain for the reason that it does not indicate a time for performance by Baker. * * *

It is only where the uncertainty or incompleteness of a contract prevents the court from knowing what to enforce that the defense of uncertainty has rationality. No such doubt exists in the instant case where the court was asked to impress a constructive trust in favor of plaintiffs based on a contract which was to be performed at some time during the life of a person who is now deceased and obviously can no longer perform his promise.

* * *

Since the law and undisputed facts require judgment to be entered for plaintiffs, the judgment is reversed. * * *

---

1. *Mutuality of Remedy*. Historically, under the mutuality of remedies doctrine, specific performance would not be available to one party unless that remedy was equally available to the other contracting party. For example, in *Horowitch v. Diamond Aircraft Ind., Inc.*, 526 F.Supp.2d 1236 (M.D. Fla. 2007), an aircraft sale contract provided that the buyer's sole remedy for breach would be the return of deposits as damages but no similar provision exclusively limited the seller's remedies. Based upon the inequality in available remedies the court found that the contract was unreasonable and lacked mutuality. Id. at 1248. *Also see* Security Land Co. v. Touliatos, 716 S.W.2d 918, 921 (Tenn. 1986) (specific performance of land sale agreement denied for lack of mutuality of remedy); *but see* Thompson v. Kromhout, 413 N.W.2d 884, 885 (Minn.App. 1987) (lack of mutuality alone in land sale contract does not render specific performance inequitable). Where a land sale contract was bargained for with services rather than money, the mutuality rule prohibited the buyer from obtaining specific performance because constitutional restraints against involuntary servitude would prevent the seller from hypothetically using specific performance to require performance of personal services.

This doctrine was distinguishable from the concept of "mutuality of obligation" as a prerequisite to the formation of a valid bilateral contract, and which itself was expressly rejected by the Restatement (Second) Contracts § 79. Northcom, Ltd. v. James, 694 So.2d 1329 (Ala. 1997) (mutuality of obligation analytically distinct from mutuality of remedy, because where consideration does not flow from one direction then no contract is formed). The mutuality of remedy doctrine flourished in the late nineteenth century co-existing with the attraction of mirror-image contracting, because it epitomized the distribution of justice with an impartial hand.

2. As the principal case reflects, the common law developed limitations to the "broken down" rule of mutuality of remedies. *See generally* 5A Corbin on Contracts § 1183 (1964). Courts did not require mutuality when the contract was fully executed, the party seeking specific performance had substantially performed, or the court was satisfied that the parties would render performance in the future. The Restatement (Second) of Contracts

§ 363 comment c explains that the principal rationale underlying the doctrine was to assure the party against whom enforcement was sought that the non-breaching party would also perform the remaining contractual obligations. Accordingly, if adequate security can be furnished to ensure full performance of executory obligations, then mutuality of remedy is not required. *See* Converse v. Fong, 159 Cal.App.3d 86, 205 Cal.Rptr. 242 (1984) (mutuality of remedy not a prerequisite to specific performance provided claimant gives adequate assurance of performance of agreed obligations).

3. Several states enacted statutes which codified the developing common law limitations on the mutuality rule. *See* Cal. Civ. Code § 3386 (1969). The modern view considers the mutuality of remedies requirement a curious historical vestige and, at most, represents just one factor in determining if specific performance is justified. This philosophy began with the realization that parties typically bargain for different things and, therefore, their respective remedies do not need to correspond precisely. *See* Humble Oil & Refining Co. v. DeLoache, 297 F.Supp. 647 (D.S.Car. 1969) (fact that remedies are not identical will not preclude specific performance for lack of mutuality) Restatement (Second) Contracts § 363 comment c.

4. Courts, on the basis of "unfairness," may decline to order specific performance because of inadequate consideration in the agreed exchange. The inadequacy between consideration received and fair market value must amount to a hard, unreasonable, or unconscionable contract, but not necessarily reaching the level of fraud. Humble Oil & Refining v. De Loache, 297 F.Supp. 647 (D.C.S.C.1969). Inadequate consideration is often found in conjunction with separate unconscionable or overreaching conduct to persuade a court to deny specific performance. If the disparity in the value is particularly large it may serve as the sole rationale for disallowing equitable enforcement of the contract. Hodge v. Shea, 252 S.C. 601, 168 S.E.2d 82 (1969).

Valuations are to be made at the time of contracting in order to include the risk inherent in any bargained-for exchange. Craven v. Williams, 302 F.Supp. 885 (D.C.S.C.1969). This rule is occasionally ignored; if the difference is great enough, the court may not allow specific performance even when the bargain was reasonable at the time of contracting. Marks v. Gates, 154 Fed. 481 (9th Cir. 1907). If one party simply made a bad bargain, the low consideration should not justify denial of specific performance.

B. Fashioning Relief

Section Coverage:

Courts weigh a variety of factors not only to determine the propriety of granting equitable relief but also to fashion the form and scope of the decree. No single factor is dispositive. The balancing process goes beyond the threshold issue of the adequacy of legal relief and encompasses the traditional equitable notions of fairness, public policy concerns, and the ability to enforce and supervise the order. Thus, a court may deny specific performance in situations involving mistake, duress, or unreasonable hardship. These factors may influence a court in exercising its remedial discretion even if none is sufficiently great to avoid the contract as a matter of substantive law.

A court will try to approximate the balance of contractual rights and duties embodied in the original bargain. A goal of the specific performance remedy is to preserve the respective interests and intentions of the parties in contracting. Sometimes a party cannot deliver the exact performance promised, but the other party still seeks specific performance. For example, a seller in a land sales contract may not have title to the full acreage as represented. A court has several alternatives: (1) decree specific performance with an abatement in the purchase price proportionate to the deficiency; (2) award damages; or (3) give restitution of money already paid. If the defect is sufficiently large, a defendant seller may object on the grounds that specific performance with damages or abatement does not resemble the original contract, or that performance would cause unreasonable hardship outweighing a marginal benefit to the buyer.

Model Case:

Danielson owns a family portrait of his grandparents and their children as they were painted eighty years ago. The artist has since become relatively famous so that the painting has market value. Danielson needed money to help his ailing farm one year, and contracted with Potter for the sale of the painting at $100,000. In anticipation of this sale, Potter arranged for a resale of the portrait to a collector for $110,000. In the meantime, two events affected Danielson: The last surviving member of the family in the portrait died, increasing Danielson's sentimental attachment to the painting, and a government loan bails out the farm. Danielson decides to keep the painting.

Potter sues for specific performance upon Danielson's breach. Although the unique portrait is the proper subject of a specific performance order, such relief is discretionary. The court could balance the interests, including the interest of the third party collector, in deciding whether to grant the order. If specific performance is denied, Potter could recover his $10,000 expectancy damages at law. The collector's rights against Potter will depend upon the terms of that separate contract.

Dover Shopping Center, Inc. v. Cushman's Sons, Inc.

63 N.J.Super. 384, 164 A.2d 785 (1960).

■ GOLDMANN, S.J.A.D.

Defendant appeals from a mandatory injunction of the Chancery Division, entered December 3, 1959, ordering it to reopen its retail bakery business at the store premises leased by it from plaintiff * * * and to keep the store open for business during the hours and on the days required by paragraph Third of the lease, with a manager or salesperson in charge and a "Cushman's" sign on the outside of the premises. * * *

On July 16, 1956 the parties entered into a written lease for one of a group of stores in plaintiff's shopping center in Dover which defendant undertook to operate as a retail bakery. The lease, a detailed and comprehensive instrument of some 29 pages, resulted from protracted negotiations between the parties during which defendant was represented by counsel. The printed form, as finally executed, contained numerous typewritten insertions and changes, obviously the result of those negotiations. Among its provisions was paragraph Third:

> "Third: As one of the inducements for the making of this lease, Tenant hereby agrees, beginning as soon after the commencement of the term as is reasonably possible and continuing during the full remaining term of this lease, to operate its business in the demised premises; to keep its store open daily for the regular conduct of its business therein during the same hours at least as are customarily employed by other similar stores in the neighborhood of the demised premises, and to keep and maintain the show window displays in an attractive and dignified manner. * * *"

The lease provided for a minimum annual rental of $7,000 plus a shifting percentage of gross sales in excess of the minimum rent.

Defendant took possession and began business on September 25, 1957, and has continued to pay the minimum rental down to the present time. * * * However, on May 1, 1959 defendant wrote plaintiff that it was permanently ceasing operations, indicating that it had found the enterprise unprofitable and had decided it would be less costly to pay the minimum rent than to resume operations.

Plaintiff subsequently instituted its action for a mandatory injunction directing defendant specifically to perform the covenants contained in paragraph Third of the lease. Defendant answered and by way of separate defenses contended, among other things, that (1) equity should not grant specific performance of a contract relating to personal services or requiring court supervision over a long period of time; (2) defendant had continued to pay its minimum rent down to date, but had not enjoyed sufficient business during its period of operation to April 1, 1959 so as to be required to pay any additional rent over and above the minimum; (3) plaintiff had not suffered any substantial or irreparable injury and had an adequate remedy at law; (4) equity should not grant specific performance where the benefits to plaintiff from the store being open would be slight in comparison to the substantial injury sustained by defendant. * * *

Defendant next contends that plaintiff should have been denied relief since money damages would be adequate, and even if that were not so, a court of equity should not direct the performance of detailed provisions of a lease, such as here, because of the necessity of continued superintendence.

π Claims

In reply, plaintiff cites paragraph Ninth (3) of the lease, which provides that "In the event of a breach or threatened breach by Tenant of any of the covenants or provisions hereof, Landlord shall have the right of injunction * * *." It argues that damages for the breach of a percentage lease arrangement are not readily measurable. Plaintiff also adduced proofs to show that the very nature of the shopping center as a cooperative enterprise, with each store's success dependent on the continued operation of the other stores, requires that defendant's bakery business be maintained in accordance with the lease for the benefit of all involved. Plaintiff further cites recent decisions showing a judicial tendency toward granting specific performance wherever feasible. It argues that the remedy is particularly feasible here because plaintiff has waived judicial superintendence and is willing to rely upon the defendant's self-interest in continuing to preserve its good reputation by conducting its business in a manner which would reflect credit upon its operation.

The mandatory injunction, as we have pointed out, does no more than require defendant to reopen and resume its retail bakery business, to display the name of "Cushman's" on the outside of the premises, to keep the store open as required by paragraph Third of the lease, and to maintain a manager or salesperson in charge.

Courts have recognized the uniqueness of a percentage lease and have generally implied therefrom an obligation on the part of the lessee to occupy the property and to use reasonable diligence in operating the business in a productive manner. But the gravamen of the complaint here is not only the possible loss of additional income by way of a percentage of defendant's increased gross sales, but the difficulty in measuring the harm that would come from the withdrawal of one of the members of a semi-cooperative enterprise like a shopping center. Plaintiff's damages cannot therefore be accurately ascertained, and remedy by way of damages at law would be impractical and unsatisfactory. [Citation.]

We turn to defendant's argument that relief should have been denied because of the necessity of continued superintendence on the part of the court. Equity will not ordinarily order specific performance where the duty to be enforced continues over a long period of time and is difficult of supervision. However, the modern tendency is to grant specific performance in the case of a clear breach, where the difficulties of enforcement are not great, particularly when compared with the inadequacy of damages at law. * * *

The specific performance granted by the court was directed at certain covenants simple of performance and supervision. The judgment expressly provided that except as specifically set forth therein, the court would "make no direction with respect to the method of operating the defendant's business on the demised premises or to the quality of the products sold and services rendered by the defendant therein * * *."

Since the court was careful to limit its order, defendant's objection to it on the ground of required continued supervision is without persuasive force. The judgment as it stands is not so difficult of enforcement that it can be said the difficulties of supervision outweigh the importance of granting specific performance because of the inadequacy of the remedy of damages at law.

Affirmed.

---

1. If a valid contract has been breached, a court of equity will order specific performance if there is no adequate remedy at law and if the court would not have to undertake a burdensome amount of supervision, such as in building or repair contracts. In *TAS Distributing Co. v. Cummins Engine Co.*, 491 F.3d 625 (7th Cir. 2007) a licensor sought specific performance of a contract which required a licensee to make "all reasonable efforts" to manufacture and market the licensor's technology. The court denied equitable relief, reasoning that oversight of the ongoing relationship of the parties and the indefinite nature of certain licensing obligations would require extensive supervision and strain judicial resources. *But see* Prudence Corp. v. Shred–It America, Inc., 2010 WL 582597 (9th Cir.) (Specific performance ordered requiring renewal of franchise agreement).

2. The Restatement (Second) of Contracts § 366 treats the potential problem of supervision as one factor for entitlement to and fashioning of the specific performance decree. Under the Restatement view, a contract will not be specifically enforced if the potential burden to the court is disproportionate to the perceived gain for the plaintiff. Conversely, if the harm from not enforcing the decree would be great, or there is a potential harm to the public, specific performance will be decreed. Thus, where faulty plumbing endangers a family's health, the court will grant specific performance. Fran Realty v. Thomas, 30 Md.App. 362, 354 A.2d 196 (1976). If, however, the only harm to the plaintiff is a delay in production, the court may decide against specific performance. Northern Delaware Indus. Dev. Corp. v. E.W. Bliss Co., 245 A.2d 431 (Del.Ch.1968).

The Restatement view also promotes specifically enforcing arbitration clauses since the court is not required to render any direct supervision. Thus, in order to ensure equity, the court will overlook a burden to itself if a serious potential harm to the plaintiff or the public would ensue.

3. *Public Interest.* In *Almetals, Inc. v. Wickeder Westfalenstah L*, 67 U.C.C.Rep.Serv.2d 562 (E.D. Mich. 2008), a company sought specific performance to require the continued delivery of specialty steel products from its supplier pursuant to a long term requirements contract. For several years, the distributor had invested significant time and resources toward developing customers who used those products. When the supplier breached, the distributor claimed that no alternative sources of supply existed and the loss of the goods would be devastating to its overall business solvency. The court awarded specific performance and an injunction, also finding that the public interest in preserving jobs favored the distributor. Similarly, in *Laclede Gas Co. v. Amoco Oil Co.*, 522 F.2d 33 (8th Cir. 1975) the court found a "manifest" public interest in maintaining a utility company's

ability to furnish propane gas to its retail customers, which supported an order of specific performance of a requirements contract with the company's supplier.

Shubert Theatrical Co. v. Rath

271 Fed. 827 (2d Cir. 1921)

■ ROGERS, CIRCUIT JUDGE.

The plaintiff corporation is organized under the laws of the state of New York, is in business as a theatrical manager and producer of plays, and for a number of years last past was and still is engaged in producing plays and attractions at various theaters in the city of New York. It likewise presents plays on the road in a tour of the United States and Canada, and among the plays so produced is one known as "The Passing Show of 1919," in which the defendants appear.

The plaintiff on July 8, 1919, entered into a written agreement with the defendants by the terms of which the plaintiff engaged them to render their exclusive services to it for a period of one year commencing from September 1, 1919. It was agreed therein that the defendants should appear at all times as directed by the plaintiff during the year, and it was guaranteed that they should be employed for 20 weeks in the minimum, and their salary was fixed at the sum of $250 per week while appearing in the city of New York and $275 per week while on the road. It was further provided that the plaintiff had an option on the services of the defendants for the theatrical year beginning September 1, 1920, and ending September 1, 1921, provided plaintiff gave notice of its desire to exercise such option prior to July 1, 1920. If the plaintiff exercised the option reserved to it, the agreement provided that the guaranty of 20 weeks should again apply for the period, but that the salary should be $300 per week while appearing in the city of New York and $325 per week while appearing on the road. On June 7, 1920, the plaintiff pursuant to its option employed the defendants for the year beginning on September 1, 1920. Notwithstanding this, the defendants advised the plaintiff that they refused to perform according to their agreement; and it appears that they have contracted with a rival manager to appear in a production to be presented in a rival theater in the city of New York.

An injunction is asked to restrain the defendants from performing for any managers other than the plaintiff, or from performing in any other theater or place of public amusement, or in any other company, except that of the plaintiff, until the expiration of the term mentioned in the agreement made between the plaintiff and the defendants. The court below granted the injunction as prayed.

The contract is found in a letter addressed by the plaintiff to the defendants and signed "Shubert Theatrical Company, by J. J. Shubert." Then follows:

"We have read the foregoing. The same contains our full understanding, and with our signatures at the bottom hereof, let this be deemed a contract between us.

Geo. & Dick Rath,

"By Geo. H. Rath."

The letter (contract) contains the following:

"You [the defendants] agree throughout the term hereof that you shall not render your services, nor will you appear publicly for any other firm or corporation, whether moving pictures or otherwise, without our written consent first had and obtained, and shall you attempt to appear for any other management or in moving pictures, we shall have the right to apply to any court having competent jurisdiction for an injunction restraining your appearance, and you agree, for the purpose of such lawsuit, that your services are extraordinary and unique, and you cannot be replaced, except for Morris Gest."

The performances which the defendants contracted to give are acrobatic in character. The testimony shows that their feats are unique and extraordinary. A prominent theatrical manager and producer of wide experience, and not associated with the plaintiff, testified. One of the feats of the defendants' performances, as he described it, is that one of the defendants with one hand raises the other defendant, a full grown man, from the floor, his body being stretched at full length upon the floor. The witness, in describing it, said this was done without apparent effort, "just as easy as you would lift a straw." In reply to a question by the court, he declared:

"It is a fact that it is the most marvelous thing that has ever been before."

He added that it had never before been done with a grown-up man in the history of this country. Another theatrical manager, of whom defendants' counsel said, "I will concede that he is a great manager and producer, and cannot be equaled in the theatrical business," and who was asked by the court whether the performances of the defendants were unique and unusual, answered, "Absolutely." He added that he did not know of any imitator in the world. Another theatrical producer, having an experience of nearly 30 years and who is widely known, testified that their performance was "absolutely unique and extraordinary." This is an excerpt from his testimony:

"One of the moves they make is taking a man underneath his body, and raising him right over his shoulder, and standing him up straight on his hands, something that has never been done, as long as my experience has been in the show business. I have never seen anything like it.

"Q.   Are you an athlete yourself? A. I am.

"Q. And do these features impress you as being peculiarly difficult? A. It has never been done as long as I remember seeing anything in the show business.

"Q. Yes. Do you know from your experience whether it would be possible to replace that act by other people? A. Absolutely impossible."

The finding of the trial court that the performances of the defendants are unique and unusual is amply justified by the testimony. The services of the defendants are extraordinary, unique and cannot be replaced.

These services were to be given to the plaintiffs exclusively, and the contract contains an express negative covenant that they would not be given under any other management during the period named. By a negative covenant the covenantor promises that something shall not be done. The relief appropriate to a breach of such a contract is an injunction. The leading authority, as respects covenants for personal service, is the well-known case of *Lumley v. Wagner*, 1 De G., M. & G. 604. In that case a famous singer agreed to sing in the opera house of the complainant for a certain time, and not to sing for any one else during that time. The opinion in that case reviews the authorities and contains what is regarded as a very able and convincing discussion of the principle applicable in such cases. As the services contracted for were those of a person possessing special and extraordinary qualifications, Lord Chancellor St. Leonards granted an injunction restraining the defendant from singing at any other theater than that belonging to the plaintiff. It was held that the fact that the court would have been unable to enforce specifically the defendant's affirmative covenant to sing at the plaintiff's theater did not affect the complainant's right to an injunction to restrain a violation of the negative covenant not to sing elsewhere.

In *McCaull v. Braham* (C.C.) 16 Fed. 37, Judge Addison Brown continued an injunction restraining Lillian Russell from the breach of a negative covenant not to sing in comic opera during the season at any other than the plaintiff's theater. In addition to the negative covenant, the contract contained an affirmative covenant to sing in the employment of the plaintiff whenever required. In the course of his opinion Judge Brown said:

"Contracts for the services of artists or authors of special merit are personal and peculiar; and when they contain negative covenants which are essential parts of the agreement, as in this case, that the artists will not perform elsewhere, and the damages, in case of violation, are incapable of definite measurement, they are such as ought to be observed in good faith and specifically enforced in equity. That violation of such covenants will be restrained by injunction is now the settled law of England."

In *Cincinnati Exhibition Co. v. Marsans*, 216 Fed. (D.C.) 269, the complainant had employed defendant as a ball player for a certain specified period, and defendant had covenanted not to render similar service to others during the continuance of the contract. An injunction issued to prevent the breach of the negative covenant. The court, by Judge Sanborn, said:

> "It is a settled rule of law that where a person agrees to render services that are unique and extraordinary, and which may not be rendered by another, and has made a negative covenant in his agreement whereby he promises not to render such service to others, the court may issue an injunction to prevent him from violating the negative covenant in order to induce him to perform his contract. The facts of this case seem to me to bring it under this rule."

In *Philadelphia Ball Club, Ltd. v. Lajoie*, 202 Pa. 210, 51 Atl. 973, 58 L.R.A. 227, 90 Am. St. Rep. 267, it was held that, where a baseball player had contracted to play with a particular club for a certain term, he would be enjoined from playing with another club during the continuance of the term, where the evidence showed that he was an expert player in any position, and had a great reputation among the patrons of the sport for his ability and skill.

In Pomeroy on Specific Performance, p. 31, the principle is stated as follows:

> "Where one person agrees to render personal services to another, which require and presuppose a special knowledge, skill and ability in the employee, so that in case of a default the same service could not easily be obtained from others, although the affirmative specific performance of the contract is beyond the power of the court, its performance will be negatively enforced by enjoining its breach."

The basis upon which the decisions rest in all such cases is that the damages for the breach of such contracts cannot be estimated with any certainty, and the employer cannot by means of any damages purchase the same services from others. The injury in such cases is irreparable. Damages which can be estimated in cases of this class only by conjecture, and not by any accurate standard, constitute such an irreparable injury as courts of equity will restrain by injunction.

In 5 Pomeroy's Equity Jurisprudence, § 289, p. 518, it is said that the doctrine of *Lumley v. Wagner* has been generally accepted, both in England and in this country, upon a similar state of facts. The author also states that—

> "The most frequent application has been in cases of actors and actresses of established reputation. Contracts for their services often stipulate that they shall not perform elsewhere during their engagement with a particular manager. Their services being extraordinary and special, and injunction is generally granted against the breach of such a stipulation. It will likewise be granted when an artist agrees to work for the complainant and for no one else."

In the argument in this court counsel for the defendants insisted that the contract between the parties is so lacking in equitable mutuality that a court of equity should not enforce it. We are not impressed by the argument. The contract binds the complainant to give the defendants employment for at least 20 weeks in the theatrical year, "not necessarily consecutive," for which the plaintiff is bound to pay a certain specific amount. The contract also binds the defendants to render their services to the plaintiff for a like number of weeks at least, and to do so for the specified salary. That there is mutuality of obligation in such an agreement is too plain for controversy, and mutuality of obligation is sufficient to justify the issuance of an injunction to restrain the breach of the agreement if the services to be rendered are unique, special, or extraordinary, and the contract be not otherwise inequitable or oppressive. Whether the contract is inequitable or oppressive will be considered in a subsequent part of this opinion.

An application for an injunction in a case like this does not depend, as counsel for the defendants in his argument in this court seemed to think, upon the principle applicable to cases for specific performance. It is not necessary in the present case for us to inquire as to what the doctrine of mutuality means in cases of specific performance. There is a distinction between actions brought to compel the specific performance of an affirmative covenant and those which are brought to restrain by injunction the breach of a negative covenant in the same agreement. It is familiar doctrine that courts of equity do not exercise their jurisdiction to grant the remedy of an affirmative specific performance of a contract for personal services. This they decline to do, because they cannot in any direct manner compel an actor to act or a singer to sing. But the rule is established in England and in this country that the courts of equity may restrain by injunction the breach of a negative covenant by which an actor or a singer of unusual gifts has agreed not to act or not to sing in a specified period, except under the management of the other party to the contract. That this may result or may not result in indirectly compelling the specific performance of the affirmative covenant is not a matter with which this court needs in the present case to concern itself. There has been a great difference of opinion, especially in the English courts, over the question whether an injunction can issue to prevent the breach of a contract unless it contains an express negative covenant. But with that question also we are not concerned in this case, as the contract here involved does contain an express negative covenant. It is sufficient for our present purpose that a distinction exists between suits brought to compel specific performance of an affirmative covenant for personal services, and suits brought to restrain by injunction the violation of a negative covenant respecting such services. McCall Co. v. Wright, 198 N.Y. 143, 91 N.E. 516, 31 L.R.A. (N.S.) 249.

* * * The contract was not induced by fraud or misrepresentation. The defendants made it of their own free will and with full knowledge of all that it contained. Contracts are made to be kept and not broken, and the parties who make them are in duty and in law bound to perform them. The injunction should issue as prayed.

Decree affirmed.

1. *Personal Service Orders*. Equity will not enforce a contract for personal services by an affirmative decree. Tucker v. Warfield, 119 F.2d 12 (D.C. Cir.1941). This rule is based on several policy considerations. First, an adequate remedy at law exists unless the services are unique. In *Pingley v. Brunson*, 272 S.C. 421, 252 S.E.2d 560 (1979) a restaurant sought an injunction to prohibit a musician from playing for competing establishments as well as specific performance of a long term contract to furnish entertainment at the restaurant. The court refused, citing the traditional rule that equity will not decree performance of a personal services contract absent special or unique circumstances. Although some evidence suggested that the musician possessed exceptional skill as an organist, several other local organists of comparable ability were available for hire. The court also recognized the difficulties inherent in compelling a close personal relationship over an extended period of time after disputes have arisen and loyalty and confidence have dissipated.

Even if there were no other bar to granting specific performance for personal services, those services must be unique enough to preclude an adequate legal remedy. Bethlehem Engineering Export Co. v. Christie, 105 F.2d 933 (2d Cir.1939) (even though agent's discharge in breach of contract gave rise to an action for damages, equity will not restore him to his position.)

Second, there is inherent difficulty in fashioning an enforceable decree and the subsequent supervision. Bach v. Friden Calculating Machine Co., 155 F.2d 361 (6th Cir.1946). It is essential to fashion a carefully tailored order in order to enforce it by contempt. If a party's conduct does not coincide with the decree, the party may be held in contempt. Thus, it is imperative to meet due process requirements that a clear and precise decree be formed.

There are obvious practical problems with forcing an unwilling employee to work. It is difficult to measure the degree of effort a worker exerts, especially in a hostile environment. Moreover, the constitutional prohibition of involuntary servitude is relevant when the order necessitates direct personal labor.

2. *Negative Injunctions*. Although equity will not compel personal services, it may prohibit giving services to others in contravention of existing contractual obligations, particularly to competitors of a former employer. The Restatement (Second) of Contracts § 367, comment b, states that the character of a personal service is one which is nondelegable. Thus, compare *Henderson v. Fisher, supra*, where the personal nature of the nursing care contracted for was considered nondelegable, but the operation of a retail bakery store in *Dover Shopping Center, Inc. v. Cushman's Sons, Inc.*, could appropriately be delegated to a hired manager.

A covenant not to compete must be reasonable in terms of function, geographic scope and duration in order to justify potential enforcement through equity. *See* Lanmark Technology, Inc. v. Canales, 454 F.Supp.2d 524 (E.D. Va. 2006); Greystone Staffing, Inc. v. Goehringer, 14 Misc. 3d 1209A, 836 N.Y.S.2d 485 (2006); Madison Square Garden v. Braddock, 19

F.Supp. 392 (D.N.J. 1937) (negative covenant unenforceable in equity because failure to fix definite time limitation placed unreasonable restraint on ability of professional boxer to earn a living in chosen occupation). The principle is based upon the strong public policy favoring competition and encouraging the individual freedom to pursue a livelihood as someone may choose. *American Broadcasting Companies, Inc. v. Wolf*, 76 A.D.2d 162, 430 N.Y.S.2d 275, 282 (1st Dept. 1980). Courts may refuse to enforce a negative covenant through equity where enforcement may be unduly harsh or burdensome. *See* Madison Square Boxing, Inc. v. Shavers, 434 F.Supp. 449, 452 (S.D.N.Y. 1977). Some jurisdictions have enacted statutes that limit or preclude injunctions to enforce negative restrictive covenants in employment contracts. *See* Montana Code Ann. § 27–19–103(5); Arizona Rev. Stat. § 12–1802(5); California Civil Code § 3423.

3. The "contract jumping" cases often involve musicians, actors, professional athletes, coaches, and others who possess special or unique skills. *See* Dallas Cowboys Football Club, Inc. v. Harris, 348 S.W.2d 37 (Tex. Civ. App.1961) (football player); Lemat Corp. v. Barry, 275 Cal. App.2d 671, 80 Cal.Rptr. 240 (Ct. 1969) (basketball); Philadelphia Ball Club, Ltd. v. Lajoie, 202 Pa. 210, 51 A. 973 (1902) (baseball); Nassau Sports v. Peters, 352 F.Supp. 870 (E.D.N.Y. 1972) (hockey); Lewis v. Rahman, 147 F.Supp.2d 225 (S.D.N.Y 2001) (boxing).

Negative injunctions may be used to prohibit other types of employees from accepting positions for competitors, however, when the circumstances demonstrate potential harm to important business interests that could not be redressed through monetary compensation. *See* Estee Lauder Companies, Inc. v. Batra, 430 F.Supp.2d 158 (S.D.N.Y. 2006) (global brand manager in prestige cosmetics industry enjoined from working for competitor pursuant to restrictive covenant). Compare AM Medica Communications Group v. Kilgallen, 90 Fed. Appx. 10 (2d Cir. 2003) (conference planner who coordinated hotels, caterers and printers did not provide special unique or extraordinary services that would justify injunctive relief to enforce a restrictive covenant in an employment contract).

4. In *Ticor Title Ins. Co. v. Cohen*, 173 F.3d 63, 65 (2d Cir. 1999), the court described the question of unique services as:

> "whether such person is extraordinary in the sense, for example, of Beethoven as a composer, Einstein as a physicist, or Michelangelo as an artist, where one can fairly say that nature made them and then broke the mold."

The court in *Ticor Title* further observed, however, that the modern inquiry focuses more on the importance of the employee's relationship to the employer's business rather than necessarily individualized special talents. Accordingly, the court upheld injunctive relief pursuant to a noncompete covenant against a senior vice president in charge of major title insurance sales accounts based on evidence that the employee had special business relationships with key clients and the potential loss of customers constituted an irreparable harm.

5. Although damages for breach of contract are the normative preferred remedy, equitable relief may be obtained where damages are difficult to calculate and the employer would be irreparably harmed if the person applied their special talents on behalf of a competitor. A negative injunction, then, effectively may indirectly achieve the result of forcing the employee to return to their previous position even though the Constitutional prohibition against involuntary servitude prevent such orders directly. *See* Beverly Glen Music, Inc. v. Warner Communications, Inc., 178 Cal. App.3d 1142, 224 Cal.Rptr. 260 (1986) (net effect of enforcing negative injunction is to pressure person to return voluntarily to employer by denying the means of earning a living).

6. A colorful description of such cases was made in *Detroit Football Co. v. Robinson*, 186 F.Supp. 933, 934 (E.D.La. 1960), where judge J. Skelly Wright observed:

> This case is but another round in the sordid fight for football players [or coaches] . . . It is a fight characterized by deception, double dealing, campus jumping, secret alumni subsidization, semi-professionalism and professionalism. It is a fight which has produced as part of its harvest this current rash of contract jumping suits. It is a fight which so conditions the minds and hearts of these athletes [and coaches] that one day they can agree to play [or coach] football for a stated amount for one group, only to repudiate that agreement the following day or whenever a better offer comes along.

Tensions may run high in these situations, as illustrated by *Northeastern University v. Brown*, 17 Mass. L. Rep. 443 (Mass. Super. 2004). In that case, a head football coach breached an employment contract by leaving his university and accepting the same position at a rival university that competed in the same conference. The court observed that the breach of contract by the coach was "obvious, brazen, and defiant" and described the actions of the competing university as a "premier higher educational institution was so callous in its duty to provide ethical and moral values for its students" such that they brought "great shame on themselves and the university." The court quoted with approval from *New England Patriots v. University of Colorado*, 592 F.2d 1196 (1st Cir. 1979) where that court observed:

> Whatever may be thought rules elsewhere, the legal rules are clear. A contract is not avoided by crossed fingers behind one's back on signing, nor by unsupported and at once inconsistently self-deprecating and self-serving protests that the breach was to the other party's benefit.

The court cited strong evidence that Northeastern would suffer irreparable harm to its football program because the coach knew its plays and procedures and could use his knowledge to gain a competitive advantage. The schools also often recruited the same student athletes and competed with each other on a regional basis for television coverage for their games. Accordingly, the court issued an injunction enforcing the negative covenant in the employment contract restraining the coach from taking the job at the other university.

7. *Reinstatement.* A court of equity will not generally grant specific performance of a personal services contract and order reinstatement of an employee where personal supervision is involved. *See* Nicholas v. Pennsylvania State University, 227 F.3d 133, 146 (3d Cir. 2000). The rule is premised on the practical recognition that once an employment relationship is fractured and an employee departs, it may be impossible to restore loyalty and confidence through forcing a return to the previous employment association. *See* Restatement (Second) of Contracts § 367(1) comment a.

In *Manila School Dist. v. Wagner*, 356 Ark. 149, 148 S.W.3d 244 (2004), the claimant brought a wrongful termination suit seeking to enjoin the defendant school district from hiring a new superintendent and also to be renewed for another contract period. The court declined to issue specific performance requiring the school to maintain the employment relationship, and found that the trial court had abused its discretion in issuing an injunction. The court reasoned that any harm to the claimant's reputation, loss of salary, and possible relocation to obtain similar employment could be recouped by money damages. Compare *Allen v. Autauga County Board of Educ.*, 685 F.2d 1302 (11th Cir. 1982) where the court ordered reinstatement of a public employee despite acknowledging high probability of encountering friction or antagonistic relationship. The court reasoned that money damages would not make the employee whole because the psychological effects of losing a job were intangible but a reality.

What about the failure to receive a promised job promotion? Would it be sufficient simply to award damages based on the difference in salaries? *See* Clark v. Pennsylvania State Police, 496 Pa. 310, 436 A.2d 1383 (1981) (Specific performance denied where claimant failed to demonstrate inadequate remedy at law because damages were calculable with reasonable certainty based on the difference in salary related to the lost promotion).

Wooster Republican Printing v. Channel 17, Inc.

533 F.Supp. 601 (W.D.Mo.1981).

■ WRIGHT, DISTRICT JUDGE.

Plaintiff, the Wooster Republican Printing Company (Wooster), is a closely-held family corporation which owns and operates daily and weekly newspapers, radio stations, and a commercial printing business. Defendant, Channel Seventeen, Inc., (Channel Seventeen), is a closely-held Missouri corporation which owns and operates a UHF television station in Columbia, Missouri, as an ABC network affiliate under the call letters, "KCBJ–TV." This diversity action was initiated by Wooster, an Ohio corporation, to enforce an alleged contract "to sell the assets, property and business of defendant, excluding bank accounts, cash-on-hand and accounts receivable." Alleging the uniqueness of the business of Channel Seventeen and an anticipatory breach of the contract by repudiation, Wooster primarily seeks specific performance of the alleged agreement. Alternatively, should specific performance be determined inappropriate, Wooster seeks damages in the amount of $912,053.02. Plaintiff also seeks attorneys fees, costs and expenses in conjunction with its claim for specific performance.

* * *

As one expert put it, Channel Seventeen is "a very unique station in itself." It is a UHF station with a national network affiliation which competes with two VHF stations also with national network affiliations. Its network, ABC, had led the industry in audience ratings for several years. The station operates with an exceptionally tall tower which is strategically placed to serve not only Columbia, Missouri, but also Sedalia, Jefferson City, and the surrounding rural areas. It services a market which is youth and government oriented with a high "per family spendable income." One national rating service, Arbitron, has recently upgraded this market from 134th in the nation to 129th. Both Columbia and Jefferson City are stable and growing communities with a high percentage of professionals residing within them.

Despite its strong markets and excellent potential, Channel Seventeen has not achieved the success it could attain. It has "one of the lowest rate cards ... in a market [of its] size," and its potential profitability has not been reached. This failure to achieve full financial potential is the result of a lack of cohesiveness and uniformity in program packaging, an unaggressive sales program and insufficient infusion of working capital. With the proper management, however, the station could achieve a high degree of profitability.

Because of the failure of Channel Seventeen to reach its potential, it is one of the few television stations in the nation which would sell for under $5,000,000. There has been no contention herein that $3,300,000 was not a fair price for the assets of Channel Seventeen on July 18, 1979. To the contrary, the testimony at trial uniformly confirmed that this price was at or above the fair market value of Channel Seventeen at that time. The station has, however, since appreciated in value to approximately $900,000 over the price established by the contract of July 18, 1979. The unrefuted expert testimony at trial established the current fair market value of Channel Seventeen at $4,200,000.

* * *

Wooster primarily seeks specific performance of the contract of July 18, 1979. Defendants, on the other hand, contend that specific performance will not lie because of the impossibility of performance of that contract, mutual mistake as to the material facts by the parties to it, and the adequacy of Wooster's remedy at law.

As an equitable remedy, "[s]pecific performance will not be ordered when the party claiming breach of contract has an adequate remedy at law." * * * In the present case, however, Wooster's remedy at law would not be adequate to afford it the benefit of the agreement which it struck with Channel Seventeen. Uniformly, the expert testimony at trial established that Channel Seventeen, and more specifically station KCBJ–TV, is a "unique" property, unique in the sense that it presents an unusual potential for future growth in a stable and growing market. Because of its potential for expansion with proper management and infusion of capital, its relative position in the local and national markets, its network affiliation, its licensing and frequency, and its physical assets, among other things, Channel Seventeen is unique. Accordingly, Wooster's remedy at law would not provide a certain, prompt, complete or efficient substitute for the specific performance of the contract. [Citations.]

But Channel Seventeen * * * argues that specific performance of the contract is not available to Wooster because of the impossibility of its performance and mutual mistakes of fact regarding certain facts upon which the contract was premised. Performance of the contract is impossible, it urges, because the site upon which the transmitter tower of KCBJ–TV is located was, and still is, owned by a third person who is not a party to this action.

"A thing is impossible in legal contemplation when it is not practicable; and a thing is impracticable when it can be done only at an excessive and unreasonable cost." [Citations.] The contract of July 18, 1979, provided, in part, that Channel Seventeen would "be able to transfer the site or cause it to be transferred in fee to [Wooster] at closing." Because title to that site is held by a third party, the land cannot be conveyed in fee to Wooster upon the closing of the contract. But Wooster states that it is willing to take less; that it is willing to take whatever title Channel Seventeen can convey, if any, with an abatement in the purchase price.

As earlier found herein, Channel Seventeen currently holds a lease to the tower site which will allow it to exercise an option to buy the land for the amount of $10,000 at the end of its term. That lease is, by its terms, assignable to a purchaser of Channel Seventeen. The performance under a decree of specific performance need not be totally identical to that which is provided by the contract as long as the agreement of the parties is substantially performed. Here, the transmitter site, a parcel of one acre of land, is but a minor part of the total agreement of the parties. Since Wooster is willing to accept the leasehold interest with the option to purchase this land at a future date, the impossibility of a present conveyance of the land in fee does not defeat the remedy of specific performance. Nor is the mutual mistake of the contracting parties, if any, sufficient to invalidate the contract or defeat the equitable remedy Wooster now seeks. Under those circumstances, the purchase price of the assets of Channel Seventeen can and should be abated by the amount necessary to exercise the option granted by the lease.

Finally, Channel Seventeen contends that a mutual mistake existed concerning the remedies for breach of the contemplating contract by the parties at the time of its execution. Channel Seventeen asserts that * * * upon breach of contract, Channel Seventeen would only be liable for the amount stated in a liquidated damages clause of the contract. Paragraph 7.1(a) of the contract of July 18, 1979, provides that Channel Seventeen may receive "Fifty Thousand Dollars ($50,000), as liquidated damages" if "closing is not achieved by reason of a breach by [Wooster] prior to closing ..." On the other hand, Paragraph 7.1(b) of the contract clearly provides that the remedies available to Wooster would include "the right to specific performance, which [Channel Seventeen] acknowledge[d] [was] an appropriate remedy because damages at law would be inadequate." * * * Based upon the testimony at trial, it cannot reasonably be found that a mutual mistake existed at the time of execution of the contract concerning the remedies available to the parties upon its breach.

* * *

For the reasons stated above, it is therefore ordered that judgment be entered in favor of plaintiff Wooster Republican Printing Company and against defendant Channel Seventeen, Inc. * * * and that a Decree of Specific Performance be entered herein.

PROBLEM: THE LAND DEFECT

Brown entered into a written agreement to purchase a 160 acre tract of farm land, Blackacre, from O for $50,000, to be paid in ten equal monthly installments. At the closing of the transaction Brown tendered a check for $5,000 in exchange for a warranty deed to Blackacre from O. The warranty deed, however, only gave clear title to 157 acres because a 3 acre strip abutting Slippery Creek on the southern part of Blackacre had been taken by the state in eminent domain proceedings. Without the 3 acres Brown had no access to a water supply for irrigating Blackacre. The cost to transport water by pipeline would be approximately $20,000.

Brown further discovered that O lacked the mineral rights to 30 acres of Blackacre. Accordingly, Brown did not make the next scheduled monthly payment but demanded rescission of the agreement and restitution of the $5,000. O counterclaimed and requested specific performance. What result? Would it make a difference if Brown was a dealer in land and had contracted to resell Blackacre to A?

─────────

1. *Exclusivity of Remedy*. Specific performance may be affected by the presence of a liquidated damages clause in the contract. Although courts will evaluate whether a liquidated damages sum constitutes an adequate remedy at law, where the parties have unambiguously provided that the agreed damages are the "sole and exclusive" remedy, courts generally will uphold the freedom of contracting parties to privately bargain for the amount of compensatory damages in the event of a material breach and deny equitable enforcement of the contract. *See* Reichert v. Rubloff Hammond, 264 Neb. 16, 645 N.W.2d 519 (2002); Ndeh v. Midtown Alexandria, L.L.C., 300 Fed.Appx. 203 (4th Cir. 2008) (presumption against finding remedies exclusive, rebutted only by language in contract clearly showing intent that remedy be exclusive).

2. *Mistake.* A mutual mistake of fact that materially affects the reasonable expectations of the contracting parties may constitute a sufficient basis to grant rescission and deny equitable relief. In *White v. Cooke*, 4 So.3d 330 (Miss. 2009) both parties were mistaken over an essential term in the contract regarding the existence of driveway that served as sole means of ingress and egress to the property. As a consequence, the court denied specific performance and rescinded the contract.

Although the standard for relief is higher, a unilateral mistake of fact made by one contracting party may prompt a court to refrain from ordering specific performance if the effect of the order would heavily penalize the mistaken party. *See* Oswald v. Allen, 285 F.Supp. 488 (S.D.N.Y.1968) (contract to sell rare coin collection not specifically enforced where mistake concerned which coins subject to contract); Brooks v. Towson Realty, 223 Md. 61, 162 A.2d 431 (1960) (no specific performance where buyer mistakenly believed contract description included an additional tract of land); Perlmutter v. Bacas, 219 Md. 406, 149 A.2d 23 (1959) (buyer mistake that land could be subdivided justified denial of specific performance). The mistake may not be sufficient to prevent formation of the contract; therefore, the court should award legal relief to which the aggrieved party may be otherwise entitled. The willingness of a court to rely upon a mistake to deny equitable relief is, of course, heightened if it was caused by misrepresentations by the other contracting party. Restatement (Second) Contracts § 364(1)(a).

3. *Contract Modification.* Equity aims to render more complete relief than that which is available at law. Although the essential function of a specific performance order is to give effect to the reasonable, justifiable expectations of the contracting parties, the court is not constrained to order the exact performance contemplated by the contract. The critical question, as examined in the principal case, is whether the equitable order will carry out the purposes of the agreement. *See* Lary v. U.S. Postal Service, 472 F.3d 1363 (Fed. Cir. 2006). When necessary, such as if the transaction is delayed beyond the originally contemplated date, the court may adjust the order to take into account rents and profits earned in the interim to place the parties in the same position they would have otherwise had. *See* Geensleeves, Inc. v. Smiley, 942 A.2d 284 (R.I. 2007).

Similarly, specific performance may be awarded with an abatement in the purchase price. If, for example, a vendor has breached by misrepresenting the acreage in a land sale contract, the vendee may specifically enforce the contract and concurrently obtain an abatement in the purchase price. This practice effectively consolidates an equitable right of specific performance and a legal right to damages for the difference in the expected land and the land received.

Generally, the treatment of specific performance with requested abatement for a breach can be broken down into three categories. If the differential is so minute as not to impair the contract substantially, then arguably no breach occurred and specific performance will lie with no abatement. If the deficiency is sufficient to rise to the level of a breach, the courts are willing to award specific performance with purchase price abatement. This willingness falters, however, when the breach is so substantial that the court would be enforcing not the parties' contract but a contract of the court's own creation. The courts perhaps believe that specific performance of such a small quantity would be "a suit in which the tail wags the dog." *See* Dobbs, Remedies § 12.10.

4. Most cases follow the reasoning that specific performance with abatement is allowed in a title defect or a deficiency in quantity but will not be permitted where the buyer knew the seller would not be able to complete the transaction, or if the breach relates to a collateral promise. A collateral promise relates not to the quantity or quality of the estate, but instead to some non-integral factor such as its earning potential. At the other end of the spectrum, where the buyer will accept whatever title the seller can offer, without abatement, the court will uphold the contract. *See* Leland v. Kligman, 160 F.2d 27 (D.C.Cir.1947) (vendor not excused from performing contract for the sale of realty on the ground that a third party had a possible interest, because the purchaser was willing to take whatever title vendor had).

C. CONTRACTS FOR THE SALE OF GOODS

Section Coverage:

The common law approach to specific performance in the sale of goods focuses upon uniqueness of the subject goods to satisfy the inadequacy at law requirement. A specific performance order is difficult to obtain under common law without a showing that the object of the contract is virtually one-of-a-kind. The Uniform Commercial Code § 2–716(1) changes and expands the specific performance remedy when goods are "unique or in other proper circumstances." Although the contours of "uniqueness" and the "other proper circumstances" provision have not been entirely drawn, the approach in U.C.C. 2–716 is intended to encompass contract matters apart from heirlooms, such as in output and requirements contracts where alternate sources or markets are not readily available.

Model Case:

Parket contracted to purchase from the Fullsail Yacht Co. a customized fiberglass "FX 160" cruising yacht with a special hull design manufactured exclusively by Fullsail. Parket gave the down payment as required under the agreement but Fullsail subsequently repudiated the contract because of a rise in the cost of its materials.

A court is likely to award specific performance of manufacture and delivery of the yacht conditioned upon compliance by Parket with the contract terms. The underlying basis for the order is that Parket cannot obtain substitute goods in the open market because only Fullsail manufactures that particular design of yacht. The inability to cover, according to comment 2 § 2–716 and relevant caselaw, is relevant not only with respect to the uniqueness of the goods but also with respect to the "other proper circumstances" test stated for specific performance under § 2–716(1).

Sedmak v. Charlie's Chevrolet, Inc.

622 S.W.2d 694 (Mo.App.1981).

■ SATZ, JUDGE.

This is an appeal from a decree of specific performance. We affirm.

In their petition, plaintiffs, Dr. and Mrs. Sedmak (Sedmaks), alleged they entered into a contract with defendant, Charlie's Chevrolet, Inc. (Charlie's), to purchase a Corvette automobile for approximately $15,000.00. The Corvette was one of a limited number manufactured to commemorate the selection of the Corvette as the Pace Car for the Indianapolis 500. Charlie's breached the contract, the Sedmaks alleged, when, after the automobile was delivered, an agent for Charlie's told the Sedmaks they could not purchase the automobile for $15,000.00 but would have to bid on it.

* * * The record reflects the Sedmaks to be automobile enthusiasts, who, at the time of trial, owned six Corvettes. In July, 1977, "Vette Vues," a Corvette fancier's magazine to which Dr. Sedmak subscribed, published an article announcing Chevrolet's tentative plans to manufacture a limited edition of the Corvette. The limited edition of approximately 6,000 automobiles was to commemorate the selection of the Corvette as the Indianapolis 500 Pace Car. The Sedmaks were interested in acquiring one of these Pace Cars to add to their Corvette collection. In November, 1977, the Sedmaks asked Tom Kells, sales manager at Charlie's Chevrolet, about the availability of the Pace Car. Mr. Kells said he did not have any information on the car but would find out about it. Mr. Kells said if Charlie's were to receive a Pace Car, the Sedmaks could purchase it.

On January 9, 1978, Dr. Sedmak telephoned Kells to ask him if a Pace Car could be ordered. Kells indicated that he would require a deposit on the car, so Mrs. Sedmak went to Charlie's and gave Kells a check for $500.00. She was given a receipt for that amount bearing the names of Kells and Charlie's Chevrolet, Inc. At that time, Kells had a pre-ordered form listing both standard equipment and options available on the Pace Car. Prior to tendering the deposit, Mrs. Sedmak asked Kells if she and Dr. Sedmak were "definitely going to be the owners." Kells replied, "yes." After the deposit had been paid, Mrs. Sedmak stated if the car was going to be theirs, her husband wanted some changes made to the stock model. She asked Kells to order the car equipped with an L82 engine, four speed standard transmission and AM/FM radio with tape deck. Kells said that he would try to arrange with the manufacturer for these changes. Kells was able to make the changes, and, when the car arrived, it was equipped as the Sedmaks had requested.

Kells informed Mrs. Sedmak that the price of the Pace Car would be the manufacturer's retail price, approximately $15,000.00. The dollar figure could not be quoted more precisely because Kells was not sure what the ordered changes would cost, nor was he sure what the "appearance package"—decals, a special paint job—would cost. * * *

On April 3, 1978, the Sedmaks were notified by Kells that the Pace Car had arrived. Kells told the Sedmaks they could not purchase the car for the manufacturer's retail price because demand for the car had inflated its value beyond the suggested price. Kells also told the Sedmaks they could bid on the car. The Sedmaks did not submit a bid. They filed this suit for specific performance.

* * *

[The court reviewed the evidence and rejected defendant's contention that no contract was made.] Without again detailing the facts, there was evidence to support the trial court's conclusion that the parties agreed the selling price would be the price suggested by the manufacturer. Whether this price accurately reflects the market demands on any given day is immaterial. The manufacturer's suggested retail price is ascertainable and, thus, if the parties choose, sufficiently definite to meet the price requirements of an enforceable contract. Failure to specify the selling price in dollars and cents did not render the contract void or voidable. As long as the parties agreed to a method by which the price was to be determined and as long as the price could be ascertained at the time of performance, the price requirement for a valid and enforceable contract was satisfied. * * *

Finally, Charlie's contends the Sedmaks failed to show they were entitled to specific performance of the contract. We disagree. Although it has been stated that the determination whether to order specific performance lies within the discretion of the trial court, this discretion is, in fact, quite narrow. When the relevant equitable principles have been met and the contract is fair and plain, "specific performance goes as a matter of right." [Citation.] Here, the trial court ordered specific performance because it concluded the Sedmaks "have no adequate remedy at law for the reason that they cannot go upon the open market and purchase an automobile of this kind with the same mileage, condition, ownership and appearance as the automobile involved in this case, except, if at all, with considerable expense, trouble, loss, great delay and inconvenience." Contrary to defendant's complaint, this is a correct expression of the relevant law and it is supported by the evidence.

Under the Code, the court may decree specific performance as a buyer's remedy for breach of contract to sell goods "where the goods are unique or in other proper circumstances." § 400.2–716(1) RSMo 1978. The general term "in other proper circumstances" expresses the drafters' intent to "further a more liberal attitude than some courts have shown in connection with the specific performance of contracts of sale," § 400.2–716, U.C.C., Comment 1. This Comment was not directed to the courts of this state, for long before the Code, we, in Missouri, took a practical approach in determining whether specific performance would lie for the breach of contract for the sale of goods and did not limit this relief only to the sale of "unique" goods. *Boeving v. Vandover,* 240 Mo.App. 117, 218 S.W.2d 175 (1949). In *Boeving,* plaintiff contracted to buy a car from defendant. When the car arrived, defendant refused to sell. The car was not unique in the traditional legal sense but, at that time, all cars were difficult to obtain because of war-time shortages. The court held specific performance was the proper remedy for plaintiff because a new car "could not be obtained elsewhere except at considerable expense, trouble or loss, which cannot be estimated in advance and under such circumstances [plaintiff] did not have an adequate remedy at law." Thus, *Boeving,* presaged the broad and liberalized language of § 400.2–716(1) and exemplifies one of the "other proper circumstances" contemplated by this subsection for ordering specific performance. § 400.2–716, Missouri Code Comment 1. The present facts track those in *Boeving.*

The Pace Car, like the car in *Boeving,* was not unique in the traditional legal sense. It was not an heirloom or, arguably, not one of a kind. However, its "mileage, condition, ownership and appearance" did make it difficult, if not impossible, to obtain its replication without considerable expense, delay and inconvenience. Admittedly, 6,000 Pace Cars were produced by Chevrolet. However, as the record reflects, this is limited production. In addition, only one of these cars was available to each dealer, and only a limited number of these were equipped with the specific options ordered by plaintiffs. Charlie's had not received a car like the Pace Car in the previous two years. The sticker price for the car was $14,284.21. Yet Charlie's received offers from individuals in Hawaii and Florida to buy the Pace Car for $24,000.00 and $28,000.00 respectively. As sensibly inferred by the trial court, the location and size of these offers demonstrated this limited edition was in short supply and great demand. We agree, with the trial court. This case was a "proper circumstance" for ordering specific performance.

Judgment affirmed.

––––––––––––

1. *Uniqueness.* The court in *Sedmak, supra,* focused on the uniqueness of the limited edition Corvette automobile in granting specific performance. *Also see* Taylor v. Hoffman Ford, Inc., 57 U.C.C. Rep.Serv.2d 805 (Conn. Super. 2005) (specific performance granted to purchase a limited edition 2005 Ford GT 40 because speculative whether similar car could be obtained in market). Compare Poltorak v. Jackson Chevrolet Co., 322 Mass. 699, 79 N.E.2d 285 (1948) where the court refused to award specific performance of contract to purchase an automobile whose delivery was delayed by World War II. The court reasoned:

> The scarcity of automobiles, which went no farther than to occasion considerable delay in delivery, is not sufficient basis for a decree of specific performance in favor of one who sought the completion of a contract for the sale of an ordinary passenger vehicle, and who showed

no substantial harm of a kind of character which could not be adequately compensated by an award of damages in an action at law. Id. at 702.

2. Although the U.C.C. is intended to promote a more liberal attitude with respect to specific performance, the Code retains "emphasis on the commercial feasibility of replacement" as the most desirable approach and retains traditional equitable principles in consideration of the proper remedy. *See* Comment 2, 2–716. *Also see* In re Bullet Jet Charter, Inc., 177 B.R. 593, 27 U.C.C. Rep. Serv.2d 1256 (Bankr.N.D.Ill. 1995) (used aircraft deemed unique for specific performance because not similar to other aircraft available on the market and special work already done on to suit buyer's particular needs); King Aircraft Sales, Inc. v. Lane, 68 Wash.App. 706, 846 P.2d 550 (1993) (aircraft rare in terms of exceptional condition that impossible to obtain alternative planes of similar quality); *but see* Klein v. PepsiCo, Inc., 845 F.2d 76 (4th Cir. 1988) (used corporate jet not unique where comparable aircraft available in market, although at higher price).

For a representative sampling of other cases finding goods unique for purposes of equitable relief under the Code see Ruddock v. First National Bank, 201 Ill.App.3d 907, 147 Ill.Dec. 310, 559 N.E.2d 483 (1990) (rare astronomical clock); Fast v. Southern Offshore Yachts, 587 F.Supp. 1354 (D.Conn.1984) and Gay v. Seafarer Fiberglass Yachts, Inc., 14 U.C.C. Rep.Serv. 1335 (N.Y.Sup.1974) (customized yachts); Schweber v. Rallye Motors, Inc., 12 U.C.C. Rep.Serv. 1154 (N.Y.Sup.1973) (Rolls Royce Corniche convertible); Colorado–Ute Electric Assoc., Inc. v. Envirotech Corp., 524 F.Supp. 1152 (D.Colo.1981) (electrostatic precipitator air pollution control equipment); But compare the following cases in which the subject goods were not considered unique and specific performance was denied Pierce–Odom, Inc. v. Evenson, 5 Ark.App. 67, 632 S.W.2d 247 (1982) (mobile home); Hilmor Sales Co. v. Helen Neushaefer Division of Supronics Corp., 6 U.C.C. Rep.Serv. 325 (N.Y.Sup.1969) (lipsticks and nail polish containers); Scholl v. Hartzell, 20 Pa.D. & C.3d 304 (Pa.Com.Pl.1981) (1962 Chevrolet Corvette).

3. The claimant bears the burden of demonstrating an inability to obtain a reasonable substitute without unnecessary burden, expense or delay. *See* Structural Polymer Group, Ltd. v. Zoltek Corp., 61 U.C.C. Rep. Serv.2d 506 (E.D. Mo. 2006) (record failed to show specific evidence regarding shortage of large-tow carbon fiber, identity of other suppliers, and likelihood of obtaining replacement goods).

4. The issue in determining whether potential replacement goods may suffice for effective cover is not merely their availability but also considers whether they are of the same quality and will be functional equivalents to the goods subject to the contract. In *International Casings Group, Inc. v. Premium Standard Farms, Inc.*, 358 F.Supp.2d 863 (W.D. Mo. 2005), for example, the court granted specific performance of a long-term contract to furnish hog casings to a pork supplier. The buyer showed that it could not obtain replacement casings of the same quality and specifications because the goods produced by the seller were not fungible and not readily available

on the spot market. The buyer supported its claim for an injunction by showing that it would suffer harm to its goodwill and reputation in the industry, which could affect its business relationships and cause the loss of customers. *Also see* Slidell, Inc. v. Millenium Inorganic Chemicals, Inc., 53 U.C.C. Rep. Serv. 2d 829 (D. Minn. 2004) (relevant factors regarding uniqueness included whether an item is custom built, has historical or sentimental significance, and whether it was designed to particular specifications).

5.   In some instances, an apparently rare item may still not be deemed a proper subject for specific performance due to changes in market conditions or excessive delays by the non-breaching party in seeking a remedy. *See* Bander v. Grossman, 161 Misc.2d 119, 611 N.Y.S.2d 985 (1994) (specific performance denied for purchase of rare, limited edition Astin–Martin automobile where buyer delayed in seeking equitable relief); Ziebarth v. Kalenze, 238 N.W.2d 261 (N.D.1976) (delay in transferring cattle).

In an interesting twist, *Semi–Materials Co. v. MEMC Electronic Materials, Inc.*, 341 Fed. Appx. 259 (8th Cir. 2009), market conditions changed dramatically and suitable substitutes became more plentiful subsequent to issuance of an order of specific performance. Based upon the change in circumstances, both parties requested that equitable relief be withdrawn and the court vacated.

PROBLEM: THE JILTED BUYER

Able owns Puppy Acres, a championship dog breeding farm. Able entered into a written requirements contract for a five year term with Chowhound, Inc. ("CI"), manufacturer of a dog food called "Puppy Lite," which provided that CI would deliver between 50 and 100 cartons of Puppy Lite at $1.00 each, every month to Able. The contract contained the following liquidated damages clause:

> "In the event that either party materially breaches this contract, the breaching party shall pay the non-breaching party the sum of $2,500."

The contract further provided that neither party could cancel the contract without obtaining the written consent of the other party.

Puppy Lite is a specially blended dog food which helps dogs have soft and shiny coats, a particularly important factor in dog show judging. A prominent trade journal called Puppy Lite "a unique blend, unmatched in the industry."

The owner of Pups Ltd., and a competitor of Able, induced CI to break the contract with Able, without obtaining the necessary consent, and to begin supplying Pups Ltd. with Puppy Lite.

Able learned of the breach of contract by CI on February 1st. He tried to negotiate with CI to continue supplying him but his efforts were unsuccessful, culminating in a final cancellation letter from CI dated March 10th. During the months of February and March the cost to obtain the closest substitute dog food, Brand X, in the market was $1.05 per carton.

However, due to seasonal demand forces, by the time that Able purchased Brand X in April, the cost had risen to $1.20 per carton. Because Brand X was manufactured in Taiwan, Able also had to pay $500 in transportation and insurance costs for each shipment.

Able seeks specific performance of the contract by CI. Should it be granted?

Weathersby v. Gore

556 F.2d 1247 (5th Cir.1977).

■ Clark, Circuit Judge:

This Mississippi-based diversity action was brought by Frank Weathersby, a Memphis, Tennessee cotton buyer doing business as Weathersby Cotton Company, against Y.B. Gore, a Webster County, Mississippi cotton farmer. Weathersby contended he had a valid contract with defendant Gore which obliged Gore to sell the cotton produced by him on 500 acres of land during the 1973 crop year. Two months after the contract was entered and many months before the cotton was to be picked, Gore gave notice that he was cancelling the contract and indicated his intention of selling his cotton elsewhere. After a jury verdict favoring Weathersby, the district court ordered specific performance of the contract. We reverse and remand.

* * * The genesis of this litigation is to be found in the volatility of the cotton futures market during 1972 and 1973. In 1972 Gore entered into a forward contract for the sale of his cotton, but his experience was not a happy one. The price at the time the cotton was picked was lower than that provided in the contract, and the buyer refused to purchase the cotton. Gore chose to sell at the lower price rather than to bring suit.

* * * As a consequence of his 1972 experience, Gore insisted that any future purchaser provide a performance bond ensuring Gore against loss in the event of a similar breach. The contract in suit was negotiated at a price of 30 cents per pound. Throughout the subsequent months the price rose, until at the time performance was due the price had soared to 80 cents per pound.

* * *

Throughout the period following May 3, and before commencement of suit on September 28, 1973, no attempt was made by Weathersby, Starke Taylor, or Fieldcrest to effect cover. It was stipulated that any party could have purchased other cotton to cover the contract expectancy on the open market.

* * * The parties are in considerable disagreement over the meaning of Miss.Code Ann. § 75–2–716(1) (1973): "Specific performance may be decreed where the goods are unique or in other proper circumstances." Various authorities have been cited to the court indicating that crop contracts historically have been treated as susceptible to specific performance treatment more readily than other types of contracts. [Citations.]

However, cotton contracts have not been given such treatment in Mississippi when other cotton was readily available on the open market. In Austin v. Montgomery, 336 So.2d 745 (Miss.1976), the Mississippi Supreme Court permitted without discussion the specific performance of a cotton output contract that had been entered in March 1973 and breached by the farmer-seller in July. The plaintiff buyer contended that it was impossible to obtain cotton elsewhere when notice was given in July that the farmer would refuse to deliver at harvest. The farmer did not attempt to refute this contention. Consequently the seller would have had to default on his contract to deliver the cotton to a textile mill. Since the parties here are in agreement that other cotton was available when the notice of cancellation was sent in May by Gore, the *Austin* decision is not in point.

Far predating Mississippi's adoption of the Uniform Commercial Code, but indicating the reasons why specific performance is not suitable here, is Scott v. Billgerry, 40 Miss. 119 (1866). Billgerry was the purchaser of seventy-five bales of cotton from Scott. The purchase price of $3900 was paid at the time the contract was entered. Upon Scott's subsequent refusal to deliver, Billgerry sought specific performance. Though the court was not referring to an output contract but rather to the simple purchase of cotton bales, the language is equally applicable here:

> It is altogether immaterial whether there was a sale of certain specific bales of cotton, or an agreement to sell and deliver a certain number of bales out of a particular lot, or a general agreement to sell and deliver a certain number of bales, without any designation of the specific bales, or of the particular lot out of which they are to come. All such cases depend upon the same general principle. The rule is, not to entertain jurisdiction in equity for a specific performance of agreements respecting goods, chattels, stock, choses in action, and other things of a personal nature, unless, under the particular circumstances of the case, there can be no adequate compensation in damages at law.

Id. at 140.

The adoption of the Uniform Commercial Code by Mississippi does not suggest the considerations expressed in *Scott v. Billgerry* are now to be rejected. Other than to indicate that the Code is intended to "further a more liberal attitude than some courts have shown in connection with the specific performance of contracts of sale," the comments accompanying UCC § 2–716 are of little guidance. The comments also state that "[o]utput and requirements contracts involving a particularly or peculiarly available source of market present today the typical commercial specific performance situation," but the interpretation of this language appears to range from suggesting all output contracts should be specifically enforceable to a mere observation that output contracts form a suitable factual background in most cases in which specific performance may be sought.

The general rule applicable when specific performance is requested has been stated in Roberts v. Spence, 209 So.2d 623, 626 (Miss.1968): "specific performance of a contract will not be awarded where damages may be recovered and the remedy in a court of law is adequate to compensate the injured party." Considering the reluctance expressed in *Roberts* to authorization of the specific performance remedy we hold that the Mississippi Supreme Court would apply a restrictive reading of § 75–2–716. A similar interpretation of the Code provision was adopted by the Georgia Supreme Court in Duval & Co. v. Malcom, 233 Ga. 784, 214 S.E.2d 356 (1975). There a buyer attempted to get specific performance of a cotton output contract entered into with a cotton farmer. Specific performance was rejected with the statement damages would be sufficient unless cotton could not be obtained in the open market. Thus the Georgia court, as did the Mississippi Supreme Court in *Austin,* would have permitted specific performance if the buyer could not otherwise obtain the needed cotton. Absent this fact, specific performance was not an available remedy. The Georgia court gave considerable attention to the Code language that specific performance should be permitted when goods are unique and "in other proper circumstances." The vague language was held not to authorize wholesale granting of the remedy when output contracts were involved. The remedy of damages—the difference between the market price at the time of the breach and the contract price—adequately compensated the buyer for his inability to procure the cotton from the farmer with whom he had contracted. Likewise Weathersby was adequately protected from any damages occasioned by Gore's breach of the contract, if any occurred. He could have acquired additional cotton on the open market when Gore informed him he would no longer perform under the contract. He did not do so and thus, if entitled to damages at all, must settle for the difference between the contract and the market price at the time Gore cancelled. *See* Miss.Code Ann. § 75–2–712 (1973).

* * * Finally, specific performance was not an appropriate remedy in the present case. If Weathersby is successful in proving that Gore improperly cancelled the contract, he is limited to recovery of damages.

Reversed and Remanded.

---

1. The court in *Weathersby* denied specific performance because the buyer failed to show the inadequacy of its remedy at law for damages, even though the cotton market was extremely volatile. Similarly, in *Duval & Co. v. Malcom,* 233 Ga. 784, 214 S.E.2d 356 (1975), and *Tower City Grain Co. v. Richman,* 232 N.W.2d 61 (N.D.1975), the courts denied specific performance after finding, as a threshold matter, that damages would adequately compensate the aggrieved buyers in an output contract to supply cotton. On the other hand, in *R. L. Kimsey Cotton Co. v. Ferguson,* 233 Ga. 962, 214 S.E.2d 360 (1975), the Georgia Supreme Court reached a different result than in *Duval* by granting specific performance of a similar cotton output contract because the parties had stipulated that the cotton involved was unique.

2. Section 2–716(1) does not require a finding that available legal remedies are inadequate, but attempts to provide an expanded test for

specific performance when the goods are "unique or in other proper circumstances." It is uncertain whether these courts have considered inadequacy of legal remedies as an additional test for entitlement to specific performance or whether it is just another factor to be weighed in the court's equitable discretion. Since the U.C.C. policy was to expand the availability of the specific performance remedy by its "more liberal attitude," the better view is that inadequacy of legal remedies does not present an independent requirement beyond the § 2–716(1) statutory language. A balanced approach is necessary, however, as demonstrated by the *Weathersby* court stating that specific performance would not automatically issue simply because it involved an output contract.

3. In *Weathersby*, should the court have considered the viability of recovering damages as a factor influencing its discretion in awarding equitable relief? For example, in *In re Bullet Jet Charter, Inc.*, 177 B.R. 593, 27 U.C.C. Rep. Serv.2d 1256 (Bankr.N.D.Ill. 1995) the court found that a used aircraft was unique for specific performance because it was not similar to other aircraft available on the market and special work had already been done on it to meet the buyer's specifications. Also, "other proper circumstances" existed because the buyer could not cover and then recover the difference in cost from an insolvent, bankrupt seller.

4. In *Laclede Gas Co. v. Amoco Oil Co.*, 522 F.2d 33 (8th Cir. 1975) the court ordered specific performance of a long term requirements contract involving the shipment of propane gas to a utility company for distribution to its customers. The court, observing that a remedy at law "must be as certain, prompt, complete and efficient to attain the ends of justice as a decree of specific performance", found that damages would be inadequate. The court noted that the utility could not own and operate a separate distribution system to another supplier's storage tanks without substantially altering supply routes to or incurring substantial costs.

Ace Equipment Co., Inc. v. Aqua Chem., Inc.

20 U.C.C.Rep.Serv. 392, 73 Pa.D. & C.2d 300 (1975).

■ Gates, Justice.

This matter comes before the court on defendant's preliminary objections to plaintiff's complaint in equity. The preliminary objections complain that plaintiff has an adequate remedy at law for damages and, in addition, demurs to the complaint for substantially the same reason.

It is defendant's contention that plaintiff has not stated a case for equitable relief in the nature of specific performance of a contract for the sale, inter alia, of a used 6000 KVA General Electric Transformer. Defendant contends that plaintiff has a complete and adequate remedy at law for money damages.

In this posture of the record, the following facts are deemed to be admitted. On or about March 30, 1973, plaintiff's written offer to purchase a used 6000 KVA General Electric Transformer was accepted in writing by defendant for the price of $1,800. * * *

However, plaintiff tells us that on April 12, 1973, the transformer was loaded on board a truck supplied by plaintiff, intending to deliver it to one Frank Lunney with whom plaintiff had an agreement to sell it for the price of $7,500. But plaintiff says that defendant wrongfully, and without prior notice to plaintiff, refused to allow the truck to leave and that defendant has retained possession of the transformer since that time.

Plaintiff further alleges that defendant was made aware of the transaction between plaintiff and Lunney and that defendant is aware that plaintiff is still obligated to perform its contract to Lunney and has not only lost the benefit of the sale, but is subject to consequential damages as a result of the failure to perform.

We agree with defendant that ordinarily a bill for specific performance for the sale of personalty will not be entertained by a court of equity. However, the Uniform Commercial code provides, in pertinent part, as follows:

"(1) Specific performance may be decreed where the goods are unique or in other proper circumstances." * * *

True it is that, as between the parties, there would be an adequate remedy at law and the measure of damages fixed by the term of the agreement and the content of the complaint. However, in light of the fact that plaintiff has entered into an agreement to sell the transformer to a third party and defendant is aware of that fact, we have a different situation than is ordinarily the case. Here, we are dealing with a huge piece of used equipment. It was purchased at a relatively low price when compared to the resale price plaintiff has contracted to sell it to Lunney. This is unlike the ordinary purchase of goods and merchandise for resale. It is unlikely that there is a substantially identical piece of used equipment which plaintiff could locate in order to perform its contract with a third party.

It is defendant's breach which renders plaintiff unable to perform its contract to the third party. This failure of performance for an item of service equipment may render plaintiff liable to damages, in addition to those for breach of contract, of a consequential nature for failing to perform. The nature of these damages is speculative and conceivably could be extensive. It is this state of affairs which, in our judgment, is the "... other proper circumstances" contemplated by the Uniform Commercial Code. These facts render a legal remedy inadequate.

Thus, we conclude that plaintiff has stated a case for specific performance and we shall dismiss the preliminary objections.

---

1. *Other Proper Circumstances.* The liberalization of the specific performance remedy under the U.C.C. may be reflected in the "other proper circumstances" prong for considering equitable relief. By expanding the

inquiry beyond measurement of damages and the viability of cover, this allows courts flexibility to consider a wide range of factors affecting commercial transactions. In *Ace Equipment*, the court interprets the "other proper circumstances" test in § 2–716 to encompass a contract to buy used equipment at a bargain price with a contract to resell at a higher price to a third party. The court is persuaded by the plaintiff's assertion that, absent equitable relief, plaintiff will incur liability for consequential damages which may be "speculative and conceivably could be extensive." Difficulties in measurement, though, should not necessarily mean that damages would be an inadequate remedy. This result may represent the outer limits of the Code's "more liberal attitude" with respect to granting specific performance.

2. *Business Necessity.* The importance of the goods to the buyer's business can be an influential factor in granting specific performance. For instance, in *Kaiser Trading Co. v. Associated Metals & Minerals Corp.*, 321 F.Supp. 923 (N.D.Cal. 1970) an aluminum manufacturing corporation contracted to purchase a supply of cryolite, an indispensable mineral used in the production of aluminum. The seller breached and the buyer sought injunctive relief. Evidence showed that the mineral was extremely scarce, as it was found naturally only in one location in Greenland, although a synthetically produced substitute was potentially available from several sources. The court recognized the "growing tendency" favoring specific performance and observed that the U.C.C. no longer limited specific performance to goods which are already specific or ascertained at the time of contracting. Accordingly, because the buyer would have difficulty in effecting cover due to the scarcity of supply, the court granted an injunction to compel performance of the contract.

Similarly, in *Eastern Air Lines, Inc. v. Gulf Oil Corp.*, 415 F.Supp. 429 (S.D.Fla.1975), the court specifically enforced a contract for supplying aviation fuel to an airline company during the 1973 Arab oil embargo. *See also* Sherwin Alumina L.P. v. AluChem, Inc., 512 F.Supp.2d 957 (S.D.Tex. 2007) (specific performance granted because products were both unique and necessary for business); Copylease Corp. of America v. Memorex Corp., 408 F.Supp. 758 (S.D.N.Y.1976) (specific performance of a contract to supply a certain brand of toner and developer for use in copy machines).

On the other hand, in *I.lan Systems, Inc. v. Netscout Service Level Corp.*, 183 F.Supp.2d 328 (D.Mass. 2002) a licensee sought specific performance to continue its business relationship with the licensor of a business software system. The licensee claimed that the software package was unique because it was copyrighted and that it had tailored its business around the software. Further, the licensee asserted that money damages would be inadequate because of the uncertainty of future needs for similar services. The court disagreed, cautioning not to "conflate reliance with uniqueness", found that other software vendors could furnish virtually interchangeable systems.

3. What if the breaching seller in *Ace Equipment* had resold to another party for a still higher price? Proponents of the efficient contract

breach theory might suggest that this hypothetical situation is economically sound to all concerned. First, the aggrieved buyer may owe damages on its third party contract but will be compensated fully by the breaching seller. The seller, although not in a sympathetic role, pays the first buyer his damages but offsets that loss by the profits received on the resale. The ultimate purchaser, willing to pay the highest price for the goods, receives what it bargained for as well. The view opposing the efficient breach approach is that certainty and confidence in contractual relations is undermined by shifting goods to the highest bidder. Moreover, the transaction costs are difficult to ascertain and are often ignored or arguably underestimated by proponents of efficiency theory. Finally, the moralist view considers that the non-breaching buyer is not above reproach as he stands to make a tidy profit on an immediate resale. Which vision of contract law is most persuasive in this context? Are there alternative approaches?

CHAPTER 5

EQUITABLE DEFENSES

Equitable defenses strongly reflect the origin of equity as the Chancellor's law of conscience. The Chancellor would not give relief to a suitor whose behavior concerning the claims was "tainted" in some respect. The Chancellor would deny equitable relief if the claimant had "unclean hands" or had engaged in unconscionable conduct in securing the right being asserted, or if the defendant had been prejudiced by prior inconsistent conduct or by undue delay by the suitor in pursuing the claim. Even in a case where the defendant's behavior was much worse by comparison, the Chancellor was unsupportive of rights tainted by improper conduct and the plaintiff would be sent away from equity to seek redress from a court of law. Equity would not sully itself by lending aid to a someone who had a questionable moral posture with regard to the claim.

Modern equity preserves the equitable defenses even in the merged system of law and equity. Moreover, the defenses still have a moralistic foundation; a court will not grant equitable relief if the plaintiff has behaved in a way prejudicial to the defendant or offensive to public policy. As in the past, there is no entitlement to equitable relief in modern law and the plaintiff's conduct in the case still affects the court's decision. Equity is guided by principled discretion but its orders still bear the name "extraordinary relief." Whenever the plaintiff seeks equitable remedies, the court may apply the doctrines of laches, estoppel, unconscionability, or unclean hands.

A. LACHES AND ESTOPPEL

Section Coverage:

The equitable defense of laches bars a plaintiff who has not acted promptly in bringing the action. It is reflected in the maxim: "Equity aids the vigilant, not those who slumber on their rights." In contrast with a statute of limitations which has a definitive length of time in which claims must be filed, laches is a flexible doctrine and focuses on whether the claimant delayed unreasonably in asserting the action. Certain factors, such as the inability to determine the facts upon which the claim is based, may excuse or toll the running of the period of delay. Laches also considers whether the delayed claim would likely produce a substantial prejudice to the defendant, such as from loss of material evidence, faded memories of witnesses, or economic losses. The underlying policy reflects the social benefit of bringing repose to stale claims, encouraging parties to act with diligence in asserting rights, and preventing one party from gaining an unfair advantage in litigation.

Laches typically operates as an equitable defense to equitable actions, such as injunctions. Accordingly, even where laches precludes equitable relief a plaintiff may potentially still seek legal remedies. Thus, a plaintiff who is denied specific performance because of laches may still seek contract damages.

The laches defense is a negative bar to what otherwise may be a meritorious claim, and thus is closely related to the doctrine of estoppel. In both instances, a party may be foreclosed from a right or remedy because the delay may result in prejudice to another who has objectively relied to their detriment on a certain state of facts. Whereas laches concerns delay, estoppel involves actions inconsistent with the rights the plaintiff now asserts. The classic example is that a person cannot first stand outside and watch a neighbor build a fence, and then go to equity and demand its removal because the fence is over the property line.

Courts have traditionally drawn a distinction to application of equitable defenses when the government is one of the parties. Even when the government has waived sovereign immunity it is not completely equivalent to a private party. As a defendant, the government more easily shows prejudice to itself when it asserts equitable defenses. As a plaintiff, the sovereign historically could not be estopped nor barred by laches in asserting claims effectuating the public interest. Modern cases have made some modifications to this principle, ordinarily in situations where the government is asserting rights based on commercial or business interests.

Model Case:

A smooth-talking and attractive young stockbroker befriended an elderly person who had little business experience. This elderly client agreed to invest in highly speculative commodities and stocks. The broker and client were in daily personal contact to discuss investments. The client agreed to the transactions recommended by the broker and thus traded very frequently. The heavy trading generated high commissions for the broker. These practices continued for years until a series of bad trades left the client's account depleted. In the end there was barely enough money for this elderly person to live comfortably.

The investor's complaint alleges that the broker took improper advantage of the client's naivete and created a speculative account out of a previously blue-chip portfolio. The broker then allegedly "churned" the speculative account with excessive trades for the purpose of generating high commissions. The broker's defense is that the client knew and approved of every aspect of the account management. Moreover, the broker argues, even if the original conversion of the portfolio from blue-chip to speculative investments was improper, the client has waited for too many years before making this protest.

The defenses of laches and estoppel will turn on a number of factual assessments. Did the plaintiff understand the true nature of the account and approve of the change? Most people in later life do not want to do heavy trading with a speculative portfolio, but some people want to take risks for big gains or big losses at any age. Was this plaintiff such a person? Did the plaintiff's acts of apparent approval prejudice the defendant's position, or was the broker exploiting the plaintiff's lack of business experience to achieve uninformed approvals? Did the plaintiff act promptly to sue as soon as the wrong was discovered, or only when the gamble on big investments was lost?

If the plaintiff did not pursue the claim soon after discovering the broker's misconduct, and if the court finds that the delay prejudiced the defendant, the claim will be barred by laches. If the plaintiff's approvals actually misled the broker into justifiable reliance upon them with resulting detriment to the broker's position, estoppel will bar the claim.

Stone v. Williams

873 F.2d 620 (2d Cir.1989).

■ CARDAMONE, CIRCUIT JUDGE:

Cathy Yvonne Stone brought this action in the United States District Court for the Southern District of New York (Keenan, J.) for her purported share of copyright renewal rights to songs composed by Hank Williams, Sr., her natural father. The defendants in this action are Hank Williams, Jr., the son of Hank Williams and stepson of Billie Jean Williams Berlin, who was married to Hank Williams at the time of his death, and a number of music companies or individuals that have obtained an interest in the copyright proceeds of the Williams' songs. * * * The sole issue presented is whether the district court abused its discretion when it granted defendants' motion for summary judgment and dismissed appellant's complaint on the grounds of laches. Even granting to Ms. Stone's situation the fullest stretch of sympathy, her own delay and procrastination in the end bars her suit. The district court's judgment, therefore, is affirmed.

I. Factual Background

The dispute arises over copyright renewal proceeds for 60 published and copyrighted songs written or performed by country and western singer Hank Williams (Williams, Sr.) who died intestate on January 1, 1953 at the age of 29. During his lifetime the well-known singer and composer wrote such popular hits as "Your Cheatin' Heart" and "Hey Good Lookin' ". We set forth the facts briefly in chronological order.

Appellant Stone was born on January 6, 1953 in Alabama, five days after Williams, Sr. died. While Ms. Stone's biological mother, Bobbie Jett, was pregnant with her in October of 1952, she and Williams, Sr. executed an agreement under which he acknowledged that he might be the father of appellant, but specifically did not admit paternity. The agreement further provided that Williams, Sr. pay Bobbie Jett for Ms. Stone's support, and placed the infant's custody until age 2 in Lillian Williams Stone, mother of Williams, Sr., who was present at the drafting and the execution of the agreement together with the two principals. Pursuant to its terms, Lillian Stone adopted plaintiff, and Bobbie Jett left for California. Until her death in 1955 Mrs. Stone cared for appellant. At that point, Williams, Sr.'s sister, Irene Smith, reneged on her promise to care for Cathy Stone if anything happened to Lillian Stone. As a result, appellant became a ward of the State of Alabama, and at age three in 1956 a foster child of the Deupree family. The Deuprees adopted her in 1959.

Williams, Sr. had a son, Hank Williams, Jr. The assignment of Hank Williams, Jr.'s copyright interests in his father's music generated litigation in 1967 and 1968 in the Circuit Court of Montgomery County, Alabama. That court appointed a guardian *ad litem*, attorney Drayton Hamilton, to ascertain any unknown potential heirs to the Williams' estate and to represent their interests. After investigating, Hamilton concluded that the only such person was appellant Stone. Unbeknownst to Ms. Stone, her adoptive family, the Deuprees, had asked Hamilton to leave her out of the 1967 proceedings, because they thought it unlikely that she would win and were worried that their then 14-year-old daughter would be subjected to embarrassing publicity because of her status as the illegitimate child of a famous country western singer. Nonetheless, Hamilton zealously litigated Ms. Stone's interests, but to no avail. The Alabama court determined that Hank Williams, Jr. was the sole heir of his father, and further held that appellant, as a natural child who had been adopted by another family, had no rights in any proceeds from the Williams, Sr.'s songs or their renewal rights. * * *

After the disruptive first few years of her life, Ms. Stone appears to have enjoyed an ordinary childhood, and developed a closely bonded relationship with the Deuprees, with no knowledge of her natural parents. Then, in late 1973, shortly before appellant's 21st birthday, Mrs. Deupree told her of the rumors regarding the identity of her natural father, but added that everything had been decided against her. This disclosure was necessary because, upon turning age 21, Ms. Stone was entitled to a small inheritance from Williams, Sr.'s mother, Lillian Stone. The Deuprees were concerned that appellant might encounter reporters while claiming the inheritance and wanted to arm her with knowledge. After picking up the inheritance check (about $3,800) at the Mobile County Courthouse, Ms. Stone went to a library and read a biography on Williams, Sr., entitled *Sing a Sad Song*, written by Roger Williams. This book mentioned the possibility that Williams, Sr. had fathered an illegitimate daughter, and the author speculated on the child's entitlement to a renewal interest in his songs. Ms. Stone surmised that she might be that daughter.

In the following years, appellant asked the Deuprees about her background and talked to some attorney acquaintances, but did little else to ascertain her connection to Williams. She recalls that the Deuprees told her that there was nothing more to do. In 1979, she met with personnel from the state agency responsible for adoptions—the Alabama Department of Pensions and Securities—but states that she no longer remembers the substance of the conversation. The record, including appellant's deposition, suggests that her feelings about Williams' parentage were ambivalent.

Her attitude crystallized in 1980 when she received a telephone call from her adoptive father, George Deupree. Evidently alluding to his decision not to pursue Ms. Stone's rights in the 1967–68 lawsuits, Deupree told her that he had undergone a change of heart after seeing Hank Williams, Jr. on a television show. Deupree has since died, but appellant related the conversation in her deposition: "I want to ask you if you would like to find out if Hank Williams is your father. He said think about it. And he said I will help you in any way that I can. And he said I think I was wrong in withholding information from you and not discussing it. And I will do everything I can to help you."

Following this call, Ms. Stone stepped up her efforts to learn about her relationship to Williams, Sr. She looked up newspaper articles about him, and sought out his relatives and those of her natural mother, Bobbie Jett, who had also since died. She met with attorney Hamilton, her former guardian *ad litem*, and discussed with him the 1952 custody and support agreement between Bobbie Jett and Williams, Sr., and obtained the records from the 1967 and 1968 Circuit Court proceedings. But Ms. Stone did not examine those documents until after she met attorney Keith Adkinson (who later became her husband) in 1984.

Appellant filed the original declaratory judgment complaint in this action on September 12, 1985 which, as amended to include all of the above-named defendants, contains two claims. The first claim against all the defendants arises under the Copyright Acts of 1909 and 1976 and seeks a number of declarations, including that Ms. Stone is the natural daughter of Williams, Sr., and as such is entitled to a proportionate share of the renewal rights from his songs. The second claim alleges that certain of the defendants committed a conspiracy to defraud her.

In addition to this federal action, Hank Williams, Jr. and Ms. Stone sued each other in Alabama state court in 1985, each seeking a declaratory judgment on appellant's status vis-a-vis Hank Williams, Sr. That court held that even though Ms. Stone was the natural child of Williams, Sr., she was not his heir under Alabama law. Thus, it gave preclusive effect to the prior 1967 and 1968 Alabama Circuit Court state ruling.

Appellant and defendants moved for summary judgment in the instant action on a number of grounds including statute of limitations and res judicata. The district court, in granting defendants' motion for summary judgment and dismissing her complaint, relied on the doctrine of laches and did not reach the other issues.

II. Discussion

Historically laches developed as an equitable defense based on the maxim *vigilantibus non dormientibus aequitas subvenit* (equity aids the vigilant, not those who sleep on their rights). [Citation] In contrast to a statute of limitations that provides a time bar within which suit must be instituted, laches asks whether the plaintiff in asserting her rights was guilty of unreasonable delay that prejudiced the defendants. The answers to these questions are to be drawn from the equitable circumstances peculiar to each case.

A ruling on the applicability of laches is overturned only when it can be said to constitute an abuse of discretion. Because this is an appeal from a motion for summary judgment that dismissed appellant's complaint, we construe the record in the light most favorable to appellant. We therefore presume the correctness of the 1985 holding of the State Court of Alabama that Cathy Stone is the natural daughter of Hank Williams, Sr.

We must analyze the reasonableness of delay and the resulting prejudice to see whether there was a material issue of fact that should have been submitted to a jury.

A. *Delay*

Although laches promotes many of the same goals as a statute of limitations, the doctrine is more flexible and requires an assessment of the facts of each case—it is the reasonableness of the delay rather than the number of years that elapse which is the focus of inquiry. *See Gardner v. Panama Railroad Co.*, 342 U.S. 29, 31–32 (1951) (the matter should not be determined by reference to mechanical application of statute of limitations; equities of parties must be considered). In holding that Ms. Stone unreasonably delayed in bringing this action to have her rights declared, the district court focused on the years 1974–85, beginning with Mrs. Deupree's conversation with appellant regarding the inheritance, and ending with the filing of the complaint that initiated the instant case.

In our view, the delay for the period from 1974 to 1980 may well have been entirely excusable under the circumstances. First, her relationship with the Deuprees is by all indications the paradigm of a successful adoption. Thus, it is not surprising that loyalty and gratitude to Mr. and Mrs. Deupree, whom she considered her real parents, gave her pause at doing anything that might hurt their feelings. For this reason, George Deupree's telephone call to Ms. Stone is significant. Only after he called in 1980 could appellant be sure that investigating her natural parentage would not damage the only family bonds she knew. Second, Ms. Stone's embarrassment at asserting her relationship to Williams, Sr. is also understandable, because his notoriety would have made publicity almost impossible for her to avoid. This is substantiated by the extensive press coverage of the 1967 and 1968 court proceedings.

Third, only in recent years have courts and the general public come to recognize that children born of unmarried parents should not be penalized by being accorded a status for which they are not to blame. In the 1967 and 1968 proceedings, attorney Hamilton argued on Ms. Stone's behalf that discriminating against illegitimate children violated the Federal Constitution. Unfortunately for appellant, Hamilton was before his time; the case that would remove much of the stigma associated with illegitimacy was then pending before the Supreme Court, but not decided until after appellant's rights had been adjudicated. [Citation]

But even though Ms. Stone might arguably be excused for the reasons just stated from filing suit until 1980, there is simply no plausible explanation for delay in filing the instant complaint until September 1985, after five more years had passed. Appellant's filial loyalty is admirable, and one can sympathize with her feelings of embarrassment and trepidation attendant upon widespread personal publicity. But these reasons for delay cannot last forever for purposes of laches. A point arrives when a plaintiff must either assert her rights or lose them. Here Ms. Stone's procrastination and delay, which silently allowed time to slip away, remain as the only reason for her failure to bring suit earlier.

Where plaintiff has not slept on her rights, but has been prevented from asserting them based, for example, on justified ignorance of the facts constituting a cause of action, personal disability, or because of ongoing settlement negotiations, the delay is reasonable and the equitable defense of laches will not bar an action. There is no such reasonable excuse, or any issue of fact presented in the instant case that would permit a jury to excuse appellant's delay for the five years beginning in 1980 and ending in September 1985.

B. *Prejudice*

Laches is not imposed as a bar to suit simply because a plaintiff's delay is found unexcused; it must also be determined whether the defendants have been prejudiced as a result of that delay.

Although an evaluation of prejudice is another subject of focus in laches analysis, it is integrally related to the inquiry regarding delay. Where there is no excuse for delay, as here, defendants need show little prejudice; a weak excuse for delay may, on the other hand, suffice to defeat a laches defense if no prejudice has been shown. Defendants may be prejudiced in several different ways. One form of prejudice is the decreased ability of the defendants to vindicate themselves that results from the death of witnesses or on account of fading memories or stale evidence. Another type of prejudice operates on the principle that it would be inequitable in light of some change in defendant's position to permit plaintiff's claim to be enforced. Defendants here were prejudiced in both ways.

As the district court noted, some of the key people having knowledge of the events preceding Ms. Stone's birth have died since 1974—George Deupree, Bobbie Jett and Audrey Mae Williams. All of their deaths are not equally prejudicial. For example, Bobbie Jett died in 1974, so absence of her testimony cannot be found to prejudice defendants because she would not have been alive to testify even if appellant had filed suit immediately. Nevertheless, the circumstances giving rise to this appeal have already spanned over two decades and the additional five years of Ms. Stone's unexcused delay doubtless would hamper the defense further—appellant's deposition reveals that even her memory has faded significantly in the interim. We conclude that the defendants were prejudiced to some degree by evidence that was lost by death or weakened during the delay. Because the defendants were injured in other ways by the delay, we need not hold that a finding of this kind of prejudice is alone sufficient to support the laches defense.

Prejudice may also be found if, during the period of delay, the circumstances or relationships between the parties have changed so that it would be unfair to let the suit go forward. The defendants have entered into numerous transactions involving Williams, Sr.'s songs. Ms. Stone responds that these transactions need not be unravelled—she could simply share in the profits. But that argument ignores the fact that the transactions were premised on the apparent certainty of the ownership of the songs' renewal rights—attributable to appellant's delay. This procrastination prejudiced defendants by lulling them into a false sense of security that the renewal rights were as they appeared and that she would not contest the 1967 and 1968 court rulings. [Citations]

We cannot be sure that defendants would have struck the bargains they did had they anticipated the dimunition in their profits that Ms. Stone seeks. This result is logically not altered by whether the defendants made actual expenditures or whether they simply incurred the opportunity costs implicated in foregoing other ventures. As Judge Learned Hand wrote as a district court judge in a copyright case in which the plaintiff delayed for 16 years before filing suit, it would be unfair for a plaintiff "to stand inactive while the proposed infringer spends large sums of money in its exploitation, and to intervene only when his speculation has proved a success. Delay under such circumstances allows the owner to speculate without risk with the other's money; he cannot possibly lose, and he may win." *Haas v. Leo Feist, Inc.*, 234 F. 105, 108 (S.D.N.Y. 1916). We therefore agree with the district court that the change in relationships and circumstances that occurred while Ms. Stone delayed would prejudice the defendants if the case were allowed to proceed at this late date.

Finally, we note that the underlying value of the laches doctrine, as with statutes of limitations, is that of repose. Even assuming that appellant's claims are meritorious, the availability of the laches defense represents a conclusion that the societal interest in a correct decision can be outweighed by the disruption its tardy filing would cause. Thus, courts, parties and witnesses "ought to be relieved of the burden of trying stale claims when a plaintiff has slept on his rights." *See Burnett v. New York Central R.R. Co.*, 380 U.S. 424, 428, 13 L. Ed. 2d 941, 85 S. Ct. 1050 (1965).

III. Conclusion

We hold therefore that Ms. Stone's delay in filing suit until September 1985 was unexcused and has prejudiced defendants. Accordingly, the order of the district court is affirmed.

---

1. The family feud over song royalties proceeded along other lines in a separate state court proceeding where Stone sought to re-open her father's estate. The trial court, however, granted summary judgment to the defendants. On appeal the Alabama Supreme Court reversed, finding that the defendants had intentionally, willfully and fraudulently concealed plaintiff's identity. The court further held that laches did not bar the claim because the defendant's fraudulent conduct excused the delay in asserting her claim. In response to that state court finding, the Second Circuit Court of Appeals granted her petition for rehearing, vacated its prior judgment, and remanded. Stone v. Williams, 891 F.2d 401 (2d Cir.1989) ("Stone II"). The court found that the equities with respect to the contest over the copyright renewal rights favored Stone, observing:

> To allow defendants to bar plaintiff from claiming her rights when the availability of the laches defense was obtained by them in such an unworthy manner would not only grant defendants a windfall in this suit to which they are not entitled, but would also encourage a party to deliberately mislead a court. Courts of equity exist to relieve a party from the defense of laches under such circumstances.

> * * * The figure representing justice is blindfolded so that the scales are held even, but justice is not blind to reality. Plaintiff therefore should have her day in court and an opportunity to have a jury determine the merits of her claim. 891 F.2d at 405.

On remand, the district court found that the claims were time-barred by the applicable statute of limitations. Stone appealed, and in Stone v. Williams, 970 F.2d 1043 (2d Cir.1992) ("Stone III") the court once again reversed and remanded. The matter was ultimately settled.

2. Under the Federal Rules of Civil Procedure § 8(c), laches is an affirmative defense; the burden of proving it belongs to the defendant. Sall v. Sall, 804 N.W.2d 378 (N.D. 2011) (party invoking laches bears burden of proving prejudice due to change of position during the delay that could not be restored to status quo).

The Supreme Court articulated the fundamental premise of laches one hundred years ago in *Mackall v. Casilear*, 137 U.S. 556, 11 S.Ct. 178, 34 L.Ed. 776 (1890). These principles guide modern laches law with equal force:

> The doctrine of laches is based upon grounds of public policy, which requires for the peace of society the discouragement of stale demands. And where the difficulty of doing entire justice by reason of the death of the principal witness or witnesses, or from the original transactions having become obscured by time, is attributable to gross negligence or deliberate delay, a court of equity will not aid a party whose application is thus destitute of conscience, good faith and reasonable diligence. 137 U.S. at 566.

3. When a statute contains a limitations period, courts generally will not apply laches to deny potential equitable relief as long as the claim is timely filed within the statutory period. Baptist Physician Hospital Organi-

zation, Inc. v. Humana Military Healthcare, 481 F.3d 337, 353 (6th Cir. 2007). The rationale is predicated on separation of powers as the doctrine of laches is a judicially created equitable defense and statutes of limitations are legislative enactments. Lyons Partnership, L.P. v. Morris Costumes, Inc., 243 F.3d 789, 798 (4th Cir.2001); United States v. Rodriguez–Aguirre, 264 F.3d 1195, 1208 (10th Cir.2001) (motion brought within operative statute of limitations not time-barred by laches).

4.   In certain instances, courts may borrow the most relevant statute of limitations and look to that statutory period by analogy to apply the laches defense. For example, in *Doyle v. Huntress, Inc.*, 513 F.3d 331 (1st Cir. 2008) several seamen brought an admiralty claim for wages against vessel owners. The court found that the three year limitations period for unpaid wage claims under Rhode Island law provided the most salient guidance to assess the reasonableness of the delay in bringing the claims. Since the plaintiffs brought suit outside the statutory period, the court held that they failed to rebut the presumption of laches and barred the claims.

Some courts have applied laches even where a statute of limitations has not expired. *See* Armstrong v. Maple Leaf Apartments, 622 F.2d 466, 472 (10th Cir.1979). Laches may be applied to bar equitable claims brought pursuant to statutes which contain no express limitations period. Holmberg v. Armbrecht, 327 U.S. 392, 395, 66 S.Ct. 582, 90 L.Ed. 743 (1946). The failure of a claimant to bring a claim within the period of an analogous statute of limitations may influence a court in determining whether the delay was reasonable in deciding whether the claims should be barred by laches. Whittington v. Dragon Group, L.L.C., 991 A.2d 1,9 (Del. 2009).

5.   In contrast with a statute of limitations, laches is a flexible doctrine which ordinarily requires a highly fact intensive evaluation of the length of the delay, reasons for waiting to initiate the claim and the changing conditions of the parties during the pendency of the delay. Township of Piscataway v. Duke Energy, 488 F.3d 203, 214–16 (3d Cir. 2007) (utility company's laches defense to claim for injunction brought by homeowners to bar utility from removing trees from right of way created genuine issue for trial to resolve conflicting evidence). There are no mechanical rules for proof of unreasonable delay and prejudice to the defendant. Waddell v. Small Tube Products, Inc., 799 F.2d 69, 79 (3d Cir.1986) (In contrast with a statute of limitations, laches offers the courts more flexibility, eschewing mechanical rules).

6.   Particular problems of application of the laches defense may occur when the nature of the claim itself develops over a long period of time. For example, the Supreme Court has recognized that a civil rights claims alleging a hostile work environment may implicate historical patterns of behavior and therefore also potentially give rise to the equitable defense of laches by an employer. National Railroad Passenger Corp. v. Morgan, 536 U.S. 101, 121, 122 S.Ct. 2061, 153 L.Ed.2d 106 (2002).

In *Pruitt v. City of Chicago*, 472 F.3d 925 (7th Cir.2006), the court held that laches barred city employees civil rights claims based upon alleged discriminatory treatment by a supervisor over a 20 year period. The court found that the city employer would be prejudiced by the delay because key witnesses were unavailable and the supervisor, in anticipation of retirement, had moved and reported severe memory problems from a stroke. The court noted that the employer did not need to show detrimental reliance related to the delay, such as destruction of records in the belief that an employee would not sue.

7. The running of the time period for evaluating delay in laches may be tolled in certain instances. For example, in *Pro–Football, Inc. v. Harjo*, 415 F.3d 44 (D.C.Cir.2005), a group of Native Americans sought to cancel the registrations of trademarks used by the Washington Redskins professional football team, claiming that the marks were disparaging and therefore violated provisions of the Lanham Trademark Act. The district court found that a 25 year delay from the first registered trademark until filing the suit justified summary judgment to the defendant football team on the grounds that laches barred the claim. On appeal, the court remanded, on the basis that one of the petitioners was a minor during a significant portion of the period of delay in question. The court held that the factor of delay for laches purposes would not run until all petitioners had reached the age of majority.

8. What if the delay is caused by an administrative agency? Should a court attribute the inefficiency of a governmental entity to a private plaintiff? *See* Whitfield v. Anheuser–Busch, Inc., 820 F.2d 243 (8th Cir. 1987) (ten year delay of Equal Employment Opportunity Commission was unreasonable delay to bar subsequent suit by alleged discrimination victim where defendant's witnesses no longer recalled event); EEOC v. Liberty Loan Corp., 584 F.2d 853 (8th Cir.1978) (four year administrative delay unreasonable, absent any excuse other than heavy workload, if prejudicial to defendant).

Various factors may justify and excuse a delay in bringing a claim, including the pursuit of other litigation, ongoing negotiations between the parties, incapacity, or dispute over property rights. *See* Expert Microsystems, Inc. v. University of Chicago, 712 F.Supp.2d 1116, 1120 (E.D. Cal. 2010). *Also see* Frank F. Smith Hardware Co. v. S.H. Pomeroy Co., 299 F. 544 (2d Cir. 1924) (poverty and illness); Armstrong v. Motorola, Inc., 374 F.2d 764 (7th Cir. 1967) (wartime conditions).

PROBLEM: THE INNOCENT INFRINGER

Poymer, Inc. is a small company whose major asset is a patent on a special catalyst useful in certain types of manufacturing. Poymer has been marketing its patented catalyst to several manufacturers. Several other companies, however, have devised their own similar types of catalysts since the Poymer patent. Poymer claims that the similar catalysts are an infringement of its patent, but these companies maintain that they use additional components in the catalysts to produce a different product, and therefore there is no patent infringement.

Five years ago Poymer sued one of these companies for infringement. At the time the suit was initiated Poymer notified every company known to be using a similar catalyst about this suit. No other company was sued, however, until the first suit was successfully completed. During this five year interim there was no further communication between Poymer and any other alleged infringer. After the success of the first suit, Poymer sued the other companies.

Should a court sitting in equity refuse to grant Poymer injunctive relief against these other companies on the grounds that too many years have passed before filing suit? Should the five year delay be excused by the pending relevant litigation against a different company? What if one of these new defendants is a company that assumed that Poymer had abandoned the claim of infringement because there had been no further communication for five years?

Vineberg v. Bissonnette

548 F.3d 50 (1st Cir. 2008).

■ SELYA, CIRCUIT JUDGE. This case has its roots in one of history's bleakest periods: the Holocaust. It began with the de facto confiscation of a valuable work of art by the Third Reich, which eventually led to the litigation that confronts us today.

In its present form, the case presents a narrow legal question concerning the viability of a laches defense asserted by the current possessor of the work of art in an effort to fend off an action for replevin. After the close of discovery, the district court granted summary judgment in favor of the original owner's successors in interest. *See Vineberg v. Bissonnette*, 529 F. Supp. 2d 300 (D.R.I. 2007). We affirm.

I. Background

The abecedarian facts are not seriously disputed. In 1934, Dr. Max Stern inherited an art gallery located in Dusseldorf, Germany. Dr. Stern, who was of Jewish ancestry, quickly became an object of Nazi persecution. The Reich Chamber for the Fine Arts, an organ of the Nazi government, determined that Dr. Stern lacked the requisite personal qualities to be a suitable exponent of German culture. For that reason, it directed Dr. Stern to liquidate the gallery and its inventory.

After unsuccessfully appealing this edict, Dr. Stern surrendered to the inevitable. He consigned most of the affected works of art to the Lempertz Auction House (LAH), a government-approved purveyor. The consignment included a painting by Franz Xaver Winterhalter known as "Madchen aus den Sabiner Bergen" (the Painting). In November of 19 #7, LAH auctioned the consigned pieces (including the Painting) at prices well below their fair market value.

Fearing for his life, Dr. Stern fled Germany shortly after the forced sale. He eventually settled in Canada. The Nazi government prevented him from retrieving the auction proceeds.

During World War II, many of LAH's records were destroyed by bombing. That circumstance hampered post-war searches to identify and locate the purchasers of Dr. Stern's collection. Nevertheless, Dr. Stern made various efforts to find the works of art that had been wrested from him.

In the immediate aftermath of World War II, Dr. Stern recovered some of his paintings through the Canadian Military Mission. He also filed a restitutionary claim with the military government in the British zone of occupied Germany.

Having achieved only limited success, Dr. Stern placed advertisements in *Canadian Art* and *Die Weltkunst* in 1948 and 1952, respectively. In addition, he visited Europe in 1949 to hunt for his missing artworks.

In 1958, Dr. Stern initiated judicial proceedings in Germany regarding paintings seized by the Nazi government. Among other things, he later pursued claims for monetary compensation in the German restitution courts. In 1964, a German court awarded Dr. Stern damages for profits lost due to the forced sale of his art collection.

When Dr. Stern died in 1987, he bequeathed the residue of his estate, including any interest in the Painting, to what the parties have called the Stern Estate. In April of 2004, the Stern Estate contracted the Art Loss Register (the Register), an art recovery company and databank, to assist in the search for the missing works of art. For good measure, the estate also listed the Painting on Germany's Lost Art Internet Database.

As matters turned out—none of this was known to Dr. Stern or his successors in interest until the end of 2004—the Painting had been purchased from LAH in 1937 by Dr. Karl Wilharm. For more than six decades, it remained sequestered in the private collection of Dr. Wilharm and his descendants, with the exception of a single brief exhibition in Kassel, Germany in the early 1950s. Defendant-appellant Baroness Maria–Louise Bissonnette, Dr. Wilharm's step-daughter, took possession of the Painting in 1959 and formally inherited it as part of her mother's estate in 1991.

The defendant has resided in the United States since 1956. She brought the Painting with her when she moved to Rhode Island in 1991. In April of 2003, she consigned the Painting to Estates Unlimited, a Rhode Island auction house. After verifying the Painting's authenticity, Estates Unlimited scheduled an auction for January 6, 2005. Promotional activities began.

Shortly before the appointed auction date, the Register informed the Stern Estate about what was transpiring. It simultaneously notified Estates Unlimited of the Stern Estate's claimed interest in the Painting. As a prudential measure, Estates Unlimited withdrew the Painting from the scheduled auction.

In January of 2005, the Stern Estate filed a claim for the Painting with the New York Holocaust Claims Processing Office (HCPO). HCPO demanded that the defendant return the Painting. Although the defendant refused to honor that demand, negotiations ensued. When the talks failed, the defendant shipped the Painting to Germany and instituted an action in a German court to determine ownership. That led to the institution of the instant action in Rhode Island's federal district court. The named plaintiffs are Robert S. Vineberg, Michael D. Vineberg, and Sydney Feldhammer, in their capacities as trustees of the Dr. and Mrs. Stern Foundation. They sought to replevy the Painting or, in the alternative, to recover damages.

Following a period of discovery, the trustees moved for summary judgment. In a comprehensive rescript, the district court granted the motion and ordered replevin. *See Vineberg*, 529 F. Supp. 2d at 311. In so holding, the court rejected a proffered laches defense, concluding (i) that Dr. Stern and the Stern Estate had exercised reasonable diligence in searching for the Painting and (ii) that in all events, the defendant had not been prejudiced by any delay in the filing of suit. This timely appeal followed.

II.   Discussion

* * *

Laches is an affirmative defense. *See* Fed. R. Civ. P. 8(c). Under Rhode Island law, it is also an equitable defense.[3] The defense has two elements; that is, it "involves not only delay but also a party's detrimental reliance on the status quo." *Adam v. Adam*, 624 A.2d 1093, 1096 (R.I. 1993). Thus, a successful showing of laches requires proof both that the plaintiff delayed prosecution of the claim and that the resulting delay prejudiced the defendant's substantial rights.

Proof of these elements necessarily requires a fact-sensitive inquiry into the particular circumstances of the case at hand. *See Raso v. Wall*, 884 A.2d 391, 396 (R.I. 2005). For that reason, a laches defense is normally not susceptible to pretrial resolution. Nevertheless, when the record is sufficiently clear, even elusive concepts like delay and prejudice may be evaluated conclusively on a pretrial motion. Thus, in an appropriate case a court may summarily dispose of a laches defense. *See Kunstsammlungen Zu Weimar v. Elicofon*, 536 F. Supp. 829, 849–52 (E.D.N.Y. 1981) (concluding on motion for summary judgment that plaintiff had not unreasonably delayed pursuit of claims for paintings stolen during World War II and, thus, his claims were not barred by statute of limitations), *aff'd*, 678 F.2d 1150, 1165 (2d Cir. 1982).

Here, the court below found the laches defense to be doubly deficient. First, the court held that Dr. Stern and his successors in interest had

---

3. Although laches historically had force under Rhode Island law only in equitable proceedings, *see, e.g., Jonklaas v. Silverman*, 117 R.I. 691, 370 A.2d 1277, 1280 (R.I. 1977), the district court assumed, without deciding, that it could be invoked in a replevin action, *Vineberg*, 529 F. Supp. 2d at 308 n.16. As the parties have not raised this issue on appeal, we indulge the same assumption.

pursued their claim to the Painting diligently. *Vineberg*, 529 F. Supp. 2d at 310. Second, the court held that the defendant had failed to adduce any probative evidence of prejudice. The defendant protests both holdings.

We deal first with the matter of prejudice. Concluding, as we do, that the district court did not err in finding a dearth of evidence anent prejudice, we do not reach the issue of undue delay (and, thus, take no view as to the degree of diligence exercised by the plaintiffs and their predecessors in interest).

Typically, the kind of prejudice that will support a laches defense arises out of a loss of evidence, the unavailability of important witnesses, the conveyance of the property in dispute for fair market value to a bona fide purchaser, or the expenditure of resources in reliance upon the status quo ante.Looked at more globally, prejudice in this context is normally either evidence-based or expectations-based. [Citations.]

In this venue, the defendant suggests, without the slightest elaboration, that potential witnesses and evidence are likely unavailable at this late date. This suggestion is deeply flawed.

For one thing, the court of appeals is not a place in which a party should be allowed to pull a rabbit out of a hat. New arguments are not ordinarily permitted on appeal. That maxim applies in this instance because the defendant wholly failed to raise the possibility of evidence-based prejudice in the district court. * * *

Even were we to consider this evidence-based contention, it would not serve the defendant's ends. In making this belated reference, she fails to point to any particular witnesses (or types of witnesses) whom she might have consulted or to any particular documents (or types of documents) that she might have located but for the delayed commencement of the action. She has not even adumbrated the nature of the witnesses or evidence that might have been marshaled if not for the passage of time. Proving prejudice requires more than the frenzied brandishing of a cardboard sword; it requires at least a hint of what witnesses or evidence a timeous investigation might have yielded. *See, e.g., Adidas–Am., Inc. v. Payless Shoesource, Inc.*, 546 F. Supp. 2d 1029, 1072 (D. Or. 2008) (rejecting laches defense at summary judgment stage on ground that defendant had failed to identify any specific missing evidence or witnesses).

If more were needed—and we doubt that it is—there is a structural defect in the defendant's belated assertion of evidence-based prejudice: she has not explained how the acquisition of further testimony or documents might assist her defense. Where courts have allowed a laches defense to be premised on an evidence-based predicate, they have done so because that evidence would have been relevant to one or more essential issues in dispute between the parties. Here, however, the defendant has chosen not to contest ownership of the Painting. Given that choice and the defendant's failure to identify any other controverted issue to which difficult-to-locate witnesses or evidence might be pertinent, she cannot make a credible showing of evidence-based prejudice.

In the court below, the defendant advanced two additional grounds for a prejudice finding: (i) that she had been forced to defend protracted litigation, which tarnished her good name; and (ii) that she had lost the opportunity to sell the Painting. The district court turned a deaf ear to these plaints. *Vineberg*, 529 F. Supp. 2d at 311. Because the defendant has not resurrected either argument on appeal, we deem these plaints abandoned.

To recapitulate, because the burden of proving laches rests with the proponent of that defense, the defendant had an obligation to adduce specific evidence of prejudice in order to thwart the plaintiffs' motion for summary judgment. The defendant failed to carry this burden; the record before the district court contained no legally cognizable evidence of prejudice. That is the end of the line. *See Chase v. Chase*, 20 R.I. 202, 37 A. 804, 805 (R.I. 1897) (noting that "[l]aches, in legal significance, is not mere delay, but delay that works a disadvantage to another").

III. Conclusion

A de facto confiscation of a work of art that arose out of a notorious exercise of man's inhumanity to man now ends with the righting of that wrong through the mundane application of common law principles. The mills of justice grind slowly, but they grind exceedingly fine.

* * *

Affirmed.

1. *Delay.* A principal consideration in application of the doctrine of laches concerns whether a plaintiff has acted with reasonable diligence in asserting their claims. The Supreme Court has stated that laches is intended to be flexible and that "no arbitrary or fixed period of time has been, or will be, established as an inflexible rule." The Key City, 81 U.S. (14 Wall.) 653, 660, 20 L.Ed. 896 (1871). The principle has remained unchanged. *See, e.g.,* Costello v. United States, 365 U.S. 265, 81 S.Ct. 534, 5 L.Ed.2d 551 (1961). In *Robinson v. Estate of Harris*, 388 S.C. 616, 698 S.E.2d 214, 221 (2010), for example, the court held that a 39 year delay in bringing a claim to set aside a quiet title action was a "flagrant and egregious" and represented the "quintessential situation that the doctrine of laches was intended to protect." *Also see* City of Sherrill v. Oneida Indian Nation of New York, 544 U.S. 197, 125 S.Ct. 1478, 161 L.Ed.2d 386 (2005), where the Court applied laches to claims by the Oneida Indian Nation that its acquisition of fee title to certain parcels of historic reservation land revived its ancient sovereignty over those lands and therefore exempted the Tribe from property taxes. The Supreme Court rejected that claim, finding that the Tribe could not unilaterally revive its ancient sovereignty over the land at issue.

2. Claimants are charged with a duty of inquiry based upon an assessment of actual or constructive knowledge of the material facts that would form the foundation of their claims. Chattanoga Mfg. v. Nike, Inc., 301 F.3d 789, 793 (7th Cir.2002) (Plaintiff had constructive notice of Nike's advertising of Michael Jordan-endorsed products, and analogous state statute of limitations created a presumption of laches which claimant failed to rebut); In re Estate of Bovey, 358 Mont. 14, 244 P.3d 716, 721 (2010) (Potential heirs who had specific knowledge of estate were barred by laches when they unreasonably delayed in petitioning for redistribution of residue of testamentary trust proceeds).

3. Delay alone is not sufficient for laches; the delay must be prejudicial. *See* Gardner v. Panama R. Co., 342 U.S. 29, 72 S.Ct. 12, 96 L.Ed. 31 (1951) (laches is not a bar if there is no prejudice to the defendant from the passage of time); In re Beaty, 306 F.3d 914, 924 (9th Cir.2002) (Party must show both an unreasonable delay and prejudice for laches defense); Blue Cross & Blue Shield v. American Express, 467 F.3d 634, 640 (7th Cir.2006) (Unwarranted delay not enough to foreclose relief, but must show detriment based upon belief that delay signaled approval of the acts in question).

The party asserting laches must show that the prejudice potentially experienced if the equitable claim were allowed would affect substantial rights to a material degree. Nature Conservancy v. Wilder Corp., 656 F.3d 646, 651 (7th Cir. 2011). For example, in *Gabriel v. Gabriel*, 947 N.E.2d 1001 (Ind.App. 2011) a wife continued to manage a family pizza restaurant for 10 years following her husband's death. When she learned that another family member asserted an interest in the restaurant, the wife brought a claim to determine the husband's heirs and ownership of the business. The court held that the delay in seeking the petition did not prejudice other parties because they knew that the wife had worked at the restaurant and handled its daily business affairs.

4. *Evidentiary Prejudice*. Courts have historically recognized that prejudice can take various forms in the laches context. One of the most common concerns is that, as a consequence of the excessive delay in bringing a claim, the defendant may be disadvantaged in the ability to marshal an effective defense. This evidentiary prejudice considers whether critical records and documents had been lost or destroyed and if witnesses were no longer available or had faded memories.

For example, *Danjaq LLC v. Sony Corp.*, 263 F.3d 942 (9th Cir. 2001) involved a copyright infringement dispute over the rights to movie scripts of James Bond movies. The court found that the period of 19 to 36 years between release of the movies and filing the copyright claim was unreasonable and prejudicial and barred by laches. The court observed that many of the relevant records pertaining to the copyright issues were missing and that the principal screenwriters, producers and other key figures who had been involved in creating the Bond movies had died. Consequently, laches was applied to bar the claim. Id. at 955–956.

Also see Smith v. Caterpillar, 338 F.3d 730, 733–34 (7th Cir.2003) where the court upheld a district court decision that the defendant company would be materially prejudiced by eight year delay by employee in filing Title VII claim. The court observed that the unavailability or faded memories of key witnesses, the inadvertent loss or destruction of personnel documents in the ordinary course of business, and exposure to liability for back pay collectively constituted sufficient prejudice for the laches defense. The court also applied a sliding scale approach, where the lengthy unexcused delay correspondingly justified a lesser showing of prejudice.

5. *Economic Prejudice.* Economic considerations also may factor into the calculus of prejudice to support a laches defense. In *United States v. City of Loveland*, 621 F.3d 465, 470 (6th Cir. 2010) a city sought to collaterally attack a consent decree which provided for the expansion of a sewage treatment facility. During the course of the five year period from when the city learned of the agreement and instituting suit, the county had commenced multi-year infrastructure improvements to the facility. Additionally, the county demonstrated reliance upon the income stream from city ratepayers who used the system to finance the obligations incurred. As a result, the action was held barred by laches. *Also see* School Comm. of City of Cranston v. Bergin–Andrews, 984 A.2d 629, 644 (R.I. 2009) (School committee delay in instituting a statutory claim for a supplemental appropriation to address a budget shortfall was barred by laches due to potential detrimental economic impact to other educational institutions).

6. Courts historically have held that the laches defense cannot be invoked against the government. *See* Costello v. United States, 365 U.S. 265, 81 S.Ct. 534, 5 L.Ed.2d 551 (1961); United States v. Summerlin, 310 U.S. 414, 416, 60 S.Ct. 1019, 84 L.Ed. 1283 (1940). The traditional rule that laches cannot run against the sovereign originated from the concept of royal privilege, but the modern rationale rests on the public policy of preserving rights and property from the negligent acts of public officials. Guaranty Trust Co. v. United States, 304 U.S. 126, 132, 58 S.Ct. 785, 82 L.Ed. 1224 (1938) (recognizing the continuing vitality of the traditional rule that the sovereign is exempt from application of the laches defense).

The rule is limited to situations in which the government acts in its representative capacity effectuating and protecting public interest, however, but not where the suit essentially involves rights common to private individuals, such as business or commercial interests. *See* Clearfield Trust Co. v. United States, 318 U.S. 363, 369, 63 S.Ct. 573, 87 L.Ed. 838 (1943) (United States not immune from laches defense when asserting claim involving commercial paper); United States v. National Exchange Bank, 270 U.S. 527, 534, 46 S.Ct. 388, 70 L.Ed. 717 (1926) (United States does business on business terms).

7. Some jurisdictions have invoked the doctrine of laches sparingly in environmental cases. Grand Canyon Trust v. Tucson Electric Power Co., 391 F.3d 979, 987 (9th Cir.2004) (laches applied sparingly to citizen suit enforcement action brought pursuant to Clean Air Act); *But see* Allens Creek/Corbetts Glen Preservation Group, Inc. v. West, 2 Fed.Appx. 162 (2d

Cir.2001) (laches barred suit by residents challenging construction project as violating Clean Water Act). Courts reason that citizens are justified in assuming that federal officials will comply with applicable law and ordinarily the plaintiff will not be the only party affected by alleged environmental damage. Montana Wilderness Ass'n v. Fry, 310 F.Supp.2d 1127, 1139 (D.Mont.2004). Also, certain federal environmental statutes are strictly interpreted and defenses that are not enumerated in the statutory text are considered unavailable. *See* Western Properties Service Corp. v. Shell Oil Co., 358 F.3d 678, 692–93 (9th Cir.2004) (equitable defenses not available to bar claim but may be considered in assessing amount of liability).

Geddes v. Mill Creek Country Club

196 Ill.2d 302, 256 Ill.Dec. 313, 751 N.E.2d 1150 (2001).

■ JUSTICE FREEMAN:

Plaintiffs, Larry and Choh–Ying Geddes, filed a complaint in the circuit court of Kane County against defendants, Mill Creek Country Club, Inc., and American Golf Corporation. The complaint contained actions for intentional trespass and intentional private nuisance based on errant golf balls hit onto their property from defendants' adjacent golf course. Following a bench trial, the trial court entered judgment in favor of defendants. * * *

* * * In 1986, plaintiffs bought 16.5 acres in Kane County. The property is rectangular in shape, with the north-south dimension slightly larger than the east-west dimension.

In the same area, Sho–Deen was developing approximately 1,450 acres as a planned unit development. A planned unit development is a land use control device that often combines subdivision regulations and zoning for the unified development of a large geographic area. Rather than seeking piecemeal variances or rezoning, a coordinated plan is drawn up and approved as a special use for the entire proposed area. The concept of this development, known as the Mill Creek Development, was to combine open space with residential areas. A golf course was to constitute part of that open space. The development surrounds plaintiffs' property. A public road, Bartelt Road, adjoins the east side of the property. The land adjoining plaintiffs' western boundary was formerly a cornfield. * * *

In 1991, the Mill Creek Country Club, Inc., was created as a subsidiary to Sho–Deen, with Shodeen as the country club's sole shareholder. Its purpose was to design and build a golf course.

In April 1992, Shodeen invited plaintiffs and other neighbors to review the concept plan for the development. For the next two years, plaintiffs and Shodeen negotiated. However, they now disagree as to the subject of their negotiations and the result thereof. * * *

Plaintiffs told Shodeen that they did not want housing adjoining their property. Shodeen then permitted plaintiffs to choose between the housing, a bicycle path, or the fairway. Plaintiffs chose the fairway to abut their property's western boundary and made other requests that he granted.

Accordingly, Shodeen changed the development plan by removing the housing on the east side of the fairway and relocating the fairway to adjoin plaintiffs' western boundary. * * *

On June 3, 1994, plaintiffs and Sho–Deen signed an agreement, which stated in pertinent part:

"Sho–Deen, Inc., will provide and install at its expense an eight foot (8′) high chain link fence with two (2) fourteen foot (14′) entrance gates on Bartelt Road along the complete common border of the Mill Creek Development with the Geddes' property. The fence and gates will be installed *when the golf course fairway that borders the Geddes' western property line is constructed * * *.*" (Emphasis added.)

The agreement further provides as follows. Sho–Deen would plant a landscape border along the Mill Creek side of the fence. Sho–Deen would not plan a bicycle path along any border of plaintiffs' property, or construct any houses within 100 feet of the south and west boundaries thereof. Sho–Deen would provide for a 40–foot "green area and landscape easement" along the south boundary of plaintiffs' property. The agreement made several references to a "golf course." The agreement concludes that plaintiffs agree not to protest the development as long as Sho–Deen complies with the agreement. * * *

The fairway for the fifth hole is 300 feet wide, and is separated from plaintiffs' property by a 25–foot "rough" area. An asphalt golf cart path lies between the fairway and the rough. As noted earlier, an eight-foot-high chain link fence and landscaping, which includes trees over that height, surround plaintiffs' property. * * *

Mill Creek Golf Course began operating in 1996. The course is open to the public. In 1997, approximately 21,000 rounds of golf were played there; in 1998, approximately 23,500 rounds were played. An average of approximately 30,000 rounds of golf are played on courses in the greater Chicagoland area.

When the course opened, plaintiffs began to find golf balls on their property. During the 1997 and 1998 golf seasons, plaintiffs collected 2,128 golf balls on their property. Some of these had landed as far away as 300 feet from the property's western boundary.

Plaintiffs testified as to how the invading golf balls harmed them. Plaintiffs previously grew alfalfa in the area where the golf balls landed. Indeed, a golf ball once struck Larry's tractor while he was mowing the alfalfa field. Plaintiffs planned to use the affected area to grow plants for sale, cultivate "pick-your-own" vegetables, and build greenhouses and similar structures. Plaintiffs had drilled a well and had hired an architect to plan a retail nursery building. Plaintiffs feared that the golf balls would injure themselves, their family, and their customers, and would damage their planned greenhouses. * * *

Plaintiffs contend that the evidence at trial demonstrated that defendants' conduct resulted in an intentional trespass and an intentional private nuisance. Defendants contend that the evidence demonstrated that plaintiffs should be estopped from bringing their claims. We first consider defendants' contention.

Equitable Estoppel

Defendants invoke the doctrine of equitable estoppel. Defendants claim that plaintiffs, by their conduct, are estopped from bringing their action. According to defendants, plaintiffs chose the fairway over other options that Sho–Deen presented to them and made other requests that Sho–Deen granted. Sho–Deen, at great expense, redesigned the development plan to accommodate plaintiffs. The agreement between plaintiffs and Sho–Deen, which contains several references to a golf course and a specific reference to the fairway, memorializes plaintiffs' requests. Defendants argue that plaintiffs' conduct prevents them from maintaining this action.

Defendants pled this affirmative defense and presented supporting evidence and argument in the trial court and argued it in the appellate court. The trial court made no findings regarding this issue and the appellate court did not address it. However, "the appellee may urge any point in support of the judgment on appeal, even though not directly ruled on by the trial court, so long as the factual basis for such point was before the trial court." [Citations] Since the record contains the factual basis for the defense of equitable estoppel, we will address the merits of this contention.

The general rule is that where a person by his or her statements and conduct leads a party to do something that the party would not have done but for such statements and conduct, that person will not be allowed to deny his or her words or acts to the damage of the other party. Equitable estoppel may be defined as the effect of the person's conduct whereby the person is barred from asserting rights that might otherwise have existed against the other party who, in good faith, relied upon such conduct and has been thereby led to change his or her position for the worse. [Citations]

To establish equitable estoppel, the party claiming estoppel must demonstrate that: (1) the other person misrepresented or concealed material facts; (2) the other person knew at the time he or she made the representations that they were untrue; (3) the party claiming estoppel did not know that the representations were untrue when they were made and when they were acted upon; (4) the other person intended or reasonably expected that the party claiming estoppel would act upon the representations; (5) the party claiming estoppel reasonably relied upon the representations in good faith to his or her detriment; and (6) the party claiming estoppel would be prejudiced by his or her reliance on the representations if the other person is permitted to deny the truth thereof. [Citation]

Regarding the first two elements, the representation need not be fraudulent in the strict legal sense or done with an intent to mislead or deceive. Although fraud is an essential element, it is sufficient that a fraudulent or unjust effect results from allowing another person to raise a claim inconsistent with his or her former declarations. The following corollary must be remembered:

"Estoppel may arise from silence as well as words. It may arise where there is a duty to speak and the party on whom the duty rests has an opportunity to speak, and, knowing the circumstances, keeps silent. It is the duty of a person having a right, and seeing another about to commit an act infringing upon it, to assert his right. He cannot by his silence induce or encourage the commission of the act and then be heard to complain." [Citation].

The question of estoppel must depend on the facts of each case. The party claiming estoppel has the burden of proving it by clear and unequivocal evidence.

Applying these principles to this case, we conclude that defendants' estoppel defense is meritorious. Injustice would result in allowing plaintiffs to bring these claims. Plaintiffs, by their conduct, induced or encouraged defendants to design and build the fifth hole. For plaintiffs to assert these claims now would be inequitable and damage defendants.

Plaintiffs attempt to avoid the consequences of their conduct with Sho–Deen. Initially, plaintiffs claim in their reply brief that they "never *requested* that the golf course be located next to their property." (Emphasis added.) This is beside the point. The record clearly and unequivocally shows that plaintiffs knowingly *agreed* to the placement of the fairway. The original concept plan provided for single-family residences to adjoin the western boundary of the property. Sometime during the following two years, Sho–Deen and plaintiffs agreed on the placement of the fifth hole fairway next to plaintiffs' property. The record contains unrebutted testimony that, prior to signing the formal agreement, Larry Geddes informed a county development planning committee meeting of his work with Shodeen and asked the board not to alter any of the proposed plans as they related to him. Finally, plaintiffs signed the 1994 agreement, which refers throughout to a golf course, and once specifically to "the golf course fairway that borders the Geddes' western property line."

Acknowledging that they agreed to the placement of the fifth hole adjacent to their property, plaintiffs contend that their decision was not a knowing one. In their reply brief, plaintiffs argue that "the agreement is silent as it relates to golf balls," and "the concept of golf balls is never addressed in the 1994 agreement." Plaintiffs testified that when they signed the agreement, and during the construction of the golf course, they knew nothing about the game of golf. They had no idea of the number of errant golf balls that would enter their property.

This contention lacks merit. That golfers do not always hit their golf balls straight is a matter of common knowledge; it is a fact that needs no supporting evidence, a principle that needs no citation of authority. Courts have long acknowledged this axiom: " 'It is well known that not every shot played by a golfer goes to the point where he intends it to go. If such were the case, every player would be perfect and the whole pleasure of the sport would be lost.' " [Citations] Indeed, "it is a matter of common knowledge that on practically all golf courses, including those constructed on vast acreages where the fairways are wide and well separated by rough and shrubs," a golfer can slice or hook a ball off of the fairway. * * * This condition is as natural as gravity or ordinary rainfall.

We repeat: it is a matter of common knowledge that golfers do not always hit their shots straight. Defendants knew it. This axiomatic proposition is evidenced by Shodeen's assumption that plaintiffs would have some golf balls on their property. However, plaintiffs also knew it. This is evidenced by the agreement provision that plaintiffs' property be surrounded by an eight-foot-high fence with landscaping that includes trees over that height. Even assuming that plaintiffs did not know of this fact of life, they reasonably should have. Plaintiffs cannot avoid the reasonable results of their conduct.

Regarding the third element of equitable estoppel, defendants did not know, either at the time of the agreement or during the construction of the fifth hole, that plaintiffs would act in a manner contrary to the agreement. Fourth, plaintiffs, of course, expected that Sho–Deen would perform all of the provisions of the 1994 agreement. Plaintiffs' promise not to protest the construction of the golf course, specifically the fifth hole, was conditional on Sho–Deen's compliance with the agreement.

Fifth, defendants reasonably relied upon plaintiffs' conduct to their detriment. All agreements between adults should be entered into thoughtfully. This admonition takes on increased significance in the context of a planned unit development:

> "*Obtaining approval for a planned unit development can involve considerable negotiation*: with other developers on a project, *with the community*, and with the local zoning board. * * * Often more amenities, such as open space or recreational facilities, are provided under a PUD [planned unit development] than could be required by local law." (Emphasis added.) 9 Real Property Service: Illinois § 49:1, at 8 (1989).

The creation of the golf course, specifically the fifth hole, required considerable negotiation with many public and private parties, including plaintiffs. Sho–Deen obtained their approval and, based thereon, built the fifth hole.

Regarding the sixth element of equitable estoppel, defendants would be prejudiced if plaintiffs were permitted to deny their conduct. Initially, the original concept plan had residences adjoining the fifth hole on the east, between the fairway and plaintiffs' property. The record contains unrebutted evidence that there would have been approximately 14 of these lots, and Shodeen would have charged an additional $15,000 for each lot because it would have adjoined the fairway. Thus, Sho–Deen lost approximately $210,000 in lot "premiums" by placing these residences elsewhere. Additionally, the record contains evidence that Sho–Deen incurred other costs in relocating the fifth hole, *e.g.*, $25,000 for re-engineering the area.

Not only did Sho–Deen incur costs in relocating the fifth hole, it now would be problematic to move it or close it. Residences were planned for the west side of the fifth hole. The price of those lots include the additional "premium" for adjoining the fairway. If Sho–Deen now moved or closed the fifth hole, it could be liable for violating the PUD agreement with other lot owners. [Citations.]

"An injunction will be refused where the complainant has actively encouraged defendant to undertake the work and then has silently, without protest, permitted defendant to go ahead with the work in disregard of the right of complainant." [Citation.] In this case, plaintiffs are equitably estopped from bringing their claims.

For the foregoing reasons, the judgment of the appellate court is affirmed.

————————

1. As reflected in the principal case, the party asserting equitable estoppel must show that they would be materially prejudiced if another were allowed to change their position after inducing the claimant to reasonably rely on their prior representations or the concealment of material information. The nature and extent of prejudice may include personal hardship or substantial inconvenience, financial detriment, or the loss of valuable legal rights. Price v. Fox Entertainment Group, Inc., 473 F.Supp.2d 446 (S.D.N.Y.2007); Mesa Air Group, Inc. v. Delta Air Lines, Inc., 573 F.3d 1124 (11th Cir. 2009) (airline carrier would be prejudiced by changing its position with respect to completion rate of service in reliance upon another airline's false representations that encouraged and coordinated cancellations); Lopez v. Patel, 407 N.J.Super. 79, 969 A.2d 510 (App.Ct. 2009) (defendants were equitably estopped from withholding an affirmative defense and waiting until day of trial to surprise the plaintiff).

In *Hubbard v. Hubbard*, 44 P.3d 153 (Alaska 2002), a putative father sought to disestablish paternity of his stepson. The court applied equitable estoppel to bar the claim, finding that the custodial parent's reliance on representations of paternity and support would result in significant future financial detriment if the father were allowed to change his paternity status.

2. The doctrine of equitable estoppel may apply where the defendant takes active steps to prevent the plaintiff from suing within the applicable statutory limitations period, such as by misrepresentation or fraudulent concealment of facts necessary to support a claim. See Christy v. Miulli; Iowa Neurological Surgery, 692 N.W.2d 694 (Iowa 2005). For example, in *John R. v. Oakland Unified School Dist.*, 48 Cal.3d 438, 256 Cal.Rptr. 766, 769 P.2d 948 (1989), a junior high school student claimed that he was a victim of sexual molestation by a teacher. Due to threats of retaliation by the teacher and embarrassment associated with the molestation, the student delayed in disclosing the incidents and filing a claim. When the school district raised the statute of limitations as a defense, the court invoked equitable estoppel. The court held that the time for filing the claim was tolled during the period that the teacher's threats prevented the student from pursuing the claims.

3. Parties claiming estoppel must exercise reasonable care in ascertaining the relevant facts which form the foundation of their claim. In *Fluke Corp. v. LeMaster*, 306 S.W.3d 55 (Ky. 2010), the court held that equitable estoppel did not bar a manufacturer from relying upon the statute of limitations in a products liability action. The plaintiffs claimed that the manufacturer should have been estopped for its failure to disclose product defects to government regulatory agencies. The court disagreed and observed that the circumstances of the accident gave sufficient notice of the nature of the product defect to the injured workers and did not relieve the plaintiffs from exercising reasonable diligence to discover the cause of action and the identity of the tortfeasor.

4. Equitable estoppel is distinguishable from equitable tolling, which does not necessarily involve wrongdoing. Rather, the propriety of whether a limitations period should be tolled focuses on whether the plaintiff had a justifiable excuse for failing to meet the statutory deadline. Huseman v. Icicle Seafoods, Inc., 471 F.3d 1116, 1121 (9th Cir.2006). Equitable tolling applies to situations where a litigant may be prevented from filing in a timely manner despite the exercise of due diligence. Bensman v. U.S. Forest Service, 408 F.3d 945, 964 (7th Cir.2005) (Court refused to equitably toll the regulatory filing requirements where claimant failed to exercise due diligence).

In *Koczor v. Melnyk*, 407 Ill.App.3d 994, 944 N.E.2d 345, 348 Ill.Dec. 392 (2011), plaintiffs brought a claim for legal malpractice based upon an attorney's failure to record a deed. The defendant asserted that the statute of limitations and repose barred the claim, but the plaintiffs claimed that equitable estoppel tolled the statute because they had reasonably relied upon the attorney's promise that he would record the deed. The court rejected the estoppel argument, finding that the attorney had not made any misrepresentations or failed to disclose material facts and did not know of the error until contacted by the plaintiffs.

5. In *Major League Baseball v. Morsani*, 790 So.2d 1071 (Fla.2001), the court held that the relevant state statutes did not prohibit application of equitable estoppel to an action filed outside applicable statute of limitations. The court made the following observations about the purpose of the doctrine:

> "Estoppe," says Lord Coke, "cometh of the French word estoupe, from whence the English word stopped; and it is called an estoppel or conclusion, because a man's own act or acceptance stoppeth or closeth up his mouth to allege or plead [otherwise]." Lancelot Feilding Everest, Everest and Strode's Law of Estoppel 1 (3d ed. 1923).

> Equitable estoppel is based on principles of fair play and essential justice and arises when one party lulls another party into a disadvantageous legal position.

> "Equitable estoppel is the effect of the voluntary conduct of a party whereby he is absolutely precluded, both at law and in equity, from asserting rights which perhaps have otherwise existed, either of prop-

erty or of contract, or of remedy, as against another person, who has in good faith relied upon such conduct and has been led thereby to change his position for the worse, and who on his part acquires some corresponding right, either of property, or of contract or of remedy."

The doctrine of estoppel is applicable in all cases where one, by word, act or conduct, willfully caused another to believe in the existence of a certain state of things, and thereby induces him to act on this belief injuriously to himself, or to alter his own previous condition to his injury. State ex rel. Watson v. Gray, 48 So.2d 84, 87–88 (Fla.1950) (quoting 3 Pomeroy's Equity Jurisprudence § 804 (5th ed. 1941)).

Equitable estoppel differs from other legal theories that may operate to deflect the statute of limitations, such as accrual, tolling, equitable tolling, and waiver. Equitable estoppel presupposes a legal shortcoming in a party's case that is directly attributable to the opposing party's misconduct. The doctrine bars the wrongdoer from asserting that shortcoming and profiting from his or her own misconduct. Equitable estoppel thus functions as a shield, not a sword, and operates against the wrongdoer, not the victim.

790 So.2d at 1076–77.

6.   Although courts have not adopted a *per se* rule barring application of equitable estoppel against the government, the traditional rule holds that the government cannot be estopped on the same terms as private individuals. *See* Heckler v. Community Health Serv. of Crawford, 467 U.S. 51, 104 S.Ct. 2218, 81 L.Ed.2d 42 (1984) (left open the question of whether any case in which estoppel may be applied against the government). The rationale for disparate treatment of the government has been variously justified on grounds of sovereignty and in the public interest of ensuring obedience to the rule of law. The Court in *Office of Personnel Management v. Richmond*, 496 U.S. 414, 433, 110 S.Ct. 2465, 110 L.Ed.2d 387 (1990) observed: "To open the door to estoppel claims would only invite endless litigation over both real and imagined claims of misinformation by disgruntled citizens, imposing an unpredictable drain on the public fisc."

The prevailing view among federal courts requires a showing of "affirmative misconduct" in addition to the traditional elements of estoppel to invoke the doctrine against the government. *See* Lewis v. Washington, 300 F.3d 829, 834 (7th Cir.2002) (affirmative misconduct requires an act to misrepresent or mislead, not an omission amounting to ordinary negligence); Nagle v. Acton–Boxborough Regional School Dist., 576 F.3d 1 (1st Cir. 2009) (Uninformed reassurances by a school official did not equitably estop government employer from raising employee's ineligibility to take leave under Family and Medical Leave Act to care for her husband); United States v. Philip Morris, Inc., 300 F.Supp.2d 61, 70 (D.D.C.2004) (application of estoppel against government must be rigid and sparing and only in compelling circumstances). *But see* Florida Dept. of Health and Rehabilitative Services v. S.A.P, 835 So.2d 1091 (Fla.2002) (equitable estoppel barred a state agency from asserting that a negligence claim was untimely filed).

7. In *Beacom v. Equal Employment Opportunity Comm'n.*, 500 F.Supp. 428 (D.Ariz.1980), the plaintiff claimed that the government was equitably estopped from applying a federal hiring freeze to his employment as a trial attorney with the EEOC. The federal agency had assured the plaintiff that the freeze did not apply to him, so he concluded his law practice of sixteen years in anticipation of assuming the new position. Only then was he told that he had no job because there had never been a formal appointment and the freeze applied. The court held that the government was equitably estopped for failing to inform the plaintiff that he was not protected by a formal appointment, its misleading confirmation of the appointment and undue delay in notifying him that the freeze would affect the job status. Despite the strong policy favoring the government, the court found that the detriment to the claimant from relying upon assurances of a job significantly outweighed any potential harm to the public interest from applying equitable estoppel.

B.   Unclean Hands and Unconscionability

Section Coverage:

The conscience defenses—unclean hands and unconscionability—bar plaintiffs whose claims are in some way morally tainted even if they are legally sound. The foundation of these defenses is that the court will not lower its dignity by granting equitable relief in such cases. These conscience defenses do not require a showing of prejudice to the defendant, unlike the defenses of laches and estoppel. It is the interest of the court and the public, rather than relative fairness between the parties that creates the bar.

The unclean hands defense applies when the party seeking relief has behaved inequitably with respect to the rights being asserted in the case. The maxim accompanying this defense is: "He who comes into a court of equity must come with clean hands." The uncleanliness that bars relief must be serious, yet need not rise to the level of fraud or illegality. The policy underlying the defense is that the court will not lend its assistance to a wrongdoer, so the central inquiry is whether the behavior is offensive to the court. If so, the plaintiff is left only the legal claim and cannot receive equitable relief.

The taint must be specifically related to the matter before the court, not collateral to it. It is often said that "equity does not require its suitors to lead blameless lives." In other words, a plaintiff's questionable behavior concerning unrelated matters is not relevant.

Unconscionability is conceptually related to unclean hands, but its history is slightly different. This defense is limited specifically to contract remedies. When a judge finds, as a matter of law, that the contractual terms are so one-sided to be oppressive, several options exist. The court can find the entire contract unenforceable, remove the objectionable provision, or simply limit its effect. The defense does not create rights to support a claim for damages, however. The evaluation of unconscionability raises both substantive and procedural issues. The procedural question considers the manner of contract formation and whether the bargain struck was inherently flawed by sharp practices or the lack of meaningful choice. The substantive question looks at the terms themselves to determine if the consideration exchanged was excessively lopsided. The difficulty, of course, is that contracts often are entered by parties with unequal bargaining strength and hindsight analysis may reveal that one side made a particularly poor bargain. Therefore, the test of unconscionability is measured at the time of contract formation and attempts to ensure that the agreement was the product of a fair bargaining process.

Although the concept of unconscionability arose in equity, in modern law its force is primarily at law. U.C.C. 2–302 adopted the concept as a defense to the legal enforcement of objectionable contracts. It has been particularly useful with respect to nonfraudulent but shockingly unfair sales practices directed at relatively unsophisticated consumers.

Model Case:

Tina Lee is an aspiring teenage actress who recently came to national attention when an appealing photograph of her won a cereal box contest. A television network approached her and offered her a contract with very unfavorable terms. She had no agent and her family was as unsophisticated and star-struck as she was. She signed the network's contract in which she further promised not to act or model for anyone else for a specific period of time.

Tina Lee appeared in a successful mini-series on this network. She was received very well by the public. When she was at a party after this success, an acquaintance casually commented to her that her contract with the network was invalid because she was underage at the time she signed it. This comment may or may not have been legally correct. There was a significant legal question whether the contract was voidable because she was a minor in the jurisdiction where the contract was to be performed, but not where she signed it. Nonetheless, Tina Lee was unaware of this conflict of laws issue. Without further inquiry into this matter, she believed this casual comment.

A movie studio called her and asked if she were free to contract. She replied that she was, and negotiations began. The network learned this fact and told the studio it would sue if Tina Lee acted for anyone else. The studio then withdrew from negotiations. Tina Lee then filed suit to enjoin the network from asserting its contract claims.

The court in equity need not resolve the conflicts issue if the judge finds that Tina Lee had "unclean hands" when she represented she was "free" to contract. The judge will consider her moral obligation rather than her legal one. Her dealing with the studio would not be "collateral" to the case because they are central to the claim asserted. Denied an injunction, she still could seek a remedy at law.

If the case arises differently, the role of the equitable defenses would change also. If the network had gone to court as plaintiff instead of Tina Lee, then the focus would be on the network's behavior. The conscience defenses relate only to the plaintiff's conduct precisely because they are defenses. Tina Lee might defend enforcement of the network's contract on the grounds that it was unconscionable. If the judge finds the terms of the contract are shockingly oppressive, the court can deny its enforcement for unconscionability.

Senter v. Furman

245 Ga. 483, 265 S.E.2d 784 (1980).

■ HILL, JUSTICE.

This is suit in equity to declare that a house and lot which Dr. James Senter, a dentist, conveyed by warranty deed to his nursing assistant, Anna Louise Furman, is held by her under a constructive trust. Dr. Senter contends that it was error to grant summary judgment to Ms. Furman on his complaint seeking to have the constructive trust imposed, because, he contends, there were genuine issues of material fact to be tried by a jury.

Dr. Senter executed the warranty deed on his Powers Ferry home, reciting a consideration of "Ten dollars and other good and valuable consideration," when he was 74 and in poor health. He contends that due to his weakened physical and mental condition he was induced to execute the deed by the fraud and undue influence of Ms. Furman at a time when he was facing a malpractice claim which could have cost him all his assets, and that she promised to return the property to him after that exposure was over.[4]

* * *

Regarding the claim of fraud and insofar as Dr. Senter's motive for conveying the property to Ms. Furman in trust is concerned, equity will not enforce the alleged trust arrangement.

* * *

In Whitley v. Whitley, 220 Ga. 471, 139 S.E.2d 381 (1964), plaintiff sought cancellation of contracts and creation of a trust, alleging that he had transferred control of his corporation to his sons to avoid estate taxes but that it was understood that his sons would cancel the contracts at his request. This court denied relief, saying (220 Ga. at 473, 139 S.E.2d at 382): "According to the petitioner's own allegations, he comes into equity with unclean hands. Therefore, he must fail." [Citations.]

The holding of *Whitley v. Whitley, supra,* is equally applicable to conveyances used to conceal assets from creditors. In Bagwell v. Johnson,

---

4. Ms. Furman testified that Dr. Senter said he was giving the land to her for her services rendered over the years. However, on motion for summary judgment, we consider the evidence most favorable to the respondent to the motion.

116 Ga. 464, 468, 42 S.E. 732, 734 (1902), the court said: "... this is simply a case where two persons complotted to hinder, delay, and defeat a creditor of one of them, with the result that one of the wrongdoers himself falls a victim to the wiles of the other. In all such cases this court has uniformly held that no relief can be afforded the victimized wrongdoer, but that the parties are to be left as they stand." * * *

Judgment affirmed.

---

1.   In *Precision Instrument Manufacturing Co. v. Automotive Maintenance Machinery Co.*, 324 U.S. 806, 65 S.Ct. 993, 89 L.Ed. 1381 (1945), the Court invoked the unclean hands defense to bar a patent infringement claim. Employees of the plaintiff manufacturing company invented certain wrenches and the company subsequently sought to obtain a patent on the design. One of the employees, however, secretly arranged to form a competing corporation with third parties for the purpose of obtaining patent rights on the same wrench design. Their application to the Patent Office used false data and showed a prior date for the invention. When the fraud was discovered by the plaintiff, the companies reached a settlement agreement which assigned the rights to the plaintiff. The Patent Office was not notified of the fraudulent scheme, however. The plaintiff later claimed infringement of the patents and breach of the settlement agreement and the defendant company raised the defense of unclean hands.

The Court held that the claims were barred by unclean hands because the plaintiff had knowledge that the patents had been obtained by submitting false data to the Patent Office, yet rather than exposing the fraud, acquired the rights for itself. The Court observed:

> The guiding doctrine in this case is the equitable maxim that "he who comes into equity must come with clean hands." This maxim is far more than a mere banality. It is a self-imposed ordinance that closes the doors of a court of equity to one tainted with inequitableness or bad faith relative to the matter in which he seeks relief, however improper may have been the behavior of the defendant. That doctrine is rooted in the historical concept of court of equity as a vehicle for affirmatively enforcing the requirements of conscience and good faith. This presupposes a refusal on its part to be "the abettor of iniquity." *Bein* v. *Heath*, 6 How. 228, 247. Thus while "equity does not demand that its suitors shall have led blameless lives," *Loughran* v. *Loughran*, 292 U.S. 216, 229, as to other matters, it does require that they shall have acted fairly and without fraud or deceit as to the controversy in issue. *Keystone Driller Co.* v. *General Excavator Co.*, 290 U.S. 240, 245; *Johnson* v. *Yellow Cab Co.*, 321 U.S. 383, 387; 2 Pomeroy, Equity Jurisprudence (5th Ed.) §§ 379–399.

> This maxim necessarily gives wide range to the equity court's use of discretion in refusing to aid the unclean litigant. It is "not bound by formula or restrained by any limitation that tends to trammel the free

and just exercise of discretion." *Keystone Driller Co.* v. *General Excavator Co., supra*, 245, 246. Accordingly one's misconduct need not necessarily have been of such a nature as to be punishable as a crime or as to justify legal proceedings of any character. Any willful act concerning the cause of action which rightfully can be said to transgress equitable standards of conduct is sufficient cause for the invocation of the maxim by the chancellor.

Moreover, where a suit in equity concerns the public interest as well as the private interests of the litigants this doctrine assumes even wider and more significant proportions. For if an equity court properly uses the maxim to withhold its assistance in such a case it not only prevents a wrongdoer from enjoying the fruits of his transgression but averts an injury to the public. The determination of when the maxim should be applied to bar this type of suit thus becomes of vital significance. See *Morton Salt Co.* v. *Suppiger Co.*, 314 U.S. at 492–494.

In the instant case Automotive has sought to enforce several patents and related contracts. Clearly these are matters concerning far more than the interests of the adverse parties. The possession and assertion of patent rights are "issues of great moment to the public."

* * * The public policy against the assertion and enforcement of patent claims infected with fraud and perjury is too great to be overridden by such a consideration. Automotive knew of and suspected the perjury and failed to act so as to uproot it and destroy its effects. Instead, Automotive acted affirmatively to magnify and increase those effects. Such inequitable conduct impregnated Automotive's entire cause of action and justified dismissal by resort to the unclean hands doctrine. 65 S.Ct. at 997–98.

2.   The trial court retains broad discretion of invoking the unclean hands defense to promote the public policy of ensuring fairness in litigation and to preserve its own integrity from aiding a wrongdoer. Fenn v. Yale University, 283 F.Supp.2d 615, 635 (D.Conn.2003). The underlying principle is that when a party who has set the judicial machinery in motion to obtain a remedy acts inequitably, "then the doors of the court will be shut" and the court will refuse to acknowledge the rights asserted. Keystone Driller Co. v. General Excavator Co., 290 U.S. 240, 244–45, 54 S.Ct. 146, 78 L.Ed. 293 (1933). The defense is not related to the liabilities or the substance of the claims, and may extinguish otherwise meritorious claims. A court may raise the doctrine of unclean hands sua sponte to ensure that it does not lend aid to a wrongdoer. Karpenko v. Leendertz, 619 F.3d 259 (3d Cir. 2010).

3.   If the unconscionable conduct occurs during the process of litigation, a court may rely upon unclean hands to dismiss specific causes of action or the entire claim. Underlying property rights remain unaffected, however. Hoffman–La Roche, Inc. v. Promega Corp., 319 F.Supp.2d 1011, 1018 (N.D.Cal.2004) (litigation misconduct does not affect the viability of property rights in patents). The traditional view holds that the defense is equitable and therefore limited to barring equitable claims. In some juris-

dictions the unclean hands defense may be applied both to legal and equitable claims. *See* Burger v. Kuimelis, 325 F.Supp.2d 1026, 1040 (N.D.Cal.2004).

4. The unclean hands defense traditionally requires that the offending conduct be of a sufficiently egregious character that the equitable claim would be tainted by the fraud or misconduct. See Hardy v. Hardy, 910 N.E.2d 851 (Ct. App. Ind. 2009) (unclean hands barred a claim for reformation of a warranty deed because prior conveyance of property was made to defraud potential governmental creditors). Although the type of conduct supporting application of unclean hands need not be punishable as a crime or justify legal proceedings, most courts require misconduct that is intentional and of a serious magnitude. Motorola Credit Corp. v. Uzan, 561 F.3d 123, 129 (2d Cir. 2009) (unclean hands closes the doors of a court of equity where one is tainted with inequitableness or bad faith relative to the relief sought); Honeywell International, Inc. v. Universal Avionics Systems Corp., 398 F.Supp.2d 305, 310 (D.Del.2005) (conduct for unclean hands must shock the moral sensibilities of the judge or be offensive to dictates of natural justice).

In *Bank of Saipan* v. CNG Financial Corp., 380 F.3d 836 (5th Cir. 2004), a borrower defaulted on a loan and the lender asserted the claims against the seller of a corporate subsidiary claiming fraud and for money had and received. The court held that the assertion that the lending bank had negligently failed to investigate credit and collateral did not, as a matter of law, justify application of the unclean hands defense to completely bar recovery. The court observed that the doctrine applies where plaintiff's conduct has been "unconscientious, unjust, marked by a want of good faith or violates the principles of equity and righteous dealing." Id. at 840. Accord Jarrow Formulas, Inc. v. Nutrition Now, Inc., 304 F.3d 829, 841–42 (9th Cir.2002) (unclean hands no bar to equitable claim absent showing of fraudulent or serious misconduct to mislead competitor).

5. Other courts have not required willfulness and have applied the unclean hands doctrine where the plaintiff acted with recklessness, gross negligence, or a blatant disregard for the rights of others. For example, in *Saudi Basic Industries Corp. v. ExxonMobil Corp.*, 401 F.Supp.2d 383, 396–97 (D.N.J.2005) the court found that a pattern of royalty overcharges over a twenty year period with a blatant or reckless disregard for property rights amounted to unconscionable behavior that shocked the integrity of the court. A specific finding by the jury of willfulness was not required to apply unclean hands to bar various contract and tort claims. Further, payment of the funds due by the plaintiff did not purge the previous inequitable conduct nor tip the equities in its favor.

PROBLEM: THE COLLEGE STAR'S SECRET

A star senior football player at the University of Metro City enters into a promotional contract with a local car dealer. The contract provides that immediately following any post-season games the dealer will run a series of advertisements featuring this player. The contract provides that the advertisements shall be filmed and appearance fees paid prior to the end of the season, but that no publicity will be made until after the season. Moreover, the contract stipulates that the arrangement shall be entirely secret. The contract further provides that for one year the player may not engage in any other promotional activity for other cars or car dealers.

This contract is in violation of the rules issued by the governing national association of college athletics. Neither the star nor the dealer tell anyone about the contract because of this violation. As provided by the contract, the star films the advertisements secretly.

In a post-season game the team from University of Metro City is a dramatic victor over a more prominent national football team. Overnight the star is a national figure. Because of this new prominence, a major automobile manufacturer offers the star a contract to make advertisements for national distribution. The star accepts this contract, in violation of the first contract with the local car dealer in Metro City.

The dealer sues to enjoin the star from performing the second contract. Should the deceitful conduct of the dealer and the star be relevant in the dealer's suit to enforce the no-competitor endorsement provision in the first contract?

North Pacific Lumber Co. v. Oliver

286 Or. 639, 596 P.2d 931 (1979).

■ Holman, Justice.

Plaintiff, North Pacific Lumber Co., is a wholesaler of lumber products. Plaintiff's employees conduct almost all of its trading activities over the telephone from its principal office in Portland, Oregon. In February 1967 plaintiff hired defendant Oliver as a lumber trader in its hardwood division. As part of his employment contract, defendant agreed to refrain from competing with plaintiff for two years following termination of his employment. * * * In April 1976 defendant voluntarily terminated his employment. Soon thereafter he went to work for Tree Products Company. Tree Products competes with plaintiff, under the terms of the contract.

[North Pacific Lumber Co. promptly filed suit. There was a lengthy trial at which the defendant employee produced considerable evidence concerning the work environment. The trial court found: (1) the traders were paid by an ill-defined salary system whose secrecy produced an atmosphere of restraint and oppressiveness; (2) some managers who had special telephones engaged in eavesdropping which sometimes went beyond the avowed "training" purpose and which was illegal to the extent it was not consented; (3) fictitious names were more than occasionally used for deception, although it is not clear anyone was damaged by this "shoddy practice"; (4) most seriously, department managers encouraged a practice of fraudulent misrepresentation when traders settled disputes between suppliers and customers. The amount of settlement would be misrepresented when possible to leave a difference between the parties which the company kept as undisclosed profit. On the basis of these findings the trial court denied enforcement of the contract on the grounds of unclean hands. The employer appeals.]

* * *

Covenants binding a person not to exercise his trade or profession for a period of time in a particular area are contracts in restraint of trade disfavored at common law. Nonetheless, courts will uphold them where they are reasonably necessary to protect a legitimate interest of the person in whose favor they run, do not impose an unreasonable hardship upon the person against whom they are asserted, and are not injurious to the public interest. * * *

The threshold issue in this case is whether the trial court properly refused plaintiff all requested relief in a suit based on an otherwise valid contract because of what the trial court viewed as plaintiff's unclean hands. * * * It is therefore necessary to have some general understanding of the operation of the clean hands maxim.

In his treatise, Pomeroy describes the concept underlying the clean hands maxim, as follows:

> * * * [T]he principle was established from the earliest days, that while the court of chancery could interpose and compel a defendant to comply with the dictates of conscience and good faith with regard to matters outside of the strict rules of the law, or even in contradiction to those rules, while it could act *upon the conscience* of a defendant and force him to do right and justice, it would never thus interfere on behalf of a plaintiff whose own conduct in connection with the same matter or transaction had been unconscientious or unjust, or marked by a want of good faith, or had violated any of the principles of equity and righteous dealing which it is the purpose of the jurisdiction to sustain. * * * This fundamental principle is expressed in the maxim, He who comes into a court of equity must come with clean hands * * *. 2 Pomeroy, Equity Jurisprudence § 398 at 93–94 (5th ed. 1941).

The maxim is applied for the protection of the court and not for the benefit of the defendant, who may in fact be equally affected with the improper transaction. McClintock, Principles of Equity at 60 (1948). The plaintiff may have a perfectly valid claim, but he will nevertheless be denied relief where the doctrine applies.

* * *

Broad as the principle seems to be in its operation, it still has some reasonable limitations. In quantitative terms, the misconduct must be serious enough to justify a court's denying relief on an otherwise valid claim. Even equity does not require saintliness. Perhaps more importantly, the misconduct must bear a certain kind of relationship to the subject matter of the suit before a court will consider it. * * * Dobbs speaks of the clean hands doctrine, as follows:

[T]his is not a license to destroy the rights of persons whose conduct is unethical. The rule is that unrelated bad conduct is not to be considered against the plaintiff. It is only when the plaintiff's improper conduct is the source, or part of the source, of his equitable claim, that he is to be barred because of this conduct. "What is material is not that the plaintiff's hands are dirty, but that he dirties them in acquiring the right he now asserts. * * *" Dobbs, Remedies § 2.4 at 46 (1973).

* * *

The critical question here is whether the employer's improper conduct "sufficiently affected the equitable relations between the parties" to justify the trial court's refusal to grant relief. Since this suit arises out of an employment relationship we believe the question can best be answered by seeking to determine whether, under the circumstances, the continued existence of that relationship made it necessary for the defendant to participate with the plaintiff in the improper conduct. We are unwilling to permit an employee to terminate his employment contract without obligation whenever his employer commits some indiscretion and the improper conduct concerns a matter with which the employee is not directly concerned. Such a rule would render many contracts unenforceable in equity. * * *

The trial court felt that the most serious charge against plaintiff was that plaintiff made a practice of making improper profits on the resolution of claims. Plaintiff, as a lumber wholesaler, matched up buyers with sellers. The seller of a lumber product generally bore legal responsibility for any deficiency in an order. When a shipment was unsatisfactory, the buyer would register its complaint with plaintiff's traders. The trader then attempted to negotiate a settlement. By downplaying the seriousness of the deficiency, the trader sought to obtain the buyer's consent to a low settlement figure. The trader could then turn around and tell the supplier that the deficiency was very serious and the buyer demanded a large settlement. Once agreement was reached, plaintiff pocketed the difference between the two figures as additional profit on the transaction.

* * *

It is our conclusion that the trial judge was correct in ruling that this conduct sufficiently affected the relations between the parties to justify invocation of the clean hands rule. The making of profits on customer claims against manufacturers was a common practice in the department in which defendant was employed. It continued over a long period of time during seven and one-half years of which defendant was assistant manager of the department and had responsibility for the supervision of such activities. He derived a personal profit from the misconduct since it affected department earnings and his compensation as assistant manager of the department. Defendant could not occupy the position of assistant manager and avoid participating in his employer's improper practices because he was responsible for carrying out and overseeing department policy. A court of equity should not lend its aid to an employer who attempts to enforce a contract of employment the performance of which involves participation by the employee in such wrongdoing. We do not refuse the court's aid in order to punish plaintiff or reward defendant but only to avoid involving ourselves in settling accounts arising from a tainted relationship.

* * * [Affirmed.]

---

1.   Although the unclean hands doctrine bars a party that has acted inequitably from obtaining equitable relief, the offending conduct must be directly related to the merits of the case. The nature of the misconduct must affect the equitable relations of the parties with respect to the particular controversy, not a collateral matter. Worthington v. Anderson, 386 F.3d 1314, 1319 (10th Cir.2004). Although the doctrine "does not demand that its suitors shall have led blameless lives.... it does require that they shall have acted fairly and without fraud or deceit as to the controversy in issue." Precision Instrument Manufacturing Co. v. Automotive Maintenance Machinery Co., 324 U.S. 806, 814–15, 65 S.Ct. 993, 89 L.Ed. 1381 (1945); PenneCom B.V. v. Merrill Lynch & Co., Inc., 372 F.3d 488, 493 (2d Cir.2004) (unconscionable conduct must be directly related to the subject matter in litigation and has injured the party attempting to invoke the unclean hands doctrine).

In *Stokely–Van Camp, Inc. v. Coca–Cola Co.*, 646 F.Supp.2d 510 (S.D.N.Y. 2009), a sports drink manufacturer brought a trademark action seeking an injunction to prevent a competitor from making allegedly false and misleading advertising claims about its product. The court barred the equitable claim on the basis of unclean hands because the claimant had made virtually identical claims about its own product. See Salas v. Sierra Chemical Co., 129 Cal.Rptr.3d 263 (2011) (claimant's wrongful use of another person's Social Security number to obtain a job went to the heart of the employment relationship and was directly related to claims of discrimination, so barred by unclean hands doctrine).

2.   The defendant's lack of "cleanliness" is not an issue for the unclean hands defense; only the plaintiff's posture is at issue. Is it equally offensive to the court's dignity for a defendant such as the one in the principal case to openly participate in the very conduct which is used against the plaintiff? Compare *Robinson v. Boohaker*, 767 So.2d 1092 (Ala.2000), where a former employee sought to prevent the employer from enforcing an illegal covenant not to compete. The employee was a party to the drafting of the clause, when both parties knew that the provision was contrary to Alabama law.

3.   In *Byron v. Clay*, 867 F.2d 1049 (7th Cir.1989), a fired public employee sought reinstatement with back pay, alleging that the dismissal for political reasons violated the First Amendment. The court disagreed, noting that the former employee described himself as "a political hack employed in a make-work position doing virtually nothing in an unnecessary job." Finding that the claim for reinstatement was barred by unclean

hands, the court observed that the claimant was "like the highwayman who sued his partner in crime for an accounting of the profits—and was hanged for his efforts." *See* Note, The Highwayman's Case, 35 L.Q.Rev. 197 (1893) (Everet v. Williams, Ex. 1725).

4. The problem of identifying direct and collateral matters appeared in a highly political case involving the affairs of a foreign government, in a suit by a foreign government brought in a New York court. In *Islamic Republic of Iran v. Pahlavi*, 116 Misc.2d 590, 455 N.Y.S.2d 987 (1982), the government of Iran brought an action against the sister of the former shah of that country. The complaint alleged breach of fiduciary obligations, seeking equitable remedies of an accounting, constructive trust, and an injunction.

The defendant asserted that the plaintiff, Iran's then current government, had unclean hands because of its involvement in the seizure of hostages from the personnel in the American embassy shortly after the Shah's necessary departure from the country. The United States historically had supported the Shah and was therefore considered an enemy by the succeeding government, who was the plaintiff in the case. The hostile takeover of the American embassy was not done directly by the government, but it was substantially involved during the many months the hostages were held before their eventual release.

The court agreed that the government's activities concerning the hostages were immoral and unconscionable. Nonetheless, the judge rejected the unclean hands defense on the ground that the Iranian government's conduct concerning the American hostages was unrelated to the subject matter of the lawsuit, specifically the money held by the sister of the former Shah.

5. The use of the unclean hands defense against a governmental plaintiff failed in a case where the conduct in question occurred during the litigation. In *S.E.C. v. Electronics Warehouse, Inc.*, 689 F.Supp. 53 (D.Conn. 1988), the issue was the unclean hands defense asserted against the plaintiff agency which is a part of the United States government. The defendant, an underwriter accused of violating federal securities laws, alleged that the government had unclean hands by harassing the defendant's attorney in connection with a current securities offering. The court rejected the unclean hands argument partly on the rationale that the basis of the defense cannot be conduct which occurs during the litigation of a lawsuit; rather, the conduct must occur during accrual of the action. The court also noted that equitable defenses against governmental agencies are strictly limited to instances where the agency's misconduct is egregious and the resulting prejudice to the defendant rises to a constitutional level.

Is it sound to distinguish improper conduct before litigation and during it? Does the court have other tools for sanctioning conduct during the time the parties are litigating? Could the *Electronics Warehouse* case have been decided instead on the collateral matter exception to the unclean hands defense?

6. *In Pari Delicto.* A legal concept closely related to unclean hands is called *in pari delicto*, which literally means "in equal fault." The doctrine historically has applied to situations where the plaintiff bore at least substantially equal responsibility for their own injury and where culpability of both parties arose out of the same illegal or fraudulent act. United States v. Philip Morris, Inc., 300 F.Supp.2d 61, 75 (D.D.C.2004) quoting 1 J. Story, Equity of Jurisprudence 399–400 (14th ed. 1918). In such instances, courts will decline to provide relief to either party. The policy justification is that courts should not lend aid to resolving disputes among wrongdoers and that the denial of judicial relief helps deter illegality. *See* Official Comm. of Unsecured Creditors of Allegheny Health Education v. Price Waterhouse Coopers, LLP, 605 Pa. 269, 296, 989 A.2d 313 (2010).

In *Kirschner v. KPMG LLP*, 938 N.E.2d 941, 912 N.Y.S.2d 508, 15 N.Y.3d 446 (2010) the court stated:

The doctrine of in pari delicto mandates that the courts will not intercede to resolve a dispute between two wrongdoers. This principle has been wrought in the inmost texture of our common law for at least two centuries (*see e.g. Woodworth v Janes*, 2 Johns Cas 417, 423 [N.Y. 1800] [parties in equal fault have no rights in equity]; *Sebring v Rathbun*, 1 Johns Cas 331, 332 [NY 1800] [where both parties are equally culpable, courts will not "interpose in favour of either"]). The doctrine survives because it serves important public policy purposes. First, denying judicial relief to an admitted wrongdoer deters illegality. Second, in pari delicto avoids entangling courts in disputes between wrongdoers. As Judge Desmond so eloquently put it more than 60 years ago, "[N]o court should be required to serve as paymaster of the wages of crime, or referee between thieves. Therefore, the law will not extend its aid to either of the parties or listen to their complaints against each other, but will leave them where their own acts have placed them" (*Stone v Freeman*, 298 N.Y. 268, 271, 82 N.E.2d 571 [1948] [internal quotation marks omitted]).

The justice of the in pari delicto rule is most obvious where a willful wrongdoer is suing someone who is alleged to be merely negligent. A criminal who is injured committing a crime cannot sue the police officer or security guard who failed to stop him; the arsonist who is singed cannot sue the fire department. But, as the cases we have cited show, the principle also applies where both parties acted willfully. 938 N.E.2d at 950.

7. The Supreme Court has considered the application of the doctrine of *in pari delicto* on several occasions with respect to enforcement of antitrust and securities laws. In *Perma Life Mufflers, Inc. v. International Parts Corp.*, 392 U.S. 134, 88 S.Ct. 1981, 20 L.Ed.2d 982 (1968) the Court declined to apply the defense to an antitrust enforcement action. Several dealers brought an action for damages against their franchisor claiming that the franchise agreement created a conspiracy to restrain trade and involved illegal price discrimination. The Court, recognizing the public interest in strong antitrust enforcement, declined to apply the doctrine.

The Court found that the franchisees were merely passive or involuntary violators of the antitrust laws and should not be denied recovery where the illegal arrangements were formulated and carried out by others.

In *Bateman Eichler, Hill Richards, Inc. v. Berner*, 472 U.S. 299, 306, 105 S.Ct. 2622, 2626, 86 L.Ed.2d 215 (1985), investors brought a private action for damages resulting from alleged violations of federal securities laws. They alleged that a securities broker-dealer and company official induced them to purchase stock by disseminating materially false insider information, which caused them financial losses when the stock price declined. The Court stated that "in its classic formulation, the in pari delicto defense was narrowly limited to situations where the plaintiff bore at least substantially equal responsibility for the injury." 105 S.Ct. at 2627. The Court declined to apply the *in pari delicto* doctrine to bar the claimants from recovery, reasoning that the broker had masterminded the scheme to manipulate the market and the tippees were not equally culpable. Also, denying the defense promoted the objectives of the federal securities laws by protecting the investing public and national economy through high standards of business ethics. Id. at 2631. The Court observed that application of the *in pari delicto* defense to causes of action pursuant to federal statutes requires a showing that the plaintiff bears at least substantially equal responsibility for the violations sought to be redressed, and that preclusion of the suit would not interfere with the implementation of the policy goals of the statute. Id. at 2629. *See also* Pinter v. Dahl, 486 U.S. 622, 632–33, 108 S.Ct. 2063, 2071, 100 L.Ed.2d 658 (1988) (*in pari delicto* defense available in federal securities action); Official Committee of Unsecured Creditors of PSA, Inc. v. Edwards, 437 F.3d 1145 (11th Cir. 2006) (doctrine of *in pari delicto* barred trustee of bankruptcy estate of debtor corporation that operated a Ponzi scheme barred from recovery on federal racketeering claims).

Lhotka v. Geographic Expeditions, Inc.

181 Cal.App.4th 816, 104 Cal.Rptr.3d 844 (2010).

■ SIGGINS, J. * * *

Jason Lhotka was 37 years old when he died of an altitude-related illness while on a GeoEx expedition up Mount Kilimanjaro with his mother, plaintiff Sandra Menefee. GeoEx's limitation of liability and release form, which both Lhotka and Menefee signed as a requirement of participating in the expedition, provided that each of them released GeoEx from all liability in connection with the trek and waived any claims for liability "to the maximum extent permitted by law." The release also required that the parties would submit any disputes between themselves first to mediation and then to binding arbitration. It reads:

> "I understand that all Trip Applications are subject to acceptance by GeoEx in San Francisco, California, USA. I agree that in the unlikely event a dispute of any kind arises between me and GeoEx, the following conditions will apply: (a) the dispute will be submitted to a

neutral third-party mediator in San Francisco, California, with both parties splitting equally the cost of such mediator. If the dispute cannot be resolved through mediation, then (b) the dispute will be submitted for binding arbitration to the American Arbitration Association in San Francisco, California; (c) the dispute will be governed by California law; and (d) the maximum amount of recovery to which I will be entitled under any and all circumstances will be the sum of the land and air cost of my trip with GeoEx. I agree that this is a fair and reasonable limitation on the damages, of any sort whatsoever, that I may suffer.

I agree to fully indemnify GeoEx for all of its costs (including attorneys' fees) if I commence an action or claim against GeoEx based upon claims I have previously released or waived by signing this release." Menefee paid $16,831 for herself and Lhotka to go on the trip.

A letter from GeoEx president James Sano that accompanied the limitation of liability and release explained that the form was mandatory and that, on this point,

> "our lawyers, insurance carriers and medical consultants give us no discretion. A signed, unmodified release form is required before any traveler may join one of our trips.

> Ultimately, we believe that you should choose your travel company based on its track record, not what you are asked to sign. ... My review of other travel companies' release forms suggests that our forms are not a whole lot different from theirs."

After her son's death, Menefee sued GeoEx for wrongful death and alleged various theories of liability including fraud, gross negligence and recklessness, and intentional infliction of emotional distress. GeoEx moved to compel arbitration. [The trial court found the arbitration provision was both substantively and procedurally unconscionable. Further, the court held that the unconscionability was so extensive that it could not sever a single provision and order arbitration.] * * *

We turn first to GeoEx's contention that the court erred when it found the arbitration agreement unconscionable. Although the issue arises here in a relatively novel setting, the basic legal framework is well established. " '[U]nconscionability has generally been recognized to include an absence of meaningful choice on the part of one of the parties together with contract terms which are unreasonably favorable to the other party.' [Citation.] Phrased another way, unconscionability has both a 'procedural' and a 'substantive' element." [Citation.] " 'The procedural element requires oppression or surprise. Oppression occurs where a contract involves lack of negotiation and meaningful choice, surprise where the allegedly unconscionable provision is hidden within a prolix printed form. The substantive element concerns whether a contractual provision reallocates risks in an objectively unreasonable or unexpected manner.' [Citation.] Under this approach, both the procedural and substantive elements must be met before a contract or term will be deemed unconscionable. Both, however, need not be present to the same degree. A sliding scale is applied so that 'the more substantively oppressive the contract term, the less evidence of procedural unconscionability is required to come to the conclusion that the term is unenforceable, and vice versa.' " [Citations] This notion of a "sliding scale," as will be seen, figures centrally in the analysis of the agreement at issue here.

A. *Procedural Unconscionability*

GeoEx argues the arbitration agreement involved neither the oppression nor surprise aspects of procedural unconscionability. GeoEx argues the agreement was not oppressive because plaintiffs made no showing of an "industry-wide requirement that travel clients must accept an agreement's terms without modification" and "they fail[ed] even to attempt to negotiate" with GeoEx. We disagree. GeoEx's argument cannot reasonably be squared with its own statements advising participants that they must sign an *unmodified* release form to participate in the expedition; that GeoEx's "lawyers, insurance carriers and medical consultants give [it] no discretion" on that point; and *that other travel companies were no different*. In other words, GeoEx led plaintiffs to understand not only that its terms and conditions were nonnegotiable, but that plaintiffs would encounter the same requirements with any other travel company. This is a sufficient basis for us to conclude plaintiffs lacked bargaining power.

GeoEx also contends its terms were not oppressive, apparently as a matter of law, because Menefee and Lhotka could have simply decided not to trek up Mount Kilimanjaro. It argues that contracts for recreational activities can *never* be unconscionably oppressive because, unlike agreements for necessities such as medical care or employment, a consumer of recreational activities *always* has the option of foregoing the activity. The argument has some initial resonance, but on closer inspection we reject it as unsound.

While the nonessential nature of recreational activities is a factor to be taken into account in assessing whether a contract is oppressive, it is not necessarily the dispositive factor. *Szetela v. Discover Bank* (2002) 97 Cal. App.4th 1094 [118 Cal. Rptr. 2d 862] is informative. The defendant, a credit card company, argued the plaintiff could not establish procedural unconscionability because there were "market alternatives" to its product—i.e., the plaintiff had the option of taking his business to a different bank. The court disagreed and held the customer's ability to walk away rather than sign the offending contract was not dispositive. "The availability of similar goods or services elsewhere may be relevant to whether the contract is one of adhesion, but even if the clause at issue here is not an adhesion contract, it can still be found unconscionable. Moreover, 'in a given case, a contract might be adhesive even if the weaker party could reject the terms and go elsewhere.' [Citation.] Therefore, whether Szetela could have found another credit card issuer who would not have required his acceptance of a similar clause *is not the deciding factor*." [Citation] The focus of procedural unconscionability in *Szetela*, rather, was on the manner in which the disputed clause was presented. Faced with the options of either closing his account or accepting the credit card company's "take it or leave it" terms, Szetela established the necessary element of procedural unconscionability despite the fact that he could have simply taken his business elsewhere.

* * *

B. *Substantive Unconscionability*

With the "sliding scale" rule firmly in mind, we address whether the substantive unconscionability of the GeoEx contract warrants the trial court's ruling. *Harper v. Ultimo, supra*, 113 Cal.App.4th 1402, is analogous. The Harpers hired a contractor to perform work on their property. The contractor allegedly broke a sewer pipe, causing concrete to infiltrate the plaintiffs' soil, plumbing and sewer and wreak havoc on their backyard drainage system. Unfortunately for the Harpers, the arbitration provision in the construction contract limited the remedies against their contractor to a refund, completion of work, costs of repair or any out-of-pocket loss or property damage—and then capped any compensation at $2,500 unless the parties agreed otherwise in writing.

In the words of Justice Sills, substantive unconscionability was "so present that it is almost impossible to keep from tripping" over it. [Citation] "Substantive unconscionability focuses on the one-sidedness or overly harsh effect of the contract term or clause. In the present case) the operative effect of the arbitration is even more one-sided against the customer than the clauses in any number of cases where the courts have found substantive unconscionability. * * * [T]he limitation of damages provision here is yet another version of a 'heads I win, tails you lose' arbitration clause that has met with uniform judicial opprobrium." The arbitration provision in the Harpers' contract did not allow even a theoretical possibility that they could be made whole, because there was no possibility of obtaining meaningful compensation unless the contractor agreed—which, not surprisingly, it did not.

The arbitration provision in GeoEx's release is similarly one-sided as that considered in *Harper*. It guaranteed that plaintiffs could not possibly obtain anything approaching full recompense for their harm by limiting any recovery they could obtain to the amount they paid GeoEx for their trip. In addition to a limit on their recovery, plaintiffs, residents of Colorado, were required to mediate and arbitrate in San Francisco—all but guaranteeing both that GeoEx would never be out more than the amount plaintiffs had paid for their trip, and that any recovery plaintiffs might obtain would be devoured by the expense they incur in pursing their remedy. The release also required plaintiffs to indemnify GeoEx for its costs and attorney fees for defending any claims covered by the release of liability form. Notably, there is no reciprocal limitation on damages or indemnification obligations imposed on GeoEx. Rather than providing a neutral forum for dispute resolution, GeoEx's arbitration scheme provides a potent disincentive for an aggrieved client to pursue any claim, in any forum—and may well guarantee that GeoEx wins even if it loses. Absent reasonable justification for this arrangement—and none is apparent—we agree with the trial court that the arbitration clause is so one-sided as to be substantively unconscionable. [Citation]

GeoEx argues that, even if the limitation of liability provision was unconscionable, the court abused its discretion when it refused to strike it and enforce the remainder of the arbitration clause. We disagree.

Civil Code section 1670.5, subdivision (a) gives the trial court discretion to either refuse to enforce a contract it finds to be unconscionable, or to strike the unconscionable provision and enforce the remainder of the contract. It provides: "If the court as a matter of law finds the contract or any clause of the contract to have been unconscionable at the time it was made the court may refuse to enforce the contract, or it may enforce the remainder of the contract without the unconscionable clause, or it may so limit the application of any unconscionable clause as to avoid any unconscionable result." The trial court has discretion under this statute to refuse to enforce an entire agreement if the agreement is "permeated" by unconscionability. An arbitration agreement can be considered permeated by unconscionability if it "contains more than one unlawful provision.... Such multiple defects indicate a systematic effort to impose arbitration ... not simply as an alternative to litigation, but as an inferior forum that works to the [stronger party's] advantage." "The overarching inquiry is whether ' "the interests of justice ... would be furthered" ' by severance." [Citations].

Here, the trial court identified multiple elements of the agreement that indicate GeoEx designed its arbitration clause to impose arbitration "not simply as an alternative to litigation, but as an inferior forum" that would give it an advantage. In addition to limiting plaintiffs' recovery, the agreement required them to indemnify GeoEx for its legal costs and fees if they pursued any claims covered by the release agreement. These one-sided burdens were compounded by the requirements that plaintiffs pay half of any mediation fees and mediate and arbitrate in San Francisco, GeoEx's choice of venue, far from plaintiffs. It was within the court's discretion to conclude this agreement was so permeated by unconscionability that the interests of justice would not be furthered by severing the damages limitation clause and enforcing the remainder.

The order denying GeoEx's motion to compel arbitration is affirmed.

---

1.   As reflected in the principal case, arbitration clauses have been a fertile ground for raising the issue of unconscionability. In *Cordova v. World Finance Corp. of New Mexico*, 208 P.3d 901, 146 N.M. 256 (2009) a loan company's standard form contract restricted a borrower to mandatory arbitration to resolve disputes yet gave the lender the exclusive option to broadly pursue any and all legal and equitable remedies in court, including judicial foreclosure or repossession. The court held such a self-serving

scheme to be substantively unconscionable. Also see McKee v. AT & T Corp., 191 P.3d 845, 164 Wash.2d 372 (2008) (a consumer services agreement with telephone company with a mandatory arbitration provision and class action waiver, confidentiality clause, abbreviated statute of limitations and restrictions on attorney's fees were substantively unconscionable); But see AT & T Mobility LLC v. Concepcion, ___ U.S. ___, 131 S.Ct. 1740, 1753, 179 L.Ed.2d 742 (2011) (Federal Arbitration Act preempted California judicial rule classifying most collective arbitration waivers found in consumer adhesion contracts as unconscionable).

2. The doctrine of unconscionability is a narrow one and applied sparingly by courts because of the strong deference to principles of freedom of contract. Merely the presence of unequal bargaining power or hindsight evidence that one side struck a poor bargain are insufficient to find unconscionability. Sander v. Alexander Richardson Investments, 334 F.3d 712, 720 (8th Cir.2003). A contract is considered oppressive if the inequality of bargaining power between the parties effectively prevents the weaker party from having a meaningful opportunity to negotiate and choose the terms of the agreement. Ingle v. Circuit City Stores, Inc., 328 F.3d 1165, 1171 (9th Cir. 2003). In such an event, the theory is that the bargain itself was flawed because it was not entered into voluntarily with an appropriate understanding of the nature of the risks and duties assumed. Scovill v. WSYX/ABC, 425 F.3d 1012, 1017 (6th Cir. 2005). Whether a contract or contractual provision is unconscionable is a question of law. Cooper Tire & Rubber Co. v. Farese, 423 F.3d 446, 458 (5th Cir. 2005).

3. Courts will exercise supervisory control over the contracting process by ensuring fundamental fairness in the bargain where the inequality of the exchange "shocks the conscience". Faber v. Menard, Inc., 367 F.3d 1048, 1053 (8th Cir.2004) (Iowa courts will invalidate contract terms as unconscionable where it is a nefarious provision, inimical to the public good).

In *Walnut Producers of California v. Diamond Foods, Inc.*, 114 Cal. Rptr.3d 449, 459, 187 Cal.App.4th 634 (2010) the court observed that phrases such as "harsh", "oppressive", and "shock the conscience" for purposes of substantive unconscionability were not synonymous with "unreasonable". As such, the court cautioned that basing the already nebulous doctrine of unconscionability on an evaluation of the reasonableness of a contract provision would inappropriately inject judicial subjectivity into the analysis and undermine freedom of contract. Also see Cooper v. MRM Investment Co., 367 F.3d 493, 503 (6th Cir.2004) (Unconscionability under Tennessee law where inequality of the bargain shocks the judgment of a person of common sense, and where the terms are so oppressive that no reasonable person would make them on one hand, and no honest and fair person would accept them on the other); Caley v. Gulfstream Aerospace Corp., 428 F.3d 1359, 1378 (11th Cir.2005) (Georgia law holds that an unconscionable contract is an agreement that "no sane man not acting under a delusion would make and that no honest man would take advantage of.").

4. *Procedural Unconscionability*. Procedural unconscionability focuses on the manner of contract formation. The procedural inquiry considers the relative sophistication and bargaining power of the parties and whether one party lacked a meaningful choice when entering the agreement. Courts may consider whether the stronger party knew of the limited financial resources or lack of knowledge of the weaker party. Other factors may include the use of sharp practices or high pressure techniques, lack of education, sophistication or wealth, and scarcity of the subject matter of the contract. Society of Lloyd's v. Reinhart, 402 F.3d 982, 996 (10th Cir.2005); Caley v. Gulfstream Aerospace Corp., 428 F.3d 1359, 1377 (11th Cir.2005) (procedural unconscionability factors include age, education, intelligence, business acumen and experience of the parties, the conspicuousness and comprehensibility of the contract language, and the presence or absence of meaningful choice).

In *Woebse v. Health Care and Retirement Corp. of America*, 977 So.2d 630 (Ct. App. Fla. 2008) a daughter brought an action for wrongful death of her father and violation of certain state statutes against a nursing home. The defendant sought to compel arbitration in accordance with the nursing home admission agreement. The court denied arbitration, finding procedural unconscionability because the daughter did not receive the agreement before her father was admitted to the nursing home, was not given an opportunity to read the contract prior to signing it, was not informed of the arbitration clause and was not furnished with a copy of the agreement. *Also see* Ting v. AT & T, 319 F.3d 1126, 1148–49 (9th Cir.2003) (procedurally unconscionable if contract of adhesion or standardized form contract, drafted by party of superior bargaining strength and gives weaker party the choice of "take it or leave it"); Miller v. Corinthian Colleges, Inc., 769 F.Supp.2d 1336, 1346 (D. Utah 2011) (whether stronger party employed deceptive practices to obscure key contractual provisions).

5. *Substantive Unconscionability*. The substantive question for unconscionability focuses on whether the terms are unreasonably favorable to one party. Numerous factors may be considered in evaluating the substantive fairness of the exchange, including industry standards, risks of default, availability of alternatives, the importance of the subject matter to the parties, the objective difference in the consideration exchanged for the nature of the product or services rendered, the commercial reasonableness of the contract terms, trade usage, the purpose and effect of the terms, the allocation of risks between the parties, and public policy concerns. Jenkins v. First American Cash Advance of Georgia, 400 F.3d 868, 876 (11th Cir.2005).

6. As reflected in the principal case, some courts adopt a sliding scale approach where the more substantively oppressive the terms, less evidence of procedural unconscionability is required to render the contract unenforceable. *See* Evans v. Linden Research, Inc., 763 F.Supp.2d 735, 740 (E.D.Pa. 2011) (applying California law); Jacada Ltd. v. International Marketing Strategies, Inc., 401 F.3d 701, 713 (6th Cir.2005) (Michigan courts employ a balancing approach to require a certain amount of both procedural and substantive unconscionability). Other courts hold that evi-

dence of either substantive or procedural unconscionability may support that defense. *See* McKee v. AT & T Corp., 191 P.3d 845, 857, 164 Wash.2d 372, 397 (2008).

7. *Campbell Soup Co. v. Wentz*, 172 F.2d 80 (3d Cir. 1948), is the classic case that developed the defense of unconscionability as an equitable defense. It involved an output contract for the delivery of carrots. The market price skyrocketed and the grower breached and resold the carrots to a third party. Campbell sought to enjoin further sales and to compel specific performance of the remainder of the goods. The court refused equitable relief, finding that the standard form contract drafted by Campbell was too one-sided in favor of the buyer, such as with respect to rights of refusal and entitlement to damages. In modern language, the court found the contract was substantively unconscionable.

See also Simar Holding Corp. v. GSC, 928 N.Y.S.2d 592, 595, 87 A.D.3d 688 (2011) (substantive unconscionability illustrated by inflated prices, unfair termination clauses, unfair limitations on consequential damages and improper disclaimers of warranty); *But see* Telecom Intern. America, Ltd. v. AT & T Corp., 280 F.3d 175, 189 (2d Cir.2001) (allocation of risks and maximizing business opportunities in a rational, informed manner not deemed unconscionable).

PROBLEM: THE GULLIBLE COMPUTER GENIUS

Cory Dexter, an eighteen-year-old student who excels at computers, wrote an excellent program and wished to market it. Distributech is a venture firm that caters to unsophisticated individuals who want to sell their computer programs. Distributech charges a fee to do a "market evaluation" of a program, but promises no results. For most individuals the company collects the fee and does little or no work except to send a standard glossy report that indicates the market is "not quite ready" for the program. The Distributech contract, however, not only provides for this fee but it further provides that the company is entitled to one-third of the gross sales of any program for which it did a market evaluation.

Dexter paid the fee to Distributech and received the standard glossy report. Subsequently Dexter managed to market the program individually with the help of an older friend. The program sold so successfully that Dexter was interviewed by a computer magazine in a feature on successful young programmers. The article alerted Distributech to Dexter's profits from the program.

Distributech sued Dexter to enforce the agreement for one-third of all past and future sales. Could Dexter defend with Distributech's unconscionability? Does it matter if Dexter's claims are legal, equitable, or mixed claims in law and equity?

Jones v. Star Credit Corp.

59 Misc.2d 189, 298 N.Y.S.2d 264 (1969).

■ WACHTLER, JUSTICE.

On August 31, 1965 the plaintiffs, who are welfare recipients, agreed to purchase a home freezer unit for $900 as the result of a visit from a salesman representing Your Shop At Home Service, Inc. With the addition of the time credit charges, credit life insurance, credit property insurance, and sales tax, the purchase price totalled $1,234.80. Thus far the plaintiffs have paid $619.88 toward their purchase. The defendant claims that with various added credit charges paid for an extension of time there is a balance of $819.81 still due from the plaintiffs. The uncontroverted proof at the trial established that the freezer unit, when purchased, had a maximum retail value of approximately $300. The question is whether this transaction and the resulting contract could be considered unconscionable within the meaning of Section 2–302 of the Uniform Commercial Code which provides in part:

(1) If the court as a matter of law finds the contract or any clause of the contract to have been unconscionable at the time it was made the court may refuse to enforce the contract, or it may enforce the remainder of the contract without the unconscionable clause, or it may so limit the application of any unconscionable clause as to avoid any unconscionable result.

(2) When it is claimed or appears to the court that the contract or any clause thereof may be unconscionable the parties shall be afforded a reasonable opportunity to present evidence as to its commercial setting, purpose and effect to aid the court in making the determination. L.1962, c. 553, eff. Sept. 27, 1964.

There was a time when the shield of "caveat emptor" would protect the most unscrupulous in the marketplace—a time when the law, in granting parties unbridled latitude to make their own contracts, allowed exploitive and callous practices which shocked the conscience of both legislative bodies and the courts.

The effort to eliminate these practices has continued to pose a difficult problem. On the one hand it is necessary to recognize the importance of preserving the integrity of agreements and the fundamental right of parties to deal, trade, bargain, and contract. On the other hand there is the concern for the uneducated and often illiterate individual who is the victim of gross inequality of bargaining power, usually the poorest members of the community.

* * *

Section 2–302 of the Uniform Commercial Code enacts the moral sense of the community into the law of commercial transactions. It authorizes the court to find, as a matter of law, that a contract or a clause of a contract was "unconscionable at the time it was made," and upon so finding the court may refuse to enforce the contract, excise the objectionable clause or limit the application of the clause to avoid an unconscionable result. "The principle," states the Official Comment to this section, "is one of the prevention of oppression and unfair surprise." It permits a court to accomplish directly what heretofore was often accomplished by construction of language, manipulations of fluid rules of contract law and determinations based upon a presumed public policy.

* * *

Fraud, in the instant case, is not present; nor is it necessary under the statute. The question which presents itself is whether or not, under the circumstances of this case, the sale of a freezer unit having a retail value of $300 for $900 ($1,439.69 including credit charges and $18 sales tax) is unconscionable as a matter of law. The court believes it is.

* * *

Having already paid more than $600 toward the purchase of this $300 freezer unit, it is apparent that the defendant has already been amply compensated. In accordance with the statute, the application of the payment provision should be limited to amounts already paid by the plaintiffs and the contract be reformed and amended by changing the payments called for therein to equal the amount of payment actually so paid by the plaintiffs.

---

1.   *Unconscionability at Law and in Equity.* The principal case, *Jones v. Star Credit Co.,* involved enforcement of a contract at law. The concept of unconscionability is equitable in nature because of its close relationship to "unclean hands." The concept has been absorbed into law to affect enforcement of contract damages, most notably through U.C.C. 2–302. Virtually all unconscionability claims arise in claims for legal damages rather than for equitable relief. The rhetoric nonetheless reflects the equitable roots of the concept, as *Star Credit* illustrates.

2.   A 1965 case that was decided before the U.C.C. was effective in the District of Columbia found a common law basis for an unconscionability defense at law. *Williams v. Walker–Thomas* held that a court could refuse legal remedies under common law when a contract is unreasonably favorable to one party and when the other party lacks meaningful choice on harsh contract terms. In the *Williams* case there were hidden important terms in a printed consumer form contract. 350 F.2d 445 (D.C.Cir.1965).

3.   Distinguish fraud from unconscionability. Fraud is a tort cause of action that can provide a variety of remedies, such as damages or rescission. Fraud has several specific elements that are difficult to prove. Notably, the seller must make a misrepresentation of a material fact—an element often not present in cases involving overreaching by one party. Transactions that do not have the elements of fraud nonetheless may be unconscionable.

4.   Upon a finding of unconscionability the court may invalidate the entire agreement, excise the offending provision, or, as in *Jones v. Star Credit*, limit its effect. A finding of unconscionability does not establish a claim for damages suffered. In *Vom Lehn v. Astor Art Galleries, Ltd.*, for

example, a dealer charged $67,000 for jade carvings worth less than $15,000. The purchasers could not use unconscionability as a basis for damages; damages require proof of fraud. The dealer's unconscionable conduct was relevant in his counterclaim for the $18,000 unpaid balance because the court refused to enforce the contract. 86 Misc.2d 1, 380 N.Y.S.2d 532 (1976).

C.   ELECTION OF REMEDIES

Section Coverage:

In some instances an injured party may have several available remedies to redress the violation of a single right. A classic example would be where a purchaser of a used car later discovers that the dealer fraudulently misrepresented the condition of the car. The buyer must choose whether to affirm the transaction and seek damages for fraud or to disaffirm the contract and seek restitution. The remedies are necessarily inconsistent; therefore the act of choosing or "electing" one remedy will preclude recovery on the other.

The two policies that gave rise historically to recognition of the doctrine of election of remedies were sensible: to prevent double recovery and to avoid undue prejudice to the defendant. Some courts, however, have applied the doctrine in situations where neither policy concern is furthered and the result appears perfectly insensible. Thus, some courts have allowed the doctrine to extinguish a substantive cause of action even before the plaintiff filed suit and even though the plaintiff never intended to make an election. For example, if the defrauded car purchaser takes the car back to the dealer, that action may be considered an election to rescind the contract. Alternatively, if the car buyer sent a letter to the dealer demanding damages as a consequence of the fraud, a court may characterize the conduct as an election to affirm the contract. Unfortunately for the car purchaser, either "election" may very likely not be upon the advice of counsel and probably does not reflect a meaningful choice. Nonetheless, the buyer may be deemed bound by the election even if the seller would not be unduly prejudiced by a later change of heart.

Critics of the doctrine cite occasions where it worked harsh results upon unwary plaintiffs who unwittingly manifested a choice of remedies by action or delay of action. Some courts have not agreed that the election should be final and irrevocable where no prejudice would actually accrue to the other party if the plaintiff were allowed to change remedies. Consequently, the Uniform Commercial Code has reacted to the unsubstantiated harshness and inequities of the election of remedies doctrine by rejecting it outright. [U.C.C. § 2–703 Comment 1; § 2–711 and § 2–721]. Similarly, the Restatement (Second) of Contracts § 378 severely circumscribes the common law doctrine by stating that the manifestation of a choice of inconsistent remedies does not bar another remedy unless the other party "materially changes his position in reliance on the manifestation." Thus, although the election of remedies doctrine survives, its vitality has been substantially weakened and its application replaced by the principles of res judicata, merger, and estoppel.

Model Case:

The Beyers are antique dealers who want to purchase a distinctive older home as their personal residence. They own many fine pieces of antique furniture as their personal property and they are quite particular about the kind of house appropriate for them.

One day they saw exactly the house they wanted, but it was not for sale. The Beyers rang the doorbell and spoke to the homeowners, the Owens. At first the Owens refused to sell, but after several days negotiations the two parties reached an agreement. Each couple was represented by counsel and signed a contract for the sale of the property.

A short time later the Owens called the Beyers and said they would not go through with the sale because they had just learned that their daughter was engaged and she wanted the wedding in the family's old home. The Beyers happened to be having marital difficulties at the time and responded, "Fine. You keep it. But you'll be hearing from our lawyer about our costs."

The Owens proceeded to repair the house in anticipation of the wedding. The front porch was removed and completely replaced with an expensive new entrance; a gazebo was built in the backyard; and extensive renovations were made throughout the house. In the meantime the Owens refused to pay the costs claimed by the Beyers, so the attorney for the Beyers filed a complaint in state court. The prayer for relief asked for damages.

After these events the Beyers reconciled their marital difficulties. As a reaffirmation of their marriage, they decided that they wanted to purchase the Owens' house as originally planned. The Beyers' attorney seeks to amend the complaint to ask for specific performance of the land sales contract.

In jurisdictions that strictly apply election of remedies the Beyers' claim may be barred even if the Owens were not prejudiced by the inconsistent demands. The initial demand for damages could be a binding election, since damages and specific performance could not both be recovered. The Restatement (Second) of Contracts has modified the doctrine by basing it on estoppel principles. Jurisdictions following this approach would preclude specific performance if Owens' change in position is material. The extensive renovations are likely to be a sufficient change in position to bar the belated specific performance request.

Head & Seemann, Inc. v. Gregg

104 Wis.2d 156, 311 N.W.2d 667 (1981).

■ Voss, Presiding Judge. * * *

Defendant Bettye J. Gregg offered to buy a Brookfield home from plaintiff corporation. She represented, verbally and in writing, that she had

$15,000 to $20,000 of equity in another home and would pay this amount to plaintiff after selling the other home. She knew, however, that she had no such equity. Relying on these intentionally fraudulent representations, plaintiff accepted defendant's offer to buy, and the parties entered into a land contract. After taking occupancy, defendant failed to make any of the contract payments. Plaintiff's investigation then revealed the fraud.

Plaintiff commenced this action seeking one of two alternative forms of relief. Based on the fraud, plaintiff sought rescission, ejectment and recovery for five months of lost use of the property and out-of-pocket expenses. Alternatively, based on defendant's breach of contract, plaintiff sought rescission, foreclosure and ejectment.

The trial court granted partial summary judgment for plaintiff, rescinding the contract for fraud. The court ordered ejectment but stayed the order for two weeks pending defendant's voluntary removal. The court also obtained plaintiff's stipulation that, if defendant removed herself within the two weeks, the plaintiff's claim for damages would be dismissed. Defendant failed to vacate the property, and the court entered an interlocutory judgment of ejectment.

Defendant later sought dismissal of the damages claim based on the election of remedies doctrine. The court determined that the judgment for ejectment was an election of remedies barring recovery of damages and, therefore, dismissed the cause of action based on fraud. * * *

Plaintiff contends that it is entitled to recover for the lost use of the property and out-of-pocket expenses during defendant's possession of the property. It contends that recovery for these items, in addition to the rescission and return of the real estate, is necessary to restore plaintiff to his status before the fraud and execution of the contract. Since these "damages" would only restore plaintiff to its previous position and would not give plaintiff the purchase price or the benefit of the bargain, plaintiff argues that the remedies are not inconsistent, and the doctrine of election of remedies should not be applied. We agree.

The election of remedies doctrine is an equitable principle barring one from maintaining inconsistent theories or forms of relief. Its underlying purpose is to prevent double recovery for the same wrong. The label "election of remedies" is frequently used as a cloak for an estoppel or ratification where, for example, it bars a suit for rescission of a contact *subsequent* to some act of affirmance of the contract. [Citation.] Wisconsin courts have been attempting to restrict the doctrine to reduce its harsh effects. [Citations.]

The classic application of the election of remedies doctrine is that a defrauded party has the election of either rescission or affirming the contract and seeking damages. The choice is forced with respect to alternative theories in a single lawsuit because of inconsistency of both rescinding and affirming the contract.

Thus, it superficially appears that if a claimant chooses to seek rescission, he may not sue for damages. But the word "damages," like the label "election of remedies," impedes rather than aids the inquiry into the types of relief appropriate in a given case. Rescission is always coupled with restitution: the parties return the money, property or other benefits so as to restore each other to the position they were in prior to the transaction.
* * *

In Carpenter v. Mason, 181 Wis. 114, 193 N.W. 973 (1923), plaintiff entered into a land contract in reliance on defendant's fraudulent statements. The trial court entered judgment of rescission and ordered recovery of the money paid toward the purchase plus $140 for plaintiff's costs in moving from another state as a result of the fraud. The Wisconsin Supreme Court disallowed the moving costs. The court stated that placing the parties *in status quo* "does not mean that the parties are to be restored to the situation which existed previous to their entering into the contract." It means, the court indicated, only that each party must return what he has actually received. Defendants did not receive plaintiff's expenditures for moving. "To require them to restore more than they received would be to permit the plaintiff to recover *damages for breach of the contract.* The plaintiff does not affirm the contract but disaffirms it and seeks rescission. He may not do both." (emphasis added).

* * * *Carpenter v. Mason* has become a somewhat infamous horror story cited as a good reason why the election of remedies doctrine ought to be abolished:

> The best example that I can recall to show the need for the fraud statute [abolishing election of remedies in fraud cases in New York] is a case decided in Wisconsin during an earlier boom period. * * *

> What substantial reason can be given for such a decision? Did not the defendants' wrong proximately cause the plaintiff all of the losses that he sustained? Did not the plaintiff allege and prove all of the facts necessary to entitle him to all of the items of recovery claimed? Was there any *duplication* of items of recovery? Certainly not. Was the defendant misled prejudicially by the plaintiff's suing to get his money "back," and also his money paid out for moving? No prejudicial reliance appears. Then is not the doctrine of election of remedies here merely a requirement of formal consistency? * * *

Patterson, *Improvements in the Law of Restitution,* 40 Cornell L.Q. 667, 679–80 (1955). * * *

A host of commentators support elimination of the election of remedies doctrine. A common theme is that the doctrine substitutes labels and formalism for inquiry into whether double recovery results in *fact.* The rigid doctrine goes to the other extreme, actually resulting in the under-compensation of fraud victims and the protection of undeserving wrongdoers. * * *

It appears that the commentators and the modern trend of the law support abandonment of the formalistic shell of the doctrine of election of remedies. The law can prevent windfalls to claimants without going overboard by requiring that fraud victims bear part of the loss, absolving defrauding parties of their proper responsibility.

Elimination of the formal doctrine would permit courts to focus on the rule of one satisfaction and deemphasize theoretical consistency of remedies. In the instant case, plaintiff might have its rescission and consequential damages for the *tort* of fraud or deceit. Since the tort system is designed to make one whole to the extent possible through a monetary award, plaintiff would receive such damages in tort which in addition to return of the land would restore it to its preinjury position. No double recovery would result in this case.

* * *

Order reversed.

---

1.   The requirements for the election of remedies doctrine traditionally include:

> [T]hree elements must be present for a party to be bound to an election of remedies: (1) two or more remedies must have existed at the time of the election, (2) these remedies must be repugnant and inconsistent with each other, and (3) the party to be bound must have affirmatively chosen, or elected between the available remedies.

Latman v. Burdette, 366 F.3d 774, 782 (9th Cir. 2004). Once a party has "elected" a remedy, whether intentionally or constructively, the action is irrevocable and binding. Lucente v. International Business Machines Corp., 310 F.3d 243, 259 (2d Cir. 2002) (Once party elected remedy for contract breach, that election is binding and cannot be changed).

2.   One of the primary purposes of the doctrine is to avoid double recovery for a single harm. For example, in *Hickson Corp. v. Norfolk Southern Railway Co.*, 260 F.3d 559, 567 (6th Cir. 2001), a rail carrier sought damages against a manufacturer for breach of contract and negligence associated with costs incurred as a result of a chemical spill. The court, relying on the election of remedies doctrine, held that the carrier could not receive damages under both contract and tort theories. There was only one distinct injury underlying both claims and the carrier could only receive a single recovery for each item of compensable damage. *Also see* United Vaccines, Inc. v. Diamond Animal Health, 409 F.Supp.2d 1083, 1097 (W.D. Wis. 2006) (plaintiff may seek rescission of contract or choose to affirm agreement and seek damages, but not both).

But see Plumbing Service Co. v. Progressive Plumbing, Inc., 46 So.3d 144 (Ct.App. Fl. 2010) (plaintiff that had already recovered reasonable value of labor and services rendered in action against surety bond not barred by election of remedies in bringing contract claim for lost profits against subcontractor because no risk of double recovery); Loughridge v.

Chiles Power Supply Co., Inc., 431 F.3d 1268, 1283 (10th Cir. 2005) (election of remedies did not bar products liability claims by homeowner against seller and manufacturer of heating systems where claimant only sought one damages remedy for defective product).

3. A key issue with respect to the election of remedies doctrine is whether several remedies are "inconsistent" with each other. In *Villeneuve v. Atlas Yacht Sales, Inc.*, 483 So.2d 67, 69–70 (Fla.App.1986), for example, the election of remedies doctrine precluded a claim to recover title to a yacht; the facts that supported a judgment for damages for loss of the purchase price were inconsistent with the facts necessary to obtain title.

See also Pennsylvania National Mutual Casualty Ins. Co. v. City of Pine Bluff, 354 F.3d 945, 951 (8th Cir. 2004) (seeking declaration of priority to funds and pursuing judgment in equal amount not an assertion of inconsistent remedies); In Re Reaves, 285 F.3d 1152, 1158 (9th Cir. 2002) (no election of remedies bar where party claimed exemptions in response to execution of levy and subsequently claimed special exemptions after filing bankruptcy party because remedies were complementary and not inconsistent); Macola v. Government Employees Ins. Co., 410 F.3d 1359, 1364 (11th Cir. 2005) (under Florida law, no election of remedies preclusion where statutory and common law bad faith claims depended upon similar factual allegations); Baker v. Superior Court, 150 Cal.App.3d 140, 197 Cal.Rptr. 480, 483 (1983) (no election of remedies where fraud in the inducement and breach of contract actions involved different obligations and different operative facts); Trahan v. Trahan, 455 A.2d 1307, 1312 (R.I.1983) (action of debt on judgment not inconsistent with contempt proceedings); North American Graphite Corp. v. Allan, 184 F.2d 387, 389 (D.C.Cir.1950) (no election required between contract and quasi-contract); *contra* Wynyard v. Beiny, 919 N.Y.S.2d 165, 82 A.D.3d 665 (2011) (recovery of money judgment inconsistent with claim seeking recovery of goods); Boyd v. Margolin, 421 S.W.2d 761, 768 (Mo.1967) (action on express contract factually dissimilar from quantum meruit, and thus "inconsistent" for election of remedies).

4. There cannot be an "election" barring an inconsistent remedy unless two or more remedies for the same claim in fact coexist. In *Davis v. Cleary Building Corp.*, 143 S.W.3d 659 (Mo.App. 2004), the plaintiffs sought to rescind a contract to build a barn on their property on the basis of fraudulent misrepresentation by the builder. The court found that rescission of the construction contract was improper because the parties could not be returned to the status quo without undue prejudice. Although the plaintiff had attempted unsuccessfully to rescind, the election of remedies doctrine did not bar a claim for damages for benefit of the bargain. The court observed, "Unlike pursuit of one of two or more inconsistent remedies, pursuit of an imaginary or mistaken remedy does not bar the subsequent pursuit of a viable remedy." Id. at 669.

5. Courts have split over whether the pursuit of a worker's compensation claim constitutes an election which forecloses an employee from subsequently asserting a common law tort cause of action. Some courts

have focused on the policy of avoiding double recovery for a single harm to deny recovery. *See* Martinkowski v. Carborundum Co., 108 Misc.2d 184, 437 N.Y.S.2d 237 (1981) (election by filing for and collecting workmens' compensation benefits precludes action against employer for intentional tortious conduct); Medina v. Herrera, 927 S.W.2d 597, 600 (Tex. 1996) (election of remedies barred worker from receiving benefits under workers' compensation act and then filing tort claim for damages).

Other jurisdictions find no bar by looking to the policies of the workers' compensation statutes and reconciling the differing purposes of benefits received under the act with potential recovery of damages for tort claims. *See* Jones v. Martin Electronics, Inc., 932 So.2d 1100 (Fla. 2006) (employee who received compensation benefits for a workplace injury not barred from filing a tort claim against an employer for the harm suffered where damages did not constitute double compensation); Salazar v. Torres, 141 N.M. 559, 158 P.3d 449 (2007) (worker not barred by election of remedies from receiving benefits under workers' compensation statute and subsequently filing claim for intentional tort). *Also see* Williams v. Johnson Custom Homes, 374 Ark. 457, 288 S.W.3d 607 (2008) (no election of remedies when claimant applied for benefits under both Ohio and Arkansas workers' compensation laws because only sought one remedy).

6. The common law doctrine of election of remedies has been expressly repudiated by the Uniform Commercial Code with respect to the sale of goods. U.C.C. § 2–703 comment a. The Code's liberal treatment of inconsistent demands is illustrated by *Melby v. Hawkins Pontiac, Inc.,* 13 Wash. App. 745, 537 P.2d 807 (1975). The plaintiff, after several months of repair difficulties following the purchase of a new automobile, filed suit against the dealership claiming damages for breach of warranty. The trial court granted the plaintiff rescission of the purchase agreement and restitution of amounts paid on the contract. On appeal, the dealership asserted that rescission was an inappropriate remedy because the plaintiff had affirmed the contract by electing to pursue only the damages remedy.

The appellate court acknowledged that an affirmance of a contract and a demand for damages is inconsistent with disaffirmance by a claim for rescission, but rejected a "harsh application" of election of remedies. The court reasoned that (1) a harsh application is not necessary to prevent double recovery, and (2) the doctrine as sometimes applied is inconsistent with modern rules of pleading which allow demands for alternative relief and amendments to the pleadings to conform to the evidence. The court added, however, that the doctrine should not be ignored when the defendant has relied detrimentally on the plaintiff's prayer for relief or has been otherwise prejudiced by the plaintiff's actions.

7. Several states have enacted statutes that abrogate the election of remedies doctrine in cases other than those involving the sale of goods. For example, Georgia Code § 3–1.4 provides "A plaintiff may pursue any number of consistent or inconsistent remedies against the same person or different persons until he shall obtain a satisfaction from some of them."

New York Civil Practice Law § 3002(e) (McKinney) rejects the election of remedies doctrine in cases involving fraud or misrepresentation. Similarly, California Civil Code § 1692 provides that a claim for damages is not inconsistent with rescission. The aggrieved party may be awarded "complete relief," including restitution of benefits and any consequential damages as long as there are no duplicate or inconsistent items of recovery.

In *Cobian v. Ordonez*, 103 Cal.App.3d Supp. 22, 163 Cal.Rptr. 126 (1980), the buyer of an automobile sued the seller demanding rescission, restitution and damages based upon fraudulent misrepresentations. The jury awarded the plaintiff rescission of the contract and damages for fraud. The appellate court rejected the seller's contention that the plaintiff, by electing to rescind, gave up the right to damages. The court stated that the plaintiff's recovery of his down payment did not foreclose the availability of punitive damages, and noted that Civil Code section 1692 provided that a damages claim was not inconsistent with a claim for rescission as long as no double recovery resulted.

PROBLEM: THE FRAUDULENT SALE

Abrams purchased all the shares of stock in a small goldmining company, Klondike King, Inc., from Meyers for $10,000. Several weeks after the sale was completed, Abrams' accountant discovered that the financial disclosures given by Meyers in connection with the transaction substantially understated the liabilities of Klondike. The accountant estimated that the current fair market value of Klondike King was only $4,500. Based upon the accountant's information, Abrams sent a letter to Meyers demanding $5,500 as damages for the difference in the value of the company as promised and the value actually received.

Negotiations between the parties proved unsuccessful and, six months after the closing date, Abrams filed suit seeking, in the alternative: (a) damages for breach of contract for lost expectancy, (b) tort damages based upon common law fraud, or (c) rescission and restitution.

1. Should the doctrine of election of remedies bar any of Abrams' asserted claims?

2. Assume instead that Abrams initially demanded rescission and restitution rather than damages. Does that make a difference?

3. What if Abrams, during the six months period of ownership of the company, made several personnel changes and instituted a different system of bookkeeping?

4. What if the price of gold declined from $400 per ounce at the time of the transaction to $300 per ounce, resulting in a corresponding decline in the fair market value of Klondike King to approximately $2,000 at the time of trial?

Altom v. Hawes

63 Ill.App.3d 659, 20 Ill.Dec. 330, 380 N.E.2d 7 (1978).

■ JONES, JUSTICE.

* * * [O]n or about February 10, 1976, the plaintiff, Janice Altom, and her then husband, Melvin Altom, entered into a separation agreement

which provided that Janice Altom was to have exclusive possession of the marital home and of the household furniture and furnishings, except such items as the parties might agree would be Melvin Altom's. On March 7, 1976, Melvin Altom called Tracy Hawes, a longtime friend, and asked if he wanted to buy some furniture. Tracy Hawes went to the marital residence where he found Melvin Altom and Melvin's brother. He chose several items of furniture, agreed to pay the asking price of $1,500 and took the items away that same afternoon. Mr. Altom gave him a bill of sale. * * *

On March 18, the plaintiff filed a complaint for divorce. A default hearing was held and a decree was entered on May 6, 1976. The decree recited that Melvin Altom had appropriated and sold certain household furniture belonging to Janice Altom in violation of the separation agreement of the value of $1,500 and judgment was entered against Melvin Altom in that amount.

Approximately one month after the entry of the decree of divorce Janice Altom filed her complaint in replevin against the Haweses.

Defendants contend that the granting of the motion for summary judgment was proper in that the plaintiff has elected her remedy in choosing to pursue her claim against Melvin Altom to judgment and may not seek a double recovery by now proceeding against them in replevin. The plaintiff counters that the judgment against Melvin Altom is unsatisfied and further that the doctrine of election of remedies does not apply as the prior judgment and the instant replevin action are not inconsistent remedies. * * *

Plaintiff's arguments on the issue of election of remedies are two. First, the remedies sought must be inconsistent in order for the doctrine to apply and second, that in order to act as a bar to a subsequent suit the prior suit must be pursued not only to the rendering of a judgment but to full satisfaction of the judgment.

The doctrine of election of remedies has proved to be confusing and difficult of application, no less so to the courts of Illinois than to the courts of other states. * * *

There is little question here that the remedies pursued by the plaintiff are inconsistent. She initially obtained a judgment for damages against her husband for a tortious sale of her furniture, a judgment that presupposes plaintiff's affirmance of the sale. By this later action of replevin she seeks a return of the furniture, an action in which she necessarily disaffirm the sale. It is this circumstance of inconsistency of remedies that prompted the defendant to advance the election of remedies argument and seek summary judgment.

Although we do not cite them here, many cases can be found which would sustain the granting of summary judgment upon these facts. Too, logic would repel the notion that a litigant could on the one hand say the sale was good but on the other say it was bad.

Research has disclosed to us, however, that the courts of Illinois, as well as those of other jurisdictions, have ameliorated the harsh results that have often flowed from a strict application of the election of remedies doctrine. Rather than follow a literal application of the rule, an approach has been derived whereby courts endeavor to determine not whether by the nature of the remedies invoked they are inconsistent, but whether the party should be estopped to bring the second action. We think the policy is best expressed by Prof. Corbin in his treatise on *Contracts,* Vol. 5A, sec. 1220:

> "The view with respect to election of remedies that is now becoming the prevailing one and that ought to be accepted is that, where a party injured by a breach definitely manifests a choice of a remedy that is actually available to him, in the place of some other alternative remedy, such a manifestation will bar an action for the latter remedy, provided that the party against whom the remedy is asked makes a substantial change of position in reliance on the manifestation of intention before notice of its retraction. This makes the conclusiveness of an 'election' depend upon the existence of facts sufficient to create an 'estoppel.' Cases stating this view are now very numerous and hold either that the remedy asked was not barred because there was no basis for an estoppel, or that an election was conclusive only because such a basis had been proved. The mere bringing of a suit asking one remedy rather than another practically never affords ground for an estoppel and is not sufficient reason to deny an application for an alternative remedy."

* * *

Of the same import as Prof. Corbin's statement is sec. 381 of the Restatement of the Law, Contracts. Comment b of that section states:

> "b. A mere manifestation of intention to pursue one remedy rather than the other is not an irrevocable election; but it becomes such as soon as the other party has materially changed his position in reasonable reliance thereon. The bringing of a suit for one remedy is a manifestation of choice of that remedy; but it does not preclude the plaintiff from seeking the other remedy instead, if he has a reasonable ground for so doing, so long as the defendant has not so altered his position as to make it unjust to permit the change."

* * *

In the case under consideration there is no threat of double recovery (plaintiff's judgment for damages against her husband has not been collectible and, in fact, appears uncollectible), defendant was not misled and did not change his position by reason of plaintiff's action for damages against her husband so that he would suffer some prejudice thereby, and there is nothing about the action for damages that would serve to bar the subsequent action by reason of *res judicata* or collateral estoppel.

For the foregoing reasons, the summary judgment rendered in defendant's behalf is reversed and this cause remanded for trial on the replevin issue.

———————

1. A key issue regarding the election of remedies doctrine involves determining at what time a person must elect between existing, inconsistent remedies. Under the modern rules of civil procedure a party should not be barred from asserting alternate counts. F.R.C.P. 8(e)(2). Additionally, F.R.C.P. 15(a) liberally permits a party to amend pleadings.

Despite the liberalization of pleading, some courts may apply the election of remedies doctrine to extinguish a substantive cause of action prior to trial. For example, in *Hipp v. Kennesaw Life & Accident Insurance Co.*, 301 F.Supp. 92, 94 (D.S.C.1968), an insured sent a letter to the insurance company demanding cancellation of a policy and reinstatement of a savings account based on alleged false representations by an agent. After the insurance company complied, the insured instituted suit seeking damages for fraud. The court held that the pretrial letter which demanded rescission was a "decisive act" which indicated an unequivocal election and thus precluded the subsequent suit for fraud.

2. Some jurisdictions have held that a binding election among inconsistent remedies occurs at the time the suit is filed. In *Radiophone Service, Inc. v. Crowson Well Service, Inc.*, 309 So.2d 393 (La.App.1975) a landlord commenced an action to rescind a lease for nonpayment of rent. Before the tenant answered, the landlord sought to amend the complaint to eliminate the rescission claim but the court held that an irrevocable election had occurred. As a consequence, the landlord was denied potential recovery of amounts reflecting subsequently arising delinquencies under the lease agreement.

Similarly, in *Morris Plan Leasing Company v. Karns*, 197 Kan. 150, 415 P.2d 291 (1966), a lessor repossessed certain equipment and then commenced an action against the lessee to recover amounts for rental due but unpaid. The court held that the pre-suit actions of the lessor in repossession did not constitute an election of remedies, but determined that the "filing of a petition * * * gives finality to the election." The court further stated that the election upon commencement of a suit would be irrevocable "even though it is later dismissed without prejudice and not prosecuted to a finality." Later authority in Kansas, however, has suggested later stages in the proceedings when an election must be made. Lehigh, Inc. v. Stevens, 205 Kan. 103, 468 P.2d 177, 182 (1970) (plaintiff must elect while case is pending); Scott v. Strickland, 10 Kan.App.2d 14, 691 P.2d 45, 50 (1984) (election required prior to submission of claim to jury).

3. Other jurisdictions have not found an election of remedies based solely upon the commencement of an action, but have followed widely varied approaches as to what stage in the proceeding an election between inconsistent remedies must be made. *See* Jacobson v. Yaschik, 249 S.C. 577,

155 S.E.2d 601, 607 (1967) (elect at any stage of proceedings but not before defendant answers); Wills v. Regan, 58 Wis.2d 328, 206 N.W.2d 398, 407 (1973) (discretion of the court whether to require election before close of the case); TVT Records v. Island Def Jam Music Group, 250 F.Supp.2d 341, 348 (S.D.N.Y. 2003) (election between equitable and monetary relief can occur after a verdict is rendered); Liddle v. Dozer, Inc., 777 So.2d 421, 422 (Fla. App. 2000) (an election between mutually exclusive remedies can be made at any time before entry of judgment); Coldwell Banker Commercial Group, Inc. v. Nodvin, 598 F.Supp. 853, 856 (N.D.Ga.1984) (elect prior to entry of judgment); Frazier v. Metropolitan Life Insurance Co., 169 Cal. App.3d 90, 214 Cal.Rptr. 883 (1985) (no election until one of inconsistent rights satisfied by res judicata or estoppel); Taylor Rental Corp. v. J.I. Case Co., 749 F.2d 1526, 1529 (11th Cir.1985) (no election until debt actually satisfied).

4. The court in the principal case treated election of remedies as functionally delimited by the other preclusion doctrines of estoppel, double recovery, and res judicata. This treatment, although gaining many adherents, raises a number of semantic and substantive problems. Notably, if the election of remedies doctrine serves no useful purpose distinct from other preclusion doctrines, it should be expressly rejected by courts rather than receive "lip service" but never functionally applied.

In *Bocanegra v. Aetna Life Insurance Co.*, 605 S.W.2d 848, 851 (Tex. 1980), the court noted that equitable estoppel differs from the election of remedies doctrine because it requires some deception that is relied upon by another resulting in prejudice. The court posited that election of remedies was a viable preclusion doctrine which would constitute a bar to relief when a plaintiff successfully exercises an informed choice between two or more remedies, rights, or states of facts that are so inconsistent as to constitute manifest injustice. The court failed to explain what significance "manifest injustice" has apart from the sort of prejudice involved in traditional estoppel theory.

5. In *Roam v. Koop*, 41 Cal.App.3d 1035, 116 Cal.Rptr. 539 (1974) a homeowner filed suit against a contractor alleging fraud, unlawful misappropriation of funds, breach of contract, and money had and received. After filing the multiple count complaint, the plaintiff obtained a writ of attachment and levied against various bank accounts, a safety deposit box, and certain real property belonging to the defendant.

The appellate court noted that the plaintiff can plead inconsistent causes of action in tort and in contract, but that obtaining an attachment constituted a positive act in pursuit of his contractual remedy. By levying under the writ, the plaintiff deprived Koop of the use of his property. The court held that because plaintiff was pursuing two inconsistent remedies and took unequivocal action under only one of them whereby he gained an advantage over the defendant the doctrine of election of remedies applied. However, since the appellate court viewed the election of remedies defense as a form of estoppel, the defendant was deemed to have waived the defense by failing to raise it in the trial court. Like estoppel, it could not be raised for the first time on appeal.

6. Some courts have inartfully interchanged the doctrines of res judicata and election of remedies to explain preclusion of claims by judgment. For example, in *Family Bank of Commerce v. Nelson*, 72 Or.App. 739, 697 P.2d 216 (1985) the court noted that an "election" occurs at the time of judgment. In contrast, in *Frazier v. Metropolitan Life Insurance Co.*, 169 Cal.App.3d 90, 101, 214 Cal.Rptr. 883, 888 (1985), the court differentiated among the doctrines by stating that "A person should be entitled to change his alternative remedies until one of his inconsistent rights is vindicated by application of the doctrines of res judicata or estoppel."

7. The Restatement (Second) of Judgments § 25, comment m (1982) further explains the interrelationship of election of remedies and res judicata:

> Sometimes it is held that the mere beginning of an action for one remedy is itself an election preventing recourse to another remedy deemed in some sense "inconsistent." In a mature procedural system the mere commencement of an action for a given remedy should not of itself prevent the granting of a different remedy when warranted by the facts proved (perhaps after amendment in the course of trial). Ordinarily a plaintiff may pursue alternative remedies, however "inconsistent," with final "election" postponed to a late stage of the action—after the proof is in or even after the fact-finder, court or jury, has made its findings on both alternatives. In such circumstances, if the plaintiff seeks but one remedy, and judgment is entered for or against him, he should be precluded from a second action by the rules of merger or bar. This is properly explained on res judicata principles rather than on any notions of election of remedies.

8. For additional commentary on the election of remedies doctrine *see*: Brill, The Election of Remedies Doctrine in Arkansas, 37 Ark.L.Rev. 385 (1983); Corbin, Waiver of Tort and Suit in Assumpsit, 19 Yale L.J. 221 (1910); Deinard & Deinard, Election of Remedies, 6 Minn.L.Rev. 341 (1922); Dobbs, Pressing Problems for the Plaintiff's Lawyer in Rescission: Election of Remedies and Restoration of Consideration, 26 Ark.L.Rev. 322 (1972); Fraser, Election of Remedies: An Anachronism, 29 Okla.L.Rev. 1 (1976); Hine, Election of Remedies, A Criticism, 26 Harv.L.Rev. 707 (1913); Mendelsohn, Election of Remedies and Settlement—New Lyrics to an Outworn Tune, 12 St. Mary's L.J. 367 (1980); Merrem, Election of Remedies in Texas, 8 Sw.L.J. 109 (1954); Oesterle, Restitution & Reform, 70 Mich.L.Rev. 336 (1980); Patterson, Improvements in the Law of Restitution, 40 Cornell L.Q. 667 (1955); Pray, Election of Remedies: A Judicial Weed?, 16 Okla.L.Rev. 193 (1963); Rothschild, A Remedy for Election of Remedies, 14 Cornell L.Q. 141 (1929); Yerkes, Election of Remedies in Cases of Fraudulent Misrepresentation, 26 S.Cal.L.Rev. 157 (1963).

CHAPTER 6

INTERLOCUTORY INJUNCTIONS

[handwritten: Forclosure Forietiire a at spec ial '78]

Interlocutory relief is expedited relief for a short term that a court may give before final adjudication of a case on the merits. This chapter concerns two important forms of interlocutory relief: the temporary restraining order (TRO) and the preliminary injunction. These equitable orders are available in special circumstances when a plaintiff needs immediate court action to avoid irreversible losses while waiting for the trial on the merits.

Courts generally are reluctant to act when there has not been time for careful deliberation of the full facts of a case. Interlocutory injunctions are considered extraordinary relief that require a strong showing of its necessity. Moreover, a plaintiff must be prepared to compensate a wrongfully enjoined defendant for losses caused by the order unless the plaintiff is ultimately victorious in the underlying case. The plaintiff's good faith in seeking the TRO or preliminary injunction is not a defense; a defendant who finally wins the case can recover any proven losses resulting from the interlocutory order. This rule serves to deter plaintiffs who doubt the strength of their claims from asking courts to grant extraordinary relief in advance of trial.

The primary differences between temporary restraining orders and preliminary injunctions are the speed with which they are acquired and their duration. A TRO is a brief stop-gap measure for a truly urgent situation. It can be replaced with a preliminary injunction after the court has had a few days to receive some greater amount of evidence in the case. A preliminary injunction, which is appealable, then lasts until the full trial.

States vary slightly in the names, procedures, and requirements for interlocutory injunctions. They are constrained by Constitutional requirements, and the Supreme Court has held that there are limits on the issuance of an *ex parte* TRO under state law, at least when First Amendment rights are at stake.

The primary focus of this chapter is on common law substantive requirements and the procedures in Federal Rule of Civil Procedure 65. Rule 65 concerns interlocutory relief in federal courts, and many states have identical or similar rules. Particularly noteworthy in modern law is the split among the federal circuit courts concerning the substantive requirements for a preliminary injunction, as explored in the first section below.

A. SUBSTANTIVE REQUIREMENTS

Section Coverage:

The common law has developed several substantive requirements for temporary injunctive orders. Although Federal Rule of Civil Procedure 65 covers only procedural requirements, federal courts have interpreted Rule 65 to incorporate common law substantive requirements.

A plaintiff must convince the court that an interlocutory order is necessary to preserve the *status quo* pending trial because otherwise irreparable harm will result. The plaintiff further must make some showing of the strength of the claim in the underlying suit. This section examines differing formulations for tests combining these elements for relief under federal law. Notably, the rules differ on whether the plaintiff must always show a "probability" of success on the merits of the underlying claim, or whether a lesser standard is appropriate when the degree of potential harm without the order is especially great. The federal circuit courts are split on the best approach, and the United States Supreme Court has not squarely addressed the issue.

Model Case:

The Tufts own a fruit orchard neighboring on the Jones Chemical Company (Jones). Jones is a repacking plant for various chemicals. The company's business is to transfer chemicals from large containers received from the manufacturers to small packages for consumer distribution. Both the orchard and the Jones plant are lawful activities in the area.

This year the Tufts suddenly have noticed a sharp deterioration in the trees adjacent to the chemical plant. Expert evidence establishes the cause to be chlorine gas and fumes escaping from the Jones plant. The Tufts sue in state court pursuant to a statute modeled after the Federal Rule of Civil Procedure 65 that governs temporary restraining orders and preliminary injunctions. They seek a preliminary and permanent injunction and damages. After a brief hearing the judge determines that continuous and irreparable damage will occur to the orchard unless the plant is enjoined from emitting the fumes.

The substantive legal issue under nuisance law is whether the activity of the defendant constitutes a substantial and unreasonable interference with the use and enjoyment of the plaintiff's property. Although there is insufficient time at a preliminary injunction hearing to determine this issue, each side can present some evidence to give the judge a general idea of the strength of the position of each party. The defendant can also introduce evidence of the degree of hardship that will occur to the plant if a preliminary injunction is issued.

The traditional test for a preliminary injunction is that the judge must find the plaintiff's claim is likely to be successful on the merits, that there will be irreparable harm to a significant portion of the orchard, and that the balance of hardships and public interest favor an injunction. If the court does not find the strength of the plaintiff's claim to amount to a "probability" of success on the merits at the full trial, then there will be no preliminary relief unless this court follows the alternative test.

Under the sliding scale alternative test the court will grant the preliminary injunction for a weaker substantive claim (but still a "substantial question") only if the showing of irreparable harm is exceptionally strong. Conversely, if the substantive claim is exceptionally strong, a preliminary injunction may be issued under the alternative test upon a weaker showing of irreparable harm (but still a showing of "irreparable harm"). Either way, the balance of hardships and public interest must be considered.

The public interest factor here may favor either side. If the escaping gas threatens people or things in addition to the orchard, it will likely favor the plaintiffs. If the defendant is a large employer and if an injunction will close operations, then it may favor the defendant.

Ride the Ducks of Philadelphia, LLC v. Duck Boat Tours, Inc.

138 Fed.Appx. 431 (3d Cir.2005).

■ NYGAARD, CIRCUIT JUDGE.

Duck Boat Tours, Inc. t/a Super Ducks appeals from the grant of a preliminary injunction by the District Court in favor of Ride The Ducks of Philadelphia, LLC. We will affirm.

Ride The Ducks, a Missouri corporation, operates a tourist attraction in Philadelphia using amphibious vehicles known as "ducks boats." These duck boats take tourists on a ride through the historic streets of Philadelphia and then enter the Delaware River via a ramp at the end of Race Street near the Benjamin Franklin Bridge for a water tour. Ride The Ducks built the ramp pursuant to a ten-year license agreement with Penn's Landing Corporation, a Pennsylvania non-profit corporation empowered by the City of Philadelphia to contract for the redevelopment of the area fronting the Delaware River.

The license states in relevant part:

> Exclusivity: Provided that RTD is not under default hereunder, RTD agrees that during the Term hereof, PLC will not directly enter into an agreement for an amphibious tour boat operation substantially similar to RTD's at Penn's Landing–Stage I or Penn's Landing–Stage II, *and RTD shall be the exclusive user of the ramping system which was constructed as part of RTD's work.*

(emphasis added). Ride The Ducks spent approximately $585,000 to build the ramp, and in addition to a $50,000 yearly license fee, Ride The Ducks pays Penn's Landing Corporation a portion of its gross revenues for the right to use the ramp it built.

Like Ride The Ducks, Super Ducks, a Pennsylvania corporation, is the owner of a number of duck boats. But unlike Ride The Ducks, Super Ducks has no license agreement with Penn's Landing Corporation for access to the Delaware River. Thus, in order to compete in the Philadelphia amphibious tour market, in early June 2004, Super Ducks sought to negotiate with Ride The Ducks for shared used of the ramp. Ride The Ducks declined. In response, Super Ducks representative T. Milton Street wrote a letter to the Director of Penn's Landing Corporation stating that Super Ducks intended to begin using Ride The Ducks's ramp on June 26, 2004, with or without the consent of Ride The Ducks or Penn's Landing Corporation.

On June 25, 2004, Ride The Ducks filed a motion for a preliminary injunction and a petition for a temporary restraining order. According to Ride The Ducks, Super Ducks' threatened use of the ramp would constitute trespass, conversion, and a tortious interference with the exclusivity provision of the license agreement between itself and Penn's Landing Corporation. The District Court granted the temporary restraining order pending a hearing on the preliminary injunction, which it held on July 1, 2004. The following day, the District Court granted Ride The Ducks's motion, enjoining Super Ducks from using or interfering with Ride The Ducks's ramp into the Delaware River. The District Court agreed with Ride The Ducks that Super Ducks' use of the ramp would be a tortious interference with the license agreement. Super Ducks now appeals.

* * *

In deciding whether to grant a preliminary injunction, a court must consider the following four factors:

(1) the likelihood that the moving party will succeed on the merits;

(2) the extent to which the moving party will suffer irreparable harm without injunctive relief;

(3) the extent to which the nonmoving party will suffer irreparable harm if the injunction is issued; and

(4) the public interest.

[Citation.] A balance of these factors leads us to hold that the District Court did not abuse its discretion in granting the preliminary injunction.

Ride The Ducks is likely to succeed on the merits of its tortious interference with contract and trespass claims. * * *

* * * Super Ducks knew Ride The Ducks had been granted the right to exclusive use of the ramp by the lease agreement. By seeking to use the ramp, Super Ducks necessarily intended to deprive Ride The Ducks of that right. * * * If forced to share the ramp with a competitor, Ride The Ducks would likely lose customers and, in turn, income. Although such injury has not yet occurred, because the purpose of a preliminary injunction is to prevent the occurrence of injuries, the demonstration by Ride The Ducks of a "presently existing actual threat" of injury suffices at this stage of the proceedings. [Citation] For these reasons, Ride The Ducks is likely to succeed on the merits of its tortious interference claim.

Ride The Ducks is equally—if not more—likely to prevail on its trespass claim. Under Pennsylvania Law, trespass is an unprivileged, intentional intrusion upon land in possession of another. * * * The terms of the license grant Ride The Ducks exclusive use of the ramp. Intrusion by Super Ducks onto the ramp would violate the exclusivity provision of the license. Accordingly, Ride The Ducks has a strong likelihood of success on the merits of its trespass claim.

If forced to share with a competitor the ramp it built with its own funds and for which it continues to pay Penn's Landing Corporation for exclusive use, Ride The Ducks would suffer irreparable harm. Having to share property so vital to its business with a competitor would almost certainly diminish Ride The Ducks's share of the amphibious tour market. We have held in other contexts that the loss of market share may be an irreparable injury. We see no reason not to apply that rule here. By contrast, Super Ducks asserts that it has "expended considerable sums in acquiring state-of-the-art amphibious crafts" and would be unable to compete in the Philadelphia market without access to the Delaware River via the ramp, which is located in a historic area. To the extent such harm is irremediable, it must be discounted by the fact that Super Ducks has brought the harm upon itself. * * *

The public interest favors Ride The Ducks as well. The public has a strong interest in seeing that contract and property rights are respected. * * *

Review of the four-factor preliminary injunction test compels the conclusion that the District Court did not abuse its discretion by granting the preliminary injunction. Ride The Ducks is likely to succeed on the merits of its claims for tortious interference with contract and trespass. If forced to share the ramp it built, Ride The Ducks would suffer irreparable harm in the form of a loss of market share. On the other hand, any irreparable harm to Super Ducks is of its own doing. And, finally, the public interest favors enforcing the property and contractual rights of Ride The Ducks.

* * * The District Court did not abuse its discretion in granting Ride The Ducks's motion for a preliminary injunction. We will affirm.

---

1. The four traditional prerequisites for issuance of a preliminary injunction are: 1) a substantial likelihood that movant will ultimately prevail on the merits; 2) a showing that movant will suffer irreparable injury unless the injunction issues; 3) proof that the threatened injury to movant outweighs whatever damage the proposed injunction may cause the opposing party; and 4) a showing that the injunction, if issued, would not

be adverse to the public interest. The burden of proof on each of these four elements rests with the movant.

2. *Likelihood of Success on the Merits.* The traditional requirements for granting a preliminary injunction begin with likelihood of success on the merits. As the court in the principal case notes, such a determination indicates only a probability. A different result may obtain after a full trial on the merits. This determination of probability has a tremendous effect on the negotiating positions of the parties with respect to any settlement of the suit, however. Many suits are won or lost as a practical matter at the preliminary injunction stage. Is there any alternative to this approach?

3. *Irreparable Harm.* The presence of irreparable harm is a requirement for a preliminary injunction. In *Narragansett Indian Tribe v. Guilbert*, 934 F.2d 4 (1st Cir.1991), for example, the defendant had purchased a lot from a Narragansett Indian for the construction of a private residence. After receiving all the necessary state and local permits, he began construction. The Tribe then filed a complaint alleging that the property encroaches on the Reservation in various ways and seeking to enjoin the work. The district court's denial of the injunction was affirmed, despite the fact that an interest in real property was involved. Although alteration to real property is usually considered irreparable, in this case the court found the possibility of irreparable damage in the absence of an injunction was "very faint" because there had already been extensive site preparation work at the time of suit. Trees and underbrush had already been cleared, the excavation for the foundation was complete, and the invasive work for the installation of a septic system had been done. The plaintiff failed to convince the court that completion of the dwelling would do further irreparable harm, given the significant transformation of the land that was already complete.

4. The inability to wait for monetary relief can occasionally, but rarely, constitute irreparable harm. In *DiDomenico v. Employers Co–op. Ind. Trust*, 676 F.Supp. 903 (N.D.Ind.1987), the plaintiff sought a preliminary order to enjoin the defendant health insurer from denying coverage for a liver transplant operation. The health plan specifically excluded "experimental" liver transplants and said that transplants for patients under the age of twelve were not experimental. Other parts of the insurance plan were ambiguous concerning the coverage of organ transplants for adults. The plaintiff's doctors testified at the preliminary injunction hearing that the contemplated operation was medically necessary for the plaintiff's diseased liver condition and that adult liver transplants recently have become accepted and were no longer considered experimental by the medical community.

The plaintiff could not afford the operation without the insurance coverage that the defendant denied. The district court found that the plaintiff had made a sufficient showing of irreparable harm in addition to the other requirements for a preliminary injunction. Irreparable harm was established because the plaintiff showed that he could not "easily wait" to get relief until the end of a full trial on the merits which might be several years in the future.

Gonzales v. O Centro Espírita Beneficente União do Vegetal

546 U.S. 418, 126 S.Ct. 1211, 163 L.Ed.2d 1017 (2006).

■ CHIEF JUSTICE ROBERTS delivered the opinion of the Court.

A religious sect with origins in the Amazon Rainforest receives communion by drinking a sacramental tea, brewed from plants unique to the region, that contains a hallucinogen regulated under the Controlled Substances Act by the Federal Government. The Government concedes that this practice is a sincere exercise of religion, but nonetheless sought to prohibit the small American branch of the sect from engaging in the practice, on the ground that the Controlled Substances Act bars all use of the hallucinogen. The sect sued to block enforcement against it of the ban on the sacramental tea, and moved for a preliminary injunction.

It relied on the Religious Freedom Restoration Act of 1993, which prohibits the Federal Government from substantially burdening a person's exercise of religion, unless the Government "demonstrates that application of the burden to the person" represents the least restrictive means of advancing a compelling interest. 42 U.S.C. § 2000bb–1(b). The District Court granted the preliminary injunction, and the Court of Appeals affirmed. We granted the Government's petition for certiorari. Before this Court, the Government's central submission is that it has a compelling interest in the *uniform* application of the Controlled Substances Act, such that no exception to the ban on use of the hallucinogen can be made to accommodate the sect's sincere religious practice. * * *

O Centro Espírita Beneficente União do Vegetal (UDV) is a Christian Spiritist sect based in Brazil, with an American branch of approximately 130 individuals. Central to the UDV's faith is receiving communion through *hoasca* (pronounced "wass-ca"), a sacramental tea made from two plants unique to the Amazon region. One of the plants, *psychotria viridis*, contains dimethyltryptamine (DMT), a hallucinogen whose effects are enhanced by alkaloids from the other plant, *banisteriopsis caapi*. DMT, as well as "any material, compound, mixture, or preparation, which contains any quantity of [DMT]," is listed in Schedule I of the Controlled Substances Act. § 812(c), Schedule IC.

In 1999, United States Customs inspectors intercepted a shipment to the American UDV containing three drums of *hoasca*. A subsequent investigation revealed that the UDV had received 14 prior shipments of *hoasca*. The inspectors seized the intercepted shipment and threatened the UDV with prosecution.

The UDV filed suit against the Attorney General and other federal law enforcement officials, seeking declaratory and injunctive relief. The complaint alleged, *inter alia,* that applying the Controlled Substances Act to the

UDV's sacramental use of *hoasca* violates RFRA. Prior to trial, the UDV moved for a preliminary injunction, so that it could continue to practice its faith pending trial on the merits.

At a hearing on the preliminary injunction, the Government conceded that the challenged application of the Controlled Substances Act would substantially burden a sincere exercise of religion by the UDV. [Citation.] The Government argued, however, that this burden did not violate RFRA, because applying the Controlled Substances Act in this case was the least restrictive means of advancing three compelling governmental interests: protecting the health and safety of UDV members, preventing the diversion of *hoasca* from the church to recreational users, and complying with the 1971 United Nations Convention on Psychotropic Substances, a treaty signed by the United States and implemented by the Act. [Citation.]

The District Court heard evidence from both parties on the health risks of *hoasca* and the potential for diversion from the church. The Government presented evidence to the effect that use of *hoasca,* or DMT more generally, can cause psychotic reactions, cardiac irregularities, and adverse drug interactions. The UDV countered by citing studies documenting the safety of its sacramental use of *hoasca* and presenting evidence that minimized the likelihood of the health risks raised by the Government. With respect to diversion, the Government pointed to a general rise in the illicit use of hallucinogens, and cited interest in the illegal use of DMT and *hoasca* in particular; the UDV emphasized the thinness of any market for *hoasca,* the relatively small amounts of the substance imported by the church, and the absence of any diversion problem in the past.

The District Court concluded that the evidence on health risks was "in equipoise," and similarly that the evidence on diversion was "virtually balanced." [citation]. In the face of such an even showing, the court reasoned that the Government had failed to demonstrate a compelling interest justifying what it acknowledged was a substantial burden on the UDV's sincere religious exercise. [Citation.] The court also rejected the asserted interest in complying with the 1971 Convention on Psychotropic Substances, holding that the Convention does not apply to *hoasca*. [Citation.]

The court entered a preliminary injunction prohibiting the Government from enforcing the Controlled Substances Act with respect to the UDV's importation and use of *hoasca*. The injunction requires the church to import the tea pursuant to federal permits, to restrict control over the tea to persons of church authority, and to warn particularly susceptible UDV members of the dangers of *hoasca*. [Citation.]. The injunction also provides that "if [the Government] believe[s] that evidence exists that *hoasca* has negatively affected the health of UDV members," or "that a shipment of *hoasca* contain[s] particularly dangerous levels of DMT, [the Government] may apply to the Court for an expedite[d] determination of whether the evidence warrants suspension or revocation of [the UDV's authority to use *hoasca*]." [Citation.]

The Government appealed the preliminary injunction and a panel of the Court of Appeals for the Tenth Circuit affirmed, [Citation.] as did a majority of the Circuit sitting en banc, [Citation.] We granted certiorari. [Citation.]

Although its briefs contain some discussion of the potential for harm and diversion from the UDV's use of *hoasca,* the Government does not challenge the District Court's factual findings or its conclusion that the evidence submitted on these issues was evenly balanced. Instead, the Government maintains that such evidentiary equipoise is an insufficient basis for issuing a preliminary injunction against enforcement of the Controlled Substances Act. We review the District Court's legal rulings *de novo* and its ultimate decision to issue the preliminary injunction for abuse of discretion. [Citation.]

The Government begins by invoking the well-established principle that the party seeking pretrial relief bears the burden of demonstrating a likelihood of success on the merits. [Citation.] The Government argues that the District Court lost sight of this principle in issuing the injunction based on a mere tie in the evidentiary record.

A majority of the en banc Court of Appeals rejected this argument, and so do we. Before the District Court, the Government conceded the UDV's prima facie case under RFRA. * * *

The Government argues that, although it would bear the burden of demonstrating a compelling interest as part of its affirmative defense at trial on the merits, the UDV should have borne the burden of disproving the asserted compelling interests at the hearing on the preliminary injunction. * * * [The Court noted that the Government has the burden under the Act of showing the compelling state interest.] The point remains that the burdens at the preliminary injunction stage track the burdens at trial.

* * *

We have no cause to pretend that the task assigned by Congress to the courts under RFRA is an easy one. * * * But Congress has determined that courts should strike sensible balances, pursuant to a compelling interest test that requires the Government to address the particular practice at issue. Applying that test, we conclude that the courts below did not err in determining that the Government failed to demonstrate, at the preliminary injunction stage, a compelling interest in barring the UDV's sacramental use of *hoasca.*

The judgment of the United States Court of Appeals for the Tenth Circuit is affirmed, and the case is remanded for further proceedings consistent with this opinion.

It is so ordered.

1.   The essence of a preliminary injunction hearing is a mini-trial on the merits. The procedural requirements under FRCP 65 are explored further later in this chapter. As the principal case illustrates, the mini-trial can be extremely significant.

The idea of "likelihood" of success on the merits has been interpreted in different ways. *See generally* Anthony DiSarro, Freeze Frame: The Supreme Court's Reaffirmation of the Substantive Principles of Preliminary Isnjunctions, 47 Gonz. L. Rev. 51(2011).

2.   Consider the difference between summary judgment and a preliminary injunction. Although in both circumstances the judge considers the application of the law, the grant of summary judgment is the substantive determination of a case. A preliminary injunction, however, is an interim determination of the relative merits of the claims of the parties producing, in conjunction with other factors, a decision whether to prevent further harm to the plaintiff pending a full trial on the merits.

Given this difference, what would you expect to be the difference in standard of review upon appeal of a summary judgment versus a preliminary injunction? The Supreme Court noted in the principal case that the standard for review for a preliminary injunction is whether the district court abused its discretion, except that issues of law are reviewed *de novo*. The Sixth Circuit offered the following explanation in *International Dairy Foods Ass'n v. Boggs*, 622 F.3d 628 (6th Cir. 2010):

> We review de novo a district court's grant of summary judgment. [Citation.] Summary judgment is proper where no genuine issue of material fact exists and the moving party is entitled to judgment as a matter of law. Fed.R.Civ.P. 56(c)(2). In considering a motion for summary judgment, the district court must draw all reasonable inferences in favor of the nonmoving party. [Citation.] The central issue is "whether the evidence presents a sufficient disagreement to require submission to a jury or whether it is so one-sided that one party must prevail as a matter of law." [Citation.]

> By contrast, the decision of whether to grant a motion for a preliminary injunction is "left to the sound discretion of the district court." [Citation.] "A district court, in deciding whether to grant an injunction, abuses its discretion when it applies the incorrect legal standard, misapplies the correct legal standard, or relies upon clearly erroneous findings of fact," [citation]. 622 F.3d at 635.

Tom Doherty Associates, Inc. v. Saban Entertainment, Inc.

60 F.3d 27 (2d Cir.1995).

■ Winter, Circuit Judge: * * *

Saban is a creator, producer, and distributor of video entertainment for children. Its library of properties in 1991 included more than 1,200 titles of children's television programming. Saban decided that it wanted to feature its characters and stories in children's books and approached a number of publishers, including TOR[.] * * * TOR is only a minor publisher of children's books. However, it was, and is, eager to expand its role in this specialized area of publishing and viewed a relationship with Saban as a means of doing so.

The ensuing negotiations between TOR and Saban concerned both TOR's immediate publication of six titles and the contours of a long-term relationship between the parties. The present dispute concerns that long-term relationship and TOR's right to publish additional children's books based on Saban properties. * * *

Like most parties to a commercial contract, Saban and TOR had substantial mutual interests that bound the relationship. Saban was a moderately successful children's television programmer that saw a chance for expansion in forming a relationship with a publisher. TOR saw such a relationship as a means of becoming a major publisher of children's books, particularly if Saban characters increased in popularity. As often happens, an unexpected event altered the mutual interests that bound the relationship. That event was the conception and development of the Mighty Morphin Power Rangers (the "Power Rangers").

After execution of the Agreement, the Power Rangers, a Saban property introduced in a Saturday morning television program, became a huge success—almost an obsession—with children. According to the record (there is no danger of this panel resorting to personal experience), an entire generation is caught up in the Power Rangers' unique ability to "morph"— to transform themselves from normal teenagers into superheroes who fight evil aliens. Saban's ownership of the Power Rangers clearly ended any need it had for TOR's publication and promotion of books based on its characters. Moreover, the exclusive rights provisions were now an albatross rather than a necessary inducement to get TOR to publish books based on Saban characters. Saban now had a property that was urgently sought after by companies in all fields of children's merchandising, including children's book publishing.

* * *

Saban thereafter entered into a number of licensing agreements relating to Power Rangers books with other publishing houses. * * *

TOR thereafter brought the present action for breach of contract and moved for a preliminary injunction. TOR contended that an injunction was required because the Power Rangers presented a unique opportunity for it to establish itself as a major player in the children's book publishing industry. The district court found that TOR demonstrated it would suffer irreparable harm unless Saban was ordered to license to it publishing rights to a Power Rangers book and that TOR had demonstrated a likelihood of success on the merits. * * *

Saban contends that, as a matter of law, a loss of future goodwill cannot constitute irreparable harm justifying injunctive relief.

Irreparable harm is an injury that is not remote or speculative but actual and imminent, and "for which a monetary award cannot be adequate compensation." [Citation] We have found irreparable harm where a party is threatened with the loss of a business. In *Semmes Motors, Inc. v. Ford Motor Co.*, 429 F.2d 1197 (2d Cir. 1970), a father-and-son car dealership was threatened with termination of its franchise by the manufacturer. We affirmed a finding of irreparable injury on the grounds that termination of the franchise would "obliterate" the dealership and that the right to continue a business "is not measurable entirely in monetary terms." Id. at 1205. We have also found irreparable harm in the loss of a relatively unique product. In *Reuters Ltd. v. United Press Int'l, Inc.*, 903 F.2d 904, 908–09 (2d Cir. 1990), a supplier of foreign news pictures threatened to stop providing those pictures to a wire service. We overturned a finding of no irreparable injury because the wire service had demonstrated that some customers would cease dealing with it for news from any source if it was unable to continue supplying those particular foreign news pictures. Id.; see also Interphoto Corp. v. Minolta Corp., 417 F.2d 621, 622 (2d Cir. 1969) (per curiam) (affirming finding of irreparable harm because plaintiff "would be unable to calculate its damages since it would suffer not merely loss of profits with respect to [defendant's] goods but loss of good will from the lack of a 'full line' ").

On the other hand, we have reversed a finding of irreparable harm where the facts demonstrate no loss of goodwill, but only provable monetary damages from the loss of a profitable line of business. See Jack Kahn Music Co. v. Baldwin Piano & Organ Co., 604 F.2d 755, 763 (2d Cir. 1979) (no irreparable harm where piano manufacturer attempted to terminate its dealership contract with a retail seller that sold many brands of musical instruments).

These cases stand for the general proposition that irreparable harm exists only where there is a threatened imminent loss that will be very difficult to quantify at trial. Generally, where we have found no irreparable harm, the alleged loss of goodwill was doubtful, and lost profits stemming from the inability to sell the terminated product could be compensated with money damages determined on the basis of past sales of that product and of current and expected future market conditions. [Citations] In contrast, where we have found irreparable harm, the very viability of the plaintiff's business, or substantial losses of sales beyond those of the terminated product, have been threatened.

We believe that the governing principle is as follows. Where the availability of a product is essential to the life of the business or increases business of the plaintiff beyond sales of that product—for example, by attracting customers who make purchases of other goods while buying the product in question-the damages caused by loss of the product will be far more difficult to quantify than where sales of one of many products is the sole loss. In such cases, injunctive relief is appropriate. This rule is necessary to avoid the unfairness of denying an injunction to a plaintiff on the ground that money damages are available, only to confront the plaintiff at a trial on the merits with the rule that damages must be based on more than speculation. Where the loss of a product with a sales record will not affect other aspects of a business, a plaintiff can generally prove damages on a basis other than speculation. Where the loss of a product will cause the destruction of a business itself or indeterminate losses in other business, the availability of money damages may be a hollow promise and a preliminary injunction appropriate.

It is true that TOR does not fit the usual factual scenario. TOR will not suffer any loss of existing sales and its existence will not be endangered if it is unable to publish a book based on the Power Rangers. However, the instant case is analytically the same. If preliminary relief is not available, TOR will lose an opportunity to become a major publisher of children's books—that is to say, it will lose an opportunity to become a sufficiently well-known publisher of children's books to attract additional authors and owners of characters. Our cases to date involve the loss of existing business rather than adding a unique product line that will allow the overall business to expand. Although we have never held that a loss of prospective goodwill that is both imminent and non-quantifiable can constitute irreparable injury, nothing in our cases precludes such a conclusion and their logic supports it. Here, the value of a Power Rangers book to TOR's fortunes as a children's publisher is beyond ready calculation. It is a wholly unique opportunity, and the amount of damages—in particular, the loss of prospective business from additional children's authors or owners of characters—will be largely indeterminate if the opportunity is denied.

Although we hold that a loss of prospective goodwill can constitute irreparable harm, we also hold that there must be a clear showing that a product that a plaintiff has not yet marketed is a truly unique opportunity for a company. New products as yet unmarketed by anyone would simply not qualify. Nor would products that are successful but have reasonable substitutes. A "clear showing" standard incorporates the primary requirements of irreparable injury because it assures that the harm—although not quantifiable—is not speculative.

We expect the "clear showing" standard to be infrequently met but conclude that TOR has made such a showing in the present case. The Power Rangers are a unique product with an established exceptional appeal to children. There are other popular children's characters, but we believe that they are not reasonably substitutable. * * * Here, the district court found that the Power Rangers are likely to transform TOR's fortunes in the children's book publishing field.

* * *

The preliminary injunction entered by the district court is affirmed.

1. Irreparable injury is a prerequisite for temporary injunctive relief as it is for permanent orders. Even if the plaintiff has a high probability of success on the merits, and even if the balance of hardships favors the plaintiff, a court should not issue an injunction without a showing of loss beyond economic loss compensable with damages. *See* Frank's GMC Truck Center, Inc. v. General Motors Corp., 847 F.2d 100 (3d Cir.1988) (only economic loss from refusal of manufacturer discontinuing line of trucks to supply parts to retailer losing service business).

2. In Classic Components Supply, Inc. v. Mitsubishi Electronics America, Inc., 841 F.2d 163 (7th Cir.1988), the plaintiff distributor sought an injunction to compel the defendant manufacturer to continue using it as a distributor. The defendant complained to the court that the plaintiff had promised by contract to arbitrate disputes of this character. The trial court ordered the plaintiff to arbitrate and denied the request for a preliminary injunction. The plaintiff appealed and argued that it was being irreparably injured because

> customers have already started to cancel their orders for Mitsubishi products. [Classic's] market development for Mitsubishi products will be totally lost if there is any significant interruption in its Dealership Agreement. This will effect [sic] not only the portion of [Classic's] business represented by the Mitsubishi line, but its entire customer base which Classic has traditionally serviced by holding itself out as a source for a broad range of its customers' needs.

The Court of Appeals for the Seventh Circuit held for the defendant. Judge Easterbrook, writing for the majority, noted that this assertion of irreparable harm

> shows only that Classic may suffer injury. Injuries of this sort, common consequences of broken contracts, yield damages. Any injury compensable in money is not "irreparable," so an injunction is unavailable. [Citation.] Classic does not acknowledge the existence, let alone the force, of this principle. Classic therefore has not appealed to the exception: that a terminated supply arrangement may create irreparable injury if the interruption bids fair to propel one firm into bankruptcy and frustrate later attempts to compute or collect damages. [Citations.] Classic does not suggest that the injury it confronts is harder to quantify than the injury in any other contract case. Perhaps Classic abjured the exception because it offered no shelter. Classic distributes the lines of about 65 manufacturers; Mitsubishi's semiconductors accounted for only 1.5% of its sales in 1986 and 3.4% in early 1987; Classic can purchase Mitsubishi products (with Mitsubishi's blessing) from its distributors even if not directly from Mitsubishi.

Judge Easterbrook opined that the plaintiff's motive in bringing the appeal was solely for the purpose of delay to avoid its contractual duty to arbitrate. Believing that the plaintiff misused the legal process as "a crowbar for obtaining concessions that the merits of the case do not support," the court found that the action was frivolous and awarded attorneys' fees to the defendant. 841 F.2d 163 (7th Cir.1988).

3. The standard for review of a district court's grant or denial of a preliminary injunction is whether there was an abuse of discretion by the trial judge. The standard is a very deferential one because the balancing process for issuance of a preliminary injunction is highly discretionary. The question before the appellate court is whether the judge "exceeded the bounds of permissible choice in the circumstances" rather than what the appellate court would have done in the trial court's place. Adams v. Attorney Registration and Disciplinary Com'n, 801 F.2d 968 (7th Cir.1986).

Abuse of discretion in the issuance of a preliminary injunction can occur in several ways. (1) The trial judge's decision must be based on relevant factors so as not to be a clear error in judgment. Citizens to Preserve Overton Park, Inc. v. Volpe, 401 U.S. 402, 91 S.Ct. 814, 28 L.Ed.2d 136 (1971). (2) The trial court must apply the correct legal standard for the federal circuit. Benda v. Grand Lodge of Int'l Ass'n of Machinists & Aerospace Workers, 584 F.2d 308 (9th Cir.1978), *cert. dismissed,* 441 U.S. 937, 99 S.Ct. 2065, 60 L.Ed.2d 667 (1979). (3) The trial judge must apply the correct law with respect to the underlying issues in the case. Sports Form, Inc. v. United Press Int'l, Inc., 686 F.2d 750 (9th Cir.1982). (4) The findings of fact must not be clearly erroneous. United States v. United States Gypsum Co., 333 U.S. 364, 68 S.Ct. 525, 92 L.Ed. 746 (1948).

PROBLEM: THE FRUSTRATED BOOK PUBLISHER

Pearson Publishing, Co. has the exclusive rights to publish and distribute a very popular series of books that have captured a wide following among both children and adults alike. When the last book in the series was scheduled for distribution, there was considerable media attention for the event. The book was to be released at midnight on a certain summer date and the retail book chains were advertising in-store parties and events surrounding the release.

Pearson had contracts with book sellers throughout the world for the distribution of this anticipated book. Every contract carefully specified that the book was to remain confidential until the release date. A week before the release date, however, Solo Books mailed copies of the book to a few hundred individuals before realizing the mistake and halting the shipments. Pearson seeks an preliminary injunction against Solo to prevent further distribution.

Solo does not contest that it distributed some books in breach of contract. Solo defends against the motion on the grounds that it voluntarily stopped the leak when it was discovered. Pearson argues that Solo leaked deliberately in order to attain the media coverage that resulted because that coverage amounted to free advertising for this obscure book seller. Pearson concedes, however, that it cannot prove any loss attributable to the leak because there have been other leaks as well from parties unrelated to Solo. Pearson also concedes that it cannot prove that it will sell any fewer books as a result of the leak.

Should the court grant the preliminary injunction? Consider the requirements of likelihood of success on the merits of the contract claim and irreparable harm.

Cassim v. Bowen

824 F.2d 791 (9th Cir.1987).

■ SKOPIL, CIRCUIT JUDGE:

M.M. Cassim is a Medicare participating physician. He argues that as a matter of due process he is entitled to a full evidentiary hearing before the Secretary of Health and Human Services [HHS] can suspend him from Medicare and publish notice of his suspension in a local newspaper. The district court denied Cassim's motion for a preliminary injunction. We affirm.

* * *

Cassim argues that the district court improperly balanced the hardships. First, he emphasizes that his livelihood, reputation, and professional career will be irreparably harmed. He contends the stigma of exclusion and publication could not be removed even if the ALJ [Administrative Law Judge] completely exonerated him. Second, he asserts that the district court mistakenly believed he threatened the lives or health of his patients. Instead, he claims, OIG [Office of Inspector General] accused him of skillfully performing excessive surgery.

We reject Cassim's argument even though we recognize the possibility of irreparable harm created by the Secretary's sanctions. Cassim is simply mistaken in asserting that HHS did not believe he threatened the health of his patients. OIG charged Cassim with doing unnecessary surgery in eight cases culled from a six-month period. In those eight cases, Cassim's patients ranged in age from 66 to 86. In each case, OIG concluded that Cassim had placed his patients in "high risk" situations or in "imminent danger." The Secretary persuasively argues that unnecessary surgery on elderly patients endangers their health.

Against the harm Cassim might suffer we must balance the harm his patients might suffer. We affirm the district court's finding that the balance of hardships neither tips sharply in Cassim's favor, nor favors him.
* * *

Cassim's interests are substantial. * * * Cassim may still treat Medicare patients. If he prevails in his administrative appeal, he must be reimbursed. A successful appeal would also help restore his reputation and practice. The Secretary would have to reinstate Cassim as a Medicare participating physician, 42 C.F.R. § 1004.120(b) (1986), and give notice of his reinstatement to the public, 42 C.F.R. § 1001.134(a)(2) (1986). On the other hand, even that vindication may not remove all of the stigma associated with the Secretary's sanctions. Some damage might remain. Cassim's patients and members of the public may distrust him.

The Government's interests, however, are compelling. In the judgment of OMPRO [Oregon Medical Profession Review Organization] and OIG, Cassim performed unnecessary surgery. Such surgery wastes public resources and, even more important, threatens the patient's health. * * *

Affirmed.

Recall that the traditional rule for awarding a preliminary injunction is the four-part test: the plaintiff must show each of the elements of (1) a probability of prevailing on the merits, (2) irreparable injury if relief is denied, (3) the balance of hardships favoring the plaintiff, and (4) the public interest favoring the relief.

The alternative test, followed in some federal circuits, allows a plaintiff the choice of establishing the four traditional factors or of satisfying a sliding scale test: the greater the potential irreparability of the harm and the clearer the balance of hardships without the order, the lesser the required showing of strength on the merits of the case. *See* Caribbean Marine Services Co. v. Baldrige, the next case *infra*. Consider what difference the tests make by considering the application of the traditional rule in the Problem that follows.

PROBLEM: THE THREATENED LANDMARK

Riverdale is a small rural town that has one main street with businesses and shops. At the end of this quaint street is an old railroad depot. The depot has been closed for years, but it is a handsome building constructed of limestone. It provides an attractive end to the street and it contributes an essential element to the quaint atmosphere of the town.

The depot is owned by the Rapid Railway Co. [RR]. The empty building has not been used for years, but RR has kept it reasonably maintained. An employee regularly visits the Riverdale depot to inspect and repair it.

Recently RR decided to raze all its closed buildings in order to save maintenance costs. The Riverdale depot was scheduled for demolition on July 14. RR made no public announcement of this plan.

On July 10 a member of the Riverdale town council learned of this secret plan from a relative in Metropolis who works in the RR main office. The town council immediately sought legal advice and formed a plan to save the depot. The council declared it a "landmark" and passed an ordinance prohibiting destruction of town landmarks without council approval.

The lawyer who proposed this plan explained to the council that these ordinances may not be enforceable. There is a substantial question under state law whether the town has the power to restrict land use by such an ordinance without state legislative delegation. There is scant law on the question and, although the law is unclear, existing authority is somewhat unfavorable to the council. When the council asked for an estimate on the probability of success, the lawyer said there is probably one chance in twenty that a court would uphold the validity of such ordinances.

The council decided that, even with that slight chance of success, it was worth paying the lawyer to draft the ordinances immediately. Another council meeting to pass the ordinances was scheduled for July 13. The council notified RR of this impending action in order to prevent the dispatch of the demolition crew. The response of RR was to change secretly the demolition date to July 13. The council member's relative who works for RR in Metropolis learned of this change and spread the news. The Riverdale council and its lawyer then speeded up the process and passed the ordinance just a few hours before the demolition crew arrived.

The council promptly notified RR that the ordinance had been passed, but RR said that the demolition crew should proceed anyway. The council's lawyer drove to the nearest state courthouse and sought an injunction to halt the demolition immediately. Should the judge grant the order?

Caribbean Marine Services Co. v. Baldrige

844 F.2d 668 (9th Cir.1988).

■ Wallace, Circuit Judge: * * *

The owners and certain crew members (crew) fish for yellow fin tuna using purse seine nets. To locate the tuna, they scan the water looking for porpoises, which for unknown reasons often swim with the tuna. Nets are set around the porpoises, and the tuna swimming beneath them are captured when the net is closed or "pursed" around them. During this procedure, many porpoises may be caught in the nets and drowned. In 1970 and 1971, for example more than 600,000 porpoises were killed in the course of such operations. [Citation.]

In 1972, Congress enacted the Marine Mammal Protection Act (Act), 16 U.S.C. §§ 1361–1406. One of the declared goals of the Act is to reduce the number of incidental kills and injuries to marine mammals permitted in the course of commercial fishing operations. * * *

Pursuant to section 1373, the Secretary promulgated regulations requiring permit holders to allow an employee of the National Oceanic and Atmospheric Administration (Administration) to accompany fishing vessels "for the purpose of conducting research and observing operations, including collecting information which may be used in civil or criminal penalty proceedings, forfeiture actions, or permit or certificate sanctions." * * *

The Administrator's new policy of hiring female, as well as male, observers to accompany selected fishing vessels on their voyages prompted the present litigation. * * *

The owners were notified in December 1986 and January 1987 that a female observer would be assigned to accompany their vessels, the M/V Mariner and the M/V Apure, on their next voyages. In two separate actions, the owners and crew filed these actions for declaratory and injunctive relief. In each action, the owners and crew alleged that the Administrator's directive requiring the presence of female observers threatened a violation of the crew members' constitutional privacy rights and a violation of regulations requiring the observer to carry out his duties so as to minimize interference with fishing operations, 50 C.F.R. § 216.24(f)(2) (1986). The owners and crew sought and obtained temporary restraining orders prohibiting the government from implementing its new directive. The owners and crew then moved for preliminary injunctive relief. They supplemented their motions with various declarations describing the living and working condition on the vessels. We now summarize these declarations.

A fishing voyage may last three months or longer, depending upon fishing conditions. During this period, the crew members work together on the deck of the boat, eat and drink together in the small galley, and are otherwise forced to interact with one another in their bunkrooms, in the passageways, and in the common showers and toilets.

The crew members allegedly enjoy little or no privacy with respect to intimate bodily functions. They share small, dormitory-style bunkrooms and common toilets and showers. Because the bunkrooms are cramped, the crew members usually undress in the common area of the bunkroom, rather than behind curtains in their bunks. Moreover, because the common toilets and showers lack partitions or curtains, they usually bathe and perform other bodily functions in view of their cabinmates. Though single and double cabins equipped with private bathrooms exist on the vessels, these are assigned to officers. Porpoise observers usually bunk with the crews and share their bathroom facilities; thus, these observers may both observe and be observed by the crew members while undressing or performing bodily functions.

* * *

Finally, the declarations state that the West Coast tuna fishing industry has suffered severe financial losses in the past few years. The declarations contend that the presence of a female observer could destroy morale and distract the crew, thus affecting the crew's efficiency and decreasing the vessel's profits. The declarations also express the owners' concern that the crew members, some of whom are allegedly crude men with little formal education, may harass or sexually assault a female observer. Such tortious conduct could subject the owners to uninsurable liability, and further endanger their profits. To support this allegation, the owners referred to an incident which occurred aboard a foreign vessel involving an assault by a Korean officer upon an American female who served as a foreign fishing observer. Finally, the owners claimed that officers would have to devote time to protecting the female observer from the crew, thus distracting them from their primary duty of locating and catching tuna.

* * *

The owners also contended that declarations stating that the presence of a female would create conflicts that would disrupt fishing operations raised a serious legal question regarding the legality of assigning females as observers under 50 C.F.R. § 216.24(f)(2) (1986). This regulation requires that the duties of the observer be performed in a manner that minimizes interference with fishing operations. * * *

The government responded to these averments by submitting declarations challenging the owners' and crew's assertion that an invasion of the crew members' privacy interests was unavoidable and that the female observer would disrupt fishing operations. With respect to the crew members' privacy claim, the government submitted declarations pointing out that Administration regulations do not require that observers be placed in shared bunkrooms, that private quarters on tuna vessels may remain vacant throughout a fishing voyage, and that both male and female observers had been assigned private accommodations on boats in the past. Declarations from both male and female observers stated that crew members were always partially dressed while performing their duties, and that they had never observed crew members taking showers on deck.

With respect to the owners' claim that the presence of a female would disrupt fishing operations and provoke jealousy and fights, the government submitted the declaration of Wendy Townsend, a female Administrator observer, who completed a 48–day voyage aboard a tuna seiner, which, like the owners' vessels, is subject to the Administration's directive. * * * Townsend also stated that she established amicable relations with the crew members, that no harassment or other disturbing incidents took place during her voyage, and that the crew members succeeded in capturing a hold-full of fish during the voyage.

* * * The government also submitted the declaration of Janet Wall, a foreign fisheries observer since 1978, who stated that approximately one-third, or about 150, of the observers serving on foreign vessels each year are women, and that in the past ten years there had been only six instances of physical or verbal abuse of female observers on these vessels. * * *

The district court granted the motions of the owners and crew for preliminary injunctions in each case. The district court found that the parties raised serious privacy questions, and a serious question concerning the legality of placing women on the vessels under 50 C.F.R. § 216.24(f)(2) (1986). The district court determined that the balance of hardships tipped sharply in favor of the owners and crew. The court decided that the injunction would merely preserve the status quo, and this was important considering "the fact that the tuna industry is not as viable as it once was." In addition, the court concluded that maintenance of the status quo allowing only male observers "will not adversely effect the purpose of the [Act], namely the preservation of porpoise."

* * *

Because our review of the district court's decision is generally limited to whether the district court abused its discretion, our disposition of an appeal from a preliminary injunction ordinarily will not dispose of the merits of the litigation. "Because of the limited scope of our review of the law applied by the district court and because the fully developed factual record may be materially different from that initially before the district court, our disposition of appeals from most preliminary injunctions may provide little guidance as to the appropriate disposition on the merits."

* * * [U]nder the "traditional test" typically used in cases involving the public interest, the district court should consider (1) the likelihood that the moving party will prevail on the merits, (2) whether the balance of irreparable harm favors the plaintiff, and (3) whether the public interest favors the moving party. [Citation.] We have allowed the district court some latitude in assessing the first two factors as it fashions appropriate relief. In some cases, we have stated that a plaintiff may meet its burden by demonstrating a combination of probable success on the merits and a possibility of irreparable injury. *E.g.*, Los Angeles Memorial Coliseum Commission v. National Football League, 634 F.2d 1197, 1201 (9th Cir. 1980) (*L.A. Coliseum*). At other times, we have stated that where the balance of hardships tips decidedly toward the plaintiff, the district court need not require a robust showing of likelihood of success on the merits, and may grant preliminary injunctive relief if the plaintiff's moving papers raise "serious questions" on the merits. This latter formulation is known as the "alternative test." Under either test, however, the district court must consider the public interest as a factor in balancing the hardships when the public interest may be affected. [Citations.]

In the case before us, the district court did not find that the owners and crew were likely to prevail on the merits. Instead, it only considered the seriousness of the questions raised and the balance of the hardships between the parties. After examining the moving papers, the court concluded that the owners and crew raised serious questions on the merits and that the balance of hardships tipped sharply in their favor. The government urges us to find that the district court erred in each of these determinations. However, we need not reach the question whether the owners and crew raised serious questions on the merits before the district court. Our review of the legal questions, as important as they are, will need to await a trial on the merits of this case and any subsequent appeal. We may properly dispose of the appeal before us by considering whether the district court properly evaluated and weighed the relevant harms in this case.

In his Memorandum Decision, the district judge cited four findings in support of his conclusion that the balance of harm tipped sharply in favor of the owners and crew: (1) the preliminary injunction would do no more than "preserve the status quo"; (2) the tuna industry "has been plagued with financial problems"; (3) the female observer would "disturb the domestic aspect of the tuna seiner"; and (4) the declarations submitted by the owners and crew "speculate that accommodation of a female federal observer may be costly."

These findings do not support the district court's conclusion that the balance of harm tipped decidedly in favor of the owners and crew. First, and perhaps most important, the owners and crew did not demonstrate, and the district court did not find, that the alleged harms will be irreparable. At a minimum, a plaintiff seeking preliminary injunctive relief must demonstrate that it will be exposed to irreparable harm. [Citation.] Speculative injury does not constitute irreparable injury sufficient to warrant granting a preliminary injunction. [Citation.] A plaintiff must do more than merely allege imminent harm sufficient to establish standing; a plaintiff must *demonstrate* immediate threatened injury as a prerequisite to preliminary injunctive relief. [Citation.]

The district court did not require a showing that the harms alleged by the owners and crew were imminent or likely. For example, the district court did not require them to demonstrate that the economic losses they alleged would result from a female observer's presence were likely to occur. Instead, the court merely stated that "the declarations submitted by the [owners] *speculate* that accommodation of a female observer *may be costly*" (emphasis added). * * *

The owners' and crew's claim that they will catch fewer fish if a woman is on board is similarly unsupported. The only materials submitted to the district court describing the impact of women on fishing operations were declarations the government filed stating that women have served successfully on numerous voyages on both foreign and American fishing vessels. Subjective apprehensions and unsupported predictions of revenue loss are not sufficient to satisfy a plaintiff's burden of demonstrating an immediate threat of irreparable harm. Moreover, there was no showing that the threat to the owners' revenues constituted an irreparable injury. No consideration was given to whether any lost revenues might be compensable in a damage award, and thus not irreparable. * * *

The district court similarly failed to find a threat of immediate, irreparable harm to the privacy interests alleged by the crew. The district court did not find, for example, that the female observer would have to bunk in the crew's quarters or observe their intimate bodily activities. Instead, the district judge stated in conclusory fashion that though a "male federal observer did not disturb the domestic aspect of the tuna seiner, a female would." It is unclear from this description whether the "harm" the court found consisted of an invasion of any constitutionally protected privacy interests or mere inconvenience to the crew members. * * *

Finally, the district court failed to identify and weigh the public interests at stake in its balance of harms analysis. * * *

The owners and crew argue that delaying either temporarily or permanently the use of women in the Act's observer program would not have any impact on the interests of the public. This argument rests on two premises: first, that the only public interest implicated by this dispute is the interest in preserving marine mammals, and second, that excluding qualified women from the observer program will not negatively affect that interest. * * *

The argument that the injunction would have no impact on the interests of the public fails to take into account both the government's and the public's interest in ensuring equal employment opportunities for women. This interest, as well as the interest in protecting and preserving marine mammals, is clearly implicated by the issuance of the preliminary injunction in this case. * * *

When the governmental and public interest in gender neutral hiring is balanced against the privacy interests asserted in this case, it is by no means apparent that the balance tips decidedly in the crew members' favor. Some courts have held that the privacy interest in remaining free from involuntary viewing of private parts of the body by members of the opposite sex should not impair employment rights unless the threatened invasion of privacy is serious and there are no means by which both interests can be reasonably accommodated. * * *

In conclusion, after careful review of the record and the district court's decision, we hold that the district court abused its discretion by ordering preliminary relief in this case. Under the alternate approach articulated in *L.A. Coliseum,* the moving party must first demonstrate an immediate threat of irreparable injury to itself and that the balance of hardships tips decidedly in its favor. The district court did not determine that the injuries alleged by the owners and crew were serious, immediate, and irreparable. Moreover, it failed to identify the harm which a preliminary injunction might cause to the government, its employees, and the public and to weigh this harm against any irreparable injuries alleged by the owners and crew. We therefore reverse the orders granting preliminary injunctions.

---

1. During the last decades of the twentieth century, the federal Courts of Appeals reconsidered the traditional standard. Some reaffirmed the traditional four part standard, but most adopted various forms of a flexible standard, as exemplified by the alternative test in the principal case. Notably, the Second Circuit first adopted a flexible standard that required a party seeking a preliminary injunction to show "(a) irreparable harm and (b) either (1) likelihood of success on the merits or (2) sufficiently serious questions going to the merits to make them a fair ground for litigation and a balance of hardships tipping decidedly toward the party requesting the preliminary relief." Jackson Dairy, Inc. v. H.P. Hood & Sons, Inc., 596 F.2d 70, 72 (2d Cir.1979).

The Seventh Circuit adopted its own flexible test in *American Hospital Supply Corp. v. Hospital Products Ltd.*, 780 F.2d 589, 593–94 (7th Cir. 1986). The standard allowed a preliminary injunction where "the harm to the plaintiff if the injunction is denied, multiplied by the probability that the denial would be an error (that the plaintiff, in other words, will win at trial), exceeds the harm to the defendant if the injunction is granted, multiplied by the probability that granting the injunction would be an error." The opinion by Justice Richard Posner provided the formula as follows: If $[P \times H_p] > (1-P) \times H_d$ then the preliminary injunction should be granted. P is the probability that the denial is an error because plaintiff will win on the substance; H_p is the harm to the plaintiff if the injunction is denied; H_d is the harm to the defendant if the injunction is granted. Id. at 593.

Judge Posner characterized this formula as the procedural counterpart to Judge Learned Hand's famous negligence formula in *United States v. Carroll Towing Co.*, 159 F.2d 169 (2d Cir.1947). Does this formula make a change? *See* Silberman, Injunctions by the Numbers: Less than the Sum of its Parts, 63 Chicago–Kent L.Rev. 279 (1987).

2. How often is the alternative test likely to alter the outcome of a motion for a preliminary injunction? How would the problem of the Threatened Landmark, *supra*, change with the use of the alternative test articulated by the principal case?

Contrast the principal case and *Cassim v. Bowen, supra*, with *Chalk v. U.S. District Court*, 840 F.2d 701 (9th Cir.1988). In *Chalk* a teacher who was reassigned to an administrative position successfully obtained a preliminary injunction for reinstatement with a classroom assignment. The teacher's removal from the classroom occurred after a medical leave when he was diagnosed with AIDS (Acquired Immune Deficiency Syndrome).

The alternative test for preliminary injunctions governed the motion in *Chalk* as it did in the principal case because both arose in the same federal circuit. The district court denied the order, and the Court of Appeals reversed. The plaintiff had established a strong likelihood of success on the merits because medical testimony established that there was little risk of his infecting the children with the virus in the classroom setting.

The trial court had found that the teacher suffered no irreparable harm because the administrative position paid the same salary as the classroom assignment. On appeal this finding was reversed as clearly erroneous. The appellate opinion said that the focus should not be on the potential monetary loss alone but on the nature of the alternative work. The teacher's original employment was in the area of his special skills, teaching hearing-impaired children. He derived great personal satisfaction from working closely with his small class. The reassigned administrative work involved writing grant proposals and he had no special training nor interest in this work.

The public expressed fear about the risk of AIDS exposure in schools. The Court of Appeals held that the public interest factor could not be grounded on unreasonable fears without frustrating the legislative purpose behind the act on which the claim was founded. The trial court could retain jurisdiction to remove the teacher from student contact at whatever point qualified medical opinion might determine that his condition poses a risk to the children. For example, as the teacher's immune system deteriorates, he may contract some opportunistic infection capable of transmission. Until then, the preliminary injunction should preserve the *status quo* with the classroom teaching assignment pending the full trial on the merits of the case.

How do this teacher's case and the principal case differ from *Cassim v. Bowen, supra*, involving the Medicare doctor? Was the interpretation of the public interest controlling in each case? Are the different results best explained by the differences in the tests for preliminary injunctions?

3. The public interest factor in the standard for interlocutory relief is an elusive one. The opposing parties often can make reasonable arguments that the public interest favors each side of the dispute. Consider the case of Adams v. Vance, 570 F.2d 950 (D.C.Cir.1978). In this case the Inupiat Eskimos challenged a decision by the Secretary of State. The International Whaling Commission (IWC) had banned Eskimo hunting of the bowhead whale, but the United States could stay the ban by timely objection. The Commission was concerned about the survival of the whale, but subsistence hunting of the bowhead had been the vital element of a millenia-old Eskimo culture.

The Secretary of State decided against making an objection to the IWC just four days before the deadline. Plaintiffs sued the Secretary and, after a short hearing one afternoon, the district court issued a temporary restraining order requiring the Secretary to file an objection. The judge accepted the plaintiffs' contention that an objection would not substantially harm the United States' efforts at international environmental cooperation because the International Whaling Convention allows objections to be withdrawn freely any time after they are made. Without the objection, however, the plaintiffs would be subject to criminal penalties if they continued their subsistence fishing.

The Court of Appeals held an emergency session on a federal holiday to reverse the order. The per curiam opinion characterized the district court's order as an unwarranted intrusion on executive discretion in the field of foreign policy. It criticized the lower court for treating this application for immediate injunctive relief as an ordinary one because it deeply intruded into the core concerns of the executive branch. The opinion observed that no other nation has entered an objection to an IWC action since 1973, so that the symbolic impact of the United States being the first nation to break that pattern could be grave. Therefore, it was clear error for the district court to find that an objection, provisional or otherwise, would not substantially endanger the interests of the United States.

Winter v. Natural Resources Defense Council, Inc.

555 U.S. 7, 129 S.Ct. 365, 172 L.Ed.2d 249 (2008).

■ Mr. Chief Justice Roberts delivered the opinion of the Court.

[At issue in this case were some Navy antisubmarine training exercises off the coast of California. The plaintiffs, who had conservation and commercial interests, sought to enjoin the exercises pending the Navy's compliance with environmental regulations and filing of an Environment Impact Statement as required under National Environmental Policy Act (NEPA). The Navy argued that it was exempt because there was no environmental impact in the use of active sonar. Sonar emits pulses of sound underwater and then receives the acoustic waves that echo off the target, and there was a scientific dispute as to whether it had or would adversely affect marine life.

The district court issued a preliminary injunction that required measures to mitigate any possible effect on marine animals, and the Court of Appeals affirmed with modification. The Supreme Court reversed on several grounds, including that the district court had given insufficient weight to the public interest in national security through a properly trained antisubmarine force. Another ground for the reversal is reprinted below.]

* * *

A plaintiff seeking a preliminary injunction must establish that he is likely to succeed on the merits, that he is likely to suffer irreparable harm in the absence of preliminary relief, that the balance of equities tips in his favor, and that an injunction is in the public interest. [Citations.]

The District Court and the Ninth Circuit concluded that plaintiffs have shown a likelihood of success on the merits of their NEPA claim. * * *

The District Court and the Ninth Circuit also held that when a plaintiff demonstrates a strong likelihood of prevailing on the merits, a preliminary injunction may be entered based only on a "possibility" of irreparable harm.[Citations.] The lower courts held that plaintiffs had met this standard because the scientific studies, declarations, and other evidence in the record established to "a near certainty" that the Navy's training exercises would cause irreparable harm to the environment.[Citation.]

The Navy challenges these holdings, arguing that plaintiffs must demonstrate a likelihood of irreparable injury—not just a possibility—in order to obtain preliminary relief. On the facts of this case, the Navy contends that plaintiffs' alleged injuries are too speculative to give rise to irreparable injury, given that ever since the Navy's training program began 40 years ago, there has been no documented case of sonar-related injury to marine mammals in [Southern California]. And even if [sonar] does cause a limited number of injuries to individual *marine mammals,* the Navy asserts that plaintiffs have failed to offer evidence of species-level harm that would adversely affect *their* scientific, recreational, and ecological interests. For their part, plaintiffs assert that they would prevail under any formulation of the irreparable injury standard, because the District Court found that they had established a "near certainty" of irreparable harm.

We agree with the Navy that the Ninth Circuit's "possibility" standard is too lenient. Our frequently reiterated standard requires plaintiffs seeking preliminary relief to demonstrate that irreparable injury is *likely* in the absence of an injunction. * * *

* * * [E]ven if plaintiffs have shown irreparable injury from the Navy's training exercises, any such injury is outweighed by the public interest and the Navy's interest in effective, realistic training of its sailors. A proper consideration of these factors alone requires denial of the requested injunctive relief. For the same reason, we do not address the lower courts' holding that plaintiffs have also established a likelihood of success on the merits. * * *

It is so ordered.

––––––––––

1. The Supreme Court addressed a related issue in a case decided shortly before *Winter*. In Munaf v. Geren, 553 U.S. 674, 128 S.Ct. 2207, 171 L.Ed.2d 1 (2008), the Court noted that equitable principles have traditionally governed substantive habeas law. The case involved two American citizens alleged to have violated Iraqi law by committing acts of insurgency. They were being held by United States military forces in Iraq under a security agreement with the Iraqi government. Petitioners sought a preliminary injunction prohibiting their transfer to Iraqi authorities. After the Court addressed the jurisdictional issues, it held that the district court could not grant the preliminary injunction without considering the underlying merits of the habeas petition. In this case, it was found insufficient and the defendants were entitled to judgment. The Court further noted that the petitioners' concern that their transfer would result in torture is a serious matter, but one best addressed by the political branch rather than the judiciary.

2. Subsequent to *Winter* and *Munaf*, the Supreme Court again touched on related issues in Nken v. Holder, 556 U.S. 418, 129 S.Ct. 1749, 1761, 173 L.Ed.2d 550 (2009). In this case, the Court considered the differences between a preliminary injunction and a stay. The Court noted that they serve different purposes: whereas an injunction directs "the conduct of a particular actor," a stay operates upon the judicial proceeding. The Court then articulated the appropriate test that a federal appellate court should use to determine whether to hold a final order in abeyance while it evaluates the legality of that order. (1) whether the stay applicant has made a strong showing that he is likely to succeed on the merits; (2) whether the applicant will be irreparably injured absent a stay; (3) whether issuance of the stay will substantially injure the other parties interested in the proceeding; and (4) where the public interest lies. 129 S.Ct. at 1756–58.

How does this test compare with the traditional federal test for issuing a preliminary injunction?

3. Does the Supreme Court's discussion of the federal standard for preliminary injunctions in the principle case, *Winter*, invalidate all of the alternative tests adopted by circuits? Consider the Court's initial outline of requirements as well as its specific holding before reading the next case, which addresses the issue for the Second Circuit.

Citigroup Global Markets, Inc. v. VCG Special Opportunities Master Fund Ltd.

598 F.3d 30 (2d. Cir. 2010).

■ WALKER, J.

[A broker, CGMI, brought an action against a hedge fund, VCG, with which it had a prime brokerage services agreement. The action sought to enjoin arbitration before the Financial Industry Regulatory Authority (FINRA) of VCG's claims arising from an alleged violation of a credit default swap agreement by the broker's affiliate, Citibank. VCG had lost in earlier litigation against Citibank and was now seeking to arbitrate with CGMI, who sought to enjoin the arbitration. The substantive question was whether VCG was "customer" of CGMI with respect to the credit swap transactions.]

* * * [T]he district court granted CGMI's motion for a preliminary injunction. In granting the injunction, the district court applied this circuit's long-established standard for the entry of a preliminary injunction, under which the movant is required to show " 'irreparable harm absent injunctive relief, and either a likelihood of success on the merits, or a serious question going to the merits to make them a fair ground for trial, with a balance of hardships tipping decidedly in plaintiff's favor.' " [Citation.] The district court held that CGMI had demonstrated a likelihood of irreparable harm, but had failed to make a showing of "probable success" on the merits based on its claim that there was no customer relationship between CGMI and VCG with respect to the credit default swap transactions. The district court found, however, that CGMI had provided evidence that raised "serious questions" as to whether VCG was in fact a customer of CGMI with respect to the swap transaction and granted the preliminary injunction on that basis.

* * * Finally, the district court found that the balance of hardships tipped decidedly in CGMI's favor given that an injunction would simply freeze the arbitration without destroying VCG's ability to continue that arbitration in the event that the district court determined that the dispute fell within the scope of the FINRA rules.

On May 29, 2009, the district court denied VCG's motion for reconsideration, rejecting VCG's argument that *Winter v. Natural Resources Defense Council, Inc.,* 555 U.S. 7, 129 S.Ct. 365, 172 L.Ed.2d 249 (2008), had eliminated the "serious questions" prong of this circuit's preliminary injunction standard. This appeal followed. * * *

* * * VCG first contends that the district court abused its discretion by applying the wrong legal standard to CGMI's request for a preliminary injunction. VCG argues that three recent decisions of the Supreme Court— *Munaf v. Geren,* 553 U.S. 674, 128 S.Ct. 2207, 171 L.Ed.2d 1 (2008); *Winter,* 555 U.S. 7, 129 S.Ct. 365, 172 L.Ed.2d 249; and *Nken v. Holder,* 556 U.S. 418, 129 S.Ct. 1749, 173 L.Ed.2d 550 (2009)—have eliminated this circuit's "serious questions" standard for the entry of a preliminary injunction, and that, in light of the district court's finding that CGMI failed to demonstrate its likelihood of success on the merits, the entry of a preliminary injunction in this case must be reversed. * * *

Although not stated explicitly in its briefs, we take VCG's position to be that the standard articulated by these three Supreme Court cases requires a preliminary injunction movant to demonstrate that it is more likely than not to succeed on its underlying claims, or in other words, that a movant must show a greater than fifty percent probability of success on the merits. Thus, according to VCG, a showing of serious questions that are a fair ground for litigation will not suffice. * * *

For the last five decades, this circuit has required a party seeking a preliminary injunction to show "(a) irreparable harm and (b) either (1) likelihood of success on the merits or (2) sufficiently serious questions going to the merits to make them a fair ground for litigation and a balance of hardships tipping decidedly toward the party requesting the preliminary relief." [Citations.] The "serious questions" standard permits a district court to grant a preliminary injunction in situations where it cannot determine with certainty that the moving party is more likely than not to prevail on the merits of the underlying claims, but where the costs outweigh the benefits of not granting the injunction. [Citation.] Because the moving party must not only show that there are "serious questions" going to the merits, but must additionally establish that "the balance of hardships tips *decidedly*" in its favor, [citation], its overall burden is no lighter than the one it bears under the "likelihood of success" standard.

If the Supreme Court had meant for *Munaf, Winter,* or *Nken* to abrogate the more flexible standard for a preliminary injunction, one would expect some reference to the considerable history of the flexible standards applied in this circuit, seven of our sister circuits, and in the Supreme Court itself. We have recognized this flexible standard since at least 1953, [citation], and our standard has survived earlier instances in which the Supreme Court described the merits prerequisite to a preliminary injunction as a "likelihood of success" without specifically addressing the content of such a "likelihood," [citation]. We have found no command from the Supreme Court that would foreclose the application of our established "serious questions" standard as a means of assessing a movant's likelihood of success on the merits. Our standard accommodates the needs of the district courts in confronting motions for preliminary injunctions in factual situations that vary widely in difficulty and complexity. Thus, we hold that our venerable standard for assessing a movant's probability of success on the merits remains valid and that the district court did not err in applying the "serious questions" standard to CGMI's motion. * * *

---

1. When the Supreme Court enters a field with a new case, as it did in *Winters, supra,* it takes the lower courts many years to work through the implications. Only occasionally will the Court take another case quickly to speed the process. The principal case is an example of the slow process of resolution of the meaning of a new Supreme Court case. The question of whether *Winters* has eliminated the alternative test will remain open in other circuits as each one works through the analysis.

2. Assuming that the principal case is correct that *Winters* is not inconsistent with the "serious question" approach of the alternative test in

the ordinary case, what about the use of the alternative test for a copyright case after *eBay Inc. v. MercExchange*, 547 U.S. 388, 126 S.Ct. 1837, 164 L.Ed.2d 641 (2006)., reprinted in Chapter 3? The Supreme Court in *eBay* articulated the tradition test for a *permanent* injunction in a copyright case, so the question is whether the same traditional test must be used for a *preliminary* injunction in a copyright case. The Second Circuit has held that the traditional test in *eBay* governs all copyright cases and the alternative test for a preliminary injunction does not apply in that circumstance. Salinger v. Colting, 607 F.3d 68 (2d Cir.2010).

B. PROCEDURAL REQUIREMENTS

Section Coverage:

Federal Rule of Civil Procedure 65 contains specific procedural provisions that have been interpreted strictly. Most notable are the differences in the time limitations and notice requirements for temporary restraining orders (TRO) and preliminary injunctions.

A TRO can be entered *ex parte,* but only upon a specific showing that immediate and irreparable harm will result before the opposing party could be notified and heard. The order can last only fourteen days, with a second fourteen-day extension for good cause. The preliminary injunction hearing is expedited on the calendar, and both sides must have a reasonable opportunity to present some evidence. A preliminary injunction then lasts until the full trial on the merits of the case.

Model Case:

Able is a professional athlete under contract with a team named the Reps in Washington, D.C. The contract between Able and the Reps provides, in addition to the usual contractual terms, that Able's services are exclusive to the Reps such that he may not play for any other professional team in that sport during the duration of the contract. The term of the contract is three years.

Although the contract with the Reps is still in effect, Able has received an irresistible offer from a team in nearby Baltimore. That team is part of a newly formed competitive league in the same sport. Able accepted the Baltimore offer and started practicing yesterday with the Baltimore team in anticipation of the opening of the new season today.

The Reps want to enjoin Able from violating the exclusivity of services provision of his contract. The first game of the season for the Baltimore team is only hours away. The Reps' season does not begin for a few more days. The new league is trying to capture publicity by having the first games before the old league starts its season.

The attorney for the Reps seeks a temporary restraining order to prevent Able from breaching the negative covenant in the contract. Able should be notified of the motion if possible. The Reps' theory of irreparable harm should focus on the immediate loss of fans to the nearby Baltimore franchise. The strength of that showing probably will determine the availability of the TRO.

If the court issues the TRO, it can last only a few days. As soon as possible the court must hold a hearing for the preliminary injunction. Since such an injunction would last until trial on the merits—probably after the season—the hearing would be crucial to both parties. Although it is not clear whether the *status quo* is best described as Able playing for the Reps or practicing with the Baltimore team, the last uncontested status was when Able was with the Reps. If the Reps can make a substantial showing of irreparable harm and the probable enforceability of the contract, the court may grant this preliminary injunction to enforce the exclusivity portion of the contract between Able and the Reps. A preliminary injunction is appealable whereas a TRO is not.

Sims v. Greene

160 F.2d 512 (3d Cir.1947).

■ BIGGS, CIRCUIT JUDGE.

On December 2, 1946, the plaintiff, David H. Sims, filed a complaint against the defendant, Sherman L. Greene, alleging that he, Sims, is a citizen of Pennsylvania and a bishop of the African Methodist Episcopal Church and that he was assigned by a General Conference of the AME Church held in 1944 to the First Episcopal District to serve as the presiding bishop of that district until the next General Conference to be held in 1948; that the defendant, another bishop of the same church, has appeared in the First Episcopal District and within the jurisdiction of the court below and has proclaimed that he is the presiding bishop of the First District and is attempting to function as such; that by reason of the foregoing the plaintiff's office and functions as presiding bishop and his salary and emoluments are threatened as is the administration of the church and its conferences in the district; and that irreparable injury will result to the church, to its property and to the plaintiff unless the defendant is enjoined from pursuing the course complained of. An affidavit supporting the allegations of the complaint was filed with it.

On December 2, 1946, the court below, *ex parte*, issued an order restraining the defendant from interfering with the plaintiff as the presiding bishop of the district. The restraint originally imposed was continued by order for an additional ten days, to expire on December 22, 1946. On December 20 the defendant consented to the restraint being extended until January 14, 1947 and the court made an order to such effect on December 20, 1946.

On December 24, 1946 the defendant filed his answer and with it a counterclaim containing prayers for affirmative relief. He * * * asserted that the plaintiff was no longer a bishop of the AME Church because he had been unfrocked by an extra session of the General Conference and by the Episcopal Committee meeting in Little Rock, Arkansas, about November 20, 1946; that he, the defendant, had been assigned by the extra session of the General Conference and by the Bishops' Council to the First Episcopal District as its presiding bishop; that by virtue of the foregoing he is the lawful presiding bishop of the district and his right to that office and its emoluments and his administration of the church and its property within the district are imperiled by the plaintiff's actions. The counterclaim ends with a prayer that the plaintiff be enjoined from interfering with the defendant.

On January 13, 1947 the court below extended the restraining order until January 24 and proceeded to a hearing on the question of whether or not a preliminary injunction should be granted. This hearing continued from January 13 to January 17, inclusive, and twelve hundred pages of argument, colloquy and testimony were taken down and have been transcribed. On January 17, at the close of the day the defendant's counsel made a motion to dissolve the restraint. The court directed him to withhold his motion, stating that he would renew the order "in due time." * * *

On January 23, 1947, the defendant appealed to this court from the restraining order and moved for a stay of all proceedings in the District Court. We stayed the proceedings in the District Court and restrained the defendant from acting as the presiding bishop of the First Episcopal District pending the disposition of the appeal, setting February 13 as the day for argument.

* * * [The defendant contends] that the temporary restraining order, continued without the consent of the defendant after January 14, is in substance a temporary injunction issued illegally since no findings of fact and conclusions of law were made by the court below as required by Rule 52(a) of the Federal Rules of Civil Procedure, 28 U.S.C.A. following section 723c. * * *

We come * * * to questions respecting the nature and effect of the restraining order issued first upon December 2, 1946 and still in force. In extending the restraint the court below did not observe that provision of Rule 65(b) of the [Federal] Rules of Civil Procedure, 28 U.S.C.A. following section 723c, which states, "The reasons for the extension shall be entered of record." The court also disregarded the following provision of Rule 65(b), "In case a temporary restraining order is granted without notice, the motion for a preliminary injunction shall be set down for hearing at the earliest possible time * * *." It is settled that no temporary restraining order may be continued beyond twenty days unless the party against whom the order is directed consents that it may be extended for a longer period. *See* Section 381 or 28 U.S.C.A. and Rule 65(b). The consent of the defendant in the instant case to the extension of the restraining order was not continued past January 14, 1947. It is also the law that the relief to be afforded by Section 129 of the Judicial Code, 28 U.S.C.A. § 227, providing for appeals from injunctions, is not limited by the terminology employed by the trial court. The relief to be afforded by the section looks to the substantial effect of the order made. [Citation.]

When a restraining order, purporting to be "temporary" is continued for a substantial length of time past the period prescribed by Section 381 of 28 U.S.C.A. without the consent of the party against which it issued and without the safeguards prescribed by Rule 65(b) it ceases to be a "temporary restraining order" within the purview of that section and becomes a preliminary injunction which cannot be maintained unless the court issuing it sets out the findings of fact and the conclusions of law which constitute the grounds for its action as required by Rule 52(a).

In our opinion the restraining order now in effect in the District Court must be treated as a temporary injunction, issued without the consent of the defendant, in the face of his motion to dissolve it, and contrary to the provisions of Rule 52(a). It is clear that an appeal lies from a temporary injunction. * * *

In view of the fact that the defendant has filed an answer and a counterclaim we can perceive no reason why the court below should not, as it itself suggested, proceed to final hearing. A prompt disposition of the cause is necessary in the public interest. The witnesses should not be permitted to give extended irrelevant testimony. Counsel should be restricted to relevant examination and cross-examination. The proceedings in the court below, as the record shows, were repeatedly interrupted by demonstrations by the spectators and the learned trial judge took no strong step to prevent such demonstrations. The dignity and decorum of a court of the United States must be maintained at all times.

The court below should sit from day to day and without unnecessary interruptions until the hearing is concluded.

The motion to dismiss the appeal will be denied. The order appealed from will be reversed. The stay order entered by this court on January 31, 1947 will be vacated. The court below will be directed to sit from day to day until the hearing is concluded.

---

1. The first two parts of the Federal Rule of Civil Procedure 65 concern preliminary injunctions and temporary restraining orders, as reprinted below. Notice that this modern version of FRCP 65(b) has a 14–day expiration and renewal time rather than the 10–day rule present at the time of the principal case. If the 14–day period had been in effect at the time the principal case was tried, would that have changed the result?

Federal Rule of Civil Procedure 65(a) and (b)

(a) Preliminary Injunction.

(1) *Notice.* The court may issue a preliminary injunction only on notice to the adverse party.

(2) *Consolidating the Hearing with the Trial on the Merits.* Before or after beginning a hearing on a motion for a preliminary injunction, the court may advance the trial on the merits and consolidate it with

the hearing. Even when consolidation is not ordered, evidence that is received on the motion and that would be admissible at trial becomes part of the trial record and need not be repeated at trial. But the court must preserve any party's right to a jury trial.

(b) Temporary Restraining Order.

(1) *Issuing Without Notice.* The court may issue a temporary restraining order without written or oral notice to the adverse party or its attorney only if:

(A) specific facts in an affidavit or a verified complaint clearly show that immediate and irreparable injury, loss, or damage will result to the movant before the adverse party can be heard in opposition; and

(B) the movant's attorney certifies in writing any efforts made to give notice and the reasons why it should not be required.

(2) *Contents; Expiration.* Every temporary restraining order issued without notice must state the date and hour it was issued; describe the injury and state why it is irreparable; state why the order was issued without notice; and be promptly filed in the clerk's office and entered in the record. The order expires at the time after entry—not to exceed 14 days—that the court sets, unless before that time the court, for good cause, extends it for a like period or the adverse party consents to a longer extension. The reasons for an extension must be entered in the record.

(3) *Expediting the Preliminary–Injunction Hearing.* If the order is issued without notice, the motion for a preliminary injunction must be set for hearing at the earliest possible time, taking precedence over all other matters except hearings on older matters of the same character. At the hearing, the party who obtained the order must proceed with the motion; if the party does not, the court must dissolve the order.

(4) *Motion to Dissolve.* On 2 days' notice to the party who obtained the order without notice—or on shorter notice set by the court—the adverse party may appear and move to dissolve or modify the order. The court must then hear and decide the motion as promptly as justice requires.

2. The remainder of Federal Rule of Civil Procedure 65 addresses issues covered in future sections. Section (c) concerns the injunction bond, covered in section C of this chapter. Section (d) specifies who is bound by an injunction, covered in the next chapter.

PROBLEM: FENDING OFF THE FENCE

Your office receives a call from a longstanding client, Thompson, who is distressed that a neighbor is about to erect a fence on the wrong side of the property line. The neighbor was "sure" about the property line and therefore did not have the land surveyed. Thompson believes the neighbor is wrong and is about to erect the fence in Thompson's yard.

This error is particularly disturbing because near the disputed line Thompson has a tree that is one hundred years old and in poor health. A specialist has been giving the tree an expensive nursing treatment. Thompson fears that digging for the fence posts would disturb the roots and jeopardize the life of the tree. The tree is far enough away from the real property line, Thompson believes, that a properly located fence would pose no danger.

The fencing crew arrived this morning and was about to begin work near the tree when your client spotted the activity. An immediate conference with the neighbor revealed the dispute about the boundary. The neighbor said that the crew has been hired to work for two days, and the contract requires that they be paid unless delayed by the weather. The neighbor agreed to start the fence at the other end of the property if Thompson wants to get a surveyor today, but the crew will put the fence along the tree side tomorrow. The neighbor is positive about the property line and insists that a surveyor is unnecessary.

Thompson cannot get a surveyor to come until next week. Is there any legal action that can be taken today?

Fengler v. Numismatic Americana, Inc.

832 F.2d 745 (2d Cir.1987).

■ ALTIMARI, CIRCUIT JUDGE:

Stuart Bochner and his law firm, Bochner and Berg ("Bochner"), appeal from an order of the United States District Court for the Southern District of New York, Kevin Thomas Duffy, Judge, which preliminarily enjoined all defendants from engaging in any business transactions with respect to Stationers Supply Co., Inc. ("Stationers"). Because this preliminary injunction was issued without holding an evidentiary hearing and was not supported by any findings of fact, we vacate the injunction and remand to the district court with instructions to hold an evidentiary hearing.

In December 1986, appellee Iris Fengler ("Fengler") contracted to sell 60% of the stock in her financially-troubled office supply company, Stationers, to defendant Numismatic Americana, Inc. ("Numismatic"). Defendant John Cameron ("Cameron") was the president of Numismatic. Preliminary negotiations for the sale had been conducted by defendant Jerry Simon ("Simon"), who was the Senior Acquisitions Director of U.S. Rare Gold Eagles, Inc.

According to Fengler, Simon orally promised that his company would invest $50,000 into Stationers; would pay Fengler a salary of $1,100 weekly; would satisfy all of Stationers' outstanding checks issued to creditors; and would conduct an audit of Stationers so that the business could be restored to financial health.

The contract which was ultimately signed provided for the audit, for the investment of $50,000 into Stationers, and for the payment of a $1,100 weekly salary to Fengler. The contract was executed on December 24, 1986. Both Simon and Cameron were present, and were represented by counsel. Fengler was unrepresented by counsel. She had not retained her own counsel, and she alleges that Simon assured her that his own attorney, Bochner, would adequately represent the interests of all parties to the transaction. Fengler further alleges that Bochner informed her it would be very difficult to obtain her own counsel on the day before Christmas.

Fengler contends that within two weeks after the contract was executed, defendants removed all the inventory, business records and furnishings of Stationers, leaving Fengler with only a desk, chair, and telephone. Defendants also allegedly converted all the cash assets of Stationers to their personal use, and refused to satisfy the claims of Stationers' creditors. Fengler herself received only one weekly salary check, and needless to say, was unable to get defendants to return her phone calls.

In February 1987, Fengler commenced the present action, asserting claims under the federal securities laws, RICO, and common-law fraud, and requesting both monetary and injunctive relief. Defendants Simon and Cameron disappeared to parts unknown before they could be served with process. The two corporate defendants were served, but did not appear and are currently in default. Bochner and Bochner and Berg were also properly served and are the only defendants appealing the district court's grant of injunctive relief.

Fengler alleged in her complaint that Bochner breached his duty of care to her by failing to advise her to obtain independent counsel. She claimed that "Bochner and Bochner and Berg participated in such a plan or scheme with the other defendants to knowingly and maliciously engage in acts of fraud and deceit against plaintiffs...." Fengler did not claim, however, that Bochner actively participated in the looting of the corporate assets.

On February 11, Judge Robert Ward issued an *ex parte* temporary restraining order against defendants, enjoining them from engaging in any business dealings on behalf of Stationers. The return date on plaintiffs' motion for preliminary injunction was set for February 17, 1987. On that date, counsel for Fengler and Bochner appeared to argue the motion before Judge Duffy; these proceedings were not transcribed. Prior to the arguments, Bochner had not submitted any papers to the court. Immediately following argument, however, Bochner submitted an affidavit which stated that his firm no longer represented the corporate defendants, and that neither he nor his firm was in a position to engage in any acts on behalf of Stationers. The affidavit concluded:

> [T]here is no reason to issue the preliminary injunction as against me or my law firm.... *Absent an evidentiary hearing,* the court should not do an unnecessary act, which can have no effect, might yet have damaging implications and might be used by plaintiff at a later date to

cast a light on these proceedings that were (sic) never intended (emphasis added).

The district court did not hold the requested evidentiary hearing. Instead, the court issued a preliminary injunction, unsupported by any factual findings, which restrained all defendants from engaging in the following activities with respect to Stationers: "Checking transactions, solicitation of customers, collection of outstanding corporate obligations, payment of corporate accounts receivable, sale or purchase of inventory, and sale and purchase of any securities."

Bochner contends that the preliminary injunction must be vacated because of the district court's failure to hold an evidentiary hearing, as well as its failure to make findings of fact. We agree with appellants on both counts.

On a motion for preliminary injunction, where "essential facts are in dispute, there must be a hearing . . . and appropriate findings of fact must be made." Visual Sciences, Inc. v. Integrated Communications, Inc., 660 F.2d 56, 58 (2d Cir.1981) (Citing Forts v. Ward, 566 F.2d 849 (2d Cir. 1977)).

In the present case, "essential facts" were unquestionably in dispute with respect to Bochner. Although Fengler alleged that Bochner was a participant in the scheme to defraud her, Bochner denied any knowledge of his codefendants' intentions. He contended, rather, that his firm's relationship with Numismatic and the other codefendants consisted solely of drafting the contract of sale and attending the closing. He claimed, moreover, that his firm no longer represented the codefendants and was not in a position to exercise any control over the assets of Stationers. Because the material facts were clearly in dispute, the district court erred by not holding an evidentiary hearing before granting the injunction.

Fengler argues that Bochner waived any right to an evidentiary hearing by failing to demand one during argument of the motion. We will never know, of course, if Bochner in fact failed to request a hearing at that time, since there is no transcript of the oral argument. Nevertheless, Bochner submitted an affidavit on the day of argument, in which he expressly urged the court not to order injunctive relief without holding a hearing.

A party against whom an injunction is sought will be found to have waived its right to a hearing only where that party was demonstrably "content to rest" on affidavits submitted to the court. [Citations.]

In this case, Bochner did not opt to wage a battle of affidavits. Indeed, the first (and only) affidavit which Bochner submitted to the court contained an explicit request for a hearing. Bochner did not, therefore, waive his right to an evidentiary hearing.

Finally, the district court's failure to make findings of fact is also reversible error. Fed.R.Civ.P. 52(a) provides that "in granting or refusing interlocutory injunctions the court *shall* . . . set forth the findings of fact and conclusions of law which constitute the grounds of its action" (emphasis added).

In a recent decision this court stated emphatically that "Rule 52(a)'s requirement that the trial court find facts specifically and state its conclusions of law is mandatory and cannot be waived." * * *

The preliminary injunction granted by the district court is hereby vacated. The case is remanded with instructions that the district court hold an evidentiary hearing regarding the propriety of injunctive relief. The district court's ultimate decision following the outcome of this hearing must be supported by adequate findings of fact, in compliance with Fed. R.Civ.P. 52(a).

---

1. Federal Rule of Civil Procedure Rule 52(a) requires the court, in "an action tried on the facts without a jury or with an advisory jury," to make findings of fact "specially" and to state "separately" its conclusions of law. Further: "The findings and conclusions may be stated on the record after the close of the evidence or may appear in an opinion or a memorandum of decision filed by the court."

2. Compare the principal case with the second appeal in the case of the defrocked bishop, *Sims v. Greene, supra.* After the case was remanded to the district court, the trial judge entered a preliminary injunction that was substantially identical to the previously invalidated temporary restraining order. On appeal from that order the Court of Appeals again set aside the new order as an insufficient preliminary injunction. Sims v. Greene, 161 F.2d 87 (3d Cir.1947). The deficiency this time was with the hearing required under Rule 65(b) for a preliminary injunction. The court observed:

> * * * The preliminary injunction was issued on the identical record which was before this court on the prior appeal. The allegations of the pleadings and affidavits filed in the cause are conflicting. Such conflicts must be resolved by oral testimony since only by hearing the witnesses and observing their demeanor on the stand can the trier of fact determine the veracity of the allegations made by the respective parties. If witnesses are not heard the trial court will be left in the position of preferring one piece of paper to another. Greene was given no opportunity to present oral testimony on his behalf except for one witness whose testimony was immaterial to any issue presented by the pleading. * * * The truth of the matter is that Greene was given no fair opportunity to present testimony prior to the issuance of the preliminary injunction.
>
> The issuance of a preliminary injunction under such circumstances is contrary not only to the Rules of Civil Procedure but also to the spirit which imbues our judicial tribunals prohibiting decision without hearing. Rule 65(a) provides that no preliminary injunction shall be

issued without notice to the adverse party. Notice implies an opportunity to be heard. Hearing requires trial of an issue or issues of fact. Trial of an issue of fact necessitates opportunity to present evidence and not by only one side to the controversy. * * *

Carroll v. President and Com'rs of Princess Anne

393 U.S. 175, 89 S.Ct. 347, 21 L.Ed.2d 325 (1968).

■ MR. JUSTICE FORTAS delivered the opinion of the Court.

Petitioners are identified with a "white supremacist" organization called the National States Rights Party. They held a public assembly or rally near the courthouse steps in the town of Princess Anne, the county seat of Somerset County, Maryland, in the evening of August 6, 1966. The authorities did not attempt to interfere with the rally. Because of the tense atmosphere which developed as the meeting progressed, about 60 state policemen were brought in, including some from a nearby county. They were held in readiness, but for tactical reasons only a few were in evidence at the scene of the rally.

Petitioners' speeches, amplified by a public address system so that they could be heard for several blocks, were aggressively and militantly racist. Their target was primarily Negroes and, secondarily, Jews. It is sufficient to observe with the court below, that the speakers engaged in deliberately derogatory, insulting, and threatening language, scarcely disguised by protestations of peaceful purposes; and that listeners might well have construed their words as both a provocation to the Negroes in the crowd and an incitement to the whites. The rally continued for something more than an hour, concluding at about 8:25 p.m. The crowd listening to the speeches increased from about 50 at the beginning to about 150, of whom 25% were Negroes.

In the course of the proceedings it was announced that the rally would be resumed the following night, August 7.

On that day, the respondents, officials of Princess Anne and of Somerset County, applied for and obtained a restraining order from the Circuit Court for Somerset County. The proceedings were *ex parte,* no notice being given to petitioners and, so far as appears, no effort being made informally to communicate with them, although this is expressly contemplated under Maryland procedure. The order restrained petitioners for 10 days from holding rallies or meetings in the county "which will tend to disturb and endanger the citizens of the County." As a result, the rally scheduled for August 7 was not held. * * *

* * * We turn to the constitutional problems raised by the 10-day injunctive order.

* * *

We need not decide the thorny problem of whether, on the facts of this case, an injunction against the announced rally could be justified. The 10–

day order here must be set aside because of a basic infirmity in the procedure by which it was obtained. It was issued *ex parte,* without notice to petitioners and without any effort, however informal, to invite or permit their participation in the proceedings. There is a place in our jurisprudence for *ex parte* issuance, without notice, of temporary restraining orders of short duration; but there is no place within the area of basic freedoms guaranteed by the First Amendment for such orders where no showing is made that it is impossible to serve or to notify the opposing parties and to give them an opportunity to participate.

* * *

In the present case, the record discloses no reason why petitioners were not notified of the application for injunction. They were apparently present in Princess Anne. They had held a rally there on the night preceding the application for an issuance of the injunction. They were scheduled to have another rally on the very evening of the day when the injunction was issued. And some of them were actually served with the writ of injunction at 6:10 that evening. In these circumstances, there is no justification for the *ex parte* character of the proceedings in the sensitive area of First Amendment rights.

The value of a judicial proceeding, as against self-help by the police, is substantially diluted where the process is *ex parte,* because the Court does not have available the fundamental instrument for judicial judgment: an adversary proceeding in which both parties may participate. The facts in any case involving a public demonstration are difficult to ascertain and even more difficult to evaluate. Judgment as to whether the facts justify the use of the drastic power of injunction necessarily turns on subtle and controversial considerations and upon a delicate assessment of the particular situation in light of legal standards which are inescapably imprecise. In the absence of evidence and argument offered by both sides and of their participation in the formulation of value judgments, there is insufficient assurance of the balanced analysis and careful conclusions which are essential in the area of First Amendment adjudication.

The same is true of the fashioning of the order. An order issued in the area of First Amendment rights must be couched in the narrowest terms that will accomplish the pin-pointed objective permitted by constitutional mandate and the essential needs of the public order. * * * In other words, the order must be tailored as precisely as possible to the exact needs of the case. The participation of both sides is necessary for this purpose. Certainly, the failure to invite participation of the party seeking to exercise First Amendment rights reduces the possibility of a narrowly drawn order, and substantially imperils the protection which the Amendment seeks to assure.

* * *

We need not here decide that it is impossible for circumstances to arise in which the issuance of an *ex parte* restraining order for a minimum period could be justified because of the unavailability of the adverse parties or their counsel, or perhaps for other reasons. In the present case, it is clear that the failure to give notice, formal or informal, and to provide an opportunity for an adversary proceeding before the holding of the rally was restrained, is incompatible with the First Amendment. Because we reverse the judgment below on this basis, we need not and do not decide whether the facts in this case provided a constitutionally permissible basis for temporarily enjoining the holding of the August 7 rally.

Reversed.

C. INJUNCTION BONDS AND APPEALS

Section Coverage:

Federal Rule of Civil Procedure 65(c) provides for security to be provided by the applicant before a court issues a restraining order or preliminary injunction. The amount of a bond is in the discretion of the court, but the enjoined party has an opportunity to request an increase in the bond. Since a plaintiff may obtain interlocutory relief based upon a showing of probabilities, the bond serves an important role in ensuring fairness to the enjoined party and to check the zeal of the movant.

The bond assures that the defendant will be compensated for any losses occasioned by the TRO or preliminary injunction in the event that the plaintiff does not ultimately prevail in the underlying case. It functions as an exception to the general rule that litigation losses and expenses are borne by the parties themselves.

The bond requirement indirectly preserves the dignity of the court. Judges dislike acting in haste, as they must for interlocutory orders, because of the greater danger of injustice. Through the bond requirement a plaintiff guarantees to compensate for losses caused by that hasty decision.

Compensable losses include measurable harms caused specifically by the wrongful order but not including distress and humiliation. Recovery is usually limited to the amount of the bond; "open bonds" do not limit recovery. The bond provides a convenient repository of funds against which the wrongfully enjoined party can collect actual damages. Thus, the enjoined party does not have to run the risk of nonrecovery if the plaintiff is judgment proof.

This section also concerns the standard on appeal for stays of injunctions and for grants of preliminary injunctions denied by the trial court. The standard for such relief at the circuit level in federal court is higher than the standard at the trial level, but the exact level is not free from doubt.

Model Case:

The A–1 Sales Corp. employs many sales representatives to market its product. The employment contract contains an anti-competition clause that prohibits a former employee from selling a similar product in the same geographical area for a certain period of time.

B.J. Babb is a former A–1 sales representative who promptly took employment with a nearby competitor. A–1 seeks a preliminary injunction to prohibit Babb from working for the competitor. A–1 argues that it will be irreparably harmed without the injunction because customers will follow Babb to the competitor and, even if Babb is eventually enjoined from competition, the customers may not return to A–1.

If the court grants the preliminary injunction, A–1 should post a bond to assure a source of payment to Babb if A–1 loses on the merits of the case. If A–1 is a substantial corporation in financially sound condition, the bond may be waived. If the court ultimately holds the anti-competition clause is not enforceable, Babb can recover under the bond for lost income during the period of the injunction.

Federal Rule of Civil Procedure 65(c)

(c) Security. The court may issue a preliminary injunction or a temporary restraining order only if the movant gives security in an amount that the court considers proper to pay the costs and damages sustained by any party found to have been wrongfully enjoined or restrained. The United States, its officers, and its agencies are not required to give security.

Coyne–Delany Co. v. Capital Development Board

717 F.2d 385 (7th Cir.1983).

■ Posner, Circuit Judge. * * *

[The State of Illinois Capital Development Board (Board) contracted to replace plumbing fixtures in one of the state prisons. A portion of the contract which involved valves was subcontracted to the Coyne–Delany Company. The valves installed in the first phase of the project malfunctioned and replacement valves also proved unsatisfactory. The Board decided to solicit bids from other contractors to complete the project.]

Bids were received, but on May 7, 1979, two days before they were to be opened, Coyne–Delany sued the Board under section 1 of the Civil Rights Act of 1871, 42 U.S.C. § 1983, and on May 8 it obtained a temporary restraining order against the Board's opening the bids. The state asked that Coyne–Delany be ordered to post a $50,000 bond, pointing out that the temporary restraining order was preventing it from proceeding with the entire project and that indefinite delay could be extremely costly. But Judge Perry, the emergency motions judge, required a bond of only $5,000, in the belief that the temporary restraining order would be in effect for only a week until Judge Bua could hear the motion for a preliminary injunction.

However, at the preliminary-injunction hearing Judge Bua issued the injunction but refused to increase the bond.

[The court issued the preliminary injunction upon determining that Coyne–Delany, under existing state law, was likely to prevail on its civil rights claim. Subsequently the state law precedent favoring the plaintiff was appealed to the state supreme court and reversed. Accordingly, the Court of Appeals reversed in this case because the law no longer allowed such claims against the Board. The delay from the preliminary injunction resulted in the Board awarding a replacement contract for a $56,000 higher amount than the original bid.] * * *

The Board then joined Hanover Insurance Company, the surety on the injunction bond, as an additional defendant in Coyne–Delany's civil rights suit, pursuant to Rule 65.1 of the Federal Rules of Civil Procedure, and moved the district court to award the Board damages of $56,000 for the wrongfully issued preliminary injunction and statutory costs (filing fees and the like, *see* 28 U.S.C. § 1920) of $523 which the Board had incurred in the district court. Judge Bua refused to award either costs or damages. His opinion states, "the Court must weigh the equitable factors of the case, including whether the case was filed in good faith or is frivolous. . . . [T]he parties have stipulated that the case was filed in good faith and without malice. Further, it is apparent that the case was not frivolous. The law as it existed at the time the case was filed clearly favored the plaintiffs. It would be unreasonable to require a party to anticipate a change in the law and would be unconscionable to label a suit filed in good faith as frivolous where there is such a subsequent change."

There is no dispute over the amount of costs claimed by the Board; and while Coyne–Delany has not conceded that the Board incurred damages of $56,000 as a result of the delay of the project and the district court made no finding with respect to those damages, they undoubtedly exceeded $5,000, the amount of the injunction bond. * * *

Although the district court has unquestioned power in an appropriate case not to award costs to the prevailing party and not to award damages on an injunction bond even though the grant of the injunction was reversed, the district court's opinion suggests that the court may have believed it had to deny both costs and damages because the lawsuit had not been brought in bad faith and was not frivolous. This would be the proper standard if the question were whether to award a prevailing defendant his attorney's fees. * * * In the absence of statute, an award of attorney's fees is proper only where the losing party has been guilty of bad faith, as by bringing a frivolous suit—frivolousness connoting not just a lack of merit but so great a lack as to suggest that the suit must have been brought to harass rather than to win. [Citations.]

The rule is different for costs. Rule 54(d) of the Federal Rules of Civil Procedure provides that "costs shall be allowed as of course to the prevailing party unless the court otherwise directs. . . ." This language creates a presumption in favor of awarding costs. * * *

The language of Rule 65(c), governing damages on an injunction bond, is only a little less clear than that of Rule 54(d): "No restraining order or preliminary injunction shall issue except upon the giving of security by the applicant, in such sum as the court deems proper, for the payment of such costs and damages as may be incurred or suffered by any party who is found to have been wrongfully enjoined or restrained." The court is not told in so many words to order the applicant to pay the wrongfully enjoined party's damages. But it is told to require a bond or equivalent security in order to ensure that the plaintiff will be able to pay all or at least some of the damages that the defendant incurs from the preliminary injunction if it turns out to have been wrongfully issued. The draftsmen must have intended that when such damages were incurred the plaintiff or his surety, pursuant to Rule 65.1's summary procedure, which despite its wording is applicable to the principal as well as the surety on the bond, would normally be required to pay the damages, at least up to the limit of the bond.

Yet some courts treat the district court's discretion to award or deny damages under an injunction bond as completely open-ended unless the plaintiff acted in bad faith in seeking the preliminary injunction. * * *

Most cases hold * * * that a prevailing defendant is entitled to damages on the injunction bond unless there is a good reason for not requiring the plaintiff to pay in the particular case. [Citations.] We agree with the majority approach. Not only is it implied by the text of Rule 65(c) but it makes the law more predictable and discourages the seeking of preliminary injunctions on flimsy (though not necessarily frivolous) grounds.

When rules prescribe a course of action as the norm but allow the district court to deviate from it, the court's discretion is more limited than it would be if the rules were nondirective. Rules 54(d) and 65(c) establish what Judge Friendly recently called "a principle of preference" guiding the exercise of the district judge's discretion. [Citation.] The judge must have a good reason for departing from such a principle in a particular case. It is not a sufficient reason for denying costs or damages on an injunction bond that the suit had as in this case been brought in good faith. That would be sufficient only if the presumption were against rather than in favor of awarding costs and damages on the bond to the prevailing party, as it would be if the issue were attorney's fees under the American rule, which in the absence of bad faith leaves each party to bear his own attorney's fees. The award of damages on the bond is not punitive but compensatory.

A good reason for not awarding such damages would be that the defendant had failed to mitigate damages. The district court made no reference to any such failure in this case and we can find no evidence that there was any; the Board's requesting and obtaining a 30–day extension of time for filing its appeal brief, the factor stressed by Coyne–Delany, did not create material or unreasonable delay. A good reason not for denying but for awarding damages in this case, unmentioned by the district court, was that the bond covered only a small fraction of the defendant's damages.

The Board asked for and should have been granted a much larger bond; and when the heavy damages that the Board had predicted in asking for the larger bond materialized, it had a strong equitable claim to recover its damages up to the limit of the bond. Nor could $5,000 be regarded as excessive because the plaintiff was a poor person. The plaintiff is not a poor person but a substantial corporation that will not be crushed by having to pay $5,523 in damages and costs. It is particularly difficult in the circumstances of this case to understand the judge's refusal to award *any* damages, or the trivial amount of costs, conceded to be reasonable in amount, asked by the defendant.

In deciding whether to withhold costs or injunction damages, not only is the district court to be guided by the implicit presumption in Rules 54(d) and 65(c) in favor of awarding them, but the ingredients of a proper decision are objective factors—such as the resources of the parties, the defendant's efforts or lack thereof to mitigate his damages, and the outcome of the underlying suit—accessible to the judgment of a reviewing court. * * *

Although the district court's decision cannot stand, both because it applies an incorrect standard and because it fails to consider and evaluate the full range of factors (which might in an appropriate case include, but is not exhausted by, the plaintiff's good faith) that would be relevant under the proper standard, we are not prepared to hold that the Board is entitled as a matter of law to its costs and to its injunction damages up to the limit of the bond. The district court did allude to one factor, besides mere absence of bad faith, that supported its ruling—the change in the applicable law after the preliminary injunction was issued. The law on which the court had relied in issuing the injunction was contained in an intermediate state appellate court decision and of course such decisions are reversed with some frequency. We do not believe that a change in the law is always a good ground for denying costs and injunction damages to a prevailing party, but it is a legitimate consideration, perhaps especially where the prevailing party is a state agency that benefited from a change in the law of its state. * * * In any event, a remand is necessary to allow Judge Bua to consider and weigh all the relevant factors identified in this opinion— bearing in mind the principle of preference that we have indicated should guide his equitable determination.

It remains to consider whether on remand the Board should be allowed to seek injunction damages above the limit of the bond. The surety cannot be required to pay more than the face amount of the bond, but it is a separate question whether the plaintiff can be. However, the Ninth Circuit has held in a scholarly opinion that the bond is the limit of the damages the defendant can obtain for a wrongful injunction, even from the plaintiff, provided the plaintiff was acting in good faith, which is not questioned here. Buddy Systems, Inc. v. Exer–Genie, Inc., 545 F.2d 1164, 1167–68 (9th Cir.1976). * * * Although there was a bond in the present case, it states unequivocally: "The obligation of this bond is limited to $5,000.00." * * *

Rightly or wrongly, American common law, state and federal, does not attempt to make the winner of a lawsuit whole by making the loser reimburse the winner's full legal expenses, even when the winner is the defendant, who unlike a prevailing plaintiff does not have the consolation of a damage recovery. In noninjunctive suits, except those brought (or defended) in bad faith, the winner can recover only his statutory costs, invariably but a small fraction of his expenses of suit. It would be incongruous if a prevailing defendant could obtain the full, and potentially the staggering, consequential damages caused by a preliminary injunction. The preliminary injunction in this case halted work on a major construction project for a year; it could easily have been two or three years, and the expenses imposed on the defendant not $56,000 but $560,000. * * * [I]f the plaintiff's damages are limited to the amount of the bond, at least he knows just what his exposure is when the bond is set by the district court. It is not unlimited. If the bond is too high he can drop the suit.

A defendant's inability to obtain damages in excess of the bond * * * can have unfortunate results, which are well illustrated by this case where the district court required too small a bond. But a defendant dissatisfied with the amount of bond set by the district court can, on appeal from the preliminary injunction, ask the court of appeals to increase the bond, which the defendant here did not do. * * *

Reversed and Remanded.

---

1. The rationale for the security requirement is to compensate defendants who have suffered loss from the issuance of a preliminary injunction. The First Circuit, noting that there is a presumption of recovery for losses in such cases, explains in *Global Naps, Inc. v. Verizon New England, Inc.*, 489 F.3d 13 (1st Cir. 2007).

> Since a preliminary injunction may be granted on a mere probability of success on the merits, generally the moving party must demonstrate confidence in his legal position by posting bond in an amount sufficient to protect his adversary from loss in the event that future proceedings prove that the injunction issued wrongfully. The bond, in effect, is the moving party's warranty that the law will uphold the issuance of the injunction. 489 F.3d at 21.

2. Neither Fed. R. Civ. P. 65(c) nor 65.1 specify what damages may be recovered by an improperly enjoined party in an action on a preliminary injunction bond. Even when the court allows recovery on the bond, damages are not awarded automatically; the wrongfully enjoined party must prove injury resulted from the issuance of the injunction. Attorney's fees, absent statutory authorization, are generally not recoverable in federal court in an action on the bond. *See* Fireman's Fund Ins. Co. v. S.E.K. Constr. Co., 436 F.2d 1345 (10th Cir.1971). In *Matek v. Murat*, 862 F.2d 720 (9th Cir.1988), the court noted that interest on the money held for the

duration of the injunction may be a recoverable item of damages, provided that the total damages did not exceed the amount of the surety bond.

3. Must a court require a party seeking injunctive relief to post a bond or can a court dispense with the bond requirement? The court in the principal case notes that Federal Rule of Civil Procedure 65(c) appears to require a bond. However, many courts have concluded that the trial court has discretion to dispense with the bond requirement in limited circumstances. *See, e.g.,* Doctor's Assoc., Inc. v. Stuart, 85 F.3d 975 (2d Cir.1996).

For example, a court may dispense with the bond requirement where requiring a bond would effectively deny access to judicial review. Thus, in *Van De Kamp v. Tahoe Regional Planning Agency,* 766 F.2d 1319 (9th Cir.1985), the Ninth Circuit upheld the trial court decision to dispense with the bond requirement in a challenge to a development plan for parts of the Lake Tahoe shoreline because the plaintiff, a non-profit public interest group, would be unable to post a substantial bond, and, hence, would be effectively denied an appeal.

A court also may dispense with the requirement of posting a preliminary injunction bond if the party seeking injunctive relief has sufficient assets to assure its ability to pay damages. In Monroe Division, Litton Business Sys. v. De Bari, 562 F.2d 30 (10th Cir.1977), for example, a large corporation obtained a preliminary injunction against a former employee and the court did not order the posting of security. When the defendant later sought to enforce liability on the wrongfully issued injunction, the plaintiff argued that no liability existed because there was no bond. The court disagreed and held that Fed. R. Civ. P. 65(c) creates a cause of action for damages suffered by a wrongfully enjoined party. The defendant, who had convinced the trial court to waive security because of its corporate solvency, could not later argue that there is no liability without a bond.

4. What effect does the trial court's failure to require the posting of a bond have on the underlying order granting a preliminary injunction? In *Coquina Oil Corp. v. Transwestern Pipeline Co.,* 825 F.2d 1461 (10th Cir.1987), the Tenth Circuit held that the trial court's failure to rule on the defendant's motion to set a bond rendered the underlying injunctive order unenforceable and deprived the appellate court of jurisdiction. The court recognized that the trial court may, in the exercise of its discretion, decline to require a bond. However, the court held that the trial court must at least give consideration to whether the circumstances justified dispensing with the bond requirement by ruling on the defendant's motion. The court concluded that the trial court's failure to do so deprived it of jurisdiction. The court also recognized that most courts would have assumed jurisdiction to review the merits of the injunction then remanded for consideration of the defendant's motion to set a bond.

5. If a defendant demands that a bond be set, must the judge accede to the demand? Most courts have interpreted the force of the language in Rule 65(c) to require the district court judge at least to make a decision on the propriety of the bond in the case and not to ignore the demand entirely. *See* Reinders Bros. v. Rain Bird Eastern Sales Corp., 627 F.2d 44 (7th

Cir.1980). *See also* System Operations, Inc. v. Scientific Games Dev. Corp., 555 F.2d 1131 (3d Cir.1977) (although the trial judge has substantial discretion in setting the amount of the bond, it is reversible error to refuse a bond unless there is no risk of monetary loss).

6.   For additional commentary on injunction bonds, *see* Dobbs, Should Security Be Required as a Pre–Condition to Provisional Injunctive Relief?, 52 N.C.L.Rev. 1091 (1974); Friendly, Indiscretion About Discretion, 31 Emory L.J. 747 (1982).

Cavel International, Inc. v. Madigan

500 F.3d 544 (7th Cir.2007).

■ Posner, Circuit Judge.

Cavel International [principal appellant] produces horsemeat for human consumption. The plant at which it slaughters the horses is in Illinois. Americans do not eat horsemeat, but it is considered a delicacy in Europe and Cavel exports its entire output. Its suit challenges the constitutionality of a recent amendment to the Illinois Horse Meat Act, 225 ILCS 635/1.5, that makes it unlawful for any person in the state to slaughter a horse for human consumption * * * [.] Cavel lost in the district court, has appealed, and, after unsuccessfully moving the district court for an injunction pending appeal, has asked us for such an injunction, emphasizing the disastrous consequences for its business if the decision of the district court stands.

An affidavit by the firm's general manager states that it is a virtual certainty that if the injunction is denied the result will be the "permanent closure" of its plant. * * * Should the judgment of the district court upholding the constitutionality of the new statutory amendment be reversed, Cavel could not obtain monetary relief from the defendants. They are state officials sued in their official capacities because the only relief sought against them is an injunction. They therefore are not subject to liability for damages; a suit against state officials in their official capacity is treated as a suit against the state itself.

Cavel has made a compelling case that it needs the injunction pending appeal to avert serious irreparable harm—the uncompensated death of its business. * * * The state * * * responds that the state will incur irreparable harm, too, if the injunction is granted, because a "slaughter cannot be undone." But the statute does not seem to be intended to protect horses. (The object of the statute is totally obscure.) For it is only when horsemeat is intended for human consumption—the niche market that Cavel serves (less that 1 percent of its output is sold for other consumption)—that a horse cannot be killed for its meat. Were Cavel or a successor able to find a market in pet-food companies, the slaughter of horses at its plant would continue without interference from the state. And, if not, all that will happen is that horses will be slaughtered elsewhere to meet the demands of the European gourmets.

The state argues that the injunction will diminish "the scope of democratic governance." That is a powerful reason for judicial self-restraint when a statute, state or federal, is sought to be invalidated by a court. A *rule* barring state statutes from going into effect until any challenges to their validity were litigated to completion would be offensive on that ground; it would amount to rewriting the effective date in all Illinois statutes. But at issue is a *stay,* based on a showing in a particular case that the harm to the challenger from denial of a stay would greatly exceed the harm to the state from its grant, that would delay the application of the statute to the challenger for a few months (the appeal in this case has been expedited and will be argued on August 16). Such a stay does not operate as a statutory revision or significantly impair democratic governance. It is a detail that because the statute in question is applicable to only a single entity, a stay of enforcement against that entity acts to postpone the effective date of the statute rather than just to postpone the statute's application to one entity subject to it. * * *

Even though denying the injunction pending appeal would do far more harm to Cavel than granting it would do to the state, we must consider whether the appeal has any merit. If an appeal has no merit at all, an injunction pending the appeal should of course be denied. But if the appeal has some though not necessarily great merit, then the showing of harm of the magnitude shown by Cavel in this case would justify the granting of an injunction pending appeal provided, as is also true in this case, that the defendant would not suffer substantial harm from the granting of the injunction. This is the "sliding scale" approach to decisions on motions for preliminary injunction that we have endorsed in previous cases, [citations]. It amounts simply to weighting harm to a party by the merit of his case.

In denying the motion for an injunction pending appeal, the district court did not apply this test or indeed any other. He said only that Cavel had failed to make a "strong showing" that the horsemeat amendment is unconstitutional. He ignored the balance of harms. Cavel's failure to make a strong showing is certainly relevant to the granting of relief, but it is not decisive. The judge did not exercise the required discretion in determining whether to grant the injunction, and so his decision is not entitled to the deference to which discretionary rulings are entitled. Nor is his ruling that Cavel failed to make a strong showing of likelihood to prevail entitled to deference. It was a legal ruling the appellate review of which is plenary. [Citation.].

There is a difference between asking a district court for a preliminary injunction and asking a court of appeals for a stay of, or other relief from, the district court's ruling. But the sliding-scale approach is also applied in such a case. * * *

Cavel, it is true, is not seeking a stay; it is seeking to enjoin the enforcement of the horsemeat statute against it pending appeal. But Rule 8(a)(1)(C), (2), of the appellate rules explicitly authorizes the court of appeals to grant an injunction pending appeal and does not suggest that the standard is different from that applicable to a motion to stay the district court's judgment. We are mindful that Chief Justice Rehnquist, in a chambers opinion (and thus speaking only for himself and not for any of the other Justices), *Brown v. Gilmore,* 533 U.S. 1301 (2001), held that the authority to grant such an injunction is conferred not by Rule 8 but by the All Writs Act, 28 U.S.C. § 1651. Traditionally of course the applicant for relief under the Act must show an incontrovertible right to relief, and not merely some likelihood of prevailing. The Chief Justice required the same high showing by an applicant for an injunction pending appeal. As the 1967 Committee Note to Rule 8 points out, however, the Supreme Court had held that the power was an inherent judicial power; and so it doesn't have to be grounded in the All Writs Act.

The approach proposed in *Brown* has not caught on. * * * In *Purcell v. Gonzalez,* 127 S.Ct. 5 (2006) (per curiam), the Supreme Court vacated an injunction against a state statute pending appeal without suggesting that any special standard applied to such injunctions and without citing *Brown v. Gilmore.* * * *

The sliding scale justifies the injunction sought by Cavel. The argument for the invalidity of the horsemeat statute is not negligible. A state can without violating the commerce clause in Article I of the U.S. Constitution (which has been interpreted to limit the power of states to regulate foreign and interstate commerce even in the absence of applicable federal legislation) forbid the importation into the state of dangerous or noxious goods. E.g., *Maine v. Taylor,* 477 U.S. 131, 151–52 (1986). But this case involves a limitation on exports, because Cavel has no domestic market; and the only ground that Illinois advances for the horsemeat amendment is "public morality." The state has a recognized interest in the humane treatment of animals within its borders, and we can assume that this interest embraces the life of the animals and not just a concern that they not be killed gratuitously or in a painful manner. But as we noted earlier, the Illinois statute does not forbid the killing of horses, but only the killing of them for human consumption of their meat. If Cavel could (as apparently it cannot) develop a market for its horsemeat as pet food, there would be no violation of the statute. So it is possible that the burden that the statute places on the foreign commerce of the United States is not offset by a legitimate state interest, in which event the statute is unconstitutional. * * *

We do not suggest that Cavel has a winning case or even a good case [citation], but only that it has a good enough case on the merits for the balance of harms to entitle it to an injunction pending an expedited appeal that will enable the merits to be fully briefed and argued. It is important to note in this regard that the sliding-scale approach that governs Cavel's request for an injunction pending appeal does not require a "strong showing" that the applicant will win his appeal. The Supreme Court was precise in stating in *Hilton v. Braunskill, supra,* 481 U.S. at 776, that among "the factors regulating the issuance of a stay are ... whether the stay applicant has made a strong showing that he is likely to succeed on the merits." Certainly that is one of the factors to be considered, but it has to be balanced against the harms to the parties of granting or denying the injunction.

■ EASTERBROOK, CHIEF JUDGE, dissenting.

My colleagues assume that, when deciding whether to issue an injunction pending appeal, both the trial and appellate courts should use the same sliding scale that a district judge uses when deciding the case as an initial matter. This is a mistake. Once a plaintiff has litigated and lost, a higher standard is required for an injunction pending appeal.

That's one conclusion of *Hilton v. Braunskill*, 481 U.S. 770, 776 (1987). *Hilton* holds that a stay of a district court's order pending appeal requires a "strong showing" that the appellant is likely to prevail. * * *

So I ask (as my colleagues do not) whether plaintiff has made out a "strong showing" that this court is likely to reverse on the merits. It has not done so. * * * [Illinois] does not discriminate against foreign (or interstate) commerce. No one in Illinois may slaughter a horse for human consumption, no matter where the meat will be eaten. 225 ILCS 635/1.5(a). That no one in Illinois *wants* to eat horse flesh means that all of Cavel's product is exported, but this does not convert a law regulating horse slaughter (an intra-state activity) into one that discriminates against commerce.

* * *

Although a "strong showing" on the merits is required for any injunction pending appeal, insisting on a significant likelihood of success is especially apt when the subject is enforcement of a statute. An injunction pending appeal does not permanently frustrate attainment of the state's goal. It does, however, permanently discard the statute's effective date. * * *

Almost all laws cause injury; very few statutes are Pareto-superior (meaning that no one loses in the process, and at least some people gain). When a rule benefits some persons without injuring others, there is no need for legislation; the people involved will reach the accommodation on their own. Laws that cause loss to some persons (Cavel, for example) create transition effects. How these should be accommodated is itself a question for democratic choice. * * *

No state of which I am aware-and no federal law or serious student of the subject-has advocated the rule: "Laws that impose losses large enough to prompt people to hire lawyers take effect only at the conclusion of federal judicial review." Such a rule not only denies states part of their legislative power but also leads to strategic behavior: people hire lawyers and file suits not because they expect to win, but just because they can benefit from delay. That's a fair characterization of this suit. Just as the state won't compensate Cavel for losses in the interim if Cavel wins in the end, Cavel does not propose to compensate Illinois for any injury caused by delayed effectiveness of the statute. The majority does not require Cavel to post an injunction bond. Requiring an applicant to back its position with a promise to pay would curtail strategic claims.

Federal courts should allow states to select and enforce effective dates for their statutes. Equitable relief is appropriate only when the plaintiff shows a substantial likelihood of winning. Cavel has not met this standard and is not entitled to an injunction pending appeal.

---

1. After the expedited appeal, the same panel of judges on the Seventh Circuit affirmed the district court in Cavel Intern., Inc. v. Madigan, 500 F.3d 551 (7th Cir. 2007). The United States Supreme Court denied *certiorari*, 554 U.S. 902, 128 S.Ct. 2950, 171 L.Ed.2d 863 (2008).

Does this result necessarily mean that the Court of Appeals should not have issued the stay? Was Judge Easterbrook correct? Or is the issue unchanged, even with 20–20 hindsight?

2. The principal case focuses on the propriety of awarding a stay pending appeal. A stay differs slightly from the other interlocutory orders discussed in this chapter. A stay takes effect only after the trial court has reached a determination on the merits and prevents the prevailing party from enforcing the trial court's order. The majority and the dissent in the principal case dispute whether a movant must make a stronger showing of success on the merits to obtain a stay than a preliminary injunction. Should a court require a stronger showing on the merits to grant a stay?

3. The stay issued in the principal case will prevent the State from enforcing a validly enacted statute until the conclusion of the plaintiffs' appeal. As the dissent notes, this will have the effect of delaying the effective date provided in the statute and by state constitution. The dissent argued that this was an inappropriate interference with the state's legislative process and was likely to lead to strategic maneuvering. Every statute poses burdens on some individuals or entities such as the plaintiffs in this case. Delaying the effectiveness of the statute allows those individuals an opportunity to position themselves to better absorb the burdens and costs of the new law. However, delay does so at a cost to the benefits to be gained by the statute. Thus, the effective date is part of the legislatively struck balance between the costs and benefits of the law. If a party can obtain an interlocutory order delaying the effectiveness of a statute based on a lesser showing of a likelihood of success, a party may be more likely to bring weak claims or seek stays pending appeal of weak claims. How likely are parties to engage in this type of strategic behavior? Do other effective devices exists for policing dilatory tactics and frivolous claims?

4. A federal court maintains jurisdiction over interlocutory appeals pursuant to 28 U.S.C. § 1292(a)(1). A related issue involves the propriety of issuing an anti-suit injunction to restrain parties subject to the court's jurisdiction from proceeding with an action in the courts of a foreign country. In such instances, the court must examine issues of international

comity, and will enjoin the foreign litigation only when it would: (1) frustrate a policy of the forum issuing the decree; (2) be vexatious or oppressive; (3) threaten the issuing court's *in rem* or *quasi in rem* jurisdiction; or (4) where the proceedings prejudice other equitable considerations. The initial step in applying such equitable principles is to ensure that the identity of the parties and the issues are the same. The court will exercise considerable restraint in issuing an anti-suit injunction. *See* E. & J. Gallo Winery v. Andina Licores S.A., 446 F.3d 984, 990–91 (9th Cir.2006) (anti-suit injunction issued because enforcing forum selection clause would frustrate policy of United States courts, and parallel proceedings in Ecuador were potentially vexatious and oppressive).

CHAPTER 7

CONTEMPT

[handwritten annotations: CIVIL — Coercive — Jail, equivalents / Compensatory; CRIM — Direct / Indirect —]

Contempt is the method by which courts enforce equitable orders. The maxim "equity acts in personam" refers to the nature of an equitable decree as a personal directive. When a defendant fails to comply with an order, the disobedience is punishable as contempt. The defendant must have disobeyed a specifically detailed, unequivocal judicial command and the defendant must have had the ability to obey the order. Thus, a defendant who lacks the financial resources or the ability to earn money to pay child support cannot be jailed for disobeying the support decree.

Contempt proceedings may be characterized as either civil or criminal depending principally on their function. A civil contempt order is analogous to a civil tort claim. It is instituted by a private party, as part of an underlying action, to recover damages occasioned by the disobedience of the equitable order or to coerce the opposing party into compliance with the order. In contrast, the criminal contempt proceeding is like any criminal action brought by the government to punish errant behavior. Its purpose is to vindicate the integrity of the court which was offended by the defendant's contumacious conduct.

Another significant difference between the types of contempt orders is that civil contempt will fall if the underlying order is vacated, whereas a criminal contempt decree will stand even if the order was erroneously issued. Significant differences also appear in the nature and extent of the procedural safeguards given to the defendant, including rights to jury trial, right to counsel, and the burden of proof. The process and principles involved in that characterization are explored in the following materials.

A. CRIMINAL CONTEMPT

Section Coverage:

A criminal contempt proceeding is brought by a state or federal prosecutor to vindicate society's interest in the obedience of lawful orders. A defendant who is capable of complying with an order but who nonetheless fails to obey it can be punished criminally for that failure. The function of criminal contempt is to uphold the dignity of the court.

Like all criminal cases, a defendant in a criminal contempt proceeding is entitled to the full panoply of Constitutional safeguards. The same standards and requirements of criminal procedure are applicable.

If a defendant is found guilty of criminal contempt, the court can draw upon the usual punishments for criminal behavior: imprisonment or fine. Any fine paid by the defendant goes to the public coffers; courts give plaintiffs compensation only under civil contempt.

Criminal contempt may be further classified as direct or indirect depending upon where the defendant's offensive conduct takes place. If the defendant shows disrespect in the presence of the court, in most cases the judge may punish the conduct summarily without according all the traditional Constitutional protections, such as the right to counsel. The purpose of granting judges such extraordinary power is to ensure the proper administration of the judicial process.

Model Case:

Pat Boyle is a political activist fighting for the rights of oppressed youth. A dispute over the nature of some new proficiency exams in the local high school caught Boyle's attention. In protest, Boyle pitched a tent on the lawn of the school superintendent's personal residence and stayed there.

The superintendent obtained an injunction against this continuing trespass. Boyle disobeyed the order. During one point of the criminal contempt hearing Boyle shouted to the judge, "You are a cowardly tyrant! Try to face the truth for once!"

Boyle's outburst in the presence of the court can be punished immediately as summary criminal contempt. The disobedience of the injunction is indirect criminal contempt. It is punishable by fine or imprisonment if there are no Constitutional infirmities in the criminal hearing.

Walker v. City of Birmingham

388 U.S. 307, 87 S.Ct. 1824, 18 L.Ed.2d 1210 (1967).

■ MR. JUSTICE STEWART delivered the opinion of the Court.

On Wednesday, April 10, 1963, officials of Birmingham, Alabama, filed a bill of complaint in a state circuit court asking for injunctive relief against 139 individuals and two organizations. The bill and accompanying affidavits stated that during the preceding seven days:

> "[R]espondents [had] sponsored and/or participated in and/or conspired to commit and/or to encourage and/or to participate in certain movements, plans or projects commonly called 'sit-in' demonstrations, 'kneel-in' demonstrations, mass street parades, trespasses on private property after being warned to leave the premises by the owners of said property, congregating in mobs upon the public streets and other public places, unlawfully picketing private places of business in the City of Birmingham, Alabama; violation of numerous ordinances and statutes of the City of Birmingham and State of Alabama. * * * "

It was alleged that this conduct was "calculated to provoke breaches of the peace," "threaten[ed] the safety, peace and tranquility of the City," and placed "an undue burden and strain upon the manpower of the Police Department."

The bill stated that these infractions of the law were expected to continue and would "lead to further imminent danger to the lives, safety, peace, tranquility and general welfare of the people of the City of Birmingham," and that the "remedy by law [was] inadequate." The circuit judge granted a temporary injunction as prayed in the bill, enjoining the petitioners from, among other things, participating in or encouraging mass street parades or mass processions without a permit as required by a Birmingham ordinance.

Five of the eight petitioners were served with copies of the writ early the next morning. Several hours later four of them held a press conference. There a statement was distributed, declaring their intention to disobey the injunction because it was "raw tyranny under the guise of maintaining law and order." At this press conference one of the petitioners stated: "That they had respect for the Federal Courts, or Federal Injunctions, but in the past the State Courts had favored local law enforcement, and if the police couldn't handle it, the mob would."

That night a meeting took place at which one of the petitioners announced that "[i]njunction or no injunction we are going to march tomorrow." The next afternoon, Good Friday, a large crowd gathered in the vicinity of Sixteenth Street and Six Avenue North in Birmingham. A group of about 50 or 60 proceeded to parade along the sidewalk while a crowd of 1,000 to 1,500 onlookers stood by "clapping and hollering, and [w]hooping." Some of the crowd followed the marchers and spilled out into the street. At least three of the petitioners participated in this march.

Meetings sponsored by some of the petitioners were held that night and the following night, where calls for volunteers to "walk" and go to jail were made. On Easter Sunday, April 14, a crowd of between 1,500 and 2,000 people congregated in the midafternoon in the vicinity of Seventh Avenue and Eleventh Street North in Birmingham. One of the petitioners was seen organizing members of the crowd in formation. A group of about 50, headed by three other petitioners, started down the sidewalk two abreast. At least one other petitioner was among the marchers. Some 300 or 400 people from among the onlookers followed in a crowd that occupied the entire width of the street and overflowed onto the sidewalks. Violence occurred. Members of the crowd threw rocks that injured a newspaperman and damaged a police motorcycle.

The next day the city officials who had requested the injunction applied to the state circuit court for an order to show cause why the petitioners should not be held in contempt for violating it. At the ensuing hearing the petitioners sought to attack the constitutionality of the injunction on the ground that it was vague and overbroad, and restrained free speech. They also sought to attack the Birmingham parade ordinance upon similar grounds, and upon the further ground that the ordinance had previously been administered in an arbitrary and discriminatory manner.

CHAPTER 7 CONTEMPT **259**

The circuit judge refused to consider any of these contentions, pointing out that there had been neither a motion to dissolve the injunction, nor an effort to comply with it by applying for a permit from the city commission before engaging in the Good Friday and Easter Sunday parades. Consequently, the court held that the only issues before it were whether it had jurisdiction to issue the temporary injunction, and whether thereafter the petitioners had knowingly violated it. Upon these issues the court found against the petitioners, and imposed upon each of them a sentence of five days in jail and a $50 fine, in accord with an Alabama statute.

The Supreme Court of Alabama affirmed. * * *

Howat v. State of Kansas, 258 U.S. 181, 42 S.Ct. 277, 66 L.Ed. 550, was decided by this Court almost 50 years ago. That was a case in which people had been punished by a Kansas trial court for refusing to obey an antistrike injunction issued under the state industrial relations act. They had claimed a right to disobey the court's order upon the ground that the state statute and the injunction based upon it were invalid under the Federal Constitution. The Supreme Court of Kansas had affirmed the judgment. * * *

This Court, in dismissing the writ of error, * * * [held]:

"An injunction duly issuing out of a court of general jurisdiction with equity powers, upon pleadings properly invoking its action, and served upon persons made parties therein and within the jurisdiction, must be obeyed by them, however erroneous the action of the court may be, even if the error be in the assumption of the validity of a seeming, but void law going to the merits of the case. It is for the court of first instance to determine the question of the validity of the law, and until its decision is reversed for error by orderly review, either by itself or by a higher court, its orders based on its decision are to be respected, and disobedience of them is contempt of its lawful authority, to be punished." 258 U.S., at 189–190, 42 S.Ct. at 280.

The rule of state law accepted and approved in *Howat v. Kansas* is consistent with the rule of law followed by the federal courts.

In the present case, however, we are asked to hold that this rule of law, upon which the Alabama courts relied, was constitutionally impermissible. We are asked to say that the Constitution compelled Alabama to allow the petitioners to violate this injunction, to organize and engage in these mass street parades and demonstrations, without any previous effort on their part to have the injunction dissolved or modified, or any attempt to secure a parade permit in accordance with its terms. Whatever the limits of *Howat v. Kansas,* we cannot accept the petitioners' contentions in the circumstances of this case.

Without question the state court that issued the injunction had, as a court of equity, jurisdiction over the petitioners and over the subject matter of the controversy. And this is not a case where the injunction was transparently invalid or had only a frivolous pretense to validity. * * *

The generality of the language contained in the Birmingham parade ordinance upon which the injunction was based would unquestionably raise substantial constitutional issues concerning some of its provisions. [Citations.] The petitioners, however, did not even attempt to apply to the Alabama courts for an authoritative construction of the ordinance. Had they done so, those courts might have given the licensing authority granted in the ordinance a narrow and precise scope. * * *

The breadth and vagueness of the injunction itself would also unquestionably be subject to substantial constitutional question. But the way to raise that question was to apply to the Alabama courts to have the injunction modified or dissolved. The injunction in all events clearly prohibited mass parading without a permit, and the evidence shows that the petitioners fully understood that prohibition when they violated it.

The petitioners also claim that they were free to disobey the injunction because the parade ordinance on which it was based had been administered in the past in an arbitrary and discriminatory fashion. In support of this claim they sought to introduce evidence that, a few days before the injunction issued, requests for permits to picket had been made to a member of the city commission. One request had been rudely rebuffed, and this same official had later made clear that he was without power to grant the permit alone, since the issuance of such permits was the responsibility of the entire city commission. Assuming the truth of this proffered evidence, it does not follow that the parade ordinance was void on its face. The petitioners, moreover, did not apply for a permit either to the commission itself or to any commissioner after the injunction issued. Had they done so, and had the permit been refused, it is clear that their claim of arbitrary or discriminatory administration of the ordinance would have been considered by the state circuit court upon a motion to dissolve the injunction.

This case would arise in quite a different constitutional posture if the petitioners, before disobeying the injunction, had challenged it in the Alabama courts, and had been met with delay or frustration of their constitutional claims. But there is no showing that such would have been the fate of a timely motion to modify or dissolve the injunction. There was an interim of two days between the issuance of the injunction and the Good Friday march. The petitioners give absolutely no explanation of why they did not make some application to the state court during that period. The injunction had issued *ex parte;* if the court had been presented with the petitioners' contentions, it might have dissolved or at least modified its order in some respects. If it had not done so, Alabama procedure would have provided for an expedited process of appellate review. It cannot be presumed that the Alabama courts would have ignored the petitioners' constitutional claims. * * *

The rule of law that Alabama followed in this case reflects a belief that in the fair administration of justice no man can be judge in his own case, however exalted his station, however righteous his motives, and irrespective of his race, color, politics, or religion. This Court cannot hold that the petitioners were constitutionally free to ignore all the procedures of the law and carry their battle to the streets. One may sympathize with the petitioners' impatient commitment to their cause. But respect for judicial process is a small price to pay for the civilizing hand of law, which alone can give abiding meaning to constitutional freedom.

Affirmed.

---

1. *Criminal Contempt as "Crime".* The Supreme Court has frequently affirmed the principle that criminal contempt is a "crime in the ordinary sense." Bloom v. Illinois, 391 U.S. 194, 201, 88 S.Ct. 1477, 1481, 20 L.Ed.2d 522 (1968). Therefore, "criminal penalties may not be imposed on someone who has not been afforded the protections that the Constitution requires of such criminal proceedings." Hicks v. Feiock, 485 U.S. 624, 632, 108 S.Ct. 1423, 1429–30, 99 L.Ed.2d 721 (1988).

Those Constitutional protections for crimes that also apply to criminal contempts include privilege against self-incrimination, right to proof beyond a reasonable doubt, right to a jury trial, double jeopardy, rights to notice of charges, assistance of counsel, summary process, and to present a defense. *See* In re Bradley, 318 U.S. 50, 63 S.Ct. 470, 87 L.Ed. 608 (1943); Cooke v. United States, 267 U.S. 517, 537, 45 S.Ct. 390, 395, 69 L.Ed. 767 (1925); Gompers v. Buck's Stove & Range Co., 221 U.S. 418, 444, 31 S.Ct. 492, 499, 55 L.Ed. 797 (1911).

The Constitutional protections for criminal contempt apply only to disobedience of a court's order outside the presence of the court. These contempts are known as indirect contempts. Direct contempts that occur in the court's presence may be immediately adjudged and sanctioned summarily. *See* Ex parte Terry, 128 U.S. 289, 9 S.Ct. 77, 32 L.Ed. 405 (1888). If a court delays punishing a direct contempt until the completion of trial, however, due process requires notice and a hearing. Taylor v. Hayes, 418 U.S. 488, 94 S.Ct. 2697, 41 L.Ed.2d 897 (1974).

2. *Jury Trial Rights in Contempt Cases.* In contempt cases the right to a jury trial depends upon the type of contempt. There is no right to a jury trial in a civil contempt case because the plaintiff receives this remedy as a part of the underlying equitable remedy, such as a specific performance order. For criminal contempts the Supreme Court held in *Bloom v. Illinois, supra,* that the sixth amendment right to jury trial applies to serious criminal contempts. This Constitutional requirement was also applied to the states through the Fourteenth Amendment. Serious criminal contempts are ones where the penalty actually imposed exceeds six months' imprisonment. 391 U.S. at 199, 88 S.Ct. at 1481. See also Taylor v. Hayes, 418 U.S. 488, 495, 94 S.Ct. 2697, 2701–02, 41 L.Ed.2d 897 (1974).

The consecutive imposition of shorter sentences that aggregate to more than six months' imprisonment also triggers the jury trial right. *See* United States v. Seale, 461 F.2d 345 (7th Cir.1972) (three months' imprisonment sentenced for each of sixteen acts of misbehavior in the presence of the court).

Where a defendant at the end of a trial is further tried for contempt concerning his personal attacks on the integrity of the judge during the trial, the trial judge should avoid the possibility of prejudice by not presiding over the contempt hearing. *Id.* In a typical summary contempt imposed during the course of a trial, however, the contempt is imposed immediately by the trial judge who witnesses the acts.

3. *Willfulness—Criminal Contempt.* Criminal contempt requires intentional conduct violating the court order. For a good discussion of the principles of willfulness, *see* United States v. Greyhound Corp., 508 F.2d 529 (7th Cir.1974). In one interesting fact pattern, a defendant claimed that he had been lured into believing that a court order was no longer in effect and thus that the disobedience was not willful. An ex-wife obtained an order of protection against her ex-husband pursuant to a state Domestic Violence Act, but then later falsely told the defendant that the order no longer existed because she was hoping to reconcile. The defendant then engaged in acts that were in violation of the order and defended the subsequent contempt citation by challenging the willfulness of the disobedience. The court concluded that the conduct was nonetheless willful because the defendant knew that the order came from the court and not from the ex-wife. Because the Domestic Violence Act is intended to protect society as well as individual victims, it did not offend public policy to enforce the order even in the face of the victim's invitation to violate the court's order. The court concluded that "[a] contrary result would lead to mockery of the powers granted the courts under the Act." People v. Townsend, 183 Ill.App.3d 268, 131 Ill.Dec. 741, 538 N.E.2d 1297 (1989).

4. *Willfulness—Civil Contempt.* In contrast to criminal contempt, willfulness or intentional disobedience is not a necessary element of civil contempt. The court in Morales Feliciano v. Hernandez Colon, 697 F.Supp. 26 (D.Puerto Rico 1987), explained the distinction:

> [T]he absence of willfulness does not relieve a party from civil contempt. Civil, as distinguished from criminal contempt, is a sanction to enforce compliance with an order of the court or to compensate for losses for damages sustained by reason of noncompliance. Since the purpose is remedial, it matters not with what intent the defendant did the prohibited act.

5. *Inability to Comply.* A party must be reasonably diligent in attempting to comply with an order. Good faith is not an absolute defense to civil contempt when the effort to obey a court's order was unsuccessful. If the order itself involves wording invoking wilfulness, however, then the motivation becomes part of the analysis of whether the order was violated. For example, in *Goluba v. School District of Ripon*, 45 F.3d 1035 (7th Cir. 1995), a federal district court ordered a school as follows:

> IT IS HEREBY ORDERED that the defendant, the School District of Ripon, and its officers, agents, servants, employees and all of those

persons in active concert or participation with it, shall be and hereby are, permanently enjoined and restrained from authorizing, conducting, sponsoring or intentionally allowing or permitting religious prayer to be conducted at school commencement proceedings.

The issue was whether the school officials had violated the order by "intentionally allowing or permitting" a prayer when they failed to interfere with a group of students who recited the Lord's Prayer aloud five minutes before the graduation ceremony began. The plan was student-initiated and school officials had heard about it second-hand a day or two before it happened but made no effort to stop it. The plaintiff argued that by knowing of the plan in advance and making no effort to stop it, the school officials had acted "intentionally" within the mean of the order. The district court disagreed and the Court of Appeals affirmed on the grounds that the officials had not encouraged or sanctioned the conduct.

The wording of the order itself governed the analysis because the issue was whether the order had been violated at all, and not whether the manner in which an order was violated met the standard for a sanction. If the order had prohibited any prayer at graduation, then the analysis would have been different. Then the attorneys for the school officials could have challenged the constitutionality of the order, and the attorneys for the plaintiff would have challenged whether the officials had acted with due diligence in preventing the students from praying independently at graduation, causing a violation of the order.

6. *Impossibility.* Impossibility or incapacity to comply with the order are defenses, but the burden of proof rests with the defendant. United States v. Rylander, 460 U.S. 752, 103 S.Ct. 1548, 75 L.Ed.2d 521 (1983).

This defense is frequently introduced in cases where a parent is in arrears making child support payments. Unwillingness to earn income to make the payments is not a defense, in contrast with the inability to do so. The California Supreme Court clarified this difference in *Moss v. Superior Court*, 17 Cal.4th 396, 71 Cal.Rptr.2d 215, 950 P.2d 59 (1998). Noting that the inability to pay is an affirmative defense, the court said that the defendant father had to prove by a preponderance of the evidence that he cannot comply. The court found no constitutional impediment to courts using the contempt power against parents who willfully refuse to seek available employment that would permit them to meet their support obligation.

The Supreme Court held in Turner v. Rogers, ___ U.S. ___, 131 S.Ct. 2507, 180 L.Ed.2d 452 (2011), reprinted *infra* in this chapter, addressed the due process requirements in cases involving the ability of a parent to pay a child support order.

7. *Standard of Proof.* Criminal contempt is governed by the Constitutional requirements for a criminal conviction, including proof beyond a reasonable doubt. Civil contempt usually requires "clear and convincing" evidence. *See* Williamson v. Recovery Ltd. Partnership, ___ F.3d ___, 2012 WL 171385 (2012) (clear and convincing standard for contempt in the

violation of an order related to disputes over the recovery of gold and other treasure in a ship that was sunk in the Atlantic in 1857, found in 1988 and still in litigation in 2012).

8. Some actions may constitute both criminal and civil contempt when defendants violate the duty to obey. In *State v. Rosse*, 18 A.D.3d 982, 794 N.Y.S.2d 721 (3d Dept. 2005), for example, the trial court ordered defendant developers to remediate defective septic and drinking water systems that tests showed contaminated with E. coli bacteria. The defendants agreed to the plan but did not follow it nor move to modify or vacate the order. Their defense in the contempt hearings was that the order to require action that would violate Public Health Law. The developers were subject to both criminal and civil sanctions, regardless of whether the order required illegal action, because they had agreed to the plan and never moved to modify or vacate it.

In re Stewart

571 F.2d 958 (5th Cir.1978).

■ Godbold, Circuit Judge.

The appellant Murray Stewart was adjudged guilty of civil contempt by the district court and sentenced to a fine and a period of probation. The fine has been paid and the period of probation has run its course. The judgment of contempt is invalid and is reversed.

* * *

Stewart is county engineer for Hinds County, Mississippi. Thomas Stubblefield was a county employee working as a laborer on the bridge crew. Stubblefield was summoned to serve as a civil juror in the United States District Court for the Southern District of Mississippi, sitting at Jackson, Hinds County, and was selected to sit on a case which ended January 13. On January 13 an unidentified member of the court personnel told District Judge Harold Cox, presiding, that Stubblefield was having some difficulty with his employer because he was serving on the jury. Judge Cox talked with Stubblefield. * * *

* * * Judge Cox's position is clear from the comments which he directed to Stewart during the hearing:

> * * * I told him [Stubblefield] to tell you when I had some word that there was some irregularity about whether or not he had been demoted—I understood that yesterday, and I told him to tell you that I didn't want anything like that to happen, that he was on the jury up here. * * *

When Stubblefield reported for work on January 14, he was told by the overseer of the solid waste crew that he (Stubblefield) had been transferred to the solid waste crew. Stubblefield went at once to see Stewart and objected, as Stubblefield phrased it, to being put on jury duty and coming back and finding his job gone. In the contempt hearing Stubblefield was asked if he had told Stewart what Judge Cox had told him to say, and he answered affirmatively, but at no time did Stubblefield testify to the content of either the message given to him or his restatement of it to Stewart. In answer to more specific questions Stubblefield testified as follows. He asked Stewart if being on the jury had any bearing on the transfer, and Stewart said it did not. Stubblefield inquired whether the transfer had any relation to a rumor that he had been loafing and hauling firewood while off work for jury duty, and Stewart stated it did not. Stewart told Stubblefield that the pay for the two jobs was the same. Finally Stewart told Stubblefield that he could accept the transfer or be dismissed. Stubblefield told Stewart he would call Judge Cox and get the matter straightened out. To this Stewart responded that Judge Cox had nothing to do with him or with running the county.

* * *

Stewart was arrested during the morning and held in custody until his trial. Judge Cox directed the U.S. Attorney to serve as prosecutor. A hearing was conducted during the afternoon of the 14th. Stewart had no counsel. The record does not show that he was advised that he had a right to counsel nor does it reveal a waiver of right to counsel. Stewart subpoenaed no witnesses, and nothing in the record shows that he was told he could do so. Stubblefield testified and Stewart cross-examined him. Stewart gave his testimony, and both the U.S. Attorney and Judge Cox cross-examined Stewart.

At the conclusion of the brief testimony Judge Cox announced that he found Stewart guilty of contempt. He gave oral findings and reasons. * * *

The judge orally imposed a sentence of $100 fine and costs and put Stewart on probation for six months conditioned upon his paying the fine and costs, upon his restoring Stubblefield to his former position, and upon Stewart's not violating any law of the state, county or municipality and "any rules or regulations of this court like this particular regulation." The judge ordered Stewart committed until the fine and costs were paid. A formal order was entered the same day adjudging Stewart to be in civil contempt and setting out the sentence, except that the condition on probation of Stewart's obeying the law and the rules and regulations of the court was omitted. A few days later Judge Cox amended the sentence by changing the probation to three months unsupervised probation but leaving the other terms in effect.

We understand a district judge's concern if he has evidence that a juror has been treated adversely by his employer because he has served on the jury. But judicial concern cannot explain the injustice that permeates this case. The proceedings did not meet rudimentary standards of due process guaranteed by our Constitution. They did not comply with the Federal Rules of Criminal Procedure. The court erroneously handled the case as a civil contempt case when in fact it was a criminal contempt proceeding. There was no proof that Stewart transferred Stubblefield because Stubblefield had been on the jury. Even if there had been such proof, Stewart's action would not have been contempt of court.

The beginning point is to determine whether the nature of the contempt proceeding was civil or criminal. [Citation.] The district judge's order recited that Stewart was found in civil contempt of the court, but the judge's characterization is not conclusive.[1] [Citation.] The nature of the proceeding may be determined from the purpose of the penalty. Civil contempt is remedial; the penalty serves to enforce compliance with a court order or to compensate an injured party. Criminal contempt is punitive; the penalty serves to vindicate the authority of the court and does not terminate upon compliance with a court order. [Citations.] Further, civil contempt is a facet of a principal suit, while criminal contempt is a separate action brought in the name of the United States. [Citation.] In this case the district judge imposed a penalty that was unconditional[2] and not subject to being lifted if Stewart purged himself. The penalty was meant to punish defiance of the court and deter similar actions.[3] The district judge's statements, particularly "I haven't had this to contend with too much, but I think I might as well just make an example out of this fellow so I won't have to bother with this matter again," make crystal clear the intent to impose punishment. Finally, while the proceeding was tangentially related to the civil suit on which Stubblefield had sat as juror and nominally did not involve the United States, it was docketed, captioned and treated as a separate case and on order of the court was prosecuted by the U.S. Attorney. The contempt proceeding against Stewart was criminal in nature.

The contempt proceeding did not comply with basic and elementary constitutional requirements of due process. The Supreme Court spelled out the procedural due process protections required in contempt proceedings in Re Oliver, 333 U.S. 257, 275, 68 S.Ct. 499, 508, 92 L.Ed. 682, 695 (1948).

> Except for a narrowly limited category of contempts, due process of law * * * requires that one charged with contempt of court be advised of the charges against him, have a reasonable opportunity to meet them by way of defense or explanation, have the right to be represented by counsel, and have a chance to testify and call other witnesses in his behalf, either by way of defense or explanation.

This proceeding does not fall within the narrow exception where summary disposition is constitutionally permissible.

---

1. A reviewing court's inability to determine whether a proceeding is civil or criminal is in itself a ground for reversal. *In re Monroe*, 532 F.2d 424 (5th Cir.1976); *Skinner v. White*, 505 F.2d 685 (5th Cir.1974).

2. The probation had conditions attached, but this is another matter.

3. Part of the penalty, the reinstatement of Stubblefield, was remedial. In *Nye v. U.S.*, 313 U.S. 33, 42–43, 61 S.Ct. 810, 813, 85 L.Ed. 1172, 1177 (1941), the Supreme Court said that a contempt proceeding is considered civil only when the punishment is wholly remedial. When the punishment is partly remedial and partly punitive, "the criminal feature of the order is dominant and fixes its character for purposes of review." *Id., quoting Union Tool Co. v. Wilson*, 259 U.S. 107, 110, 42 S.Ct. 427, 428, 66 L.Ed. 848, 850 (1922).

The narrow exception to these due process requirements includes only charges of misconduct, in open court, in the presence of the judge, which disturbs the court's business, where all of the essential elements of the misconduct are under the eye of the court, are actually observed by the court, and where immediate punishment is essential to prevent 'demoralization of the court's authority before the public'. If some essential elements of the offense are not personally observed by the judge, so that he must depend upon statements made by others for his knowledge about these essential elements, due process requires, * * * that the accused be accorded notice and a fair hearing as above set out.

Re Oliver, 333 U.S. at 275, 68 S.Ct. at 509, 92 L.Ed. at 695.

Stewart was tried without counsel and without being informed by the court that he had a right to counsel. He was not given a meaningful opportunity to call witnesses or advised of his right to do so. * * *

The proceeding also failed to comply with Federal Rule of Criminal Procedure 42(b), governing criminal contempts. This rule requires that, except for conduct committed in the presence of and seen or heard by the judge, a criminal contempt shall be prosecuted on notice given to the alleged contemnor. The notice "shall state the time and place of hearing, allow a reasonable time for the preparation of the defense, and shall state the essential facts constituting the criminal contempt charged and describe it as such." Here the judge issued a show cause and arrest order, which under 42(b) may be the means of notice. It did not allow a reasonable time for preparation of a defense. It did not even state the time and place of hearing.

* * *

Turning to the merits of the case, Stewart's contempt conviction was clearly erroneous. As in any other criminal case, proof of guilt beyond reasonable doubt is required. [Citations.] The evidence did not even come close to sustaining the district judge's factual conclusion that Stewart demoted or mistreated Stubblefield because he was serving on the jury. * * *

Finally, even if the foregoing gaps in the evidence had been filled, Stewart would not have been guilty of contempt under 18 U.S.C. § 401. That section provides:

A court of the United States shall have power to punish by fine or imprisonment, at its discretion, such contempt of its authority, and none other, as—

(1) Misbehavior of any person in its presence or so near thereto as to obstruct the administration of justice;

(2) Misbehavior of any of its officers in their official transactions;

(3) Disobedience or resistance to its lawful writ, process, order, rule, decree, or command.

Subsection (1) does not apply. Stewart's acts were outside the presence of the court, and they were not "so near thereto as to obstruct the administration of justice." The words "so near thereto" are meant as geographic terms that limit the subsection's application to acts within the immediate vicinity of the courtroom, such as the adjoining hallway or the jury room. *Nye v. U.S.*, 313 U.S. 33, 48–49, 61 S.Ct. 810, 815–816, 85 L.Ed. 1172, 1180 (1941).

Subsection (2) is obviously inapplicable. Stewart is not an officer of the court.

Subsection (3) was not violated. Stewart disobeyed no writ, process, or decree of the district court. Even if the proof had established the content of Judge Cox's message to Stubblefield and had established that Stubblefield accurately relayed it, an oral "message" such as this, not stated in open court where it could be taken down by a court reporter, addressed to a person not before the court, never entered upon the records of the court, and relayed by word of mouth through a person without official status, is not an "order" or "command" within the meaning of subsection (3). * * *

The conviction is reversed and the cause remanded with directions that the clerk be ordered to repay Stewart the fine he paid and that the proceedings be dismissed.

---

1.   *Criminal/civil Contempt Distinction.* As the principal case illustrates, the difference between criminal and civil contempt is essential, but often elusive. Scholars have criticized the distinction as unworkable, but the Supreme Court has adhered to the distinction. *See* Dudley, Getting Beyond the Civil/Criminal Distinction: A New Approach to Regulation of Indirect Contempts, 79 Va.L.Rev. 1025, 1033 (1993); Martineau, Contempt of Court: Eliminating the Confusion between Civil and Criminal Contempt, 50 U.Cin.L.Rev. 677 (1981); Moskovitz, Contempt of Injunctions, Civil and Criminal, 43 Colum.L.Rev. 780 (1943); R. Goldfarb, The Contempt Power 58 (1963).

2.   Some conduct can result in multiple penalties. In *Henning v. Ritz,* 22 A.D.3d 524, 801 N.Y.S.2d 768 (2d Dept. 2005), an attorney was held in both criminal and civil contempt after she forged a judge's signature on a document while she was representing herself pro se in a divorce action. Then she was disbarred for the conduct. *In re* Henning, 32 A.D.3d 161, 819 N.Y.S.2d 540 (2d Dept. 2006).

3.   *Specificity of the Order.* As the principal case demonstrates, a criminal contempt conviction based upon 18 U.S.C. § 401(3) must be premised upon the violation of an identifiable court order. That order must be sufficiently specific that the defendant has an opportunity to know that his behavior is disobedience.

The specificity requirement for the framing of injunctive orders is contained in F.R.Civ.P. 65(d)(1):

Contents. Every order granting an injunction and every restraining order must:

(A) state the reasons why it issued;

(B) state its terms specifically; and

(C) describe in reasonable detail—and not by referring to the complaint or other document—the act or acts restrained or required.

The necessity of careful compliance with the specificity requirement is noted as follows in H.K. Porter Co. v. National Friction Products, 568 F.2d 24, 27 (7th Cir.1977):

Rule 65(d) is no mere extract from a manual of procedural practice. It is a page from the book of liberty.

* * * Because of the risks of contempt proceedings, civil or criminal, paramount interests of liberty and due process make it indispensable for the chancellor or his surrogate to speak clearly, explicitly, and specifically if violation of his direction is to subject a litigant * * * to coercive or penal measures, as well as to payment of damages.

One of the problems in the principal case is the uncertainty of the "message" that Judge Cox apparently sent to Stewart through the juror Stubblefield. What could Judge Cox have done instead?

4. *Who Is Bound by Injunctions?* The contempt power is premised upon the disobedience of a binding court order. F.R.Civ.P. 65(d)(2) provides:

Persons Bound. The order binds only the following who receive actual notice of it by personal service or otherwise:

(A) the parties;

(B) the parties' officers, agents, servants, employees, and attorneys; and

(C) other persons who are in active concert or participation with anyone described in Rule 65(d)(2)(A) or (B).

The Supreme Court has interpreted this rule to include not only party defendants but those in "privity" with them, at least to the extent that they are in "active concert" with the defendants. Regal Knitwear Co. v. NLRB, 324 U.S. 9, 65 S.Ct. 478, 89 L.Ed. 661 (1945). *See also* Golden State Bottling Co. v. NLRB, 414 U.S. 168, 94 S.Ct. 414, 38 L.Ed.2d 388 (1973) (a bona fide purchaser of a company who acquired it with knowledge that an order to remedy an unfair labor practice had not been fulfilled may be considered in privity with its predecessor for purposes of Rule 65(d)).

5. Many state courts have been historically more willing to bind nonparties to an injunction and to find them in contempt for violation of the order when they have notice. *See* Silvers v. Traverse, 82 Iowa 52, 47 N.W. 888 (1891) (injunction barring sale of alcohol on certain property bound a nonparty who sold liquor on the premises).

Similarly, a few other courts have taken the extreme position that once jurisdiction is acquired over the *res,* an order can protect the *res* against all, such as an injunction against trespass on a parcel of land. *See* State v. Porter, 76 Kan. 411, 91 P. 1073 (1907); State v. Terry, 99 Wash. 1, 168 P. 513 (1917). *But see* Kean v. Hurley, 179 F.2d 888 (8th Cir.1950) (trespass injunction against world at large impermissible under Rule 65(d)). The *res* approach has been justly criticized as an over-extension of the court's powers. An injunction that binds all the world would be functionally indistinguishable from a statute, thus allowing the court to usurp legislative functions and to punish with a minimal check on its power. *See* discussions in Dobbs, Contempt of Court: A Survey, 56 Cornell L.Rev. 183, 249–52 (1971); Note, Binding Nonparties to Injunction Decrees, 49 Minn. L.Rev. 719, 729–31 (1965).

6. A related problem has appeared in some cases involving school desegregation decrees where the court has wanted to bind nonparties to an order not to interfere with an orderly desegregation process. The Fifth Circuit has upheld a contempt conviction of a nonparty, Hall, who was served with a noninterference order that purported to bind anyone with notice not to obstruct school entrances. Hall was arrested for blocking a high school entrance in express defiance of the court order. The district court found him in criminal contempt, and the Fifth Circuit upheld the court's "inherent power" to preserve its judgment. The opinion states that Rule 65(d) acts as a "codification rather than a limitation of courts' common-law powers [and] cannot be read to restrict the inherent power of a court to protect its ability to render a binding judgment." United States v. Hall, 472 F.2d 261, 267 (5th Cir.1972). This case is criticized in Rendleman, "Beyond Contempt: Obligors to Injunctions," 53 Tex.L.Rev. 873 (1975). *See also* on this general topic Dobbyn, Contempt Power of the Equity Court Over Outside Agitators, 8 St. Mary's L.J. 1 (1976).

Ex parte Daniels

722 S.W.2d 707 (Tex.Cr.App.1987).

■ McCORMICK, JUDGE.

This is an application for writ of habeas corpus filed pursuant to the provisions of Article 11.06, V.A.C.C.P.

Applicant was held to be in direct criminal contempt of court by the Honorable Max W. Boyer, sitting by assignment in the 308th District Court in Harris County. The contempt order was the result of an incident which occurred on January 22, 1985, while applicant was appearing pro se.

In the course of the proceedings, applicant became involved in an argument with Judge Boyer. The judge ordered applicant to leave the courtroom and to not return until she obtained counsel. When applicant failed to leave the courtroom immediately, the bailiff was ordered to escort her out.

Applicant apparently went peacefully with the bailiff until they reached the doorway of the courtroom. At that point, applicant is alleged to have physically attacked the master of the court. The bailiff then moved to restrain applicant and a general disturbance erupted in which several people were involved.

The record indicates that at some point after this occurrence the trial judge ordered applicant brought before him for a summary contempt proceeding. During the course of this hearing, applicant did not have the benefit of retained counsel but instead continued to act in a pro se capacity. Applicant was found to be in direct criminal contempt and ordered to be confined in jail for a period of thirty days. No fine was imposed. Applicant was ordered to pay thirty-three dollars in court costs.

Applicant, now represented by retained counsel, * * * argues that her confinement is illegal because she was denied due process of law in that she was denied counsel during the contempt proceedings. * * *

Contempt power is a necessary and integral component of judicial authority. [Citation.] While it is clear the exercise of this authority should be tempered with common sense and sound discretion, contempt power is accorded wide latitude because it is essential to judicial independence and authority. [Citations.]

At the outset of any discussion or judicial determination of the right of due process in a contempt case, it is necessary to distinguish "direct" contempt from "constructive" contempt. Direct contempt is contempt which is committed or occurs in the presence of the court. In direct contempt cases the court has direct knowledge of the facts which constitute contempt. Constructive or indirect contempt involves actions outside of the presence of the court. Constructive contempt refers to acts which require testimony or the production of evidence to establish their existence.

The distinction is important because due process imposes different standards for the proceedings in which the contempt is adjudicated. In cases of constructive contempt in which factual issues relating to activities outside the court's presence must be resolved, due process requires the accused be afforded notice and a hearing. [Citations.] In a situation involving indirect or constructive contempt, the contemner cannot be legally confined without a reasonable opportunity to obtain counsel. [Citations.]

In cases of direct contempt, however, the behavior constituting contempt has occurred in the presence of the court. The judge has personal knowledge of the events in question and the court is allowed to conduct a summary proceeding in which the contemner is not accorded notice nor a hearing in the usual sense of the word. [Citations.]

Furthermore, in cases of direct contempt, the accused has no right to counsel. [Citation.] The right to counsel is, of course, one of the most fundamental protections guaranteed under the United States Constitution. The rationale for this very limited exception to the basic principle of the right to counsel was explained in the case of *Cooke v. United States*:

"To preserve order in the courtroom for the proper conduct of business, the court must act instantly to suppress disturbance or violence or physical obstruction or disrespect to the court, when occurring in open court. There is no need of evidence or assistance of counsel before punishment, because the court has seen the offense. Such summary vindication of the court's dignity and authority is necessary. It has always been so in the courts of the common law, and the punishment imposed is due process of law...." 267 U.S. at 394, 45 S.Ct. at 534.

* * *

Applicant has argued that the acts of contempt which she is accused of having committed did not take place in the judge's presence. Applicant states that the judge did not actually see much of the activity which took place at the door of the courtroom. Applicant states that the judge required testimony before he could make a complete determination that contemptuous actions occurred. Therefore, applicant argues her contempt was constructive rather than direct and applicant therefore argues that she was denied due process because she was denied the right of counsel.

The record reflects that the activities which gave rise to applicant's being held in contempt occurred in the 308th District Court while Judge Boyer was present and seated at the bench. Applicant states in effect that due to the rapid and confusing sequence of events the judge did not actually see everything that occurred, but only witnessed a general disturbance. Applicant urges this Court to accept the proposition that this means the actions constituting contempt did not occur in the presence of the court.

Applicant overlooks the fact that "in the presence of the court" does not necessarily mean in the immediate presence of the trial judge. Ex parte Aldridge, 169 Tex.Cr.R. 395, 334 S.W.2d 161, 168 (1959). As we stated above, the rationale justifying the harsh remedy of direct contempt adjudications is that the authority and ability of the courts to conduct the peoples' business is compromised by the disruptive actions of the alleged contemner. [Citations.] It is for this reason that this Court has held that the court is present whenever any of its constituent parts, the courtroom, the jury and the jury room are engaged in pursuing the work of the court. It was for this reason that the applicant in *Ex parte Aldridge, supra,* was properly determined to have committed direct contempt when he placed contemptuous publications in the corridors of the courthouse where prospective jurors would necessarily see them.

In the case before us it is clear that applicant's behavior was sufficiently "before the court" to justify a determination that she was in direct contempt of the court. Her actions took place in the presence of the trial judge. Even though some details of the disturbance were not noted by the trial judge due to the confusion and rapid sequence of the events, that does not mean the incident did not occur in the presence of the court. It is undisputed that the judge witnessed what he considered a disturbance and felt compelled to interrupt court business and intervene in the activities which took place at the courtroom entrance. The judge felt it was necessary to further interrupt the court's business by calling a recess.

The bailiff and the master of the court are court officers. The ability of the 308th District Court to conduct its duties was compromised by the direct physical attack on one of its officers in the courtroom and in the physical presence of the trial judge. As such, applicant's actions constitute direct contempt.

* * *

■ CLINTON, JUDGE, dissenting. * * *

The written order of contempt recites, *inter alia,* that after a hearing in the family law matter applicant "was ordered by this Court to be removed from the Courtroom for causing a disturbance at the bench."[3] According to the brief on behalf of the judge, at the courtroom door applicant "tried to strike the Master of the Court in the head with her purse or briefcase at which time the bailiff threw [applicant] against the wall and had to tackle [applicant]."

* * *

In her brief applicant contends "that it was only after being *told* of an alleged incident in the doorway to the courtroom—only after relying on the word of the bailiff, the Master, and possibly others—that the judge found Applicant in contempt." [emphasis by applicant]. To that the brief for the

---

3. An exchange immediately preceding that order went to a stated determination by the court to pass the case until applicant retained counsel; she objected and announced she would "refuse to leave until I get justice," only to be told by the judge that she would be taken bodily from the courtroom; applicant rejoined that she could not afford to hire an attorney and said, "I appeal right now." Then came the following:

"THE COURT: From what you were saying, you don't think you will get justice from me, do you, the way I am acting?

[APPLICANT]: I thought I would.

[APPLICANT]: Is this a democratic court?

THE COURT: There is no politics in this court.

[APPLICANT]: I pay my taxes.

THE COURT: This Court tries to deal in dispatch and there is no way I can deal in dispatch with a person like you.

Remove her from the courtroom. I order you to remove this woman from the courtroom and don't permit her to come back in. The only way you can permit her to come back in is to have counsel with her.

[The bailiff asked applicant to leave with him; she protested that 'he can't do that to me,' but was informed 'he can;' the judge told the bailiff to get help if needed and to 'remove her without further activity.']

[APPLICANT]: I want to take a picture of this. I don't believe this and I object. This is not justice and I don't accept it.

* * *

THE BAILIFF: Let's go.

THE COURT: And don't let her back in this courtroom unless she has counsel.

(Mrs. Daniels took a picture of the Judge.)

(Recess)."

judge correctly responds that the record does not reflect he had any discussion with anyone, but elsewhere states:

> "Although Judge Boyer expressed *no knowledge* of the attempt to assault the Master of the Court, Judge Boyer was aware that Applicant had done *something* at the courtroom door which disrupted the Court's business."

* * *

In the instant cause alleged contemptuous conduct took on a form that is not susceptible to easy classification as either constructive contempt or direct contempt. Clearly a "disturbance" occurred at an entrance to the courtroom in which applicant was involved. While the majority opinion says that the judge felt "compelled to interrupt court business and intervene in the activities which took place at the courtroom entrance," and that "it was necessary to further interrupt the court's business by calling a recess," I find no support for that conclusion—unless the majority means that the judge recessed to investigate the matter by speaking to the bailiff and others and then prepared his order of contempt. After a lapse of time the judge did reconvene court, state his findings of fact and conclusions of law and order of contempt he rendered for the court. What is presented here is at best a hybrid form of contempt, and a proceeding which the brief for the judge concedes was not "a hearing as to the issue of contempt."

Regardless of its label, the ultimate question is whether the proceeding comported with requisites of due process in the premises. *Codispoti v. Pennsylvania*, 418 U.S. 506, 94 S.Ct. 2687, 41 L.Ed.2d 912 (1974) and *Taylor v. Hayes*, 418 U.S. 488, 94 S.Ct. 2697, 41 L.Ed.2d 897 (1974), have taught us that when a trial judge does not convict and sentence for various disruptive acts "as they occur," "there is no overriding necessity for instant action to preserve order and no justification for dispensing with the ordinary rudiments of due process," *Codispoti, supra*, 418 U.S. at 513, 515, 94 S.Ct. at 1692. "On the other hand, where conviction and punishment are delayed, 'it is difficult to argue that action without notice or hearing of any kind is necessary to preserve order and enable [the court] to proceed with its business.' " [Citations.]

* * *

Applicant was not convicted and sentenced for creating the second disturbance "as it occurred." The bailiff had been ordered by the judge only to remove her from the courtroom, and that was done. Though the majority says the judge "witnessed what he considered to be a disturbance," clearly the judge did not then and there summarily hold her in contempt. Rather, under authority not revealed by this record, she was detained elsewhere for an extended period—four hours, according to her brief, or the time taken while the court was in recess in order for the judge to prepare and include written findings and conclusions in the order of contempt, according to the brief for the judge—before being taken back into court. By then "action without notice or hearing of any kind [was not] necessary to preserve order and enable [the court] to proceed with its business.''

* * *

Accordingly, I respectfully dissent.

Matter of Contempt of Greenberg

849 F.2d 1251 (9th Cir.1988).

■ PREGERSON, CIRCUIT JUDGE:

Stanley I. Greenberg was counsel for the defendant in a criminal trial in the district court. The district judge summarily convicted Greenberg of criminal contempt and fined him $500 pursuant to 18 U.S.C. § 401. Two issues are presented on appeal: first, whether the district judge certified that he ''saw or heard'' the alleged contemptuous conduct as required by Fed.R.Crim.P. 42(a); second, whether Greenberg's courtroom conduct constituted sufficient grounds for a summary criminal contempt conviction.

The district court convicted Stanley I. Greenberg of criminal contempt for his courtroom behavior in defending former FBI agent Richard W. Miller, who was convicted on charges of espionage. The verbal exchange for which the district judge held Greenberg in contempt occurred during the government's rebuttal to the defendant's closing argument. The exchange appears in the transcript of June 13, 1986 as follows:

> Mr. Bonner: . . . And up got Mr. Greenberg and he objected, ''No, we're not going into that.''

> Mr. Greenberg: I object to that. I didn't say that. I said that's not proper opening statement.

> The Court: Sit down, Mr. Greenberg. Please, sit down. That's improper Mr. Greenberg.

> Mr. Greenberg: I respectfully disagree.

> The Court: You're not being respectful and you're going to be very, very much in trouble.

> Mr. Greenberg: May I have a ruling on my objection? That misstated the opening statement.

> The Court: You sit down Mr. Greenberg, period.

> Mr. Bonner: Ladies and Gentlemen—Your honor, may I continue?

> Mr. Greenberg: May we have a ruling, your honor?

> The Court: I told you to sit down. I'm now going to tell you to be quiet, period.

> Mr. Greenberg: I'm sitting, your honor.

> The Court: Now, you proceed.

After a recess, the district judge stated the following for the record:

There was an outburst in the courtroom. And again, unfortunately one of the lawyers, Mr. Greenberg, lost his composure. The court finds that Mr. Greenberg was in contempt, after having had time to consider it through this short while.

The Court had warned Mr. Greenberg, and all the lawyers, that the court was not going to tolerate one more outburst of the temper. It was a slamming of something and Mr. Greenberg shouted out at the court in anger and it was very disruptive. And no matter whether Mr. Bonner's argument was correct or not, the court had on more than one occasion warned all lawyers, and specifically Mr. Greenberg.

The court hereby finds Mr. Greenberg for interrupting the court and disrupting the proceedings in an unethical manner, finds him in contempt and a fine of $500 is imposed at this time payable within the next 48 hours.

On July 8, 1986, the district judge filed an order of contempt memorializing the summary proceeding in which Greenberg was convicted of contempt. The order stated that on June 13, 1986, during the government's rebuttal argument before the jury, Greenberg

suddenly interrupted the proceedings by stating, at the top of his voice, an objection to something government counsel had said. The court ordered Mr. Greenberg to be seated and also stated that Mr. Greenberg was acting improperly. Mr. Greenberg then slammed his hand on the counsel table in an angry manner, demanding a ruling from the court. The court then told Mr. Greenberg that he was not being respectful and that he was going to find himself in trouble with the court. Mr. Greenberg then again asked for a ruling from the court, and the court again told Mr. Greenberg to sit down "period." When government counsel attempted to continue its argument, Mr. Greenberg again asked for a ruling, and the court told Mr. Greenberg to be quiet "period." Government counsel then resumed his argument.

We review summary contempt convictions for abuse of discretion. [Citation.]

The district court convicted Greenberg in a summary contempt proceeding under Fed.R.Crim.P. 42(a). Rule 42(a) states in full:

A criminal contempt may be punished summarily if the *judge certifies that the judge saw or heard the conduct constituting the contempt* and that it was committed in the actual presence of the court. The order of contempt shall recite the facts and shall be signed by the judge and entered of record.

(Emphasis added.)

Greenberg argues that the district judge erred by not certifying that the judge "saw or heard" the conduct held to be contemptuous. The July 8 order of contempt, which constitutes the certificate required by Rule 42(a), describes Greenberg as stating an objection "at the top of his voice," slamming "his hand on the counsel table in an angry manner," twice asking for a ruling on his objection, and not sitting down until asked to do so twice. The order, however, does not certify that the district judge "saw or heard" the conduct constituting the contempt. Thus, under Rule 42(a), the order cannot serve as a basis for a summary criminal contempt conviction.

The government contends that if the July 8 order itself does not fulfill the certification requirement of Rule 42(a), then the trial transcript could serve as a certification of the district court's actual knowledge. The trial transcript in this case, however, does not fulfill the function of the certificate. Although the transcript casts some light on the proceedings, to be valid a summary contempt conviction under Rule 42(a) must be supported by a certificate that satisfies the requirements of the rule by clearly identifying the specific facts constituting the contempt and by stating that the judge "saw or heard" the contemptuous conduct. [Citation.] The transcript fails to meet these requirements.

Additionally, the government urges in its brief that even without the explicit certification of first-hand knowledge required in Rule 42(a), this court may affirm the conviction because "there can be [no] serious question that the district court *saw* appellant's behavior. The outburst occurred in a courtroom in which the district court was then present and presiding over an ongoing jury trial." Appellee's brief at 24 (emphasis in original).

This argument is unpersuasive for two reasons. First, it appears that the district court judge did not see or hear at least part of the behavior giving rise to the summary contempt conviction. The judge's recounting of the incident immediately following the recess was that "[i]t was a slamming of something and Mr. Greenberg shouted out at the court in anger and it was very disruptive." Arguably from that statement it does not appear that the court knew precisely what was slammed or who slammed it.

More importantly, the government's contention ignores the importance of procedural safeguards mandated in summary criminal contempt proceedings. The summary criminal contempt procedure in Rule 42(a) dispenses with the hearing and notice requirements mandated by the general contempt scheme set forth in Fed.R.Crim.P. 42(b).[1] Rule 42(a) combines the "otherwise inconsistent functions of prosecutor, jury and judge . . . in one individual." [Citation.] This procedure "represents a significant departure

---

1. Rule 42(b) states:

(b) Disposition upon Notice and Hearing. A criminal contempt except as provided in subdivision (a) of this rule shall be prosecuted on notice. The notice shall state the time and place of hearing, allowing a reasonable time for the preparation of the defense, and shall state the essential facts constituting the criminal contempt charged and describe it as such. The notice shall be given orally by the judge in open court in the presence of the defendant or, on application of the United States attorney or of an attorney appointed by the court for that purpose, by an order to show cause or an order of arrest. The defendant is entitled to a trial by jury in any case in which an act of Congress so provides. The defendant is entitled to admission to bail as provided in these rules. If the contempt charged involves disrespect to or criticism of a judge, that judge is disqualified from presiding at the trial or hearing except with the defendant's consent. Upon a verdict or finding of guilt the court shall enter an order fixing the punishment.

from the accepted standards of due process," and is to be used only "where instant action is necessary to protect the judicial institution itself." Harris v. United States, 382 U.S. 162, 167, 86 S.Ct. 352, 355–56, 15 L.Ed.2d 240 (1965).

The certification requirement in Rule 42(a) is essential to safeguard the proper use of summary criminal contempt procedure. The requirement is not simply a legal formality. Rather, the certificate provides the basis for informed appellate review. We see no reason to depart from existing Ninth Circuit law requiring "that the procedural safeguards that [Rule 42(a)] provides must be strictly adhered to lest the drastic power authorized escape the permissible limits of reason and fairness." [Citation.]

Greenberg also argues that the acts referred to in the July 8 contempt order do not constitute an "open, serious threat to orderly procedure" justifying "instant and summary punishment." [Citation.] As noted above, the July 8 order describes the improper conduct as Greenberg stating an objection "at the top of his voice," slamming "his hand on the counsel table in an angry manner," twice asking for a ruling on his objection, and refusing to sit down until asked to do so twice. Although we recognize the importance of maintaining courtroom decorum, we find that the acts attributed to Greenberg do not standing alone constitute sufficient basis for a summary criminal contempt conviction.

"Rule 42(a) was reserved for 'exceptional circumstances,' such as acts threatening the judge or disrupting a hearing or obstructing court proceedings." [Citation.] Using summary criminal contempt proceedings to punish attorneys for overzealous advocacy is contrary to the important principle of maintaining an independent and assertive bar. * * * Thus summary criminal contempt procedure should be used only in exceptional circumstances where there is an immediate threat to the judicial process. Otherwise the procedure may deter vigorous representation by conscientious attorneys. Accordingly, a district court should not summarily convict an attorney of criminal contempt unless that attorney "create[s] an obstruction which blocks the judge in the performance of his judicial duty." [Citation.]

In this case, the acts of counsel did not cause an obstruction of the judicial process serious enough to justify a summary criminal contempt conviction. We agree with the Seventh Circuit that "where the line between vigorous advocacy and actual obstruction defie[s] strict delineation, doubts should be resolved in favor of vigorous advocacy." [Citation.] That Greenberg twice asked for a ruling on his objection is not a threat to orderly judicial procedure. Greenberg's client had a right to a ruling on the objection. [Citation.] Although the court arguably overruled the objection by asking Greenberg to sit down, Greenberg was entitled to a formal ruling for the record. Moreover, Greenberg's other acts were insufficient to support a summary criminal contempt conviction. That Greenberg continued to stand is not inconsistent with the custom of attorneys in the federal courts to stand when making an objection or addressing the court. Similarly, Greenberg's loud voice and hand slamming during the heat of a long and hard fought trial, although annoying and not condoned by this court, do not constitute the type of "exceptional circumstances" that pose an immediate threat to the judicial process, thereby justifying a summary criminal contempt conviction. [Citation.]

Accordingly, the judgment of the district court holding Greenberg in criminal contempt is reversed.

---

1.   The concept of the court's "presence" has been variously interpreted. In *In re Adams,* 421 F.Supp. 1027 (E.D.Mich.1976), an employer was held in contempt by the trial court for threatening to fire a juror. Relying on the provision in 18 U.S.C. § 401(1) for contempt to punish misbehavior in the presence of the court, the court found such threats to be in the "presence" of the court even though not occurring in the vicinity of the courtroom.

The United States Supreme Court had previously held that geographical proximity to the court is necessary under § 401(1) in Nye v. United States, 313 U.S. 33, 61 S.Ct. 810, 85 L.Ed. 1172 (1941). The district court in *Adams* nonetheless found the proximity rule satisfied on the theory that a juror carries a part of the court with him wherever he goes. A threat to a juror anywhere is thus "in the presence of the court." The case was not appealed.

Compare *Adams* with the preceding two summary contempt cases and with *In re Stewart, supra,* which involved firing a juror. Should the judge in *Stewart* have used summary criminal contempt powers instead of either regular criminal contempt or civil contempt? If he had, what arguments would you make on appeal if you represented Stewart?

2.   Another curious construction of "the presence of the court" is found in *People v. Higgins,* 173 Misc. 96, 16 N.Y.S.2d 302 (1939). In that case a male deputy sheriff and a woman juror had a private sexual encounter that interfered with jury deliberations. This act was found to be a criminal contempt in the "immediate view and presence" of the court.

3.   Are these various interpretations of "presence" justifiable? What power is necessary to assure the integrity of the court and the jury system? Is contempt the appropriate tool for judges to use to avoid courtroom disruptions? To avoid an obstruction of justice by interference with jurors?

PROBLEM: THE ENJOINED CONSTRUCTION PROJECT

An active environmentalist group known as SAVE has been protesting construction projects that commit new land to concrete. When a project threatens to convert an area with existing vegetation to concrete, SAVE attempts to stop the construction. SAVE uses a variety of tactics, some of which the group intends as "headline grabbers," such as sit-ins in front of bulldozers. Other methods are legal maneuvers to get projects enjoined, at least temporarily, while the group tries to attract public attention to the cause. Most of the projects targeted by SAVE are state construction. A few state projects even have been cancelled after the SAVE campaign called the public attention to particularly bad situations. The perception of state legislators, however, is that the overall effect of SAVE's tactics has been simply to delay and increase the cost of many projects.

The state legislature therefore passed a statute designed to prevent SAVE from delaying costly projects. The statute provided that no court in the state has "jurisdiction" to issue an injunction against a state "construction project."

After passage of this statute, SAVE targeted another construction project and sued to enjoin it. The defendant moved to dismiss under the statute. SAVE argued to the court that the statute does not apply in this case because this project is not financed entirely with public funds and therefore is not a "state" construction project. The judge has enjoined the project pending determination of the statute's applicability. Consider:

(1) If the trial judge finds the statute does apply to this project, the injunction will be dissolved. What if the defendant contractors disobeyed the injunction before its dissolution? Is that disobedience contempt?

(2) What if the trial judge finds the statute does not apply and continues the injunction against the project? Must the defendant obey pending appeal? Can the defendant contractor "take its chances" and continue building pending appeal with the hope of winning ultimately?

(3) The statute deprived the court of "jurisdiction" to enjoin state construction projects. Who has jurisdiction to decide the jurisdictional issue whether the construction is a state project?

United States v. United Mine Workers of America

330 U.S. 258, 67 S.Ct. 677, 91 L.Ed. 884 (1947).

■ MR. CHIEF JUSTICE VINSON delivered the opinion of the Court.

[The President ordered the seizure of the bituminous coal mines pursuant to his constitutional and statutory powers during a national emergency. A dispute arose between the Government and the union over interpretation of the labor contract, and the union threatened to strike. The Government obtained from the federal district court a temporary restraining order against the United Mine Workers and its president, John L. Lewis, to prevent the strike. A walk-out nonetheless occurred and mines producing the major part of the country's bituminous coal were idle. The United States petitioned the court to punish the defendants for contempt because of their willful disobedience of the restraining order. The defendants were found guilty of both civil and criminal contempt, and they appealed.

The defendants challenged the district court's jurisdiction to issue the restraining order under Section 4 of the Norris–LaGuardia Act which provides: "No court of the United States shall have jurisdiction to issue any restraining order or temporary or permanent injunction in any case involving or growing out of any labor dispute to prohibit any person or persons participating in such dispute from doing [any of several enumerated acts] * * *."

The first part of the Supreme Court's opinion held that the United States was not an "employer" within the meaning of the Act in this situation, so the district court did have the power to issue the order. The remainder of the opinion, from which excerpts follow, concerned alternative grounds for upholding the criminal contempt, but not the civil contempt, even if the Court had found the Norris–LaGuardia Act to apply.]

Supreme ct opinion

* * *

Although we have held that the Norris–LaGuardia Act did not render injunctive relief beyond the jurisdiction of the District Court, there are alternative grounds which support the power of the District Court to punish violations of its orders as criminal contempt.

* * *

In the case before us, the District Court had the power to preserve existing conditions while it was determining its own authority to grant injunctive relief. The defendants, in making their private determination of the law, acted at their peril. Their disobedience is punishable as criminal contempt.

Although a different result would follow were the question of jurisdiction frivolous and not substantial, such contention would be idle here. * * *

* * * [A]n order issued by a court with jurisdiction over the subject matter and person must be obeyed by the parties until it is reversed by orderly and proper proceedings. This is true without regard even for the constitutionality of the Act under which the order is issued. * * * Violations of an order are punishable as criminal contempt even though the order is set aside on appeal, or though the basic action has become moot. [Citations.]

We insist upon the same duty of obedience where, as here, the subject matter of the suit, as well as the parties, was properly before the court; where the elements of federal jurisdiction were clearly shown; and where the authority of the court of first instance to issue an order ancillary to the main suit depended upon a statute, the scope and applicability of which were subject to substantial doubt. The District Court on November 29 affirmatively decided that the Norris–LaGuardia Act was of no force in this case and that injunctive relief was therefore authorized. Orders outstanding or issued after that date were to be obeyed until they expired or were set aside by appropriate proceedings, appellate or otherwise. Convictions for criminal contempt intervening before that time may stand.

It does not follow, of course, that simply because a defendant may be punished for criminal contempt for disobedience of an order later set aside on appeal, that the plaintiff in the action may profit by way of a fine imposed in a simultaneous proceeding for civil contempt based upon a violation of the same order. The right to remedial relief falls with an injunction which events prove was erroneously issued, and *a fortiori* when the injunction or restraining order was beyond the jurisdiction of the court. * * * If the Norris–LaGuardia Act were applicable in this case, the conviction for civil contempt would be reversed in its entirety.

Assuming, then, that the Norris–LaGuardia Act applied to this case and prohibited injunctive relief at the request of the United States, we would set aside the preliminary injunction of December 4 and the judgment for civil contempt; but we would, subject to any infirmities in the contempt proceedings or in the fines imposed, affirm the judgments for criminal contempt as validly punishing violations of an order then outstanding and unreversed. * * *

As *United Mine Workers* reveals, the importance of the distinction between civil and criminal contempt is not just the difference in constitutional protections. The dependence of the contempt penalties on the validity of the underlying order also depends upon whether the contempt is civil or criminal. Recall the problem of void orders and the duty to obey erroneous orders, especially *Walker v. City of Birmingham, supra.*

B. CIVIL CONTEMPT AND COERCIVE CIVIL CONTEMPT

Section Coverage:

The primary function of civil contempt is not to vindicate the authority of the court, although such vindication is a derivative benefit. The purpose of civil contempt is to benefit the plaintiff who received the original equitable order. When the defendant disobeyed that order, the plaintiff no longer had the protection from harm that the original remedy was designed to provide. Civil contempt is available to compensate for the resulting losses if any occur, and sometimes to coerce the defendant into compliance to prevent any further losses.

There are two kinds of civil contempt: compensatory and coercive. The compensatory form of civil contempt is damages. The damages must be specifically caused by the defendant's disobedience of the court order. The losses must be actual ones and the plaintiff must prove them with reasonable certainty. In most jurisdictions such losses may include the attorneys' fees incurred by the plaintiff to enforce the order.

The second kind of civil contempt is coercive civil contempt. This form is a close cousin of criminal contempt because under coercive civil contempt judges impose fines paid to the state or order imprisonment. The distinction between criminal and coercive civil contempts lies in their different purposes. Whereas criminal contempt punishes defendants for past disobedience, coercive civil contempt seeks to compel present and future compliance with the court's order. Plaintiffs can seek coercive civil contempt sanctions to protect from future losses.

Model Case:

A court determines in a divorce proceeding that certain out-of-state property held in the husband's name should be deeded to the wife. The husband refuses to obey the order directing him to make the conveyance.

The court may jail the husband until he complies. The imprisonment is not punishment for past disobedience; it is to compel an act in the present for the benefit of the wife. The husband has the "jail keys in his pocket" because he will be out of jail as soon as he makes the conveyance. This imprisonment is coercive civil contempt.

The wife can recover in a civil contempt claim any losses occasioned by the disobedience. In most jurisdictions such damages would include reasonable attorneys' fees to enforce the order, but not fees incurred in the underlying divorce action.

Federal Trade Commission v. Trudeau ["Trudeau I"]

579 F.3d 754 (7th Cir. 2009).

■ TINDER, CIRCUIT JUDGE.

If you have a problem, chances are Kevin Trudeau has an answer. For over a decade, Trudeau has promoted countless "cures" for a host of human woes that he claims the government and corporations have kept hidden from the American public. Cancer, AIDS, severe pain, hair loss, slow reading, poor memory, debt, obesity-you name it, Trudeau has a "cure" for it. To get his messages out, Trudeau has become a marketing machine. And the infomercial is his medium of choice. He has appeared in dozens of them, usually in the form of a staged, scripted interview where Trudeau raves about the astounding benefits of the miracle product he's pitching. But Trudeau's tactics have long drawn the ire of the Federal Trade Commission ("FTC"). By promoting his cures, Trudeau claims he is merely exposing corporate and government conspiracies to keep Americans fat and unhealthy. But the FTC accuses Trudeau of being nothing more than a huckster who preys on unwitting consumers—a 21st-century snake-oil salesman. For years Trudeau has dueled with the FTC in and out of court.

Trudeau's latest run-in concerns his cure for weight loss, which he explains in his book, *The Weight Loss Cure "They" Don't Want You to Know About.* By the time Trudeau began promoting the book, courts had sharply curbed his marketing activities. A consent decree banned Trudeau from appearing in infomercials for any products, except for books, provided that he did not "misrepresent the content of the book."

That proviso forms the basis for this latest lawsuit. The FTC claimed that Trudeau's *Weight Loss Cure* infomercial misled consumers by describing a weight loss program that was "easy," "simple," and able to be completed at home, when in fact it was anything but. The program requires a diet of only 500 calories per day, injections of a prescription hormone not approved for weight loss, and dozens of dietary and lifestyle restrictions. The district court sided with the FTC, concluded that Trudeau had misrepresented his book, and held Trudeau in contempt. As sanctions, the court ordered Trudeau to pay $37.6 million[.] * * *.

Trudeau and the FTC then duked it out over remedies. The FTC requested reimbursement for all consumers who purchased the book[.] * * *

* * * Trudeau argues that his infomercials didn't misrepresent anything and thus didn't violate the Consent Order. In Trudeau's view, describing the protocol as "easy" and saying dieters who complete the protocol can eat "anything you want" merely quoted or paraphrased the book.

In sum, Trudeau misrepresented the content of his *Weight Loss Cure* book. Trudeau may have quoted parts of his book, but he did so deceptively. These selective quotations mislead because they present consumers with an incomplete picture of what the protocol requires, thereby inducing consumers to purchase the book on false hopes and assumptions. True, Trudeau's belief that the protocol is "easy" is his subjective opinion. But without giving consumers a fuller picture of what the protocol entails while claiming that the protocol is "the easiest method known on planet Earth," consumers are led to believe that Trudeau's statements are more than just his beliefs; they appear as objective facts. Moreover, Trudeau did more than just quote his book; he outright lied. In one infomercial, Trudeau claimed the protocol was "not a diet, not an exercise program, not portion control, not calorie counting, . . . no crazy potions, powder or pills . . . ." None of that is true. Dieters "MUST" eat only 100% organic food, walk an hour a day, eat six meals per day, eat only 500 calories per day for up to 45 days, drink organic raw apple vinégar cider, and take probiotics, krill oil, Vitamin E, digestive enzymes, and Acetyl–L Carnitin. Consequently, we conclude Trudeau violated the 2004 Consent Order by misrepresenting the content of his book. * * *

* * * Trudeau seeks greater procedural protections, such as a jury trial and a proof-beyond-a-reasonable-doubt standard, on remand. We decline to find such safeguards required in this case. * * *

The differences between criminal and civil contempt sanctions are not always easy to discern. [Citations.] In terms of monetary sanctions, civil sanctions fall in two categories. They can *compensate* the complainant for his losses caused by the contemptuous conduct. Or they can *coerce* the contemnor's compliance with a court order. A coercive sanction must afford the contemnor the opportunity to "purge," meaning the contemnor can avoid punishment by complying with the court order. * * *

Trudeau argues that the sanction imposed was neither coercive nor compensatory and thus not civil. We think Trudeau is clearly right on the coercive part. * * * As the order stands now, Trudeau has no opportunity to purge any of the $37.6 million judgment by representing his books truthfully from here on out. Without a purge provision, the order is not coercive.

So for the sanction to stand, it must "compensate the complainant for losses sustained." The FTC explicitly sought a compensatory remedy. * * *

[The court found inadequate the explanation for the district court's calculation and remanded the case for further findings.]

Beyond explaining its calculations, the court must also outline how the sanction should be administered. As it stands now, the court's order is silent on this point. The order merely commands Trudeau to pay $37.6 million to the FTC. Simply ordering money to be paid to the U.S. Treasury rather than to reimburse consumers looks more like a criminal fine than a compensatory sanction. * * *

[The case was remanded to the district court and returned to the Court of Appeals again in the case excerpted below.]

F.T.C. v. Trudeau ["Trudeau II"]

662 F.3d 947 (7th Cir. 2011).

* * * On remand, the district court reinstated the $37.6 million remedial fine. This time, however, the court explained that it reached that figure by multiplying the price of the book by the 800–number orders, plus the cost of shipping, less returns. Addressing our questions about administration, the court instructed the FTC to distribute the funds to those who bought Trudeau's book using the 800–number; any remainder not paid to those victims or used in the administration of the sanction was to be returned to Trudeau. * * *

Trudeau appeals the sanctions. He argues that the $37.6 million remedial sanction was improperly based on consumer loss rather than his unjust gain. * * *

We disagree and therefore affirm the district court. The consent order was intended to protect customers from deceptive infomercials. The protections, unfortunately, were too weak: Trudeau aired infomercials in violation of the order at least 32,000 times. He should not now be surprised that he must pay for the loss he caused. At a minimum, it was easily within the district court's discretion to conclude that he should. And $37.6 million correctly measures the loss. The figure is *conservative*—it only considers sales from the 800–number, not sales in bookstores[.] * * *

* * * Trudeau misunderstands a Second Circuit case, *FTC v. Verity Int'l, Ltd.*, 443 F.3d 48 (2d Cir.2006), to require a different conclusion. *Verity* was not a contempt case, but a direct action under section 13(b) of the FTC Act. * * *

Affirmed.

1. Contempt is a broad remedy with varying functions. Acts that interfere directly with the judicial process or affront the dignity of the court are punishable as summary criminal contempt. Failure to comply with a court order, such as an injunctive order to convey a certain parcel of land, is punishable as criminal contempt for disobedience. The same act can also be subject to civil contempt, a private remedy to the wronged plaintiff who is entitled to have the land conveyed to him. The civil contempt can be either in the form of money damages for the delay or a coercive fine or imprisonment until the disobedient defendant complies.

2. The plaintiff must prove the amount of loss with reasonable certainty. In *Allied Materials Corp. v. Superior Products Co.*, for example, the Court of Appeals upheld the district court's refusal to allow $12,000 in compensatory damages because of insufficient proof. The defendant had violated the terms of a consent decree, but the plaintiff presented no proof of the cost of that noncompliance to its company except for the testimony of one manager who said the damages were "probably" $10,000 to $12,000. The court made an award of $7000 in attorneys' fees because it was the only definite sum. 620 F.2d 224 (10th Cir.1980). If the loss to a business is the time of salaried employees, how could such loss be substantiated? What kind of proof should the company in this case have submitted?

3. In *Time–Share Systems, Inc. v. Schmidt*, 397 N.W.2d 438 (Minn. App.1986), a defendant was held in contempt for defiance of an order not to delete anything from a certain computer. The parties had litigated the ownership of certain software and the plaintiff had obtained an order of replevin for it. The defendant failed to deliver the software, so the court issued a further order that enjoined him from deleting anything from a certain computer and required him to allow the plaintiff to do a file save on it. Upon learning of the order, a programmer for the defendant immediately began making deletions from the system for the purpose of preventing plaintiff's access to some programs and data. The court found these actions were in contempt of the order.

The trial court ordered a compensatory civil contempt sanction of $3000 for costs and attorneys' fees and $2500 to indemnify for the wrongful activities. On appeal, the court noted that although attorney fees are a proper element of damages in compensatory civil contempt, they must be related only to the contempt proceeding and not the underlying case. Second, the award of $2500 in general losses was appropriate only if the plaintiff's losses were proven with specificity. Like tort damages, the contempt award compensates for actual losses. It is compensatory in character and not punitive.

4. Civil contempts are appealable when they are final orders. Thus, a compensatory contempt award can be appealed when the trial court has ordered an unconditional award. A conditional order is not appealable because the contempt can be purged by the defendant's voluntary conduct. *See* Tell v. Tell, 383 N.W.2d 678 (Minn.1986).

United States v. Darwin Construction Co.

680 F.Supp. 739 (D.Md.1988).

■ YOUNG, DISTRICT JUDGE.

On the date its payment was due on the civil contempt fine levied by this Court, respondent Darwin Construction Company filed a motion to set aside or reduce the fine. * * * This memorandum will resolve respondent's doubts that the Court carefully considered appropriate factors in determining that respondent was in contempt of the Court's order to comply with the IRS summons for six days. * * *

On June 23, 1986, the Court ordered respondent to comply with the IRS summons or face penalties of $5000 per day for noncompliance. The order was not designed to compensate the petitioner for its expenses in bringing the suit, nor has the petitioner ever pled or proven such expenses. Rather the purpose of this second-stage contempt order was coercive, but not punitive: it was chosen to encourage respondent to produce documents which they continued to withhold even after this Court's initial order was affirmed on interlocutory appeal. * * * The Court based its determination of contempt upon the respondent's preferred theory of substantial compliance, but also made a finding upon respondent's good faith defense.

The essence of respondent's argument is that "it is clear that Darwin did everything it possibly could after the order was entered" and that the "order served its purpose, and Darwin should not now be subject to an inordinately severe fine that in effect punishes Darwin for what the Court feels Darwin failed to do prior to the entry of the contempt order." The Court rejects both assertions.

* * * Specifically, Darwin claims that the items produced six days late were "lost" and that "considering only the period from the contempt order forward, immediate production of the lost items was impossible." * * *

Darwin was required to comply substantially with the Court's order. Substantial compliance is found where "all reasonable steps" have been taken to ensure compliance: inadvertent omissions are excused only if such steps were taken. [Citation.] Darwin argues only that there were "difficulties in arranging compliance.... Darwin could not reasonably be expected to find financial records that were labelled with the wrong year or that were located in a closed box of engineering materials buried behind dozens of other boxes in Darwin's cramped quarters." But Darwin does not assert that the documents missing from the first production on June 24, 1986, were beyond its possession or control. * * * It is clear that Darwin did not take "all reasonable steps" to ensure complete production until *after* it was notified by Agent Kohorst [on June 27] that some documents were still unproduced and additional efforts to find the missing documents were made. Darwin's efforts to achieve complete production between June 27 and June 30 do not transform its initial failure to make substantial compliance at the time of the first production. Thus, compliance was insubstantial until the second production occurred on June 30, 1986. This finding is based solely upon Darwin's inattentiveness after the June 23 order was issued.

Darwin's good faith defense is also rejected on the basis of its indifference regarding the completeness of the initial production, but particularly in light of the opportunity it had to prepare for production before the Court's order on June 23, 1986. * * * The evidence produced at the assessment hearing leaves no doubt that Darwin either knew that documents were missing or took no special steps to find out before the June 23 hearing. Darwin's initial production, grounded in indifference and ignorance as to the completeness, did not show good faith where Darwin had over one year to ensure that all the documents listed in the summons were located and more than eight weeks' notice that this Court's contempt order would be enforced. * * *

The $5000 per day penalty was pre-specified at a rate determined by the Court to be reasonable based upon the non-complying party's previous reluctance to obey the Court's directives, the corporate character of the non-complying party, and the injury to justice which further contempt would invite. * * * The Court found that substantial compliance occurred only after six days of insubstantial compliance.

The subject of a conditional contempt order cannot expect the Court to threaten to fine the party for non-compliance with a court order at a certain rate and then later find that party to be non-complying but yet deserving of a lesser penalty. The coercive power of a threatened penalty is nullified if the Court is unable to enforce the penalty later at the pre-specified rate. That the factual circumstances under which the Court will find compliance or non-compliance are unclear *ex ante* does not necessitate *ex post* adjustment of the penalty at the assessment stage of the proceedings. The object of the order is to encourage full compliance by setting a known cost for non-compliance. If the Court were required to adjust the cost downward according to the degree of compliance, then the $5000 per day penalty would be indeterminant and therefore less effective in encouraging compliance.

* * *

The Court today rules that a pre-specified daily contempt fine for non-compliance need not be adjusted at the assessment stage. The only mitigating factors are the defenses raised by respondent: substantial compliance and, perhaps, good faith. These defenses were rejected in the Court's February 4, 1988 memorandum and order and are rejected again today. The Court will not consider reduction of the fine, nor, does it find that a $5000 per day fine was then, or is now, unreasonable in light of the appropriate considerations. * * *

----

1. Compare coercive civil contempt fines with criminal contempt fines. Whereas a criminal contempt fine for past disobedience is a fixed sum

determined after the acts are complete, a coercive civil contempt fine is predetermined by the court as a daily penalty for future non-compliance. The coercive civil contempt fine is not specified, however, until after the defendant has manifested a reluctance to obey the court's initial order. Would it be a good idea for every equitable order to indicate a date for compliance and a coercive contempt fine for each day thereafter? Why should a court wait until a defendant shows recalcitrance?

2.   The United States Supreme Court has held that determination of the amount of the daily civil contempt fine should be guided by certain factors: "the character and magnitude of the harm threatened by continued contumacy, and the probable effectiveness of any suggested sanctions in bringing about the result desired." United States v. United Mine Workers, 330 U.S. 258, 304, 67 S.Ct. 677, 701, 91 L.Ed. 884 (1947). *See also* Dole Fresh Fruit Co. v. United Banana Co., 821 F.2d 106 (2d Cir.1987); General Signal Corp. v. Donallco, 787 F.2d 1376 (9th Cir.1986).

3.   The court in the principal case refused to adjust the amount of the pre-set fine after the disobedience. A Court of Appeals decision from the District of Columbia indicated that in cases with "complicating factors" such an adjustment is appropriate. Such factors in a back-to-work labor dispute include the complexity of the outstanding order, possible ambiguities, and difficulties in arranging compliance. Brotherhood of Locomotive Firemen and Enginemen v. Bangor & Aroostook Railroad Co., 380 F.2d 570 (D.C.Cir.), *cert. denied*, 389 U.S. 327, 88 S.Ct. 437, 19 L.Ed.2d 560 (1967).

PROBLEM: THE PERSISTENT PROTESTER

Jim Lofton is a college student who is an activist on environmental issues. You represent him in a case where the Newprod Company has obtained an injunction against Lofton to prohibit him from trespassing and interfering with Newprod employees in the company parking lot. Lofton had been going there every night to hand to the employees leaflets about the company's pollution. On occasion Lofton has been sufficiently pushy and argumentative with some individuals that they complained to the company. One night Lofton blocked the president's car and would not get out of the way until the president had read through the leaflet. The company then sought and obtained against Lofton an injunction prohibiting further trespass on the company's property.

Lofton ignored the injunction and returned to distribute new flyers in the company's parking lot. After a hearing, the judge found him in contempt and fined him $100. The episode was repeated a second time, and contempt was again found. This time the fine was $200. The judge told Lofton that if he again defied the court order, the fine would be $500 the next time *and* Lofton would go to jail for thirty days.

Lofton, undaunted, again violated the order. The judge imposed the fine and jail term as previously indicated. When the sentence was announced, Lofton looked straight in the judge's eye and muttered an obscene reference to the judge's ancestry. For this offense the judge summarily sentenced Lofton to six months in jail for contempt of the court.

Throughout these events you have advised Lofton to obey the court's orders, but your advice has not been heeded. The question now is whether you can appeal successfully any of these contempts. Lofton has protested all along that he wanted a jury to hear his case because he believes a jury would be sympathetic. There have been many complaints in the community about Newprod's unresponsiveness to the problem of the factory odor. Lofton also believes that his First Amendment right to free speech has been violated because the parking lot is used in part by the public as well as the company employees. Assuming that the First Amendment argument is a substantial claim, and that a jury trial would be desirable, what can you do for Lofton?

United Mine Workers v. Bagwell

512 U.S. 821, 114 S.Ct. 2552, 129 L.Ed.2d 642 (1994).

■ JUSTICE BLACKMUN delivered the opinion of the Court.

We are called upon once again to consider the distinction between civil and criminal contempt. Specifically, we address whether contempt fines levied against a union for violations of a labor injunction are coercive civil fines, or are criminal fines that constitutionally could be imposed only through a jury trial. We conclude that the fines are criminal and, accordingly, we reverse the judgment of the Supreme Court of Virginia.

I

Petitioners, the International Union, United Mine Workers of America and United Mine Workers of America, District 28 (collectively, the union) engaged in a protracted labor dispute with the Clinchfield Coal Company and Sea "B" Mining Company (collectively, the companies) over alleged unfair labor practices. In April 1989, the companies filed suit in the Circuit Court of Russell County, Virginia, to enjoin the union from conducting unlawful strike-related activities. The trial court entered an injunction which, as later amended, prohibited the union and its members from, among other things, obstructing ingress and egress to company facilities, throwing objects at and physically threatening company employees, placing tire-damaging "jackrocks" on roads used by company vehicles, and picketing with more than a specified number of people at designated sites. The court additionally ordered the union to take all steps necessary to ensure compliance with the injunction, to place supervisors at picket sites, and to report all violations to the court.

On May 16, 1989, the trial court held a contempt hearing and found that petitioners had committed 72 violations of the injunction. After fining the union $642,000 for its disobedience, the court announced that it would fine the union $100,000 for any future violent breach of the injunction and $20,000 for any future nonviolent infraction, "such as exceeding picket numbers, [or] blocking entrances or exits." The Court early stated that its purpose was to "impos[e] prospective civil fines[,] the payment of which would only be required if it were shown the defendants disobeyed the Court's orders."

In seven subsequent contempt hearings held between June and December 1989, the court found the union in contempt for more than 400 separate violations of the injunction, many of them violent. Based on the court's stated "intention that these fines are civil and coercive," each contempt hearing was conducted as a civil proceeding before the trial judge, in which the parties conducted discovery, introduced evidence, and called and cross-examined witnesses. The trial court required that contumacious acts be proved beyond a reasonable doubt, but did not afford the union a right to jury trial.

As a result of these contempt proceedings, the court levied over $64,000,000 in fines against the union, approximately $12,000,000 of which was ordered payable to the companies. Because the union objected to payment of any fines to the companies and in light of the law enforcement burdens posed by the strike, the court ordered that the remaining roughly $52,000,000 in fines be paid to the Commonwealth of Virginia and Russell and Dickenson Counties, "the two counties most heavily affected by the unlawful activity."

While appeals from the contempt orders were pending, the union and the companies settled the underlying labor dispute, agreed to vacate the contempt fines, and jointly moved to dismiss the case. * * * The trial court granted the motion to dismiss, dissolved the injunction, and vacated the $12,000,000 in fines payable to the companies. After reiterating its belief that the remaining $52,000,000 owed to the counties and the Commonwealth were coercive, civil fines, the trial court refused to vacate these fines, concluding they were "payable in effect to the public."

* * * [T]he court appointed respondent John L. Bagwell to act as Special Commissioner to collect the unpaid contempt fines on behalf of the counties and the Commonwealth.

The Court of Appeals of Virginia reversed and ordered that the contempt fines be vacated pursuant to the settlement agreement. Assuming for the purposes of argument that the fines were civil, the court concluded "that civil contempt fines imposed during or as a part of a civil proceeding between private parties are settled when the underlying litigation is settled by the parties and the court is without discretion to refuse to vacate such fines."

On consolidated appeals, the Supreme Court of Virginia reversed. The court held that whether coercive, civil contempt sanctions could be settled by private parties was a question of state law, and that Virginia public policy disfavored such a rule, "if the dignity of the law and public respect for the judiciary are to be maintained." The court also rejected petitioners' contention that the outstanding fines were criminal and could not be imposed absent a criminal trial. * * * This Court granted certiorari.

II

A

"Criminal contempt is a crime in the ordinary sense," Bloom v. Illinois, 391 U.S. 194, 201, 88 S.Ct. 1477, 1481, 20 L.Ed.2d 522 (1968), and "criminal penalties may not be imposed on someone who has not been afforded the protections that the Constitution requires of such criminal proceedings." [Citations.] In contrast, civil contempt sanctions, or those penalties designed to compel future compliance with a court order, are considered to be coercive and avoidable through obedience, and thus may be imposed in an ordinary civil proceeding upon notice and opportunity to be heard. Neither a jury trial nor proof beyond a reasonable doubt is required.

civil ←

Although the procedural contours of the two forms of contempt are well established, the distinguishing characteristics of civil versus criminal contempts are somewhat less clear. In the leading early case addressing this issue in the context of imprisonment, Gompers v. Bucks Stove & Range Co., 221 U.S., at 441, 31 S.Ct., at 498, the Court emphasized that whether a contempt is civil or criminal turns on the "character and purpose" of the sanction involved. Thus, a contempt sanction is considered civil if it "is remedial, and for the benefit of the complainant. But if it is for criminal contempt the sentence is punitive, to vindicate the authority of the court." * * *

The paradigmatic coercive, civil contempt sanction, as set forth in Gompers, involves confining a contemnor indefinitely until he complies with an affirmative command such as an order "to pay alimony, or to surrender property ordered to be turned over to a receiver, or to make a conveyance." Gompers, 221 U.S., at 442, 31 S.Ct., at 498[.] * * *

By contrast, a fixed sentence of imprisonment is punitive and criminal if it is imposed retrospectively for a "completed act of disobedience," Gompers, 221 U.S., at 443, 31 S.Ct., at 498, such that the contemnor cannot avoid or abbreviate the confinement through later compliance. * * *

This dichotomy between coercive and punitive imprisonment has been extended to the fine context. A contempt fine accordingly is considered civil and remedial if it either "coerce[s] the defendant into compliance with the court's order, [or] . . . compensate[s] the complainant for losses sustained." United States v. United Mine Workers of America, 330 U.S. 258, 303–304, 67 S.Ct. 677, 701, 91 L.Ed. 884 (1947). Where a fine is not compensatory, it is civil only if the contemnor is afforded an opportunity to purge. [Citation.] Thus, a "flat, unconditional fine" totalling even as little as $50 announced after a finding of contempt is criminal if the contemnor has no subsequent opportunity to reduce or avoid the fine through compliance.

A close analogy to coercive imprisonment is a per diem fine imposed for each day a contemnor fails to comply with an affirmative court order. Like civil imprisonment, such fines exert a constant coercive pressure, and once the jural command is obeyed, the future, indefinite, daily fines are purged.

Less comfortable is the analogy between coercive imprisonment and suspended, determinate fines. In this Court's sole prior decision squarely addressing the judicial power to impose coercive civil contempt fines, *United Mine Workers*, *supra*, it held that fixed fines also may be considered purgable and civil when imposed and suspended pending future compliance.

* * *

This Court has not revisited the issue of coercive civil contempt fines addressed in *United Mine Workers*. Since that decision, the Court has erected substantial procedural protections in other areas of contempt law, such as criminal contempts. [Citations.] Lower federal courts and state courts such as the trial court here nevertheless have relied on *United Mine Workers* to authorize a relatively unlimited judicial power to impose noncompensatory civil contempt fines.

B

Underlying the somewhat elusive distinction between civil and criminal contempt fines, and the ultimate question posed in this case, is what procedural protections are due before any particular contempt penalty may be imposed. Because civil contempt sanctions are viewed as nonpunitive and avoidable, fewer procedural protections for such sanctions have been required. To the extent that such contempts take on a punitive character, however, and are not justified by other considerations central to the contempt power, criminal procedural protections may be in order.

* * *

For a discrete category of indirect contempts, civil procedural protections may be insufficient. Contempts involving out-of-court disobedience to complex injunctions often require elaborate and reliable factfinding. [Citation.] Such contempts do not obstruct the court's ability to adjudicate the proceedings before it, and the risk of erroneous deprivation from the lack of a neutral factfinder may be substantial. Under these circumstances, criminal procedural protections such as the rights to counsel and proof beyond a reasonable doubt are both necessary and appropriate to protect the due process rights of parties and prevent the arbitrary exercise of judicial power.

C

In the instant case, neither any party nor any court of the Commonwealth has suggested that the challenged fines are compensatory. * * * The issue before us is limited to whether these fines, despite their noncompensatory character, are coercive civil or criminal sanctions.

* * *

Despite respondent's urging, we are not persuaded that dispositive significance should be accorded to the fact that the trial court prospectively announced the sanctions it would impose. Had the trial court simply levied the fines after finding the union guilty of contempt, the resulting determinate and unconditional fines would be considered solely and exclusively punitive. [Citation.] Respondent nevertheless contends that the trial court's announcement of a prospective fine schedule allowed the union to avoid paying the fines simply by performing the act required by the court's order, [citations], and thus transformed these fines into coercive, civil ones. Respondent maintains here, as the Virginia Supreme Court held below, that the trial court could have imposed a daily civil fine to coerce the union into compliance, and that a prospective fine schedule is indistinguishable from such a sanction.

Respondent's argument highlights the difficulties encountered in parsing coercive civil and criminal contempt fines. * * * The trial court here simply announced the penalty—determinate fines of $20,000 or $100,000 per violation—that would be imposed for future contempts. The union's ability to avoid the contempt fines was indistinguishable from the ability of any ordinary citizen to avoid a criminal sanction by conforming his behavior to the law. The fines are not coercive day fines, or even suspended fines, but are more closely analogous to fixed, determinate, retrospective criminal fines which petitioners had no opportunity to purge once imposed. We therefore decline to conclude that the mere fact that the sanctions were announced in advance rendered them coercive and civil as a matter of constitutional law.

* * *

III

Our decision concededly imposes some procedural burdens on courts' ability to sanction widespread, indirect contempts of complex injunctions through noncompensatory fines. Our holding, however, leaves unaltered the longstanding authority of judges to adjudicate direct contempts summarily, and to enter broad compensatory awards for all contempts through civil proceedings. [Citation.] Because the right to trial by jury applies only to serious criminal sanctions, courts still may impose noncompensatory, petty fines for contempts such as the present ones without conducting a jury trial. We also do not disturb a court's ability to levy, albeit through the criminal contempt process, serious fines like those in this case.

Ultimately, whatever slight burden our holding may impose on the judicial contempt power cannot be controlling. * * * Where, as here, "a serious contempt is at issue, considerations of efficiency must give way to the more fundamental interest of ensuring the even-handed exercise of judicial power." [citing *Bloom*] at 209, 88 S.Ct., at 1486.

The judgment of the Supreme Court of Virginia is reversed.

■ Justice Scalia, concurring.

I join the Court's opinion classifying the $52,000,000 in contempt fines levied against petitioners as criminal. As the Court's opinion demonstrates, our cases have employed a variety of not easily reconcilable tests for differentiating between civil and criminal contempts. Since all of those tests would yield the same result here, there is no need to decide which is the correct one—and a case so extreme on its facts is not the best case in which to make that decision. I wish to suggest, however, that when we come to making it, a careful examination of historical practice will ultimately yield the answer.

That one and the same person should be able to make the rule, to adjudicate its violation, and to assess its penalty is out of accord with our usual notions of fairness and separation of powers. [Citations.] And it is worse still for that person to conduct the adjudication without affording the protections usually given in criminal trials. Only the clearest of historical practice could establish that such a departure from the procedures that the Constitution normally requires is not a denial of due process of law. * * *

The order at issue here provides a relatively tame example of the modern, complex decree. The amended injunction prohibited, inter alia, rock-throwing, the puncturing of tires, threatening, following or interfering with respondents' employees, placing pickets in other than specified locations, and roving picketing; and it required, inter alia, that petitioners provide a list of names of designated supervisors. Although it would seem quite in accord with historical practice to enforce, by conditional incarceration or per diem fines, compliance with the last provision—a discrete command, observance of which is readily ascertained—using that same means to enforce the remainder of the order would be a novelty.

* * * We will have to decide at some point which modern injunctions sufficiently resemble their historical namesakes to warrant the same extraordinary means of enforcement. We need not draw that line in the present case, and so I am content to join the opinion of the Court.

■ JUSTICE GINSBURG, with whom THE CHIEF JUSTICE joins, concurring in part and concurring in the judgment.

The issue in this case is whether the contempt proceedings brought against the petitioner unions are to be classified as "civil" or "criminal." As the Court explains, if those proceedings were "criminal," then the unions were entitled under our precedents to a jury trial, and the disputed fines, imposed in bench proceedings, could not stand.

* * *

Two considerations persuade me that the contempt proceedings in this case should be classified as "criminal" rather than "civil." First, were we to accept the logic of Bagwell's argument that the fines here were civil, because "conditional" and "coercive," no fine would elude that categorization. * * *

Second, the Virginia courts' refusal to vacate the fines, despite the parties' settlement and joint motion, is characteristic of criminal, not civil proceedings. In explaining why the fines outlived the underlying civil dispute, the Supreme Court of Virginia stated: "Courts of the Commonwealth must have the authority to enforce their orders by employing coercive, civil sanctions if the dignity of the law and public respect for the judiciary are to be maintained." * * *

Concluding that the fines at issue "are more closely analogous to ... criminal fines" [citation], than to civil fines, I join the Court's judgment and all but Part II–B of its opinion.

---

1. What policy reason can justify treating any coercive order to compel obedience as civil rather than criminal? Is there a meaningful distinction between a routine injunction against trespass and a daily fine for continued trespass? If so, should criminal procedure safeguards attach only to the latter? Both? Neither? Does the principal case answer these questions?

2. Does the principal case implicitly expand the definition of criminal contempt? For a thoughtful discussion of this question and an argument that the Court has unduly restricted plaintiffs from obtaining prompt and reliable equitable relief, see Margit Livingston, *Disobedience and Contempt*, 75 Wash. L. Rev. 345 (2000).

3. The Court in the principal case found it unnecessary to define a "serious contempt" when the punishment is by fine rather than imprisonment. In a previous case the Court found that a $10,000 criminal fine imposed upon a union with 13,000 dues paying members was a petty punishment that did not warrant a jury trial. Muniz v. Hoffman, 422 U.S. 454, 95 S.Ct. 2178, 45 L.Ed.2d 319 (1975).

One court found it necessary to reach a related issue in application of *Bagwell*. In Evans v. Williams, 206 F.3d 1292 (D.C.Cir.2000), the court considered the character of fines paid for failure to comply with a consent decree's bill payment schedule. Because they were considered non-petty and criminal, the Constitutional safeguards applied: there was a right to a jury trial; noncompliance must be willful; and proof must be beyond a reasonable doubt.

4. Does the Court suggest in *Bagwell* that all predetermined sanctions in coercive civil contempt are criminal in nature? Compare N.O.W. v. Operation Rescue, 37 F.3d 646 (D.C.Cir.1994) (all noncompensatory fines should be afforded criminal protections) with People v. Operation Rescue National, 80 F.3d 64 (2d Cir.1996) (noncompensatory fines may be civil under *Bagwell*).

Latrobe Steel Co. v. United Steelworkers of America

545 F.2d 1336 (3d Cir.1976).

■ Adams, Circuit Judge.

This appeal presents two principal issues. First, we must decide whether the district court had jurisdiction to enjoin the appellant union from refusing to cross a "stranger picket line."[1] Then, if that question is

---

1. A "stranger picket line" is a picket line established by a union other than the one against which the injunction is sought.

answered in the negative, we must determine whether a coercive civil contempt decree, based on a violation of the injunction, can survive the invalidation of the underlying order.

United Steelworkers of America and its Local Union No. 1537 have for many years represented the production and maintenance employees of the Latrobe Steel Company. Local 1537 and Latrobe Steel were signatories to a collective bargaining agreement that contained a broad no-strike clause and an expansive grievance-arbitration provision.

The Steelworkers and another local union have been the certified representatives of the office, clerical and technical employees at the Latrobe plant since 1974. After efforts to negotiate a collective bargaining agreement between the office workers local and Latrobe Steel proved unsuccessful, the office employees established a picket line outside of the Latrobe facility at about 11:00 P.M. on September 4, 1975. As a result of the picket line, the production workers on the midnight shift refused to enter the plant.

Early the next morning, September 5th, Latrobe Steel brought an action in the district court under section 301 of the Labor Management Relations Act of 1947 [29 U.S.C. § 185 (1970)], seeking a temporary restraining order against the refusal of the production employees to cross the picket line. * * *

When the production workers did not report for work on September 10th, Latrobe Steel moved the district court to hold Local 1537 and certain of its officers and members in "civil contempt." Following a full hearing the district court ruled that the union was "adjudged in civil contempt."
* * *

The district court's contempt order levied a two-part fine on the union. An assessment of $10,000 was imposed, payable to the United States, if the production employees did not report for work at the next shift beginning midnight, September 12th. The court's adjudication also provided that the union would have to pay an additional $10,000, again to the United States, for each subsequent day the union failed to comply with the preliminary injunction. * * *

After a careful review of the facts and the authorities, we conclude that the preliminary injunction as well as the contempt judgment in this case must be vacated.

[The court concludes that the anti-injunction provision of the Norris–LaGuardia Act is applicable and "the district court was without jurisdiction to enter a preliminary injunction." The court further determined that the contempt was coercive civil contempt rather than indirect criminal contempt.] * * *

The remaining issue, whether a civil contempt order that is coercive in nature falls with the underlying injunction, is one which has received scant judicial consideration. The paucity of analysis of this problem, which is critical to the disposition of this case, is particularly surprising, given the wealth of precedent on the effect generally of the invalidation of a prior injunction on subsequent criminal and compensatory civil contempts.

With regard to criminal contempt, the Supreme Court's opinions in *Walker v. Birmingham* [388 U.S. 307, 87 S.Ct. 1824 (1967) reproduced *supra*] and *United States v. United Mine Workers* [330 U.S. 258, 67 S.Ct. 677 (1947) reproduced *supra*] clearly hold that a criminal contempt judgment does survive the voiding of an injunction. * * *

Although the cases do not fully explicate the reasoning behind the general principle that compensatory civil contempt does not survive the abrogation of the underlying decree, the precept is, in our opinion, a sound one. A compensatory contempt proceeding is similar in several particulars to an ordinary damage action, since it is in essence an action between private parties, with rights created by the injunctive order rather than by a statute or the common law. The invalidation of an injunction in such a setting is equivalent to a holding that the plaintiff never had a legally cognizable interest which the defendant was obliged to respect, a conclusion which should be distinguished from the nearly unconditional duty of obedience owed by a defendant to a court. The *United Mine Workers'* doctrine thus recognizes that a private party should not profit as a result of an order to which a court determines, in retrospect, he was never entitled.

* * *

* * * [O]ur task, as often the case in litigation, is to reconcile two legal principles, in order to prevent either from destroying the other. Here, the importance of each of the principles can be acknowledged by recognizing that a court may uphold respect for law through the utilization of the criminal contempt process, while preventing litigants from benefiting from void court orders through the medium of either remedial or coercive civil contempt.

* * *

Accordingly, the injunction and the order of contempt will be vacated and the cause remanded for proceedings consistent with this opinion.

---

1. The reversal of a civil contempt upon the reversal of the underlying injunctive order has been explained as follows:

> It is true that the reversal of the decree does not retroactively obliterate the past existence of the violation; yet on the other hand it does more than destroy the future sanction of the decree. It adjudges that it never should have passed; that the right which it affected to create was no right at all. To let the liability stand for past contumacy would be to give the plaintiff a remedy not for a right but for a wrong, which the law should not do.

Salvage Process Corp. v. Acme Tank Cleaning Process Corp., 86 F.2d 727, 727 (2d Cir.1936).

2. The United States Supreme Court once suggested that a test to distinguish the nature of contempt penalties is whether the conduct was "refusing to do an act commanded" or "doing an act prohibited." The former contempts are civil whereas the latter ones are criminal. Gompers v. Buck's Stove & Range Co., 221 U.S. 418, 443, 31 S.Ct. 492, 55 L.Ed. 797 (1911).

Is this distinction useful? Is the conduct in the principal case best characterized as refusing the commanded act to return to work or as doing the prohibited act of striking?

The Supreme Court subsequently rejected this simply dichotomy in complex cases:

> * * * The distinction between mandatory and prohibitory orders is easily applied in the classic contempt scenario, where contempt sanctions are used to enforce orders compelling or forbidding a single, discrete act. In such cases, orders commanding an affirmative act simply designate those actions that are capable of being coerced.

> But the distinction between coercion of affirmative acts and punishment of prohibited conduct is difficult to apply when conduct that can recur is involved, or when an injunction contains both mandatory and prohibitory provisions. Moreover, in borderline cases injunctive provisions containing essentially the same command can be phrased either in mandatory or prohibitory terms. Under a literal application of petitioners' theory, an injunction ordering the union: "Do not strike," would appear to be prohibitory and criminal, while an injunction ordering the union: "Continue working," would be mandatory and civil. Dobbs, Contempt of Court: A Survey, 56 Cornell L.Rev. 183, 239 (1971).

United Mine Workers v. Bagwell, 512 U.S. 821, 114 S.Ct. 2552, 129 L.Ed.2d 642 (1994).

3. Consider the usefulness of the following attempt to distinguish between contempts:

> Contempts may be civil or criminal. In a civil contempt the contemnor violates a decree or order of the court made for the benefit of an adverse party litigant. In a criminal contempt a court's process is violated or disobeyed and disrespect of the court is manifested.

State *ex rel.* Oregon State Bar v. Lenske, 243 Or. 477, 480, 405 P.2d 510, 512 (1965), *cert. denied,* 384 U.S. 943, 86 S.Ct. 1460, 16 L.Ed.2d 541 (1966). A helpful discussion is in Dobbs, Contempt of Court: A Survey, 56 Cornell L.Rev. 183, 239–41 (1971).

4. Does *United Mine Workers,* reproduced *supra,* compel the result reached by the court in the principal case? *United Mine Workers* phrased the issue addressed by that opinion as whether "the plaintiff may profit by way of a fine imposed" for violation of an order erroneously issued. 330 U.S. 258, 294–5, 67 S.Ct. 677, 696, 91 L.Ed. 884 (1947). Should "profit" be interpreted broadly?

Should the Court's reasoning in *United Mine Workers v. Bagwell*, reproduced *supra*, affect the result in cases posing the issue in the principal case?

Turner v. Rogers

___ U.S. ___, 131 S.Ct. 2507, 180 L.Ed.2d 452 (2011).

■ JUSTICE BREYER delivered the opinion of the Court.

South Carolina's Family Court enforces its child support orders by threatening with incarceration for civil contempt those who are (1) subject to a child support order, (2) able to comply with that order, but (3) fail to do so. We must decide whether the Fourteenth Amendment's Due Process Clause requires the State to provide counsel (at a civil contempt hearing) to an *indigent* person potentially faced with such incarceration. * * *

South Carolina family courts enforce their child support orders in part through civil contempt proceedings. Each month the family court clerk reviews outstanding child support orders, identifies those in which the supporting parent has fallen more than five days behind, and sends that parent an order to "show cause" why he should not be held in contempt. * * * At the hearing that parent may demonstrate that he is not in contempt, say, by showing that he is not able to make the required payments. [Citation.] If he fails to make the required showing, the court may hold him in civil contempt. And it may require that he be imprisoned unless and until he purges himself of contempt by making the required child support payments (but not for more than one year regardless). [Citation.]

In June 2003 a South Carolina family court entered an order, which (as amended) required petitioner, Michael Turner, to pay $51.73 per week to respondent, Rebecca Rogers, to help support their child. (Rogers' father, Larry Price, currently has custody of the child and is also a respondent before this Court.) Over the next three years, Turner repeatedly failed to pay the amount due and was held in contempt on five occasions. The first four times he was sentenced to 90 days' imprisonment, but he ultimately paid the amount due (twice without being jailed, twice after spending two or three days in custody). The fifth time he did not pay but completed a 6–month sentence.

After his release in 2006 Turner remained in arrears. On March 27, 2006, the clerk issued a new "show cause" order. And after an initial postponement due to Turner's failure to appear, Turner's civil contempt hearing took place on January 3, 2008. Turner and Rogers were present, each without representation by counsel.

The hearing was brief. The court clerk said that Turner was $5,728.76 behind in his payments. The judge asked Turner if there was "anything you want to say." Turner replied,

"Well, when I first got out, I got back on dope. I done meth, smoked pot and everything else, and I paid a little bit here and there. And, when I finally did get to working, I broke my back, back in September. I filed for disability and SSI. And, I didn't get straightened out off the dope until I broke my back and laid up for two months. And, now I'm off the dope and everything. I just hope that you give me a chance. I don't know what else to say. I mean, I know I done wrong, and I should have been paying and helping her, and I'm sorry. I mean, dope had a hold to me." * * *

[The judge found Turner in wilful contempt.] The court made no express finding concerning Turner's ability to pay his arrearage (though Turner's wife had voluntarily submitted a copy of Turner's application for disability benefits, [citation]). Nor did the judge ask any followup questions or otherwise address the ability-to-pay issue. * * *

While serving his 12–month sentence, Turner, with the help of *pro bono* counsel, appealed. He claimed that the Federal Constitution entitled him to counsel at his contempt hearing. The South Carolina Supreme Court decided Turner's appeal after he had completed his sentence. And it rejected his "right to counsel" claim. The court pointed out that civil contempt differs significantly from criminal contempt. * * *

Turner sought certiorari. In light of differences among state courts (and some federal courts) on the applicability of a "right to counsel" in civil contempt proceedings enforcing child support orders, we granted the writ. * * *

We must decide whether the Due Process Clause grants an indigent defendant, such as Turner, a right to state-appointed counsel at a civil contempt proceeding, which may lead to his incarceration. This Court's precedents provide no definitive answer to that question. This Court has long held that the Sixth Amendment grants an indigent defendant the right to state-appointed counsel in a *criminal* case. Gideon v. Wainwright, 372 U.S. 335, 83 S.Ct. 792, 9 L.Ed.2d 799 (1963). And we have held that this same rule applies to *criminal contempt* proceedings (other than summary proceedings). [Citations.]

But the Sixth Amendment does not govern civil cases. Civil contempt differs from criminal contempt in that it seeks only to "coerc[e] the defendant to do" what a court had previously ordered him to do. Gompers v. Bucks Stove & Range Co., 221 U.S. 418, 442, 31 S.Ct. 492, 55 L.Ed. 797 (1911). A court may not impose punishment "in a civil contempt proceeding when it is clearly established that the alleged contemnor is unable to comply with the terms of the order." Hicks v. Feiock, 485 U.S. 624, 638, n. 9, 108 S.Ct. 1423, 99 L.Ed.2d 721 (1988). And once a civil contemnor complies with the underlying order, he is purged of the contempt and is free. Id., at 633, 108 S.Ct. 1423 (he "carr[ies] the keys of [his] prison in [his] own pockets" (internal quotation marks omitted)).

Consequently, the Court has made clear (in a case not involving the right to counsel) that, where civil contempt is at issue, the Fourteenth Amendment's Due Process Clause allows a State to provide fewer procedural protections than in a criminal case. * * * Civil contempt proceedings in child support cases constitute one part of a highly complex system designed to assure a noncustodial parent's regular payment of funds typically necessary for the support of his children. Often the family receives welfare support from a state-administered federal program, and the State then seeks reimbursement from the noncustodial parent. * * *

The "private interest that will be affected" argues strongly for the right to counsel that Turner advocates. That interest consists of an indigent defendant's loss of personal liberty through imprisonment. The interest in securing that freedom, the freedom "from bodily restraint," lies "at the core of the liberty protected by the Due Process Clause." * * *

Given the importance of the interest at stake, it is obviously important to assure accurate decisionmaking in respect to the key "ability to pay" question. Moreover, the fact that ability to comply marks a dividing line between civil and criminal contempt, *Hicks*, 485 U.S., at 635, n. 7, 108 S.Ct. 1423, reinforces the need for accuracy. That is because an incorrect decision (wrongly classifying the contempt proceeding as civil) can increase the risk of wrongful incarceration by depriving the defendant of the procedural protections (including counsel) that the Constitution would demand in a criminal proceeding. * * *

On the other hand, the Due Process Clause does not always require the provision of counsel in civil proceedings where incarceration is threatened. [Citation.] And in determining whether the Clause requires a right to counsel here, we must take account of opposing interests, as well as consider the probable value of "additional or substitute procedural safeguards." [Citation.]

Doing so, we find three related considerations that, when taken together, argue strongly against the Due Process Clause requiring the State to provide indigents with counsel in every proceeding of the kind before us.

First, the critical question likely at issue in these cases concerns, as we have said, the defendant's ability to pay. That question is often closely related to the question of the defendant's indigence. But when the right procedures are in place, indigence can be a question that in many—but not all—cases is sufficiently straightforward to warrant determination *prior* to providing a defendant with counsel, even in a criminal case. * * *

Second, sometimes, as here, the person opposing the defendant at the hearing is not the government represented by counsel but the custodial parent *un*-represented by counsel. * * * A requirement that the State provide counsel to the noncustodial parent in these cases could create an asymmetry of representation that would "alter significantly the nature of the proceeding." * * *

Third, as the Solicitor General points out, there is available a set of "substitute procedural safeguards," [citation], which, if employed together, can significantly reduce the risk of an erroneous deprivation of liberty. They can do so, moreover, without incurring some of the drawbacks inherent in recognizing an automatic right to counsel. Those safeguards include (1) notice to the defendant that his "ability to pay" is a critical issue in the contempt proceeding; (2) the use of a form (or the equivalent) to elicit relevant financial information; (3) an opportunity at the hearing for the defendant to respond to statements and questions about his financial status, (*e.g.,* those triggered by his responses on the form); and (4) an express finding by the court that the defendant has the ability to pay. * * *

While recognizing the strength of Turner's arguments, we ultimately believe that the three considerations we have just discussed must carry the day. In our view, a categorical right to counsel in proceedings of the kind before us would carry with it disadvantages (in the form of unfairness and delay) that, in terms of ultimate fairness, would deprive it of significant superiority over the alternatives that we have mentioned. We consequently hold that the Due Process Clause does not *automatically* require the provision of counsel at civil contempt proceedings to an indigent individual who is subject to a child support order, even if that individual faces incarceration (for up to a year). In particular, that Clause does not require the provision of counsel where the opposing parent or other custodian (to whom support funds are owed) is not represented by counsel and the State provides alternative procedural safeguards equivalent to those we have mentioned (adequate notice of the importance of ability to pay, fair opportunity to present, and to dispute, relevant information, and court findings).

We do not address civil contempt proceedings where the underlying child support payment is owed to the State, for example, for reimbursement of welfare funds paid to the parent with custody. [Citation.] Those proceedings more closely resemble debt-collection proceedings. The government is likely to have counsel or some other competent representative. * * *

The record indicates that Turner received neither counsel nor the benefit of alternative procedures like those we have described. He did not receive clear notice that his ability to pay would constitute the critical question in his civil contempt proceeding. No one provided him with a form (or the equivalent) designed to elicit information about his financial circumstances. The court did not find that Turner was able to pay his arrearage, but instead left the relevant "finding" section of the contempt order blank. The court nonetheless found Turner in contempt and ordered him incarcerated. Under these circumstances Turner's incarceration violated the Due Process Clause.

We vacate the judgment of the South Carolina Supreme Court and remand the case for further proceedings not inconsistent with this opinion.

It is so ordered.

■ JUSTICE THOMAS, with whom JUSTICE SCALIA joins, and with whom THE CHIEF JUSTICE and JUSTICE ALITO join as to Parts IB and II, dissenting.

The Due Process Clause of the Fourteenth Amendment does not provide a right to appointed counsel for indigent defendants facing incarceration in civil contempt proceedings. Therefore, I would affirm. Although the Court agrees that appointed counsel was not required in this case, it nevertheless vacates the judgment of the South Carolina Supreme Court on a different ground, which the parties have never raised. Solely at the invitation of the United States as *amicus curiae,* the majority decides that Turner's contempt proceeding violated due process because it did not include "alternative procedural safeguards." Consistent with this Court's longstanding practice, I would not reach that question. * * *

B.

Even under the Court's modern interpretation of the Constitution, the Due Process Clause does not provide a right to appointed counsel for all indigent defendants facing incarceration in civil contempt proceedings. Such a reading would render the Sixth Amendment right to counsel—as it is currently understood—superfluous. * * *

III.

* * * Although I think that the majority's analytical framework does not account for the interests that children and mothers have in effective and flexible methods to secure payment, I do not pass on the wisdom of the majority's preferred procedures. Nor do I address the wisdom of the State's decision to use certain methods of enforcement. * * *

I would affirm the judgment of the South Carolina Supreme Court because the Due Process Clause does not provide a right to appointed counsel in civil contempt hearings that may lead to incarceration. As that is the only issue properly before the Court, I respectfully dissent.

———————

1. Indefinite jail terms or continuing fines under coercive civil contempt pose particular difficulty with respect of contemnors who have demonstrated that they will never comply with the court's order. Recalcitrant witnesses, for example, may demonstrate by their continued silence that they will never testify. Typically such witnesses fear for their physical safety or for the safety of their families. When coercion is impossible, is it permissible for the court to continue to try to coerce?

Some courts have accepted the idea of "exhausted coercion" and have permitted contemnors to demonstrate that their continued incarceration is punitive because there is no meaningful possibility of compliance. Others have refused to allow such a demonstration because future compliance is always theoretically possible. *Compare* Lambert v. Montana, 545 F.2d 87 (9th Cir.1976), *with* In re Grand Jury Investigation, 600 F.2d 420 (3d Cir.1979). *See also* In re Grand Jury Proceedings, 894 F.2d 881 (7th Cir.1989); Catena v. Seidl, 65 N.J. 257, 321 A.2d 225 (1974).

One celebrated case of this type involved Dr. Elizabeth Morgan, who refused to reveal the location of her child for the father to have visitation rights because she was convinced that the father had sexually molested the child. She remained imprisoned for two years before her release under a special statutory provision enacted for her benefit. *See* Morgan v. Foretich, 564 A.2d 1 (D.C.App.1989).

2. Another consequence of the distinction between civil and criminal contempt is the timing of the appeal. Criminal contempts are immediately appealable, whereas civil contempts are appealable with the underlying claim.

CHAPTER 8

Modern Injunction Forms and Functions

In modern law there are four types of injunctions: preventive, restorative, prophylactic, and structural. The last three have become common enough to receive labels only in the latter part of the twentieth century. The preventive injunction, previously studied in Chapter 3, has roots deep in the common law. Its purpose is to prevent the defendant from inflicting future injury on the plaintiff. The plaintiff must prove that the defendant was likely to do harm absent the order, that legal remedies would be inadequate, and that such harm would be irreparable.

The other types of injunctions are similar in the sense that in all of them the court makes an order that the defendant must do some act or refrain from doing some act. It is their different functions that distinguish them. This chapter explores those differences.

A. Restorative and Prophylactic Injunctions

Section Coverage:

Restorative and prophylactic injunctions are close cousins of preventive injunctions. A restorative injunction principally operates to correct the present by undoing the effects of a past wrong. The notion of "restoring" means that it focuses not only prospectively, as does the traditional preventive injunction, but also retroactively. For example, a tainted election process affects future governance; the wrong can only be corrected by turning back time, in some sense, and redoing the election.

A prophylactic injunction seeks to safeguard the plaintiff's rights by directing the defendant's behavior so as to minimize the chance that wrongs might recur in the future. For example, if an employer maintains an integrated work force where the social atmosphere is so pervasively prejudiced that it violates federal law, the court may order the employer to take specific steps to monitor complaints and to educate the employees on their responsibility not to harass co-workers on the basis of race. The lack of such procedures are not themselves a violation of federal law in the absence of a court order. The court would order the measures only if it seemed that future infractions of the plaintiffs' rights are likely without extra protections. Violation of a prophylactic injunction is not necessarily a legal wrong in itself, except that the injunction makes it so.

Model Case:

Officials in a small town are prejudiced against the members of a new group that has started a utopian community on the outskirts of town. The founders of community, known as The Kolony, force members to adhere to strict rules of dress and behavior. They do not believe in private ownership of property as a general principle, although they own the land where The Kolony is situated.

During the last election the town officials adopted unusually strict voting procedures. The ballots in this small town are hand-counted. Election judges can declare as "spoiled" any ballot where the marks in the boxes exceed the printed bounds sufficient to raise an ambiguity about the vote. In the election in question, election judges in the precinct exclusively containing The Kolony found ninety percent of the ballots were "spoiled." In all the other precincts only one ballot was declared "spoiled."

The Kolony sued and the judge found the behavior of the election judges was founded in prejudice. The court declared the election so tainted that it was invalid. An injunction against election officials required a new election. This order is a restorative injunction.

Because of the pervasive prejudice against members of The Kolony, the court issued additional orders to safeguard their right to vote. The order mandated certain registration practices that were not otherwise required by law. The court also ordered that precincts be drawn such that The Kolony is not exclusively in one. These orders are prophylactic injunctive measures.

Vasquez v. Bannworths, Inc.

707 S.W.2d 886 (Tex.1986).

■ McGEE, JUSTICE.

This is a suit for wrongful discharge brought by an employee, Maria Guadalupe Vasquez, against her employer, Bannworths, Inc. The issue on this appeal is whether the district court abused its discretion in failing to order Bannworths, Inc. to rehire Mrs. Vasquez, who was wrongfully discharged because of her union affiliation. Although the trial court awarded Mrs. Vasquez lost wages and enjoined Bannworths, Inc. from discriminating against Mrs. Vasquez if she was ever employed by Bannworths again, the trial court refused to order Bannworths to rehire Mrs. Vasquez. The court of appeals, in an unpublished opinion, affirmed the judgment of the trial court. We hold that the trial court abused its discretion and, therefore, we reverse the judgment of the court of appeals. The cause is remanded to the trial court to reform its judgment to include a mandatory injunction ordering Bannworths, Inc. to rehire Mrs. Vasquez in the same or similar capacity to the one she held prior to her unlawful discharge.

Mrs. Vasquez was first employed by Bannworths, Inc. as a farm worker in 1973. Although the nature of the work does not provide for permanent employment, Mrs. Vasquez worked for Bannworths for several different seasons each year for nine consecutive years. While employed by Bannworths, she usually worked five to six days a week for up to ten hours a day at minimum wage.

In January 1982, while employed by Bannworths, Mrs. Vasquez sought assistance through the local United Farm Workers office to obtain permanent resident status in the United States. She became an active member in the UFW, a labor union, about a month later. Subsequently, Mrs. Vasquez began to complain to UFW representatives about the lack of sanitation at Bannworth's facilities. Mrs. Vasquez charged that all employees were required to share a common drinking cup and that the portable restroom facilities provided for the workers in the fields were filthy and did not comply with certain minimum health and sanitation standards which had been promulgated by the Texas Health Commissioner. On November 5, 1982, two Hidalgo County Health Department sanitation engineers came to Bannworth's fields where Mrs. Vasquez's crew was working to inspect the bathroom facilities. Later that same day, Mrs. Vasquez was fired from her job with Bannworths.

Mrs. Vasquez brought this suit seeking damages for lost wages and an injunction to refrain Bannworths from violating the Texas Right-to-Work Law (hereinafter the Act). Tex.Rev.Civ.Stat.Ann. art. 5154g (Vernon 1971). That statute prohibits an employer from denying a person the right to work on account of membership or non-membership in a labor union. Tex.Rev.Civ.Stat.Ann. art. 5154g, sec. 1 (Vernon 1971). A jury found that Mrs. Vasquez had been fired by Bannworths because of her union membership and her complaints concerning the restroom facilities. Although the jury failed to find that Bannworths's act of firing Mrs. Vasquez was done with malice or in gross disregard of her rights, the jury did find that Bannworths would not hire Mrs. Vasquez again because of her union membership. The jury awarded Mrs. Vasquez $3000 in lost wages from the time she was fired until suit was filed.

Based on the jury's finding of probable, continuing, future injury and recognizing that the plaintiff would suffer continuing, immediate and irreparable harm without an adequate remedy at law, the trial court awarded injunctive relief. That relief, however, falls short of remedying the harm recognized by the court. While the trial court enjoined Bannworths from terminating, suspending, discriminating against, or threatening to terminate, suspend or discriminate against the plaintiff because of her union membership, the court conditioned the injunction on Bannworth's voluntary reemployment of Mrs. Vasquez. In other words, unless Mrs. Vasquez actually began working for Bannworths again, the injunction was of no consequence because it neither required Bannworths to rehire Mrs. Vasquez nor required Bannworths to not discriminate against Mrs. Vasquez if she chose to reapply for employment with Bannworths. Considering the jury's finding in this case, that Bannworths would continue to discriminate against Mrs. Vasquez because of her union membership, it became mandatory for the trial court to issue an injunction which would remedy the violation of the Act. Section 4 of article 5154g mandates that the trial court enjoin an employer whenever it is shown that the employer has violated the Act. Tex.Rev.Civ.Stat.Ann. art. 5154g, sec. 4 (Vernon 1971).

Although a trial court may have some discretion in fashioning the relief to be granted by the injunction, we hold that article 5154g, section 4 limits that discretion by requiring that the remedy devised be one which will effectuate the policy of the Act and which will undo the effects of violations of the Act. Tex.Rev.Civ.Stat.Ann. art. 5154g, sec. 4 (Vernon 1971). The injunction issued by the trial court does not alleviate the violation that occurred in this case. The violation to be enjoined in this case was Bannworths's firing of Mrs. Vasquez because of her union membership. The trial court failed to address this violation in the injunction it issued.

* * *

The right to injunctive relief, when such is necessary to afford a party full protection of his established right, is clear under Texas decisions. [Citations.] When faced with the twin findings of firing because of impermissible discrimination and a refusal to rehire on that basis, as well as a request by the plaintiff for reinstatement, we can see no reason which would justify a court's refusal to order reemployment. [Citation.] Based on the findings in this case and plaintiff's request to be rehired, there was only one remedy available to the trial court which would rectify the harm caused by Bannworths's violation of the Act. The remedy was to order Bannworths to rehire Mrs. Vasquez. The trial court abused its discretion in failing to order Mrs. Vasquez's rehiring because, in effect, the court's order allows Bannworths to continue to discriminate against Mrs. Vasquez by refusing to hire her because of her union membership.

The cause is remanded to the trial court to reform its judgment to include a mandatory injunction ordering Bannworths, Inc. to rehire Mrs. Vasquez in the same or similar capacity to the one she held prior to her unlawful discharge.

---

1. Courts are generally reluctant to require an employer to accept the services of a worker for many reasons. One is that it is difficult to supervise the relationship and the parties are likely to return to court with additional disputes. Another is that it is generally offensive to public policy to require receipt of services. These issues were explored previously in the context of specific performance of service contracts in Chapter 4. As noted in that chapter, courts cannot order the performance of services for both constitutional and practical reasons, but those considerations are different when the order involves the receipt of services. No constitutional constraint forbids such an order, but the problem is the practical one of court supervision of an employment relationship.

Courts are willing to order receipt of services in a context where important rights are at stake and no other remedy will accomplish that goal, as the principal case illustrates. This case involves a state court enforcing a state statute, but federal courts now routinely grant hiring orders in cases involving labor and employment rights under federal law. By definition, the federal law only applies to employers of a certain size such that very small employers are not covered. This fact alters the offensiveness of such orders to public policy because the defendant employer is rarely in a personal working relationship with the plaintiff. Contrast the one-on-one nursing services discussed in Chapter 4 with the more impersonal working relationship involved in the principal case.

2. Consider the problem faced by the court in *Siegel v. LePore*, 234 F.3d 1163 (11th Cir.2000). In that case the presidential election of 2000 turned on the result in the state of Florida and one candidate sought to restrain the manual recount of ballots obtained by the other candidate on the grounds that there were no uniform standards to accomplish that result. In light of tools available to courts to remedy conditions with a restorative injunctions, consider whether the plaintiff could show irreparable harm sufficient to support a preliminary injunction. The function of a preliminary injunction is to prevent irreparable harm that cannot be remedied with a permanent injunction. Should the concept of harm in this context be limited to counting votes to see who won the election, and if so, was the court correct that it could provide meaningful remedy later if the plaintiff prevailed?

PROBLEM: THE FALSIFIED TEST RESULTS

Genstore Company has a chain of retail stores marketing general merchandise. It is a regional chain employing hundreds of non-unionized employees. The top level Genstore management decided three years ago to require all applicants and current employees to submit to a "personality" test.

One of the purposes of testing current employees was to probe the loyalty of each to the company. Management believed that indications of disloyalty would be relevant in determining which employees should be promoted. The policy was that only employees displaying a high degree of loyalty to the company should be promoted.

A top manager unknowingly hired a disreputable company to conduct these tests. The operator was dishonest and took bribes from some employees to falsify their test results. Moreover, part of the bribery scheme involved falsifying the test results of some rival employees to reflect disloyalty. The bribers' purpose was to eliminate those individuals for future promotions. As a result of this bribery, the records of some two dozen employees were altered to show disloyalty.

The victims of this scheme had no immediate knowledge of their test results. The company kept all results private and fired no one. When the company did not choose any of the victims for promotions, each assumed it was for other reasons. The bribers fared better, but not all of them were promoted. Some promotions went to employees who became contenders after the bribery scheme was completed.

The bribery was recently discovered. Genstore immediately fired all the bribers. Although the bribers told the company managers which records were falsified, Genstore has refused all demands of the victims. The victims want the removal of the adverse loyalty notation from their files or retesting. They also want priority for the next promotions.

Rebuffed by management, the victims now wish to sue. They have a cause of action under state law for the violation of a statute that limits the questions an employer can ask in personality tests. The restrictive list of acceptable questions includes honesty but not loyalty. The remedy provision in this statute allows damages and "such relief as the court deems appropriate."

Is there any "appropriate relief" for the court to give these individual plaintiffs? Should the court order Genstore to take steps to prevent future violations of the act? Genstore has continued to administer personality tests, although now with a different company. Given that Genstore once failed to adhere to the statute's limited list of permissible questions, would it be appropriate for the court to prevent future violations by ordering Genstore to educate its managers concerning the requirements of the statute? In the case that follows, note the type of relief given to right the wrong. Consider whether the court went beyond the specific wrong to order broad relief to prevent future wrongs to unknown individuals.

Bundy v. Jackson

641 F.2d 934 (D.C.Cir.1981).

■ J. SKELLY WRIGHT, CHIEF JUDGE:

* * *

Appellant Sandra Bundy is now, and was at the time she filed her lawsuit, a Vocational Rehabilitation Specialist, level GS-9, with the District of Columbia Department of Corrections (the agency). * * * In recent years Bundy's chief task has been to find jobs for former criminal offenders.

The District Court's finding that sexual intimidation was a "normal condition of employment" in Bundy's agency finds ample support in the District Court's own chronology of Bundy's experiences there. Those experiences began in 1972 when Bundy, still a GS-5, received and rejected sexual propositions from Delbert Jackson, then a fellow employee at the agency but now its Director and the named defendant in this lawsuit in his official capacity. It was two years later, however, that the sexual intimidation Bundy suffered began to intertwine directly with her employment, when she received propositions from two of her supervisors, Arthur Burton and James Gainey.

* * * Burton began sexually harassing Bundy in June 1974, continually calling her into his office to request that she spend the workday afternoon with him at his apartment and to question her about her sexual proclivities. Shortly after becoming her first-line supervisor Gainey also began making sexual advances to Bundy, asking her to join him at a motel and on a trip to the Bahamas. Bundy complained about these advances to Lawrence Swain, who supervised both Burton and Gainey. Swain casually dismissed Bundy's complaints, telling her that "any man in his right mind would want to rape you," and then proceeding himself to request that she begin a sexual relationship with him in his apartment. Bundy rejected his request.

We add that, although the District Court made no explicit findings as to harassment of other female employees, its finding that harassment was "standard operating procedure" finds ample support in record evidence that Bundy was not the only woman subjected to sexual intimidation by male supervisors.[3]

In denying Bundy any relief, the District Court found that Bundy's supervisors did not take the "game" of sexually propositioning female employees "seriously," and that Bundy's rejection of their advances did not evoke in them any motive to take any action against her. The record, however, contains nothing to support this view, and indeed some evidence directly belies it. For example, after Bundy complained to Swain, Burton began to derogate her for alleged malingering and poor work performance, though she had not previously received any such criticism. * * *

The relevance of * * * "discriminatory environment" cases to sexual harassment is beyond serious dispute. Racial or ethnic discrimination against a company's minority clients may reflect no intent to discriminate directly against the company's minority employees, but in poisoning the atmosphere of employment it violates Title VII. Sexual stereotyping through discriminatory dress requirements may be benign in intent, and may offend women only in a general, atmospheric manner, yet it violates Title VII. Racial slurs, though intentional and directed at individuals, may still be just verbal insults, yet they too may create Title VII liability. How then can sexual harassment, which injects the most demeaning sexual stereotypes into the general work environment and which always represents an intentional assault on an individual's innermost privacy, not be illegal?

* * *

---

3. Carolyn Epps, who worked for the agency between 1967 and 1974, testified that after she asked her supervisor, Lawrence Swain, about the possibility of a promotion he began making unsolicited physical and verbal advances toward her, and that she received verbal sexual advances from supervisor Claude Burgin after she discussed her promotion with him. Epps also testified that she heard Swain ask other female employees to come to his apartment for drinks and saw him pressing his body against their bodies in his office. In 1974 Epps applied to become an administrative aide-stenographer, which would have meant a promotion from GS–6 to GS–7. She testified that, although she was qualified for the job, it went instead to another female employee who had received sexual advances from Swain and who, unlike Epps, did not know stenography.

Ann Blanchard worked for the agency from 1971 to 1973, supervised by James Gainey and Arthur Burton. Burton made sexual advances toward her and also apparently intimidated her by stating that another employee whom he would not identify had told Burton that Blanchard had been conducting a sexual relationship with one of her clients.

Indeed, so long as women remain inferiors in the employment hierarchy, they may have little recourse against harassment beyond the legal recourse Bundy seeks in this case. The law may allow a woman to prove that her resistance to the harassment cost her her job or some economic benefit, but this will do her no good if the employer never takes such tangible actions against her.

* * *

The employer can thus implicitly and effectively make the employee's endurance of sexual intimidation a "condition" of her employment. The woman then faces a "cruel trilemma." She can endure the harassment. She can attempt to oppose it, with little hope of success, either legal or practical, but with every prospect of making the job even less tolerable for her. Or she can leave her job, with little hope of legal relief and the likely prospect of another job where she will face harassment anew.

Bundy proved that she was the victim of a practice of sexual harassment and a discriminatory work environment permitted by her employer. Her rights under Title VII were therefore violated. We thus reverse the District Court's holding on this issue and remand it to that court so it can fashion appropriate injunctive relief.[12] And on this novel issue, we think it advisable to offer the District Court guidance in framing its decree.[13]

The Final Guidelines on Sexual Harassment in the Workplace (Guidelines) issued by the Equal Employment Opportunity Commission on November 10, 1980, 45 Fed.Reg. 74676–74677 (1980) (to be codified at 29 C.F.R. § 1604.11(a)–(f)), offer a useful basis for injunctive relief in this case. Those Guidelines define sexual harassment broadly:

> Unwelcome sexual advances, requests for sexual favors, and other verbal or physical conduct of a sexual nature constitute sexual harassment when (1) submission to such conduct is made either explicitly or implicitly a term or condition of an individual's employment, (2)

---

12. Title VII allows the courts to award a victorious plaintiff reinstatement, back pay, or "any other equitable relief as the court deems appropriate." 42 U.S.C. § 2000e–5(g) (1976). Back pay and reinstatement are, of course, irrelevant to the discriminatory environment issue, and we follow the great majority of the federal courts in construing "equitable relief" to preclude any award of damages for emotional harm resulting from a Title VII violation. [Citations.] We add that, since our holding makes Bundy a prevailing party in this suit, the District Court on remand may entertain a request for attorney's fees. 42 U.S.C. § 2000e–5(k) (1976).

13. Appellee has argued that an injunction is improper and unnecessary in this case since Bundy has complained of no instances of sexual harassment since 1975 and there is therefore no reason to think further harassment will occur. Common sense tells us that the men who harassed Bundy may well have ceased their actions solely because of the pendency of her complaint and lawsuit. Moreover, the law tells us that a suit for injunctive relief does not become moot simply because the offending party has ceased the offending conduct, since the offending party might be free otherwise to renew that conduct once the court denied the relief, [citation]. The request for injunctive relief will be moot only where there is no reasonable expectation that the conduct will recur, [citation] or where interim events have "completely and irrevocably eradicated the effects of the alleged violation" [citation.] We perceive no such certainty here, most obviously because Bundy's agency has taken no affirmative steps to prevent recurrence of the harassment, and because all the harassing employees still work for the agency. * * *

submission to or rejection of such conduct by an individual is used as the basis for employment decisions affecting such individual, or (3) such conduct has the purpose or effect of unreasonably interfering with an individual's work performance or creating an intimidating, hostile, or offensive work environment.

* * * The general goal of these Guidelines is *preventive*. An employer may negate liability by taking "immediate and appropriate corrective action" when it learns of any illegal harassment, but the employer should fashion rules within its firm or agency to ensure that such corrective action never becomes necessary.

Applying these Guidelines to the present case, we believe that the Director of the agency should be ordered to raise affirmatively the subject of sexual harassment with all his employees and inform all employees that sexual harassment violates Title VII of the Civil Rights Act of 1964, the Guidelines of the EEOC, the express orders of the Mayor of the District of Columbia, and the policy of the agency itself. The Director should also establish and publicize a scheme whereby harassed employees may complain to the Director immediately and confidentially. The Director should promptly take all necessary steps to investigate and correct any harassment, including warnings and appropriate discipline directed at the offending party, and should generally develop other means of preventing harassment within the agency.

Perhaps the most important part of the preventive remedy will be a prompt and effective procedure for hearing, adjudicating, and remedying complaints of sexual harassment within the agency. Fortunately, the District Court need not establish an entire new procedural mechanism for harassment complaints. Under regulations promulgated by the Equal Employment Opportunity Commission, 29 C.F.R. §§ 1613.201–1613.283 (1979), the Department of Corrections, like all other federal and District of Columbia agencies, is required to establish procedures for adjudication of complaints of denial of equal employment opportunity, whether the ground of discrimination is race, color, religion, sex, or national origin. The required procedures guarantee the complainant a prompt and effective investigation, an opportunity for informal adjustment of the discrimination, and, if necessary, a formal evidentiary hearing. Moreover, if the complaint proves meritorious the agency may be required to take disciplinary action against any employee found to have committed discriminatory acts. Finally, the agency must inform any employee denied relief within the agency of his or her right to file a civil action in the District Court.

Since we have held that sexual harassment, even if it does not result in loss of tangible job benefits, is illegal sex discrimination, the District Court may simply order the Director of the agency to ensure that complaints of sexual harassment receive thorough and effective treatment within the formal process the agency has already established to comply with the Civil Service Commission regulations. Finally, we believe the District Court should retain jurisdiction of the case so that it may review the Director's plans for complying with the injunction.

* * * [Remanded to the district court.]

The court in the principal case further suggested the following language for the district court to consider "as appropriate for the injunction":

The court decrees that the defendant Delbert Jackson, Director of the District of Columbia Department of Corrections, along with his supervising employees, agents, and all those subject to his control or acting in concert with him, are enjoined from causing, encouraging, condoning, or permitting the practice of sexual harassment of female employees by male supervisors and employees within the Department: to wit, any unwelcome sexual advances, requests for sexual favors, or other verbal or physical conduct of a sexual nature when submission to such conduct is explicitly or implicitly a requirement of the individual's employment, or used as a basis for any employment decision concerning that individual, or when such conduct has the purpose or effect of unreasonably interfering with the individual's work performance or creating an intimidating or hostile or offensive work environment.

Defendant is further required:

1. To notify all employees and supervisors in the Department, through individual letters and permanent posting in prominent locations throughout Department offices, that sexual harassment, as explicitly defined in the previous paragraph, violates Title VII of the Civil Rights Act of 1964, regulatory guidelines of the Equal Employment Opportunity Commission, the express orders of the Mayor of the District of Columbia, and the policy of the Department of Corrections.

2. To ensure that employees complaining of sexual harassment can avail themselves of the full and effective use of the complaint, hearing, adjudication, and appeals procedures for complaints of discrimination established by the Department of Corrections pursuant to Equal Employment Opportunity Commission regulations 29 C.F.R. §§ 1613–201–1613.283 (1979).

3. To develop appropriate sanctions or disciplinary measures for supervisors or other employees who are found to have sexually harassed female employees, including warnings to the offending person and notations in that person's employment record for reference in the event future complaints are directed against that person.

4. To develop other appropriate means of instructing employees of the Department of the harmful nature of sexual harassment.

Defendant shall return to this court within 60 days to report on the steps he has taken in compliance with this order and to present his plans for the additional measures required by Paragraph 4 above. The court shall retain jurisdiction of this case.

B.   STRUCTURAL INJUNCTIONS

Section Coverage:

Structural injunctions are a modern phenomenon born of necessity from developments in Constitutional law. The United States Supreme Court has identified substantive rights whose enforcement requires substantial judicial supervision. These rights concern the treatment of individuals by institutions, such as the right not to suffer inhumane treatment in a prison or public mental hospital. Enforcement of such rights by injunction has become an implicit part of the Constitutional guarantee.

Such injunctions are categorized "structural" because courts undertake supervision over the institutional policies and practices. If defendants do not respond cooperatively to orders requiring reform proposals, then judges often undertake to mandate particular changes. Structural injunctions are often long and costly battles with persistent class plaintiffs, recalcitrant defendants, and frustrated judges.

Model Case:

The city of Springdale has a public school system that serves children of many racial and ethnic identities. Twenty-five years ago the city voluntarily ended its policy of neighborhood schools because officials perceived that the effect was legally impermissible racial and ethnic segregation. There were also noticeable differences in the quality and conditions of the schools. Although this effect had long existed with apparent community approval by the majority who benefitted from it, officials were mindful of the Constitutional rights of the minority students. The Supreme Court declared in *Brown v. Board of Education* that segregated schools violated the equal protection guarantee. Its 1955 decree in the same case required district courts to make orders as necessary in school cases to end segregation "with all deliberate speed."

In the decade following the decision, the Springdale officials became aware that districts failing to take voluntary action often became defendants in school desegregation actions. The Springdale School Board adopted a busing plan that produced some integration, and some schools that previously were populated with only minority children became new magnet schools. The magnet schools specialized in particular programs and required application; they attracted a racial and ethnic mix of children.

In the years since these changes the neighborhoods have correspondingly changed and the magnet schools were less successful. "Special talents" programs within other schools replaced interest in the magnet schools, and the effect was new racial and ethnic segregation within programs and disproportionate representation within schools. The School Board discussed these effects but made no changes.

A suit is filed against the School Board. After a lengthy trial the court finds unlawful segregation. The Board is ordered to propose a plan to correct the Constitutional violations. Months pass and the Board submits only one half-hearted plan to the court. The judge rejects the plan as inadequate and orders the Board to produce a plan addressing specific issues. A temporary plan allowing some voluntary transfers is adopted for the immediate school year. The court receives complaints from individuals who believe the plan was not administered in good faith.

The Board fails to satisfy the court. The judge begins to take a more active role in monitoring school policies and practices. The affirmative orders that result are structural injunctions.

Modern injunctions received their names from Yale Professor Owen Fiss in his book *The Civil Rights Injunction* (Indiana University Press 1978). He distinguished three types of modern civil rights injunctions from the traditional preventive injunction, as examined in Chapter 3 of this course book, which is designed to prevent future harm. Professor Fiss identified the three modern forms as structural, reparative, and prophylactic injunctions.

Two of these forms—structural and reparative injunctions—are particularly unusual because they are not future-oriented like a preventive injunction at all; they are backward-looking. The structural injunction seeks to reform a social institution, such as a school system, mental institution or prison. By ordering a reorganization of such a social institution, a court may vindicate a claim of racial inequality, the right to treatment, or the right against cruel or unusual punishment. A structural injunction tries to reconfigure the organizational foundation that produced these violations in the past.

The other backward looking civil rights injunction is what Professor Fiss called the reparative injunction. Through this form, a court seeks to undo the effects of a past wrong. For example, in *United States v. Louisiana,* 380 U.S. 145 (1965), the Supreme Court identified as a proper use of an injunction to eliminate the effects of a past wrong in an election case. When an election is tainted by racial discrimination, a court may order not only a preventive injunction to prevent discrimination in future elections, but also a reparative injunction to set aside the results of the tainted election and hold a new election. With this additional tool of the reparative injunction, a court may remove the lingering effects of past discrimination. The reparative injunction was later called a restorative injunction.

A prophylactic injunction is forward-looking like a preventive injunction, but Professor Fiss found it distinguishable in the civil rights context. Whereas a preventive injunction seeks to prohibit future behavior that would be wrongful in itself—such as a future trespass—a prophylactic injunction prohibits behavior that is not in itself wrongful but which is part of a pattern that contributes to a civil rights violation. For example, ordering an employer to educate its employees about the requirements of a civil rights statute is a prophylactic injunction because failure to educate employees is not itself a wrongful act. When a work place is riddled with violations of the statute, however, the purpose of ordering such education is to prevent future violations of the statute.

Vasquez v. Bannworths, Inc., reprinted *infra* in this chapter, provides an example of a reparative injunction, which is also called a restorative injunction. *Bundy v. Jackson*, reprinted *infra* in this chapter, exemplified a prophylactic injunction. The next case, the Supreme Court's 1955 remedial decision in *Brown v Board of Education*, begins the coverage of the structural injunction.

Brown v. Board of Education

349 U.S. 294, 75 S.Ct. 753, 99 L.Ed. 1083 (1955).

[The Supreme Court in 1954 decided in *Brown v. Board of Education* and companion cases that racial segregation in public schools violated the Constitution. That liability decision is known as *Brown I.* The following term the Court addressed the appropriate remedy for this Constitutional wrong. This opinion, known as *Brown II,* is reprinted in part below.]

■ MR. CHIEF JUSTICE WARREN delivered the opinion of the Court.

These cases were decided on May 17, 1954. The opinions of that date,[1] declaring the fundamental principle that racial discrimination in public education is unconstitutional, are incorporated herein by reference. All provisions of federal, state, or local law requiring or permitting such discrimination must yield to this principle. There remains for consideration the manner in which relief is to be accorded.

Because these cases arose under different local conditions and their disposition will involve a variety of local problems, we requested further argument on the question of relief.[2] * * *

---

1. 347 U.S. 483; 347 U.S. 497.

2. Further argument was requested on the following questions, 347 U.S. 483, 495–496, n. 13, previously propounded by the Court:

"4. Assuming it is decided that segregation in public schools violates the Fourteenth Amendment

"(a) would a decree necessarily follow providing that, within the limits set by normal geographic school districting, Negro children should forthwith be admitted to schools of their choice, or

"(b) may this Court, in the exercise of its equity powers, permit an effective gradual adjustment to be brought about from existing segregated systems to a system not based on color distinctions?

"5. On the assumption on which questions 4(a) and (b) are based, and assuming further that this Court will exercise its equity powers to the end described in question 4(b),

"(a) should this Court formulate detailed decrees in these cases;

"(b) if so, what specific issues should the decrees reach;

"(c) should this Court appoint a special master to hear evidence with a view to recommending specific terms for such decrees;

"(d) should this Court remand to the courts of first instance with directions to frame decrees in these cases, and if so what general directions should the decrees of this Court include and what procedures should the courts of first instance follow in arriving at the specific terms of more detailed decrees?"

Full implementation of these constitutional principles may require solution of varied local school problems. School authorities have the primary responsibility for elucidating, assessing, and solving these problems; courts will have to consider whether the action of school authorities constitutes good faith implementation of the governing constitutional principles. Because of their proximity to local conditions and the possible need for further hearings, the courts which originally heard these cases can best perform this judicial appraisal. Accordingly, we believe it appropriate to remand the cases to those courts.

In fashioning and effectuating the decrees, the courts will be guided by equitable principles. Traditionally, equity has been characterized by a practical flexibility in shaping its remedies and by a facility for adjusting and reconciling public and private needs. These cases call for the exercise of these traditional attributes of equity power. At stake is the personal interest of the plaintiffs in admission to public schools as soon as practicable on a nondiscriminatory basis. To effectuate this interest may call for elimination of a variety of obstacles in making the transition to school systems operated in accordance with the constitutional principles set forth in our May 17, 1954, decision. Courts of equity may properly take into account the public interest in the elimination of such obstacles in a systematic and effective manner. But it should go without saying that the vitality of these constitutional principles cannot be allowed to yield simply because of disagreement with them.

While giving weight to these public and private considerations, the courts will require that the defendants make a prompt and reasonable start toward full compliance with our May 17, 1954, ruling. Once such a start has been made, the courts may find that additional time is necessary to carry out the ruling in an effective manner. The burden rests upon the defendants to establish that such time is necessary in the public interest and is consistent with good faith compliance at the earliest practicable date. To that end, the courts may consider problems related to administration, arising from the physical condition of the school plant, the school transportation system, personnel, revision of school districts and attendance areas into compact units to achieve a system of determining admission to the public schools on a nonracial basis, and revision of local laws and regulations which may be necessary in solving the foregoing problems. They will also consider the adequacy of any plans the defendants may propose to meet these problems and to effectuate a transition to a racially nondiscriminatory school system. During this period of transition, the courts will retain jurisdiction of these cases.

The judgments below * * * are accordingly reversed and the cases are remanded to the District Courts to take such proceedings and enter such orders and decrees consistent with this opinion as are necessary and proper to admit to public schools on a racially nondiscriminatory basis with all deliberate speed the parties to these cases. * * *

It is so ordered.

———————

1. Historically courts of equity frequently said that equitable relief would not be granted if the enforcement of the injunction would require extensive supervision by the court. Thus it is still common to refuse an injunction requiring the specific performance of a construction contract on the ground that supervision would be too complex.

In the second half of the twentieth century there has been a major departure from that principle in the area of the civil rights injunction. Beginning with the school desegregation cases, courts have frequently responded to the necessity of issuing and supervising a complex injunction despite the many hours of judicial time necessary for the task.

Professor Philip Kurland considered the effect of the *Brown II* decision in his article " '*Brown v. Board of Education* Was the Beginning'—The School Desegregation Cases in the United States Supreme Court: 1954–1979," 1979 Washington University Law Quarterly 309. He characterized the question in *Brown II* as whether the Court should act in its ordinary judicial mode or in a novel legislative mode to respond to the special problem. Rather than grant the plaintiff's request for an order immediately ending all school segregation by race, the Court accepted the defendants' premise that such a fundamental change could not be accomplished immediately. Therefore, the opinion emphasized the breadth of equity powers available to the district court judges as well as the wide range of issues that they could consider in effecting the social revolution required by the *Brown I* decision. The essence of *Brown II*, Professor Kurland argues, is that the federal courts were to substitute themselves for the local governing bodies with regard to the management of schools. As a result, every one of the Court's list of relevant factors, such as transportation and redistricting, led to lengthy and complex litigation. *Brown II* was thus the first case to make the federal courts the "overseers" of local government, which today is not regarded as unusual.

2. Modern forms of injunctions has been an ongoing area of substantial and controversial scholarship. See Tracy A. Thomas, The Prophylactic Remedy: Normative Principles and Definitional Parameters of Broad Injunctive Relief, 52 Buff. L. Rev. 301 (2004) (prophylactic relief is appropriately broad); Myriam E. Gilles, In Defense of Making Government Pay: The Deterrent Effect of Constitutional Tort Remedies, 35 Ga. L. Rev. 845 (2001) (structural reform injunctions are uniquely appropriate for constitutional wrongs); Daryl J. Levinson, Making Government Pay: Markets, Politics, and the Allocation of Constitutional Costs, 67 U. Chi. L. Rev. 345 (2000) (courts should rely even more heavily on injunctions); John Choon Yoo, Who Measures the Chancellor's Foot? The Inherent Remedial Authority of the Federal Courts, 84 Calif. L. Rev. 1121 (1996) (prophylactic injunctions violate core state functions); Paul Gewirtz, Remedies and Resistance, 92

Yale L.J. 585 (1983) (arguing that a prophylactic injunctions reduce risk of ineffective remedies).

PROBLEM: THE MERGED CITIES

Plaintiffs are minority city residents who have proven that the city of Metroside discriminated against the minority community in the allocation of city services. The trial judge has found this discrimination to be a denial of equal protection under the state and federal Constitutions. The dilemma facing the judge is how to fashion an order to remedy this unconstitutional condition.

The present city of Metroside developed from the merger of two smaller cities. A dozen years ago the two cities voted to merge into one larger city. It was provided in the proposition accepted by the voters that the city services for each of the old cities would remain separate with no centralized control for a period of ten years. This provision was politically necessary to avoid the opposition of the separate city workers. The proposition further provided that after ten years a commission appointed by the mayor of the new city would determine whether to merge the two city-services departments or to leave them separate.

The two old cities originally developed side by side when a railroad was built through the area in the 19th century. By the time of the merger one of the old cities, Riverside, was dominated by one major factory employer. Most of the workers at this shoe factory, both blue collar and white collar workers, lived in Riverside. The other city, Arborside, contained office buildings and some light industry. The residents of Arborside were generally wealthier than those of Riverside, but Riverside had the advantage of the shoe factory in its tax base.

A few years after the merger, however, the shoe factory closed. This unforeseen development dramatically changed the character of Riverside. The white collar workers moved elsewhere to new jobs. There were fewer opportunities for the blue collar workers, and unemployment rose in Riverside. At the end of the ten year period Riverside's population declined, and the percentage of minority residents was much larger than it had been before. Arborside, on the other hand, prospered. New high-technology industries were attracted there and the population grew with affluent, and predominately non-minority, residents.

The city services budget of Riverside at the time of the merger was a small one but the Arborside budget was fairly large. Riverside had no separate Park District; the city parks were simply included in the general public maintenance division. Arborside, in contrast, had a separate Park District with extensive recreational programs for residents of all ages. Similarly, the library in Arborside had always had a large budget with funds for various programs; the Riverside library was poorer. During the ten years after the merger, the Metroside government increased the budget of the Arborside city services in response to the growth in its population. The Riverside budget was not increased and did not even keep up with the high inflation present in the economy at the time. Accordingly, the differences in city services between the two communities grew more disparate. When the Mayor appointed a commission at the end of the ten years to determine whether to merge the city services, the vote was no. The trial judge found that the commission had discriminated racially in this decision, following the city's pattern of racial discrimination in the budget allocation of city services in recent years.

The problem is how to fashion a remedy for this violation. There is no simple way to achieve equality by ordering an increase in the Riverside budget, even if the judge has the power to make such an order to a city government. Only unification of the city services could result in equality, and then only if done in a way to provide all residents with all services. How can the court order the city to achieve this goal without having the judge virtually become the administrator of the city services? Consider *Brown II* as well as the case and notes that follow.

Brown v. Plata

___ U.S. ___, 131 S.Ct. 1910, 179 L.Ed.2d 969 (2011).

■ MR. JUSTICE KENNEDY delivered the opinion of the Court.

This case arises from serious constitutional violations in California's prison system. The violations have persisted for years. They remain uncorrected. The appeal comes to this Court from a three-judge District Court order directing California to remedy two ongoing violations of the Cruel and Unusual Punishments Clause, a guarantee binding on the States by the Due Process Clause of the Fourteenth Amendment. * * *

After years of litigation, it became apparent that a remedy for the constitutional violations would not be effective absent a reduction in the prison system population. The authority to order release of prisoners as a remedy to cure a systemic violation of the Eighth Amendment is a power reserved to a three-judge district court, not a single-judge district court. * * * The State in this Court has not objected to consolidation, although the State does argue that the three-judge court was prematurely convened. The State also objects to the substance of the three-judge court order, which requires the State to reduce overcrowding in its prisons.

The appeal presents the question whether the remedial order issued by the three-judge court is consistent with requirements and procedures set forth in a congressional statute, the Prison Litigation Reform Act of 1995 (PLRA). 18 U.S.C. § 3626. The order leaves the choice of means to reduce overcrowding to the discretion of state officials. But absent compliance through new construction, out-of-state transfers, or other means—or modification of the order upon a further showing by the State—the State will be required to release some number of prisoners before their full sentences have been served. High recidivism rates must serve as a warning that mistaken or premature release of even one prisoner can cause injury and harm. The release of prisoners in large numbers—assuming the State finds no other way to comply with the order—is a matter of undoubted, grave concern.

At the time of trial, California's correctional facilities held some 156,000 persons. This is nearly double the number that California's prisons were designed to hold, and California has been ordered to reduce its prison population to 137.5% of design capacity. By the three-judge court's own estimate, the required population reduction could be as high as 46,000 persons. Although the State has reduced the population by at least 9,000 persons during the pendency of this appeal, this means a further reduction of 37,000 persons could be required. As will be noted, the reduction need not be accomplished in an indiscriminate manner or in these substantial numbers if satisfactory, alternate remedies or means for compliance are devised. The State may employ measures, including good-time credits and diversion of low-risk offenders and technical parole violators to community-based programs, that will mitigate the order's impact. The population reduction potentially required is nevertheless of unprecedented sweep and extent.

Yet so too is the continuing injury and harm resulting from these serious constitutional violations. For years the medical and mental health care provided by California's prisons has fallen short of minimum constitutional requirements and has failed to meet prisoners' basic health needs. Needless suffering and death have been the well-documented result. Over the whole course of years during which this litigation has been pending, no other remedies have been found to be sufficient. Efforts to remedy the violation have been frustrated by severe overcrowding in California's prison system. Short term gains in the provision of care have been eroded by the long-term effects of severe and pervasive overcrowding.

Overcrowding has overtaken the limited resources of prison staff; imposed demands well beyond the capacity of medical and mental health facilities; and created unsanitary and unsafe conditions that make progress in the provision of care difficult or impossible to achieve. The overcrowding is the "primary cause of the violation of a Federal right," 18 U.S.C. § 3626(a)(3)(E)(i), specifically the severe and unlawful mistreatment of prisoners through grossly inadequate provision of medical and mental health care.

This Court now holds that the PLRA does authorize the relief afforded in this case and that the court-mandated population limit is necessary to remedy the violation of prisoners' constitutional rights. The order of the three-judge court, subject to the right of the State to seek its modification in appropriate circumstances, must be affirmed.

* * *

If government fails to fulfill this obligation, the courts have a responsibility to remedy the resulting Eighth Amendment violation. See Hutto v. Finney, 437 U.S. 678, 687, n. 9, 98 S.Ct. 2565, 57 L.Ed.2d 522 (1978). Courts must be sensitive to the State's interest in punishment, deterrence, and rehabilitation, as well as the need for deference to experienced and expert prison administrators faced with the difficult and dangerous task of housing large numbers of convicted criminals. * * * Courts may not allow constitutional violations to continue simply because a remedy would involve intrusion into the realm of prison administration.

Courts faced with the sensitive task of remedying unconstitutional prison conditions must consider a range of available options, including appointment of special masters or receivers and the possibility of consent decrees. When necessary to ensure compliance with a constitutional mandate, courts may enter orders placing limits on a prison's population. By its terms, the PLRA restricts the circumstances in which a court may enter an order "that has the purpose or effect of reducing or limiting the prison population." 18 U.S.C. § 3626(g)(4). The order in this case does not necessarily require the State to release any prisoners. The State may comply by raising the design capacity of its prisons or by transferring prisoners to county facilities or facilities in other States. Because the order limits the prison population as a percentage of design capacity, it nonetheless has the "effect of reducing or limiting the prison population." * * *

This Court's review of the three-judge court's legal determinations is *de novo,* but factual findings are reviewed for clear error. * * * The three-judge court oversaw two weeks of trial and heard at considerable length from California prison officials, as well as experts in the field of correctional administration. The judges had the opportunity to ask relevant questions of those witnesses. Two of the judges had overseen the ongoing remedial efforts of the Receiver and Special Master. The three-judge court was well situated to make the difficult factual judgments necessary to fashion a remedy for this complex and intractable constitutional violation. The three-judge court's findings of fact may be reversed only if this Court is left with a " 'definite and firm conviction that a mistake has been committed.' " * * *

Before a three-judge court may be convened to consider whether to enter a population limit, the PLRA requires that the court have "previously entered an order for less intrusive relief that has failed to remedy the deprivation of the Federal right sought to be remedied." 18 U.S.C. § 3626(a)(3)(A)(i). This provision refers to "an order." It is satisfied if the court has entered one order, and this single order has "failed to remedy" the constitutional violation. The defendant must also have had "a reasonable amount of time to comply with the previous court orders." § 3626(a)(3)(A)(ii). This provision refers to the court's "orders." It requires that the defendant have been given a reasonable time to comply with all of the court's orders. Together, these requirements ensure that " 'the last resort remedy' " of a population limit is not imposed " 'as a first step.' " * * *

The PLRA should not be interpreted to place undue restrictions on the authority of federal courts to fashion practical remedies when confronted with complex and intractable constitutional violations. Congress limited the availability of limits on prison populations, but it did not forbid these measures altogether. * * *

Courts should presume that Congress was sensitive to the real-world problems faced by those who would remedy constitutional violations in the prisons and that Congress did not leave prisoners without a remedy for violations of their constitutional rights. * * *

Even if out-of-state transfers could be regarded as a less restrictive alternative, the three-judge court found no evidence of plans for transfers in numbers sufficient to relieve overcrowding. The State complains that the [district court] slowed the rate of transfer by requiring inspections to assure that the receiving institutions were in compliance with the Eighth Amendment, but the State has made no effort to show that it has the resources and the capacity to transfer significantly larger numbers of prisoners absent that condition.

Construction of new facilities, in theory, could alleviate overcrowding, but the three-judge court found no realistic possibility that California would be able to build itself out of this crisis. At the time of the court's decision the State had plans to build new medical and housing facilities, but funding for some plans had not been secured and funding for other plans had been delayed by the legislature for years. Particularly in light of California's ongoing fiscal crisis, the three-judge court deemed "chimerical" any "remedy that requires significant additional spending by the state." * * *

The three-judge court also rejected additional hiring as a realistic means to achieve a remedy. The State for years had been unable to fill positions necessary for the adequate provision of medical and mental health care, and the three-judge court found no reason to expect a change. * * * The three-judge court found that violence and other negative conditions caused by crowding made it difficult to hire and retain needed staff. The court also concluded that there would be insufficient space for additional staff to work even if adequate personnel could somehow be retained. Additional staff cannot help to remedy the violation if they have no space in which to see and treat patients.

The three-judge court also did not err, much less commit clear error, when it concluded that, absent a population reduction, continued efforts by the Receiver and Special Master would not achieve a remedy. Both the Receiver and the Special Master filed reports stating that overcrowding posed a significant barrier to their efforts. * * *

* * * At one time, it may have been possible to hope that these violations would be cured without a reduction in overcrowding. A long history of failed remedial orders, together with substantial evidence of overcrowding's deleterious effects on the provision of care, compels a different conclusion today.

The common thread connecting the State's proposed remedial efforts is that they would require the State to expend large amounts of money absent a reduction in overcrowding. The Court cannot ignore the political and fiscal reality behind this case. California's Legislature has not been willing or able to allocate the resources necessary to meet this crisis absent a reduction in overcrowding. There is no reason to believe it will begin to do so now, when the State of California is facing an unprecedented budgetary shortfall. * * *

Nor is the order overbroad because it limits the State's authority to run its prisons, as the State urges in its brief. While the order does in some respects shape or control the State's authority in the realm of prison administration, it does so in a manner that leaves much to the State's discretion. The State may choose how to allocate prisoners between institutions; it may choose whether to increase the prisons' capacity through construction or reduce the population; and, if it does reduce the population, it may decide what steps to take to achieve the necessary reduction. The order's limited scope is necessary to remedy a constitutional violation.

As the State implements the order of the three-judge court, time and experience may reveal targeted and effective remedies that will end the constitutional violations even without a significant decrease in the general prison population. The State will be free to move the three-judge court for modification of its order on that basis, and these motions would be entitled to serious consideration. * * *

In reaching its decision, the three-judge court gave "substantial weight" to any potential adverse impact on public safety from its order. The court devoted nearly 10 days of trial to the issue of public safety, and it gave the question extensive attention in its opinion. Ultimately, the court concluded that it would be possible to reduce the prison population "in a manner that preserves public safety and the operation of the criminal justice system." [Citation.]

The PLRA's requirement that a court give "substantial weight" to public safety does not require the court to certify that its order has no possible adverse impact on the public. A contrary reading would depart from the statute's text by replacing the word "substantial" with "conclusive." * * *

This inquiry necessarily involves difficult predictive judgments regarding the likely effects of court orders. Although these judgments are normally made by state officials, they necessarily must be made by courts when those courts fashion injunctive relief to remedy serious constitutional violations in the prisons. These questions are difficult and sensitive, but they are factual questions and should be treated as such. * * *

* * * The medical and mental health care provided by California's prisons falls below the standard of decency that inheres in the Eighth Amendment. This extensive and ongoing constitutional violation requires a remedy, and a remedy will not be achieved without a reduction in overcrowding. The relief ordered by the three-judge court is required by the Constitution and was authorized by Congress in the PLRA. The State shall implement the order without further delay.

The judgment of the three-judge court is affirmed.

It is so ordered.

■ Justice Scalia, with whom Justice Thomas joins, dissenting.

Today the Court affirms what is perhaps the most radical injunction issued by a court in our Nation's history: an order requiring California to release the staggering number of 46,000 convicted criminals. * * *

Structural injunctions depart from that historical practice, turning judges into long-term administrators of complex social institutions such as schools, prisons, and police departments. Indeed, they require judges to play a role essentially indistinguishable from the role ordinarily played by executive officials. Today's decision not only affirms the structural injunction but vastly expands its use, by holding that an entire system is unconstitutional because it *may produce* constitutional violations.

The drawbacks of structural injunctions have been described at great length elsewhere. [Citations.] This case illustrates one of their most pernicious aspects: that they force judges to engage in a form of factfinding-as-policymaking that is outside the traditional judicial role. * * * In a very limited category of cases, judges have also traditionally been called upon to make some predictive judgments: which custody will best serve the interests of the child, for example, or whether a particular one-shot injunction will remedy the plaintiff's grievance. When a judge manages a structural injunction, however, he will inevitably be required to make very broad empirical predictions necessarily based in large part upon policy views—the sort of predictions regularly made by legislators and executive officials, but inappropriate for the Third Branch.

* * *

■ Justice Alito, with whom The Chief Justice joins, dissenting.

* * * Here, the majority and the court below maintain that no remedy short of a massive release of prisoners from the general prison population can remedy the State's failure to provide constitutionally adequate health care. This argument is implausible on its face and is not supported by the requisite clear and convincing evidence. * * *

The prisoner release ordered in this case is unprecedented, improvident, and contrary to the PLRA. In largely sustaining the decision below, the majority is gambling with the safety of the people of California. Before putting public safety at risk, every reasonable precaution should be taken. The decision below should be reversed, and the case should be remanded for this to be done.

I fear that today's decision, like prior prisoner release orders, will lead to a grim roster of victims. I hope that I am wrong.

In a few years, we will see.

———————

1. The majority opinion in the principal case refers to its 1978 opinion involving Eighth Amendment violations in a state prison, *Hutto v. Finney*, 437 U.S. 678, 98 S.Ct. 2565, 57 L.Ed.2d 522 (1978). In that case, a district

court had obtained evidence for years on the inhumane conditions in Arkansas state prisons, mostly concerning cruel punishments for misbehavior, as well as inadequate hygiene and nutrition. The majority opinion, authored by Justice Stevens, approved the use of specific remedial orders, such as a limitation on the number of days that a prisoner could spend consecutively in solitary confinement. One of the Constitutional issues was whether a federal court could make a remedial order with regard to changing a condition that was not in itself a violation of the Eighth Amendment. In this circumstance, the number of days in solitary confinement was not unconstitutional by itself, but only as part of a pattern.

In dissent in *Hutto*, Justice Rehnquist took the position that a remedial order cannot be broader than an unconstitutional condition. If all the other conditions in the prison system were reformed and this one remained, it would not be unconstitutional and yet would still be enjoined. Whereas the majority found the order justifiable as part of a "comprehensive order" supportable by the "interdependence of the conditions producing the remedy," Justice Rehnquist found the order to be a prophylactic rule that exceeds the constitutional authority of the federal courts.

The litigation in *Hutto* lasted for more than a decade, beginning with a 1965 district court opinion. For many times the court continued the cases that arose from the conditions in the Arkansas state prisons. The judge who heard the first case, Judge Henley, became quite an expert on the prison conditions and the litigation that stretched over the years. Even when he was appointed to the Court of Appeals, he was specially designated to continue to hear this case as a district judge because of his familiarity with its extensive history.

2. In 1996, Congress enacted the Prison Litigation Reform Act (PLRA), which governed the principal case, in an attempt to reduce the number of prison condition cases in the federal courts. Among other provisions, the PLRA restricts the equitable remedies available in such cases. Under the terms of the PLRA, injunctions and consent decrees may extend "no further than necessary to correct violations of the Federal right of a particular plaintiff or plaintiffs" and must be "narrowly drawn" and the "least intrusive means necessary to correct the violation." Additionally, the court must "give substantial weight to any adverse impact on public safety or the operation of a criminal justice system caused by the relief." 18 U.S.C. § 3626(a). Any preliminary injunctive relief must automatically expire after 90 days unless the court issues a permanent injunction before the expiration of the 90 day period. *Id.* Injunctions must terminate within 2 years of entry unless the court makes written findings that the injunction remains necessary. 18 U.S.C. § 3626(b).

The PLRA also reduces the amount of attorneys fees available in prison condition cases; imposes an exhaustion of administrative remedies requirement on prisoners; and limits the court's ability to waive filing fees for prisoners who file successive suits. *See* David S. Udell & Rebekah Diller, Access to the Courts: An Essay for the Georgetown University Law Center Conference on the Independence of the Courts 95 GEO. L. J. (2007).

Research has indicated a significant drop in filings since the PLRA went into effect. *Id.*

3.   Who should determine which rights are sufficiently important to consume such an enormous amount of judicial energy and societal expense? Would one solution be to consider the remedy at law adequate and to give damages to the wrongfully treated prisoners or their families? What about damages for school children who attend an unconstitutionally segregated school? Would a damages approach be likely to change conditions in the future or not?

Consider also that injunctions can produce damage remedies through civil contempt when there is noncompliance with the injunction. See Chapter 7. *See also* Gordon G. Young, *Enforcement of Federal Private Rights Against States after Alden v. Maine: The Importance of Hutto v. Finney and Compensation via Civil Contempt Proceedings,* 59 Md. L. Rev. 440 (2000).

4.   Failure to comply with an injunction is punishable by contempt, as covered in Chapter 7. Contempt sanctions against an individual defendant are more direct in their force and effect than sanctions against a governmental entity, as the principal case reflects. For an interesting contempt case pitting one government entity against another, see Chairs v. Burgess, 143 F.3d 1432 (11th Cir.1998) (county government sought contempt sanctions against the state for failure to comply with court order to state prisoners from county jail to state prisons within thirty days of convictions).

CHAPTER 9

SPECIAL ISSUES IN EQUITY

A. STATUTORY LIMITATIONS ON DISCRETION

Section Coverage:

A statute may affect equitable discretion in several ways: (1) by enumerating some remedies but not others, leaving a question of interpretation whether additional remedies may be implied; or (2) by prohibiting courts from issuing injunctions in a narrowly defined type of dispute; or (3) by requiring a court to enjoin certain types of conduct upon a showing that the statutory elements are met. The materials in Chapter 2 explored the first two of these restraints; this section focuses on the third—statutes mandating injunctions.

A statute may mandate explicitly that a court issue an injunction upon the plaintiff's showing that the defendant's conduct has contravened the statutory prohibitions. Because such statutes dramatically alter equitable remedies by removing the judge's discretion in awarding them, courts do not readily impute a legislative intent to do so. If the statute is clear that the legislature has already balanced the equities in favor of injunctive relief, however, the court will enjoin conduct upon a demonstration of statutory conditions. The court's traditional equitable discretion in determining entitlement to injunctive relief is withdrawn by the legislative action. The court nevertheless retains its discretion in fashioning the injunction to implement the intent of the legislature and to accommodate the respective interests of the parties.

Model Case:

Congress enacts a statute that creates a new federal right for private sector employees in service or industry affecting interstate commerce. That new right in this hypothetical act is to receive upon termination a "service letter" indicating the length and nature of employment and the reason for severance. The Secretary of Labor is empowered to make regulations concerning the form of the letter, its contents, and similar matters. The Secretary is further empowered to investigate complaints and to make findings of noncompliance when an employer demonstrates a pattern or practice of violating the act.

This hypothetical new act further provides that whenever the Secretary makes a finding of "wilful noncompliance" by an employer, the Secretary will bring an action in federal district court to compel compliance. The act specifies that in such an action the court "will enter an injunction" requiring the employer to comply with the act once the Secretary establishes the fact of "noncompliance."

In a suit brought by the Secretary under this act, the federal district court has a problem of interpretation. Although the Secretary found the defendant employer to be willfully in noncompliance, the judge found the noncompliance not willful. The judge, unlike the Secretary, found credible the employer's excuses and believed that there would be compliance in the future without an injunction to require it. Ordinarily the judge would not grant an order under such findings, but the statute appears to mandate an injunction.

Congress may not have contemplated that if the judge confirmed the Secretary's finding of noncompliance the two could disagree on willfulness. The act requires only the Secretary to find noncompliance willful. Was this an oversight, or did Congress mean that it had already weighed the equities in such a situation and the injunction is mandatory?

Courts do not interpret statutes to remove the judge's traditional equitable discretion unless the intent of Congress to do so is clear. The problem under this new hypothetical act would be to determine the Congressional intent. The court would consult legislative history, other portions of the act, and opinions interpreting similar wording in other acts.

Tennessee Valley Authority v. Hill

437 U.S. 153, 98 S.Ct. 2279, 57 L.Ed.2d 117 (1978).

■ MR. CHIEF JUSTICE BURGER delivered the opinion of the Court.

The questions presented in this case are (a) whether the Endangered Species Act of 1973 requires a court to enjoin the operation of a virtually completed federal dam—which had been authorized prior to 1973—when, pursuant to authority vested in him by Congress, the Secretary of the Interior has determined that operation of the dam would eradicate an endangered species. * * *

* * * [T]he Tennessee Valley Authority, a wholly owned public corporation of the United States, began constructing the Tellico Dam and Reservoir Project in 1967, shortly after Congress appropriated initial funds for its development. Tellico is a multipurpose regional development project designed principally to stimulate shoreline development, generate sufficient electric current to heat 20,000 homes, and provide flatwater recreation and flood control, as well as improve economic conditions in "an area characterized by underutilization of human resources and outmigration of young people." [Citation.] Of particular relevance to this case is one aspect of the project, a dam which TVA determined to place on the Little Tennessee, a short distance from where the river's waters meet with the Big Tennessee. When fully operational, the dam would impound water covering some 16,500 acres—much of which represents valuable and productive farmland—thereby converting the river's shallow, fast-flowing waters into a deep reservoir over 30 miles in length.

The Tellico Dam has never opened, however, despite the fact that construction has been virtually completed and the dam is essentially ready for operation. Although Congress has appropriated monies for Tellico every year since 1967, progress was delayed, and ultimately stopped, by a tangle of lawsuits and administrative proceedings. * * *

* * * [A] discovery was made in the waters of the Little Tennessee which would profoundly affect the Tellico Project. Exploring the area around Coytee Springs, which is about seven miles from the mouth of the river, a University of Tennessee ichthyologist, Dr. David A. Etnier, found a previously unknown species of perch, the snail darter, or *Percina (Imostoma) tanasi*. This three-inch, tannish-colored fish, whose numbers are estimated to be in the range of 10,000 to 15,000, would soon engage the attention of environmentalists, the TVA, the Department of the Interior, the Congress of the United States, and ultimately the federal courts, as a new and additional basis to halt construction of the dam.

Until recently the finding of a new species of animal life would hardly generate a cause célèbre. This is particularly so in the case of darters, of which there are approximately 130 known species, 8 to 10 of these having been identified only in the last five years. The moving force behind the snail darter's sudden fame came some four months after its discovery, when the Congress passed the Endangered Species Act of 1973 (Act), 87 Stat. 884, 16 U.S.C. § 1531 *et seq.* (1976 ed.). This legislation, among other things, authorizes the Secretary of the Interior to declare species of animal life "endangered" and to identify the "critical habitat" of these creatures. * * *

* * * After receiving comments from various interested parties, including TVA and the State of Tennessee, the Secretary formally listed the snail darter as an endangered species on October 8, 1975. 40 Fed.Reg. 47505–47506; *see* 50 CFR § 17.11(i) (1976). In so acting, it was noted that "the snail darter is a living entity which is genetically distinct and reproductively isolated from other fishes." More important for the purposes of this case, the Secretary determined that the snail darter apparently lives only in that portion of the Little Tennessee River which would be completely inundated by the reservoir created as a consequence of the Tellico Dam's completion. * * *

In February 1976, pursuant to § 11(g) of the Endangered Species Act, 87 Stat. 900, 16 U.S.C. § 1540(g) (1976 ed.), respondents filed the case now under review, seeking to enjoin completion of the dam and impoundment of the reservoir on the ground that those actions would violate the Act by directly causing the extinction of the species *Percina (Imostoma) tanasi*. The District Court denied respondents' request for a preliminary injunction and set the matter for trial. * * *

Trial was held in the District Court on April 29 and 30, 1976, and on May 25, 1976, the court entered its memorandum opinion and order denying respondents their requested relief and dismissing the complaint. The District Court found that closure of the dam and the consequent impoundment of the reservoir would "result in the adverse modification, if not complete destruction, of the snail darter's critical habitat," making it "highly probable" that "the continued existence of the snail darter" would be "jeopardize[d]." Despite these findings, the District Court declined to embrace the plaintiffs' position on the merits: that once a federal project was shown to jeopardize an endangered species, a court of equity is compelled to issue an injunction restraining violation of the Endangered Species Act.

In reaching this result, the District Court stressed that the entire project was then about 80% complete and, based on available evidence, "there [were] no alternatives to impoundment of the reservoir, short of scrapping the entire project." The District Court also found that if the Tellico Project was permanently enjoined, "some $53 million would be lost in nonrecoverable obligations," meaning that a large portion of the $78 million already expended would be wasted. The court also noted that the Endangered Species Act of 1973 was passed some seven years after construction on the dam commenced and that Congress had continued appropriations for Tellico, with full awareness of the snail darter problem. Assessing these various factors, the District Court concluded:

> "At some point in time a federal project becomes so near completion and so incapable of modification that a court of equity should not apply a statute enacted long after inception of the project to produce an unreasonable result.... Where there has been an irreversible and irretrievable commitment of resources by Congress to a project over a span of almost a decade, the Court should proceed with a great deal of circumspection." * * *

Thereafter, in the Court of Appeals, respondents argued that the District Court had abused its discretion by not issuing an injunction in the face of "a blatant statutory violation." The Court of Appeals agreed, and on January 31, 1977, it reversed, remanding "with instructions that a permanent injunction issue halting all activities incident to the Tellico Project which may destroy or modify the critical habitat of the snail darter." The Court of Appeals directed that the injunction "remain in effect until Congress, by appropriate legislation, exempts Tellico from compliance with the Act or the snail darter has been deleted from the list of endangered species or its critical habitat materially redefined."

* * *

We granted certiorari, 434 U.S. 954 (1977), to review the judgment of the Court of Appeals.

* * * [T]wo questions are presented: (a) would TVA be in violation of the Act if it completed and operated the Tellico Dam as planned? (b) if TVA's actions would offend the Act, is an injunction the appropriate remedy for the violation? For the reasons stated hereinafter, we hold that both questions must be answered in the affirmative.

It may seem curious to some that the survival of a relatively small number of three-inch fish among all the countless millions of species extant would require the permanent halting of a virtually completed dam for which Congress has expended more than $100 million. The paradox is not minimized by the fact that Congress continued to appropriate large sums of public money for the project, even after congressional Appropriations Committees were apprised of its apparent impact upon the survival of the snail darter. We conclude, however, that the explicit provisions of the Endangered Species Act require precisely that result.

One would be hard pressed to find a statutory provision whose terms were any plainer than those in § 7 of the Endangered Species Act. Its very words affirmatively command all federal agencies "to *insure* that actions *authorized, funded,* or *carried out* by them do not *jeopardize* the continued existence" of an endangered species or "*result* in the destruction or modification of habitat of such species. . . ." 16 U.S.C. § 1536 (1976 ed.). (Emphasis added.) This language admits of no exception. * * *

Concededly, this view of the Act will produce results requiring the sacrifice of the anticipated benefits of the project and of many millions of dollars in public funds. But examination of the language, history, and structure of the legislation under review here indicates beyond doubt that Congress intended endangered species to be afforded the highest of priorities.

* * * [T]he totality of congressional action makes it abundantly clear that the result we reach today is wholly in accord with both the words of the statute and the intent of Congress. The plain intent of Congress in enacting this statute was to halt and reverse the trend toward species extinction, whatever the cost. This is reflected not only in the stated policies of the Act, but in literally every section of the statute. * * *

It is not for us to speculate, much less act, on whether Congress would have altered its stance had the specific events of this case been anticipated. In any event, we discern no hint in the deliberations of Congress relating to the 1973 Act that would compel a different result than we reach here.

* * *

One might dispute the applicability of these examples to the Tellico Dam by saying that in this case the burden on the public through the loss of millions of unrecoverable dollars would greatly outweigh the loss of the snail darter. But neither the Endangered Species Act nor Art. III of the Constitution provides federal courts with authority to make such fine utilitarian calculations. On the contrary, the plain language of the Act, buttressed by its legislative history, shows clearly that Congress viewed the value of endangered species as "incalculable." Quite obviously, it would be difficult for a court to balance the loss of a sum certain—even $100 million—against a congressionally declared "incalculable" value, even assuming we had the power to engage in such a weighing process, which we emphatically do not.

* * *

Having determined that there is an irreconcilable conflict between operation of the Tellico Dam and the explicit provisions of § 7 of the

Endangered Species Act, we must now consider what remedy, if any, is appropriate. It is correct, of course, that a federal judge sitting as a chancellor is not mechanically obligated to grant an injunction for every violation of law. This Court made plain in Hecht Co. v. Bowles, 321 U.S. 321, 329 (1944), that "[a] grant of *jurisdiction* to issue compliance orders hardly suggests an absolute duty to do so under any and all circumstances." As a general matter it may be said that "[s]ince all or almost all equitable remedies are discretionary, the balancing of equities and hardships is appropriate in almost any case as a guide to the chancellor's discretion." [Citation.] Thus, in *Hecht Co.* the Court refused to grant an injunction when it appeared from the District Court findings that "the issuance of an injunction would have 'no effect by way of insuring better compliance in the future' and would [have been] 'unjust' to [the] petitioner and not 'in the public interest.'"

But these principles take a court only so far. Our system of government is, after all, a tripartite one, with each branch having certain defined functions delegated to it by the Constitution. While "[i]t is emphatically the province and duty of the judicial department to say what the law is," Marbury v. Madison, 1 Cranch 137, 177 (1803), it is equally—and emphatically—the exclusive province of the Congress not only to formulate legislative policies and mandate programs and projects, but also to establish their relative priority for the Nation. Once Congress, exercising its delegated powers, has decided the order of priorities in a given area, it is for the Executive to administer the laws and for the courts to enforce them when enforcement is sought.

Here we are urged to view the Endangered Species Act "reasonably," and hence shape a remedy "that accords with some modicum of common sense and the public weal." [Citation.] But is that our function? We have no expert knowledge on the subject of endangered species, much less do we have a mandate from the people to strike a balance of equities on the side of the Tellico Dam. Congress has spoken in the plainest of words, making it abundantly clear that the balance has been struck in favor of affording endangered species the highest of priorities, thereby adopting a policy which it described as "institutionalized caution."

Our individual appraisal of the wisdom or unwisdom of a particular course consciously selected by the Congress is to be put aside in the process of interpreting a statute. Once the meaning of an enactment is discerned and its constitutionality determined, the judicial process comes to an end. We do not sit as a committee of review, nor are we vested with the power of veto. The lines ascribed to Sir Thomas Moore by Robert Bolt are not without relevance here:

> "The law, Roper, the law. I know what's legal, not what's right. And I'll stick to what's legal.... I'm *not* God. The currents and eddies of right and wrong, which you find such plain-sailing, I can't navigate, I'm no voyager. But in the thickets of the law, oh there I'm a forester.... What would you do? Cut a great road through the law to get after the Devil? ... And when the last law was down, and the Devil

turned round on you—where would you hide, Roper, the laws all being flat? ... This country's planted thick with laws from coast to coast— Man's laws, not God's—and if you cut them down ... d'you really think you could stand upright in the winds that would blow them? ... Yes, I'd give the Devil benefit of law, for my own safety's sake." R. Bolt, A Man for All Seasons, Act I, p. 147 (Three Plays, Heinemann ed. 1967).

We agree with the Court of Appeals that in our constitutional system the commitment to the separation of powers is too fundamental for us to pre-empt congressional action by judicially decreeing what accords with "common sense and the public weal." Our Constitution vests such responsibilities in the political branches.

Affirmed.

---

1. Prior to *TVA v. Hill,* the Supreme Court had previously considered similar statutory wording in the Emergency Price Control Act of 1942. The Act concerned maximum price control of commodities and services during World War II. It provided:

Whenever in the judgment of the Administrator any person has engaged or is about to engage in any acts or practices which constitute a violation of any provision [of this Act] * * * he may make application to the appropriate court for an order enjoining such acts or practices * * * and upon a showing by the Administrator that such person has engaged or is about to engage in any such acts or practices a permanent or temporary injunction, restraining order, or other order shall be granted without bond.

The question before the Supreme Court in *Hecht Co. v. Bowles*, 321 U.S. 321, 64 S.Ct. 587, 88 L.Ed. 754 (1944), was whether the Administrator was automatically entitled to an injunction upon a showing of a violation, or whether the court had some discretion to grant or withhold relief. The case concerned the Hecht Company's violations found during a spot check. The regulations under the Act were complex and confusing to apply, and the good faith effort of the defendant to comply with the Act was not questioned. The violations were corrected immediately and voluntarily by the store and vigorous steps were taken to prevent further mistakes. The district court had concluded that an injunction against the store would be pointless and unjust, and dismissed the complaint. The Court of Appeals reversed because it construed the Act as requiring the issuance of the injunction as a matter of course once violations were found.

The Administrator argued to the Supreme Court that the language "shall be granted" is not permissive. The Court nonetheless found that there is room for discretion under the statute. The reference in the Act to the possibility of some type of "other order" suggests that a court may conclude that it is more appropriate to issue some type of order other than the type sought by the Administrator. Therefore an injunction was not mandatory simply because the Administrator asked for it.

Moreover, the Court found unlikely an intent by Congress to make a drastic departure from the traditions of equity practice by removing discretion in the issuance of an injunction. Justice Douglas' opinion for the Court observed: "The historic injunctive process was designed to deter, not to punish. The essence of equity jurisdiction has been the power of the Chancellor to do equity and to mould each decree to the necessities of the particular case. Flexibility rather than rigidity have distinguished it. * * * We do not believe that such a major departure from that long tradition as is here proposed should be lightly implied." The Court of Appeals was therefore reversed.

2. The consideration of the role of public interest and equitable discretion in statutory interpretation was revisited by the Supreme Court recently in *United States v. Oakland Cannabis Buyers' Cooperative*, 532 U.S. 483, 121 S.Ct. 1711, 149 L.Ed.2d 722 (2001) reproduced in Chapter 6. A federal statute, the Controlled Substances Act, prohibits the manufacture and sale of certain drugs. The State of California sought to reconcile one of its statutes with the federal legislation by finding a medical necessity exception within the federal scheme. The Court rejected that argument, distinguishing TVA v. Hill and its progeny:

> As an initial matter, * * * when district courts are properly acting as courts of equity, they have discretion unless a statute clearly provides otherwise. For "several hundred years," courts of equity have enjoyed "sound discretion" to consider the "necessities of the public interest" when fashioning injunctive relief. *Hecht Co. v. Bowles,* 321 U.S. 321, 329–330, 64 S.Ct. 587, 88 L.Ed. 754 (1944) ("The essence of equity jurisdiction has been the power of the Chancellor to do equity and to mould each decree to the necessities of the particular case. Flexibility rather than rigidity has distinguished it"); *Weinberger v. Romero–Barcelo,* 456 U.S. 305, 312, 102 S.Ct. 1798, 72 L.Ed.2d 91 (1982) ("In exercising their sound discretion, courts of equity should pay particular regard for the public consequences in employing the extraordinary remedy of injunction"). Such discretion is displaced only by a "clear and valid legislative command." * * *

> The Controlled Substances Act vests district courts with jurisdiction to enjoin violations of the Act, 21 U.S.C. § 882(a). But a "grant of jurisdiction to issue [equitable relief] hardly suggests an absolute duty to do so under any and all circumstances. Because the District Court's use of equitable power is not textually required by any 'clear and valid legislative command,' the court did not have to issue an injunction."

> *TVA v. Hill,* 437 U.S. 153, 98 S.Ct. 2279, 57 L.Ed.2d 117 (1978), does not support the Government's contention that the District Court lacked discretion in fashioning injunctive relief. In *Hill,* the Court held that the Endangered Species Act of 1973 required the District Court to enjoin completion of a dam, whose operation would either eradicate the known population of the snail darter or destroy its critical habitat. The

District Court lacked discretion because an injunction was the "only means of ensuring compliance." Congress' "order of priorities," as expressed in the statute, would be deprived of effect if the District Court could choose to deny injunctive relief. In effect, the District Court had only a Hobson's choice. By contrast, with respect to the Controlled Substances Act, criminal enforcement is an alternative, and indeed the customary, means of ensuring compliance with the statute. Congress' resolution of the policy issues can be (and usually is) upheld without an injunction.

But the mere fact that the District Court had discretion does not suggest that the District Court, when evaluating the motion to modify the injunction, could consider any and all factors that might relate to the public interest or the conveniences of the parties, including the medical needs of the Cooperative's patients. On the contrary, a court sitting in equity cannot "ignore the judgment of Congress, deliberately expressed in legislation." [Citation] A district court cannot, for example, override Congress' policy choice, articulated in a statute, as to what behavior should be prohibited. "Once Congress, exercising its delegated powers, has decided the order of priorities in a given area, it is ... for the courts to enforce them when enforcement is sought." Courts of equity cannot, in their discretion, reject the balance that Congress has struck in a statute. Their choice (unless there is statutory language to the contrary) is simply whether a particular means of enforcing the statute should be chosen over another permissible means; their choice is not whether enforcement is preferable to no enforcement at all. Consequently, when a court of equity exercises its discretion, it may not consider the advantages and disadvantages of nonenforcement of the statute, but only the advantages and disadvantages of "employing the extraordinary remedy of injunction," over the other available methods of enforcement. [Citations] To the extent the district court considers the public interest and the conveniences of the parties, the court is limited to evaluating how such interest and conveniences are affected by the selection of an injunction over other enforcement mechanisms.

Id. at 121 S.Ct. at 1720–1722.

3. Statutes affect remedies in many ways. They more typically limit remedies than mandate relief. Recall *Orloff v. Los Angeles Turf Club*, 30 Cal.2d 110, 180 P.2d 321 (1947), reprinted *supra* in Chapter 2, where the court considered a statute that provided only a small and specific damages remedy. Is it permissible for a court to grant equitable relief if the statute provides only for damages? When the statutory remedies are limited, a court must decide whether the legislature intended to foreclose other remedies or whether an additional remedy, such as an injunction, may be properly implied to carry out the purposes of the statute.

4. In contrast to the statutes that mandate injunctions, some statutes completely prohibit them in certain circumstances. For example, one such anti-injunction provision is Internal Revenue Code § 7421(a), which effec-

tively prohibits injunctions against the Internal Revenue Service from collecting taxes. Another example is the Norris–LaGuardia Act, 29 U.S.C. § 104, reprinted in part *supra* in Chapter 2. This Act prevents federal courts from enjoining labor disputes by removing federal "jurisdiction" over such issues. Recall the problems with interpreting this prohibition in United States v. United Mine Workers of America, 330 U.S. 258, 67 S.Ct. 677, 91 L.Ed. 884 (1947), reprinted *supra* in Chapter 7.

PROBLEM: THE HOSPITAL DISCLOSING PATIENT RECORDS

Assume that Congress passed new legislation designed to further protect the privacy of medical records in all clinics and hospitals receiving federal funds. The Act provides that no records concerning the health of any individual can be released by such an institution without the express written consent of the patient on a specified form. The Act further provides that such consent must be obtained for each specific request for release, such as for a scientific study, and that the patient's rights under the statute cannot be otherwise waived. For minors the consent of parent or guardian is needed.

Penalties for violation of the hypothetical Act include compensatory and punitive damages, plus attorneys' fees to prevailing plaintiffs. The Act gives jurisdiction in federal district court without regard to the amount in controversy. Moreover, the Act provides that if a hospital or clinic threatens to release information without the proper authorization from the patient, the federal district court "shall issue" an injunction prohibiting such disclosure until the Act has been complied with. The only exception to the Act is that proper local or national health authorities may seek information concerning "any communicable disease that seriously threatens the health and welfare of the surrounding community" without consent of the patients.

There is a controversy in one community with respect to health studies following a radiation leak from a nearby nuclear power plant last year. Local and national health officials wish to study the effects of the leak on babies who were *in utero* at the time of the leak. The local newspaper, which has followed all aspects of the leak incident closely, reported that these health authorities were going to obtain data from the local hospital. The article quoted a hospital official who said that although the hospital generally respects the privacy of its patients, it intends to continue full cooperation with the authorities on this matter of profound public importance.

Several parents who had babies born in the hospital during the time in question object to the threatened release of their babies' records. They have sued under the Act in federal district court to prohibit the hospital, a recipient of federal funds, from releasing the information without their consent. The complaint does not indicate the reason why the parents object; it simply invokes the language of the Act that an injunction "shall issue" to prevent unauthorized disclosure.

The question is whether the judge may use discretion in the issuance of an injunction in this case. Is it proper to balance the equities between the individuals' right of privacy and the public need? The communicable disease exception to the Act does not apply. Should the court nonetheless use traditional equitable principles to decide the case or is the order mandatory upon the plaintiffs' proof of threatened disclosure in violation of the Act? Should the court dismiss the complaint unless the plaintiffs reveal the reasons for their objections, at least *in camera?*

B. ENJOINING SPEECH OR LITIGATION

Section Coverage:

Special problems arise when the object of an injunction is to inhibit free speech, to restrict access to civil courts, or to interfere with the function of the criminal law system. A judge should not lightly enjoin conduct involving any of these important aspects of a free society.

Such restraints are sometimes necessary. When freedom of speech is exercised in a way that seriously interferes with other important rights, a court may restrain it with a narrowly tailored order. Similarly, when a defendant greatly abuses the civil litigation system with harassing litigation, the judge may restrict access to the normal court process with a limited order.

Injunctions against criminal prosecutions are very rare. A state civil court will enjoin a threatened or existing criminal case in its jurisdiction only upon a strong showing of improper prosecutorial motivation. When the prosecution is in another state, only a showing of greatest urgency will support an injunction against it because the court has no practical means of enforcing an order against the out-of-state parties.

Federal court plaintiffs face further difficulties when they seek an injunction against a state prosecution. The Supreme Court has held that principles of "our Federalism" caution against the exercise of this power except in cases where the state officials' clearly improper motivation threatens fundamental freedoms. Otherwise plaintiffs must seek their remedies at law by defending themselves in the criminal cases.

Model Case:

A city ordinance provides that vendors, in order to sell food and beverages either at retail or wholesale, must obtain a license by paying a fee of $300. The ordinance further provides that violators would be subject to a fine of $50. Marty Mitchell sells popcorn from a moveable cart on the streets of the city without a license. Like other street vendors, Mitchell had sold on the street for years without a license on the assumption that the ordinance applied only to stores.

The city prosecuting attorney recently decided to interpret the ordinance to apply to the city's increasing number of street vendors. Marty

Mitchell became the test case. Rather than pursue criminal penalties against Mitchell, however, the city instead sought an injunction to prohibit any future business transactions in violation of the ordinance. The case is pending, but the court is unlikely to grant the injunction because the city has an adequate remedy at law, namely criminal prosecution under the ordinance. Because the ordinance did not specifically provide for injunctive relief, the court would need either to imply the remedy from the ordinance or to rely upon common law nuisance. Even if the court finds such a source of injunctive power, however, it is unlikely to grant the relief. Not only is the legal remedy adequate, but equity will not ordinarily enjoin a crime without proof that the defendant's conduct is a public nuisance.

Mitchell is supported by a civil rights group that fears the city wants to reduce the number of vendors on the street because recently their numbers have swelled with immigrants from an ethnic minority. This group arranged legal representation for Mitchell by a young attorney named Alexis Rosch. Rosch's theory is that the city wants to discourage the vendors with a highly public case and that Mitchell, a non-minority and long-established vendor, was targeted to hide the city official's prejudiced motives. Rosch further theorizes that the official's purpose in seeking an injunction was twofold: If it is granted, the contempt penalties for continued violations by Mitchell on principle can be much larger than the fine provided by statute. If it is not granted, the case will get daily publicity for a while as the city then seeks a criminal prosecution.

Rosch therefore files a claim for Mitchell in federal district court seeking an injunction against the civil suit and against the threatened criminal prosecution. The court is unlikely to grant either request. The remedy at law is adequate for the civil suit; Mitchell cannot show that the court would act improperly in the matter. Mitchell also cannot show irreparable harm because the harm normally incident to prosecution is not sufficient. The threatened criminal prosecution does not seriously endanger important rights to allow a federal court to interfere with the state's process. Principles of federalism require abstention under these facts. The state court will be left to rectify any injustice that may occur if the city officials are indeed acting with wrongful motives.

Willing v. Mazzocone

482 Pa. 377, 393 A.2d 1155 (1978).

■ MANDERINO, JUSTICE.

On Monday, September 29, and Wednesday, October 1, 1975, appellant, Helen Willing, demonstrated in the pedestrian plaza between building number two and building number three, Penn Center Plaza, downtown Philadelphia, Pennsylvania. The plaza is bounded by 15th and 16th Streets, Market Street, and John F. Kennedy Boulevard, and is a well traveled pedestrian pathway between the two court buildings located at City Hall and at Five Penn Center Plaza. While engaged in this activity, which lasted for several hours each day, appellant wore a "sandwich-board" sign around her neck. On the sign she had hand lettered the following:

LAW–FIRM

of

QUINN–MAZZOCONE

Stole money from me—and

Sold-me-out-to-the

INSURANCE COMPANY

As she marched back and forth, appellant also pushed a shopping cart on which she had placed an American flag. She continuously rang a cow bell and blew on a whistle to further attract attention.

Appellees in this case are two members of the legal profession, Carl M. Mazzocone and Charles F. Quinn, who are associated in the two member law firm of Mazzocone and Quinn, p.c. When appellant refused appellees' efforts to amicably dissuade her from further activity such as that described above, appellees filed a suit in equity in the Court of Common Pleas of Philadelphia County seeking to enjoin her from further demonstration. Three hearings were held at which the following factual history emerged.

In 1968, appellees, who have specialized in the trial of workmen's compensation matters for several years, represented appellant in such a case. Pursuant to appellees' representation, appellant was awarded permanent/partial disability benefits which she collected for a number of years. At the time of the initial settlement distribution with appellant, appellees deducted the sum of $150.00 as costs of the case. This sum, according to appellees' evidence, was paid in full to Robert DeSilverio, M.D., a treating psychiatrist who testified on appellant's behalf in the Workmen's Compensation matter. Appellees presented copies of their records covering the transaction with Dr. DeSilverio. A cancelled check for the amount of the payment, and the testimony of Dr. DeSilverio himself, confirmed appellees' account of the transaction. Appellant offered no evidence other than her testimony that the cause of her antagonism towards appellees was not any dissatisfaction with the settlement, but rather, her belief that appellees had wrongfully diverted to themselves $25.00 of the $150.00 that was supposed to have been paid to Dr. DeSilverio.

Based on this evidence, the equity court concluded that appellant was "... a woman firmly on the thrall of the belief that [appellees] defrauded her, an *idee fixe* which, either by reason of eccentricity or an even more serious mental instability, refuses to be dislodged by the most convincing proof to the contrary." The Court then enjoined appellant from

"... further unlawful demonstration, picketing, carrying placards which contain defamatory and libelous statements and or uttering, publishing and declaring defamatory statements against the [appellees] herein."

On appeal, the Superior Court modified the trial court's order to read,

"Helen R. Willing, be and is permanently enjoined from further demonstrating against and/or picketing Mazzocone and Quinn, Attorneys-at-Law, by uttering or publishing statements to the effect that Mazzocone and Quinn, Attorneys-at-Law stole money from her and sold her out to the insurance company." [Citation.]

We granted appellant's petition for allowance of appeal, and now reverse.

[The majority opinion reversed on the ground that the injunction was an unconstitutional prior restraint on rights of free speech under the Pennsylvania Constitution. The court also said that the indigency of the appellant was irrelevant to the consideration of whether the remedy at law was adequate. The following concurrence of Justice Roberts elaborates on the indigency consideration and considers the prior restraint question under federal constitutional law.]

■ ROBERTS, JUSTICE, concurring.

I agree with the opinion of Mr. Justice Manderino that appellant's indigency does not justify the Superior Court's radical departure from the long-standing general rule that equity will not enjoin a defamation. In Heilman v. Union Canal Company, 37 Pa. 100, 104 (1860), this Court said:

"The fact, if it be so, that this remedy may not be successful in realizing the fruits of a recovery at law, on account of the insolvency of the defendants, is not of itself a ground of equitable interference. The remedy is what is to be looked at. If it exist [sic], and is ordinarily adequate, its possible want of success is not a consideration."

[Citations.] Money damages are adequate to recompense the plaintiffs for any losses they have suffered as a consequence of the defendant's defamatory publication. Thus, it was improper to grant equitable relief based on appellant's presumed inability to pay a money judgment.

As a consequence of holding that the defendant's indigency creates equitable jurisdiction, the Superior Court conditions appellant's right to trial by jury on her economic status. One of the underlying justifications for equity's traditional refusal to enjoin defamatory speech is that in equity all questions of fact are resolved by the trial court, rather than the jury. Thus, it deprives appellant of her right to a jury trial on the issue of the truth or falsity of her speech. [Citations.] The right to trial by jury is more than mere form. * * *

Furthermore, despite this Court's traditional practice of avoiding constitutional questions where a non-constitutional ground is dispositive [citation], it is appropriate in this case to reaffirm expressly the settled law governing the first amendment issue before us. The injunction in this case is a classic example of a prior restraint on speech. Protection of the citizenry from prior restraints is one of the leading principles on which the first amendment is based. [Citations.] Thus, there is a heavy presumption against the constitutional validity of any prior restraint on speech. [Citations.]

In *Organization for a Better Austin* [402 U.S. 415 (1971)], the Supreme Court held unconstitutional an injunction restraining members of a citizen group from leafletting and picketing outside a real estate broker's home. In doing so the Court stated:

> "Respondent thus carries a heavy burden of showing justification for the imposition of such a restraint. He has not met that burden. No prior decisions support the claim that the interest of an individual in being free from public criticism of his business practices in pamphlets or leaflets warrants use of the injunctive power of a court."

Id., 402 U.S. at 419. That rationale is equally applicable here. Appellees' interest in protecting their reputations is insufficient to justify enjoining appellant's speech, particularly where there is a legal remedy available. Thus, under the first amendment and the Supreme Court cases involving prior restraints, no basis exists for permitting the injunction in this case to stand.

---

1. Note that the intermediate appellate court in the principal case found it necessary to modify the trial court's order even though the intermediate court believed the restraint was constitutional. Is the trial court's wording overly broad? Is the modified wording too narrow? The intermediate appellate court has a good discussion at 246 Pa.Super. 98, 369 A.2d 829.

2. Compare the principal case to the result in *Martin v. Reynolds Metals Company*, 224 F.Supp. 978 (D.Or.1963). In *Martin* a rancher believed that a nearby alumina reduction plant was damaging human and animal health by allowing large quantities of fluorides to escape from the plant. He erected a billboard that said the company had contaminated his ranch and killed 831 cattle in the past six years. The district court judge found the allegations were actionable libel and a jury trial was scheduled for the company's past damages claim. The court held further that pending adjudication of the damage claim the rancher would be enjoined to take down the sign. The court noted that the legal remedy was inadequate because "the mere existence of a concurrent legal remedy does not bar equitable relief. Rather ' * * * the legal remedy must be equally effectual with the equitable remedy, as to all the rights of the complainant.'" Lewis v. Cocks, 90 U.S. 466, 23 L.Ed. 70, 23 Wall. 466 (1874). 224 F.Supp. at 984.

The injunction against the rancher was in effect only until the adjudication of the damages claim. What if the rancher erects the billboard again immediately after paying damages? Would a permanent injunction be appropriate?

3. In the exceptional cases where courts grant prior restraints of speech, the injunctions must be narrowly tailored not only to withstand Constitutional scrutiny but also to meet due process standards to enforce them with contempt. In *Madsen v. Women's Health Center, Inc.*, 512 U.S.

753, 114 S.Ct. 2516, 129 L.Ed.2d 593 (1994), operators of a health clinic that performed abortions sought to broaden a previously entered injunction against anti-abortion protestors. The state court injunction established a 36–foot buffer zone around the clinic entrances, driveway and surrounding private property. It also imposed limited noise restrictions and provided for a 300–foot no-approach zone around the clinic and staff residences. The Court held that the provisions establishing a 36–foot buffer zone around the clinic entrances and driveway and imposing noise restrictions did not violate the First Amendment. It further held that the buffer zone on private property and the no-approach zone burdened more speech than necessary.

The Court rejected the argument that any injunction that restricts speech of protesters is necessarily content or viewpoint based. The Court observed:

> An injunction, by its very nature, applies only to a particular group (or individuals) and regulates the activities, and perhaps the speech, of that group. It does so, however, because of the group's past actions in the context of a specific dispute between real parties. 512 U.S. at 762.

The Court also explained the attributes of injunctions, in contrast with legislative restrictions on conduct:

> There are obvious differences * * * between an injunction and a generally applicable ordinance [that restricts conduct]. Ordinances represent a legislative choice regarding the promotion of particular societal interests. Injunctions, by contrast, are remedies imposed for violations (or threatened violations) of a legislative or judicial decree. Injunctions also carry greater risk of censorship and discriminatory application than do general ordinances. * * * Injunctions, of course, have some advantages over generally applicable statutes in that they can be tailored by a trial judge to afford more precise relief than a statute where a violation of the law has already occurred. 512 U.S. 764–765.

The Court further noted that the injunction served governmental interests in protecting woman's freedom to seek lawful medical and counseling services. After implementing the amended injunction, the protestors could still be seen and heard from the clinic parking lots. Also the noise restrictions were necessary to ensure health and well-being of the patients. However, the Court stated that the injunction interfered with state's interest in protecting the privacy of homes by prohibiting the protestors from demonstrating within 300 feet of residences, recognizing the unique nature of the home as "the last citadel or the tired, the weary, and the sick." [Citations] The limitation on time, duration of picketing, and number of pickets could have accomplished the desired result.

4.　In *Schenck v. Pro–Choice Network of Western N.Y.*, 519 U.S. 357, 117 S.Ct. 855, 137 L.Ed.2d 1 (1997), health care providers sought a preliminary injunction prohibiting abortion protestors from engaging in allegedly illegal efforts to prevent women from obtaining abortions. The injunction banned "demonstrating within 15 feet ... of ... doorways or doorway entrances, parking lot entrances, driveways and driveway entrances of [clinic] facilities" (fixed buffer zones), or "within 15 feet of any person or vehicle seeking access to or leaving such facilities" (floating buffer zones). Another provision allowed two sidewalk counselors inside the buffer zones, but required them to "cease and desist" their counseling if the patient so requested.

The Supreme Court held the injunction provisions imposing "fixed buffer zone" limitations constitutional, but the provisions imposing "floating buffer zone" limitations violated the First Amendment. The Court noted that "floating buffer zones" would require protestors to move with various people entering and leaving the clinic in order to communicate their messages. The resulting lack of certainty on how to comply would lead to substantial risk that much more speech would be burdened than prohibited by the injunction's terms. The fixed buffer zones were upheld against the First Amendment challenge as necessary to ensure that people and vehicles trying to enter or exit the clinic could do so freely. In addition, the "cease and desist" provision was not contrary to the respective First Amendment rights and protections. Even though the patient was allowed to terminate the protestor's right to speak, the counselors remained free to espouse their message outside the 15–foot buffer zones.

Mabe v. City of Galveston

687 S.W.2d 769 (Tex.App.1985).

■ EVANS, CHIEF JUSTICE.

The appellant, James Mabe, appeals from a temporary injunction entered in favor of appellees, The City of Galveston and Park Board of Trustees, prohibiting him from distributing pamphlets that list the names and phone numbers of certain members of the City Council and Park Board. The City and Park Board petitioned for injunctive relief, claiming that Mabe's publication of his pamphlet invaded the privacy of the individual members of the Council and Park Board. * * * The trial court * * * issued an injunction prohibiting Mabe from directly or indirectly publishing in writing any list of the names of members of the City Council or Park Board, coupled with their home telephone numbers. We reverse and render, directing that the temporary injunction be dissolved.

In his one point of error, Mabe challenges the constitutionality of the trial court's action, arguing that the injunction is void because it operates as a prior restraint of the exercise of his first amendment right to freedom of speech. * * *

Mabe owns a gift shop on Seawall Boulevard, the beachfront in Galveston. He is a Galveston native and has been in business on the island for seven years. Because of comments made by his customers and other visitors, he became concerned that there were no public restroom facilities on the Seawall. On a number of occasions, he appeared before the Galveston City Council and the Park Board and made his complaints known to those governmental bodies. Mabe finally reached the conclusion that the City Council and Park Board officials lacked concern about the matter, and in midsummer 1984, he printed and distributed 2000 pamphlets, which read:

THE BUSINESS OPERATORS ON SEAWALL BOULEVARD APOLO-GIZE FOR NO PUBLIC RESTROOM FACILITIES ON OUR BEACH-FRONT.

The Persons to Contact Are:

Council Members:
Lou Muller (409) 744–7444
John L. Sullivan (409) 744–5632
Mayor:
Jan Coggeshall (409) 744–5918

Park Board Members:
Mrs. Marilyn Schwartz (409) 744–3531
Mr. Meyer Reiswerg (409) 762–7540
Mr. Roby Burkett (409) 744–3686
Mr. Tom Wiseheart (409) 762–8434

Shortly after these pamphlets were distributed, the named members of City Council and Park Board of Trustees began receiving phone calls at home from persons who complained about the lack of restroom facilities. Some of the calls were received during the day, some in the evening, and three or four calls were received in the very late evening or early morning hours. The phone numbers of each person listed on the pamphlet could be found in the Galveston telephone directory, and some were also listed in documents published by the Park Board.

Any system of prior restraints bears a heavy presumption against its constitutional validity. [Citations.] Although in exceptional cases prior restraints may be constitutionally permissible, [citation] prior restraint against distribution of pamphlets is particularly suspect. [Citation.]

In 1973, the Supreme Court of Texas followed the practice of most other American jurisdictions and recognized a legally enforceable right of privacy. [Citation.] However, this right of privacy has never been considered unlimited. In certain circumstances, an individual's right of privacy must yield to other overriding constitutional mandates. [Citations.] This is particularly true where an individual is a public official, and the distributed information is critical of the conduct of public business or bears on some matter of public concern. In such an instance, the interest in privacy is outweighed by the larger, fundamental interest in free discussion and the dissemination of truth. [Citations.] Thus, courts are extremely reluctant to allow a prior restraint on free speech merely to protect a perceived threat to a public official's limited right of privacy.

In the case at bar, the pamphlets merely published the names and telephone numbers of certain public officials. These same telephone numbers were listed in the telephone directory and in other public documents. The pamphlets had a direct relationship to the public interest, *i.e.,* the lack of public restroom facilities on the Seawall. Thus, Mabe had the constitutional right to publish the pamphlets, regardless of whether the particular public officials were, in fact, empowered to take corrective action with respect to his complaint. [Citation.] The evidence does not suggest that Mabe's actions were taken solely to harass the public officials, nor was there evidence that the officials could not have taken measures, such as having their phone numbers unlisted, to protect themselves against unwanted telephone calls. We conclude that the trial court's injunctive order constituted an unwarranted prior restraint on the exercise of Mabe's first amendment right of freedom of speech, and we accordingly sustain his point of error.

The trial court's temporary injunctive order is reversed, and the injunction is ordered dissolved.

PROBLEM: THE LITIGIOUS NEIGHBOR

Cotter and a neighbor named Baxter had a dispute one night during a card game. Since then they have not spoken to each other. Baxter, knowing that Cotter hated to have cars parked on the street in this suburban neighborhood, began parking his car on the street in front of Cotter's house for the purpose of annoying Cotter. It was otherwise permissible to park there.

Cotter, an attorney, filed a civil complaint against Baxter for parking in front of the house. Baxter was a dentist and therefore needed to hire an attorney to get the complaint dismissed for failure to state a cause of action. Baxter has learned from neighbors that Cotter plans to repeat this procedure if Baxter continues to park in front of Cotter's house.

Baxter wants to get a court order against Cotter to prohibit such future complaints from being filed against Baxter. Is a court likely to protect Baxter from Cotter's harassment with such an injunction?

Pavilonis v. King

626 F.2d 1075 (1st Cir.1980).

■ Bownes, Circuit Judge.

Anne M. Pavilonis appeals from the dismissal of two civil rights actions she filed against various people connected with the Boston schools. She also challenges the district court's entry of an order enjoining her from filing any lawsuit in the federal district court of Massachusetts—and prohibiting the clerk of court from accepting for filing any paper submitted by her—without authorization by a district judge.

Pavilonis' first lawsuit was commenced on December 9, 1977, by a complaint against the then Governor Michael Dukakis, Boston School Committee President Kathleen Sullivan, and Solomon Lewenberg School Principal William I. O'Connell. The body of the complaint read, in its entirety, as follows:

1. This is an action to redress the deprivation under color of a law of the state of Massachusetts of a right secured to plaintiff by Article V

Amendment 14 of the Constitution of the United States. Jurisdiction is conferred on this Court by 28 U.S.C. Section 1343.

2. Plaintiff brings this action under 42 U.S.C. Section 1986 to recover damages for defendant's failure to prevent a wrong mentioned in 42 U.S.C. Section 1985, which defendant knew was about to occur and which defendants had the power to prevent, as hereinafter more fully appears. Jurisdiction is conferred on this Court by 28 [U.S.C.] Section 1343.

The second complaint, filed on December 19, 1977, was nearly identical, but named Northeastern University President Kenneth G. Ryder as an additional defendant.

When Pavilonis moved for appointment of counsel, these cases were referred to a magistrate. Consulting the district court docket, the magistrate found five other complaints filed by Pavilonis, against various defendants including Michael Dukakis and Kenneth Ryder, in which the language contained in paragraph 2 of the instant complaints was used, apparently without significant elaboration. Of the opinion that the two complaints before him, even read liberally, were "completely devoid of any information that would assist the defendants ... [in] answer[ing]," were "completely violative of Rule 8 of the Federal Rules of Civil Procedure," and "appear[ed] frivolous," the magistrate denied the motions for appointment of counsel. Finding that Pavilonis had filed "numerous unsupported actions" that placed an undue burden on the court and deprived other legitimate litigants of a hearing, the magistrate also recommended that she be restricted from filing new actions without permission of a district judge.

* * *

The district judge approved the magistrate's recommendation and, on April 12, 1978, issued an order enjoining Pavilonis from filing new lawsuits without permission of a judge of the District Court of Massachusetts, and ordering the clerk to refuse to file additional papers submitted by her without such permission. * * *

We have little difficulty upholding the district court's dismissal of the complaints. Although pro se complaints are to be read liberally, [citations], these complaints are so hopelessly general that they could give no notice of Pavilonis' claims. * * *

Whether Pavilonis was properly enjoined from filing additional pleadings or new lawsuits without permission from a district judge is a closer question. In recommending an injunction against her filing new actions without permission, the magistrate relied on *Rudnicki v. McCormack*, 210 F.Supp. 905 (D.R.I.1962), *appeal dismissed sub nom.* Rudnicki v. Cox, 372 U.S. 226, 83 S.Ct. 679, 9 L.Ed.2d 714 (1963), and Rudnicki v. Department of Massachusetts Attorney General, 362 F.2d 337 (1st Cir.1966). In *Rudnicki v. McCormack,* such an injunction was entered against a plaintiff who had filed "baseless, vexatious, and repetitive" suits against judges, judicial officers, and attorneys, in an effort to relitigate cases that had been dismissed. The court ruled that it had equitable and supervisory power to protect the defendants from harassment and the court itself from the burden of processing frivolous and unimportant papers. In *Rudnicki v. Department of Massachusetts Attorney General,* we noted the existence of the injunction against Rudnicki and upheld the district court's denial of leave to file a new action. More recently, a similar injunction was entered against another litigant who had filed complaints comprised of vituperative attacks against judges who had ruled against him; upholding the district court's refusal to allow a new complaint of a similar ilk to be filed, we said, "The law is well established that it is proper and necessary for an injunction to issue barring a party, such as appellant, from filing and processing frivolous and vexatious lawsuits." *Gordon v. United States Department of Justice,* 558 F.2d 618 (1st Cir.1977).

While we reject Pavilonis' argument that enjoining litigation is unconstitutional, we do not think her case fits into the classic *Rudnicki–Gordon* mold. Those cases, like many others from other jurisdictions, involved plaintiffs bent on reopening closed cases and evidently also intent on harassing defendants, often judges who had ruled against them. Here, the magistrate determined only that Pavilonis had filed "numerous unsupported" actions, using the same deficient complaints. It does not appear that Pavilonis was attempting to reopen closed cases; according to the magistrate's report, when injunctive relief was recommended at least four of Pavilonis' five other lawsuits were still pending. Likewise, although Pavilonis is obviously dissatisfied with the Boston school system and certain individuals connected with it, it is not clear that her litigation was malicious and designed to harass. Furthermore, it is possible that her use of the same complaint in several cases resulted from a misunderstanding of Rule 8, rather than a desire to mask repetitive litigation or to make response by the defendants difficult.

Nevertheless, Pavilonis' lawsuits were at least to some extent duplicative; for example, in the two cases now on appeal, she sued certain defendants twice in two weeks and there is no apparent difference between the actions. In addition, all her complaints suffered from the same deficiencies. Faced with a situation where its docket was being burdened and defendants were being called upon to answer multiple, impenetrable complaints, the district court was justified in taking action. * * *

Affirmed.

---

1. As reflected in the principal case, a pre-suit screening injunction may be issued to abate a pattern of frivolous, duplicative or vexatious litigation. A pattern of excessive claims imposes fiscal and administrative burdens on the courts and opposing litigants and lessens opportunities of other litigants to obtain timely judicial consideration of legitimate claims. Public policy, though, favors the liberal access to the judicial system and provides a degree of latitude to parties who may lack the sophistication or resources to properly marshal a well-crafted lawsuit. *See* Dantzler v.

E.E.O.C., 810 F.Supp.2d. 312 (D.D.C. 2011) (in fashioning a remedy to abate frivolous actions the court must exercise great care not to unduly impede a litigant's constitutional right of access to courts).

2. Commonly accepted considerations affecting whether to impose pre-filing injunctive relief against duplicative litigation include:

> (1) the litigant's history of litigation and in particular whether it entailed vexatious, harassing, or duplicative suits; (2) the litigant's motive in pursuing the litigation, for example, whether the litigant had a good faith expectation of prevailing; (3) whether the litigant is represented by counsel; (4) whether the litigant has caused unnecessary expense to the parties or placed a needless burden on the courts; and (5) whether other sanctions would be adequate to protect the courts and parties.

Safir v. United States Lines, Inc., 792 F.2d 19, 24 (2d Cir. 1986). *See* In Re Kinney, 201 Cal.App.4th 951, 135 Cal.Rptr.3d 471 (2011) (imposition of attorney fees needlessly incurred in prior cases did not deter litigant from becoming a vexatious litigant).

3. No bright line exists to determine the point at which a "serial" litigator should be enjoined or restricted from future court filings. An extreme example was addressed in *Srivastava v. Daniels*, 409 Fed. Appx. 953 (7th Cir. 2011) where a litigant brought suit against 70 defendants, alleging more than 190 theories of recovery. The district court dismissed the suit after characterizing the complaint as "kitchen-sink style", "confusing, repetitious and baseless" and contained "pages of nonsense" with "outlandish and frivolous arguments". Noting that the litigant had previously filed 32 pro se lawsuits and appeals, all of which had been dismissed, the district court also entered an injunction requiring that any new filings be screened to determine they were not frivolous or duplicative of other suits. The Seventh Circuit affirmed and warned of monetary fines and a possible complete bar forbidding any future filings in federal court if the litigant did not desist from making frivolous claims.

Also see Watson v. Justice of Boston Div. Of Housing Court Dept., 458 Mass. 1025, 941 N.E.2d 593 (2011) (court barred additional filings from litigator who brought five separate actions in various courts and filed sixteen meritless appeals over four year period); Hastings v. State, 79 So. 3d 739, 2011 WL 5573935 (Fla. 2011) (inmate who filed 27 pro se claims enjoined from future filings related to his conviction unless the filings were signed by a licensed attorney); Hofland v. LaHaye, ___ F.Supp.2d ___, 2011 WL 5511661 (D.Me. 2011) (7 prior suits regarding same dispute justified injunction); Malcolm v. Board of Educ. of the Honeoye Falls–Lima Central School, 737 F.Supp.2d 117 (W.D.N.Y. 2010) (pre-filing injunction issued against employee who filed 5 previous cases alleging discrimination). *But see* Stimac v. Wieking, 785 F.Supp.2d 847 (N.D. Cal. 2011) (two actions in ten years insufficient to support a pre-filing order).

4. In balancing the rights of litigants to the broad access to courts with the needs to prevent abuse of the judicial system, certain guidelines

are followed by courts. Those include providing adequate notice and an opportunity to be heard, an adequate record by the trial court for appellate review, clear terms advising the litigant regarding what is required to file future claims, careful scrutiny of new filings and determination that they are repetitive, specific findings that past filings were frivolous or harassing, and narrowly tailoring the order to remedy the particular abuses. *See generally* Parish v. Parish, 412 N.J.Super. 39, 988 A.2d 1180 (2010); Stimac v. Wieking, 785 F.Supp.2d 847 (N.D. Cal. 2011); Hill v. Carpenter, 323 Fed. Appx. 167 (3d Cir. 2009) (injunction barring litigant from ever bringing another lawsuit in the district was overbroad); In re GMS Mgt. Co., Inc. v. Unpaid Court Costs, Fees and Delinquencies, 187 Ohio App.3d 426, 932 N.E.2d 405 (2010) (order barring court clerk from accepting new pleadings from corporation violated constitutional right of access to courts because entered without notice or opportunity to be heard).

Norcisa v. Board of Selectmen of Provincetown

368 Mass. 161, 330 N.E.2d 830 (1975).

■ QUIRICO, JUSTICE.

This is an appeal by the defendants, the board of selectmen of Provincetown (selectmen) and their agent, from a decree entered by the judge of the Probate Court * * * declaring that the plaintiff and her retail clothing business in the town of Provincetown (town) are not within the scope of G.L. c. 101, §§ 1–12, the Transient Vendor Statute, and ordering that the town and its agents, servants, and employees "are hereby restrained and permanently enjoined from enforcing .·. any of the provisions of Mass. G.L. c. 101, §§ 1–12, against the Petitioner or the retail business she operates." * * * Prior to the commencement of this suit in equity, a criminal complaint had issued in the Second District Court of Barnstable County charging the plaintiff with violating G.L. c. 101, §§ 6, 8. This criminal complaint was still pending when the decree appealed from issued. The obvious purpose and effect of the decree was to enjoin the pending criminal prosecution. We reverse.

* * * [I]n 1973 the plaintiff, who was a resident of Provincetown, opened a retail clothing business in that town under the name of The Town Crier Wearhouse. At the time she opened her business, the plaintiff was informed by the agent for the selectmen "that she would not be able to open and operate her business unless she paid to Provincetown a license fee of two hundred dollars ($200.00), furnished a bond of five hundred dollars ($500.00) to the Commonwealth, and applied for both a state and town Transient Vendor's License, all of the above pursuant to and authorized by G.L. c. 101, § 3."

General Laws c. 101, § 3, requires that anyone "before commencing business in the commonwealth as a transient vendor" shall apply for a State license, good for one year, to do business as a transient vendor, subject to local rules and regulations. * * *

The plaintiff's position as stated in the "Agreed Statement of Facts" is that she was not a transient vendor at the time the selectment sought to categorize her as one, that she had not been a transient vendor in the past, and that she would not be a transient vendor in the future. She further asserted that she had performed no acts which could be construed as classifying her as anything except a retailer of clothes, that she intended to conduct her business as a full time retail clothing shop, and that she would take no action inconsistent with these assertions. * * * The defendants' position, in the court below as well as in their brief here, has been "that under the terms of the statute petitioner is required to take out a transient vendor's license unless she *has been* 'open for business during usual business hours for a period of at least twelve consecutive months'" (emphasis added).

* * * [W]e conclude that the judge should not have enjoined the pending criminal prosecution.

At one time, it was common for courts to express the view that an equity court had no "jurisdiction" to enjoin a criminal prosecution. In In re Sawyer, 124 U.S. 200, 8 S.Ct. 482, 31 L.Ed. 402 (1888), the court said, "The office and jurisdiction of a court of equity, unless enlarged by express statute, are limited to the protection of rights of property. It has no jurisdiction over the prosecution, the punishment, or the pardon of crimes or misdemeanors.... To assume such a jurisdiction, or to sustain a bill in equity to restrain or relieve against proceedings for the punishment of offences, ... is to invade the domain of the courts of common law, or of the executive and administrative department of the government." * * *

In this Commonwealth, however, it was early established that courts with general equity powers have the power to restrain criminal prosecutions. In Shuman v. Gilbert, 229 Mass. 225, 118 N.E. 254 (1918), for example, this court recognized the "general rule" that criminal prosecutions are not to be enjoined, but pointed out, "[T]here is an exception to this comprehensive statement. Jurisdiction in equity to restrain the institution of prosecutions under unconstitutional or void statutes or local ordinances has been upheld by this court when property rights would be injured irreparably, and when other elements necessary to support cognizance by equity are present." [Citations.]

As pointed out in the *Shuman* case, the occasions when an equity court may properly enjoin a criminal prosecution remain the exception to the "general rule" of non-intervention. Some of the basic policy reasons underlying the rule of nonintervention were well-expressed by the Supreme Court of Hawaii: "Courts of equity are not constituted to deal with crimes and criminal proceedings. They have no power to punish admitted offenders of a challenged penal statute after holding it to be valid, or to compensate those injured by the violations thereof while the hands of the officers of the law have been stayed by injunction. To that extent such courts are incapable of affording a complete remedy. Equity, therefore, takes no part in the administration of the criminal law. It neither aids, restrains, nor obstructs criminal courts in the exercise of their jurisdiction.

Ordinarily a court of equity deals only with civil cases involving property rights where it can afford a complete remedy by injunctive relief. Hence it does not interfere in the enforcement of penal statutes even though invalid unless there be exceptional circumstances and a clear showing that an injunction is urgently necessary to afford adequate protection to rights of property so as to circumvent great and irreparable injury until the validity of the particular penal statute is sustained." Liu v. Farr, 39 Hawaii 23, 35–36 (1950).

Both the *Shuman* and *Liu* cases quoted above indicated that equity would act only to protect "property rights" from irreparable damage by criminal prosecution. In the leading case of Kenyon v. Chicopee, 320 Mass. 528, 70 N.E.2d 241 (1946), however, we largely rejected the personal rights-property rights distinction as a factor in considering whether an injunction should issue. We considered this question and said at 534, 70 N.E.2d at 244: "We believe the true rule to be that equity will protect personal rights by injunction upon the same conditions upon which it will protect property rights by injunction. In general, these conditions are, [1] that unless relief is granted a substantial right of the plaintiff will be impaired to a material degree; [2] that the remedy at law is inadequate; and [3] that injunctive relief can be applied with practical success and without imposing an impossible burden on the court or bringing its processes into disrepute." This, then, is the test which the probate judge should have applied in considering the request for an injunction, and it is the test which we now apply to the facts before us. In so doing, we assume without deciding that parts (1) and (3) of the *Kenyon* test are satisfied and concentrate on part (2), that is, whether the remedy at law would be adequate in this case.

The plaintiff variously claims that G.L. c. 101, §§ 1–12, is either unconstitutional on its face or as applied, or that the statute, properly construed, does not apply to her at all. In accordance with these claims, she asserts that she cannot be prosecuted for failure to comply with the statute. If we assume, again without deciding the question, that the plaintiff indeed cannot properly be prosecuted under this statute, the issue resolves itself simply to whether the available defenses to the District Court criminal complaint amount to an adequate remedy at law. In the circumstances of this case, we think they plainly do.

In both the *Shuman* and *Kenyon* cases, the question was considered whether, in the circumstances of those cases, the defense to the criminal prosecution provided an adequate remedy at law. Since the injunction was denied in the former case and granted in the latter, it is instructive to compare them.

In the *Shuman* case, six merchants alleged that the defendant chief of police of Northampton threatened to prosecute them for conducting a business without a license, which they claimed they were not obligated to obtain. The plaintiffs' bill sought to make out a case of irreparable damage and inadequacy of legal remedy by alleging, inter alia, that it would take several months to obtain a decision on the case from an appellate court and that in the intervening period the loss of profits and advantageous business relations would cause the plaintiffs great and irreparable damage. To these averments, a demurrer was sustained. This court upheld the sustaining of the demurrer. After noting that in the event of multiple, oppressive, and wrongful prosecutions, an injunction might properly issue, we said: "A possibility that complaints may be lodged against six persons is not enough under these circumstances to make out a case of multiplicity. The allegations as to repeated complaints are not sufficient to warrant the inference that the courts of this commonwealth will countenance continued and oppressive prosecutions when once a genuine test case open to fair question has been presented and is on its way to final decision[.] * * * Simply that one is in business and may be injured in respect of his business by prosecution for an alleged crime, is no sufficient reason for asking a court of equity to ascertain in advance whether the business as conducted is in violation of a penal statute." [Citation.]

In the *Kenyon* case, by contrast, we reversed interlocutory decrees sustaining demurrers where the bill alleged that members of Jehovah's Witnesses had been repeatedly, on different dates, arrested, prosecuted, and convicted under an unconstitutional ordinance, prohibiting distribution of handbills, that on at least two occasions a defendant judge had convicted some of the plaintiffs despite being shown United States Supreme Court decisions holding such an ordinance unconstitutional, that the defendants well knew that the ordinances were unconstitutional and void, that the plaintiffs' means of paying bail fees and of posting bail and appeal bonds were exhausted, and that the defendants had threatened to and would continue to make false arrests, all to the irreparable damage of the plaintiffs' attempts to exercise their constitutional rights. In these circumstances, we held that an injunction against further prosecutions could properly issue, if the allegations were ultimately proved. We observed: "The plaintiffs' rights are of the most fundamental character. According to the bill they have been violated repeatedly. It is plain that the legal remedies by defending against repeated complaints and bringing successive actions for malicious prosecution or false arrest are not adequate." [Citation.]

In the present case, the plaintiff is the subject of a complaint charging a single violation of the statute. She avers that the statute is either unconstitutional on its face or as applied, or that, properly construed, it is inapplicable to her. These averments, of course, would, if established, each constitute a complete defense to the violation charged. We repeat here a passage from a United States Supreme Court case which applies equally to the matter before us: "It is a familiar rule that courts of equity do not ordinarily restrain criminal prosecutions. No person is immune from prosecution in good faith for his alleged criminal acts. Its imminence, even though alleged to be in violation of constitutional guarantees, is not a ground for equity relief since the lawfulness or constitutionality of the statute or ordinance on which the prosecution is based may be determined as readily in the criminal case as in a suit for injunction.... It does not appear from the record that petitioners have been threatened with any injury other than that incidental to every criminal proceeding brought lawfully and in good faith, or that a ... court of equity by withdrawing the determination of guilt from the ... [criminal] courts could rightly afford petitioners any protection which they could not secure by prompt trial and appeal pursued to this Court." [Citation.]

* * *

Our decision would not be different if we were considering only those portions of the proceedings below which involved a request for and grant of declaratory relief under G.L. c. 231A, §§ 1, 2. The fundamental jurisprudential considerations underlying the general prohibition against enjoining a pending criminal prosecution apply with full force to support a prohibition against issuing declaratory decrees concerning a pending criminal prosecution. To conclude otherwise would encourage fragmentation and proliferation of litigation and disrupt the orderly administration of the criminal law.[6]

The rule we adopt today in regard to the issuance of declaratory judgments when criminal litigation is pending is merely a logical extension of our rules which generally proscribe the issuance of such a judgment when an appropriate administrative proceeding is in progress, or when a civil proceeding in which the same issue is or can be raised is already pending between the parties. * * *

For the reasons given above, the injunction and declaratory relief should not have been granted. The final decree is reversed and a new judgment is to be entered dismissing the bill.

So ordered.

---

1. *Timing.* For declaratory relief in federal courts an issue must be presented with sufficient clarity and concreteness in order to satisfy the requirement of a "case or controversy" for Article III jurisdiction. Consequently, at an early stage the parties may not have a definitive controversy to merit declaratory relief. If litigation has already ensued, however, then a court may decline to exercise jurisdiction to render a declaratory judgment on the basis that an adequate remedy at law exists in the nature of a defense regarding the scope of a statute in the pending criminal action. Although courts generally view declaratory relief liberally and not as an "extraordinary" remedy like an injunction, parties nevertheless are confronted with a difficult decision in protecting their interests at an early stage before the incurrence of harm while ensuring that the dispute fits

---

6. "The modern declaratory action to construe or invalidate a penal statute bears the important distinction that it does not disrupt a pending prosecution, but seeks to resolve legal issues to prevent prosecution. Whereas prosecution can only follow conduct, the modern declaratory action precedes it, and in that difference lies its cardinal function. Cases do appear in which the plaintiff seeks a declaratory judgment after having acted, either racing to the court ahead of the prosecutor or with prosecution formally pending, but the courts refuse the remedy to prevent needless proliferation of litigation. Once the disputed conduct has taken place, the equities of the statute itself can be at least as well litigated in defense to the prosecution thus ripened." Note, Declaratory Relief in the Criminal Law, 80 Harv.L.Rev. 1490, 1503–1504 (1967).

within the jurisdictional requirements of Article III. This topic is examined in greater detail in Chapter 20.

2. A battle of conflicting constitutional interests was presented in *United States v. Noriega*, 917 F.2d 1543 (11th Cir.1990), where a district court enjoined the Cable News Network (CNN) from broadcasting taped communications between counsel and a defendant in a pending criminal proceeding. When CNN sought relief from the order, the Court of Appeals for the Eleventh Circuit noted the "delicate, difficult and important task" involved in balancing the press and the public's First Amendment rights, the Sixth Amendment rights of the accused, and the public expectation that the trial be conducted in a fair and impartial manner. The court observed that this balance could only be achieved by the trial court's inspection of the tapes, which CNN had refused to provide. The court found that withholding these tapes made it impossible for the trial court to make the requisite factual findings to resolve the constitutional conflicts at stake.

Justice Marshall dissented from the Supreme Court's denial of CNN's petition for certiorari. His dissenting opinion, joined by Justice O'Connor, noted that the court entered the injunctive order "without any finding that suppression of the broadcast was necessary to protect Noriega's right to a fair trial, reasoning that no such determination need to be made unless CNN surrendered the tapes for the court's inspection." 498 U.S. 976, 111 S.Ct. 451, 112 L.Ed.2d 432 (1990).

3. In *Hill v. Colorado*, 530 U.S. 703, 120 S.Ct. 2480, 147 L.Ed.2d 597 (2000), abortion opponents sought an injunction against enforcement of a state criminal statute's enforcement. The statute prohibited persons near a health care facility from knowingly approaching another person within eight feet for the purposes of displaying signs, engaging in oral protest, or passing leaflets without that person's consent. The Court held the statute did not impose an unconstitutional restraint on speech because it did not require the speaker to cease communication, but only to remain outside the proscribed distance from the listener. The Court further noted that the statute left open ample channels of communication and thus was narrowly tailored to serve the state's interests. It also did not place any limitations on the number, size, text or images on placards, or on the number of speakers or noise level.

C.   ENJOINING CRIMES AND NUISANCES

Section Coverage:

A considerable amount of litigation has dealt with whether a court should enjoin activity which constitutes a public or private nuisance. The threshold inquiry concerns the substantive entitlement to relief; the plaintiff must establish that the defendant's conduct was a substantial and unreasonable interference with the use and enjoyment of the plaintiff's property or public interests. The court evaluates "unreasonable interference" by weighing the gravity of the harm against the utility of the conduct. If this standard is met, the plaintiff must further demonstrate (1) that the threatened harm is immediate, (2) that the injury is irreparable, (3) that no adequate remedy at law exists, and (4) that equitable considerations balance in its favor. Two factors are particularly significant in the balancing process: the extent to which a damages award will redress the injury and considerations of the nature and extent of public interest implicated. Injunctions against a nuisance are never automatic nor a matter of right; it rests within the discretion of the judge sitting in equity. An injunction case always involves some degree of future prediction. The judge must determine both the probability and degree of future threatened harm absent the injunction. The legal consequence of a particular prediction is easily applied only at the two extremes: Equity will not enjoin a completed act, but injunctions are granted to halt clearly continuous invasions of an important interest where the remedy at law is inadequate.

Nuisance cases sometimes involve activities that also fall within the scope of criminal law. The problem then becomes whether a civil court should issue an injunction to prohibit behavior that could be sanctioned by the criminal justice system. The modern approach generally holds that equity will not enjoin conduct merely because it offends a criminal statute. Conversely, if the activity constitutes a public nuisance, an injunction is not automatically precluded because of potential penal sanctions. Rather, the principal inquiry involves whether an adequate remedy at law exists to address the conduct through application of the ordinary penal sanctions available through the criminal law. Related issues involve the concern that no jury trial right exists in an equity proceeding and that a civil action requires a lower standard of proof for issuance of an injunction than beyond a reasonable doubt under the applicable criminal statutes.

Model Case:

Dunlop, a contractor, is constructing a large building near a college dormitory. The construction is very noisy; pneumatic drills and riveting machines operate 24 hours a day. The noise substantially interferes with the students' studying in the dormitory during the day and with their sleeping at night.

In a suit to enjoin the construction, the court would take evidence on the nature of the construction and on the alternatives available to both parties. It is found as a fact that the operation of the drills and riveting machines could be discontinued during the night without delaying the ultimate construction of the building more than a few days. It is further found that the cost of the delay would not be unduly burdensome to Dunlop. The court also concludes that the students can study in a relatively quiet near-by library during the day.

A court would weigh the competing interests of the parties and determine that a damages award for the past harm would not be effective in curtailing the interference with the plaintiff's use and enjoyment of their property. Accordingly, the court could issue an injunction which would prohibit future construction operations during certain evening and early morning hours. The court would not have difficulties in retaining a supervisory role for the limited duration of the building construction. Potential enforcement of the decree should not present an obstacle since the order could be narrowly tailored to the specific harm.

1. ENJOINING NUISANCES

Harrison v. Indiana Auto Shredders Co.

528 F.2d 1107 (7th Cir.1975).

■ CLARK, ASSOCIATE JUSTICE.

This is an appeal from a judgment of the United States District Court for the Southern District of Indiana in a nuisance action, permanently enjoining appellant-Indiana Auto Shredders Company from operating its shredding plant for the recycling of automobiles in the Irish Hill section of Indianapolis, Indiana, and awarding $176,956 in compensatory and $353,912 in punitive damages to plaintiffs and interveners. The suit was filed by appellee-Russell Harrison (d/b/a Indiana Coldweld Company) and some 33 other "claimants" who reside or work in the Irish Hill section, alleging: (1) that the dust, vibration, and noise generated by the company's shredding plant constituted a common law and statutory nuisance under Indiana law by damaging property and endangering the health and safety of residents and workers in the area; and (2) that the company's shredding plant violated various local air pollution regulations.

This case presents the very difficult question of how to balance the legitimate demands of an urban neighborhood for clean air and a comfortable environment against the utility and economic enterprise of a beneficial, but polluting, industry. * * *

In recent years, the abandoned and junked automobile has become recognized as one of this country's major solid waste disposal problems. Auto "graveyards" represent not only an aesthetic blight that mars the natural beauty of the land, but also a scandalous waste of energy and resources that produced those cars. * * *

This case is representative of the new breed of lawsuit spawned by the growing concern for cleaner air and water. The birth and burgeoning growth of environmental litigation have forced the courts into difficult situations where modern hybrids of the traditional concepts of nuisance law and equity must be fashioned. Nuisance has always been a difficult area for the courts; the conflict of precedents and the confusing theoretical foundations of nuisance, led Prosser to tag the area a "legal garbage can." In any case, environmental consciousness may be the saving prescript for our age. Thus the right of environmentally aggrieved parties to obtain redress in the courts serves as a necessary and valuable supplement to legislative efforts to restore the natural ecology of our cities and countryside.

Judicial involvement in solving environmental problems does, however, bring its own hazards. Balancing the interests of a modern urban community like Indianapolis may be very difficult. Weighing the desire for economic and industrial strength against the need for clean and livable surroundings is not easily done, especially because of the graduations in quality as well as quantity that are involved. There is the danger that environmental problems will be inadequately treated by the piecemeal methods of litigation. It is possible that courtroom battles may be used to slow down effective policymaking for the environment. Litigation often fails to provide sufficient opportunities for the expert analysis and broad perspective that such policymaking often requires.

As difficult as environmental balancing may be, however, some forum for aggrieved parties must be made available. If necessary, the courts are qualified to perform the task. The courts are skilled at "balancing the equities," a technique that traditionally has been one of the judicial functions. Courts are insulated from the lobbying that gives strong advantages to industrial polluters when they face administrative or legislative review of their operations. The local state or federal court, because of its proximity to the individual problem, is often in a better position to judge the effect of a pollution nuisance upon a locality. For all of these reasons, the balancing in this case, although difficult, was nonetheless a proper function for the court below to perform. All other forums for obtaining relief were cut-off from the claimants and they understandably turned to the courts for relief.

The problem of balancing the equities in this case, however, was compounded by the fact that the company was not the ordinary industrial polluter. Usually, industrial polluters bring only their proprietary rights to be balanced on the scale opposite the community interests in a cleaner environment. The polluter asks the court to give due weight to the contributions that the business enterprise makes to the community by its economic achievements: payroll, taxes, investment of profits. Although when contrasted with the direct damage caused by uncontrolled pollution, such contributions may seem indirect, they are nonetheless entitled to serious consideration. No court could lightly decide to shut down a business that was the sole or principal livelihood of a community's citizens. Economic and property interests are entitled to significant weight. But here, the Indiana Auto Shredders Company makes more than only those economic contributions to the Indianapolis community; it is making a direct contribution toward improving the environment and conserving its natural resources by the recycling of abandoned automobiles. In curtailing the company's operations, the court below chose a very serious course of action. It is our view that such a course of action must be based upon conspicuous facts and reasonable standards of law.

* * * [E]nvironmental litigation of this type, whether based upon the Indiana nuisance statute or the common law of nuisance, logically will involve two stages of adjudication. First, the court or trier of fact will determine whether the facts alleged actually constitute a nuisance and a nuisance of what type. Second, having determined the nature of the alleged nuisance, the court will fashion relief appropriate to the equities of the case. Each of these two stages implicate their own legal standards.

Some activities, occupations, or structures are so offensive at all times and under all circumstances, regardless of location or surroundings, that they constitute "nuisance per se." Activities that imminently and dangerously threaten the public health fall into this category. It is more often the case, however, that the activities challenged by suitors in a nuisance case fall short of this standard of imminent and dangerous harm. Such activities as cause more remote harm to people or are the source of inconvenience, annoyance, and minor damage to property are labeled "nuisance in fact" or "nuisance per accidens." These latter activities are nuisances primarily because of the circumstances or the location and surrounding of the activities, rather than the nature of the activities themselves. Most air and water pollution, when their effects are only minimally or remotely harmful to the public health, will be nuisances of this second type. Obviously, it is this second type that more frequently occurs. Very often this second type will present the offensive activities of an otherwise lawful business, activities that are being conducted in such a manner so as to become a nuisance.

* * *

If a pollution nuisance has been found to exist, the court must then decide what relief to grant to those suffering the nuisance. In this second stage in the adjudication of environmental nuisance suits, balancing the equities becomes all important. The court must decide whether injunctive relief, damages, or some combination of the two best satisfies the particular demands of the case before it. This is the difficult but necessary work the court must perform.

Of course, where the pollution from a mill or factory creates hazards that imminently and dangerously affect the public health, the appropriate relief is a permanent injunction against the continuation of the polluting activities. It would be unreasonable to allow a private interest in the profits and product of such a polluting menace to outweigh the community's interests in the health of its citizens. However, a permanent injunction that shuts down a mill or factory without consideration of the extent of the harm that its pollution caused would be equally unreasonable. Pollution nuisance cases present no special features that should exempt them from the equitable requirements for injunctive relief, including proof of irreparable harm and inadequate remedy at law. * * * Ordinarily a permanent injunction will not lie unless (1) either the polluter seriously and imminently threatens the public health or (2) he causes non-health injuries that are substantial and the business cannot be operated to avoid the injuries apprehended. Thus the particular situation facts of each pollution nuisance case will determine whether a permanent injunction should be issued. When a business' offensive activities fall short of that standard, only the combination of both reckless disregard of substantial annoyances caused to adjoining property owners plus the impossibility of mitigating the offensive characteristics of the business will justify the granting of permanent injunctive relief.

* * *

We can well appreciate and fully sympathize with the unhappiness of the appellees over their situation. However, the problem of zoning is a local one, governed by local law; it must be solved in local perspective. The appropriate local authority has zoned the property specifically for shredder use; and appellant has been issued a permit to so use the property. After careful and continued tests by reputable experts as well as public officials, appellant's operation has met all the required standards. Under these circumstances and in the absence of an imminent hazard to health or welfare—none of which was established or found present here, the appellant cannot be prevented from continuing to engage in the operation of its shredding. [Citation.] The national environmental policy, as announced by Congress, allows offending industries a reasonable period of time to make adjustments to conform to standards. [Citations.] Appellant is a new undertaking in Irish Hill; it too is entitled to a reasonable period of time to correct any defects not of imminent or substantial harm. If there is damage to property, of course, it is recoverable here as in any other case.

The trial court based its action on the existence of a common nuisance but even if such were present, the drastic remedy of closing down the operation without endeavoring to launder its objectionable features would be impermissible under our law. [Citation.] In applying the test of the cases, we find no ground on which to base a permanent injunction here.

This is not to say that those features of the appellant's operation that are found to be offensive should not be remedied. We only say that the offender shall have time to correct the evil. If the appellant does not correct the infractions presently existing within a reasonable period, the district court may take action that will require the appellant so to do. * * *

The judgment is reversed, the permanent injunction is dissolved, and the case is remanded for further proceedings in accordance herewith.

---

1. *Zoning.* As the principal case reflects, a zoning ordinance may affect the availability and the nature of injunctive relief. The defendant's compliance with governmental regulations should be relevant to the reasonableness of the activity and its suitability to the locale. Compliance with all pertinent regulations is not necessarily sufficient to defeat an injunction, however. What about activities that a court finds extremely hazardous and presenting a serious threat to public health? Should such activity be enjoined as a public nuisance if the defendant has obtained all necessary permits? Does it matter how imminent is the threat to health?

2. Courts traditionally have accorded a heavy presumption of validity to legislative determinations that certain activities offend the public health, safety, or welfare. Nonetheless, judicial deference to the legislative police power is not without limits. In *Ace Tire Co. v. Municipal Officers of Waterville,* an operator of a junkyard challenged the constitutionality of a statute concerning junkyard licensing fees. It provided that junkyards and automobile graveyards within 100 feet of a highway must pay a $500

licensing fee, whereas those located farther away had to pay only a $10 fee. The court acknowledged that a legislature may take into account aesthetic values, such as preserving scenic beauty, when enacting measures for the public welfare. However, the court determined that the statutory licensing scheme arbitrarily and unreasonably favored some operators of junkyards over others, and bore no rational relationship to the stated objectives of preventing distractions to highway travelers. The court therefore held it unconstitutional and noted: "The legislature may not, under the guise of protecting the public interests, arbitrarily interfere with private legitimate businesses or impose unusual and unnecessary restrictions upon lawful occupations by labeling them nuisances." 302 A.2d 90 (Me.1973).

Similarly, *Kadash v. City of Williamsport*, 19 Pa.Cmwlth. 643, 340 A.2d 617 (1975), held that the legislature could not declare an activity to be a nuisance per se when it did not constitute a nuisance in fact. Accordingly, the court interpreted an ordinance regulating junked automobiles as involving a reasonableness test: Is the defendant's operation reasonable in light of the locale and attendant circumstances?

3. *Anti-injunction Acts.* Some jurisdictions have passed anti-injunction acts affecting nuisance cases. They typically preclude courts from restraining business activities that are being reasonably conducted in compliance with zoning regulations if the only injury is a nuisance to the plaintiff in the operations. Thus, in *Kornoff v. Kingsburg Cotton Oil Co.*, 45 Cal.2d 265, 288 P.2d 507 (1955), the court held that California Code Civ.Proc. § 731a shielded the defendant from an injunction against the operation of its cotton gin because it was conducted in a location properly zoned for business and commercial activity. However, the court found that § 731a did not operate to bar a recovery for damages. Also see Holland v. United States, 94 F.Supp.2d 787, 792 (S.D.Tex.2000) (nuisance claim denied where alleged injury results from lawful operation of business).

An anti-injunction act does not necessarily end the court's equitable power but may simply affect its exercise of discretion. Consider *Sierra Screw Products v. Azusa Greens, Inc.*, 88 Cal.App.3d 358, 151 Cal.Rptr. 799 (1979), where landowners sought damages and injunctive relief against a neighboring golf course. The complaint sought abatement of the nuisance caused by stray golf balls damaging the plaintiff's property. The defendants contended that its conditional use permit which authorized operation of the golf course constituted an automatic bar to injunctive relief. The court found that the defendants had employed unnecessary and injurious methods in operating the course and therefore issued an injunction mandating that the defendants redesign two holes. Compare Nussbaum v. Lacopo, 27 N.Y.2d 311, 317 N.Y.S.2d 347, 265 N.E.2d 762 (1970) (no injunction against golf course where errant golf balls landed on neighboring plaintiff's property only once or twice a week); Gleason v. Hillcrest Golf Course, 148 Misc. 246, 265 N.Y.S. 886 (1933) (damages awarded to the driver of an automobile who sustained injury when a golf ball struck and shattered the windshield of her car).

4. When a nuisance cannot be sufficiently abated, the question becomes whether the court should order the cessation of the offending

activity. Requests for such orders pose difficult problems when the defendant operates an established, lawfully conducted business. An order to cease operations in the current location forces the business to relocate or shut down. The order is likely to impose heavy economic losses, cost some number of jobs and may defeat the justifiable expectations of those who invested in the business.

Further losses are likely if the order to cease operations requires prompt action. In *Pendoley v. Ferreira*, 345 Mass. 309, 187 N.E.2d 142 (1963), the court enjoined the operation of a piggery. In drafting the decree, the court gave consideration to alleviating the economic hardship on the defendant by providing a reasonable period of time for the defendant either to liquidate its stock or to find new premises.

5. *Public Interest.* A significant factor affecting the entitlement and selection of the remedy chosen for public or private nuisance can include whether an injunction may affect the public interest. For example, in *Oglethorpe Power Corp. v. Forrister*, 289 Ga. 331, 711 S.E.2d 641 (2011) neighboring property owners brought a nuisance claim against a power plant operated by a public utility. The complaint pointed to the substantial interference with the use and enjoyment of their property from noise and vibrations emanating from the regular operation of the plant's gas turbines. The noise could not be abated without a complete tear-down and rebuilding of the exhaust stacks. The court declined to issue an injunction shutting down the plant because of the importance of providing utility service; however, damages were awarded to compensate for a permanent nuisance.

6. A court is faced with an especially difficult task of prediction when the activity sought to be enjoined is causing no current harm and poses only an uncertain future threat. An injunction is not justified if its basis is solely that a tort may possibly occur. For example, in *Nicholson v. Connecticut Half-Way House, Inc.*, 153 Conn. 507, 218 A.2d 383 (1966), residents sought to enjoin the prospective use of defendant's property as a temporary residence for selected parolees from state prison. The plaintiffs claimed that the parolees might commit criminal acts in their neighborhood and that the half-way house would cause their property values to depreciate. The court denied injunctive relief because unsubstantiated fears could not justify the intervention of equity. Are there circumstances where prospective harm is so potentially devastating that a lower probability of such injury should suffice to support an injunctive? Are there problems with a sliding scale approach that weighs the seriousness of the harm against the likelihood of its occurrence?

7. Where an offending activity has ceased a court will not impose injunctive relief to prohibit an uncertain future harm. *See* City of West St. Paul v. Krengel, 768 N.W.2d 352 (Minn. 2009) (court denied permanent injunction against homeowner where resident had abated nuisance activities which previously interfered with neighboring landowners).

8. *Coming to the Nuisance.* The character of a locale may change over time, which may influence the relative suitability of surrounding uses for

nuisance purposes. For example, in the famous case *Spur Industries, Inc. v. Del E. Webb Development Co.*, 108 Ariz. 178, 494 P.2d 700 (1972) the outskirts of a city gradually expanded until a residential development became located in near proximity to a large cattle feedlot. The developer brought suit to enjoin the feedlot operation as a public and private nuisance. The court granted the injunction, forcing the feedlot to relocate, but conditioned the order upon the developer paying for the costs of the move. The court considered the investment expectations of the cattle farm owners and that the agricultural use was previously established before the city grew near its operations.

Early authorities often denied equitable assistance to parties who chose to locate within close proximity to the operation of an established industry. The rationale was that the later arriving parties either implicitly had consented to the offending trade or they should have foreseen that the business would constitute a nuisance. *See* Rex v. Cross, 2 C. & P. 483, 172 Eng.Rep. 219; Wittman, First Come, First Served: An Economic Analysis of "Coming to the Nuisance," 9 J.Leg.Stud. 557 (1980).

As reflected in *Spur*, the parties' order of arrival still serves as a persuasive factor in determining the availability of equitable relief for a nuisance and the scope of the relief granted but does not foreclose other equitable considerations.

9.   What should happen if the nuisance activity comes to the plaintiff? In *Bove v. Donner–Hanna Coke Corporation*, 236 A.D. 37, 258 N.Y.S. 229 (1932), the plaintiff purchased a house and grocery store in a light industrial area and lived there several years before the defendant built a factory nearby. The court denied the plaintiff's request for an injunction against the factory on the basis that the plaintiff should have reasonably foreseen that the area was adapted for industrial purposes rather than residential uses.

10.   The requirement that an activity substantially and unreasonably interfere with the use and enjoyment of another's property for nuisance is a relative concept. The court may properly consider the uses of adjoining land and the general character of the area. In *Mahlstadt v. City of Indianola*, 251 Iowa 222, 100 N.W.2d 189 (1959), the court determined that a long-established city trash dump itself partially defined the character of the area. The court held that the dump served a useful public service, and that the long run costs and benefits made it appropriate to remain in existence with some modifications in the manner of its operations. Compare Whittle v. Weber, 243 P.3d 208 (Alaska 2010) (junkyard on property violated subdivision covenants and constituted continuing nuisance to neighboring landowner).

PROBLEM: THE POLLUTING PLANT

The Browns live with their family on Blackacre and raise wheat and corn crops. They also have a fruit orchard which they cultivate for a small commercial profit each year.

Their neighbors, the Websters, live on Greenacre and operate a chicken processing plant on the premises. The Websters have operated the plant for five years without any significant interference with the Browns' property. Recently the Websters decided to expand the plant by adding another smokestack. Immediately after the new smokestack was installed a large quantity of noxious fumes escaped from a crack caused by improper sealant. The fumes scorched the leaves on the Browns' lemon trees and damaged the majority of the fruit. At harvest they had a significantly reduced yield on the fruit crop, although the other crops were unaffected.

The Browns complained bitterly to the Websters and demanded that they close the plant. The Websters repeatedly promised repairs, but each effort to fix the problem during that summer failed. After the harvest the Websters said that the problem had finally been repaired permanently. The quantity of fumes was indeed reduced, although not eliminated. The Browns are skeptical and worried about next year's lemon crop. They sue to enjoin the operation of the plant as a private nuisance.

(a) What result?

(b) Assume instead that the normal operation of the plant results in the periodic emission of some noxious fumes and feather particles which settle on Blackacre, partially damaging the Browns' crops and the orchard. The estimated damage to the crops and the trees is approximately $10,000 per year. The cost to replace the orchard itself would be $80,000. The chicken plant cost the Websters $100,000, and its only employees are family members. The plant is located outside the city and thus not subject to any zoning ordinances. The Browns called the state environmental protection agency and learned that the state does have an air pollution control statute which prohibits the discharge of toxic pollutants into the air. The agency is overburdened with enforcement of the statute and could not help the Browns any time soon. Meanwhile, the Browns discovered that several of their livestock had become diseased as a result of drinking water contaminated by the plant's discharge of various chemicals. Should a court issue an injunction? If so, how should it be drafted?

Fancher v. Fagella

274 Va. 549, 650 S.E.2d 519 (2007).

■ Opinion by SENIOR JUSTICE CHARLES S. RUSSELL

This is an interlocutory appeal taken pursuant to Code § 8.01–670(B)(1) from an order denying injunctive relief. The dispositive question is whether an injunction may issue to compel an adjoining landowner to remove a tree, the roots of which intrude into, and cause significant, continuous and increasing structural damage to the plaintiff's property. The appeal requires us to revisit our holding in *Smith v. Holt*, 174 Va. 213, 5 S.E.2d 492 (1939).

Facts and Proceedings

The essential facts are not in dispute. Richard A. Fancher and Joseph B. Fagella are the owners of adjoining townhouses in the Cambridge Court subdivision in Fairfax County. Fagella's property is higher in elevation than Fancher's and a masonry retaining wall running along the property line behind the townhouses supports the grade separation. There is a sunken patio behind Fancher's townhouse, covered by masonry pavers.

Fancher brought this suit against Fagella, alleging that Fagella has on his property a large sweet gum tree that constitutes a noxious nuisance; the tree's invasive root system has damaged and displaced the retaining wall between the parties' properties, displaced the pavers on Fancher's patio, caused blockage of his sewer and water pipes and has impaired the foundation of his house. Fancher also complained that the tree's overhanging branches grow onto his roof, depositing leaves and other debris onto his roof and rain gutters. He contended that he had attempted self-help, by trying to repair the damage to the retaining wall and the rear foundation of the house, as well as trying to cut back the overhanging branches, but that these steps were ineffectual because of the continuing expansion of the root system and branches. Fancher prayed for an injunction compelling Fagella to remove the tree and its invading root system entirely, and an award of damages to cover the cost of restoring the property to its former condition.

The circuit court heard the evidence ore tenus. At the hearing, Fancher testified that the tree's trunk was on Fagella's property, about "two to three feet from the party/common wall." Fancher estimated the tree was about 60 feet high at the present time and two feet in trunk diameter at its base.

Fancher presented the testimony of an arborist who qualified as an expert witness and testified that the sweet gum is native to the area, that it grows to "incredible heights of 120 to 140 feet" at maturity and would eventually reach a trunk diameter of 4 to 6 feet. The arborist testified that the tree was deciduous, dropped "spiky gumballs," had a "heavy pollen load," an "extremely invasive root system" and a "high demand for water." His opinion was that the tree was presently "only at mid-maturity," that it would continue to grow, and that "[n]o amount of concrete would hold the root system back." The root system was, in his opinion, the cause of the damage to the retaining wall and the pavers and "in the same line as those cracks to the wall and the foundation." The arborist stated that the tree was "noxious" because of its location and that the only way to stop the continuing damage being done by the root system was to remove the tree entirely, because the roots, if cut, would grow back.

Fancher also presented the expert testimony of two engineers, who opined that the pressure of the tree's expanding root system was the cause of the structural damage to the retaining wall. At the conclusion of Fancher's case, Fagella moved to strike the prayer for injunctive relief. The court, relying on our decision in *Smith v. Holt*, granted the motion to strike and entered an order denying injunctive relief, retaining for further adjudication Fancher's claim for damages. We awarded Fancher an interlocutory appeal.

Analysis

A. *Right of action*

The issues raised by vegetation encroaching across property lines have frequently confronted courts throughout the country, leading to results that are less than harmonious. The earlier decisions, including our own, were decided in times when the population was far less densely concentrated than at present, and more often engaged in agriculture. More recent cases have been concerned with problems arising in more urban settings. A thorough review and analysis of those cases was recently made by the Supreme Court of Tennessee in *Lane v. W.J. Curry & Sons,* 92 S.W.3d 355, 360–63 (Tenn. 2002), and it would serve no purpose to repeat that discussion here.

Suffice it to say that, as the Tennessee court explained in *Lane,* several rules have evolved. (1) The "Massachusetts Rule," holds that a landowner's right to protect his property from the encroaching boughs and roots of a neighbor's tree is limited to self-help, i.e., cutting off the branches and roots at the point they invade his property. That rule was based on *Michalson v. Nutting,* 275 Mass. 232, 175 N.E. 490 (Mass. 1931), where the court observed that "the common law has recognized that it is wiser to leave the individual to protect himself, if harm results to him from this exercise of another's right to use his property in a reasonable way, than to subject that other to the annoyance, and the public to the burden, of actions at law, which would be likely to be innumerable and, in many instances, purely vexatious." *Id.* at 491. (2) The "Virginia Rule," holds that the intrusion of roots and branches from a neighbor's plantings which were "not noxious in [their] nature" and had caused no "sensible injury" were not actionable at law, the plaintiff being limited to his right of self-help. That rule was based on our holding in *Smith v. Holt,* 174 Va. 213, 5 S.E.2d 492 (1939), where we also said, "when it appears that a sensible injury has been inflicted by the protrusion of roots from a noxious tree or plant onto the land of another, he has, after notice, a right of action at law for the trespass committed." *Id.* at 219, 5 S.E.2d at 495. We affirmed the trial court's order sustaining a demurrer in that case, holding that neither equitable relief nor damages were warranted because the invading roots came from a privet hedge that was not "noxious" in nature and had caused no "sensible injury." *Id.* at 220, 5 S.E.2d at 495. (3) The "Restatement Rule," based on *Restatement (Second) of Torts* §§ 839, 840 (1979), imposes an obligation on a landowner to control vegetation that encroaches upon adjoining land if the vegetation is "artificial," i.e., planted or maintained by a person, but not if the encroaching vegetation is "natural." (4) The "Hawaii Rule," holds that living trees and plants are ordinarily not nuisances, but can become so when they cause actual harm or pose an imminent danger of actual harm to adjoining property. That rule is based upon *Whitesell v. Houlton,* 2 Haw. App. 365, 632 P.2d 1077 (Haw. Ct. App.

1981), where the court said: "[W]hen overhanging branches or protruding roots actually cause, or there is imminent danger of them causing, [substantial] harm to property other than plant life, in ways other than by casting shade or dropping leaves, flowers, or fruit, the damaged or imminently endangered neighbor may require the owner of the tree to pay for the damages and to cut back the endangering branches or roots and, if such is not done within a reasonable time, the . . . neighbor may cause the cutback to be done at the tree owner's expense." *Id.* at 1079. The Tennessee court, in *Lane,* after considering the merits and weaknesses of the foregoing rules, decided to adopt the Hawaii approach, partially overruling an earlier Tennessee decision that had generally adhered to the "Massachusetts Rule." *Lane,* 92 S.W.3d at 363–64.

The "Massachusetts Rule" has been criticized on the ground that it is unsuited to modern urban and suburban life, although it may still be suited to many rural conditions. The "Restatement Rule" has been criticized on the grounds that it is often impossible to determine whether a plant has originated naturally or has been introduced or nurtured by human activity; further, that rule illogically imposes liability on a landowner who carefully maintains his property and spares one who neglects his land and permits his vegetation to "run wild."

Our "Virginia Rule" is subject to the just criticism that the classification of a plant as "noxious" depends upon the viewpoint of the beholder. "Noxious" has been defined as "Hurtful; offensive; offensive to the smell. The word 'noxious' includes the complex idea both of insalubrity and offensiveness. That which causes or tends to cause injury, especially to health or morals." Black's Law Dictionary 1065 (6th ed. 1990). Many would agree that poison ivy meets that definition because of its proclivity to cause personal injury. Some would include kudzu because of its tendency toward rampant growth, smothering other vegetation. Few would include healthy shade trees, although they may cause more damage, and be more expensive to remove, than the others. We conclude that continued reliance on the distinction between plants that are "noxious," and those that are not, imposes an unworkable standard for determining the rights of neighboring landowners.

Accordingly, we now overrule *Smith v. Holt,* insofar as it conditions a right of action upon the "noxious" nature of a plant that sends forth invading roots or branches into a neighbor's property. We find the reasoning of the Tennessee court in *Lane* persuasive, and adopt the Hawaii approach as expressed in that case:

> Accordingly, we hold that encroaching trees and plants are not nuisances merely because they cast shade, drop leaves, flowers, or fruit, or just because they happen to encroach upon adjoining property either above or below the ground. However, encroaching trees and plants may be regarded as a nuisance when they cause actual harm or pose an imminent danger of actual harm to adjoining property. If so, the owner of the tree or plant may be held responsible for harm caused to [adjoining property], and may also be required to cut back the en-

croaching branches or roots, assuming the encroaching vegetation constitutes a nuisance. We do not, however, alter existing . . . law that the adjoining landowner may, at his own expense, cut away the encroaching vegetation to the property line whether or not the encroaching vegetation constitutes a nuisance or is otherwise causing harm or possible harm to the adjoining property. Thus, the law of self-help remains intact. . . .

Lane, 92 S.W.3d at 364. We also overrule *Smith v. Holt* insofar as its language may be read to imply that equitable relief is precluded even when a nuisance is found to exist.

B. *Remedy*

In a proper application of *stare decisis,* the circuit court followed *Smith v. Holt* in denying injunctive relief in the present case. Because of the rule we now adopt, it becomes necessary to consider the appropriate remedy. The facts pleaded, if proved by Fancher, would constitute a continuing trespass, resulting in actual harm to his property. Under traditional equitable principles, a chancellor may enjoin a continuing trespass, even when each increment of trespass is trivial or the damage is trifling, in order to avoid a multiplicity of actions at law. Thus, on remand, the circuit court may properly consider injunctive relief in the present case.

Not every case of nuisance or continuing trespass, however, may be enjoined. The decision whether to grant an injunction always rests in the sound discretion of the chancellor, and depends on the relative benefit an injunction would confer upon the plaintiff in contrast to the injury it would impose on the defendant. Any burden imposed on the public should also be weighed.

In weighing the equities in a case of this kind, the chancellor must necessarily first consider whether the conditions existing on the adjoining lands are such that it is reasonable to impose a duty on the owner of a tree to protect a neighbor's land from damage caused by its intruding branches and roots. In the absence of such a duty, the traditional right of self-help is an adequate remedy. It would be clearly unreasonable to impose such a duty upon the owner of historically forested or agricultural land, but entirely appropriate to do so in the case of parties, like those in the present case, who dwell on adjoining residential lots.

Further, if such a duty is found to exist on the part of the tree owner, the chancellor must determine the extent of the remedy. Under the circumstances of the case, will self-help by cutting off the invading roots and branches, followed by an award of damages to compensate the plaintiff for his expenses, afford an adequate and permanent remedy, obviating the need for an injunction? If not, will complete removal of the defendant's tree be the appropriate remedy when the equities are balanced? An affirmative answer to the latter question will necessitate a mandatory injunction. As in all cases in which equitable relief is sought, the chancellor's decision must necessarily depend on the particular facts shown by the evidence, guided by traditional equitable principles.

Conclusion

Because the circuit court, following our decision in *Smith v. Holt,* did not consider equitable relief to be available, we will reverse the order appealed from and remand the case for further proceedings consistent with this opinion.

Reversed and remanded.

---

1.   As reflected in the principal case, the growth of trees and shrubs can cause a sufficient interference with the use and enjoyment of neighboring property interests to constitute a private nuisance. The interference can also affect the ground and subsurface. *See* Scheckel v. NLI, Inc., 953 N.E.2d 133 (Ind. App. 2011) (growth of tree trunk and roots of landowner infringed upon fence and walkway of adjoining property and constituted a private nuisance). *But see* Pesaturo v. Kinne, 161 N.H. 550, 20 A.3d 284 (N.H. 2011) (overhang of decaying tree limbs across fence found insubstantial to constitute private nuisance); Rogers v. Ford, 57 So.3d 681 (Miss. App. 2011) (property owner not liable under private nuisance for damages caused by pecan tree which uprooted during heavy rains and fell on neighbor's garage).

2.   In *Peters v. O' Leary*, 30 A.3d 825 (Me. 2011) a landowner brought a private nuisance claim on the basis that a neighboring property owner intentionally planted a row of trees for the purpose of obstructing the claimant's view of the ocean from their newly constructed home. The court found that the dense row of tall trees forming a continuous barrier adjacent to the neighboring property constituted a structure in the nature of a fence and therefore fit within the scope of the spite fence statute. The court upheld the trial court's finding of malice in the planting and failure to prune numerous trees justified injunctive relief. *See also* Vanderpol v. Starr, 194 Cal.App.4th 385, 123 Cal.Rptr.3d 506 (2011) (although row of trees could be characterized as a structure under spite fence statute, claimant failed to demonstrate a sufficient injury to justify injunctive relief).

3.   To what extent in a nuisance case should a court consider subjective factors, such as the motive behind using property in a certain way? In *Sundowner, Inc. v. King*, 95 Idaho 367, 509 P.2d 785 (1973), the plaintiff sought an injunction to remove an 85 foot long and 18 foot high sign which had been erected between two adjacent hotels. The sign blocked 80 percent of the plaintiff's building and restricted the passage of light and air. The court acknowledged that the so-called English rule, followed by many 19th century American courts, gave a property owner the unfettered right to maintain such structures. The court instead chose to follow the American rule which enjoins "spite" fences that serve no useful purpose and are intended to annoy and inconvenience neighboring landowners.

Similarly, in *Hutcherson v. Alexander*, 264 Cal.App.2d 126, 70 Cal.Rptr. 366 (1968), the court ordered the defendant restaurant owner to remove a 14 foot high "menu board" which obstructed the public view of a nearby competing business. The court determined that the sign was not essential to the defendant's business but was constructed as part of a general scheme to interfere with the reasonable use and enjoyment of the plaintiff's property. *Also see* Green Acres Trust v. Wells, 72 So.3d 1123 (Miss. App. 2011) (landowners obtained injunction against adjoining property owner to remove spite fence which purposefully obstructed the claimant's view of a lake).

4.   What if a person acts in a spiteful or angry manner? In *Connors v. Lake Dexter Woods Homeowners Ass'n. Inc.*, 50 So.3d 1212 (Fla. App. 2d Dist. 2010), a homeowners association sought an injunction against a developmentally disabled adult who had an "angry" personality, used abusive language and drove an automobile in a threatening manner around other residents. The court found that the activities violated the restrictive covenants governing the neighborhood and issued an injunction against the defendant and his legal guardian.

Michigan v. U.S. Army Corps of Engineers

667 F.3d 765 (7th Cir. 2011).

■ Wood, Circuit Judge.

Ambitious engineering projects that began at the time that the City of Chicago was founded have established a waterway in northeastern Illinois that connects Lake Michigan to the Mississippi watershed. (Additional links between the Mississippi and the Great Lakes exist elsewhere, from northern Minnesota to New York.) The system of canals, channels, locks, and dams, with which we are concerned, known today as the Chicago Area Waterway System (or CAWS, as the parties call it in their briefs), winds from the mouth of the Chicago River and four other points on Lake Michigan to tributaries of the Mississippi River in Illinois. The navigable link has been a boon to industry and commerce, and it supports transportation and recreation. Public health crises that once were common because the Chicago River emptied the City's sewage into the lake—the City's freshwater supply—vanished thanks to the Chicago Sanitary and Ship Canal, which reversed the flow of the Chicago River so that it now pulls water from the lake, into the CAWS, and down toward the Mississippi. During heavy rains and seasonal high waters in the region, the CAWS is used to control flooding.

This effort to connect the Great Lakes and Mississippi watersheds has not been without controversy. * * * Nor has opening a pathway between these bodies of fresh water come without costs. This appeal requires us to consider one of those costs: the environmental and economic harm posed by two invasive species of carp, commonly known as Asian carp, which have migrated up the Mississippi River and now are poised at the brink of this man-made path to the Great Lakes. The carp are voracious eaters that consume small organisms on which the entire food chain relies; they crowd out native species as they enter new environments; they reproduce at a high rate; they travel quickly and adapt readily; and they have a dangerous habit of jumping out of the water and harming people and property.

In an attempt to stop the fish, Michigan, Minnesota, Ohio, Pennsylvania, and Wisconsin, all states bordering the Great Lakes, filed this lawsuit against the U.S. Army Corps of Engineers (the Corps) and the Metropolitan Water Reclamation District of Greater Chicago (the District), which together own and operate the facilities that make up the CAWS. The plaintiff states allege that the Corps and the District are managing the CAWS in a manner that will allow invasive carp to move for the first time into the Great Lakes. The states fear that if the fish establish a sustainable population there, ecological disaster and the collapse of billion-dollar industries that depend on the existing ecosystem will follow. They say that the defendants' failure to close down parts of the CAWS to avert the crisis creates a grave risk of harm, in violation of the federal common law of public nuisance, see *American Electric Power Co., Inc. v. Connecticut*, 131 S. Ct. 2527, 180 L. Ed. 2d 435 (2011). The states asked the district court for declaratory and injunctive relief and moved for a preliminary injunction that would require the defendants to put in place additional physical barriers throughout the CAWS, implement new procedures to stop invasive carp, and expedite a study of how best to separate the Mississippi and Great Lakes watersheds permanently. Other parties intervened to protect their interests—the Grand Traverse Band of Ottawa and Chippewa Indians on the side of the plaintiffs, and the City of Chicago, Wendella Sightseeing Company, and the Coalition to Save Our Waterways as defendants. The district court denied the motion for a preliminary injunction, and the states appealed immediately. See 28 U.S.C. § 1292(a)(1).

* * *

To justify a preliminary injunction, the plaintiff states must show that they are likely to succeed on the merits of their claims, that they are likely to suffer irreparable harm without an injunction, that the harm they would suffer without the injunction is greater than the harm that preliminary relief would inflict on the defendants, and that the injunction is in the public interest. *Winter v. Natural Res. Def. Council, Inc.*, 555 U.S. 7, 20, 129 S. Ct. 365, 172 L. Ed. 2d 249 (2008). We will affirm the decision to deny a preliminary injunction unless the district court has abused its discretion. * * *

The states' public nuisance action here is based on allegations that non-native species of carp (specifically, bighead and silver carp) will migrate through waterworks operated by the defendants from rivers connected to the Mississippi into Lake Michigan and on to the other Great Lakes. "When we deal with air and water in their ambient and interstate aspects, there is a federal common law." *Milwaukee I*, 406 U.S. at 103. We know that this body of law applies in a dispute about "the pollution of a body of water such as Lake Michigan bounded, as it is, by four States," *id.* at 105 n.6. But the Court has cautioned that it has never "held that a State may sue to abate any and all manner of pollution originating outside its borders." *American Electric Power*, 131 S. Ct. at 2536. The Corps and the District contend that the common law does not extend to the allegations in this case. They stress that they are not emitting "traditional pollutants"; all they have done, they say, is to operate facilities in the CAWS through which invasive species already living in local rivers might travel on their own. We can dismiss the latter part of this argument without much discussion: the defendants bear responsibility for nuisances caused by their operation of a manmade waterway between the Great Lakes and Mississippi watersheds. That they are not themselves physically moving fish from one body of water to the other does not mean that their normal operation of the CAWS cannot cause a nuisance. See, *e.g.*, RESTATEMENT (SECOND) TORTS § 834 ("One is subject to liability for a nuisance caused by an activity, not only when he carries on the activity but also when he participates to a substantial extent in carrying it on.") & cmt. (b) (defining "activity" to include acts "that create physical conditions that are harmful to neighboring land after the activity that created them has ceased").

Similarly, we know of no rule saying that the defendants must emit a "traditional pollutant" in order for federal common law to apply. While it may be true that the introduction of an invasive species of fish into a new ecosystem does not fit the concept of nuisance as neatly as a spill of toxic chemicals into a stream, we do not think the Supreme Court has limited the concept of public nuisance as much as the defendants suggest. A public nuisance is defined as a substantial and unreasonable interference with a right common to the general public, usually affecting the public health, safety, peace, comfort, or convenience. RESTATEMENT (SECOND) TORTS § 821B; DAN B. DOBBS, THE LAW OF TORTS § 467, at 1334 (2000). It would be arbitrary to conclude that this type of action extends to the harm caused by industrial pollution but not to the environmental and economic destruction caused by the introduction of an invasive, nonnative organism into a new ecosystem (assuming that the states have correctly forecast the depletion of the Great Lakes fishery and the corresponding damage to the multi-billion-dollar sports fishing industry). Public nuisance traditionally has been understood to cover a tremendous range of subjects:

> It includes interferences with the public health, as in the case of a hogpen, the keeping of diseased animals, or a malarial pond; with the public safety, as in the case of the storage of explosives, the shooting of fireworks in the streets, harboring a vicious dog, or the practice of medicine by one not qualified; with public morals, as in the case of houses of prostitution, illegal liquor establishments, gambling houses, indecent exhibitions, bullfights, unlicensed prize fights, or public profanity; with the public peace, as by loud and disturbing noises, or an opera performance which threatens to cause a riot; with the public comfort, as in the case of bad odors, smoke, dust and vibration; with public convenience, as by obstructing a highway or a navigable stream, or creating a condition which makes travel unsafe or highly disagreeable, or the collection of an inconvenient crowd; and in addition, such

unclassified offenses as eavesdropping on a jury, or being a common scold. [Citations.]

* * * We conclude that the federal common law of public nuisance extends to the problem that the plaintiff states have identified.

The district court began with the definition of public nuisance found in the *Restatement (Second) of Torts*, which has been a common reference point for courts considering cases arising under federal common law. The *Restatement* provides that "[a] public nuisance is an unreasonable interference with a right common to the general public," RESTATEMENT (SECOND) OF TORTS § 821B(1), and it goes on to explain that conduct meets this standard when it interferes significantly with the public health, safety, peace, comfort, or convenience, *id*. § 821B(2)(a). We described above the reasons why the federal common law of public nuisance is available to redress the type of harm that the states have alleged. And all sides agree that if invasive carp were to achieve a sustainable population in the Great Lakes, the environmental and economic impact would qualify as an unreasonable interference with a public right. * * * As a result, the central question on the merits of the states' public nuisance claim will be whether the harm that the states have described is sufficiently close to occurring that the courts should order the defendants to take some new action that will be effective to abate the public nuisance. * * *

A court may grant equitable relief to abate a public nuisance that is occurring or to stop a threatened nuisance from arising. See *Tennessee Copper*, 206 U.S. at 238–39 (requiring the plaintiff to show that a defendant's actions "cause and threaten damage"). In *Missouri v. Illinois*, 200 U.S. at 518, the Court wrote that the threatened harm underlying the nuisance claim "must be shown to be real and immediate." We have read the Court's cases to say that "[t]he elements of a claim based on the federal common law of nuisance are simply that the defendant is carrying on an activity that is causing an injury or significant threat of injury to some cognizable interest of the complainant," *Illinois v. City of Milwaukee*, 599 F.2d 151, 165 (7th Cir. 1979), *rev'd on other grounds, Milwaukee II*, 451 U.S. 304, 101 S. Ct. 1784, 68 L. Ed. 2d 114. Additional statements about averting threatened nuisances appear in the *Restatement*, see RESTATEMENT (SECOND) TORTS § 821B cmt. (i)("[F]or damages to be awarded [in public nuisance cases] significant harm must have been actually incurred, while for an injunction harm need only be threatened and need not actually have been sustained at all."); *id*. § 821F cmt. (b) ("[E]ither a public or a private nuisance may be enjoined because harm is threatened that would be significant if it occurred."), and in other treatises, see, *e.g.*, 5 J. POMEROY, A TREATISE ON EQUITY JURISPRUDENCE AND EQUITABLE REMEDIES, § 1937 (§ 523), at 4398 (2d ed. 1919) (noting that while "a mere possibility of a future nuisance will not support an injunction," relief will be warranted when "the *risk* of its happening is greater than a reasonable man would incur").

* * * As the district court rightly noted, the magnitude of the potential harm here is tremendous, and the risk that this harm will come to pass may be growing with every passing day. (It certainly has grown since the

ill-fated day around 1970 when the carp escaped from various aquaculture facilities and began their march up the Mississippi River). Given the magnitude of the harm, we are inclined to give the benefit of the doubt to the states on the question whether they have shown enough of a risk of nuisance to satisfy the likelihood-of-success requirement at this preliminary stage. In addition, the nature of the threat—an ecological harm—suggests that a broader perspective on the problem might be necessary. It is hard to see 60 miles of separation between the carp invasion front and the Great Lakes (and remember this was the estimated distance more than two years ago) as a particularly safe margin, even with functioning electric barriers to deter fish and efforts to reduce propagule pressure (the volume of invasive carp in the water downstream of the front). It is especially chilling to recall that in just 40 years the fish have migrated all the way from the lower Mississippi River to within striking distance of the lakes and have come to dominate the ecosystem in the process. * * *

In our view, the proper inference to draw from the evidence is that invasive carp are knocking on the door to the Great Lakes. We need not wait to see fish being pulled from the mouth of the Chicago River every day before concluding that a threat of a nuisance exists. It is enough that the threat is substantial and that it may be increasing with each day that passes. Unlike many nuisances that can be eliminated after they are discovered, this one in all likelihood cannot be. The fact that it would be impossible to un-ring the bell in this case is another reason to be more open to a conclusion that the threat is real. In our view, the plaintiff states presented enough evidence to establish a good or even substantial likelihood of success on the merits of their public nuisance claim.

* * * [W]e have very little trouble concluding that the environmental and economic harm that the states have shown might come to pass would be genuinely irreparable if it did occur. * * * "Environmental injury, by its nature, can seldom be adequately remedied by money damages and is often permanent or at least of long duration, *i.e.*, irreparable." [Citation.] Harms like those the states allege here are irreparable because they are difficult—if not impossible—to reverse.

For preliminary relief to be granted, the irreparable harm must also be likely. That is, there must be more than a mere possibility that the harm will come to pass, but the alleged harm need not be occurring or be certain to occur before a court may grant relief. [Citations.] Commentators describe the required level of certainty this way: "[A] preliminary injunction will not be issued simply to prevent the possibility of some remote future injury. A presently existing actual threat must be shown. However, the injury need not have been inflicted when application is made or be certain to occur." [Citation.] * * *

The balancing process to which we now turn is a classic part of any preliminary injunction inquiry. How much of the danger forecast by the states would be avoided by the particular injunction they have asked for? And what harm would the injunction impose on the defendants? Typically, after we balance these party-specific equities, we evaluate whether the injunction would advance or impede the public interest. That additional analysis is not necessary in this case, however, because the parties themselves, with the exception of two intervenors, are governmental entities that represent the interests of the public.

* * * [W]e conclude that a preliminary injunction would cause significantly more harm that it would prevent. We reach this result for two reasons, which we summarize here before explaining the balance of harms in more detail. First, there are a number of problems with various line items in the plaintiffs' proposed package of relief. Taken together, these problems leave us doubting whether the proposed injunction would reduce by a significant amount the risk that invasive carp will gain a foothold in the Great Lakes between now and the time that a full trial on the merits is completed. It is clear, on the other side, that the requested measures would impose substantial costs on the defendants and the public interests they represent, as well as added expenses for commerce, recreation, and tourism. Second, as circumstances currently stand, there is a more fundamental reason that the states' requested injunction is unlikely to prevent much harm and actually may impose costs. The courts would not be acting alone. As we have explained, there is a powerful array of expert federal and state actors that are engaged in a monumental effort to stop invasive carp from entering the Great Lakes. The last thing we need is an injunction operating at cross-purposes with their efforts or imposing needless transactional costs that divert scarce resources from science to bureaucracy. Furthermore, from an institutional perspective courts are comparatively ill situated to solve this type of problem. The balance of harms favors the defendants and the public interests they represent to such an extent that we conclude that the district court's decision to deny preliminary relief was not an abuse of discretion.

* * *

If the requested preliminary injunction were to issue, we can be sure that it would impose significant costs. First, we would have the expenses of implementing all of the measures that the states have recommended. In addition, funds that the defendants spend complying with the injunction likely would be diverted from other agency efforts to curb invasive carp. If we required the Corps to complete its long-term study within 18 months, the Corps suggests that it would not have time study the problem comprehensively and that the study might not adequately support any proposed solutions. The prospect of closing the locks permanently, installing screens on sluice gates, and placing block nets in the CAWS increases the risk of flooding, which (to the extent that it occurs) would impose costs throughout the region. * * * Meanwhile, closing the locks to boat traffic would have a tremendous impact. Police and fire services on which the City of Chicago relies would not be able to move from the Chicago River and other points in the CAWS to Lake Michigan, which means that the city would have to establish redundant emergency response fleets on either side of the locks. The same goes for Coast Guard operations around the CAWS. Recreational and tourist vessels would be stopped. And last but certainly not least, closed locks would mean that all commercial shipping in the area between the Great Lakes and the Mississippi would have to find alternative routes.

We can stop there. This overview demonstrates that the preliminary injunction the states have requested would impose substantial costs, yet given the current state of the record, we are not convinced that the preliminary injunction would assure much of a reduction in the risk of the invasive carp establishing themselves in Lake Michigan in the near future. That the balance of harms at this stage of the litigation favors the defendants might be enough by itself to support a conclusion that preliminary relief is not warranted, even though we have concluded that the states have demonstrated a likelihood of success on the merits and a threat of irreparable harm. * * *

None of this means that courts can no longer craft remedies designed to abate a public nuisance. In light of the general approach the Supreme Court took in *American Electric Power*, however, it does mean that the court should not blind itself to other remedies that are available under the law or to other measures that are actively being pursued to solve the problem. Even if legal displacement like that found in *American Electric Power* does not exist, the practical effect of agency actions might add up to displace as a matter of fact any role that equity might otherwise play. Efforts of other branches of government might be so complete that additional action ordered by a court would risk undermining agency efforts to abate the nuisance. How much the equitable power of the court has been limited by agency action will be a factual question that turns on the quality and quantity of the agency's (or, as here, agencies') efforts. This kind of institutional consideration of the court's relative ability to craft meaningful relief fits naturally in the balance-of-harms analysis. For if an injunction might hamper agency efforts or can improve upon them only slightly, that is all the more reason to conclude that the equities tilt in favor of the defendant.

* * *

We take very seriously the threat posed by the invasive species of carp that have come to dominate parts of the Mississippi River basin and now stand at the border of one of the most precious freshwater ecosystems in the world. Any threat to the irreplaceable natural resources on which we all depend demands the most diligent attention of government. As the case proceeds, the district judge should bear in mind that the risk of harm here depends upon both the probability of the harm and the magnitude of the problem that would result. In the end, however, the question whether the federal courts can offer meaningful equitable relief—either preliminary or permanent—to help abate a public nuisance in the face of agency action is factual in nature. It depends on the actual measures that the agencies have implemented already and those that they have committed to put in place going forward. Our ruling today is tied to our understanding of the current state of play. We recognize that the facts on the ground (or in the water) could change. The agencies currently working hard to solve the carp problem might find themselves unable to continue, for budgetary reasons, because of policy changes in Washington, D.C., or for some other reason. If that happens, it is possible that the balance of equities would shift. Similarly, new evidence might come to light which would require more drastic action, up to and including closing locks on Lake Michigan for a period of time. If either situation comes to pass, then the district court would have the authority to revisit the question whether an exercise of its equitable powers is warranted, taking into account the principles we have discussed in this opinion. As things stand now, however, preliminary relief is not appropriate. The district court's judgment is AFFIRMED.

———————

1.   What role should the common law of nuisance play in relation to various statutory schemes for environmental protection? In *Illinois v. Milwaukee*, 406 U.S. 91, 92 S.Ct. 1385, 31 L.Ed.2d 712 (1972) (*Milwaukee I*), the Supreme Court recognized a federal common law of nuisance to abate pollution of interstate or navigable waters. The Court intimated that a comprehensive federal regulatory scheme could preempt the field of federal common law of nuisance. Congress subsequently enacted the Federal Water Pollution Control Act Amendments of 1972.

Almost a decade later the Court then held in *Milwaukee v. Illinois*, 451 U.S. 304, 101 S.Ct. 1784, 68 L.Ed.2d 114 (1981) (*Milwaukee II*), that the federal legislation occupied the field of water pollution regulation and left no room for federal common law. In *International Paper Company v. Ouellette*, 479 U.S. 481, 107 S.Ct. 805, 93 L.Ed.2d 883 (1987), the plaintiffs sought damages and an injunction to require the defendant to restructure part of the water treatment system of its pulp and paper mill. The plaintiffs claimed that the defendant's New York operations had caused a significant interference with their property interests in Vermont through the discharge of waste materials into Lake Champlain. The Court held that the federal Clean Water Act precluded the application of the Vermont state law against an out of state source. However, the Court further held that New York nuisance law would not be preempted by the federal regulation. The opinion observes that states could properly use their own common laws in setting permit standards consistent with the Clean Water Act. The decision effectively rejuvenated the role of state nuisance law to complement federal pollution control regulations.

Most recently, in *American Electric Power Co. v. Connecticut*, ___ U.S. ___, 131 S.Ct. 2527, 180 L.Ed.2d 435 (2011) the Court reaffirmed federal common law suits brought by one State to redress the effects of pollution emanating from another State. The Court also emphasized that "public nuisance law, like common law generally, adapts to changing scientific and factual circumstances." 131 S.Ct. at 2536. The question remained, however, of whether federal legislation effectively displaced common law with respect to issues relating to carbon-dioxide emissions from fossil-fuel fired power plants. Finding that the Clean Air Act required the EPA to establish performance standards for all carbon-dioxide emitters and the statute provided various avenues for enforcement, the Court held that claims based on public nuisance law against the power companies was foreclosed by the Act.

2. *Standing.* The majority rule provides that a private individual must demonstrate suffering harm of a different kind from members of the general public in order to have standing to maintain an action to abate a public nuisance. The rationale for requiring a showing of special injury involves the difficulty in drawing a satisfactory line between public and private nuisance and to avoid multiplicity of suits. *See* Allegheny General Hospital v. Philip Morris, Inc., 228 F.3d 429 (3d Cir.2000); Restatement (Second) of Torts section 821C cmt. b. (1979). The traditional view is reflected, for example, in California Civil Code § 3493; a private person is allowed to bring a public nuisance suit if the activity is "specially injurious to himself, but not otherwise." *Contra* Akau v. Olohana Corp., 65 Hawaii 383, 652 P.2d 1130 (1982) (individual had standing to sue to enforce the rights of the public even though their injury was not different in kind from the public's generally; provided showing made of suffering an injury in fact, and that the concerns of a multiplicity of suits were satisfied).

3. A current illustration of the principle requiring special harm to maintain a public nuisance claim was shown in *Burton v. Dominion Nuclear Connecticut, Inc.*, 300 Conn. 542, 23 A.3d 1176 (2011). The plaintiff landowner brought a public nuisance claim seeking to restrain a nuclear power plant from implementing an increase in its electric power generating capacity on the basis that the excess pollution produced would contribute to detrimental global warming effects on marine life. The court held that the plaintiff lacked standing because she failed to demonstrate how her swimming, boating or consumption of seafood would be affected by increased temperatures of the water or how her interest differed from those of the general public.

Also, in *Burns Jackson Miller Summit & Spitzer v. Lindner*, 464 N.Y.S.2d 712, 59 N.Y.2d 314, 451 N.E.2d 459 (1983), the court held that a law firm lacked standing to assert a public nuisance claim for lost business profits resulting from a mass transit strike because all members of the public had been affected by the strike. The court reasoned that any interference with the law firm's business was only an incidental result of the transit union's conduct rather than a special kind of harm.

4. The general requirement that a plaintiff suffer special harm, rather than merely a greater degree of harm, has proved troublesome in some cases. For example, in *Stop & Shop Companies, Inc. v. Fisher*, 387 Mass. 889, 444 N.E.2d 368 (1983), the plaintiff claimed it lost profits because the negligent obstruction of a public bridge cut off access to the plaintiff's business premises for customers. The court held that the plaintiff had standing to assert a public nuisance claim. On similar facts, the court in *Nebraska Innkeepers, Inc. v. Pittsburgh–Des Moines Corp.*, 345 N.W.2d 124 (Iowa 1984), denied standing. The plaintiff's claim was made on behalf of the retail business community for losses attributed to a bridge's closing. That court denied the claim because the plaintiff suffered no "special"

harm. *Also see* Goldhirsch v. Majewski by Majewski, 87 F.Supp.2d 272 (S.D.N.Y.2000) (plaintiff denied recovery under public nuisance theory when injured as business invitee to paintball field and not exercising a public right).

2.   ENJOINING CRIMES

Meyer v. Seifert

216 Ark. 293, 225 S.W.2d 4 (1949).

■ LEFLAR, JUSTICE.

Appellant G.A. Meyer on behalf of himself and other property owners filed this bill in equity for a mandatory injunction to require the removal of a non-fireproof building erected by defendants Seifert and Mahle, under a permit granted by the other defendants (City of Stuttgart, Ark., and the Mayor, City Clerk, and Aldermen of said city, in their official capacities) within a fire zone in which the erection of such buildings was prohibited by city ordinances. The Chancery Court refused to issue the injunction, and plaintiff appeals.

[The court first recognized that the relevant city ordinances (Nos. 277 and 286) flatly prohibited the construction of non-fireproof frame buildings, such as the type built by the defendants Seifert and Mahle. Additionally, the building permit relied upon by the defendants had been invalidly issued by the city council.]

* * *

A second contention urged by the defendants is that equity is without power, or should not exercise the power, to enjoin maintenance of the prohibited structure. The argument is that the ordinance prescribes criminal punishments, making violation a misdemeanor punishable by fine of not less than $10 nor more than $100 for each day of violation, and that this remedy is exclusive. That equity will not act to restrain ordinary violations of the criminal law, but will leave the task of enforcing the criminal laws to courts having criminal jurisdiction, is basic learning in our legal system. But it is equally basic that if grounds for equity jurisdiction exist in a given case, the fact that the act to be enjoined is incidentally violative of a criminal enactment will not preclude equity's action to enjoin it.

In one of the most publicized cases that ever arose in Arkansas, Chancellor Martin enjoined the holding at Hot Springs of a world championship heavyweight prizefight between James J. Corbett and Robert Fitzsimmons. Judge Martin conceded that ordinarily equity does not enjoin the commission of crimes, but pointed out that it does issue such injunctions where property interests are involved, and emphasized the prospective property injuries threatened by the prizefight, notably the payment of money by purchasers of tickets of admission to the illegal enterprise, losses by bettors, the use and congestion of some buildings which might be harmful to other adjoining buildings, and the possible loss of property to thieves, pick-pockets and similar gentry who might come to the state for the fight. The most frequently quoted statement of the rule in Arkansas appears in State v. Vaughan, 81 Ark. 117, 126, 98 S.W. 685, 690, 7 L.R.A., N.S., 899, 118 Am.St.Rep. 29, 11 Ann.Cas. 277, where, after denying the injunction in the particular case, Chief Justice Hill added: "On the other hand, if the public nuisance is one touching civil property rights or privileges of the public, or the public health is affected by a physical nuisance, or if any other ground of equity jurisdiction exists calling for an injunction, a chancery court will enjoin, notwithstanding the act enjoined may also be a crime. The criminality of the act will neither give nor oust jurisdiction in chancery." * * *

It is characteristic of most instances in which injunctions against criminal acts are sustained that the threat of punishment after the event will not have a very strong deterrent effect upon the offender. As to some acts, this is because the criminal punishment is small and unimportant as compared with the benefits or profits expected to be gained from the criminal act. Oftentimes the act is a recurrent or continuing one, necessitating numerous successive petty prosecutions if the regular criminal procedure is to be followed. Frequently the acts are such that it is difficult to get jury convictions, either because local juries are prejudiced against the enforcement of the particular law involved, or for some other equally practical reason. In effect these considerations point to (1) the practical inadequacy of the available legal (criminal) remedy, and (2) interference with property or other equitably protectible interests of the plaintiff or, if he has sued in a representative capacity, of a substantial group of the general public.

The decisions on the specific type of invasion of rights involved in the instant case are in accord with these principles. Many cases hold that a nearby property owner, for himself and others similarly situated, may enjoin the violation of building codes, zoning laws or similar enactments, on showing substantial threat of injury to his and their property. [Citations.] The case of Lewis v. A. Hirsch & Co., 192 Ark. 209, 90 S.W.2d 976, is not contrary to these cases. The *Hirsch* case merely held that one who sued as a citizen and taxpayer only, who did not claim to own any property or show any prospective injury to himself, would not be granted an injunction against construction of a building in violation of a fire zone ordinance. * * * And in Van Hovenberg v. Holeman, 201 Ark. 370, 144 S.W.2d 718, 722, this court held squarely that an injunction should be sustained on behalf of a plaintiff property owner restraining defendant's erection of a filling station in a restricted zone in violation of a city ordinance. There we said: "But the primary and fundamental purpose of the ordinance was to prohibit operation—not to punish. It is definitely settled that equity will not interfere to stay proceedings in a criminal matter. Here, however, the relief sought is abatement of unauthorized conduct. If it should be held that penalty of the ordinance deprived equity of jurisdiction, then any person desiring to proceed in violation of law could pay the maximum fine and become immune thereafter except as to damages. This is not the law."

The plaintiff made a substantial showing of probable damage to his own and other adjoining properties through increased fire hazards arising from maintenance of defendants' building where they have placed it in violation of the Stuttgart fire zone ordinance. This constitutes a proper case for equitable relief, as against defendants Seifert and Mahle. As to them, the decree is reversed and remanded. It is not shown that a decree against the City of Stuttgart, its Mayor, City Clerk and Board of Aldermen would afford any relief to the plaintiff, therefore the decree is affirmed as to them.

---

1.   In *State v. Red Owl Stores*, 253 Minn. 236, 92 N.W.2d 103 (1958), the state sought to enjoin the defendant corporations from continuing to sell and distribute certain drugs without obtaining the necessary registration and licenses required by the state's Pharmacy Act. The trial court had denied the injunctive relief on the grounds that the exclusive remedy in the Act was enforcement by criminal prosecution. The Minnesota Supreme Court reversed because the state lacked an adequate remedy at law to enforce a public health measure. The legal remedy was inadequate because enforcement through the sanctions in the Act would require a multiplicity of actions.

The state in *Red Owl* had not even attempted to enforce the Act by criminal prosecution. Did the court act too hastily in concluding that criminal sanctions would be ineffective? How should equity courts balance public interest concerns with the rights of defendants to the safeguards of trial by jury and the reasonable doubt standard of proof? Would a better alternative have been for the court to defer to the legislature by refusing the injunction simply because the Act failed to offer such a remedy?

2.   A number of courts have issued injunctions prohibiting the practice of a profession without a license on the basis of characterizing the activity as a public nuisance or by finding that a property right of the claimant was invaded. *See* State ex rel. Commission on Unauthorized Practice of Law v. M.A. Yah, 281 Neb. 383, 796 N.W.2d 189 (2011) (injunction issued against unlicensed practice of law); Geauga Cty. Bar Assn. v. Haig, 129 Ohio St.3d 601, 955 N.E.2d 352 (2011) (loan officer enjoined from unauthorized practice of law); Arizona State Bd. of Dental Examiners v. Hyder, 114 Ariz. 544, 562 P.2d 717 (1977) (injunction granted prohibiting practicing dentistry without a license even though criminal penalties were also available for unauthorized practice); People ex rel. Bennett v. Laman, 277 N.Y. 368, 14 N.E.2d 439 (1938) (practicing medicine without a license). *But see* Massachusetts Society of Optometrists v. Waddick, 340 Mass. 581, 165 N.E.2d 394 (1960) (action to enjoin optician from engaging in unlawful practice as public nuisance denied).

In *Missouri Veterinary Medical Ass'n. v. Glisan*, 230 S.W.2d 169 (Mo.App.1950), the court denied the Association's request to enjoin the defendant from the unlicensed practice of veterinary medicine. The court stated that equity would not enjoin the commission of a crime absent a showing that the Association had property rights which were being violated by the defendant's conduct. The court further held that the Association was not a proper party to bring a public nuisance action without demonstrating that it suffered a special injury as a consequence of the unlicensed practice.

People v. Lim

18 Cal.2d 872, 118 P.2d 472 (1941).

■ GIBSON, CHIEF JUSTICE.

The district attorney of Monterey county commenced this action on behalf of the People of the State of California to restrain defendants from continuing the operation of a gambling establishment in the city of Monterey. The complaint set forth the manner in which the various games were played and alleged that the operation of this gambling house constituted a public nuisance by encouraging idle and dissolute habits, by disturbing the public peace and by corrupting the public morals. It was further alleged that previous attempts to eradicate this evil by prosecutions under the penal laws had proven ineffective and that the aid of equity was necessary to accomplish its suppression. A preliminary injunction was asked to restrain defendants from conducting and operating gambling games pending a trial of the action. Defendants interposed both general and special demurrers. The trial court sustained the demurrers and denied plaintiff's motion for a temporary injunction. After plaintiff's refusal to amend the complaint, the court entered its judgment in favor of defendants.

Upon this appeal it is contended in behalf of the People that the complaint states a proper cause of action and that it was error on the part of the trial court to sustain the general demurrer. The authority of a district attorney to bring such an action is found in the Code of Civil Procedure, section 731, which provides: "A civil action may be brought in the name of the people of the State of California to abate a public nuisance, as the same is defined in section thirty-four hundred and eighty of the Civil Code, by the district attorney of any county in which such nuisance exists * * *." Civil Code, section 3480 provides: "A public nuisance is one which affects at the same time an entire community or neighborhood, or any considerable number of persons, although the extent of the annoyance or damage inflicted upon individuals may be unequal." The definition of "nuisance", as the term is used in section 3480, is found in the provisions of the preceding section, Civil Code, section 3479: "Anything which is injurious to health, or is indecent or offensive to the senses, or an obstruction to the free use of property, so as to interfere with the comfortable enjoyment of life or property, * * * is a nuisance." It is stated in the allegations of the complaint that the action was instituted under statutory provisions. Thus, it is alleged that the gambling house operated by defendants constitutes a public nuisance "for the reason that it tends to and does in fact debauch and corrupt the public morals, encourage idle and dissolute habits, draws together great numbers of disorderly persons, disturbs the public peace, brings together idle persons and cultivates dissolute habits among them, creates traffic and fire hazards, and is thereby injurious to health, indecent and offensive to the senses and impairs the free enjoyment of life and property.''

Although this proceeding purports to have been brought under the code provisions governing such actions, the plaintiff upon this appeal relies rather upon the theory that the statutory definition of ''public nuisance'' is not intended to be exclusive and that gaming houses, which were recognized as public nuisances at common law, are inherently public nuisances apart from the provisions of our statute. Plaintiff cites those statutes which provide that the common law must be given effect as the rule of decision where not repugnant to or inconsistent with the constitution or laws of the state. Pol.Code, § 4468; Civ.Code, § 5. Thus, it is said, a gambling house constitutes an inherent public nuisance in this state and equity will enjoin such a public nuisance in an action brought on behalf of the People. Defendants argue, however, that the authority conferred upon a district attorney to bring such an action in equity extends only to those nuisances specified by statute and that their activities are not within the terms of our statute.

It must be conceded that the cases cited by plaintiff, as well as many others, demonstrate that a gambling house constituted a public nuisance at common law for the purposes of a criminal prosecution. [Citations.] While these cases indicate that gambling houses were recognized as public nuisances in criminal prosecutions, they do not hold that an equity action on behalf of the state might be maintained at common law to enjoin the operation of a gambling house. On the contrary, it is clear that the jurisdiction of equity was very sparingly exercised on behalf of the sovereign to enjoin public nuisances. The attitude of the early English cases is expressed by Chancellor Kent in a leading case: ''I know that the court is in the practice of restraining private nuisances to property, and of quieting persons in the enjoyment of private right; but it is an extremely rare case, and may be considered, if it ever happened, as an anomaly, for a court of equity to interfere at all, and much less, preliminarily, by injunction, to put down a public nuisance which did not violate the rights of property, but only contravened the general policy.'' [Citation.] The authorities support the conclusion that this statement accurately represents the attitude of the earlier courts of equity where the sovereign sought injunctions against public nuisances. [Citations.] The common law recognized various types of wrongful activity as indictable public nuisances, including such miscellaneous acts as eavesdropping, being a common scold and maintaining for hire a place of amusement which served no useful purpose. [Citation.] The kinds of public nuisance at common law, however, where injunctions were granted on behalf of the sovereign included only those cases of public nuisance in which the sovereign's rights were given the same protection that would have been given to the rights of a private person. An action on behalf of the state, therefore, to enjoin activity which violates general concepts of public policy finds no basis in the doctrines of the common law.

It has been recognized that the tendency to utilize the equity injunction as a means of enforcing public policy is a relatively recent development in the law. [Citations.] Courts have held that public and social interests, as well as the rights of property, are entitled to the protection of equity. [Citations.] This development has resulted in a continuous expansion of the field of public nuisances in which equitable relief is available at the request of the state. It has been held, for example, that the legislature may properly define the term "public nuisance" for the purposes of an equity injunction so as to include activity which was not a nuisance at common law or activity which offends concepts of public policy even though no rights of property are involved. [Citations.] Where particular activity, such as gambling or horse-racing, has been held to come within the language of a statute defining the term "public nuisance" for the purposes of equity jurisdiction on behalf of the state, courts have granted injunctions, or indicated that they would grant them, even though the acts were also criminal. Upon at least two occasions the legislature of this state has passed statutes authorizing an action in equity to enjoin particular activity contrary to the public policy as a "public nuisance". Thus, houses of prostitution and houses where narcotics are illegally sold may be enjoined in an action brought by the district attorney of the county in which they are located. [Citations.]

It must be admitted, however, that the authorities are divided as to whether the expansion of the field of public nuisances in which equity will grant injunctions must be accomplished by an act of the legislature. [Citations.] Some courts have attempted by judicial action alone to define "public nuisance" very broadly in order to grant injunctions on behalf of the state. Thus, it has been said that any place where a public statute is continuously flouted constitutes a public nuisance which may be enjoined by the state. [Citations.] Other courts have flatly stated that a particular form of activity, such as bullfighting, is so objectionable as to constitute a public nuisance for the purposes of an equity injunction without the aid of a statute. [Citations.] The courts of this state, however, have refused to sanction the granting of injunctions on behalf of the state merely by a judicial extension of the definition of "public nuisance". * * * In Weis v. Superior Court, 30 Cal.App. 730, 159 P. 464, it was held that the district attorney of San Diego county was authorized, under Code of Civil Procedure, section 731, to enjoin the performance of a public exhibition which was shown to have been indecent, and thus within the statutory definition of public nuisance in Civil Code, section 3479. In People v. Seccombe, 103 Cal.App. 306, 284 P. 725, however, the court refused to permit the maintenance of a suit in equity on behalf of the state to restrain defendant's continued practice of usury. It was held that though reprehensible, the practice of usury could not be brought within any of the sections of the statute defining public nuisances. The courts have thus refused to grant injunctions on behalf of the state except where the objectionable activity can be brought within the terms of the statutory definition of public nuisance. Where the legislature has felt that the summary power of equity was required to control activity contrary to public policy, it has enacted statutes specifying that such activity constitutes a public nuisance which may be enjoined in an action brought on behalf of the state.

We think the proper rule, therefore, and the one to which this state is committed is expressed in the following language from State v. Ehrlick, 65 W.Va. 700, 64 S.E. 935, 940, 23 L.R.A., N.S., 691: "It is also competent for the Legislature, within the constitutional limits of its powers, to declare any act criminal and make the repetition or continuance thereof a public nuisance * * * or to vest in courts of equity the power to abate them by injunction; but it is not the province of the courts to ordain such jurisdiction for themselves." [Citations.]

In addition to the historical precedents which we have considered, compelling reasons of policy require that the responsibility for establishing those standards of public morality, the violations of which are to constitute public nuisances within equity's jurisdiction, should be left with the legislature. "Nuisance" is a term which does not have a fixed content either at common law or at the present time. [Citations.] Blackstone defined it so broadly as to include almost all types of actionable wrong, that is, "any thing that worketh hurt, inconvenience or damage". 2 Cooley's Blackstone, 4th ed. 1899, p. 1012. We have already referred to those modern definitions which seek to make of equity an additional remedy for the enforcement of the criminal law by defining "public nuisance" for the purposes of an injunction as any repeated and continuous violation of the law. In a field where the meaning of terms is so vague and uncertain it is a proper function of the legislature to define those breaches of public policy which are to be considered public nuisances within the control of equity. Activity which in one period constitutes a public nuisance, such as the sale of liquor or the holding of prize fights, might not be objectionable in another. Such declarations of policy should be left for the legislature.

Conduct against which injunctions are sought in behalf of the public is frequently criminal in nature. While this alone will not prevent the intervention of equity where a clear case justifying equitable relief is present, it is apparent that the equitable remedy has the collateral effect of depriving a defendant of the jury trial to which he would be entitled in a criminal prosecution for violating exactly the same standards of public policy. The defendant also loses the protection of the higher burden of proof required in criminal prosecutions and, after imprisonment and fine for violation of the equity injunction, may be subjected under the criminal law to similar punishment for the same acts. For these reasons equity is loath to interfere where the standards of public policy can be enforced by resort to the criminal law, and in the absence of a legislative declaration to that effect, the courts should not broaden the field in which injunctions against criminal activity will be granted. Thus, for the reasons set forth, the basis for an action such as this must be found in our statutes rather than by reference to the common law definitions of public nuisance.

* * * In support of the court's ruling on the general demurrer, defendants argue that the allegations of the complaint are insufficient because no facts are alleged from which the court could conclude that a

nuisance existed under the provisions of Civil Code, sections 3479, 3480, and Code of Civil Procedure, section 731. It is contended that the allegations of the complaint present merely conclusions of the pleader, framed in the language of the statute.

* * *

Although the defendants' contention that particular allegations of fact are required is therefore correct, we think that the allegations of the present complaint are adequate as against a general demurrer. The complaint alleges that the gambling house operated by defendants "draws together great numbers of disorderly persons, disturbs the public peace, brings together idle persons and cultivates dissolute habits among them, creates traffic and fire hazards, and is thereby injurious to health, indecent and offensive to the senses and impairs the free enjoyment of life and property". Crowds of disorderly people who disturb the peace and obstruct the traffic may well impair the free enjoyment of life and property and give rise to the hazards designated in the statute. In cases of a similar nature pleadings which are not essentially different from the one here involved have been held to state facts sufficient to constitute a cause of action. [Citations.] It follows that the trial court was in error in sustaining the general demurrer.

[Reversed.]

———————

1. In *United States v. Menominee Indian Tribe of Wisconsin*, a 1988 federal district court opinion concerning gambling activities on an Indian reservation. The government sought declaratory and injunctive relief under the Organized Crime Control Act to prohibit gambling operations conducted by an Indian tribe. The court denied the government's request and followed the general rule that equity will not enjoin the commission of a crime. The court observed:

> To use an analogy: suppose the government wanted to prosecute a bank robber who was using a toy gun to convince tellers to hand over the cash, but first the government wanted to know whether by using a toy gun, the robber committed "armed" rather than simple robbery. Should a court issue a declaratory judgment that the robber committed an armed robbery, or should that issue be litigated in a criminal case? I think the latter. The essence of the request for both declaratory and injunctive relief is that a crime is being committed. As framed, the issue is not one which should be decided in a civil proceeding. A criminal proceeding, where proof beyond a reasonable doubt is necessary for a conviction, is the place where these issues should be decided. 694 F.Supp. 1373, 1377 (E.D.Wis.1988).

Also see State of Oklahoma v. Twin C Convenience Store, 218 P.3d 529 (Okla. Civ. App. 2009) (court lacked equity jurisdiction over suit brought by

State seeking declaratory judgment that defendant's telephone card vending machines constituted illegal gambling devices under penal code).

2.   In *West Allis Memorial Hospital, Inc. v. Bowen*, 852 F.2d 251 (7th Cir.1988), the plaintiff hospital sought a preliminary injunction against a competitor. The complaint alleged that the defendant's waiver of deductible and coinsurance program violated the anti-fraud provisions of Medicare and various state and federal antitrust laws. The plaintiff apparently perceived that it faced a Hobson's choice: implement a similar program and potentially face criminal prosecution for violating the anti-fraud provisions or refrain from acting and lose business to its competitor. The district court denied the injunction.

The Court of Appeals agreed with the trial judge that the Medicare statute did not create an implied private right of action to give the plaintiff standing to sue and that equity would not enjoin criminal activity. The court noted that the plaintiff's claims did not fit within one of the three recognized exceptions which would warrant an injunction against crimes: cases of national emergencies, public nuisances, and specific statutory authorization.

The court reversed and remanded to the district court with respect to the plaintiff's antitrust claims and common law claims of unfair competition. In contrast to the Medicare statute, the relevant statutes did provide for injunctive relief to enjoin criminal activity in violation of the acts.

3.   Compare the principal case with *Goose v. Commonwealth*, 305 Ky. 644, 205 S.W.2d 326 (1947), where the court issued an injunction against the proprietors of a gambling establishment. The court observed that numerous arrests of the owners and employees on various charges during a five year period had not been effective in abating the criminal conduct. The state thus had no adequate remedy at law which in turn caused irreparable harm to the public. The court stated:

> These men confess a general course of criminality at this place. They have in some way been able to set the law at naught and to continue their criminal project. The processes of the criminal courts seem to have broken down in dealing with this place and these men. At least, they have failed to accomplish their primary purposes of protecting society, reforming the wayward and preventing future offenses of the same kind. As a consequence, the Commonwealth has invoked the processes of the court of equity and obtained an injunction against the named persons to abate their use of the property for the unlawful purposes. * * *
>
> Courts of equity will not ordinarily enjoin the commission of a crime. The statutes themselves are standing injunctions. But the mere fact that the act constituting a nuisance is also a crime does not hinder the use of the civil processes to procure its abatement where the use of property is a part. There may also be a remedy by indictment and upon conviction an abatement by order of the criminal court where the nuisance may be of a continuing character. This remedy is sometimes confused with the other. But there is a clear distinction between enjoining an individual from committing a crime and enjoining him

from using his or another's property so as to make it a nuisance to others, and between a proceeding in equity to abate a nuisance and a criminal prosecution to punish the offender for maintaining it. [Citations.]

It is a historic function of courts of equity to grant preventive as well as remedial relief. Irreparable injury to property rights is perhaps the most common of causes for injunctive relief. Surely irreparable injury to public morals and individual character is of as grave concern as mere loss of dollars and cents. The ground of the jurisdiction is the ability of the chancellor to give a more complete and perfect remedy by a perpetual injunction. It is a weapon from the arsenal of equity to be used to protect Society—to meet the social need that continuation of the offenses at a given place shall be repressed. This abatement by injunction, independent of the criminal prosecution, is supported by ancient precedents and modern instances. * * *

Stronger and stronger has become the disposition of the legislatures and the courts to extend the law of nuisances to every sort of gambling irrespective of its connection with other offenses, or of its potentiality of spawning them, or of other conditions which brought it within the classification of a nuisance in former days. It long ago ceased to be essential to injunctive redress that the gambling should be in view of the public or that the public be disturbed by noise therefrom. Nor is it requisite to show that dissolute or criminal characters frequent the premises or that respectable citizens have been "forced to come in contact with a lower strata of society", as appellants submit. However, we suspect that none of the habitues of this place wore the halo of a saint or the wings of an angel. * * *

Neither principle nor precedent supports the absolution claimed by these defendants. If the moral fiber of its manhood and womanhood is not a state concern, we may ask, what is? The court does not falter for an answer. 305 Ky. 644, 205 S.W.2d 326 (1947).

4. What kind of causal connection is required in order to justify equitable relief against conduct as a public nuisance? In *City of Little Rock v. Rhee*, 375 Ark. 491, 292 S.W.3d 292 (2009), a city brought a public nuisance claim seeking an injunction and order of abatement against the owner, mortgagee and tenants of a shopping mall. The complaint alleged that numerous criminal violations had occurred on mall property, including loitering, public intoxication and illegal possession of weapons and drugs. The court denied injunctive relief, finding that the city had failed to establish a link between the criminal activities by third parties and the defendants. The court drew support for declining equity by noting that the mall owner had undertaken extensive measures designed to curb the criminal activity on the premises, such as expanding security guard services, building a fence and installing flood lights and surveillance cameras. *Also see* Jones v. Starnes, 150 Idaho 257, 245 P.3d 1009 (2011) (bar not held responsible for public nuisance where its owners had no control or affiliation with persons responsible for brawl which occurred outside its premises).

PART III

DAMAGES

CHAPTER 10

CONTRACT DAMAGES

A. INTRODUCTION

Section Coverage:

The law of damages for breach of contract recognizes and protects an injured party's expectancy, reliance, and restitutionary interests. The measure of recovery often will vary depending upon which remedial interest is asserted. Expectancy damages provide a monetary substitute for the promised but undelivered performance. Therefore, compensation is calculated by the amount necessary to place the injured plaintiff in as good a position financially as that party would have occupied if the defendant had rendered the remaining performance.

In some instances, the plaintiff may seek reliance damages or restitutionary relief as an alternative to expectancy damages. The nature of the circumstances that give rise to the various remedial options varies. In some cases the reliance or restitution measures may be appropriate because the plaintiff cannot prove expectancy damages with reasonable certainty. These alternative measures are also appropriate in cases where the contract ultimately proved to be a losing one for the plaintiff, so there are no expectancy damages. The most fortunate plaintiffs can prove damages under all measures and thus they have a choice.

Model Case:

Clark contracted with American Restaurants, Inc. to buy a franchise of a Ribs & Stuff Restaurant. The principal terms of the franchise agreement required Clark to pay a $25,000 non-refundable franchise fee, including an obligation to purchase from American all of Clark's requirements of certain "secret ribs sauce," and a 6% royalty based on gross sales payable monthly. Clark paid the $25,000 fee and expended another $10,000 for advertising and marketing services in a promotional campaign introducing the opening of the restaurant.

American's senior management decided to terminate the Clark's franchise agreement because they thought that the business had expanded into new geographical areas too quickly to service all of them. Assuming that the cancellation by American constituted a breach of contract, Clark may seek compensatory damages to protect the expectancy, reliance, and restitution interests in the agreement. Clark probably would have difficulty in proving expectancy damages with reasonable certainty because the business had no established track record, thus making claims for lost profits too speculative. A court probably would award the $25,000 franchise fee as restitution, together with the $10,000 expenditures as reliance damages.

Eastlake Construction Co. v. Hess

102 Wash.2d 30, 686 P.2d 465 (1984).

■ PEARSON, JUSTICE.

* * *

Plaintiff Eastlake Construction Company (Eastlake) brought this action in King County Superior Court to recover $13,719 allegedly owing on a construction contract. Eastlake had entered the contract with defendants Leroy and Jean Hess to erect a 5–unit condominium building in Issaquah. Defendants counterclaimed, alleging damages for breach of the contract * * *. The trial court awarded defendants damages for breach of contract, less the amount owing to Eastlake under the contract. * * *

* * * The trial court found that Eastlake had breached the construction contract in a number of respects. These findings, and the damages allowed by the trial court, may be summarized as follows.

A. *Breaches for which the trial court allowed damages.*

1. Eastlake wrongfully abandoned the project in February 1978, and defendants were allowed the reasonable cost of completing construction to make the condominiums habitable, $7,979.90.

2. Defendants were allowed the reasonable rental value of the condominiums from the time construction should have been completed until the actual completion date, $4,262.50.

3. Defendants were allowed damages for the reasonable cost of work specified in the plans, but not completed by Eastlake: insulating waste pipes, $807.44; installing recirculating fans, $1,031.10.

4. Defendants were allowed damages for the reasonable cost of repairing and replacing work performed by Eastlake which did not conform to the specifications: repairing the roof, $4,414.01; replacing balcony guardrails, $1,580.76; repairing and replacing washer and dryer closets, $751.84; replacing nonvented kitchen hood fans, $926.53; and replacing interior doors, $787.22.

5. Defendants were also allowed $75 for installation of cable television and $200 for light fixture underrun.

6. Defendants were also allowed damages for the installation of kitchen cabinets not in accordance with contract specifications.

The court declined to award the cost of replacement of these cabinets because this would constitute unreasonable economic waste. Instead, the measure of damages was the difference between the value of the specified cabinets ($8,725.50) and the cost of the cabinets actually installed ($3,700): $5,0252.50.

B.   *Breaches for which the trial court allowed no damages.*

The trial court found that Eastlake had breached the construction contract in a number of other respects, but that these breaches "did not result in substantial damage to the building nor result in a substantial loss of value to the building". Defendants were not allowed damages for these breaches.

* * *

The trial court found a total of $27,841.70 in damages to defendants, against which was offset the $13,719 owing on the construction contract, for an award on the counterclaim of $14,122.70.

* * *

The general measure of damages for breach of contract is that the injured party is entitled (1) to recovery of all damages that accrue naturally from the breach, and (2) to be put into as good a pecuniary position as he would have had if the contract had been performed. [Citation.] In the case of construction contracts, special problems have been encountered in putting the injured party in the pecuniary position he would have enjoyed had the contract been properly performed by the builder. These special problems have led to the creation of special rules for measuring damages in such cases.

* * * [D]amages should put the injured party in the position which he would have enjoyed without the breach. In many cases this will be achieved by awarding the costs of repairing defective construction so as to conform to the contract. Some defects, however, cannot be remedied without great expense and substantial damage to the rest of the structure (for instance, the cracked foundations in Forrester v. Craddock, 51 Wash.2d 315, 317 P.2d 1077, or the nonconforming insulation beneath the concrete floor in the present case). In such cases the cost of remedying the defect would far exceed the value to the injured party of the improvement. An award of the cost of repairs in such cases would therefore constitute a substantial windfall to the injured party. The cost of repairs should not be awarded if that cost is clearly disproportionate to the value to the injured party of those repairs.

This idea was recognized by Professor McCormick in his treatise on damages:

> In whatever way the issue arises, the generally approved standards for measuring the owner's loss from defects in the work are two: First in cases where the defect is one that can be repaired or cured *without undue expense,* so as to make the building conform to the agreed plan, then the owner recovers such amount as he has reasonably expended, or will reasonably have to spend, to remedy the defect. Second if, on the other hand, the defect in material or construction is one that cannot be remedied without an *expenditure for reconstruction disproportionate to the end to be attained,* or without endangering unduly other parts of the building, then the damages will be measured not by

the cost of remedying the defect, but by the difference between the value of the building as it is and what it would have been worth if it had been built in conformity with the contract.

(Footnotes omitted. Italics ours.) C. McCormick, *Damages* § 168, 648–49 (1935).

The crux of the determination of which measure of damages to apply is therefore the proportionality of the cost to the corresponding benefits. This is a factual question which must be resolved, as Professor Corbin points out, according to "prevailing practices and opinions (the mores) of men, involving their emotions as well as reason and logic". A. Corbin, *Contracts* § 1089, at 492 (1964).

The authors of the Restatement have recently recognized in Restatement (Second) of Contracts (1981) that the concept of unreasonable economic waste is unhelpful in determining damages, and have turned instead to consider the proportionality of the cost of repairs to the value conferred. The second Restatement provides a convenient and effective means of clarifying and regularizing the rules governing this issue.

The general rule of damages is stated in Restatement (Second) of Contracts § 347, at 112:

> Subject to the limitations stated in §§ 350–53, the injured party has a right to damages based on his expectation interest as measured by
>
> (a) the loss in the value to him of the other party's performance caused by its failure or deficiency, plus
>
> (b) any other loss, including incidental or consequential loss, caused by the breach, less
>
> (c) any cost or other loss that he has avoided by not having to perform.

Comment *a* to this rule explains the rationale for damages under the second Restatement.

> a. *Expectation interest.* Contract damages are ordinarily based on the injured party's expectation interest and are intended to give him the benefit of his bargain by awarding him a sum of money that will, to the extent possible, put him in as good a position as he would have been in had the contract been performed.

Further comments to section 347 recognize that in some cases it may be difficult to determine with sufficient certainty the damage to the injured party's expectation interest. Comment *b* states, in part:

> Where the injured party's expected advantage consists largely or exclusively of the realization of profit, it may be possible to express this loss in value in terms of money with some assurance. In other situations, however, this is not possible and compensation for lost value may be precluded by the limitation of certainty. *See* § 352. In order to facilitate the estimation of loss with sufficient certainty to award damages, the injured party is sometimes given a choice between alternative bases

of calculating his loss in value. The most important of these are stated in § 348.

The alternatives set out in Restatement (Second) of Contracts § 348, at 119–20, include measures of damages specifically applicable to construction contracts.

(1) If a breach delays the use of property and the loss in value to the injured party is not proved with reasonable certainty, he may recover damages based on the rental value of the property or on interest on the value of the property.

(2) If a breach results in defective or unfinished construction and the loss in value to the injured party is not proved with sufficient certainty, he may recover damages based on

> (a) the diminution in the market price of the property caused by the breach, or

> (b) the reasonable cost of completing performance or of remedying the defects if that cost is not clearly disproportionate to the probable loss in value to him.

The comments to section 348 include a helpful discussion of the considerations applicable to a determination of damages for a breach of the construction contract. Comment *c* at 121 is especially relevant to this case and is here set out in full:

c. Incomplete or defective performance. If the contract is one for construction, including repair or similar performance affecting the condition of property, and the work is not finished, the injured party will usually find it easier to prove what it would cost to have the work completed by another contractor than to prove the difference between the values to him of the finished and the unfinished performance. Since the cost to complete is usually less than the loss in value to him, he is limited by the rule on avoidability to damages based on cost to complete. *See* § 350(1). If he has actually had the work completed, damages will be based on his expenditures if he comes within the rule stated in § 350(2).

Sometimes, especially if the performance is defective as distinguished from incomplete, it may not be possible to prove the loss in value to the injured party with reasonable certainty. In that case he can usually recover damages based on the cost to remedy the defects. Even if this gives him a recovery somewhat in excess of the loss in value to him, it is better that he receive a small windfall than that he be undercompensated by being limited to the resulting diminution in the market price of his property.

Sometimes, however, such a large part of the cost to remedy the defects consists of the cost to undo what has been improperly done that the cost to remedy the defects will be clearly disproportionate to the probable loss in value to the injured party. Damages based on the cost to remedy the defects would then give the injured party a recovery greatly in excess of the loss in value to him and result in a substantial windfall. Such an award will not be made. It is sometimes said that the award would involve "economic waste," but this is a misleading expression since an injured party will not, even if awarded an excessive amount of damages, usually pay to have the defects remedied if to do so will cost him more than the resulting increase in value to him. If an award based on the cost to remedy the defects would clearly be excessive and the injured party does not prove the actual loss in value to him, damages will be based instead on the difference between the market price that the property would have had without the defects and the market price of the property with the defects. This diminution in market price is the least possible loss in value to the injured party, since he could always sell the property on the market even if it had no special value to him.

The Restatement formulation of the rule represents a sensible and workable approach to measuring damages in construction contract cases. It achieves a fair measure of damages while avoiding the potentially confusing concepts of substantial completion and unreasonable economic waste. We therefore adopt Restatement (Second) of Contracts § 348 as the appropriate rule for determining damages in cases such as the present one.

This conclusion requires us to remand the issue of damages to the trial court for reconsideration in light of section 348. The trial court should award defendants the cost of replacing defective items, unless the cost of replacement is "clearly disproportionate" to the value of the benefit conferred by replacement. Section 348(2)(a) and (b).

Of course, we do not disturb the trial court's award of damages for the loss of rental value, the costs of completing the project, and the costs of remedying various defects. These items of damages are clearly recoverable under Section 348. The trial court, therefore, need only apply the "clearly disproportionate" test to the kitchen cabinets and to the 9 breaches for which the trial court allowed no damages.

* * *

1. *Cost of Completion v. Diminution in Value.* The expectancy interest of the injured party may be measured in a variety of ways. Traditionally, courts have awarded the cost to complete the performance which has been promised. However, as indicated in the principal case, in some circumstances the cost to remedy the defects in performance may be disproportionately greater than the difference in value of what was promised and what was actually received. In that event, courts may award the diminution in value to the injured party in order to prevent economic waste.

In the leading case of *Jacob & Youngs v. Kent*, 230 N.Y. 239, 129 N.E. 889 (1921), a contractor built a residence, but mistakenly installed a brand of plumbing pipe which differed from the specifications. Judge Cardozo held that the proper measure of damages would be the difference in value between the pipe specified and the type actually installed because it would be economically wasteful to tear down the house for the small benefit of substituting a different brand of pipe.

Contrast the result in *O.W. Grun Roofing & Const. Co. v. Cope*, 529 S.W.2d 258 (Tex.Civ.App.1975). In that case the plaintiff sued a roofing company to set aside a mechanic's lien and for damages sustained as a result of the defendant's failure to install properly a new roof on the plaintiff's home. After the defendant had installed the roof, the plaintiff noticed it had "streaks" due to a difference in color of some of the shingles. The defendant's attempts to remedy the problem by replacing certain shingles proved unsuccessful. The court awarded the homeowner damages to compensate for installing a completely new roof.

Can the result in *O.W. Grun Roofing & Const. Co. v. Cope* be reconciled with *Jacob & Youngs v. Kent?* To what extent is the object and purpose of the contract relevant in selecting the appropriate measure of damages?

2. *Bad Faith.* Some courts have awarded damages for the cost to complete performance even where that measure is clearly disproportionate to the diminution in value because the defendant breached the contract willfully or in bad faith. *See* Groves v. John Wunder Co., 205 Minn. 163, 286 N.W. 235 (1939). The majority of courts, though, have rejected the factor of an intentional or willful breach as affecting the remedial consequences. The latter view reflects the philosophy that the goal in contract damages is compensating for losses and that the domain for punishing certain behavior is exemplary damages.

3. *Economic Theory.* Moreover, in some instances a party may choose to breach a contract and pay the resulting damages in order to move goods to a higher bidder. This process accords with traditional notions of economic theory by distributing assets to maximize resources in the most efficient manner. For an examination of the competing interests involved in the economic theory of contract damages *see generally* Macneil, Efficient Breach of Contract: Circle in the Sky, 68 Va.L.Rev. 947 (1982); Linzer, On the Amorality of Contract Remedies—Efficiency, Equity, and the Second Restatement, 81 Colum.L.Rev. 111 (1981); Farber, Reassessing the Economic Efficiency of Compensatory Damages for Breach of Contract, 66 Va.L.Rev. 1443 (1980); Kronman, Specific Performance, 45 U.Chi.L.Rev. 351 (1978); Polinsky, Economic Analysis as a Potentially Defective Product: A Buyer's Guide to Posner's Economic Analysis of Law, 87 Harv.L.Rev. 1655 (1974); Barton, The Economic Basis of Damages for Breach of Contract, 1 J.Leg.Studies 277 (1972); Birmingham, Breach of Contract, Damage Measures, and Economic Efficiency, 24 Rutgers L.Rev. 273 (1970).

PROBLEM: THE PORTRAIT CONTRACT

The Anderson family wished to have individual portraits painted for each of seven family members. The portraits were wanted as an integral set with similar style and design so that they may be hung as a group on the living room wall. Cavender, a locally well-known artist, was sought for the job. They contracted to have the seven portraits painted for a total of $14,000. By custom the parties expected Cavender to furnish all supplies.

The Andersons became dissatisfied with Cavender after the completion of two of the portraits. The work was progressing much more slowly than they had been led to expect, and they did not find the two finished portraits sufficiently flattering. They notified Cavender that they did not want to continue the contract. No money had been paid at that point except a $1000 advance, and the Andersons refused to pay any more.

Cavender had expended $300 on each of the two portraits on supplies. The overhead costs in running the commercial studio add another $200 in expenditures attributable to painting each of these portraits.

The Andersons turned the unwanted portraits over to an art auctioneer for sale. An out-of-town art collector who was intrigued by Cavender's refreshing and honest portrait style bid up the price on each. The collector ultimately paid $7000 for one of the portraits and $9000 for the other. The auctioneer's commission was $1600, so the Andersons netted $14,400 from this sale.

Cavender sues the Andersons. Assuming the court decides that the contract did not require the satisfaction of the Andersons, what should be the measure of damages for their breach? If Cavender enters into a contract to paint portraits for another family for $10,000 shortly after the Andersons breach, should that affect the measure of Cavender's damages? Does Cavender have any duty to seek out another contract? If Cavender does not seek out another contract, should Cavender be entitled to recover the full profit on the contract with the Andersons?

The doctrine of avoidable consequences, which is examined more fully in Chapter 13, obligates the non-breaching party to a contract to take reasonable steps to avoid the losses caused by the breach. In the employment setting, if an employer wrongfully discharges an employee, the employee is required to take reasonable steps to secure substitute employment. The employee's damages will be limited to the difference between the salary the employee would have earned from the contract with the employer and the salary the employee will or could have earned from substitute employment. Difficult issues arise when an employee can perform contracts with several employers simultaneously.

For example, in Gianetti v. Norwalk Hospital, 266 Conn. 544, 833 A.2d 891 (2003), a surgeon sued a hospital after the hospital wrongfully failed to renew his staff privileges. The surgeon held staff privileges at four other hospitals at the same time and earned more income in the year following his termination than he had earned the last year he held privileges at the defendant hospital. The hospital contended that under the avoidable consequences doctrine, the surgeon was required to offset the earnings he made from surgeries performed at other hospitals against the income he lost from surgeries he was unable to perform at the defendant hospital and, thus he had no damages as a result of the breach. On appeal, the Connecticut Supreme Court concluded that the avoidable consequences doctrine would not require the surgeon to offset his income from the other hospitals if the surgeon could prove that he would have been able to perform the surgeries at the other hospitals even if he had remained on staff at the defendant hospital. The court recognized this as the common law analog to the lost volume seller doctrine discussed in the next section of this chapter.

Gruber v. S–M News Company

126 F.Supp. 442 (S.D.N.Y.1954).

■ MURPHY, DISTRICT JUDGE.

[Plaintiffs] seek damages for breach of contract. Plaintiffs allege * * * that a contract between them and defendant was made [whereby plaintiffs] promised to manufacture in conformity with samples approved by defendant, 90,000 sets of twelve Christmas greeting cards for the impending Christmas season; to pack every set in a box of design approved by defendant and be ready for shipment to a list of wholesalers to be furnished by defendant not later than the second week in October; to give defendant exclusive sale and distribution rights to these sets. According to plaintiffs' complaint, in consideration of their promises, defendant bound itself to exercise reasonable diligence to sell all of the sets and use its resources for scientific sales promotion, national advertising, newsstand outlets and sales organization. Defendant further agreed, plaintiffs claim, to pay eighty-four cents for each set f.o.b. its wholesalers' respective places of business where, according to defendant's regular checkup, the cards had been sold at retail. Credit was to be allowed for all sets returned to plaintiffs unsold. It is further alleged that plaintiffs manufactured and packed the sets in accordance with the agreement, notified the defendant to this effect on October 2, 1945, and that defendant then refused its promised performance. Damages for $101,800 are demanded.

* * *

For breach of a contract of exclusive distribution and return, plaintiffs should be entitled to damages measured by the difference between what they actually obtained for their cards and what they would have obtained had defendant exercised its promised reasonable diligence. On this, plaintiffs have the burden of proof to the extent of a reasonably certain and definite factual basis of computation. Under the evidence, such basis in this case is too speculative for an award in a sum certain. The past experience of the defendant in distribution of a high proportion of jig-saw puzzles, maps and cleaning fluids is hardly a basis for prophecy with respect to Christmas cards. And a single retailer's opinion that he would have disposed of 50 boxes of the cards is a precarious foundation for generalization with respect to 90,000 such boxes. Accordingly, plaintiffs have not sustained their burden of proof with respect to their expectation under the breached agreement.

However, alternative to damages for loss of their expectation, plaintiffs have demanded at the close of trial at least their out-of-pocket expenses. The basis for these damages is not plaintiffs' expectation of profits but rather their expenditures made in "essential reliance" upon defendant's promise. Defendant, for its part, insists that there can be no recovery upon this theory of essential reliance because there would have been a loss to plaintiffs had defendant fully performed its promise of distribution.

The few cases in point in New York are apparently not entirely in accord with respect to the relationship between anticipated loss in event of full performance by the defendant, on one hand, and a plaintiff's recovery of his out-of-pocket expenses in reliance on defendant's unperformed promise, on the other. There are situations where there is no such relationship, and a plaintiff may recover his expenditures in reliance upon defendant's promise without regard to profit if that promise had been fully performed by defendant, as in actions for restitution and ones based upon fraud. The Restatement has suggested that if full performance by defendant would have resulted in loss to a plaintiff, then this loss must be deducted from plaintiff's expenditures. * * *

We accept as the rule that plaintiffs' recovery for their out-of-pocket expenses must be diminished by any loss that would result from defendant's full performance. We are not persuaded that defendant has established the probability of such loss. True plaintiffs were able to obtain merely six cents per box on a sale of 40,000 boxes in 1949, rather than the promised eighty-four cents for sale in 1945 under their agreement with defendant. But the Christmas cards had a novelty appeal, designed as they were to exploit a dozen different nations at the time of the newly-formed United Nations in 1945. The glamour of the caricatures may well have been clouded by the worsening world situation that gathered in the succeeding years.

The burden of proving loss in event of performance properly rests on the defendant who by its wrong has made the question relevant to the rights of the plaintiffs. We do not find that defendant has sustained this burden.

Only the amount of plaintiffs' expenditures reasonably made in performance of the contract or in necessary preparation therefore, may be recovered. This does not include, as plaintiffs have requested, the cost of making the plates from which the cards were printed since these had already been fabricated prior to making the contract with defendant. The amount of plaintiffs' expenditures for labor and material reasonably made in essential reliance on defendant's promise was $19,934.44. From this sum must be deducted the *net* amount realized by plaintiffs from sale of 40,000 sets at six cents a set which was $2,080. Accordingly plaintiffs are entitled to $17,854.44 in damages.

Judgment accordingly.

---

1. *The Reliance Alternative.* In the principal case, the manufacturer's expectancy interest for breach of the exclusive distributorship agreement would have been measured by the difference in value between the performance promised by the defendant and that which was actually received. However, since the plaintiff could not sustain its burden of proof on expectancy damages with reasonable certainty, the alternative measure of reliance damages was sought. The reliance damages often will be less than the expectancy damages because the profit of the non-breaching party is not included. Moreover, the recovery is further reduced to the extent that the breaching party can prove the plaintiff would have sustained losses in the event of full performance. How difficult would it be for the defendant to demonstrate such losses would have resulted? What information would be relevant as evidence on the issue of the plaintiff's potential losses?

2. *Losing Contract.* Courts will limit the amount of reliance damages recoverable not to exceed the contract price. The rationale for such a limitation is that expenses incurred above the contract price certainly would have been losses sustained by the plaintiff, and therefore are properly deducted from the total recovery.

3. *Essential Reliance.* The court in the principal case awarded damages for "essential" reliance. These damages typically include expenses incurred in preparation for performance or in the actual performance of the contract. "Incidental" reliance damages, in contrast, may be described as expenditures made in preparing for collateral transactions apart from the contract.

The difference in classification may be seen in cases involving new business ventures. For example, assume that O entered into a contract with the XYZ Construction Company to build a restaurant. If O breached the contract after XYZ had partly performed, the builder could recover as essential reliance damages the expenditures made in preparing to perform and in commencing performance. If, on the other hand, the builder breached the contract, purchases made by O toward furnishing the restaurant would be characterized as incidental reliance. The significance of the distinction lies in the role that foreseeability plays as a limitation on incidental reliance damages. *See generally* Fuller and Perdue, The Reliance Interest in Contract Damages, 46 Yale L.J. 52 (1936).

Johnson v. Penny

779 N.W.2d 412 (S.D. 2010).

■ KONENKAMP, JUSTICE

In this breach of contract, conversion, and unjust enrichment case, the circuit court held that defendants were unjustly enriched by plaintiff's services, after a jury rendered a verdict in favor of defendants on plaintiff's breach of contract and conversion claims. On appeal, we reverse the court's damages award against one defendant because two express contracts govern the rights between that defendant and plaintiff. In regard to the defendant with no express contractual relationship with plaintiff, we affirm the court's finding of unjust enrichment, but reverse and remand for a proper calculation of damages.

In early March 2005, Michael Johnson and Robert Larson entered into an oral contract whereby Johnson agreed to remove rock from Larson's farmland in exchange for Johnson receiving the value of the rock removed. Larson is a retired farmer who owns farm and pasture land near Madison, South Dakota. Johnson operates Michael Johnson Construction and owns two mining pits, one east, and one west, of Madison. Shortly after Johnson began removing rock from Larson's land, the two entered into a second oral agreement. In exchange for Johnson's right to keep the excavated rock extracted from Larson's land, Johnson agreed to install drain tile in a low lying area of Larson's farmland.

From March 16, 2005 through April 15, 2005, Johnson removed rock from Larson's land. He also installed drain tile. Johnson claimed that he extracted approximately 1,100 tons of rock. Of that amount, Johnson only removed between three to five semi-truck loads from Larson's land. The rest Johnson stored on Larson's land to the west of Larson's home, for removal at a later date. According to Johnson, Larson permitted him to store the rocks on his land until Johnson needed them.

Joel Penny is a farmer in Decatur, Nebraska. While visiting Flandreau in July 2006, Penny learned that Larson had rock on his land that he wanted removed. Penny contacted Larson. Larson informed Penny that he and Johnson had previously agreed that Johnson would remove the rock from his land. Larson told Penny that after excavating the rock, Johnson had not come back to actually remove the rock he had stockpiled since the spring of 2005. Larson told Penny that he had inquired several times about when Johnson intended to remove the stockpiles. Larson also told Penny that he would contact Johnson to ask whether Johnson intended on removing the rock.

In August 2006, Penny again contacted Larson about removing the rock. Larson believed Johnson had no intention of removing the stockpiled rock, based on the fact he had not heard from Johnson, even after leaving his number with Johnson's bookkeeper. Ultimately, Larson gave Penny permission to remove the rock. Penny paid Larson nothing for the rock. He removed approximately 50 semi-truck loads from Larson's land. Penny estimated that he took approximately 25 loads from the rock pile stocked by Johnson.

In October 2006, Johnson learned that his rock piles were no longer on Larson's land. He sent an invoice to Larson on October 24, 2006, for his services in excavating and removing the rock. Johnson also included an invoice for the installation of the drain tile. He enclosed a letter with the invoices reminding Larson of the parties' oral agreement that Johnson was to receive the rocks in exchange for clearing them from Larson's land. Larson neither responded to the letter nor paid the invoice.

On January 11, 2007, Johnson brought suit against Larson for breach of contract, conversion, restitution, constructive trust, and unjust enrichment. He amended his complaint in April 2007, to include Penny as a defendant and removed the restitution cause of action. A jury trial was held November 17 through November 20, 2008, on the breach of contract and conversion claims. The jury returned a verdict in favor of Larson and Penny. On January 8, 2009, a hearing was held in the circuit court to consider Johnson's equitable claims. On May 13, 2009, the court entered a judgment against Larson and Penny jointly and severally. The court concluded that Larson and Penny were unjustly enriched by the labor, equipment, and materials provided by Johnson for the removal of the rock. The court further concluded that Larson was unjustly enriched by the labor, equipment, and materials provided for the installation of drain tile. On appeal, Larson and Penny assert that the court erred when it concluded that they were unjustly enriched by Johnson.

Penny and Larson claim, among other things, that because the jury rendered a verdict against Johnson on his breach of contract and conversion claims, the court erred in allowing Johnson unjust enrichment damages on the same facts. We recently held that the equitable remedy of unjust enrichment is unwarranted when the rights of the parties are controlled by an express contract. [Citation.] Unjust enrichment contemplates an involuntary or nonconsensual transfer, unjustly enriching one party. The equitable remedy of restitution is imposed because the transfer lacks an adequate legal basis.

When there is a valid and enforceable contract, however, liability for compensation or other resolution of the breach is fixed exclusively by the contract. [Citations.] In the contract framework, benefits are voluntarily conferred and transfers are consensual.

No one disputes that Johnson and Larson entered into two valid and enforceable contracts. The first permitted Johnson to remove rock from Larson's farmland in exchange for Johnson receiving the value of the rock removed. The second permitted Johnson to remove rock and receive the value of that rock in exchange for installing drain tile on Larson's land. Because there existed two express contracts, and the benefit conferred on Larson was specified as part of the parties' contracts, Johnson had a valid remedy at law. *See* Restatement (Third) Restitution § 2 (unjust enrichment can apply in a contract context when the performance received was not specified by the contract). Johnson voluntarily and consensually conferred the benefit of drain tile and rock removal to Larson as part of the parties' valid and enforceable contracts. Therefore, there was no room for a court to imply a promise by Larson to pay Johnson, as the parties expressly fixed their rights and obligations: Johnson's remedy lay in a claim for breach of contract. The court erred when it acted in equity to impose restitution against Larson.

As between Johnson and Penny, however, there was no express contract controlling the parties' relationship. Therefore, an equitable remedy was available. To prevail on a claim for unjust enrichment, Johnson was required to prove that Penny received a benefit, Penny was aware he was receiving a benefit, and it would be inequitable to allow Penny to retain the benefit without paying for it. Here, the court found that Penny received the benefit of Johnson's excavation services. The court further found that Penny was aware he was receiving the benefit. Larson had told Penny that the rock was removed and stored by Johnson as part of an agreement between Johnson and Larson. Finally, the court concluded that it would be inequitable to allow Penny to retain the benefit of Johnson's services without having to pay for them.

The transfer between Johnson and Penny is the very type of event contemplated by the doctrine of unjust enrichment. Johnson expended many hours and employed the use of expensive heavy machinery to excavate tons of rock from Larson's land. He stored the rock to be removed at a later date. It was not left for anyone's taking. Penny was aware of Johnson's efforts and removed and retained the rock without Johnson's knowledge or consent. The transfer of Johnson's efforts and Johnson's rock to Penny was involuntary and nonconsensual. Also, because there was no express contract between Johnson and Penny, Johnson had no remedy at law to recover for the rock removed. Thus, based on our review of the record, there was ample support for the court to find that Penny was unjustly enriched by Johnson's efforts.

What is the appropriate measure of damages when one is unjustly enriched by another's efforts? According to Penny, the proper measure of restitution for an unjust enrichment claim is the value to the person receiving the benefit rather than the cost to the person providing it. Relying on the doctrine of quantum meruit, Johnson argues that when one benefits by the labor and materials of another the proper measure of restitution is the reasonable value of labor and materials furnished. [Citation.] In the circuit court's view, Johnson was entitled to the reasonable value of labor and materials he provided to Penny. In reaching this conclusion, the court held that "[q]uantum meruit is an equitable remedy to provide restitution for unjust enrichment."

While unjust enrichment and quantum meruit are similarly based on an inequity in allowing a person to retain a benefit without having to pay for it, the two doctrines are not interchangeable. [Citations.] Quantum meruit implies a contract where none exists and awards restitution for the value of the services provided under that implied contract. To recover under quantum meruit, the plaintiff must prove, among other things, that the defendant requested the plaintiff's services and the plaintiff reasonably expected to be paid. [Citations.] Further, damages may be awarded even if the plaintiff's services conferred no benefit.

Unjust enrichment, on the other hand, allows an award of restitution for the value of the benefit unjustly received, rather than the value of the service provided. The defendant must be unjustly *enriched*. However, the

Quantum meruit vs. unjust enrichment

reasonable cost of the services provided can be evidence of the value of the benefit conferred. [Citations.]

Here, there was no basis to find an implied contract between Johnson and Penny. As the court recognized, Johnson was unaware that Penny removed the rock. Moreover, neither Johnson nor Penny were wrongdoers: the court found that Penny had no intent to deprive Johnson of the value of his rock. Therefore, although the court was correct in finding that Penny was unjustly enriched, it erred when it further held that quantum meruit was the proper remedy to provide Johnson restitution. The proper measure of damages in this case is the benefit conferred on Penny.

In summary, the court erred when it acted in equity to impose a judgment against Larson for unjust enrichment when two valid and enforceable contracts controlled the parties' relationship and a jury had previously found for Larson on Johnson's breach of contract claim. The court did not abuse its discretion when it found that Penny was unjustly enriched by Johnson's services. But the court erred when it applied the remedy of quantum meruit to an unjust enrichment claim. Accordingly, we reverse the court's judgment against Larson, affirm the court's finding of unjust enrichment against Penny, and remand for the court to determine the proper measure of damages against Penny consistent with this opinion.

Affirmed in part, reversed in part, and remanded.

---

1. The Restatement (Third) of Restitution and Unjust Enrichment (2011) states in § 1:

> A person who is unjustly enriched at the expense of another is subject to liability in restitution.

The Reporter's Comment to that section notes:

> Liability in restitution derives from the receipt of a benefit whose retention without payment would result in the unjust enrichment of the defendant at the expense of the claimant. While the paradigm case of unjust enrichment is one in which the benefit on one side of the transaction corresponds to an observable loss on the other, the consecrated formula "at the expense of another" can also mean "in violation of the other's legally protected rights," without the need to show that the claimant has suffered a loss. See § 3. The usual consequence of a liability in restitution is that the defendant must restore the benefit in question or its traceable product, or else pay money in the amount necessary to eliminate unjust enrichment.
>
> The identification of unjust enrichment as an independent basis of liability in common-law legal systems—comparable in this respect to a liability in contract or tort—was the central achievement of the 1937 Restatement of Restitution. That conception of the subject is carried forward here. The use of the word "restitution" to describe the cause of action as well as the remedy is likewise inherited from the original

Restatement, despite the problems this usage creates. There are cases in which the essence of a plaintiff's right and remedy is the reversal of a transfer, and thus a literal "restitution," without regard to whether the defendant has been enriched by the transfer in question. Conversely, there are cases in which the remedy for unjust enrichment gives the plaintiff something—typically, the defendant's wrongful gain—that the plaintiff did not previously possess. The Restatement (Third) of Restitution and Unjust Enrichment § 1, comment a (2011).

2.   The Restatement (Third) of Restitution and Unjust Enrichment (2011) attempts to resolve some of the confusion by delineating separately the principles governing restitution that is based on unjust enrichment and restitution that is based on an enforceable contract. Principles governing restitution for unjust enrichment appear in sections 31–36. Principles governing restitution for breach of an enforceable contract appear in sections 37–38 and are expressly termed "restitutionary remedies for breach of an enforceable contract." Finally, section 39 proposes a remedy for "opportunistic breach" that would permit a plaintiff to disgorge the profit a defendant earns from certain breaches of contract. *See* Joseph M. Perillo, Restitution in a Contractual Context and the Restatement (Third) of Restitution & Unjust Enrichment, 68 Wash. & Lee L. Rev. 1007 (2011).

B.   SALE OF GOODS CONTRACTS

Section Coverage:

The damages remedies with respect to contracts for the sale of goods are governed by Article 2 of the Uniform Commercial Code. The remedies available to non-breaching buyers mirror in large part those available to non-breaching sellers. An aggrieved buyer may make a reasonable purchase of substitute goods and recover damages measured by the excess of the cost to cover and the contract price, plus any incidental or consequential damages less expenses saved. [*See* U.C.C. § 2–712]. If the buyer declines to purchase replacement goods, the same formula for calculating damages is used by substituting the market price at the time the buyer learned of the breach for the market price actually paid when effecting cover. [*See* U.C.C. § 2–713]. If the buyer chooses to accept the goods, then damages may be recovered for the difference between the value as promised and the value of the goods as accepted. [*See* U.C.C. § 2–714].

Similarly, a seller may seek either the contract price minus the market price at the time and place for tender under U.C.C. § 2–708(1), or the difference in the contract price less the resale price (equivalent to buyer's cover) under U.C.C. § 2–706. Although sellers are not entitled to consequential damages, they may recover lost profits and reasonable overhead if the ordinary measure of damages under § 2–708(1) is "inadequate to put the seller in as good a position as performance." [*See* U.C.C. § 2–708(2)]. The seller may also be entitled to incidental damages, such as expenses incurred in transportation or storage of the goods, with an adjustment for expenses saved as a result of the buyer's breach.

Finally, Article 2 provides buyers and sellers with corresponding remedies of rescission and restitution [U.C.C. §§ 2–702, 2–711] and specific performance (action for the price) [U.C.C. §§ 2–716, 2–709, respectively]. The remedies are considered cumulatively available to the non-breaching party, as the U.C.C. rejects the election of remedies doctrine "as a fundamental policy." [U.C.C. § 2–703, comment 1].

Model Case:

On January 1, Jones contracts to purchase 1,000 widgets from Widget Co. for $1.00 each, and makes a $200 down payment with the balance due at the time of the scheduled delivery on March 1. On February 1, Widget Co. notifies Jones that it is repudiating the contract because the current market value of widgets has skyrocketed to $1.30 each.

Jones "covers" by purchasing substitute widgets on the open market for $1.30 each and also incurs $250 expenses for transportation and storage in connection with the transaction. Assuming that Widget Co. breached the contract without a legally recognized excuse, Jones may claim damages against Widget Co. in the amount of $750. These damages reflect: (a) multiplication of 1,000 times the market price in effecting cover ($1.30) less the contract price ($1.00) = $300 (following U.C.C. § 2–712(2)); (b) the $250 additional expenses as "incidental" damages under U.C.C. § 2–715(1); and (c) restitution of the down payment of $200 pursuant to U.C.C. § 2–711(1).

1.   BUYER'S REMEDIES

Wilson v. Hays

544 S.W.2d 833 (Tex.Civ.App.1976).

■ JAMES, JUSTICE.

This is a suit by the buyer against the seller for breach of an oral contract to sell and deliver used bricks. Trial was had to a jury, which rendered a verdict favorable to the Plaintiff buyer, pursuant to which verdict the trial court entered judgment. We affirm in part and reverse and render in part.

Plaintiff–Appellee W.D. Hays was in the business of buying and selling used building materials. Defendant–Appellant Bobby Wilson doing business as Wilson Salvage Co. was in the business of wrecking or demolishing buildings. * * * Hays and Wilson entered into an oral agreement whereby Wilson agreed to sell and deliver 600,000 used uncleaned bricks to Hays at a price of one cent per brick, and Hays agreed to buy said bricks at said price. Hays paid Wilson $6,000.00 in advance. Wilson delivered the uncleaned brick to a designated area where Hays had people hired to clean and stack the brick. Wilson delivered a lesser number of brick than 600,000, thereby precipitating this suit.

Plaintiff–Appellee Hays brought this suit for the return of the proportionate part of the purchase price paid for the bricks he did not get, plus
damages. In answer to special issues the jury found:

(1) That Bobby Wilson orally agreed with Hays that he, Bobby Wilson,
would sell and deliver to Hays at least 600,000 bricks at a price of one cent
per brick; * * *

(6) That Bobby Wilson did not deliver 600,000 uncleaned bricks to
Hays (but)

(6A) delivered only 400,000 bricks to Hays;

(7) The market value of used bricks in Midland, Texas in April 1972,
was five cents per brick;

(8) Hays suffered lost profits in the amount of $6250.00 by virtue of
the failure of Bobby Wilson to deliver to Hays at least 600,000 bricks;

(9) That Hays saved $2605.00 in expenses in consequence of the
failure of Bobby Wilson to deliver to him (Hays) at least 600,000 bricks.

Pursuant to the jury verdict, the trial court entered judgment in favor
of Plaintiff Hays against Defendant Bobby Wilson in the amount of
$13,645.00, plus accrued interest at 6% per annum from and after May 15,
1972, up to Jan. 27, 1976, same being the date of the trial court's judgment,
plus interest at 9% per annum from and after the date of said judgment.
From this judgment, Defendant Wilson appeals.

* * * [Appellant] challenges the $13,645.00 judgment upon the ground,
among other things, that there is no evidence to support the jury's findings
in answer to Special Issues No. 8 (lost profits) and No. 9 (expenses). We
sustain these points of error insofar as they assert no evidence to support
the jury's findings concerning lost profits less expenses, and in all other
respects we overrule such points.

Plaintiff–Appellee Hays's remedies and measures of damages as a
buyer of goods in the case at bar are governed by Sections 2.711, 2.712,
2.713, and 2.715 of the Texas Business and Commerce Code. We herewith
quote the portions of said sections that bear upon the case at bar:

"*Sec. 2.711.   Buyer's Remedies in General;* * * *.

"(a) Where the seller fails to make delivery or repudiates * * * the
buyer may cancel and whether or not he has done so may in addition to
recovering so much of the price as has been paid

"(1) 'cover' and have damages under the next section as to all the
goods affected whether or not they have been identified to the contract; or

"(2) recover damages for non-delivery as provided in this chapter
(Section 2.713)."

* * *

"*Section 2.712.   'Cover'; Buyer's Procurement of Substitute Goods*

"(a) After a breach within the preceding section the buyer may 'cover'
by making in good faith and without unreasonable delay any reasonable

purchase of or contract to purchase goods in substitution for those due from the seller.

"(b) The buyer may recover from the seller as damages the difference between the cost of cover and the contract price together with any incidental or consequential damages as hereinafter defined (Section 2.715), but less expenses saved in consequence of the seller's breach.

"(c) Failure of the buyer to effect cover within this section does not bar him from any other remedy."

"Section 2.713.   Buyer's Damages for Non–Delivery or Repudiation

"(a) * * * the measure of damages for non-delivery or repudiation by the seller is the difference between the market price at the time when the buyer learned of the breach and the contract price together with any incidental and consequential damages provided in this chapter (Sec. 2.715), but less expenses saved in consequence of the seller's breach."

* * *

"Section 2.715.   Buyer's Incidental and Consequential Damages

"(a) Incidental damages * * * (not applicable).

"(b) Consequential damages resulting from the seller's breach include

"(1) any loss resulting from general or particular requirements and needs of which the seller at the time of contracting had reason to know and which could not reasonably be prevented by cover or otherwise; * * *."

Let us analyze the verdict and judgment in the light of the foregoing statutory provisions. In the first place, it is established that Plaintiff Hays paid $6000.00 for 600,000 used brick at the rate of one cent per brick, whereas he received only 400,000 brick. Therefore he paid $2000 for 200,000 brick that he never got, and he is thereby entitled to recover $2000.00 under Section 2.711 for "recovering so much of the price as has been paid."

Next, under Section 2.713, he is entitled to damages for "non-delivery or repudiation," and here his measure of damages is the difference between the market price and the contract price. The contract price of the 200,000 brick not delivered is established at $2000.00. The market price at the appropriate time and place of the undelivered brick was five cents per brick or $10,000.00. This jury finding of market value (five cents per brick) although challenged by Appellant for legal and factual insufficiency, is amply supported by the evidence and is well within the range of probative testimony. Therefore under Section 2.713 and appropriate jury findings, Plaintiff is entitled to $8000.00 damages (or $10,000.00 market price less $2000.00 contract price) for non-delivery.

Now we come to the problem of "consequential damages * * * less expenses saved in consequence of the seller's breach" as mentioned in Sec. 2.713 and which damages are provided for in Sec. 2.715. As stated, the jury found Hays sustained lost profits of $6250.00 (Special Issue No. 8) and saved $2605.00 expenses (No. 9), thereby suffering a lost profits net of

$3645.00, which last-named amount was included in the $13,645.00 judgment total. This $3645.00 lost profits amount has no support in the evidence. Under Sec. 2.715, "consequential damages" includes "any loss * * * which could not reasonably be prevented by cover or otherwise." There is no evidence in the record whatever that Plaintiff Hays at any time made any effort to cover or in any other manner attempt to prevent or mitigate a loss resulting from the Defendant Wilson's non-delivery of the 200,000 brick in question. In the absence of such a showing these consequential damages are unauthorized under Section 2.715. The burden of proving the extent of loss incurred by way of consequential damage is on the buyer. [Citations.] This being so, we are of the opinion that there is no evidence to support these jury findings concerning consequential damages, and that the trial court's judgment insofar as it awarded Plaintiff Hays $3645.00 lost profits is improper and this amount should be deleted from said judgment.

As stated before, the judgment is proper and should be affirmed for the amount of $10,000.00, same being composed of $2000.00 paid by Plaintiff for which he received no bricks plus $8000.00 damages for non-delivery. * * *

1. *Expectancy Interest.* The Uniform Commercial Code, like the common law, attempts to protect the expectancy interests of non-breaching parties. The damages remedy attempts to place non-breaching parties in the same position they would have occupied but for the breach.

The buyer's expectancy interest is compensated with three principal elements of damages: (1) contract-market differential damages; (2) incidental losses incurred in reasonable efforts to avoid losses occasioned by the breach; and (3) consequential losses reasonably foreseeable by the breaching party, including items such as lost profits.

Contract-market differential damages are measured differently depending upon whether the buyer accepts non-conforming goods or whether the seller fails to deliver goods or anticipatorily repudiates the contract. When the buyer accepts non-conforming goods, the buyer's contract-market differential damages are measured by the difference between the value of the goods as accepted and the value of the goods as warranted. When the seller anticipatorily repudiates the contract or fails to deliver goods, the buyer's contract-market differential damages are measured in one of two different ways. If the buyer purchases reasonable substitute goods, in other words, if the buyer "covers," the buyer may recover the difference between the cover price and the contract price. If, however, the buyer does not cover, the buyer may recover the difference between the market price at the time that the buyer learned of the breach and the contract price.

2. *Goods that Fluctuate in Value.* A particularly troublesome problem is the determination of the appropriate time to measure a buyer's damages when the seller has anticipatorily repudiated a contract and the buyer does

not cover. This determination is most significant when market prices for the goods are fluctuating. In a rising market the determination may significantly affect the size of the buyer's damage award and also may provide an incentive to the seller to repudiate or a disincentive to the buyer to cover.

The version of section 2–713 currently enacted in most states provides that the damages for a seller's repudiation are calculated at the time the buyer "learned of the breach." Courts and commentators interpret this phrase in three ways in this context. First, some courts hold that a buyer learns of the breach when the seller anticipatorily repudiates. *See, e.g.,* Fredonia Broad. Corp. v. RCA Corp., 481 F.2d 781 (5th Cir.1973); Farmers Comm'n Co. v. Burks, 130 Ohio App.3d 158, 719 N.E.2d 980 (1998); Palmer v. Idaho Peterbilt, Inc., 102 Idaho 800, 641 P.2d 346 (1982).

Second, some courts and commentators have suggested that a buyer "learns of the breach" at the time at which the contract called for delivery. *See, e.g.,* Cargill, Inc. v. Stafford, 553 F.2d 1222 (10th Cir.1977) (damages should be measured from the time performance is due unless cover is readily available at the time of repudiation); 1 James J. White & Robert S. Summers, Uniform Commercial Code § 6–7 (4th ed. 1995). These courts and commentators argue, in part, that this reading is more consistent with other Code provisions and gives meaning to the entire Code. For example, section 2–708 measures the seller's market damages for repudiation as the difference between the contract price and the market price at the time and place for tender. Measuring the buyer's damages at the time for performance would make the buyer's damages mirror the seller's damages. Also, section 2–723 expressly provides that if an action based on anticipatory repudiation comes to trial before the time for performance, the market price shall be measured as the market price at the time of repudiation. Courts and commentators reason that if "learned of the breach" meant the time of repudiation, section 2–723 would be meaningless.

Finally, some courts hold that the buyer's damages should be measured at the expiration of some commercially reasonable period after the seller repudiates. This reading is consistent with Section 2–610 which allows the buyer to await the repudiating seller's performance despite the repudiation but to do so for a commercially reasonable time only. As the Fifth Circuit explained in Cosden Oil v. Karl O. Helm Aktiengesellschaft, 736 F.2d 1064 (5th Cir.1984), the commercially reasonable time approach also attempts to balance competing concerns about the seller's incentive to repudiate and the buyer's disincentive to cover. In *Cosden Oil*, the court observed:

> Typically, [the] question will arise where the parties to an executory contract are in the midst of a rising market. To the extent that market decisions are influenced by a damages rule, measuring market price at the time of seller's repudiation gives seller the ability to fix buyer's damages and may induce seller to repudiate rather than abide by the contract. By contrast, measuring buyer's damages at the time of performance will tend to dissuade the buyer from covering, in the

hopes that the market price will continue upward until performance time.

Allowing the aggrieved buyer a commercially reasonable time, however, provides him with an opportunity to investigate his cover possibilities in a rising market without fear that, if he is unsuccessful in obtaining cover, he will be relegated to a market-contract damage remedy measured at the time of repudiation. * * *

Article 2 of the Code was revised in 2003. Among other revisions, section 2–713 was revised to expressly adopt the commercially reasonable time approach. Under the revisions, section 2–713(2) provides:

> the measure of damages for repudiation by the seller is the difference between the market price at the expiration of a commercially reasonable time after the buyer learned of the repudiation * * * together with any incidental or consequential provided in this Article (Section 2–710), but less expenses saved in consequence of the seller's breach.

As of 2012, no states have adopted this revision. *See* Uniform Law Commissioners: The National Conference of Commissioners on Uniform State Laws,http://www.nccusl.org/Act.aspx?title=UCC Article 2, Sales and Article 2A, Leases (2003).

3. *Cover Damages.* One of the significant ways in which the Code differs from the common law is the allowance of cover damages. The Code, unlike the common law, expressly permits an aggrieved buyer to effectuate cover by purchasing goods in substitute for those due under the contract. When the buyer covers, it may recover the difference between the cost of cover and the contract price even if the cover price differs from the market price. In making cover, the buyer must act in good faith and without unreasonable delay. The Code does not require the buyer to purchase goods that are identical to those due under the contract. However, the substitute goods must be "likekind substitutes." In other words, the goods must be commercially useable as reasonable substitutes under the circumstances of the particular case. *See* U.C.C. § 2–712 cmt. 2. Whether the goods are reasonable substitutes is a question of fact for the trier of fact, but the buyer must offer sufficient evidence to establish that the goods are reasonable substitutes.

Should a buyer be able to recover the cost of cover if the buyer substitutes with improved goods? Some courts have held that recovery of costs for an improved product depends on the availability of more comparable substitutes. *See, e.g.* Mueller v. McGill, 870 S.W.2d 673 (Tex.App.Ct. 1994) (trial court improperly directed the verdict on the grounds that a 1986 Porsche was not a commercially reasonable substitute for the 1985 Porsche described in the contract where the evidence presented to the jury showed that it was very difficult to obtain a 1985 Porsche so late in the year); Freitag v. Bill Swad Datsun, 3 Ohio App.3d 83, 443 N.E.2d 988 (1981) (plaintiff not entitled to cover damages based on his purchase of a 1980 Datsun when no evidence indicated that the 1979 model for which he contracted was unavailable elsewhere).

4. *Internal Cover.* Should a buyer be able to recover the cost of producing a comparable good in-house? Should the buyer be able to recover damages for the profits it could have made from manufacturing and selling the good to third parties during the time it was manufacturing the good for itself? In Dura–Wood Treating Company v. Century Forest Industries, 675 F.2d 745 (5th Cir.1982), the Fifth Circuit held that a manufacturer-buyer effectuated cover by manufacturing the contracted for goods itself. However, the court noted that internal cover was reasonable because the buyer was already in the marketplace and could produce the goods at a price approximating or lower than market price. Moreover, the court denied the buyer's request for lost "potential profits" from goods it could have made and sold to other customers if it had not had to manufacture the contracted for goods itself. The court observed that while the cost of producing the goods internally was less than the cost to purchase replacement goods on the market, the cost of manufacturing the goods combined with the lost potential profits exceeded the market price of replacement goods. Noting that the seller "should not be obligated to pay for [the buyer's] poor choice," the court reasoned that a different form of cover could have prevented the lost potential profits.

See also Cives Corp. v. Callier Steel Pipe & Tube, 482 A.2d 852 (Me.1984) (buyer was justified in producing goods in-house where buyer did not resort to in-house cover until after conducting a thorough search for an alternate supplier); *but see* Chronister Oil Co. v. Unocal Refining & Mktg., 34 F.3d 462 (7th Cir.1994) (rejecting cover damages where the buyer covered by substituting goods from its own inventory for the goods due under the contract).

Gerwin v. Southeastern Cal. Ass'n of Seventh Day Adventists

14 Cal.App.3d 209, 92 Cal.Rptr. 111 (1971).

■ Tamura, Associate Justice.

Plaintiff brought an action seeking specific performance and damages for breach of an alleged contract for the sale from defendant to plaintiff of certain restaurant and bar equipment. Following a nonjury trial the court found in favor of plaintiff and entered judgment which (1) decreed specific performance, or, in the event defendant fails or is unable to deliver the property, ordered payment of damages in the sum of $15,000 in lieu of specific performance, and (2) awarded plaintiff consequential damages for loss of anticipated profits in the sum of $20,000. Defendant appeals from the judgment.

* * *

The court found that Cunningham's [agent for plaintiff] written bid was received and accepted by defendant; that the bid was definite and certain respecting the items bid upon; * * * that defendant refused to deliver; that plaintiff performed all of the required conditions; * * * that the reasonable value of the equipment as of July 12, 1965, was $25,000; and that plaintiff, in addition, suffered consequential damages of $20,000. The judgment decree ordered specific performance or, in lieu thereof, ordered payment of $25,000, and, in addition, awarded consequential damages of $20,000. Defendant moved for a new trial. The court denied the motion but amended the judgment by reducing the award in lieu of specific performance from $25,000 to $15,000.

[The court concluded that the evidence was sufficient to support the finding that the parties had entered into a contract.] * * *

We next consider the damage issues. As heretofore noted the court awarded $15,000 direct or general damages as an alternative to specific performance and, in addition, $20,000 consequential damages for loss of anticipated profits. Defendant contends that the $15,000 award was excessive and that the award of consequential damages based upon loss of anticipated profits was improper.

* * * Where the seller refuses to deliver, the buyer may "cover" by making, in good faith and without unreasonable delay, a reasonable purchase of goods in substitution for those due from the seller and recover from the seller as damages the difference between the cost of "cover" and the contract price, together with any incidental or consequential damages. (Comm.Code, § 2712.) If the buyer elects not to "cover," he may sue for breach in which event the measure of damages is the difference between market price and the contract price (Comm.Code, § 2713) and any consequential damages "which could not reasonably be prevented by cover or otherwise, * * *" (Comm.Code, § 2715).

Although plaintiff failed to "cover," failure to do so did not bar him from the right to recover damages for the difference between market price and the contract price under section 2713 of the Commercial Code. (Comm. Code, § 2712.)

There was substantial evidence to support the amount of the alternative award of $15,000. Plaintiff testified he had owned and operated bars, was familiar with the cost of bar equipment and cash registers, and that his investigation disclosed that the cost of obtaining "similar type of equipment" ranged from $25,000 to $75,000. His testimony was uncontradicted. Evidence of cost, uncontradicted by other evidence, is sufficient to support a finding of value. * * *

We turn next to the award of $20,000 for consequential damages for loss of anticipated profits.

As noted earlier herein, if a buyer elects not to "cover" and sues for damages for breach, the measure of damages is the difference between market value and the contract price (Comm.Code, § 2713), and any consequential damage "resulting from general or particular requirements and needs of which the seller at the time of contracting had reason to know and which could not reasonably be prevented by cover or otherwise; * * *" (Comm.Code, § 2715.) Paragraph 2 of the Uniform Commercial Code Comment to section 2715 states: "Although the older rule at common law which made the seller liable for all consequential damages of which he had 'reason to know' in advance is followed, the liberality of that rule is modified by refusing to permit recovery unless the buyer could not reasonably have prevented the loss by cover or otherwise. * * * '' Thus, in order to recover consequential damages other than those which could not have been avoided by cover or otherwise, the buyer must have made a good faith attempt to mitigate his losses by "cover." The concept of "cover" thus serves two purposes; it enables the buyer to make reasonable substitute purchases and to recover the cost thereof rather than the difference between market value and contract price and, at the same time, protects the seller from consequential damages which could have been mitigated by the purchase of substitute goods. [Citations.]

In the present case plaintiff did not cover. But it does not follow that he was thereby precluded from recovering consequential damages. Plaintiff was unable to purchase substitute items because of their unavailability at prices within his financial ability. Ordinarily a duty to mitigate does not require an injured party to take measures which are unreasonable or impractical or which require expenditures disproportionate to the loss sought to be avoided or which are beyond his financial means. [Citations.] That principle should govern in determining whether a buyer acted reasonably in failing to cover or otherwise mitigate his losses. [Citation.] In the circumstances here presented plaintiff's failure to purchase substitute goods did not, in and of itself, preclude his recovery of consequential damages. By ordering specific performance, the court impliedly found that after reasonable effort plaintiff was either unable to effect cover or the circumstances reasonably indicated that such effort would be unrewarding. (Comm.Code, § 2716(3).) There was substantial evidence to support such an implied finding.

Nevertheless the evidence in the instant case is insufficient to support the award of damages for loss of prospective profits. The Commercial Code permits recovery of consequential damages for "[a]ny loss resulting from general or particular requirements and needs of which the seller at the time of contracting had reason to know[.] * * * '' (Sec. 2715) Paragraph 3 of Uniform Commercial Code Comment to section 2715 states in part: "Particular needs of the buyer must generally be made known to the seller while general needs must rarely be made known to charge the seller with knowledge." In substance, the section modifies the rule enunciated in Hadley v. Baxendale, 9 Ex. 341, 156 Eng.Rep. 145; the test is one of reasonable foreseeability of probable consequences. [Citations.] Foreseeability, however, is to be determined as of the time the contract was entered into and not as of the time of the breach or some other subsequent event. [Citations.]

In the present case the court found that defendant knew "that plaintiff intended to use the assets to run a restaurant, hotel and cocktail lounge." * * * At the time it accepted the bid, defendant could not reasonably have foreseen the probable consequences of its breach upon plaintiff when it didn't even know it was contracting with him. Although plaintiff made known to defendant his particular need for the equipment when he went to pick up the items on July 12, 1965, knowledge on the part of the seller at the time of breach is insufficient.

Apart from the foregoing, the evidence discloses deficiency in proof of anticipated profits.

It has been frequently stated that if a business is new, it is improper to award damage for loss of profits because absence of income and expense experience renders anticipated profits too speculative to meet the legal standard of reasonable certainty necessary to support an award of such damage. [Citations.] However, the rule is not a hard and fast one and loss of prospective profits may nevertheless be recovered if the evidence shows with reasonable certainty both their occurrence and the extent thereof. [Citations.] In the present case the question is whether the evidence of loss of prospective profits meets that standard.

* * *

[The] evidence fails to measure up to that degree of reasonable certainty required to support the award for loss of anticipated profits. The business being new, plaintiff was obviously unable to produce evidence of operating history of the proposed venture. But neither did he introduce even evidence of operating history of comparable businesses in the locality. Although plaintiff expressed his opinion that the Turners could have paid the $1500 per month rental for the operation of the hotel, bar and restaurant, plaintiff had no prior experience in the operation of a hotel or of a bar in the locality in question. In these circumstances it was speculative and conjectural whether the venture would have generated the business necessary to enable the Turners to pay the $1500 per month.

Moreover, there was no showing that the rental income from the lease would have constituted net profit to plaintiff. Under the terms of the proposed lease plaintiff was required to provide and install the necessary equipment, furniture and furnishings. Amortization of such costs as well as interest on his capital investment, taxes, and cost of maintenance should have been deducted. When loss of anticipated profits is an element of damages, it means net and not gross profits. * * * An award of consequential damages based on loss of anticipated profits, particularly in a new venture, may not be sustained on such evidence.

* * *

For the foregoing reasons that portion of the amended judgment awarding plaintiff $20,000 as consequential damages (Paragraph II of Judgment) is reversed; the remainder of the judgment is affirmed.

———————

1. *Foreseeability.* An aggrieved buyer may recover consequential damages under § 2–715(2) if the seller had reason to know of the buyer's general or particular requirements and needs at the time of contracting,

assuming the losses could not have been prevented by cover or otherwise. The "reason to know" test has two elements: an objective inquiry of what a reasonable person in the seller's position would know and a subjective test of what the seller actually knew. *See* R.I. Lampus Co. v. Neville Cement Products Corp., 474 Pa. 199, 378 A.2d 288 (1977).

The adoption of the reasonable foreseeability test in Section 2–715(2) is a rejection of the so-called tacit agreement test; the latter test required a buyer to prove that the seller specifically contemplated and consciously assumed the risk of consequential damages. Globe Refining Co. v. Landa Cotton Oil Co., 190 U.S. 540, 23 S.Ct. 754, 47 L.Ed. 1171 (1903); Keystone Diesel Engine Co. v. Irwin, 411 Pa. 222, 191 A.2d 376 (1963).

2. *Foreseeability of Amount.* What should be the appropriate measure of damages when the market price of goods changes dramatically? In *Sun–Maid Raisin Growers of California v. Victor Packing Co.*, 146 Cal.App.3d 787, 194 Cal.Rptr. 612 (1983), buyers of raisins sought damages for lost profits from the sellers who failed to deliver the contracted quantity when the market price doubled due to "disastrous" rains which caused a 50 percent crop loss. The sellers claimed that the extraordinarily high price of raisins caused by the destruction of crops was unforeseeable. The court disagreed, holding that the breaching party was not required to foresee the *amount* of lost profits at time of entering contract, only that they objectively contemplated that *some* profits could be lost as consequence of non-performance. Further, the court found that the raisin packers should have understood the risk in contracting to sell raisins at a fixed price over a period of time extending into the next crop year, knowing that the market price could change dramatically based on consumer demand and supply and quality of raisins. The court awarded the buyer lost profits, reasoning that otherwise the seller could effectively speculate on the direction of the market price as compared to the contract price.

3. *Duty to Mitigate.* Consequential damages may be precluded or limited to the extent that the loss could "reasonably be prevented by cover or otherwise." This limitation reflects the principle of mitigation of damages whereby the non-breaching party must take reasonable steps to avoid damages. The buyer need not undertake extraordinary measures in attempting to mitigate, such as incurring substantial expenses or assuming excessive risk.

In *R.E.B., Inc. v. Ralston Purina Co.*, 525 F.2d 749 (10th Cir.1975), a hog farmer sued an animal feed manufacturer for damages for lost profits and diminished value of producing business as result of defective feed which injured or killed numerous animals. The court allowed lost profits for the diminished herd, finding that the farmer satisfied the standard for mitigation by obtaining replacement animals within his financial capability and using reasonable efforts to cull the affected herd.

4. *Mitigation Alternatives.* Cover is not the only mitigating option available to an aggrieved buyer who may want to recover consequential damages. In *Waters v. Massey–Ferguson,* 775 F.2d 587 (4th Cir.1985), a buyer of a defective tractor hired local area farmers to assist in planting his

fields. In several other cases buyers have continued to use the defective goods in order to preserve their rights to consequential damages where replacement goods were not readily available or the buyers could not reasonably effect cover. *See, e.g.,* Chatlos Systems, Inc. v. National Cash Register Corp., 479 F.Supp. 738 (D.N.J.1979); Prutch v. Ford Motor Co., 618 P.2d 657 (Colo.1980).

5. *New Business Rule.* The requirement that damages be established with reasonable certainty has been articulated frequently as a key basis for denying a new or unestablished business any recovery of lost profits for breach of contract. The rationale for precluding recovery simply was the assumption that the lack of sufficient operating history for new businesses necessarily made prospective profits too speculative, contingent, and remote to satisfy the legal standard of reasonable certainty. *See* Thrift Wholesale v. Malkin–Illion Corp., 50 F.Supp. 998, 1000 (E.D.Pa.1943).

This distinction drawn between new business ventures and existing operations for awards of future profits became so prevalent that some courts elevated it to virtually a *per se* rule. *See* Evergreen Amusement Corporation v. Milstead, 206 Md. 610, 112 A.2d 901, 905 (1955) ("While this Court has not laid down a flat rule ... nevertheless, no case has permitted recovery of lost profits under comparable circumstances.") A growing number of courts, however, have recognized no sound policy basis to automatically preclude lost profits solely on the characterization that a "new business" was involved and instead have focused on whether the damages were established by sufficient evidence. These courts acknowledge that a new business faces a greater burden of proof in establishing the loss of anticipated profits but allow the claimant an opportunity to produce evidence to meet the reasonable certainty standard. *See, e.g.,* Handi Caddy, Inc. v. American Home Products Corporation, 557 F.2d 136, 139 (8th Cir.1977). The Restatement (Second) of Contracts § 352 comment b acknowledges this shift in the law by stating that the difficulty of proving lost profits should vary depending upon the nature of the transaction.

Illustrative of the modern trend is *In re Merritt Logan, Inc.*, 901 F.2d 349 (3d Cir.1990), where a buyer of a defective refrigeration system sought lost profits of its grocery store business. The court rejected a *per se* rule against potential recovery of lost profits simply because the business had a brief operating history.

AM/PM Franchise Assn. v. Atlantic Richfield Co.

526 Pa. 110, 584 A.2d 915 (1990).

■ CAPPY, JUDGE.

[ARCO entered into franchise agreements with the plaintiffs to operate mini-markets. The contract mandated that the franchisees sell only ARCO petroleum products. Plaintiffs claimed that many of their customers who purchased an oxinol gasoline blend produced by ARCO experienced various engine problems. The franchisees asserted that they suffered a decline in business and attendant loss of profits as a consequence of the defective gasoline. The plaintiff class sought damages for breach of warranty by ARCO. The Superior Court affirmed the trial court's dismissal of the franchisees' complaint, holding that damages for loss of goodwill in a breach of warranty action were not recoverable.]

The point at which we start our inquiry is the Uniform Commercial Code ("the U.C.C."), codified at 13 Pa.C.S. § 1101 *et seq.* Section 2714, entitled "Damages of buyer for breach in regard to accepted goods" is one of the governing provisions in the case before us, and provides, in pertinent part:

(b) Measure of damages for breach of warranty.—The measure of damages for breach of warranty is the difference at the time and place of acceptance between the value of the goods accepted and the value they would have had if they had been as warranted, unless special circumstances show proximate damages of a different amount.

(c) Incidental and consequential damages.—In a proper case any incidental and consequential damages under section 2715 (relating to incidental and consequential damages of buyer) may also be recovered.

Section 2715 is entitled "Incidental and Consequential Damages of Buyer" and provides, in pertinent part:

(a) Incidental damages.—Incidental damages resulting from the breach of the seller include:

(3) any other reasonable expenses incident to the delay or other breach.

(b) Consequential damages.—Consequential damages resulting from the breach of the seller include:

(1) any loss resulting from general or particular requirements and needs of which the seller at the time of contracting had reason to know and which could not reasonably be prevented by cover or otherwise.

Pursuant to the provisions of the U.C.C., plaintiffs are entitled to seek "general" damages, so-called, under section 2714(b), and consequential damages as provided by section 2714(c).

There has been substantial confusion in the courts and among litigants about what consequential damages actually are and what types of consequential damages are available in a breach of warranty case. Where a buyer in the business of reselling goods can prove that a breach by the seller has caused him to lose profitable resales, the buyer's lost profits constitute a form of consequential damages. We now hold that in addition to general damages, there are three types of lost profit recoverable as consequential damages that may flow from a breach of warranty: (1) loss of primary profits; (2) loss of secondary profits; and (3) a loss of good will damages (or prospective damages, as they are sometimes termed). * * *

General damages in the case of accepted goods (such as occurred here) are the actual difference in value between the goods as promised and the goods as received. Thus, suppose a buyer bought five hundred tires from a wholesaler that were to be delivered in good condition, and in that condition would be worth $2,500. The tires were delivered with holes in them which rendered them worthless. The buyer would be entitled to $2,500 from the seller—the difference between the value of the tires as warranted and the value of the tires as received; those would be the general damages.

Consequential damages are generally understood to be other damages which naturally and proximately flow from the breach and include three types of lost profit damages: (1) lost primary profits; (2) lost secondary profits; and (3) loss of prospective profits, also commonly referred to as good will damages.

Lost primary profits are the difference between what the buyer would have earned from reselling the goods in question had there been no breach and what was earned after the breach occurred. Thus, if the buyer of the tires proved that he would have resold the tires for $5,000, he would be able to claim an additional $2,500 for loss of tire profits; the difference between what he would have earned from the sale of the tires and what he actually did earn from the sale (or lack of sales) from the tires.

If the buyer of the tires also sold, for example, hubcaps with every set of tires, he would also suffer a loss of hubcap profits. These types of damages are what we term "loss of secondary profits."

If the buyer's regular customers were so disgruntled about the defective tires that they no longer frequented the buyer's business and began to patronize a competitor's business, the buyer would have suffered a "loss of good will" beyond the direct loss of profits from the nonconforming goods; his future business would be adversely affected as a result of the defective tires. Thus, good will damages refer to profits lost on future sales rather than on sales of the defective goods themselves. * * *

In addition to recognizing general damages under § 2714 of the Code, Pennsylvania allows consequential damages in the form of lost profits to be recovered. [Citations.]

Pennsylvania has, however, disallowed good will damages; finding them to be too speculative to permit recovery. In the cases disallowing good will damages, part of the reason we found them too speculative is that the damages were not contemplated by the parties at the time the contract was made.

In 1977, this court had occasion to re-examine sections 2714 and 2715 of the Uniform Commercial Code in the case of R.I. Lampus Co. v. Neville Cement Products Corp., 474 Pa. 199, 378 A.2d 288 (1977). Before the *Lampus* case, we required the party seeking consequential damages in the form of lost profits to show that there were "special circumstances" indicating that such damages were actually contemplated by the parties at the time they entered into the agreement. This rule, termed the "tacit-agreement" test, "permit[ed] the plaintiff to recover damages arising from special circumstances only if 'the defendant fairly may be supposed to have assumed consciously, or to have warranted the plaintiff reasonably to suppose that it assumed, [such liability] when the contract was made.'" [Citation.]

In *Lampus*, we overruled the restrictive "tacit agreement" test and replaced it with the "reason to know" test; which requires that "[i]f a seller knows of a buyer's general or particular requirements and needs, that seller is liable for the resulting consequential damages whether or not that seller contemplated or agreed to such damages." *Id.*, 474 Pa. at 209, 378 A.2d at 292 (1977) (emphasis supplied).[6] Thus, in order to obtain consequential damages, the plaintiff need only prove that the damages were reasonably foreseeable at the time the agreement was entered into.

Turning to the case at hand, we must determine whether the plaintiffs have alleged sufficient facts to permit them to proceed with a claim for consequential damages.

* * * [T]he plaintiffs have alleged: that ARCO expressly warranted through its agreements, mailgrams and brochures that its oxinol gasoline was of high quality, better for the environment and would not damage new or older automobiles; that the oxinol gasoline was not merchantable because it damaged engines; that it was not fit for the ordinary purpose for which it was intended; that ARCO knew that the plaintiffs were relying on the skill of the defendants to select or furnish suitable gasoline; that ARCO's actions constituted a breach of express warranties which resulted in harm to the plaintiffs in the form of lost profits, incidental and consequential damages. [The court found that plaintiffs had shown sufficient facts to state a cause of action under the breach of warranty counts.]

The plaintiffs seek lost profits, incidental and consequential damages.[8] The defendants and the lower courts, however, considered these damages to be lost good will. We believe that the lower courts and the defendants are in error in categorizing all the claimed damages as good will damages. * * *

Loss of Profits for Gasoline Sales

The first claim the plaintiff makes for damages is for the profits lost from the sales of gasoline. The plaintiffs claim that the breach of warranty by the defendant concerning the gasoline caused the plaintiffs to lose sales during a three and one half year period while they received nonconforming gasoline from ARCO. In the case of Kassab v. Central Soya, 432 Pa. 217, 246 A.2d 848 (1968), we permitted lost profits for cattle sales when the plaintiff showed that the defective feed caused harm to their cattle, causing the public to stop buying their cattle. The allegation here is similar. When the gasoline buying public discovered that the gasoline was defective, many stopped purchasing ARCO gasoline.

---

6. *Lampus* is in accord with section 2–715 of the U.C.C., comment 2 (1978), which states; "[t]he 'tacit agreement' test for the recovery of consequential damages is rejected."

8. The plaintiffs claim "lost profits, incidental and consequential damages." As we noted herein, however, "lost profits" are a type of consequential damage; not a separate category of damages.

Employing the reasoning of *Kassab* and taking it one step further, we believe that the plaintiffs here are entitled to show that the gasoline buying community did not buy their gasoline from 1982 through 1985 because of the reasonable belief that the gasoline was defective and would harm their engines. The lost gasoline sales are comparable to the lost cattle sales in *Kassab*. The distinction between the two cases is that the Kassabs had bought the feed all at one time and thus all their livestock was affected. The instant plaintiffs bought their gasoline in regular intervals and could only earn a profit on what they could sell per month. The defendant's argument—that the plaintiffs sold all the gasoline they bought—misses the point. While they may have sold every gallon, they sold significantly fewer gallons during the period that ARCO allegedly delivered nonconforming gasoline. Thus, during this period, the plaintiffs' lost sales were just as directly attributable to the defective gasoline as the lost profits were attributable to the defective tires in the example we used previously.[9]

Thus, if prior to the manufacture of defective gasoline the plaintiffs sold 100,000 gallons per month every month and then as a result of the defective gasoline, they sold only 60,000 gallons per month every month until ARCO discontinued that gasoline, then the plaintiffs have lost the profits they would have received on 40,000 gallons per month for the three year claimed period. Lost profits are, in fact, the difference between what the plaintiff actually earned and what they would have earned had the defendant not committed the breach. Because the gasoline was allegedly not in conformance with the warranties, the plaintiffs may be entitled to lost profits for the gasoline on a breach of warranty theory. The lost gasoline sales are what we have termed "loss of primary profits," and they are recoverable pursuant to § 2715 of the U.C.C. upon proper proof.

We note, furthermore, that the remedy of cover was unavailable to the plaintiffs. Section 2715 of the U.C.C. limits a plaintiff's ability to recover when he could have prevented such damage "by cover or otherwise". Pursuant to the code, cover is defined as the buyer's purchase of substitute goods at a commercially reasonable price. The buyer can recover from the seller the difference between the contract price and the cost of goods bought as cover. 13 Pa.C.S. § 2712, defining "cover" and damages recoverable, provides, in pertinent part:

> (a) Right and manner of cover.—After a breach within section 2711 (relating to remedies of buyer in general; security interest of buyer in rejected goods) the buyer may "cover" by making in good faith and without unreasonable delay any reasonable purchase of or contract to purchase goods in substitution for those due from the seller.

---

9. The current case, unlike the tire example, involves a requirements contract rather than a fixed quantity agreement. In a requirement contract, profits lost during the period of time in which the seller supplies nonconforming goods constitute lost primary profits. The Code does not require that the buyer prove he would have purchased the same amount as usually required, for § 2715 permits the buyer to mitigate his damages by "cover or otherwise." Thus the buyer need not buy his usual amount of goods and then be unable to sell them before he can claim a loss of profits.

The plaintiffs here, by their allegations, could not "cover;" they were contractually required to purchase all their gasoline from ARCO. In effect, they had to accept the allegedly nonconforming gasoline and had no possible way to avoid the attendant loss of profits. Thus, since they could not cover, the only remedy that was available to them was to file suit. * * *

The Code itself compels us to be liberal in our interpretation of the types of damages we permit. We would therefore allow the plaintiffs to proceed with their claims for lost gasoline profits during the period ARCO supplied allegedly nonconforming gasoline.

Loss of Profits for Items Other Than Gasoline Sales

The plaintiffs allege that in addition to a loss of profits for sales of gasoline, they had a concomitant loss of sales for other items that they sold in their mini-marts during the period of time that ARCO supplied noncon-forming gasoline. Their rationale is that when the number of customers buying gasoline decreased, so did the number of customers buying items at the mini-mart. In other words, related facets of their business suffered as a result of the defective gasoline. This type of injury is what we characterize as "loss of secondary profits;" meaning that the sales of other products suffered as a result of the breach of warranty.

* * * [T]he essence of plaintiffs' allegations is that customers frequent the mini-marts because it is convenient to do so at the time they purchase gasoline. Customers of the mini-mart are foremost gasoline buying patrons; gasoline is their primary purchase and sundries are their incidental pur-chases. Here, the plaintiffs claim that the primary product sales so affected the incidental sales as to create a loss in other aspects of their business. It is reasonable to assume that if the gasoline sales dropped dramatically, there was a ripple effect on the mini-mart sales. Additionally, when a primary product does not conform to the warranty, we believe that it is foreseeable that there will be a loss of secondary profits. Thus, permitting these damages would correspond with the requirement of foreseeability as set forth in *Lampus*, *supra*, and the Code. It is much less foreseeable to assume there will be a loss of secondary profits when the nonconforming products are not the primary ones. We believe that unless it is a primary product that does not conform to the warranty, the causal relationship between the breach and the loss is too attenuated to permit damages for the loss of secondary profits.

We also find that the fact situation before us presents a further problem in that the plaintiffs were not able to mitigate the harm in any way by buying substitute goods or "cover." Thus, the plaintiffs' primary product was defective and they were unable to remedy the situation by buying gasoline from another supplier.

We find that the present case presents compelling reasons for permit-ting damages for loss of secondary profits. Henceforth, in a breach of warranty case, when a primary product of the plaintiff is alleged to be nonconforming and the plaintiff is unable to cover by purchasing substitute goods, we hold that upon proper proof, the plaintiff should be entitled to sue for loss of secondary profits.[13]

Loss of Good Will

Historically, Pennsylvania has disallowed recovery for loss of good will damages or prospective profits in breach of warranty cases. [Citations.]

The defendant and the lower courts rely on these cases for the proposition that the plaintiffs claims are for "good will damages" and thus too speculative as a matter of law to permit recovery. * * *

With the advent of the *Lampus* "reason-to-know" test—which is a test of foreseeability—the holdings under each of these cases have much less precedential effect, since the *Lampus* test is much less restrictive than the tacit-agreement test.

Although the plaintiffs do not style their claim as one for good will damages, the Superior Court, the trial court, and the defendant have all characterized the claim for lost profits in this case as good will damages. What actually constitutes good will damages has caused much consternation to the courts and litigants. * * *

As one commentator aptly noted, "[l]oss of good will is a mercurial concept and, as such, is difficult to define. In a broad sense, it refers to a loss of future profits." [Citation.] Other jurisdictions have considered loss of good will to be a loss of profits and reputation among customers. Generally, good will refers to the reputation that businesses have built over the course of time that is reflected by the return of customers to purchase goods and the attendant profits that accompanies such sales. Thus the phrase "good will damages" is coextensive with prospective profits and loss of business reputation.

Secondly, we must decide when good will damages arise in a breach of warranty situation. Essentially, damage to good will in a case in which the seller supplies a quantity dictated by the buyer's requirements arises only after the seller has ceased providing nonconforming goods—or the buyer has purchased substitute goods. Damage to good will in this case would refer to the loss of business sales that occurred after the buyer was able to provide acceptable goods to his customers; it does not refer to the period of time during which he is forced to sell the nonconforming goods.

Thirdly, we must address whether good will damages are too speculative to permit recovery, as we held in [previous cases]. Although we disallowed good will damages in those cases, they are not recent. They were written in a time when business was conducted on a more simple basis, where market studies and economic forecasting were unexplored sciences.

We are now in an era in which computers, economic forecasting, sophisticated marketing studies and demographic studies are widely used

---

13. What constitutes a "primary product" will be dependent on the facts of each case. However, we would define a "primary product" as an item upon which the aggrieved party relies for a substantial amount of its revenue. The plaintiff must show that without that product, his business would be severely incapacitated.

and accepted. As such, we believe that the rationale for precluding prospective profits under the rubric of "too speculative" ignores the realities of the marketplace and the science of modern economics. We believe that claims for prospective profits should not be barred *ab initio*. Rather, plaintiffs should be given an opportunity to set forth and attempt to prove their damages. * * *

We believe the time has come to reconsider [our] rule. In doing so, we find our position on recovery for good will damages (or prospective profits) to be out of step with modern day business practices and techniques, as well as the law of other jurisdictions.

* * * In reviewing our case law on the issue of prospective profits, we have not had a significant case come before us since [1968]. Since that time, astronauts have walked on the moon, engineers have developed computers capable of amazing feats and biomedical engineers and physicians have made enormous strides in organ transplantation and replacement. * * * While these rapid technological developments have not been without their concomitant problems, they have made possible many things that were not possible before; including the calculation of prospective profits. For these reasons, we overrule [previous cases] to the extent they prohibit a plaintiff from alleging a claim for damage to good will as a matter of law.

Inextricably entwined with the issue of speculation is the difficulty in proving the damages are causally related to the breach. As we stated earlier, difficulty in proving causation should not operate as a bar to permitting plaintiffs to claim the damages. Furthermore, we note that pursuant to our case law and the Uniform Commercial Code, damages need not be proved with mathematical certainty. As long as the plaintiffs can provide a reasonable basis from which the jury can calculate damages, they will be permitted to pursue their case.

Thus, we now hold that plaintiffs should be entitled to try to prove good will damages; provided they are able to introduce sufficient evidence (1) to establish that the such profits were causally related to a breach of warranty and (2) to provide the trier of fact with a reasonable basis from which to calculate damages.

Turning to the facts of this case, we note that the plaintiffs have made no claim for good will damages, since none was incurred; ARCO having cured the breach by stopping the supply of the nonconforming gasoline. The damages claimed are only for the period of time that the plaintiffs were forced to purchase the gasoline with oxinol. Thus, we reverse the decision of the lower courts in holding that the plaintiffs' claim was for good will damages.

Conclusion

We now hold that there are three types of lost profits recoverable as consequential damages available under § 2714 and § 2715 of the Uniform Commercial Code: (1) loss of primary profits; (2) loss of secondary profits; and (3) good will damages, defined as a loss of prospective profits or business reputation. While this categorization of damages represents a new direction for the court, we believe it is the better direction.

---

1. *Difference-in-Value Damages.* When a buyer accepts non-conforming goods, the buyer is entitled to recover general damages as well as any consequential or incidental damages occasioned by the breach. The buyer's general damages are measured by the difference between the actual value of the non-conforming goods as accepted and the value that the goods would have had if they had been as warranted. *See* U.C.C. § 2–715; Beyond the Garden Gate, Inc. v. Northstar Freeze–Dry Mfg., 526 N.W.2d 305 (Iowa 1995). Should a buyer be able to offer evidence of the cost to repair nonconforming goods as evidence of the difference in value? *Compare* In re Fried Group, Inc., 218 Bankr. 247 (Bkrtcy.M.D.Ga.1998) (evidence of cost to repair defective farm equipment persuasive where the mechanical condition of the equipment was important to their value, the repairs were necessary to realize the value of the equipment as warranted and the cost to repair did not exceed the purchase price) *with* Litton Microwave Cooking Prod. v. Leviton Mfg., 15 F.3d 790 (8th Cir.1994) (additional cost of repairs unrecoverable where buyer's own auditors found the additional costs to be unreasonable).

2. *Certainty under the Code.* The Uniform Commercial Code specifically addresses the requirement of certainty in the context of a buyer's ability to recover consequential damages for a breach by a seller in the sale of goods. Comment 4 to U.C.C. § 2–715 states, in pertinent part:

> The burden of proving the extent of loss incurred by way of consequential damage is on the buyer, but the section on liberal administration of remedies rejects any doctrine of certainty which requires almost mathematical precision in the proof of loss. Loss may be determined in any manner which is reasonable under the circumstances.

In addition, comment 1 to U.C.C. § 1–106 provides that in order to effectuate the liberal administration of remedies under the code, it rejects the view that "damages must be calculable with mathematical accuracy." Rather, the code's approach favors a flexible policy where compensatory damages need only "be proved with whatever definiteness and accuracy the facts permit, but no more." Finally, the common law doctrinal limitation which demands only "reasonable" certainty may be considered incorporated through U.C.C. § 1–103.

3. *Past Profits.* Compare the principal case to *In Migerobe, Inc. v. Certina USA, Inc.*, 924 F.2d 1330 (5th Cir.1991), where a buyer that owned and operated jewelry counters at department stores brought an action for lost profits resulting from the seller's refusal to ship orders of watches. The buyer had planned to sell the watches as a "loss leader" item (sold at or below cost) and featured them in a "doorbuster" Thanksgiving advertisement at a 50 percent discount. The buyer claimed losses of corollary sales of other items at its jewelry counters was a foreseeable consequence of the

seller's breach of contract to sell the watches. The court upheld the jury verdict awarding lost profits, finding that historical data showing the buyer's profits made in past promotions of different items was the best evidence available and provided a reasonable basis for estimating the loss.

4. *Proof of Lost Goodwill.* As the principal case reflects, recovery of damages for loss of goodwill is inherently difficult because it relates to the future; no actual profit base will be available for evidentiary use at trial. Where the aggrieved party can show the fact of damage, however, uncertainty regarding the amount of lost goodwill does not automatically preclude recovery. *See* Lewis River Golf v. O.M. Scott & Sons, 120 Wash.2d 712, 845 P.2d 987, 989 (1993) (damage to business reputation or goodwill and resulting loss in the value of business properly recoverable as an element of consequential damages); Consolidated Data Terminals v. Applied Digital Data Systems, Inc., 708 F.2d 385 (9th Cir.1983) (loss of goodwill among customers of distributor caused by problems with defective computer terminals compensable).

5. *Consequential Damages Caused by Non–Conforming Goods.* In *Cole Energy Development Co. v. Ingersoll–Rand Co.*, 913 F.2d 1194 (7th Cir. 1990), a lessee of gas compressors brought a breach of warranty claim against the lessor/manufacturer. The lessee did not lose actual production as a result of the decreased effectiveness of the equipment, but experienced a delay in its realization of profits. The court held that the lost opportunity costs in delaying expected profits were properly compensable, measured by the costs of actual production compared to costs the lessee would have incurred if defective equipment had worked as warranted at full capacity. *See also* Horizons, Inc. v. Avco Corp., 551 F.Supp. 771, 781 (D.C.S.D.1982) (buyer of business equipment could recover lost profits, calculated by the down-time caused by period of equipment failure).

6. *Foreseeability of Special Damages.* The different treatment of foreseeability with respect to general and special damages has been carried forward from the common law to the Uniform Commercial Code. Because general damages flow directly and immediately as a natural consequence of the kind of wrongful act by the breaching party, they are conclusively presumed foreseeable. This approach is reflected in section 2–714(1) which concerns accepted but nonconforming goods, in section 2–712 which pertains to cover, and in section 2–713 which gives the market price-contract price differential to an aggrieved buyer.

Hess Die Mold Inc. v. American Plasti–Plate Corp., 653 S.W.2d 927 (Tex.App.1983), illustrates the treatment of foreseeability with respect to general damages. The case involved a contract to purchase a plastic mold for use in the buyer's business. The seller failed to deliver a mold conforming to the contract and the buyer obtained a replacement from another manufacturer at a higher price. The court found that the cost to cover was equivalent to an item of common law general damages, and therefore did not require specific findings that the breaching seller had contemplated the buyer's losses at the time of entering the contract.

Compare the requirements for special damages in section 2–715(2), which requires reference to the particular character, condition, or circumstances of the non-breaching party and foreseeability by the breaching party. Accordingly, special damages must be specially pleaded to give the defendant fair notice of the claim and must be specially proved rather than being implied by law.

Aries v. Palmer Johnson, Inc.

153 Ariz. 250, 735 P.2d 1373 (1987).

■ HOWARD, P.J.

This is an action by the purchaser of a yacht (Aries) against the manufacturer/seller [Palmer Johnson, Inc. (PJ)] for breach of contract, breach of warranty, and fraud. * * *

The action was tried to the court, sitting without a jury, which found that PJ breached its contractual promise concerning time of delivery, breached express and implied warranties as to description and quality, and defrauded Aries in regard to the boat's promised delivery date. The court awarded Aries $218,795.58 in damages. * * *

In August of 1982, Aries sent PJ $100,000 as a deposit toward the purchase of an Alden 75 yacht, to be called "Scheherazade." * * * On September 1, 1982, Aries sent a letter to PJ which contained a list of specifications for the new yacht. He also inquired about a queen-size bunk for the master stateroom and asked Kelsey's opinion as to whether it could be done. Fifteen days later, PJ signed and mailed one of its standard form contracts for Aries' signature. The contract price was $1,237,500. The delivery date was "on or about June 25, 1983" in accordance with prior discussions between Aries and Kelsey wherein Aries told Kelsey of his intended use of the yacht for the summer of 1983. One day after mailing the contract, PJ wrote Aries in response to his September 1 letter. PJ did not address the issue of the queen-size bunk, but stated that construction was already under way and that PJ expected no problem in completing the yacht by the scheduled delivery date of June 25, 1983.

[Aries paid PJ all sums of money that were due under the contract.] * * *

From the fall of 1982 until early spring of 1983, Aries had regular conversations with Kelsey and Johansen concerning the progress of the construction. It was uncontradicted that in these conversations Aries was advised that construction was proceeding on schedule and that the contract delivery date would be met. * * *

The boat was not delivered until November 23, 1983, five months late, depriving Aries of all use during the summer and fall of 1983. After delivery, it promptly broke down. It was dry-docked in a repair facility for approximately 168 days during the year following delivery. Defects in quality and material were wide ranging, from delaminating paint, to drill holes in the hull, to a jerry-rigged sewage tank system which was vented near the cabin portholes.

Aries informed PJ repeatedly, both before and after executing the contract, of his intended use of the boat during the summer and fall of 1983, which included the "shakedown cruise" in Lake Michigan, attendance at the quadrennial America's Cup races in August and September, and then on to the Caribbean. From the time the contract was executed in the fall of 1982, to the early spring of 1983, PJ's president and construction superintendent repeatedly assured Aries that construction was proceeding in a timely manner and that delivery would be timely. The record shows that Aries relied on those representations to his detriment. For example, he decommissioned the yacht he then owned and did not secure a substitute vessel for his intended use during the summer and fall of 1983.

* * *

Damages for Loss of Use

The trial court awarded Aries $100,000 for loss of use of the yacht before delivery and $20,000 for loss of use after delivery. PJ contends the trial court erred in awarding any damages for loss of use because (1) they were speculative, (2) PJ had no knowledge of Aries' intended use of the boat when it entered into the contract, (3) no substitute vessel was actually rented, and (4) the loss of rental value used to compute the damages for loss of use failed to take into account expenses which were necessary in order to rent the vessel.

Damages for loss of use are appropriate under the Uniform Commercial Code if the seller had knowledge of the buyer's intended use of the goods at the time of contracting and the buyer proves that there are periods when the goods would have been used but were not because of defects that the buyer, in good faith, was waiting for the seller to cure. Damages are recoverable for only those days the goods would have been in use. [Citation.] This would also apply to the failure to deliver the goods on the date promised in the contract. [Citation.] One is entitled to use his property for pleasure as well as business, and a loss of use recovery is allowed as to pleasure vehicles as well as to business vehicles. [Citation.]

Aries' damages for loss of use of his yacht are measured by its reasonable rental value at the time of the loss. [Citation.] His failure to actually rent a substitute yacht does not preclude him from recovering such damages.

An excellent discussion on the loss of use of a motor home and entitlement to damages under the Uniform Commercial Code is contained in the Minnesota case of *Jacobs v. Rosemount Dodge–Winnebago South*, 310 N.W.2d 71, 78 (Minn.1981):

> * * * It is for the trier of fact, in this case the jury, to assess damages for loss of use so long as that assessment is reasonable and not punitive.... Where the measure of damages is not easily amenable to mathematical precision, the trier of fact must consider the general or

particular needs of the buyer which the seller could have known at the time of contracting. In considering the needs of the buyer, the specific buyer's needs and circumstances must be considered, not those of the average buyer. [Citations omitted.]

There was ample evidence of Aries' intended use of the yacht during the five months' period of delayed delivery, and there was evidence that PJ knew of Aries' intended use of the yacht when the contract was entered into. Aries testified that had the ship been delivered on time or reasonably close, he would have used it for a one-month shakedown cruise on Lake Michigan and then a trip up the St. Lawrence Seaway and on to Newport, Rhode Island to attend the quadrennial America's Cup trials and finals in August and September. After the America's Cup, Aries intended to take the yacht to the Caribbean, where it was his habit to spend at least ten days per month. Aries' intended use was consistent with the trial court's finding of his substantial use of his prior yacht, Varuna. Aries testified that he used Varuna approximately ten days per month during the winter season in the Caribbean, took numerous trips from the east to the west coast of the United States through the Panama Canal, as well as cruises in the Mediterranean. He testified that his boat was his sanctuary and refuge and that he intended to use it as much as reasonably possible. The trial court did not award loss of use for all five months; instead, it awarded loss of use for two-thirds of this time.

As for post-delivery loss, the trial court awarded Aries $20,000 for loss of use for 20 of the 168 days that the yacht was being repaired during the year after its delivery. Aries' expert witness, Johnson, testified that 30 days' downtime for repair ("warranty") was normal during the first year, and that 60 days was excessive. PJ's expert estimated that 50 to 80 of the 168 days were attributable to warranty work, as distinguished from items such as owner preference work.

We believe there was sufficient evidence of postdelivery loss of time to support the court's award. Furthermore, as to the predelivery loss, the court did not award damages for the entire five months, but only for two-thirds of that time.

Aries testified that, based on his long experience as the owner of a charter company, $1,500 per day was at the low end of the reasonable range to charter a comparable boat under normal circumstances. He further testified that the cost of a comparable boat during the America's Cup would have been $5,000 to $7,000 per day. Finally, he testified that he would have charged $2,000 per day to charter his boat for business purposes.

Johnson testified that $1,500 per day was a reasonable charter rate for a comparable boat under normal circumstances without consumable and crew expenses. Johnson testified that the minimum charter rate for a comparable vessel during the America's Cup would be $3,000 per day.

PJ's executive vice president, Parsons, testified that the reasonable charter value under normal circumstances was $8,500 per week or $1,200 per day averaged on a weekly rate. He also testified, however, that the loss of use in 1983 could have been $1,500 per day. There was also evidence that Ondine, one of the other boats that was being built, contained a $2,000 per day penalty provision that was personally guaranteed by PJ's shareholders. The $2,000 per day rate was a negotiated estimate of loss of daily use for late delivery of that boat. There was evidence as to the daily cost of consumables and crew expenses that would have to be deducted against the rental rate. We presume the trial court took these sums into account, and we find no error in its award of $1,000 per day damages.

* * *

Aries testified that his original intended delivery route was from Lake Michigan out the St. Lawrence Seaway to the North Atlantic and then south, but because of the delay in delivery from early summer to late fall and the prospect of taking an untested pleasure craft into a northern seaway that freezes in winter, the route south was changed to the Mississippi River. This decision was made in consultation with PJ's representatives.

The boat, when finally delivered, had the masts in place, but the masts had to be removed and placed on deck due to the rerouting because they were too tall to pass under some of the bridges on the Mississippi. PJ charged Aries $5,731 to take the masts down, and it cost Aries $2,378.21 to have the masts put up again when he reached New Orleans. This would not have occurred if the boat had been delivered on time. The trial court awarded damages to reimburse him for the cost of the masts' removal and replacement. PJ contends that this was erroneous because there was evidence that the St. Lawrence Seaway did not freeze over and close until December 15, 1983, and there was, therefore, no necessity to remove the masts. We do not agree. The question was whether it was unreasonable for Aries and defendant's employees to change the route at the time they did, not having the power to predict when the St. Lawrence Seaway was going to freeze. The trial court found that Aries acted reasonably in changing the route after delivery; we cannot gainsay the trial court's determination.
* * *

---

1. *Rental Expenses.* Compare the principal case with *McGinnis v. Wentworth Chevrolet Co.*, 295 Or. 494, 668 P.2d 365 (1983). In this case an aggrieved buyer justifiably revoked acceptance of a nonconforming automobile and then rented a substitute vehicle rather than purchasing a replacement. The buyer then sought damages for her rental expense. The court held that the rental expenses were not recoverable as an expense in effecting "cover" and that loss of bargain damages must be computed by a market price formula.

The court found that the rental expenses did not translate into a comparable figure for loss of bargain. Moreover, the rental expenses were not recoverable as incidental damages because they related to the particular circumstances of this buyer rather than being necessarily incident to the breach of contract. The court ultimately remanded for the trial court to determine if the rental costs were recoverable as consequential damages under these circumstances because the contract contained a limitation of liability clause.

2. *Contractual Limitation of Damages.* Although incidental items of damages are usually identifiable, there are often problems with the distinction between difference-in-value losses and consequential damages. Although this distinction normally would not be critical in contract cases because all expectancy damages are recoverable, it becomes so when the parties have excluded consequential damages by agreement.

For example, in *Reynolds Metals Co. v. Westinghouse Electric Corp.*, 758 F.2d 1073 (5th Cir.1985), Westinghouse contracted to manufacture and install an electric transformer for Reynolds Metals. The seller breached the contract by improperly installing the equipment and thereby causing extensive harm to the transformer. The court recognized that the damages were a foreseeable consequence of the breach which ordinarily would be recoverable as consequential damages. In this contract, however, the parties had specifically limited such damages. Reynolds could only recover damages under section 2–714 for the difference in value of the performance promised and what had been received.

3. *Additional Commentary.* For additional commentary on damages in contracts for the sale of goods see the following references: Farnsworth, Legal Remedies for Breach of Contract, 70 Colum.L.Rev. 1145 (1970); Harris, A Radical Restatement of the Law of Seller's Damages, 18 Stan. L.Rev. 66 (1965); Peters, Remedies for Breach of Contracts Relating to the Sale of Goods Under the Uniform Commercial Code: A Roadmap for Article Two, 73 Yale L.J. 199 (1963); Macneil, Power of Contract and Agreed Remedies, 47 Cornell L.Q. 495 (1962); Van Hecke, Changing Emphasis in Specific Performance, 40 N.C.L.Rev. 1 (1961); Gilmore, The Commercial Doctrine of Good Faith Purchase, 63 Yale L.J. 1057 (1954); Fuller & Perdue, The Reliance Interest in Contract Damages, 46 Yale L.J. 52 (1936); Llewellyn, What Price Contract?, 40 Yale L.J. 704 (1931).

4. *Emotional Distress Damages.* In *Kwan v. Mercedes–Benz of North America, Inc.*, 23 Cal.App.4th 174, 28 Cal.Rptr.2d 371 (1994), a buyer of a new $46,000 Mercedes sought damages under California's consumer protection act for emotional distress associated with difficulties he experienced in getting the dealership to repair the vehicle. The buyer claimed that the operational problems made the car unsafe and made him "frustrated and mad," "sad," "nervous," and "worried about the safety for the family." The categories and principles of measurement of compensatory damages available to a buyer under the consumer act paralleled comparable provisions normally available to a buyer for a seller's breach of a contract for sale of goods under the U.C.C. Although a jury awarded the buyer emotional distress damages, the appellate court reversed, following the general rule

disallowing damages for mental suffering in contracts independent of physical injury.

The court found that the case did not fit within an exception awarding distress damages for breach of contracts "very personal in nature," in which emotional concerns are closely linked to the essence of contractual performance. The court observed:

> In our view, a contract for sale of an automobile is not essentially tied to the buyer's mental or emotional well-being. Personal as the choice of a car may be, the central reason for buying one is usually transportation. In the words of the Restatement, a breach of such a contract is not "particularly likely" to result in "serious" emotional distress. (Rest.2d Contracts, § 353.) The purchase of an automobile ordinarily does not "so affect the vital concerns of the individual that severe mental distress is a foreseeable result of breach."

> In spite of America's much-discussed "love affair with the automobile," disruption of an owner's relationship with his or her car is not, in the normal case, comparable to the loss or mistreatment of a family member's remains, an invasion of one's privacy, or the loss of one's spouse to a gambling addiction. In the latter situations, the contract exists primarily to further or protect emotional interests; the direct and foreseeable injuries resulting from a breach are also primarily emotional. In contrast, the undeniable aggravation, irritation and anxiety that may result from breach of an automobile warranty are secondary effects deriving from the decreased usefulness of the car and the frequently frustrating process of having an automobile repaired. While purchase of an automobile may sometimes lead to severe emotional distress, such a result is not ordinarily foreseeable from the nature of the contract. 23 Cal.App.4th at 190.

2.   SELLER'S REMEDIES

Sprague v. Sumitomo Forestry Co.

104 Wash.2d 751, 709 P.2d 1200 (1985).

■ DORE, JUSTICE.

This action involves a claim by Clyde Sprague against Sumitomo Forestry Company, Ltd. for breach of contract arising from Sumitomo's unconditional cancellation of a log purchase contract. A jury trial resulted in a judgment of $280,693.03 for Sprague. Except for one element of damages that we hold should have been excluded, we affirm.

Sprague is a logger located in Enumclaw, Washington who has been active in buying, selling, harvesting and milling timber in various capacities. As it relates to the issues involved in this lawsuit, Sprague's business has two distinct aspects: the harvesting of timber on a contract basis for various timberland owners, and the purchase of United States Forest Service timber sales from which Sprague harvests and sells logs.

Sprague purchased a tract of timber, known as the Flip Blowdown from the United States Forest Service (USFS) in June 1979. * * *

[Sprague entered into a written contract to sell timber to the Sumitomo Forestry Company, which was engaged in the purchase and export of logs and lumber to Japan. Sprague commenced performance and delivered approximately 100,000 board feet of logs on the Flip Blowdown site to Sumitomo's specifications. In October, 1980, however, Sumitomo sent a letter to Sprague unequivocally canceling the contract. Sprague brought suit for breach of contract, and attempted to mitigate his damages by reselling the timber to various purchasers at private sales. Sprague sought to recover the difference between the contract price and the resale price of the timber, together with incidental damages.]

Via a special verdict form, the jury found * * * (2) that there was a breach and no waiver; (3) that the contract price was $197,204 and the resale price was $144,924 with net contractual damages of $52,280; (4) that Sprague sustained incidental damages of $216,498 for the following items: (a) cost of refinancing, $39,674; (b) extra transportation cost, $5,612; (c) loss of revenue on Flip Blowdown not covered by contract, $9,121; (d) loss of logging time, 11 weeks, $171,200; and (e) cost of moving tower, $2,115.

The major thrust of Sumitomo's appellate argument here is that Sprague did not give the requisite notice of intention to resell the canceled goods as required by RCW 62W.2–706(3) and, therefore, Sprague is not entitled to recover the difference between the contract price and the resale price.

Resale Price Differential

The catalogue of a seller's remedies in a breach of contract case governed by the sale of goods provisions of the Uniform Commercial Code is found in RCW 62A.2–703. In the present case, the catalogue of available remedies can quickly be reduced to two; these are:

> (1) resale and recovery under RCW 62A.2–706, or

> (2) recovery of the difference between the contract price and the market price under RCW 62A.2–708(1).

At trial Sprague apparently proceeded, pursuant to RCW 62A.2–706, to recover as damages the difference between the resale price and contract price. RCW 62A.2–706(1) provides that if the seller acts in good faith and in a commercially reasonable manner, he may recover the difference between the resale price and the contract price, together with any incidental damages allowed under RCW 62A.2–710, less expenses saved.

RCW 62A.2–706(2) goes on to permit resale at public or private sale. Of critical importance here is the requirement of RCW 62A.2–706(3) which provides that where an aggrieved seller resells goods which are the subject of a breach at a private sale, he must give the buyer "reasonable notification of his intention to resell."

In response to his failure to give specific notice of intention to resell, and in support of his judgment, Sprague argues: that the lack of notice was an affirmative defense which the buyer failed to plead, or that the buyer, from all the surrounding facts and circumstances, knew or should have known that the seller was going to resell the logs.

We deal first with whether the buyer needed to plead affirmatively as a defense the admitted lack of actual notice. This issue has not been previously addressed in Washington and only a few courts have reached this issue. Notice has been termed a "prerequisite" and a "condition precedent" to section 2–706 damage claims. [Citations.] The burden of showing compliance with the notice requirement has been placed on the seller. [Citations.]

Williston has analyzed the issue as follows:

> Assuming that the seller has an affirmative duty to meet the requirements of § 2–706, a showing by the seller of compliance with this section would make it unnecessary for the buyer to raise a defense of lack of notice. All the buyer need do is show contradictory evidence of seller's statement that he gave notice of his intention to resell.

3 A. Squillante & J. Fonseca, *Williston on Sales* § 24–7, at 418 (4th ed. 1974). This analysis, which finds notice as a prerequisite to bringing the claim, fits well with Washington law on affirmative defenses. CR 8(c) enumerates certain specific affirmative defenses which must be pleaded, but includes a general clause "and any other matter constituting an avoidance or affirmative defense." While this language is very general, it clearly contemplates matters which are in avoidance or are a specific affirmative defense. It would follow, therefore, that if notice of intent to resell is part of the seller's prima facie case, then lack of such notice would not have to be affirmatively denied.

To recover under RCW 62A.2–706, Sprague was required to give notice of intent to resell. This is an element of the seller's right to invoke the remedies of RCW 62A.2–706. Therefore, the buyer need not plead as an affirmative defense those elements which seller must prove.

Next, can the notice requirement be satisfied by the fact that the buyer knew or should have known that the seller intended to resell? From the plain language of RCW 62A.2–706, the giving by the seller of notice of intention to resell is a specific requirement to entitle seller to claim as damages the difference between resale price and the contract price. The words of subsection (3) are precise: "The seller *must* give the buyer reasonable notification of his intention to resell." (Italics ours.) RCW 62A.2–706(3).

Sprague contends Sumitomo knew or should have known that Sprague would make a resale and hold Sumitomo liable for the difference in resulting recovery. Thus, he argues that there was substantial compliance with the notice requirement. Sprague would have us hold that his filing of a lawsuit is sufficient notice. Whether such filing could ever be adequate notice is not before us. Factually, what is before us is a complaint that alleges a breach of contract and subsequent damages. It gives no notice of the remedy claimed other than damages. It was not an adequate substitute for the statutorily required notice of intent to resell.

Market Price Differential

* * * Although the jury verdict cannot be upheld under the resale method of determining damages, we find that the record supports the verdict under the alternate method of establishing damages, computed by measuring the difference between the market price and the contract price as provided in RCW 62A.2–708. This provision states:

> (1) Subject to subsection (2) and to the provisions of this Article with respect to proof of market price (RCW 62A.2–723), the measure of damages for non-acceptance or repudiation by the buyer is the difference between the market price at the time and place for tender and the unpaid contract price together with any incidental damages provided in this Article (RCW 62A.2–710), but less expenses saved in consequence of the buyer's breach.

> (2) If the measure of damages provided in subsection (1) is inadequate to put the seller in as good a position as performance would have done then the measure of damages is the profit (including reasonable overhead) which the seller would have made from full performance by the buyer, together with any incidental damages provided in this Article (RCW 62A.2–710), due allowance for costs reasonably incurred and due credit for payments or proceeds of resale.

It is fundamental under RCW 62A.2–703 and the sections that follow that an aggrieved seller is not required to elect between damages under RCW 62A.2–706 and 62A.2–708. RCW 62A.2–703 cumulatively sets forth the remedies available to a seller upon the buyer's breach. The pertinent commentary thereto indicates specifically that the remedies provided are cumulative and not exclusive and that as a fundamental policy Article 2 of the U.C.C. rejects any doctrine of election of remedy.

The seller has the burden of proof with respect to market price or market value. A seller cannot avail himself of the benefit of RCW 62A.2–708 when he has not presented evidence of market price or market value. However, the resale price of goods may be considered as appropriate evidence of the market value at the time of tender in determining damages pursuant to RCW 62A.2–708. [Citations.]

While, admittedly, Sprague's resale came after the time for tender, it can still be utilized as a market price. RCW 62A.2–723(2) states:

> (2) If evidence of a price prevailing at the times or places described in this Article is not readily available the price prevailing within any reasonable time before *or after* the time described or at any other place which in commercial judgment or under usage of trade would serve as a reasonable substitute for the one described may be used . . . (Italics ours).

The court is granted a "reasonable leeway" (Official Comments to RCWA 62A.2–723) in measuring market price. During the trial of this action, not only was there testimony to the effect that in an effort to mitigate damages, respondent Sprague sold the Flip Blowdown logs to five purchasers at private sales in 1981 and 1982, there was also testimony that the market price remained at the same level as at the time and place of tender in late 1980.

The net contractual damages of $52,280 ($197,204 contract price − $144,924 resale price) which was awarded respondent under the jury verdict thus equaled the measure of damages available under RCW 62A.2–708(1). We affirm this award.

Incidental Damages

Sprague is entitled also to incidental damages. RCW 62A.2–708 provides that the seller is entitled to the difference between the market price and contract price "together with any incidental damages provided in this Article (RCW 62A.2–710), but less expenses saved in consequence of the buyer's breach." Incidental damages are defined in RCW 62A.2–710 as follows:

> Incidental damages to an aggrieved seller include any commercially reasonable charges, expenses or commissions incurred in stopping delivery, in the transportation, care and custody of goods after the buyer's breach, in connection with return or resale of the goods or otherwise resulting from the breach.

At trial, the jury found that respondent sustained incidental damages of $216,498 for the following items: (a) cost of refinancing, $39,674; (b) extra transportation cost, $5,612; (c) loss of revenue on Flip Blowdown not covered by contract, $9,121; (d) loss of logging time, 11 weeks, $171,200; and (e) cost of moving tower, $2,115.

Sumitomo contends that some of these items are not incidental damages but more properly classified as consequential. Consequential damages are *not* allowed except as specifically provided in RCW Title 62A or by other rule of law. RCW 62A.1–106. Washington Comment to section 2–710 indicates that consequential damages are denied to sellers under the Uniform Commercial Code. RCWA 62A.2–710.

The distinction between consequential and incidental damages was made in Petroleo Brasileiro, S.A. Petrobras v. Ameropan Oil Corp., 372 F.Supp. 503, 508 (E.D.N.Y.1974):

> While the distinction between the two is not an obvious one, the Code makes plain that incidental damages are normally incurred when a buyer (or seller) repudiates the contract or wrongfully rejects the goods, causing the other to incur such expenses as transporting, storing, or reselling the goods. On the other hand, *consequential damages* do not arise within the scope of the immediate buyer-seller transaction, but rather *stem from losses incurred by the non-breaching party in its dealings, often with third parties*, which were a proximate result of the breach, and which were reasonably foreseeable by the breaching party at the time of contracting. (Citations omitted. Italics ours.)

We find that the loss of logging time is an inappropriate item of incidental damages. Sprague's damage claim for loss of logging time is essentially a claim for lost profits on a contract with Mt. Baker Plywood. In *Petroleo Brasileiro,* the court stated that "consequential damages do not arise within the scope of the immediate buyer-seller transaction [as do incidental damages], but rather stem from losses incurred by the non-breaching party in its dealings, often with third parties . . .". Applying this test to Sprague's claim for loss of logging time, Sprague's loss clearly did not arise within the scope of his contract with Sumitomo; instead, Sprague incurred this loss as a consequence of his delay in performing his contract with Mt. Baker Plywood, a third party. The fact that Sumitomo's conduct proximately caused Sprague's loss is irrelevant to this analysis. The focus is upon losses arising within the scope of the immediate contract. Accordingly, Sprague's loss can only be characterized as consequential. Therefore, the judgment awarded Sprague is reduced by $171,200.

* * *

1. *Consequential Damages.* Although the Code does not permit a seller to recover consequential damages, as the principal case reflects, recent amendments to Article 2 would change this rule. Amended section 2–708(1) would allow a seller to recover consequential damages as well as contract-market differential damages when a buyer wrongfully rejects or repudiates. Amended section 2–710 would adopt a definition of the seller's consequential damages that mirrors the existing definition of the buyer's consequential damages. A notable exception is that section 2–710 would preclude a seller from recovering consequential damages from a consumer. As of 2007, no state had adopted these amendments to section 2–708 and 2–710. *See* Scott J. Burnham, *Is Article 2 Regulatory or Facilitatory? A Socratic Dialogue*, 68 Ohio St. L. J. 57 (2007).

2. *Contract–Market Differential Damages.* U.C.C. 2–708(1) provides that a seller's benefit of the bargain damages are determined by the differential between the contract price and the market price at the time and place for tender. When proof of prices in the relevant market at tender is lacking, courts have some flexibility in using a reasonable substitute to make the necessary calculations. *See* U.C.C. 2–723(2).

In *Buchsteiner Prestige Corp. v. Abraham & Straus*, 107 Misc.2d 327, 433 N.Y.S.2d 972 (1980), the contract provided for tender of goods in 1978 for a contract price of $8,764.80. The seller established a market price of $865.20 by offering evidence of a resale offer in July, 1979. The court found the 1979 market figure to be acceptable, reasoning that a "reasonable leeway" should be allowed when proving the market price. Is this result justifiable? What additional facts might be useful in determining what constituted a reasonable substitute market?

3. *Limitations on Contract–Market Differential Damages.* As indicated in the principal case, a seller's failure to conduct a resale of goods within the requirements of section 2–706 will preclude recovery of the resale-contract price differential as damages. Additionally, courts may place limitations on the amount of damages available under section 2–708(1).

In *Coast Trading Co. v. Cudahy Co.*, 592 F.2d 1074 (9th Cir.1979), the court held that a seller should not be allowed a greater award under 2–708(1) than was actually lost in effecting the resale, but that the burden would be on the buyer to establish the actual loss. This case involved several contracts for the sale of barley in Oregon. The seller had sought damages based on section 2–706 contract price less resale price but was not allowed to do so since the resale was not deemed to be commercially reasonable. The buyer provided evidence of the seller's actual receipts on resale of the barley and the damages award was thus limited.

4. *Commercially Reasonable Resale.* The purpose of the resale provision in section 2–706 is to provide evidence of the market price at the time and place performance should have been rendered by the buyer. Consequently, as more time elapses between the breach and the resale, the probative value of the resale price is similarly reduced. For example, in *McMillan v. Meuser Material & Equipment*, 260 Ark. 422, 541 S.W.2d 911 (1976), an equipment dealer waited fourteen months after the buyer's breach to resell a bulldozer. The court held that the delay was commercially unreasonable, and therefore precluded recovery of damages under 2–706. A significant fact was that the market had been declining due to a recession in the construction industry and high fuel prices.

Should a seller be forced to resell in a declining market or be given leeway to wait for more favorable market conditions? If the seller does resell in a weak market, can the buyer argue that the seller acted unreasonably by not waiting for a stronger market? How long should a seller wait during a declining market before it should be apparent that the decline is not just a temporary downturn in an otherwise strong market? Should the subjective belief of the seller about the prospect for the market price in the near future be relevant?

Collins Entertainment Corp. v. Coats and Coats Rental Amusement

368 S.C. 410, 629 S.E.2d 635 (2006).

■ JUSTICE WALLER:

We granted a writ of certiorari to review the Court of Appeals' opinion in *Collins Ent. Corp. v. Coats & Coats Rental Amuse.*, 355 S.C. 125, 584 S.E.2d 120 (Ct.App.2003). The sole issue on certiorari is whether the Court of Appeals erred in utilizing the "lost volume seller" doctrine to calculate damages. We affirm.

Facts

In 1996, Collins Entertainment Corporation (Collins) contracted to lease video poker machines to two bingo hall operations known as Ponderosa Bingo and Shipwatch Bingo. The six-year lease required that any purchaser of the premises assume the lease. In 1997, American Bingo and Gaming Corporation (American) purchased the assets of the bingo parlors. American failed to assume the lease and removed Collins' machines from the premises. Collins brought this action against American alleging * * * intentional interference with contract. The matter was referred to a master in equity for trial. The master found American liable for intentional interference with contract and awarded Collins actual damages of $157,449.66 and punitive damages of $1,569,013.00. The Court of Appeals affirmed. *Collins Ent. Corp. v. Coats & Coats Rental Amuse.*, 355 S.C. 125, 584 S.E.2d 120 (Ct.App.2003).

Issue

Did the Court of Appeals err in utilizing the "lost volume seller" doctrine to hold Collins did not have a duty to mitigate its damages?

Discussion

Comment f to Section 347 of the Restatement (Second) of Contracts states, in part, "if the injured party could and would have entered into the subsequent contract, even if the contract had not been broken, and could have had the benefit of both, he can be said to have lost volume and the subsequent transaction is not a substitute for the broken contract." This theory of damages has come to be known as the "lost volume seller" doctrine. A lost volume seller is one whose willingness and ability to supply is, as a practical matter, unlimited in comparison to the demand for the product. Thus, "[t]he lost volume seller theory allows [for the] recovery of lost profits despite resale of the services that were the subject of the terminated contract if the seller ... can prove that he would have entered into both transactions but for the breach." [Citations.] Although the lost volume seller theory is commonly understood to apply to contracts involving the sale of goods, it applies with equal force to contracts involving the performance of personal services. [Citations.] Whether a seller is a lost volume seller is a question of fact. [Citations.]

American asserts adoption of the lost volume seller doctrine eliminates a seller's duty to mitigate damages. It contends we should adopt the position advanced by the Pennsylvania Supreme Court in Northeastern Vending Company v. PDO, Inc., 414 Pa.Super. 200, 606 A.2d 936 (1992), in which the court declined to adopt the lost volume seller doctrine stating, summarily, that it would erode the duty to mitigate damages. We decline to adopt the Pennsylvania approach because we do not find the doctrine erodes the duty to mitigate damages. On the contrary, the doctrine realizes that in certain situations, even where a [seller] does mitigate, if the seller would have made the second sale in any event, then the "lost volume" measure of damages places him in the same position he would have been had the buyer not repudiated. As the Court in *Davis Chemical v. Diasonics Inc.*, 826 F.2d 678, 683, n. 3 (7th Cir.1987), stated, "by definition, a lost volume seller cannot mitigate damages through resale. Resale does not reduce a lost volume seller's damages because the breach has still resulted in its losing one sale and a corresponding profit." [Citations.]

Further, we find the legislature's adoption of S.C.Code Ann. § 36–2A–528(2) is consistent with adoption of the lost volume seller doctrine. Section 36–2A–528(2) (dealing with leased goods) tracks the language of S.C.Code Ann. § 36–2–708(2) (seller's damages for sales). Section 36–2–708 clearly tracks the provisions of the Uniform Commercial Code section (UCC § 2–708(2)) upon which the lost volume seller doctrine is premised. [Citations.] By adoption of S.C.Code Ann. § 36–2A–528(2), we find the Legislature has tacitly approved of the lost volume seller doctrine.

American next asserts there is insufficient evidence in the record to demonstrate that Collins is a lost volume seller. We disagree. There is no one set test to determine whether one is a lost volume seller. According to one commentator:

> Professor Harris has developed three main requirements that a lost volume seller must meet: (1) the person who bought the resold entity would have been solicited by the plaintiff had there been no breach or resale; (2) the solicitation would have been successful; and (3) the plaintiff could have performed that additional contract.

Most American courts and commentators have adopted these requirements.

Here, there is testimony in the record which indicates that Collins had surplus machines on hand and that, had another location been available, it could and would have supplied those locations with video machines. Further, Collins did place 19 of the 20 machines which were removed from Shipwatch and Ponderosa into other premises. As found by the Master, it is patent that Collins had excess inventory with which to supply and rotate machines through all of its customers.

American argues there has been no showing by Collins that the specific type of machines removed from the Shipwatch and Ponderosa were available at its warehouses, such that it has failed in its burden to demonstrate it had excess capacity. We disagree. Initially, although American argued there was insufficient evidence of excess capacity below, it made no argument with respect to the specific types of machines at issue. Accordingly, as this specific argument was not raised below, it is not preserved. In any event, Collins presented testimony from its assistant comptroller for accounting that, although there were ten machines in each location (i.e., the Shipwatch and Ponderosa), a total of 48 machines rotated through the locations. Livingston also testified that "we had machines in the warehouse that could have easily replaced these 48 at the 130 locations." Livingston's testimony is sufficient to establish that Collins had more supply capacity of these machines than it had demand. Moreover, the lease agreement between Collins and Coats and Coats Rental gives Collins the right to furnish "all video game terminals and all coin operated music and amusement machines, to include a special multi-player Black Jack/Poker unit." We find no requirement (other than one multi-player poker unit) that Collins place any particular machines on the premises, such that Collins was free to have utilized any of its machines at the Ponderosa and Shipwatch. Accordingly, Collins was not required to demonstrate excess capacity as to a specific type of machine.

Conclusion

Contrary to the arguments raised by American, we find adoption of the lost volume seller doctrine does not eliminate a seller's duty to mitigate his damages. The doctrine simply recognizes that, in situations in which the seller has excess capacity and would, in any event, have made both sales, the lost volume measure of damages is necessary to place the seller in the same position he would have been had the buyer not repudiated. Further, there is sufficient evidence to demonstrate that Collins was, in fact, a lost volume seller in this case. Accordingly, the opinion of the Court of Appeals utilizing the lost volume seller doctrine is affirmed.

---

1. *Contracts for Services.* Courts and commentators generally recognize that UCC § 2–708(2) codifies the lost volume seller doctrine as applied to contracts for the sale of goods. However, like the court in the principal case, other courts have applied the lost volume seller doctrine to contracts for services and lease agreements. *See, e.g.,* Bitterroot Int'l Sys. v. Western Star Trucks, 336 Mont. 145, 153 P.3d 627 (2007) (lost volume seller theory applied to contract to provide freight hauling and transportation logistics even though the contract was one for services rather than goods); Gianetti v. Norwalk Hosp., 266 Conn. 544, 833 A.2d 891 (2003) (applying the lost volume seller doctrine to an employment contract between a surgeon and a hospital); Jetz Serv. Co. v. Salina Properties, 19 Kan.App.2d 144, 865 P.2d 1051 (1993) (applying the doctrine to a lessor in the business of leasing coin-operated laundry equipment). Indeed, as the *Collins Entertainment* Court recognized, Comment f to the Restatement (Second) Contracts § 347, like UCC § 2–708(2), recognizes the lost volume seller theory.

2. *Definition of Lost Volume Seller.* As the principal case reflects, most courts require a seller seeking to recover lost profits as a lost volume seller to demonstrate three elements: (1) the seller would have solicited the person who bought the "resold" good even if there had been no breach; (2) the solicitation would have been successful; and (3) the seller could have performed both the original contract and the contract for resale. These courts focus on the seller's capacity to perform both contracts. Some courts have added an additional requirement. These courts require the seller to demonstrate not only that it had the capacity to make the additional sale but also that it would have been profitable for the seller to make the additional sale. *See, e.g.,* R.E. Davis Chemical Corp. v. Diasonics, Inc., 826 F.2d 678 (7th Cir.1987).

3. *New Businesses.* Prospective profits are ordinarily not recoverable for a newly established business with no track record or for a business operated at a loss. What if the business is established on the basis of a contract specifically to furnish a particular product? In *Fiberlok, Inc. v. LMS Enterprises, Inc.*, 976 F.2d 958 (5th Cir.1992), a manufacturer of resins initiated a new business which involved output and processing contracts with a buyer for a special product. The seller sought to recover lost profits under 2–708(2) when the buyer failed to purchase goods pursuant to the contracts. The court found that the seller was unable to mitigate damages because the buyer's breach prevented the seller from maintaining its overhead expenses, supplies and materials and caused the seller to cease production entirely of the special items. The seller was awarded lost profits based upon estimates associated with the prior course of dealing of parties.

4. *Never Produced Goods.* Should a seller be compensated for breach of contract involving a product never produced? In *Oral–X Corp. v. Farnam Companies, Inc.*, 931 F.2d 667 (10th Cir.1991), a manufacturer of horse care products sought to recover lost royalties both for products shipped and destroyed after risk of loss passed to the buyer as well as for orders cancelled by the buyer before manufacture of the remaining goods. The court awarded the seller lost profits for both the delivered products and for the cancelled orders, reasoning that to do otherwise would defeat the reasonable expectations of the seller of royalties for the entire supply of goods. *See also* Jewish Federation of Greater Des Moines v. Cedar Forest Prod. Co., 796 N.W.2d 456, 52 U.C.C. Rep.Serv.2d 422 (Iowa App.2003) (awarding lost profits on a construction contract even though seller had merely purchased materials and had not begun assembly at the time of the breach).

5. *Calculating Lost Profits.* Assuming that a seller demonstrates that it is entitled to lost profits under section 2–708(2), how does one measure lost profits? Section 2–708(2) provides that lost profits should be calculated as the profit (including reasonable overhead) that the seller would have made from full performance with due allowance for costs reasonably incurred and due credit for payments or proceeds of re-sale. Profit generally is measured as the difference between the contract price and the seller's cost to perform under the contract. *See, e.g.,* RKR Motors, Inc. v. Associated Uniform Rental Linen Supply, 2006 WL 3019582 (Fla.App. 3 Dist.2006); Sterling Freight Lines, Inc. v. Prairie Material Sales, Inc., 285 Ill.App.3d 914, 221 Ill.Dec. 155, 674 N.E.2d 948 (1996). The seller's costs can be divided into two types of costs: fixed costs or overhead and variable costs. Fixed costs or overhead are considered to be those expenses that will be incurred by a business regardless of whether it performs a particular contract. Examples include secretarial and executive salaries, property taxes, general administrative expenses, rent and insurance. Grand Trunk W.R.R. Co. v. H.W. Nelson Co., 116 F.2d 823, 839 (6th Cir.1941); Magnet Resources, Inc. v. Summit MRI, Inc., 318 N.J.Super. 275, 295, 723 A.2d 976, 986 (App.Div.1998). Section 2–708(2) expressly allows the seller to recover that portion of overhead which is reasonably incurred. Variable

costs are considered to be those costs that can be identified to the specific contract and can be avoided if the contract is not performed. Examples of variable costs include the cost of materials, labor, transportation and storage. *See, e.g.,* R & A, Inc. v. Kozy Korner, Inc., 672 A.2d 1062 (D.C.App.1996) (food, liquor and state sales taxes for a restaurant).

6. *Proceeds of Resale.* As noted above, section 2–708(2) requires the seller to deduct any proceeds earned on resale from its lost profits. This language has proven problematic in cases involving lost volume sellers because deducting the proceeds from the resale of the contracted for goods to a third party would eliminate the seller's recovery. Courts universally have concluded that this language does not apply to lost volume sellers because the sale to the third party is independent of and would have occurred regardless of the breach. *See, e.g.,* Auto Shine Car Wash Systems, Inc. v. Nice 'N Clean Car Wash, Inc., 58 Mass.App.Ct. 685, 792 N.E.2d 682 (2003); National Controls v. Commodore Business Machines, 163 Cal. App.3d 688, 209 Cal.Rptr. 636 (1985).

Kenco Homes Inc. v. Williams

94 Wash.App. 219, 972 P.2d 125 (1999).

■ MORGAN, J.

Kenco Homes, Inc., sued Dale E. Williams and Debi A. Williams, husband and wife, for breaching a contract to purchase a mobile home. After a bench trial, the trial court ruled primarily for Williams. Kenco appealed, claiming the trial court used an incorrect measure of damages. We reverse.

Kenco buys mobile homes from the factory and sells them to the public. Sometimes, it contracts to sell a home that the factory has not yet built. It has "a virtually unlimited supply of product," according to the trial court's finding of fact.

On September 27, 1994, Kenco and Williams signed a written contract whereby Kenco agreed to sell, and Williams agreed to buy, a mobile home that Kenco had not yet ordered from the factory. The contract called for a price of $39,400, with $500 down.

The contract contained two conditions pertinent here. According to the first, the contract would be enforceable only if Williams could obtain financing. According to the second, the contract would be enforceable only if Williams later approved a bid for site improvements. Financing was to cover the cost of the mobile home and the cost of the land on which the mobile home would be placed.

* * *

In early October, Williams accepted Kenco's bid for site improvements. * * * Also in early October, Williams received preliminary approval on the needed financing.

On or about October 12, Williams gave Kenco a $600 check so Kenco could order an appraisal of the land on which the mobile home would be located. Before Kenco could act, however, Williams stopped payment on the check and repudiated the entire transaction. His reason, according to the trial court's finding of fact, was that he "had found a better deal elsewhere."

When Williams repudiated, Kenco had not yet ordered the mobile home from the factory. After Williams repudiated, Kenco simply did not place the order. As a result, Kenco's only out-of-pocket expense was a minor amount of office overhead.

On November 1, 1994, Kenco sued Williams for lost profits. After a bench trial, the superior court found that Williams had breached the contract; that Kenco was entitled to damages; and that Kenco had lost profits in the amount of $11,133 ($6,720 on the mobile home, and $4,413 on the site improvements). The court further found, however, that Kenco would be adequately compensated by retaining Williams' $500 down payment * * * Kenco filed this appeal.

In this court, Williams does not contest the trial court's finding that he breached the contract. Thus, the only issues are (1) whether the superior court used the correct measure of damages * * *.

Under the Uniform Commercial Code (UCC), a nonbreaching seller may recover "damages for non-acceptance" from a breaching buyer. The measure of such damages is as follows:

> (1) Subject to subsection (2) and to the provisions of this Article with respect to proof of market price (RCW 62A.2–723), the measure of damages for non-acceptance or repudiation by the buyer is the difference between the market price at the time and place for tender and the unpaid contract price together with any incidental damages provided in this Article (RCW 62A.2–710), but less expenses saved in consequence of the buyer's breach.
>
> (2) *If the measure of damages provided in subsection (1) is inadequate to put the seller in as good a position as performance would have done* then the measure of damages is the profit (including reasonable overhead) which the seller would have made from full performance by the buyer, together with any incidental damages provided in this Article (RCW 62A.2–710), due allowance for costs reasonably incurred and due credit for payments or proceeds of resale.[10]

As the italicized words demonstrate, the statute's purpose is to put the nonbreaching seller in the position that he or she would have occupied if the breaching buyer had fully performed (or, in alternative terms, to give the nonbreaching seller the benefit of his or her bargain). A party claiming damages under subsection (2) bears the burden of showing that an award of damages under subsection (1) would be inadequate.

---

10. RCW 62A.2–708 (emphasis added).

In general, the adequacy of damages under subsection (1) depends on whether the nonbreaching seller has a readily available market on which he or she can resell the goods that the breaching buyer should have taken. When a buyer breaches before either side has begun to perform, the amount needed to give the seller the benefit of his or her bargain is the difference between the contract price and the seller's expected cost of performance. Using market price, this difference can, in turn, be subdivided into two smaller differences: (a) the difference between the contract price and the market price, and (b) the difference between the market price and the seller's expected cost of performance. So long as a nonbreaching seller can reasonably resell the breached goods on the open market, he or she can recover the difference between contract price and market price by invoking subsection (1), and the difference between market price and his or her expected cost of performance by reselling the breached goods on the open market. Thus, he or she is made whole by subsection (1), and subsection (1) damages should be deemed "adequate." But if a nonbreaching seller cannot reasonably resell the breached goods on the open market, he or she cannot recover, merely by invoking subsection (1), the difference between market price and his or her expected cost of performance. Hence, he or she is not made whole by subsection (1); subsection (1) damages are "inadequate to put the seller in as good a position as performance would have done;" and subsection (2) comes into play.

The cases illustrate at least three specific situations in which a nonbreaching seller cannot reasonably resell on the open market. In the first, the seller never comes into possession of the breached goods; although he or she plans to acquire such goods before the buyer's breach, he or she rightfully elects not to acquire them after the buyer's breach. In the second, the seller possesses some or all of the breached goods, but they are of such an odd or peculiar nature that the seller lacks a post-breach market on which to sell them; they are, for example, unfinished, obsolete, or highly specialized. In the third situation, the seller again possesses some or all of the breached goods, but because the market is already oversupplied with such goods (i.e., the available supply exceeds demand), he or she cannot resell the breached goods without displacing another sale. Frequently, these sellers are labelled "jobber," "components seller," and "lost volume seller," respectively; in our view, however, such labels confuse more than clarify.

To illustrate the first situation, we examine *Copymate Marketing v. Modern Merchandising,* a case cited and discussed by both parties. In that case, Copymate had an option to purchase three thousand copiers from Dowling for $51,750. Before Copymate had exercised its option, it contracted to sell the copiers to Modern for $165,000. It also promised Modern that it would spend $47,350 for advertising that would benefit Modern. It told Dowling it was exercising its option, but before it could finish its purchase from Dowling, Modern repudiated. Acting with commercial reasonableness, Copymate responded by cancelling its deal with Dowling and never acquiring the copiers. It then sued Modern for its lost profits and prevailed in the trial court. Modern appealed, but this court affirmed. Because Copymate had rightfully elected not to acquire the copiers, it had no way to resell them on the open market; subsection (1) was inadequate; and subsection (2) applied. Thus, Copymate recovered its contract price with Modern ($165,000), minus the expected cost of performing its contract with Modern ($51,750 for Dowling, $47,350 for advertising, and $180 for a miscellaneous import fee), for a total of $65,720.

To illustrate the second situation, we again examine *Copymate*. Based on substantial evidence, the *Copymate* trial court found that after Modern's repudiation, Copymate had "no active or reasonably available market for the resale of the ... copiers." One reason was that the copiers had been in storage in Canada for nine years; thus, they seem to have been obsolete. Again, then, Copymate could not resell the copiers on the open market; subsection (1) was inadequate; and subsection (2) provided for an award of "lost profits."

To illustrate the third situation, we examine *R.E. Davis Chemical Corp. v. Diasonics*. In that case, Davis breached his contract to buy medical equipment from Diasonics. Diasonics was in possession of the equipment, which it soon resold on the open market. Diasonics then sued Davis for "lost profits" under subsection (2), arguing that "it was a 'lost volume seller,' and, as such, it lost the profit from one sale when Davis breached its contract." The trial court granted summary judgment to Davis, but the appellate court reversed and remanded for trial. Other courts, the appellate court noted, "have defined a lost volume seller as one that has a predictable and finite number of customers and that has the capacity either to sell to all new buyers or to make the one additional sale represented by the resale after the breach." This definition, the appellate court ruled, lacks an essential element: whether the seller *would* have sold an additional unit but for the buyer's breach. On remand, then, Diasonics would have to prove (a) that it *could* have produced and sold the breached unit in addition to its actual volume, and (b) that it *would* have produced and sold the breached unit in addition to its actual volume.

In this case, Kenco did not order the breached goods before Williams repudiated. After Williams repudiated, Kenco was not required to order the breached goods from the factory; it rightfully elected not to do so; and it could not resell the breached goods on the open market. Here, then, "the measure of damages provided in subsection (1) is inadequate to put [Kenco] in as good a position as [Williams'] performance would have done;" subsection (2) states the applicable measure of damages; and Kenco is entitled to its lost profit of $11,133.

* * *

Reversed with directions to enter an amended judgment awarding Kenco its lost profit of $11,133; * * * and any ancillary amounts required by law.

1. *Loss of Market.* In the principal case, the court awarded the seller lost profits because 2–708(1) implicitly requires that the seller have the contracted for goods to resell in the market. Section 2–708(1) also implicitly requires that a market for the contracted goods exist. Thus courts have awarded aggrieved sellers lost profits even when the seller retains the completed contracted for goods because no market exists in which to sell the goods.

Timber Access Industries v. U.S. Plywood–Champion Papers, Inc., 263 Or. 509, 503 P.2d 482 (1972), illustrates the problem of "loss of market." In this case there was a contract for the sale of timber, but the market price had fallen so low as to not justify the seller's manufacturing the requested product. The court held that this would constitute a loss of market, requiring the use of section 2–708(2) measure of damages.

2. *Specialty Items.* As the principal case notes, Section 2–708(2) has been used in other situations when the contract-market price differential would be inappropriate. For example, in *Capital Steel Co. v. Foster and Creighton Co.*, 264 Ark. 683, 574 S.W.2d 256 (1978), the seller's damages were measured by loss of profits under 2–708(2) when there was an anticipatory repudiation of a contract for steel and the seller had not fabricated the product. The court held that since the seller could not and did not "tender" actual performance, damages were limited to the contract price less the proposed manufacturing cost as the measure of lost profits.

3. *Duty to Mitigate.* In *Madsen v. Murrey & Sons Co., Inc.*, 743 P.2d 1212 (Utah 1987), the seller sought to recover the lost profits under 2–708(2) for customized pool tables which were manufactured in accordance with special electronic features designed by the buyer. The seller had completed the manufacture of the pool tables when the buyer repudiated the agreement. The court found that the seller failed to mitigate damages in a commercially reasonable manner by dismantling the pool tables and using the materials for salvage and firewood, rather than attempting to sell or market tables at a full or discounted price. Since the seller failed to mitigate damages properly by attempting to sell the pool tables on the open market, the court disallowed lost profits and limited damages to the contract price-market price differential under 2–708(1), less restitution to the buyer of amounts paid on the contract.

4. *Lost Profits as a Limit on Damages.* Should courts apply the lost profits measure of damages under section 2–708(2) in cases where the seller would be overcompensated by the traditional damages formula in section 2–708(1)? Whether and in what circumstances to limit a seller to damages under section 2–708(2) has proved a troublesome issue for courts. As the court explained in *Purina Mills v. Less*, 295 F.Supp.2d 1017 (N.D.Iowa 2003), courts focus on whether the seller assumed the risk of market fluctuations and whether the seller is contractually obligated to acquire the contracted for goods in determining whether to limit the seller to lost profits. For example, in *Trans World Metals, Inc. v. Southwire Co.*, 769 F.2d 902 (2d Cir.1985), the seller sued when the buyer repudiated a long-term commodity supply contract after the market price of the supply

contract fell dramatically. The seller sought the difference between the contract and market prices, but the buyer claimed that the 2–708(1) measure gave the seller an unwarranted windfall. Instead the buyer argued for a limitation of the damages to the seller's lost profits under 2–708(2). The court recognized that the contract-market price differential would seldom be equivalent to the seller's actual economic loss from the breach. Nonetheless, the court noted the parties entered into a long-term supply contract in a volatile market. In so doing, the court reasoned that both parties had assumed the risk of market fluctuations. As such, the court concluded that the seller should not be denied the benefit of its bargain.

Compare *Union Carbide Corp. v. Consumers Power Co.*, 636 F.Supp. 1498 (E.D.Mich.1986), where the court allowed such a limitation. The case involved a contract for fuel oil which the buyer breached after a substantial drop in the price of oil. The seller's damages under section 2–708(1) were limited to a "fair profit" under 2–708(2). The court explained that a windfall to the seller might be appropriate when risks of price fluctuation were assumed in the contract because this would leave the parties with the benefit of their bargain. Here, however, the contract price was tied to the seller's cost in acquiring the oil. Thus, the seller had not assumed any such risk of market fluctuation but, instead, was guaranteed a profit on the goods accepted by the buyer. Similarly, in *Purina Mills*, the seller entered into a contract to supply weanling pigs to a farmer at a fixed price. The seller then entered into a fixed price supply contract with a third party. In this way, the seller insulated itself from the risk that the market price would rise above the contract price. When the market price instead fell and the farmer breached the contract, the seller was theoretically exposed to the risk that it would be forced to resell the pigs at a price below the market price. However, because the supplier offered to release the seller from its obligation to purchase pigs, the court concluded that the seller had an obligation to mitigate its damages by accepting the buyout and as such would be limited to recovering its lost profits only.

5. *Proof Problems.* Proof of damages under section 2–708(2) is often more difficult than under other U.C.C. provisions because proving lost profits may be complicated. Lost profits under 2–708(2) are considered an item of special damages and must be pleaded with particularity. *See* Great Western Sugar Co. v. Mrs. Allison's Cookie Co., 563 F.Supp. 430 (E.D.Mo. 1983).

Problems arise both from the typical complexity of the accounting and from legal uncertainties. *Compare* Nederlandse Draadindustrie NDI B.V. v. Grand Pre–Stressed Corp., 466 F.Supp. 846 (E.D.N.Y.1979) (calculation of the company's expenses includes only the manufacturer's variable costs and not fixed costs because the contract did not require the seller to incur additional fixed costs) *with* Scullin Steel Co. v. Paccar, Inc., 708 S.W.2d 756 (Mo.App.1986) (overhead expenses were awarded separately from lost profits).

6. *Fungible Goods.* Resale under section 2–706 is not limited to the resale of the goods "identified" to the contract when the goods are

fungible. For example, in *Servbest Foods v. Emessee Ind.*, 82 Ill.App.3d 662, 37 Ill.Dec. 945, 403 N.E.2d 1 (1980), the buyer rejected a particular lot of beef. In calculating damages from the mitigating resale, the seller was allowed to use the resale price of a different lot of beef because there was no evidence that the lots were not identical in quantity, quality and description.

PROBLEM: THE COINS

A state Centennial Commission contracted to purchase 100,000 silver-colored commemorative coins at $.50 each from the American Manufacturing Company. The Commission planned to distribute the coins in connection with the celebration of the state's one hundredth anniversary.

The Commission ran low on funds and repudiated the contract. American had already manufactured 60,000 coins but the Commission had not yet paid any amounts on the contract.

No ready market exists in which American Manufacturing can resell the coins. The company has also incurred storage charges of $800 for the coins. Assuming the coins cost American $.30 each to manufacture, what would be the proper measure of damages for the seller:

(a) With respect to the 60,000 manufactured coins;

(b) For the remaining 40,000 coins which have not been manufactured?

C.R. Daniels, Inc. v. Yazoo Mfg. Co.

641 F.Supp. 205 (S.D.Miss.1986).

■ LEE, DISTRICT JUDGE.

This cause came before the court for trial on the complaint of the plaintiff, C.R. Daniels, Inc. (Daniels), and the counterclaim of the defendant, Yazoo Manufacturing Company, Inc. (Yazoo). * * *

In June 1981, Charles Silvernail, who was then vice president of Daniels, and James Kerr, who was at that time president of Yazoo, began negotiating an agreement whereby Daniels would design and manufacture grass catcher bags for "S" series lawn mowers to be manufactured by Yazoo. Daniels was to begin manufacture upon approval by Yazoo of a design and sample of the proposed bag. * * *

The agreement between Daniels and Yazoo was reduced to writing in the form of a series of purchase orders issued by defendant and signed by Kerr, with each replacing earlier purchase orders. The initial purchase order was issued on October 23, 1981, prior to final approval of the designs, so that Daniels could begin ordering raw materials. In the October 23 purchase order, Yazoo contracted for 20,000 bags. * * *

Kerr testified that in June 1982, he began to see evidence of a problem with cracking chutes on the bags. He sent a damaged bag to Stavinoha who informed Kerr that, based on the presence of tire marks on the bag, Daniels had determined the problem to be caused by abuse.[5] Kerr also testified that he sent two other bags to Stavinoha in 1982 and 1983, apparently without a cover letter. Stavinoha denied receipt and Kerr offered neither physical proof that the bags were sent nor explanation for his failure to contact Stavinoha when no response was forthcoming.

* * * Throughout this time, Daniels continued to manufacture bags and frames. On October 14, 1982, Kerr sent to Daniels a photocopy of the July 5 purchase order with "cancelled" written on its face. Kerr offered no explanation at that time for the attempted cancellation. * * *

Daniels' attorney wrote Yazoo on May 18 demanding payment. Yazoo's counsel responded and notified Daniels for the first time of the specific complaints which Yazoo had with the bags and frames. Following initiation of this suit, Daniels' attorney was invited to view inspection of the bags in Yazoo's inventory. The inspection revealed that ninety-two percent of the bags had cracked chutes. Until this time, Daniels had been unaware that the chutes were defective in a substantial number of bags. Upon learning the results of Yazoo's inspection, Daniels found that approximately seventy-five percent of the bags that it held were also faulty.

Daniels brought this suit to recover the price of the goods pursuant to Miss.Code Ann. § 75–2–709 (1972), which provides in part:

(1) When the buyer fails to pay the price as it becomes due the seller may recover, together with any incidental damages under the next section, the price

(a) of goods accepted or conforming goods lost or damaged within a commercially reasonable time after risk of their loss is passed to the buyer; and

(b) of goods identified to the contract if the seller is unable after reasonable effort to resell them at a reasonable price or the circumstances reasonably indicate that such effort will be unavailing.

Yazoo argues that it never accepted the bags and frames. * * * It is undisputed that at least by December 1982, Kerr was aware of the tremendous magnitude of the problem with cracked chutes. Thereafter, however, he continued to indicate to Daniels that Yazoo would attempt to sell the bags it had in stock and anticipated delivery of bags some time in the future. By his action, Kerr signified to Daniels that the bags were accepted in spite of his knowledge of their nonconformity. Additionally, Yazoo's continued attempts to sell the bags, as well as its destruction of the defective bags, were inconsistent with an effective rejection. Accordingly, this court is of the opinion that Yazoo accepted the bags. * * *

The amount of damages to which plaintiff is entitled is governed by Miss.Code Ann. § 75–2–709 (1972) which is set out above. At trial, plaintiff established that the bags and frames were specially designed and manufac-

---

5. At trial, Kerr testified that the tire marks were the result of his driving over the bag to test it. There was no evidence that he told Stavinoha of this.

tured for Yazoo and cannot be used for any other purpose and that the raw materials have no other use and cannot be resold. Plaintiff computed its damages for bags and frames in different stages of production without challenge by defendant. Plaintiff's computations, which include materials cost, labor and overhead, selling and administrative expense and profit relating to manufacture of the bags and frames, and incidental damages, are as follows:

Bags, completed: 6,953 bags @ $12.05	83,783.65
Bags, various stages of production 2,220 units @ $10.68	23,709.60
Bags, raw material 2,459 units @ $7.50	18,442.50
Frames, complete 764 units @ $4.88	3,728.32
Frames, in process 5,270 units @ $4.26	22,450.20
Incidental Damages	2,379.68
TOTAL	$154,493.95

* * *

Daniels contends that Yazoo's action for breach of warranties is foreclosed by failure to give adequate notice of the breach. * * * Daniels had no reason even to suspect that Yazoo considered the contract to be breached. In fact, it was not until initiation of this litigation that Daniels learned of the magnitude of the problem. Such conduct on the part of Yazoo can hardly be viewed as notification of breach. [Citation.] Accordingly, this court is of the opinion that Yazoo's counterclaim should be dismissed. * * *

---

1. *Price, Resale Damages and Lost Profits.* The seller in the principal case had not completed production of all of the grass catcher bags and frames. Should the court have awarded the seller price under section 2–709 for bags that were not completed at the time of the breach? Review the plaintiff's computation of damages. Did the plaintiff seek to recover the price of the unfinished bags?

2. Compare the principal case with *City of Louisville v. Rockwell Manufacturing Co.*, 482 F.2d 159 (6th Cir.1973), where the manufacturer sought damages for breach of contract for the purchase and installation of 7,650 parking meters for the municipality. The company completed the manufacture of the initial purchase order of 1,000 parking meters when the city repudiated the entire contract. The court allowed recovery pursuant to 2–709 of the purchase price for the already completed meters which remained "unsold and unsalable" and the loss of profit under 2–708(2) for the remaining meters. *See also* S.N.A. Nut Co. v. The Haagen–Dazs Co., 247 Bankr. 7 (Bkrtcy.N.D.Ill.2000) (seller of processed nuts entitled to recover from buyer the difference between the contract price and resale price for those finished nuts that could be resold; the contract price for those specially manufactured finished nuts for which no market for resale

existed; and lost profits for the remaining nuts called for under the contract which had not been completed at the time of the breach).

C. LIQUIDATED DAMAGES

Section Coverage:

Contracting parties may stipulate a specified sum of money which would be payable as damages to the non-breaching party for a material breach of the contract. Liquidated damages serve to remove the uncertainties and difficulties involved in proving actual damages in the event of a breach, and they thereby function to reduce litigation expenses and expedite the trial process.

The principle of freedom of contract is not an absolute concept; it is limited by the refusal of courts to enforce extortionate or unconscionable bargains. Therefore, a liquidated damages provision is valid only if it corresponds with general notions of damages as a substitutionary measure for performance in the event of breach. If the court perceives the purpose of the clause as an attempt to compel performance through the threat of onerous damages, the provision will be considered a penalty and thus unenforceable. Labels applied by the parties to describe the provision as a penalty or an enforceable liquidated damages clause are not controlling.

The law of liquidated damages is consistent with the common law policy of allowing efficient contract breach. This substantive policy is that a contracting party should be permitted to pay compensatory damages for a breach in exchange for the opportunity to shift goods or services to a different source in order to maximize economic resources. To the extent that a contractual damages provision operates to punish a contract breach, the goal of maximizing resources is undermined. Conversely, a liquidated damages provision that specifies a reasonable estimate of actual damages upon breach is consistent with that goal.

The traditional test to evaluate the validity of a liquidated damages provision is whether, at the time the parties entered the contract, (1) damages resulting from a breach would be difficult to determine, and (2) the stipulated amount had a reasonable relationship to the potential damages if a breach occurred. The two criteria are not necessarily inconsistent or contradictory because the reasonableness of the liquidated sum is determined in light of the anticipated harm rather than in hindsight looking at the amount of actual damages. Thus, courts do not require precise estimates; the amount of actual damages will almost certainly vary from that stipulated in the contract. The very uncertainty in predicting future harm militates against requiring a precise matching of actual to liquidated damages.

The Uniform Commercial Code § 2–718(1) and the Restatement (Second) of Contracts § 356(1) carry forward the common law approach in a slightly modified fashion by providing that reasonableness of a liquidated damages clause may be shown based upon either the anticipated or actual harm from the breach. Section 2–718 further provides an insight into the meaning of "reasonableness" by considering the "difficulties of proof of loss, inconvenience or infeasibility of otherwise obtaining an adequate remedy." Under both the U.C.C. and the common law, whether the parties made a good faith pre-estimate of damages should be objectively evaluated rather than inquiring into the subjective intentions of the parties.

Finally, courts may consider whether the parties intended the liquidated damages provision to serve as the exclusive or an alternative remedy in the event of a breach. Unless the contract expressly provides otherwise, courts generally will construe the contract to allow the non-breaching party to pursue other available remedies, such as specific performance. In that regard, however, the party seeking specific performance still must demonstrate the requisite elements for entitlement to equitable relief, including that damages were not an adequate remedy, despite the existence of the liquidated damages clause.

Model Case:

John Harrell, who had fifteen years of experience in the jewelry business working for several companies, decided to open his own jewelry store. He acquired a small tract of land in a developing commercial area of the city and entered into a contract with Parsons' Engineering Company to construct a building for the store.

Harrell wanted the building to be completed by September 1 in order to take advantage of the historically strong sales which take place at the end of the year. Accordingly, the parties placed a clause in their construction agreement which provided that Parsons agreed to pay, as liquidated damages, a sum in the amount of $200 per day for every day that the completion of the building was delayed past September 1. Correspondingly, Parsons would receive a bonus payment from Harrell of $1,000 if the building was finished by August 15.

A court would probably uphold the validity of the stipulated damages provision because the loss of business which Harrell would sustain by a delay in opening the new business would be difficult to estimate. Therefore, a liquidated damages clause serves the function of compensating where proof of damages would be otherwise uncertain. Harrell also would need to show a reasonable basis for arriving at the $200 per day figure as a good faith pre-estimate of the anticipated harm which would potentially result from a breach by Parsons. Mathematical precision would not be required; rather the inquiry is whether the stipulated amount was objectively reasonable as a substitute for performance or had an oppressive character to compel performance.

Boyle v. Petrie Stores Corporation

136 Misc.2d 380, 518 N.Y.S.2d 854 (1985).

■ GREENFIELD, JUSTICE.

This is an action for wrongful discharge, but unlike many such cases which have besieged the courts of late, this one involves an executive employee who in fact had a carefully worked out written contract, and now, claiming a breach, insists on a literal application of that contract.

* * * Under the contract, Boyle was to become President and Chief Executive Officer of the corporation as of Nov. 1, 1982. * * * The Board approved the agreement, which was duly executed, and amended the corporate by-laws to reflect the fact that Milton Petrie, the Chairman of the Board, was to preside at director's meetings, but that he was no longer to be the Chief Executive Officer. Boyle, as Chief Executive Officer and President was, subject to the control of the Board, to "have general supervision over the business of the corporation."

* * *

Boyle in fact reported for work at the corporate headquarters in Secaucus on Nov. 8, 1982. While Boyle informed the other Petrie executives that he was now the Chief Executive Officer, and they should take their directions from him, Petrie continued to give operating directions just as he always had. * * *

On January 6, a formal real estate meeting and review, with Petrie present, was held. As various items were taken up, Petrie said, "leave it to me, I'll take care of it." When Boyle pressed him for details, Petrie repeated, "I'll take care of it". At the conclusion of the meeting Petrie confronted Boyle in his office. With mounting anger, he said, "Where the hell do you get off to question my authority on these leases and embarrass me in front of all my organization?" He told Boyle he was moving in too fast. Boyle challenged him, and impertinently replied, "If you didn't have 63 percent of this stock, I would take you to the Board of Directors and have you removed as Chairman." This was too much for Petrie. He exploded, "You're fired!"

A special meeting of the Board of Directors was held on January 13, 1983. * * * The Board did not discuss the terms of Boyle's employment agreement or ask to hear Mr. Boyle, but acceded to Mr. Petrie's demand that he be terminated effective immediately. Mr. Petrie retook the titles of Chief Executive Officer and President. A press release announced these changes and stated that "The reason for the change was due to policy differences on the way the business should be run."

Boyle had served but two months of his five year contract. Claiming that the contract had been improperly breached by Petrie Stores Corporation, he brought this action seeking recovery of over $2,000,000 as liquidated damages he is entitled to under the contract. * * *

 The employment agreement is quite specific about the damages which are to be payable for termination other than for "material breach or just cause". Section 7(a) of the agreement provides that in the event of a termination other than for "material breach or just cause", the corporation is to pay "in one lump sum the amounts otherwise payable to Employee ... discounted to present value at the rate of 15 percent per annum." Calculation of the lump sum payable thus works out to $1,439,352.44 in lieu of lost salary, and $166,689.39 in guaranteed bonus claims, for a total of $1,606,041.83.

While this is a very substantial figure to pay a man who was on the job for 8 weeks, and was fired within days after his orientation period, when he tried to take over the reins of management, we are dealing here with a provision for liquidated damages designed to provide some precision for the calculation of otherwise speculative damages.

Parties may properly agree to a dollar figure representing the injuries they agree the plaintiff would sustain if the contract were breached. [Citation.] So long as the liquidated damages provisions are neither unconscionable nor contrary to public policy, they will be enforced as written by a court. [Citations.]

Defendant contends that the contractual provisions for liquidated damages are, in fact, a penalty. Stipulated contractual damages will be considered a penalty only if the amount provided for is clearly disproportionate to the actual loss, and as an *in terrorem* effort to assure performance regardless of economic loss. Those cases urged by the defendant as standing for the proposition that stipulated damages such as those here involved should be considered a "penalty", are readily distinguishable. Since courts have traditionally, from the time of the Merchant of Venice, viewed a forfeiture out of all proportion to the breach of contract as an unenforceable penalty, our courts have attempted to strike out the clear penalties while upholding agreement which clarified amounts of damage which could otherwise be in dispute. * * * In this case, a termination of Boyle's employment contract could result in damages well over $500,000 a year, and the parties could reasonably agree that instead of litigating the question of damages after the event, which would leave uncertainties such as the employee's efforts to mitigate damages by securing other employment, and the question as to how long the other employment might last, and whether the benefits were comparable, they could reasonably agree beforehand as to what damages would be payable. The amounts fixed do not exceed the total compensation provided in the five year contract.

Both parties to the contract were sophisticated and were represented by able counsel. This is a factor to be taken into consideration in determining whether one side is now exacting an unconscionable penalty. [Citations.]

It is to be recalled that Boyle was aware of Mr. Petrie's mercurial reputation, and wanted some concrete assurances of security before giving up the well-paid position he had worked himself up to with Federated Stores. An involuntary discharge from Petrie Stores would cast a considerable shadow on Mr. Boyle's reputation as a young super-achieving executive, and possibly diminish his prospects for the future. The agreement was carefully negotiated at arms-length by reputable attorneys for both parties, and it was clearly understood that a precipitate firing of Mr. Boyle could result in very substantial contractual damages. The fact that the parties agreed to limit liability to $2,100,000 excluding stock options demonstrates a realization that without such a ceiling the actual damages could go even higher.

* * *

The lump sum payment provision here clearly was a liquidated damages provision and not a penalty. In the bargaining neither party had the ability to overreach the other. The sum provided for was not disproportionate to the damages which could be incurred. * * * The damage provisions are valid and enforceable pursuant to their terms.

The fact that subsequent to his termination Boyle took a position with another corporation—General Mills—as one of six executive vice-presidents rather than as Chief Executive Officer, does not serve to mitigate the liquidated damages.

Once the parties have provided for valid liquidated damages, the sum payable becomes fixed and there is no further inquiry to be made as to possible mitigation by subsequent employment. * * *

Here, a formula was set forth to calculate damages without regard to subsequent extrinsic facts. At the time the parties could not know how long plaintiff would be unemployed if terminated. We still do not know how long the subsequent employment will continue, or whether it will give the same net to Mr. Boyle as his Petrie Stores contract over a 5 year span, since his subsequent General Mills contract is terminable at will. We need not wait to the conclusion of the five year contract period to find out what Boyle's aggregate loss of earnings might be, because the agreement requires the liquidated damages to be paid "forthwith". That clearly contemplates that damages were to be fixed as of the date of termination, regardless of events thereafter.

* * * [Judgment for the plaintiff.]

_____

1. Compare the principal case with *Vanderbilt University v. DiNardo*, 174 F.3d 751 (6th Cir.1999), where the university sought to enforce a liquidated damages clause for an alleged breach of an employment agreement by its head football coach, triggered by resigning his position and taking a job at another school. The clause provided that the coach would be obligated to pay the school an amount equal to the number of years remaining on the contract multiplied times the annual salary. The court found the clause enforceable, reasoning that the university's interest in maintaining a stable football program, coupled with the difficulty of estimating the potential losses in revenues associated with ticket sales, alumni relations, and public support satisfied the test of reasonableness. The court further noted that the clause was the product of bargaining and operated in a reciprocal fashion, whereby the university would have liability for a breach of the agreement on an equal basis as the coach. A strong dissenting opinion objected that the clause was simply a disguised penalty functioning to deter the coach from taking a position at another school. The dissent

observed that "the use of a 'take-home pay' measuring stick suggests that the function of the stick was to rap the coach's knuckles and not to measure the university's loss." Id. at 761.

2.   The law of liquidated damages reflects a tension between conflicting goals. It is socially desirable for parties to fix damages in the event of breach when the amount bears a reasonable proportion to the probable loss and the actual loss is difficult to estimate with precision. Such a provision, however, should not have the effect of deterring breach through compulsion because of the potential high economic loss. *See* Leasing Service Corp. v. Justice, 673 F.2d 70, 73 (2d Cir.1982) (liquidated damages may serve useful purpose, but cannot have an *in terrorem* effect and the promisee may reap a windfall well in excess of just compensation).

3.   A threshold requirement for enforceability of a liquidated damages clause is that the terms must be expressly stated in the contract. *See* ABI, Inc. v. City of Los Angeles, 153 Cal.App.3d 669, 200 Cal.Rptr. 563 (1984) (city's claim to retain a developer's fee as liquidated damages not allowed because the contract did not effectively express such a designation). *See also* Polish American Machinery Corp. v. R.D. & D. Corp., 760 F.2d 507 (3d Cir.1985). Also, liquidated damages will not be awarded absent material breach of the contract. *See* Woodbridge Place Apts. v. Washington Square Capital, 965 F.2d 1429 (7th Cir.1992) (liquidated damages provision in loan commitment agreement unenforceable where borrower did not breach contract but rather failed to satisfy conditions precedent to funding of loan).

4.   Whether a contractual provision is characterized as a valid liquidated damages clause or a penalty does not depend upon the label given by the parties. *See* American Multi–Cinema, Inc. v. Southroads, L.L.C., 115 F.Supp.2d 1257, 1264 (D.Kan.2000) (parties' own characterization of clause as liquidated damages or as a penalty does not control). A handful of courts, though, will give some weight to the terminology chosen by the parties as a factor in interpreting a provision fixing damages. Thus, in *Zeppenfeld v. Morgan*, 185 S.W.2d 898 (Mo.App.1945), the court recognized that the mere fact that the parties styled the sum "liquidated damages" was not conclusive of its character yet was considered very persuasive evidence to that effect. Some courts have considered the intentions of the parties as a criterion for enforcement in addition to the traditional two-prong test of reasonableness and difficulty in estimating damages. ADP–Financial Computer Services v. First National Bank, 703 F.2d 1261 (11th Cir.1983).

The prevailing view, though, rejects the intention element as being surplusage. *See* Wilmington Housing Authority v. Pan Builders, Inc., 665 F.Supp. 351 (D.Del.1987) (the intention criterion adds nothing because it validates a provision only if the other two criteria are met and invalidates a provision only when they are not). Koenings v. Joseph Schlitz Brewing Co., 126 Wis.2d 349, 377 N.W.2d 593 (1985) (courts should consider the circumstances which give rise to the formation of the contract rather than the intent of the parties). *See also* Restatement (Second) of Contracts § 356 comment C; Williston, Contracts § 272 (3d ed. 1961); Corbin, Contracts § 1058 (1964); Clarkson, Miller & Muris, Liquidated Damages v. Penalties: Sense or Nonsense, 1978 Wis.L.Rev. 351.

5. Why was Boyle's subsequent employment irrelevant? Consider also *Musman v. Modern Deb, Inc.*, 50 A.D.2d 761, 377 N.Y.S.2d 17 (1975), where the plaintiff sued for wrongful termination of a five year employment contract. The contract provided that he would receive full compensation and bonuses to the end of the five year term if he was terminated without cause. The trial court reduced the amount of liquidated damages by the amount plaintiff earned from other employment. This deduction was reversed on appeal and the court restored the full amount of liquidated damages without deduction. Why should a liquidated damages clause remove the ordinary rule requiring an employee to mitigate damages?

6. In *Space Master International, Inc. v. City of Worcester*, 940 F.2d 16 (1st Cir.1991), a contractor entered into an agreement to install modular classroom buildings at city school sites. The contract specified that if the contractor delayed performance beyond a certain date, the city was entitled to retain $250 per day plus $100 per day per site as liquidated damages. When the contractor failed to meet the stated deadline to build the classrooms, children were forced to attend classes in hallways, gymnasiums, auditoriums and libraries. Morale among teachers, students and administrators suffered as a result of the dislocation. The court upheld the validity of the liquidated damages clause, observing that the injury to the public was inherently difficult to quantify in monetary terms.

Truck Rent–A–Center, Inc. v. Puritan Farms 2nd, Inc.

41 N.Y.2d 420, 361 N.E.2d 1015, 393 N.Y.S.2d 365 (1977).

■ JASEN, JUDGE. * * *

Defendant Puritan Farms 2nd, Inc. (Puritan), was in the business of furnishing milk and milk products to customers through home delivery. In January, 1969, Puritan leased a fleet of 25 new milk delivery trucks from plaintiff Truck Rent–A–Center for a term of seven years commencing January 15, 1970. Under the provisions of a truck lease and service agreement entered into by the parties, the plaintiff was to supply the trucks and make all necessary repairs. Puritan was to pay an agreed upon weekly rental fee. * * * The lessee was granted the right to purchase the trucks, at any time after 12 months following commencement of the lease, by paying to the lessor the amount then due and owing on the bank loan, plus an additional $100 per truck purchased.

Article 16 of the lease agreement provided that if the agreement should terminate prior to expiration of the term of the lease as a result of the lessee's breach, the lessor would be entitled to damages, "liquidated for all purposes", in the amount of all rentals that would have come due from the date of termination to the date of normal expiration of the term less the "re-rental value" of the vehicles, which was set at 50% of the rentals that would have become due. In effect, the lessee would be obligated to pay the lessor, as a consequence of breach, one half of all rentals that would have become due had the agreement run its full course. The agreement recited that, in arriving at the settled amount of damages, "the parties hereto have considered, among other factors, Lessor's substantial initial investment in purchasing or reconditioning for Lessee's service the demised motor vehicles, the uncertainty of Lessor's ability to re-enter the said vehicles, the costs to Lessor during any period the vehicles may remain idle until re-rented, or if sold, the uncertainty of the sales price and its possible attendant loss. The parties have also considered, among other factors, in so liquidating the said damages, Lessor's saving in expenditures for gasoline, oil and other service items."

[After three years, the lessee Puritan terminated the lease agreement. Puritan complained that the lessor had failed to repair and maintain the trucks as provided in the lease agreement. The lessor sued for payment of the liquidated damages on the grounds that the lessee had breached the contract. The defendant lessee counterclaimed for return of the security deposit on the basis that the lessor had breached the contract. At the time of termination of the agreement, the plaintiff owed $45,134.17 on the outstanding bank loan.]

* * * The home milk delivery business was on the decline and plaintiff's president testified that efforts to either re-rent or sell the truck fleet to other dairies had not been successful. Even with modifications in the trucks, such as the removal of the milk racks and a change in the floor of the trucks, it was not possible to lease the trucks to other industries, although a few trucks were subsequently sold.

* * *

At the close of the trial, the court found, based on the evidence it found to be credible, that plaintiff had substantially performed its obligations under the lease and that defendant was not justified in terminating the agreement. Further, the court held that the provision for liquidated damages was reasonable and represented a fair estimate of actual damages which would be difficult to ascertain precisely. * * * The court calculated that plaintiff would have been entitled to $177,355.20 in rent for the period remaining in the lease and, in accordance with the liquidated damages provision, awarded plaintiff half that amount, $88,677.60. * * *

* * * A liquidated damage provision has its basis in the principle of just compensation for loss. A clause which provides for an amount plainly disproportionate to real damage is not intended to provide fair compensation but to secure performance by the compulsion of the very disproportion. A promisor would be compelled, out of fear of economic devastation, to continue performance and his promisee, in the event of default, would reap a windfall well above actual harm sustained. [Citations.] As was stated eloquently long ago, to permit parties, in their unbridled discretion, to utilize penalties as damages, "would lead to the most terrible oppression in pecuniary dealings." [Citations.]

4 FACTORS TALK ABOUT ON THE BAR.

The rule is now well established. A contractual provision fixing damages in the event of breach will be sustained if the amount liquidated bears a reasonable proportion to the probable loss and the amount of actual loss is incapable or difficult of precise estimation. [Citations.] If, however, the amount fixed is plainly or grossly disproportionate to the probable loss, the provision calls for a penalty and will not be enforced. [Citations.] In interpreting a provision fixing damages, it is not material whether the parties themselves have chosen to call the provision one for "liquidated damages", as in this case, or have styled it as a penalty. [Citations.] Such an approach would put too much faith in form and too little in substance. Similarly, the agreement should be interpreted as of the date of its making and not as of the date of its breach. [Citation.]

In applying these principles to the case before us, we conclude that the amount stipulated by the parties as damages bears a reasonable relation to the amount of probable actual harm and is not a penalty. Hence, the provision is enforceable and the order of the Appellate Division should be affirmed.

Looking forward from the date of the lease, the parties could reasonably conclude, as they did, that there might not be an actual market for the sale or re-rental of these specialized vehicles in the event of the lessee's breach. To be sure, plaintiff's lost profit could readily be measured by the amount of the weekly rental fee. However, it was permissible for the parties, in advance, to agree that the re-rental or sale value of the vehicles would be 50% of the weekly rental. Since there was uncertainty as to whether the trucks could be re-rented or sold, the parties could reasonably set, as they did, the value of such mitigation at 50% of the amount the lessee was obligated to pay for rental of the trucks. This could take into consideration the fact that, after being used by the lessee, the vehicles would no longer be "shiny, new trucks", but would be used, possibly battered, trucks, whose value would have declined appreciably. The parties also considered the fact that, although plaintiff, in the event of Puritan's breach, might be spared repair and maintenance costs necessitated by Puritan's use of the trucks, plaintiff would have to assume the cost of storing and maintaining trucks idled by Puritan's refusal to use them. Further, it was by no means certain, at the time of the contract, that lessee would peacefully return the trucks to the lessor after lessee had breached the contract.

* * * [T]he existence of the option clause has absolutely no bearing on the validity of the discrete, liquidated damages provision. The lessee could have elected to purchase the trucks but elected not to do so. In fact, the lessee's letter of termination made a point of the fact that the lessee did not want to purchase the trucks. The reality is that the lessee sought, by its wrongful termination of the lease, to evade all obligations to the plaintiff, whether for rent or for the agreed upon purchase price. Its effort to do so failed. That lessee could have made a better bargain for itself by purchasing the trucks for $48,134.17 pursuant to the option, instead of paying $92,341.79 in damages for wrongful breach of the lease is not availing to it

now. Although the lessee might now wish, with the benefit of hindsight, that it had purchased the trucks rather than default on its lease obligations, the simple fact is that it did not do so.

We attach no significance to the fact that the liquidated damages clause appears on the preprinted form portion of the agreement. The agreement was fully negotiated and the provisions of the form, in many other respects, were amended. There is no indication of any disparity of bargaining power or of unconscionability. The provision for liquidated damages related reasonably to potential harm that was difficult to estimate and did not constitute a disguised penalty. * * *

[Affirmed.]

---

1.   The traditional common law test for upholding a liquidated damages clause is that the potential damages which might accrue as a result of a breach must be uncertain and difficult to ascertain. What should "difficulty" mean: Difficulty in forecasting all possible damages that may be caused by breach? Difficulty of producing proof of damages? Difficulty of proving causally the link between the breach and the loss? Difficulty of meeting the foreseeability limitations for contract damages? Difficulty from lack of any standardized measure of the damages for a certain breach? *See* PYCA Industries v. Harrison County, 177 F.3d 351, 368 (5th Cir.1999) (inherent difficulty in affixing actual damages resulting from a potential breach is a factor favoring the use of a liquidated damages clause). *See* an excellent analysis in Macneil, Power of Contract and Agreed Remedies, 47 Cornell L.Q. 495, 502 (1962).

2.   Although courts have tended to apply sparingly the rule that potential damages must be uncertain to enforce liquidated damages clauses, the rule has determined some cases. A case illustrating the force of the rule is *Semico, Inc. v. Pipefitters Local No. 195*, 538 S.W.2d 273 (Tex.Civ.App. 1976). A clause in a collective bargaining agreement provided that if the employer failed to make certain specified union contributions, the employer would be required to pay 15% of the contribution total for each month the payments were delinquent. The court held that the provision was invalid as a penalty because damages for the nonpayment of money could easily be calculated and therefore presented no difficulty in estimation at the time of contracting. Also see Checkers Eight Ltd. Partnership v. Hawkins, 241 F.3d 558, 562 (7th Cir.2001) (absent exceptional circumstances, liquidated damages clause was invalid where actual damages caused by monetary payments being late are not difficult to measure, because interest rates can be used to estimate the time value of money)

Why should it matter if the damages in the event of breach are difficult to ascertain? Even if the damages are exactly and readily foreseen, why not let the parties agree to the amount in advance? Is there any difference between such a liquidated damages provision and a settlement before trial? *See* McCormick, Damages § 148, at 605 (1935).

3. California has codified the uncertainty element regarding liquidated damages by statute, which provides in pertinent part:

> * * * a provision in a contract liquidating damages for the breach of the contract is void except that the parties to such a contract may agree therein upon an amount which shall be presumed to be the amount of damage sustained by a breach thereof, when, from the nature of the case, it would be impracticable or extremely difficult to fix the actual damage.

California Civil Code § 1671(d). An example of the operation of the California rule may be found in *Cook v. King Manor and Convalescent Hospital*, 40 Cal.App.3d 782, 115 Cal.Rptr. 471 (1974). A seller sought to recover the stipulated amount of $25,000 for a buyer's breach of a contract to purchase certain real property for approximately $2,000,000. The liquidated damages provision recited that it would be "extremely difficult and impractical to determine the amount and extent of detriment to seller" if the buyer failed to perform its obligations. The court held that the provision constituted a penalty because the seller had failed to plead and prove that the potential damages contemplated by the parties in the event of a breach were in fact difficult to estimate. *See generally* Sweet, Liquidated Damages in California, 60 Calif.L.Rev. 84 (1972).

4. The Restatement (Second) of Contracts § 356 comment b approaches the uncertainty of loss factor with a flexible test:

> The greater the difficulty either of proving that loss has occurred or of establishing its amount with the requisite certainty (*see* § 351), the easier it is to show that the amount fixed is reasonable. To the extent that there is uncertainty as to the harm, the estimate of the court or jury may not accord with the principle of compensation any more than does the advance estimate of the parties. A determination whether the amount fixed is a penalty turns on a combination of these two factors. If the difficulty of proof of loss is slight, less latitude is allowed in that approximation. If, to take an extreme case, it is clear that no loss at all has occurred, a provision fixing a substantial sum as damages is unenforceable.

5. The Uniform Commercial Code test in § 2–718(1) has reduced difficulty of loss from being treated as a separate factor to serving as one consideration regarding the reasonableness of the clause:

> Damages for breach by either party may be liquidated in the agreement but only at an amount which is reasonable in the light of the anticipated or actual harm caused by the breach, the difficulties of proof of loss, and the inconvenience or nonfeasibility of otherwise obtaining an adequate remedy.

The U.C.C. approach has been described by one pair of commentators as a continuum: The latitude of the contracting parties in setting damages for breach increases with the degree of uncertainty facing them. Goetz & Scott, Liquidated Damages, Penalties and the Just Compensation Principle:

Some Notes on an Enforcement Model and a Theory of Efficient Breach, 77 Colum.L.Rev. 554, 560 (1977).

6. A valid liquidated damages provision must reflect a *reasonable estimate* of the uncertain damages in the event of breach. In *Southpace Properties, Inc. v. Acquisition Group*, 5 F.3d 500 (11th Cir.1993), the court held that a stipulated damages clause in a real estate listing agreement which provided that the broker was entitled to full 6% commission plus costs and expenses if the property owner breached the agreement was void under Alabama law as a penalty. The court found that the damages provision was not a reasonable pre-breach estimate of the probable loss because the broker would actually recover *more* if the contract were breached than if fully performed. *See also* Ashcraft & Gerel v. Coady, 244 F.3d 948, 955 (D.C.Cir.2001) (liquidated damages clause in employment contract between attorney and law firm was not unreasonable where damages amount was adjusted annually with increasing increments, reflecting the lawyer's greater responsibilities and value to the firm); Atel Financial Corp. v. Quaker Coal Co., 132 F.Supp.2d 1233, 1241 (N.D.Cal. 2001) (formula requiring a defaulting lessee to pay the present value of all monies due for balance of lease term plus anticipated residual value of equipment unreasonably disproportionate to loss and constituted a penalty); A.V. Consultants, Inc. v. Barnes, 978 F.2d 996 (7th Cir.1992) (liquidated damages clause unenforceable as a penalty where provision would give party expected profit plus the value of its services).

7. What if the stipulated amount of damages for breach of a contract is considered an unreasonably low estimate of the anticipated harm? Some courts focus on the time of contracting to assess the reasonableness of the agreed amount and the uncertainty of damages because that approach is consistent with the traditional test for liquidated damages.

In *Better Food Markets v. American Dist. Tel. Co.*, 40 Cal.2d 179, 253 P.2d 10 (1953), for example, the plaintiff sought actual damages of $35,930 to compensate for merchandise stolen as a result of the defendant security company's failure to properly transmit burglar alarm signals in accordance with its contractual duties. The court nonetheless limited the plaintiff's recovery to the contractually agreed amount of only $50. Following the statutory provision regarding liquidated damages, California Civil Code § 1671, the court found it would have been impracticable or extremely difficult to fix the actual damage in the event of a breach. The court reasoned that the parties had exercised their business judgment that the actual loss resulting from a breach might be greater or lesser than the $50 sum, and therefore it also satisfied the requirement that the sum must bear a reasonable relationship to the losses contemplated.

8. Unreasonably low stipulated damages for breach of contract may reflect overreaching by the favored party. A defense of overreaching requires an inquiry into unconscionability rather than the examination of unreasonableness that is necessary to invalidate a liquidated damages clause. *See* Wedner v. Fidelity Security Systems, Inc., 228 Pa.Super. 67, 307 A.2d 429 (1973).

9. Distinguish a contractual provision that *limits* damages from a provision for liquidated damages. For example, in *Tharalson v. Pfizer Genetics, Inc.*, 728 F.2d 1108 (8th Cir.1984), the buyer's damages for the seller's breach of warranty was limited to the sale price of seed under a limitation of damages provision in the contract of sale. The court relied upon U.C.C. § 2–719(3) which provides, in part, "consequential damages may be limited or excluded unless the limitation or exclusion is unconscionable." The court noted that liquidated damages provisions usually threaten unjustifiably large recoveries, such that the judicial role is to contain them with a test of reasonableness. There is an opposite concern with limitation of damages provision; the danger is unjustifiably small recoveries. The official comments to Uniform Commercial Code § 2–718 indicate that where the concern is unreasonably small recoveries the proper test is unconscionability.

Lake River Corporation v. Carborundum Co.

769 F.2d 1284 (7th Cir.1985).

POSNER, CIRCUIT JUDGE.

This diversity suit between Lake River Corporation and Carborundum Company requires us to consider questions of Illinois commercial law, and in particular to explore the fuzzy line between penalty clauses and liquidated-damages clauses.

Carborundum manufactures "Ferro Carbo," an abrasive powder used in making steel. To serve its midwestern customers better, Carborundum made a contract with Lake River by which the latter agreed to provide distribution services in its warehouse in Illinois. Lake River would receive Ferro Carbo in bulk from Carborundum, "bag" it, and ship the bagged product to Carborundum's customers. The Ferro Carbo would remain Carborundum's property until delivered to the customers.

[Carborundum insisted that Lake River install a new bagging system to handle the contract. In order to be sure of being able to recover the cost of the new system and make a profit, Lake River insisted on a minimum-quantity guarantee and an agreement that if Carborundum had not shipped the minimum quantity in three years, Lake River would receive the full contract price minus the amount already shipped.]

* * *

After the contract was signed in 1979, the demand for domestic steel, and with it the demand for Ferro Carbo, plummeted, and Carborundum failed to ship the guaranteed amount. When the contract expired late in 1982, Carborundum had shipped only 12,000 of the 22,500 tons it had guaranteed. Lake River had bagged the 12,000 tons and had billed Carborundum for this bagging, and Carborundum had paid, but by virtue of the formula in the minimum-guarantee clause Carborundum still owed Lake River $241,000—the contract price of $533,000 if the full amount of Ferro

Carbo had been shipped, minus what Carborundum had paid for the bagging of the quantity it had shipped.

* * *

Lake River brought this suit for $241,000, which it claims as liquidated damages. * * *

The hardest issue in the case is whether the formula in the minimum-guarantee clause imposes a penalty for breach of contract or is merely an effort to liquidate damages. Deep as the hostility to penalty clauses runs in the common law, we still might be inclined to question, if we thought ourselves free to do so, whether a modern court should refuse to enforce a penalty clause where the signator is a substantial corporation, well able to avoid improvident commitments. Penalty clauses provide an earnest of performance. The clause here enhanced Carborundum's credibility in promising to ship the minimum amount guaranteed by showing that it was willing to pay the full contract price even if it failed to ship anything. On the other side it can be pointed out that by raising the cost of a breach of contract to the contract breaker, a penalty clause increases the risk to his other creditors; increases (what is the same thing and more, because bankruptcy imposes "deadweight" social costs) the risk of bankruptcy; and could amplify the business cycle by increasing the number of bankruptcies in bad times, which is when contracts are most likely to be broken. But since little effort is made to prevent businessmen from assuming risks, these reasons are no better than makeweights.

A better argument is that a penalty clause may discourage efficient as well as inefficient breaches of contract. Suppose a breach would cost the promisee $12,000 in actual damages but would yield the promisor $20,000 in additional profits. Then there would be a net social gain from breach. After being fully compensated for his loss the promisee would be no worse off than if the contract had been performed, while the promisor would be better off by $8,000. But now suppose the contract contains a penalty clause under which the promisor if he breaks his promise must pay the promisee $25,000. The promisor will be discouraged from breaking the contract, since $25,000, the penalty, is greater than $20,000, the profits of the breach; and a transaction that would have increased value will be foregone.

On this view, since compensatory damages should be sufficient to deter inefficient breaches (that is, breaches that cost the victim more than the gain to the contract breaker), penal damages could have no effect other than to deter some efficient breaches. But this overlooks the earlier point that the willingness to agree to a penalty clause is a way of making the promisor and his promise credible and may therefore be essential to inducing some value-maximizing contracts to be made. It also overlooks the more important point that the parties (always assuming they are fully competent) will, in deciding whether to include a penalty clause in their contract, weigh the gains against the costs—costs that include the possibility of discouraging an efficient breach somewhere down the road—and will include the clause only if the benefits exceed those costs as well as all other costs.

On this view the refusal to enforce penalty clauses is (at best) paternalistic—and it seems odd that courts should display parental solicitude for large corporations. But however this may be, we must be on guard to avoid importing our own ideas of sound public policy into an area where our proper judicial role is more than usually deferential. The responsibility for making innovations in the common law of Illinois rests with the courts of Illinois, and not with the federal courts in Illinois. And like every other state, Illinois, untroubled by academic skepticism of the wisdom of refusing to enforce penalty clauses against sophisticated promisors, continues steadfastly to insist on the distinction between penalties and liquidated damages.
* * *

Mindful that Illinois courts resolve doubtful cases in favor of classification as a penalty * * * we conclude that the damage formula in this case is a penalty and not a liquidation of damages, because it is designed always to assure Lake River more than its actual damages. The formula—full contract price minus the amount already invoiced to Carborundum—is invariant to the gravity of the breach. When a contract specifies a single sum in damages for any and all breaches even though it is apparent that all are not of the same gravity, the specification is not a reasonable effort to estimate damages; and when in addition the fixed sum greatly exceeds the actual damages likely to be inflicted by a minor breach, its character as a penalty become unmistakable. [Citations.] This case is within the gravitational field of these principles even though the minimum-guarantee clause does not fix a single sum as damages.

* * *

The fact that the damage formula is invalid does not deprive Lake River of a remedy. The parties did not contract explicitly with reference to the measure of damages if the agreed-on damage formula was invalidated, but all this means is that the victim of the breach is entitled to his common law damages. *See, e.g.*, Restatement, Second, Contracts § 356, comment a (1981). In this case that would be the unpaid contract price of $241,000 minus the costs that Lake River saved by not having to complete the contract (the variable costs on the other 45 percent of the Ferro Carbo that it never had to bag). The case must be remanded to the district judge to fix these damages.

* * *

Affirmed in part, reversed in part, and remanded.

———

1. The principal focus in determining the validity of a liquidated damages clause is the reasonableness of the relationship that the stipulated damages bear to the potential harm which the parties contemplate may

accrue as a result of a breach. Another question concerns what relevance the provable actual damages have when measured against the liquidated amount. The Restatement (Second) of Contracts § 356 and Uniform Commercial Code § 2–718(1) both provide that the reasonableness of the liquidated damages clause may be shown either by its proportionality to the anticipated or actual harm. Thus, the amount fixed may be considered valid if it approximates either alternative. *See* Reliance Ins. v. Utah Dept. of Transp., 858 P.2d 1363, 1367 (Utah 1993) (whether an amount constitutes a reasonable forecast is determined by reference to the time of contract formation, not the date of breach).

2. *Exclusivity of remedy.* Courts differ with respect to whether a liquidated damages clause serves as the exclusive remedy for contract breach. Compare Entergy Services, Inc. v. Union Pac. R. Co., 35 F.Supp.2d 746, 753 (D.Neb.1999) (liquidated damages clause does not preclude other remedies available at law or equity, absent the clear expression of the parties to the contrary) with MCA Television Ltd. v. Public Interest Corp., 171 F.3d 1265, 1272 (11th Cir.1999) (a stipulated damages provision that allows the non-breaching party a choice of options in the event of a breach is generally recognized as a penalty). Clearly double recovery of the liquidated amount and compensatory damages is precluded by ordinary principles of contract damages, but the preclusion of specific performance is more problematic. The liquidated damages provision functions as a surrogate for the actual damages; therefore, the liquidated damages becomes the focus in the consideration of the adequacy of the remedy at law. Recall the discussion of these issues in Chapters 3 and 4.

3. *Burden.* The prevailing view is that the party challenging the enforceability of a liquidated damages clause has the burden of proving that it is a penalty. *See* Honey Dew Associates, Inc. v. M & K Food Corp., 241 F.3d 23, 27 (1st Cir.2001) (party who stands to benefit from determination that clause is an unenforceable penalty bears burden of proof, similar to burden of raising and proving defense when challenging contract enforcement on basis of illegality or public policy). *See also* Melvin Aron Eisenberg, The Limits of Cognition and the Limits of Contract, 47 Stan. L.Rev. 211 (1995).

4. What if the liquidated sum is characterized as a reasonable approximation of the contemplated losses but the proof of actual harm is significantly less? Most courts have held that the liquidated amount must satisfy only one of the alternative tests, not both. Accordingly, evidence of the actual losses resulting from the breach would be considered irrelevant, assuming damages could reasonably be anticipated at the time of contracting. Southwest Engineering Co. v. United States, 341 F.2d 998 (8th Cir.1965); United States v. Bethlehem Steel Co., 205 U.S. 105, 27 S.Ct. 450, 51 L.Ed. 731 (1907).

The justification for the enforceability of a liquidated damages clause despite the lack of actual damages has been predicated on freedom of contract principles:

Courts have now become strongly inclined to allow parties to make their own contracts, and to carry out their intentions, even when it would result in the recovery of an amount stated as liquidated damages, upon proof of the violation of the contract, and without proof of the damages actually sustained.

United States v. Bethlehem Steel Co., 205 U.S. 105, 119, 27 S.Ct. 450, 455, 51 L.Ed. 731 (1907).

For example, in *In re Lion Overall Co.*, 55 F.Supp. 789 (S.D.N.Y.1943), *aff'd sub nom.* United States v. Walkof, 144 F.2d 75 (2d Cir.1944), the government sought enforcement of a liquidated damages clause for a contractor's failure to deliver clothing for soldiers in a timely manner. The contract recited that the stipulated damages for each day's delay were necessary because the actual damages which the government might sustain as a result of delays were impossible to calculate. The court upheld as reasonable the $20,000 liquidated damages amount in relation to $53,000 as the total contract price for the goods, despite evidence that the government actually incurred an excess cost of only $3.56 as a result of the breach. The court concluded that the only relevant time to evaluate the reasonableness of the clause was when the contract was entered and that the stipulated damages were "not out of all proportion to any possible loss."

5. Certainly to some extent courts may be influenced by public interest considerations to give particular deference to the validity of liquidated damages provisions in government contracts. *See generally* Gant & Breslauer, Liquidated Damages in Federal Government Contracts, 47 B.U.L.Rev. 71 (1967); Note, The Use and Abuse of Liquidated Damages in Federal Defense Contracts: An Analysis, 8 Okla. City U.L.Rev. 261 (1983); Peckar, Liquidated Damages in Federal Construction Contracts: Time for a New Approach, 5 Pub.Cont.L.J. 129 (1972). Thus, the court in *In re Lion Overall Co.*, 55 F.Supp. 789, 791 (S.D.N.Y.1943) stated:

The contract was made for an article of military equipment for our troops at a time when the war clouds from Europe were gathering ominously about this country and when it could reasonably be anticipated, certainly by the Army and Navy Departments, that sooner or later we might be embroiled in the conflict. While there were others in the country who were manufacturing similar garments, what damage might result from a delayed delivery could not be ascertained with accuracy. In any event, the agreement was made without any overreaching or fraud, and as an obvious spur to prompt performance.

6. The validation of a liquidated damages clause as reasonably proportionate to the anticipated harm but significantly disproportionate to the provable actual losses is not limited to the context of government contracts. For instance, in *Robbins v. Finlay*, 645 P.2d 623 (Utah 1982), the court held that an employer was entitled to recover $5,000 as liquidated damages for an employee's breach of a covenant not to misuse customer leads even though the employer had not introduced any direct evidence of actual losses incurred and had shown that only five potential customers were involved.

In contrast, some courts have held that evidence of little or no actual losses may invalidate a liquidated damages clause as a penalty even if the stipulated amount was otherwise reasonably related to the anticipated harm. For example, in *Gorco Construction Co. v. Stein*, 256 Minn. 476, 99 N.W.2d 69 (1959), the court determined that a contract provision which designated damages in the amount of 15% of the total contract price to cover expenses for advertising, labor, equipment, and commissions was invalid where the plaintiff did not prove any actual loss because of the breach. Similarly, in *S.O.G.–San Ore–Gardner v. Missouri Pacific Railroad*, 658 F.2d 562, 570 (8th Cir.1981), the court invalidated a clause which stipulated $600 per day liquidated damages to cover estimated losses from delayed performance where the party asserting the claim sustained no actual damages from the breach.

7.   A liquidated damages clause which provides for payment of the sum to the non-breaching party in the event of a breach of covenants that have varying degrees of importance typically has been invalidated as an unreasonable forecast of the anticipated harm. McCormick, Damages § 151 (1935); Corbin, Contracts § 1066 (1964). Thus, a liquidated damages clause which fixes a payment of $200 per day for late delivery in the shipment of goods may be justifiable as an appropriate compensation for the contemplated disruption in the purchaser's business operations. However, the $200 figure may be considered invalid as a penalty if sought by the seller for a breach of a covenant requiring certain insurance for the goods. In *Coe v. Thermasol, Ltd.*, 615 F.Supp. 316, 320 (W.D.N.C.1985), though, the court upheld the enforceability of a liquidated damages clause even though it could be triggered by a breach of several covenants because the covenants were "interdependent and call for acts with one primary purpose."

D.   LAND SALES CONTRACTS

Section Coverage:

The damages remedy is important to vendors and vendees in contracts for the sale of land even though the equitable remedy of specific performance is generally available. Equity courts historically have deemed that every parcel of land is unique and that an award of damages is therefore inadequate. Nonetheless, the specific performance remedy is not automatic; a court must still evaluate the relative hardships of the parties. Moreover, that remedy is not practical in all cases, depending upon the cause for the breach and changes in the parties' positions between breach and trial.

The usual damages award for breach of a contract to convey land is based upon the expectancy interest. It is measured by the difference between the contract price and the fair market value of the property on the date of the breach. The damages award also includes any consequential damages proved with reasonable certainty. There is a further adjustment for benefits received or expenses saved by the plaintiff.

The majority of jurisdictions follow the "American" rule of damages for a vendor's breach which results from a deficiency in title. This rule provides for an award of the benefit of the bargain to a vendee for a vendor's breach of an executory contract to convey title. A minority of courts follow the "English" rule derived from Flureau v. Thornhill, 2 W.Bl. 1078, 96 Eng.Rep. 635 (C.P.1776). It provides a vendee with restitution of amounts paid on the contract plus reliance expenditures, but denies recovery for the vendee's expectancy interest unless the vendor's breach was characterized as made in bad faith.

Model Case:

The Larsons contracted to purchase from Ross for $80,000 a 100 acre tract of land which contained a small farmhouse and barn. The contract provided for a down payment of $8,000 and monthly installments in the principal amount of $1,000 plus interest for six years. The earnest money of $8,000 was designated by the parties as "liquidated damages in all respects in the event of a material breach by the purchaser, and not as a penalty."

The Larsons paid the $8,000 and moved their family into the farmhouse. Almost immediately after assuming possession the Larsons noticed that the well water had a foul smelling odor and was a greenish-yellow color. They notified the state environmental protection agency. Tests revealed that a dangerous level of toxic chemical waste products had contaminated the water. The agency officials located an open landfill near the well which contained a number of barrels of highly toxic chemicals, many of which were improperly sealed. Cracks in the barrels had allowed chemicals to seep into the water supply. The officials informed the Larsons that the landfill site violated both state and federal environmental statutes.

The Larsons stopped making the monthly payments and instituted suit against Ross demanding rescission and restitution. Ross counterclaimed seeking alternatively the specific performance of the contract or enforcement of the $8,000 liquidated damages clause.

A court would probably find that the contaminated water supply constituted a material breach of the executory contract which justified rescission, restitution of the $8,000 down payment, and compensatory damages for the excess, if any, of the market value of the land versus the contract price.

Alternatively, assume that no toxic chemicals were located on the property, and that the Larsons had stopped making payments for personal reasons. Ross seeks specific performance of the contract or, if equitable relief is denied, enforcement of the liquidated damages clause. Specific performance of the land sale contract may be granted a vendor if the legal remedies are inadequate and if the balance of hardships favor the party requesting relief.

The liquidated damages clause was not designated as the exclusive remedy for breach of the contract; however, a court may still consider it to be an adequate remedy for Ross. The clause would not be automatically enforceable based solely on the parties' description that it was not a penalty. Rather, the court will inquire whether at the time of contracting the potential actual damages in the event of a breach were difficult to determine and the $8,000 sum had a reasonable relationship to the potential damages. An amount of liquidated damages of ten percent of the total contract price will be presumed reasonable for a land sale contract in most jurisdictions, especially if Ross is likely to have difficulty in reselling the tract.

Uzan v. 845 UN Limited Partnership

10 A.D.3d 230, 778 N.Y.S.2d 171 (2004).

■ MAZZARELLI, J.

This appeal presents the issue of whether plaintiffs, who defaulted on the purchase of four luxury condominium units, have forfeited their 25% down payments as a matter of law. Because the governing purchase agreements were a product of lengthy negotiation between parties of equal bargaining power, all represented by counsel, there was no evidence of overreaching, and upon consideration of the fact that a 25% down payment is common usage in the new construction luxury condominium market in New York City, we hold that upon their default and failure to cure, plaintiffs forfeited all rights to their deposits pursuant to the rule set forth in *Maxton Bldrs., Inc. v Lo Galbo* (68 NY2d 373 [1986]).

Facts

In October 1998, defendant 845 UN Limited Partnership (sponsor or 845 UN) began to sell apartments at the Trump World Tower (Trump World), a luxury condominium building to be constructed at 845 United Nations Plaza. Donald Trump is the managing general partner of the sponsor. Plaintiffs Cem Uzan and Hakan Uzan, two brothers, are Turkish billionaires who sought to purchase multiple units in the building.

In April 1999, plaintiffs and an associate executed seven purchase agreements for apartments in Trump World. Only four of those units (the penthouse units) are the subject of this lawsuit and appeal. As relevant, Cem Uzan defaulted on contracts to buy two penthouse units on the 90th floor of the building, and Hakan defaulted on contracts to purchase two other penthouse units on the 89th floor.

The building had not been constructed when plaintiffs executed their purchase agreements. In paragraph 17.4 of those contracts, the sponsor projected that the first closing in the building would occur on or about April 1, 2001, nearly two years after the signing of the agreements.

The condominium offering plan included a section titled "Special Risks to be Considered by Purchasers," which stated:

"Purchasers will be required to make a down payment upon execution of a Purchase Agreement in an amount equal to 10% of the purchase price, and within 180 days after receipt of the executed Purchase

Agreement from Sponsor or 15 days after Purchaser receives a written notice or amendment to the Plan declaring the Plan effective, whichever is earlier, an additional down payment equal to 15% of the purchase price. . . .''

* * * [The] offering plans prominently disclosed the sponsor's right to retain the *entire down payment* should there be an uncured default.

Negotiations Preceding Execution of the Purchase Agreements

Plaintiffs were represented by experienced local counsel during the two-month-long negotiation for the purchase of the apartments. There were numerous telephone conversations between counsel, and at least four extensively marked-up copies of draft purchase agreements were exchanged. In consideration for plaintiffs' purchase of multiple units, the sponsor reduced the aggregate purchase price of the penthouse units by more than $7 million from the list price in the offering plan for a total cost of approximately $32 million. Plaintiffs also negotiated a number of revisions to the standard purchase agreement, including extensions of time for payment of the down payment. As amended, each purchase agreement obligated plaintiffs to make a 25% down payment: 10% at contract, an additional 7½% down payment 12 months later, and a final 7½% down payment 18 months after the execution of the contract. At no time did plaintiffs object to the total amount required as a nonrefundable down payment.

There were other significant amendments to the standard purchase agreement which benefitted plaintiffs. * * *

The executed purchase agreements provide, at paragraph 12 (b), that:

"[u]pon the occurrence of an Event of Default . . . [i]f Sponsor elects to cancel . . . [and i]f the default is not cured within . . . thirty (30) days, then this Agreement shall be deemed canceled, and Sponsor shall have the right to retain, as and for liquidated damages, the Down payment and any interest earned on the Down payment.''

Plaintiffs paid the first 10% down payment installment for the penthouse units on April 26, 1999 when they signed the purchase agreements. They paid the second 7½% installment in April 2000, and the third 7½% installment in October 2000. The total 25% down payment of approximately $8 million was placed in an escrow account.

Default, Failure to Cure, and this Action

On September 11, 2001, terrorists attacked New York City by flying two planes into the World Trade Center, the City's two tallest buildings, murdering thousands of people. Plaintiffs, asserting concerns of future terrorist attacks, failed to appear at the October 19, 2001 closing, resulting in their default. By letter dated October 19, 2001, plaintiffs' counsel stated:

"[W]e believe that our clients are entitled to rescind their Purchase Agreements in view of the terrorist attack which occurred on September 11 and has not abated. In particular, our clients are concerned that the top floors in a 'trophy' building, described as the tallest residential building in the world, will be an attractive terrorist target. The situation is further aggravated by the fact that the building bears the name of Donald Trump, perhaps the most widely known symbol of American capitalism. Finally, the United Nations complex brings even more attention to this location."

That day 845 UN sent plaintiffs default letters, notifying them that they had 30 days to cure. On November 19, 2001, upon expiration of the cure period, the sponsor terminated the four purchase agreements.

Plaintiffs then brought this action. They alleged that Donald Trump had prior special knowledge that certain tall buildings, such as Trump World, were potential targets for terrorists. Plaintiffs also alleged that Trump World did not have adequate protection for the residents of the upper floors of the building. * * * [The plaintiffs] sought a declaratory judgment that the down payment was an "unconscionable, illegal and unenforceable penalty." * * *

Motions for Summary Judgment

After exchanging discovery and conducting various depositions, plaintiffs moved for summary judgment on their third cause of action, arguing that forfeiture of the down payments was an unenforceable penalty. * * *

Defendant opposed the motion and cross-moved for summary judgment, asserting that defaulting vendees on real estate contracts may not recover their down payments. * * *

The Role of the 25% Down Payment

In his affidavit in support of the cross motion, Donald Trump stated that he sought 25% down payments from preconstruction purchasers at the Trump World Tower because of the substantial length of time between contract signing and closing, during which period the sponsor had to keep the units off the market, and because of the obvious associated risks. Trump also affirmed that down payments in the range of 20% to 25% are standard practice in the new construction luxury condominium submarket in New York City. He cited three projects where he was the developer, the Trump Palace, 610 Park Avenue and Trump International Hotel and Tower, all of which had similar down payment provisions. Trump also noted that,

"[i]n new construction condominium projects, purchasers often speculate on the market by putting down initial down payments of 10% and 15% and watching how the market moves. If the market value increases, they will then make the second down payment. If the market prices drop, they may then walk away from their down payment."

[The affidavit of Marilyn Weitzman, the president of a nationwide real estate consulting firm] echoed Trump's opinion that 20% to 25% down payments are customary in New York City for new construction condominium apartments, because of the volatility of the market. Weitzman also discussed other risk factors specific to developers of newly constructed luxury condominium projects. She concluded that from the sponsor's perspective, future competition is largely unknown, requiring an educated guess by the developer of the appropriate level of services and amenities to be provided at the building. Weitzman also noted that the demographic profile for potential purchasers in the luxury condominium submarket includes many foreign nationals, who are inherently high risk purchasers because their incomes and assets are often difficult to measure, and to reach. Both Weitzman and Martin stated, based upon research detailed in their affidavits, that the volatility of individual real estate transactions increases with the size of the unit involved, and that price swings for three- and four-bedroom units, such as the penthouse units plaintiffs sought to purchase here, were greater than for smaller apartments.

Defendant also presented a compilation of 16 recent condominium offering plans, all of which required down payments of either 20% or 25% of the purchase price for the unit. Fourteen of the 16 offering plans required 25% down payments. Further, defendant provided proof that in July 2001, plaintiff Cem Uzan closed on the purchase of an apartment on the 80th floor of Trump World after making a 25% down payment, and that he had previously purchased another apartment at 515 Park Avenue, also with a 25% down payment provision.

The Order Appealed

After hearing oral argument on the motion, the IAS court granted defendant partial summary judgment, finding that plaintiffs forfeited the portion of their down payment amounting to 10% of the purchase price, pursuant to *Maxton Bldrs., Inc. v. Lo Galbo* (68 N.Y.2d 373 [1986], *supra*). The court held that the remainder of the down payment was subject to a liquidated damages analysis to determine whether it bore a reasonable relation to the sponsor's actual or probable loss. Defendant appeals from that portion of the order which denied it full relief.

Discussion

More than a century ago, the Court of Appeals, in *Lawrence v. Miller* (86 N.Y. 131 [1881]), held that a vendee who defaults on a real estate contract without lawful excuse cannot recover his or her down payment. It reaffirmed this holding in *Maxton* (*supra*), again in 1986. * * *

For over a century, courts have consistently upheld what was called the *Lawrence* rule and recognized a distinction between real estate deposits and general liquidated damages clauses. Liquidated damages clauses have traditionally been subject to judicial oversight to confirm that the stipulated damages bear a reasonable proportion to the probable loss caused by the breach. By contrast, real estate down payments have been subject to limited supervision. They have only been refunded upon a showing of disparity of bargaining power between the parties, duress, fraud, illegality or mutual mistake (*see Cipriano v. Glen Cove Lodge #1458*, 1 N.Y.3d 53 [2003]).

In *Maxton*, plaintiff had contracted to sell defendants a house, and accepted a check for a 10% down payment. When defendants canceled the contract and placed a stop payment on the check, plaintiff sued for the down payment, citing the *Lawrence* rule. Defendants argued that plaintiff's recovery should be limited to its actual damages. In ruling for the vendor, the Court of Appeals identified two legal principles as flowing from *Lawrence*. First, that the vendor was entitled to retain the down payment in a real estate contract, without reference to his actual damages. Second, the "parent" rule, upon which the first rule was based, that one who breaches a contract may not recover the value of his part performance.

The Court noted that the parent rule had been substantially undermined in the 100 years since *Lawrence*. Many courts had rejected the parent rule because of criticism that it produced a forfeiture "and the amount of the forfeiture increases as performance proceeds, so that the penalty grows larger as the breach grows smaller" (*Maxton*, 68 NY2d 373, 379 [1986] [citation omitted]).

The Court also noted that since *Lawrence*, the rule of allowing recovery of down payments of not more than 10% in real estate contracts continues to be followed by a "majority of jurisdictions," including in New York (*Maxton*, 68 NY2d at 380). Thereafter, the Court noted the long and widespread reliance on the *Lawrence* rule in real estate transactions, and it concluded that, based upon notions of efficiency and avoiding unnecessary litigation, the rule should remain in effect (*id.* at 381).

After acknowledging that "real estate contracts are probably the best examples of arm's length transactions," the Court broadly concluded:

> "Except in cases where there is a real risk of overreaching, there should be no need for the courts to relieve the parties of the consequences of their contract. *If the parties are dissatisfied with the rule of [Lawrence], the time to say so is at the bargaining table.*" (*Maxton*, 68 NY2d 373, 382 [1986] [emphasis supplied].)

The *Maxton/Lawrence* rule has since been followed by this Court as well as the other departments to deny a refund of a down payment when a default has occurred [citations].

Further, other departments have specifically applied the *Maxton/Lawrence* rule, where, as here, a real estate down payment of greater than 10% of the purchase price is at issue. * * *

Applying the reasoning of these cases to the facts of the instant matter, it is clear that plaintiffs are not entitled to a return of any portion of their down payment. Here the 25% down payment was a specifically negotiated element of the contracts. There is no question that this was an arm's length transaction. The parties were sophisticated businesspeople, represented by counsel, who spent two months at the bargaining table before executing the amended purchase agreements.

Further, the record evidences that it is customary in the preconstruction luxury condominium industry for parties to price the risk of default at 25% of the purchase price. The purchase agreements included a detailed

nonrefundable down payment clause to which plaintiffs' counsel had negotiated a specific amendment. That amendment allowed for the payment of
25% of the purchase price in three installments: 10% at contract, an
additional 7½% 12 months later, and a final 7½% 18 months later. Clearly,
plaintiffs were fully aware of and accepted the requirement of a nonrefundable 25% down payment for these luxury preconstruction condominiums. In
fact, Cem Uzan has purchased two other condominiums, one in the same
building, with similar down payment provisions.

Plaintiffs negotiated the payment of the 25% down payments in
installments to spread their risk over time [citation]. In the event of a
severe economic downturn, plaintiffs were free to cancel the deal, capping
their losses at the amount paid as of the date of their default. For the
sponsor, the 25% deposit served to cover its risk for keeping the apartments
off the market should the purchaser default.

Finally, there was no evidence of a disparity of bargaining power, or of
duress, fraud, illegality or mutual mistake by the parties in drafting the
down payment clause of the purchase agreements. The detailed provision
concerning the nonrefundable deposit was integral to the transaction. If
plaintiffs were dissatisfied with the 25% nonrefundable down payment
provision in the purchase agreements, the time to have voiced objection
was at the bargaining table (*see Maxton*, 68 NY2d 373, 382 [1986], *supra*).
Because they chose to accept it, they are committed to its terms. Thus,
upon plaintiffs' default and failure to cure, defendant was entitled to retain
the full 25% down payments.

Accordingly, the order of the Supreme Court, New York County (Alice
Schlesinger, J.), entered July 21, 2003, which, to the extent appealed from,
denied defendant 845 UN Limited Partnership's motion for summary
judgment, should be reversed, on the law, with costs, defendant's motion
granted and the complaint dismissed. The Clerk is directed to enter
judgment in favor of defendant-appellant dismissing the complaint as
against it.

---

1. The court in the principal case observes that the rule in a majority
of jurisdictions is that a non-breaching seller is entitled to retain the
breaching buyer's down payment regardless of the seller's actual damages.
Thus, in a majority of jurisdictions a seller may be entitled to retain the
buyer's down payment even if the seller later resells the property for more
than the purchase price or even if the down payment exceeds the difference
between the purchase price and the resale price. This is particularly true if
the down payment is no more than 10% of the purchase price or if the real
estate contract expressly provides the seller the right to retain the down
payment. *See* James O. Pearson, Jr., *Modern Status of Defaulting Vendee's
Right to Recover Contractual Payments Withheld by Vendor as Forfeited*, 4
A.L.R. 4th 993 (1981).

Some courts, such as the court in the principal case, distinguish earnest money provisions in real estate contracts from liquidated damages clauses in other contracts and subject to earnest money provisions to limited scrutiny. Other courts subject earnest money clauses to judicial scrutiny but have found difficulty in determining the seller's actual damages because of difficulty in determining the market value of real property, *see, e.g.,* Liberty Life Ins. Co. v. Thomas B. Hartley Constr. Co., 258 Ga. 808, 809, 375 S.E.2d 222, 223 (1989) or because of difficulty in anticipating costs that may accrue to the seller as a result of maintaining possession of the property for longer than anticipated, *see, e.g.,* Growney v. CMH Real Estate Co., 195 Neb. 398, 238 N.W.2d 240 (1976).

Other courts allow the defaulting purchaser to recover some or all of the down payment if it exceeds the seller's actual damages. For example, in *Vines v. Orchard Hills, Inc.,* 181 Conn. 501, 435 A.2d 1022 (1980), the defaulting would-be purchasers of a condominium brought a claim for unjust enrichment against the seller, seeking a return of their down payment on the ground that the condominium had increased in value after the buyers' breach. The Connecticut Supreme Court concluded that a breaching purchaser may be entitled to restitution despite a forfeiture clause in the contract if the down payment exceeds the seller's actual damages. However, the Court noted that the buyer would bear the burden of establishing that the down payment exceeded the actual damages. The Court remanded the case to the trial court to allow the purchasers to present evidence of the seller's actual damages. *See also* Shanghai Inv. Co. v. Alteka Co., 92 Haw. 482, 993 P.2d 516 (Hawaii 2000); Kutzin v. Pirnie, 124 N.J. 500, 591 A.2d 932 (1991).

Some courts have also invalidated forfeiture clauses in real estate contracts because the clauses attempt to preserve the sellers' ability to elect between forfeiture of the down payment and actual damages. *See, e.g.,* Grossinger Motorcorp v. American Nat'l Bank & Trust, 240 Ill.App.3d 737, 180 Ill.Dec. 824, 607 N.E.2d 1337 (1992).

2. The traditional equitable rule holds that damages provide an inadequate remedy at law in land sales contracts because every parcel of land is considered unique. This traditional approach was not followed in *Centex Homes Corp. v. Boag,* 128 N.J.Super. 385, 320 A.2d 194 (1974), where the court denied specific performance to a seller of a condominium unit. Equitable relief was denied because (1) the property was virtually identical to hundreds of other units being offered for sale to the public, and (2) the damages resulting from the breach were readily measurable.

In the ordinary land sales case, the traditional assumption of the inadequacy of damages still prevails. Is it appropriate to treat remedies for land contracts unlike other types of contracts? Should the availability and measure of damages for a breach of contract to sell land play a significant role in whether a court will grant or deny specific performance?

3. Under what circumstances, if any, should punitive damages be recovered for breach of a contract to sell land? *See* Hanna v. American International Land Corp., 289 So.2d 756 (Fla.App.1974) (punitive damages

allowed because vendor's bad faith breach of contract also amounted to an independent tort of conversion where equitable title had vested in the vendee).

Donovan v. Bachstadt

91 N.J. 434, 453 A.2d 160 (1982).

■ SCHREIBER, J.

The central legal issue in this case concerns the damages to which a buyer of realty is entitled upon the breach of the executory agreement by the seller. The procedural circumstances under which the question arose are unique. The buyers, Edward Donovan and Donna Donovan, husband and wife, prevailed in a suit for specific performance * * *. When the seller, Carl Bachstadt, could not perform because of a defect in title, the Donovans instituted this action for damages [and] they were awarded reimbursement of their expenditures of $145.00 for a survey and $142.85 for title searches. * * *

The contract recited that the purchase price was $58,900. A deposit of $5,890 was paid to and held by the broker. At the closing scheduled for May 1, 1980, the Donovans were to pay an additional $9,010 in cash and the balance was to consist of a purchase money bond or note and mortgage in the principal amount of $44,000, for 30 years, at an interest rate of 13%. The conveyance was to be made subject to easements and restrictions of record and facts disclosed in an accurate survey, provided that these would not render the title unmarketable. The contract also stated that title "shall be marketable and insurable ... by any reputable title insurance company...." There was no liquidated damage provision.

* * *

When defendant could not obtain marketable title, the Donovans commenced this suit for compensatory and punitive damages. As previously observed the trial court granted plaintiffs' motion for summary judgment. It was indisputable that the defendant had breached the agreement. The only issue was damages. The trial court held that plaintiffs were entitled under N.J.S.A. 2A:29–1 to recovery of their costs for the title search and survey. Plaintiffs had apparently in the interim purchased a home in Middlesex County and obtained a mortgage loan bearing interest at the rate of 13¼% per annum. Plaintiffs sought the difference between 10½% and 13¼% as compensatory damages, representing their loss of the benefit of the bargain. The trial court denied recovery because the contract was for the sale of the property and the financing "was only incidental to the basic concept."

The Appellate Division reversed. * * *

The initial inquiry is whether plaintiffs are entitled to compensatory damages. We had occasion recently to discuss the measure of damages available when a seller breaches an executory contract for the sale of real property. St. Pius X House of Retreats v. Diocese of Camden, 88 N.J. 571, 582–87, 443 A.2d 1052 (1982). We noted that New Jersey follows the English rule, which generally limits a buyer's recovery to the return of his deposit unless the seller wilfully refuses to convey or is guilty of fraud or deceit. The traditional formulation of the English rule has been expressed by T. Cyprian Williams, an English barrister, as follows:

> Where the breach of contract is occasioned by the vendor's inability, without his own fault, to show a good title, the purchaser is entitled to recover as damages his deposit, if any, with interest, and his expenses incurred in connection with the agreement, but not more than nominal damages for the loss of his bargain. [T.C. Williams, *The Contract of Sale of Land* 128 (1930)].

In *St. Pius* we found no need to reexamine the English rule, though we raised the question whether the American rule that permits a buyer to obtain benefit of the bargain damages irrespective of the nature of the reasons for the seller's default might not be more desirable.

* * *

We are satisfied that the American rule is preferable. The English principle developed because of the uncertainties of title due to the complexity of the rules governing title to land during the eighteenth and nineteenth centuries. [Citation.] At that time the only evidence of title was contained in deeds which were in a phrase attributed to Lord Westbury, "difficult to read, disgusting to touch, and impossible to understand." The reason for the English principle that creates an exception to the law governing damages for breaches of executory contracts for the sale of property is no longer valid, and the exception should be eliminated. [Citations.] Indeed in England the rule has been modified by placing the burden of proof on the vendor to establish that he has done everything within his power to carry out the contract. * * *

There is no sound basis why benefit of the bargain damages should not be awarded whether the subject matter of the contract is realty or personalty. Serious losses should not be borne by the vendee of real estate to the benefit of the defaulting vendor. This is particularly so when an installment purchase contract is involved that extends over a period of years during which the vendee makes substantial payments upon the principal, as well as extensive improvements to the property.

The innocent purchaser should be permitted to recover benefit of the bargain damages irrespective of the good or bad faith of the seller. Contract culpability depends on the breach of the contractual promise. [Citation.] Where, as here, the seller agreed that title would be marketable, the seller's liability should depend upon his breach of that promise.

* * *

The English rule is consistent with the limitation on recovery in suits on a covenant for breach of warranty. The damages for a buyer, who has taken title and is ousted because the title is defective, are limited to the consideration paid and interest thereon. [Citation.] There appears to be no real difference between that situation and one where the vendor who does not have good title refuses to convey. In both cases the buyer loses the property because of a defect in the title. The fact that one sues for breach of a warranty covenant does not justify depriving a buyer of compensatory damages to which he is justly entitled when the seller breaches the contract of sale. Professor Corbin has suggested that any inconsistency in this respect should be resolved by awarding full compensatory damages when the action is for breach of warranty. [Citation.] Moreover, an anomaly already exists, for our courts have acknowledged that a buyer may recover such damages upon a showing of the seller's bad faith. [Citation.]

We are satisfied that a buyer should be permitted to recover benefit of the bargain damages when the seller breaches an executory contract to convey real property. Here the defendant agreed to convey marketable title. He made that bargained-for promise and breached it and is responsible to the plaintiff for the damages occasioned thereby. The next question is how to compute those compensatory damages.

Judicial remedies upon breach of contract fall into three general categories: restitution, compensatory damages and performance. Separate concepts undergird each of these remedial provisions. The rationale for restitution is to return the innocent party to his status before the contract was executed. Compensatory damages are intended to recompense the injured claimant for losses due to the breach, that is, to give the innocent party the benefit of the bargain. Performance is to effect a result, essentially other than in terms of monetary reparation, so that the innocent party is placed in the position of having had the contract performed. We have now adopted the American rule providing for compensatory damages upon the seller's breach of an executory contract to sell realty and we must examine the appropriate elements that should properly be included in an award.

"Compensatory damages are designed 'to put the injured party in as good a position as he would have had if performance had been rendered as promised.'" [Citations.] What that position is depends upon what the parties reasonably expected. It follows that the defendant is not chargeable for loss that he did not have reason to foresee as a probable result of the breach when the contract was made. * * * Further the loss must be a reasonably certain consequence of the breach although the exact amount of the loss need not be certain. [Citations.]

The specific elements to be applied in any given case of a seller's breach of an executory agreement to sell realty may vary in order to achieve the broad purposes of reparations; some items, however, will almost invariably exist. Thus the purchaser will usually be entitled to the return of the amount paid on the purchase price with interest thereon. Costs and expenses incurred in connection with the proposed acquisition, such as for the title search and survey, would fall in the same category. The traditional test is the difference between the market price of the property at the time of the breach and the contract price. * * *

The difference between market and contract price may not be suitable in all situations. Thus where a buyer had in turn contracted to sell the realty, it is reasonable to measure his damages in terms of the actual lost profit. * * * What the proper elements of damage are depend upon the particular circumstances surrounding the transaction, especially the terms, conditions and nature of the agreement.

The plaintiffs here assert that their damages are equivalent to the difference in interest costs incurred by them in purchasing a different home at another location. This claim assumes that the financial provision of the contract concerning the purchase money mortgage that the defendant agreed to accept was independent and divisible from the purchase of the land and house. The defendant contends that he did not agree to loan these funds in connection with the purchase of some other property, but that this provision was incidental to the sale of the house. Neither position is entirely sound. This financing was an integral part of the transaction. It can be neither ignored nor viewed as an isolated element.

The relationship of the financing to the purchase of a home has changed in recent years. As interest rates rose and the availability of first mortgage funds was sharply reduced, potential homeowners, though desirous of purchasing homes, found financing difficult to obtain. * * * In evaluating a contract such a financial arrangement could play an important part in determining price. * * * The interest rate is not sufficiently discrete to calculate damages in terms of it alone under these circumstances.

In some circumstances interest rate differentials are an appropriate measure of damages. Where the buyer has obtained specific performance, but because of the delay has incurred higher mortgage rates, then his loss clearly should include the higher financing cost. Godwin v. Lindbert, 101 Mich.App. 754, 300 N.W.2d 514 (1980), is illustrative. The buyers lost their commitment for a mortgage with an interest rate of 8¾% when the seller refused to convey. The buyers succeeded in obtaining specific performance but were compelled to borrow funds at 11½%. They were awarded the difference reduced to present value. * * * The particular realty might well be a secondary and incidental consideration for the loan. Therefore an interest differential occasioned by the seller's default might be a proper factor in fixing damages where the buyer shortly thereafter purchased another property financed at a higher interest rate.

This is not such a situation. The defendant's motive was to sell a house and not to lend money. In measuring the plaintiffs' loss there should be a determination of the fair market value of the property and house that could be acquired with a purchase money mortgage in the principal amount of $44,000 at an interest rate of 10½% (no appeal was taken from the judgment of reformation) for a 30–year term. The valuation should be at the time the defendant failed to comply with the judgment of specific performance. The plaintiffs would be entitled to the difference between $58,900 and that fair market value. If the fair market value was not more than the contract price, the plaintiffs would not have established any damage ascribable to the loss of the bargain. They are also entitled to their expenditures for the survey, search, and counsel fees for services rendered in preparation of the aborted closing. The plaintiffs have hitherto received the return of the deposit.

The judgment of the Appellate Division is modified and, as so modified, remanded to the trial court for further proceedings consistent with this opinion.

■ O'HERN, J., dissenting.

I must respectfully dissent from the opinion and judgment of the Court. The issue is whether out of pocket costs or benefit of the bargain damages are to be awarded for breach of an executory contract for the sale of real estate when the contract does not close because of a defect in title unknown to the seller at the time of execution of the contract.

Although commentators advocate the adoption of the "American rule" as suggested by the majority, there remains sufficient flexibility in the rule that would except its application to the circumstances of this case. While both Williston and Corbin suggest that the only rule defensible on principle is allowing the purchaser the difference between the contract price and the market value of the land, it is put this way: the rule "is applied in every case where the vendor *breaks* his contract without legal excuse." [Citations.] Most of the recent American cases cited in both treatises do not sustain a conclusion that such a rule would be applied to a case where the seller was wholly without fault with respect to the existence of a defect in title that prevents closing.

* * *

I would adhere to the rule that an award of damages should be just under the circumstances. * * * As originally stated the English rule would not allow recovery of benefit of the bargain under any circumstances, whether with or without fault on the part of the seller, the seller's liability being limited to recovery in an action at law where fraud or deceit is involved for the loss he may sustain thereby. * * *

If any modifications of existing law were to be made under the circumstances of this case, I would recommend that the Court follow the recommendations of the Commissioners on Uniform State Laws. They suggest the adoption of a rule that better conforms with prevailing American decisional law and reflects a "just method of determining damages." Zeliff v. Sabatino, 15 N.J. at 74, 104 A.2d 54. That rule is stated as follows:

Section 2–510 [Buyer's Damages for Seller's Failure to Convey]

(a) Except as provided in subsection (b), the measure of damages for a seller's repudiation or wrongful failure to convey is the difference between the fair market value at the time for conveyance and the contract price and any incidental and consequential damages (Section 2–514), less expenses avoided because of the seller's breach.

(b) Unless the title defect is an encumbrance securing an obligation to pay money which could be discharged by application of all or a portion of the purchase price, if a seller is unable to convey because of a title defect of which the seller had no knowledge at the time of entering into the contract, the buyer is entitled only to restitution of any amounts paid on the contract price and incidental damages (Section 2–514). [Unif. Land Transactions Act § 2–510, 13 U.L.A. 638 (1980)].

If I were to reach the issue of increased financing costs, I would agree with the majority that such are appropriate for consideration. * * *

1.   When a seller breaches a land sale contract, should courts award damages to compensate for the buyer's increased financing costs such as higher mortgage rates? Do you agree with the *Donovan* opinion that the financing aspect of a real estate transaction plays only an incidental role? Which view more accurately gives the aggrieved buyer the benefit of the bargain? Should it matter whether the buyer is also awarded specific performance?

2.   In *Smith v. Mady*, 146 Cal.App.3d 129, 194 Cal.Rptr. 42 (1983), the sellers contracted to sell a residence for $205,000 but the buyer defaulted. Within a few days after the breach the sellers entered into a second contract to sell the property to third parties for $215,000. The rapid resale established that the market value of the property at the time of the breach exceeded the contract price, thus precluding the sellers from recovering damages for loss of benefit of the bargain. The sellers also sought consequential damages for miscellaneous costs of insurance, taxes, utilities, and interest payments incurred between the default and the subsequent resale. The court held that defaulting buyer should receive a credit for the higher proceeds received in the resale against the damages liability. The rationale was that the seller otherwise would receive a windfall if the offset was denied. Do you agree?

In order to reach its result the court concluded that the two sales were not inherently separate. What if the resale had taken place six months after the breach instead of just a few days?

3.   When a sale of land is in gross, meaning by the tract, the vendor generally will not be liable for a deficiency in acreage absent fraud in the transaction. Conversely, where the sale is on a per acre basis, a court will charge the vendor with damages to reflect the deficiency. In *Hagenbuch v. Chapin*, 149 Ill.App.3d 572, 102 Ill.Dec. 886, 500 N.E.2d 987 (1986), for example, the purchasers of a farm at auction brought suit for damages against the sellers for a deficiency in acreage. The court noted that the presumption that sales are by the acre could be rebutted only by clear and convincing proof. Although the farm was offered for sale as a single, undivided parcel and the notice of sale at public auction described the land as "129 acres, more or less," the court held that it was not a sale in gross because the bidding was done on a per acre basis. Damages were awarded against the vendors for the 6 acre deficiency. *See also* Boswell v. Bryans, 159 Ga.App. 724, 285 S.E.2d 74 (1981).

PROBLEM: THE HOME SALE

Upon retirement the Strattons decided to sell their family home and move to a warmer climate. They entered into a contract to sell their single-family residence to the Powells for $325,000. Prior to closing, the Powells placed 10 percent of the purchase price in escrow and obtained a 30–year real estate loan at a fixed rate of 6% for $100,000 of the purchase price. Before the closing date, the Strattons had a change of heart and decided that they did not wish to move. They informed the Powells that they did not wish to sell their home. The Strattons refused to deliver title to the property at the closing date and remain in possession of the home to date.

If the Powells bring suit against the Strattons, should the Powells be entitled to specific performance? If not, what should be the measure of their damages? If the Powells lose their mortgage as a result of the Strattons' breach and are able to secure a new mortgage only at a higher rate, should the Powells be entitled to recover damages for the increased financing costs? Should their ability to recover these increased financing costs depend on whether the court grants specific performance? Should the Powells be compensated for the lost use of the home during the period from the time of the scheduled closing until specific performance can be effectuated? Should the Strattons be compensated for their lost use of the purchase price during the period from the time of the scheduled closing until specific performance can be effectuated?

Consider *Smith v. American Motor Inns of Florida,* 538 F.2d 1090 (5th Cir.1976), where the court addressed the problems of adjustment in an accounting action following rescission of a contract to sell a motel. The court determined that the seller was entitled to charge the buyer for the rental value for the period during which the buyer had operated the motel. The buyer received a credit for the actual value of improvements made to the property during occupancy, and received credit for payments made on the motel mortgage and the land lease.

CHAPTER 11

TORT DAMAGES

The function of a damages remedy in tort cases is to make the injured party whole by substituting money for tangible and intangible losses caused by the tort. In contrast, the orientation of restitution is to disgorge those benefits which the law considers it unjust for the defendant to retain. The difference in orientation of these remedies may produce different dollar amounts.

This chapter focuses exclusively on the damages remedy for torts and presents the recurring remedial themes for the most commonly suffered losses. It is divided into sections representing types of injuries to legally protected rights: personal property, real property, personal injury, and wrongful death/survival. These categories do not form an exhaustive list of rights for which tort damages are available, but they are the most common ones. Chapter 14 includes some other types of injuries that present special remedial problems and for which damages in tort are only sometimes available, such as emotional distress without personal injury and economic losses without physical injury.

Although the primary goal of tort damages is adequate compensation, other goals must be considered in choosing the measure of damages. One goal is economic efficiency and the avoidance of waste; another interest is the promotion of out-of-court settlements by fixing a predictable and objective measure of damages. In circumstances where a tension develops between apparently conflicting goals, courts will try to achieve appropriate compromises. Jurisdictions have formulated slightly different rules as a result of the process of resolving these conflicting interests, and the rules are subject to exceptions that constantly evolve. Tort damage law rules are confusing and meaningless without an understanding of the unifying principles that govern them and the conflicts in remedial goals that change them. This chapter addresses those principles and conflicts.

A. HARM TO PERSONAL PROPERTY

Section Coverage:

Tortious injury to personalty presents two major remedial issues. First, what losses are compensable? Second, how should the losses be measured? Resolution of these issues traditionally requires drawing a distinction between property that has been completely destroyed and property that is capable of repair. The difference between these two categories can be a thin line at times. It is a finding of fact whether the chattel can be repaired, and legal consequences follow accordingly.

What losses related to personal property are recoverable? A plaintiff can recover the value of a destroyed chattel at the time and place of its destruction. Injury without destruction also produces compensable losses to the chattel itself. Plaintiffs may or may not recover for the loss of the use of the property, however, before it can be replaced or repaired. Many jurisdictions follow a rule that allows loss of use awards only for injured chattel but not for those which are destroyed.

Courts generally agree that losses associated with personalty must be objective ones; consequently plaintiffs cannot recover for emotional injuries caused by the loss of items with sentimental value. Measurement of objective losses also poses difficulties. For example, should the measure of damages for a reparably injured chattel be the cost of its repair or the diminution in its value? Sometimes these measures produce the same dollar amount, but sometimes they do not. Jurisdictions vary in approach.

Another measurement problem arises with unique, irreplaceable goods such as family papers, photographs, or heirlooms. When there is no readily ascertainable fair market value, the court takes evidence on the personal value of the destroyed chattel to the plaintiff. The evidentiary problem is to establish some reasonable basis for a valuation.

Model Case:

Stuart is a graduate student who was involved in a car accident caused by the negligence of another driver. He was returning to campus in his car for the beginning of the fall semester at the time. Stuart's car was loaded with his personal possessions. The car itself was damaged but capable of repair. Things packed in the trunk survived the accident, but items in the back seat were severely damaged. Most of Stuart's clothes were destroyed; a stereo system was badly damaged; and a handmade quilt was partially damaged.

The clothes cannot be salvaged. The stereo can be fixed, but at a cost greater than the fair market value as a used system. The quilt could be repaired only by hand, at great cost. Even when repaired, the quilt would never be in as good a condition as it was prior to the accident. Nonetheless, Stuart wishes to have the quilt repaired because it was a present from his now deceased grandmother. She had made it while he was in college and presented it to him when he first left for graduate school two years ago.

Car: Courts vary in whether to measure damages for the car by cost of repair or by diminution in value. The difference in orientation often does not produce different results, but sometimes it does. *Clothes:* The general rule of valuation for personal property damaged beyond repair is the fair market value at the time and place of destruction. A few consumer items, such as clothes, escape this rule. Under this exception Stuart may be able to recover the value of the clothing to him personally rather than just its low value as used clothes. *Stereo:* If the stereo cannot be repaired for less than it is worth, then arguably it is in the "destroyed" category rather than the "reparable" one. Even if the court finds it capable of repair, however, the general rule is that damages for a reparable item cannot exceed its pre-tort fair market value as a used chattel. *Quilt:* The ceiling of fair market value presents a greater problem with items that have relatively low market value yet have a significant sentimental value to the owner. Although courts are in agreement that Stuart could not recover separately for the sentimental value of the quilt, should that sentiment at least allow repair damages? This issue is not well resolved in most jurisdictions. Should it matter if the repairs to the quilt are actually made before trial? Under existing rules in most jurisdictions Stuart would receive no more than the fair market value of the quilt.

Hewlett v. Barge Bertie

418 F.2d 654 (4th Cir.1969), *cert. denied*, 397 U.S. 1021, 90 S.Ct. 1261, 25 L.Ed.2d 531 (1970).

■ BRYAN, CIRCUIT JUDGE:

Computation of pecuniary damages recoverable for a ship's injury in a maritime collision centers this cause. The minim of the injury here, however, obscures and tempts neglect of the importance of the issue.

Without dispute, the facts are that barge BA 1401, afloat and made fast alongside a pier in the Elizabeth River at South Norfolk, Virginia, on September 28, 1960 was struck by another barge. * * *

[Hewlett, owner of BA 1401, sued the barge owner in admiralty. The only issue was damages because liability was confessed. The admiralty court awarded only $1.00 as nominal damages.]

The basis of the decision was that as the BA 1401 had been declared a constructive loss two years before, the District Court was of the opinion that a subsequent injury could not sustain a claim. The declaration followed upon her misfortune on November 11, 1958, when she foundered in Chesapeake Bay near the mouth of the Potomac River. [Citation.] Raised and refloated by the present libelant as contractor-salvor in June, 1959, the repair and recovery cost of the barge was estimated to exceed both her 1958 purchase price of $40,000.00 and current insurance of $45,000.00. In these circumstances she was released to Hewlett in satisfaction of his claim for services. After $1305.76 was expended upon her in temporary repairs, such as leak stoppages, she was brought to Norfolk.

The barge was used or useable for carrying pilings or logs weatherproof cargo. She was engaged on one occasion as a pontoon or caisson in lifting a steamer from the river bottom. In this task the barge was allowed to fill, settle beside the sunken ship and then attached to her. When pumped out, the barge's buoyancy brought the steamer to the surface.

Admittedly, the barge had no market value as an instrument of navigation and could be sold only for scrap. The skin of the barge was not pierced in the collision, and the only mark of impact was a dent in her starboard side. It produced no harmful effect upon the barge's seaworthiness or carrying capacity.

Our concern is the acceptance by the instant court of the respondent's defense to the damage claim, *i.e.* "the barge was a constructive total loss and that no real or actual damages have been shown, thus restricting the recovery to nominal damages". The decree on review purports to fix "nominal damages", but this is in reality a dismissal of the libel, for admiralty does not recognize nominal damages. [Citation.] Presently, the Court stated, "We find no precedent for allowing damages where a vessel, deemed a constructive total loss, suffers still further damage." Apparently, the award of $1.00 was the product of this proposition. It is, we think, an untenable postulate; if accepted, it could result in unjust deprivations.

Actually, the case does not commence with the barge as a constructive loss, as the admiralty judge believed. True, that was her status more than a year previous, but only as between the owner and the salvor. Even this, however, was not a decree of outlawry. She was not a derelict, to be jostled about with impunity. Indeed, as a sheer-hulk she had a demonstrated utility for the libelant. Slightly more than a year previous, to repeat, $1305.76 had been expended in restoration. The accused tugboat and tow cannot escape liability by recall of the past ill luck of the BA 1401. Nor are they relieved by showing that she has not suffered in utility value or in market value.

To illustrate, although an automobile through age or misfortune may have no value in the market save for scrap, and although still another nick in its paint or shape may not appreciably reduce the usefulness or dollar-value of the car, nevertheless its checkered career and disreputable appearance do not assure absolution to one who negligently further scars the vehicle. The owner is entitled to have the automobile free of even that dent. *De minimis non curat lex* does not, semble, apply to damages but only to injury. [Citation.]

"Restitutio in integrum" is the precept in fixing damages, and "where repairs are practicable the general rule followed by the admiralty courts in such cases is that the damages assessed against the respondent shall be sufficient to restore the injured vessel to the condition in which she was at the time the collision occurred; * * * " The Baltimore, 75 U.S. 377, 385, 19 L.Ed. 463, 8 Wall. 377 (1869).

The workable guides to this end, generally stated, are these. If the ship sinks and is beyond recovery, the damages are her value just before she sank, plus interest thereon until payment. If she is not a complete loss and repossession or repairs are both physically and economically feasible, then the reasonable cost of recovery, including repairs and an allowance for deprivation of use, is the measure. But if the reclamation expense including repairs exceeds the ship's just value at the time of the casualty, or if repairs are not both physically and economically practicable, then it is a constructive total loss, and the limit of compensation is the value plus interest. O'Brien Bros. v. The Helen B. Moran, 160 F.2d 502 (2d Cir.1947).

The case at bar comes closer to the second category the loss was not complete, repairs were physically practicable, but the question remains whether they were economically so. The answer depends on whether the repair cost was more than the value of the barge. Libelant has shown a fair estimate for the repairs to be between $2895.00 and $3000.00. If this expense was beyond the fair and reasonable monetary value of the vessel to the owner, then the recovery is limited to such value. [Citation.]

When, as here, the tortfeasors assert that the value is less than the cost of repairs, they have the burden to establish that fact. The respondents have failed to do so. Consequently, the case stands on the proof of the repair costs, and the libelant is entitled to a decree in that amount.

The District Court made no finding of value. It merely found that the BA 1401 had no value save for sale as scrap, but this is not the equivalent of fixing a figure of value. Moreover, it is erroneous. It is refuted by the other uncontested findings of her continuing utility.

Apparently, the chief factor influencing the District Judge in this determination was the absence of any market for the sale of the barge. That problem, however, cannot justify withholding all value from libelant's vessel. [Citation.] The special value to the owner is a consideration of substance. [Citation.]

* * * If there is no market value, other indicia of value must be looked to. [Citations.] Among other factors is the use value to the owner. As was said in Bishop v. East Ohio Gas Co., 143 Ohio St. 541, 56 N.E.2d 164, 166 (1944):

> "Market value is the standard which the courts insist on as a measure of direct property loss, where it is available, but that is a standard not a shackle. When market value cannot be feasibly obtained, a more elastic standard is restored to, sometimes called the standard of value to the owner. This doctrine is a recognition that property may have value to the owner in exceptional circumstances which is the basis of a better standard than what the article would bring in the open market."

> * * *

The order on appeal will be vacated, and the cause remanded with request to the District Court to enter a decree awarding the appellant Hewlett damages of $2895.00, with interest at 6% per annum from the date of the collision until paid, together with costs in the trial and appellate courts.

Reversed and remanded for entry of judgment.

■ HAYNSWORTH, CHIEF JUDGE (dissenting):

With respect to my brothers, I must dissent, for I think they misapprehend the record, the issue presented, and the legal principle which should control its resolution.

Clarity may be served if I first lay aside one area in which there is no disagreement between us. The fact that the barge had earlier been declared a total constructive loss gave no subsequent wrongdoer an immunity. The District Judge did not hold otherwise. I readily agree, too, that the fact that she was previously declared a constructive total loss has no legal significance in itself in the assessment of the damages or in the application of the governing legal principles. It has only historical significance as the basis upon which the salvor, the principal libelant, acquired her. The prior physical history of the barge, however, is highly relevant in explanation of her condition, her value and potential uses, with respect to all of which the record is far clearer with much less disagreement than the majority opinion might indicate.

The Barge 1401 had been purchased in 1958 for $40,000 and immediately insured for $45,000. One month later she sank. After salvage operations, the lowest bid for restoration to her former condition was $46,290. That was why she was declared a constructive total loss and surrendered to the salvor.

The salvor effected certain repairs costing only $1305.76, which had the effect of making her hull watertight. She was then usable as a pontoon in other salvage operations, as she was once used. It gave her a theoretical potentiality for hauling deck cargo, though she had never been used for such a purpose, and it is very doubtful that she could have been insured for such use.

The barge in her then condition had a market value of $5,616. This was her scrap value, but it was a ready market value, and it seems to me to be a mistake to approach the case as if there were no market value when everyone agrees there was.

Everyone agrees, too, that the market value of $5,616 was not affected in the slightest by the additional dent inflicted in her side when the Barge Bertie collided with her. The already battered Barge 1401 had a scrap value after the additional dent of $5,616, just as she had before.

The libelant here, of course, claimed that the Barge 1401 had a special value to him for use as a pontoon, as once he used it, and potentially, but highly theoretically, for use in carrying telephone poles or other dry deck cargo, a use in which she had never been engaged. It is true, of course, that the special value, if any, was not determined in the District Court, but everyone agrees that the additional dent placed in her side by the Barge Bertie did not effect any diminution in that value, whatever it was. She was as useful as a pontoon after she sustained this dent as she was before, and whatever potential she had for use in carrying deck cargo was not impaired in the slightest.

Under these circumstances, of course, the owner did not attempt to effect the repair of the barge for the repairs were estimated to cost $2,895, and that expenditure would not enhance the value of the barge or its usefulness to the libelant, or to anyone else, in the slightest. No one claims that any such repairs would ever be attempted. If the libelant prevails on the basis of the opinion of my brothers, his winnings will go as cash into his pocket and will not be applied to any reparation of the barge. It is thus clear beyond all dispute that repair is not economically practicable or feasible, and in no event will it be attempted.

It is thus settled in the record that the additional dent inflicted by the Barge Bertie occasioned no diminution in the market value of the Barge 1401 of $5,616; it occasioned no diminution in any special value she may have had to the libelant. Between the parties, there is no dispute about this. The conclusion is inescapable that the libelant has suffered no economic loss. The question then is whether the libelant's damages should be measured by his economic loss, as was done in the District Court, or by an estimate of the cost of economically imprudent and senseless repair which has not been and never will be incurred.

I think the damages are to be measured by the economic loss sustained by the libelant and that no different rule can be found in admiralty by looking at isolated statements lifted from their context.

* * *

If my brothers are right, the libelant is unduly enriched. He must hope greatly that another errant navigator will hit his battered barge again, and still another yet again, so that each time he may happily pocket the estimated cost of theoretical repairs which neither he nor anyone else will ever dream of undertaking while retaining all along a barge as seaworthy and useful to him and of undiminished worth if he chooses to sell it.

---

1. *General Rule.* As the majority in the principal case explains, the measure of compensatory damages differs depending on whether personal property has been damaged or destroyed. When personal property has been destroyed, the owner is entitled to recover the value of the property immediately before its destruction less any value the destroyed property has as scrap. On the other hand, when personal property has been damaged but is capable of repair, the owner is entitled to recover the cost to repair the property provided that the repairs are economically feasible. When repairs are not economically feasible, the plaintiff can recover the diminution in value of the property only.

As reflected in the majority and dissenting opinions in the principal case, jurisdictions differ as to at what point repairs become economically infeasible. The majority in *Barge Bertie* and many other jurisdictions provide that repairs are economically feasible and that, therefore, the plaintiff may recover the cost of repair as long as the cost does not exceed the pre-tort value of the damaged property. *See, e.g.,* Canal Ins. Co. v. Tullis, 237 Ga.App. 515, 515 S.E.2d 649 (1999). Some jurisdictions adopt the same approach used by the dissenter in *Barge Bertie*, however, and use the diminution in value as a ceiling on recovery. *See, e.g.,* Robert v. Aircraft Inv. Co., 575 N.W.2d 672 (N.D.1998). In these jurisdictions a plaintiff may not recover the cost of repair if that repair cost exceeds the difference in the value of the damaged property immediately before and immediately after the tort.

The competing measures demonstrate the tension in the law between the desire to fully compensate an injured party by placing the party in as good a position as the party would have been had the tort not occurred and the desire to avoid overcompensating a plaintiff and to promote economically efficient activity. Does either of these measures achieve all of these goals? Has the owner of BA–1401 been unduly enriched by receiving the cost to repair the BA–1401? Assuming the dissent is correct that the dent did not decrease the value of BA–1401 or affect the owner's ability to use it as a pontoon, is it likely that the owner of BA–1401 actually will repair the dent? If the owner of BA–1401 does not repair the dent, will the owner have received a windfall? If the owner of the BA–1401 does not receive the cost to repair the dent, will the owner be in as good a position as the owner would have been had the accident not occurred? Should a court award the cost of repair as damages only when there is proof that the plaintiff intends to make the repairs? Assuming no measure of recovery will fully compensate without overcompensating the injured party, who should bear the risk of inaccurate compensation? Should the plaintiff bear the risk of undercompensation? Should the defendant bear the risk of overcompensation? Why?

2. *Market Value.* Generally, courts insist that the fair market value of the damaged or destroyed property serve as the measure or the property's value whenever a market for the property exists. The parties in *Barge Bertie* apparently agreed that the BA–1401 had a market value of $5,616 as scrap. The majority, however, concluded that the lower court made no finding as to the value of the BA–1401 prior to the accident. Why did the majority reject the scrap value as the pre-tort market value of the BA–1401?

Consider the court's observations in *King Fisher Marine Service v. NP Sunbonnet*, 724 F.2d 1181 (5th Cir. 1984). In that case the plaintiff purchased a barge, intending to use the barge as a dry-dock platform. The plaintiff paid $30,000 for the barge. The barge sunk and was lost two days after the plaintiff purchased it while the defendant was towing it to the plaintiff. The plaintiff sought to recover the costs it incurred in purchasing a new barge and modifying it to make it similar to the destroyed barge. The defendant argued that the plaintiff was not entitled to recover the replacement costs because those costs exceeded the market value of the destroyed barge. The defendant maintained that the market value of the barge was $30,000 because that was the price the plaintiff paid to purchase the barge two days before it was destroyed. The Fifth Circuit rejected the defendant's contentions holding:

> [C]ourts have long held that where a vessel is a total loss the measure of damages is the market value at the time of the loss. Where there are insufficient sales to establish a market other evidence such as replacement costs, depreciation, expert opinion and the amount of insurance can also be considered to determine the value of the lost vessel. [Citations.]

[Defendant] claims that the evidence establishes that the market value of the barge was $30,000 because that is what [plaintiff] paid for it in an arm length's sale only two days before it was lost. As far as it goes, the argument is unassailable. The difficulty is that the barge was not purchased to perform as a barge. It was instead purchased for use as a drydock platform. The barge's price in the barge market is not determinative of its value because its unique capabilities made it valuable for use other than as a barge. 724 F.2d at 1185.

Does the BA–1401 in *Barge Bertie* differ from the barge turned drydock in *King Fisher*? Can an ordinary vehicle acquire unique status by becoming an old wreck? Should an old jalopy be treated as unique or is there a sufficient market for old jalopies such that its market value and the diminution in its value from another dent could be ascertained? What if the jalopy did not run and had value only as scrap but its owners kept it on the street as "decoration," or as a symbol, or as a means of annoying the neighbors, or as a source of spare parts? Should a court distinguish among such uses in determining the jalopy's value? Should a court make factual findings concerning the actual personal uses? How important was it to dissenting Judge Haynsworth that the uses of BA–1401 were highly theoretical except for its one-time use as a pontoon?

3. *Multiple Markets.* If damaged or destroyed property is commonly traded in more that one market and the market price differs in each market, which market price represents the market value of the damaged or destroyed property? For example, if a portion of a retailer's goods is tortiously destroyed, should the retailer be entitled to recover the fair market value as evidenced by the wholesale price for the goods or as evidenced by the retail price of the goods? If an automobile is destroyed on a dealer's lot, what is the fair market value of the car to the dealer?

In *United Truck Rental Equipment Leasing v. Kleenco Corp.*, 84 Haw. 86, 929 P.2d 99 (App.Ct.1996), a Hawaiian appellate court held that a plaintiff was entitled to recover the value of the property in the market in which the plaintiff would have to replace it. In this case the plaintiff, who operated a truck leasing business, leased to the defendant a truck which then was stolen while in the defendant's possession. The plaintiff sued to recover damages for the stolen truck. The defendant conceded that the plaintiff was entitled to recover the fair market value of the stolen truck but objected to the jury's verdict because it was based on the retail value of the stolen truck rather than the wholesale value.

The court upheld the verdict, noting that the plaintiff was not strictly a consumer or a retailer. The court acknowledged that the plaintiff purchased the stolen truck in the wholesale market. However, the court explained that the stolen truck was one of ten trucks that the plaintiff purchased in bulk in the wholesale market. The plaintiff could purchase in the wholesale market in bulk only. Since the plaintiff would have to replace only one truck, the court concluded that the plaintiff would have to purchase a replacement truck in the retail market. In reaching its holding, the court explained:

Whether the retail or wholesale price will govern when calculating damages depends on the replacement market available to the injured party. Thus, a consumer, who is usually limited to purchasing an item at retail prices, is entitled to recover the retail market value for the loss of that item. Contrastingly, when a retailer's stock-in-trade is damaged, the retailer is entitled to recover the wholesale market value of the stock because that value represents the retailer's actual replacement cost. The theory underlying this rule is that if the owner of lost or destroyed property is a retailer ... the goods may be replaced at their wholesale value and subsequently sold at retail just as the original goods would have been sold. Because a retailer purchases goods at wholesale and then sells the goods at retail, awarding a retailer the retail market value of damaged or lost goods would be tantamount to giving the retailer his or her profits without the retailer having to incur the expense of selling the goods. Therefore, the damages award should be based upon the market value, retail or wholesale which will actually or as precisely as possible compensate the injured party. 929 P.2d at 107.

PROBLEM: WINTHROP'S LOSS

Winthrop, a wealthy entrepreneur, loaned an original Picasso to a gallery for display in an exhibition. While on loan, a gallery employee accidentally tore a hole in the painting. On the day before the damage to the painting occurred, the painting was valued at $139 million. Experts estimate that the cost to repair the hole will be approximately $90,000. Even after restoration, however, experts estimate that the painting will be worth only $85 million (a $54 million loss in value) because it will be flawed and the flaw will be visible under black light. Assuming Winthrop prevails in a suit against the gallery, what should be the measure of Winthrop's damages? Should Winthrop be entitled to recover the diminished value of the painting? The cost to repair the painting? Both? Why? Assume that the gallery employee had damaged Winthrop's car rather than a precious artwork. If Winthrop's car could be repaired at a cost that was less than the pre-tort value of the car, but even after repairs the car would be less than its pre-tort value, what would be the measure of Winthrop's damages? Why?

Roxas v. Marcos

89 Hawai'i 91, 969 P.2d 1209 (1998).

■ LEVINSON, J.

[The Estate of a Philippine national Rogelio Domingo Roxas and the Golden Buddha Corporation ("GBC"), a corporation formed by Roxas and his childhood friend, sued former Philippine President Ferdinand E. Marcos and his wife Imelda Marcos. Plaintiffs asserted several causes of action, including one count for conversion.

In relevant part, Plaintiffs alleged that the decedent, Rogelio Roxas, was an amateur treasure hunter who discovered a legendary buried WWII treasure while treasure hunting in the Philippines in January 1971. Roxas claimed to have removed twenty-four bars of gold, each measuring one-inch by two-and-one-half-inches, and a three-foot tall gold-colored statue of buddha from the underground enclosure housing the treasure. Assay tests revealed that the golden buddha statue was solid 22 carat gold. Roxas also discovered that the head of the statue was filled with uncut diamonds. The plaintiffs contended that eight men wearing military uniforms and purporting to be members of various Philippine national law enforcement agencies raided Roxas' home in April 1971 and seized the golden buddha, the diamonds and seventeen of the gold bars. The plaintiffs contended that the eight men were acting on behalf of then Philippine President Ferdinand Marcos.

After Marcos was removed from office in 1986, Roxas formed the Golden Buddha Corporation with a childhood friend and transferred his rights to the gold, diamonds and golden buddha to the GBC. In 1988, GBC and Roxas brought suit against Marcos and his wife. GBC asserted claims for relief against both Ferdinand and Imelda for (1) conversion, (2) constructive trust, and (3) fraudulent conveyances. In particular, GBC's claims related to the taking of the golden buddha, the gold bars, and other items from Roxas's home. A jury awarded the plaintiffs approximately $1.4 million for conversion of the gold, diamonds and golden buddha. The defendants appealed from the judgment, and the plaintiffs cross appealed on the grounds that the court erred in instructing the jury that the proper measure of damages for the conversion of gold was the value at the time of conversion rather than the highest value of the gold between the time of the conversion and the time of trial.]

* * *

The plaintiffs-appellees argue that the circuit court erred in instructing the jury that the correct measure of damages in connection with GBC's claim for relief arising out of the conversion of Roxas's gold was the value of the gold on the date of conversion. They assert, instead, that the proper measure should have been the highest value of the gold between the time of its taking and the entry of the circuit court's amended judgment. * * *

Imelda cites to this court's opinion in *Tsuru v. Bayer,* 25 Haw. 693, 699–700 (1920), for the proposition that the measure of damages for conversion is "the fair reasonable value of the property at the time of the conversion." However, in that case, the conversion at issue was of the personal effects of the lessee of a building, which were taken and sold by the building's owner. *Id.* at 694. Accordingly, the *Tsuru* court was not concerned with the valuation of a commodity of fluctuating value, such as the gold involved in the instant case. Indeed, it appears that the issue has never been directly addressed by the Hawai'i appellate courts.

In *Brougham v. Swarva,* 34 Wash.App. 68, 661 P.2d 138, 143–44 (Wash.Ct.App.1983), a case involving the conversion of silver coins, the

Washington Court of Appeals summarized the approaches adopted by the various jurisdictions toward the valuation of fluctuating commodities as follows:

> Prior [Washington state] cases have applied the standard measure of damages for conversion of stock, *i.e.,* the fair market value at the date of conversion, [citations], but recent decisions in other jurisdictions have held otherwise.

> Some decisions have awarded damages based on the highest value reached by the stock or personal property between the time of conversion and trial. [Citations.] Other jurisdictions have awarded the highest price between the date of conversion and a reasonable time after learning thereof. [Citations.] Still other courts have applied the "New York rule [,]" which awards the highest price within a reasonable time after learning of the conversion[,] disregarding the period between conversion and learning thereof. *Klein v. Newburger Loeb & Co.,* 151 So.2d 879 (Fla.App.1963) (stock conversion) [citations.]

In line with the first approach described by the *Brougham* court, Imelda cites *Charles Selon & Assocs., Inc. v. Aisenberg,* 103 Ill.App.3d 797, 59 Ill.Dec. 457, 431 N.E.2d 1214 (Ill.Ct.App.1981). In *Aisenberg,* the Illinois Court of Appeals declined to adopt an exception to the general rule that "damages are set at the date of conversion" for converted gold. The *Aisenberg* court noted that the Illinois Supreme Court had similarly declined to make an exception for converted stock, arguing that such an exception "was based on the premises that the plaintiff originally obtained the stock for a permanent investment and would have kept it until the time of trial" and that such premises were "arbitrary and speculative." *Id.,* 59 Ill.Dec. 457, 431 N.E.2d at 1217 (citing *Sturges v. Keith,* 57 Ill. 451 (1870)). [Citation.]

We agree that some subjectivity inheres in any measure of damages that assumes that the victim of a conversion would have sold the commodity at the highest price during a particular period of time. However, [t]he hallmark of conversion cases is the interference with the plaintiff's ability to transfer [commodities] he owns or to which he is entitled. The injury that the plaintiff suffers is the deprivation of his range of elective action, and by applying the conversion measure of damages a court endeavors to restore that range of elective action. To require the plaintiff to show that he would have sold his securities, had he been able, is to require him to prove that he would have taken the very steps that defendant's wrongful act ... precluded him from taking. . . .

The defendant's acts prevent a court from determining with any degree of certainty what the plaintiff would have done with his [commodities] had they been freely alienable. Because it is the defendant who creates this uncertainty, fundamental justice requires that, as between [the plaintiff] and [the defendant], the perils of such uncertainty should be laid at defendant's door. *American Gen. Corp. v. Continental Airlines Corp.,* 622 A.2d 1, 10 (Del.Ch.), *aff'd,* 620 A.2d 856 (Del.1992) (citations and internal quotation signals omitted) (some brackets added and some in original).

On the other hand, we believe that the approach advocated by GBC and adopted in some jurisdictions—*i.e.,* that the measure of damages must be the highest value of the converted property between the time of the conversion and the time of judgment or the filing of the complaint—tips the balance too far to the other side. There is no persuasive punitive or compensatory rationale for penalizing the defendant (absent bad faith delay) or rewarding the plaintiff for the time required for the plaintiff to file a complaint or obtain a judgment. "[T]o adopt the highest value between the time of actual conversion and the trial would be to encourage the owner to delay and speculate upon the chances of higher markets, without assuming the chances of lower markets." *Newburger Cotton Co. v. Stevens,* 167 Ark. 257, 267 S.W. 777, 778 (Ark.1925). However readily ascertainable the relevant time period might be pursuant to this rule, we deem the rule's unfairness to outweigh its predictability.

On balance, we agree with the resolution at which the *Brougham* court arrived. After considering the options available to it, the *Brougham* court adopted the "New York rule," holding that "the measure of damages is the highest value of the property wrongfully and knowingly converted between the time of conversion and a reasonable time after the person learns of such conversion." *Id.* at 144. "Such a rule," declared the *Brougham* court,

> protects the victim who has invested in property for speculative purposes when the market either rises or falls subsequent to the conversion. The innocent victim should not suffer a loss because of a wrongful taking and withholding of his property. Neither should he be granted the windfall of complete umbrella protection by being awarded the highest possible valuation of the property from the time of its taking to the entry of judgment or its return.

Id. at 144 (citation omitted).[46]

The "New York rule" errs on the side of granting the unforeseen benefit of a fluctuating commodity's increase in value to the innocent victim of conversion rather than to the converter, but it does not do so to the extent of conferring an unreasonable windfall. It also avoids the foreseeable possibility that, because of a sudden and infelicitous dip in the market for a particular commodity on the date of conversion, the victim of conversion would be inadequately compensated for his or her loss by operation of the general rule. Moreover, the New York rule tempers the speculative nature of such a measurement of damages by disregarding the market prices of the converted commodity between the time of conversion and the time the plaintiff discovers the conversion. We can be relatively certain that the plaintiff would not have sold the commodity during that time period absent the defendant's wrongdoing because " 'if he had desired to dispose of [his property] in that interval, he would have learned of the conversion.' " [Citations.] We therefore expressly adopt the New York rule with respect to the valuation of fluctuating commodities.

---

46. We note that the "reasonable time" includes the date of the conversion itself. [Citation.]

With regard to how the trier of fact is to arrive at its determination of a "reasonable time," the courts applying the "New York rule" have described the object of that inquiry as the time necessary to replace the converted commodity. [Citations.] In other words, the rule sets as an outside boundary for the determination of the value of the converted commodity the latest date upon which a "reasonable investor" with adequate funds would have reentered the market by purchasing a replacement for his or her converted commodity to "cover" the damages from the conversion. [Citations.] The rule's underlying premise is that any increase in value of the commodity after that cut-off date would have been enjoyed by the reasonable investor and should therefore not be awarded to the plaintiff who (presumably) missed his or her chance to be exposed to the market. Thus, applying the New York rule to the present case, the date of close of the evidence at trial would, as a matter of law, be the absolute end-point beyond which the "reasonable time" cannot extend, inasmuch as the market values of the converted Buddha statue and gold bars beyond that date would be unknowable to the trier of fact.

Accordingly, the circuit court's jury instruction regarding the valuation of the converted gold was erroneous. Likewise, the special verdict form erroneously required the jury to value the gold as of the date of conversion. * * * [W]ith respect to the golden buddha statue and the seventeen gold bars taken from Roxas' home, a new trial on the issue of value is necessary, and we therefore vacate that portion of the circuit court's judgment regarding the damages attributable to the golden buddha statue and the seventeen golden bars and remand for further proceedings. On retrial, the circuit court should instruct the jury that the measure of damages for the conversion of the golden buddha and the seventeen gold bars is the highest value of the gold between—and including—the date of conversion and a reasonable time thereafter.[47] The reasonable time is bounded by the latest date on which a reasonable investor with adequate funds would have replaced the converted gold. The reasonable time cannot extend beyond the date of the close of evidence at trial. * * *

———

1. *The Rest of the Story.* The facts underlying the principal case as told by the Hawaii Supreme Court, *see* Roxas v. Marcos, 89 Haw. 91, 969 P.2d 1209 (1998), befit a Hollywood movie with one of the principal actors dying under mysterious circumstances, families feuding over the buried treasure and lawsuits filed in the United States and the Philippines. The buried WWII treasure that Roxas claimed to have discovered was the legendary "Yamashita Treasure." The treasure purportedly consisted of

———

47. As described *supra*, the New York rule excludes the period between the time of conversion and the plaintiff's notice of the conversion, and the "reasonable time" extends after the plaintiff has notice. On the present record, it would be unnecessary to instruct as to these distinctions, inasmuch as it was uncontroverted that Roxas was present during the conversion of the golden buddha and the gold bars, and, therefore, the moment of the conversion and Roxas's notice of it were the same.

booty, which had been plundered from various Southeast Asian countries, during World War II, by Japanese troops under the command of General Tomoyuki Yamashita and which was allegedly buried in the Philippines during the final battle for the islands in order to keep it out of the hands of the Americans.

In addition to the golden buddha and the gold at issue in the principal case, Roxas claimed to have discovered wiring, radios, bayonets, rifles, and a human skeleton wearing a Japanese army uniform as well as numerous boxes filled with gold bars. Roxas claimed these boxes were each approximately the size of a case of beer and stacked five feet high over an area six feet wide and thirty feet long. Roxas claimed to have removed the bars of gold at issue in the principal case, the golden buddha statue and some samurai swords, bayonets, and other artifacts, intending to sell the statue to finance removal of the remaining treasure. Roxas then blasted the tunnel closed.

The quest to find and recover the legendary treasure consumed a significant part of Roxas's life. After learning of the location of the treasure, he apparently spent 9 years organizing partners and laborers to help with his search and obtaining the requisite permits from the Philippine government then seven months digging "24 hours a day," before breaking into a system of underground tunnels where he eventually discovered the golden buddha and the rest of the treasure. After the raid on his home, Roxas undertook a 20–year campaign to recover the golden buddha from the Philippine government. First, he publicized the raid to the media. Shortly thereafter, he was arrested and spent 2½ years in jail. Roxas alleged that he was arrested and tortured while in custody and that the Philippine government ordered his assassination. Ultimately, Roxas filed the litigation underlying the principal case. However, Roxas died under "mysterious circumstances" shortly before the trial of his case was set to begin. Nonetheless, the jury awarded his estate $6 million for false arrest and battery in addition to the damages for conversion of the gold based largely on the deposition testimony of Roxas which was read into the record at trial.

The Roxas family encountered many obstacles in their efforts to collect the judgment from Marcos. Marcos died before the entry of judgment, and his wife, Imelda, was never properly appointed administrator of his estate for purposes of the litigation. Thus, the Hawaiian Supreme Court limited recovery to Imelda's share of the estate only. A Hawaiian court refused to institute probate proceedings in Hawaii to protect the Roxas family's claim to the estate's assets. *See* In the Matter of Marcos, 88 Haw. 148, 963 P.2d 1124 (1998). Finally, one of the lawyers who represented Roxas sued the estate and the GBC for failure to pay legal fees, and an associate of Roxas instituted an action against the estate and GBC claiming that he had an interest in the converted gold. *See* Dacanay v. Beckmann, 2007 WL 867038 (Cal.App.Ct.2007).

The existence of the golden buddha has been a matter of some controversy that has divided the Roxas family. Shortly after the raid,

Philippine police surrendered a buddha statue to a Philippine court. However, Roxas denied that it was the statue he recovered from the treasure, and tests revealed that the statue in custody was made of brass and lead rather than gold. In 1996, a Philippine court determined that the bronze statue was the statue that Roxas recovered from the treasure and ordered that the statue be returned to the Roxas family. As late as 2006, Roxas' children continued to maintain that the brass statue was a fake and refused custody of it. Roxas' brother, who was present during the 1971 raid, recanted his previous statements and claimed that the statue in custody was the statue seized in the raid. He claimed that Roxas never discovered a golden buddha. *See* Delmar Cariño, "Judge's Suspension Over Golden Buddha Reopens Old Wounds," *Inquirer.net* available at http://newsinfo.inquirer.net/breakingnews/nation/view_article.php?article_id=81195 (Aug. 2007).

2. *New York Rule.* As explained in the principal case, the general measure of damages for converted personalty is the market value of the property at the time of conversion. The problem with this rule is that it may not compensate the plaintiff fully when the converted property fluctuates in value. Theoretically, at least, in the absence of the conversion the plaintiff could have sold the property at a later date when the market value increased. Another problem with the traditional measure of market value at the time of conversion is that the plaintiff cannot become whole simply by purchasing replacement property in the market, because the price of replacement property may exceed the market value at the time of conversion.

The advantage of the traditional measure, however, is that it does not permit the plaintiff to benefit from a rising market without assuming the risk of speculation. The reasoning is that a conversion should not insulate an investor from the risk of a falling market. Thus, courts have struggled to find a measure that compensates the plaintiff for the lost opportunity to transfer the converted property at a higher market price while preventing the plaintiff from speculating without assuming any risk of loss.

Like the court in the principal case, many courts have adopted the "New York Rule." Under the New York Rule, the plaintiff is awarded the greater of (1) the market value at the time of conversion; or (2) the highest market value between the date on which the plaintiff learns of the conversion and the expiration of a reasonable period of time thereafter. The reasonable period of time is defined as the length of time necessary for a reasonable investor to purchase replacement property.

Under the New York Rule, the plaintiff may not recover the market value of the converted property during the period of time between the conversion and the date upon which the plaintiff learns of the conversion even if the value during this period exceeds the market value after the plaintiff learns of the conversion. Courts preclude a plaintiff from recovering the market value during this period on the theory that the plaintiff's failure to discover the conversion during this period demonstrates that the plaintiff did not intend to sell the property during this period. Courts reason that a plaintiff who desired to transfer the property during this period would have discovered the conversion.

Should this reasoning also invalidate the traditional rule granting the value of the property on the date of conversion in the circumstance where that measure exceeds the value after the plaintiff learns of the conversion? Doesn't the plaintiff's failure to discover the conversion on the date it happened likewise evidence the plaintiff's lack of intent to sell the property on the date of conversion? Should that matter? *See* Fawcett v. Heimbach, 591 N.W.2d 516 (Minn.App.Ct.1999) ("[W]here there is a falling market, it would be inequitable to provide the injured party with less than the value of the stock at the time of the conversion.").

3. *Determining Market Value.* Even when property has a stable market value, determining that value can be problematic. Courts define a market value as what a willing buyer under no compulsion would pay to a willing seller, each being fully informed. How does a plaintiff establish what that price would be?

Some types of property are frequently exchanged in the marketplace and have well documented exchange rates. For example, the "blue book" value of a used automobile is readily ascertainable and fairly represents the automobile's market value. *See* United Truck Rental Equip. Leasing v. Kleenco Corp., 84 Haw. 86, 929 P.2d 99 (App.Ct.1996) (recognizing the Kelly bluebook as an authoritative reference book utilized when making evaluations regarding the value of automobiles). Similarly, the market value of many stocks are listed in different indices and represent the price that a willing buyer would pay a willing seller on any given day.

How would you establish the market value of frequently traded chattel in the absence of such an index.? For example how would you establish the market value of used law textbooks?

Special difficulties occur with unique chattel. Consider chattel such as the barge in *Barge Bertie*. To what extent, should a court consider the price the owner paid for a unique chattel in determining the market value in subsequent litigation between the owner and a defendant who tortiously damages or destroys the property? If the owner negotiates a good price, should that price be considered the fair market value for purposes of later litigation with a defendant unrelated to the seller?

Consider the case of *Boston Iron & Metal Co. v. S.S. Winding Gulf*, 85 F.Supp. 806, 812 (D.Md.1949), *aff'd* 209 F.2d 410 (4th Cir.1954), *rev'd on other grounds* 349 U.S. 122, 75 S.Ct. 649, 99 L.Ed. 933 (1955). Boston Iron purchased an obsolete ship to use as scrap and then it sank in tow during delivery. Boston Iron argued that the value of the ship as scrap was much greater than the purchase price. The court awarded more than the purchase price, but less than Boston Iron's claim. The district court judge observed:

> As a practical test I think the evidence fairly leads to the view that considering all of the relevant facts some person engaged in a similar business would fairly have been willing to pay for the destroyer as an

entity at the time and place of loss substantially more than what it cost the owner up to that time. It must be remembered that the purchase was made by one skilled in the particular business taking advantage of a particular opportunity not often afforded, and resulting from skill and knowledge of when, why and how to buy. Or, in other words, it may be said that the evidence as a whole fairly indicates that in the purchase the owner made a very good bargain and is entitled under the circumstances of the loss to have the damages fixed at a sum which would fairly pecuniarily reimburse him for the loss incurred. 85 F.Supp. at 812.

What else might serve as evidence of a unique chattel's market value? To what extent would the value of an insurance policy on the chattel be relevant?

4. *Expert Testimony.* A litigant seeking to establish the fair market value of personalty generally must present testimony from an expert witness or from someone with special knowledge of the market value from experience. *See, e.g.,* Sykes v. Sin, 229 Ga.App. 155, 493 S.E.2d 571 (1997) (lay opinion as to the value of personal property must be based upon a foundation that the witness has some knowledge, experience or familiarity with the value of the property or similar property).

The exception to this rule is that an owner may testify as to the actual value of personal property without special knowledge or training. *See, e.g.,* Maryland Cas. Co. v. Therm–O–Disc, Inc., 137 F.3d 780 (4th Cir.1998) (under Maryland law, a homeowner can testify as to the fair market value of common goods, which will usually be close or equal to their replacement costs.); Dugan v. Gotsopoulos, 117 Nev. 285, 22 P.3d 205 (2001) (a party may testify as to the value of personal property, and expert testimony is not required). The owner may testify as to such matters as the cost of the item when new, its condition and age, its time in use and expense of replacement by a similarly used item. The jury determines the weight to attach to the plaintiff's own nonexpert testimony. *See* Dugan, 22 P.3d at 207.

Lane v. Oil Delivery, Inc.

216 N.J.Super. 413, 524 A.2d 405 (1987).

■ Muir, Jr., J.A.D.

Defendant appeals and plaintiffs cross appeal from a judgment entered on a jury verdict in favor of plaintiffs which was subsequently molded and corrected by the trial court into a $278,677.20 judgment * * *.

On August 10, 1983, plaintiffs, William and Betty Lane, and the American National Fire Insurance Company filed a complaint against defendant, Oil Delivery, Inc. The complaint and its later amendment sought damages for losses incurred by the Lanes in a fire at their home. * * *

The jury set the Lanes' damages at $425,985. This figure represented the total losses claimed for house reconstruction, living expenses during reconstruction, loss of jewelry and personalty replacement costs. The Lanes set out the personalty replacement costs in a 30 page list. Prior to their testimony on the value of the personalty, the trial judge ruled the measure of damages should be the market value at the time of the fire.

The value of personalty the jury accepted came from a total of the figures on the 30 page list. On that list, the Lanes set forth each item of personalty and their estimated value or the actual cost of the item. In their testimony, they did not state how they arrived at the value for each item. Instead, they selected an apparent cross section of the items.

As to the value of items specifically covered, Mr. Lane set the value based on his experience in buying the articles in the past, pricing them at stores or in newspaper ads. Mrs. Lane, who testified essentially on her clothing and furniture in the house, based her opinion on her experience as the owner of a retail clothing store and as supervisor of charity flea markets.

* * *

The measure of damages for personalty destroyed by a tortfeasor, when there is a market value, is the market value at the time of the loss. [Citations.]

When, however, the personalty is household furnishings and wearing apparel and the like, where the market value cannot be ascertained, the better measure of damages and the one we find applicable in this case, is the actual or intrinsic value of the property to the owner, excluding sentimental or fanciful value. [Citations.]

The rationale for such a rule is consonant with the goal of tort damages to fully compensate the injured party, thereby making it possible to replace the lost property with a comparable substitute. The market value of wearing apparel and household furnishings cannot compensate the owner for their loss. While there may be a second-hand market value, other items of equal value are not interchangeable. As noted in *4 Damages in Tort Actions* (MB) 37.22[a]:

> The average owner will not replace lost clothing or furniture with secondhand merchandise, but will instead be "forced" to purchase new substitutes. Consequently, the second hand price does not provide adequate compensation for the loss sustained.

That is not to say the plaintiff is entitled to full replacement cost. [Citation.] While the element of original cost is relevant, depreciation, age, wear and tear, condition, cost of replacement and cost of repair are all factors to be considered in assessing the damage sustained. [Citation.]

Where an item is brand new, proof of original cost sustains the owner's burden of proof as to value. [Citation.] Further, while the cost of repair may be the sole proof of damages, depreciation of a repaired object, adequately established, may be an additional relevant factor. [Citation.]

Proof of damages need not be done with exactitude, particularly when dealing with household furnishings and wearing apparel. It is therefore sufficient that the plaintiff prove damages with such certainty as the nature of the case may permit, laying a foundation which will enable the trier of the facts to make a fair and reasonable estimate. [Citation.]

In providing such evidence, the plaintiff, as owner, may give an opinion of worth although he or she is without expert knowledge. [Citation.] The basis for arriving at the opinion must, however, not be a matter of speculation and the witness must be required to establish the grounds for any opinion given. It is for the jury, with appropriate instructions from the court, to ascertain the probative value of the opinion. * * *

[Remanded.]

Carbasho v. Musulin

217 W.Va. 359, 618 S.E.2d 368 (2005).

■ MAYNARD, JUSTICE:

This case is before this Court upon appeal of a final order of the Circuit Court of Brooke County entered on March 31, 2004. In that order, the circuit court granted summary judgment in favor of the appellee and defendant below, Michael Musulin, finding that the measure of property damages for the loss of a pet dog is limited to the dog's fair market value. In this appeal, the appellant and plaintiff below, Helen Tracy Carbasho, contends that the damages recoverable for the loss of a pet dog must include the "true and special value" of the dog to its owner, and therefore, the circuit court erred by granting summary judgment to Mr. Musulin.

This Court has before it the petition for appeal, the entire record, and the briefs and argument of counsel. For the reasons set forth below, the final order is affirmed.

This case arises out of an accident that occurred around midnight on June 8, 2001, in Follansbee, Brooke County, West Virginia. At that time, Ms. Carbasho was walking her dog, Groucho, down an alley when both she and the dog were struck by a vehicle driven by Mr. Musulin. Both Ms. Carbasho and her dog were injured. The dog died shortly thereafter from its injuries.

On February 19, 2002, Ms. Carbasho filed suit against Mr. Musulin seeking damages for her personal injuries and the death of her dog. On March 20, 2003, the parties agreed to a settlement with regard to Ms. Carbasho's bodily injury claims. As a result, the circuit court entered an order on April 10, 2003, stating that "the only issue remaining to be determined was the property damage value of the dog, Groucho, and whether or not sentimental value, emotional distress and emotional attachment are recoverable damages in West Virginia for the loss of the dog, and if so, to what extent."

On April 22, 2003, Mr. Musulin moved for summary judgment requesting that the circuit court dismiss Ms. Carbasho's claim for damages in excess of the dog's assessed value which was estimated to be between

$100.00 and $150.00. By order dated March 31, 2004, the circuit court granted Mr. Musulin's motion limiting Ms. Carbasho's recovery for the loss of her dog to its fair market or assessed value. This appeal followed.

The issue presented in this case is the proper measure of property damages for the loss of a pet dog. As noted above, Ms. Carbasho maintains that her dog's market value is not an adequate measure of damages. She contends that the loss of companionship she has suffered must be considered as an element of the dog's actual value. She says that the "real worth" of a pet is not primarily financial, but emotional, and its value should be determined based upon the relationship between the pet and its owner, and not its market value.

In support of her argument, Ms. Carbasho relies upon *Julian v. De Vincent*, 155 W.Va. 320, 322, 184 S.E.2d 535, 536 (1971), a case in which this Court stated that a plaintiff may recover damages for the loss of a dog by proving "the market value, pecuniary value or *some special value.*" (Emphasis added). Ms. Carbasho submits that pursuant to *Julian*, the circuit court's order should be reversed and her case should be remanded to allow her to prove her dog's "special value." Ms. Carbasho's reliance upon *Julian* is misplaced, however, because this Court further held in that case that damages for sentimental value or mental suffering are not recoverable. * * *

This Court has long held that damages recoverable for the negligent destruction of personal property are limited to the fair market value. Syllabus Point 5 of *Stenger v. Hope Natural Gas Co.*, 139 W.Va. 549, 80 S.E.2d 889 (1954), states:

> The measure of recovery for property destroyed through negligence is the fair market value of the property at the time of destruction. The measure of recovery for negligent damage to property not destroyed, where the damage is of a permanent nature, is the diminution in the market value of the property by reason of the injury.

Ms. Carbasho argues that it is unfair to view pets in the same way that we do other personal property when it comes to damages for their injury or destruction. She says that the death of a pet is simply not the same as losing an inanimate object. Certainly, "labeling a dog 'property' fails to describe the value human beings place upon the companionship that they enjoy with a dog. A companion dog is not a fungible item, equivalent to other items of personal property.... This term inadequately and inaccurately describes the relationship between a human and a dog." [Citation.] While Ms. Carbasho's distress over the loss of her dog is understandable, our law categorizes dogs as personal property and as a result sentimental attachment of an owner to his or her dog cannot be considered in the computation of damages.

Our statutory law, as well as, this Court's decision in *Julian,* clearly establish that damages for sentimental value, mental suffering, and emotional distress are not recoverable for the death of a pet dog. Not only is that the law of this State, but it is also the general rule in a majority of jurisdictions.

Accordingly, for clarification purposes, we now hold that dogs are personal property and damages for sentimental value, mental suffering, and emotional distress are not recoverable for the negligently inflicted death of a dog. * * *

■ STARCHER, J., dissenting:

This opinion is simply medieval. The majority blithely says that "our law categorizes dogs as personal property"—that "damages for sentimental value, mental suffering, and emotional distress are not recoverable" when one's pet is injured or killed by the negligence of another person. In coming to this conclusion, the majority overlooks the fact that the "law" in question is the common law which is controlled by this Court. There was nothing stopping the majority from changing that common law other than their lack of concern for pet owners and the emotional bonds that exist between owners and their pets.

When the common law of the past is no longer in harmony with the institutions or societal conditions of the present, this Court is constitutionally empowered to adjust the common law to current needs. As we stated in Syllabus Point 1 of *Powell v. Sims*, 5 W.Va. 1 (1871), "the common law of England is in force in this State only so far as it is in harmony with its institutions, and its principles applicable to the state of the country and the condition of society." As Justice Holmes succinctly reflected, "the common law is not a brooding omnipresence in the sky but the articulate voice of some sovereign or quasisovereign that can be identified." *Southern Pacific Co. v. Jensen*, 244 U.S. 205, 222, 37 S. Ct. 524, 61 L. Ed. 1086 (1917) (Holmes, J., dissenting).

We have since made clear that our courts retain the power to change the common law, holding in Syllabus Point 2 of *Morningstar v. Black and Decker Mfg. Co.*, 162 W.Va. 857, 253 S.E.2d 666 (1979) that "Article VIII, Section 13 of the West Virginia Constitution and W.Va.Code, 2–1–1, were not intended to operate as a bar to this Court's evolution of common law principles, including its historic power to alter or amend the common law." * * *

Yet the majority opinion continues to maintain the primitive limits of the common law, and refuses to adjust to the realities of the modern world, and permit recovery of damages for sentimental values, mental suffering, or emotional distress.

Today, 63% of all American households have one pet, 45% have more than one. In fact, there are more pets in America than there are citizens (360 million pets, 290 million people). Americans will spend upwards of $36 billion pampering those pets this year, an amount nearly equal to the amount Americans spend on toys and candy *combined. See* American Pet Products Manufacturers Association, Inc., *Fact Sheet: Industry Statistics & Trends,* www.appma.org. Beyond question, many Americans love their cats, their dogs, their birds, as well as they love their children. But like the children of the pre-industrial revolution, the majority opinion chooses to categorize those pets as nothing more than chattel.

I was saddened when I read the majority's opinion, and was reminded of an old country music song by Red Foley called "Old Shep:"

> When I was a lad
> And old Shep was a pup
> Over hills and meadows we'd stray
> Just a boy and his dog
> We were both full of fun
> We grew up together that way.
>
> I remember the time at the old swimmin' hole
> When I would have drowned beyond doubt
> But old Shep was right there
> To the rescue he came
> He jumped in and then pulled me out.
>
> As the years fast did roll
> Old Shep he grew old
> His eyes were fast growing dim
> And one day the doctor looked at me and said
> I can do no more for him Jim.
>
> With hands that were trembling
> I picked up my gun
> And aimed it at Shep's faithful head
> I just couldn't do it
> I wanted to run
> I wish they would shoot me instead.
>
> He came to my side
> And looked up at me
> And laid his old head on my knee
> I had struck the best friend that a man ever had
> I cried so I scarcely could see.
>
> Old Shep he has gone
> Where the good doggies go
> And no more with old Shep will I roam
> But if dogs have a heaven
> There's one thing I know
> Old Shep has a wonderful home.

I'm sure Groucho has a wonderful home too. I'm sorry, however, that Ms. Carbasho has no remedy for her grief and emotional distress in our common law.

I therefore respectfully dissent.

---

1. *Unique and Irreplaceable Property.* As the principal cases reflect, when damaged or destroyed property has no real market value or the value of the property to the owner exceeds the market value, measuring damages has proved troublesome. When household goods and clothing, such as the items at issue in *Lane* are damaged or destroyed, most courts allow the owner to recover the actual value of the property to the owner. Courts also have extended this measure to cases involving the loss or destruction of family heirlooms such as trophies and photographs. *See, e.g.,* Landers v. Municipality of Anchorage, 915 P.2d 614 (Alaska 1996). Generally, the actual value to the owner excludes "sentimental or fanciful value." However, when the damaged or destroyed property has its primary value in sentiment, a few courts have allowed the owner to recover the sentimental or emotional value of the property. *See, e.g., Campins v. Capels*, 461 N.E.2d 712 (Ind.App.1984); *Bond v. A.H. Belo Corp.*, 602 S.W.2d 105 (Tex.Civ.App. 1980).

How does one prove the actual value to the owner? What constitutes the actual value excluding its sentimental or fanciful value? Is the distinction between sentimental value and value to the owner a valid one?

2. *Pets.* Measuring damages for the death of a pet has proven even more problematic. As the principal case reflects, a majority of jurisdictions measure damages for the death of a pet as the fair market value at the time of the pet's death, and courts, generally, have rejected claims for the emotional distress, sentimental attachment or loss of companionship its owner suffers. *See, e.g.,* Nichols v. Sukaro Kennels, 555 N.W.2d 689, 61 A.L.R.5th 883 (Iowa 1996); Pickford v. Masion, 124 Wash.App. 257, 98 P.3d 1232 (2004); *see also* Robin Cheryl Miller, *Damages for Killing or Injuring Dog*, 61 A.L.R. 5th 635 (1998). One commentator traced the origins of this rule to the eighteenth and nineteenth century when many animals were used for agrarian purposes and, thus, fair market value truly reflected the value of the animals to their owners. *See* Margit Livingston, The Calculus of Animal Valuation: Crafting a Viable Remedy, 82 NEB. L. REV. 783 (2004).

Although some pedigree animals young enough for breeding or show have objective value, today most family pets have little or no value in the marketplace. In light of this, should a pet owner be able to recover the personal value of a lost pet? Some jurisdictions have expanded recovery to allow damages for the actual value of the pet, including the owner's sentimental attachments to the pet. *See, e.g.,* Anzalone v. Kragness, 356 Ill.App.3d 365, 292 Ill.Dec. 331, 826 N.E.2d 472 (2005). However, even in those cases damages are limited. In cases of extreme or outrageous conduct, some courts have been willing to allow recovery for emotional distress and punitive damages. *See, e.g.,* Burgess v. Taylor, 44 S.W.3d 806 (Ky.App. 2001). If many jurisdictions were to make pets an exception to the rule excluding sentimental value, would such an exception be likely to stand alone or would it signal a significant erosion of the general rule?

3. *Cars v. Clothes.* Consumers use both cars as well as clothes and household goods. However, the law distinguishes between them in measuring damages. Clothes and household goods may be valued at the personal

value to the owner, but cars are valued at fair market value. Why distinguish? Does the market value of a used car always equal its actual value to the owner? Is it a sufficient answer that there is a greater market in used cars than used clothes or that the economic interchangeability may be ascertained with a higher degree of certainty in the used car market? To what extent does the difficulty in valuation affect settlement offers?

4. *Replacement Value.* Plaintiffs may sometimes hold items such as used clothes or used furniture for business purposes. Such plaintiffs are fully compensated by an award for the market value of any such items that are lost or destroyed. An owner of a second-hand shop, for example, would be fully compensated by an award for the market value of any inventory destroyed in a store fire.

Consumers, however, are in a different position. As a practical matter they must replace destroyed clothes and household goods rather than simply adjust their balance sheets. Nonetheless, courts have rejected replacement cost as the measure of actual value to the owner. *See, e.g.,* McConchie v. Samsung Elec. America, 2000 WL 1507442 (D.N.H.2000) Instead, replacement cost is a factor to be considered in determining the actual value to the owner along with the original cost of the property, the quality and condition at the time of loss and depreciation.

Why not give replacement cost? Is replacement overcompensation for consumers? Could any windfall be eliminated by a deduction for the depreciation of the destroyed property? Should a plaintiff be compensated for the time and inconvenience incurred in trying to purchase replacement items in used markets or at bargain sales?

5. *Objectively Sentimental.* Courts that have permitted recovery of sentimental value limit recovery to property whose primary value is sentiment. Indeed, in *Campins v. Capels*, 461 N.E.2d 712 (Ind.App.1984), the court permitted the plaintiffs to recover the actual value, including the sentimental value, of three professional automobile racing championship rings but limited recovery for one of the plaintiffs' wedding band to the value at which it is had been appraised.

Should a plaintiff be able to recover the sentimental value of any item that holds primarily sentimental value? For example, should a particularly sentimental person be entitled to recover damages for the sentimental value of a ticket stub from the first date with his or her spouse if the ticket stub is destroyed in a fire? Consider the court's observations in *Campins*:

> When we refer to sentimental value, we do not mean mawkishly emotional or unreasonable attachments to personal property. Rather, we are referring to the feelings generated by items of almost purely sentimental value, such as heirlooms, family papers and photographs, handicrafts, and trophies. [Citations.] What we are referring to basically are those items *generally* capable of generating sentimental feelings, not just the emotions peculiar to the owner. 461 N.E.2d at 721.

6. *Irreplaceable Property.* If emotional or sentimental value is excluded from the measure of actual value, how does a plaintiff establish the

actual value of the property? Courts consider factors such as the original cost, the cost to replace or reproduce and the age and condition of the item at the time of loss or destruction. Distinguish irreplaceable property from difficult to replace property. How does one establish the value of property that cannot be replaced or reproduced?

In one notable case, *Taliferro v. Augle*, 757 F.2d 157 (7th Cir.1985), a court significantly reduced the amount of damages a plaintiff recovered for destruction of an unpublished manuscript. In *Taliferro*, the plaintiff, an African–American and amateur writer who had written "on the theme of oppression of blacks by whites," filed suit after he was allegedly arrested and beaten by two Chicago police officers. The officers seized a manuscript that was in the plaintiff's possession at the time of his arrest, and the manuscript was lost or destroyed while in police custody.

A jury awarded the plaintiff $47,000 in compensatory damages for the loss of the manuscript. In an opinion authored by Judge Posner, self-described as "a sometime author of academic manuscripts," the court concluded that the plaintiff failed to offer sufficient evidence to establish the actual value of the manuscript. The court explained that proof of the cost in time or materials to reconstruct the manuscript would have been sufficient to sustain the verdict but that the plaintiff had failed to offer any such evidence. The court remitted the verdict to $25,000, noting that such an amount was the highest amount that could be justified on the record. The court offered no explanation as to how it arrived at the remitted amount.

If the plaintiff was not gainfully employed as a writer, how could the value of his time be measured? Is it clear that the plaintiff could reconstruct the manuscript? Judge Posner's experience as an author of legal manuscripts may not be the same as the plaintiff's experience as an author about oppression. The process of inspiration may work very differently and may affect the ability to reconstruct previously written work.

PROBLEM: THE CAUTIOUS RANCHER

Watt is an old Nevada rancher who has lived through a few difficult winters. He particularly remembers one hard winter years ago when he lost a significant portion of his livestock. Ever since, Watt has grown and stored enough hay to survive even such an extraordinary year. Watt has been growing and storing more hay than he has needed in recent years. Neighboring ranchers believe that his degree of caution is foolish. If Watt had not developed such a concern about exceptionally hard weather, he could have turned a larger profit on his ranch. He persists in his practice nonetheless, and warns that nature will teach a lesson of caution again one of these years. His critics observe that the amount he has lost by hoarding hay is probably equal to the entire value of his present stock. He retorts that "the past is past, but the future is uncertain."

Last fall Watt's hay crop was burned as it lay drying in the field. A negligently driven tanker truck owned by Central Trucking overturned and caught fire on the highway adjacent to Watt's ranch. The fire spread to Watt's field and destroyed the drying hay. Watt sued for this destruction of his personal property.

How should the hay be valued? Assume that the hay had a fair market value as a commodity and that, if Watt had elected to sell his hay at the market, he would have incurred transportation expenses. Conversely, if Watt were to purchase hay at the market to store on his ranch, he would incur transportation expenses.

Should the court grant the fair market value of the hay and add or subtract transportation costs? Should the hay be divided into two categories: (1) an amount reasonable to store for the winter and (2) the extra amount that Watt cautiously adds?

Long v. McAllister

319 N.W.2d 256 (Iowa 1982).

■ McCORMICK, JUSTICE.

This tort action arose from a dispute concerning adjustment of motor vehicle property damage under the liability coverage of the tortfeasor's insurance policy. In entering summary judgment for defendants, the trial court limited plaintiff's recovery to the reasonable value of his automobile at the time it was damaged. * * *

Plaintiff Arthur Long's automobile was damaged on October 19, 1978, when a farm wagon of defendants Dan McAllister and McAllister Seed Company, Inc., rolled down an incline and struck it. These defendants had property damage liability insurance covering the loss with defendant I.M.T. Insurance Company and another insurer. Although I.M.T. obtained repair estimates from plaintiff shortly after the occurrence, thirty-three days passed before the insurers agreed between themselves on how the loss would be shared. Eight days later I.M.T. offered plaintiff $1250 to settle the loss in behalf of McAllister and the seed company. No dispute existed concerning liability or the fact the vehicle was damaged beyond repair.

After first agreeing to the settlement, plaintiff later in the same day rejected it as inadequate. Eventually plaintiff employed an attorney who demanded $1500 in settlement. I.M.T. raised its offer to $1300 but received no response. * * *

[Plaintiff sued for $1300 as the fair market value of the car and for $500 as the cost of renting a substitute vehicle during the time he waited for the adjustment. The trial court refused to allow the $500 cost of renting a car on the grounds that loss of use damages were not appropriate.]

Loss of use damages. In denying damages for loss of use of the destroyed automobile, the trial court followed existing precedent. *See, e.g.,*

Aetna Casualty and Surety Co. v. Insurance Department of Iowa, 299 N.W.2d 484, 485 (Iowa 1980):

(1) When the automobile is totally destroyed, the measure of damages is its reasonable market value immediately before its destruction.

(2) Where the injury to the car can be repaired, so that, when repaired, it will be in as good condition as it was in before, the injury, then the measure of damages is the reasonable value of the use of the car while being repaired, with ordinary diligence, not exceeding the value of the car before the injury.

(3) When the car cannot, by repair, be placed in as good condition as it was in before the injury, then the measure of damages is the difference between its reasonable market value immediately before and immediately after the accident.

These rules were first distilled in Langham v. Chicago, R.I. & P. R., 201 Iowa 897, 901, 208 N.W. 356, 358 (1925). The court expressly held that loss of use damages are not allowed under the first and third rules in Kohl v. Arp, 236 Iowa 31, 33 34, 17 N.W.2d 824, 826 (1945).

The rule denying loss of use damages in these situations has not been specifically discussed in the cases. Because the rule has been challenged in the present case, we must determine its continued viability. We do so against the background "that the principle underlying allowance of damages is that of compensation, the ultimate purpose being to place the injured party in as favorable a position as though no wrong had been committed." Dealers Hobby, Inc. v. Marie Ann Linn Realty Co., 255 N.W.2d 131, 134 (Iowa 1977).

Inherent in our present rules governing damages to motor vehicles is the concept that the market value of the vehicle is the ceiling on recovery whether the vehicle can be repaired or must be replaced. In some cases the owner will be fully compensated despite that limitation. Even when the vehicle is destroyed and delay occurs before compensation is received, interest on the market value of the vehicle from the date of the accident theoretically pays the owner for the delay. The same is true when the vehicle is not destroyed but cannot be restored to its prior condition and the owner receives interest on its depreciated value. Moreover, when the vehicle can be restored by repair to its prior condition, the owner is not only entitled to compensation for the reasonable cost of repair but for reasonable loss of use damages. Although market value is nevertheless a ceiling on recovery even in this situation, full compensation is possible when the cumulated damages do not exceed the limitation.

In other cases, however, the present rules plainly do not permit full compensation. Loss of use damages will be incurred as readily when a vehicle is totally destroyed or when it cannot be restored by repair to its prior condition as when the vehicle can be restored by repair. Just as loss of use damages are necessary for full compensation when the vehicle can be restored to its prior condition, they are warranted when the vehicle is destroyed or cannot be so restored. No logical basis exists for cutting them off when the total reaches the vehicle's market value before the injury.

The origin of the market value limitation lies in history rather than logic. Damages for destruction of chattels were based on analogy to conversion. The reasonable market value of the chattel was viewed as adequate compensation under this concept in the common law action of trover. The rigidity of the analogy obscured any distinction between destruction of chattels generally and destruction of chattels of such utility that the owners incurred loss of use expense. Perhaps this distinction became important only with the advent of the motor vehicle and the practice of motor vehicle leasing and rental.

The historical basis and usual arguments for denying loss of use damages are addressed in D. Dobbs, *Remedies* 5.11 at 384 85 (1973) (footnotes omitted):

> * * * There was probably some thought that the market value of the chattel which reflected the right to use it gainfully plus interest for the time the owner was deprived of it, actually furnished full compensation. Another argument made against granting loss of use where there was total destruction sounds rather strange in modern ears. The authors of Sedgwick on Damages argued that when compensation for the whole value of the property destroyed is sought, "it is upon the theory that the plaintiff's entire interest in the property ceased at the time of the injury, and was replaced by a right to have the value of the property in money. Since therefore, the plaintiff no longer has title to the property he can no longer claim that he might make a future gain from it...." Such an argument probably would not be accepted, or even thought of, today. It is a conceptual argument that does not interest itself in whether the owner has actually lost something of value beyond the market value of his property; it interests itself only in a legal concept passage of title that is not a part of the real world of facts and has no significant relation to important facts of actual loss. * * *

The fallacy in the market value ceiling upon recovery in a destruction case was pinpointed in Bartlett v. Garrett, 130 N.J.Super. 193, 196, 325 A.2d 866, 867 (1974):

> When an automobile is damaged through the negligence of another, temporary loss of the use of such vehicle pending repair or replacement is a reasonably foreseeable consequence of the defendant's tortious conduct. Compensation for the temporary loss of use is directed at plaintiff's *economic loss,* the amount of money plaintiff had to pay for rental of a car. This is an injury different in kind from *property damage,* the amount of money necessary to repair or replace the damaged vehicle. A plaintiff in a total

destruction case deprived of his reasonable loss-of-use expenses has simply not been made whole. (emphasis in original).

* * *

We believe our motor vehicle damages rules should be modified to permit full compensation including loss of use damages. The new rules shall apply to this case, any pending case in which error has been preserved on the issue, and all cases tried after the date of filing this opinion. As modified, the rules are as follows:

(1) When the motor vehicle is totally destroyed or the reasonable cost of repair exceeds the difference in reasonable market value before and after the injury, the measure of damages is the lost market value plus the reasonable value of the use of the vehicle for the time reasonably required to obtain a replacement.

(2) When the injury to the motor vehicle can be repaired so that, when repaired, it will be in as good condition as it was in before the injury, and the cost of repair does not exceed the difference in market value of the vehicle before and after the injury, then the measure of damages is the reasonable cost of repair plus the reasonable value of the use of the vehicle for the time reasonably required to complete its repair.

(3) When the motor vehicle cannot by repair be placed in as good condition as it was in before the injury, then the measure of damages is the difference between its reasonable market value before and after the injury, plus the reasonable value of the use of the vehicle for the time reasonably required to repair or replace it.

In the present case, plaintiff alleged loss of use damages but did not get an opportunity to prove them because of the adjudication of law points denying their availability. We reverse the adjudication and order that plaintiff be accorded a trial on the issue upon demand. * * *

---

1. *Emerging Trend.* Historically, plaintiffs have been entitled to recover damages for loss of use as well as the cost of repair or diminished value when personal property has been tortiously damaged. Loss of use damages were intended to compensate plaintiffs for the loss of the use of their property while the property was being repaired. When personal property is destroyed, plaintiffs typically cannot replace the property immediately and, consequently need to rent substitute property. Traditionally, however, plaintiffs were not entitled to recover damages for loss of use when personal property was destroyed rather than damaged. Courts have begun to recognize the similarity between renting substitutes during repair time and during replacement time, especially for automobiles. Since World War II, the trend of state courts has been to allow loss of use damages in destruction cases as well as damage cases. *See* Annot., "Recovery for Loss of Use of Motor Vehicle Damaged or Destroyed," 18 A.L.R.3d 497 (1968). Some courts, however, continue to adhere to the traditional rule. *See, e.g.,*

Boral Bricks, Inc. v. Old South Trans. Mgmt., 198 Ga.App. 678, 402 S.E.2d 777 (1991). The Restatement (Second) of Torts § 927 endorses recovery for loss of use.

2. *Evidence of Loss of Use.* Plaintiffs need not actually obtain a substitute to recover loss of use damages. Moreover, courts permit plaintiffs to establish the value of the loss of use of their property through several mutually exclusive measures. Plaintiffs can demonstrate (1) the reasonable cost of renting a substitute; (2) the rental value of the damaged property; or (3) the profits that could have been made from the use of the property. If a plaintiff seeks to recover the rental value of the damaged property or the lost profits, however, the rental value or the value of the lost profits must be adjusted to account for any expenses the plaintiff saved by not having possession of the property.

3. *Duty to Mitigate.* Plaintiffs have a duty to mitigate their damages, including damages from loss of use. Thus, plaintiffs may only recover those damages that could not have been reasonably avoided. With respect to loss of use damages, this means a plaintiff's damages are limited to recovery for the period of time reasonably necessary to secure a substitute.

In *Doughty v. Sullivan*, 661 A.2d 1112 (Me.1995), for example, the plaintiff purchased a lobster boat from a would-be seller. Before the plaintiff could take possession of the boat, the original owner repossessed it from the seller. The plaintiff sued the original owner, seeking damages for his loss of profits during the season that he was unable to use the boat because it was in the original owner's possession. The lower court awarded the plaintiff more than $3,000 for loss of use, but the Maine Supreme Court reduced the damage award to $500 because the plaintiff failed to mitigate his damages. In reaching its holding, the court noted that the plaintiff first learned that the original owner claimed title to the boat six months before the lobster season began. The plaintiff did not seek to obtain a replacement boat for the season but chose to forgo lobster fishing that season. On those facts, the court reduced the plaintiff's damages to $500 on the reasoning that the plaintiff would have lost only $500 in profits during the time it would have taken a reasonable person to replace the boat.

4. *Expenses Incurred in Mitigation.* Because plaintiffs have a duty to mitigate damages, it follows that plaintiffs should be entitled to recover damages for any expenses reasonably incurred in trying to mitigate damages. Applying this principle, the Seventh Circuit held that a plaintiff was entitled to recover the cost of failed repairs in addition to the diminished value of its damaged property. *See* Toledo Peoria & Western Ry. v. Metro Waste Sys., 59 F.3d 637 (7th Cir.1995). The court explained that although the damage to the property ultimately proved irreparable, entitling the plaintiff to recover the diminished value of the property, the cost of the repairs if successful would have been less than the diminished value of the property. Thus, the plaintiff had a duty to attempt the repairs and avoid the cost of scrapping the damaged property. Because the plaintiff had a duty to attempt the repairs, the court reasoned that the plaintiff was entitled to recover the cost of those repairs.

5. *Cost of Repairs and Diminution in Value.* Should a plaintiff be entitled to recover both the cost of repairs and the diminished value of the property under any other circumstances? The two measures are usually considered inconsistent or duplicative. However, a repaired chattel often has diminished value even after repair. Consider that an automobile that has been in a serious accident is worth less after full repair than an otherwise equivalent automobile. The fact that a chattel has undergone major repair may create doubt in a buyer's mind because of the fear that latent problems may exist. Should any such loss in fair market value be compensable in addition to the full cost of repair?

In *Ellis v. King*, 184 W.Va. 227, 400 S.E.2d 235 (1990), the court permitted the plaintiffs to recover damages for the cost to repair their damaged automobile as well as for its diminution in value after the repairs. In permitting recovery for both the cost of repairs and diminution in value, the court recognized that once an automobile incurs structural damage, no amount of repairs may be able to return the vehicle to the value it had prior to the accident. Thus, the court allowed recovery for both the cost of repairs and diminished value under the limited circumstances where a plaintiff could show actual proof of diminished value following repair and that the automobile had significant value prior to the accident. *See also* Unitrust, Inc. v. Jet Fleet Corp., 673 S.W.2d 619 (Tex.App.Ct.1984) (the value of an aircraft in its repaired condition was not necessarily the same as its fair market value prior to the crash); *but see* Sullivan v. Pulkrabek, 611 N.W.2d 162 (N.D.2000) (rejecting claim for diminished value because vehicle owner had already received the cost of repairs); Papenheim v. Lovell, 553 N.W.2d 328 (Iowa 1996) (rejecting claim for diminished value after repairs; if an automobile has diminished value after repairs, proper measure of recovery is the difference in value before and after the accident).

B. HARM TO REAL PROPERTY

Section Coverage:

The practical problems and policy conflicts that affect damages for tortious injury to personal property emerge also in cases involving tortious injury to real property. For example, is it appropriate to award cost of repair damages greater than the overall diminution in value of the property? Should a plaintiff be awarded loss of use damages during repairs?

It is useful to distinguish between injuries to the land itself and injuries to structures on the land. Another important distinction separates permanent injuries from reparable ones. Land itself is rarely "destroyed," of course, unless it is submerged under water. Some critical feature of the land, such as its productivity, could be effectively ruined in certain instances. The leaching of toxic chemicals into the soil and water supply, for example, may permanently render the land unfit for growing crops. The distinction between temporary and permanent harms is often elusive, however. If negligent blasting causes a well to run dry such that a new one must be drilled, is the well injured or destroyed?

Model Case:

A negligent truck driver runs into a homeowner's yard and smashes a free-standing garage. The structure is very substantially damaged. Repair estimates are close to the value of an entirely new garage. A real estate appraisal shows a fair market value reduction in the value of the home-owner's property that is less than either the cost of repair or replacement of the garage.

Jurisdictions vary in damage rules. Some would give the cost of repair. Others would limit a cost of repair recovery to the diminution in the fair market value of the overall property unless the plaintiff can prove that the structure has a separate value and that cost of repair does not exceed that separate value. Yet other jurisdictions distinguish between permanent and reparable injuries to improvements on land. If the plaintiff establishes that the injury to the garage is not permanent, even though substantial, then cost of repair is appropriate. Some courts distinguish between a homeowner who needs the garage and a real estate investor who buys and sells property regularly.

Miller v. Cudahy Co.

858 F.2d 1449 (10th Cir.1988).

■ BALDOCK, CIRCUIT JUDGE.

In this diversity action, plaintiffs-appellees claimed that the American Salt Company's (American Salt) salt mining operations caused the pollution of an underground aquifer passing under their farms, resulting in their inability to utilize the water in the aquifer for irrigation. At the time appellees filed their complaint, American Salt was an operating division of defendant-appellant Cudahy Company (Cudahy), which is a wholly-owned subsidiary of defendant-appellant General Host Corporation (General Host). The district court concluded that the pollution emanating from the salt plant constituted a continuing, abatable nuisance causing temporary damages and found appellants liable for $3.06 million in actual damages and $10 million in punitive damages. * * *

Appellees are owners and lessees of real property located in Rice County, Kansas. The land is used primarily for agricultural production. American Salt, along with its predecessor, has operated a salt manufactur-ing plant near Lyons, Kansas since 1908.

Located two miles south of Lyons is Cow Creek, which flows in a southeasterly direction and is a minor tributary of the Arkansas River. Below Cow Creek is the Cow Creek Valley Aquifer (the aquifer), an underground fresh-water stratum which occupies a width of one to two miles and lies at depths of between approximately ten and seventy feet. The aquifer also flows in a southeasterly direction, at a rate of between one-and-a-half and five feet per day. The water in the aquifer passes under the land owned or leased by appellees after it has passed under American Salt's brine fields and plant.

Salt concentrations of over 30,000 parts per million have been recorded in water samples drawn from the aquifer. Concentrations of 250 parts per million are sufficient to render water unfit for domestic or irrigation use. As found by the district court, the salt present in the aquifer escaped from the property and control of American Salt. The majority of the salt escaped through subsurface leaks, while the remainder percolated downward from surface spills.

Due to insufficient rainfall, farmers in Rice County are unable to grow corn without irrigating their land. Appellees alleged that because of the salt pollution of the aquifer, they are unable to irrigate and therefore can grow only dryland crops such as wheat and milo, which do not produce the revenues generated by corn crops.

The district court, in commenting on the more than half-century of disputes between American Salt and area farmers, described the historical background of this case as "Dickensian" in nature. [Citation.] Final resolution of this lawsuit itself required nearly a decade. * * *

The district court denied appellants' motion for summary judgment, which was predicated on their contention that appellees' claims were barred by the statute of limitations. The court concluded that appellees' showing was sufficient to categorize the American Salt operation as a continuing, abatable nuisance causing temporary damages and giving rise to a continuing series of causes of action. The court also concluded that the two-year statute of limitations did operate to preclude appellees from recovering for injuries sustained more than two years prior to the filing of their complaint. The court stated that appellees were entitled to attempt to prove and recover their damages accruing between a date two years before the complaint was filed (May 31, 1975) and the date of judgment.

Following a bench trial, the court found appellants liable for temporary damages to annual crops and awarded appellees $3.06 million in actual damages for the period of 1975 through 1983. The court arrived at the amount of lost crop profits by calculating the difference between the net value of corn crops and the net value of the wheat and milo crops which were actually grown. The court also awarded $10 million in punitive damages; however, it retained jurisdiction over the award and held final judgment in abeyance, pending appellants' "good-faith efforts to define and remedy the pollution they have caused." Pursuant to Fed.R.Civ.P. 54(b), the court entered final judgment on the issues of liability and actual damages. * * *

Appellants first argue that appellees' claims are time-barred, the primary thrust of their argument being that the injuries suffered by appellees are permanent in nature and were ascertained long before the statute of limitations began to run. * * *

The applicable Kansas statute of limitations, Kan.Stat.Ann. 60 513 (1983), provides in pertinent part:

(a) The following actions shall be brought within two (2) years: (1) An action for trespass upon real property.

* * *

(4) An action for injury to the rights of another, not arising on contract, and not herein enumerated.

The crucial question in regard to the applicability of the two-year statute of limitations is whether the injuries sustained by appellees are permanent or temporary in nature. Drawing a distinction between permanent and temporary damages resulting from a nuisance is at best problematical.[3] The district court, upon surveying Kansas nuisance law from 1876 to the present, noted that the relevant cases addressing the distinction between permanent and temporary injuries are somewhat unclear and inconsistent.

The Kansas Supreme Court likewise has recognized the rather confused state of the law concerning the distinction between permanent and temporary nuisances. [Citation.] The supreme court recently indicated that the distinction between temporary and permanent damages remains a viable concept, however, while emphasizing that "no hard and fast rule can be adopted as to when the damages are deemed permanent and when they are deemed temporary." Olson v. State Highway Comm'n of Kan., 235 Kan. 20, 679 P.2d 167, 172 (1984). Noting that some cases refer not only to the permanent or temporary nature of the damages, but also to the permanent or temporary nature of the causative factor, the court stressed that "[e]ach case must be considered in its own factual setting."

* * *

Under Kansas law, the plaintiff has the option of suing for either permanent or temporary damages. [Citation.] If permanent damages are sought, an action claiming such damages must be brought within two years. [Citation.] "Permanent damages are given on the theory that the cause of injury is fixed and that the property will always remain subject to that injury." McAlister v. Atlantic Richfield Co., 233 Kan. 252, 662 P.2d 1203, 1211 (1983). They "are damages for the entire injury done past, present and prospective and generally speaking [are] those which are practically irremediable."

If the injury or wrong is classified as temporary, the limitation period starts to run only when the plaintiff's land or crops are actually harmed, and for purposes of the statute of limitations, each injury causes a new cause of action to accrue, at least until the injury becomes permanent.

---

3. As described in one torts treatise, "[t]here is perhaps no more impenetrable jungle in the entire law than that which surrounds the word 'nuisance.'" W. Keeton, D. Dobbs, R. Keeton & D. Owen, Prosser and Keeton on Torts 616 (5th ed. 1984). In regard to the specific issue presented here, another treatise notes the general confusion surrounding the distinction the courts have drawn between permanent and temporary nuisances. F. Harper, F. James & O. Gray, The Law of Torts 1.30 (2d ed. 1986).

[Citations.] This rule is especially applicable if the situation involves elements of uncertainty, "such as the possibility or likelihood of the alteration or abatement of the causative condition." [Citation.] The rule is predicated upon the defendant's ability and duty to abate the existing conditions which constitute the nuisance. [Citations.]

Appellants rely primarily on *McAlister v. Atlantic Richfield Co.* in arguing that the damages caused by their admitted pollution of the aquifer will last indefinitely (at least 200 years) and therefore are permanent for purposes of the statute of limitations. In *McAlister*, the plaintiff sued for temporary damage to his water well caused by the defendant's oil fields. The plaintiff alleged "that not less than 150 nor more than 400 years will pass before the well water will be once again fit for drinking." [Citation.] Under the circumstances of that case, in which there was no indication that the pollution was abatable and the relevant defendants had discontinued oil well operations in the 1940's, the Kansas Supreme Court held that portion of the claim to be barred by the two-year statute of limitations because the injury was "fixed" and "the property will always remain subject to that injury."

* * *

The trial evidence indicates that the damage to the aquifer is remediable if the salt pollution is abated. While it is true that no conclusive time frame for the cleansing of the aquifer has been established, it is apparent to this court that, contrary to appellants' contention, the cleanup process can be accelerated by intervention measures and can be achieved within a reasonable time. Further, appellants' argument focusing solely on the nature of the injuries resulting from the salt pollution of the aquifer disregards the fact that we must look at the nature of the causative factor of the pollution.[7] [Citation.] Appellants do not contend that there is no "possibility or likelihood" that the causative condition, namely American Salt's mining operations, can be altered or abated. [Citation.] The record indicates that the cause of the injuries can be terminated, and indeed appellants state that they have already undertaken measures to do so. [Citation.] Nor do appellants argue that they have no duty to abate the existing conditions which constitute the nuisance. [Citations.] The conclu-

---

7. In pointing out the inconsistent use of the terms "temporary" and "permanent" in the Kansas cases, the district court notes

> that, when realty is damaged by pollution, the terms "temporary" and "permanent" can be applied to three quite distinct facets of the situation. First, the *pollution itself,* or the causal chemistry of the injury to the land, may be either temporary or permanent. Second, the *damage or loss* caused by the injury may be temporary or permanent. Last, the *source or origin of the pollution,* be it a sewage plant, an oil well, or a salt mine, may be temporary or permanent. The possibilities for inconsistencies are, of course, multiplied when different labels are applied to these facets, such as, for example, calling the source of the pollution a nuisance and then characterizing the nuisance as temporary or permanent.

Miller I, 567 F.Supp. at 899 900 (emphasis in original). The district court's analysis is helpful to our determination of the legal nature of the nuisance and serves to reinforce our interpretation of the Kansas nuisance cases, namely that appellants' argument is deficient by virtue of focusing solely on the nature of the injuries resulting from the salt pollution of the aquifer.

sion that the damages are temporary is bolstered by the evidence that the salt pollution actually continued during the course of this litigation, further indicating the existence of a continuing nuisance.

The damage to the aquifer is remediable and the cause of the damage is abatable. Upon considering all the facts and circumstances, including the nature of the pollution and the nature of the causative factor, as well as the continuing pollution of the aquifer, we conclude, as did the district court, that American Salt's operation constitutes a continuing nuisance causing temporary damages.

Having rejected appellants' assertion that the damages resulting from their pollution of the aquifer are permanent for statute of limitations purposes, we also reject their claim that *all* of appellees' claims are time-barred. The fact that salt pollution has existed in the aquifer for many years does not negate the district court's limitation of appellees' recovery to temporary damages. By limiting their potential recovery to those damages incurred not more than two years prior to the filing of their complaint, the court implicitly determined that the two-year statute of limitations precluded any claims for permanent damages.

* * *

Arguing that the district court's method of calculating actual damages was erroneous as a matter of law, appellants assert that the amount of temporary damages awarded cannot exceed the potential recovery for permanent damages. They alternatively contend that, assuming the propriety of an award of temporary damages, the proper measure of such damages is the reduced rental value of appellees' land.

* * *

The temporary-permanent distinction which is determinative in regard to the running of the statute of limitations is also relevant to the question of the proper measure of damages resulting from an actionable nuisance. [Citations.] In Kansas, the measure of damages for permanent injury to real property is the difference in the fair market value of the land before and after the injury. [Citations.] Diminished fair market value is not used as the measure of recovery, however, if an injury to real property is temporary in nature. Temporary damages represent the reasonable cost of repairing the property, "which may include the value of the use thereof during the period covered by the suit, or it may be the diminution in the rental value of the property, together with such special damages to crops, improvements, etc." [Citations.]

Appellants' assertion that temporary damages may not exceed the value of the property injured, or essentially that there must be a "cap" on an award of temporary damages, is unsupported by pertinent Kansas authority. Their alternative contention, that the sole measure of such damages is reduced rental value, is likewise unsupported. While reduced rental value of the property injured is indeed one measure of temporary damages, the value of the *use* of the property is also a proper measure of damages. The Kansas Supreme Court has treated the value of the use of property and the diminution of rental value as separate and distinct bases for awarding temporary damages. [Citations.]

The district court found that because irrigated corn crops would be more profitable than the dryland crops appellees were forced to grow because of the salt pollution of the aquifer, appellees "have been damaged by the pollution to the extent of these lost crop profits." In so finding, the court applied the proper legal standard under Kansas law for measuring temporary damages. [Citation.] The court's calculation of actual damages, made upon consideration of the similar formulas presented by the various expert witnesses, was based upon the difference between the net value of the lost corn production and the net value of the wheat and milo crops actually grown. That calculation is supported by the evidence and is not clearly erroneous.

* * *

Roman Catholic Church of the Archdiocese of New Orleans v. Louisiana Gas Serv. Co.

618 So.2d 874 (La.1993).

■ DENNIS, JUSTICE.

[In August 1981, the Roman Catholic Church of the Archdiocese of New Orleans ("Archdiocese") purchased the Villa D'Ames Apartment complex from the Department of Housing and Urban Development ("HUD") to further the Archdiocese's interest in providing housing for poor families affiliated with its newly placed parish church. The Archdiocese had been managing the apartment complex for almost five years prior to the sale. The Archdiocese and HUD agreed that if the Archdiocese failed to maintain the complex as low income rental housing for 200 families over the next 15 years, the property would revert to HUD.]

* * * On the night of December 24, 1983, a fire occurred at the Villa D'Ames apartment complex. The complex consisted of 13 detached apartment buildings as well as an office/laundry building and a community building. The fire was restricted to building 3 of that complex.

* * * The defendant, Louisiana Gas Service Company (hereinafter referred to as "Louisiana Gas") supplied natural gas to the apartments in the complex. On the evening of December 24, 1983, there was a hard freeze, which caused a malfunction of the natural gas regulating equipment utilized by Louisiana Gas to supply gas to the apartment units. As a result of this malfunction, dangerous amounts of gas surged into the apartments, eventually causing the fire and resulting damages.

[The Archdiocese filed suit against Louisiana Gas for recovery of the damages sustained as a result of the fire.] [T]he trial court ruled that since the cost of restoration exceeded the market value of the building before the damage, plaintiffs' recovery was limited to the amount expended to restore the building to its pre-fire condition reduced by depreciation. The plaintiffs appealed. The Court of Appeal affirmed, 592 So.2d 14 (La.App. 5th Cir. 1991). We granted certiorari, 592 So.2d 1321 (1992).

* * * One injured through the fault of another is entitled to full indemnification for damages caused thereby. [Citations.] In such a case, "[t]he obligation of defendant . . . is to indemnify plaintiff—to put him in the position that he would have occupied if the injury complained of had not been inflicted on him." [Citations.]

Consequently, "[w]hen property is damaged through the legal fault of another, the primary objective is to restore the property as nearly as possible to the state it was in immediately preceding the damage. . . ." [Citation.] Accordingly, "the measure of damages is the cost of restoring the property to its former condition. In assessing damage to property, generally, courts have considered the cost of restoration as the proper measure of damage where the thing damaged can be adequately repaired." [Citations.] "[N]o mechanical rule can be applied with exactitude in the assessment of property damage under Article 2315." [Citations.]

These basic precepts have been reaffirmed and strengthened indirectly by the Declaration of the Right to Property of our state constitution. * * * Thus, our constitution does not simply require that the owner of condemned or damaged property be compensated with the market value of the property taken and severance damage to his remainder, but that he be "compensated to the full extent of his loss" and "placed in as good a position pecuniarily as [he] enjoyed prior to the taking." *State v. Bitterwolf*, 415 So.2d 196, 199 (La.1982), quoting *State v. Constant*, 369 So.2d 699, 702 (La.1979). * * *

In contrast with these fundamental principles, some jurisdictions have placed more restrictive limits on when an owner whose property has been tortiously damaged can recover the full cost to repair or restore. Although expressed in differing ways, many of these courts essentially limit the owner's damage to the lesser of cost to repair and diminution in market value caused by the damage. [Citations.] Other courts, although applying cost to restore as the appropriate measure of damages in all cases of reparable injury to property, use the fair market value of the property before the injury, rather than the diminution in value, as a ceiling on the damage award. [Citations.] * * *

Recently, courts and commentators have criticized these types of simplistic tests which require the automatic application of limitations on an owner's recovery of the cost to restore or repair his damaged property. See generally, D. Dobbs, Handbook on the Law of Remedies §§ 5.1 (1973). "Such ceilings on recovery not only seem unduly mechanical but also seem wrong from the point of view of reasonable compensation. If the plaintiff wishes to use the damaged property, not sell it, repair or restoration at the expense of the defendant is the only remedy that affords full compensation. To limit repair costs to diminution in value is to either force a landowner to sell the property he wishes to keep or to make repairs partly out of his own pocket." *Id.* at 317. * * * " 'To hold that appellant is without remedy merely because the value of the land has not been diminished, would be to decide that by the wrongful act of another, an owner of land may be compelled to accept a change in the physical condition of his property, or else perform the work of restoration at his own expense.'" *Heninger v. Dunn,* 101 Cal.App.3d 858, 863, 162 Cal.Rptr. 104, 108 (1980), quoting *Dandoy v. Oswald Bros. Paving Co.,* 113 Cal.App. 570, 572–73, 298 P. 1030, 1031 (1931).

In recognition of the need for a more flexible approach, particularly with respect to damages to immovable property, the Restatement (Second) of Torts provides, in pertinent part, that whenever there is injury to land, damages should include "the difference between the value of the land before the harm and the value after the harm, or at [the owner's] election in an appropriate case, the cost of restoration that has been or may be reasonably incurred...." Restatement (Second) of Torts §§ 929 (1977). The official comment on this section indicates that (i) costs of restoration are ordinarily allowable as the measure of damages (ii) but that courts will use diminution in value when the cost of restoring the land to its original condition is "disproportionate" to the diminution in value—(iii) "unless there is a reason personal to the owner for restoring the original condition." *Id.* §§ 929, comment b. In the latter case, the damages will ordinarily include the amount necessary for repairs, even though this amount might be greater than the total value of the property. *Id.*

Increasingly, courts in Louisiana and elsewhere have articulated standards approximating the Restatement (Second) of Torts provisions. Reasons "personal to the owner" frequently are pointed to as justification for allowing high damage awards, often in excess of diminution in market value. [Citations.] The "personal reasons" usually are the owners' desires to enjoy and live in their homes, but several courts have accepted "special reasons" related to the non-homestead use of property. [Citations.]

However, the courts often state that some limits exist to the amount that can be recovered: e.g., the repair must be "practical" and "reasonable." [Citations.] But extensive damages are often awarded as cost of restoration. [Citations.]

In only a few cases have courts refused to award the full cost to restore because the expense was truly exorbitant. [Citations.]

The teachings of the cases approximating Restatement (Second) of Torts §§ 929 and its comments, when applied as flexible guides rather than as arbitrary formulae, tend to foster the same goals established by our Civil Code and state constitutional property damage principles, i.e., they tend to compensate the victim to the full extent of his loss and restore him to as good a position as he held prior to the damage. [Citations.] Accordingly, we conclude that, as a general rule of thumb, when a person sustains property damage due to the fault of another, he is entitled to recover damages including the cost of restoration that has been or may be reasonably incurred, or, at his election, the difference between the value of the property before and after the harm. If, however, the cost of restoring the property in its original condition is disproportionate to the value of the property or economically wasteful, unless there is a reason personal to the owner for restoring the original condition or there is a reason to believe that the plaintiff will, in fact, make the repairs, damages are measured only by the difference between the value of the property before and after the harm. Consequently, if a building such as a homestead is used for a purpose personal to the owner, the damages ordinarily include an amount for repairs, even though this might be greater than the entire value of the building.

Applying these precepts, we decide that plaintiffs are entitled to recover from the defendants the full $232,677.00 cost of restoration that has been reasonably incurred. First, the cost of restoring the property in its original condition is not economically wasteful or disproportionate to the value of the property. The value of the apartment complex far exceeds the restoration cost. The complex was acquired by HUD at a cost of $3.3 million, renovated at a cost of $3.0 million, and sold to the Archdiocese for $1.7 million upon the condition that it maintain the complex for 200 poor families for 15 years. Despite the fact that the building destroyed by fire was separate from the other twelve buildings, it contained 16 family units and was a necessary and integral part of the 200 family low income rental project. * * * Second, even if the foregoing reason did not exist, there is a reason personal to the owner for restoring the property to its original condition. The interest of the Archdiocese harmed by the fault of the defendant was not purely financial. The Archdiocese did not purchase the complex as a business investment with an eye towards speculation and does not hold the property solely for the production of income. Its object in acquiring and maintaining the facility was to provide housing for its low income parishioners. Moreover, the continuance of the Archdiocese's ownership and housing mission is conditioned upon its removal of the property from commerce and providing housing for 200 poor families during a fifteen year period. In choosing between the cost of repair measure and some other measure of damages, it is important to know how the property is used and what interest in it is asserted, so that the measure can be adopted that will afford compensation for any legitimate use that the owner makes of his property. See D. Dobbs, supra at §§ 5.1 p. 315. Finally, even in the absence of either of the foregoing reasons, the plaintiff in the present case is clearly entitled to recover the full cost of restoration because it has, in fact, made the repairs by replacing the building in its original condition.

For the reasons assigned, the judgments of the trial and appellate court are amended to award plaintiffs * * * the reasonable cost of restoring the building. As amended, the judgments below are affirmed.

––––––––––

1. *Reasonable Repairs.* When damage to real property cannot be repaired so that the real property is restored to its original condition, measuring damages is relatively simple. The plaintiff is entitled to recover the diminution in value of the land, measured as the difference between the

market value of the property immediately before the damage and its market value immediately thereafter. As *Louisiana Gas* illustrates, the difficulty arises when the damage to the property is repairable but only at a substantial cost. Generally, a plaintiff is entitled to recover the cost of restoration or repair only if that cost is reasonable.

How does one determine when repairs become unreasonable? Jurisdictions differ. Some jurisdictions allow a plaintiff to recover the cost of repairs only when the cost does not exceed the diminution in value to the property. Other jurisdictions, permit the plaintiff to recover the cost of restoration even where it exceeds the diminution in value as long as the cost of restoration does not exceed the pre-tort value of the property.

Why place any ceiling on recovery of restoration costs? Why limit a plaintiff's recovery to the diminution in value? Why permit recovery of restoration costs beyond diminution in value? Consider the courts' observations in the following cases:

In *General Outdoor Advertising Company v. La Salle Realty Corporation*, 141 Ind.App. 247, 218 N.E.2d 141 (1966), a building owner brought an action to recover damages for injuries to the building caused by the large advertising sign the defendant erected on the roof of the building. An Indiana appellate court refused to limit the owner's damages to the diminution in value to the building. In reaching its holding, the court reasoned:

> In advocating the use of this rule of damages, the appellant states that if a plaintiff is allowed repair costs without the limitation of the "before and after" test, then he might be placed in a better position than he was before the damage. If a plaintiff is to be allowed repair costs when they exceed the market value of the property before the injury less the market value after the injury, plaintiff could choose not to repair the building and sell it, profiting to the extent of such excess of repair costs.
>
> Although this view seems equitable from a defendant's position, it is rather discriminate against a plaintiff. What if a plaintiff does not desire to sell his property? In this posture the effect of the rule would be that where the restoration costs exceed the "before and after" measure, a plaintiff would receive the latter. Consequently, if he did not desire to sell the building, he would not receive damages sufficient to restore the building to its original condition. The "before and after" test, if used in cases of non-permanent injury, is in reality forcing the plaintiff to sell the building in order to restore himself to the same position enjoyed before the injury. Certainly, such a measure of damages partially compensates a plaintiff for injury done to his building and affords some protection to a part of his property rights. However, it would seem more proper to place the plaintiff in a position where he could be unrestricted in the exercise of his property rights of continued ownership or alienation. When these considerations are weighed against the possible "windfall" that might be given to the plaintiff, the former seems to take precedence over the latter. It is the defendant

who places the plaintiff in such a position. Consequently, this court is of the opinion that under the above stated issues, the rights and equities of a plaintiff should be determinative, within defined legal limits.

* * * In the facts at bar, it would seem reasonable to define permanent injury as being one wherein the cost of restoration exceeds the market value of the building prior to the injury. By adhering to such a definition, we as a matter of law, raise a safeguard against a windfall while additionally protecting the property rights involved. Such a rule is protective of the interests of both parties in their proper perspectives. 218 N.E.2d at 151–52.

In contrast, in *Duquesne Light Company v. Woodland Hills School District*, 700 A.2d 1038 (Pa.Cmwlth.1997) *appeal denied* 555 Pa. 722, 724 A.2d 936 (1998), a Pennsylvania appellate court reversed a trial court decision to exclude evidence of diminution in value and permit the plaintiffs to recover restoration costs. In reaching its holding, the court noted:

> Under Pennsylvania law, "the purpose of damages for injury or destruction of property by tortious conduct of another is to compensate the injured owner for the actual loss suffered" by making him whole. [Citation.] Thus, the purpose is not to award a windfall. To the extent that a property owner is allowed to recover the cost of restoration that is greater than the diminution in market value, there is a possibility that the owner will receive a monetary windfall. By choosing to sell the property rather than restore it, the owner will profit to the extent that restoration costs recovered exceed the diminution in market value. The problem is exaggerated ... where the restoration costs would be permitted to approach the value of the property.
>
> In keeping with the purpose of compensatory damages and in prevention of windfall awards, we find it necessary to interpret "permanency" in terms of whether or not the cost of repair would be unfair or inappropriate under the circumstances. Where the cost of repair is shown to be reasonable, the injury to real property is not permanent and the cost of repair would be the appropriate measure of damages. However, where the cost of replacing the real property in its original condition disproportionately exceeds the diminution in the value of the property, the injury to real property is permanent and the cost of repair would not be fair or appropriate. Rather, the proper measure of damages for permanent injury would be the difference between the value of the property before and after the harm. 700 A.2d at 1053.

The Restatement (Second) of Torts recognizes that either limitation can have inequitable results when a plaintiff holds injured property for personal use. Under such circumstances, no replacement property will adequately compensate the plaintiff, and the plaintiff has an incentive to make repairs that exceed the pre-tort market value of the property because the actual value of the property to the plaintiff exceeds the market value. Thus, the Restatement and courts adopting the Restatement, like the *Louisiana Gas* court, allow a property owner who holds property for personal reasons to recover reasonable restoration costs even if those costs exceed the diminished value of the property and the pre-tort value of the property.

2. *Practical Good Sense.* Under the Restatement's "reason personal" rule, an owner may elect to recover restoration costs rather than diminution in value to the land only in *appropriate cases* and only to the extent the restoration costs are *reasonable*. In general, this means the plaintiff's reason personal must be objectively reasonable. Additionally, the restoration costs must be objectively reasonable in light of the plaintiff's reason personal and the diminution in value to the land. *See* Osborne v. Hurst, 947 P.2d 1356 (Alaska 1997).

The reason personal rule, however, can be difficult for courts to apply because no clear guideline exists for distinguishing objectively reasonable reasons personal from unreasonable reasons personal and reasonable restoration costs from unreasonable restoration costs. Instead, courts must be guided by what Professor Dobbs termed as "practical good sense" in determining when to award restoration costs under the reason personal rule. *See* 1 Dan B. Dobbs, Law of Remedies § 5.2(2), 720 (2d ed. 1993).

Accordingly, courts have reached varying results in applying the reason personal rule. *Compare* St. Martin v. Mobil Exploration & Producing U.S., Inc., 224 F.3d 402 (5th Cir.2000) (plaintiffs entitled to recover costs to restore marsh where plaintiffs' efforts to create and maintain a wildlife refuge on the marsh and plaintiffs' use of the marsh for hunting and recreational purposes evidenced genuine personal reasons for restoring the marsh but restoration costs reduced from plaintiffs' initial proposal of $39,000 per acre to $10,000 per acre) *with* Heninger v. Dunn, 101 Cal. App.3d 858, 162 Cal.Rptr. 104 (1980) (plaintiff not entitled to recover $241,000 restoration cost where the pre-tort value of the property was $179,000 and the plaintiff testified as follows concerning his personal reason for restoration: "I think the land is beautiful, the natural forest beautiful, and I would like to see it remain that way"); *and compare* Leonard Missionary Baptist Church v. Sears, Roebuck & Co., 42 S.W.3d 833 (Mo.App.Ct.2001) (church entitled to recover $2 million cost of restoration even though the pre-tort fair market value of the destroyed church building was $198,000 where witnesses described the church as "old but in good condition," "majestic," "awesome," and a "community church") *with* Heidorf v. Town of Northumberland, 985 F.Supp. 250 (N.D.N.Y.1997) (plaintiff not entitled to recover cost to restore church building that was designated as a state and national landmark where church building had not been specially used as a church since 1958).

3. *Commercial Uses.* Should a plaintiff's use of injured property for commercial purposes preclude the plaintiff from recovering restoration costs under the reason personal rule? What if the plaintiff uses the property for both commercial and residential purposes? For example, should an owner of a duplex who lives in half and rents the other half be entitled to recover the cost to restore the duplex even if it exceeds the diminution in value to the property?

Would it be a good solution to award cost of repair only if the plaintiff has already undertaken repair? Consider the effect of such a rule to require plaintiffs to borrow money for the repair expense in the face of the uncertainty of any recovery in litigation. Does this result matter? Consider further what rule should attach if the plaintiff tries and fails to borrow money for the cost of repair. Alternatively, what if the plaintiff has taken steps before trial incompatible with repair, such as demolishing the injured structure?

4. *Permanent and Temporary.* Can an injury to real property be both temporary and permanent? Should a plaintiff ever be able to recover both the diminution in value to the land and the cost of restoration? A majority of courts that have faced this issue have allowed recovery of both restoration costs and diminution in value when a defendant's nuisance or trespass has caused some temporary physical injury to the property but, despite the temporary injury's remediation, the property's market value remains depressed. *See, e.g.,* In re Paoli R.R. Yard PCB Litig., 35 F.3d 717 (3d Cir.1994); Walker Drug Co. v. La Sal Oil Co., 972 P.2d 1238 (Utah 1998).

The cases presenting this issue have typically involved the contamination of the plaintiff's property as a result of the defendant's spilling or mishandling of hazardous substances. Plaintiffs have been entitled to recover the costs to remove the hazardous substances from their property and to restore their property to its pre-contamination condition. Further, they are often permitted "stigma damages" when the market value of the plaintiffs' property remains depressed because of lingering buyer concerns about the effect of environmental contamination on the property even after it has been cleaned. Such "stigma damages" compensate for loss to the property's market value resulting from this long-term negative perception of the property. These stigma damages are in excess of any recovery the plaintiff receives for the temporary injury itself.

5. *Statute of Limitations.* As the *Miller* case illustrates, the nature of the trespass determines when the statute of limitations begins to run as well as the damages a plaintiff may recover at trial. The nuisance or trespass is classified for these purposes as either permanent or temporary (often called continuous). If the trespass or nuisance that causes injury to the plaintiff's property is permanent, the plaintiff must seek to recover all damages—whether for past, present or prospective injuries—in a single action. If the trespass is continuous or temporary, the plaintiff may seek to recover damages for only those injuries that have already occurred, and the plaintiff is limited to recovery for injuries that occurred during the applicable limitations period. However, the plaintiff may file successive actions to recover damages for each new injury. To determine whether a trespass or nuisance is permanent or temporary, courts consider different factors, including the abatability of the nuisance or the trespass, the continuous or sporadic nature of the injury caused by the nuisance or the trespass, and the ability to determine or estimate damages.

PROBLEM: THE DAMAGED LAWN

Albertson drove his car over the front lawn of the Hudsons' house as a prank late one Saturday night. A neighbor identified Albertson's car, so the Hudsons sued Albertson in small claims court.

Albertson's car left ruts in the lawn that were six inches deep and twenty-five feet long. The Hudsons, a couple with modest means, restored the lawn themselves by filling in the ruts and replanting. The work was substantial and time-consuming with daily monitoring of the growth, but the out-of-pocket expense was $50.

What should be the measure of damages and what evidence should plaintiffs produce on the issue of damages? What if one professional landscaping company in the city would ordinarily charge $300 for performing a similar job and another company had quoted $450 to restore the yard?

Laube v. Thomas

376 N.W.2d 108 (Iowa 1985).

■ HARRIS, JUSTICE.

This appeal presents a straightforward damages question. What is the proper measure of damages for the wrongful destruction of walnut trees? The trial court, rejecting plaintiffs' claim for their future productive value, fixed the award on the basis of their current market value as lumber. We affirm.

In 1983 defendants contracted to sell a farm in Floyd County to plaintiffs. Possession was to pass on March 1, 1984. Although no timber rights were reserved to the sellers, they cut down and removed about one hundred walnut trees from the tract during August and September 1983. This suit followed. There is no question of liability; at trial defendants offered to confess judgment for $1,000. The offer was refused.

Plaintiffs conceded the trees were timber or forest. They were not a part of any windbreak or used for any ornamental purposes. The trees had stood at two sites on the farm, one a low-level area near a stream and the other in a permanent pasture. Both sites had been timbered, that is, other trees had been removed from the area some five years previously. According to plaintiffs' expert witness, the prior removal of the other trees is significant because it indicates the one hundred trees in question were smaller, presumably inferior for marketing purposes.

Plaintiffs' expert made a strong showing that it was not a practical marketing time for the trees in question. At an age of twenty years they would not mature so as to reach their reasonable marketing potential for another twenty years. Plaintiffs' damages estimate was computed by taking the current market price, considering the size and quality of trees twenty years hence, then discounting the figure appropriately to reach the present value.

On these facts, especially the showing of the inappropriateness of cutting the trees at their stage of semi-maturity, there is at first blush an attractiveness in plaintiffs' contention that a routine allowance of only log value is inadequate. On the other hand their suggested recovery does not conform with any recognized measure of damages for loss of trees.

It is impossible to state a simple, all-purpose measure of recovery for loss of trees. Because of the wide variety in their uses the law has devised a number of alternative measures, to be applied according to the location and use of the loss of trees. [Citations.] These authorities and our own cases provide rather standard recoveries.

Where the trees were put to a special purpose, such as for windbreaks, shade or ornamental use, the measure is usually the difference in value of the realty before and after the destruction of the trees. [Citation.] Where the trees had no such special use the measure is the commercial market value of the trees at the time of taking. *Grell v. Lumsden*, 206 Iowa 166, 169, 220 N.W. 123, 125 (1928) (ordinary forest trees on hillside). Another measure mentioned in *Grell* applies where the trees can be replaced. It is the reasonable cost of replacement. [Citation.] That measure would obviously be inappropriate here and neither party urges its application. We do not consider fruit trees, which produce a marketable crop. Neither do we consider trees with special aesthetic value.

We have already explained plaintiffs' assertion that the standard measure of damages was inadequate to compensate them for their full loss. It was perhaps to address this criticism that the legislature provided for treble damages in Iowa Code section 658.4 (1985), [citations.] In an appropriate case either punitive damages or treble damages can be sought, though not both. We find no basis to disturb the measure of recovery allowed by the trial court.

* * * [Affirmed.]

Kroulik v. Knuppel

634 P.2d 1027 (Colo.App.1981).

■ KIRSHBAUM, JUDGE.

Defendants, Raymond F. Knuppel, Jr. and Burnett Construction Co. (Burnett), appeal from a judgment entered by the trial court granting title to plaintiffs, Charles W. Kroulik and Claire L. Kroulik, and plaintiffs cross-appeal the trial court's award of damages and assessment of costs. We modify the trial court's judgment in part and, as modified, affirm.

* * *

[Defendant Knuppel in 1973 purchased property adjoining plaintiffs' land. The gravel bar between them was part of the land purchased by Knuppel, but the court held that it belonged to plaintiffs by adverse possession. In the meantime, Knuppel had leased the gravel bar to Burnett, who conducted mining operations for two years.]

The trial court concluded * * * that defendants had damaged plaintiffs' property by removing gravel and by destroying certain vegetation, including a 73 year old pine tree. Defendants were ordered to render an accounting of the gravel removed from the property, and the parties subsequently stipulated as to the amount of gravel removed and the royalty payments received by Knuppel from Burnett.

At the commencement of the hearing on damages, the trial court ruled that the amount of royalties received by Knuppel was the proper measure of damages. Plaintiffs then made an offer of proof of evidence to support their theory that they were entitled to an award of damages based on the value of the gravel extracted less the extraction costs. The trial court entered judgment for plaintiffs in the amount of $14,189.54 for the gravel extraction, $1,500 for destruction of the pine tree, $10 for damage to real property, and costs of $114.35.

* * * [Defendants] contend that the trial court erred in awarding damages for the destruction of the pine tree on the basis of the aesthetic value of the tree. We agree in part, and modify the damages awarded for the loss of the tree.

Damage to growing trees is generally measured by the diminution in the market value of the real property. [Citations.] However, aesthetic value may be considered in establishing the replacement cost of certain unique property. * * *

The tree here involved was a 50 foot tall pine tree located on a promontory overlooking the river. No other trees of that size were visible in that locale. Several witnesses testified with respect to the particular grace, majesty and beauty of this isolated tree in that setting. We conclude that the trial court did not commit error here by considering aesthetic value to determine the amount of damages to which plaintiffs were entitled as a result of the defendants' uprooting of the pine tree.

However, the only evidence of the value of the tree introduced at trial was the uncontroverted testimony of an expert witness who valued the pine at $8.40 for lumber and $229.63 for aesthetic value. There is no evidence to support the trial court's award of $1,500 as damages for the destruction of the pine tree. Findings not supported by any evidence cannot stand on appeal. [Citation.] As the only evidence offered respecting the pine tree's value was not contradicted * * * the judgment shall be modified to reflect the damages of $238.03 for such loss.

Plaintiffs assert that the trial court erred in ruling that the royalties received by Knuppel constituted the proper measure of damages. We disagree.

When a non-willful trespasser appropriates minerals, the measure of damages is the value of the minerals in place. [Citations.] Such value may be calculated by ascertaining the amount of royalties the landowner would receive or could have received from the trespassing appropriator. [Citations.] Use of a royalty-based valuation permits the landowner to recover the amount the landowner would have realized by contracting for removal of the minerals, without unduly penalizing the merely negligent trespasser. However, this damages measure permits the extractor to retain the profit, if any, realized from the mining venture.

Another means for determining the value of the minerals in place, calculation of the value at the surface less the direct costs of extracting them, does not allow the excavator to retain profits. This measure of value has been employed in trespasser cases. [Citations.] Furthermore, a willful or intentional trespasser may be required to recompense the landowner for the value of the minerals at the surface without deductions for extraction costs. [Citation.]

Here, the trial court concluded that defendants were not willful trespassers. * * * Plaintiffs at no time attempted to mine the gravel pit, and had themselves previously obtained royalty payments pursuant to a mineral lease. Under all the circumstances of this case, we find no error in the trial court's conclusion that the royalty payments received by Knuppel constituted the appropriate measure of plaintiffs' damages.

* * *

The judgment of the trial court is modified to reflect the sum of $238.03 as the damage to which plaintiffs are entitled for the loss of the pine tree, and, as modified, the judgment is affirmed.

----

1. *Removal of Property with Commercial Value.* Many cases have presented the problem of valuing commercially marketable property taken from land by trespass (intentional, negligent, or innocent invasions of real property without legal right) or through other wrongs. When trees, shrubbery or vegetation are removed from the land, courts generally award the landowner the market value of the trees, shrubbery or vegetation at the time of removal.

When the property has commercial value, courts have employed different measures of that value based on the nature of the property and its intended use. *See, e.g.,* Semenza v. Bowman, 268 Mont. 118, 885 P.2d 451 (1994) (measure of damages is net value of crop loss usually measured by market value at the time of harvest but plaintiffs entitled to use market value at the time of sale where plaintiffs established a common practice of selling crops at a later date); Elwood v. Bolte, 119 N.H. 508, 403 A.2d 869 (1979) (plaintiff entitled to market value of apple trees at time of removal plus lost profits during period of regeneration); Davis v. Jefferson Savings & Loan Assoc., 820 S.W.2d 549 (Mo.Ct.App.1991) (normal measure of damages for the partial destruction of a growing crop is the difference between the maturity value immediately before and after its destruction); Sadler v. Duvall, 815 S.W.2d 285 (Tex.App.Ct.1991) (holding stumpage value proper measure of damages for timber removed from property where defendants acted in good faith in removing the timber but suggesting that the manufactured value of timber might have been the proper measure if the defendants acted in bad faith); Baker v. Ramirez, 190 Cal.App.3d 1123, 235 Cal.Rptr. 857 (1987) (plaintiff entitled to costs of replacing damaged orange trees); Sparks v. Douglas County, 39 Wash.App. 714, 695 P.2d 588 (1985) (proper measure is lost production value of fruit trees while replacement trees are maturing less production costs); Henriksen v. Lyons, 33 Wash.App. 123, 652 P.2d 18 (1982) (plaintiff entitled to stumpage value of removed trees and diminution in value of her land); Pearce v. G.R. Kirk Co., 92 Wash.2d 869, 602 P.2d 357 (1979) (plaintiff entitled to lost profits where she established that she intended to sell the damaged trees as Christmas trees); Hill v. Morrison, 88 Cal.App. 405, 263 P. 573 (1928) (measure of damages for destruction of productive trees is value of the orchard before and after destruction).

When the property removed is minerals or oil, courts generally have applied three different measures. The lowest award usually results if the court uses a royalty measure (the royalty commonly paid to landowners in the vicinity for the right to mine on their land). The highest award ordinarily results from a measure of market value without any deduction for expenditures in extracting the minerals or bringing them to market. In between these extremes, a court might award the value of the minerals at the mouth of the mine less the cost of extracting the minerals and bringing them to market.

As *Knuppel* indicates, the measure of damages in this area sometimes reflects the defendant's good or bad faith. If a defendant is innocent and believes in good faith to have a legal right to remove the minerals from the land, courts generally will award a low measure of damages such as a royalty measure or the value of the mineral in the ground less extraction costs. *See, e.g.,* Payne v. Consolidation Coal Co., 607 F.Supp. 378 (W.D.Va. 1985) (proper measure of damages where coal is mined innocently and in good faith is its royalty value); Hunt v. HNG Oil Co., 791 S.W.2d 191 (Tex.App.Ct.1990) (a good faith trespasser is liable in damages only for the value of the minerals removed less drilling and operating costs); Alaska Placer Co. v. Lee, 553 P.2d 54 (Alaska 1976) (a good faith trespasser must pay the owner damages based either on a royalty rate or on the market value of the materials less the cost of extraction).

Some courts look to whether the landowner could have mined the land himself or herself in choosing between a royalty measure and an in-place value. *See, e.g.,* Deltic Timber Corp. v. Great Lakes Chem. Corp., 2 F.Supp.2d 1192 (W.D.Ark.1998) (Where the plaintiff would have mined the mineral himself, he is awarded the value of the mineral less retrieval costs; as to a landowner who has not the opportunity nor the equipment to develop minerals, the value for which he can lease them, or royalty value, is the accepted measure of damages.). If the defendant acted willfully and in knowing disregard of a landowner's rights, courts generally award a high measure of damages such as market value without deductions for costs. *See* Imperial Colliery Co. v. Oxy USA Inc., 912 F.2d 696 (4th Cir.1990) (bad faith trespasser is liable for the fair market value of all the resources extracted without any deduction for removal costs).

2. *Multiple Damage Statutes.* Many states now have statutes that protect landowners from the removal or destruction of trees, minerals or crops on their property. Some of these statutes prescribe the measure of damages for the destruction or removal of these items. For example, Maine's timber trespass statute permits owners to recover as damages for the removal of agricultural or forest products the greater of the market value of the removed property or the diminution in value to the land as whole as a result of removal. Alternatively, for lost trees owners may elect to recover civil penalties ranging from $25 to $150 per tree and the costs for regeneration. Me. Rev. Stat. Ann. Tit. 14 § 7552 (West 1999).

Further, as *Laube* indicates, many of these statutes, including the Maine statute, award the landowner double or treble damages for trespass under some circumstances, such as where a defendant recklessly or willfully disregards the plaintiff's rights. The standard in a state's statute is not necessarily the same as its standard for punitive damages. *See* Denoyer v. Lamb, 22 Ohio App.3d 136, 490 N.E.2d 615 (1984) ("recklessness" standard in trespass treble damage statute for injuries to trees and shrubs is lower standard than "actual malice" required for punitive damages); Auburn Harpswell Association v. Day, 438 A.2d 234 (Me.1981) (double damages statute for willfully and knowingly cutting tree is remedial in nature rather than punitive and need not be specially pleaded).

3. *Removal of Property Without Commercial Value.* Courts agree that the loss of a tree in a homeowner's front yard cannot reasonably be measured by the timber value of the tree because that value is usually close to zero. *See, e.g.,* Manitou & Pike's Peak Ry. v. Harris, 45 Colo. 185, 101 P. 61 (1909). Courts lack agreement on the measure of damages for destruction or injury to trees or shrubs without commercial value. What measure is appropriate in lieu of the market value of the removed tree?

The general rule for injuries to trees and shrubs without market value is to award the diminution in market value to the land as a whole. *See, e.g.,* Kebschull v. Nott, 220 Mont. 64, 714 P.2d 993 (1986); Kapcsos v. Hammond, 13 Ohio App.3d 140, 468 N.E.2d 325 (1983) (the proper measure of damages is the diminution in value of the property when the trees are not unique to the parcel or in any way ornamental or rare). This measure often produces a low award.

Some courts, consistent with Restatement § 929, have awarded the landowner the reasonable cost of replacing the trees or shrubbery and restoring the land to its original condition when the land is held for personal use. *See, e.g.,* Keitges v. VanDermeulen, 240 Neb. 580, 483 N.W.2d 137 (1992) (when the landowner intends to use the property for residential or recreational purposes, the owner may recover the cost of reasonable restoration not to exceed the pre-tort market value of the property); Otto v. Cornell, 119 Wis.2d 4, 349 N.W.2d 703 (App.1984) (proper measure of damages for the destruction of fruit, ornamental or shade trees is the replacement value of the trees when the owner holds the land for personal use) However, courts generally require the replacement costs to be reasonable and require the landowner to replace the destroyed trees with identical or substantially similar trees. When restoration is impossible or impracticable, some courts allow the landowner to recover the aesthetic value or intrinsic value of the trees. *See* Heninger v. Dunn, 101 Cal.App.3d 858, 162 Cal.Rptr. 104 (1980).

One court has permitted recovery of emotional distress damages in an action for trespass based on the defendant's wrongful removal vegetation. *See* Birchler v. Castello Land Co., 133 Wash.2d 106, 942 P.2d 968 (1997).

4. Injury to an ornamental tree in a car accident was the subject of the humorous decision in Fisher v. Lowe, 122 Mich.App. 418, 333 N.W.2d 67 (1983). Judge Gillis wrote the opinion in verse, beginning:

We thought that we would never

see a suit to compensate a tree.

A suit whose claim in tort is prest

upon a mangled tree's behest.

In a footnote the court explained that the Michigan no-fault insurance act provided the exclusive remedy for the landowner's tree.

Commonwealth of Puerto Rico v. SS Zoe Colocotroni

628 F.2d 652 (1st Cir.1980), *cert. denied* 450 U.S. 912, 101 S.Ct. 1350, 67 L.Ed.2d 336 (1981).

■ CAMPBELL, CIRCUIT JUDGE.

In the early morning hours of March 18, 1973, the SS ZOE COLOCOTRONI, a tramp oil tanker, ran aground on a reef three and a half miles off the south coast of Puerto Rico. To refloat the vessel, the captain ordered the dumping of more than 5,000 tons of crude oil into the surrounding waters. An oil slick four miles long, and a tenth of a mile wide, floated towards the coast and came ashore at an isolated peninsula on the southwestern tip of the island—a place called Bahia Sucia. The present appeal concerns an action in admiralty brought by the Commonwealth of Puerto Rico and the local Environmental Quality Board (EQB) to recover damages for harm done to the coastal environment by the spilled oil.

Defendants have raised numerous objections to the district court's judgment awarding plaintiffs $6,164,192.09 in damages for cleanup costs and environmental harm. * * *

The following facts found by the district court are not in serious dispute. On March 15, 1973, the ZOE COLOCOTRONI departed La Salina, Venezuela, carrying 187,670 barrels of crude oil en route to Guayanilla, Puerto Rico. * * * As the vessel approached the south coast of Puerto Rico, it was, the district court stated, "hopelessly lost." At 0300 hours on March 18, the ship grounded on a reef. Efforts to free the tanker by alternately running the engines in forward and reverse were unsuccessful. After ten minutes, the captain ordered the crew to lighten ship by emptying the cargo of crude oil into the sea. By the time the vessel refloated, some 1.5

million gallons of crude oil—5,170.1 tons—had poured into the surrounding waters.

The oil floated westward from the site of the spill throughout the daylight hours of March 18, and began coming ashore after nightfall. Bahia Sucia is a crescent-shaped bay facing southeastward from the Cabo Rojo peninsula, which forms the southwest tip of Puerto Rico. The oil entered Bahia Sucia, washed onto the beaches, and penetrated the mangrove forests that line the western edge of the bay. The oil was particularly thick in three areas: around the rocky tip of the peninsula, in a section of mangroves known as West Mangrove between a point called "Hermit One" and an inlet called "Dogman's Cove,"[5] and on the open beach area stretching along the northern edge of the bay. In addition, as the tide ebbed and flowed, oil entered the tidal flats behind the mangrove fringe, coating the roots of mangroves growing deeper in the forest and soaking into the sediments.

A massive cleanup operation, coordinated by the United States Coast Guard and several Commonwealth agencies, commenced on the morning of March 19. Cleanup crews, hampered to some extent by variable winds that blew oil back and forth across the bay, used booms to attempt to contain oil floating on the surface. Much of this oil was pumped out, either directly from the water or from large holes dug in the beach into which oil was channeled by the cleanup crews. By March 29, approximately 755,000 gallons of oil, or about half the amount spilled, had been recovered. * * *

By April, cleanup activities had switched from large-scale removal of oil to small-scale activities such as manual beach cleanup and bailing of oil from tidal pockets with buckets and small boats. Large amounts of contaminated sands—totalling about 4,500 cubic yards—were removed from the beach area by bulldozer and by hand. At the end of April, the major remaining cleanup efforts were halted, and all further efforts were discontinued after September 24. Despite the cleanup, oil continued to be present in Bahia Sucia, especially in the stand of mangroves on the west side of the bay.

One of plaintiffs' expert witnesses, Dr. Ariel Lugo Garces, a wetlands specialist, testified that the ecological functions of a mangrove forest such as that at Bahia Sucia included: (1) protecting the shoreline from erosion, storms, tides, and high winds; (2) providing a habitat for wildlife, especially birds; (3) providing a protected breeding ground for fish and shellfish; and (4) acting as a food source for aquatic creatures of all kinds. * * *

Finally, Dr. Philip E. Sorenson, an economist specializing in natural resources, discussed the economic theory that shippers of oil should be required to bear such external social costs as oil spill damages in order to prevent underpricing of their product. "If the producers and consumers of oil are able to conduct their affairs in such a way as to transfer to society a

---

5. Two hermits—Hermit One and the Dogman—lived in the West Mangrove area at the time of trial, the Dogman being so called because of his large collection of canine acquaintances. Neither hermit claimed any legal interest in the property. Various local topographical features were identified in court by reference to these two eponymous individuals.

large part of the real cost of producing and consuming their product." Dr. Sorenson said, "we'll be in an inefficient economic situation: one in which the market price of the commodity will be less than the full social cost of producing it." Dr. Sorenson also presented a summary of plaintiff's claims for damages, including *inter alia* the Commonwealth's uncontested claim for cleanup expenses of $78,108.89, the $7.5 million for sediment removal and mangrove replanting, and Dr. Sorenson's own estimate of $5,526,583 as the replacement value of the invertebrate organisms killed by the oil spill.

Dr. Sorenson testified he arrived at the latter figure by * * * [extrapolating] the differences in number of organisms found in the ten—centimeter core samples over a square meter area to determine the net difference in creatures per square meter. * * * The net difference was calculated to be 1,138 creatures per square meter. This figure in turn yielded the sum of 4,605,486 creatures per acre, and a total of 92,109,720 creatures of the 20 acres of mangroves allegedly impacted by oil. * * *

To arrive at an estimate of damages, Dr. Sorenson testified he consulted catalogs from biological supply houses. From these catalogs he determined that "[m]any of these species sell at prices ranging from $1 to $4.50" and "that no animal on the list sold for less than 10 cents."[10] Dr. Sorenson assigned an average replacement value to each creature, regardless of species, of six cents. Multiplying 92,109,720 times .06 resulted in an estimate of $5,526,583 as the replacement value of the organisms "missing" from the Bahia Sucia sediments. * * *

[The Commonwealth of Puerto Rico held the land in trust for the people. Pursuant to statutory powers, the Commonwealth sued the SS ZOE COLOCOTRONI. The statute provides that the Commonwealth may sue to recover "the total value of the damages caused to the environment and/or natural resources."]

The district court made the following findings on the issue of damages:

1.   Plaintiffs' proven claim of damage to marine organisms covers an approximate area of about 20 acres in and around the West Mangrove. The surveys conducted by Plaintiffs reliably establish that there was a decline of approximately 4,605,486 organisms per acre as a direct result of the oil spill. This means that 92,109,720 marine animals were killed by the COLOCOTRONI oil spill. The uncontradicted evidence establishes that there is a ready market with reference to biological supply laboratories, thus allowing a reliable calculation of the cost of replacing these organisms. The lowest possible replacement cost figure is $.06 per animal, with many species selling from $1.00 to $4.50 per individual. Accepting the lowest replacement cost, and attaching damages only to the lost marine animals in the West Mangrove area, we find the damages caused by Defendants to amount to $5,526,583.20.

---

10. Dr. Sorenson did not testify that the biological supply houses actually procured specimens at Bahia Sucia or that the Bahia Sucia animals were marketable through such outlets. He only stated that creatures similar to those killed could be replaced by purchasing them from the catalogs.

2. The evidence is overwhelming to the effect that the sediments in and around the West Mangrove continue to be impregnated with oil. * * * The most affected spots in the West Mangrove cover an area of approximately 23 acres. It is the Court's opinion that these areas can best be reestablished by the intensive planting of mangrove and restoration of this area to its condition before the oil spill. The evidence shows that the planting of mangrove runs at about $16,500 per acre, thus bringing the cost of replanting 23 acres to $379,500. The evidence further demonstrates that the planting will require a five year monitoring and fertilizing program which will cost $36,000 per year or $180,000 for five years. The total damages thus suffered by Plaintiffs by reason of the pollution of the mangrove in the West Mangrove amount to $559,500.

3. Plaintiffs incurred in cleanup costs in the amount of $78,108.89 which were not reimbursed from any source, and they are entitled to recover said damages from Defendants.

* * * [Defendants] argue the district court erred in failing to apply the common law "diminution in value" rule in calculating damages. Under the traditional rule, the measure of damages for tortious injury to real property is the difference in the commercial or market value of the property before and after the event causing injury. *See* Restatement (Second) of Torts § 929(1)(a) (1979). Where the property can be restored to its original condition for a sum less than the diminution in value, however, the cost of restoration may be substituted as a measure of damages. [Citation.] Defendants introduced evidence at trial tending to show that the market value of comparable property in the vicinity of Bahia Sucia was less than $5,000 per acre, based on recent sales. Thus, defendants contend, damages here could not have exceeded $5,000 per affected acre even if the land were shown to have lost all value.

We believe that defendants have misconceived the character of the remedy created [by the statute]. The EQB is not concerned with any loss in the market or other commercial value of the Commonwealth's land. In point of fact, the EQB concedes the land has no significant commercial or market value. The claim, rather, is for the injury—broadly conceived—that has been caused to the natural environment by the spilled oil. The question before us is not whether in a typical land damage case a claim of this sort could be successfully advanced—we assume it could not—but rather whether Puerto Rico's statute * * * envisions the awarding of damages on a different basis than would have been traditionally allowed.

* * * Many unspoiled natural areas of considerable ecological value have little or no commercial or market value. Indeed, to the extent such areas have a commercial value, it is logical to assume they will not long remain unspoiled, absent some governmental or philanthropic protection. A strict application of the diminution in value rule would deny the state any right to recover meaningful damages for harm to such areas, and would frustrate appropriate measures to restore or rehabilitate the environment.

* * * [W]e think that limitation of recovery to those damages recoverable under the common law "diminution in value" rule would be inconsistent with the manifest intent of Puerto Rico's environmental statute. In enacting section 1131, Puerto Rico obviously meant to sanction the difficult, but perhaps not impossible, task of putting a price tag on resources whose value cannot always be measured by the rules of the market place. Although the diminution rule is appropriate in most contexts, and may indeed be appropriate in certain cases under section 1131, it does not measure the loss which the statute seeks to redress in a context such as the present. No market exists in which Puerto Rico can readily replace what it has lost. The loss is not only to certain plant and animal life but, perhaps more importantly, to the capacity of the now polluted segments of the environment to regenerate and sustain such life for some time into the future. That the Commonwealth did not intend, and perhaps was unable, to exploit these life forms, and the coastal areas which supported them, for commercial purposes should not prevent a damages remedy in the face of the clearly stated legislative intent to compensate for "the total value of the damages caused to the environment and/or natural resources." 12 L.P.R.A. § 1131(29). In recent times, mankind has become increasingly aware that the planet's resources are finite and that portions of the land and sea which at first glance seem useless, like salt marshes, barrier reefs, and other coastal areas, often contribute in subtle but critical ways to an environment capable of supporting both human life and the other forms of life on which we all depend. The Puerto Rico statute is obviously aimed at providing a damages remedy with sufficient scope to compensate for, and deter, the destruction of such resources; and while we can see many problems in fashioning such a remedy, we see no reason to try to frustrate that endeavor. We therefore do not limit damages herein to the loss of market value of the real estate affected.

We turn now to whether the damages awarded by the district court were appropriate. To review the court's award, we must ascertain what a fair and equitable damages measure would be in these circumstances. * * *

* * * [W]e think the appropriate primary standard for determining damages in a case such as this is the cost reasonably to be incurred by the sovereign or its designated agency to restore or rehabilitate the environment in the affected area to its pre-existing condition, or as close thereto as is feasible without grossly disproportionate expenditures. The focus in determining such a remedy should be on the steps a reasonable and prudent sovereign or agency would take to mitigate the harm done by the pollution, with attention to such factors as technical feasibility, harmful side effects, compatibility with or duplication of such regeneration as is naturally to be expected, and the extent to which efforts beyond a certain point would become either redundant or disproportionately expensive. Admittedly, such a remedy cannot be calculated with the degree of certainty usually possible when the issue is, for example, damages on a commercial contract. On the other hand, a district court can surely calculate damages under the foregoing standard with as much or more certainty and accuracy as a jury determining damages for pain and suffering or mental anguish.

There may be circumstances where direct restoration of the affected area is either physically impossible or so disproportionately expensive that it would not be reasonable to undertake such a remedy. Some other measure of damages might be reasonable in such cases, at least where the process of natural regeneration will be too slow to ensure restoration within a reasonable period. * * * Alternatives might include acquisition of comparable lands for public parks or, as suggested by defendants below, reforestation of a similar proximate site where the presence of oil would not pose the same hazard to ultimate success. As with the remedy of restoration, the damages awarded for such alternative measures should be reasonable and not grossly disproportionate to the harm caused and the ecological values involved. The ultimate purpose of any such remedy should be to protect the public interest in a healthy, functioning environment, and not to provide a windfall to the public treasury. In emphasizing the above measures, we do not mean to rule out others in appropriate circumstances. There may indeed be cases where traditional commercial valuation rules will afford the best yardstick, as where there is a market in which the damaged resource could have been sold that reflects its actual value. Much must necessarily be left to the discretion of courts, especially before a body of precedent has arisen.

But while the district court's discretion is extensive, we are unable to agree with the approach taken by the court here in placing a value on the damaged resources. Plaintiffs presented two principal theories of damages to the court. The first theory was somewhat analogous to the primary standard we have enunciated above, focusing on plaintiffs' plan to remove the damaged mangrove trees and oil-impregnated sediments from a large area and replace them with clean sediment and container-grown mangrove plants. This plan was estimated to cost approximately $7 million. The district court sensibly and correctly rejected this plan as impractical, inordinately expensive, and unjustifiably dangerous to the healthy mangroves and marine animals still present in the area to be restored. We can find no fault with the district court's conclusion that this draconian plan was not a step that a reasonable trustee of the natural environment would be expected to take as a means of protecting the corpus of the trust.

Plaintiffs' second theory, which the court accepted, focused on the supposed replacement value of the living creatures—the epibenthic and infaunal animals—alleged to have been permanently destroyed or damaged by the oil spill. Plaintiffs repeatedly disavowed any connection between this theory and an actual restoration plan. In other words, plaintiffs did not represent that they proposed to purchase 92 million invertebrate animals for actual introduction into the sediments (which, being contaminated with oil, would hardly support them), but rather wished to use the alleged replacement value of these animals as a yardstick for estimating the quantum of harm caused to the Commonwealth. * * * [Replacement cost is an appropriate recovery only] as a component in a practicable plan for actual restoration. Thus, for example, if a state were seeking to restore a damaged area of forest, a portion of the damages sought might be allocated to replacement of wild birds or game animals or such other creatures as would not be expected to regenerate naturally within a relatively finite period of time even with appropriate restoration. This is a far different matter from permitting the state to recover money damages for the loss of small, commercially valueless creatures which assertedly would perish if returned to the oil-soaked sands, yet probably would replenish themselves naturally if and when restoration—either artificial or natural—took place.

* * * We thus hold that it was error to award $5,526,583.20 for the replacement value of the destroyed organisms.

We come finally to the disposition of this case. Defendants argue that, having rejected plaintiffs' damages theories, we should reverse the district court's judgment, except as to the Commonwealth's undisputed cleanup costs. While this is superficially an attractive course, we do not think the matter is quite so simple. To say that the law on this question is unsettled is vastly to understate the situation. The parties in this lawsuit, and we ourselves, have ventured far into uncharted waters. We do not think plaintiffs could reasonably have been expected to anticipate where this journey would take us. Though we have affirmed the district court's rejection of the Commonwealth's original, rather grandiose restoration plan, we believe the EQB should still have an opportunity to show, if it can, that some lesser steps are feasible that would have a beneficial effect on the West Mangrove ecosystem without excessive destruction of existing natural resources or disproportionate cost. The costs projected for carrying out of such reasonable lesser steps would be an appropriate award of damages. Plaintiffs may wish, at the same time, to reopen the question of alternative-site restoration, as to which the district court initially declined to take evidence, although we hasten to add that we do not now rule on whether the concept of alternative site restoration would make sense in this case as a measure of damages. We therefore, remand the case to the district court with instructions to reopen the record for further evidence on the issue of damages in line with our discussion of the principles governing recovery in cases of this sort.

* * * [Reversed and remanded.]

———————

1. If the Bahia Sucia had been privately owned, the landowner would have a common law tort action in which recovery would probably be limited to the value of the land. Assume as correct the evidence that such value was $5,000 per acre. Why should a private owner be restricted by the economic value of the land? Do the prior cases in this section support an extension of common law to allow more creative measures, such as the ones discussed in this case? Why does it matter that the harm is covered by an environmental statute?

2. Many environmental statutes provide for specific types of recovery like the ones discussed in the case. *See, e.g.,* The Clean Water Act, 22 U.S.C. § 1321(f)(4) (as amended 1977); Outer Continental Shelf Lands Act, 43 U.S.C. § 1813(b)(3) (as amended 1978).

3. The criminal law also seeks to deter oil dumping by providing statutory penalties. The captain of the SS ZOE COLOCOTRONI was tried and convicted of violating 33 U.S.C. § 1321(b)(5) in connection with the dumping of the oil. 456 F.Supp. at 1333 n.9. Does the deterrent effect of criminal sanctions affect the goals of civil damages remedies?

C. PERSONAL INJURY DAMAGES

Section Coverage:

Personal injury tort claims involve bodily injury to the person of the plaintiff proximately resulting from the defendant's tortious conduct. Chapter 13 explores the foreseeability limitation represented by proximate cause; this section examines the basic elements of personal injury damages.

Damage rules for personal injury are independent of the basis of the claim. The focus is upon the plaintiff's condition, without regard to whether the injuries resulted from a bar-room fight or a defective product. The tort may be based upon negligence, strict liability, or intentional conduct. It is only with respect to punitive damages (Chapter 15) that the nature of the defendant's conduct affects personal injury recovery. The cases in the section concern the elements of damages for physical injuries. Not included are shock cases, such as the suits by accident bystanders who suffer injuries from watching tortious harm to loved ones. (Chapter 14) Distress, even with physical consequences, is distinguished from physical harm.

There is a distress component, however, in damages for physical harm. Recovery for bodily injury includes compensation for the plaintiff's physical pain and mental suffering. Pain and suffering are characterized as general damages in personal injury cases because bodily injury necessarily involves some degree of physical pain and suffering. Therefore, the complaint does not need to allege pain and suffering in order to present evidence of it. All other losses are considered special damages, and require special pleading, because they are the particular losses of each plaintiff.

It is helpful to distinguish between past (pre-trial) losses and future losses, if any. Elements of personal injury damages include: loss of earnings or of earning capacity, medical expenses, pain and suffering, and special expenses attributable to the injury. Most states require future losses to be reduced to their present value. This topic is covered in the chapter immediately following this one, Chapter 12, concerning the use and value of money.

A derivative action for loss of consortium with a personal injury victim is available for spouses. There is no uniformity among jurisdictions on the availability of consortium claims for other family relationships, such as for parents whose child is personally injured or for children whose parents have suffered personal injury. Loss of consortium should not be confused with other emotional intangibles, such as grief or distress.

Several state legislatures have enacted statutes affecting personal injury damages, especially in the area of medical malpractice. A common provision is to limit the dollar amount of the pain and suffering component. Some statutes alter the collateral source rule (Chapter 13) or limit the availability of punitive damages. (Chapter 15).

Model Case:

A speeding motorist negligently injured a young child on a bicycle. The child's damages for permanent personal injury can include the following components for both past losses and reasonably established future expenses: medical expenses, pain and suffering, rehabilitation costs, special education costs, lost earning capacity, and psychiatric expense to recover from the trauma.

The parents might separately claim damages for loss of society with their child from the injuries. Such a claim for loss of consortium is a derivative action from the child's personal injury suit. It should not be confused with any claims the parents may have as shock victims if they witnessed the accident. Claims for loss of society with a child are an outgrowth of the consortium claims allowed when a husband or wife is injured. Although jurisdictions widely recognize loss of consortium with an injured spouse, only a few state courts have recently accepted parents' loss of consortium with a child.

Frankel v. United States

321 F.Supp. 1331 (E.D.Pa.1970).

■ SHERIDAN, CHIEF JUDGE.

[As a result of an automobile collision with a car driven by an employee of the Department of the Army, Marilyn Heym sustained serious, irreversible personal injuries. Her guardian instituted a negligence suit against the United States pursuant to the Federal Tort Claims Act, 28 U.S.C. 1346(b), 2671 *et seq.* seeking damages for her medical expenses and personal injuries.]

The hospital and medical bills to the time of trial totaled $17,325.69. These expenses were fair, reasonable and necessary for the treatment of her injuries. Under Pennsylvania law, her father is entitled to recover for the expenses incurred before she reached the age of 21. * * *

At the time of the accident, Marilyn, born November 6, 1946, was 19 years of age, had completed two years of a four year course in commercial art at the Academy of Fine Arts in Philadelphia and intended and was expected to continue to graduation, after which she intended to enter upon a career as a commercial artist. She did generally well in school, and excelled in art. Before the accident she was normal, accident free and in good health, and enjoyed the usual activities of persons in her social and economic situation, including membership in the Girl Scouts, 4 H activities and the like. She was an accomplished and a well-known rider of horses, and an instructress in all phases of horsemanship. * * *

Plaintiff claims past loss of earning capacity from shortly after the time Marilyn would have completed school, or July 1, 1968, to the time of the award. She would have been 21 years of age in July of 1968. The evidence showed that she would have completed school and embarked on a career as a commercial artist. Her progress in school, her family background and her paintings indicated that she was making excellent progress. The evidence convincingly demonstrated that she would have earned an average of $5,000.00 a year commencing July 1, 1968. * * *

* * * [Her earning capacity] to age 65 is $125,000.00 which when reduced to present worth at 6% simple interest under the Pennsylvania rule is $62,000.00, which will be awarded for this item.

Other items of damage are physical and mental pain and suffering, loss of enjoyment of life's pleasures, inconvenience, disfigurement, and permanent injuries. The Government argues that a large part of Marilyn's pain and suffering was not conscious because she was in a coma or semi-coma. Even while in a coma she responded to painful stimuli. For many weeks when she was in a semi-coma she recognized members of her family but could not communicate with them. During this time she undoubtedly appreciated pain. In the future she will experience pain from her arm, the use of the prosthesis and from the therapy that she must undergo for the rest of her life. She frequently falls "with a thud," making no attempt to break her fall. She is suffering and will continue to suffer mentally. * * * She realizes that her sudden and uncontrollable outbursts are wrong and she feels badly that she cannot explain her actions and apologizes for them. In addition, she has lost the ability to engage in those activities which normally contribute to the enjoyment of life. The possibility of marriage and motherhood are gone. [Citation.] She cannot continue in the art career that she so enjoyed, or engage in horseback riding. She has lost peace of mind and well-being. * * * In short, she has lost almost every enjoyment that life can offer. An award of $650,000.00 will be made for these items. [Citations.]

A final item of damage is what plaintiff has characterized as future hospitalization and related medical and incidental expense. Plaintiff contends that: Marilyn is reasonably expected to live out her life expectancy of 54.7 years; she will need constant care for life, both physical and psychiatric; this care cannot be provided at home; only one private institution, Fairmount Farm, near Marilyn's residence, is prepared to accept her and to render this care; and at the present rate of $75.00 a day and taking into account projected increases, an award of at least $8,046,379.00 should be made for this item. A much larger amount is requested if any part is taxable.

* * * While Marilyn is presently being maintained at home, there is no doubt that her parents will not be able to cope with her much longer, much less give her the physical and emotional therapy she needs. Fairmount Farm has 130 employees, including 40 nurses, nurses aides and attendants,

servicing 114 patients. In addition, there are 50 doctors on the staff. If Marilyn were admitted to this hospital, she would have the individual attention and help she needs in her everyday activities such as washing, dressing, bathing and the like. While there is no hope for improvement in her mentality, emotional improvement is possible. This will require close individual attention. Public and most private institutions are not equipped to give this attention. Her program in these institutions would consist largely of sedation in an effort to control her outbursts. The medical testimony clearly shows that heavy sedation is not the proper course of treatment of Marilyn. There is no evidence that the regime in a public institution would be adequate or comparable to that of Fairmount Farm. There is no evidence of the costs of other private institutions, or of the comparative costs of private and public institutions. Plaintiff's claim for private institutional care is a proper item of damage.

The Government suggests that the traditional lump-sum award should not be made because of the uncertainties in forecasting the cost of long-term institutional care, and the large amount of money necessary to pay for this care; it suggests that the court order the Government to establish a $500,000.00 trust fund under the control of a fiduciary which would pay all the institutional costs, and that the court retain jurisdiction to resolve any questions of administration of the trust and order the Government to replenish the corpus if the occasion should arise. Upon Marilyn's death, the balance in the fund would revert to the United States.

The common law provides for a single lump-sum judgment. [Citation.] There can be no judgment for an indefinite amount, or a judgment payable in installments. [Citation.] The single lump-sum judgment as it relates to future damages has been criticized.[9] On the other hand, if the single recovery rule were discarded, final disposition of cases could be delayed for years, and the courts would have to assume the added burden of supervision of their awards. In ordinary cases involving private parties there are practical considerations of insurance policy limits and the ability of defendants to pay. Frequently, cases are settled or disposed of for less than they are worth because of these. In Federal Tort Claims Act actions the ability of the Government to pay is never in question. An amendment to the

---

9.   Schreiber, Damages in Personal Injury and Wrongful Death Cases (Practicing Law Institute, 1965) at page 21:

"There are two important practical consequences of the single recovery rule. For one thing it means that all damages, future as well as past, must be taken account of at the time of trial. This in turn faces the tribunal with the difficult and uncertain task of prophesy, with no chance for second-guessing where the prophesy turns out to be mistaken or where the parties have failed to present all items of their claims.

"Another important aspect of a single recovery is the burden it casts on the successful plaintiff of wise investment and of providence, wherever the recovery must be relied on to take care of future needs.

" * * *

"These features mean that the single recovery rule is often both capricious and inflexible in its operation so that damages in accident cases, even where they are awarded and actually paid, often fail to do the job they should if accident law is to perform its function of administering accident losses efficiently in the public interest."

Federal Tort Claims Act to provide for periodic payments when future, long range damages are significant seems desirable. If such an amendment were passed, the Government would pay more in some cases and less in others, than it would under a single recovery. In all cases justice through just compensation, no more no less, would be achieved. Such drastic changes must come from the Congress, however, and not from the courts. The Government's suggestion is rejected.

* * *

Plaintiff presented evidence that institutionalization costs have been increasing, and that the cost of mental institutional care in the Philadelphia area has increased about 5¼ percent each year over the past ten years. Thus, plaintiff's original request for damages of $1,497,412.50 ($75.00 a day × 365 days = $27,375.00 per year × life expectancy of 54.7 years = $1,497,412.50) becomes $8,046,071.00 with the application of a factor for future cost increases. Inflationary considerations have most commonly been used in the justification of awards. In many instances the consideration has been an evaluation of an award considering present inflationary trends as compared to awards *in the past.* * * *

The projected inflationary trend is speculation. Plaintiff has used the decade of the 1960's, one of the more inflationary times in the history of our country, as the basis for a projection of over fifty years. It is common knowledge that our Government is and has been attempting to control inflation, even to the point of considering wage and price controls. Economists differ on their predictions. Moreover, plaintiff will have money that can be invested and if inflation continues, the return on the money will be greater, and this would have an offsetting effect. Increased costs for institutional care will not be considered.

The Government urges that an award for private institutional care must be reduced to present worth. Plaintiff relies on *Yost v. West Penn Railways Co.,* 1939, 336 Pa. 407, 9 A.2d 368, for the proposition that present worth does not apply to future medical expenses, and that the institutionalization required for Marilyn falls into this category. Many of the costs which make up the daily rate of care and maintenance are not future medical expenses but rather are custodial in nature. The Pennsylvania rule that future medical expenses are not to be reduced to present worth is based on the theory as expressed in *Yost* that:

> " * * * Future medical attention presupposes an out-of-pocket expenditure by the plaintiff. She was entitled to have defendant presently place in her hands the money necessary to meet her future medical expenses, as estimated by the jury based upon the testimony heard, so that she will have it ready to lay out when the service is rendered. * * * "

Yost expresses a sound general rule, although the kind of medical attention to be rendered does not appear from the facts. In the usual case, future medical expenses are sought to remedy a specific malady. If an accident victim will be required to undergo surgery, he should have the money to pay for the service if it is rendered shortly after the verdict. To apply the present worth rule to future medical expenses in most instances would necessitate the resolution of many collateral, variable and imponderable factors such as whether the victim intended to have medical attention immediately or whether his health would permit immediate treatment and if not, when it would permit it. Clearly, there would be no workable way in which to apply the present worth rule.

Here, the expenses of institutionalization will recur periodically in the same manner as future earnings are payable periodically. If the rule of *Yost* were applied and the sum not reduced to present worth, plaintiff would have the money to "lay out" *far before* "the service is rendered." Moreover, the return on any non-reduced sum, properly invested, would exceed the cost of the institutional care. Thus, Marilyn would not only be compensated for her institutionalization, but would reap a windfall. Damages means compensation for a legal injury sustained. [Citation.] The purpose of damages is not to make people wealthy. * * * The general rule of *Yost*, as in the case with many general rules, must yield to exceptional circumstances. The award for institutionalization will be reduced to present worth. The amount so computed is $461,084.00 ($75.00 a day × 365 days = $27,375.00 per year × 30 years = $821,250.00 reduced to present worth = $461,084.00).

* * *

To summarize, the damages to be awarded for the injuries suffered by Marilyn are $1,202,909.69:

To Alvin H. Frankel, Guardian of Marilyn Heym, an incompetent:

Past medical and related expenses	$ 1,414.00
Loss of earning capacity, past and future	74,500.00
Pain, suffering, inconvenience, disfigurement and loss of life's pleasures	650,000.00
Future institutionalization expense	461,084.00
	$1,186,998.00

To Herbert Heym, her father:

Medical and other expenses incurred during Marilyn's minority	$ 15,911.69

* * *

---

1. *Inflation.* Note that the principal case was decided in 1970. We thus have the benefit of hindsight to evaluate the judge's comments about the future. We now know that the court's refusal to consider inflation with respect to the plaintiff's future medical care left her badly undercompensated. Since 1970, inflation in medical costs has been even greater than in the overall cost of living. Every $1 of medical costs in 1970 now costs approxi-

mately $12. In the overall cost of living, goods and services purchased with every $1 now cost approximately $6.

The judge was hopeful that the inflationary trend during the decade of the 1960s was over, but his prediction was wrong. He referred to governmental efforts to control inflation "even to the point of considering wage and price controls." Ironically, the Nixon administration began wage and price controls shortly after this opinion. Inflation was nonetheless rampant. By 1975 prices were up 38 percent.

The judge further commented that even if inflation continued, the plaintiff would be protected by a greater return on her money. This reassuring statement depends upon how the guardian invested the award. If the guardian shared the judge's sanguine view of future trends, he or she would have purchased long term investments in order to take advantage of existing interest rates before they would fall with lower inflation. If the award was put in such investments, the plaintiff's money was not "protected" because their value fell rapidly during the ensuing high inflation. These issues are developed further in Chapter 12.

Future economic trends cannot be predicted with certainty today any more than in 1970. What is the solution for personal injury victims?

2. *Periodic Payments.* A periodic payment system poses an alternative to lump sum payment of a personal injury award. Both injured plaintiffs and defendants may benefit from periodic payments. As the government suggested in the principal case, the use of a periodic payment system can offset uncertainties in calculating future damages. For example, under the periodic payment system, a defendant may recover or avoid paying any amount awarded for future damages that exceeds the actual cost of the plaintiff's future expenses.

There are also advantages to periodic payments from the plaintiff's perspective. Unlike a lump sum payment, periodic payments cannot be lost completely through mismanagement or misfortune. Additionally, just as the defendant is protected from overcompensation, the plaintiff is protected from undercompensation. The injured plaintiff is assured a constant stream of payments, even if the plaintiff outlives his or her normal life expectancy. Certain tax advantages may accompany a periodic payment system as well. Although a lump sum award is not taxable itself, the interest earned on investment of the lump sum award is taxable.

Many states have enacted legislation providing for periodic payment of personal injury awards. Most statutes set forth a threshold amount that is payable to the plaintiff in a lump sum award. Portions of the damage award in excess of this threshold amount are then payable in periodic payments. Some statutes provide for periodic payment of all future damages while other statutes limit periodic payments to damages for future economic losses. *Compare* Fla. Stat. § 768.78 (West 2001) (court may order periodic payment of future economic damages in excess of $250,000) *with* Calif. Code Civ. Pro. § 667.7 (West 2001) (court may order periodic payments if future damages exceed $50,000).

Statutes also vary as to whether periodic payments are mandatory. Some statutes require defendants to make periodic payments. *See, e.g.,* Ala. Stat. § 6–5–543 (2001) (in any action for injury or damages against a health care provider the court shall enter judgment requiring the defendant to pay future damages in excess of $150,000 by periodic payments); Colo. Rev. Stat. § 13–64–205 (West 2001) (in medical malpractice actions the court shall enter judgment for the periodic payment of future damages). Others allow the court to award periodic payments at the parties' election or in the court's discretion. *See, e.g.,* Ark. Code § 16–114–208 (1987) (in an action arising out professional services rendered by a health care provider, the court may order future damages exceeding $100,000 be paid in part or in whole by periodic payments at the request of either party); Ohio Rev. Code § 2323.56 (West 2001) (at the request of either party and upon the court's determination that periodic payments would better compensate the plaintiff, the court may order payment of future damages in excess of $250,000 by periodic payments).

State schemes also differ on the issue of whether a defendant's obligation to make periodic payments abates at the plaintiff's death. *Compare* Colo. Rev. Stat. § 13–64–206 (West 2001) (payments for future damages other than loss of future earnings cease at the plaintiff's death); Md. Code § 11–109 (2000) (if the plaintiff dies before the final periodic payment is made any unpaid balance of the award for future loss of earnings reverts to the plaintiff's estate while any unpaid balance for future medical expenses reverts to the defendant) *with* Fla. Stat. § 768.78 (West 2001) (any liability remaining after the plaintiff's death is reduced to present value and paid in lump sum to the estate); Conn. Gen. Stat. § 52–225d (West 2001) (the defendant's obligation to make periodic payments shall not cease upon the plaintiff's death).

Constitutional challenges to these periodic payment schemes have met with mixed results. *Compare* American Bank & Trust Co. v. Community Hosp., 36 Cal.3d 359, 204 Cal.Rptr. 671, 683 P.2d 670 (1984) (statute providing for periodic payment of future damages in medical malpractice actions did not violate equal protection or due process) *with* Galayda v. Lake Hosp. Sys., 71 Ohio St.3d 421, 644 N.E.2d 298 (1994) (statute requiring periodic payment of future damages in medical malpractice actions violated constitutional right to a jury trial and due process); Smith v. Myers, 181 Ariz. 11, 887 P.2d 541 (1994) (statute allowing for periodic payment of future damages in medical malpractice actions violated state constitutional prohibition against statutorily reducing personal injury damage awards). *See also* Russell G. Donaldson, Validity of State Statutes Providing for Periodic Payment of Future Damages in Medical Malpractice Actions, 41 A.L.R. 4th 275 (1985).

In the absence of an express statutory directive, most courts continue to reject requests for periodic payments and insist upon lump sum awards. *See, e.g.,* Lozada v. United States, 140 F.R.D. 404 (D.Neb.1991) (damages should be distributed in the form of a lump sum payment); Reilly v. United States, 665 F.Supp. 976 (D.R.I.1987) (in the absence of agreement by the parties the court must order payment of a lump sum judgment), *aff'd in part and remanded on other grounds* 863 F.2d 149 (1st Cir.1988) (lower court was correct in insisting that its award of damages be rendered in lump sum form) *but see* Hull v. United States, 971 F.2d 1499 (10th Cir.1992) (court has inherent authority to order that damages be paid into a reversionary trust as long as payment in trust form is in the plaintiff's best interest).

Periodic payments also are used in private structured settlements. By way of settlement, the parties can agree to periodic payments with or without adjustments for changes in the plaintiff's condition.

3. *Unemancipated Minors.* Note that in the principal case, the court awarded damages to both Marilyn (through her guardian) and her father. Although Marilyn was 19, at that time the age of majority was 21 in most states. When an unemancipated minor is injured, both the parents and the child have a cause of action. Courts generally divide the elements of damages between the actions appropriately. For example, when parents have paid medical expenses, those losses can be part of their damages. Parrott v. Mallett, 262 Ark. 525, 558 S.W.2d 152 (1977) (two distinct actions; parent entitled to recover expenses incurred and to be incurred by parent on account of injury to child). If the child actually pays the medical expenses personally, only the child is entitled to recover those damages. Sommers v. Hartford Accident & Indemnity Co., 277 S.W.2d 645 (Mo.App. 1955). If the parents do not bring a separate action, the child's action may include medical expenses paid by the parents because the child is also liable for them. White v. Moreno Valley Unified School Dist., 181 Cal.App.3d 1024, 226 Cal.Rptr. 742 (1986). Courts do not allow double recovery for the same expenses in two actions, however. Alaskan Village, Inc. v. Smalley, 720 P.2d 945 (Alaska 1986) (mother waived right to recover damages for past medical expenses incurred by allowing child to assert claim and testifying on her behalf).

When both minors and parents have claims, some elements of damages are not shared and require separate actions. The child's pain and suffering and lost adult earning capacity belong only to the child's action. The parent's action claims loss of services or earnings of a child during minority. Emanuel v. Clewis, 272 N.C. 505, 158 S.E.2d 587 (1968). Parents may have special damages, such as travel, lodging, and telephone expenses to establish contact with the injured child. Mancino v. Webb, 274 A.2d 711 (Del.Super.1971) (allowing those elements but not parents' mental anguish or lost wages). Punitive damage claims belong to the child rather than the parent. Hughey v. Ausborn, 249 S.C. 470, 154 S.E.2d 839 (1967).

4. *Substantive Reform.* Public dissatisfaction with the operation of the tort system has produced a variety of reforms. Some changes are directed at the substantive law, others at remedies.

Fundamental substantive changes began with the workers' compensation movement at the beginning of the century. *See* Weinstein, The Corporate Ideal in the Liberal State, 1900–1918 (1968). In every state there is now a no-fault compensation scheme for workers' injuries. An injured worker no longer needs to prove that the employer was negligent, and is no longer barred by any defense such as assumption of the risk. In exchange for the substantive changes favorable to workers, the damage scheme provides for lower recoveries than a successful personal injury tort claimant ordinarily would recover. The merits of this trade-off and any effect the workers' compensation scheme may have on overall industrial safety are the subject of debate. For a critical view of the history of workers' compensation acts in the context of injuries from asbestos *see* M. Brodeur, Outrageous Misconduct (1985).

In the second half of this century public attention turned to injuries from automobile accidents. Responding to dissatisfaction with the tort system, scholars advocated no-fault auto accident legislation. Particularly notable is the 1965 book by R. Keeton & J. O'Connell, Basic Protection for Accident Victims A Blueprint for Reforming Automobile Insurance. Central to this reform movement is recognition of the role of insurance. Potential defendants seek "third party" insurance to protect them from losses occasioned by tort liability. The no-fault scheme for auto accidents relies upon a "first party" insurance whereby insureds recover directly from their own insurers.

Proponents of no-fault plans identify as major advantages the guaranteed recoveries for injury victims and savings in the transactional costs of litigation. Opponents question the amount of savings and argue that traditional tort law has a deterrent effect on drivers.

About half of the states have passed some form of automobile no-fault legislation. There is wide variation among them. Unlike workers' compensation acts, the no-fault plans for auto accidents replace only part of the tort system. *See* U.S. Dept. of Transportation, Compensating Auto Victims: A Follow-up Report on No Fault Auto Insurance Experiences (1985).

Wilburn v. Maritrans GP Inc.

139 F.3d 350 (3d Cir.1998).

■ ALARCON, CIRCUIT JUDGE.

Michael T. Wilburn ("Wilburn") was injured when he was swept off the deck of the tug, the *Enterprise,* by a huge wave during a storm. He filed an action against his employer, Maritrans GP Inc. ("Maritrans") to recover damages for negligence pursuant to the Jones Act, 46 U.S.C.App. § 688, and for the unseaworthiness of the *Enterprise* under general maritime law.

* * * Regarding damages, we hold that the evidence was sufficient to show a narrowing of Wilburn's economic opportunities, however, it was insufficient to support the jury's award of damages. We therefore reverse the district court's judgment as a matter of law and affirm the order granting a new trial with respect to damages.

In setting forth its reasons for granting the judgment as a matter of law, the district court separately concluded that the evidence was insufficient to support an award of damages for loss of future earning capacity. The district court explained its ruling as follows:

> Wilburn produced no evidence regarding what, if any, positions as barge captain were available to him and his prospect of attaining such a position in relation to other qualified individuals. There was no evidence as to when Wilburn could expect to attain such a position, what his anticipated work-life as a barge captain would be, or what salary he would receive.

A plaintiff may recover compensatory damages for loss of future earning capacity in Jones Act and FELA cases. The plaintiff must produce, however, "competent evidence" suggesting that his injuries have narrowed the range of economic opportunities available to him. [Citation]

Under the law of this circuit, a plaintiff may recover an award for future lost earning capacity,

> if he has produced competent evidence suggesting that his injuries have narrowed the range of economic opportunities available to him. This means that a plaintiff need not, as a prerequisite to recovery, prove that in the near future he will earn less money than he would have but for his injury. Rather, a plaintiff must show that his injury has caused a diminution in his ability to earn a living. Such a diminution includes a decreased ability to weather adverse economic circumstances, such as a discharge or lay-off, or to voluntarily leave the defendant employer for other employment.

[Citation.]

* * *

At trial Wilburn introduced evidence of both physical and psychological limitations caused by his traumatic experience that limit his economic opportunities. Dr. Steven Newman testified that Wilburn has permanent injury to his left shoulder resulting in mobility and functional limitations in both his shoulder and arm. With these permanent injuries, Wilburn is restricted from performing activities that involve overhead or repetitive reaching and stretching, pushing or pulling, and very strenuous activities. Performing these activities is both painful for Wilburn and can be expected to exacerbate the injury. Despite his injuries, Wilburn has continued to work as an AB tankerman. He compensates for his limitations by using his right arm and hand.

Wilburn testified that as a result of his harrowing experience, he has a fear of sailing coastwise—that is leaving the sight of land. Although he has made eight to ten coastwise trips during good weather, he fears that if he were on a coastwise trip during bad weather, he would be unable to go out on deck to perform his mariner's duties even if he were ordered to do so.

Dr. Robert Sadoff, a forensic psychiatrist, testified that Wilburn suffers from post-traumatic stress syndrome, and his fears of sailing coastwise are consistent with that diagnosis. While Wilburn has made progress in overcoming his fears, and has made some voyages coastwise, he would need to undergo a behavioral desensitization program in order to overcome his "realistic reasons for being afraid." Such a program, however, is "not practical because you have to deal with companies who own ships and they're not there for [Wilburn's] therapy." In absence of a desensitization program, Dr. Sadoff testified "I just don't think that without treatment, as I have outlined it, he's going to go much further than he is now.... [H]e's gone pretty far in what he's done, but he's limited and he's reached a kind of plateau at this point...."

Wilburn testified that he made a bid for a barge captain position, but withdrew his name when Richard Steady, Maritrans's port captain, told him he would never get a barge captain position as long as he would not go coastwise. Wilburn also stated that he was concerned about bidding on barge captain positions because as a barge captain, he would lose his union protection; therefore, even if he were successful in obtaining a barge captain position on an inland barge, the company could transfer him to a coastwise barge or fire him if he refused to go coastwise. Although Steady denied telling Wilburn that he would never become a barge captain if he were unwilling to go coastwise, Steady testified that an inland barge could be required to go coastwise.

We conclude that the evidence, when viewed in the light most favorable to Wilburn, demonstrates a narrowing of Wilburn's economic opportunities and provides a sufficient basis upon which the jury could have decided to compensate Wilburn for loss of future earning capacity. The fact that Wilburn has continued to work as an AB tankerman since the accident and has compensated for his physical injuries by using his right arm does not preclude a recovery for loss of future earning capacity. Rather, those were factors the jury could consider in deciding whether Wilburn's economic prospects have been narrowed or whether he "is chained to his present job in a kind of economic servitude." Finally, while there is a conflict in testimony as to whether Wilburn was told he could never become a barge captain due to his psychological limitation, "[i]t was the duty of the jury to resolve the conflicting testimony and it did so in favor of [Wilburn]." * * *

The district court concluded that the award of one million dollars for loss of future earning capacity was excessive and not supported by the evidence. We agree.

We use the shockingly excessive standard to review jury verdicts, but "review the calculation methods of a jury in cases which are 'susceptible to mathematical formula.' [Citation] Loss of future earnings capacity is subject to mathematical calculation." Although the determination of such damages often involves a host of uncertain contingencies, the verdict must still have its basis in evidence, not conjecture. [Citation]

Wilburn was thirty-eight years old at the time he was injured. The evidence showed that he had been receiving $44,000 a year as an AB tankerman. The pay for a barge captain is $50,000 a year. Assuming a retirement age of 65, the gross loss of earnings would be approximately $162,000. That is far less than the one million dollars awarded by the jury.

* * *

The district court also held that the jury's award of one million dollars for Wilburn's physical and psychological damage was excessive and not supported by the evidence. Wilburn suffered injuries to his left shoulder and knee. Physical therapy has improved the condition of his knee. His left shoulder has not responded to treatment. He has continued to work for Maritrans as an AB tankerman. In performing his duties, however, he must compensate for his limitations by using his right arm and hand. He is unable to participate in the recreational activities he formerly enjoyed such as wind-surfing, softball, and basketball.

Wilburn's experience in being thrown overboard by a giant wave has caused him to suffer from a post-traumatic stress disorder. He is now afraid of ocean storms. He will not leave the sight of land if there is a chance of bad weather. As a result of his fear, he believes that he could not go on deck to perform his job if he were in a storm off the coast. * * *

With respect to his psychological trauma, Dr. Sadoff testified that the symptoms Wilburn experienced after the accident—flashbacks, nightmares, difficulty sleeping, and depression—have all improved. His symptoms of irritability, withdrawal, and excessive startle reaction have also improved and are likely to continue to do so.

Regarding Wilburn's fear of storms at sea, Dr. Sadoff testified that Wilburn has a good prognosis for a complete recovery if he undergoes the behavioral sensitization program that Dr. Sadoff outlined. While Dr. Sadoff testified that the program is not practical to implement because it requires the cooperation of a company that owns ships, Dr. Sadoff also testified that Wilburn might be able to overcome his fear of storms at seas in the same manner that has allowed him to take several coastwise trips during good weather. Dr. Sadoff testified as follows:

> There may be some other steps that he could take. I don't think he's going to get to the point where anybody is going to take him out on an excursion just for the point of helping him deal with his anxieties. But if, for example, if he's on board and there is a storm and they have to go out or they are out at sea, maybe going to Norfolk or up to New York, and a storm comes up unexpectedly and he's on board and if he handles it and deal with it—doesn't panic and doesn't run below deck—it may be that would be an impetus for the next step after that.... But I just can't plan for that. * * *

Under these circumstances, we are persuaded that the district court did not abuse its discretion in finding that an award of one million dollars for Wilburn's physical and psychiatric disorders is excessive.

1. *Lost Future Earnings.* Damages for lost or diminished earning capacity, like those that the plaintiff sought to recover in the principal case, must be distinguished from damages for lost future earnings. As the principal case illustrates, damages for lost or diminished earning capacity compensate injured plaintiffs for reductions in the market value of their services in the workplace in general. Many factors affect a person's market-ability. These factors include education, age, experience, talents, general health and physical capacity. When a person's health or physical capacity is permanently impaired, the market value of that person's services may be diminished. Damages for diminished earning capacity seek to redress this loss. Put another way, diminished earning capacity is measured by the reduction in value of the power to earn rather than the difference in earnings received for a specific occupation before and after the injury. *See* Stephens v. Crown Equip. Corp., 22 F.3d 832 (8th Cir.1994).

In contrast, damages for lost future earnings compensate the plaintiff for loss of earnings from the time of trial until some point in the future when the plaintiff will be able to return to work. A plaintiff usually seeks to recover lost future earnings when he or she has not suffered a permanent injury, but the plaintiff will be unable to work for some period of time while recovering from a temporary injury.

2. *Proof of Earning Capacity.* Lost or diminished earning capacity is measured by the difference between the injured plaintiff's earning capacity before the injury and after the injury. Evidence concerning the plaintiff's past employment history may be helpful in determining pre-tort earning capacity and, hence, the diminished earning capacity. However, proof of past earnings is not necessary to establish diminished earning capacity. Indeed, a person who was unemployed at the time of injury still may recover damages for lost or diminished capacity. *See, e.g.,* Bishop v. Poore, 475 So.2d 486 (Ala.1985) (unemployed worker alleging permanent injury may present evidence of lost earning capacity).

On the other hand, the injured plaintiff must prove with reasonable certainty that there is a loss in earning capacity and must provide some reasonable basis upon which to estimate those damages. A plaintiff who was employed with a predictable income stream of income at the time of injury can use expert testimony to project what similarly situated workers are likely to earn for some reasonable distance in the future and, thus, establish the diminished earning capacity with reasonable certainty. *See, e.g.,* Knight v. Texaco, Inc., 786 F.2d 1296 (5th Cir.1986) (defendant employed injured roustabout at another job with higher wage, but testimony suggested job was to be eliminated after trial and expert testimony established future losses based on probable future wages of a successful roustabout).

Consider how a plaintiff who has no established earnings history would prove pre-tort earning capacity with reasonable certainty. What if the plaintiff has not even completed the level of education that was planned before the tort? How should a court or jury calculate the diminished earning capacity of a child who is severely injured? What factors might a court or jury consider in determining whether the child's anticipated employment was too speculative to permit recovery? Consider *Athridge v. Iglesias*, 950 F.Supp. 1187 (D.D.C.1996), *affirmed* 1997 WL 404854 (D.C.Cir.1997).

In *Athridge*, a 15–year–old high school student sought to recover damages, including damages for lost earning capacity, after he was struck by a car during a game of "chicken" and severely injured. Evidence clearly established that the plaintiff suffered severe permanent brain damage and that as a result of this he would be limited to relatively low-wage jobs with a high risk of unemployment. The difficulty for the court was determining what his earning capacity would have been but for his injuries. Ultimately, the court accepted the estimate of the plaintiff's expert with a minor reduction in the amount of the expert's estimate for lost fringe benefits and vacation pay.

Based on information the expert received from the plaintiff's high school, the expert then concluded that but for his injuries the plaintiff had a 16% chance of obtaining only a high school degree, a 60% chance of obtaining a college degree and a 24% chance of obtaining a professional degree. The expert computed the plaintiff's diminished earning capacity as the difference between his earning capacity at low wage jobs and a weighted average of his projected income at each of the three potential education levels. In adopting the expert's conclusion, the court observed that each of the plaintiff's siblings was enrolled in professional degree programs and that the plaintiff had expressed an interest in becoming a lawyer. The court concluded that the plaintiff most likely would have obtained a college degree and that a significant probability existed that the plaintiff would have obtained a professional degree.

3. *Expenses*. In calculating the plaintiff's diminished earning capacity, the trier of fact must deduct any expenses the plaintiff avoided as a result of the injury. Thus, in *Athridge*, *supra*, the court deducted the reasonable costs the plaintiff would have incurred in obtaining a college degree and a professional degree from his projected income at each education level. Generally, plaintiffs need not deduct everyday living expenses because they will still incur them despite the injury. Indeed, the plaintiff often must pay ordinary living expenses out of the award for lost earning capacity. However, if the plaintiff receives an award for future medical costs that includes the cost of extended hospitalization or institutional care, the plaintiff may be required to deduct the cost of ordinary living expenses from any award for lost earnings or lost earning capacity. Under these circumstances, the plaintiff's award for hospitalization or institutional care also compensates him or her for ordinary living expenses as housing and food will be provided as part of the hospitalization or institutional care. To allow the plaintiff to recover the full lost earning capacity essentially would require the defendant to pay the plaintiff's living expenses twice. Thus, some courts have required the plaintiff to offset awards for future hospitalization and lost earnings. *See, e.g.*, Lozada v. United States, 140 F.R.D. 404 (D.Neb. 1991).

Some courts have refused to require such an offset. *See, e.g.,* Reilly v. United States, 863 F.2d 149 (1st Cir.1988). In *Reilly,* the court explained:

* * * Every time a tort claimant is hospitalized for treatment of injuries, she "saves" on certain personal expenditures. Her meals are provided by the hospital, thus reducing her food budget; she spends her time in a hospital gown, thus reducing her dry cleaning expenses; utilities come with the accommodations, thus minimizing the costs of heat, light, and power at her residence. Despite this "duplications," it has never been suggested that the tortfeasor should be allowed to insist that his victim account for these savings and deduct them from the amount of the hospital bill when proving damages.

The reasons why such offsets are not accepted practice, we suggest, have both pragmatic and equitable roots. From a practical standpoint, the difficulties in attempting to prove such offsets are enormous. Unless we are prepared to say that damages must now be proved with sliderule precision—an approach this court has never adopted—it makes very little sense to devote the overtaxed resources of court, jury, and litigants to a search designed to sanitize every penny of consequential expense and certify it as altogether free from taint of duplication. Once that rationale is accepted, equity comes into play. As a matter of simple justice, it is far fairer to give the injured plaintiff the benefit of what small duplication may inevitably occur than to confer the trouvaille upon the wrongdoer.

How does this issue of duplication relate to the collateral source rule? If the plaintiff has health insurance that covers the hospital costs, those costs can still be recovered from the tortfeasor. *See* Chapter 13. How many times can a plaintiff recover the expense of the same meal?

If the plaintiff is hospitalized for a year, how much money is likely to be involved in such a setoff? What proportion is it likely to be to the damages as a whole for someone hospitalized that long? Would it be useful to distinguish between plaintiffs who are temporarily hospitalized and plaintiffs who are permanently institutionalized because of injuries? If that distinction is useful, is it nonetheless offensive to our sense of justice to allow the setoff only for the more injured plaintiffs, or is it a logical and justifiable ground for reducing some plaintiffs' awards for the savings in personal expenses?

4. *Taxes.* Personal injury awards are exempt from federal tax and most state income taxes. Should a plaintiff's award for lost earnings or lost earning capacity be reduced by the amount of income taxes the plaintiff avoids? In other words, should lost income be measured by gross earnings or net earnings after taxes? Jurisdictions are divided. Had a plaintiff not been injured, the plaintiff would have been required to pay taxes on the earnings received and, thus, only the plaintiff's net earnings would be available. However, the plaintiff will not be obligated to pay taxes on any damage award representing lost earnings. Thus, most courts recognize, at least in theory, that net earnings more truly reflect the injured plaintiff's losses.

Nonetheless, many jurisdictions hold that tax deductions from income are improper and that gross income is the proper measure of the plaintiff's damages for lost future earnings and diminished future earning capacity. These courts reason that estimating future tax liability is too speculative. For example, while recognizing that "abstract logic could favor the defendant's view" that after-tax income was the correct measure of damages, the New York Court of Appeals rejected such a rule. *See* Johnson v. Manhattan & Bronx Surface Transit Operating Auth., 71 N.Y.2d 198, 524 N.Y.S.2d 415, 519 N.E.2d 326 (1988). Instead, the Court held that practical policy and sound jurisprudence dictated that gross income was the proper measure of damages. The court explained:

> No crystal ball is available to juries to overcome the inevitable speculation concerning future tax status of an individual or future tax law itself. Trial strategies and tactics in wrongful death actions should not be allowed to deteriorate into battles between a new wave of experts consisting of accountants and economists in the interest of mathematical purity and of rigid logic over common sense. Countless numbers of unknown and unpredictable variables for tax purposes alone include, as mere examples, future marital and family status, changes in rates, exemption and deduction provisions of overlapping tax codes. All sides to this issue would no doubt agree at least that this could produce much guesswork. 524 N.Y.S.2d at 418.

Other courts also have reasoned that the defendant rather than the plaintiff should suffer the consequences of such speculation. *See* Paducah Area Public Library v. Terry, 655 S.W.2d 19 (Ky.App.Ct.1983) ("There appears to be no reason for abating damages in favor of a wrongdoer by deducting tax payments solely for his benefit.").

In contrast, some courts have held that net earnings are the proper measure of damages despite any uncertainty in estimating future taxes. These courts reason that awarding the plaintiff gross earnings would provide the plaintiff with a windfall and decline to permit the plaintiff a windfall merely because determining tax liability may be uncertain. As the New Jersey Supreme Court explained in *Ruff v. Weintraub*, 105 N.J. 233, 519 A.2d 1384 (1987):

> We recognize that a plaintiff's future tax liability is uncertain and that the jury will be asked to arrive at a figure without knowing what change may occur in the tax laws or in the plaintiff's tax status. * * * However, * * * "[w]e decline to give simplicity paramount significance in fashioning damages. Such an approach might aid the judiciary but hardly justice." [Citation.]

> Estimating future tax liability is no more speculative or complicated than many of the other factors a jury considers in setting damages for future losses. Although, as a result of this decision, some testimony on the plaintiff's future tax liability will be necessary, protracted battles between tax experts will not inevitably result. Juries are already considering evidence regarding issues as complicated as future inflationary trends and interest rates without being hopelessly confused or

engaging in unwarranted speculation. [Citations.] We are confident that the same can be done with evidence on the plaintiff's future taxes. 519 A.2d at 1387–88.

See also Norfolk & Western Ry. v. Liepelt, 444 U.S. 490, 100 S.Ct. 755, 62 L.Ed.2d 689 (1980) (after-tax income proper measure of damages under FELA) ("Admittedly there are many variables that may affect the amount of a wage earner's future income tax liability. * * * But future employment itself, future health, future personal expenditures, future interest rates and future inflation are also matters of estimate and prediction.").

Healy v. White

173 Conn. 438, 378 A.2d 540 (1977).

■ SPEZIALE, ASSOCIATE JUSTICE.

This personal injury action was tried to the jury as a hearing in damages, the issue of the defendants' liability having been determined by summary judgment. The defendants have appealed from the judgments rendered on the verdicts for the plaintiffs.

On July 24, 1973, the plaintiff Brian Healy, then seven and a half years old, was riding as a passenger in an automobile operated by his mother, Mary Jane Healy. At the intersection of Routes 25 and 202 in Newtown, their automobile was struck by a tractor-trailer truck owned by the defendant Silliman Company and operated by its employee, the defendant Allen H. White. As a result of the impact, Brian was thrown from the car onto the pavement. He was taken by ambulance to Danbury Hospital and, subsequently, to Yale New Haven Hospital.

On July 11, 1974, the present negligence action was begun. After summary judgment on liability was rendered against the defendants, the plaintiffs filed a substituted complaint in two counts. The first count, claiming $750,000 in damages, was in behalf of Brian Healy and alleged, inter alia, that, as a result of the defendants' negligence, Brian had been violently thrown from his car and had suffered various physical injuries which included the "aggravation and worsening of a specific learning disability" and resulted in a "permanent minimal brain dysfunction syndrome [brain damage] with associated multiple psychomotor seizures [permanent epilepsy]." The second count was on behalf of Brian's father, Bartholomew Healy. It alleged that, as a result of the injuries sustained by his minor son, he had incurred and would in the future incur expenses for Brian's hospitalization, physicians' care and other medical needs, as well as expenses for private tutors and teaching specialists. The ad damnum to this second count claimed $125,000 damages.

In answering the substituted complaint, the defendants admitted their negligence and the allegations that Brian had suffered "fractured ribs, and multiple contusions and abrasions." The granting of the plaintiffs' motion for summary judgment eliminated any consideration of liability during the trial. The jury returned a verdict of $350,000 damages on the first count and $60,000 on the second count. Thereafter, the court denied the defendants' motion to set aside the verdicts, judgments were entered, and the defendants appealed.

* * * [The court reviewed the medical evidence on the permanency of the epilepsy and found sufficient evidence in expert testimony that the odds of permanency were greater than fifty percent.]

Our final consideration is whether the evidence was sufficient to support the verdict on the second count insofar as Brian's father claimed damages for future medical and educational expenses to be incurred because of Brian's injuries. There was sufficient qualified and undisputed testimony from which the jury could conclude that it was reasonably probable that Brian's conditions would, for a long time, necessitate future treatment, medications, medical therapy and supervision and would even require neurosurgery.

There was also evidence from which the jury could find that following his accident, Brian received a lower score in his I.Q. testing; his school work deteriorated badly; the epilepsy medications would continue to affect his learning adversely; these medications, combined with the problems from his brain damage, would severely limit his functioning in school; and special education would be essential for a very long time. [A medical expert] specifically testified that Brian "certainly is doing very poorly. The only hope that this youngster has to at least gain enough academic skills to make him competitive is for him to get special education." * * *

There was strong evidence that Brian would need special schooling for a long time; the actual cost of such education in private schools was established by testimony; and the defendants took no exception to the court's charge to the jury on this item of damages. From this evidence the jury could reach a valid conclusion as to (1) the reasonable probability of Brian's continued need for special schooling and (2) the reasonable value of such schooling. This evidence alone, without regard to Brian's future medical needs, fully supports the jury's award of damages to his father for future expenses during Brian's minority.

The defendants make no claim that the amount of damages on either count is excessively high in and of itself. The claim is, rather, one of insufficient evidence. The jurors could reasonably have found in accordance with the verdicts as rendered on both counts, giving the evidence the most favorable construction in support of the verdicts to which it is reasonably entitled. The verdicts could, therefore, not be set aside as being against the evidence and should stand. [Citations.]

There is no error.

———————

1. *Difficulty in Predicting Future Disability.* Prediction of future disability, such as Brian's future epilepsy in the principal case, is often difficult. What if there is a fifty-fifty chance of a future medical condition?

Consider the observation of the Oregon Supreme Court in *Crawford v. Seufert:* "For medical testimony to have any probative value, it must at least advise the jury that the inference drawn by the doctor is more probably correct than incorrect. If the probabilities are in balance, the matter is left to speculation. Speculation filtered through a jury is still speculation." 236 Or. 369, 388 P.2d 456, 459 (1964).

What if the testimony had been that only ten percent of the people in Brian's position still have epilepsy by the age of sixteen? No damages for this unlikely occurrence would be awarded, but what if Brian was one of the unlucky ten percent? Should judgments not be final? Should plaintiffs be able to reopen cases years later and seek more damages? If the issue were to arise in a child support suit against a parent in a domestic relations case, the court would retain jurisdiction and allow a change in support to meet changing conditions. Is it desirable to treat personal injury claims differently?

Conversely, reconsider the fact that Brian actually did receive damages for the future condition because the odds were greater than fifty percent. If Brian turns out to be among the lucky minority that are cured, should the defendant be able to reopen the case to recover the excess compensation?

2.   *Latent Disease.* What about medical conditions that the plaintiff does not currently suffer but probably will suffer later? For example, consider a plaintiff who has been exposed to toxic chemicals and who has some probability of developing cancer sometime in the future. If the plaintiff is suffering current physical injuries from the exposure, the statute of limitations and the "single action" rule combine to put the plaintiff in a difficult position. Generally, the plaintiff's claim accrues and the statute of limitations begins to run when the plaintiff knows or reasonably should know that he or she has been injured. Thus, if the plaintiff suffers physical injuries at the time of exposure, the statute of limitations will begin to run on the plaintiff's claim at that time. The plaintiff must bring a lawsuit against the defendant to avoid having the claim be time barred.

The problem in this situation is that at the time of bringing the claim, the plaintiff does not know the full extent of future injuries. In particular, the plaintiff does not know whether or not he or she will develop cancer and frequently cannot demonstrate with any reasonable certainty that he or she will develop cancer. Nonetheless, the "single action" rule requires plaintiffs to seek damages for all injuries—past, present or future—in a single action. Thus, the plaintiff is put in the difficult, often impossible, position of establishing that he or she will more likely than not develop cancer in the future. Even if the plaintiff is unsuccessful, the plaintiff will be precluded from bringing a subsequent action if and when cancer develops in the future.

How should a court best deal with the difficulties encountered in compensating a plaintiff for latent medical conditions? Should a court award damages for the fear and distress the plaintiff suffers as a result of the increased risk of cancer? For the increased risk of cancer itself? For the cost of medical monitoring to attempt early detection of any cancer? Should a court, instead, permit a plaintiff to bring a subsequent action if and when he or she actually develops cancer? Courts have employed several of these remedies in seeking to compensate victims of toxic torts.

Most courts have rejected claims for damages based on the increased risk of cancer itself unless the plaintiff can demonstrate a reasonable possibility that he or she will develop cancer. *See, e.g.,* Sterling v. Velsicol Chem. Corp., 855 F.2d 1188 (6th Cir.1988); Eagle–Picher Indus. v. Cox, 481 So.2d 517 (Fla.Ct.App.1985). However, a growing number of jurisdictions now allow a plaintiff to seek damages for the cost of any future medical monitoring that is a reasonably certain consequence of exposure to the toxic substance. *See, e.g.,* Bower v. Westinghouse Elec. Corp., 206 W.Va. 133, 522 S.E.2d 424 (1999); Bourgeois v. A.P. Green Indus., 716 So.2d 355 (La.1998); Hansen v. Mountain Fuel Supply Co., 858 P.2d 970 (Utah 1993); Potter v. Firestone Tire & Rubber Co., 6 Cal.4th 965, 25 Cal.Rptr.2d 550, 863 P.2d 795 (1993). Most of these courts allow a plaintiff to recover the costs of medical monitoring even in the absence of a present physical injury. *See, e.g.,* Potter, 863 P.2d 795.

Courts limit recovery of medical monitoring costs to plaintiffs who have been exposed to a proven hazardous substance at levels greater than normal background levels through tortious conduct and who as a result of that exposure suffer an increased risk of disease when compared to the plaintiffs' pre-exposure risk and the risk of the public at large. Courts also require plaintiffs to demonstrate the clinical value of medical monitoring in leading to early detection and the clinical value of early detection. Finally, some courts allow recovery for the emotional distress the plaintiff suffers as a result of the fear of developing cancer. *See, e.g.,* Hagerty v. L & L Marine Serv., 788 F.2d 315 (5th Cir.1986). However, some courts restrict recovery for emotional distress to situations in which the plaintiff has suffered a present physical injury as well or situations in which the plaintiff can show he or she is more likely than not to develop cancer in the future. *See, e.g.,* Potter, 863 P.2d 795 (in the absence of physical injury, a plaintiff must show that a plaintiff will more likely than not develop cancer).

Courts also have attempted to deal with the problem of compensating plaintiffs for latent medical conditions by relaxing the single action rule and rules governing tolling of the statute of limitations. For example, several courts have held that the statute of limitations does not begin to run on a plaintiff's claim when he or she is initially diagnosed with some physical injuries from toxic exposure but rather only upon diagnosis of serious medical condition. *See, e.g.,* Sopha v. Owens–Corning Fiberglas, 230 Wis.2d 212, 601 N.W.2d 627 (1999) (diagnosis of non-malignant asbestos-related lung pathology does not trigger the statute of limitations with respect to an action for a later diagnosed, distinct malignant asbestos-related condition); Potts v. Celotex Corp., 796 S.W.2d 678 (Tenn.1990) (same). Additionally, some courts have recognized that even when the plaintiff brings an initial claim for damages suffered as a result of toxic exposure, the plaintiff should be able to bring a subsequent action for a separate disease that had not manifested itself at the time of the original action. *See, e.g.,* Hagerty v. L & L Marine Serv., 788 F.2d 315 (single action rule should not preclude subsequent action if plaintiff develops cancer even though plaintiff brought action to recover for initial physical injuries caused by toxic exposure).

3.   *Loss of Chance and Shortened Life Expectancy.* Should plaintiffs be permitted to recover damages for a decrease in the chance of survival? What if the plaintiff had less than a 50% chance of surviving before the tortious conduct? Should a plaintiff be permitted to recover for shortened life expectancy? Consider a cancer patient whose physician negligently fails to diagnose the condition in time for treatments that might possibly have helped. If the patient had a 40% chance of survival had the cancer been timely diagnosed but the patient's chance of survival was reduced to 20% as a result of the doctor's negligent delay in diagnosis, should the plaintiff be entitled to recover damages? How should those damages be measured? What if the patient had a life expectancy of 10 years had the cancer been timely diagnosed but as a result of the doctor's delay in diagnosis, the patient's life expectancy is reduced to 5 years?

Many courts have rejected recovery for loss of chance. *See, e.g.,* Wright v. St. Mary's Medical Center, 59 F.Supp.2d 794 (S.D.Ind.1999); Jones v. Owings, 318 S.C. 72, 456 S.E.2d 371 (1995). However, several courts have permitted a plaintiff to recover damages for loss of a chance of survival. Some of these jurisdictions award the plaintiff a proportion of the total amount of death-related damages that reflects the reduction of the victim's chance of survival. *See, e.g.,* Delaney v. Cade, 255 Kan. 199, 873 P.2d 175 (1994); Wollen v. DePaul Health Center, 828 S.W.2d 681 (Mo.1992). Other jurisdictions relax the causation standard, allowing the plaintiff to recover full damages if the plaintiff establishes that the defendant's conduct substantially increased the risk of harm. *See, e.g.,* McKellips v. Saint Francis Hosp., 741 P.2d 467 (Okla.1987).

Some courts have allowed shortened life expectancy as a separate compensable element of damages. For example, in *Morrison v. Stallworth,* 73 N.C.App. 196, 326 S.E.2d 387 (1985), a 45–year–old woman saw her gynecologist, complaining of a lump in her breast. The doctor twice negligently failed to detect cancer before a subsequent biopsy revealed a malignancy. The North Carolina appellate court remanded the case to the trial court after the trial court improperly excluded evidence of shortened life expectancy as an element of damages.

4.   *Court–Appointed Experts.* A federal district court is authorized by Federal Rule of Evidence 706 to appoint expert witnesses of its own selection. In *Reilly v. United States*, 863 F.2d 149 (1st Cir.1988). the Court of Appeals for the First Circuit recognized an inherent judicial power to appoint technical advisors, apart from the statutory authorization. The court cautioned:

> [S]uch appointments should be the exception and not the rule, and should be reserved for truly extraordinary cases where the introduction of outside skills and expertise, not possessed by the judge, will hasten

the just adjudication of a dispute without dislodging the delicate balance of the juristic role.

* * * Appropriate instances, we suspect, will be hen's teeth rare. The modality is, if not a last, a near-to-last resort, to be engaged only where the trial court is faced with problems of unusual difficulty, sophistication, and complexity, involving something well beyond the regular questions of fact and law with which judges routinely grapple. Although a technical advisor can be valuable in an appropriate case, the judge must not be eager to lighten his load without the best of cause. 863 F.2d at 156–57.

See generally, Sink, "The Unused Power of a Federal Judge to Call His Own Expert Witnesses," 29 S.Cal.L.Rev. 195 (1956).

Debus v. Grand Union Stores of Vermont

159 Vt. 537, 621 A.2d 1288 (1993).

■ JOHNSON, JUSTICE.

Defendant Grand Union appeals from a jury verdict and award of personal injury damages made to plaintiff on her premises-liability claim. Defendant contends the trial court erred by allowing plaintiff to make a per diem damage argument to the jury, and claims that such arguments are overly prejudicial and should not be allowed. We disagree, and affirm. * * *

Plaintiff was injured while shopping at defendant's store on August 23, 1985, when a pallet of boxes, piled high and imbalanced, toppled over and fell upon her. The boxes, containing cans of pet food, tumbled off the pallet and onto plaintiff when a store clerk, engaged in routine shelf-restocking, attempted to move the overloaded pallet. Plaintiff suffered injuries resulting in a 20% permanent disability. The jury awarded plaintiff damages of $346,276.23.

During closing argument, plaintiff suggested that the jury think about plaintiff's injury in terms of daily pain and suffering, and then determine what amount of damages would be appropriate compensation for each day of suffering. An average daily figure was suggested to the jury, which it could then multiply by the number of days plaintiff would live, counting from the day of the accident until the end of her life expectancy, some thirty-five years. The jury was told to consider the figure only if it found the calculations useful in quantifying plaintiff's damages. Defendant contends that such per diem arguments are unduly prejudicial and should have been disallowed by the trial court. Defendant further contends that if per diem arguments are permissible, the court should give cautionary instructions.

A per diem argument is a tool of persuasion used by counsel to suggest to the jury how it can quantify damages based on the evidence of pain and suffering presented. [Citation.] Other jurisdictions are divided as to whether to allow such arguments. [Citations.] The principal reason advanced against per diem arguments is that a jury's verdict must be based on the evidence before it, and a per diem figure, which is not in evidence, allows the jury to calculate damages based solely on the argument of counsel. [Citation.] Further, courts have reasoned that a per diem argument unfairly assumes that pain is constant, uniform, and continuous, and that the pain will prevail for the rest of plaintiff's life. Therefore, it creates an "illusion of certainty" in a disability that is more likely to be subject to great variation. [Citations.] Finally, some courts conclude that the jury will be too easily misled by the plaintiff's argument. [Citation.]

On the other hand, jurisdictions that have allowed per diem arguments counter that sufficient safeguards exist in the adversarial system to overcome the objections to its use. They point out that a plaintiff's hypothesis on damages, even if presented on a per diem basis, must be reasonable or suffer serious and possibly fatal attack by opposing counsel; further, the notion that pain is constant and uniform may be easily rebutted by reference to the evidence or the jury's own experience. [Citation.] Most importantly, they note that juries are entitled to draw inferences from the evidence before them and that the extent of damages attributable to pain and suffering is a permissible inference.

After review of the arguments and authorities, we are persuaded that there is nothing inherently improper or prejudicial about per diem arguments if they are made under the ordinary supervision and control of the trial court. In cases where claims for pain and suffering are made, juries are forced to equate pain with damages. The jury can benefit by guidance offered by counsel in closing argument as to how they can construct that equation. [Citation.] We permit counsel reasonable latitude in this phase of the trial to summarize the evidence, to persuade the jury to accept or reject a plaintiff's claim, and to award a specific lump sum. If a lump sum is to be suggested to the jury,* it cannot be impermissible to explain how the lump sum was determined. [Citation.]

Nor do we agree with defendant that per diem arguments must be accompanied by specific instructions. Juries are routinely instructed that arguments and suggestions by counsel are not evidence, whether or not a party makes a per diem argument. It may well be that other instructions may be required when per diem arguments are used, but we leave to the trial courts the fashioning of instructions and controls appropriate to the cases before them.

Our holding should not be taken to grant the plaintiff carte blanche to depart from any reasonable view of the evidence. Rather, it reflects our confidence that the defendant's opportunity to refute the plaintiff's closing argument will ensure that an absurd hypothesis will be rejected. Even if it is not, and a verdict is excessive, the trial court has adequate mechanisms, such as remittitur, to deal with it.

---

* Counsel's request that the jury award a lump sum amount is not error per se. [Citations.] Although the lump sum may be more consistent with counsel's hope than with the reality of the evidence, use of a lump sum, like a per diem damages argument, is not reversible error unless shown to be prejudicial.

The question remains as to whether the per diem argument in the present case was improper. In closing argument, plaintiff's counsel told the jury the per diem figure was only a suggestion for its consideration, and that determining a fair amount would be entirely up to the jury. He did not argue that plaintiff's pain was constant, uniform, and easy to quantify on a daily basis. In fact, counsel told the jury that pain fluctuates and that he was only suggesting an average figure for their consideration, and told them to "[d]isregard it if it is not helpful." Defendant had a full opportunity to rebut the per diem argument and did so. We cannot conclude that this argument invaded the province of the jury.

The case was submitted to the jury with appropriate instructions. The trial court cautioned the jury that "the arguments of the attorneys and any statements which they made in their arguments or in their summation is not evidence and will not be considered by you as evidence," and that "it is your recollection of the witness's testimony and not the attorney's statements which shall control you in reaching your decision."

The court made it clear to the jury that the final determination of damages was to be made on the evidence alone and not on persuasive arguments for any particular formulas. That the jury was able to make this distinction between presented evidence and suggested formulas is demonstrated by their arriving at a total damages award $166,194 below the figure suggested by plaintiff's counsel, which figure counsel calculated in part by using the per diem formula. There was no error. * * *

Affirmed.

■ ALLEN, CHIEF JUSTICE, dissenting.

The majority reasons that if a lump sum award may be suggested to a jury, it cannot be impermissible to explain how the lump sum was determined. The difficulty with this rationale, however, is that, until today, it has been improper in Vermont to mention to the jury the lump sum being sought. [Citations.] * * * [T]he amount which the plaintiff hopes to recover is not evidence, proof of the amount due, or a standard for estimating the damages. It is unnecessary here to set forth the various arguments in favor of or against per diem arguments as they have been thoroughly and exhaustively discussed in opinions from virtually every other jurisdiction over the past thirty years. [Citation.] I believe the better answer is to permit counsel to argue to the trier of fact the appropriateness of employing a time-unit calculation technique for fixing damages for pain and suffering, but to prohibit any suggestion by counsel of specific monetary amounts either on a lump sum or time-unit basis. * * *

The ultimate objective should be to aid the jury in determining what sum of money will reasonably compensate the plaintiff for the pain and suffering endured. The attainment of this goal is not enhanced by counsel arguing the dollar amounts that they desire to have a jury return. The fair and practical solution is to permit the jury to hear about the methodology and to apply its dollar amounts from the evidence rather than sums suggested in argument.

I further disagree with the majority in its reluctance to require a specific cautionary instruction, beyond the general language offered that "the arguments of the attorneys and any statements which they made in their arguments or in their summation [are] not in evidence and will not be considered by you as evidence." The instruction approved by the majority may be adequate to deal with remarks of an attorney that are plainly argumentative. The difficulty is that remarks regarding numbers or dollar amounts may not appear to be argument, but rather evidence itself. Hence, an instruction not to consider argument as evidence does not cure the problem.

* * *

The majority relies on the proposition that "[i]n closing argument, plaintiff's counsel told the jury the per diem figure was only a suggestion for its consideration, and that determining a fair amount would be entirely up to the jury." The majority is overly generous. Counsel's remarks are at best ambiguous and come at the beginning of a lengthy and detailed mathematical presentation. That presentation, stated in part, follows:

> What award will it take to tell Grand Union what accountability means and that this is what the people in Bennington County think a human life and human suffering is worth[?] Now, let's just take one element. We have talked about pain and suffering. What would be fair compensation for pain and suffering? *Entirely up to you.* I have a suggestion. If you think about what it is like for Susanne to go through one day with the pain that she has and think about what would be fair compensation for that one day, what do you think it would be? Would it be $100 to go through that in a day? Would it be $75? Would it be $50, $40?
>
> Ladies and gentlemen, we want to be scrupulously fair about our request to you. So I am going to suggest to you that you award Susanne $30 a day for the loss of those three elements: pain and suffering, mental anguish, and loss of enjoyment of life. That is $10 a day for each one. *I put it to you for your consideration to follow that through.*
>
> You would do it this way, there are 365 days a year. I am just going to put here pain and suffering, mental anguish, loss of enjoyment of life. Now there are 365 days in a year. And Susanne's six years she has already suffered in these ways and 29 more, that is 35 years total that she should be compensated for. And if you multiply 35 times 365, there are 12,775 days. And if you multiply that figure by the $30 per day I just suggested, it comes out to $383,250—sorry. $383,250.
>
> Now, another way of thinking of that is if you divide 35 years into this figure of $383,250 it comes out to slightly under $11,000 a year. Maybe that would be a help to think for you $11,000 a year to live the way she lives, to lose what she has lost. *Perhaps that would be a help for you; I don't know.* (Emphasis added.)

The caveats in this argument are nearly invisible, and an additional statement in rebuttal is no better. The residue is a set of specific numbers that are, by the majority's holding, proper, but which at least deserve a specific cautionary instruction. Yet the majority would substitute counsel's at best ambiguous message for a clear instruction from the bench about the use of the numbers.

I would not, and I dissent.

---

1. *Variations on the Per Diem Argument.* Per diem arguments take many forms. In addition to the "pure" per diem argument employed in the principal case, counsel sometimes employ a "job offer" per diem approach. For example, in one famous case, *Faught v. Washam*, 329 S.W.2d 588 (Mo.1959), the plaintiff's counsel had argued:

> "In considering what is an adequate sum for this young man, suppose I was to meet one of you ladies on the street and I say to you, 'I want to offer you a job and I want to tell you a little bit about this job before you say you are going to accept it; one peculiar thing, if you take it you have to keep it for the rest of your life, you work seven days a week, no vacations, work daytime and night. The other thing is, you only get paid $3.00 a day. Here is your job—your job is to suffer Mr. Faught's disability.' " 329 S.W.2d at 602.

The Missouri Supreme Court reversed a jury verdict, ruling that the job offer argument unfairly prejudiced the jury.

Counsel sometimes employ the "golden rule" approach, asking jurors to award damages in an amount they would want for their own suffering or its avoidance. For example, the following argument was not permitted in New Jersey in *Henker v. Preybylowski*, 216 N.J.Super. 513, 524 A.2d 455 (1987):

> Remember the wisdom tooth, a little canker sore in your mouth. You can't get rid of it. You may take Tylenol. Or take a fractured tooth, finger, a cut, a burn. What is pain worth for one hour? You've gone to doctors and dentists. An anesthesiologist, you know how much he charges just to limit or prevent pain during the course of an operation. You know how much a dentist charges to give a shot of Novocain so you don't feel pain for ten, fifteen minutes. How much is that pain worth for one hour? When you get that hour, think about the thousands of hours that Ken Henker has suffered pain just the last three years ... The jury is going to tell how much is owed him for that pain, thousands of hours in the past and thousand of hours in the future. 524 A.2d at 458.

2. *Arguments Against Per Diem Arguments.* The majority in the principal case highlighted some of the reasons courts have prohibited per diem arguments. The arguments usually advanced in support of prohibiting per diem arguments include the following:

- The attorney is giving impermissible testimony by suggesting a formula for pain and suffering;

- The suggestion of a formula produces an illusion of certainty and discourages reasonable and practical consideration;
- The formula has no evidentiary basis;
- Juries are misled and deceived by the effect of multiplication; and
- Defense counsel is placed in a very difficult position following such an argument.

What are the most persuasive arguments for prohibiting per diem arguments? Are there other reasons that per diem arguments should not be allowed? Are per diem arguments fundamentally unfair? Why?

3. *Arguments in Favor of Per Diem Arguments.* The majority in the principal case ultimately concluded that per diem arguments are not inherently prejudicial and, instead, offer juries guidance as to how they can translate pain into monetary damages. In addition to advancing this reason in support of allowing per diem arguments, supporters commonly offer the following points to rebut arguments against per diem arguments:

- The judge can explain to the jury the difference between evidence and argument;
- Jury instructions counsel the jury that arguments of counsel are not evidence and guide the jury to estimate the proper amount based upon the evidence; and
- Defense attorneys can anticipate per diem arguments and be prepared to counter them.

Do other reasons support permitting per diem arguments? Is a jury any more likely to return an unreasonable award after hearing a per diem argument than in the absence of a per diem argument? Consider the comments of Kansas Supreme Court Justice Wertz in dissent from the court's decision in *Caylor v. Atchison*, T. & S.F. Ry., 190 Kan. 261, 374 P.2d 53 (1962). to prohibit per diem arguments:

> I consider it a fair argument and rational approach to treat damages for pain in the way it is endured—month by month—year by year. The concept of totality pronounced by the majority opinion has no counterpart in the world of human affairs. Society recognizes "the day" as a basic unit of humanity. We rise in the morning and go to bed at night, and our institutions function accordingly. No judge's salary is computed or paid in a lifetime lump and there are no lifetime meals, no lifetime drinks, no lifetime haircuts, nor anything else; nor has any living human being ever lived a lifetime of pain in the whole. Pain is lived by the hour and the day and is ticked off the same clock that sends one to work in the morning and home at night.
>
> Although the jurors will eat their daily meals and live their daily lives, they must now think of pain and suffering as a lifetime lump. Such a coerced concept will have no more meaning than lifetime rent, lifetime shoes, or lifetime meals. This court's logic would now force jurors to value steak by the herd, cars by the fleet, and pain by the life. Forcing

jurors to think in a language they never heard cannot be designed or expected to produce just results. 374 P.2d at 64.

The Kansas Supreme Court eventually reversed *Caylor*, expressly adopting Justice Wentz' dissent, in *Wilson v. Williams*, 261 Kan. 703, 933 P.2d 757 (1997).

4. *Lump Sum Arguments.* Many jurisdictions permit counsel to suggest a total lump sum to compensate for pain and suffering even if the jurisdictions prohibit per diem arguments. *See, e.g.,* Caley v. Manicke, 24 Ill.2d 390, 182 N.E.2d 206 (1962) (Although it is permissible for counsel to suggest to the jury a total sum to compensate for pain and suffering, it is improper to suggest a mathematical formula, such as an award of a specific sum per day, to calculate those damages.) *but see* Botta v. Brunner, 26 N.J. 82, 138 A.2d 713 (1958) (improper to suggest either formula to calculate pain and suffering or amount that would be reasonable compensation for pain and suffering). The distinction between lump sump arguments and per diem arguments becomes blurred when counsel suggests a lump sum for a specific period of time (e.g., We think $4,000 is a fair amount for 40 days in the hospital). Nonetheless, some courts have rejected challenges to these types of arguments. *See, e.g.,* Graeff v. Baptist Temple of Springfield, 576 S.W.2d 291 (Mo.1978) (counsel's suggestion of a lump sum for specific periods of hospitalization, the period of time from injury to trial and future life expectancy was not an impermissible per diem argument).

5. *Expert Testimony.* How can plaintiffs prove the value of their pain and suffering? Should plaintiffs be permitted to introduce expert testimony to assign value to such noneconomic losses? Some plaintiffs have sought to introduce economists to testify as to the amount of damages they sustained as a result of their loss of enjoyment of life. These economists typically employ a "willingness-to-pay" method of valuation. The method measures the value of human life and the value of the loss of enjoyment of life by examining what people pay to avoid loss of life. For example, the economist examines what amount individuals will pay for safety devices such as smoke detectors and airbags; what amount individuals accept as payment for high-risk employment; and the willingness of governments to regulate with respect to safety features.

Most courts have rejected willingness-to-pay estimates. *See, e.g.,* Mercado v. Ahmed, 974 F.2d 863 (7th Cir.1992); Livingston v. United States, 817 F.Supp. 601 (E.D.N.C.1993); Anderson v. Nebraska Dep't of Social Serv., 248 Neb. 651, 538 N.W.2d 732 (1995); Scharrel v. Wal–Mart Stores, Inc., 949 P.2d 89 (Colo.App.Ct.1997). These courts note that the willingness-to-pay estimates estimate the anonymous value of a statistical life rather than the loss of enjoyment of life suffered by a specific plaintiff. Additionally, the estimates fail to account for factors other than risk reduction that often play an important role in decisions regarding consumer purchasing, employment and governmental regulation. *See* Scharrel, 949 P.2d at 92.

6. *Remittitur and Additur.* Most jurisdictions provide for judicial review of damage awards, including awards for noneconomic losses like

pain and suffering. Because the amount of a damage award is an issue of fact peculiarly within the province of the jury, however, most jurisdictions provide only deferential review, allowing a reviewing court to disturb a jury verdict only when it is "excessive," or "shocks the judicial conscience" or "is obviously the result of passion or prejudice." *See, e.g.,* Kimberlin v. DeLong, 637 N.E.2d 121, 129 (Ind.1994) (the award "must appear to be so outrageous as to impress the Court at 'first blush' with its enormity"); Coulthard v. Cossairt, 803 P.2d 86, 92 (Wyo.1990) ("jury's determination of the amount of damages is inviolate absent an award so excessive or inadequate as to shock the judicial conscience and to raise an irresistible inference that passion, prejudice, or other improper cause had invaded the trial"); DeWitt v. Schuhbauer, 287 Minn. 279, 177 N.W.2d 790 (1970) (test for setting aside a verdict as excessive by the trial court is whether it shocks the conscience)

If the reviewing court determines that a jury award is excessive, it generally does not set aside the entire verdict. Instead, the court sets aside only that portion of the verdict which the court concludes is excessive. In many jurisdictions, the plaintiff then has the option of accepting the remitted verdict or seeking a new trial on damages. *See, e.g.,* Spence v. Maurice H. Hilliard, Jr. P.C., 260 Ga. 107, 389 S.E.2d 753 (1990) (statute codifying additur and remittitur did not give the court the right to reduce a jury's damage award without granting the parties the option of a new trial). Because the amount of damages is an issue of fact, the Seventh Amendment mandates that federal courts give plaintiffs the option of seeking a new trial in lieu of consenting to a remittitur. *See* Hetzel v. Prince William County, 523 U.S. 208, 118 S.Ct. 1210, 140 L.Ed.2d 336 (1998) (ordering district court to enter judgment for amount lesser than jury verdict violated plaintiff's Seventh Amendment right to a jury trial).

A plaintiff also may seek review of a damage award if the plaintiff believes that a jury verdict is inadequate. Generally, a reviewing court will consider a jury award to be inadequate only if the verdict fails to include an element of damage that was specifically proven in an uncontroverted amount or if, viewing the evidence in the light most favorable to the defendant, the verdict fails to award the plaintiff a substantial amount of compensation for pain and suffering. *See, e.g.,* Hewett v. Frye, 184 W.Va. 477, 401 S.E.2d 222 (1990); *see also* Maddox v. Muirhead, 738 So.2d 742 (Miss.1999) ("Additurs represent a judicial incursion into the traditional habitat of the jury, and therefore should never be employed without great caution."). If a court determines an award is inadequate, the court orders an additur, increasing the verdict by the amount necessary to render an adequate verdict.

7. *Objective or Subjective Standard.* Should a pain and suffering award be only for pain that any person would feel, or should it reflect this particular plaintiff's pain? Some individuals have a higher or lower threshold for pain than most people. Consider also phantom pain. In *Jarrell v. Fort Worth Steel & Mfg. Co.*, 666 S.W.2d 828 (Mo.App.1984), a man lost his right arm to an ice conveyor. In the violent accident the machine totally

and traumatically tore off the arm and part of the back at the shoulder. He later suffered phantom limb pain at the stump, in addition to other emotional disorders from the trauma.

PROBLEM: BABY ALISSA AND THE CONFUSED DOCTOR

Jim and Anna Pegman were expecting their first child to be born on August 6, but the due date passed uneventfully. The obstetrician explained that first babies are often late and assured them that all was normal. When the baby was eleven days late, Anna Pegman awoke with excruciating pain. Her husband rushed her to the hospital, but she was sent home again after examination by the physician in charge, Dr. Hill. Although the nurse had attached a fetal monitor and the instrument recorded a heartbeat indicating infant distress, Dr. Hill did not undertake the necessary surgical delivery. The reason the patient was sent home instead was that Dr. Hill, a medical resident, did not know how to read the fetal monitor and was too embarrassed to call the supervising physician or to make an inquiry of the experienced nurse.

When Anna Pegman delivered by normal birth the next day, a baby girl named Alissa was born. Baby Alissa was not normal, however. The failure to deliver her the preceding day caused brain damage from insufficient oxygen. Assume that there is a finding of fact that this deprivation of oxygen caused Anna to have cerebral palsy, although medical experts provided conflicting testimony on this causation issue. She is expected to live a normal life span as a severely retarded and partially paralyzed person who will suffer constant physical discomfort. Experts testify that she will never be able to walk, talk, or feed herself, nor will she gain bladder and bowel control. Otherwise she will grow to normal adult size.

By the time of the malpractice trial on these facts, Alissa is three. She is unable to lift her head, turn herself over, or lift a bottle. She requires special chairs, special swings, and special toys. Assuming liability is established, how should damages be measured? Should Alissa's parents be able to recover for the loss of Alissa's companionship and society? What about parental recovery for the household services Alissa would have performed for them? Consider the next case and the notes that follow.

White Construction Co. v. Dupont

430 So.2d 915 (Fla.App.1983), *modified on other grounds* 455 So.2d 1026 (1984).

■ ERVIN, JUDGE.

Appellants, White Construction Company, Inc. (White) and Limerock Industries, Inc. (Limerock) appeal a jury verdict awarding $5,550,000.00 in compensatory and punitive damages to appellees, Nathaniel and Janey Dupont, in an action for personal injuries and loss of consortium. Of the five points raised on appeal, we find merit only with point two, challenging the award of $1,025,000.00 to Janey Dupont, Nathaniel's wife, for loss of consortium as excessive. * * *

The record discloses that Nathaniel Dupont, a 55 year old independent truck owner/operator, arrived at Limerock's mine on September 13, 1977 to pick up a load of rock. Dupont parked his four-axle tractor-trailer, with the motor running, to wait his turn for loading, and he stepped out of the cab and went between the trailer and the cab for the purpose of cleaning the cab. A Limerock employee, driving a CAT 988 loader, weighing some forty tons and standing approximately 22 feet high, proceeded to *back* the loader around a large pile of limerock toward Dupont's trailer. As the loader, proceeding at top speed, approached Dupont's trailer, the driver looked back, and realizing he was going to hit the trailer, shouted a warning to Dupont. The loader struck the back end of the trailer and the impact apparently caused its gear to pop into forward position, forcing the trailer to advance about one and half times its length, and in the process to roll over Dupont, who in turn suffered permanent disability as a result of his injuries.

Dupont brought an action against Limerock, the corporation that owns the mine, and White, the corporation that owns the loader which was then leased to Limerock, seeking compensatory and punitive damages for his personal injuries. Janey Dupont joined in the action, seeking damages for her loss of consortium. The jury returned a verdict in favor of the Duponts for the following damages: $1,025,000.00 in compensatory damaged to Nathaniel Dupont, $1,025,000.00 in damages to Janey Dupont for loss of consortium, $2,000,000.00 in punitive damages against Limerock, and $1,500,000.00 in punitive damages against White.

Appellants contend that the award of $1,025,000.00 for loss of consortium must be reversed as excessive because the jury could only have arrived at that figure through motivations of passion or prejudice, or because the award amounts to a double recovery of damages properly awarded to Mr. Dupont. Although we find nothing in the record substantiating the former argument, we find that the record supports appellants' claim of double recovery, requiring that the award be reversed. * * *

Before 1971 a wife could not maintain an action for loss of consortium in Florida when her husband was injured due to the negligent or intentional acts of another. In *Gates v. Foley,* 247 So.2d 40 (Fla.1971), the Florida Supreme Court, rejecting precedent and the common law rule, elected to follow the trend in other jurisdictions by recognizing that a wife is entitled to recover for loss of consortium in the same manner as her husband if she were injured. [Citations.]

An action for loss of consortium is, of course, a derivative action and the jury must first find that the husband has sustained compensable injuries at the hands of another before the wife's action may be considered. If that threshold is met, the wife must then "present competent testimony concerning the impact which the accident had on the marital relationship and, more specifically, evidence concerning her loss of consortium." [Citation.] Upon such a showing, the wife is thus entitled to, at the very minimum, nominal damages. [Citations.]

We are not confronted with a situation in which only nominal damages were awarded, but rather with an award which appellants contend is excessive and amounts to a double recovery. In Florida, because the types of losses which the spouse may recover have not been clearly defined, the potential danger of a double recovery is always lurking. One commentator has observed that "[t]he concept of 'consortium' embraces two contrasting types of elements. The *tangible* elements include support and services provided by the other spouse, while *intangible* elements encompass such items as love, companionship, affection, society, sexual relations, comfort, and solace." [Citation.] In Florida, there is no question that recovery may be had for the intangible elements of loss of consortium, which, as defined by *Gates,* consist of

> the companionship and fellowship of husband and wife and the right of each to the company, cooperation and aid of the other in every conjugal relation. Consortium means much more than mere sexual relation and consists, also, of that affection, solace, comfort, companionship, conjugal life, fellowship, society and assistance so necessary to a successful marriage.

247 So.2d at 43. Contrasted against these elements, *Gates* forbids, however, recovery by the wife for the tangible loss of "support or earnings which the husband might recover in his own right." The law of consortium in Florida is less clear as to the wife's right to recover for "services" which the husband is no longer able to perform.

In an earlier decision addressing the issue of what services the jury may consider in an action for wrongful death and loss of consortium brought by a husband after the death of his wife, it was held that the composition of this element includes the

> pecuniary value of services which the husband might reasonably expect to have received from the deceased wife if she had not been killed, less maintenance costs, of course; this includes the value of such services as the wife was accustomed to perform in the household and which will have to be replaced by hiring services; services ordinarily performed by the deceased wife in the care and moral training of the minor children in the household; and any special service which the wife was accustomed to perform for the husband in the household, and in his business without compensation, which will have to be replaced by hired services.

Lithgow v. Hamilton, 69 So.2d 776, 778 (Fla.1954). Because the plaintiff in *Lithgow* was able to substantiate the actual cost of obtaining the services of a "combination housekeeper-governess-counsellor", the award of damages, including those for loss of services, was affirmed.

* * * *

In this case we find that there was insufficient evidence to justify the $1,025,000.00 award for loss of consortium. Although Mrs. Dupont has undoubtedly suffered a loss of the intangible elements of consortium as defined in *Gates,* that loss alone cannot explain or justify an award of this magnitude. Nor can the award be sustained on the theory of loss of services, since the only evidence to support such loss consists of Mrs. Dupont's statement that her husband was no longer able to help her with routine household chores. Because no evidence was presented as to the reasonable value of such services or to show that it was necessary to hire someone else to perform such services, the award may not be justified on the basis of such unsubstantiated, non-pecuniary loss.

Our review of the record causes us to conclude that the jury's award does in fact amount to a double recovery of the sums included in the jury's verdict of damages to the husband. Mrs. Dupont was allowed to testify at length concerning financial losses incurred by her husband's trucking business since the accident and the fact that she had been forced to take a more active role in the operation of that business as a result of her husband's injuries. Because any losses relating to the business were properly recoverable by Mr. Dupont, his wife's testimony as to such losses could only have served to confuse the jury as to the proper measure of damages in considering her claim for loss of consortium. Because we find insufficient evidence in the record to support the award of $1,025,000.00 for loss of consortium, we reverse the trial court's judgment as to that award only.

Accordingly, we reverse in part, affirm in part, and remand this cause for purposes of a new trial on the issue only of Mrs. Dupont's damages for loss of consortium.

---

1. *Origins of the Claim.* Loss of consortium was historically a claim held only by men for injuries to wives. As the principal case indicates, the modern approach allows claims by women for injuries to their husbands. *See* Annot. 36 A.L.R.3d 900.

The first change occurred with the passage of the Married Women's Acts. Courts then allowed a wife to recover for loss of consortium when her husband was intentionally injured by third parties. The major case to establish the claim for negligent injuries was not until 1950. Hitaffer v. Argonne Co., 183 F.2d 811 (D.C.Cir.1950), *cert. denied,* 340 U.S. 852, 71 S.Ct. 80, 95 L.Ed. 624 (1950). In the decades since then, especially the 1970s, virtually all jurisdictions recognized the claim of the wife as identical to the claim of the husband.

2. *Filial and Parental Consortium.* Some jurisdictions have expanded loss of consortium claims beyond the spousal relationship. Should a child recover for loss of society with an injured parent? What if the child is an adult child? Should a parent recover for the loss of society with an injured child? Should a stepparent or grandparent be permitted to recover for loss of society with an injured child?

Jurisdictions disagree over the scope of loss of consortium claims. *Compare* Lee v. Colorado Dep't of Health, 718 P.2d 221 (Colo.1986) (Colorado does not recognize a child's right to recover consortium damages for loss of an injured parent's society) *with* Reagan v. Vaughn, 804 S.W.2d 463 (Tex.1990) (child may recover for loss of consortium of seriously injured parent); Elgin v. Bartlett, 994 P.2d 411 (Colo.1999) (refusing to recognize a parent's claim for loss of filial consortium of injured child) *with* United States v. Dempsey, 635 So.2d 961 (Fla.1994) (parents may recover for loss of child's filial consortium as a result of significant injury); Estate of Wells v. Mount Sinai Medical Center, 183 Wis.2d 667, 515 N.W.2d 705 (1994) (allowing parents to recover for loss of consortium of minor child but refusing to extend recovery to loss of consortium of adult child) *with* Masaki v. General Motors Corp., 71 Haw. 1, 780 P.2d 566 (1989) (parents can maintain an action for loss of consortium of a severely injured adult child); Fernandez v. Walgreen Hastings Co., 126 N.M. 263, 968 P.2d 774 (1998) (recognizing a grandparent's right to recover for loss of consortium due to death or serious injury of minor child) *with* Hutchinson v. Broadlawns Medical Center, 459 N.W.2d 273 (Iowa 1990) (rejecting granddaughter's claim for loss of consortium of grandfather).

3. *Excessiveness.* There is no easy test for the excessiveness of consortium awards, as with other intangible losses. One common test is whether the amount "shocks" the court. *See, e.g.,* Jackson v. Magnolia Brokerage Co., 742 F.2d 1305 (11th Cir.1984); Clissold v. St. Louis S.F.R., 600 F.2d 35 (6th Cir.1979).

An award generally should be in some reasonable proportion to the damages of the injured spouse, but there is no fixed rule. In *General Electric Co. v. Bush,* for example, a wife was awarded half a million dollars for loss of consortium with her husband after a mining accident. The husband was awarded over three million dollars for his injuries, and there was evidence that the accident had left him "among the living dead." 88 Nev. 360, 498 P.2d 366 (1972).

D. DAMAGES FOR INJURIES RESULTING IN DEATH

Section Coverage:

Wrongful death and survival actions are almost exclusively statutory actions with limited damages. There is little agreement among jurisdictions on appropriate damages when a tortfeasor's conduct results in death rather than personal injury short of death.

Two old common law rules with little justification explain modern developments. First, the death of a person was not considered an actionable injury. Second, personal tort actions died with the plaintiff. The result of these rules was harsh for dependents who consequently had no claim for the tortious death of a family member. In modern law these rules have been changed, usually by statutes. The odd patchwork of current law is attributable to this history.

Most state legislatures now have provided Survival Acts that allow the decedent's estate to bring at least some tort actions. Many jurisdictions allow the victim's personal injury claims to survive under these acts. The orientation of these actions is upon the decedent's losses rather than upon the family's losses. The estate recovers the damages and distribution is by will or intestacy.

Many state and federal statutes provide for wrongful death actions in addition to or as an alternative to the survival of personal injury claims. A typical Wrongful Death Act names specific beneficiaries with some relationship to the decedent who may sue and limits the types of recoverable damages, such as to "pecuniary" losses sustained by the statutory beneficiaries. Jurisdictions with both a Survival Act and a Wrongful Death Act allow both actions and use rules such as collateral estoppel to avoid double recovery by family members.

Model Case:

A speeding motorist negligently injured and killed a young child on a bicycle. In some jurisdictions the child's estate has a cause of action against the motorist. In other jurisdictions the wrongful death act would name close relatives, such as the child's parents, who could sue the motorist for the loss of the family member.

Damages in the survival or wrongful death actions vary by jurisdiction. Some or all of the following elements may be permitted: loss of future income, loss of child's services in minority and support of parents in their elderly years, the child's pain and suffering before death, medical expenses, funeral expenses, loss of society with the child, and parents' grief.

Moragne v. States Marine Lines, Inc.

398 U.S. 375, 90 S.Ct. 1772, 26 L.Ed.2d 339 (1970).

■ MR. JUSTICE HARLAN delivered the opinion of the Court.

We brought this case here to consider whether *The Harrisburg,* 119 U.S. 199, 7 S.Ct. 140 30 L.Ed. 358, in which this Court held in 1886 that maritime law does not afford a cause of action for wrongful death, should any longer be regarded as acceptable law.

The complaint sets forth that Edward Moragne, a longshoreman, was killed while working aboard the vessel *Palmetto State* in navigable waters within the State of Florida. Petitioner, as his widow and representative of his estate, brought this suit in a state court against respondent States Marine Lines, Inc., the owner of the vessel, to recover damages for wrongful death and for the pain and suffering experienced by the decedent prior to his death. The claims were predicated upon both negligence and the unseaworthiness of the vessel.

States Marine removed the case to the Federal District Court for the Middle District of Florida on the basis of diversity of citizenship, *see* 28 U.S.C. 133, 1441, and there filed a third-party complaint against respondent Gulf Florida Terminal Company, the decedent's employer, asserting that Gulf had contracted to perform stevedoring services on the vessel in a workmanlike manner and that any negligence or unseaworthiness causing the accident resulted from Gulf's operations.

Both States Marine and Gulf sought dismissal of the portion of petitioner's complaint that requested damages for wrongful death on the basis of unseaworthiness. They contended that maritime law provided no recovery for wrongful death within a State's territorial waters. * * *

* * * We granted certiorari * * * to reconsider the important question of remedies under federal maritime law for tortious deaths on state territorial waters.

* * *

The first explicit statement of the common-law rule against recovery for wrongful death came in the opinion of Lord Ellenborough, sitting at *nisi prius,* in *Baker v. Bolton,* 1 Camp. 493, 170 Eng.Rep. 1033 (1808). That opinion did not cite authority, or give supporting reasoning, or refer to the felony-merger doctrine in announcing that "[i]n a Civil court, the death of a human being could not be complained of as an injury."

* * * [D]espite some early cases in which the rule was rejected as "incapable of vindication," [citations], American courts generally adopted the English rule as the common law of this country as well. Throughout the period of this adoption, * * * the courts failed to produce any satisfactory justification for applying the rule in this country.

Some courts explained that their holdings were prompted by an asserted difficulty in computation of damages for wrongful death or by a "repugnance * * * to setting a price upon human life." [Citations.] However, other courts have recognized that calculation of the loss sustained by dependents or by the estate of the deceased * * * does not present difficulties more insurmountable than assessment of damages for many nonfatal personal injuries. * * *

We need not, however, pronounce a verdict on whether *The Harrisburg,* when decided, was a correct extrapolation of the principles of decisional law then in existence. A development of major significance has intervened, making clear that the rule against recovery for wrongful death is sharply out of keeping with the policies of modern American maritime law. This development is the wholesale abandonment of the rule in most of the areas where it once held sway, quite evidently prompted by the same sense of the rule's injustice that generated so much criticism of its original promulgation.

* * * [L]egislatures both here and in England began to evidence unanimous disapproval of the rule against recovery for wrongful death. The first statute partially abrogating the rule was Lord Campbell's Act, 9 & 10 Vict., c. 93 (1846), which granted recovery to the families of persons killed by tortious conduct, "although the Death shall have been caused under such Circumstances as amount in Law to Felony."

In the United States, every State today had enacted a wrongful-death statute. [Citation.] The Congress has created actions for wrongful deaths of railroad employees, Federal Employers' Liability Act, 45 U.S.C. 51–59; of merchant seamen, Jones Act, 46 U.S.C. 688; and of persons on the high seas, Death on the High Seas Act, 46 U.S.C. 761, 762. Congress has also, in the Federal Tort Claims Act, 28 U.S.C. 1346(b), made the United States subject to liability in certain circumstances for negligently caused wrongful death to the same extent as a private person. [Citation.]

These numerous and broadly applicable statutes, taken as a whole, make it clear that there is no present public policy against allowing recovery for wrongful death. The statutes evidence a wide rejection by the legislatures of whatever justifications may once have existed for a general refusal to allow such recovery. This legislative establishment of policy carries significance beyond the particular scope of each of the statutes involved. The policy thus established has become itself a part of our law, to be given its appropriate weight not only in matters of statutory construction but also in those of decisional law. * * *

Respondents argue that overruling *The Harrisburg* will necessitate a long course of decisions to spell out the elements of the new "cause of action." We believe these fears are exaggerated, because our decision does not require the fashioning of a whole new body of federal law, but merely removes a bar to access to the existing general maritime law. In most respects the law applied in personal-injury cases will answer all questions that arise in death cases.

Respondents argue, for example, that a statute of limitations must be devised or "borrowed" for the new wrongful-death claim. However, petitioner and the United States respond that since we have simply removed the barrier to general maritime actions for fatal injuries, there is no reason in federal admiralty suits at least that such actions should not share the doctrine of laches immemorially applied to admiralty claims. * * *

The one aspect of a claim for wrongful death that has no precise counterpart in the established law governing nonfatal injuries is the determination of the beneficiaries who are entitled to recover. General maritime law, which denied any recovery for wrongful death, found no need to specify which dependents should receive such recovery. * * *

We do not determine this issue now, for we think its final resolution should await further sifting through the lower courts in future litigation. For present purposes we conclude only that its existence affords no sufficient reason for not coming to grips with *The Harrisburg*. If still other subsidiary issues should require resolution, such as particular questions of the measure of damages, the courts will not be without persuasive analogy for guidance. Both the Death on the High Seas Act and the numerous state wrongful-death acts have been implemented with success for decades. The experience thus built up counsels that a suit for wrongful death raises no problems unlike those that have long been grist for the judicial mill.

* * *

We accordingly overrule *The Harrisburg,* and hold that an action does lie under general maritime law for death caused by violation of maritime duties. * * *

Reversed and remanded.

----

1. *Historical Origins.* As the principal case explains, at common law "the death of a human being could not be complained of as an injury." This common law rule originated as a comment by Lord Ellenborough in *Baker v. Bolton*, 1 Camp. 493, 170 Eng. Rep. 1033 (1808). For the most part, legislatures rather than courts acted to abrogate this common law rule. Beginning in 1846 with the British Parliament's enactment of Lord Campbell's Act, legislatures worked to ameliorate the harsh effects of the common law rule by creating statutory rights to recovery for wrongful death. As a result, most claims for damages arising from negligence resulting in death are governed by statute. In this respect, *Moragne* is highly unusual in that the Supreme Court created a common law claim for wrongful death in admiralty.

CALIFORNIA CODE OF CIVIL PROCEDURE

§ 377.20   Cause of action survives; limitations; loss or damage simultaneous with death

(a) Except as otherwise provided by statute, a cause of action for or against a person is not lost by reason of the person's death, but survives subject to the applicable limitations period.

* * *

§ 377.30   Surviving cause of action; person to whom passes; commencement of action

A cause of action that survives the death of the person entitled to commence an action or proceeding passes to the decedent's successor in interest * * * and an action may be commenced by the decedent's personal representative or, if none, by the decedent's successor in interest.

§ 377.34   Damages recoverable

In an action or proceeding by a decedent's personal representative or successor in interest on the decedent's cause of action, the damages recoverable are limited to the loss or damage that the decedent sustained or incurred before death, including any penalties or punitive or exemplary damages that the decedent would have been entitled to recover had the decedent lived, and do not include damages for pain, suffering, or disfigurement.

§ 377.60   Persons with standing

A cause of action for the death of a person caused by the wrongful act or neglect of another may be asserted by any of the following persons or by the decedent's personal representative on their behalf:

(a) The decedent's surviving spouse, domestic partner, children, and issue of deceased children, or, if there is no surviving issue of the decedent, the persons, including the surviving spouse or domestic partner, who would be entitled to the property of the decedent by intestate succession.

* * *

§ 377.61   Damages recoverable

In an action under this article, damages may be awarded that, under all the circumstances of the case, may be just, but may not include damages recoverable under Section 377.34. The court shall determine the respective rights in an award of the persons entitled to assert the cause of action.

----

1. *Two Claims.* Negligence resulting in death gives rise to two types of claims—survival claims and wrongful death claims. Survival act claims are merely the claims the decedent would have prosecuted in a personal injury action had the decedent survived. Survival damages compensate the decedent's estate for the damages the decedent suffered as a result of the tortious conduct between the time of the tortious conduct and the time of the decedent's death. Wrongful death claims are the claims of the decedent's beneficiaries. Wrongful death damages compensate the decedent's beneficiaries for the losses that the beneficiaries suffer as a result of the decedent's death.

Most states permit recovery of both of these types of damages. Some states, like California, have enacted two different statutory provisions—a "survival act" and a "wrongful death act." The two statutes create two distinct causes of action for survival damages and wrongful death damages. Other states have enacted one statute which is a hybrid statute providing for recovery of survival damages and wrongful death damages in a single action.

2. *Beneficiaries.* Wrongful death acts generally name the decedent's next of kin, heirs at law, or spouse, parent or child as the beneficiaries of the wrongful death action. Interpreting these family terms sometimes can be problematic. For example, are adopted children or stepchildren beneficiaries to actions seeking damages for the wrongful death of their adoptive parents or stepparents? What about grandchildren? Should an illegitimate child be a beneficiary to an action seeking damages for the wrongful death of her natural mother? Natural father? Should the natural father be a beneficiary to an action seeking damages for the wrongful death of his illegitimate child?

Jurisdictions have taken varied approaches. *See, e.g.,* Otero v. City of Albuquerque, 125 N.M. 770, 965 P.2d 354 (App.1998) (stepchild must show that he was formally or legally adopted to recover under New Mexico wrongful death statute); Osborne v. Martin, 2000 WL 235144 (Tex.App.Ct. 2000) (unpublished opinion holding that grandchildren are not considered children under the Texas wrongful death statute); Jenkins v. Mangano Corp., 774 So.2d 101 (La.2000) (an illegitimate child must prove that the deceased parent acknowledged the child during his lifetime to maintain a wrongful death and survival action); In the Matter of the Estate of Patterson, 798 So.2d 347 (Miss.2001) (father of illegitimate child was not a wrongful death beneficiary because he failed to openly acknowledge the child during the child's lifetime and failed to support the child); Guard v. Jackson, 132 Wash.2d 660, 940 P.2d 642 (1997) (statute requiring father of an illegitimate child to prove that he contributed regularly to the financial support of the child before recovering in a wrongful death action violated the state Equal Rights Amendment).

3. *Unborn Children.* Should parents or other heirs be permitted to bring an action seeking damages for the wrongful death of an unborn child? Jurisdictions differ. *Compare* Shelton v. DeWitte, 271 Kan. 831, 26 P.3d 650 (2001) (as sole heirs at law, grandparents were entitled to maintain an action for the wrongful death of their deceased daughter's unborn viable fetus); *with* Giardina v. Bennett, 111 N.J. 412, 545 A.2d 139 (1988) (New Jersey Wrongful Death Act does not permit recovery for damages attributable to the wrongful death of a fetus).

4. *Allocation.* When states recognize distinct survival act claims and wrongful death act claims, allocation of damages between the two claims can become important. Generally, all survival acts award damages to the decedent's estate. The damages then get distributed pursuant to the testamentary plan the decedent left in place. Wrongful death acts, however, may provide a different method of distribution. Wrongful death acts provide for distribution of damages to an enumerated group of beneficiaries. This class of beneficiaries may be different from the takers under the decedent's testamentary plan. For example, the California wrongful death act provides that damages should be distributed to the decedent's surviving spouse, children and issue of any deceased children or, if the decedent has no surviving children, those who would take decedent's property if decedent died intestate. Thus, if the decedent dies leaving a will that distributes property differently than the statutory method of intestate succession, allocation of damages will be important to the competing claimants. Likewise, allocation may be important when the statute of limitations has run on only one claim or when no beneficiaries are alive to sue under the wrongful death act.

Jurisdictions disagree over the proper allocation of some potentially duplicitous damages. For example, jurisdictions vary as to whether the decedent's estate recovers for lost future earning capacity or whether the wrongful death beneficiaries recover for lost financial support.

5. *Damages.* What losses do family members suffer when a fellow family member is killed as a result of a third party's negligence? Which of those losses should be compensable? How should the value of those losses be measured? Consider the following case and notes.

Jordan v. Baptist Three Rivers Hospital

984 S.W.2d 593 (Tenn.1999).

■ Holder, J.

We granted this appeal to determine whether spousal and parental consortium losses should be permissible in wrongful death actions. Tennessee law previously permitted the anomalous result of allowing spousal consortium losses in personal injury cases but not in cases of wrongful death. Upon review of the modern trend of authority and careful scrutiny of our statutory scheme, we hold that loss of consortium claims should not be limited to personal injury suits. We hold that the pecuniary value of a deceased's life includes the element of damages commonly referred to as loss of consortium.

* * * [The estate of decedent Mary Sue Douglas and her surviving adult child sued the defendant doctors for medical malpractice.] The plaintiff's complaint sought damages for loss of consortium and for the decedent's loss of enjoyment of life or hedonic damages. The defendants filed a motion to strike and a motion for judgment on the pleadings asserting that Tennessee law does not permit recovery for loss of parental consortium and for hedonic damages.

* * * We granted appeal to determine whether claims for loss of spousal and parental consortium in wrongful death cases are viable in Tennessee under Tenn.Code Ann. § 20–5–113.[2] We express no opinion as to whether the loss of parental consortium may be recovered in personal injury actions in which the parent or parents survive. That issue will be addressed in an appropriate case.

A wrongful death cause of action did not exist at common law. [Citation.] Pursuant to the common law, actions for personal injuries that resulted in death terminated at the victim's death because "in a civil court the death of a human being could not be complained of as an injury." [Citation.] "The [legal] result was that it was cheaper for the defendant to kill the plaintiff than to injure him, and that the most grievous of all injuries left the bereaved family of the victim ... without a remedy." [Citation.] This rule of non-liability for wrongful death was previously the prevailing view in both England and in the United States. [Citations.]

In 1846, the British Parliament enacted a wrongful death statute designed to abrogate the common law rule's harsh effect of denying recovery for personal injuries resulting in death. The English statute was

---

2. This Court has previously held that claims for hedonic damages are not viable in Tennessee in wrongful death cases. [Citation.]

referred to as "Lord Campbell's Act" and created a cause of action for designated survivors that accrued upon the tort victim's death. [Citations.]

Jurisdictions in the United States were quick to follow England's lead. [Citation.] In 1847, New York became the first American jurisdiction to enact a wrongful death statute. [Citation.] Presently, every jurisdiction in the United States has a wrongful death statute. [Citations.] These statutes, including that of Tennessee, embody the substantive provisions of Lord Campbell's Act and permit designated beneficiaries to recover losses sustained as a result of the tort victim's death. * * *

After more than a century of piecemeal revision by the legislature and interpretation by the courts, Tennessee's modern wrongful death law has taken shape. [Citation.] Specifically, Tenn.Code Ann. § 20–5–102 * * * provides that

> [n]o civil action commenced, whether founded on wrongs or contracts, except actions for wrongs affecting the character of the plaintiff, shall abate by the death of either party ...; nor shall any right of action arising hereafter based on the wrongful act or omission of another, except actions for wrongs affecting the character, be abated by the death of the party wronged; but the right of action shall pass in like manner as [described in Tenn.Code Ann. § 20–5–106].

Moreover, Tenn. Code Ann. § 20–5–106 * * * provides in part:

> The right of action which a person, who dies from injuries received from another, or whose death is caused by the wrongful act, omission, or killing by another, would have had against the wrongdoer, in case death had not been ensued, shall not abate or be extinguished by the person's death but shall pass to the person's surviving spouse and, in case there is no surviving spouse, to the person's children or next of kin; or to the person's personal representative, for the benefit of the person's surviving spouse or next of kin.

Tenn.Code Ann. § 20–5–106(a). Thus, an examination of the development of Tennessee's wrongful death law, from its inception to the present, establishes that the right of recovery in a wrongful death case is strictly a creation of statute. [Citations.]

Because a cause of action for wrongful death is a creation of statute, recoverable damages must be determined by reference to the particular statute involved. Although all states have abolished the rule of non-liability when personal injury results in death, the statutory methods of doing so fall into two distinct categories—wrongful death statutes and survival statutes. [Citation.]

The majority of states have enacted "survival statutes." These statutes permit the victim's cause of action to survive the death, so that the victim, through the victim's estate, recovers damages that would have been recovered *by the victim* had the victim survived. [Citations.] Survival statutes do not create a new cause of action; rather, the cause of action vested in the victim at the time of death is transferred to the person designated in the statutory scheme to pursue it, and the action is enlarged to include damages for the death itself. [Citation.] "[T]he recovery is the same one the decedent would have been entitled to at death, and thus included such items as wages lost after injury and before death, medical expenses incurred, and pain and suffering," and other appropriate compensatory damages suffered by the victim from the time of injury to the time of death. [Citation.]

In contrast to survival statutes, "pure wrongful death statutes" create a *new* cause of action in favor of the survivors of the victim for *their* loss occasioned by the death. [Citation.] These statutes proceed "on the theory of compensating the individual beneficiaries for the loss of the economic benefit which they might reasonably have expected to receive from the decedent in the form of support, services or contributions during the remainder of [the decedent's] lifetime if [the decedent] had not been killed." [Citation.] Hence, most wrongful death jurisdictions have adopted a "pecuniary loss" standard of recovery, allowing damages for economic contributions the deceased would have made to the survivors had death not occurred and for the economic value of the services the deceased would have rendered to the survivors but for the death. [Citation.]

Tennessee's approach to providing a remedy for death resulting from personal injury is a hybrid between survival and wrongful death statutes, resulting in a statutory scheme with a "split personality." [Citation.] The pertinent damages statute, Tenn.Code Ann. § 20–5–113, has been in existence in one form or another since 1883. It provides:

> Where a person's death is caused by the wrongful act, fault, or omission of another, and suit is brought for damages . . . the party suing shall, if entitled to damages, have the right to recover the mental and physical suffering, loss of time, and necessary expenses resulting to the deceased from the personal injuries, *and also the damages resulting to the parties for whose use and benefit the right of action survives from the death consequent upon the injuries received.* Tenn.Code Ann. § 20–5–113 (emphasis added).

The plain language of Tenn.Code Ann. § 20–5–113 reveals that it may be classified as a survival statute because it preserves whatever cause of action was vested in the victim at the time of death. [Citations.] The survival character of the statute is evidenced by the language "the party suing shall have the right to recover [damages] resulting *to the deceased from the personal injuries.*" [Citation.] Tennessee courts have declared that the purpose of this language is to provide "for the continued existence and passing of the right of action of the deceased, and not for any new, independent cause of action in [survivors]." [Citations.] Accordingly, Tenn. Code Ann. § 20–5–113 "in theory, preserve[s] the right of action which the deceased himself would have had, and . . . [has] basically been construed as falling within the survival type of wrongful death statutes for over a century" because it continues that cause of action by permitting recovery of damages for the death itself. [Citation.]

Notwithstanding the accurate, technical characterization of Tenn.Code Ann. § 20–5–113 as survival legislation, the statute also creates a cause of action that compensates survivors for their losses. The statute provides that damages may be recovered *"resulting to the parties for whose use and benefit the right of action survives from the death." Id.* (emphasis added). Hence, survivors of the deceased may recover damages for *their* losses suffered as a result of the death as well as damages sustained by the deceased from the time of injury to the time of death. [Citation.]

Loss of Spousal Consortium

In 1903, this Court held in *Davidson Benedict Co. v. Severson,* 109 Tenn. 572, 72 S.W. 967 (Tenn.1903), that consortium damages were not available under Tennessee's wrongful death statute. The plaintiff urges this Court to revisit and reverse the holding in *Davidson* based on the following assertions: (1) that the *Davidson* holding was contrary to the plain language of the wrongful death statute; (2) that permitting consortium damages in personal injury but not in wrongful death cases is illogical; (3) that the majority of jurisdictions now permit loss of consortium damages in wrongful death cases; and (4) that the doctrine of stare decisis should not commit this Court "to the sanctification of ancient fallacy." Upon careful review, we agree with the plaintiff.

* * *

The defendant argues that this Court has previously held that Tenn. Code Ann. § 20–5–113 is a survival statute and that survival statutes generally do not permit recovery under consortium theories. While this Court in *Jones v. Black,* 539 S.W.2d 123 (Tenn.1976), previously classified Tennessee's wrongful death statute as a survival statute for purposes of limitations of action, we are not confined to interpret the statute according to the strictures of a judicially imposed classification when such an interpretation would ignore unambiguous statutory language. Accordingly, our analysis of Tenn.Code Ann. § 20–5–113 shall focus on the statute's language and not on what damages "survival" statutes in other states generally permit. It must be remembered that, notwithstanding the accurate, technical characterization of Tenn.Code Ann. § 20–5–113 as survival legislation, the statute also provides for a cause of action that compensates survivors for *their* losses.

Damages under our wrongful death statute can be delineated into two distinct classifications. [Citations.] The first classification permits recovery for injuries sustained by the deceased from the time of injury to the time of death. Damages under the first classification include medical expenses, physical and mental pain and suffering, funeral expenses, lost wages, and loss of earning capacity. *See* Tenn.Code Ann. § 20–5–113 ("right to recover the mental and physical suffering, loss of time, and necessary expenses resulting to the deceased from the personal injuries").

The second classification of damages permits recovery of incidental damages suffered by the decedent's next of kin. *See* Tenn.Code Ann. § 20–5–113 ("***and*** also the damages resulting to the parties for whose use and benefit the right of action survives from the death consequent upon the injuries received.'') (emphasis added); [Citations.] * * *

The wrongful death statute neither explicitly precludes consortium damages nor reflects an intention to preclude consortium damages. The statute's language does not limit recovery to purely economic losses. To the contrary, the statute's plain language appears to encompass consortium damages.

Indeed, this Court has recognized that pecuniary value cannot be defined to a mathematical certainty as such a definition "would overlook the value of the [spouse's] personal interest in the affairs of the home and the economy incident to [the spouse's] services." [Citation.] We further believe that the pecuniary value of a human life is a compound of many elements. An individual family member has value to others as part of a functioning social and economic unit. This value necessarily includes the value of mutual society and protection, i.e, human companionship. Human companionship has a definite, substantial and ascertainable pecuniary value, and its loss forms a part of the value of the life we seek to ascertain. While uncertainties may arise in proof when defining the value of human companionship, the one committing the wrongful act causing the death of a human being should not be permitted to seek protection behind the uncertainties inherent in the very situation his wrongful act has created. Moreover, it seems illogical and absurd to believe that the legislature would intend the anomaly of permitting recovery of consortium losses when a spouse is injured and survives but not when the very same act causes a spouse's death.

* * * Accordingly, we reverse *Davidson Benedict v. Severson,* 109 Tenn. 572, 72 S.W. 967 (Tenn.1902), to the extent that *Davidson Benedict* prohibits consideration of spousal consortium losses when calculating the pecuniary value of a deceased's life under the wrongful death statute.

Loss of Parental Consortium

The wrongful death statute precludes neither a minor child nor an adult child from seeking compensation for the child's consortium losses. Moreover, Tenn.Code Ann. § 20–5–110 provides that "a suit for the wrongful killing of the spouse may be brought in the name of the surviving spouse for the benefit of the surviving spouse and the children of the deceased." This provision when read in pari materia with Tenn.Code Ann. § 20–5–113 seemingly permits consideration of parental consortium damages. [Citation.]

A review of case law in other jurisdictions indicates a trend to expand consortium claims to include the impairment of a child's relationship with a parent. [Citation.] In cases involving a parent's death, "[t]he general rule ... followed is that a child's loss of nurture, education and moral training which it probably would have received from a parent wrongfully killed is a pecuniary loss to be considered as an element of the damages suffered by the child." [Citations.]

A basis for placing an economic value on parental consortium is that the education and training which a child may reasonably expect to receive from a parent are of actual and commercial value to the child. Accordingly, a child sustains a pecuniary injury for the loss of parental education and training when a defendant tortiously causes the death of the child's parent. Moreover, we recognize that:

> "normal home life for a child consists of complex incidences in which the sums constitute a nurturing environment. When the vitally important parent-child relationship is impaired and the child loses the love, guidance and close companionship of a parent, the child is deprived of something that is indeed valuable and precious. No one could seriously contend otherwise."

[Citation.]

The additional considerations employed for spousal consortium may be applicable to parental consortium claims. We agree with the observation of one court that "companionship, comfort, society, guidance, solace, and protection . . . go into the vase of family happiness [and] are the things for which a wrongdoer must pay when he shatters the vase." [Citation.]

Adult children may be too attenuated from their parents in some cases to proffer sufficient evidence of consortium losses. Similarly, if the deceased did not have a close relationship with any of the statutory beneficiaries, the statutory beneficiaries will not likely sustain compensable consortium losses or their consortium losses will be nominal. The age of the child does not, in and of itself, preclude consideration of parental consortium damages. The adult child inquiry shall take into consideration factors such as closeness of the relationship and dependence (i.e., of a handicapped adult child, assistance with day care, etc.).

Conclusion

We hold that consortium-type damages may be considered when calculating the pecuniary value of a deceased's life. This holding does not create a new cause of action but merely refines the term "pecuniary value." Consortium losses are not to limited to spousal claims but also necessarily encompass a child's loss, whether minor or adult. Loss of consortium consists of several elements, encompassing not only tangible services provided by a family member, but also intangible benefits each family member receives from the continued existence of other family members. Such benefits include attention, guidance, care, protection, training, companionship, cooperation, affection, love, and in the case of a spouse, sexual relations. Our holding conforms with the plain language of the wrongful death statutes, the trend of modern authority, and the social and economic reality of modern society.

The decision of the of the trial court granting the defendants' motion to strike is reversed. Costs of this appeal shall be taxed to the defendants for which execution may issue if necessary.

1. *Damage Provisions.* The damages provisions in Wrongful Death Acts are generally one of three types: (1) the all-inclusive type that lists particular elements of damages, (2) the pecuniary loss type that restricts recoveries to economic losses, and (3) the general loss type that provides for damages in a vague way, such as "damages as are just."

The express language of the wrongful death act is not always conclusive as to what type of damages beneficiaries may recover. For example, the wrongful death statutes of several states limit recovery to "fair and just compensation with reference to the pecuniary injuries resulting from such death." *See, e.g.,* 740 ILCS 180.2 (West 2001); N.J. Stat. Ann. § 2A:31–5 (West 2001); N.Y. Est. Powers & Trusts § 5–4.3 (McKinney 2001). However, courts have interpreted the scope of permissible damages under these statutes differently. The Illinois Supreme Court has permitted spouses, parents of minor and adult children and siblings to recover damages for loss of companionship and society. *See* Finley v. Zemmel, 151 Ill.2d 95, 176 Ill.Dec. 1, 601 N.E.2d 699 (1992). On the other hand, courts interpreting New York and New Jersey law expressly preclude recovery for loss of society or companionship. *See, e.g.,* Alexander v. Whitman, 114 F.3d 1392 (3d Cir.1997) (under New Jersey law damages are awarded for pecuniary loss only, and not for injury to feelings, mental suffering, or loss of society or companionship); Gonzalez v. New York City Housing Auth., 77 N.Y.2d 663, 569 N.Y.S.2d 915, 572 N.E.2d 598 (1991) (New York steadfastly denies recovery for grief, loss of society, affection, conjugal fellowship and consortium). When a parent or a child dies, New York and New Jersey courts do allow recovery for loss of guidance. *See* Carey v. Lovett, 132 N.J. 44, 622 A.2d 1279 (1993); Gonzalez, 569 N.Y.S.2d at 668. However, that loss must be measured by the economic value of the loss such as by reference to increased expenditures to continue the guidance lost. *See* Gonzalez, 569 N.Y.S.2d at 668; Gangemi v. National Health Labs., 291 N.J.Super. 569, 677 A.2d 1163 (1996) (using as an example the price of hired companions who may provide assistance to aged parents with shopping and household management). No recovery is permitted for the mental or emotional loss of the parent or child.

2. *Loss to Survivors v. Loss to Estate.* The orientation of the death statute toward the survivors or the decedent may affect recovery for intangible losses. For example, New Hampshire refused to allow parents to recover for loss of society with an injured or killed child, in part, because the state's wrongful death statute is not based on loss to the survivors but focuses on losses suffered by the decedent. The court also invoked public policy reasons. *See* Siciliano v. Capitol City Shows, Inc., 124 N.H. 719, 475 A.2d 19 (1984).

Similarly, Georgia also has a statute focused on the losses suffered by the decedent rather than the survivors. The Georgia statute measures damages as the full value of the life of the decedent. Intangible losses are measured by loss to the decedent such as the decedent's loss of enjoyment of life and the decedent's loss of companionship and society with his or her family.

3. *Loss of Consortium*. Even in jurisdictions where the wrongful death statute precludes recovery for a surviving spouse's loss of consortium, the spouse may have a common law cause of action for any loss of consortium the spouse suffered after the decedent's injuries but before the decedent's death. For example, in *Thalman v. Owens–Corning Fiberglas Corporation*, 290 N.J.Super. 676, 676 A.2d 611 (1996), the New Jersey appellate court reversed a trial court order remitting the loss of consortium award to the surviving wife of a pipe fitter who died 11 months after the onset of mesothelioma, an asbestos-related disease. Although the surviving wife could not recover for the loss of consortium after her husband's death, the surviving wife was entitled to recover for loss of consortium during her husband's illness. The court noted that the jury was instructed to limit its consortium award to the period of the husband's life and concluded that nothing suggested that the jury had disregarded that instruction.

4. *Economic Losses*. In wrongful death actions the beneficiaries can recover the value of the decedent's support and services in the home. Evidence of the decedent's work history, if any, and contribution to household is relevant. Such contributions can include wages from work outside the home, performance of routine household tasks, and advice, counsel, or guidance for other family members, especially children. The amount that would have been spent from earnings toward the personal support of the decedent are deducted. *See, e.g.,* Wentling v. Medical Anesthesia Services, P.A., 237 Kan. 503, 701 P.2d 939 (1985) (assistance in spouse's work and care of handicapped child); Henneman v. McCalla, 260 Iowa 60, 148 N.W.2d 447 (1967) (housework, care of minor child, assistant to husband in farm work, income outside home as nurse's aide).

Where the decedent had no legal obligation to support the beneficiary, such as an adult child whose parent seeks to recover wrongful death damages, the beneficiary also must present evidence that the decedent would have volunteered to provide support to the beneficiary. Evidence of the decedent's past contributions, including financial support and services performed for the beneficiary may be relevant. However, the beneficiary also must introduce evidence of a firm commitment to support the beneficiary. *See* Datskow v. Teledyne Continental Motors Aircraft Prod., 826 F.Supp. 677 (W.D.N.Y.1993).

5. *Punitive Damages*. Jurisdictions vary as to whether punitive damages are available in wrongful death and survival actions. *See, e.g.,* Durham v. U–Haul Int'l, 745 N.E.2d 755 (Ind.2001) (punitive damages are not recoverable in a wrongful death action); Simeone v. Charron, 762 A.2d 442 (R.I.2000) (same); State v. Izzolena, 609 N.W.2d 541 (Iowa 2000) (estate can recover punitive damages on behalf of the decedent); Lewis v. Hiatt, 683 So.2d 937 (Miss.1996) (punitive damages are allowable in wrongful death action); Roach v. Jimmy D. Enter., Ltd., 912 P.2d 852 (Okla.1996) (same).

6. *Survival Act Losses*. In addition to economic losses the decedent suffers prior to death, such as medical expenses, lost wages and lost earning capacity, some jurisdictions permit an estate to recover for noneconomic

losses the decedent suffers before death. For example, some jurisdictions allow damages for the decedent's pain and suffering. Usually, the estate must establish that the decedent was consciously in pain before death. *See, e.g.,* Brereton v. United States, 973 F.Supp. 752 (E.D.Mich.1997) (Michigan Wrongful Death Act expressly limits recoverable pain and suffering to that consciously suffered by the decedent between the time of injury and death); Murphy v. Martin Oil Co., 56 Ill.2d 423, 308 N.E.2d 583 (1974).

Some courts also have allowed recovery for pre-injury fear and apprehension of death. *See, e.g.,* Nelson v. Dolan, 230 Neb. 848, 434 N.W.2d 25 (1989) (claim for conscious prefatal-injury fear and apprehension of death survives decedent's death and inures to the benefit of the decedent's estate); *but see* In re Air Crash Disaster Near Chicago, Illinois, 507 F.Supp. 21 (N.D.Ill.1980) (refusing to recognize claim for pre-injury fright and terror under Illinois law).

Finally, a few jurisdictions have recognized damages for decedent's loss of enjoyment of life, sometimes call hedonic damages. *See, e.g.,* Thomas v. Ford Motor Co., 70 F.Supp.2d 521 (D.N.J.1999) (applying New Jersey law). Unlike damages for pain and suffering, a decedent's estate may recover hedonic damages whether or not the decedent regained consciousness before death. *See* Thomas, 70 F.Supp.2d at 526.

Should an award of hedonic damages in a survival action be allowed only if intangible losses are not recoverable in a corresponding wrongful death action? Is the logical answer different from the practical answer? Are such losses equivalent, parallel or independent of one another?

E. TORT REFORM

Section Coverage:

In some sense, tort law is always being reformed. As a creature of common law, tort law is reformed whenever a court distinguishes or overrules precedent or applies precedent to a new factual setting. However, during the latter half of the twentieth century, a concentrated movement began to reform the civil justice system through legislation. This movement focused on altering and restricting traditional common law tort remedies through legislative action. As part of this movement, many states have enacted "tort reform acts." The acts employ a variety of measures in an attempt to reduce verdicts awarded in tort cases, and in particular, personal injury cases. The most common of these measures include limitations on the availability and amount of punitive damages and limitations on damages for noneconomic losses. Many tort reform acts also modify or abolish the collateral source rule, allowing evidence of any benefits a plaintiff receives from a collateral source to be admitted at trial. Some statutes also require courts to offset benefits received from collateral sources against any jury verdict the plaintiff receives. Additionally, many tort reform acts abolish or limit joint and several liability.

Plaintiffs have challenged tort reform acts in state courts on the grounds that tort reform measures violate a number of state constitutional provisions, including provisions ensuring the right to a jury trial, open access to the courts, due process and equal protections as well as provisions prohibiting special legislation. State courts are divided over the constitutionality of tort reform measures.

Key proponents of tort reform include insurance companies, small businesses, product manufacturers, municipalities and professional service providers. They argue that tort reform is necessary to ensure consistency and predictability in damage awards. Proponents also argue that tort reform produces fairer results by ensuring that defendants are forced to pay only that portion of the plaintiff's damages for which the defendant is responsible, that plaintiffs do not receive double recoveries and that funds remain available to compensate plaintiffs who file their claims later in time.

Key opponents of tort reform include trial lawyers and consumers' rights advocates. They argue that tort reform is unnecessary because large verdicts are awarded in rare cases only and are frequently reduced on appeal. Opponents argue that tort reform does not produce any more consistency or predictability in verdicts and that tort reform unfairly burdens the most seriously injured plaintiffs.

Judd v. Drezga

103 P.3d 135 (Utah 2004).

■ WILKINS, ASSOCIATE CHIEF JUSTICE:

Plaintiff Heidi J. Judd, personally and as the parent and guardian of Athan Montgomery, appeals the trial court's reduction of a jury's general damage award from $1,250,000 to $250,000. We affirm.

Background

In 1997, Athan Montgomery was born with severe brain damage as a result of Dr. Gregory Drezga's incompetence in his failed attempt to deliver Athan with the use of forceps. Athan's mother, Heidi J. Judd, sued Dr. Drezga on Athan's behalf. Athan, who is now six, was three at the time of trial. The jury, having heard the evidence presented on behalf of Athan and Dr. Drezga, awarded Athan $22,735.30 for amounts already expended to maintain his life, and $1,000,000 as the amount necessary to maintain his life during his expected-although shortened-life span. The jury also awarded Athan $1,250,000 of so-called "noneconomic" damages in recognition of the difference between a life as a normal, healthy boy, and a life as he must now live it: severely brain damaged, with drastically reduced life experiences and expectations.

In 1986, the legislature enacted a statutory limitation on some forms of damages recoverable by victims in medical malpractice actions. Utah Code Ann. § 78–14–7.1 (2002). * * * For injuries occurring before July 1, 2001, as Athan's did, the limit applies only to those who have sustained over

$250,000 in damages. [Citation.] * * * Upon motion by Dr. Drezga, the trial court reduced the jury's award to $250,000 pursuant to section 78–14–7.1(1)(a).

The damages that the statute limits are commonly referred to by various names, but amount to the same measure: pain and suffering, noneconomic loss, or general damages. The terms "noneconomic loss" and "general damages" merely euphemize what the damages truly represent-diminished capacity for the enjoyment of life. The measure is actually the difference between what life would have been like without the harm done by the medical professional, and what it is like with that additional burden. In Athan's case, the difference is dramatic in terms of his abilities, his joys, his opportunities, and his life expectancy. These damages are often called "noneconomic" because they are a measure of the cost neither of medical and other necessary care the malpractice caused nor of decreased earning ability. Those damages are considered more finite, measurable, and "economic" because they are more easily calculated on the basis of projected life expectancy, expected medical difficulties, and reduced earning capacity. Economic damages on the other hand, are not restricted, presumably because they are less likely to be exaggerated by a jury, and also because they are "hard" amounts, subject to careful calculation.

* * *

Judd asks us to consider whether the legislature's limitation on Athan's recovery of quality of life damages from Dr. Drezga is constitutionally infirm. * * *

Specifically, Judd * * * claims that, first, the cap violates the protections of the open courts provision of article I, section 11; [and] second, the cap violates Athan's right to the uniform operation of laws under article I.

On appeal, * * * Dr. Drezga argues that the trial court correctly reduced Athan's quality of life damages based on the statutory cap on such damages imposed by the legislature, and on our historic deference to the decisions of the legislature on questions of public policy. * * *

Analysis

I.   Standard of Review

We review the trial court's reduction of Athan's judgment for correctness given the constitutional questions Judd raises. [Citation.]

II.   Open Courts Clause

This court has held, since our decision in Berry ex rel. Berry v. Beech Aircraft Corp., 717 P.2d 670 (Utah 1985), that citizens of Utah have a right to a remedy for an injury. Article I, section 11 of the Utah Constitution provides: "All courts shall be open, and every person, for an injury done to him in his person, property or reputation, shall have remedy by due course of law, which shall be administered without denial or unnecessary delay." Utah Const. art. I, § 11. * * *

Our past jurisprudence has clearly and firmly established the following test for violations of the Open Courts Clause:

* * *

... [I]f there is no substitute or alternative remedy provided, abrogation of the remedy ... may be justified only if there is a clear social or economic evil to be eliminated and the elimination of an existing legal remedy is not an arbitrary or unreasonable means for achieving the objective.

Berry, 717 P.2d at 680. * * *

A. Substitute Remedy

* * * [I]t is self-evident that the cap on quality of life damages, which does nothing more than reduce Athan's recovery, does not provide a substitute remedy substantially equal to that abrogated. Accordingly, we must consider * * * whether the damage cap represents a reasonable, nonarbitrary method of reducing increasing health care costs and other dangers that the legislature views as clear social or economic evils.

B. Clear Social or Economic Evil

Recovery of quality of life damages in Athan's case is limited to $250,000 by Utah Code section 78–14–7.1(1)(a). [Citation.] The legislature's stated purpose in enacting the cap is [to reduce health care costs and to ensure the continued availability of health care].

* * *

Although the empirical truth of these findings is a matter of some dispute, we will not undertake the same investigation as the legislature, reviewing its data-gathering methods and conclusions to determine whether the stated legislative findings are perfectly correct. A court is ill-suited to undertake investigation of such a nature. Our inquiry under the "clear social or economic evil" portion of the Berry test is more limited.

* * *

Our job as this state's court of last resort is to determine whether the legislature overstepped the bounds of its constitutional authority in enacting the cap on quality of life damages, not whether it made wise policy in doing so. Although there are indications that overall health care costs may only be minimally affected by large damage awards, there is also data that indicates otherwise. [Citations.] When an issue is fairly debatable, we cannot say that the legislature overstepped its constitutional bounds when it determined that there was a crisis needing a remedy. Accordingly, we next consider whether the elimination of Athan's right to collect unlimited quality of life damages is a reasonable, nonarbitrary method for achieving the legislature's stated purpose of controlling medical malpractice premiums and health care costs.

C. Nonarbitrary, Reasonable Nature of Cap

We cannot conclude that the cap on quality of life damages is arbitrary or unreasonable. The legislature's determination that it needed to respond to the perceived medical malpractice crisis was logically followed by action designed to control costs. Although malpractice insurance rates may not be entirely controlled by such matters, they are undoubtedly subject to some measure of fluctuation based on paid claims. [Citation.] Thus, one nonarbitrary manner of controlling such costs is to limit amounts paid out. Intuitively, the greater the amount paid on claims, the greater the increase in premiums. Limiting recovery of quality of life damages to a certain amount gives insurers some idea of their potential liability. [Citation.] While we recognize that such a cap heavily punishes those most severely injured, it is not unconstitutionally arbitrary merely because it does so. Rather, it is targeted to control costs in one area where costs might be controllable.

Despite this court's concerns about the wisdom of depriving a few badly injured plaintiffs of full recovery, the cap is also constitutionally reasonable. Rather than cap all damages, like the cap struck down in Condemarin v. University Hospital, 775 P.2d 348 (Utah 1989), the limitation on recoverable damages in this case is narrowly tailored, by limiting quality of life damages alone. While Judd notes that Utah has not seen large damage awards in significant numbers, this position ignores at least one important factor. Although quality of life damages are very real, they are also less susceptible to quantification than purely economic damages. As amici point out, "[t]he estimated value of future costs forms the basis of the [insurance] rate-setting process." The difficulty of predicting quality of life damages must be considered by insurers when setting rates and planning reserves. At least in some measure, then, predicting and controlling future costs can result in lower insurance rates. Taken as one of a number of measures enacted to help control health care costs, the cap on quality of life damages is thus a reasonable approach.

Having determined that the damage cap is designed to eliminate a social or economic evil, and that it is a reasonable, nonarbitrary means for doing so, we conclude that Utah Code section 78–14–7.1 does not violate article I, section 11 of the Utah Constitution.

III. Uniform Operation of Laws

Judd next argues that section 78–14–7.1 violates the Utah Constitution's uniform operation of laws provision found in article I, section 24. This provision guards against discrimination within the same class and helps ensure that statutes establishing or recognizing rights for certain classes do so reasonably given the statutory objectives. [Citation.] We employ heightened scrutiny under article I, section 24 when reviewing legislation that "implicates" rights under article I, section 11. [Citation.] Sustaining legislation against an article I, section 24 challenge alleging that one's rights under the Open Courts Clause are constitutionally discriminated against requires the court to find that the challenged legislation "(1) is reasonable, (2) has more than a speculative tendency to further the legislative objective and, in fact, actually and substantially furthers a valid legislative purpose, and (3) is reasonably necessary to further a legitimate legislative goal." [Citation.] Although it causes great hardship for a small, severely injured group of plaintiffs, we find that the damage cap is reasonable, and it substantially furthers and is reasonably necessary to the legislative goal of decreasing health care costs and ensuring the continued availability of health care.

Judd's arguments before this court identify three important ways that the cap on quality of life damages might be unconstitutionally discriminatory. First, Judd notes that the limitation applies only to victims of medical malpractice, not to victims of other torts. Second, Judd points out that only medical malpractice victims with significant quality of life damages, as opposed to special damages, are affected. Last, Judd recognizes that the cap impacts only those who are most severely injured. We evaluate the damage cap under the heightened scrutiny standard with reference to these classifications.

In connection with our discussion of the Open Courts Clause, supra, we determined that the damage cap was a reasonable method of implementing the legitimate legislative purpose of limiting health care costs and ensuring the continuing availability of health care resources. That discussion bears on this section as well. However, in order to sustain the damage cap under article I, section 24, a higher standard must be met. The cap on quality of life damages must be reasonably necessary to achieve the goals, and, in fact, actually and substantially further them.

As we recognized above in connection with our analysis under the Open Courts Clause, we do not proceed in our analysis under article I, section 24 as if we were called upon to answer these questions in the first instance. Instead, we carry out our role as the state's court of last resort, called upon to identify the boundaries of the constitution, giving appropriate deference to the policy choices of the citizens' elected representatives. Our review of the arguments and information presented by the parties and amici reveals that the cap meets the standard for constitutionality set by article I, section 24.

With regard to controlling health care costs, a report authored by Congress's Office of Technology Assessment evaluated six different empirical studies and concluded that "caps on damage awards were the only type of State tort reform that consistently showed significant results in reducing the malpractice cost indicators." [Citation.] This reveals that such caps may be considered reasonably necessary to implement the legislature's policy of controlling malpractice insurance costs, and thus health care costs. However, the caps appear not only to be reasonably necessary, but to have an actual and substantial impact. This can be seen from a review of the actions and experiences of other states.

[The court then discussed two studies relied upon by the legislature that found that a cap on noneconomic damages in California had stabilized local malpractice insurance rates. The court concluded that these studies provided sufficient evidence that caps on quality of life damages do have an actual impact on the cost of malpractice insurance.] * * *

While the damage cap does indeed discriminate against medical malpractice victims with the most severe noneconomic injuries, it does so reasonably, given the statute's purpose. In order to control costs and provide for the continuing availability of health care resources, the legislature was faced with a number of choices. By deciding which reforms to enact, it necessarily discriminated. However, the classifications established by the statute meet the heightened scrutiny test.

Although the classifications deny some victims a full recovery while allowing such a recovery to others, the classifications are not unconstitutional. While medical malpractice victims are deprived of a measure of their remedy where other tort victims are not, enacting damage caps on all tort victims would be imprudent and overbroad given that the legislature's goal was to control health care costs. Additionally, although medical malpractice victims, those with primarily noneconomic, or quality of life, damages, are punished by the limitation when compared with those whose injuries are largely economic, this discrimination is permissible given the cap's purpose of controlling costs. As noted above, "caps on noneconomic damages tend to be particularly effective in reducing costs because of the extreme variability of damage award[s] attributable to pain and suffering." [Citation.] Thus, it appears there is support for the proposition that a large measure of the problem identified by the legislature results from fluctuation in cases with high noneconomic damages, and a cap which targets just those problems is therefore not unconstitutional. Because the crisis identified by the legislature is primarily precipitated by the potential for large, unpredictable judgments, establishing a cap that prevents only those types of judgments is reasonably necessary to achieve the legislative purpose, despite punishing the most severely injured victims.

When attempting to resolve problems of policy, the legislature is inevitably forced to draw lines. In this instance the legislature has chosen to enact a cap, limiting the right to recover quality of life damages to $250,000. This cap severely injures young Athan, who will live a life greatly diminished by Dr. Drezga's negligence. But that is a policy choice made by the legislative branch, and we cannot say that it is unconstitutional. The legislature's purpose in enacting the damage cap is a valid and legitimate one. The cap is a reasonably necessary means of achieving that purpose, and it actually and substantially furthers it. Therefore, the damage cap is permissible under article I, section 24 of the Utah Constitution.

[The court also concluded that the statutory limit on noneconomic damages did not violate Judd's rights to due process and a jury trial and did not violate separation of powers under the Utah constitution.]

Conclusion

We affirm the trial court's ruling limiting Athan's recovery of quality of life damages to $250,000 because the constitution does not prohibit it, despite its consequences to Athan.

The cap is designed to reduce health care costs, increase the availability of medical malpractice insurance, and secure the continued availability of health care resources—all legitimate legislative goals given the clear social and economic evil of rising health care costs and a shortage of qualified health care professionals. In attempting to meet its goals, the legislature has not unreasonably or arbitrarily limited recovery. Rather, it has chosen to place a limit on the recovery of "noneconomic" quality of life damages-one area where legislation has been shown to actually and substantially further these goals. Applying each individual test, we conclude that the open courts, uniform operation of laws, and due process provisions of our constitution are not offended by the damage cap. Additionally, neither the right to a jury trial nor the constitutional guarantee of separation of powers is offended by the cap. Affirmed.

■ DURHAM, CHIEF JUSTICE, dissenting:

I respectfully dissent. The majority opinion analyzes the plaintiff's constitutional claims under the wrong standard of review and reaches the wrong result. The plaintiff has challenged the statute in question as a violation of due process, equal protection, the remedies clause of Utah's "open courts" provision, the separation of powers doctrine, and the right to a jury trial. Despite the protection each of these rights receives in the Utah Constitution, and despite this court's clear precedent requiring a heightened standard of review in such challenges, the majority instead identifies a need for "deference to legislative judgments in a Berry review" and specifically rejects heightened scrutiny in favor of a "rational basis" standard. * * * Under the proper standard of review, this statute fails. Because that result is required under sections 10 and 11 of article I, and under article V, I will discuss only the issues raised under those provisions.

I. Remedy By Due Course of Law

* * * In Berry, as we later explained, we determined that legislative attempts to abrogate section 11 rights should "be closely examined by this Court and struck down when the disability they seek to impose on individual rights is too great to be justified by the benefits accomplished or when the legislation is simply an arbitrary and impermissible shifting of collective burdens to individual citizens." [Citation.]

The collective burden this statute imposes on individual citizens is significant. To be clear about the nature of the capped damages at issue, noneconomic damages are real; they are intended to compensate victims of negligence for such things as chronic pain, disfigurement, and (as in this case) the loss of a normal life. The suggestion that they are somehow "soft" damages, or less quantifiable than economic damages, is, in my view, a red herring. Projected earnings and costs of future treatment and care, to name two typical elements of "economic" damages, are by no means exempt from uncertainty and the need for guesswork by juries (who regularly hear extensively from competing experts on these questions). Once one acknowledges the fact that noneconomic damages, fully as much as economic ones, are truly compensatory, not "extras" or "freebies," for individual injured plaintiffs, the degree of the legislature's invasion of an individual's right under section 11 to a remedy is apparent.

Furthermore, I regard as extremely problematic the majority's wholesale acceptance of the rationale that, because damage awards for noneconomic damages are unpredictable, they are more acceptable targets for legislative diminution or destruction. The unpredictability of a jury's determination of the value of all losses, including noneconomic losses, has been, from the earliest beginnings of our tort system, an essential part of the deterrent function of tort law. One need go no further than the Ford Pinto case, where the evidence disclosed that Ford Motor had actually calibrated the relative costs of fixing its defective cars versus paying a few adverse verdicts—and opted to pay the verdicts—to be confronted with the flaw in the predictability argument. [Citation.]

Lastly, the majority opinion takes insufficient account, I believe, of the arbitrary method by which the statute distributes the cost of its solution to the so-called malpractice crisis. The most seriously harmed plaintiff is likely to receive the smallest fraction of his or her actual damages, while the less injured are likely to receive much higher, or even total, compensation for the injuries they suffer. A more graphic illustration of the "impermissible shifting of collective burdens to individual citizens," [citation], is hard to imagine, and it is the most vulnerable and voiceless citizens who bear the brunt of this shift.

Against this extreme cost to the few victims whose injuries and suffering are severe and perhaps (as with this plaintiff) lifelong is to be considered the legislature's rationale for inflicting such damage on individual rights. The majority defers entirely to the legislature's "fact-finding" process and cites rather extensively to specific sources supporting the legislature's conclusions that high jury verdicts are the major cause of high medical malpractice premiums. This conclusion is entirely inconsistent with Utah's long experience with juries in these cases. [The dissent cited a recent study purporting to document Utah's low median awards.] While we owe deference to legislative judgments on policy questions generally, we do not grant immunity to constitutional review on the basis of legislative assertions of "fact" that have no demonstrated basis in reality. * * *

In addition to its uncritical acceptance of the legislature's perception that high jury verdicts in Utah are the cause of the problem this statute purports to address, the majority fails to acknowledge the numerous recent studies attributing rises in insurance premiums to phenomena within the insurance industry itself, rather than to the size of jury verdicts. * * *

Given the extensive debate and the lack of empirical or expert consensus on the cause of increasing insurance costs, the legislature, however persuaded it may be by one set of assertions, may not properly deprive individual victims of their constitutional right to receive jury-determined compensation for their losses in the absence of overwhelming evidence that the public interest can only be protected by the deprivation. Such a state of affairs currently does not exist; indeed, many thoughtful experts have propounded numerous responses to the situation that would involve no infringement of constitutional rights of citizens. [Citations.] * * * As we said in Berry, the basic purpose of article I, section 11 is "to impose some limitation on that power for the benefit of those persons who are injured in their persons, property, or reputations since they are generally isolated in society, belong to no identifiable group, and rarely are able to rally the political process to their aid." * * *

Conclusion

Notwithstanding the preeminent role in policymaking that belongs to the legislature, this court's responsibility to uphold the individual rights guaranteed by the Utah Constitution requires us from time to time to scrutinize legislative choices regarding the implementation of policy to ensure that they do not violate those rights. The mandatory cap on noneconomic damages contained in Utah Code section 78–14–7.1 violates the right to a remedy for personal injury under article I, section 11 and the right to a jury trial under article I, section 10 of the Utah Constitution. * * *

---

1. *Tort Reform Measures.* During the past 30 years, states have enacted a variety of measures aimed at restricting tort remedies in personal injury actions. Some states have targeted recoveries in all personal injury actions, while other states have limited restrictions to medical malpractice actions specifically. Statutory limits on the amount a party can recover as noneconomic damages, like the caps at issue in the principal case, are one of the most prevalent forms of tort reform. *See, e.g.,* Kan. Stat. § 60–19a02 (2007) (total amount recoverable for noneconomic losses shall not exceed $250,000); Md. Cts. & Jud. Pro. § 11–108 (2007) (an award for noneconomic damages in any personal injury or wrongful death action may not exceed $500,000).

Rules regarding joint and several liability have been another prevalent focus of reform efforts. Many states have limited joint liability based on the defendant's fault, *see e.g.,* Tex. Civ. Prac. & Rem. § 33.013 (West 2007) (a defendant is jointly and severally liable only if the defendant is greater than 50% at fault) or limited joint liability to economic damages only. *See, e.g.,* Calif. Civ. Code § 1431.1 (West 2007) (liability of each defendant for noneconomic damages is several only and not joint). *See also* N.Y. Civ. Prac. L. R. § 1601 (West 2001) (any defendant found to be no more than 50% liable shall not be jointly liable for noneconomic damages).

The collateral source rule also has been a frequent target for reform. Under the collateral source rule, defendants were not permitted to offset from their own liability compensation or benefits that an injured plaintiff received from an independent or collateral source, such as insurance coverage, nor were defendants permitted to introduce evidence of such benefits. (See Chapter 13.) Many states now permit defendants to introduce evidence of payments from collateral sources for consideration by the jury.

See, e.g., Ind. Stat. (West 2001) § 34–44–1–2 (parties may introduce proof of collateral source payments except payments of life insurance or death benefits or insurance benefits for which plaintiff or plaintiff's family have paid). Some states permit or require courts to deduct collateral source benefits from a plaintiff's damage award. Alaska Stat. § 9.17.070 (2000) (court shall deduct from plaintiff's award the amount by which payments from any collateral source exceed plaintiff's attorneys fees and insurance premiums).

Other prevalent reforms include caps on punitive damages, limitations on evidence admissible to show liability for or the amount of punitive damages, statutes providing for periodic payment of future damages, *see* pp. 533–535, creation of patient compensation funds, caps on total damages and restrictions on contingency fees. For a more complete summary of state tort reform measures, see Ronen Avraham, *Database of State Tort Law Reforms*, Northwestern University Law & Economics Research Paper Series Paper No. 06–08 (2006) available at http://papers.ssrn.com/sol3/papers.cfm?abstract_id=902711 and F. Patrick Hubbard, *The Nature and Impact of the "Tort Reform" Movement*, 35 HOFSTRA L. REV. 437 (2006).

2. *Constitutional Challenges.* As the principal case illustrates, opponents of statutes limiting noneconomic damages and other tort reform measures have challenged such statutes as violative of a variety of state and federal constitutional provisions. Opponents have argued that statutes limiting noneconomic damages violate federal and state equal protection rights, the right to a jury trial, state constitutional prohibitions on special legislation, the separation of powers doctrine and state constitutional rights of access to courts. Courts have greeted these constitutional challenges with mixed responses. *Compare* Kirkland v. Blaine County Medical Center, 134 Idaho 464, 4 P.3d 1115 (2000) (rejecting state separation of powers, special legislation and jury trial challenges); *with* Ferdon v. Wisconsin Patients Compensation Fund, 284 Wis.2d 573, 701 N.W.2d 440 (2005) (violates equal protection); Lakin v. Senco Prod., 329 Or. 62, 987 P.2d 463 (1999) (violates right to a jury trial); Lucas v. United States, 757 S.W.2d 687 (Tex.1988) (violates state right to access to the courts).

3. *Policy Debate.* Proponents raise the following arguments in support of tort reform:

- Tort reform is necessary to ensure consistency and predictability of jury verdicts, thereby increasing availability of liability insurance and reducing the cost of liability insurance.

- The excessive verdicts arbitrarily awarded by juries in personal injury cases erode the public's confidence in the civil justice system. Tort reform restores the public's confidence in the civil justice system by reducing seemingly unfair and arbitrary large verdicts.

- Tort reform promotes fairness by ensuring that each defendant pays only its proportionate share of the plaintiff's losses.

- Tort reform is necessary to provide compensation for all injured parties by ensuring that when multiple parties file claims against the same defendant adequate funds remain available to compensate later filing claimants.

- The large verdicts awarded in personal injury cases are a "hidden tax" on the American economy because the cost of these verdicts is passed on to consumers through higher costs for goods and services. Tort reform is necessary to ensure the availability of reasonably priced goods and services.

- Large jury verdicts discourage new product innovation.

- Tort reform will reduce the burden on the court system by weeding out frivolous claims.

Opponents raise the following arguments against tort reform:

- Claims that jury verdicts are out-of-control are greatly exaggerated. Plaintiffs lose the majority of personal injury cases, punitive damages are rarely awarded, and jury awards are usually modest. The few large awards are reduced on appeal or through settlement.

- No evidence suggests that insurance premiums will decrease or have decreased as a result of tort reform.

- Jury verdicts are often the only way to police consumer product safety.

- Tort liability provides incentives for safety and innovation.

- Tort reform unfairly burdens the most severely injured parties.

- No evidence exists that tort reform will reduce court costs or improve efficiency.

- If any windfall must be had in the tort system, it should inure to the benefit of the injured party. Tort reform grants the wrongdoer any windfall resulting in the system.

4. *Historical Origins.* As the principal case notes, the tort reform movement arose in response to a perceived insurance crisis. Proponents of tort reform argue that providers of goods and services in certain industries such as health care have experienced steep increases in insurance premiums during the past few decades and that the increase in insurance costs is due to an increase in the number of lawsuits filed against these providers and the size of jury verdicts awarded in these claims. As the principal case also reflects, the existence of an insurance crisis and to what extent lawsuits affect insurance premiums has been a source of much controversy. Recently, observers have turned their attention to studying what effect, if any, tort reform measures such as the damage cap at issue in the principal case have had on insurance premiums, jury verdicts and the availability and cost of targeted goods and services. Results from these studies have been mixed. *See Ferdon*, 284 Wis.2d 573, 701 N.W.2d 440 (examining several conflicting studies on the impact of damage caps on insurance premiums); Paul H. Rubin & Joanna M. Shepherd, Tort Reform and Accidental Deaths, 50 J. L. & Econ. 221, 226 (2007) (discussing studies concluding that damage caps disproportionately affect women, children, the

elderly and minorities and concluding that damage caps also disproportionately increase female death rates).

5.   Recall from Chapter 2 that limitations on remedies are a limit on the scope of the underlying cause of action. Consider the effect of the legislation described in this chapter on the common law tort claims to which they apply.

CHAPTER 12

ADJUSTMENTS TO COMPENSATORY DAMAGES

A. PRESENT VALUE AND INFLATION

Section Coverage:

The purpose of compensatory damages in personal injury actions is to restore the injured party, as nearly as practicable, to the position held prior to incurring the harm. A principal component of the damages awarded often will be to replace projected lost wages, calculated by the injured party's diminished earning capacity over the period of their work life expectancy. Typically, the future earning stream is awarded in a lump sum rather than in periodic payments.

An adjustment to the damages awarded is necessary to take into consideration the amount of interest that an investment of the lump sum itself will earn over time. The task confronting the trier of fact is to calculate what amount of money at the date of the judgment will equal the lost wages when placed in safe investments. Several critical issues play a role in making the appropriate adjustments to the final total of damages given.

First, determining which percentage rate should be used for discounting the damages has evoked considerable controversy among courts, commentators, and experts. A high discount rate functions to the defendant's advantage by lowering the total liability; conversely, the plaintiff benefits from applying the lowest possible percentage rate.

Second, no consensus has developed regarding the extent, if any, to consider the impact of inflation on the projected earning stream. Proponents of including it as an adjustment factor contend that, unless the damages award reflects estimated future inflationary trends, a plaintiff will be undercompensated because inflation will erode the purchasing power of the substituted wages. Critics of adjusting damages for inflation argue that predicting future inflation is akin to crystal ball gazing; it is too speculative and unreliable to be fairly applied. Moreover, forecasting such trends is too complex for accurate assessment by jurors, even with the aid of expert testimony.

The inflation factor must be distinguished from other individualized and societal factors which may affect the computation of damages. For example, apart from inflation, estimated wage increases may be entirely attributable to projected job promotions or industry growth.

In the final analysis, predicting future inflationary trends, future market interest rates, and future industrial trends is an inexact science. The final lump sum damages award almost certainly will, in hindsight, turn out to be either overcompensation or undercompensation. Consequently, there is a growing interest in periodic payment of damages in a series of installments rather than in a lump sum.

Model Case:

Smith sustained personal injuries in an automobile accident, including a partial but permanent disability in Smith's arms. Prior to the accident Smith had been employed in a skilled position as a machine press operator earning $18,000 per year. As a result of the injuries, however, Smith could be expected to earn approximately $12,000 annually as an unskilled laborer.

The jury accepted expert evidence showing the difference in earning capacity, including projected job promotions and societal factors, over Smith's work life expectancy at a total of $140,000. A special verdict showed this amount of damages for the lost wages.

Courts have employed numerous methods to evaluate the respective roles of the discount rate and future inflation rate. One approach acknowledges that both the discount and inflation factors are relevant yet not susceptible of being accurately predicted. Therefore, both factors are simply offset and cancel each other out. Another method allows the introduction of expert testimony with respect to each factor, leaving the trier of fact to evaluate the evidence and make any adjustments as deemed appropriate. Other courts have disregarded inflation but have adjusted the damages award downward by some discount rate. Many courts are now following the lead of the United States Supreme Court with a varied offset approach. Under this method courts discount the damages award only by the "real" rate of interest. This method considers that market interest rates include two components: an estimate of anticipated inflation and the lender's desired real return on investment. The first element concerning inflation is offset against projected future inflation. The real interest rate, which essentially remains constant over time (between 1 and 3%), is then applied to reduce the damages award into present value.

Budge v. Post

643 F.2d 372 (5th Cir.1981).

■ Per Curiam:

This [is a] diversity suit for breach of contract. * * *

Don Budge, a former Wimbeldon tennis champion and winner of the Davis Cup, contracted with Troy Post to serve as tennis professional at Post's clubs, resorts and hotels for five years working for seven months each year. * * * Post discontinued payments to Budge under the contract and notified Budge that he was terminating their business relationship, claiming that Budge had violated the contract by failing properly to perform the duties required of the tennis professional under the agreement. Budge subsequently instituted this action contending that Post, not he, had breached the contract by failing to pay him the agreed compensation and by terminating the contract.

After a three-day trial, the jury returned a verdict in Budge's favor awarding him $353,800 as the compensation he would have received under the contract for the remaining fifty-eight months after Post discontinued payments to Budge, plus $85,500 for the value of the living accommodations and meals that Post had contracted to provide to Budge. To an interrogatory asking the jury what amount of money Budge had earned or, in the exercise of due diligence, could earn in similar employment during the contract period after Post terminated the agreement, the jury responded $1,500. The court entered a judgment for a total of $455,041, the sum of the amounts awarded for compensation and living expenses, minus the $1,500. * * *

In a diversity case, the determination of damages is substantive and is, therefore, governed by state law. [Citations.] Thus, whether an award of future damages must be reduced to its present value is an issue controlled by state law. [Citations.]

The Texas cases are not ambiguous. Discounting of future damage awards is adequately handled by the trial judge if he simply instructs the jury that damages are equal to the "sum of money, if any, if paid now in cash" that would compensate the plaintiff. [Citations.] Texas courts refuse to amplify this simple instruction because they believe that further explanation would confuse the jury. [Citation.] We might think an instruction further explaining the theory of discount would clarify the matter, but we are obliged to accept the decision of the Texas courts. Moreover, no evidence was presented at trial from which a discount rate could be computed. Therefore, the trial court's instruction to the jury to measure damages as the "present cash value" of the contract was an adequate charge under Texas law.

However, although the instruction was correct, the jury evidently did not follow it. The award patently reflected that, to arrive at the figure for earnings due, the jury simply multiplied the monthly compensation contracted for by the parties times the number of months of the contract period for which Budge was not paid. * * * The jury's failure to discount the award of earnings under the contract is an obvious oversight that must be corrected to prevent a manifest miscarriage of justice. Accordingly, we remand the case so that the trial judge, after considering such evidence as he may deem appropriate, may determine an appropriate discount rate and compute the present value of the award for contract earnings.

[Affirmed and remanded for recomputation.]

1. *Discounting Future Losses.* The calculation of future lost income requires first a determination of the amount of income that would have been earned each future year. Then that amount is reduced to present value. The present value of a sum is the amount of money that the plaintiff must have today in order to have the amount equal to the loss at the future date. It is assumed that the plaintiff will invest the money prudently and that it will compound annually until it equals the correct sum at the right time in the future.

2. *Calculation.* Discounting is difficult arithmetically, but there are present value tables available to simplify the task. *See, e.g.,* 1 Speiser § 8:4. When a sum is discounted to present value, the interest rate determines the result. If a low interest rate is used, the discounted result will be more money than if a high interest rate is used. For example, consider a plaintiff who will need $1000 at the end of next year. If this sum is discounted by 10%, then the plaintiff must have approximately $909 this year to equal $1000 with simple interest in a year. If, however, the sum is discounted by 20%, then the plaintiff must have approximately $833 this year to equal $1000 with simple interest in a year.

In *Shealy v. City of Albany, Ga.,* 137 F.Supp.2d 1359, 1367–68 (M.D.Ga.2001), the court followed the "below market discount rate," defined as the rate that reflects the estimated market interest rate that the plaintiff would earn on the monies received after final judgment, adjusted for the effect of income taxes they would pay on the interest and then offset by the expected rate of general wage and price inflation. The court further observed that a widely accepted method of determining the below market discount rate is to subtract the average annual change in the Consumer Price Index over a period of years from the annual interest rate on corporate bonds held during the same period. The opinion explained:

> The precise formula for this calculation is: $PV = x/(1 + i)n$ where PV represents present value; x represents the amount of money to be awarded; i represents the interest or discount rate; and n represents the number of periods or years in the future. This formula must be applied to each year separately rather than applied to the damages award as a whole. Id. at 1368, n.5.

3. *Lost Future Wages.* The starting place for calculating each annual installment in the lost stream of income is the actual wage or base salary. The worker may have fringe benefits to add, or work related expenses and taxes to subtract. For simplicity the parties often agree that the elements affecting the basic wage cancel out each other.

The major adjustment in wages that is not related to merit or productivity is inflation. As inflation makes dollars worth less, wages tend to increase an equal amount to preserve the worker's buying power. It is this adjustment that has attracted the greatest legal debate, as reflected in the following landmark case.

Jones & Laughlin Steel Corp. v. Pfeifer

462 U.S. 523, 103 S.Ct. 2541, 76 L.Ed.2d 768 (1983).

■ JUSTICE STEVENS delivered the opinion of the Court.

Respondent was injured in the course of his employment as a loading helper on a coal barge. As his employer, petitioner was required to compensate him for his injury under § 4 of the Longshoremen's and Harbor Workers' Compensation Act (Act). 44 Stat. 1426, 33 U.S.C. § 904. * * * We granted certiorari to decide * * * whether the Court of Appeals correctly upheld the trial court's computation of respondent's damages.

* * *

The District Court's calculation of damages was predicated on a few undisputed facts. At the time of his injury respondent was earning an annual wage of $26,025. He had a remaining work expectancy of 12½ years. On the date of trial (October 1, 1980), respondent had received compensation payments of $33,079.14. If he had obtained light work and earned the legal minimum hourly wage from July 1, 1979, until his 65th birthday, he would have earned $66,352.

The District Court arrived at its final award by taking 12½ years of earnings at respondent's wage at the time of injury ($325,312.50), subtracting his projected hypothetical earnings at the minimum wage ($66,352) and the compensation payments he had received under § 4 ($33,079.14), and adding $50,000 for pain and suffering. The court did not increase the award to take inflation into account, and it did not discount the award to reflect the present value of the future stream of income. The court instead decided to follow a decision of the Supreme Court of Pennsylvania, which had held "as a matter of law that future inflation shall be presumed equal to future interest rates with these factors offsetting." Kaczkowski v. Bolubasz, 491 Pa. 561, 583, 421 A.2d 1027, 1038–1039 (1980). * * *

The District Court found that respondent was permanently disabled as a result of petitioner's negligence. He therefore was entitled to an award of damages to compensate him for his probable pecuniary loss over the duration of his career, reduced to its present value. It is useful at the outset to review the way in which damages should be measured in a hypothetical inflation-free economy. We shall then consider how price inflation alters the analysis. Finally, we shall decide whether the District Court committed reversible error in this case.

In calculating damages, it is assumed that if the injured party had not been disabled, he would have continued to work, and to receive wages at periodic intervals until retirement, disability, or death. An award for impaired earning capacity is intended to compensate the worker for the diminution in that stream of income. The award could in theory take the form of periodic payments, but in this country it has traditionally taken the form of a lump sum, paid at the conclusion of the litigation. The appropriate lump sum cannot be computed without first examining the stream of income it purports to replace.

The lost stream's length cannot be known with certainty; the worker could have been disabled or even killed in a different, non-work-related accident at any time. The probability that he would still be working at a given date is constantly diminishing. Given the complexity of trying to make an exact calculation, litigants frequently follow the relatively simple course of assuming that the worker would have continued to work up until a specific date certain. In this case, for example, both parties agreed that the petitioner would have continued to work until age 65 (12½ more years) if he had not been injured.

* * * [T]he first stage in calculating an appropriate award for lost earnings involves an estimate of what the lost stream of income would have been. The stream may be approximated as a series of after-tax payments, one in each year of the worker's expected remaining career. In estimating what those payments would have been in an inflation-free economy, the trier of fact may begin with the worker's annual wage at the time of injury. If sufficient proof is offered, the trier of fact may increase that figure to reflect the appropriate influence of individualized factors (such as foreseeable promotions) and societal factors (such as foreseeable productivity growth within the worker's industry).

Of course, even in an inflation-free economy the award of damages to replace the lost stream of income cannot be computed simply by totaling up the sum of the periodic payments. For the damages award is paid in a lump sum at the conclusion of the litigation, and when it—or even a part of it—is invested, it will earn additional money. It has been settled since our decision in *Chesapeake & Ohio R. Co. v. Kelly,* 241 U.S. 485, 36 S.Ct. 630, 60 L.Ed. 1117 (1916), that "in all cases where it is reasonable to suppose that interest may safely be earned upon the amount that is awarded, the ascertained future benefits ought to be discounted in the making up of the award."

The discount rate should be based on the rate of interest that would be earned on "the best and safest investments." Once it is assumed that the injured worker would definitely have worked for a specific term of years, he is entitled to a risk-free stream of future income to replace his lost wages; therefore, the discount rate should not reflect the market's premium for investors who are willing to accept some risk of default. * * *

Thus, although the notion of a damages award representing the present value of a lost stream of earnings in an inflation-free economy rests on some fairly sophisticated economic concepts, the two elements that determine its calculation can be stated fairly easily. They are: (1) the amount that the employee would have earned during each year that he could have been expected to work after the injury; and (2) the appropriate discount rate, reflecting the safest available investment. The trier of fact should apply the discount rate to each of the estimated installments in the lost stream of income, and then add up the discounted installments to determine the total award.

Unfortunately for triers of fact, ours is not an inflation-free economy. Inflation has been a permanent fixture in our economy for many decades, and there can be no doubt that it ideally should affect both stages of the calculation described in the previous section. The difficult problem is how it can do so in the practical context of civil litigation under § 5(b) of the Act.

The first stage of the calculation requires an estimate of the shape of the lost stream of future income. For many workers, including respondent, a contractual "cost-of-living adjustment" automatically increases wages each year by the percentage change during the previous year in the consumer price index calculated by the Bureau of Labor Statistics. Such a contract provides a basis for taking into account an additional societal factor—price inflation—in estimating the worker's lost future earnings.

The second stage of the calculation requires the selection of an appropriate discount rate. Price inflation—or more precisely, anticipated price inflation—certainly affects market rates of return. If a lender knows that his loan is to be repaid a year later with dollars that are less valuable than those he has advanced, he will charge an interest rate that is high enough both to compensate him for the temporary use of the loan proceeds and also to make up for their shrinkage in value.

* * *

Our sister common-law nations generally continue to adhere to the position that inflation is too speculative to be considered in estimating the lost stream of future earnings; they have sought to counteract the danger of systematically undercompensating plaintiffs by applying a discount rate that is below the current market rate. Nevertheless, they have each chosen different rates, applying slightly different economic theories. * * *

In this country, some courts have taken the same "real interest rate" approach as Australia. [Citations.] They have endorsed the economic theory suggesting that market interest rates include two components—an estimate of anticipated inflation, and a desired "real" rate of return on investment—and that the latter component is essentially constant over time. They have concluded that the inflationary increase in the estimated lost stream of future earnings will therefore be perfectly "offset" by all but the "real" component of the market interest rate.

Still other courts have preferred to continue relying on market interest rates. To avoid undercompensation, they have shown at least tentative willingness to permit evidence of what future price inflation will be in estimating the lost stream of future income. * * *

Within the past year, two Federal Courts of Appeals have decided to allow litigants a choice of methods. Sitting *en banc*, the Court of Appeals for the Fifth Circuit has overruled its prior decision in Johnson v. Penrod Drilling Co., 510 F.2d 234 (1975), and held it acceptable either to exclude evidence of future price inflation and discount by a "real" interest rate, or to attempt to predict the effects of future price inflation on future wages and then discount by the market interest rate. Culver v. Slater Boat Co., 688 F.2d 280, 308–310 (1982). A panel of the Court of Appeals for the Seventh Circuit has taken a substantially similar position. O'Shea v. Riverway Towing Co., 677 F.2d 1194, 1200 (1982).

Finally, some courts have applied a number of techniques that have loosely been termed "total offset" methods. What these methods have in common is that they presume that the ideal discount rate—the after-tax market interest rate on a safe investment—is (to a legally tolerable degree of precision) completely offset by certain elements in the ideal computation of the estimated lost stream of future income. They all assume that the effects of future price inflation on wages are part of what offsets the market interest rate. The methods differ, however, in their assumptions regarding which if any other elements in the first stage of the damages calculation contribute to the offset.

* * *

The litigants and the *amici* in this case urge us to select one of the many rules that have been proposed and establish it for all time as the exclusive method in all federal trials for calculating an award for lost earnings in an inflationary economy. We are not persuaded, however, that such an approach is warranted. [Citation.] For our review of the foregoing cases leads us to draw three conclusions. First, by its very nature the calculation of an award for lost earnings must be a rough approximation. Because the lost stream can never be predicted with complete confidence, any lump sum represents only a "rough and ready" effort to put the plaintiff in the position he would have been in had he not been injured. Second, sustained price inflation can make the award substantially less precise. Inflation's current magnitude and unpredictability create a substantial risk that the damages award will prove to have little relation to the lost wages it purports to replace. Third, the question of lost earnings can arise in many different contexts. In some sectors of the economy, it is far easier to assemble evidence of an individual's most likely career path than in others.

These conclusions all counsel hesitation. Having surveyed the multitude of options available, we will do no more than is necessary to resolve the case before us. We limit our attention to suits under § 5(b) of the Act, noting that Congress has provided generally for an award of damages but has not given specific guidance regarding how they are to be calculated. Within that narrow context, we shall define the general boundaries within which a particular award will be considered legally acceptable.

The Court of Appeals correctly noted that respondent's cause of action "is rooted in federal maritime law." [Citations.] The fact that Pennsylvania has adopted the total offset rule for all negligence cases in that forum is therefore not of controlling importance in this case. * * *

In calculating an award for a longshoreman's lost earnings caused by the negligence of a vessel, the discount rate should be chosen on the basis of the factors that are used to estimate the lost stream of future earnings. If the trier of fact relies on a specific forecast of the future rate of price inflation, and if the estimated lost stream of future earnings is calculated to include price inflation along with individual factors and other societal factors, then the proper discount rate would be the after-tax market interest rate. But since specific forecasts of future price inflation remain too unreliable to be useful in many cases, it will normally be a costly and ultimately unproductive waste of longshoremen's resources to make such forecasts the centerpiece of litigation under § 5(b). As Judge Newman has warned: "The average accident trial should not be converted into a graduate seminar on economic forecasting." Doca v. Marina Mercante Nicaraguense, S.A., 634 F.2d, at 39. For that reason, both plaintiffs and trial courts should be discouraged from pursuing that approach.

On the other hand, if forecasts of future price inflation are not used, it is necessary to choose an appropriate below-market discount rate. As long as inflation continues, one must ask how much should be "offset" against the market rate. Once again, that amount should be chosen on the basis of the same factors that are used to estimate the lost stream of future earnings. If full account is taken of the individual and societal factors (excepting price inflation) that can be expected to have resulted in wage increases, then all that should be set off against the market interest rate is an estimate of future price inflation. This would result in one of the "real interest rate" approaches described above. Although we find the economic evidence distinctly inconclusive regarding an essential premise of those approaches, we do not believe a trial court adopting such an approach in a suit under § 5(b) should be reversed if it adopts a rate between 1 and 3% and explains its choice.

* * *

We do not suggest that the trial judge should embark on a search for "delusive exactness." It is perfectly obvious that the most detailed inquiry can at best produce an approximate result. And one cannot ignore the fact that in many instances the award for impaired earning capacity may be overshadowed by a highly impressionistic award for pain and suffering. But we are satisfied that whatever rate the District Court may choose to discount the estimated stream of future earnings, it must make a deliberate choice, rather than assuming that it is bound by a rule of state law.

The judgment of the Court of Appeals is vacated, and the case is remanded for further proceedings consistent with this opinion.

It is so ordered.

---

1. *The Adjustment Dilemma.* At one time many courts refused to adjust future lost wages for anticipated inflation or deflation because of the speculative nature of such adjustment. The problem was that the same courts used current market interest rates to reduce future losses to their present value. To the extent that the current market interest rate reflects anticipated inflation reducing the value of the dollar upon maturity, plaintiffs were disadvantaged. Such rules incorporated inflation into only one stage of the calculation but not the other. *See* Johnson v. Penrod Drilling

Co., 510 F.2d 234 (5th Cir.1975); Sleeman v. Chesapeake and Ohio R. Co., 414 F.2d 305 (6th Cir.1969).

The effect of this rule was to deny the plaintiff the benefit of inflationary increases to calculate future earnings, while giving the defendant the benefit of inflation's impact on the interest rate that is used to discount those earnings to present value. This inequity was not serious during periods of relatively low rates of inflation. The nation's economic history since the middle of the 1960's has forced courts to reevaluate this policy. A personal injury victim who received a judgment in 1967 now has dollars worth approximately one third as much in purchasing power.

2. *Merit Increases in Wages.* An individual worker may receive "real" wage increases, beyond inflationary adjustments. Such increases are usually reflected in "seniority" or "experience" raises, "merit" raises, or promotions. It is difficult to prove whether a particular injured worker might have received such increases, or when they might occur. Some types of employment lend themselves to such proof more easily than others. There has been little dispute that such adjustments should be included in the stream if they can be established with reasonable certainty. *See* State v. Guinn, 555 P.2d 530 (Alaska 1976).

3. *Societal Factors.* A plaintiff's wages may change for societal reasons unrelated to price inflation or the individual worker's advancement on merit. The wages of workers in plaintiff's class may increase or decrease over time. Changes in society bring about such adjustments. New technology, growth in industrial productivity, and successful collective bargaining are all factors that can contribute to changes in wages. Some cases have allowed evidence of the probable effect of such societal factors. *See* Kaczkowski v. Bolubasz, 491 Pa. 561, 421 A.2d 1027 (1980).

4. *Future Price Inflation.* Persistently high inflation rates during a period of recent history convinced many courts that plaintiffs were being seriously undercompensated. Judicial refusal to acknowledge price inflation left many personal injury victims and wrongful death dependents with reduced purchasing power. The problem was that courts refused to allow evidence of future inflation to compute lost future income, yet allowed discounting with current interest rates that reflected anticipated future price inflation.

Judge Posner explained this problem in *O'Shea v. Riverway Towing Co.*, 677 F.2d 1194 (7th Cir.1982): "[I]f there is inflation it will affect wages as well as prices. Therefore to give Mrs. O'Shea $2318 today because that is the present value of $7200 10 years hence, computed at a discount rate—12 percent—that consists mainly of an allowance for anticipated inflation, is in fact to give her less than she would have been earning then if she was earning $7200 on the date of the accident, even if the only wage increases she would have received would have been those necessary to keep pace with inflation." 677 F.2d at 1199.

5. *Methods of Adjustment for Inflation.* As the Supreme Court noted in the principal case, there are several ways to adjust damages awards to

account for the effect of wage and price inflation. Courts have generally used one of three methods.

(1) In the "case-by-case" method, the fact-finder first predicts all of the wage increases a plaintiff would have received during each future year of work lost by the injury. These wage increases include expected adjustments for future inflation. These predictions allow calculation of the future income stream the plaintiff has lost. The fact-finder then discounts that income stream to present value using the market interest rate, which reflects future predicted price inflation. The resulting figure is the plaintiff's damages for lost wages.

(2) Another approach is the "real interest rate" method, also called the below-market-discount method. The fact-finder predicts wage increases attributed to merit or industry productivity, but does not attempt to predict the wage increases that might result from inflationary pressures on wages. Then the resulting income stream is discounted by a below-market discount rate between 1% and 3%. The "real interest rate" subtracts the amount attributable to future price inflation. This is the method used in *Pfeifer*.

(3) Another method is based on the "total-offset" theory. In this approach future wage increases, including the effects of future inflation, are presumed to offset exactly the interest a plaintiff would earn by investing the lump-sum damage award. A court thus awards a plaintiff the amount of estimated lost wages. The fact-finder neither discounts the award nor adjusts it for inflation.

6. *Taxes.* The United States Supreme Court had said previous to *Pfeifer* that the lost stream of income in a Federal Employers' Liability Act (FELA) case should be estimated in after-tax dollars and that the discount rate should also represent the after-tax rate of return to the injured worker. Norfolk & Western R. Co. v. Liepelt, 444 U.S. 490, 100 S.Ct. 755, 62 L.Ed.2d 689 (1980). In *Walden v. United States*, 31 F.Supp.2d 1230, 1235 (S.D.Cal.1998) the court held that an award for lost income, past and future, must be discounted to reflect lost wage income after both state and federal taxes have been deducted. It must also be discounted to reflect amounts otherwise paid in social security taxes.

7. *Choice of Discount Rate.* The Court in *Pfeifer,* drawing from its previous decision in *Chesapeake & Ohio Railway v. Kelly*, 241 U.S. 485, 36 S.Ct. 630, 60 L.Ed. 1117 (1916), suggested that the discount rate should be based on the interest rate available on the "best and safest investments" but failed to explain the meaning of that phrase. Certainly United States government issued securities would be considered the only completely "risk-free" investment. See Espana v. United States, 616 F.2d 41 (2d Cir.1980) (6 percent rate based on short-term government securities). Contrast the approach followed in *Hoskie v. United States*, 666 F.2d 1353 (10th Cir.1981), where the court applied a 9.5 percent discount rate based on the current yield of triple-A rated corporate bonds as satisfying the court's standard of a "reasonably safe long-term investment available to the average person." How does that test differ from the *Pfeifer* standard?

8. *Investment Risks.* Even securities issued by the federal government are only risk-free in the sense that the debtor is unlikely to default. The holder still will be subject to fluctuations in the current value of the bond which, if the need arises for liquidation of the bond prior to maturity, could result in a net loss. Consider the following illustration:

Plaintiff is a child personal injury victim who has suffered serious internal injuries from swallowing a toxic drain cleaner. At the time of trial the expert medical testimony established that one more operation would probably be necessary, but that it should be postponed as long as possible during the growing years. The testimony further established that the operation would simply have to be done whenever it was absolutely necessary, and that time could be anytime within the next seven years. In the meantime, the child must continue to have expensive treatments until an internal problem can be cured by the operation.

The cost of this future operation was determined to be $10,000. The treatments until the operation are $800 annually. The compensation allowed purchase of a seven year United States government bond with a coupon (yield) of 8% at par ($10,000). Thus the child will receive the necessary $800 interest annually to pay for the treatments and will have $10,000 upon maturity in seven years to pay for the operation.

As the medical expert feared, however, the operation became absolutely necessary after only two years. The bond had to be sold immediately to pay for the operation. The problem is that even though the investment is a conservative one, the change in interest rates in the market during the intervening time period will affect the price of the bond. Consider two possibilities: (1) If interest rates have risen and 11% is the rate for similar bonds, then the bond will sell for approximately $8870. The child will not have enough money from this sale for the $10,000 operation. Moreover, the high interest rate may reflect an inflation rate that is unexpectedly high, which would also be likely to increase the cost of the operation beyond the estimated $10,000. (2) If interest rates have fallen and 5% is the rate for similar bonds, then the bond will sell for approximately $11,310. Then there is more than enough money for the operation. Moreover, the cost of the operation may have been overestimated if this low interest rate reflects low inflation.

9. In *Colleen v. United States*, 843 F.2d 329 (9th Cir.1987), the court held that the use of a zero discount rate to find the present value of a lump-sum award in a medical malpractice suit, absent support by credible expert testimony, constituted an abuse of the trial court's discretion. Compare that result with *Monaghan v. Uiterwyk Lines, Ltd.*, 607 F.Supp. 1020 (E.D.Pa.1985), where no economic evidence regarding discounting to present value was introduced, but the court took "judicial notice of historical interest and inflation rates" and determined the appropriate discount rate was 2%. *See also* Self v. Great Lakes Dredge & Dock Co., 832 F.2d 1540, 1552 (11th Cir.1987) (2% rate acceptable).

10. The approach of awarding damages in a lump sum to compensate for future losses in personal injury and wrongful death cases is, at best, a

system of calculated guesswork involving a "battle of the experts." A complex formula that incorporates numerous projections of individual and societal factors will certainly result in a lump-sum total which will either overcompensate or undercompensate. An alternative method is to award payments in installments over the time period during which the losses will accrue in the future. The Model Periodic Payment of Judgments Act provides a system for the payment of damages for bodily injury in periodic installments, at the election of any party, subject to certain safeguards. The Model Act is designed to pay damages as losses actually accrue, thus eliminating the need to discount awards of future damages to present value. Also, the Act suggests that the installment method removes the burden of making difficult investment decisions for those claimants who are unsophisticated in financial matters. For a contrary view *see* Conklin, Wrongful Death Damages Expansion, Inflation; Discounts and Taxes—The Numbers Game, 28 Trial Law.Guide 249 (1984).

11.   Should courts be addressing these damages adjustments issues or are legislatures better equipped to resolve them? If the legislative branch does not provide guidance, should appellate courts give clear mandates to the trial courts, or leave them wide discretion?

PROBLEM: THE FRUSTRATED JUDGE

You are a clerk for a federal district court judge who is hearing without a jury a wrongful death case under federal jurisdiction. The decedent was a privately employed pilot who crashed over the ocean because of a defect in the manufacture of the aircraft.

The plaintiff presented evidence on the future lost earnings of the pilot, B.J. Raull. At the time of death, Raull was earning $37,680, not including certain benefits supplied by the employer, such as food and shelter while Raull was on the job. An econometrist testified about projected pilot earnings compounded on a 4% basis and on an 6% basis, and discounted at a 3% basis. There were two models: one projected continued work with the same employer; the other assumed that after five years Raull would enter the more lucrative profession of commercial pilots. The expert testified that all projections were based upon several conservative assumptions: employment was assumed only to age sixty; no fringe benefits were included in the calculations; and the value of personal household services and future inheritances were not included.

The expert had several charts showing the projections. The district court judge was very upset with the testimony and with the charts that showed very high damages. The judge tells you privately that this testimony is useless. You listen to the following lecture:

"I am unconvinced that anyone can foretell economic conditions years down the road; it is nothing but crystal ball gazing. I read recently that in 1930, a transcontinental telephone call cost about $20, and for that same $20 one could mail 1,000 first class letters. Today, I make phone calls across the country for no extra charge, but one can only stamp 45 first class letters for that same $20.00, if one is communicating non-electronically at all. In other words, things change unpredictably. Some costs go up and some go down. Services come and go and so do jobs. When I was young, one of the largest of the building trades was that of the plasterers. Today plasterers are almost a curiosity. Who's to say what will happen to pilots?

"These charts assume that there will be a continuing and a growing demand for ever more high priced airline pilots. With the rapid development of automation, who is to say that by the year 2030 commercial airline pilots will not have fewer jobs instead of more?

"I don't enjoy reading that *Pfeifer* case either, but it controls here. Go read the thing again and tell me if I have to hear any more of this testimony."

What will you report?

Estevez v. United States

74 F.Supp.2d 305 (S.D.N.Y.1999).

■ SCHEINDLIN, DISTRICT JUDGE.

The defendant, The United States of America (the "Government") moves pursuant to Local Rule 6.3 and Fed.R.Civ.P. 59(e) and 60(a) for reconsideration and modification of the Court's Opinion and Order, dated July 15, 1999. The Government objects to the Opinion on three grounds: (1) that the judgment requires the Government to purchase an annuity rather than pay a lump sum damage award; (2) that the awards for future lost earnings were not reduced to account for federal income taxes; and (3) that the lump sum awards for future pain and suffering were not reduced to reflect the time value of money.

A.   The Structured Judgment

The Government disagrees with the Court's holding that the damage award should be structured. In so holding, this Court relied upon the law of New York State, which requires that for future damages in excess of $250,000, the court is to enter judgment for "the present value of an annuity contract that will provide for the payments of the remaining amounts of future damages in periodic installments." *See* Civil Practice Law and Rules ("CPLR") § 5041(e) (McKinney 1992 & Supp.1999). The Government argues that the Federal Tort Claims Act does not authorize judgments other than lump sum damage awards. [Citations] The Second Circuit has not addressed this issue.

I do not agree. In actions brought under the FTCA, damages are determined "in the same manner and to the same extent as a private individual under like circumstances, but shall not be awarded for interest prior to judgment or for punitive damages." 28 U.S.C. § 2674. The law governing the award of damages is that "of the place where the [tortious] act or omission occurred." 28 U.S.C. § 1346(b). Because the plaintiffs were injured in New York, this Court will apply New York law to determine the appropriate damage award in this action.

Moreover, the case the Government cites to support the contention that the damages award be rendered in lump sum actually supports structuring the judgment in this case. In *Reilly* [*Reilly v. United States,* 863 F.2d 149, 170 (1st Cir.1988)], the First Circuit held that "absent unusual circumstances not present here, see supra note 16, the court below was right in insisting that its award of damages be rendered in lump-sum form." Note 16 states, in pertinent part, that:

> Periodic damage awards are permissible in certain situations. For example, if a controlling statute permits, see, e.g., Fla. Stat. Ann. § 768.51(1)(b) (West 1986); Cal.Civ.Proc.Code § 667.7(a) (West 1987); Wis. Stat. Ann. § 655.015 (West 1980 & Supp.1988).... Such an outcome can also be achieved by agreement of the parties in interest ... or where a trust, annuity, or other prophylactic arrangement is necessary to ensure that the injured party will in fact receive his due....

Id. at 169 & n. 16. The court reasoned that because neither Congress nor Rhode Island has enacted legislation permitting the routine imposition of structured payouts in lieu of lump sum damage awards, the district court did not err in ruling that it was obligated to make the award of damages in the form of a lump sum.

Similar to California and Wisconsin, in 1986, the New York legislature enacted CPLR § 5041, extending the structured judgment requirement to tort actions generally, including: personal injury, injury to property, and wrongful death. Because the New York legislature, unlike that of Rhode Island, has enacted a law *requiring* structured payouts when future damages exceed $250,000, this court has discretion to structure damage awards in this case, where future damages for Joseph total $750,000. In addition, Joseph is five years old, and an annuity is necessary to ensure that when he reaches the age of majority, Joseph will in fact receive his due.

B. Income Tax

The Government also disagrees with this Court's holding that the future lost earning awards should not be reduced by federal income tax. In so holding, this Court relied upon the law of New York State, which dictates that taxes not be reduced. The Government, however, argues that it is unlike private defendants because the failure to deduct taxes subjects it to double sanctions and is thus punitive: the judgment is not reduced by the amount of the tax and the Government will not collect that amount as revenue.

This argument is unpersuasive. The Government is being treated no differently than any private defendant. The Government, like any private defendant, must pay a damage award without deduction for tax because it is a tortfeasor in a state that does not provide for any such deduction. To the extent it does not receive tax revenue from plaintiff in this case, the

Government is similarly deprived of such income in cases involving plaintiffs who sue private defendants. The failure to deduct tax from the damage awards in this case cannot be considered punitive. No private defendant in New York is able to withhold the tax, or to pay it to the Government rather than the plaintiff. Indeed, the result sought by the Government would result in a windfall to it (the payment of tax from a minuscule subset of tort victims) and a punishment to plaintiffs, the innocent victims who had the bad luck to be severely injured by a government vehicle.

C. Future Pain and Suffering

The Government finally contends that the awards for future pain and suffering were not reduced to account for the time value of money. The Government specifically requests that Joseph's future pain and suffering award be discounted by 2%, which is the approximate historic time value of money in the United States.

The Government is confused. In structuring the judgment, Joseph is awarded three-quarters of the future value of the damage award ($820,-052). Joseph's future damage award, which includes future pain and suffering, was not reduced for the time value of money because the Government is to purchase an annuity that will pay Joseph $820,052 over a ten year period. The cost or present value to the Government of such an annuity is less than $820,052. Therefore, the reduction for the time value of money is automatically accounted for when the Government purchases the annuity that will pay Joseph $820,052 over a ten year period.[1]

For the reasons set forth above, the Government's motion for reconsideration and modification of this Court's Opinion and Order, dated July 15, 1999, is denied.

---

1. The parties in a private suit may stipulate to the "total offset" method before trial, thus eliminating the need for the production of evidence on inflation and discount rates. The Supreme Court observed in *Monessen Southwestern Ry. Co. v. Morgan*, 486 U.S. 330, 108 S.Ct. 1837, 1846 n. 11, 100 L.Ed.2d 349 (1988), that Jones & Laughlin Steel Corp. v. Pfeifer, reprinted *supra* in this chapter, allows such stipulation. "[N]othing

---

1. Were Joseph's award not structured but rather paid in lump sum as the Government contends, the calculations are as follows. Joseph is entitled to a total award of $1,993,902 ($588,000 for past damages, $750,000 for future pain and suffering, $220,815 for future medical expenses, and $432,887 for future lost earnings.) Applying a 2% discount rate over 13 years, the present value of Joseph's future pain and suffering is $576,767. Using the Government's growth rate (6.21%) and discount rate (5%) for medical services, the present value of Joseph's future medical services is $272,052. After applying the Government's requested discount rate of 2% for a period of 48 years (the sum of 31 years (Joseph's reduced work life expectancy according to Mr. Gluck) and 17 years (the difference between his present age and age 22)), the present value of Joseph's lost earnings is $164,144. Thus, the total present value of Joseph's future damages is $1,012,963. Joseph's total lump sum award is $1,600,963, (the sum of the past damages ($588,000) and the present value of the future damages ($1,012,963)), inclusive of both attorney's fees (25% or $400,241) and actual and necessary expenses.

prevents parties interested in keeping litigation costs under control from stipulating to [the total offset method's] use before trial." 462 U.S. 523, 550, 103 S.Ct. 2541, 2557, 76 L.Ed.2d 768 (1983).

Monessen held that if the parties do not so stipulate, the trial judge in a FELA case may not require the jury to accept one method of calculation, as some state courts do as a matter of common law. The trial court had applied the state rule mandating the total offset method, but the Supreme Court held that the mandatory instruction to the jury was reversible error in a FELA case. The Court reasoned that the judge improperly took from the jury the factual question of the appropriate rate for discounting the award. In *Monessen* the Court explained that its previous decision in *Pfeifer* required that the present value calculation had to be made as a "deliberate choice" by the trier of fact. Since no right to a jury trial existed in the Longshoremen's and Harbor Workers' Compensation Act claim involved in *Pfeifer*, the trier of fact was necessarily the judge. For the FELA claim in *Monessen*, the Court said the judge could not preempt the jury's function by mandating one method of computing present value, although the opinion notes that it is permissible for the judge to assist the jury by recommending a method. 486 U.S. 330, 108 S.Ct. 1837, 1846, 100 L.Ed.2d 349 (1988).

In *Conde v. Starlight I, Inc.*, 103 F.3d 210, 214–215 (1st Cir.1997), the court observed that calculating a future stream of lost income typically involved "unknowable and unquantifiable factors," and therefore upheld a 3% per annum adjustment for inflation in wages of non-agricultural workers as not "excessive to shock conscience." The court also allowed the parties to stipulate that some present value reduction (1 or 2 percent) would be appropriate, although reserving the precise discount rate.

2.   The Supreme Court in *St. Louis Southwestern Railway Company v. Dickerson*, 470 U.S. 409, 105 S.Ct. 1347, 84 L.Ed.2d 303 (1985), held that the refusal to give a present value instruction in a FELA case constituted reversible error. Although FELA cases are adjudicated in state courts and are subject to state procedural rules, the substantive law which governs the actions is federal. In contrast, in *Kokesh v. American Steamship Company*, 747 F.2d 1092 (6th Cir.1984), the court held that the trial court had not committed plain error by not instructing the jury on reducing future personal injury damages to present value in a negligence action under the Jones Act. The court of appeals noted that one approach acknowledged in *Pfeifer* was to assume that the market interest rate exactly offsets price inflation and productivity gains. Accordingly, the court concluded that the failure to request a present value instruction may have been an intentional trial strategy.

In *Kasper v. Saint Mary of Nazareth Hosp.*, 135 F.3d 1170 (7th Cir.1998) the court used a computational procedure whereby both inflation and discounting were ignored, but did not exclude the possibility of a successful challenge based on a factual showing that the assumptions were incorrect. Further, the court stated that the failure to mention present value to the jury was not fatal to plaintiff's case. The court applied a "bottom-line" test to a jury's assessment of damages: if the jury could by a proper procedure have arrived at the amount it awarded, "the court would not insist on a showing that it followed a proper procedure." Id. at 1177.

B.   Prejudgment Interest

Section Coverage:

There are three types or categories of interest: conventional, prejudgment, and postjudgment. Conventional interest, or *eo nomine* ("in name only"), is contractual; an example is the amount payable by a borrower on a home mortgage loan. Postjudgment interest is statutory. All jurisdictions have enacted an interest rate payable on a judgment. Interest accrues at that rate from the date of entry to judgment satisfaction.

Prejudgment interest is somewhat of a mirror-image of its postjudgment counterpart. It too is interest payable upon the judgment, but from the time period running from accrual of a cause of action until entry of the judgment. The basis for imposing prejudgment interest may be pursuant to the agreement of the parties, by statute, or in equity as a restitutionary device to prevent unjust enrichment. Unlike postjudgment interest which accrues automatically, prejudgment interest is not always awarded.

Several competing policies exist with respect to the propriety of prejudgment interest. From the plaintiff's perspective, prejudgment interest provides a form of compensation for the loss of use of money damages until the date of judgment. If a defendant knows that the court will award prejudgment interest, there is no longer any incentive to delay paying a valid claim or to delay engaging in good faith settlement negotiations.

From the defendant's perspective, it is unfair to award interest on a claimed sum when it is uncertain whether the plaintiff would prevail at trial and uncertain as to the size of the ultimate verdict after trial. The threat of prejudgment interest presents a defendant with a Hobson's choice: either pay a contested claim in order to halt accrual of prejudgment interest or wait until judgment and pay interest for the time period from accrual of the claim until satisfaction of the judgment.

Courts, and sometimes legislatures, have resolved this conflict by placing several limitations on the allowability of prejudgment interest. The usual limitations are that prejudgment interest is recoverable when (1) the date the claim accrued was definite and (2) the amount of damages was readily ascertainable at that time. The first requirement recognizes that some damages, such as medical expenses, may be incurred intermittently from the occurrence of the harm until trial. The second criterion provides that prejudgment interest should be assessed only in the event that the damages were "liquidated" or calculable with some precision at the time the cause of action accrued. Consequently, courts historically have denied prejudgment interest in personal injury cases because certain elements, such as pain and suffering, inherently are unliquidated until determined by the trier of fact. Prejudgment interest awards typically have been reserved for breach of contract actions involving a definite sum of money or performance with an ascertainable pecuniary value and for those tort cases involving harm to land or chattels where valuation may be established by market prices.

Model Case:

On January 1 Baker entered into a contract to purchase 1,000 bushels of wheat at $3.00 per bushel from Peterson, payment and delivery to take place on October 1. On September 1 Peterson wrongfully repudiated the contract and Baker immediately obtained replacement wheat in the open market for $4.00 per bushel.

Baker sent a notice to Peterson demanding the $1,000 differential between the cost to cover and the contract price, reimbursement of expenses incidental to effecting cover, and lost profits. Peterson refused to pay any amount and Baker filed suit for breach of contract claiming each of the stated elements as damages.

The trial is concluded two years later and the court awards Baker the $1,000 plus incidental damages and an additional $500 as lost profits. Prejudgment interest would be properly assessed on the $1,000 and the incidental damages but the court, in its discretion, could justifiably deny it with respect to the lost profits. The claim for lost profits would typically be much more difficult to ascertain with certainty at the time of the breach, and therefore less appropriate to expect Peterson to satisfy in advance of trial. The assessment of prejudgment interest on the other two elements of damages serves two functions: Baker is wholly compensated for the damages for the loss of use of his money until the court's order and, the corollary, Peterson is denied the benefits of holding and being able to earn interest on the damages from the date of breach until judgment. Peterson could have tolled the running of prejudgment interest by promptly tendering payment of the $1,000 and the incidental expenses incurred as a result of the breach but should not be penalized for validly contesting the lost profits claim.

Kansas v. Colorado

533 U.S. 1, 121 S.Ct. 2023, 150 L.Ed.2d 72 (2001).

■ JUSTICE STEVENS delivered the opinion of the Court.

The Arkansas River rises in the mountains of Colorado just east of the Continental Divide, descends for about 280 miles to the Kansas border, then flows through that State, Oklahoma, and Arkansas and empties into the Mississippi River. On May 20, 1901, Kansas first invoked this Court's original jurisdiction to seek a remedy for Colorado's diversion of water from the Arkansas River. In opinions written during the past century we have described the history and the importance of the river. [Citations] For present purposes it suffices to note that two of those cases * * * led to the negotiation of the Arkansas River Compact (Compact), an agreement between Kansas and Colorado that in turn was approved by Congress in 1949. See 63 Stat. 145. The case before us today involves a claim by Kansas for damages based on Colorado's violations of that Compact.

The Compact was designed to "[s]ettle existing disputes and remove causes of future controversy" between the two States and their citizens concerning waters of the Arkansas River and to "[e]quitably divide and apportion" those waters and the benefits arising from construction and operation of the federal project known as the "John Martin Reservoir." * * *

In 1986, we granted Kansas leave to file a complaint alleging three violations of the Compact by Colorado. After taking evidence in the liability phase of the proceeding, Special Master Arthur L. Littleworth filed his first report, in which he recommended that two of the claims be denied, but that the Court find that post-Compact increases in groundwater well pumping in Colorado had materially depleted the waters of the river in violation of Article IV–D. * * * We remanded the case to the Special Master to determine an appropriate remedy for the violations of Article IV–D.

[The Special Master filed a second report recommending an award of damages. Colorado filed various exceptions, including arguing that the report improperly recommended the recovery of prejudgment interest on an unliquidated claim. The Court overruled those exceptions without prejudice to their renewal after the Special Master made a more specific recommendation for a remedy.] He did so in his third report, and we are now confronted with exceptions filed by both States.

In the third report, the Special Master recommends that damages be measured by Kansas' losses, rather than Colorado's profits, attributable to Compact violations after 1950; that the damages be paid in money rather than water; and that the damages should include prejudgment interest from 1969 to the date of judgment. [Colorado again filed various objections to the report, including that the damages award should not include prejudgment interest, and that the amount of interest awarded was excessive. Kansas also filed an objection, contending that prejudgment interest should be paid from 1950, rather than 1969.] * * * The United States, which intervened because of its interest in the operation of flood control projects in Colorado, submits that both States' objections should be overruled.

II

Colorado next excepts to the Special Master's conclusion that the damages award should include prejudgment interest despite the fact that Kansas' claim is unliquidated.[2] At one point in time, the fact that the claim

---

2. Though final damages have not yet been calculated, the importance of this issue is illustrated by breaking down the damages claimed by Kansas. Of $62,369,173 in damages so claimed, $9,218,305 represents direct and indirect losses in actual dollars when the damage occurred. Of the remaining $53,150,867, about $12 million constitutes an adjustment for inflation (a type of interest that Colorado concedes is appropriate) while the remaining amount (approximately $41 million) represents additional interest intended to compensate for

was unliquidated would have been of substantial importance. As a general matter, early common-law cases drew a distinction between liquidated and unliquidated claims and refused to allow interest on the latter. This rule seems to have rested upon a belief that there was something inherently unfair about requiring debtors to pay interest when they were unable to halt its accrual by handing over to their creditors a fixed and unassailable amount.

This common-law distinction has long since lost its hold on the legal imagination. Beginning in the early part of the last century, numerous courts and commentators have rejected the distinction for failing to acknowledge the compensatory nature of interest awards. This Court allied itself with the evolving consensus in 1933, when we expressed the opinion that the distinction between cases of liquidated and unliquidated damages "is not a sound one." *Funkhouser v. J.B. Preston Co.*, 290 U.S. 163, 168, 54 S.Ct. 134, 78 L.Ed. 243 (1933). The analysis supporting that conclusion gave no doubt as to our reasoning: "Whether the case is of the one class or the other, the injured party has suffered a loss which may be regarded as not fully compensated if he is confined to the amount found to be recoverable as of the time of breach and nothing is added for the delay in obtaining the award of damages." Our cases since 1933 have consistently acknowledged that a monetary award does not fully compensate for an injury unless it includes an interest component. [Citation]

Relying on our cases, the Special Master "concluded that the unliquidated nature of Kansas' money damages does not, in and of itself, bar an award of prejudgment interest." In reaching that conclusion, the Special Master was fully cognizant of both the displaced common-law rule and the subsequent doctrinal evolution. In addition, he gave careful consideration to equitable considerations that might mitigate against an award of interest, concluding that "considerations of fairness,"supported the award of at least some prejudgment interest in this case.

We find no fault in the Special Master's analysis of either our prior cases or the equities of this matter. While we will deal with the amount of prejudgment interest below, to answer Colorado's second objection it is sufficient to conclude that the Special Master was correct in determining that the unliquidated nature of the damages does not preclude an award of prejudgment interest

Colorado's second exception is overruled.

III

Colorado's third exception takes issue with both the rate of interest adopted by the Special Master and the date from which he recommended that interest begin to accrue. As to the second of these two concerns, Colorado submits that, if any prejudgment interest is to be awarded, it should begin to accrue in 1985 (when Kansas filed its complaint in this

---

lost investment opportunities. Third Report of Special Master 87–88 (hereinafter Third Report). The magnitude of prejudgment interest ultimately awarded in this case will, of course, turn on the date from which interest accrues.

action), rather than in 1969 (when, the Special Master concluded, Colorado knew or should have known that it was violating the Compact). On the other hand, Kansas has entered an exception, arguing that the accrual of interest should begin in 1950. We first address the rate question, then the timing issue.

A

The Special Master credited the testimony of Kansas' three experts who calculated the interest rates that they thought necessary to provide full compensation for the damages caused by Colorado's violations of the Compact in the years since 1950. As a result of inflation and changing market conditions those rates varied from year to year. In their calculation of the damages suffered by Kansas farmers, the experts used the interest rates that were applicable to individuals in the relevant years rather than the (lower) rates available to States.

Colorado argues that the lower rates should have been used because it is the State, rather than the individual farmers, that is maintaining the action and will receive any award of damages. But if, as we have already decided, it is permissible for the State to measure a portion of its damages by losses suffered by individual farmers, it necessarily follows that the courts are free to utilize whatever interest rate will most accurately measure those losses. The money in question in this portion of the damages award is revenue that would—but for Colorado's actions—have been earned by individual farmers. Thus, the Special Master correctly concluded that the economic consequences of Colorado's breach could best be remedied by an interest award that mirrors the cost of any additional borrowing the farmers may have been forced to undertake in order to compensate for lost revenue.

B

Although the Special Master rejected Colorado's submission that there is a categorical bar to the award of prejudgment interest on unliquidated claims, he concluded that such interest should not " 'be awarded according to any rigid theory of compensation for money withheld,' " but rather should respond to " 'considerations of fairness.' " Kansas argues that our decisions subsequent to *Jackson County* have effectively foreclosed the equities—balancing approach that the Special Master adopted. There is some merit to Kansas' position. [Citation]

However, despite the clear direction indicated by some of our earlier opinions, we cannot say that by 1949 our caselaw had developed sufficiently to put Colorado on notice that, upon a violation of the Compact, we would automatically award prejudgment interest from the time of injury. Given the state of the law at that time, Colorado may well have believed that we would balance the equities in order to achieve a just and equitable remedy, rather than automatically imposing prejudgment interest in order to achieve full compensation. See *Jackson Cty.*, 308 U.S., at 352, 60 S.Ct. 285 (prejudgment interest award limited by "considerations of fairness"); *Mil-*

ler v. Robertson, 266 U.S. 243, 258, 45 S.Ct. 73, 69 L.Ed. 265 (1924) ("[W]hen necessary in order to arrive at fair compensation, the court in the exercise of a sound discretion may include interest or its equivalent as an element of damages" on unliquidated claims); Restatement of Contracts § 337, p. 542 (1932) (prejudgment interest on unliquidated claims "may be allowed in the discretion of the court, if justice requires it"). While we are confident that, when it signed the Compact, Colorado was on notice that it might be subject to prejudgment interest if such interest was necessary to fashion an equitable remedy, we are unable to conclude with sufficient certainty that Colorado was on notice that such interest would be imposed as a matter of course. We, therefore, believe that the Special Master acted properly in carefully analyzing the facts of the case and in only awarding as much prejudgment interest as was required by a balancing of the equities.

We also agree with the Special Master that the equities in this case do not support an award of prejudgment interest from the date of the first violation of the Compact, but rather favor an award beginning on a later date. In reaching this conclusion, the Special Master appropriately considered several factors. In particular, he relied on the fact that in the early years after the Compact was signed, no one had any thought that the pact was being violated. In addition, he considered the long interval that passed between the original injuries and these proceedings, as well as the dramatic impact of compounding interest over many years.

In its exception, Kansas argues that the Special Master's reasoning would be appropriate if damages were being awarded as a form of punishment, but does not justify a refusal to provide full compensation to an injured party. Moreover, Kansas argues, a rule that rewards ignorance might discourage diligence in making sure that there is full compliance with the terms of the Compact. Kansas' argument is consistent with a "rigid theory of compensation for money withheld," but, for the reasons discussed above, we are persuaded that the Special Master correctly declined to adopt such a theory. The equitable considerations identified by the Special Master fully justify his view that in this case it would be inappropriate to award prejudgment interest for any years before either party was aware of the excessive pumping in Colorado. In its third exception, Colorado argues that, if prejudgment interest is to be awarded at all, the equities are best balanced by limiting such interest to the time after the complaint was filed, rather than the time after which Colorado knew or should have known that it was violating the Compact. Specifically, Colorado suggests that prejudgment interest should begin to accrue in 1985 rather than 1969. The choice between the two dates is surely debatable; it is a matter over which reasonable people can—and do—disagree. After examining the equities for ourselves, however, a majority of the Court has decided that the later date is the more appropriate.

When we overruled Colorado's objections to the Special Master's second report, we held that Kansas was not guilty of inexcusable delay in failing to complain more promptly about post-Compact well-pumping. In saying that the delay was not inexcusable, we recognized that the nature and extent of Colorado's violations continued to be unclear even in the years after which it became obvious that the Compact was being violated. That conclusion is something of a two-edged sword, however. While Kansas' delay was understandable given the amorphous nature of its claims, there is no doubt that the interests of both States would have been served if the claim had been advanced promptly after its basis became known. Once it became obvious that a violation of the Compact had occurred, it was equally clear that the proceedings necessary to evaluate the significance of the violations would be complex and protracted. Despite the diligence of the parties and the Special Master, over 15 years have elapsed since the complaint was filed. Given the uncertainty over the scope of damages that prevailed during the period between 1968 and 1985 and the fact that it was uniquely in Kansas' power to begin the process by which those damages would be quantified, Colorado's request that we deny prejudgment interest for that period is reasonable.

For these reasons, we overrule Kansas' exception. We also overrule Colorado's third exception insofar as it challenges the interest rates recommended by the Special Master, but we sustain that objection insofar as it challenges the award of interest for the years prior to 1985.

We remand the case to the Special Master for preparation of a final judgment consistent with this opinion.

It is so ordered.

■ JUSTICE O'CONNOR, with whom JUSTICE SCALIA and JUSTICE THOMAS join, concurring in part and dissenting in part.

* * * We are dealing with an interstate compact apportioning the flow of a river between two States. A compact is a contract. It represents a bargained-for exchange between its signatories and "remains a legal document that must be construed and applied in accordance with its terms." [Citations] It is a fundamental tenet of contract law that parties to a contract are deemed to have contracted with reference to principles of law existing at the time the contract was made. [Citations] * * * [T]he question is whether, at the time the Compact was negotiated and approved, Colorado and Kansas could fairly be said to have intended, or at least to have expected or assumed, that Colorado might be exposing itself to liability for prejudgment interest in the event of the Compact's breach.

I fail to see how Colorado and Kansas could have contemplated that prejudgment interest would be awarded. The "venerable ... rule" at common law was that prejudgment interest was unavailable on claims for unliquidated or, even more significantly, unascertainable damages. * * * [I]n the absence of a statute providing for such interest, many courts, including our own, still denied and would continue to deny prejudgment interest on claims for unliquidated and unascertainable damages in a great many, and probably most, circumstances. * * *

There is nothing fair about awarding prejudgment interest as a remedy for the Compact's breach when all available evidence suggests that the signatories to the Compact neither intended nor contemplated such an unconventional remedy. Many compacts between States are old; suits involving compacts concerning water rights are late in starting and are invariably long pending; and, because statutes of limitation or the doctrine of laches is rarely available to preclude the steady buildup of prejudgment interest, the amount of such interest can become quite large, as Kansas' claim for approximately $41 million illustrates. One would think that, particularly in such circumstances, even the most rudimentary conception of fairness would dictate that the Court ought not to interpret a contract between two States as exposing one of them to liability under a novel legal principle some 50 years later without some indication that the States might have contemplated such exposure in conjunction with the contractual rights and duties expressed in their compact. * * *

1. *Policy Arguments for Prejudgment Interest.* The policy arguments in favor of awarding prejudgment interest are based on considerations of both fairness and practicality. The fairness argument is that such awards, whether predicated on agreement, statute or general principles of equity, fundamentally advance the goal of compensatory damages to make the injured party whole by accounting for the time value of money or the "loss of use" of the funds ultimately determined as damages. The practicality argument is that such awards promote settlements and discourage delay tactics, especially in situations where liability and the amount of damages are fairly certain.

2. *Liquidated Sums.* As described in the principal case, the common law has traditionally followed an apparently simple dichotomy for whether to award prejudgment interest—ascertainable or "liquidated" versus claims which are unascertainable or unliquidated in character. Thus, where the amount of damages is readily calculable, such as the amount due to be paid on a contract claim, courts routinely allow prejudgment interest. Where the amount of damages is unascertainable, such as for pain and suffering, courts generally have not allowed prejudgment interest.

In *Greater Westchester Homeowners Association v. City of Los Angeles,* 26 Cal.3d 86, 160 Cal.Rptr. 733, 603 P.2d 1329 (1979), the Supreme Court of California court articulated the rationale for this distinction, observing that prejudgment interest represents the accretion of wealth which could have been produced by the money during the period between loss and trial. A fact-finder can use established techniques for computing with fair accuracy the amount of interest on a specific sum of money or specially valued property when the date of loss is known.

"However," the court observed, "damages for the intangible, non-economic aspects of mental and emotional injury are of a different nature. They are inherently non-pecuniary, unliquidated and not readily subject to precise calculation. The amount of such damages is necessarily left to the subjective discretion of the trier of fact. Retroactive interest on such damages adds uncertain conjecture to speculation." Moreover, when an injury is of a continuous nature, as many tort claims are, it is difficult to determine when any particular increment of intangible loss has occurred.

Despite increasing criticism, the view that claims must be liquidated as a prerequisite for prejudgment interest survives. *See* Moncrief v. Williston Basin Interstate Pipeline, 174 F.3d 1150, 1177 (10th Cir.1999) (prejudgment interest recoverable on liquidated claims only, as defined as readily determined by basic mathematical calculation which are certain by computation from the face of the contract or by reference to well-established market values). Some of the reasons for the ascertainability or liquidated rule historically have included:

(a) A court should not require payment of interest on an unknowable sum because the defendant could not stop the accrual of that interest by paying the sum immediately to the plaintiff.

(b) In contract cases involving a fixed debt or a performance with an ascertainable value, the purposes of the contract are best met by providing lost interest after the breach.

(c) Where intangible losses occur, the uncertainty in their calculation is so great that adding prejudgment interest is a pretention to precision that never exists.

(d) Prejudgment interest is not really a "loss" suffered by the plaintiff except in cases involving specific debts or other analogous situations.

(e) Interest should never be allowed except where it is clearly an injustice to preclude it; that clear injustice occurs only in cases involving ascertainable sums.

3. *Rate*. An important question also involves the determination of the appropriate rate of interest assigned to the damages awarded. Absent specific guidance from statute or agreement, the prevailing view is that the rate of prejudgment interest rests with the broad discretion of the trial court. Different courts have considered a variety of market-based mechanisms for guidance. See Guardian Pipeline, L.L.C. v. 950.80 Acres of Land, 486 F.Supp.2d 741, 765–66 (N.D. Ill. 2007) (interest rate awarded at rate that a reasonably prudent person would receive by investing funds to produce a reasonable return while maintaining safety; looked to yields on highly rated long term corporate bonds); New York Marine & General Ins. Co. v. Tradeline, 266 F.3d 112, 131 (2d Cir. 2001) (measured by interest rate on short-term, risk-free obligations such as United States Treasury Bills); Pimentel v. Jacobsen Fishing Co., Inc., 102 F.3d 638, 640 (1st Cir. 1996) (affirmed district court use of variable interest rate based on average price of 52–week Treasury Bills for each year within the relevant prejudgment interest period); Dishman v. Unum Life Ins. Co., 250 F.3d 1272, 1284 (9th Cir. 2001) (16% prejudgment interest rate constituted abuse of discretion as exceeding range of fair compensation).

4. *Timing/Accrual.* Another significant issue involves determining the proper date for commencement of accrual of interest. See AMHS Ins. Co. v. Mutual Ins. Co. of Arizona, 258 F.3d 1090, 1103 (9th Cir.2001) (accrual

based on date when creditor provided to debtor sufficient information and supporting data to ascertain the amount owed).

5. *Contract.* The principal case dealt with an interstate compact, which effectively functions as a contract assigning various rights and duties of the respective state parties. Consider other contract-based predicates for justifying prejudgment interest awards. In Perez v. Z Frank Oldsmobile, Inc., 223 F.3d 617, 620 (7th Cir.2000), the plaintiff claimed damages for odometer fraud in a vehicle sale transaction. The court added prejudgment interest based on the difference between the fair market value of the car with actual mileage compared to the contract purchase price. The court used the interest rate based upon availability of capital whether the car was purchased on credit or for cash. *See also* Medcom Holding Co. v. Baxter Travenol Laboratories, Inc., 200 F.3d 518, 520 (7th Cir.1999) (prejudgment interest allowed at market rate on legal expenses incurred in action for damages for breach of contract); Reilly v. Natwest Markets Group Inc., 181 F.3d 253, 265 (2d Cir.1999) (prejudgment interest and liquidated damages are not functional equivalents, so not double recovery if award both). In Illinois, no right to prejudgment interest generally exists unless expressly authorized by statute or by existing agreement.

City of Milwaukee v. Cement Div., National Gypsum Co.

515 U.S. 189, 115 S.Ct. 2091, 132 L.Ed.2d 148 (1995).

■ JUSTICE STEVENS delivered the opinion of the Court.

This is an admiralty case in which the plaintiff's loss was primarily attributable to its own negligence. The question presented is whether that fact, together with the existence of a genuine dispute over liability, justified the District Court's departure from the general rule that prejudgment interest should be awarded in maritime collision cases.

I

Respondents are the owner and the insurers of the *E.M. Ford,* a ship that sank in Milwaukee's outer harbor on Christmas Eve 1979. At the time of this disaster, the *Ford* was berthed in a slip owned by the city of Milwaukee (City). In the course of a severe storm, she broke loose from her moorings, battered against the headwall of the slip, took on water, and sank. She was subsequently raised and repaired.

In 1980 the *Ford*'s owner, the Cement Division of National Gypsum Co. (National Gypsum), brought suit against the City, invoking the District Court's admiralty and maritime jurisdiction. The complaint alleged that the City had breached its duty as a wharfinger by assigning the vessel to a berthing slip known to be unsafe in heavy winds and by failing to give adequate warning of hidden dangers in the slip. The plaintiff sought damages of $4.5 million, later increased to $6.5 million. The City denied fault and filed a $250,000 counterclaim for damage to its dock. The City alleged that National Gypsum was negligent in leaving the ship virtually unmanned in winter, with no means aboard for monitoring weather conditions or summoning help.

In 1986 the District Court conducted a 3–week trial on the issue of liability. Finding that both National Gypsum and the City had been negligent, the court determined that the owner bore 96% of the responsibility for the disaster, while the City bore 4% of the fault. Given the disparity in the parties' damages, a final judgment giving effect to that allocation (and awarding the damages sought in the pleadings) would have essentially left each party to bear its own losses.

Respondents took an interlocutory appeal from the District Court's ruling. The Court of Appeals for the Seventh Circuit agreed with the District Court's conclusion that both parties were at fault, and that the owner's negligence was "more egregious" than the City's, but it rejected the allocation of 96% of the responsibility to the owner as clearly erroneous. After making its own analysis of the record, the Court of Appeals apportioned liability two-thirds to National Gypsum and one-third to the City.

Thereafter the parties entered into a partial settlement fixing respondents' damages, excluding prejudgment interest, at $1,677,541.86. The parties agreed that any claim for interest would be submitted to the District Court for decision. A partial judgment for the stipulated amount was entered and satisfied.

Respondents then sought an award of over $5.3 million in prejudgment interest. The District Court denied respondents' request. It noted that "an award of prejudgment interest calculated from the date of the loss is the rule rather than the exception in cases brought under a district court's admiralty jurisdiction," but held that special circumstances justified a departure from that rule in this case. The court explained:

> In the instant case the record shows that from the outset there has been a genuine dispute over [respondents'] good faith claim that the City of Milwaukee was negligent for failing to warn the agents of [National Gypsum] (who were planning to leave the FORD unmanned during the Christmas holidays) that a winter storm could create conditions in the outer harbor at Milwaukee which could damage the ship. The trial court and the court of appeals both found mutual fault for the damage which ensued to the ship and to the [City's] dock. The court of appeals ascribed two-thirds of the negligence to [National Gypsum]. Thus, in this situation the court concludes that [National Gypsum's] contributory negligence was of such magnitude that an award of prejudgment interest would be inequitable.

The Court of Appeals reversed. It noted that prior to this Court's announcement of the comparative fault rule in *United States v. Reliable Transfer Co.,* 421 U.S. 397, 95 S.Ct. 1708, 44 L.Ed.2d 251 (1975), some courts had denied prejudgment interest in order to mitigate the harsh effects of the earlier rule commanding an equal division of damages whenever a collision resulted from the fault of both parties, even though one party was only slightly negligent. In the court's view, however, after the divided damages rule was "thrown overboard" and replaced with comparative fault, mutual fault could no longer provide a basis for denying prejudgment interest. The Court of Appeals also read our decision in *West Virginia v. United States,* 479 U.S. 305, 311, n. 3, 107 S.Ct. 702, 706, n. 3, 93 L.Ed.2d 639 (1987), as disapproving of a "balancing of the equities" as a method of deciding whether to allow prejudgment interest.

The Court of Appeals' decision deepened an existing Circuit split regarding the criteria for denying prejudgment interest in maritime collision cases. We granted certiorari, 513 U.S. 1072, 115 S.Ct. 714, 130 L.Ed.2d 622 (1995), and now affirm.

II

Although Congress has enacted a statute governing the award of postjudgment interest in federal court litigation, see 28 U.S.C. § 1961, there is no comparable legislation regarding prejudgment interest. Far from indicating a legislative determination that prejudgment interest should not be awarded, however, the absence of a statute merely indicates that the question is governed by traditional judge-made principles. [Citation] Those principles are well developed in admiralty, where "the Judiciary has traditionally taken the lead in formulating flexible and fair remedies." [Citation]

Throughout our history, admiralty decrees have included provisions for prejudgment interest. In *Del Col v. Arnold,* 3 U.S. (3 Dall.) 333, 1 L.Ed. 624, a prize case decided in 1796, we affirmed a decree awarding the libellant interest from "the day of capture." In *The Amiable Nancy,* 16 U.S. (3 Wheat.) 546, 4 L.Ed. 456 (1818), we considered a similar decree. In augmenting the damages awarded by the lower court, we directed that the additional funds should bear prejudgment interest, as had the damages already awarded by the lower court. *The Amiable Nancy* arose out of the "gross and wanton" seizure of a Haitian vessel near the island of Antigua by the *Scourge,* an American privateer. In his opinion for the Court, Justice Story explained that even though the "loss of the supposed profits" of the *Amiable Nancy*'s voyage was not recoverable, "the prime cost, or value of the property lost, at the time of the loss, and in case of injury, the diminution in value, by reason of the injury, *with interest upon such valuation,* afforded the true measure for assessing damages." Id. at 560 (emphasis added). We applied the same rule in *The Umbria,* 166 U.S. 404, 421, 17 S.Ct. 610, 617, 41 L.Ed. 1053 (1897), explaining that "in cases of total loss by collision damages are limited to the value of the vessel, *with interest thereon,* and the net freight pending at the time of the collision." (Emphasis added.)

The Courts of Appeals have consistently and correctly construed decisions such as these as establishing a general rule that prejudgment interest should be awarded in maritime collision cases, subject to a limited exception for "peculiar" or "exceptional" circumstances. [Citations]

The essential rationale for awarding prejudgment interest is to ensure that an injured party is fully compensated for its loss.[7] Full compensation has long been recognized as a basic principle of admiralty law, where "*[r]estitutio in integrum* is the leading maxim applied by admiralty courts to ascertain damages resulting from a collision." [Citation] By compensating "for the loss of use of money due as damages from the time the claim accrues until judgment is entered, an award of prejudgment interest helps achieve the goal of restoring a party to the condition it enjoyed before the injury occurred." [Citation]

Despite admiralty's traditional hospitality to prejudgment interest, however, such an award has never been automatic. In *The Scotland*, 118 U.S. 507, 518–519, 6 S.Ct. 1174, 1175, 30 L.Ed. 153 (1886), we stated that the "allowance of interest on damages is not an absolute right. Whether it ought or ought not to be allowed depends upon the circumstances of each case, and rests very much in the discretion of the tribunal which has to pass upon the subject, whether it be a court or a jury." Although we have never attempted to exhaustively catalog the circumstances that will justify the denial of interest, and do not do so today, the most obvious example is the plaintiff's responsibility for "undue delay in prosecuting the lawsuit." [Citation] Other circumstances may appropriately be invoked as warranted by the facts of particular cases.

In this case, the City asks us to characterize two features of the instant litigation as sufficiently unusual to justify a departure from the general rule that prejudgment interest should be awarded to make the injured party whole. First, the City stresses the fact that there was a good-faith dispute over its liability for respondents' loss. In our view, however, this fact carries little weight. If interest were awarded as a penalty for bad-faith conduct of the litigation, the City's argument would be well taken. But prejudgment interest is not awarded as a penalty; it is merely an element of just compensation.

The City's "good-faith" argument has some resonance with the venerable common-law rule that prejudgment interest is not awarded on unliquidated claims (those where the precise amount of damages at issue cannot be computed). If a party contests liability in good faith, it will usually be the case that the party's ultimate exposure is uncertain. But the liquidated/unliquidated distinction has faced trenchant criticism for a number of years. Moreover, that distinction "has never become so firmly entrenched in admiralty as it has been at law." [Citation] Any fixed rule allowing prejudgment interest only on liquidated claims would be difficult, if not impossible, to reconcile with admiralty's traditional presumption. Yet unless we were willing to adopt such a rule—which we are not—uncertainty about the outcome of a case should not preclude an award of interest.

---

7. We have recognized the compensatory nature of prejudgment interest in a number of cases decided outside the admiralty context. [Citations] But cf. *Blau v. Lehman*, 368 U.S. 403, 414, 82 S.Ct. 451, 457, 7 L.Ed.2d 403 (1962) (" 'interest is not recovered according to a rigid theory of compensation for money withheld, but is given in response to considerations of fairness' ") (quoting *Board of Comm'rs of Jackson Cty. v. United States*, 308 U.S. 343, 352, 60 S.Ct. 285, 289, 84 L.Ed. 313 (1939)).

In sum, the existence of a legitimate difference of opinion on the issue of liability is merely a characteristic of most ordinary lawsuits. It is not an extraordinary circumstance that can justify denying prejudgment interest.

The second purportedly "peculiar" feature of this case is the magnitude of the plaintiff's fault. Leaving aside the empirical question whether such a division of fault is in fact an aberration, it is true in this case that the owner of the *E.M. Ford* was primarily responsible for the vessel's loss. As a result, it might appear somewhat inequitable to award a large sum in prejudgment interest against a relatively innocent party. But any unfairness is illusory, because the relative fault of the parties has already been taken into consideration in calculating the amount of the loss for which the City is responsible.

In *United States v. Reliable Transfer Co.*, 421 U.S. 397, 95 S.Ct. 1708, 44 L.Ed.2d 251 (1975), we "replaced the divided damages rule, which required an equal division of property damage whatever the relative degree of fault may have been, with a rule requiring that damages be assessed on the basis of proportionate fault when such an allocation can reasonably be made." [Citation] Thus, in this case, before prejudgment interest even entered the picture, the total amount of respondents' recovery had already been reduced by two-thirds because of National Gypsum's own negligence. The City's responsibility for the remaining one-third is no different than if it had performed the same negligent acts and the owner, instead of also being negligent, had engaged in heroic maneuvers that avoided two-thirds of the damages. The City is merely required to compensate the owner for the loss for which the City is responsible. In light of *Reliable Transfer,* we are unmoved by the City's contention that an award of prejudgment interest is inequitable in a mutual fault situation. Indeed, the converse is true: a *denial* of prejudgment interest would be unfair. As JUSTICE KENNEDY noted while he was sitting on the Ninth Circuit, "under any rule allowing apportionment of liability, denying prejudgment interest on the basis of mutual fault would seem to penalize a party twice for the same mistake." [Citation] Such a double penalty is commended neither by logic nor by fairness; the rule giving rise to it is a relic of history that has ceased to serve any purpose in the wake of *Reliable Transfer.*

Accordingly, we hold that neither a good-faith dispute over liability nor the existence of mutual fault justifies the denial of prejudgment interest in an admiralty collision case. Questions related to the calculation of the prejudgment interest award, including the rate to be applied, have not been raised in this Court and remain open for consideration, in the first instance, by the District Court.

The judgment of the Court of Appeals is *Affirmed.*

1. *Admiralty.* As recognized in the principal case, prejudgment interest is awarded in cases under admiralty law at the discretion of the court to ensure full compensation of the injured party, and is ordinarily granted

unless exceptional or peculiar circumstances exist. See Kirksey v. P & O Ports Texas, Inc., 488 F.Supp.2d 579, 589 (S.D. Tex. 2007) (under maritime law awarding prejudgment interest is the rule, not the exception; applied 6% rate as equitable); ConAgra, Inc. v. Inland River Towing Co., 252 F.3d 979, 985 (8th Cir.2001) (allowed on claims for lost profits, loss of use damages and repair costs of vessel); Great Lakes Dredge & Dock Co. v. City of Chicago, 260 F.3d 789, 796 (7th Cir.2001) (interest considered an aspect of full compensation under admiralty law; neither equitable considerations nor existence of a bona fide dispute about liability affect the running of interest); also see Simeonoff v. Hiner, 249 F.3d 883, 894 (9th Cir.2001) (granted in personal injury cases under admiralty jurisdiction unless peculiar circumstances justify denial).

2. *Calculation of Interest.* Should courts use a simple or compound interest method for prejudgment interest awards? Generally courts have assessed just simple interest. *See* Restatement (Second) of Contracts § 354; Restatement (Second) of Torts § 913. Would compound interest more closely approximate the loss of investment opportunity in the market? Are there any reasons to chose simple interest over compound as a matter of policy? *See* Audiovisual Publishers, Inc. v. Cenco Inc., 185 F.3d 93, 97 (2d Cir.1999) (compound interest may be awarded under New York law where defendant acts in bad faith); also see Bogosian v. Woloohojian, 158 F.3d 1,9 (1st Cir.1998) (Rhode Island does not allow award of compound interest; however, allowed 11 per cent rate to stand as within boundary of reasonableness, so not affected by difference between simple and compound interest). Where an express contract provision unambiguously provides for compound interest, however, courts will uphold the contractual provision rather than award simple interest. See Exxon Corp. v. Crosby–Mississippi Resources, Ltd., 40 F.3d 1474, 1489 (5th Cir.1995). In *Stovall v. Illinois Central Gulf R.R. Co.*, 722 F.2d 190 (5th Cir.1984), the court compounded the prejudgment interest but computed postjudgment interest on a simple interest basis. The second choice was based upon certain amendments to Mississippi's legal interest statutes. The Court Improvement Act of 1982, 28 U.S.C. § 1961 (Supp. I 1988) provides for compound interest for post-judgment interest but is silent regarding prejudgment interest. Is there any policy reason for distinguishing the two?

3. A recurrent problem of statutory interpretation is the propriety of awarding prejudgment interest where a federal statute provides remedial relief but is silent with respect to interest. *See* In re Doctors Hosp. of Hyde Park, Inc., 360 B.R. 787, 878 (Bkrtcy. N.D. Ill. 2007) (under Bankruptcy Code, calculate prejudgment interest by average of prime rate for years in question); Crider v. Highmark Life Ins. Co., 458 F.Supp.2d 487, 514 (W.D. Mich. 2006) (ERISA case awarded prejudgment interest based 52–week Treasury Bill rate as equitable amount); Blankenship v. Liberty Life Assur. Co. of Boston, 486 F.3d 620, 627–28 (9th Cir. 2007) (for ERISA claim court awarded 10.01% rate where evidence showed that wrongful nonpayment of benefits forced claimant to replace lost amounts with personal funds invested in mutual funds, which earned that rate for relevant time period).

Courts attempt to determine Congressional intent in order to decide whether an interest award would further the statutory policies. The Supreme Court explained in *Rodgers v. United States*, 332 U.S. 371, 373, 68 S.Ct. 5,7, 92 L.Ed. 3 (1947):

> [T]he failure to mention interest in statutes which create obligations has not been interpreted by this Court as manifesting an unequivocal congressional purpose that the obligation shall not bear interest. For in the absence of an unequivocal prohibition of interest on such obligations, this Court has fashioned rules which granted or denied interest on particular statutory obligations by an appraisal of the congressional purpose in imposing them and in the light of general principles deemed relevant by the Court.
>
> As our prior cases show, a persuasive consideration in determining whether such obligations shall bear interest is the relative equities between the beneficiaries of the obligation and those upon whom it has been imposed. And this Court has generally weighed these relative equities in accordance with the historic judicial principle that one for whose financial advantage an obligation was assumed or imposed, and who has suffered actual money damages by another's breach of that obligation, should be fairly compensated for the loss thereby sustained. [Internal citations omitted].

The determination of legislative intent is a difficult process and courts use a variety of tools to assess the whether an award of prejudgment interest would be consistent with an act's purpose. Such consideration has included:

1) the need to fully compensate the wronged party for actual damages suffered,

2) considerations of fairness and the relative equities of the award,

3) the remedial purpose of the statute involved,

4) encouragement of prompt settlement of disputes,

5) the need to conform to historical legislative and judicial precedent,

6) other general principles as are deemed relevant by the court.

See generally Gierlinger v. Gleason, 160 F.3d 858 (2d Cir.1998); Gore, Inc. v. Glickman, 137 F.3d 863 (5th Cir.1998); Poleto v. Consolidated Rail Corp., 826 F.2d 1270 (3d Cir.1987).

4. *Unjust enrichment.* Courts may award prejudgment interest in restitution to prevent the unjust enrichment of the defendant. For example, the court in *Sack v. Feinman*, 489 Pa. 152, 413 A.2d 1059 (1980). held that prejudgment interest may be allowed on a constructive trust. In that case, one sister sought to impress a constructive trust on savings bonds allegedly converted fraudulently by another sister from their mother. The Pennsylvania Supreme Court reversed the trial court's denial of prejudgment interest and noted that pre-verdict interest may be necessary in order to disgorge completely any profits which a fiduciary might otherwise gain from abusing a confidential relationship. The decision whether to grant or

deny prejudgment interest in such a restitution case rests within the court's sound discretion to prevent unjust enrichment.

The Restatement (Third) of Restitution and Unjust Enrichment (2011) provides that in the absence of a statute specifying the interest rate, the court should apply the rate that most closely reflects the value to the defendant of the interim use of the claimant's funds. This result is reached as a matter of preventing unjust enrichment rather than compensation to the claimant. *See* Restatement (Third) of Restitution § 53, cmt. e.

5. *Employment law.* Prejudgment interest may be awarded in connection with back pay damages or may serve a restitutionary basis to accompany equitable reinstatement orders. Frazier v. Iowa Beef Processors, Inc., 200 F.3d 1190 (8th Cir.2000) (prejudgment interest awarded on back pay damages under state and federal laws proper unless exceptional or unusual circumstances exist making the award inequitable); Trustmark Life Ins. v. University of Chicago Hospitals, 207 F.3d 876, 885 (7th Cir.2000) (allowed in ERISA cases to fully compensate victim and to prevent unjust enrichment); Also see Shelby County Health v. Southern Council, 203 F.3d 926, 937 (6th Cir.2000) (ERISA does not require prejudgment interest to a prevailing plan participant, although district court has discretion to grant such an award in accordance with equitable principles); Mary Helen Coal Corp. v. Hudson, 235 F.3d 207, 210 (4th Cir.2000) (prejudgment interest not precluded by ERISA but allowed on basis that "interest follows principal").

Consider the prejudgment interest award on back pay that the court awarded for violation of the Fair Labor Standards Act in *Donovan v. Sovereign Security, Ltd.* The case concerned a violation of the Act by a private sector employer. The court allowed the interest award as part of a restitutionary injunction provided under section 17. The court reasoned that the purposes of the restitutionary injunction are to make whole employees who have been underpaid. The Act was intended to eliminate the competitive advantage of employers who violate the federal wage restrictions. The court continued, "Pre-judgment interest also serves to remedy the competitive disadvantage inflicted on law-abiding businesses by denying the errant employer the free use of the money it should have paid out in wages. Failure to award interest would create an incentive to violate the FLSA, because violators in effect would enjoy an interest-free loan for as long as they could delay paying out back wages." 726 F.2d 55 (2d Cir.1984).

Would the same rationale apply to a common law claim of wrongful discharge? If the defendant employer discharges the plaintiff for refusing to decline jury duty, for example, the court may order reinstatement and back pay. Should prejudgment interest be awarded under the unjust enrichment theory? Under the competitive edge theory? Under the ascertainability rule? *See* Diggs v. Pepsi–Cola Metropolitan Bottling Co., 861 F.2d 914 (6th Cir.1988) (wrongfully discharged employee entitled to prejudgment interest on back pay award). In response to the perceived inequity between employees of the public and private sector with respect to prejudgment interest,

Congress amended the Back Pay Act. It now specifically provides for prejudgment interest in suits by federal agency employees covered by the Act. 5 U.S.C. § 5596(b)(1)(A).

6. *Delay.* The court may exercise its discretion to limit or deny prejudgment interest if the plaintiff has delayed unduly in pursuing the lawsuit. *See* General Motors Corp. v. Devex Corp., 461 U.S. 648, 103 S.Ct. 2058, 76 L.Ed.2d 211 (1983); also see Jones v. Spentonbush–Red Star Co., 155 F.3d 587, 593 (2d Cir.1998) (undue delay in bringing negligence action under general maritime law and non-compliance with discovery schedule precluded award of prejudgment interest). The court may require that the defendant be prejudiced by the delay before denying prejudgment interest. *See* Lummus Industries, Inc. v. D.M. & E. Corp., 862 F.2d 267 (Fed.Cir. 1988) (prejudgment interest should not be denied in a patent infringement claim absent a showing that the plaintiff's delay prejudiced the defendant).

7. *Tolling Interest.* Courts have recognized that valid, good faith offers to settle a dispute or actually tendering money to the claimant may toll or limit the running of prejudgment interest. *See* Bogosian v. Woloohojian, 158 F.3d 1, 8–9 (1st Cir.1998) (debtor could stop running of prejudgment interest by tendering a portion of debt to creditor or paying into registry of court).

States also use prejudgment interest to encourage good faith offers of settlement. For example, California added § 3291 to its Civil Code which provides that prejudgment interest will be awarded in personal injury actions at the legal rate of 10 percent per annum on the portion of the judgment which exceeds the plaintiff's settlement offer. The interest is calculated from the date of the plaintiff's initial offer and accrues until judgment is satisfied. Ohio law permits a plaintiff to recover prejudgment interest if the court determines that "the party required to pay the money failed to make a good faith effort to settle the case and that the party to whom the money is to be paid did not fail to make a good faith effort to settle the case." Ohio Rev. Code Ann. § 1343.03(C). In *Conte v. General Housewares Corp.*, 215 F.3d 628, 633 (6th Cir.2000), the court interpreted the Ohio law to permit the following considerations: 1) full cooperation in discovery proceedings, 2) rational evaluation of respective risks and potential liability, 3) lack of attempts to unnecessarily delay any of the proceedings, and 4) making a good faith monetary settlement offer or responding in good faith to an offer from the other party. Finally, if the party has a good faith, objectively reasonable belief that she has no liability, she need not make a monetary settlement offer.

Campbell v. Metropolitan Property and Cas. Ins.

239 F.3d 179 (2d Cir.2001).

■ KEARSE, CIRCUIT JUDGE:

Defendants Metropolitan Property and Casualty Insurance Company *et al.* (collectively "Metropolitan") appeal from a judgment entered in the

United States District Court for the Southern District of New York follow-ing a bench trial before Naomi Reice Buchwald, *Judge,* awarding plaintiffs Faith Campbell ("Campbell") and her children Jazmin, Alteasha, and Clarence (collectively the "children" or "Campbell children") $300,000 on a policy of insurance covering bodily injury, plus prejudgment interest. The district court found that the Campbell children suffered injuries from exposure to lead paint during the policy period September 5, 1992, to September 5, 1993. On appeal, Metropolitan contends that the district court erred * * * in awarding prejudgment interest. For the reasons that follow, we affirm the district court's finding of liability and reverse the award of prejudgment interest.

The Insurance Policies and the Campbells' Apartment

* * * From January 1993 to March 22, 1995, Campbell and her children lived in a Bronx, New York apartment in a building owned by Kormal and Tajwattie Singh (collectively "Singh"). In January 1994, the children were tested for lead poisoning and were found to have lead levels in their blood ranging from 18 to 22 micrograms of lead per deciliter of blood. Later blood tests showed that the children's blood lead levels had risen and ranged from 29 to 44 micrograms per deciliter. Under the New York City Health Code, "a blood lead level of 10 micrograms per deciliter or higher" is classified as "lead poisoning." N.Y.C. Health Code, Tit. 24, § 11.03. *See also* Centers for Disease Control, *Preventing Lead Poisoning in Children* 1–2 (October 1991) ("Epidemiologic studies have identified harm-ful effects of lead in children at blood lead levels as low as 10 mb/dcl."). Campbell brought an action against Singh in state court, alleging that her apartment contained cracked, chipped, and peeling lead-based paint, and that exposure to it had caused the children injuries, including brain damage, attention deficit disorder, developmental delay, decreases in IQ, and lead intoxication.

With respect to the period in which the Campbells lived in that apartment, Metropolitan issued liability insurance policies covering Singh's building for the periods September 5, 1992, to September 5, 1993 ("first policy period" or "Period One"), September 5, 1993, to September 5, 1994 ("second policy period" or "Period Two"), and September 5, 1994, to September 5, 1995 ("third policy period" or "Period Three"). In the policies, Metropolitan agreed to "pay all sums for bodily injury and proper-ty damage to others for which the law holds [Singh] responsible because of any occurrence. This includes prejudgment interest awarded against [Singh]." (Emphasis omitted.) The policies defined "occurrence" to include "continuous or repeated exposure to substantially the same general harm-ful conditions, resulting in bodily injury . . . during the term of the policy" (emphasis omitted); "bodily injury" was defined to mean "any bodily harm, sickness or disease." Each policy provided a maximum of $300,000 in coverage. Campbell's action against Singh was settled pursuant to a stipu-lation dated April 20, 1998 (the "Stipulation"), entered into by Campbell, Singh, and Metropolitan. The Stipulation recited, *inter alia,* that during each of the three policy periods the Campbell children "were exposed to lead based paint", and Metropolitan agreed to pay Campbell the full policy liability limit of $300,000 for the second policy period, *i.e.*, September 5, 1993, to September 5, 1994. The parties agreed that the state-court action against Singh would be discontinued, that Campbell would bring a declaratory judgment action against Metropolitan with respect to the first and third policy periods, and that Metropolitan would pay plaintiffs the maximum policy amount for any period within which the court finally determined, after all appeals were concluded, that bodily injury had occurred.

[Metropolitan eventually conceded liability with respect to Period Three and agreed to pay the full policy limit. Therefore, the only issue remaining was whether the plaintiffs sustained a bodily injury during the first policy period.] * * * Metropolitan argued that there was no injury during the first policy period because plaintiffs could not show that the children " 'sustained an adverse effect on the bone marrow where the red blood cell is formed (heme biosynthesis) or any other cellular or subcellular injury during the first policy period.' "

At trial, plaintiffs introduced New York City Department of Health ("Health Department") records showing that on February 15, 1994, and July 28, 1994, the Campbells' apartment had contained lead-based paint in numerous locations. The lead level was so high as to constitute a nuisance, and the Health Department ordered its abatement. [The court then discusses the testimony of the respective experts. The district court found that Metropolitan was liable under the first policy period, and was ordered to pay the full policy amount plus prejudgment interest.] * * *

Prejudgment Interest

Under New York law, which governs the substantive issues in this diversity action, including that of the availability of prejudgment interest, *see, e.g., Schwimmer v. Allstate Ins. Co.*, 176 F.3d 648, 650 (2d Cir.1999), prejudgment interest is recoverable only in certain types of actions.

> *Actions in which recoverable.* Interest shall be recovered upon a sum awarded because of a breach of performance of a contract, or because of an act or omission depriving or otherwise interfering with title to, or possession or enjoyment of, property, except that in an action of an equitable nature, interest and the rate and date from which it shall be computed shall be in the court's discretion.

N.Y. C.P.L.R. § 5001(a) (2000). Actions for personal injury are not mentioned in § 5001(a), and "[i]t has long been the established rule that in all personal injury actions, whether resulting from intentional tort or not, the plaintiff has not been entitled in any circumstance to recover interest on the damages assessed," *Gillespie v. Great Atlantic & Pacific Tea Co.*, 44 Misc.2d 670, 671, 255 N.Y.S.2d 10, 11 (N.Y.Sup.1964) (action to recover damages on breach of warranty theory). Prejudgment interest on a recovery for personal injury is "barr[ed]," "irrespective of the form of action pursued—contract-related as in the present instance—or otherwise." *Id.* at 671, 255 N.Y.S.2d at 12; *see also Schwimmer v. Allstate Ins. Co.*, 176 F.3d at 650 (not recoverable on award for pain suffering pursuant to policy's uninsured/underinsured motorist coverage); *Alkinburgh v. Glessing,* 240 A.D.2d 904, 906, 658 N.Y.S.2d 735, 737 (3d Dep't 1997) (not recoverable on award of medical costs in action to recover for personal injury); *Hyatt v. Pepsi–Cola Albany Bottling Co.,* 32 A.D.2d 574, 574–75, 298 N.Y.S.2d 1005, 1006–07 (3d Dep't 1969) (not recoverable in breach of warranty action based on personal injury).

The present action is not one grounded in equity or on any theory that Metropolitan breached a contract. Rather, it is simply an action to recover damages for which Singh would be held accountable for the Campbell children's personal injuries. As such, it does not fall within § 5001(a).

Plaintiffs' reliance on *United States Fire Insurance Co. v. Federal Insurance Co.,* 858 F.2d 882 (2d Cir.1988), for the contrary result is misplaced. That suit revolved around a person who had multiple insurance coverages and had received an insurance payment from the plaintiff; the plaintiff sued a coinsurer to recover part of the insurance payout. The district court had denied prejudgment interest on the theory that the plaintiff's suit was analogous to a claim for contribution among persons jointly liable for personal injury—a claim that does not arise from contract, and as to which prejudgment interest is barred. We rejected that analogy, noting that New York law "makes plain that an insurer's right to contribution does have its origin in contract, to wit, the contracts between the insured and the various insurers," *id.* at 887. We thus concluded that "where the insurance contracts reveal multiple coverage, the court exercises its equity powers to imply a contract between the coinsurers to contribute," *id.* at 888, and that the claim of the insurer against its coinsurer was thus within the scope of § 5001(a). That rationale provides no basis for an award of prejudgment interest in the present case, where plaintiffs sued to recover for personal injuries.

We have considered all of Metropolitan's arguments against liability, and all of plaintiffs' arguments in favor of prejudgment interest, and have found them to be without merit. The judgment of the district court is affirmed insofar as it requires Metropolitan to pay plaintiff $300,000 for the first policy period, and is reversed insofar as it awards prejudgment interest.

---

1. In *Baker v. Dorfman,* 239 F.3d 415 (2d Cir.2000), the Second Circuit Court of Appeals, applying the same New York statute at issue in the principal case, upheld the district court ruling allowing prejudgment interest. The plaintiff in *Baker* sued in federal court for legal malpractice and resume fraud in connection with the dismissal of a state court case against the city which alleged negligence associated with a false positive HIV test administered at a city agency. The district court justified the award of prejudgment interest by characterizing the loss of a claim as the deprivation of "property" within the meaning of the statute in order to "make the plaintiff whole." The court further observed that interest should

be awarded as a matter of right in order to make the plaintiff whole whenever tortious conduct causes pecuniary damage to tangible or intangible property interests. Id. at 425. Which is the better view?

2. As recognized in the principal case, the ascertainability or liquidated requirement often poses a stumbling block in tort cases, except ones involving tangible or quantifiable injury such as taking of land, taking or detention of personal property, and destruction of personal property or some part of real property. Conversely, unascertainable losses in tort typically include: pain and suffering, emotional distress, and injury to reputation. Amounts due for lost wages or medical expenses in personal injury cases lose their ascertainability by the uncertainty about the specific time each loss occurs.

The Restatement (Second) of Torts § 913 accepts this distinction. It further states that except for cases where prejudgment interest should never be allowed—bodily injury, emotional distress, or injury to reputation—the court should allow interest if it is required "to avoid an injustice." Does this provision add any predictability for litigants or guidance for courts? Would it serve to promote good faith settlement discussions? In contract cases the same distinction occurs, but it less often acts to preclude recovery of prejudgment interest. The Restatement (Second) of Contracts § 354 reflects the rule for breach of contract cases: Prejudgment interest is permissible when the breach consists of a failure to pay a definite sum of money or a failure to do acts with ascertainable monetary value. In other circumstances, courts should award interest "as justice requires."

3. Contrary to the statute in the principal case and the Restatement (Second) of Torts § 913, some states allow recovery of prejudgment interest in personal injury actions. For example, Nevada allows prejudgment interest on all damages awarded in personal injury actions except any amount representing future damages. Under the statute, a judgment draws interest from the time of service of summons and complaint until satisfied. Nev. Rev. Stat. 17.130. West Virginia allows prejudgment interest on any portion of an award that compensates for "special damages." The statute defines special damages to include lost wages and income, medical expenses, damages to tangible personal property and similar out-of-pocket expenditures, as determined by the court. W. Va. Code § 56–6–31.

4. *Punitive Damages.* Prejudgment interest is rarely awarded on punitive damages. *See* Dunbar Medical Systems Inc. v. Gammex Inc., 216 F.3d 441, 455 (5th Cir.2000) (prejudgment interest not allowed on punitive damages under Texas law). The typical rationale is that the purpose behind prejudgment interest is to compensate for the loss of the use of the compensatory damages rather than to punish or deter the defendant. *See* Restatement (Second) of Torts § 913, comment d. Also see Ambassador Hotel Co., Ltd. v. Wei–Chuan Investment, 189 F.3d 1017, 1031 (9th Cir.1999) (both punitive damages and pre-judgment interest may be awarded on successful fraud claims under California law, but since punitive damages sound in tort, no award of pre-judgment interest calculated at contract rate because of double recovery).

5. *Future Losses.* Courts routinely recognize that an award of prejudgment interest is not appropriate with respect to an award of damages for future injuries because those losses have not yet been incurred. Therefore, the claimant has not been deprived of the loss of use of their money nor the defendant unjustly enriched. *See* Gordon v. Matthew Bender & Co., Inc., 186 F.3d 183, 186 (2d Cir.1999). For example, in *Verdin v. C & B Boat Co., Inc.,* 860 F.2d 150 (5th Cir.1988), the district court erred in an admiralty case by allowing prejudgment interest on future losses as well as on past ones. The action was against a barge owner for the wrongful death of a tugboat captain. On appeal the court denied prejudgment interest for future losses and allowed it only on damages for past ones: the past loss of support, the pain and suffering of the decedent before death, and the medical and funeral expenses for the decedent. *See also* Cummings v. Standard Register Co., 265 F.3d 56, 69 (1st Cir.2001) (no prejudgment interest awarded on front pay award).

6. *Conflict of Laws.* The general rules on prejudgment interest do not apply in every jurisdiction or in every circumstance. Significant conflict of laws problems thus can occur. In *Draper v. Airco, Inc.,* 580 F.2d 91 (3d Cir.1978), for example, there was a conflicts issue concerning prejudgment interest in a wrongful death and survival action. This diversity case was brought in a federal district court in New Jersey. The judge determined that Pennsylvania substantive law governed in accordance with the choice of law rules but that New Jersey Law should control prejudgment interest. As a result, the jury verdict of $430,000 was increased to $585,000. The Third Circuit Court of Appeals disagreed and held that, as a matter of conflicts law, Pennsylvania law should govern the issue of prejudgment interest. Consequently, the award of prejudgment interest was reversed because Pennsylvania law disallows it in tort actions claiming unliquidated damages.

CHAPTER 13

LIMITATIONS ON COMPENSATORY DAMAGES

A. FORESEEABILITY

Section Coverage:

A significant limitation on the extent of compensatory damages recoverable for breach of contract is that the loss must be reasonably "foreseeable" from the perspective of the breaching party at the time the contract was formed. The requirement of foreseeability reflects a policy that a party should be held accountable only for those risks that were foreseeable at the time of making contractual promises.

The role of foreseeability in tort differs significantly from its function in contracts. It affects first the nature of the duty imposed by law upon the actors. Once that duty is established, the actor is responsible for all the ensuing harm proximately caused by conduct in breach of that duty. The limitation of "proximate cause" is also defined by foreseeability, although jurisdictions differ on when and what injuries must be foreseeable for this "legal cause" concept.

As a result, the recoverable damages in tort are usually greater than in contract once the tortfeasor's duty has been established. This difference has received criticism because it invites characterization of certain conduct as tortious simply to gain greater damages than if couched as a breach of contract. Despite the different treatment of foreseeability in tort and contract, the shared underlying policy goal is limiting or excluding recovery of damages that are too remote.

Model Case:

On January 1 Baker contracted to purchase 10,000 gallons of high-grade aircraft fuel oil from the Energon Company for $100 per gallon with delivery scheduled for July 1. In April Energon repudiated the contract, asserting that new government tariffs had increased its costs dramatically, making it commercially impracticable to perform under the contract. The market price for fuel oil at the time of Energon's repudiation had risen to $150 per gallon.

Baker, prior to entering its contract with Energon, had effected a resale contract of the fuel oil to Industri Chem for $200 per gallon. Assuming that the repudiation constituted a breach of contract which was not excused, Baker would be entitled to recover damages measured by the cost to cover or the difference between the market price and the contract price for the oil in April. However, Baker would not be allowed to recover damages for lost profits under its resale contract to Industri Chem absent a showing that Energon would have reasonably foreseen those consequences of its potential breach on January 1.

Redgrave v. Boston Symphony Orchestra

855 F.2d 888 (1st Cir.1988).

■ COFFIN, CIRCUIT JUDGE. * * *

The plaintiffs, actress Vanessa Redgrave and Vanessa Redgrave Enterprises, Ltd. (hereinafter Redgrave), brought suit against the Boston Symphony Orchestra (hereinafter the BSO) for cancelling a contract for Redgrave's appearance as narrator in a performance of Stravinsky's "Oedipus Rex." The cancellation occurred in the wake of protests over Redgrave's participation because of her support of the Palestine Liberation Organization. * * * [A jury awarded Redgrave $100,000 in consequential damages caused by the BSO's breach of contract, but the district court granted the BSO's motion for judgment notwithstanding the verdict.]

In response to special interrogatories, the jury found that the BSO's cancellation of the "Oedipus Rex" concerts caused consequential harm to Redgrave's professional career and that this harm was a foreseeable consequence within the contemplation of the parties at the time they entered the contract. A threshold question is whether Massachusetts contract law allows the award of such consequential damages for harm to a claimant's professional career.

Redgrave's consequential damages claim is based on the proposition that a significant number of movie and theater offers that she would ordinarily have received in the years 1982 and following were in fact not offered to her as a result of the BSO's cancellation in April 1982. The BSO characterizes this claim as one for damage to Redgrave's reputation, and argues that the recent Massachusetts state court decisions in McCone v. New England Telephone & Telegraph Co., 393 Mass. 231, 471 N.E.2d 47 (1984), and Daley v. Town of West Brookfield, 19 Mass.App.Ct.1019, 476 N.E.2d 980 (1985), establish that Massachusetts law does not permit plaintiffs in breach of contract actions to recover consequential damages for harm to reputation.

In *McCone v. New England Telephone & Telegraph Co.*, plaintiffs alleged that their employer's breach of an implied covenant of good faith had caused them loss of salary increases, loss of pension benefits, and "damage to their professional reputations, disruption of their personal lives, and great pain of body and mind." The Massachusetts Supreme Judicial Court held that the claims for damages to reputation and other emotional injury could not be sustained in the suit because "these additional damages are not contract damages." In *Daley v. Town of West Brookfield*, a Massachusetts appellate court observed that "[d]amages for injury to reputation are usually not available in contract actions," noting that the rationale most often given is that "such damages are remote and not within the contemplation of the parties." [Citation.]

The BSO notes that Massachusetts is in agreement with virtually all other jurisdictions in holding that damages for reputation are not available in contract actions. * * *

In cases that have analyzed the reasons for disallowing a contract claim for reputation damages, courts have identified two determinative factors. First, courts have observed that attempting to calculate damages for injury to reputation is "unduly speculative." [Citations.] In many cases, the courts have viewed the claims for damages to reputation as analogous to claims for physical or emotional distress and have noted the difficulty in ascertaining such damages for contract purposes. * * *

The second factor that courts identify is that damages for injury to reputation "cannot reasonably be presumed to have been within the contemplation of the parties when they entered into the contract." These courts state that the basic rule of Hadley v. Baxendale, 9 Ex. 341, 156 Eng.Rep. 145 (1854), which requires that contract damages be of the kind that arise naturally from the breach of a contract or be of a kind that reasonably may have been in the contemplation of the parties when they entered the contract, cannot possibly be met in a claim for general damages to reputation occurring as the result of a breach of contract. [Citations.] The Massachusetts Supreme Judicial Court seems to have accepted this rationale as a legitimate one for disallowing claims for injury to reputation as a contract damage. * * *

The claim advanced by Redgrave is significantly different, however, from a general claim of damage to reputation. Redgrave is not claiming that her general reputation as a professional actress has been tarnished by the BSO's cancellation. Rather, she claims that a number of specific movie and theater performances that would have been offered to her in the usual course of events were not offered to her as a result of the BSO's cancellation. This is the type of specific claim that, with appropriate evidence, can meet the *Hadley v. Baxendale* rule, as adopted by the Massachusetts Supreme Judicial Court in John Hetherington & Sons, Ltd. v. William Firth Co., 210 Mass. 8, 21, 95 N.E. 961, 964 (1911) (in breach of contract action, injured party receives compensation for any loss that follows as a natural consequence from the breach, was within the contemplation of reasonable parties as a probable result of breach, and may be computed by "rational methods upon a firm basis of facts"). * * *

The jury was given appropriate instructions to help it determine whether Redgrave had suffered consequential damages through loss of future professional opportunities. They were told to find that the BSO's cancellation was a proximate cause of harm to Redgrave's professional career only if they determined that "harm would not have occurred but for the cancellation and that the harm was a natural and probable consequence of the cancellation." *Redgrave v. BSO,* 602 F.Supp. at 1211. In addition, they were told that damages should be allowed for consequential harm "only if the harm was a foreseeable consequence within the contemplation of the parties to the contract when it was made." In response to special interrogatories, the jury found that the BSO's cancellation caused consequential harm to Redgrave's career and that the harm was a foreseeable consequence within the contemplation of the parties.

Although we find that Redgrave did not present sufficient evidence to establish that the BSO's cancellation caused consequential harm to her professional career in the amount of $100,000, we hold that, as a matter of Massachusetts contract law, a plaintiff may receive consequential damages if the plaintiff proves with sufficient evidence that a breach of contract proximately caused the loss of identifiable professional opportunities. This type of claim is sufficiently different from a nonspecific allegation of damage to reputation that it appropriately falls outside the general rule that reputation damages are not an acceptable form of contract damage.

* * *

The requirements for awarding consequential damages for breach of contract are designed to ensure that a breaching party pays only those damages that have resulted from its breach. Thus, to receive consequential damages, the plaintiff must establish a "basis for an inference of fact" that the plaintiff has actually been damaged, and the factfinder must be able to compute the compensation "by rational methods upon a firm basis of facts." * * *

In order for Redgrave to prove that the BSO's cancellation resulted in the loss of other professional opportunities, she must present sufficient facts for a jury reasonably to infer that Redgrave lost wages and professional opportunities subsequent to April 1982, that such losses were the result of the BSO's cancellation rather than the result of other, independent factors, and that damages for such losses are capable of being ascertained "by reference to some definite standard, either market value, established experience or direct inference from known circumstances." [Citation.] During trial, evidence was presented regarding losses Redgrave allegedly suffered in film offers and American theater offers. Based on this testimony, the jury found that the BSO's cancellation of its contract with Redgrave caused Redgrave $100,000 in consequential damages. We find that the evidence presented by Redgrave was not sufficient to support a finding of damages greater than $12,000, less expenses.

Most of Redgrave's annual earnings prior to April 1982 were derived from appearances in films and the English theater. Redgrave presented evidence at trial that she earned more than $200,000 on the average since her company's fiscal year 1976, and she testified that she had a constant stream of offers from which she could choose films that had secure financial backing. After the BSO's cancellation in April 1982, Redgrave contended, her career underwent a "startling turnabout." Redgrave testified that she did not work at all for the fourteen months following the cancellation and that the only offers she received during that time were for films with insufficient financial backing.

The evidence demonstrates that Redgrave accepted three firm film offers in the fourteen months following the BSO cancellation. If these three films had been produced, Redgrave would have earned $850,000 during that period. The first offer, for a film entitled *Annie's Coming Out,* was for a role in which Redgrave had expressed interest in February 1982, two months prior to the BSO cancellation. The offer for the role was made in July 1982, a short time after the BSO's cancellation, and was finalized in August 1982. The film was to be financed by Film Australia, a government production company, and no evidence was presented that Redgrave believed the film might experience financial difficulties. Redgrave's fee for the film was to be $250,000.

From July 1982 until approximately the end of October 1982, Redgrave believed that she would be filming *Annie's Coming Out* sometime during the fall. Because of that commitment, Redgrave turned down other firm offers that had secure financial backing. These included an offer received in July 1982 to do a cameo appearance in a Monty Python film entitled *Yellowbeard* for $10,000 and an offer received in September 1982 to star in the television film *Who Will Love My Children?* for $150,000. In late October or early November 1982, Redgrave was informed that *Annie's Coming Out* would not be produced because of financial difficulties. No evidence was presented that the film's financial failure was related to the BSO cancellation.

* * *

Although there is no doubt that Redgrave did not have a successful financial year following the BSO cancellation, we cannot say that she presented sufficient evidence to prove that her financial difficulties were caused by the BSO cancellation. No evidence was presented that, at the time she accepted the offer for *Annie's Coming Out,* Redgrave believed the film would experience financial difficulties. In addition, there was no allegation that the offers Redgrave turned down because of her commitment to *Annie's Coming Out,* such as offers to appear in *Yellowbeard* and *Who Will Love My Children?,* did not have firm financial backing. If *Annie's Coming Out* had been produced, Redgrave would have earned $250,000 in the year following the BSO cancellation an amount equal to Redgrave's average earnings before April 1982.

Redgrave contends, however, that the film offers she received following the BSO cancellation lacked secure financial backing and were thus significantly different from offers she had received prior to the cancellation. Thus, although Redgrave would have received $600,000 had *No Alternatives* and *Track 39* been produced, she argues that the fact that she had to accept two films that ultimately were not produced was itself a result of the BSO cancellation.

* * *

Even if we accept, however, that Redgrave proved she had experienced a drop in the quality of film offers following the BSO cancellation, Redgrave must also prove that the drop was proximately caused by the BSO cancellation and not by other, independent factors. Redgrave failed to carry her burden of presenting evidence sufficient to allow a jury reasonably to infer this causal connection.

The defense introduced evidence that Redgrave's political activities and statements had generated much media attention prior to the incident with the BSO. Redgrave conceded that her agents had informed her, prior to April 1982, that certain producers were hesitant to hire her because of the controversy she generated. And, in a newspaper interview in February 1982, Redgrave stated that she "had lost a lot of work because of her political beliefs" but that every time there had been a move to stop her working, "an equally terrific response [came] forward condemning any witch hunts."

To the extent that Redgrave may have experienced a decline in the quality of film offers received subsequent to April 1982, that decline could have been the result of Redgrave's political views and not the result of the BSO's cancellation. Even if the cancellation highlighted for producers the potential problems in hiring Redgrave, it was Redgrave's burden to establish that, in some way, the cancellation itself caused the difference in film offers rather than the problems as highlighted by the cancellation. Redgrave produced no direct evidence from film producers who were influenced by the cancellation. Thus, the jury's inference that the BSO cancellation had caused Redgrave consequential damages was one based more on "conjecture and speculation" than on a sufficient factual basis.

* * *

Redgrave contends that, as a result of the BSO cancellation, she no longer received offers to appear on Broadway. She testified that in April 1983 she was appearing in a successful English theater production of *The Aspern Papers* and was led to believe by the producers that the show would move to New York. Although it was Redgrave's opinion that the reason the play did not move to Broadway was because of the "situation" caused by the BSO cancellation, there was no testimony from the producers or others as to why the production did not go to Broadway. * * * Finally, Redgrave testified that Theodore Mann had considered offering her a role in *Heartbreak House* at Circle in the Square, but decided not to extend the offer because of the ramifications of the BSO cancellation.

Theodore Mann was the one producer who testified regarding his decision not to employ Redgrave in a Broadway production. He explained that

> the Boston Symphony Orchestra had cancelled, terminated Ms. Redgrave's contract. This had a—this is the premier or one of the premier arts organizations in America who, like ourselves, seeks support from foundations, corporations, individuals; have subscribers; sell individual tickets. I was afraid ... and those in my organization were afraid that this termination would have a negative effect on us if we hired her. And so we had conferences about this. We were also concerned about if there would be any physical disturbances to the performance.... And

it was finally decided ... that we would not hire [Redgrave] because of all the events that had happened, the cancellation by the Boston Symphony and the effects that we felt it would have on us by hiring her.

The evidence presented by Redgrave concerning her drop in Broadway offers after April 1982, apart from Mann's testimony, is not sufficient to support a finding of consequential damages. We do not, of course, question Redgrave's credibility in any way. Our concern is with the meager factual evidence. Redgrave had to introduce enough facts for a jury reasonably to infer that any drop in Broadway offers was proximately caused by the BSO cancellation and not by the fact that producers independently were concerned with the same factors that had motivated the BSO. Mann's testimony itself reflects that fact that many producers in New York may have been hesitant about hiring Redgrave because of a feared drop in subscription support or problems of physical disturbances. Apart from Mann's testimony, Redgrave presented nothing other than the fact that three expected offers or productions did not materialize. This type of circumstantial evidence is not sufficient to support a finding of consequential damages.

* * *

Mann's testimony reveals that, in considering whether to hire Redgrave, he and his partners were concerned about losing support from foundations and subscribers, having difficulty selling tickets, and dealing with possible physical disruptions. These are factors that result from the community response to Redgrave's political views. They are the same factors that apparently motivated the BSO to cancel its contract with Redgrave and are not the result of that cancellation. Thus, one possibly could infer from Mann's testimony that the BSO cancellation was not a proximate cause of the damage suffered by Redgrave in being denied the part in *Heartbreak House*.

Mann also testified, however, that he and his partners were affected by the BSO cancellation because the BSO was a premier arts organization and was dependent on the same type of support as Circle in the Square. A jury reasonably could infer that the BSO's cancellation did more than just highlight for Mann the potential problems that hiring Redgrave would cause but was actually a cause of Mann's decision, perhaps because Mann's theater support was similar to that of the BSO or because Mann felt influenced to follow the example of a "premier arts organization." Because this is a possible inference that a jury could draw from Mann's testimony, we defer to that inference. We therefore find that Redgrave presented sufficient evidence to prove consequential damages of $12,000, the fee arrangement contemplated by Mann for Redgrave's appearance in *Heartbreak House,* minus expenses she personally would have incurred had she appeared in the play.

* * *

1. The principle that the breaching party bears responsibility for damages contemplated when the contract was made found early expression in *Hadley v. Baxendale,* 156 Eng.Rep. 145, 151 (1854):

> Where two parties have made a contract which one of them had broken, the damages which the other party ought to receive in respect of such breach of contract should be such as may fairly and reasonably be considered either arising naturally, *i.e.,* according to the usual course of things, from such breach of contract itself, or such as may reasonably be supposed to have been in the contemplation of both parties, at the time they made the contract, as the probable result of the breach of it.

The *Hadley* formulation, adopted by the Restatement (Second) of Contracts 351, sets forth an objective test for determining the recoverability of damages based upon what the breaching party had reason to foresee as the probable result of the breach.

2. The *Hadley* rule has been applied with varying degrees of restrictiveness. The strictest application requires that the defendant "tacitly agreed," by implication or expressly at the time of contracting, to accept the risk of the particular type of loss. Most courts, however, use the concept for foreseeability from *Hadley* more generally and have rejected the tacit agreement test for the recovery of consequential damages. *See* Restatement (Second) of Contracts 351 comment a; U.C.C. § 2–715 comment 2.

3. The foreseeability principle has varied application with respect to determining "general" and "special" or "consequential" damages. General damages, according to *Hadley,* are those which flow directly and immediately as a natural consequence of the kind of wrongful act by the breaching party; therefore, the law conclusively presumes them to be foreseen or contemplated by the defendant. Special damages, in contrast, although actually caused by the defendant's acts, would not necessarily always follow from such conduct. Accordingly, liability attaches only by reference to the special character, condition or circumstances of the non-breaching party, and the loss must be foreseen by the breaching party rather than implied by law. The least restrictive interpretation of the *Hadley* foreseeability requirement is that the loss must have been "foreseeable" at the time of contracting even if it was not actually "foreseen."

Although the terms "general" and "special" damages have fallen gradually out of favor in some jurisdictions, the essence of the special damages criteria has been embraced by the Uniform Commercial Code 2 715(2) with respect to the availability of consequential damages to an aggrieved buyer of goods. Section 2 715(2) determines recoverability of damages depending upon whether the seller, at the time of contracting, had "reason to know" of general or particular requirements of the buyer.

Spang Industries, Inc. v. Aetna Casualty and Surety Co.

512 F.2d 365 (2d Cir.1975).

■ MULLIGAN, CIRCUIT JUDGE:

[Torrington Construction Co. (Torrington) successfully bid to reconstruct a highway in New York. Prior to submitting its bid, Torrington received a quotation from Spang Industries, Inc., Fort Pitt Bridge Division (Fort Pitt) for the fabrication, furnishing and erection of structural steel to construct a bridge. The delivery date was "to be mutually agreed upon", and Torrington subsequently notified Fort Pitt of the required delivery schedule. Fort Pitt subcontracted the unloading and erection of the steel to Syracuse Rigging Co. (Syracuse) but neglected to notify it of the delivery schedule. As a result, Syracuse delayed in unloading and Torrington did the work itself. The delays also resulted in completion of the structure during the winter. Since the job site was in northern New York and the danger of freezing temperatures was imminent, Torrington arranged for the pouring of concrete on an expedited basis at increased expense.

Fort Pitt instituted suit in federal court against Torrington's surety, Aetna, to recover the balance due on the subcontract. Torrington commenced suit in state court against Fort Pitt for damages caused by the delays in performance. The suit was removed to federal court, and in the consolidated action the district court held that Fort Pitt was entitled to recover the contract balance of $23,290.12, reduced by $7,653.57 in damages sustained by Torrington caused by the delays in performance.]

Fort Pitt on this appeal does not take issue with any of the findings of fact of the court below but contends that the recovery by Torrington of its increased expenses constitutes special damages which were not reasonably within the contemplation of the parties when they entered into the contract.

While the damages awarded Torrington are relatively modest ($7,653.57) in comparison with the subcontract price ($132,274.37), Fort Pitt urges that an affirmance of the award will do violence to the rule of Hadley v. Baxendale, 156 Eng.Rep. 145 (Ex.1854), and create a precedent which will have a severe impact on the business of all subcontractors and suppliers.

While it is evident that the function of the award of damages for a breach of contract is to put the plaintiff in the same position he would have been in had there been no breach, *Hadley v. Baxendale* limits the recovery to those injuries which the parties could reasonably have anticipated at the time the contract was entered into. If the damages suffered do not usually flow from the breach, then it must be established that the special circumstances giving rise to them should reasonably have been anticipated at the time the contract was made.

* * *

The gist of Fort Pitt's argument is that, when it entered into the subcontract to fabricate, furnish and erect the steel in September, 1969, it had received a copy of the specifications which indicated that the total work was to be completed by December 15, 1971. It could not reasonably have anticipated that Torrington would so expedite the work (which was accepted by the State on January 21, 1971) that steel delivery would be called for in 1970 rather than in 1971. Whatever knowledge Fort Pitt received after the contract was entered into, it argues, cannot expand its liability, since it is essential under *Hadley v. Baxendale* and its Yankee progeny that the notice of the facts which would give rise to special damages in case of breach be given at or before the time the contract was made. The principle urged cannot be disputed. [Citations.] We do not, however, agree that any violence to the doctrine was done here.

* * * [A]t the time when the parties, pursuant to their initial agreement, fixed the date for performance which is crucial here, Fort Pitt knew that a June, 1970 delivery was required. It would be a strained and unpalatable interpretation of *Hadley v. Baxendale* to now hold that, although the parties left to further agreement the time for delivery, the supplier could reasonably rely upon a 1971 delivery date rather than one the parties later fixed. * * *

We conclude that, when the parties enter into a contract which, by its terms, provides that the time of performance is to be fixed at a later date, the knowledge of the consequences of a failure to perform is to be imputed to the defaulting party as of the time the parties agreed upon the date of performance. This comports, in our view, with both the logic and the spirit of *Hadley v. Baxendale*. * * * At the time Fort Pitt did become committed to a delivery date, it was aware that a June, 1970 performance was required by virtue of its own acceptance. * * *

Having proceeded thus far, we do not think it follows automatically that Torrington is entitled to recover the damages it seeks here; further consideration of the facts before us is warranted. Fort Pitt maintains that, under the *Hadley v. Baxendale* rubric, the damages flowing from its conceded breach are "special" or "consequential" and were not reasonably to be contemplated by the parties. Since Torrington has not proved any "general" or "direct" damages, Fort Pitt urges that the contractor is entitled to nothing. We cannot agree. * * *

It must be taken as a reasonable assumption that, when the delivery date of June, 1970 was set, Torrington planned the bridge erection within a reasonable time thereafter. It is normal construction procedure that the erection of the steel girders would be followed by the installation of a poured concrete platform and whatever railings or super-structure the platform would require. Fort Pitt was an experienced bridge fabricator supplying contractors and the sequence of the work is hardly arcane. Moreover, any delay beyond June or August would assuredly have jeopardized the pouring of the concrete and have forced the postponement of the work until the spring. The work here, as was well known to Fort Pitt, was to be performed in northern New York near the Vermont border. The court below found that continuing freezing weather would have forced the pouring to be delayed until June, 1971. Had Torrington refused delivery or had it been compelled to delay the completion of the work until the spring of 1971, the potential damages claim would have been substantial. Instead, in a good faith effort to mitigate damages, Torrington embarked upon the crash program we have described. It appears to us that this eventuality should have reasonably been anticipated by Fort Pitt as it was experienced in the trade and was supplying bridge steel in northern climes on a project requiring a concrete roadway.

Torrington's recovery under the circumstances is not substantial or cataclysmic from Fort Pitt's point of view. It represents the expenses of unloading steel from the gondola due to Fort Pitt's admitted failure to notify its erection subcontractor, Syracuse Rigging, that the steel had been shipped, plus the costs of premium time, extra equipment and the cost of protecting the work, all occasioned by the realities Torrington faced in the wake of Fort Pitt's breach. In fact, Torrington's original claim of $23,290.81 was whittled down by the court below because of Torrington's failure to establish that its supervisory costs, overhead and certain equipment costs were directly attributable to the delay in delivery of the steel.

Professor Williston has commented:

> The true reason why notice to the defendant of the plaintiff's special circumstances is important is because, just as a court of equity under circumstances of hardship arising after the formation of a contract may deny specific performance, so a court of law may deny damages for unusual consequences where the defendant was not aware when he entered into the contract *how serious an injury would result from its breach*.

11 S. Williston, *supra,* at 295 (Footnote omitted) (emphasis added).

In this case, serious or catastrophic injury was avoided by prompt, effective and reasonable mitigation at modest cost. Had Torrington not acted, had it been forced to wait until the following spring to complete the entire job and then sued to recover the profits it would have made had there been performance by Fort Pitt according to the terms of its agreement, then we might well have an appropriate setting for a classical *Hadley v. Baxendale* controversy. As this case comes to us, it hardly presents that situation. We therefore affirm the judgment below permitting Torrington to offset its damages against the contract price. * * *

Evra Corp. v. Swiss Bank Corp.

673 F.2d 951 (7th Cir.1982).

■ POSNER, CIRCUIT JUDGE.

The question one of first impression in this diversity case is the extent of a bank's liability for failure to make a transfer of funds when requested by wire to do so. The essential facts are undisputed. In 1972 Hyman Michaels Company, a large Chicago dealer in scrap metal, entered into a two-year contract to supply steel scrap to a Brazilian corporation. Hyman Michaels chartered a ship, the *Pandora,* to carry the scrap to Brazil. The charter was for one year, with an option to extend the charter for a second year; specified a fixed daily rate of pay for the hire of the ship during both the initial and the option period, payable semi-monthly "in advance"; and provided that if payment was not made on time the *Pandora's* owner could cancel the charter. Payment was to be made by deposit to the owner's account in the Banque de Paris et des Pays Bas (Suisse) in Geneva, Switzerland.

The usual method by which Hyman Michaels, in Chicago, got the payments to the Banque de Paris in Geneva was to request the Continental Illinois National Bank and Trust Company of Chicago, where it had an account, to make a wire transfer of funds. Continental would debit Hyman Michaels' account by the amount of the payment and then send a telex to its London office for retransmission to its correspondent bank in Geneva Swiss Bank Corporation asking Swiss Bank to deposit this amount in the Banque de Paris account of the *Pandora's* owner. The transaction was completed by the crediting of Swiss Bank's account at Continental by the same amount.

When Hyman Michaels chartered the *Pandora* in June 1972, market charter rates were fixed in the charter for its entire term two years if Hyman Michaels exercised its option. Shortly after the agreement was signed, however, charter rates began to climb and by October 1972 they were much higher than they had been in June. The *Pandora's* owners were eager to get out of the charter if they could. * * *

* * * On the morning of April 25, 1973, [Hyman Michaels] telephoned Continental Bank and requested it to transfer $27,000 to the Banque de Paris account of the *Pandora's* owner in payment for the charter hire period from April 27 to May 11, 1973. Since the charter provided for payment "in advance," this payment arguably was due by the close of business on April 26. The requested telex went out to Continental's London office on the afternoon of April 25, which was nighttime in England. Early the next morning a telex operator in Continental's London office dialed, as Continental's Chicago office had instructed him to do, Swiss Bank's general telex number, which rings in the bank's cable department. But that number was busy, and after trying unsuccessfully for an hour to engage it the Continental telex operator dialed another number, that of a machine in Swiss Bank's foreign exchange department which he had used in the past when the general number was engaged. We know this machine received the telexed message because it signaled the sending machine at both the beginning and end of the transmission that the telex was being received. Yet Swiss Bank failed to comply with the payment order, and no transfer of funds was made to the account of the *Pandora's* owner in the Banque of Paris.

No one knows exactly what went wrong. One possibility is that the receiving telex machine had simply run out of paper, in which event it would not print the message although it had received it. Another is that whoever took the message out of the machine after it was printed failed to deliver it to the banking department. Unlike the machine in the cable department that the Continental telex operator had originally tried to reach, the machines in the foreign exchange department were operated by junior foreign exchange dealers rather than by professional telex operators, although Swiss Bank knew that messages intended for other departments were sometimes diverted to the telex machines in the foreign exchange department.

At 8:30 a.m. the next day, April 27, Hyman Michaels in Chicago received a telex from the *Pandora's* owner stating that the charter was canceled because payment for the April 27 May 11 charter period had not been made. Hyman Michaels called over to Continental and told them to keep trying to effect payment through Swiss Bank even if the *Pandora's* owner rejected it. * * * Days passed while the missing telex message was hunted unsuccessfully. Finally Swiss Bank suggested to Continental that it retransmit the telex message to the machine in the cable department and this was done on May 1. The next day Swiss Bank attempted to deposit the $27,000 in the account of the *Pandora's* owner at the Banque de Paris but the payment was refused.

[The matter was referred to arbitration, in accordance with the charter. The arbitrators agreed that this delay was sufficient to entitle *Pandora's* owner to cancel the agreement.]

Hyman Michaels then brought this diversity action against Swiss Bank seeking to recover its expenses in the * * * arbitration proceeding plus the profits that it lost because of the cancellation of the charter. The contract by which Hyman Michaels had agreed to ship scrap steel to Brazil had been terminated by the buyer in March 1973 and Hyman Michaels had promptly subchartered the *Pandora* at market rates, which by April 1973 were double the rates fixed in the charter. Its lost profits are based on the difference between the charter and subcharter rates.

* * *

The case was tried to a district judge without a jury. * * * [He ruled] that Swiss Bank had been negligent and under Illinois law was liable to Hyman Michaels for $2.1 million in damages. This figure was made up of about $16,000 in arbitration expenses and the rest in lost profits on the subcharter of the *Pandora*. * * * The case comes to us on Swiss Bank's appeal from the judgment. * * *

When a bank fails to make a requested transfer of funds, this can cause two kinds of loss. First, the funds themselves or interest on them may be lost, and of course the fee paid for the transfer, having bought nothing, becomes a loss item. These are "direct" (sometimes called "general") damages. Hyman Michaels is not seeking any direct damages in this case and apparently sustained none. It did not lose any part of the $27,000; although its account with Continental Bank was debited by this amount prematurely, it was not an interest-bearing account so Hyman Michaels lost no interest; and Hyman Michaels paid no fee either to Continental or to Swiss Bank for the aborted transfer. A second type of loss, which either the payor or the payee may suffer, is a dislocation in one's business triggered by the failure to pay. Swiss Bank's failure to transfer funds to the Banque de Paris when requested to do so by Continental Bank set off a chain reaction which resulted in an arbitration proceeding that was costly to Hyman Michaels and in the cancellation of a highly profitable contract.

It is those costs and lost profits "consequential" or, as they are sometimes called, "special" damages that Hyman Michaels seeks in this lawsuit, and recovered below. It is conceded that if Hyman Michaels was entitled to consequential damages, the district court measured them correctly. The only issue is whether it was entitled to consequential damages.

* * *

Hadley v. Baxendale, 9 Ex. 341, 156 Eng.Rep. 145 (1854), is the leading common law case on liability for consequential damages caused by failure or delay in carrying out a commercial undertaking. The engine shaft in plaintiffs' corn mill had broken and they hired the defendants, a common carrier, to transport the shaft to the manufacturer, who was to make a new one using the broken shaft as a model. The carrier failed to deliver the shaft within the time promised. With the engine shaft out of service the mill was shut down. The plaintiffs sued the defendants for the lost profits of the mill during the additional period that it was shut down because of the defendants' breach of their promise. The court held that the lost profits were not a proper item of damages, because "in the great multitude of cases of millers sending off broken shafts to third persons by a carrier under ordinary circumstances, such consequences [the stoppage of the mill and resulting loss of profits] would not, in all probability, have occurred; and these special circumstances were here never communicated by the plaintiffs to the defendants." 9 Ex. at 356, 156 Eng.Rep. at 151.

The rule of *Hadley v. Baxendale* that consequential damages will not be awarded unless the defendant was put on notice of the special circumstances giving rise to them has been applied in many Illinois cases, and *Hadley* cited approvingly. [Citations.] In *Siegel* [*Siegel v. Western Union Tel. Co.,* 312 Ill.App. 86, 92 93, 37 N.E.2d 868, 871 (1941)], the plaintiff had delivered $200 to Western Union with instructions to transmit it to a friend of the plaintiff's. The money was to be bet (legally) on a horse, but this was not disclosed in the instructions. Western Union misdirected the money order and it did not reach the friend until several hours after the race had taken place. The horse that the plaintiff had intended to bet on won and would have paid $1650 on the plaintiff's $200 bet if the bet had been placed. He sued Western Union for his $1450 lost profit, but the court held that under the rule of *Hadley v. Baxendale* Western Union was not liable, because it "had no notice or knowledge of the purpose for which the money was being transmitted." [Citation.]

The present case is similar, though Swiss Bank knew more than Western Union knew in *Siegel;* it knew or should have known, from Continental Bank's previous telexes, that Hyman Michaels was paying the Pandora Shipping Company for the hire of a motor vessel named *Pandora.* But it did not know when payment was due, what the terms of the charter were, or that they had turned out to be extremely favorable to Hyman Michaels. And it did not know that Hyman Michaels knew the *Pandora's* owner would try to cancel the charter, and probably would succeed, if Hyman Michaels was * * * late in making payment, or that despite this peril Hyman Michaels would not try to pay until the last possible moment and in the event of a delay in transmission would not do everything in its power to minimize the consequences of the delay. Electronic funds transfers are not so unusual as to automatically place a bank on notice of extraordinary consequences if such a transfer goes awry. Swiss Bank did not have enough information to infer that if it lost a $27,000 payment order it would face a liability in excess of $2 million. [Citations.]

It is true that in both *Hadley* and *Siegel* there was a contract between the parties and here there was none. * * * We must therefore ask what difference it should make whether the parties are or are not bound to each other by a contract. On the one hand, it seems odd that the absence of a contract would enlarge rather than limit the extent of liability. * * * Privity is not a wholly artificial concept. It is one thing to imply a duty to one with whom one has a contract and another to imply it to the entire world.

On the other hand, contract liability is strict. A breach of contract does not connote wrongdoing; it may have been caused by circumstances beyond the promisor's control a strike, a fire, the failure of a supplier to deliver an essential input. [Citation.] And while such contract doctrines as impossibility, impracticability, and frustration relieve promisors from liability for some failures to perform that are beyond their control, many other such failures are actionable although they could not have been prevented by the exercise of due care. The district judge found that Swiss Bank had been negligent in losing Continental Bank's telex message and it can be argued that Swiss Bank should therefore be liable for a broader set of consequences than if it had only broken a contract. But *Siegel* implicitly rejects this distinction. Western Union had not merely broken its contract to deliver the plaintiff's money order; it had "negligently misdirected" the money order. "The company's negligence is conceded." Yet it was not liable for the consequences.

Siegel, we conclude, is authority for holding that Swiss Bank is not liable for the consequences of negligently failing to transfer Hyman Michaels' funds to Banque de Paris; reason for such a holding is found in the animating principle of *Hadley v. Baxendale,* which is that the costs of the untoward consequence of a course of dealings should be borne by that party who was able to avert the consequence at least cost and failed to do so. In *Hadley* the untoward consequence was the shutting down of the mill. The carrier could have avoided it by delivering the engine shaft on time. But the mill owners, as the court noted, could have avoided it simply by having a spare shaft. Prudence required that they have a spare shaft anyway, since a replacement could not be obtained at once even if there was no undue delay in carting the broken shaft to and the replacement shaft from the manufacturer. The court refused to imply a duty on the part of the carrier to guarantee the mill owners against the consequences of their own lack of prudence, though of course if the parties had stipulated for such a guarantee the court would have enforced it. The notice requirement of *Hadley v. Baxendale* is designed to assure that such an improbable guarantee really is intended.

This case is much the same, though it arises in a tort rather than a contract setting. Hyman Michaels showed a lack of prudence throughout. * * * It was imprudent for Hyman Michaels * * * to wait till arguably the last day before payment was due to instruct its bank to transfer the necessary funds overseas. And it was imprudent in the last degree for Hyman Michaels, when it received notice of cancellation on the last possible day payment was due, to fail to pull out all the stops to get payment to the Banque de Paris on that day, and instead to dither while Continental and Swiss Bank wasted five days looking for the lost telex message. * * *

This is not to condone the sloppy handling of incoming telex messages in Swiss Bank's foreign department. But Hyman Michaels is a sophisticated business enterprise. It knew or should have known that even the Swiss are not infallible; that messages sometimes get lost or delayed in transit among three banks, two of them located 5000 miles apart, even when all the banks are using reasonable care; and that therefore it should take its own precautions against the consequences best known to itself of a mishap that might not be due to anyone's negligence.

* * *

The rule of *Hadley v. Baxendale* links up with tort concepts. * * * The rule is sometimes stated in the form that only foreseeable damages are recoverable in a breach of contract action. *E.g.*, Restatement (Second) of Contracts 351 (1979). So expressed, it corresponds to the tort principle that limits liability to the foreseeable consequence of the defendant's carelessness. * * * To estimate the extent of its probable liability in order to know how many and how elaborate fail-safe features to install in its telex rooms or how much insurance to buy against the inevitable failures, Swiss Bank would have to collect reams of information about firms that are not even its regular customers. It had no banking relationship with Hyman Michaels. It did not know or have reason to know how at once precious and fragile Hyman Michaels' contract with the *Pandora's* owner was. These were circumstances too remote from Swiss Bank's practical range of knowledge to have affected its decisions as to who should man the telex machines in the foreign department or whether it should have more intelligent machines or should install more machines in the cable department, any more than the falling of a platform scale because a conductor jostled a passenger who was carrying fireworks was a prospect that could have influenced the amount of care taken by the Long Island Railroad. *See Palsgraf v. Long Island R.R.*, 248 N.Y. 339, 162 N.E. 99 (1928).

In short, Swiss Bank was not required in the absence of a contractual undertaking to take precautions or insure against a harm that it could not measure but that was known with precision to Hyman Michaels, which could by the exercise of common prudence have averted it completely. * * *

* * * The undisputed facts, recited in this opinion, show as a matter of law that Hyman Michaels is not entitled to recover consequential damages from Swiss Bank.

* * * [So Ordered.]

---

1. In tort law, foreseeability operates in the initial determination of liability for negligence. A reasonably prudent person acts in accordance with the foreseeable consequences of voluntary conduct. If an injury occurs as a result of an unforeseeable consequence from an otherwise prudent act, there is no liability for negligence. Once liability is found, however, the tortfeasor is liable for all damage that is "proximate."

2. The role of foreseeability in tort to determine what injuries are "proximate" is a continuing subject of debate. It is universally agreed that foreseeability does not limit damages in cases where the extent of a personal injury is greater than anticipated. This is the "thin-skulled plaintiff" rule, based on the frequent illustration in the case law that if a negligent defendant injures a person with an eggshell skull so that death results, the tortfeasor is liable for all the loss even though a normal person would only have a bump on the head. This example originated in *Dulieu v. White*, 2 K.B. 669 (1901).

For other types of unforeseeable consequences, however, courts have not been in agreement on the role of foreseeability in proximate cause. The famous case *In re Polemis*, 3 K.B. 560 (1921), articulates the extreme position that all direct consequences of negligence are compensable regardless of the unforeseeability of the consequences. The contrary position is represented in the case known as The Wagon Mound, No. 1, [1961] A.C. 388. Viscount Simmons noted there that "it does not seem consonant with current ideas of justice or morality for an act of negligence ... which results in some trivial foreseeable damage, the actor should be liable for all consequences however unforeseeable and however unforeseeable and however grave, so long as they can be said to be 'direct.' "

3. Justice Cardozo approached the issue of foreseeability in terms of liability analysis rather than damages limitation in his celebrated opinion *Palsgraf v. Long Island R. Co.*, 248 N.Y. 339, 162 N.E. 99 (1928). There must be a duty established toward the injured party first, *Palsgraf* holds, and that duty arises from the foreseeability of harm to that person. In the absence of such foreseeability, there is no duty and thus no liability. In *Palsgraf* the plaintiff was injured by a firecracker explosion on a railway platform. The defendant railroad's employees had acted negligently toward another passenger by helping him board a moving train. A package that passenger was carrying dropped and the fireworks inside went off. Plaintiff Palsgraf, standing several feet away, was injured. She was denied recovery on the grounds that the negligent act endangered only the boarding passenger and did not foreseeably threaten someone remote. She was an "unforeseen plaintiff" and thus there was no liability to her.

The *Palsgraf* approach uses foreseeability in negligence analysis to determine liability, but it does not settle the problem of when to deny damages for unseen losses caused to foreseen plaintiffs. *See* Petition of Kinsman Transit Co., 338 F.2d 708 (2d Cir.1964).

B.   CERTAINTY

Section Coverage:

A limiting factor on the compensatory damages recoverable in contract or tort is the requirement that the injured party must prove damages with reasonable certainty. The first facet of the certainty limitation pertains to substantive entitlement to damages. Has the plaintiff shown with sufficient definiteness that the defendant acted in a manner which invaded a legally protected duty and caused resulting harm? If so, the certainty requirement secondarily functions to determine the extent to which the defendant should be held accountable for the consequences of the misconduct. A plaintiff may satisfy this burden upon producing a reasonable evidentiary basis that would allow damages to be calculated without speculation or conjecture. Mathematical exactitude is not required. An injured party who fails to meet the requisite burden of proof with reasonable certainty may be entitled to nominal damages.

Traditionally courts have demanded a higher level of certainty with respect to damages for breach of contract than for torts. One explanation for the differentiation is that certain elements of tort awards, such as pain and suffering or emotional distress, are inherently difficult to quantify into dollar amounts, while loss of earnings may be more precisely determined. The Restatement (Second) of Torts 912 suggests a flexible test for certainty "as the nature of the tort and the circumstances permit."

Model Case:

Carter planned to open a new restaurant to be named Pizzatown. He contracted to purchase furnishings for the restaurant from the Interior Supply Company with delivery and installation scheduled in time for the grand opening on September 1. Carter expended $5,000 for promotional materials which advertised the September 1 opening.

The furnishings did not arrive when scheduled, resulting in the delay of the restaurant opening until January 1. Carter brings suit for breach of contract against Interior Supply. Carter seeks reliance damages for the advertising expenditures and also requests prospective lost profits for the four month period during which the restaurant could not operate.

A court would typically find that the promotional expenses would be a compensable item of damages capable of being reasonably ascertained. The claim for lost profits would be viewed as speculative or conjectural, even if the foreseeability test is passed, because Carter had no prior operating history to satisfy the requirement of certainty. Consider, in light of the following materials, whether it should make a difference if Carter could introduce evidence of operating histories of comparable restaurants at similar stages of development. What if Carter could produce such evidence of other Pizzatown restaurants in similar locales?

Cannon v. Yankee Products Co., Inc.

59 Mass.App.Dec. 169 (1977).

■ WALSH, J.

In this claim for lost profits a restaurant owner originally brought an action of contract against Yankee Products Co., Inc. (Yankee) for breach of express and breach of implied warranty. * * *

The plaintiff purchased vegetables from Yankee on a weekly basis and dealt with the same route salesman for three years. The plaintiff had purchased the same brand of canned sweet peas packed by Oco, from Yankee, for a period of six months to one year and on January 7, 1970 had purchased one-half of a case of such peas packed in sealed cans. The salesman told plaintiff that the peas were a good product, a big pea, good tasting, not hard and that he and his customers would be satisfied with them and this is the very best brand you can buy, good flavor, wholesome and will please your customers thus increasing your business.

The plaintiff prepared and sold to his customers some of the canned peas purchased on January 7, 1970 on Friday, January 23, 1970 as part of the ninety-nine cent special. He opened a can of peas, placed the peas in a colander, strained them and washed them off. He then put the peas in a pot which had just been cleaned and wiped dry, heated the peas and put them in another pot designed for use in a steam table. He then served the peas to customers.

A worm was discovered by a customer in the "99 cent special" purchased by him. The plaintiff, having had his attention called to the presence of the worm, saw it in the peas on the customer's plate. The worm was skinny, green, dead and $1\frac{1}{3}$ inches in length.

The said male customer "made a stink" thereover in the presence of about fifty-five fellow patrons; that other customers exclaimed "oh! oh!"; that the plaintiff commented that the incident or occurrence was just an accident; that he refunded the price of the specially priced meals which had been served with the peas in question to the respective purchasers but the "word spread" and about thirty patrons walked out and the plaintiff refunded the price of their dinners to them. The plaintiff could neither remember the name of or remember the last time he saw the customer who found the worm on his plate.

After this incident the plaintiff observed a reduction in the number of customers patronizing his restaurant, particularly at the lunch hour. He took a ride around the area and observed many of his former customers eating elsewhere at other dining establishments.

Subsequent to the incident the plaintiff increased the number of hours of doing business. He remained open until 11:00 P.M., hiring a night man to do so. However, all of his efforts to increase the volume of his business were futile. According to the plaintiff "the word spread—the news got around." Consequently, he sold the business on February 1, 1971 and the place has changed hands three times since.

[Plaintiff produced evidence of the gross sales of the plaintiff's business from July, 1969, through November, 1970. The trial court found that the incident caused patrons to remain away from the restaurant, and that Yankee's breaches of warranty rendered it liable for damages for lost profits. The court awarded plaintiff damages of $7,622.80 based upon the average diminution of sales for a twelve month period following the incident.]

It is recognized that loss of profits may be recovered as an element of damages for breach of contract, but it may be difficult to fit the applicable law to a particular case. "The loss of prospective profits may be allowed . . . where it appears that the loss was the natural, primary and probable consequence of the breach, that the profits arising from the performance of the contract or the loss likely to result from its non-performance were within the contemplation of the parties, and the profits were not so uncertain or contingent as to be incapable of reasonable proof." [Citation.] They must be the proximate result of the breach and cannot be recovered when they are remote or so uncertain, contingent or speculative as not to be susceptible of trustworthy proof. A claimant cannot prevail when any essential element is left to conjecture, surmise or hypothesis. "The difficulty is not so much in the statement of the general principle as in applying it. A comparatively insignificant incident may be in such combination with others as to lead to a conclusion in one decision apparently at variance with that reached in others. Each case must be decided on its own facts under this necessarily somewhat broad and comprehensive proposition." [Citations.]

A leading case allowing recovery for lost profits involving the sale of food and relied on by the plaintiff is Hawkins v. Jamrog, 277 Mass. 540, 179 N.E. 224 (1931). The plaintiff in that case was the proprietor of a boarding house conducted for college students. The defendant sold dressed turkeys to the plaintiff, knowing their intended use as food in the boarding house. The turkeys were unwholesome and after eating them the plaintiff, all the student waiters and almost all of the boarders were made ill. There was evidence that of the seventy original boarders only thirty returned despite plaintiff's efforts to induce them to do so and also evidence of the average weekly profit per boarder. It was held that an award of loss of prospective profits to the end of the school year was neither too remote to be allowed as an element of damage nor merely speculative or conjectural in nature.

The Uniform Commercial Code is also applicable here and GL § 2–714(3) provides that in addition to damages for loss recoverable from a seller's breach in the ordinary course of events, consequential damages may also be recovered in a proper case under § 2–715. Section 2–715(2) provides that "consequential damages resulting from the seller's breach include (a) any loss resulting from general or particular requirements and needs of which the seller at the time of contracting had reason to know and which could not reasonably be prevented by cover or otherwise; and (b) injury to person or property proximately resulting from any breach of warranty."

We think the case at bar is distinguishable from *Hawkins v. Jamrog, supra.* In both cases the plaintiffs purchased food products for resale and their respective vendors had reason to know it. However, in *Hawkins* the plaintiff's customers ate the unwholesome food and a substantial number became ill. Such was not the case here. The customer who saw the worm probably would not have had a cause of action for personal injury. [Citations.] Certainly those who didn't see it would not have had any such claim.

The fact that the exodus of the customers was caused as much by the utterances of the obviously upset customer as by the presence of the worm and the fact that no one was made ill by the alleged unwholesome food would seem to take the loss of customers out of the natural and probable consequences of the breach. If for no other reason we feel these are incidents, not necessarily insignificant, which render a finding of loss of profits in this case not warranted. On the same grounds we do not think this is, in the words of GS § 2–714(3), "a proper case" for the recovery of consequential damages under the provisions of GS § 2–715.

With respect to the amount of the loss of profit, we do not find in the report any direct evidence of that nature. Prospective profits need not be proved to mathematical certainty, but in order to recover they must be proved. Here there was evidence of diminution of receipts or sales but no evidence of how much of this constituted loss of profit. There was basis for an opinion, perhaps, but no opinion or calculation.

The plaintiff fares no better in his complaint alleging negligence on the part of the canner of the product since he has the burden to establish that the defendant's breach of duty was the proximate cause of his claimed loss of profit. "One is bound to anticipate and provide against what usually happens and what is likely to happen, but is not bound in like manner to guard against what is unusual and unlikely to happen, or what, as is sometimes said, is only remotely and slightly probable." [Citations.]

We find that on the complaint for negligence against the defendant canning company the plaintiff is not entitled to recover damages. Even though negligence may be found, there is no invasion of rights and no right of action unless legal damage is caused. [Citation.] With respect to the counts in contract against the vendor the situation is different. The plaintiff alleged in his declaration loss of customers and business, but apparently offered no evidence on any out-of-pocket loss for the purchase of the goods or money refunded to his customers. However, the breach, once established, entitled the plaintiff to at least nominal damages.

It is our determination that there has been prejudicial error in the denial of defendants' request for ruling relating to loss of profit. Accordingly, the judgments entered in counts 1 and 2 are modified and judgment is to be entered for nominal damages in each count. On the complaint, judgment for the plaintiff is vacated and judgment is to be entered for the defendant.

––––––––––

1. The Uniform Commercial Code rejects requiring mathematical precision in the proof of loss, but provides that damages may be determined in "any manner which is reasonable under the circumstances." See Comment 4 to U.C.C. § 2–715. Such an approach effectuates the liberal administration of remedies under the Code. Comment 1 to U.C.C. § 1–106. The Code's approach favors a flexible policy where compensatory damages need only "be proved with whatever definiteness and accuracy the facts permit, but no more." Id. The common law doctrinal standard which demands only "reasonable" certainty may be considered incorporated through U.C.C. § 1–103.

2. *New Businesses.* In order to satisfy the requirement of reasonable certainty, new businesses have drawn from several methods suggested by the Supreme Court in *Bigelow v. RKO Radio Pictures*, 327 U.S. 251, 66 S.Ct. 574, 90 L.Ed. 652 (1946), in an antitrust context to establish lost profits for breach of contract. The Fifth Circuit in *Lehrman v. Gulf Oil Corp.*, 500 F.2d 659 (5th Cir.1974). explained as follows:

> There are two generally recognized methods of proving lost profits: (1) the before and after theory; and (2) the yardstick test. The before and after theory compares the plaintiff's profit record prior to the violation with that subsequent to it. The before and after theory is not easily adaptable to a plaintiff who is driven out of business before he is able to compile an earnings record sufficient to allow estimation of lost profits. Therefore, the yardstick test is sometimes employed. It consists of a study of the profits of business operations that are closely comparable to the plaintiff's. Although allowances can be made for differences between the firms, the business used as a standard must be as nearly identical to the plaintiff's as possible. 500 F.2d at 667.

See also Guard v. P & R Enterprises, Inc., 631 P.2d 1068 (Alaska 1981); Chung v. Kaonohi Center Co., 62 Haw. 594, 618 P.2d 283 (1980); El Fredo Pizza, Inc. v. Roto–Flex Oven Co., 199 Neb. 697, 261 N.W.2d 358 (1978); Comment, Remedies Lost Profits as Contract Damages for an Unestablished Business: The New Business Rule Becomes Outdated, 56 N.C.L.Rev. 693 (1978).

3. The limitation that damages be established with reasonable certainty is consistent with the policy that compensatory damages should be awarded to make an injured party whole but not to punish. Just as the notion of what constitutes fair compensation is variable with the circumstances of the nature and extent of harm, the sort of evidence which satisfies the burden of "reasonable certainty" similarly must be flexible and pragmatic. In order to accommodate the differences in torts and contracts, and within those broad categories the range of harms, courts have recognized modifications of the rule of certainty. The court in *M & R*

Contractors & Builders v. Michael, 215 Md. 340, 138 A.2d 350 (1958) observed:

> Courts have modified the "certainty" rule into a more flexible one of "reasonable certainty." In such instances, recovery may often be based on opinion evidence, in the legal sense of that term, from which liberal inferences may be drawn. Generally, proof of actual or even estimated costs is all that is required with certainty. 138 A.2d at 355.

4. The doctrine of certainty in the law of damages draws a clear distinction between the level of proof required to demonstrate entitlement to recovery and to measure the amount of damages once liability has been established. Consider the Supreme Court's classic statement in *Story Parchment Co. v. Paterson Parchment Paper Co.,* 282 U.S. 555, 51 S.Ct. 248, 75 L.Ed. 544 (1931), regarding entitlement and measurement of damages:

> It is sometimes said that speculative damages cannot be recovered, because the amount is uncertain; but such remarks will generally be found applicable to such damages as it is uncertain whether sustained at all from the breach. Sometimes the claim is rejected as being too remote. This is another mode of saying that it is uncertain whether such damages resulted necessarily and immediately from the breach complained of. * * *

> Where the tort itself is of such a nature as to preclude the ascertainment of the amount of damages with certainty, it would be a perversion of fundamental principles of justice to deny all relief to the injured person, and thereby relieve the wrongdoer from making any amend for his acts. In such case, while the damages may not be determined by mere speculation or guess, it will be enough if the evidence show the extent of the damages as a matter of just and reasonable inference, although the result be only approximate. The wrongdoer is not entitled to complain that they cannot be measured with the exactness and precision that would be possible if the case, which he alone is responsible for making, were otherwise. [Citation.] As the Supreme Court of Michigan has forcefully declared, the risk of the uncertainty should be thrown upon the wrongdoer instead of upon the injured party. Allison v. Chandler, 11 Mich. 542, 550–556. * * *

> To deny the injured party the right to recover any actual damages in such cases, because they are of a nature which cannot be thus certainly measured, would be to enable parties to profit by, and speculate upon, their own wrongs, encourage violence and invite depredation. Such is not, and cannot be the law, though cases may be found where courts have laid down artificial and arbitrary rules which have produced such a result.

> * * * Numerous decisions are there cited in support of the statement, that "The constant tendency of the courts is to find some way in which damages can be awarded where a wrong has been done. Difficulty of

ascertainment is no longer confused with right of recovery." 51 S.Ct. at 250–51.

5. As recognized in *Story Parchment,* where sufficient evidence of the fact of damage exists courts will not allow a tortfeasor to escape liability because the amount of damages cannot be ascertained with precision. In the torts context, the rationale for such a differentiation often is stated as being that the wrongdoer should bear the risk of uncertainty. Bastian v. King, 661 P.2d 953 (Utah 1983). That does not mean, however, that the burden of proving damages with certainty is actually shifted to the wrongdoer. One court explained the justification for relaxing the certainty limitation by observing: "It is the height of hypocrisy that a wrongdoer complain about inaccuracies or uncertainty in a jury system. One whose actions hurt another is in an extremely poor position to demand precision in measuring damages, and will have to bear whatever risk of uncertainty exists in our system of settling differences." Creason v. Myers, 217 Neb. 551, 350 N.W.2d 526 (1984) (difficulty in assessing damages did not justify abolishing the cause of action for alienation of affections).

6. Consider the case, *Grace v. Corbis–Sygma,* 487 F.3d 113 (2d Cir.2007), where a famous photographer sought damages for thousands of photographic images which were entrusted to an agent over a thirty year period and which were subsequently lost or destroyed. The plaintiff could only estimate the number of images that had been entrusted to the bailee over the term of their licensing arrangement.

The court observed that, although the burden of proving damages with reasonable certainty traditionally rested with the claimant, that burden was relaxed when the defendant's wrongdoing prevented the plaintiff from making a just and reasonable estimate of the losses suffered. The court considered the photographer's outstanding reputation in the field in evaluating the uniqueness of the lost slides, together with the claimant's earning potential. The Second Circuit Court of Appeals found that the District Court had applied an arbitrary methodology, "untethered to the facts", in assessing damages. The court suggested that, on remand, an appropriate analysis for awarding damages would be to reasonably ascertain the number of lost images, factor those to the plaintiff's diminished earning capacity, and then consider a discounted value of the stream of future income that the images would be expected to produce.

See also Fortune v. First Union Nat. Bank, 323 N.C. 146, 371 S.E.2d 483 (1988) (breach of fiduciary duty by trustee; plaintiff need only prove "the extent of the harm and the amount of money representing adequate compensation with as much certainty as the nature of the tort and the circumstances permit"); Fera v. Village Plaza, Inc., 396 Mich. 639, 242 N.W.2d 372 (1976) (recovery not precluded where precision is unattainable, especially when defendant has caused the imprecision).

Youst v. Longo

43 Cal.3d 64, 729 P.2d 728, 233 Cal.Rptr. 294 (1987).

■ LUCAS, JUSTICE.

Is a racehorse owner entitled to tort damages when the harness driver of another horse negligently or intentionally interferes with the owner's

horse during a race, thereby preventing the owner from the chance of winning a particular cash prize? It is a well-settled general tort principle that interference with the chance of winning a contest, such as the horserace at issue here, usually presents a situation too uncertain upon which to base tort liability. We agree that application of this principle should govern here. * * *

Plaintiff Harlan Youst entered his standardbred trotter horse, Bat Champ, in the eighth harness race at Hollywood Park in Inglewood, California. Also entered in the race was The Thilly Brudder, driven by defendant, Gerald Longo. During the race, defendant allegedly drove The Thilly Brudder into Bat Champ's path and struck Bat Champ with his whip, thereby causing the horse to break stride. Bat Champ finished sixth while The Thilly Brudder finished second. The Board reviewed the events of the race and disqualified The Thilly Brudder, which moved Bat Champ into fifth place, entitling plaintiff to a purse of only $5,000.[1]

Plaintiff filed a complaint for damages against defendant in the Los Angeles Superior Court, asserting three causes of action: (1) defendant *negligently* interfered with Bat Champ's progress in the race; (2) defendant *intentionally* interfered therewith; and (3) defendant and unidentified individuals (Does I through X) *conspired to interfere*. Plaintiff sought as compensatory damages the difference in prize money between Bat Champ's actual finish and the finish which allegedly would have occurred but for defendant's interference. Plaintiff requested compensatory damages in three alternative amounts, namely, the purse amount for either first, second or third place (less the fifth place prize of $5,000 which Bat Champ has already received). Ascertainment of the amount of actual damages apparently would require a finding as to the position in which Bat Champ would have finished but for defendant's interference. Punitive damages of $250,000 were also sought.

[The trial court sustained the defendant's demurrer and the court of appeal affirmed.]

* * * [T]he Court of Appeal failed to apply the threshold requirement of a probability of the prospective economic benefit. That requirement is especially appropriate to evaluate a lost economic expectancy where the facts involve a competitive contest of one kind or another. To require less of a showing would open the proverbial floodgates to a surge of litigation based on alleged missed opportunities to win various types of contests, despite the speculative outcome of many of them. In fact, it is the very "speculativeness" of the outcome that makes such competitions interesting. Further, to allow recovery without proof of probable loss would essentially eliminate the tort's element of causation, which links the wrongful act with the damages suffered.

---

1. The purse for the race was $100,000 distributed as follows: the winner received $50,000; second place received $25,000; third place received $12,000; fourth place received $8,000, and fifth place received $5,000.

Scholarly authority and cases from other jurisdictions agree that an application of the threshold requirement of probable expectancy to the area of contests in general will usually result in a denial of recovery. Prosser has generally remarked that "since a large part of what is most valuable in modern life depends on 'probable expectancies,' as social and industrial life becomes more complex the courts must do more to discover, define and protect them from undue interference." (*See* Prosser & Keeton, Torts (5th ed. 1984) 130, p. 1006, fn. omitted.) Prosser, however, has specifically addressed the area of interference with contests: "When the attempt has been made to carry liability for interference . . . into such areas as . . . *deprivation of the chance of winning a contest,* the courts have been disturbed by a feeling that they were embarking upon uncharted seas, and recovery has been denied; and *it is significant that the reason usually given is that there is no sufficient degree of certainty that the plaintiff ever would have received the anticipated benefits.*"

Notwithstanding rare cases where public policies are compelling, the tort of interference with prospective economic advantage traditionally has not protected speculative expectancies such as the particular outcome of a contest. Prosser instructs that the true source of the modern law on interference with prospective relations is the principle that tort liability exists for interference with *existing* contractual relations. (Prosser & Keeton, *supra,* at p. 1006.) "For the most part the 'expectancies' thus protected have been those of future contractual relations. . . . In such cases there is a background of business experience on the basis of which it is *possible to estimate with some fair amount of success both the value of what has been lost and the likelihood that the plaintiff would have received it if the defendant had not interfered.*"

* * *

Determining the probable expectancy of winning a *sporting* contest but for the defendant's interference seems impossible in most if not all cases, including the instant case. Sports generally involve the application of various unique or unpredictable skills and techniques, together with instances of luck or chance occurring at different times during the event, any one of which factors can drastically change the event's outcome. In fact, certain intentional acts of interference by various potential "defendant" players may, through imposition of penalties or increased motivation, actually allow the "victim" player or team to prevail. Usually, it is impossible to predict the outcome of most sporting events without awaiting the actual conclusion.

The Restatement Second of Torts specifically addresses the speculative nature of the outcome of a horse race. The relevant comment is contained in a "Special Note on Liability for Interference With Other Prospective Benefits of a Noncontractual Nature." The comment states that various possible situations may justify liability for interference with prospective economic benefits of a noncommercial character. Special mention is given to "[c]ases in which the plaintiff is wrongfully deprived of the expectancy of winning a race or a contest, when he has had *a substantial certainty or at least a high probability of success.* For example, the plaintiff is entered in a contest for a large cash prize to be awarded to the person who, during a given time limit, obtains the largest number of subscriptions to a magazine. At a time when the contest has one week more to run and the plaintiff is leading all other competitors by a margin of two to one, the defendant unjustifiably strikes the plaintiff out of the contest and rules him ineligible. In such a case there may be sufficient certainty established so that the plaintiff may successfully maintain an action for loss of the prospective benefits. *On the other hand, if the plaintiff has a horse entered in a race and the defendant wrongfully prevents him from running, there may well not be sufficient certainty to entitle the plaintiff to recover. . . .*" (Rest.2d Torts, 774B, special note, pp. 59 60, italics added.)

As indicated by the Restatement comment, certain contests may have a higher probability of ultimate success than others. To this end, the cases cited by the Court of Appeal here, awarding damages to competitors in contests, are distinguishable because in each case there was a high probability of winning.[2] In addition to the Restatement position, one older case has specifically held that the loss of a chance to win a prize purse at a trotting horse race was too speculative to support tort liability. (*See* Western Union Tel. Co. v. Crall (1888) 39 Kan. 580, 18 P. 719.)

Applying the foregoing analysis to the instant case, it seems clear that plaintiff's complaint fails adequately to allege facts showing interference with a *probable* economic gain, *i.e.*, that Bat Champ would have won this horse race, or at least won a larger prize, if defendant had not interfered. Here, the complaint only alleged in conclusory terms that defendant's wrongful interference resulted in a lost "opportunity" to finish higher in the money. The complaint merely indicated that defendant's maneuvers and whipping forced Bat Champ to break stride and fall out of contention.[3]

We conclude, as a matter of law, that the threshold element of probability for interference with prospective economic advantage was not met by the facts alleged, whether or not some "conspiracy" between a competitor and noncompetitor may have existed. It was not reasonably *probable,* on the facts alleged, that Bat Champ would have finished in a

---

2. Nor are we persuaded by the Court of Appeal's argument that damages should be allowed for the value of the lost chance of benefit. (*See* Schaefer, *Uncertainty and the Law of Damages* (1978) 19 Wm. & Mary L.Rev. 719.) Under this approach, plaintiff would not recover the full value of the lost prize but that value discounted by the probability of winning in the absence of defendant's interference. We believe this calculation is incorporated in the basic analysis for interference with prospective economic advantage; the speculative nature of the chance of winning is examined in establishing the first element of the tort as opposed to determining specific damages after recognizing a cause of action. In the instant case, the potential economic advantage is simply too speculative to allow *any recovery.*

3. Presented in plaintiff's opposition to the demurrer were the following additional facts: "As the horses entered in the eighth race rounded the last turn, Bat Champ *began to make his move* to the lead of the group. As his move progressed, Defendant drove his horse into Bat Champ's path and thereafter whipped Bat Champ with his whip. Bat Champ's advance was halted, his stride broken and his *chances* at finishing 'in the money' ended." (Italics added.) Further, at oral argument, plaintiff asserted that the alleged interference took place 100 yards from the finish line. However, despite these asserted facts, Bat Champ's chance of placing higher in the purse money remained highly speculative.

JUD. NOTICE!

better position. Indeed, we may take judicial notice of the impossibility of predicting such matters; the winner of a horserace is not always the leader throughout the race for a horse can "break the pack" at any point in the race, even as a matter of strategy. Further, many races are won by a "nose." Thus, no cause of action exists for interference with this horseracing event.

* * *

Deprivation of the *chance* of winning a horserace or any sporting event does not present a basis for tort liability for interference with prospective economic advantage. Here, the probability that plaintiff's horse would have won the race is simply too speculative a basis for tort liability. * * *

The judgment of the Court of Appeal is affirmed.

1. Should courts recognize that the reasonable certainty limitation is met when placing a value on a chance, such as to win a contest? In *Locke v. United States*, 151 Ct.Cl. 262, 283 F.2d 521 (Ct.Cl.1960), an operator of a typewriter repair business sought lost profits resulting from a breach of a requirements contract with the government. The plaintiff, together with three other unaffiliated local companies, were awarded typewriter repair contracts which entitled the contractor's names to be placed on a federal supply schedule for distribution to government installations in the area. Although the various government offices were free to select any of the four contractors, the court held that it was proper for the lower court to assess the value of the plaintiff's chance at the lost business opportunities. The court stated:

> We are here concerned with the value of a chance for obtaining business and profits. . . . Here it appears that the plaintiff did have a chance of obtaining at least one-fourth of the total typewriter-repair business let by the Government. . . . We believe that where the value of a chance for profit is not outweighed by a countervailing risk of loss, and where it is fairly measurable by calculable odds and by evidence bearing specifically on the probabilities that the court should be allowed to value that lost opportunity. 283 F.2d at 525.

What limitations, from a policy standpoint, should be placed on the ability to recover for damages based on the value of a chance? *See generally* Schaefer, Uncertainty and the Law of Damages, 19 Wm. & Mary L.Rev. 719 (1978) (suggesting that uncertainty in estimating the value of lost earnings may be overcome by combining an expected-value deduction and a discount for risk).

2. The requirement that damages be established with reasonable certainty has generally presented less of an obstacle to recovery for torts than for breaches of contract. In *Grayson v. Irvmar Realty Corp.*, 184 N.Y.S.2d 33, 7 A.D.2d 436 (1959), for example, a young musician sustained

a fractured leg and hearing impairment as a result of the defendant's negligence in failing to light properly a construction sidewalk. Although the plaintiff had never earned any money as an opera singer, the court permitted the recovery of damages based upon impaired future earning capacity because credible evidence was introduced that she had a "bright future." The court recognized the tension between denying recovery because of the difficulty in quantifying the harm balanced against the policy of compensating for the injury:

> The would-be operatic singer, or the would-be violin virtuoso, or the would-be actor, are not assured of achieving their objectives merely because they have some gifts and complete the customary periods of training. Their future is a highly speculative one, namely, whether they will ever receive recognition or the financial prerequisites that result from such recognition. Nevertheless, the opportunities exist and those opportunities have an economic value which can be assessed, although, obviously, without any precision. But a jury may not assume that a young student of the opera who has certain gifts will earn the income of an operatic singer, even in the median group.

> In determining, therefore, the amount to be recovered, the jury may consider the gifts attributed to plaintiff; the training she has received; the training she is likely to receive; the opportunities and the recognition she already has had; the opportunities she is likely to have in the future; the fact that even though the opportunities may be many, that the full realization of those opportunities is limited to the very few; the fact that there are many other risks and contingencies, other than accidents, which may divert a would-be vocal artist from her career; and, finally, that it is assessing directly not so much future earning capacity as the opportunities for a practical chance at such future earning capacity.

> The foregoing factors to be considered must reflect substantial development in the would-be artist's career. Every gleam in a doting parent's eye and every self-delusion as to one's potentialities must be skeptically eradicated. The jury is not to assess within the limits of wishful thinking but is to assess the genuine potentialities, although not yet realized, as evidenced by objective circumstances. Thus viewed, plaintiff here was undoubtedly serious about her operatic career; but, except from her teachers, she had not achieved any spectacular or extraordinary recognition for her talents. It is not the dilettante interest that has a pecuniary value, but the genuine opportunity to engage in a serious artistic career. In this context no effort has been made to consider the possible issues, sometimes tendered, as to the compensability for artistic pursuits indulged in solely for self-enjoyment, but impaired as a result of tortious injury. 7 A.D.2d 441.

3. Simply because the cause of action sounds in tort, though, does not automatically eliminate the certainty limitation on the damages recoverable. Where courts determine that no rational basis exists to measure damages, then the task of calculating any potential recovery is considered insurmountable. For example, in *Procanik v. Cillo*, 97 N.J. 339, 478 A.2d 755 (1984), the Supreme Court of New Jersey denied recovery of general damages for emotional distress or for impaired childhood in a claim for wrongful life brought on behalf of a birth-defective child. The court stated:

> The crux of the problem is that there is no rational way to measure non-existence or to compare non-existence with pain and suffering of his impaired existence. Whatever theoretical appeal one might find in recognizing a claim for pain and suffering is outweighed by the essentially irrational and unpredictable nature of that claim. Although damages in a personal injury action need not be calculated with mathematical precision, they require at their base some modicum of rationality.

> Underlying our conclusion is an evaluation of the capability of the judicial system, often proceeding in these cases through trial by jury, to appraise such a claim. Also at work is an appraisal of the role of tort law in compensating injured parties, involving as that role does, not only reason, but also fairness, predictability, and even deterrence of future wrongful acts. In brief, the ultimate decision is a policy choice summoning the most sensitive and careful judgment.

> From that perspective it is simply too speculative to permit an infant plaintiff to recover for emotional distress attendant on birth defects when that plaintiff claims he would be better off if he had not been born. 478 A.2d at 763.

On the other hand, the court allowed recovery of extraordinary medical expenses associated with the birth-defects as special damages because they were susceptible of calculation. *See also* Goldberg v. Ruskin, 113 Ill.2d 482, 101 Ill.Dec. 818, 499 N.E.2d 406 (1986); Harbeson v. Parke–Davis, Inc., 98 Wash.2d 460, 656 P.2d 483 (1983); Turpin v. Sortini, 31 Cal.3d 220, 182 Cal.Rptr. 337, 643 P.2d 954 (1982).

C.   AVOIDABLE CONSEQUENCES

Section Coverage:

The rule of avoidable consequences has two components, one negative and one affirmative. The affirmative side allows damages reasonably incurred to mitigate damages. The negative side precludes an injured party from recovering damages that could have been averted by taking reasonable steps following accrual of the harm.

The negative doctrine does not impose a restriction on a party's substantive entitlement to damages; instead it serves as a limitation on the measure of damages recoverable for a tort or contract breach. Although the rule sometimes is labeled as a "duty," that characterization is inartful because the injured party has no true legal obligation to act. Rather, the rule only operates to exclude the damages that result from a failure to minimize losses. Moreover, the avoidable consequences rule becomes operative only after the wrongdoer has caused the harm. It does not require that a party take avoidance measures in anticipation of the harm.

The avoidable consequences rule encourages an injured party to take reasonable steps to mitigate the loss caused by the defendant's tortious wrong or breach of contract. An injured party is not expected to undertake extraordinary measures or suffer undue hardship; the rule requires reasonable attempts to avoid incurring additional losses. For example, if P is injured in an automobile accident caused by the negligence of D, P is obliged to seek medical attention as reasonably necessary. Similarly, if an employer discharges an employee in breach of contract, the employee is obligated to mitigate damages by taking reasonable steps to secure equivalent employment. The principle is to avoid unnecessary losses. It reflects a public policy of fairness to breaching parties or tortfeasors by not holding them accountable to the extent that the injured party has evidenced a lack of due care after sustaining the harm.

The same principle guides the affirmative rule that any expenditures reasonably incurred to mitigate damages are recoverable. For example, if the plaintiff's doctor reasonably orders x-ray photographs after an accident, their cost is recoverable even if the results show no fractures. Similarly, a discharged employee may recover costs reasonably incurred in seeking equivalent employment after the breach of the employment contract.

Model Case:

Jones, a machine press operator, suffered minor cuts and bruises in an automobile accident caused by the negligence of an employee of ABC Trucking Company in the scope of employment. Jones unreasonably delayed in seeking medical treatment, however, and the wounds became infected. As a result, Jones missed six weeks of work. Jones sued ABC claiming damages for pain and suffering, medical expenses, and the loss of six weeks' wages. ABC filed an answer contending that Jones failed to exercise due care by delaying in taking antiseptic measures.

The avoidable consequences rule would not be a complete defense to ABC's liability, but it would serve to deny Jones' recovery for those damages which could have been averted after the accident by the exercise of reasonable care. In that regard, the lost wages would not be compensable if ABC could establish that prompt medical attention would have meant Jones would not have missed any work. In contrast, the medical expenses and the pain and suffering caused by ABC's negligence should be recoverable elements of damages to the extent that Jones could not have avoided them by reasonable measures.

Rockingham County v. Luten Bridge Co.

35 F.2d 301 (4th Cir.1929).

■ PARKER, CIRCUIT JUDGE.

[The Board of Commissioners of Rockingham county awarded a contract to the Luten Bridge Company for the construction of a bridge. Shortly after entering the contract, however, the board adopted a series of resolutions which declared the contract invalid and gave notice of cancellation to Luten. Although Luten had barely commenced performance when it received the initial notice from the county repudiating the contract, the company proceeded with construction of the bridge. Luten then instituted suit against the county to recover amounts allegedly due under the contract. The trial court excluded evidence offered by the county concerning its notice of cancellation and damages, and instructed a verdict for Luten for the full amount of its claim. The county appealed.] * * *

As the county now admits the execution and validity of the contract, and the breach on its part, the ultimate question in the case is one as to the measure of plaintiff's recovery, and * * * whether plaintiff, if the notices are to be deemed action by the county, can recover under the contract for work done after they were received, or is limited to the recovery of damages for breach of contract as of that date.

* * *

[W]e do not think that, after the county had given notice, while the contract was still executory, that it did not desire the bridge built and would not pay for it, plaintiff could proceed to build it and recover the contract price. It is true that the county had no right to rescind the contract, and the notice given plaintiff amounted to a breach on its part; but, after plaintiff had received notice of the breach, it was its duty to do nothing to increase the damages flowing therefrom. If A enters into a binding contract to build a house for B, B, of course, has no right to rescind the contract without A's consent. But if, before the house is built, he decides that he does not want it, and notifies A to that effect, A has no right to proceed with the building and thus pile up damages. His remedy is to treat the contract as broken when he receives the notice, and sue for the recovery of such damages as he may have sustained from the breach, including any profit which he would have realized upon performance, as well as any other losses which may have resulted to him. In the case at bar, the county decided not to build the road of which the bridge was to be a part, and did not build it. The bridge, built in the midst of the forest, is of no value to the county because of this change of circumstances. When, therefore, the county gave notice to the plaintiff that it would not proceed with the project, plaintiff should have desisted from further work. It had no right thus to pile up damages by proceeding with the erection of a useless bridge.

* * * The American rule and the reasons supporting it are well stated by Prof. Williston as follows:

"There is a line of cases running back to 1845 which holds that, after an absolute repudiation or refusal to perform by one party to a contract, the other party cannot continue to perform and recover damages based on full performance. * * * If a man engages to have work done, and afterwards repudiates his contract before the work has been begun or when it has been only partially done, it is inflicting damage on the defendant without benefit to the plaintiff to allow the latter to insist on proceeding with the contract. The work may be useless to the defendant, and yet he would be forced to pay the full contract price. On the other hand, the plaintiff is interested only in the profit he will make out of the contract. If he receives this it is equally advantageous for him to use his time otherwise."

The leading case on the subject in this country is the New York case of *Clark v. Marsiglia*, 1 Denio (N.Y.) 317, 43 Am.Dec. 670. In that case defendant had employed plaintiff to paint certain pictures for him, but countermanded the order before the work was finished. Plaintiff, however, went on and completed the work and sued for the contract price. In reversing a judgment for plaintiff, the court said:

"The plaintiff was allowed to recover as though there had been no countermand of the order; and in this the court erred. The defendant, by requiring the plaintiff to stop work upon the paintings, violated his contract, and thereby incurred a liability to pay such damages as the plaintiff should sustain. Such damages would include a recompense for the labor done and materials used, and such further sum in damages as might, upon legal principles, be assessed for the breach of the contract; but the plaintiff had no right, by obstinately persisting in the work, to make the penalty upon the defendant greater than it would otherwise have been."

* * * It follows that there was error in directing a verdict for plaintiff for the full amount of its claim. The measure of plaintiff's damage, upon its appearing that notice was duly given not to build the bridge, is an amount sufficient to compensate plaintiff for labor and materials expended and expense incurred in the part performance of the contract, prior to its repudiation, plus the profit which would have been realized if it had been carried out in accordance with its terms.

* * * [Reversed.]

---

1.   The avoidable consequences doctrine precludes the recovery of damages which could have been averted by the injured party undertaking reasonable steps following the harm. This avoidance principle occasionally is expressed as a "duty" on the part of a claimant to minimize damages, or as an "obligation" to take reasonable action to avoid enhancing the damages attributable to the defendant. Such characterizations are inaccurate expressions of the doctrine, however, because the failure to make reasonable efforts to limit damages creates no affirmative right in the defendant to assert an action for breach of that duty. Rock v. Vandine, 106

Kan. 588, 189 P. 157 (1920); Restatement (Second) of Torts § 918 comment a.

The only result of a failure to mitigate properly is that the court will not allow damages for those consequences of the breach of contract or tort which the injured party could have reasonably avoided. Thus, the doctrine should be viewed as a disability on the recovery of reasonably avoidable damages. Gideon v. Johns–Manville Sales Corp., 761 F.2d 1129 (5th Cir. 1985).

2. Expenditures reasonably incurred by an injured party in attempting to mitigate losses are recoverable even if the mitigation efforts prove to be unsuccessful. *See* Baker v. Dorfman, 239 F.3d 415, 427 (2d Cir.2000) (expenses of proper effort to mitigate damages recoverable even if ultimately unsuccessful). Thus, commercially reasonable expenses incurred by an aggrieved buyer in effecting cover are recoverable as incidental damages under U.C.C. § 2–715(1). In *Women's Federal Sav. & Loan v. Nevada National Bank*, 607 F.Supp. 1129 (D.Nev.1985), the court identified the following factors to evaluate the mitigation effort: (1) good faith, (2) reasonable skill, prudence and efficiency, (3) reasonably proportioned to the injury and consequences to be averted, and (4) reasonably justified belief that it will avoid or reduce the damage otherwise expected.

3. In contracts for the sale of goods the failure of the aggrieved party to take reasonable measures to mitigate damages following a material breach will limit the amount of damages potentially recoverable. *See* U.C.C. §§ 2–708; 2–713; 2–610 comment 1. For example, in *Oloffson v. Coomer*, 11 Ill.App.3d 918, 296 N.E.2d 871 (1973), a grain dealer who unreasonably delayed in effecting cover after the seller repudiated was denied damages which could have been avoided by promptly procuring substitute goods. Similarly, the court in *Whewell v. Dobson*, 227 N.W.2d 115 (Iowa 1975), held that a seller of Christmas trees should have mitigated damages by reselling the trees in a commercially reasonable time following repudiation by the buyer. The seller's damages were not reduced, however, because the buyer failed to plead mitigation as a special defense.

Parker v. Twentieth Century–Fox Film Corporation

3 Cal.3d 176, 474 P.2d 689, 89 Cal.Rptr. 737 (1970).

■ Burke, Justice.

Defendant Twentieth Century–Fox Film Corporation appeals from a summary judgment granting to plaintiff the recovery of agreed compensation under a written contract for her services as an actress in a motion picture. * * *

Plaintiff is well known as an actress, and in the contract between plaintiff and defendant is sometimes referred to as the "Artist." Under the contract, dated August 6, 1965, plaintiff was to play the female lead in defendant's contemplated production of a motion picture entitled "Bloomer Girl." The contract provided that defendant would pay plaintiff a minimum "guaranteed compensation" of $53,571.42 per week for 14 weeks commencing May 23, 1966, for a total of $750,000. Prior to May 1966 defendant decided not to produce the picture and by a letter dated April 4, 1966, it notified plaintiff of that decision and that it would not "comply with our obligations to you under" the written contract.

By the same letter and with the professed purpose "to avoid any damage to you," defendant instead offered to employ plaintiff as the leading actress in another film tentatively entitled "Big Country, Big Man" (hereinafter, "Big Country"). The compensation offered was identical, as were 31 of the 34 numbered provisions or articles of the original contract. Unlike "Bloomer Girl," however, which was to have been a musical production, "Big Country" was a dramatic "western type" movie. "Bloomer Girl" was to have been filmed in California; "Big Country" was to be produced in Australia. Also, certain terms in the proffered contract varied from those of the original. Plaintiff was given one week within which to accept; she did not and the offer lapsed. Plaintiff then commenced this action seeking recovery of the agreed guaranteed compensation.

The complaint sets forth two causes of action. The first is for money due under the contract; the second, based upon the same allegations as the first, is for damages resulting from defendant's breach of contract. Defendant in its answer admits the existence and validity of the contract, that plaintiff complied with all the conditions, covenants and promises and stood ready to complete the performance, and that defendant breached and "anticipatorily repudiated" the contract. It denies, however, that any money is due to plaintiff either under the contract or as a result of its breach, and pleads as an affirmative defense to both causes of action plaintiff's allegedly deliberate failure to mitigate damages, asserting that she unreasonably refused to accept its offer of the leading role in "Big Country."

[The court entered summary judgment for $750,000 for the plaintiff and the defendant appealed.] * * *

As stated, defendant's sole defense to this action which resulted from its deliberate breach of contract is that in rejecting defendant's substitute offer of employment plaintiff unreasonably refused to mitigate damages.

The general rule is that the measure of recovery by a wrongfully discharged employee is the amount of salary agreed upon for the period of service, less the amount which the employer affirmatively proves the employee has earned or with reasonable effort might have earned from other employment. [Citations.] However, before projected earnings from other employment opportunities not sought or accepted by the discharged employee can be applied in mitigation, the employer must show that the other employment was comparable, or substantially similar, to that of which the employee has been deprived; the employee's rejection of or failure to seek other available employment of a different or inferior kind may not be resorted to in order to mitigate damages. [Citations.]

In the present case defendant has raised no issue of *reasonableness of efforts* by plaintiff to obtain other employment; the sole issue is whether plaintiff's refusal of defendant's substitute offer of "Big Country" may be used in mitigation. Nor, if the "Big Country" offer was of employment different or inferior when compared with the original "Bloomer Girl" employment, is there an issue as to whether or not plaintiff acted reasonably in refusing the substitute offer. Despite defendant's arguments to the contrary, no case cited or which our research has discovered holds or suggests that reasonableness is an element of a wrongfully discharged employee's option to reject, or fail to seek, different or inferior employment lest the possible earnings therefrom be charged against him in mitigation of damages.

* * * [I]t is clear that the trial court correctly ruled that plaintiff's failure to accept defendant's tended substitute employment could not be applied in mitigation of damages because the offer of the "Big Country" lead was of employment both different and inferior, and that no factual dispute was presented on that issue. The mere circumstance that "Bloomer Girl" was to be a musical review calling upon plaintiff's talents as a dancer as well as an actress, and was to be produced in the City of Los Angeles, whereas "Big Country" was a straight dramatic role in a "Western Type" story taking place in an opal mine in Australia, demonstrates the difference in kind between the two employments; the female lead as a dramatic actress in a western style motion picture can by no stretch of imagination be considered the equivalent of or substantially similar to the lead in a song-and-dance production.

Additionally, the substitute "Big Country" offer proposed to eliminate or impair the director and screenplay approvals accorded to plaintiff under the original "Bloomer Girl" contract and thus constituted an offer of inferior employment. No expertise or judicial notice is required in order to hold that the deprivation or infringement of an employee's rights held under an original employment contract converts the available "other employment" relied upon by the employer to mitigate damages, into inferior employment which the employee need not seek or accept. * * *

The judgment is affirmed.

■ SULLIVAN, ACTING CHIEF JUSTICE (dissenting).

The basic question in this case is whether or not plaintiff acted reasonably in rejecting defendant's offer of alternate employment. The answer depends upon whether that offer (starring in "Big Country, Big Man") was an offer of work that was substantially similar to her former employment (starring in "Bloomer Girl") or of work that was of a different or inferior kind. To my mind this is a factual issue which the trial court should not have determined on a motion for summary judgment. The majority have not only repeated this error but have compounded it by applying the rules governing mitigation of damages in the employer-employee context in a misleading fashion. Accordingly, I respectfully dissent.

The familiar rule requiring a plaintiff in a tort or contract action to mitigate damages embodies notions of fairness and socially responsible behavior which are fundamental to our jurisprudence. Most broadly stated, it precludes the recovery of damages which, through the exercise of due diligence, could have been avoided. Thus, in essence, it is a rule requiring reasonable conduct in commercial affairs. This general principle governs the obligations of an employee after his employer has wrongfully repudiated or terminated the employment contract. Rather than permitting the employee simply to remain idle during the balance of the contract period, the law requires him to make a reasonable effort to secure other employment. He is not obliged, however, to seek or accept any and all types of work which may be available. Only work which is in the same field and which is of the same quality need be accepted.

* * * The inquiry in cases such as this should not be whether differences between the two jobs exist (there will always be differences) but whether the differences which are present are substantial enough to constitute differences in the *kind* of employment or, alternatively, whether they render the substitute work employment of an *inferior kind.*

* * *

I believe that the judgment should be reversed so that the issue of whether or not the offer of the lead role in "Big Country, Big Man" was of employment comparable to that of the lead role in "Bloomer Girl" may be determined at trial.

———————

1.   The general rule for breach of contract is that the party injured must make every reasonable effort to minimize damages and may not recover for damages which could have been avoided by reasonable efforts under existing circumstances. However, where the offer of a substitute contract is conditioned on surrender by the injured party of its claim for breach, one is not required to mitigate losses by accepting an arrangement with the repudiator which is made conditional on the surrender of rights under the repudiated contract. Teradyne, Inc. v. Teledyne Industries, Inc., 676 F.2d 865 (1st Cir.1982).

2.   In *Faragher v. City of Boca Raton,* 524 U.S. 775, 118 S.Ct. 2275, 141 L.Ed.2d 662 (1998), the Supreme Court made the following observations regarding the doctrine of avoidable consequences in a Title VII context:

Although Title VII seeks "to make persons whole for injuries suffered on account of unlawful employment discrimination," its "primary objective," like that of any statute meant to influence primary conduct, is not to provide redress but to avoid harm. * * * It would therefore implement clear statutory policy and complement the Government's Title VII enforcement efforts to recognize the employer's affirmative obligation to prevent violations and give credit here to employers who make reasonable efforts to discharge their duty. * * *

The requirement to show that the employee has failed in a coordinate duty to avoid or mitigate harm reflects an equally obvious policy imported from the general theory of damages, that a victim has a duty "to use such means as are reasonable under the circumstances to avoid or minimize the damages" that result from violations of the statute. An employer may, for example, have provided a proven, effective mechanism for reporting and resolving complaints of sexual harassment, available to the employee without undue risk or expense. If the plaintiff unreasonably failed to avail herself of the employer's preventive or remedial apparatus, she should not recover damages that could have been avoided if she had done so. If the victim could have avoided harm, no liability should be found against the employer who had taken reasonable care, and if damages could reasonably have been mitigated no award against a liable employer should reward a plaintiff for what her own efforts could have avoided.

In order to accommodate the principle of vicarious liability for harm caused by misuse of supervisory authority, as well as Title VII's equally basic policies of encouraging forethought by employers and saving action by objecting employees, we adopt the following holding in this case and in *Burlington Industries, Inc. v. Ellerth*, 524 U.S. 742, 118 S.Ct. 2257, 141 L.Ed.2d 633 (1998), also decided today. An employer is subject to vicarious liability to a victimized employee for an actionable hostile environment created by a supervisor with immediate (or successively higher) authority over the employee. When no tangible employment action is taken, a defending employer may raise an affirmative defense to liability or damages, subject to proof by a preponderance of the evidence[.] The defense comprises two necessary elements: (a) that the employer exercised reasonable care to prevent and correct promptly any sexually harassing behavior, and (b) that the plaintiff employee unreasonably failed to take advantage of any preventive or corrective opportunities provided by the employer or to avoid harm otherwise. While proof that an employer had promulgated an antiharassment policy with complaint procedure is not necessary in every instance as a matter of law, the need for a stated policy suitable to the employment circumstances may appropriately be addressed in any case when litigating the first element of the defense. And while proof that an employee failed to fulfill the corresponding obligation of reasonable care to avoid harm is not limited to showing an unreasonable failure to use any complaint procedure provided by the employer, a demonstration of such failure will normally suffice to satisfy the employer's burden under the second element of the defense. No affirmative defense is available, however, when the supervisor's harassment culminates in a tangible employment action, such as discharge, demotion, or undesirable reassignment. 118 S.Ct. at 2292–2293.

3.   In *Contempo Design v. Chicago & N.E. Illinois Carpenters*, 226 F.3d 535, 555 (7th Cir.2000), an employer sued a union for damages for breach of collective bargaining agreement. The court found that, since the employer had no alternative source for substitute labor other than the breaching union, the employer had made a reasonable effort to limit damages to the difference in contract prices and costs incurred during period of strike.

PROBLEM: THE DAMAGED FENCE

The Potters are professional breeders of show dogs. Their dogs are kept in their rural home and they are allowed to exercise in the large, fenced yard.

Davis, a neighbor, negligently damages a portion of the Potters' fence. Three puppies discover the hole in the fence and escape; they are never found again. The Potters learn of the damage to the fence after the loss of the three puppies. They take no immediate action to mend the fence, but instruct the children to keep the dogs in the house. The next day a young Potter child forgets the restriction and allows a puppy to go outside. That puppy also escapes and is found injured in the road. After a $400 treatment by the veterinarian that puppy recovers.

The Potters then erect a temporary barricade to cover the hole in the fence. The temporary materials cost $50 and have no use once the fence is permanently mended.

Davis admits liability to creating the hole in the fence and agrees to pay the permanent repair cost. The Potters and Davis dispute several other points:

1.   The Potters claim that Davis should pay the value of the three lost puppies. Davis argues that the Potters should have discovered the hole as soon as it was made.

2.   The Potters claim Davis should pay the $400 veterinarian's bill, but Davis maintains that the Potters should have blocked the hole in the fence immediately.

3.   The Potters claim $50 for the cost of the temporary barricade, whereas Davis argues there is liability only for the permanent repair.

How should the principles of avoidable consequences apply to these facts?

Garcia v. Wal–Mart Stores, Inc.

209 F.3d 1170 (10th Cir.2000).

■ LUCERO, CIRCUIT JUDGE.

* * * On January 25, 1995, appellee/cross-appellant Garcia and her husband went shopping at Wal–Mart. While Garcia searched for film in one of the aisles, she was hit by a cart pushed by a Wal–Mart employee and

knocked to the floor, hurting her back, which had already been causing her pain before the incident. Several physicians and one psychologist, each after having examined her once, determined that a portion of her back pain may have been psychological or "non-organic" in nature, i.e., not a direct result of her physiological condition. Most of them, however, did not deny that at the same time she might be suffering physical pain caused by her physical injury. Her treating physicians also testified that Garcia suffered from chronic degenerative disc disease prior to the incident at Wal–Mart.

Before she was hit, Garcia owned and operated "Mary's Burritos." Rising between 4:30 and 5:00 a.m. on weekday mornings, she would prepare, by 8:00 a.m., between twelve and eighteen dozen burritos, weighing almost forty pounds, load them into a cooler, and deliver them to local businesses. After the incident at Wal–Mart, she found herself physically unable to lift the cooler and found it very difficult to get into and out of her car. That physical incapacitation rendered her unable to continue operating her business, which she turned over to her sister-in-law, Valerie Gonzales.

An economist estimated her economic losses from her inability to pursue her business to be between approximately $631,000 and $908,000—the former figure based in part on Garcia's loss of earnings from her business, and the latter figure based in part on average earnings of someone of her age and education level. There was also testimony on the value of her business, the degree of her disability with regard to physical functioning and performance of household chores, and her projected yearly medical expenses.

At trial, Wal–Mart submitted proposed jury instructions on both mitigation of damages by Garcia and apportionment of damages contingent on the jury's ability to separate out the portion of Garcia's damages attributable to pre-existing conditions. After the close of argument, the district court furnished the parties with the set of instructions it intended to submit to the jury, admonishing them to review those instructions. The district court did not instruct on mitigation of damages, and Wal–Mart did not object to that omission before the jury retired to consider its verdict. [The jury awarded damages to Garcia in the amount of $75,000 for non-economic losses, $268,000 for economic losses, and $7,000 for physical impairment or disfigurement, for a total award of $350,000.] * * *

Because Wal–Mart did not object to the court's failure to give the mitigation of damages instruction before the jury retired, and because the absence of such an instruction did not result in a fundamental injustice, we reject Wal–Mart's claim that the district court erred by not instructing on mitigation. * * *

Absent a proper objection, we apply the plain error standard of review. But "[o]nly rarely will we reverse based on allegedly erroneous instructions to which there was no objection at trial; the party claiming plain error has the heavy burden of demonstrating fundamental injustice." "Mitigation or failure to mitigate is an affirmative defense that may be raised by the defendant and the defendant bears the burden of proving the defense." Under Colorado law, "the defense of failure to mitigate damages will not be presented to the jury unless the trial court determines there is sufficient evidence to support it." [Citations]

We discern no "fundamental injustice" in the district court's failure to submit a mitigation instruction to the jury in this case. Based on the recommendations of two pain clinic psychologists that Garcia seek psychological counseling for depression, Wal–Mart argues Garcia failed to mitigate her damages because she did not seek psychological treatment. However, Garcia's testimony that she could not afford such treatment was unchallenged, and the district court judge declared that such mitigation was not legally required, stating "[i]t isn't required under the law that she undertake a course of treatment that she couldn't pay for." Wal–Mart cites no case law to support its allegation that Colorado requires the mitigation instruction it seeks under the circumstances of this case, and we apprehend no plain error in the district court's decision.

The same can be said of Wal–Mart's assertion that Garcia failed to mitigate the economic consequences of her injury by failing to get help in operating Mary's Burritos. The court found Garcia's business was "almost a personal service business that only she could do" and implicitly that efforts to employ others to continue operating the business would be futile and therefore not reasonable mitigation. In addition, Wal–Mart offered no evidence that appropriate jobs were available for someone in Garcia's condition or that such jobs were available to someone of her educational and skill level, but instead merely presented the evidence of its medical expert that she could return to sedentary light-duty or self-paced jobs. *See Wilson v. Union Pacific R.R. Co.,* 56 F.3d 1226, 1232 (10th Cir.1995) ("[The plaintiff's] general failure to seek employment for eighteen months before trial does not alone suffice to justify a mitigation instruction; the defendant must also show that appropriate jobs were available."). It was not fundamental injustice for the district court to refuse a mitigation of economic damages instruction. * * *

Lobermeier v. General Telephone Company of Wisconsin

119 Wis.2d 129, 349 N.W.2d 466 (1984).

■ HEFFERNAN, CHIEF JUSTICE. * * *

On July 19, 1976, the plaintiff sustained a ruptured eardrum, with a resulting hearing loss, while talking on a telephone in his parents' home. The phone was installed and maintained by the defendant, General Telephone Company of Wisconsin. The plaintiff was treated for the injury by Doctors Ruben T. Aguas and Gurdon Hamilton. The doctors determined that the plaintiff sustained a traumatic tympanic membrane perforation of the left ear caused by a lightning-induced electrical charge. For the first four months after the injury, the doctors prescribed a conservative treatment of antibiotics and ear drops. On October 28, 1976, Dr. Aguas felt the tympanic membrane was not going to heal spontaneously and recommended the plaintiff have surgery on the left ear.

On November 24, 1976, Dr. Aguas performed a tympanoplasty of the left ear, which involved the grafting of a substitute membrane over the eardrum. Doctor Aguas last saw the plaintiff on June 27, 1977. The plaintiff's subsequent treating doctor, Dr. Richard L. Dobbs, first saw him on February 6, 1979, at which time the plaintiff complained of a hearing loss in the left ear since July of 1976 and of ringing in the ear. After examining the plaintiff, Dr. Dobbs concluded, to a reasonable degree of medical certainty, that the graft done in November of 1976 had lateralized, there was severe conductive hearing loss in the left ear, and there was a possibility of a cholesteatoma. A cholesteatoma is disquamated skin and tissue which collected behind the eardrum. It is a potentially threatening disease because, as it slowly enlarges, it erodes into the inner ear and may cause vertigo or deafness, or may erode the covering of the brain and cause a brain abscess, or may erode into the facial nerve canal and cause a facial paralysis.

On June 7, 1979, the plaintiff filed a complaint alleging the defendant was negligent in that the telephone system on the Lobermeier premises was inadequately grounded and that, while the plaintiff was using the telephone service, he suffered a severe shock of atmospheric electricity conducted by the telephone lines to the telephone handset into the left ear and through the eardrum, causing the plaintiff's injuries. In its answer of July 3, 1979, the defendant denied negligence in failing to ground adequately the telephone or to maintain adequately such telephone service and raised, as one of its affirmative defenses, that the plaintiff failed to mitigate his damages.

* * *

The trial court erred * * * when it ruled, as a matter of law, that the defendant had no duty to mitigate damages by undergoing a second ear operation. We agree with the conclusion of the court of appeals that it was a matter of fact to be determined by the jury whether a reasonable person under the circumstances would submit to a second surgical procedure. Because it appears that this conclusion, reached as a matter of law by the trial judge, that the defendant's damages were not to be reduced by reason of his refusal to submit to surgery had a substantial impact upon the award of damages, a new trial upon the question of damages is necessary.

The facts show that, upon objection by plaintiff, the court refused to permit a physician, hired by the telephone company, to examine the defendant and to testify in respect to the damage to the plaintiff if second surgery were not performed and the improvement in hearing that probably would result if further surgical procedures were undertaken. The court also held that the deposition of Lobermeier's treating physician could not be produced either in respect to risks for or against future surgery. The court stated:

"[I]n all fairness to a person who is injured, if there is a risk of either further harm or death, that decision should be left up to him without penalty."

The court concluded that, once it reached the conclusion based on the reasoning above that a second operation was not required, the jury had nothing to weigh in respect to further mitigation of damages by reason of not having further surgery.

It instructed the jury, "[P]laintiff's damages are not to be diminished because he did not have a second operation." Because of this instruction, the defendant objected and moved for a mistrial. The balance of the instruction included the usual admonitions in respect to mitigation of damages:

"[D]uty of plaintiff to exercise ordinary care to mitigate his damages and if you find that he did not do so, you should not include in your answer to this question any amount for consequences of his injuries which could have been averted by the exercise of such care."

The court also instructed that, in fixing damages, the jury could consider Lobermeier's failure to use a hearing aid.

The general instruction of the trial court in respect to the duty to mitigate damages was correct. Its specific ruling as a matter of law that there was no duty to submit to a second operation was not.

The duty to mitigate damages has long been standard personal injury law. McCormick, *Damages* (hornbook series, 1935), sec. 36, p. 136, states as a matter of black letter law:

"Any suffering or disability incurred by one who has sustained personal injury, when the same could have been avoided by submitting to treatment by a physician selected with reasonable care, must be excluded as a ground of recovery. It is held, however, that the victim may use his own judgment about submitting to a dangerous or serious operation."

McCormick goes on to explain that:

"If the operation is simple and not dangerous, a failure to submit when advised to do so will be deemed unreasonable." *Id.* at 137.

Nevertheless, at the time McCormick wrote, 1935, there was a considerable body of law supportive of the trial judge here that held that:

"[A] 'major,' 'dangerous,' or 'serious' operation, especially where the results are 'problematical,' involves so critical a choice between the danger of the operation and the danger of the injury ... that most courts seem to hold as a matter of law that a refusal to undergo such a danger is not ground for reducing damages." *Id.* at 137.

McCormick then went on to note that, as surgical science progresses and becomes more predictable, reasonable conduct in the future may require that the advice of physicians be followed even in respect to serious operations.

We conclude that Wisconsin law has set its course midway between these two extremes. The question is one of fact for the jury—what was a reasonable course of conduct, under the circumstances, to mitigate the injuries or damages.

* * *

Failure to mitigate damages is an affirmative defense which must be raised by the defendant in its answer. [Citations.] When the defense is properly raised, the burden of proving failure to mitigate is upon the party asserting it. [Citation.] If the defendant asserts failure to mitigate on the part of the injured party, he must prove that a person of ordinary intelligence and prudence under the same or similar circumstances would have elected to undergo the recommended medical procedure. If the defendant meets the burden of proof, the consequence of the injured party's failure to mitigate damages is that the fact finder will not allow damages for those consequences of the injury which the plaintiff could have avoided by the exercise of ordinary care.

To summarize Wisconsin law on mitigation of damages in tort actions: An injured party is obligated to exercise that care usually exercised by a person of ordinary intelligence and prudence, under the same or similar circumstances; to seek medical or surgical treatment; and to submit to and undergo recommended surgical or medical treatment, within a reasonable time, which is not hazardous and is reasonably within his means, to minimize his damages. The injured party is not *required* to submit to surgery or medical treatment but is only required to submit to those treatments to which the "reasonable person" would have submitted. Although the injured party is not required to undergo recommended treatment, a tortfeasor is not expected to pay for disability or pain if medical treatment could reasonably correct the ailment. The proper period for which damages are allowed is only for the length of time reasonably required to effect a cure.

In the instant case, the defendant attempted to assume the burden of proving that the plaintiff, if acting reasonably under the circumstances, would have followed the advice of physicians and undergone the elective surgery. The trial court erred when it refused to allow the question to go to the jury, rejected evidence on the point, and ruled as a matter of law that the plaintiff's damages were not to be diminished for the failure to have surgery. The trial judge erroneously excluded surgery from the general rule, stating that an injured person was required to seek treatment that was not hazardous, would probably improve the condition, and was within his means.

The defendant was denied a full jury trial on the question of damages. Accordingly, the cause must be remanded for retrial on damages. * * *

1. The policy underlying the doctrine of mitigation of damages is to encourage injured parties to use reasonable efforts and expense to avert further losses. The policy applies equally to tort and contract cases.

Should that policy of conserving economic and social interests apply with equal force in cases of intentional torts? A *New York decision, Clark Operating Corp. v. Yokley*, 120 Misc.2d 631, 466 N.Y.S.2d 204 (1983), held that a tenant was not required to mitigate damages by terminating a tenancy and vacating premises when the landlord's conduct constituted intentional infliction of emotional distress. The court acknowledged the potential problem of economic waste if a tort victim unreasonably increases damages following the harm, but justified its result by applying the Restatement (Second) of Torts § 918(2) which distinguishes intentional or reckless conduct, provided that the plaintiff's failure to mitigate is not itself intentional or reckless.

2. In *Lobermeier,* the court examined whether an injured party would be expected to undergo surgery in order to avoid potential future losses. Defining the limits of "reasonableness" depends on many factors, including the state of medical knowledge and the degree of possible complications arising from the elective surgery. Consider also *DiPirro v. United States*, 43 F.Supp.2d 327, 345 (W.D.N.Y.1999), where the court limited personal injury damages for past pain and suffering because they might have been avoided by having recommended corrective rotator cuff surgery. The court stated that the injured party had a duty to use reasonable and proper efforts to make the damage "as small as practicable and to act in good faith to adopt reasonable methods to restore herself." Id. at 344.

3. A person is not required to commit a tort in order to lessen the damage. For example, in *J.M. Huber Petroleum Co. v. Yake*, 121 S.W.2d 670 (Tex.Civ.App.1938), the defendant excavated a deep ditch, pursuant to its right-of-way deed, for the purpose of installing a pipeline. The ditch, however, wrongfully obstructed the access of the plaintiff-lessee's cattle to certain portions of the leasehold. Consequently the plaintiff sustained losses through "shrinkage" of his herd and incurred higher labor costs in repairing fences and in preventing the cattle from falling into the ditch. The court held that the plaintiff had no duty to fill in the ditch in mitigation because that action would have constituted an unlawful trespass upon the defendant's right-of-way. Should the same result obtain if the trespass is only technical, yet the potential losses avoided would be significant?

4. Should a claimant's failure to wear an available seat belt limit the amount of damages recoverable from an automobile accident by application of the doctrine of avoidable consequences? One view, articulated in *Spier v. Barker*, 35 N.Y.2d 444, 363 N.Y.S.2d 916, 323 N.E.2d 164 (1974), holds that the jury can properly consider the non-use of a seat belt in determining whether the plaintiff exercised due care in mitigating damages. *Also see* Estevez v. United States, 72 F.Supp.2d 205, 208 (S.D.N.Y.1999) (passenger must exercise reasonable care and mitigate damages by wearing seat belt and also must not ride in an unreasonable position).

A different approach was followed in *Thomas v. Henson*, 102 N.M. 417, 696 P.2d 1010 (1984), where the court acknowledged the merit in the avoidable consequences approach of *Spier* but decided that the factfinder could consider evidence of the failure to wear a seat belt in apportioning damages. See Restatement (Second) of Torts § 465 comment c. *See also* Milbrand v. DaimlerChrysler Corp., 105 F.Supp.2d 601, 605 (E.D.Tex.2000) (policy that damages not reduced or mitigated because of failure to wear seat belts codified by statutory prohibition of evidentiary exclusion of usage or nonusage).

D.   COLLATERAL SOURCE RULE

Section Coverage:

Defendants sometimes make payments of undisputed sums before trial. Such pre-trial payments to a plaintiff are then credited against the wrong-doer's ultimate liability. The collateral source rule states a negative corollary to that principle: compensation or other benefits which an injured party receives from a source unaffiliated or independent of the responsible party are *not* deducted from the defendant's liability. A second facet to the rule is that it serves as an evidentiary preclusion device; the defendant may not introduce evidence that the plaintiff has insurance coverage or has received gifts or benefits from some other source. Although the rule principally finds application in the tort context, it also may surface in cases of breach of contract.

Critics have attacked the collateral source rule on the basis that in certain instances an injured party actually receives double compensation for a single harm. Because the rule operates to allow a plaintiff to keep the benefits from a collateral source and to assess the wrongdoer for the same damages, it stands as an exception to the traditional goal of compensatory damages to place plaintiffs as nearly as practicable in the position they held prior to the harm. For this reason, the rule has been abolished in some states as part of tort reform legislation.

Proponents of the rule have justified it with several arguments. First, if insurance benefits were viewed as an offset to tort liability, then a plaintiff would have less incentive to obtain insurance; without the rule plaintiffs actually would be net losers because they paid the insurance premiums. Second, an injured party may not in fact receive a double recovery if the insurance policy provided for subrogation rights. Third, apart from subrogation, the collateral source rule serves as a rough offset for the attorney's contingency fee. Finally, proponents argue that as between the tortfeasor and the plaintiff, any windfall should be enjoyed by the innocent party.

The principal legal difficulty in applying the collateral source rule is determining when a source is truly "independent" from the tortfeasor. Some jurisdictions have narrowed the effect of the rule by shifting the focus away from the wrongdoer and analyzing whether the source is affiliated in some manner with the plaintiff. The private sector sources, such as personal medical insurance, are fairly easy to characterize under either approach. The more complex questions have involved trying to classify whether certain types of public sector social benefits, such as medicare or unemployment benefits, should be viewed as "collateral" for purposes of the rule.

Model Case:

Baker drove through a red light and hit a pedestrian named Penn who was attempting to cross an intersection. Penn consequently incurred various medical expenses and was forced to miss several weeks of work. The claim against Baker prays for compensatory damages, including lost wages, medical expenses, and pain and suffering. A trial court applying the collateral source rule would refuse to allow the introduction of evidence of disability payments and medical benefits which Penn received under the terms of a union contract. The union benefits would be characterized as a source wholly independent from the interests of Baker. If the union contract did not provide for subrogation rights, Penn would effectively receive a double compensation for the injuries sustained.

Helfend v. Southern California Rapid Transit Dist.

2 Cal.3d 1, 465 P.2d 61, 84 Cal.Rptr. 173 (1970).

■ TOBRINER, ACTING CHIEF JUSTICE.

Defendants appeal from a judgment of the Los Angeles Superior Court entered on a verdict in favor of plaintiff, Julius J. Helfend, for $16,400 in general and special damages for injuries sustained in a bus-auto collision that occurred on July 19, 1965, in the City of Los Angeles.

We have concluded that the judgment for plaintiff in this tort action against the defendant governmental entity should be affirmed. The trial court properly followed the collateral source rule in excluding evidence that a portion of plaintiff's medical bills had been paid through a medical insurance plan that requires the refund of benefits from tort recoveries.

* * *

Plaintiff filed a tort action against the Southern California Rapid Transit District, a public entity, and Mitchell an employee of the transit district. At trial plaintiff claimed slightly more than $2,700 in special damages, including $921 in doctor's bills, a $336.99 hospital bill, and about $45 for medicines. Defendant requested permission to show that about 80 percent of the plaintiff's hospital bill had been paid by plaintiff's Blue Cross insurance carrier and that some of his other medical expenses may have been paid by other insurance. The superior court thoroughly considered the then very recent case of City of Salinas v. Souza & McCue Construction Company (1967) 66 Cal.2d 217, 57 Cal.Rptr. 337, 424 P.2d 921, distinguished the *Souza* case on the ground that *Souza* involved a contract setting, and concluded that the judgment should not be reduced to the extent of the amount of insurance payments which plaintiff received. The court ruled that defendants should not be permitted to show that plaintiff had received medical coverage from any collateral source.

After the jury verdict in favor of plaintiff in the sum of $16,300, defendants appealed. * * *

We must decide whether the collateral source rule applies to tort actions involving public entities and public employees in which the plaintiff has received benefits from his medical insurance coverage.

The Supreme Court of California has long adhered to the doctrine that if an injured party received some compensation for his injuries from a source wholly independent of the tortfeasor, such payment should not be deducted from the damages which the plaintiff would otherwise collect from the tortfeasor. * * *

Although the collateral source rule remains generally accepted in the United States, nevertheless many other jurisdictions have restricted or repealed it. In this country most commentators have criticized the rule and called for its early demise. In *Souza* we took note of the academic criticism of the rule, characterized the rule as "punitive," and held it inapplicable to the governmental entity involved in that case.

* * *

The collateral source rule as applied here embodies the venerable concept that a person who has invested years of insurance premiums to assure his medical case should receive the benefits of his thrift. The tortfeasor should not garner the benefits of his victim's providence.

The collateral source rule expresses a policy judgment in favor of encouraging citizens to purchase and maintain insurance for personal injuries and for other eventualities. Courts consider insurance a form of investment, the benefits of which become payable without respect to any other possible source of funds. If we were to permit a tortfeasor to mitigate damages with payments from plaintiff's insurance, plaintiff would be in a position inferior to that of having bought no insurance, because his payment of premiums would have earned no benefit. Defendant should not be able to avoid payment of full compensation for the injury inflicted merely because the victim has had the foresight to provide himself with insurance.

Some commentators object that the above approach to the collateral source rule provides plaintiff with a "double recovery," rewards him for the injury, and defeats the principle that damages should compensate the victim but not punish the tortfeasor. We agree with Professor Fleming's observation, however, that "double recovery is justified only in the face of some exceptional, supervening reason, as in the case of accident or life insurance, where it is felt unjust that the tortfeasor should take advantage of the thrift and prescience of the victim in having paid the premiums." (Fleming, Introduction to the Law of Torts (1967) p. 131.) * * *

Furthermore, insurance policies increasingly provide for either subrogation or refund of benefits upon a tort recovery, and such refund is indeed called for the present case. [Citation.] Hence, the plaintiff receives no double recovery; the collateral source rule simply serves as a means of by-passing the antiquated doctrine of non-assignment of tortious actions and permits a proper transfer of risk from the plaintiff's insurer to the tortfeasor by way of the victim's tort recovery. The double shift from the tortfeasor to the victim and then from the victim to his insurance carrier can normally occur with little cost in that the insurance carrier is often intimately involved in the initial litigation and quite automatically receives its part of the tort settlement or verdict.

Even in cases in which the contract or the law precludes subrogation or refund of benefits, or in situations in which the collateral source waives such subrogation or refund, the rule performs entirely necessary functions in the computation of damages. For example, the cost of medical care often provides both attorneys and juries in tort cases with an important measure for assessing the plaintiff's general damages. [Citation.] To permit the defendant to tell the jury that the plaintiff has been recompensed by a collateral source for his medical costs might irretrievably upset the complex, delicate, and somewhat indefinable calculations which result in the normal jury verdict. [Citations.]

We also note that generally the jury is not informed that plaintiff's attorney will receive a large portion of the plaintiff's recovery in contingent fees or that personal injury damages are not taxable to the plaintiff and are normally deductible by the defendant. Hence, the plaintiff rarely actually receives full compensation for his injuries as computed by the jury. The collateral source rule partially serves to compensate for the attorney's share and does not actually render "double recovery" for the plaintiff. Indeed, many jurisdictions that have abolished or limited the collateral source rule have also established a means for assessing the plaintiff's costs for counsel directly against the defendant rather than imposing the contingent fee system. In sum, the plaintiff's recovery for his medical expenses from both the tortfeasor and his medical insurance program will not usually give him "double recovery," but partially provides a somewhat closer approximation to full compensation for his injuries.

If we consider the collateral source rule as applied here in the context of the entire American approach to the law of torts and damages, we find that the rule presently performs a number of legitimate and even indispensable functions. Without a thorough revolution in the American approach to torts and the consequent damages, the rule at least with respect to medical insurance benefits has become so integrated within our present system that its precipitous judicial nullification would work hardship. In this case the collateral source rule lies between two systems for the compensation of accident victims: the traditional tort recovery based on fault and the increasingly prevalent coverage based on non-fault insurance. Neither system possesses such universality of coverage or completeness of compensation that we can easily dispense with the collateral source rule's approach to meshing the two systems. [Citations.] The reforms which many academicians propose cannot easily be achieved through piecemeal common law development; the proposed changes, if desirable, would be more effectively accomplished through legislative reform. * * *

* * * Hence, we conclude that in a case in which a tort victim has received partial compensation from medical insurance coverage entirely independent of the tortfeasor the trial court properly followed the collateral source rule and foreclosed defendant from mitigating damages by means of the collateral payments.

* * *

Defendants would have this court create a special form of sovereign immunity as a novel exception to the collateral source rule for tortfeasors who are public entities or public employees. [Citations.] We see no justification for such special treatment. In the present case the nullification of the collateral source rule would simply frustrate the transfer of the medical costs from the medical insurance carrier, Blue Cross, to the public entity. The public entity or its insurance carrier is in at least as advantageous a position to spread the risk of loss as is the plaintiff's medical insurance carrier. To deprive Blue Cross of repayment for its expenditures on plaintiff's behalf merely because he was injured by a public entity rather than a private individual would constitute an unwarranted and arbitrary discrimination. * * *

The judgment is affirmed.

———————

1. *Policy Considerations.* Courts have recognized various reasons for the collateral source rule. Which, if any, of the following justifications are the most persuasive?

(A) A defendant tortfeasor should not gain a windfall or be unjustly enriched by reducing potential damages liability through offsetting benefits received by an injured party;

(B) An injured party who has paid premiums to obtain insurance should receive the fruits of the contract; otherwise it would undermine the incentive to obtain valuable insurance protection;

(C) As between an innocent party and a tortfeasor, equity favors receipt of benefits by the party who has not committed a wrong;

(D) Society imposes a burden upon tortfeasors to bear the full responsibility for their actions and to deter future wrongdoing;

(E) An injured party ordinarily does not receive a double recovery because insurance contracts typically provide for subrogation rights by the insurance company.

See generally McLean v. Runyon, 222 F.3d 1150, 1156 (9th Cir.2000); Halek v. United States, 178 F.3d 481, 483 (7th Cir.1999); Szedlock v. Tenet, 139 F.Supp.2d 725, 736 (E.D.Va.2001).

2. *Rule of Evidence.* Application of the collateral source rule also bars the introduction of evidence pertaining to proof of benefits or compensation that the plaintiff has received as compensation for an injury. Thus, it functions both as a rule of evidence and as a rule of damages. *See* Jacobsen, The Collateral Source Rule and the Role of the Jury, 70 Or. L. Rev. 523 (1991); *see also* Fitzgerald v. Expressway Sewerage Const., Inc., 177 F.3d 71, 73–74 (1st Cir.1999) (in diversity case, state law of collateral source rule applied regarding rule of damages while federal evidence rules govern aspects pertaining to evidence, such as involving relevancy and prejudicial effect).

In *Hassan v. United States Postal Service*, 842 F.2d 260 (11th Cir. 1988), the claimant in a Federal Tort Claims Act suit asserted that the trial court had erred by allowing the government to introduce evidence that its liability should be reduced by collateral social security and insurance payments received by the plaintiff. The state statute applicable in assessing damages under the Act had abrogated the collateral source rule in personal injury or wrongful death actions involving motor vehicles. The plaintiff argued that the government's attempt to reduce its liability by the collateral source payments was an affirmative defense which was waived when not raised in the government's pleadings. The court held that the issue did fall within the scope of Federal Rule of Civil Procedure 8(c) as an affirmative defense, but nonetheless upheld its admission into evidence. The court noted that the underlying purpose of Rule 8(c) is to guarantee the opposing party notice of an issue to avoid prejudice, and in this case the claimant knew about the government's plans to raise the issue at trial.

3. *Contracts.* The policy justifications underlying the collateral source rule do not support its application in contract cases because the expectations implicit in contract breach are simply full payment or performance. *See* Safeco v. City of White House, Tenn., 191 F.3d 675, 693 (6th Cir.1999); Garofalo v. Empire Blue Cross and Blue Shield, 67 F.Supp.2d 343, 347 (S.D.N.Y.1999); Chisholm v. UHP Projects, Inc., 205 F.3d 731, 737 (4th Cir.2000) (contractor's damages liability for breach of implied warranty of workmanlike performance properly reduced by amounts received by injured party in prior settlement as collateral source policies not implicated).

4. Who should bear the burden of proving the amount received from a collateral source when a statute abrogates the common law rule? In Reilly v. United States, 863 F.2d 149 (1st Cir.1988), the court found that burden rested with the defendant under the statute. The defendant's general allusions to the plaintiff's possible eligibility to receive benefits failed to satisfy evidentiary requirements.

5. The line between affiliated and collateral sources is often blurry. This difficulty is highlighted when one government agency has liability under the Federal Tort Claims Act while a separate branch or agency of the government renders medical services to the injured party or supplies other benefits. Courts typically have resolved the issue by allowing an offset to liability when the benefits come from unfunded general government revenues and not deducting benefits from a special fund. *See* United States v.

Gray, 199 F.2d 239 (10th Cir.1952) (disability payments under Veterans Act deductible); United States v. Harue Hayashi, 282 F.2d 599 (9th Cir. 1960) (social security payments not deductible because funded in part by the beneficiary or a relative upon whom the beneficiary was dependent); United States v. Price, 288 F.2d 448 (4th Cir.1961) (benefits under the Civil Service Retirement Act were a collateral source); United States v. Brooks, 176 F.2d 482 (4th Cir.1949) (National Service Life Insurance Policy benefits not deductible from an FTCA damages award).

6. The rationales for distinguishing special government funds for collateral source treatment are twofold: the source itself is considered independent of other federal agencies and the plaintiffs deserve any additional compensation because they have effectively contracted for it in the nature of social insurance. *See* Overton v. United States, 619 F.2d 1299 (8th Cir.1980). A more restrictive approach was taken in Steckler v. United States, 549 F.2d 1372 (10th Cir.1977), where the court held that Social Security payments constituted a non-deductible collateral source only to the extent that the claimant succeeded in tracing his contributions to the fund.

7. Courts have had particular problems applying the collateral source rule to Medicare, a federal program originally enacted as an amendment to the Social Security Act. In *Overton v. United States*, 619 F.2d 1299 (8th Cir.1980), the court held that Medicare payments were deductible from the government's liability because the Medicare Part A trust fund was not wholly independent from the general revenues of the federal treasury and the plaintiff did not show contributions to the source of the payments. In contrast, in *Siverson v. United States*, 710 F.2d 557 (9th Cir.1983), the court held that the government was not entitled to offset Medicare payments against an FTCA award where the claimant had shown that he contributed to the Medicare fund through social security payments while employed. *Accord,* Titchnell v. United States, 681 F.2d 165 (3d Cir.1982) (Medicare payments deemed collateral source because plaintiff had contributed to fund).

PROBLEM: THE GOOD SAMARITAN

Carlton was driving down a quiet two lane country road when a cement-mixer truck barreled around the corner and forced Carlton's car into a ditch. The driver of the truck sped away from the scene of the accident, leaving Carlton injured and helpless.

Fortunately, kindly Doc Miller and his teenage son, Butch, drove past just a few minutes later, saw the overturned vehicle, and stopped to render aid. Doc and Butch pulled Carlton from the car and rushed to the hospital. Doc performed emergency surgery on Carlton to stop internal hemorrhaging and he also stitched and bandaged several cuts. Carlton recovered in the hospital for three days and was then discharged.

1. Assume that Carlton had been paying premiums on a medical insurance policy for a number of years. The policy, apart from a small

deductible, provided coverage for the hospital charges as well as for surgical fees. Ignorant of this fact, Doc decided not to send Carlton a bill for the operation but considered his services to be a "favor for a friend." Meanwhile, the company that owned the cement truck, Pavco, was identified. Assume that Pavco would be liable for the tort of its driver in this instance. Should Carlton be entitled to receive payment from the insurance company for a "reasonable surgical fee" as expressly provided in the policy and to recover such fees also from Pavco?

2. What if Doc instead sent Carlton a bill for the operation and the insurance company paid the fee. Under the collateral source rule, can Carlton claim the surgical fee as a compensable item of damages against Pavco? Should the jury be instructed that the plaintiff had medical insurance which would cover the various hospital charges and doctor's fees?

Hueper v. Goodrich

314 N.W.2d 828 (Minn.1982).

■ TODD, JUSTICE.

Bruce Hueper, a minor, was seriously injured in an auto accident. A lawsuit was commenced on his behalf for his injuries and his father brought action for his medical expenses. The trial was bifurcated as to liability and damages. Following the damages trial, the court allowed the father full recovery of the reasonable value of medical expenses, including hospital services furnished without charge, under the collateral source rule.
* * *

The jury award of $37,270 to Emil Hueper was for special damages arising out of medical and hospital care provided to his son Bruce before Bruce's 18th birthday. Of that sum, $25,977 reflected the reasonable value of the medical care provided to Bruce Hueper while he was a patient at Shriner's Hospital. A physician at Shriner's Hospital testified that it was the policy of the hospital not to charge patients for care provided or to accept insurance proceeds from a third party.

* * *

The issues presented are:

I. Did the trial court err in applying the collateral source rule to allow the father of a minor son to recover the reasonable value of medical and hospital services provided free of charge by a charitable institution?

* * *

Under the collateral source rule, a plaintiff may recover damages from a tortfeasor, although the plaintiff has received money or services in reparation of the injury from a source other than the tortfeasor. [Citation.] The benefit conferred on the injured person from the collateral source is not credited against the tortfeasor's liability, although it may partially or completely reimburse the plaintiff for his injuries. Restatement (Second) of Torts, § 920A (1979). The rule has been applied where the plaintiff has received insurance proceeds, employment benefits, gifts of money or medical services, welfare benefits or tax advantages. [Citation.]

Various justifications have been given for applying the rule. Where the plaintiff has paid for the benefit such as by buying an insurance policy, the rationale is that the plaintiff should be reimbursed and the tortfeasor should not get a windfall. *See* Restatement (Second) of Torts, § 920A, comment b (1979). If the benefit is a gift from a third party, such as an employer, a relative or a charity, the argument is that the donor intended that the injured party receive the gift and not that the benefit be shifted to the tortfeasor. Other reasons for applying the rule are that the wrongdoer should be punished by being made to take full responsibility for his negligence and that the plaintiff will be more fully compensated if he is allowed to recover from the tortfeasor.

Minnesota has adopted the collateral source rule and the cases applying the rule have relied upon the policy reasons discussed above. *See* Hubbard Broadcasting, Inc. v. Loescher, 291 N.W.2d 216 (1980) (purpose of rule is punitive); Van Tassel v. Horace Mann Ins. Co., 296 Minn. 181, 207 N.W.2d 348 (1973) (insurance paid for by plaintiff should not benefit tortfeasor); Local 1140, Int'l Union of Elec., Radio & Mach. Workers, 282 Minn. 455, 165 N.W.2d 234 (1969) (benefit of reimbursement by hospital when blood was replaced by donor group to which injured plaintiffs belonged goes to plaintiffs.)

In this case the trial court correctly followed Minnesota case law in applying the collateral source rule. Emil Hueper, as the father of Bruce Hueper, a minor, had a right to recover special damages for medical expenses from the defendants. [Citations.] He could still recover the reasonable value of those medical expenses although Shriner's Hospital did not charge the Huepers anything for Bruce's medical care. In Dahlin v. Kron, 232 Minn. 312, 45 N.W.2d 833 (1950), this court held that the plaintiff could recover the reasonable value of medical services provided by a hospital even though those services were rendered gratuitously by the hospital.

We are being asked to review the policy considerations involved in our long-standing support of the collateral source rule. The facts of this case present this issue in a light most favorable to those advocating abandonment of the collateral source rule. However, the rule in its application is broader than the facts of this case. To begin limiting the application of the rule is to invite an unlimited flow of litigation seeking ad hoc determinations with the confusion that would necessarily follow. Considering the rule in its broadest sense and reviewing all of the considerations involved in such an evaluation, we decline to abandon the collateral source rule or to create limitations on its application. * * *

■ SIMONETT, JUSTICE (dissenting in part). * * *

Mr. Hueper has been compensated for his own personal injuries. He settled for $85,000. Before us is his claim for hospital and medical expenses incurred by him for his son Bruce's care during Bruce's minority. This claim is separate from, although derivative of, Bruce's claim. The jury awarded Mr. Hueper $43,847.34. This was reduced by 15% for Mr. Hueper's own fault to $37,370.24. This figure includes $24,977.14, representing the reasonable value of the services rendered by Shriners Hospital. Mr. Hueper keeps this money, since the hospital made no charge and accepts no payment for its services. The $24,977.14 is to be paid by defendants Dean Goodrich and John M. Neubauer, the owner and driver, respectively, of the other truck involved in the accident. Mr. Goodrich is not personally at fault. He is liable to Mr. Hueper for the unincurred hospital bill of $24,977.14 by reason of his vicarious liability as owner of the truck.

The collateral source rule is usually justified on one or more of the following rationales: (1) the injured party has *paid for* the collateral source benefit and deserves what he paid for; (2) a collateral source benefit is sometimes a *gift intended* by the donor to benefit the injured donee and not the tortfeasor; (3) only cumulation of collateral source benefits with amounts assessed the tortfeasor will *fully compensate* the injured person; (4) a tortfeasor deserves to be *punished,* a purpose which would be foiled if he were relieved from "total responsibility" for his wrong; and (5) since a *windfall* payment is inevitable, better it go to the injured person than the tortfeasor.

None of these reasons, it seems to me, applies in this case, or, to the extent any does, it applies with very little persuasive force.

First, Mr. Hueper did not pay for the Shriner's care in any way. He paid no insurance premium; there was no surrender of sick leave or other fringe benefits. No "consideration" was given * * *.

Second, in providing its care, the Shriners Hospital was indifferent as to whether Bruce Hueper had been in a compensable auto accident or not. He was afforded no different care than other patients. No specific gift was intended, such as where fellow employees donate blood to one of their number, as in Local 1140 v. Massachusetts Mutual Life Insurance Co., 282 Minn. 455, 165 N.W.2d 234 (1969), or where one spouse renders nursing care to the other.

Third, it cannot be said deduction of the Shriners Hospital bill will leave Mr. Hueper less than fully compensated. It is said that pain and suffering are more likely to be completely compensated if collateral source benefits are recoverable. Here, however, plaintiff's entire claim is for specific expense items; no general damages, difficult to measure, are involved. The claim is more akin to a property damage claim where often the collateral source rule is disallowed.

Fourth, there would seem to be little reason to punish the defendants. If the defendants deserve punishment, punitive damages should be the route. If the jurors had known the hospital bill was not actually incurred, it is doubtful they would have punished defendants by making them pay it nevertheless. In any event, there seems to be little need to punish defendant Goodrich, who was not personally at fault.

Fifth, the windfall rationale lacks persuasive force here. Ordinarily, other things being equal, if someone is to benefit by the generosity of the Shriners Hospital, it is better that it be the injured party rather than the wrongdoer. What this means is that it is better to assure that plaintiff is made whole than that the defendant pay less than he ought to. Here, however, "other things" are not equal. Since plaintiff's damages relate solely to "out-of-pocket" expenses, it cannot be said plaintiff is not made whole even with the collateral source benefit deducted. To say defendant should not pay less than he ought to is only another way of saying the defendant should be punished, a rationale which, as we have seen, is inappropriate in this factual setting.

While the collateral source rule has been strongly criticized, it is still true no one has really offered a better alternative. Perhaps this is the strongest rationale for its continued use. In most cases there is simply no way of knowing what is the fairest way to handle the collateral source benefit "windfall." To try and find this "equality" by admitting a multitude of collateral sources would be most confusing, prejudicial and unfair.[2] It is probably better, arbitrarily, to keep collateral source benefits out of the lawsuit and then allow the windfall to plaintiff.

But having said this, I see no need to extend this somewhat arbitrary rule to a fact situation where the policy considerations favoring it clearly do not apply. I would be willing to hold that in a parent's derivative claim for out-of-pocket expenses the parent may not recover for hospital or medical care furnished his or her minor child gratuitously and not as a specific gift. At the very least, I would hold, in this case, that plaintiff is not entitled to recover against defendant Goodrich who is not personally at fault. It should be plaintiff's option whether to prove up the reasonable value of the gratuitous services and then have the court, after the verdict, make the reduction, or to choose not to include the services in his claim.

———————

1. Courts have split over the issue whether the collateral source rule should be applied to allow an injured party to recover the reasonable value of gratuitously supplied medical services. In *Oddo v. Cardi*, 100 R.I. 578, 218 A.2d 373 (1966), the court adopted the same approach as in the

———————

2. If one starts recognizing collateral sources, where does one stop? Studies indicate that about 55% of auto accident tort victims' compensation comes from tort recoveries, the remainder being supplied by collateral sources. Birmingham, *The Theory of Economic Policy and the Law of Torts*, 55 Minn.L.Rev. 1, 9 (1970); United States Department of Transportation, *Automobile Insurance and Compensation Study*, March 1971, "Motor Vehicle Crash Losses and their Compensation in the United States." What about health insurance benefits, pensions, social security, sick leave, disability insurance and, in the case of a decedent, life insurance? And if these items are recognizable, then what about defendant's liability insurance or lack of it? Here, for example, the Goodrich truck had only $100,000 coverage for any one claim and the insurer paid the $100,000 to Bruce, so apparently the defendants have personal exposure for Mr. Hueper's verdict of $37,370.24.

principal case; the amount of recovery from a party responsible for an injury is not affected by the plaintiff's receipt of free medical care from sources collateral to the defendant. *See also* Banks v. Crowner, 694 P.2d 101 (Wyo.1985); Restatement (Second) of Torts § 920A, comment c (1979).

2. Consider the court's support of the collateral source rule in *Hudson v. Lazarus*, 217 F.2d 344 (D.C.Cir.1954):

> Usually the collateral contribution necessarily benefits either the injured person or the wrongdoer. Whether it is a gift or the product of a contract of employment or of insurance, the purposes of the parties to it are obviously better served and the interests of society are likely to be better served if the injured person is benefitted than if the wrongdoer is benefitted. Legal "compensation" for personal injuries does not actually compensate. Not many people would sell an arm for the average or even the maximum amount that juries award for the loss of an arm. Moreover the injured person seldom gets the compensation he "recovers," for a substantial attorney's fee usually comes out of it. 217 F.2d at 346.

The court, then, is justifying the potential overcompensation attributed to the collateral source rule by saying that an injured party cannot truly be compensated in monetary equivalents for personal injuries. Does that answer beg the question?

3. Compare *Coyne v. Campbell*, 11 N.Y.2d 372, 230 N.Y.S.2d 1, 183 N.E.2d 891 (1962), where the court held that the rationale underlying the collateral source rule did not allow an injured physician to recover as special damages the reasonable value of medical and nursing care and treatment which were gratuitously rendered. The court reasoned that the goal of tort law is merely compensatory rather than of a punitive character, and if the rule were otherwise applied it "would involve odd consequences, and in the end simply require a defendant to pay a plaintiff the value of a gift." *Accord* Peterson v. Lou Bachrodt Chevrolet Co., 76 Ill.2d 353, 29 Ill.Dec. 444, 392 N.E.2d 1 (1979).

4. *Tort Reform of the Collateral Source Rule.* At common law, defendants were not permitted to offset from their own liability compensation or benefits that an injured plaintiff received from an independent or collateral source, such as insurance coverage, nor were defendants permitted to introduce evidence of such benefits. Many states now permit defendants to introduce evidence of payments from collateral sources. *See, e.g.,* Ind. Stat. (West 2001) § 34–44–1–2 (parties may introduce proof of collateral source payments except payments of life insurance or death benefits or insurance benefits for which plaintiff or plaintiff's family have paid); Iowa Stat. § 668.14 (West 2001) (court shall permit evidence and argument as to previous collateral payments and future rights to collateral payments but also permit evidence and argument as to the cost to the plaintiff of procuring those collateral payments). Some states then allow the jury to consider the collateral source benefits in determining a plaintiff's damages. *See, e.g.,* Ind. Stat. (West 2001) § 34–44–13 (proof of collateral benefits shall be considered by the trier of fact is assessing damages); Iowa Stat.

§ 668.14 (West 2001) (jury shall make findings indicating the effect of evidence and argument pertaining to collateral payments on its verdict). Alternatively, some states permit or require courts to deduct collateral source benefits from a plaintiff's damage award. Alaska Stat. § 9.17.070 (2000) (court shall deduct from plaintiff's award the amount by which payments from any collateral source exceed plaintiff's attorneys fees and insurance premiums); Colo. Rev. Stat. § 13–21–111.6 (West 2000) (court shall reduce the verdict by the amount of any collateral payments not paid as a result of a contract entered into and paid for by or on behalf of the plaintiff).

In *Miller v. Sciaroni*, 172 Cal.App.3d 306, 218 Cal.Rptr. 219 (1985), the court upheld the constitutionality of California Civil Code § 3333.1. The court found that because the legislation affected only economic interests of indemnitors, rather than fundamental rights, it should be scrutinized according to whether the statutory evidentiary distinctions bore a rational relationship to a legitimate state purpose. In applying the rational basis test, the court found a legitimate state interest in "the protection of a viable state health care system," and that it was not the judiciary's role to reweigh or second-guess the facts involved in the legislative determination. Also, in *Barme v. Wood*, 37 Cal.3d 174, 207 Cal.Rptr. 816, 689 P.2d 446 (1984), the court held that another provision of the California collateral source statute which eliminated certain subrogation rights against a malpractice defendant was rationally related to the legislative purpose because it reduced costs on those defendants by shifting them to other insurers.

Finally, in *Fein v. Permanente Medical Group,* 38 Cal.3d 137, 211 Cal.Rptr. 368, 695 P.2d 665, *appeal dismissed,* 474 U.S. 892, 106 S.Ct. 214, 88 L.Ed.2d 215 (1985), the California Supreme Court held that the statutory modification of the common law collateral source rule satisfied constitutional due process objections, even though the provision admittedly affects the measure of a plaintiff's damage award, because a plaintiff has no vested property right in a particular measure of damages. In dissent from the United States Supreme Court's denial of appeal, Justice White identified the unresolved issue as: "Whether due process requires a legislatively enacted compensation scheme to be a quid pro quo for the common-law or state-law remedy it replaces, and if so, how adequate it must be[.]" 474 U.S. at 894 (White, J. dissenting).

The majority of cases that have addressed the issue have upheld the constitutionality of provisions modifying or abolishing the collateral source rule in medical malpractice cases. *See* Rudolph v. Iowa Methodist Medical Ctr., 293 N.W.2d 550 (Iowa 1980); Baker v. Vanderbilt Univ., 616 F.Supp. 330 (M.D.Tenn.1985). *See generally* McDowell, The Collateral Source Rule—The American Medical Association and Tort Reform, 24 Washburn L.J. 205 (1985). *See also* Eastin v. Broomfield, 116 Ariz. 576, 570 P.2d 744 (1977) (Arizona's statutory abrogation of collateral source rule with respect to medical malpractice actions did not deprive claimants of any property interest protected by constitutional due process, nor was it arbitrary and unreasonable to deny claimants equal protection of the laws)

Some decisions have struck down statutory abolitions of the collateral source rule on constitutional grounds. In *Graley v. Satayatham*, 74 Ohio Op.2d 316, 343 N.E.2d 832 (1976), the court held that an Ohio statute abrogating the collateral source rule only with respect to medical malpractice actions was violative of the equal protection guarantees in both the state and federal Constitutions. The statutory classification scheme which differentiated between medical malpractice claims and other tort actions failed the compelling governmental interest test.

Similarly, in *Doran v. Priddy*, 534 F.Supp. 30 (D.Kan.1981), the court upheld an equal protection challenge to a Kansas statute which applied only if the putative tortfeasor was a health care provider. The statute permitted the introduction into evidence of collateral benefits received by a plaintiff from gratuitous sources and disallowed evidence of benefits received from a plaintiff's insurance or employment. The court held that this new statutory rule did not bear a reasonable and substantial relation to the avowed legislative purpose of reducing medical costs.

CHAPTER 14

SPECIAL ISSUES IN DAMAGES

A. DISTRESS DAMAGES

Judicial reluctance to award damages for mental distress has been reflected in both substantive and remedial law. Substantive law restrictions appear when the plaintiff suffers mental distress in the absence of other injury. In tort claims this issue arises frequently when a plaintiff is distressed by witnessing an accident involving a loved one, or when a plaintiff is terrorized by a situation threatening serious injury but none results.

In contract, a party may suffer distress if a breach is anticipated but does not occur. If, for example, a photographic studio has promised to deliver wedding photos on Wednesday, and delivery does occur on Wednesday, there is no contract breach. The couple may be greatly distressed, however, if the studio indicated on Monday that the photos could not be located and may be lost. Timely location and delivery by Wednesday fulfills the contract, but the couple will have suffered noncompensable distress for two days.

The general rule is that a contract claim will not support distress damages, although there are a few exceptions. The historical rule in tort was that there is no substantive claim for negligently caused distress without physical injury. Today, most jurisdictions recognize a claim for negligently caused emotional distress, but jurisdictions place different limitations on recovery. In "direct" cases where the plaintiff suffers emotional distress because of fear of harm to herself, a common limitation restricts recovery to plaintiffs who were in the zone of danger and suffer some physical manifestation of emotional distress. Many jurisdictions allow recovery in "bystander" cases where the plaintiffs suffer distress from viewing an injury to a loved one. In these cases, some states limit recovery to those bystanders who were in the zone of danger of the accident. Some states allow recovery to distressed witnesses even if the claimant is not in the zone of danger if certain specific criteria are met.

Remedial issues with distress damages arise when the plaintiff has established an action for the invasion of another interest, such as personal injury or breach of contract. When a plaintiff has established a claim for invasion of an interest in person or property, distress damages are recoverable as "parasitic damages," meaning that they attach to the other claim rather than support a claim by themselves. The limits on such recovery are governed by the remedial limitations of foreseeability and certainty. Foreseeable distress and its consequences are usually traced quite liberally in personal injury cases, whereas in fraud cases courts generally interpret foreseeability restrictively or prohibit such damages altogether.

Model Case:

Defendant Driver negligently lost control of the car and jumped the curb. A child who was riding a tricycle on the sidewalk was seriously injured. The child's parents were both near-by and witnessed the accident.

The child's personal injury damages will include the mental distress suffered as a result of this trauma. In most jurisdictions such distress is included in the instruction on pain and suffering. Sometimes courts will consider elements of the distress separately. If, for example, the child needed psychological counselling to overcome a phobia resulting from the accident, these damages would be in a separate instruction. The child's distress damages, including subsequent problems caused by the distress, are restricted only by foreseeability and certainty limitations. A subsequent teen-age suicide from the childhood trauma, for example, would not be compensable.

One of the parents witnessing the accident suffered a nervous breakdown with physical manifestations as a result of the experience. Many jurisdictions would allow a claim as a matter of substantive law, but only if this parent was in the "zone of danger" at the time of the accident. A few states would allow this action if the parent was just near-by yet outside the zone of danger.

The other parent who witnessed the accident suffered extreme distress but without any physical manifestations. The great majority of jurisdictions deny any action to this parent.

The parents would both be able to recover if the conduct of the driver was malicious rather than negligent. As a matter of substantive law, most states would allow claims by all these victims if the driver was aiming for the sidewalk to hurt this family.

Crinkley v. Holiday Inns, Inc.

844 F.2d 156 (4th Cir.1988).

■ PHILLIPS, CIRCUIT JUDGE:

This is a civil action in which various defendants associated with the Holiday Inns enterprise appeal from jury verdicts finding them liable for personal injuries inflicted by third persons upon the plaintiffs Crinkley, while the Crinkleys were guests in a Holiday Inn Motel. * * *

Sometime before the weekend of February 27 28, 1981, the Crinkleys decided to attend a function being held during that weekend at the Charlotte, North Carolina Civic Center. * * * [T]hey selected the Holiday Inn Concord and reserved a room for the nights of February 27 and 28. The Holiday Inn Concord is located some twenty-odd miles north of Charlotte, just off Highway 29, which runs directly south into downtown Charlotte, and Interstate 85, which runs to and around the northern edge of Charlotte.

During the approximately two weeks preceding the weekend of February 27, guests at several Charlotte area motels had been assaulted and robbed on the premises by a group later dubbed the "Motel Bandits" in media reports. The motels involved were located throughout the metropolitan Charlotte area, and many of them were located close to Interstate 85. The assistant manager of the Holiday Inn Concord, Brian McRorie, was aware of the Motel Bandits from the various news media. He was contacted by several unidentified members of the local County Sheriff's Office who wanted to know if McRorie was aware of the Motel Bandits and what plans he had for security at the motel while the Motel Bandits were at large. Some of these officers also offered to serve for a fee as security guards during their off duty hours, a security measure that the motel had used in the past, but did not avail itself of in this instance.

As a result of this information, McRorie contacted Jim Van Over about the possibility of hiring security guards to patrol the motel. Van Over was the manager of the Holiday Inn on Woodlawn Road in Charlotte, and had some supervisory responsibility over the Holiday Inn Concord as an employee of defendant Travelers Management Corporation (TRAVCO), the entity in operational control of the Holiday Inn Concord. Van Over was also the president of the Metrolina Innkeepers Association and had been interviewed for a newspaper story covering the Motel Bandits. In that article, he noted that his hotel had added security personnel for night patrols. As to McRorie's requests for additional security at the Concord property, however, Van Over concluded that extra security measures were not justified. McRorie did instruct his employees to be particularly alert for anything suspicious and he periodically patrolled the premises on February 27, the last time being sometime between 8:00 and 8:30 p.m. The motel also continued its program to encourage local law enforcement personnel to frequent the premises by offering a free snack tray and discount meals in the restaurant though it did not employ any as security guards.

At approximately 8:00 p.m. on February 27, the Crinkleys arrived at the Holiday Inn Concord. After spending a short time checking in, they parked their car in front of their room and began unloading their baggage. As James Crinkley was bringing in the last of their items, Sarah Crinkley, who was standing in the doorway to their room, noticed a man come around the corner of the motel and begin walking toward them. When the man reached the Crinkleys' room, he stopped and asked to speak with James Crinkley. Almost immediately, the man began trying to push the Crinkleys into their room. Despite James Crinkley's efforts to resist him, the man succeeded in getting the Crinkleys into their room. The man was armed with a gun, and once inside he beat James Crinkley, turned on the television and called for his accomplices. He was joined in the room by two men who again beat James Crinkley, bound and gagged him, and put a mattress on top of him. After going through the Crinkleys' possessions, the men approached Sarah Crinkley. They pushed her down and asked for her money and her engagement ring. When she told them that the ring would not come off, one of the men put a gun to her head and told her that if she did not take it off, he would "blow her brains out." She got the ring off and gave it to the men. They then bound and gagged her before fleeing. She was able to free herself after a short time. She removed the mattress and gag from her husband and called the front desk for help. The desk clerk notified the Cabarras County Sheriff's Office and a deputy arrived at the Crinkleys' room within minutes.

The Crinkleys were taken to an area hospital for emergency medical care. James Crinkley sustained multiple bruises to his head and upper body region, as well as a severely broken jaw. His broken jaw was wired, a condition which lasted approximately six weeks. Sarah Crinkley's subsequent condition was more complicated. Before the assault she was under a doctor's care for hypertension and obesity. In April of 1982 approximately fourteen months after the assault she suffered a heart attack. A balloon angioplasty was performed in an effort to clear the blockage in her arteries, but was not successful. After consulting with her doctors, she opted for heart by-pass surgery to treat her condition. In addition to her cardiac problems, friends and family noted that Sarah Crinkley's personality changed drastically after the assault. She became fearful, anxious and withdrawn. Her activities also were observed to be much more restricted. In early 1984, she began seeking a psychiatrist who diagnosed her as suffering from posttraumatic stress disorder and major affective disorder.

The Crinkleys brought suit against several defendants variously associated with the Holiday Inn Concord alleging, *inter alia,* that the defendants were negligent by providing them inadequate security and that such negligence was the proximate cause of their injuries. * * *

At trial, the Crinkleys relied primarily on the testimony of Brian McRorie to show that the assault was reasonably foreseeable. They introduced testimony from a security expert that the measures in effect at the Holiday Inn Concord were inadequate to deal with the potential threat. The main deficiencies identified were inadequate fencing around the perimeter of the property, and the lack of no trespassing signs and of any security patrols. Medical experts opined that both Sarah Crinkley's heart attack and her psychological problems were due to the stress she continued to experience in the wake of the assault.

Following the denial of motions for directed verdict, the jury returned verdicts in favor of the Crinkleys against all the defendants above identified, finding in special verdicts that the criminal acts were reasonably foreseeable by the motel owners and TRAVCO, that those defendants were negligent in providing inadequate security, and that such negligence caused the Crinkleys' injuries. Holiday Inns was found vicariously liable on the basis of apparent agency. The jury awarded Sarah Crinkley $400,000 and James Crinkley $100,000 in compensatory damages.

* * *

Defendants * * * contend that there was insufficient evidence to prove the necessary causal link between the assault and Sarah Crinkley's heart attack and psychological problems and her related medical expenses, so that these should not have been submitted to the jury as potentially compensable items of damage. * * *

We are satisfied that there was sufficient evidence of a causal link between the assault and Sarah Crinkley's heart attack and psychological condition to permit the jury to award damages related to those conditions.

* * * [N]umerous witnesses testified that Sarah Crinkley showed marked personality and emotional changes following the assault. Observations included notable anxiety, fearfulness, withdrawal, sadness, lack of activity, and an inability to work. This evidence is corroborative of the medical testimony that Sarah Crinkley was suffering from a significant amount of stress caused as a result of the assault.

The Crinkleys presented expert testimony that it was medically and scientifically plausible that significant stress could produce or accelerate atherosclerosis to the point of heart attack. Further, they removed the cause of Sarah Crinkley's own heart attack from the realm of conjecture by providing competent medical testimony from which the jury would conclude that the stress from the assault was the prime causal factor. They also produced expert testimony, that the assault produced severe stress in Sarah Crinkley.

We are also satisfied that the evidence was sufficient to connect the disputed medical expenses to the assault. As noted above, there was evidence that linked the assault to Sarah Crinkley's heart attack. The evidence also showed that the heart attack itself resulted from the occlusion of an artery in her heart and that the resulting added stress on her remaining "good" arteries necessitated invasive treatment. A balloon angioplasty was attempted as a means of opening the closed artery; however, the procedure was unsuccessful. The record indicates that after this unsuccessful treatment, by-pass surgery was recommended and ultimately performed. From this evidence alone, the jury could infer that all of Sarah Crinkley's heart-related medical procedures for which expenses were claimed were linked to the assault. The district court therefore properly submitted this damages issue to the jury.

* * *

■ WILKINSON, CIRCUIT JUDGE, concurring in part and dissenting in part:

Like the majority, I am saddened by the sequence of events that has befallen Sarah Crinkley. The assault suffered by the Crinkleys was absolutely dreadful. No one disputes that the circumstances are poignant, yet there remains the need to remember that wrenching facts may wrest a body of law from its moorings and foundations. That is what had happened to North Carolina tort law in this case.

The law of tort performs important functions: it has compensated the victims of wrongful acts and enhanced, through deterrence, or basic sense of safety. It cannot, however, provide an answer to every personal misfortune and it is not intended to replace the role of non-liability insurance, private pensions, public assistance, and the like in promoting the well being of our citizens.

* * *

Plaintiff is now to recover damages, not only for the trauma and injuries that she sustained in the assault, but also for a heart attack she suffered fourteen months later as well as for hospital and medical expenses incurred in treating her heart condition for a period extending up to five and one-half years after the assault. This is highly problematic. The evidence indicates that Sarah Crinkley was sixty-six years old at the time of the assault. She was overweight and had a history of arteriosclerosis, chest pains, and high blood pressure for which she had been under a physician's care since 1978. She was clearly exposed to alternate sources of stress with the closing of the family hardware store where she worked. Although North Carolina recognizes the "thin skull" rule, making tortfeasors liable for the "unusually extensive" damages resulting from their negligence to persons of "peculiar susceptibility," *see Lockwood v. McCaskill,* 262 N.C. 663, 138 S.E.2d 541, 546 (1964), the North Carolina Supreme Court has clearly articulated the limits of a tortfeasor's liability for injuries suffered by persons with such preexisting susceptibilities.

* * *

I understand and appreciate that the expansion of this field of law owes much to genuine concern for the plight of injured persons. It is no easy thing to draw lines in the face of visible personal misfortune. However, there are claims of justice on both sides of these hard cases which find expression in the limits of state law. With all respect for the sympathetic circumstances presented here, I would reverse and remand for a new trial on damages.

———————

1. In personal injury cases damages for mental distress are routinely allowed. Even if the plaintiff is unusually susceptible to suffering distress, the "thin-skulled plaintiff" rule allows recovery on the theory that the defendant takes the plaintiff as found. Such damages include any physical or psychological consequences of the distress even if any ordinary person would not have suffered the additional injuries. *See, e.g.,* Bartolone v. Jeckovich, 103 A.D.2d 632, 481 N.Y.S.2d 545 (1984) (back injuries in car accident aggravated a pre-existing paranoid schizophrenic condition). Is there any reason to distinguish physical injuries triggered by distress, as in the principal case, from profound injuries entirely psychological in nature?

2. Distinguish physical manifestations of distress and psychological effects from "mere" distress without such complications. In negligence law, many jurisdictions preclude recovery for distress without physical manifestations. The interpretation of "physical" often includes severe psychological conditions, however.

For example, in *Toney v. Chester County Hosp.*, 2008 Pa. Super. 268 961 A.2d 192 (2008), the plaintiff mother witnessed the birth of her son who was born with profound physical abnormalities. Several months before she gave birth to her son, the defendant doctor performed an ultrasound examination on the plaintiff and informed her that the baby was normal and healthy. Plaintiff sued the defendant doctor for medical malpractice and sought damages for her emotional distress upon witnessing her son's deformities. The Superior Court concluded that plaintiff's allegations of "severe shock, nervous shock, grief, rage, humiliation, emotional pain, mental anguish, emotional trauma, and emotional distress" and "continued nausea and headaches, insomnia, depression, nightmares, flashbacks, repeated hysterical attacks, stress, hysteria, nervousness, sleeplessness, nightmares and anxiety" combined with her allegations of psychological treatment and care satisfied the physical manifestation requirement.

California repudiated the physical consequences rule in *Molien v. Kaiser Foundation Hosp.*, 27 Cal.3d 916, 167 Cal.Rptr. 831, 616 P.2d 813 (1980). In this case the defendant negligently diagnosed the plaintiff's wife with syphilis and instructed her to notify her husband. The misdiagnosis caused the couple great distress and ultimately ended their marriage. The plaintiff recovered under a negligence theory even though he suffered no physical harm. *See also* St. Elizabeth Hospital v. Garrard, 730 S.W.2d 649 (Tex.1987); Rodrigues v. State, 52 Haw. 156, 472 P.2d 509 (1970).

3.   Intentional infliction of emotional distress claims are not subject to the same physical harm requirement or the zone of danger requirement. Instead, when defendants have acted recklessly or maliciously to inflict mental distress in outrageous and socially intolerable circumstances, plaintiffs may recover if they suffer "severe distress." Courts rely on the requirement that the defendant's conduct be extreme and outrageous to filter out trivial complaints and to assure the genuineness of the plaintiff's emotional distress. Some jurisdictions have imposed other limitations to filter out trivial or fabricated claims. For example, in some jurisdictions, if the defendant's conduct has not been extreme, a plaintiff may need to offer evidence of physical manifestations to demonstrate that the distress was severe. *See e.g.*, Harris v. Jones, 281 Md. 560, 380 A.2d 611 (1977). Other courts have required the plaintiff to prove her claim with clear and convincing evidence, *see e.g.* Supervalu, Inc. v. Johnson, 276 Va. 356, 666 S.E.2d 335 (2008) or adhered to the zone of danger requirement, *see e.g.*, Goodrich v. Long Island R.R. Co., 654 F.3d 190 (2d Cir. 2011).

Camper v. Minor

915 S.W.2d 437 (Tenn. 1996).

■ Drowota, Justice.

In this negligent infliction of emotional distress case, the plaintiff Bobby L. Camper, II, appeals from the Court of Appeals' judgment granting the defendants a summary judgment. * * *

On April 14, 1992, the plaintiff Camper was driving his cement truck along South Wilcox Drive, a four-lane highway in Kingsport, Tennessee. At the same time, Jennifer L. Taylor, a 16 year old driver of a car owned by Sharon Barnett, was proceeding on Reservoir Road, a two-lane road that intersects with South Wilcox Drive. As Camper approached the South Wilcox–Reservoir Road intersection, which is controlled by a stop sign, Ms. Taylor, who had been stopped at this intersection, suddenly pulled out in front of Camper. The vehicles collided, and Ms. Taylor was killed instantly. Camper exited his truck moments after the crash, walked around the front of his vehicle, and viewed Ms. Taylor's body in the wreckage from close range.

Mr. Camper subsequently brought an action against Daniel B. Minor, the administrator of Ms. Taylor's estate, and Sharon Barnett, seeking to recover for the emotional injuries he allegedly received as a result of viewing Ms. Taylor's body soon after the accident. In his complaint, Camper did not allege that he sustained any substantial physical injury in the accident; instead, he alleged that "as a result of this accident, the plaintiff suffers from personal injuries to his nerves and nervous system[.]"
* * *

In his affidavit, Mr. Camper stated "[t]hat as a result of the collision in which I was involved, I have sustained mental and emotional injuries resulting in loss of sleep, inability to function on a normal basis, outbursts of crying and depression. It has been necessary for me to be under the care and treatment of a psychiatrist and counselors and further that I am taking medication in order to help relieve me of my suffering." Camper testified in his deposition that he never feared for his own safety during the accident, and that his emotional injuries resulted solely from seeing Ms. Taylor's body in the car immediately after the accident.

About two weeks after the accident, Mr. Camper consulted a psychiatrist about his mental problems stemming from the accident. He went to the psychiatrist's office twice; but he stated that he quit going because he could not afford it and because the medication the psychiatrist prescribed left him unable to function. * * *

After the complaint was filed, the defendants filed a motion for summary judgment, arguing that damages for emotional injuries were not recoverable because Camper did not suffer any physical injury and because he did not, at the time of the accident, fear for his own safety. The defendants relied upon Shelton v. Russell Pipe and Foundry Co., 570 S.W.2d 861 (Tenn.1978) to support this argument.

The trial court denied the defendants' motion, finding that *Shelton*—a "zone of danger" case in which a father sued for emotional injuries after learning of his daughter's injury in an automobile accident in which the father was not involved—did not apply because "the plaintiff was personally involved in the automobile accident and suffered minor injuries." The defendants then sought permission for an interlocutory appeal * * *. The trial court granted the motion * * *.

The Court of Appeals reversed the judgment of the trial court. The intermediate court reasoned that because Camper's alleged emotional injuries occurred after the accident, when he saw Ms. Taylor's body in the wreckage, the plaintiff failed to provide evidence that he was in fear for his own safety—one of the Shelton elements for recovering for mental injuries. The Court also stated that the plaintiff failed to satisfy another requirement enunciated in *Shelton*—that the plaintiff have a "close relationship" with the deceased. In the instant case, the court said, there was no proof that Camper and Ms. Taylor had such a relationship. Because it determined that the plaintiff failed to satisfy the *Shelton* requirements for a prima facie case of negligent infliction of emotional distress, the Court granted the defendants' motion for summary judgment.

Camper then filed an application for permission to appeal pursuant to Rule 11, Tenn.R.App.P. We granted the application to address these important issues of Tennessee tort law.

The first issue for our consideration concerns the viability of Camper's claim against both defendants for his emotional damages. Because the law of negligent infliction of emotional distress is one of the most disparate and confusing areas of tort law, we believe that it would be useful to briefly survey the approaches used by other jurisdictions before turning to a discussion of the germane Tennessee cases.

Negligent Infliction of Emotional Distress Law in General

Any survey of the law in this area must begin with a clear and frank recognition that the law of negligent infliction of emotional distress, however it is formulated in a specific jurisdiction, is fundamentally concerned with striking a balance between two opposing objectives: first, promoting the underlying purpose of negligence law—that of compensating persons who have sustained emotional injuries attributable to the wrongful conduct of others; and second, avoiding the trivial or fraudulent claims that have been thought to be inevitable due to the subjective nature of these injuries. The tension produced by this ongoing attempt to winnow out invalid claims at the summary judgment level has caused inconsistency and incoherence in the law; indeed, as the Washington Supreme Court aptly stated some years ago, "any attempt at a consistent exegesis of the authorities is likely to break down in embarrassed perplexity." Hunsley v. Giard, 87 Wash.2d 424, 553 P.2d 1096, 1098 (1976).

The first attempt by the courts to mediate between these competing concerns took the form of the classic "physical impact" rule. Under this rule, which was formulated in Britain in the mid to late nineteenth century, [citation], a plaintiff may not recover for emotional injuries unless he or she suffered an actual physical impact or contemporaneous physical injury caused by the defendant's negligence. In other words, if the defendant's negligence causes both a physical impact or injury *and* emotional distress then the plaintiff may recover damages not only for the physical injury but also for the emotional distress. * * * The physical impact rule was also adopted in a number of other jurisdictions in the late nineteenth and early twentieth centuries. [Citation.]

Three principal reasons were usually advanced by courts in support of the classic physical impact rule:

The first deals with medical science's difficulty in proving causation between the claimed damages and the alleged fright. The second involves the fear of fraudulent or exaggerated claims. Finally, there is the concern that such a rule [allowing recovery without a physical injury] will precipitate a veritable flood of litigation.

[Citation.]

However, as several courts and commentators have pointed out, the reasoning advanced in support of the physical impact rule is seriously flawed. First, the fact that a case may be difficult to prove does not in itself justify a prohibition on the cause of action; instead, this difficulty may be addressed in rules concerning the development of the evidence. Second, because imaginary and fraudulent claims may be just as likely in cases in which an actual physical injury occurred, there is no reason to bar this cause of action simply out a fear of such lawsuits; the trial courts, through the rules of evidence and the adversarial system, can guard against these types of cases. Finally, there are at least two reasons that the fear of a flood of litigation should not be used to completely bar a claim for negligent infliction of emotional distress: (1) courts are charged with the duty of providing a remedy to those who are injured; (2) states which have rules other than the physical impact rule have apparently not suffered any such flood of litigation.

Despite this widespread criticism of the physical impact rule, and the fact that it was been abandoned by many courts, [citations]. However, in some of these states the rigidity of the impact rule has been lessened due to the way in which it has been applied. For instance, even though a physical impact is required before a plaintiff may recover damages for emotional distress, the courts have carved out explicit exceptions to this requirement. [Citations.] The fact that courts have repeatedly found it necessary to craft formal exceptions to the rule suggests that the physical impact rule provides an arbitrary and inadequate means of reconciling the competing concerns of the law.

Another way in which the potential harshness of the physical impact rule has been ameliorated is that courts have permitted recovery for emotional injuries in cases in which the actual physical injury or impact sustained by the plaintiff was *de minimis*. [Citation.]

An approach that is closely related to, but distinct from, the classic physical impact rule may be characterized as the "physical manifestation" rule. Like the impact rule, the physical manifestation rule requires that the plaintiff sustain a "physical injury," but the requisite injury may either be shown by proof of a contemporaneous physical injury *or* by proof of physical symptoms or manifestations of the emotional injury. This approach is utilized in several jurisdictions. [Citations.] This broader approach is based upon the recognition that the physical impact rule unfairly and arbitrarily excludes plaintiffs with meritorious claims of serious emotional injury. It is thus an attempt to strike a balance between the realization that serious emotional distress can result even in the absence of a physical injury with the longstanding concerns over trivial or fraudulent claims. However, like the physical impact rule, courts have found it necessary to both make exceptions to the physical manifestation rule and to find "physical injury" in cases in which the physical component of the injury was *de minimis*. For this reason, the physical manifestation rule, like the physical impact rule, is open to criticism as an arbitrary and underinclusive approach.

Other jurisdictions do not require the plaintiff to present evidence of a physical injury at all; rather, these jurisdictions use a variety of approaches to separate the meritorious claims from the nonmeritorious ones. One such approach is the "zone of danger" doctrine. Under this doctrine, a plaintiff may recover for emotional distress if, as a result of the defendant's negligence, the plaintiff either suffered a physical injury or was placed in immediate danger of physical harm and contemporaneously feared for his or her own safety. [Citations.]

The zone of danger test is somewhat broader than either of the physical injury approaches discussed above. However, this test, which arose primarily from "near-miss" automobile accident cases, is based upon a questionable premise: that emotional injuries result *only* from fear of physical harm. While, as a practical matter, many negligent infliction of emotional distress cases may well involve either physical injuries or fear of physical harm, there are certainly cases in which neither is implicated. Examples of such cases are the failure to timely deliver telegrams concerning the imminent death or serious illness of a loved one, mishandling the corpse of a loved one, or the unauthorized dissemination of private information. In such cases, applying the zone of danger doctrine is illogical, and courts utilizing the doctrine have been compelled to create exceptions to fit these factual situations.

Another approach that does not necessarily require any evidence of a physical injury is the "foreseeability" approach. Under this approach, the key inquiry is whether it was reasonably foreseeable that the defendant's specific course of conduct would cause the plaintiff serious emotional distress. The foreseeability approach, which was first utilized by the California Supreme Court in Dillon v. Legg, 68 Cal.2d 728, 69 Cal.Rptr. 72, 441 P.2d 912 (1968), is applied in a few jurisdictions. [Citations.] Although this approach has the merit of recognizing that emotional injuries may occur without a concomitant physical injury, and is flexible enough to cover factual situations for which the zone of danger test is clearly inapposite, it provides little, if any, concrete guidelines for trial courts and juries to use in deciding how each case should be resolved.

A final approach that does not require any evidence of a physical injury might be characterized as the "general negligence approach." Courts using this approach have rejected the above-mentioned specially crafted rules and have concluded that negligent infliction of emotional distress cases should be analyzed no differently than any other negligence case; and that the proper application of the familiar elements of negligence is the preferable way in which to sort out the genuine from the false, the serious from the trivial. [Citations.]

Moreover, because of their concerns over the possibility of trivial or fraudulent lawsuits, some courts following this approach have imposed a requirement that in order to recover, the plaintiff's emotional injury must have been "serious" or "severe." [Citations.] Thus, concerns about possible frivolous or fraudulent lawsuits are dealt with by strengthening the "injury" or "loss" element of the basic negligence framework.

Tennessee Negligent Infliction of Emotional Distress Law

With these approaches and their respective strengths and weaknesses in mind, we now turn to the Tennessee cases in this area. The early Tennessee cases can clearly be placed in the "physical manifestation" category. * * *

* * * However, as the preceding general overview of the law would lead one to expect, the cases have been far from consistent. * * *

As is the case with the general overview presented above, Tennessee courts have continually found it necessary to deviate from the "physical manifestation" rule by either formally creating exceptions to the rule or by applying the rule in a nonrigorous fashion. This practice of creating *ad hoc* exceptions has made our law of negligent infliction of emotional distress confusing and unpredictable; indeed, the practice appears to have, as the plaintiff here argues, "robbed the law of logic, consistency and fairness."

Although there is some truth to this charge, the Tennessee cases in this area do contain a common thread: the courts' desire to separate, at the prima facie stage and in a meaningful and rational manner, the meritorious cases from the nonmeritorious ones. had sustained a physical injury before being allowed to recover for emotional and mental damages. * * *

Although our seemingly disparate cases in this area are thus reconcilable on a functional level, we nevertheless agree with the plaintiff here and with many other jurisdictions that the time has come to abandon the rigid and overly formulaic "physical manifestation" or "injury" rule. This rule has proved to be inflexible and inadequate in practice; and, as noted in the preceding section, it completely ignores the fact that some valid emotional injuries simply may not be accompanied by a contemporaneous physical injury or have physical consequences. Therefore, in accordance with our statement in Carroll that "[we have] realized that in some situations, whether the plaintiff has incurred a literal physical injury has little to do with whether the emotional damages complained of are reasonable," id. at

594, we conclude that the rule shall no longer be used to test the validity of a prima facie case of negligent infliction of emotional distress.

This negative conclusion logically raises its positive counterpart: what is required to make out a prima facie case? After considering the strengths and weaknesses of the options used in other jurisdictions, we conclude that these cases should be analyzed under the general negligence approach discussed above. In other words, the plaintiff must present material evidence as to each of the five elements of general negligence—duty, breach of duty, injury or loss, causation in fact, and proximate, or legal, cause,[citation]—in order to avoid summary judgment. Furthermore, we agree that in order to guard against trivial or fraudulent actions, the law ought to provide a recovery only for "serious" or "severe" emotional injury. [Citations.] A "serious" or "severe" emotional injury occurs "where a reasonable person, normally constituted, would be unable to adequately cope with the mental stress engendered by the circumstances of the case." [Citations.] Finally, we conclude that the claimed injury or impairment must be supported by expert medical or scientific proof. [Citation.]

Having so concluded, we have no alternative but to remand this case for further proceedings consistent with the approach that we adopt today. A remand is necessary because in the trial court the defendants simply argued that they were entitled to a summary judgment because (1) the plaintiff had received no physical injury—a requirement under the prior law; and (2) that the plaintiff had not been in fear for his own safety, as required by *Shelton*. Because the general negligence approach was not controlling at the time the defendants submitted their summary judgment motion, they clearly have failed to prove that no genuine issue of material fact exists as to those elements of negligent infliction of emotional distress that we adopt herein, and that they are entitled to a judgment as matter of law. [Citation.] Because the defendants failed to carry their initial burden pursuant to Rule 56, Tenn.R.Civ.P., we cannot approve of the summary judgment granted by the Court of Appeals.

---

1.   Early English and American law rejected entirely the idea of emotional distress recoveries except as parasitic damages. *See* Magruder, Mental and Emotional Distress in the Law of Torts, 49 Harv.L.Rev. 1033 (1936); Lynch v. Knight, 9 H.L.Cas. 577 (1861) (the law cannot value mental pain and anxiety and does not pretend to redress it when standing alone).

2.   The general rule continues to disallow claims for distress alone, with a few exceptions. Intentional infliction of emotional distress and negligent infliction of emotional distress are both torts allowing recovery for distress without other harm. As the principal case illustrates, courts have struggled to define the appropriate limitations on recovery for negligently inflicted emotional distress. While the court in the principal case adopted a foreseeability standard, other courts continue to adhere to other

limitations. Some courts require that the plaintiff be within the "zone of danger" while others require that the plaintiff demonstrate physical manifestations of emotional distress. Some jurisdictions require that the plaintiff be within the zone of danger and demonstrate physical manifestations of emotional distress. *See* John J. Kircher, The Four Faces of Tort Law: Liability for Emotional Harm, 90 Marq. L. Rev. 789 (2007) (collecting cases).

3. What reasons are most persuasive for denying distress damages in the absence of other harm? Consider:

(a) The subjective nature of the injury makes measurement too speculative;

(b) Allowing such actions would open the courts to a "floodgate" of litigation;

(c) The causal connection between distress and other injuries is too tenuous;

(d) The inherent difficulties of proof in such cases requires an excessive reliance on plaintiffs' testimony;

(e) Such claims are simply too speculative.

4. In subsequent cases, the Tennessee Supreme Court has further refined its foreseeability standard. The court explained that the "zone of danger" test was a relevant consideration in determining whether the plaintiff's emotional distress was foreseeable. In addition to the plaintiff's proximity to the accident, the Tennessee Supreme Court also instructed courts to consider the severity of injury to the victim of the accident and the relationship between the victim of the accident and the plaintiff suffering the emotional distress. Ramsey v. Beavers, 931 S.W.2d 527 (Tenn. 1996). In *Eskin v. Bartee*, 262 S.W.3d 727 (Tenn. 2008), the Tennessee Supreme Court emphasized that these considerations were factors to weigh rather than independent requirements that must be satisfied in all cases. In *Eskin*, the court held that a mother and brother of a child who was severely injured in a car accident could recover for emotional distress even though neither the mother or the brother were present at the time of the accident but instead arrived at the scene of the accident shortly after it occurred.

Norfolk & Western Railway Co. v. Ayers

538 U.S. 135, 123 S.Ct. 1210, 155 L.Ed.2d 261 (2003).

■ JUSTICE GINSBURG delivered the opinion of the Court.

The Federal Employers' Liability Act (FELA or Act), 35 Stat. 65, as amended, 45 U.S.C. §§ 51–60, makes common carrier railroads liable in damages to employees who suffer work-related injuries caused "in whole or in part" by the railroad's negligence. This case, brought against Norfolk & Western Railway Company (Norfolk) by six former employees now suffering from asbestosis (asbestosis claimants), presents two issues involving the

FELA's application. The first issue concerns the damages recoverable by a railroad worker who suffers from the disease asbestosis: When the cause of that disease, in whole or in part, was exposure to asbestos while on the job, may the worker's recovery for his asbestosis-related "pain and suffering" include damages for fear of developing cancer?

* * *.

The asbestosis claimants (plaintiffs below, respondents here) brought this FELA action against their former employer, Norfolk, in the Circuit Court of Kanawha County, West Virginia. Norfolk, they alleged, negligently exposed them to asbestos, which caused them to contract the occupational disease asbestosis. [Citation.] As an element of their occupational disease damages, the asbestosis claimants sought recovery for mental anguish based on their fear of developing cancer. [Citation.]

Before trial, Norfolk moved to exclude all evidence referring to cancer as irrelevant and prejudicial. [Citation.] The trial court denied the motion, [citation], and the asbestosis claimants placed before the jury extensive evidence relating to cancer, including expert testimony that asbestosis sufferers with smoking histories have a significantly increased risk of developing lung cancer. (Of the six asbestosis claimants, five had smoking histories, and two persisted in smoking even after their asbestosis diagnosis. [Citation.] Asbestosis sufferers—workers whose exposure to asbestos has manifested itself in a chronic disease—the jury also heard, have a significant (one in ten) risk of dying of mesothelioma, a fatal cancer of the lining of the lung or abdominal cavity). [Citation.]

Concluding that no asbestosis claimant had shown he was reasonably certain to develop cancer, the trial court instructed the jury that damages could not be awarded to any claimant "for cancer or any increased risk of cancer." [Citation.] The testimony about cancer, the court explained, was relevant "only to judge the genuineness of plaintiffs' claims of fear of developing cancer." [Citation.] On that score, the court charged:

> "[A]ny plaintiff who has demonstrated that he has developed a reasonable fear of cancer that is related to proven physical injury from asbestos is entitled to be compensated for that fear as a part of the damages you may award for pain and suffering." [Citation.]

In so instructing the jury, the court rejected Norfolk's proposed instruction, which would have ruled out damages for an asbestosis sufferer's fear of cancer, unless the claimant proved both "an actual likelihood of developing cancer" and "physical manifestations" of the alleged fear. * * *

The jury returned total damages awards for each asbestosis claimant, ranging from $770,000 to $1.2 million. [Citation.] After reduction for three claimants' comparative negligence from smoking and for settlements with non-FELA entities, the final judgments amounted to approximately $4.9 million [Citation.] * * *

We turn first to the question whether the trial judge correctly stated the law when he charged the jury that an asbestosis claimant, upon demonstrating a reasonable fear of cancer stemming from his present disease, could recover for that fear as part of asbestosis-related pain and suffering damages. [Citation.] In answering this question, we follow the path marked by the Court's decisions in Consolidated Rail Corporation v. Gottshall, 512 U.S. 532, 114 S.Ct. 2396, 129 L.Ed.2d 427 (1994), and Metro–North Commuter R. Co. v. Buckley, 521 U.S. 424, 117 S.Ct. 2113, 138 L.Ed.2d 560 (1997).

The FELA plaintiff in *Gottshall* alleged that he witnessed the death of a co-worker while on the job, and that the episode caused him severe emotional distress. [Citation.] He sought to recover damages from his employer, Conrail, "for mental or emotional harm . . . not directly brought about by a physical injury." [Citation.]

Reversing the Court of Appeals' judgment in favor of the plaintiff, this Court stated that uncabined recognition of claims for negligently inflicted emotional distress would "hol[d] out the very real possibility of nearly infinite and unpredictable liability for defendants." [Citation.] Of the "limiting tests . . . developed in the common law," [citation], the Court selected the zone-of-danger test to delineate "the proper scope of an employer's duty under [the] FELA to avoid subjecting its employees to negligently inflicted emotional injury," [Citation.] That test confines recovery for stand-alone emotional distress claims to plaintiffs who: (1) "sustain a physical impact as a result of a defendant's negligent conduct;" or (2) "are placed in immediate risk of physical harm by that conduct"—that is, those who escaped instant physical harm, but were "within the zone of danger of physical impact." * * *

In *Metro–North*, the Court applied the zone-of-danger test to a claim for damages under the FELA, one element of which was fear of cancer stemming from exposure to asbestos. The plaintiff in *Metro–North* had been intensively exposed to asbestos while working as a pipefitter for Metro–North in New York City's Grand Central Terminal. At the time of his lawsuit, however, he had a clean bill of health. The Court rejected his entire claim for relief. Exposure alone, the Court held, is insufficient to show "physical impact" under the zone-of-danger test. [Citation.] "[A] simple (though extensive) contact with a carcinogenic substance," the Court observed, "does not . . . offer much help in separating valid from invalid emotional distress claims." [Citation.] The evaluation problem would be formidable, the Court explained, "because contacts, even extensive contacts, with serious carcinogens are common." [Citation.] "The large number of those exposed and the uncertainties that may surround recovery," the Court added, "suggest what Gottshall called the problem of 'unlimited and unpredictable liability.' " [Citation.]

As in *Gottshall*, the Court distinguished stand-alone distress claims from prayers for damages for emotional pain and suffering tied to a physical injury: "Common-law courts," the Court recognized, "*do* permit a plaintiff *who suffers from a disease* to recover for related negligently caused emotional distress. . . ." [Citation.] When a plaintiff suffers from a disease, the Court noted, common-law courts have made "a special effort" to value related emotional distress, "perhaps from a desire to make a physically injured victim whole or because the parties are likely to be in court in any event." [Citation.]

In sum, our decisions in *Gottshall* and *Metro–North* describe two categories: Stand-alone emotional distress claims not provoked by any physical injury, for which recovery is sharply circumscribed by the zone-of-danger test; and emotional distress claims brought on by a physical injury, for which pain and suffering recovery is permitted. Norfolk, whose position the principal dissent embraces [citation.], would have us ally this case with those in the stand-alone emotional distress category, [citation.]; the asbestosis claimants urge its placement in the emotional distress brought on by a physical injury (or disease) category, [citation].

Relevant to this characterization question, the parties agree that asbestosis is a cognizable injury under the FELA. Norfolk does not dispute that the claimants suffer from asbestosis [Citation.], or that asbestosis can be "a clinically serious, often disabling, and progressive disease,". [Citation.] As *Metro–North* plainly indicates, pain and suffering damages may include compensation for fear of cancer when that fear "accompanies a physical injury." [Citation.]. Norfolk, therefore, cannot plausibly maintain that the claimants here, like the plaintiff in *Metro–North*, "are disease and symptom free." [Citation.] The plaintiffs in *Gottshall* and *Metro–North* grounded their suits on claims of negligent infliction of emotional distress. The claimants before us, in contrast, complain of a negligently inflicted physical injury (asbestosis) and attendant pain and suffering.

Unlike stand-alone claims for negligently inflicted emotional distress, claims for pain and suffering associated with, or "parasitic" on, a physical injury are traditionally compensable. The Restatement (Second) of Torts § 456 (1963–1964) (hereinafter Restatement) states the general rule:

> "If the actor's negligent conduct has so caused *any* bodily harm to another as to make him liable for it, the actor is also subject to liability for
>
> "(a) fright, shock, *or other emotional disturbance* resulting from the bodily harm or from the conduct which causes it...." (Emphases added.)

A plaintiff suffering bodily harm need not allege physical manifestations of her mental anguish. *Id.,* Comment *c.* "The plaintiff must of course present evidence that she has suffered, but otherwise her emotional distress claims, in whatever form, are fully recoverable." D. Dobbs, Law of Torts 822 (2000).

By 1908, when the FELA was enacted, the common law had evolved to encompass apprehension of future harm as a component of pain and suffering. The future harm, genuinely feared, need not be more likely than not to materialize. [Citation.] Physically injured plaintiffs, it is now recognized, may recover for "reasonable fears" of a future disease. Dobbs, *supra,* at 844. As a classic example, plaintiffs bitten by dogs succeeded in gaining recovery, not only for the pain of the wound, but also for their fear that the bite would someday result in rabies or tetanus. The wound might heal, but "[t]he ghost of hydrophobia is raised, not to down during the life-time of the victim." [Citation.]

In the course of the 20th century, courts sustained a variety of other "fear-of" claims. Among them have been claims for fear of cancer. * * * [Citation.]

Many courts in recent years have considered the question presented here—whether an asbestosis claimant may be compensated for fear of cancer. Of decisions that address the issue, a clear majority sustain recovery.[Citations.]

Arguing against the trend in the lower courts, Norfolk and its supporting *amici* assert that the asbestosis claimants' alleged cancer fears are too remote from asbestosis to warrant inclusion in their pain and suffering awards. In support of this contention, the United States, one of Norfolk's *amici*, refers to the "separate disease rule," under which most courts have held that the statute of limitations runs separately for each asbestos-related disease. [Citation.] Because the asbestosis claimants may bring a second action if cancer develops, Norfolk and the Government argue, cancer-related damages are unwarranted in their asbestosis suit. [Citation.] The question, as the Government frames it, is not *whether* the asbestosis claimants can recover for fear of cancer, but *when*. * * *

But the asbestosis claimants did not seek, and the trial court did not allow, discrete damages for their *increased risk* of future cancer. [Citations.] Instead, the claimants sought damages for their *current* injury, which, they allege, encompasses a *present fear* that the toxic exposure causative of asbestosis may later result in cancer. * * *

There is an undisputed relationship between exposure to asbestos sufficient to cause asbestosis, and asbestos-related cancer. Norfolk's own expert acknowledged that asbestosis puts a worker in a heightened risk category for asbestos-related lung cancer. * * *

Norfolk understandably underscores a point central to the Court's decision in Metro–North. [Citation.] The Court's opinion in Metro–North stressed that holding employers liable to workers merely exposed to asbestos would risk "unlimited and unpredictable liability." [Citation.] But as earlier observed, [citation], Metro–North sharply distinguished exposure-only "plaintiffs from plaintiffs who suffer from a disease," and stated, unambiguously, that "[t]he common law permits emotional distress recovery for [the latter] category." [Citation.] * * *

Norfolk presented the question "[w]hether a plaintiff who has asbestosis but not cancer can recover damages for fear of cancer under the [FELA] without proof of physical manifestations of the claimed emotional distress." [Citation.] Our answer is yes, with an important reservation. We affirm only the qualification of an asbestosis sufferer to seek compensation for fear of cancer as an element of his asbestosis-related pain and suffering damages. It is incumbent upon such a complainant, however, to prove that his alleged fear is genuine and serious. [Citations.] In this case, proof directed to that matter was notably thin, and might well have succumbed to a straightforward sufficiency-of-the-evidence objection, had Norfolk so targeted its attack.

* * *

The "elephantine mass of asbestos cases" lodged in state and federal courts, we again recognize, "defies customary judicial administration and calls for national legislation." [Citations.] Courts, however, must resist pleas of the kind Norfolk has made, essentially to reconfigure established liability rules because they do not serve to abate today's asbestos litigation crisis. * * *

Affirmed.

■ JUSTICE KENNEDY, with whom THE CHIEF JUSTICE%, JUSTICE O'CONNOR, and JUSTICE BREYER join, concurring in part and dissenting in part.

* * * The Court allows compensation for fear of cancer to those who manifest symptoms of some other disease, not itself causative of cancer, though stemming from asbestos exposure. The Court's precedents interpreting FELA neither compel nor justify this result. The Court's ruling is not based upon a sound application of the common-law principles that should inform our decisions implementing FELA. On the contrary, those principles call for a different rule, one which does not yield such aberrant results in asbestos exposure cases. These reasons require my respectful dissent.

It is common ground that the purpose of FELA is to provide compensation for employees protected under the Act. *Ante,* at 1216–1217. The Court's decision is a serious threat to that objective. Although a ruling that allows compensation for fear of a disease might appear on the surface to be solicitous of employees and thus consistent with the goals of FELA, the realities of asbestos litigation should instruct the Court otherwise.

Consider the consequences of allowing compensation for fear of cancer in the cases now before the Court. The respondents are between 60 and 77 years old. All except one have a long history of tobacco use, and three have smoked for more than 50 years. They suffer from shortness of breath, but only one testified that it affects his daily activities. As for emotional injury, one of the respondents complained that his shortness of breath caused him to become depressed; the others stated, in response to questions from their attorneys, that they have some "concern" about their health and about cancer. For this, the jury awarded each respondent between $770,640 and $1,230,806 in damages, reduced by the trial court to between $523,605 and $1,204,093 to account for the comparative negligence of the respondents' cigarette use.

Contrast this recovery with the prospects of an employee who does not yet have asbestosis but who in fact will develop asbestos-related cancer. Cancers caused by asbestos have long periods of latency. Their symptoms do not become manifest for decades after exposure. [Citations.] These cancers inflict excruciating pain and distress-pain more severe than that associated with asbestosis, distress more harrowing than the fear of developing a future illness.

* * *

Asbestos litigation has driven 57 companies, which employed hundreds of thousands of people, into bankruptcy, including 26 companies that have become insolvent since January 1, 2000. [Citation.] With each bankruptcy the remaining defendants come under greater financial strain, [citations] and the funds available for compensation become closer to exhaustion, [citation].

In this particular universe of asbestos litigation, with its fast diminishing resources, the Court's wooden determination to allow recovery for fear of future illness is antithetical to FELA's goals of ensuring compensation for injuries. [Citations.] As a consequence of the majority's decision, it is more likely that those with the worst injuries from exposure to asbestos will find they are without remedy because those with lesser, and even problematic, injuries will have exhausted the resources for payment. Today's decision is not employee protecting; it is employee threatening.

* * *

I disagree with the Court's conclusion that damages for fear of cancer may be recovered as part of the pain and suffering caused by asbestosis. *Ante,* at 1218. The majority observes that a person who suffers from "a disease" may recover for all "related" emotional distress. [Citations.] While that may be true as a general matter, it begs the question: What relationship between a disease and associated emotional distress should entitle a person to compensation for the distress as pain and suffering?

* * * I do not think the brooding, contemplative fear the respondents allege can be called a direct result of their asbestosis. Unlike shortness of breath or other discomfort asbestosis may cause, their fear does not arise from the presence of disease in their lungs. Instead, the respondents' fear is the product of learning from a doctor about their asbestosis, receiving information (perhaps at a much later time) about the conditions that correlate with this disease, and then contemplating how these possible conditions might affect their lives.

The majority nevertheless would permit recovery because "[t]here is an undisputed relationship between exposure to asbestos sufficient to cause asbestosis, and asbestos-related cancer." *Ante,* at 1222. To state that some relationship exists without examining whether the relationship is enough to support recovery, however, ignores the central issue in this case. There is a fundamental premise in this case-conceded, as I understand it, by all parties—and it is this: There is no demonstrated causal link between asbestosis and cancer. [Citation.] The incidence of asbestosis correlates with the less-frequent incidence of cancer among exposed workers, [citation,] but this does not suffice. Correlation is not causation. Absent causation, it is difficult to conceive why asbestosis is any more than marginally more suitable a predicate for recovering for fear of cancer than the fact of mere exposure. This correlation the Court relies upon does not establish a direct link between asbestosis and asbestos-related cancer, and it does not suffice under common-law precedents as a predicate condition for recovery of damages based upon fear.

* * * [I]t is important to keep in mind the nature of the Court's responsibility under FELA. The implementation of the Act is a matter of federal common law, [citation] and it is for the Court to develop and administer a fair and workable rule of decision, [citations]. State-court precedent is not dispositive. [Citation.] Instead, the Court is bound only by the terms of FELA and its own precedent giving meaning to the Act. Within those constraints, the Court must endeavor to arrive at the correct rule—a rule that is just and practical—rather than the majority rule or the rule of the Restatement.

* * *

It is beyond the ability of juries to derive from statistics like these a fair estimate of the danger caused by negligent exposure to asbestos. [Citation.] For this reason, the trial judge was correct to instruct the jury that they could not award the respondents any damages for cancer or for an increased risk of cancer. In disallowing recovery for risk but allowing recovery for fear based on that risk, however, the trial judge attempted to avoid speculation at the outset but succumbed to added speculation in the end. If instructing a jury to calculate an increased risk of cancer invites speculation, then asking the jury to infer from its estimate a rough sense of the fear based on the risk invites speculation compounded.

The damages the jury awarded in this case indicate the legitimacy of these concerns. As described above, the respondents received damages of between $500,000 and $1.2 million despite having complained only that they suffered shortness of breath and experienced varying degrees of concern about cancer. * * *

The Court's response to the possibility of speculative awards is instead to adopt common-law rules restricting the classes of plaintiffs eligible to seek recovery and the types of emotional distress for which recovery is available. See ibid.; see also Metro–North, 521 U.S., at 436, 117 S.Ct. 2113. This is not to say that allegations of emotional distress need not be genuine and serious in order to warrant compensation, but review for genuineness alone does little or nothing to prevent capricious outcomes. Instead, the responsibility of today's Court is not to review whether an individual claim alleging fear of cancer is genuine and severe, but to adopt a rule that reconciles the need to provide compensation for deserving claimants with the concerns that speculative damages awards will exhaust the resources available for recovery.

* * *

■ JUSTICE BREYER, concurring in part and dissenting in part.

* * * I would accept the majority's limitations on recovery [citation], while adding further restrictions to rule out recovery for fear of disease

when the following conditions are met: (1) actual development of the disease can neither be expected nor ruled out for many years; (2) fear of the disease is separately compensable if the disease occurs; *and* (3) fear of the disease is based upon risks not significantly different in kind from the background risks that all individuals face. Where these conditions hold, I believe the law generally rules out recovery for fear of cancer. This is not to say that fear of cancer is never reimbursable. The conditions above may not hold. Even when they do, I would, consistent with the sense of the common law, permit recovery where the fear of cancer is unusually severe—where it significantly and detrimentally affects the plaintiff's ability to carry on with everyday life and work. [Citation.] However, because I believe that the above limitations create a rule more restrictive than the jury charge here, *ante,* at 1216 (majority opinion), and, indeed, would bar recovery as a matter of law in this case, I too respectfully dissent[.] * * *

1. As the principal case notes, the Court has adopted the zone of danger test for recovery of emotional distress damages under FELA. Thus, plaintiffs can recover damages for emotional distress only if they suffer physical injury or are placed in the immediate risk of physical harm by the employer's conduct. Consolidated Rail Corp. v. Gottshall, 512 U.S. 532, 114 S.Ct. 2396, 129 L.Ed.2d 427 (1994). In *Metro–North Commuter R. Co. v. Buckley,* 521 U.S. 424, 117 S.Ct. 2113, 138 L.Ed.2d 560 (1997), the Court denied recovery for fear of cancer to a railroad worker who had been exposed to asbestos during the course of his employment. Unlike the plaintiffs in the principal case, the plaintiff in *Metro–North* was not suffering from any asbestos-related illnesses at the time he brought suit. The Court concluded that exposure to asbestos itself did not constitute a sufficient physical impact to satisfy the zone of danger test.

2. Both the majority and the dissent suggest that the award of damages may have been excessive. Damages for emotional distress, like damages for non-economic damages in personal injury cases, are subject to judicial review for excessiveness. What factors should guide a court in a case like *Ayers* in determining whether the amount of damages for fear of cancer is excessive?

3. Note that the Supreme Court allows recovery of damages for the fear of developing cancer even though the plaintiffs cannot establish that they are more likely to develop cancer than not and, hence, cannot recover damages related to any treatment for cancer or any pain and suffering associated with developing cancer. Because they cannot prove that they are more likely to develop cancer than not with reasonable certainty, the law regards damages related to the cancer itself as speculative. How likely is it that a jury will be able to draw such precise distinctions in awarding damages? At least one court has held that plaintiffs exposed to toxic substances cannot recover damages for the fear of cancer unless the plaintiffs establish by reliable medical or scientific opinion that they are

more likely to develop cancer than not as a result of their exposure to the toxic substance. Potter v. Firestone Tire and Rubber Co., 6 Cal.4th 965, 863 P.2d 795, 25 Cal. Rprt. 2d 550 (1993).

4.   Distinguish damages for fear of cancer from damages for medical monitoring. Damages for medical monitoring compensate a plaintiff who has been exposed to a toxic substance for the cost of future periodic medical examinations to facilitate early detection and treatment of diseases caused by exposure to toxic substances. Many jurisdictions permit recovery of medical monitoring damages. As with emotional distress damages, courts have imposed differing limitations. Some require plaintiffs to prove present physical injury while others do not. Jurisdictions typically require plaintiffs to show exposure to a harmful substance as a result of the defendant's actions; a significantly increased risk of developing latent disease as a result of the exposure; that diagnostic tests capable of detecting the disease exist; that the increased risk of disease due to exposure makes the diagnostic tests reasonably necessary; and that early detection can improve treatment. Manual for Complex Litigation § 22.74 (4th ed. 2004).

Rubin v. Matthews International Corp.

503 A.2d 694 (Me.1986).

■ Scolnik, Justice.

* * * The plaintiff sought to recover damages for the emotional or mental distress she claims to have suffered as the result of the defendant's failure to make timely delivery of a memorial stone. Her complaint asserts four claims: breach of contract, negligence, negligent infliction of mental distress and intentional infliction of mental distress. On the defendant's motion, the Superior Court dismissed Rubin's complaint for failure to state a claim upon which relief could be granted. We vacate only the court's dismissal of that portion of the complaint that alleges the intentional infliction of mental distress.

In determining whether the lower court erred in granting the defendant's motion to dismiss, we consider all well-pleaded material allegations of the complaint as admitted. [Citations.] Those allegations reveal that on February 2, 1984, Donna L. Rubin placed an order with the Memorial Division of Matthews for the design and provision of a memorial stone for her mother's grave. Matthews was notified that the stone was to be provided for an unveiling ceremony scheduled to occur on May 5, 1984. Representatives of Matthews were aware of the religious significance of the event and agreed to have the memorial stone delivered prior to the time for the unveiling. They repeatedly represented in the weeks prior to May 5, 1984, that the memorial stone had been shipped and would be delivered on time to Rubin through Brooklawn Memorial Park in Portland. Matthews was further aware that the delivery of the memorial stone would take at least one week. The stone was in fact not shipped until April 30, 1984, just five days before the scheduled date of the ceremony, and did not arrive on time.

The first issue presented by this appeal is whether a cause of action exists for the recovery of damages for mental or emotional distress suffered solely as the result of a breach of contract. In a breach of contract action, those damages that were "reasonably within the contemplation of the contracting parties when the agreement was made and which would naturally flow from a breach thereof" may be recovered. [Citations.] As a general rule, courts in other jurisdictions have denied recovery for mental or emotional distress suffered as a result of breach of contract unaccompanied by physical injury. [Citations.] On the facts of this case, we decline to adopt a broad exception, as urged by the plaintiff, to the general rule precluding damages for mental and emotional distress in a contract case. We also do not find that the untimely delivery of a memorial stone falls within the existing narrow exceptions to the general rule.

The judicial reluctance to award damages for emotional distress in contract actions is reflected in *Restatement (Second) of Contracts* 353:

> Recovery for emotional disturbance will be excluded unless the breach also caused bodily harm or the contract or the breach is of such a kind that serious emotional disturbance was a particularly likely result.

Common examples of the second exceptional situation are contracts 1) between carriers and innkeepers and their passengers and guests; 2) for the carriage or proper disposition of dead bodies; and 3) for the delivery of messages concerning death. [Citations.]

Rubin contends that the untimely delivery of a memorial stone falls within the second or third exception concerning death. Assuming without deciding that we recognize these narrow exceptions, the present case does not fall within their parameters. It would strain the exception for disposition of bodies and delivery of death messages to include untimely delivery of a memorial stone. * * *

Rubin alternatively proposes that we not limit ourselves to the narrow exceptions discussed above but that we adopt a broad exception to the general rule precluding such damages in contract actions. * * *

California early allowed recovery for mental distress damages in contract actions. *See, e.g.,* Westervelt v. McCullough, 68 Cal.App. 198, 228 P. 734 (1924) (plaintiff allowed mental distress damages suffered as a result of defendant's breach of promise to provide plaintiff a home for duration of plaintiff's life). Although *Westervelt* involved physical suffering resulting from mental distress, the California court, relying on contract cases from other jurisdictions in which recovery for mental distress alone was allowed, held:

> Whenever the terms of a contract relate to matters which concern directly the comfort, happiness, or personal welfare of one of the parties, or the subject-matter of which is such as directly to affect or move the affection, self-esteem, or tender feelings of that party, he may recover damages for physical suffering or illness proximately caused by its breach.

[Citation.] Subsequent California cases have applied this principle to allow recovery of mental distress damages alone in a contract action. [Citation.] However, we agree with the North Carolina Court that the California standard is overly broad and "imposes too great a burden on parties to a contract." *See* Stanback v. Stanback, 297 N.C. at 194, 254 S.E.2d at 620.

Accordingly, we are not persuaded, on the facts of this case, that the general rule precluding damages for emotional or mental distress for breach of contract should be abandoned.

Rubin argues that the tort of negligent infliction of emotional distress may rest on the underlying tort of negligence where the sole harm suffered is emotional distress. We disagree.

We stated in Packard v. Central Maine Power Co., 477 A.2d 264, 268 (Me.1984) that

> no recovery can be had on a claim for infliction of emotional distress unless the defendant is found liable on the underlying tort.

Contrary to Rubin's contention, mental distress is insufficient in and of itself to establish the harm necessary to make negligence actionable, without either accompanying physical consequences, or an independent underlying tort. *See Prosser and Keeton on Torts,* 54, at 361 62 (5th ed. 1984); 2 F. Harper & F. James, *The Law of Torts* 18.4, at 1031 32 (1956) (mental or emotional distress standing alone will not constitute the kind of legal damage needed to support an action for negligence). * * *

Rubin asserts finally that because reasonable men could differ as to the outrageousness of the defendant's conduct, it was for the jury to determine whether the conduct was sufficiently extreme and outrageous to result in liability. Because we agree, we vacate the order of dismissal as to this count.

We recognized the tort of intentional infliction of emotional distress in Vicnire v. Ford Motor Credit Co., 401 A.2d 148 (Me.1979). We held there that a defendant is subject to liability if he intentionally or recklessly inflicts severe emotional distress upon another by engaging in extreme or outrageous conduct. Accepting as true the allegations here that the defendant's conduct was intentional and the emotional distress suffered by the plaintiff was severe, the issue becomes whether Matthews' misrepresentations and failure to make a timely delivery of the monument rise to the level of "extreme and outrageous" conduct.

* * *

In *Hanke* [Hanke v. Global Van Lines, Inc., 533 F.2d 396 (8th Cir. 1976)] the defendant moving company firmly promised an August 13 delivery date for the plaintiff's goods. The moving company repeatedly misrepresented the delivery date to the plaintiff, a local newspaper publisher, a United States government agency, and two United States Senators, finally making three partial deliveries in October and November. The court found that a jury could infer that the repeated misrepresentations, absent an explanation, were knowing falsehoods made for the purpose of "stringing her along." The court concluded that reasonable persons might differ as to whether the facts supported a conclusion that the defendant was liable for intentional infliction of emotional distress.

Although Matthew's misrepresentations in this case were not so extensive, given the allegations of repeated misrepresentation of a timely delivery of the monument for the unveiling ceremony and the circumstances in which they were made, we conclude that the complaint states a cause of action for intentional infliction of emotional distress. *See Restatement (Second) of Torts* 46 comment d, at 73. Our conclusion draws further support from the alleged contractual nature of the relationship between the parties. *See* D. Givelber, *The Right to Minimum Social Recovery and the Limits of Evenhandedness: Intentional Infliction of Emotional Distress by Outrageous Conduct,* 82 Col.L.Rev. 42, 69 (1982) (courts most likely to recognize a claim of outrageousness when the parties are "apparently bound by contracts regulating an economic relationship"). Thus, the allegations of this complaint sufficiently set forth conduct upon which liability for intentional infliction of emotional distress may be predicated.

[Remanded.]

———

Courts have allowed recovery of emotional distress damages for contract breach in limited circumstances. The contract has to be of a personal nature where emotional concerns are likely to be closely linked to performance. For example, some courts have awarded damages for negligent infliction of emotional distress in cases where a funeral home mishandles the remains of a loved one. *See, e.g.,* Corrigal v. Ball & Dodd Funeral Home, 89 Wash.2d 959, 577 P.2d 580 (1978).

B.   ECONOMIC LOSS DAMAGES

Section Coverage:

Recovery of purely economic losses such as lost profits has been in general the province of contract law and special statutory areas like antitrust law. In tort, the traditional view would preclude any recovery for negligently inflicted economic losses absent physical harm to person or property.

The economic loss rule arises in two different settings. The first involves a defendant and a plaintiff who are not in a contractual or other special relationship. Under the economic loss rule, a plaintiff may not recover damages for economic losses from a "stranger" defendant when the defendant's tortious action causes economic loss only rather than injury to the plaintiff's person or property. For example, assume that a defendant negligently obstructs a roadway leading to the plaintiff's business such that the plaintiff's customers are unable to get to the plaintiff's store. The economic loss rule precludes the plaintiff from recovering damages for its lost profits because it has suffered economic loss only. Courts and commentators argue that the economic loss rule is necessary to provide predictability in an otherwise uncertain area of law and places a reasonable limit on the tortfeasor's potential liability.

The economic loss rule also applies when the plaintiff and the defendant are parties to a contract. Under the economic loss rule, a party to a contract cannot recover tort damages for economic loss absent injury to the plaintiff or property other than the property which is the subject of the contract. For example, if the defendant sells the plaintiff a tractor that does not work properly such that the plaintiff can not harvest its crops, the plaintiff cannot sue in tort to recover the profits it lost on the sale of the crops. Instead, the plaintiff is limited to whatever damages may be available in a breach of contract claim. If the lost profits were not foreseeable at the time of contracting or the contract precludes recovery for consequential damages, the plaintiff will not be permitted to recover lost profits. Courts and commentators suggest the rule protects the fundamental distinction between contract and tort law. The economic loss rule prevents a party from achieving an end-run around a contractual bargain. This, in turn, encourages parties to allocate risk of loss in the contract.

When a component of a product or a machine causes harm to the entire product or machine applying the economic loss rule can prove difficult. Courts have used various approaches to determine whether harm to other property has occurred such that the plaintiff can recover in tort. Some courts look to the see whether the component was part of an integrated whole. Some courts also distinguish between consumers and commercial purchasers.

Although unquestionably the bright-line bar to recovery of such losses has the advantage of predictability and administrative convenience, it has produced some harsh results. There has been a critical perception of past inequities, and courts have begun to recognize exceptions. Some recent law has allowed compensation by finding the parties had a "special relationship" that created a duty to protect from economic harm. Some courts have simply reconsidered the application of foreseeability and remoteness. Despite these inroads on the rule denying economic losses for negligent interference with contracts in the absence of physical harm, this traditional rule remains the prevailing one.

Model Case:

The Hawkins Dredging Company, while conducting excavation operations, negligently damaged a natural gas pipeline owned by the National Pipeline Co. The resulting closure of the pipeline for repairs forced Rexall Industries, a contract purchaser of natural gas from National, to obtain fuel from another source during the repair period at an increased cost.

Hawkins would be liable to National for both the cost of repairs and any direct economic losses it sustained. In contrast, an action brought by Rexall would be unlikely to succeed. Although Hawkins' negligence prevented National from performing its contract to supply gas to Rexall, a court typically would preclude Rexall from recovering damages for its increased fuel costs. The rationale for the disparate treatment of the pipeline company and the contract purchaser would be that the latter was outside the class of persons to whom the dredging company owed a duty of care. On the other hand, if the court found that Hawkins intentionally interfered with National's performance of its contract, then Rexall would be permitted to recover its pecuniary losses.

Clark v. International Harvester Co.

99 Idaho 326, 581 P.2d 784 (1978).

■ BAKES, JUSTICE.

This is a products liability case in which the plaintiffs seek to recover consequential damages for economic losses resulting from an allegedly defective tractor manufactured by defendant International Harvester Company and sold to the plaintiffs by defendant McVey's, Inc., an International Harvester Co. dealer. The plaintiffs alleged a breach of implied and express warranties and negligent design and manufacture of the tractor. Prior to trial the district court granted partial summary judgments in favor of the defendants on the warranty claims. After trial the district court, sitting without a jury, entered judgment against the defendants on the negligence claim and awarded the plaintiffs $26,950.15 in damages.

[The plaintiff Clark is a "custom" farmer who contracts to plow or preplant farmland for compensation related to the number of acres involved. Clark purchased a tractor from the defendant McVey's, Inc., manufactured by International Harvester, for use in his custom farming business. The plaintiff claimed damages allegedly attributable to downtime when the equipment was being repaired and asserted that the tractor failed to function as warranted.]

* * *

The defendants separately moved for summary judgment alleging that when Clark purchased the tractor he signed a sales form which provided for a 12 month warranty and which limited the buyer's remedies to the repair or replacement of defective parts by the defendant and disclaimed all other warranties. The trial court granted the motion for summary judgment on the warranty claims but ruled that the disclaimer provisions in the form did not exclude liability for negligence.

* * *

In a memorandum opinion the trial court found that "[p]laintiffs' consequential damages due to 'down' time in their operation were caused by design defect in the valve train of the engine and negligent manufacture or assembly in the torque amplifier, ... Plaintiffs are entitled to recover $24,246.00 for their down time and $2,112.00 for repair of the tractor."

The trial court denied the plaintiffs' claims for damages due to loss of "present and future" business and decreased value of the tractor. * * *

The defendant on appeal has made numerous assignments of error. They can be summarized as follows: * * *

4. The trial court erred in awarding consequential damages for purely economic loss in a tort action. * * *

We first consider assignment of error No. 4, which concerns the recovery of damages for economic loss in a negligence action, because, in our view, that is dispositive of the negligence issue. The specific question presented by this assignment of error is best demonstrated by distinguishing this case from those of our earlier and somewhat related cases. This case is not like Shields v. Morton Chemical Co., 95 Idaho 674, 518 P.2d 857 (1974), in which the plaintiff sought damages for economic loss as a result of seeds which were damaged by the defendant's chemicals. In the instant case the plaintiffs have not alleged that their economic losses were the result of any property damage caused by the defendants. This case is not like Rindlisbaker v. Wilson, 95 Idaho 752, 519 P.2d 421 (1974), in which the plaintiff sought damages for profits lost as a result of a personal injury. In the instant case the plaintiffs have not alleged any personal injury. The negligence issue in this case is not like Salmon Rivers Sportsman Camps, Inc. v. Cessna Aircraft Co., 97 Idaho 348, 544 P.2d 306 (1975), in which the plaintiffs sought damages for economic loss for breach of an implied warranty. In that case we did not rule whether such damages were recoverable in a negligence action, but held that a plaintiff who was not in privity of contract with the defendant could not recover economic losses based on a breach of an implied warranty. In this case it is conceded that there is privity.

In this action the plaintiffs seek recovery only of lost profits due to alleged "down time" and the costs of repairing and replacing allegedly defective parts. The instant case presents the very narrow question whether the purchaser of a defective product who has not sustained any property damage or personal injury, but only suffered economic losses, can recover those losses in a negligence action against the manufacturer.

This Court has not previously considered this issue. The majority of jurisdictions which have considered the issue have not permitted the recovery of purely economic loss in a products liability action sounding in tort. [Citations.] However, a small minority of jurisdictions allow the recovery of purely economic losses in strict liability actions. [Citations.]

Dean Prosser summarized this majority rule with respect to recovery of economic losses in a products liability case sounding in negligence as follows:

> "There can be no doubt that the seller's liability for negligence covers any kind of physical harm, including not only personal injuries, but also property damage to the defective chattel itself, as where an automobile is wrecked by reason of its own bad brakes, as well as damage to any other property in the vicinity. But where there is no

accident, and no physical damage, and the only loss is a pecuniary one, through loss of the value or use of the thing sold, or the cost of repairing it, the courts have adhered to the rule, to be encountered later, that purely economic interests are not entitled to protection against mere negligence, and so have denied the recovery." W. Prosser, Handbook on the Law of Torts, § 101 at 665 (4th ed. 1971).

The Restatement (Second) of Torts, § 395 (1965), states that a manufacturer is to be liable for "physical harm" caused by its negligence in the manufacture of a chattel dangerous unless carefully made, but that Restatement section does not extend the manufacturer's liability to encompass purely economic loss.

Similarly, Restatement (Second) of Torts, § 402A (1965), which states the rule of strict liability in tort adopted by this Court in *Shields v. Morton Chemical Co., supra,* provides:

"One who sells any product in a defective condition unreasonably dangerous to the user or consumer or to his property is subject to liability for physical harm thereby caused to the ultimate user or consumer, or to his property...."

Like the Restatement section concerning the manufacturer's liability for negligence, § 402A does not extend a seller's tort liability to include purely economic losses.

. One of the most fully articulated discussions of the considerations underlying this rule is found in Justice Traynor's majority opinion in Seely v. White Motor Co., 63 Cal.2d 9, 45 Cal.Rptr. 17, 403 P.2d 145 (1965), [where] * * * the plaintiff sought to recover lost profits and a refund of the purchase price of a defective truck. The California Supreme Court ruled that such damages, although recoverable in a breach of warranty action, were not recoverable in strict liability in tort. The following passage from the majority opinion is pertinent to this case:

"The distinction that the law has drawn between tort recovery for physical injuries and warranty recovery for economic loss is not arbitrary and does not rest on the 'luck' of one plaintiff in having an accident causing physical injury. The distinction rests, rather, on an understanding of the nature of the responsibility a manufacturer must undertake in distributing his products. He can appropriately be held liable for physical injuries caused by defects by requiring his goods to match a standard of safety defined in terms of conditions that create unreasonable risks of harm. He cannot be held for the level of performance of his products in the consumer's business unless he agrees that the product was designed to meet the consumer's demands. A consumer should not be charged at the will of the manufacturer with bearing the risk of physical injury when he buys a product on the market. He can, however, be fairly charged with the risk that the product will not match his economic expectations unless the manufacturer agrees that it will. Even in actions for negligence, a manufacturer's liability is limited to damages for physical injuries and there is no recovery for economic loss alone. [Citations omitted]." 45 Cal.Rptr. at 23, 403 P.2d at 151.

We believe the rule advanced by the majority of the jurisdictions and by the Restatement is sound for the reasons articulated by Justice Traynor in *Seely*. * * * The Idaho legislature, and indeed the legislatures of nearly every state in the Union, have adopted the U.C.C. which carefully and painstakingly sets forth the rights between parties in a sales transaction with regard to economic loss. This Court, in the common law evolution of the tort law of this state, must recognize the legislature's action in this area of commercial law and should accommodate when possible the evolution of tort law with the principles laid down in the U.C.C.

The economic expectations of parties have not traditionally been protected by the law concerning unintentional torts. [Citations.] We do not believe that any good purpose would be achieved by undermining the operation of the U.C.C. provisions by extending tort law to embrace purely economic losses in product liability cases. Moreover, the U.C.C. provisions provide the Court with ample room for the exercise of wide judicial discretion to ensure that substantial justice results in particular cases. *See, e.g.,* I.C. §§ 28–2–302 and –2–719(3) (concerning unconscionable clauses and contracts), and I.C. § 28–1–203 (imposing a general obligation of good faith).

* * *

The plaintiffs further argue that, in many of the cases which refused to permit the recovery of damages for economic loss in negligence actions and which are cited by the defendants, the absence of privity of contract between the parties was the determinative factor, not the nature of the damages. There is language in some cases suggesting that the absence of privity may have played a role in the reasoning of some courts which have denied the recovery of purely economic losses in negligence. [Citation.] The requirement of privity in negligence actions, an unfortunate amalgam of tort and contract principles, was for the most part laid to rest by Justice Cardozo's famous opinion in MacPherson v. Buick Motor Co., 217 N.Y. 382, 111 N.E. 1050 (1916), and we are not disposed to resurrect it in this case. Rather than obscure fundamental tort concepts with contract notions of privity, we believe it is analytically more useful to focus on the precise duty of care that the law of negligence, not the law of contract or an agreement by the parties, has imposed on the defendant International Harvester. The law of negligence requires the defendant to exercise due care to build a tractor that does not harm person or property. If the defendant fails to exercise such due care it is of course liable for the resulting injury to person or property as well as other losses which naturally follow from that injury. However, the law of negligence does not impose on International Harvester a duty to build a tractor that plows fast enough and breaks down infrequently enough for Clark to make a profit in his custom farming business. This is not to say that such a duty could not arise by a warranty—express or implied—by agreement of the parties or by representations of the defendant, but the law of negligence imposes no such duty. Accordingly the trial court erred in granting a judgment to the plaintiffs on their negligence count.

* * * [Reversed and remanded.]

1. Economic losses similarly are not recoverable under strict products liability. The leading case is *Seely v. White Motor Co.*, 63 Cal.2d 9, 403 P.2d 145, 45 Cal.Rptr. 17 (1965). Jurisdictions are split on this issue, but most follow *Seely*. Plaintiffs may recover purely economic losses under theories of express or implied warranty, although they are often barred by contract limitations or substantive limitations such as privity of contract, depending on the rules of the jurisdiction.

2. An excellent and comprehensive description of the underlying policy considerations animating the economic loss doctrine was articulated by the court in *Rich Products Corp. v. Kemutec Inc.*, 241 F.3d 915 (7th Cir.2001), quoting with approval from Daanen & Janssen, Inc. v. Cedarapids, Inc., 216 Wis.2d 395, 573 N.W.2d 842 (1998):

> [A] commercial purchaser of a product cannot recover from a manufacturer, under the tort theories of negligence or strict products liability, damages that are solely "economic" in nature. As other courts have recognized, defining "economic loss" is difficult. Economic loss is generally defined as damages resulting from inadequate value because the product is inferior and does not work for the general purposes for which it was manufactured and sold. It includes both direct economic loss and consequential economic loss. The former is loss in value of the product itself; the latter is all other economic losses attributable to the product defect. * * *
>
> Direct economic loss may be said to encompass damage based on insufficient product value; thus, direct economic loss may be "out of pocket"—the difference in value between what is given and received—or "loss of bargain"—the difference between the value of what is received and its value as represented.... Consequential economic loss includes all indirect loss, such as loss of profits resulting from inability to make use of the defective product. * * *
>
> The economic loss doctrine, however, does not bar a commercial purchaser's claims based on personal injury or damage to property other than the product, or economic loss claims that are alleged in combination with noneconomic losses. In short, economic loss is damage to a product itself or monetary loss caused by the defective product, which does not cause personal injury or damage to other property. 241 F.3d 917.

The court further explained that the doctrine, as applied to tort actions between commercial parties, is predicated on certain policies:

> (1) to maintain the fundamental distinction between tort law and contract law; (2) to protect commercial parties' freedom to allocate

economic risk by contract; and (3) to encourage the party best situated to assess the risk of economic loss, the commercial purchaser, to assume, allocate, or insure against that risk.

From its inception the economic loss doctrine has been based on an understanding that contract law and the law of warranty, in particular, is better suited than tort law for dealing with purely economic loss in the commercial arena. . . . Contract law rests on obligations imposed by bargain. The law of contracts is designed to effectuate exchanges and to protect the expectancy interests of parties to private bargained-for agreements. Contract law, therefore, seeks to hold commercial parties to their promises, ensuring that each party receives the benefit of their bargain. Accordingly, the individual limited duties implicated by the law of contracts arise from the terms of the agreement between the particular parties. * * *

The law of torts, on the other hand, rests on obligations imposed by law. Tort law is rooted in the concept of protecting society as a whole from physical harm to person or property. Products liability and negligence law, in particular, developed to protect consumers from unreasonably dangerous goods that cause personal injury and damage to other property. It is society's interest in human life, health, and safety that demands protection against defective products, and imposes a duty upon manufacturers of those products. * * *

By definition economic loss excludes claims for personal injury and damage to other property. Recovery of economic loss is intended solely to protect purchasers from losses suffered because a product failed in its intended use. As a result, the general duty of care to refrain from acts unreasonably threatening physical harm is not paralleled by any comparable duty when the harm threatened is merely economic. A manufacturer in a commercial relationship has no duty under either negligence or strict liability theories to prevent a product from injuring itself. The duty to provide a product which functions to certain specifications is contractual. Contract law, therefore, is better suited for enforcing duties in the commercial arena because it permits the parties to specify the terms of their bargain and to protect themselves from commercial risk. 241 F.3d 917–918.

3. For an interesting example of the difficulties in applying the economic loss rule see *Sommer v. Federal Signal Corp.,* 79 N.Y.2d 540, 548, 583 N.Y.S.2d 957, 593 N.E.2d 1365 (1992). In this case the employee of a fire alarm company negligently failed to alert authorities of a reported fire in a New York City skyscraper, resulting in delayed response and major property damage. The court noted the difficulty in determining whether the company owning the skyscraper could pursue a tort claim against the fire alarm company, or whether it was limited to breach of contract remedies:

Between actions plainly *ex contractu* and those as clearly *ex delicto* there exists what has been termed a border-land, where the lines of distinction are shadowy and obscure, and the tort and the contract so approach each other, and become so nearly coincident as to make their practical separation somewhat difficult. [Citation] 79 N.Y.2d at 550.

The court concluded that the claims of the skyscraper owner were not limited to breach of contract theories, but could also sound in tort. The opinion lists several factors: (1) that the fire alarm company's duty of care derived not only from contract but from the nature of its services; (2) that the fire alarm stations are franchised and regulated by the City; (3) that the fire alarm company served a significant public interest; (4) that the breach of the fire alarm company's duties could have catastrophic consequences; (5) the nature of the fire alarm company's relationship with the skyscraper owner; and (6) the sudden manner of the loss.

4.   Why might an injured party want to pursue a claim in tort even though it had a contract with the wrongdoer? One reason might be the greater remedies available in a tort action. For example punitive damages or attorneys fees are sometimes available. Under contract law, parties are permitted to contractually limit the scope and amount of liability for breach. Further, whether the claim is characterized as a tort or a contract might affect which parties can be named as defendants or might affect the availability of insurance coverage.

Grams v. Milk Products, Inc.

283 Wis.2d 511, 699 N.W.2d 167 (2005).

■ DAVID T. PROSSER, J.

Petitioners Gerald and Joliene Grams (the Grams) seek review of an unpublished court of appeals decision, affirming a grant of summary judgment to Milk Products, Inc. (Milk Products) by the circuit court for Rock County, John W. Roethe, Judge. The court of appeals affirmed the circuit court's determination that the economic loss doctrine barred the Grams' tort claims against Milk Products and Cargill, Inc. (Cargill).

The economic loss doctrine is a judicial doctrine intended to preserve the fundamental distinction between contract and tort. [Citation.] It works to prevent a party to a contract from employing tort remedies to compensate the party for purely economic losses arising from the contract. There are exceptions. For instance, we noted several years ago that "The economic loss doctrine does not preclude a product purchaser's claims of personal injury or *damage to property other than the product* itself." Wausau Tile, Inc. v. County Concrete Corp., 226 Wis.2d 235, 247, 593 N.W.2d 445 (1999) (emphasis added). Over time, however, the parameters of this "other property" exception have proved elusive. In this case, we must decide whether the Grams' claimed damages fall within the scope of the "other property" exception.

We hold that if claimed damages are the result of disappointed expectations of a bargained-for product's performance, the economic loss doctrine applies to bar the plaintiff's tort claims and the plaintiff must rely upon contractual remedies alone. In this case, the Grams allege in tort that the object of the contract, a "milk replacer" intended for livestock nourishment, did not adequately nourish their calves and that some died. Because we find that this tort claim is, at bottom, based on disappointed performance expectations, we hold that it does not fit within the "other property" exception and is therefore barred by the economic loss doctrine. * * *

Gerald and Joliene Grams have specialized in raising calves since 1992. The Grams acquire the calves when they are between three and five days old and raise them until they are approximately four months old, at which time they resell them. At the time of this dispute, the Grams were raising approximately 6000 calves each year.

For the first few weeks of their lives, the calves are fed a milk substitute which, in farming parlance, is called a "milk replacer." The Grams used a Cargill milk replacer known as "Half–Time." This product included medications designed to keep the calves healthy during the first few weeks of their lives, a critical time in which the calves' immune systems are developing. The "Half–Time" milk replacer was manufactured for Cargill by Milk Products, Inc.

In November 2000, the Grams asked a Cargill representative about obtaining a less expensive milk replacer. The representative told the Grams that they could purchase "Half–Time" milk replacer without medication at a lower price than the medicated version. The Grams began using this non-medicated version in January 2001. As with the medicated "Half–Time," the non-medicated version was sold by Cargill and manufactured by Milk Products.

Soon after they began using the non-medicated "Half–Time," the Grams noticed certain problems developing in their calves. Specifically, the calves were not gaining weight properly and appeared gaunt and hungry. In addition, the mortality rate of the calves tripled, from an average of 9 percent before the new replacer was used to a high of 34 percent after the new replacer was introduced. * * *

[The Grams filed suit against Cargill and Milk Products with claims in both tort and contract. The trial court granted summary judgment to the defendants on the tort claims, finding that they were barred by the economic loss rule. The court also granted summary judgment to Milk Products on the contract claims because there was no privity of contract. That left just the contract claims against Cargill. The Grams appealed. The court of appeals affirmed. The Wisconsin Supreme Court granted review on whether the economic loss rule barred the tort claims.]

The economic loss doctrine is a judicially created doctrine intended to preserve the boundary between tort and contract. To illustrate, the commercial purchaser of a product may not recover from the manufacturer or seller, under negligence or strict liability theories, for solely economic losses arising from that product. This is especially true when a warranty given by the manufacturer specifically precludes the recovery of such damages. [Citation.] In Wisconsin, the economic loss doctrine is based on three fundamental premises. It seeks "(1) to maintain the fundamental distinction between tort law and contract law; (2) to protect commercial parties' freedom to allocate economic risk by contract; and (3) to encourage the party best situated to assess the risk of economic loss, [that is,] the commercial purchaser, to assume, allocate, or insure against that risk." [Citation.]

Tort law generally offers a "broader array" of damages than contract. [Citation.] As a result, many products liability plaintiffs would prefer to sue in tort. It has been said that without a boundary maintaining the distinction between the two, "contract law would drown in a sea of tort." [Citations.]

Wisconsin has recognized the superior ability of contract law, and in particular the Uniform Commercial Code (UCC), to deal with certain kinds of disputes. Cease Elec., 276 Wis.2d 361, ¶ 33, 688 N.W.2d 462. In *Cease Electric,* however, we declined to apply the economic loss doctrine to contracts for services. *Id.,* ¶ 2. Central to our decision was the fact that no body of law similar to the UCC applies to contracts for services. We recognized that the UCC provides a "comprehensive system for compensating consumers for economic loss arising from the purchase of defective products." *Id.,* ¶ 28 (citing State Farm, 225 Wis.2d at 342, 592 N.W.2d 201.) When a product proves to be defective, the UCC allows the aggrieved buyer to sue for breach of warranty or (under certain circumstances) to return the goods and sue for breach of contract. [Citations.]

* * *

In addition, contract law and tort law embody distinctly different approaches to risk sharing. The UCC provides a structure that encourages parties to a contract to allocate the economic risks of a given transaction between or among themselves. [Citation.] This is especially true when a manufacturer produces a part or component that can be used in a variety of ways. In that case, a party down the supply chain—often the ultimate purchaser—may be best situated to assess the risk and guard against it by securing a warranty, buying insurance, or allocating risk in other ways. [Citation.]

Tort law, unlike contract, does not permit risk sharing. It imposes obligations. Tort law is designed "to protect society against the unreasonable risk of harm from accidental and unexpected injury." [Citation.] When a product poses these types of risks to society, "public policy demands that responsibility be fixed wherever it will most effectively reduce the hazards to life and health inherent in defective products that reach the market." [Citation.] When a manufacturer designs or produces a product that poses such a risk, responsibility for the resulting injuries will redound to the manufacturer.

This tort rationale breaks down when a loss is purely economic. When parties of roughly equal bargaining power allocate risks of loss through negotiation, society has no special interest in overturning that allocation. [Citation.] If buyers could recover purely economic losses through tort suits, manufacturers could never rely on the risk allocations they negotiated through contract. Instead, end users could circumvent unfavorable warranties simply by suing a manufacturer up the production chain, or negotiate for no warranty at all and rely on tort law as their insurer. [Citation.] This would be contrary to the public policy embodied in the UCC, which lays out a carefully constructed framework of warranties to allow manufacturers to negotiate limits on their risk. [Citation.] Tort recovery for purely economic losses would also be contrary to sound economic policy. If a manufacturer must always insure its products against economic loss, all manufacturers will be transformed "into insurers with seemingly unlimited tort liability." * * *

The economic loss doctrine has been traced to a landmark decision by the California Supreme Court, Seely v. White Motor Co., 63 Cal.2d 9, 45 Cal.Rptr. 17, 403 P.2d 145 (1965), involving a defective truck. The court allowed recovery for breach of an express warranty but refused to allow recovery on the basis of strict product liability. The court said that a manufacturer can be held liable for physical injuries caused by defects "by requiring his goods to match a standard of safety defined in terms of conditions that create unreasonable risks of harm. He cannot be held for the level of performance of his products in the consumer's business unless he agrees that the product was designed to meet the consumer's demands." [Citation.]

The law following *Seely* was summarized by Professor William K. Jones of Columbia University School of Law in 1990:

> If a product fails to function properly, the buyer usually incurs expenses in repairing or replacing the product. In addition, the buyer's business may be disrupted, resulting in lost profits. Such "economic losses" generally cannot be recovered in tort actions alleging negligence or strict product liability. If, however, the defect in the product causes *physical injury to property,* tort remedies are available. The distinction is easy to apply in some cases, but it poses severe difficulties in others.

William K. Jones, Product Defects Causing Commercial Loss: The Ascendancy of Contract over Tort, 44 U. Miami L. Rev. 731, 747–48 (1990) (emphasis added). * * *

This court has recognized the "other property" exception in Wisconsin. [Citation.] It has also acknowledged, as Professor Jones did, that "distinguishing between economic loss and physical harm to property other than the product itself is often a difficult task. . . ." [Citation.]

The economic loss doctrine has been approved in the majority of jurisdictions throughout the United States. Consequently, there is a substantial body of law showing how various states have defined and dealt with the "other property" exception. * * *

* * *

In this state, the evolution of the economic loss doctrine has been slower * * *; our appellate decisions have repeatedly used techniques to limit the scope of the "other property" exception without eliminating it. Like many other states, we have incorporated the concept of an "integrated system." If the "product" at issue is a defective component in a larger "system," the other components are not regarded as "other property" in a legal sense, even if they are different property in a literal sense.

* * *

The "integrated system" concept does not translate well to all situations involving property damage to which the economic loss doctrine logically applies. To address situations in which a different explanation is needed for delimiting the other property exception, the court of appeals adopted the "disappointed expectations" concept which entails a different analysis. This concept governs situations in which a commercial product causes property damage but the damage was within the scope of bargaining, or as the Michigan Supreme Court reasoned, "the occurrence of such damage could have been the subject of negotiations between the parties." [Citation.]

The "disappointed expectations" concept is grounded in contract principles of bargaining and risk sharing, not on a redefinition of "other property." The determination of whether particular damage qualifies as damage to "other property" turns on the parties' expectations of the function of the bargained-for product. [Citation.]

* * *

In exploring the parameters of the "other property" exception to the economic loss doctrine, we will incorporate this concept of "disappointed expectations" into our analysis, as well as the integrated system concept. This does not mean that contract principles will envelop all damages foreseeable "in a remote or general sense." [Citation.] Rather, the economic loss doctrine will apply when "prevention of the subject risk was one of the contractual expectations motivating the purchase of the defective product." [Citation.]

The Grams urge this court to resolve the "other property" conundrum by adopting a new "bright line rule," that physical damage to anything other than the product itself would be considered damage to "other property" and therefore subject to suit in tort, and this argument attracts the dissent. *See* Chief Justice Abrahamson's dissent, ¶¶ 74, 80. The Grams concede that this proposal would obliterate the distinction between literal "other property" and legal "other property" discussed in the case law. Suits in tort would be allowed whenever damage extends beyond the physical dimensions of the purchased product. If such a rule were applied to this case, the Grams' tort claims could proceed because the calves were property different from the replacer.

We decline to adopt such a rule. The proposed rule would reject inquiry into the scope of the bargain and replace it with an overly formalistic distinction based on the kind of property harmed. Such a distinction would inevitably cause the erosion of the UCC. The "fundamental distinction" between contract and tort espoused in our cases would be lost.

Under the UCC, product warranties are important and necessary vehicles for limiting a manufacturer's liability for risks associated with the possible *uses* of a product, not just diminution in value of the product itself. When a product is intended to be used as part of an integrated system, the integrated system rule allows the manufacturer to share the risk that its product will damage the rest of the system. [Citation.] In adopting the integrated system concept, we recognized that "[s]ince all but the very simplest of machines have component parts, a holding that a component of a machine was 'other property' would require a finding of 'property damage' in virtually every case where a product damages itself. Such a holding would eliminate the distinction between warranty and strict products liability." [Citations.]

The same rationale applies here. If a product is expected and intended to interact with other products and property, it naturally follows that the product could adversely affect and even damage that property. A rule that allows tort recovery based on what is damaged, rather than whether the risk of that damage was within the scope of the bargain, would leave little room for contract.

* * *

The Grams claim that the non-medicated milk replacer they bought from Cargill damaged their calves' immune systems, leading to poor growth and higher mortality. Consistent with the foregoing analysis, we ask whether, at bottom, this claim involves disappointment in the milk replacer's performance and failure of the product to fulfill the Grams' contractual expectations.

The first step in our inquiry is to determine what those expectations were. This necessitates an inquiry into the substance and the purpose of the transaction. The record shows that the expected function of the milk replacer was to provide sustenance for the Grams' calves. The Grams expected that the "Half–Time" non-medicated replacer would properly nourish the calves, much as the old replacer had, so that the calves would grow. This bargain was not about milk replacer per se; it was about a product that would foster the healthy development and growth of young calves.

The next step is to inquire whether the Grams' claim is about disappointment with those expectations. In this case, the milk replacer did not properly nourish the calves. Poor nourishment led to a number of consequences for the calves, including weakened immune systems and for some, even death. The replacer did not do what the parties expected it to do, and this caused the exact result the Grams sought to avoid. It is difficult to think of a better example of disappointed expectations than a product that is expected to nourish animals but leaves them malnourished. The Grams' expectations were disappointed; the fact that they were severely disappointed does not change the analysis.

The Grams argue that * * * the damage caused by the replacer was worse than failed expectations. The replacer not only stunted the calves' growth, it killed some of them. The Grams argue that when the replacer killed some of the calves, the result was entirely unanticipated[.] * * *.

This argument ignores the intertwined nature of calf health, nutrition, and mortality. The Grams bargained for a replacer that would nourish the calves and make them grow. Even with high quality medicated milk replacer, the mortality rate of the Grams' calves ran about 9 percent. A reasonable farmer would know that switching to an unmedicated milk replacer could cause some increase in calf mortality. The only question was how much. Obviously, the Grams expected a lower increase in calf mortality than actually occurred, but that does not change the fact that the calves' nutrition—or, unfortunately, malnutrition—was at the heart of the bargain the Grams made. * * *

We acknowledge that determining whether a case is one of disappointed performance expectations will not always be as simple as it is here. It will necessarily require interpretation of the purpose of a transaction and the expected uses of a product. * * *

The Grams have a contractually rooted claim against Cargill for breach of implied warranty that remains to be resolved at the circuit court. Because their tort claims are, at bottom, based on their disappointment with the performance of the non-medicated milk replacer, their contract claim is the proper vehicle for resolving this dispute. We therefore affirm the court of appeals.

■ SHIRLEY S. ABRAHAMSON, CHIEF JUSTICE (*dissenting*). * * *

I dissent for three reasons: (1) the policies motivating the creation of the economic loss doctrine are not furthered by dismissing the Grams' tort action against Milk Products (the manufacturer of milk replacer that killed and injured their calves), with whom the Grams have no contractual relationship; (2) the majority opinion's use of the "disappointed expectations" concept to define "other property" is so broad that the economic loss doctrine threatens the strict products liability doctrine; and (3) even under the majority opinion's standard for "other property," summary judgment was inappropriate[.] * * *

* * * As I see it, a defendant is liable when he or she places in commerce a defective product that creates an unreasonable risk of injury to property other than the product sold and that injury occurs. The purchaser should not bear this risk of injury. The Grams should have an opportunity to prove that the milk replacer was a defective product that created an unreasonable risk of injury to the calves and that injury occurred.

1. Distinguish purely economic loss from other types of harm that can be caused by a defective product:

(a) *Physical injury to person.* A defective product may cause personal injury, such as when an automobile manufactured with defective brakes is responsible for a traffic accident. A victim can recover losses under a theory of negligence, if any, or under a strict liability theory following § 402A of the Restatement (Second) of Torts.

(b) *Physical injury to property.* A defective product may cause losses to property, such as when a misdesigned room heater causes a fire. Most courts allow recovery either under a theory of negligence, if any, or under the strict liability theory of § 402A of the Restatement (Second) of Torts. Some courts have distinguished injury to the defective product itself from injury to other property.

(c) *Economic injury from loss of bargain.* The buyer of a defective product has an economic loss because a defective product is worth less than the nondefective one that the buyer contracted to purchase. The buyer may have claims in express or implied warranty under state and federal law, but most jurisdictions do not allow an action in tort without proof of actionable misrepresentation, such as fraud. Absent such exception, remedies are governed by warranty law.

(d) *Other economic injury.* There may be other pecuniary losses besides the loss of the bargain when a defective product fails to perform as expected. When equipment is needed for a business, profits may be lost if a defect in the equipment prevents its normal use.

As the principal case illustrates, distinguishing economic injury from loss of bargain from injury to property is sometimes problematical.

2. Applying the economic loss rule in construction cases has posed challenging for courts. Courts struggle to determine what constitutes the product and, thus, whether there has been physical injury to other property or merely economic injury for loss of bargain. For example, courts have reached different conclusions about whether the economic loss rule precludes recovery when a defective window causes damage to surrounding walls. *Compare* Jimenez v. Superior Court, 29 Cal.4th 473, 127 Cal.Rptr.2d 614, 58 P.3d 450 (2002) *with* Bay Breeze Condominium Assoc. v. Norco Windows, Inc., 257 Wis.2d 511, 651 N.W.2d 738 (App. Ct. 2002). In *Jimenez*, a class of homeowners brought suit against the manufacturer of the windows that had been installed in mass-produced homes in the homeowners' subdivision. The homeowners claimed that the defective windows "damaged the stucco, insulation, framing, drywall, paint, wall coverings, baseboards, and other parts of the home." The manufacturer argued that the house constituted "the product" that the homeowners purchased and, as such, damage to other parts of the house as a result of a defect in the windows was economic injury from loss of bargain. The California Supreme Court disagreed, finding that the "concept of recoverable property had expanded over time to include damage to one part of a product caused by another, defective part." In contrast, in *Bay Breeze*, the

Wisconsin Court of Appeals concluded that the economic loss doctrine precluded a condominium association's suit against a widow manufacturer, alleging that the manufacturer's windows were negligently designed and manufactured resulting in damage to walls surrounding the windows. The court concluded that the windows were part of "an integrated structure." As such, the court reasoned that the plaintiff had not suffered physical injury to any other property.

In re the Exxon Valdez v. Hazelwood

270 F.3d 1215 (9th Cir.2001).

■ KLEINFELD, CIRCUIT JUDGE:

* * * This is not a case about befouling the environment. This is a case about commercial fishing. The jury was specifically instructed that it could not award damages for environmental harm. The reason is that under a stipulation with the United States and Alaska, Exxon had already been punished for environmental harm. The verdict in this case was for damage to economic expectations for commercial fishermen. * * *

Bligh Island and Bligh Reef have been known to navigators for a long time. Captain George Vancouver charted and named the island on his third voyage to the North Pacific on the *Discovery* in 1794. The Bligh Island Reef has long been mapped on U.S. Coast and Geodetic Survey maps, shortened to Bligh Reef by the Coast and Geodetic Survey in 1930. Captain William Bligh and Vancouver had been officers together sixteen years earlier, on the *Resolution,* when Captain James Cook, among the greatest navigators in history, explored Alaska and the South Pacific.

Captain William Bligh is infamous from Fletcher Christian's mutiny on the *Bounty.* The infamy was refreshed in 1989, the 200th anniversary of the mutiny on the *Bounty,* by Captain Joseph Hazelwood of the *Exxon Valdez.*

On March 24, 1989, the oil tanker *Exxon Valdez* ran aground on Bligh Reef in Prince William Sound, Alaska. It has never been altogether clear why the *Exxon Valdez* ran aground on this long known, well-marked reef. * * *

The vessel left the port of Valdez at night. In March, it is still dark at night in Valdez, the white nights of the summer solstice being three months away. There is an established sea lane that takes vessels well to the west of Bligh Reef, but Captain Hazelwood prudently took the vessel east of the shipping lanes to avoid a heavy concentration of ice in the shipping lane, which is a serious hazard. Plaintiffs have not claimed that Captain Hazelwood violated any law or regulation by traveling outside the sea lane. The problem with being outside the sea lane was that the ship's course was directly toward Bligh Reef.

Bligh Reef was not hard to avoid. All that needed to be done was to bear west about the time the ship got abeam of the navigation light at Busby Island, which is visible even at night, some distance north of the reef. The real puzzle of this case was how the ship managed to run aground on this known and foreseen hazard. * * *

Shortly after midnight on March 24, 1989, the tanker ran onto Bligh Reef. The reef tore the hull open. Prince William Sound was polluted with eleven million gallons of oil. Exxon spent over $2 billion on efforts to remove the oil from the water and from the adjacent shores, and even from the individual birds and other wildlife dirtied by the oil. It also began an extensive program of settling with property owners, fishermen and others, whose economic interests were harmed by the spill. Some were paid cash without providing releases, some released some claims but not all, and some released all claims. Exxon spent $300 million on voluntary settlements prior to any judgments being entered against it. * * *

This case involves the action for compensatory and punitive damages by entities affected by the spill. The District Court certified a Commercial Fishing Class, a Native Class, and a Landowner Class for compensatory damages. * * * For purposes of this litigation, Exxon stipulated that its negligence caused the oil spill. The district court, which did a masterful job of managing this very complex case, tried the case to the jury in three phases. In the first phase, the jury found that Hazelwood and Exxon had been reckless, in order to determine liability for punitive damages. The second phase assessed the amount of compensatory damages attributable to the spill to commercial fishermen and Alaska Natives. The third phase established the amount of punitive damages. A fourth phase, which settled before trial, was to determine the compensatory damages of plaintiffs whose damages were not determined in Phase II, including landowners and participants in other commercial fisheries. [The jury awarded compensatory and damages, and the district court entered judgment for the plaintiffs against Hazelwood and Exxon. Exxon and Hazelwood appealed, and plaintiffs cross appealed. Plaintiffs argue that the district court erroneously granted summary judgment against the claimants who suffered purely economic injury on account of the oil spill.] * * *

Economic injury

The district court granted summary judgment against all claimants who suffered only economic injury on account of the oil spill, unaccompanied by any physical injury to their property or person. It relied on the United States Supreme Court's decision in *Robins Dry Dock & Repair Co. v. Flint,*[184] a case commonly read to hold that economic recovery is unavailable in admiralty cases absent physical harm, and our decision in *Union Oil Co. v. Oppen,* [501 F.2d 558 (9th Cir.1974)] which recognized a commercial fisherman's exception to the *Robins Dry Dock* rule. Based on the understanding that state law may not conflict with federal maritime law, the district court held that *Robins Dry Dock* preempted Alaska's strict liability statute for hazardous substances. In light of subsequent Supreme Court decisions, we are compelled to reverse the district court's ruling in part.

---

184. 275 U.S. 303, 48 S.Ct. 134, 72 L.Ed. 290 (1927).

Whether the dismissed claimants may recover depends on two inquiries: whether state law can control despite *Robins Dry Dock,* and whether Alaska law does indeed allow for recovery. The first question has been recently addressed by the United States Supreme Court [in which the Court * * *] reaffirmed the three-prong test articulated almost a century ago in *Southern Pacific Co. v. Jensen*[185] as the proper analysis for determining whether federal admiralty law preempts contrary state law. Interpreting the "saving to suitors clause" of the 1789 Judiciary Act, the Supreme Court held that, notwithstanding federal admiralty law, a state may "adopt such remedies ... as it sees fit" so long as the state remedy does not (1) "contravene[ ] the essential purpose expressed by an act of Congress;" (2) "work[ ] material prejudice to the characteristic features of the general maritime law"; or (3) "interfere[ ] with the proper harmony and uniformity of that law in its international and interstate relations." Whether contrary state law can control despite *Robins* thus depends on whether the denial of recovery for pure economic injury is the "essential purpose" of an act of Congress, a "characteristic feature" of admiralty, or a doctrine whose uniform application is necessary to maintain the "proper harmony" of maritime law. Like the First Circuit, we think it is none of these.

The first question is easily disposed of: no act of Congress directly governs our case. The second prong of the *Jensen* test requires preemption where a state remedy "works material prejudice to [a] characteristic featur[e] of the general maritime law." In *American Dredging,* the Court held that the "characteristic feature" language of *Jensen* refers only to a federal rule that either "originated in admiralty" or "has exclusive application there." Where a federal rule "is and has long been a doctrine of general application," a state's refusal to follow that rule does not "work 'material prejudice to [a] characteristic featur[e] of the general maritime law.' " [Citation]

As the First Circuit has held, the *Robins Dry Dock* rule denying purely economic losses neither "originated in admiralty" nor "had 'exclusive' application in admiralty." Justice Holmes' opinion in *Robins Dry Dock* presents the rule as a truism for which "no authority need be cited," and cites four cases that have applied the rule, only two of which are in admiralty. It is a traditional rule of tort law. Commentators trace the *Robins Dry Dock* rule to a non-admiralty case decided in 1875. And courts, including our own, have repeatedly denied liability for purely economic harm in a variety of land-based contexts. As the Fifth Circuit noted in *M/V Testbank,* "[*Robins Dry Dock*] broke no new ground but instead applied a principle, then settled both in the United States and England, which refused recovery for negligent interference with 'contractual rights.' " [Citation] Thus, a state's decision to depart from *Robins Dry Dock* does not materially prejudice a rule that "originated in" or is "exclusive to" general maritime law, and cannot be preempted on this ground.

---

185. 244 U.S. 205, 37 S.Ct. 524, 61 L.Ed. 1086 (1917).

State law allowing for recovery of purely economic damage can be preempted, therefore, only if it "interferes with the proper harmony and uniformity" of maritime law. The Supreme Court has adopted a balancing test that weighs state and federal interests on a case-by-case basis.

In undertaking this balancing test, we first look to the state interest in providing remedies for damages caused by oil spills. The Alaska Supreme Court has expressly recognized the state's "strong interest in regulating oil pollution and in providing remedies for damages caused by oil spills." The United States Supreme Court has similarly recognized that regulating oil pollution and providing for recovery of economic damages is within the state's police powers, and is not preempted by federal law. Because it is undisputed that "general maritime law may be changed, modified, or affected by state legislation," where "the state law is aimed at a matter of great and legitimate state concern, a court must act with great caution," before declaring the state remedy "potentially so disruptive as to be unconstitutional."

Accordingly, we must balance a state's "great and legitimate" interest in protecting its citizens from oil spill-related injury against the federal interest in barring recovery for pure economic harm. The federal interest in maintaining a uniform rule of recovery in admiralty is "more subtle but also not without importance." It aims to contain costs potentially imposed on maritime commerce by a regime of liability, or a diversity of regimes, that are not so difficult to administer as to prevent the efficient and predictable resolution of maritime disputes.

Two federal laws establish the absence of a federal policy against awards for purely economic harm, the Oil Pollution Act ("OPA")[207] and the Trans–Alaska Pipeline Authorization Act ("TAPAA").[208] The First Circuit concluded that OPA "almost certainly provides for recovery of purely economic damages in oil spill cases" even where the claimant does not have a proprietary interest in the damaged property or natural resources. The same has been said of TAPAA. Both OPA and TAPAA, moreover, expressly provide that they do not preempt state imposition of additional liability requirements. These statutes offer "compelling evidence that Congress does not view either expansion of liability to cover purely economic losses or enactment of comparable state oil pollution regimes as an excessive burden on maritime commerce."

In light of these considerations, the balance tips in favor of the state: "Alaska's strong interest in protecting its waters and providing remedies for damages resulting from oil spills outweighs the diminished federal interest in achieving interstate harmony through the uniform application of *Robins*." Whether the dismissed claimants can recover depends, therefore, on whether economic recovery is indeed available under Alaska law. The Alaska Supreme Court has recently addressed this issue under Alaska's strict liability statute for hazardous substances, Alaska Stat. § 46.03.822.

---

207.   Oil Pollution Act of 1990, 33 U.S.C §§ 2701–2718 (1990).

208.   Trans–Alaska Pipeline Authorization Act, 43 U.S.C. §§ 1651–1656 (1994).

This expansion of liability to purely economic harm does not establish liability for all the claims plaintiffs advance. As we held in *Benefiel v. Exxon Corp.* [959 F.2d 805, 808 (9th Cir.1992)] the requirement of proximate cause bars remote and speculative claims. There we held that Californians who claimed that their gasoline cost more as a result of the Exxon Valdez oil spill were barred from recovery because of "the remote and derivative damages" they claimed and lack of proximate cause as a matter of law.

We remand so that the district court can determine whether tender-boat operators and crews, and seafood processors, dealers, wholesalers, and processor employees can establish allowable damages. Summary judgment was appropriately granted against "area businesses," "commercial fishermen outside the closed areas," the aquaculture association, and persons claiming "stigma" damages. Even without *Robins Dry Dock,* these groups' damages were too remote.

———

1. An absolute bar to recovery for negligent interferences with contracts found an early expression in the United States in *Robins Dry Dock & Repair Co. v. Flint*, 275 U.S. 303, 309, 48 S.Ct. 134, 72 L.Ed. 290 (1927). A steamship charterer sought to recover lost profits when the vessel was delayed after the defendant negligently broke the ship's propeller. The charterer had no property interest in the ship when it was damaged, but rather had a contract with the ship's owners. The Court denied recovery of economic losses potentially attributable to the delay. Writing for the Court, Justice Holmes observed:

> [W]hile intentionally to bring about a breach of contract may give rise to a cause of action ... a tort to the person or property of one man does not make the tortfeasor liable to another merely because the injured person was under a contract with that other, unknown to the doer of the wrong. The law does not spread its protection so far. [Citations.] 48 S.Ct. at 135

2. The *Robins Dry Dock* approach of denying recovery for economic losses in negligent interference with contract cases has shown continued vitality among several federal circuit courts. In *Nautilus Marine, Inc. v. Niemela*, 170 F.3d 1195, 1197 (9th Cir.1999), the court denied recovery of damages for economic losses sought by a charterer of lost profits caused by maritime tort. The court observed that industry could obtain insurance to alleviate the potentially harsh effect of the *Robins Dry Dock* bar of economic losses in tort actions. Similarly, in *Reserve Mooring v. American Commercial Barge Line*, 251 F.3d 1069, 1072 (5th Cir.2001), the owner of a mooring facility sought recovery of lost income resulting from the negligent sinking of a barge which blocked access to plaintiff's business operations. Because the negligence only interfered with a "business expectancy" and did not result in physical damage to the facility, recovery of purely economic damages was denied.

3. In *Louisiana ex rel. Guste v. M/V TESTBANK*, 752 F.2d 1019 (5th Cir.1985), a vessel collided with another in the Mississippi River Gulf Outlet causing a major chemical spill. The spill caused the closure of the outlet for several weeks. Various businesses and individuals affected by the closure, including marina and boat rental operators, fishermen, shops and restaurants, and shipping interests claimed economic losses from loss of use of the area. The court reaffirmed the per se rule against recovery for pecuniary harm in tort absent physical injury to a proprietary interest, reasoning that a pragmatic limit was necessary to avoid disproportionate damages relative to the defendant's fault, "liability in an indeterminate amount for an indeterminate time to an indeterminate class." (quoting Justice Cardozo in Ultramares Corp. v. Touche, 255 N.Y. 170, 174 N.E. 441 (1931).) *See also* American River Transp. Co. v. KAVO KALIAKRA SS, 206 F.3d 462, 465 (5th Cir.2000) (recovery for economic damages in negligence denied where not connected to an injury to a property interest). *But see* Corpus Christi Oil & Gas Co. v. Zapata Gulf Marine Corp., 71 F.3d 198 (5th Cir.1995) (physical damage to property justified recovery of economic losses). The Restatement (Second) of Torts § 766C comment b allows recovery of lost profits or other pecuniary losses which are "parasitic to an injury to person or property."

Does the result in *Robins Dry Dock* and its progeny really devolve into a policy question of where to allocate losses in the most economically efficient manner from an insurance perspective?

4. In *Union Oil Co. v. Oppen*, 501 F.2d 558 (9th Cir.1974), the Ninth Circuit recognized a narrow exception to the bright-line rule of *Robins Dry Dock* that precludes recovery of economic losses for negligent interference with contractual relations absent physical harm. The court held that commercial fishermen could recover lost profits attributable to an oil spill caused by the defendants because there was a special duty owed to this particular class of plaintiffs. The court relied upon case law which allowed recovery of economic losses against defendants engaged in certain professions, businesses or trades: pension consultants, accountants, architects, attorneys, notaries public, test hole drillers, title abstractors, termite inspectors, soil engineers, surveyors, real estate brokers, drawers of checks, director of corporations, trustees, bailees and public weighers.

The court further justified its decision with an economic analysis. The rule would effectuate maximum allocation of resources by charging such pecuniary losses against parties that are in the best position to take cost-avoidance measures. In this situation that party was the defendant oil companies.

5. The preclusion of economic losses in negligent interference with contracts is sometimes accomplished through a per se rule and sometimes through the tort concepts of proximate cause and duty. A leading proximate cause case concerning economic losses is *In re Kinsman Transit Co.* (*Kinsman II*),388 F.2d 821 (2d Cir.1968), where Judge Kaufman noted:

In the final analysis, the circumlocution whether posed in terms of "foreseeability," "duty," "proximate cause," "remoteness," etc. seems unavoidable. As we have previously noted, 338 F.2d at 725, we return to Judge Andrews' frequently quoted statement in Palsgraf v. Long Island R.R., 248 N.Y. 339, 354–355, 162 N.E. 99, 104, 59 A.L.R. 1253 (1928) (dissenting opinion): "It is all a question of expediency * * * of fair judgment, always keeping in mind the fact that we endeavor to make a rule in each case that will be practical and in keeping with the general understanding of mankind." 388 F.2d at 825.

In *Kinsman II* the plaintiffs sought recovery for transportation and storage costs resulting from the defendant's negligent collision with a bridge. The court denied recovery on the grounds that the injuries were too remote or indirect a consequence of the defendant's negligence rather than by applying the absolute bar rule of *Robins Dry Dock. Accord,* In re Bethlehem Steel Corp., 631 F.2d 441 (6th Cir.1980), *cert. denied,* 450 U.S. 921, 101 S.Ct. 1370, 67 L.Ed.2d 349 (1981); Venore Transportation Co. v. M/V Struma, 583 F.2d 708 (4th Cir.1978). But see Reserve Mooring v. American Commercial Barge Line, 251 F.3d 1069, 1071 (5th Cir.2001) (rejected foreseeability approach to determine recovery of economic damages for unintentional torts).

People Express Airlines v. Consolidated Rail Corp.

100 N.J. 246, 495 A.2d 107 (1985).

■ HANDLER, J.

This appeal presents a question that has not previously been directly considered: whether a defendant's negligent conduct that interferes with a plaintiff's business resulting in purely economic losses, unaccompanied by property damage or personal injury, is compensable in tort. The appeal poses this issue in the context of the defendants' alleged negligence that caused a dangerous chemical to escape from a railway tank car, resulting in the evacuation from the surrounding area of persons whose safety and health were threatened. The plaintiff, a commercial airline, was forced to evacuate its premises and suffered an interruption of its business operations with resultant economic losses.

Because of the posture of the case—an appeal taken from the grant of summary judgment for the defendant railroad, subsequently reversed by the Appellant Division, we must accept plaintiff's version of the facts as alleged. The facts are straight-forward.

On July 22, 1981, a fire began in the Port Newark freight yard of defendant Consolidated Rail Corporation (Conrail) when ethylene oxide manufactured by defendant BASF Wyandotte Company (BASF) escaped from a tank car, punctured during a "coupling" operation with another rail car, and ignited. The tank car was owned by defendant Union Tank Car Company (Union Car) and was leased to defendant BASF.

The plaintiff asserted at oral argument that at least some of the defendants were aware from prior experiences that ethylene oxide is a highly volatile substance; further, that emergency response plans in case of an accident had been prepared. When the fire occurred that gave rise to this lawsuit, some of the defendants' consultants helped determine how much of the surrounding area to evacuate. The municipal authorities then evacuated the area within a one-mile radius surrounding the fire to lessen the risk to persons within the area should the burning tank car explode. The evacuation area included the adjacent North Terminal building of Newark International Airport, where plaintiff People Express Airlines' (People Express) business operations are based. Although the feared explosion never occurred, People Express employees were prohibited from using the North Terminal for twelve hours.

The plaintiff contends that it suffered business-interruption losses as a result of the evacuation. These losses consist of cancelled scheduled flights and lost reservations because employees were unable to answer the telephones to accept bookings; also, certain fixed operating expenses allocable to the evacuation time period were incurred and paid despite the fact that plaintiff's offices were closed. No physical damage to airline property and no personal injury occurred as a result of the fire.

According to People Express' original complaint, each defendant acted negligently and these acts of negligence proximately caused the plaintiff's harm. * * *

The single characteristic that distinguishes parties in negligence suits whose claims for economic losses have been regularly denied by American and English courts from those who have recovered economic losses is, with respect to the successful claimants, the fortuitous occurrence of physical harm or property damage, however slight. It is well-accepted that a defendant who negligently injures a plaintiff or his property may be liable for all proximately caused harm, including economic losses. *See* Palsgraf v. Long Island R.R., 248 N.Y. 339, 162 N.E. 99 (1928); W. Prosser & W. Keeton, *The Law of Torts* § 129, at 997 (5th ed. 1984) (Prosser & Keeton). Nevertheless, a virtually *per se* rule barring recovery for economic loss unless the negligent conduct also caused physical harm has evolved throughout this century, based, in part, on Robins Dry Dock & Repair Co. v. Flint, 275 U.S. 303, 48 S.Ct. 134, 72 L.Ed. 290 (1927) and Cattle v. Stockton Waterworks Co., 10 Q.B. 453 (1875). * * *

The reasons that have been advanced to explain the divergent results for litigants seeking economic losses are varied. Some courts have viewed the general rule against recovery as necessary to limit damages to reasonably foreseeable consequences of negligent conduct. This concern in a given case is often manifested as an issue of causation and has led to the requirement of physical harm as an element of proximate cause. In this context, the physical harm requirement functions as part of the definition of the causal relationship between the defendant's negligent act and the plaintiff's economic damages; it acts as a convenient clamp on otherwise boundless liability. [Citations.] The physical harm rule also reflects certain deep-seated concerns that underlie courts' denial of recovery for purely economic losses occasioned by a defendant's negligence. These concerns include the fear of fraudulent claims, mass litigation, and limitless liability, or liability out of proportion to the defendant's fault. * * *

It is understandable that courts, fearing that if even one deserving plaintiff suffering purely economic loss were allowed to recover, all such plaintiffs could recover, have anchored their rulings to the physical harm requirement. While the rationale is understandable, it supports only a limitation on, not a denial of, liability. The physical harm requirement capriciously showers compensation along the path of physical destruction, regardless of the status or circumstances of individual claimants. Purely economic losses are borne by innocent victims, who may not be able to absorb their losses. [Citation.] In the end, the challenge is to fashion a rule that limits liability but permits adjudication of meritorious claims. The asserted inability to fix crystalline formulae for recovery on the differing facts of future cases simply does not justify the wholesale rejection of recovery in all cases.

* * *

We may appropriately consider two relevant avenues of analysis in defining a cause of action for negligently-caused economic loss. The first examines the evolution of various exceptions to the rule of nonrecovery for purely economic losses, and suggests that the exceptions have cast considerable doubt on the validity of the current rule and, indeed, have laid the foundation for a rule that would allow recovery. The second explores the elements of a suitable rule and adopts the traditional approach of foreseeability as it relates to duty and proximate cause molded to circumstances involving a claim only for negligently-caused economic injury.

Judicial discomfiture with the rule of nonrecovery for purely economic loss throughout the last several decades has led to numerous exceptions in the general rule. Although the rationalizations for these exceptions differ among courts and cases, two common threads run throughout the exceptions. The first is that the element of foreseeability emerges as a more appropriate analytical standard to determine the question of liability than a *per se* prohibitory rule. The second is that the extent to which the defendant knew or should have known the particular consequences of his negligence, including the economic loss of a particularly foreseeable plaintiff, is dispositive of the issues of duty and fault.

One group of exceptions is based on the "special relationship" between the tortfeasor and the individual or business deprived of economic expectations. Many of these cases are recognized as involving the tort of negligent misrepresentation, resulting in liability for specially foreseeable economic losses. Importantly, the cases do not involve a breach of contract claim between parties in privity; rather, they involve tort claims by innocent third parties who suffered purely economic losses at the hands of negligent defendants with whom no direct relationship existed. Courts have justified their finding of liability in these negligence cases based on notions of a special relationship between the negligent tortfeasors and the foreseeable plaintiffs who relied on the quality of defendants' work or services, to their detriment. The special relationship, in reality, is an expression of the courts' satisfaction that a duty of care existed because the plaintiffs were particularly foreseeable and the injury was proximately caused by the defendant's negligence.

The special relationship exception has been extended to auditors, surveyors, termite inspectors, engineers, attorneys, notaries public, architects, weighers, and telegraph companies. [Citations given for each category.]

A related exception in which courts have allowed recovery for purely economic losses has been extended to plaintiffs belonging to a particularly foreseeable group, such as sailors and seamen, for whom the law has traditionally shown great solicitude. [Citations.]

Courts have found it fair and just in all of these exceptional cases to impose liability on defendants who, by virtue of their special activities, professional training or other unique preparation for their work, had particular knowledge or reason to know that others, such as the intended beneficiaries of wills [citation] or the purchasers of stock who were expected to rely on the company's financial statement in the prospectus [citation] would be economically harmed by negligent conduct. In this group of cases, even though the particular plaintiff was not always foreseeable, the particular class of plaintiffs was foreseeable as was the particular type of injury.

A very solid exception allowing recovery for economic losses has also been created in cases akin to private actions for public nuisance. Where a plaintiff's business is based in part upon the exercise of a public right, the plaintiff has been able to recover purely economic losses caused by a defendant's negligence. [Citations.] The theory running throughout these cases, in which the plaintiffs depend on the exercise of the public or riparian right to clean water as a natural resource, is that the pecuniary losses suffered by those who make direct use of the resource are particularly foreseeable because they are so closely linked, through the resource, to the defendants' behavior.

Particular knowledge of the economic consequences has sufficed to establish duty and proximate cause in contexts other than those already considered. In Clay v. Jersey City, 74 N.J.Super. 490, 181 A.2d 545 (Ch.Div.1962), aff'd, 84 N.J.Super. 9, 200 A.2d 787 (App.Div.1964), for example, a lessee-manufacturer had to vacate the building in which its business was located because of the defendant city's negligent failure to maintain its sewer line while the line was repaired. While there was some property damage, the court treated the tenant's and owner's claims separately; the tenant's claims were purely economic, stemming from the loss of use of its property right, as in the instant case. Further, the city had had notice of the leak since 1957 and should have known about it even earlier. Duty, breach and proximate cause were found to exist; the plaintiff-tenant recovered lost profits and expenses incurred during the shut-down. [Citation.]

These exceptions expose the hopeless artificiality of the *per se* rule against recovery for purely economic losses. When the plaintiffs are reasonably foreseeable, the injury is directly and proximately caused by defendant's negligence, and liability can be limited fairly, courts have endeavored to create exceptions to allow recovery. The scope and number of exceptions, while independently justified on various grounds, have nonetheless created lasting doubt as to the wisdom of the *per se* rule of nonrecovery for purely economic losses. Indeed, it has been fashionable for commentators to state that the rule has been giving way for nearly fifty years, although the cases have not always kept pace with the hypothesis. [Citations.]

One thematic motif that may be extrapolated from these decisions to differentiate between those cases in which recovery for economic losses was allowed and denied is that of foreseeability as it related to both the duty owed and proximate cause. The traditional test of negligence is what a reasonably prudent person would foresee and do in the circumstances; duty is clearly defined by knowledge of the risk of harm or the reasonable apprehension of that risk. * * *

The further theme that may be extracted from these decisions rests on the specificity and strictness that are infused into the definitional standard of foreseeability. The foreseeability standard that may be synthesized from these cases is one that posits liability in terms of where, along a spectrum ranging from the general to the particular, foreseeability is ultimately found. [Citations.] A broad view of these cases reasonably permits the conclusion that the extent of liability and degree of foreseeability stand in direct proportion to one another. The more particular is the foreseeability that economic loss will be suffered by the plaintiff as a result of defendant's negligence, the more just is it that liability be imposed and recovery allowed.

We hold therefore that a defendant owes a duty of care to take reasonable measures to avoid the risk of causing economic damages, aside from physical injury, to particular plaintiffs or plaintiffs comprising an identifiable class with respect to whom defendant knows or has reason to know are likely to suffer such damages from its conduct. A defendant failing to adhere to this duty of care may be found liable for such economic damages proximately caused by its breach of duty.

We stress that an identifiable class of plaintiffs is not simply a foreseeable class of plaintiffs. For example, members of the general public, or invitees such as sales and service persons at a particular plaintiff's business premises, or persons travelling on a highway near the scene of a negligently-caused accident, such as the one at bar, who are delayed in the conduct of their affairs and suffer varied economic losses, are certainly a foreseeable class of plaintiffs. Yet their presence within the area would be fortuitous, and the particular type of economic injury that could be suffered by such persons would be hopelessly unpredictable and not realistically foreseeable. Thus, the class itself would not be sufficiently ascertainable. An identifiable class of plaintiffs must be particularly foreseeable in terms of the type of persons or entities comprising the class, the certainty or predictability of their presence, the approximate numbers of those in the class, as well as the type of economic expectations disrupted. [Citations.]

[The court reviews the role of proximate cause to restrict recoveries and concludes that the economic losses must be reasonably foreseeable, not just generally foreseeable.] * * * If negligence is the failure to take precautions that cost less than the damage wrought by the ensuing accident, it would be unfair and socially inefficient to assign liability for harm that no reasonably-undertaken precaution could have avoided. [Citations.]

We conclude therefore that a defendant who has breached his duty of care to avoid the risk of economic injury to particularly foreseeable plaintiffs may be held liable for actual economic losses that are proximately caused by its breach of duty. In this context, those economic losses are recoverable as damages when they are the natural and probable consequence of a defendant's negligence in the sense that they are reasonably to be anticipated in view of defendant's capacity to have foreseen that the particular plaintiff or identifiable class of plaintiffs, as defined *infra,* is demonstrably within the risk created by defendant's negligence.

We are satisfied that our holding today is fully applicable to the facts that we have considered on this appeal. Plaintiff has set forth a cause of action under our decision, and it is entitled to have the matter proceed to a plenary trial. Among the facts that persuade us that a cause of action has been established is the close proximity of the North Terminal and People Express Airlines to the Conrail freight yard; the obvious nature of the plaintiff's operations and particular foreseeability of economic losses resulting from a accident and evacuation; the defendants' actual or constructive knowledge of the volatile properties of ethylene oxide; and the existence of an emergency response plan prepared by some of the defendants (alluded to in the course of oral argument), which apparently called for the nearby area to be evacuated to avoid the risk of harm in case of an explosion. We do not mean to suggest by our recitation of these facts that actual knowledge of the eventual economic losses is necessary to the cause of action; rather, particular foreseeability will suffice. The plaintiff still faces a difficult task in proving damages, particularly lost profits, to the degree of certainty required in other negligence cases. The trial court's examination of these proofs must be exacting to ensure that damages recovered are those reasonably to have been anticipated in view of the defendants' capacity to have foreseen that this particular plaintiff was within the risk created by their negligence.

    * * * [Remanded.]

---

1. Compare the economic loss suffered when a professional commits malpractice. This tort allows recovery of provable losses even though they are only economic ones without accompanying physical harm to person or property. For a recent illustration, consider *Hydro Investors, Inc. v. Trafalgar Power, Inc.,* 227 F.3d 8 (2d Cir.2000), where the owners of hydroelectric

power plants brought a professional malpractice action against an engineering firm. The court recognized the historical foundations of the economic loss preclusionary rule:

> The rule developed as a way of enforcing the dictates of privity in product liability law and preventing tort remedies from eliminating the customary limitations involved in cases addressing the sale of goods. "[T]he majority of cases enunciating the economic loss rule [have] arise[n] in the context of product liability, where the economic losses are essentially contractual in nature, and therefore the risk may be allocated by the parties, as reflected in the purchase price, UCC warranties or insurance. . . . "

> Although the doctrine survives in today's caselaw despite the increasing relaxation of privity rules, it is not always applied in negligence cases. Primarily, its continuing role is based on the recognition that "[r]elying solely on foreseeability to define the extent of liability [in cases involving economic loss], while generally effective, could result in some instances in liability so great that, as a matter of policy, courts would be reluctant to impose it." To prevent such open-ended liability, courts have applied the economic loss rule to prevent the recovery of damages that are inappropriate because they actually lie in the nature of breach of contract as opposed to tort. The difficulty in our case is determining where to draw the line. [Citations omitted] 227 F.3d at 16.

The court held that, under New York law, the economic loss preclusion rule did not bar recovery of damages for lost revenues attributable to the engineering malpractice. The court reasoned that since many types of malpractice claims against professionals regularly arise out of a contractual relationship and involve economic losses; to apply a per se rule of exclusion would potentially bar many meritorious claims.

Should purely economic losses caused by malpractice be compensable when ones from a defective product are not? Why distinguish between them? *See also* Smith v. Lewis, 13 Cal.3d 349, 530 P.2d 589, 118 Cal.Rptr. 621 (1975) ($100,000 award against attorney who represented wife in divorce proceeding and failed to claim her interest in the husband's retirement benefits).

2. The Restatement (Second) of Torts adopts the distinction made by Justice Holmes in *Robins Dry Dock*. It denies recovery for pecuniary losses resulting from a negligent interference with contractual performance (§ 766C), but allows compensation if the tortfeasor intentionally interfered with performance (§ 766A) or with prospective contractual relations (§ 766B).

Annett Holdings, Inc. v. Kum & Go, L.C.

801 N.W.2d 499 (Iowa 2011).

■ MANSFIELD, JUSTICE.

A dishonest employee of a trucking company put money in his pocket while claiming to be buying fuel for his fellow employees. This fraud was perpetrated at a truck stop, where the employee used his company credit card to obtain cash while reporting purchases of fuel. The truck stop paid out the cash, accepting the employee's bogus explanation that the money was for other employees' fuel purchases, and was reimbursed pursuant to its contract with the card issuer. The card issuer in turn was reimbursed under a separate contract with the trucking company's parent. After the fraud had been ongoing for several years, it was discovered, and the employee was arrested and convicted of theft.

The trucking company's parent now seeks to reverse the contractual flow of dollars by suing the truck stop both for negligence and as an alleged third-party beneficiary of the contract between the card issuer and the truck stop. We agree with the district court that the economic loss rule bars the negligence claim. * * *

Annett Holdings, Inc. is an Iowa holding company. One of its subsidiaries is TMC Transportation, a trucking company that employed Michael Vititoe as a shag driver at the Clow Valve plant in Oskaloosa. Vititoe's duties as a shag driver consisted of moving empty and loaded semi-tractor trailers within the yard of the Clow Valve plant, facilitating the loading and unloading of trailers, and facilitating the transportation of Clow Valve products by other TMC drivers to outside destinations. TMC provided Vititoe a truck along with a Comdata credit card to purchase fuel for the truck.

Annett and Comdata had a written agreement. Under the agreement, Comdata provided cards that could be used by authorized Annett employees to purchase fuel and obtain cash advances at any Comdata authorized service center locations. Annett agreed to accept full responsibility for all purchases made with those cards and also to be "fully responsible for the unauthorized or fraudulent use thereof until such time as Comdata has received such notification from [Annett] provided that each fraud or misuse is not attributed to Comdata." Annett also agreed to "hold Comdata harmless from any and all liability resulting from the acts of any employees or agents of [Annett] which acts shall include but are not limited to negligent acts of such persons." A separate schedule, signed by both parties, clarified that the Annett/Comdata agreement extended to Annett's TMC subsidiary.

Comdata in turn had a written contract with Kum & Go, L.C. that enabled a particular Kum & Go store in Oskaloosa to handle Comdata transactions. The agreement provided that this Kum & Go service center would lease a Comdata terminal for $80 per month, which would then be utilized for Comdata card transactions. Comdata would reimburse Kum & Go for those transactions after deducting certain fees. The agreement contained detailed procedures that Kum & Go promised to follow in processing Comdata transactions. The Comdata/Kum & Go agreement was governed by Tennessee law.

From November 2002 to April 2006, while Vititoe was employed by TMC, he went to the Kum & Go in Oskaloosa on an almost daily basis. Store personnel allowed Vititoe to operate the Comdata terminal himself. Vititoe managed to steal money by entering fuel purchases on the Comdata machine and submitting cash advance slips printed out by the machine to the store clerks—who then paid Vititoe in cash. Kum & Go personnel wondered why Vititoe was getting cash back while reporting fuel purchases. He claimed he was doing so because he was a "regional supervisor" and needed cash to pay for other employees' fuel purchases because the other employees did not have cards of their own.

Vititoe's Comdata transactions were reported, reviewed, and validated daily by TMC's fuel manager. For reasons that are not clear, the pre-March 2006 fuel manager never noticed (or at least never did anything about) Vititoe's suspicious activity. In March 2006, a new fuel manager took over. Almost immediately, he noticed Vititoe's pattern of "buying" fuel every day, even on weekends when he was supposedly not working[.] * * *

Annett filed a petition against Kum & Go alleging, among other theories, negligence and breach of contract for the monetary losses it suffered through Vititoe's theft. Annett's negligence theory asserted that Kum & Go was negligent in providing cash to Vititoe and that Vititoe did not have actual or apparent authority to receive cash back on Comdata transactions. * * *

Kum & Go moved for summary judgment. Kum & Go argued it could not be liable in negligence due to the "economic loss rule" and because it owed no duty to Annett. * * *

The district court granted summary judgment to Kum & Go. It found the negligence claim barred by the economic loss rule. [Annett appeals.] * * *

In this case, Annett seeks to recover an economic loss. No one was injured; no property was damaged or destroyed. Rather, Vititoe made unauthorized withdrawals of cash that were charged to Comdata and ultimately to Annett. Annett now claims that Kum & Go was negligent in failing to prevent this unauthorized activity, which resulted, indirectly, in economic losses to Annett.

Notably, Annett had entered into a contract with the card provider, Comdata, which in turn had entered into a contract with Kum & Go. In the contract with Comdata, Annett assumed responsibility for unauthorized or fraudulent use of Comdata cards by its own employees. Annett does not dispute that this contract bars it from recovering against Comdata, but seeks now to recover in tort from the remote party with which Comdata contracted—Kum & Go.

* * *

As a general proposition, the economic loss rule bars recovery in negligence when the plaintiff has suffered only economic loss. * * *

This rule is partly intended to prevent the "Death of Contract," *see* Grant Gilmore, The Death of Contract (2d ed.1995), or the tortification of contract law. When two parties have a contractual relationship, the economic loss rule prevents one party from bringing a negligence action against the other over the first party's defeated expectations—a subject matter the parties can be presumed to have allocated between themselves in their contract. [Citations.] This is sometimes referred to as "the contractual economic loss rule." *See* Dan B. Dobbs, An Introduction to Non–Statutory Economic Loss Claims, 48 Ariz. L.Rev. 713, 723 (2006) [hereinafter Dobbs]. Courts reason that when a party enters into a contract, that document should control the party's rights and duties. *Id.*

But the doctrine is by no means limited to the situation where the plaintiff and the defendant are in direct contractual privity. For example, in Nebraska Innkeepers, plaintiffs sought recovery from a bridge contractor for purely economic loss that occurred when the bridge had to be closed because of the contractor's negligence. 345 N.W.2d at 128–29. This is an example of what is sometimes called "the stranger economic loss rule." *See* Dobbs, 48 Ariz. L.Rev. at 715. This aspect of the economic loss rule has several underlying justifications. In a complex society such as ours, economic reverberations travel quickly and widely, resulting in potentially limitless liability. As Professor Dobbs puts it, "Stand-alone economic loss often spreads without limit. *Id.* Also, the rule encourages parties to enter into contracts." *Id.* at 716–17.

* * *

The economic loss rule is subject to qualifications. For example, purely economic losses are recoverable in actions asserting claims of professional negligence against attorneys and accountants. [Citation.] Also, negligent misrepresentation claims fall outside the scope of the economic loss rule. [Citation.] In addition, when the duty of care arises out of a principal-agent relationship, economic losses may be recoverable. [Citation.]

We need not attempt to delineate the precise contours of the economic loss rule in Iowa. For present purposes, it is enough for us to note that Annett's cause of action bears a number of characteristics that bring it within the scope of the economic loss rule. The claim does not fall under any of the recognized exceptions or qualifications to the economic loss rule. * * *

Here Annett agreed with Comdata that it would be "fully responsible" for the fraudulent or unauthorized use of credit cards. Annett knew that Comdata would be entering into agreements with service centers, that Comdata would be reimbursing service centers for charges made to the credit cards, and that Comdata would in turn expect reimbursement from Annett. Also, Annett had the capacity to prevent fraudulent or unauthorized use by its employee: Its subsidiary TMC received a daily report of Vititoe's transactions, and as soon as a new fuel manager took over, that person noticed the suspicious activity immediately. It is difficult to see why a tort remedy is needed here. Annett contracted to assume certain risks of financial loss and had the ability to minimize those risks.

* * *

AFFIRMED.

■ WIGGINS, JUSTICE (dissenting).

I dissent. * * * I cannot support the conclusion that we should bar its claim because of the economic loss rule. * * *

In examining the cause of action in the present case, it is clear to me that Annett Holdings is not trying to circumvent a contract claim by bringing a tort claim. Allowing the claim against Kum & Go to proceed will not result in a flood of litigation, speculative damages, or thwart any of the other rationales commonly asserted in association with the economic loss rule. * * *

In the summary judgment record there is a genuine issue of material fact as to whether Kum & Go was negligent in the processing of the credit card transactions. The breach of the duty to use ordinary care in the processing of the purchases made with Annett's credit cards is independent of any contractual duty. In Iowa, courts recognized that under some circumstances, a breach of a contractual duty may give rise to an independent action in tort. [Citation.] It seems incongruous to me that this court will allow independent tort actions in situations where a breach of a contractual duty gives rise to an independent tort, but will not allow such an action where an independent duty exists and there is no contract between the parties.

* * * I would not apply the economic loss rule mechanically. I would look at the nature of the action, the breach of the duty alleged, and the damages sought before I would allow the economic loss rule to bar a claim. I agree the economic loss rule should preclude recovery when the parties are in privity with the attendant opportunity to allocate the risk of loss, and no independent duty is established, because any damages incurred could have been covered by an agreement negotiated between the parties. It makes no sense to hold parties not in privity to the same standard, where a duty to process credit card transactions in a reasonable manner exists. The purpose of the rule is to prevent contract claims from being litigated as tort claims. There are no contract claims available to Annett under the facts of this case. Hence, the purpose of the economic loss rule is not frustrated by applying it under these narrow facts. Accordingly, I would reverse the district court's order granting Kum & Go's motion for summary judgment.

---

1.   For classic commentary on economic loss, *see*: McThenia & Ulrich, A Return to Principles of Corrective Justice in Deciding Economic Loss Cases, 69 Va.L.Rev. 1517 (1983); Rizzo, The Theory of Economic Loss in the Law of Torts, 11 J.Legal Stud. 281 (1982); James, Limitations on Liability for Economic Loss Caused by Negligence: A Pragmatic Appraisal, 25 Vand.L.Rev. 43 (1972); Harper, Interference with Contractual Relations, 47 Nw.U.L.Rev. 873 (1953).

CHAPTER 15

Punitive Damages

Chapter Coverage:

The area of civil damages that overlaps with criminal law is punitive damages. Unlike compensatory damages, punitive damages are not awarded to plaintiffs to compensate for their losses. Rather, punitive damages are awarded to punish defendants for egregious conduct and deter defendants and others from future offenses. Punitive damages are often referred to as "exemplary damages" because they are intended to make defendants public examples of inappropriate behavior. Punitive damages also are sometimes referred to as "smart money" because they are suppose to hurt defendants financially.

Punitive damages have a lengthy heritage in Anglo–American jurisprudence, but they also have come under sharp attack. American courts began to recognize punitive damage awards at least as early as 1791. Despite their longstanding presence, however, punitive damages remain a controversial issue. Critics complain that awarding punitive damages punishes defendants for anti-social conduct without the benefit of the constitutional safeguards that apply to the imposition of criminal sanctions and that awarding punitive damages is not in keeping with the traditional compensatory goal of damages law. When courts award punitive damages, plaintiffs receive a windfall in excess of what is necessary to compensate them for their losses. Proponents argue that punitive damages are necessary to assess the true societal costs of defendants' misfeasances. An award of punitive damages also provides a fund from which plaintiffs can recover attorneys fees and other litigation costs that are otherwise noncompensable.

Punitive damages are not available to redress all legal wrongs. Instead, punitive damages are available to punish and deter only egregious misconduct. Jurisdictions define the level of conduct that is sufficiently egregious to sustain an award of punitive damages differently. Generally, however, punitive damages are available when a defendant acts with an evil motive such as spite, ill will, intent to injure or fraud or when a defendant acts with gross recklessness or a willful disregard for the rights of others.

Punitive damages are never awarded automatically, nor are they awarded as a matter of right. The trier of fact has discretion whether to award them at all and, if so, in fixing the amount. Factors in determining the amount include: the nature and reprehensibility of the defendant's wrongdoing, the duration of the misconduct and any attempt to conceal the misconduct, and the relationship between the defendant and plaintiff.

Generally, the trier of fact also is permitted to consider the defendant's financial condition and whether the defendant profited financially from its misconduct. The financial condition of the defendant is an appropriate consideration because the purpose of an award of punitive damages is to punish and deter the defendant and others similarly situated from engaging in such conduct in the future. A reviewing court will not set aside an award of punitive damages unless it is so excessive that it appears to be the result of passion or prejudice.

Punitive damages pose special problems in mass disaster and products liability cases. Courts are challenged in those cases to accommodate the goals of punishment and deterrence without imposing ruinous liability. To the extent that punitive damage awards are imposed to disgorge a manufacturer of the profits it earned from the marketing of an unsafe product, problems arise when multiple cases seek to disgorge the defendant of the same profit. Disgorging profits from the marketing of unsafe products raises questions about one state's ability to impose sanctions for conduct occurring in another state. Furthermore, at some point the numerous awards based on the same conduct exceed the goals of deterrence and punishment and threaten the viability of the enterprise. This situation often creates a race to the courthouse among plaintiffs who file separate but similar cases. Each plaintiff wishes to be the first, and possibly the last, to get a large punitive damage award.

Many states have sought to restrict punitive damage awards through various legislative and judicial measures. Some states require plaintiffs to make a prima facie showing of liability for punitive damages before they may plead claims for punitive damages. Other states require plaintiffs to make such a showing before allowing discovery of defendants' financial condition. Numerous states require plaintiffs to prove liability for punitive damages by clear and convincing evidence. Many states require punitive damages to be assessed in bifurcated proceedings. Some states have placed ceilings on the dollar amounts allowable as punitive damage awards. Finally, some states require a portion of punitive damages awards to be paid to the state rather than plaintiffs.

Punitive damages generally are not available to remedy a breach of contract regardless of how willful, intentional or malicious the breach. However, a few jurisdictions have permitted punitive damages for wrongful breaches of contract. Additionally, most jurisdictions allow a plaintiff to recover punitive damages when a defendant's conduct in breaching a contract also constitutes an independent tort.

The Supreme Court has addressed the constitutionality of punitive damages several times. The Court has held that punitive damages do not constitute excessive fines. However, the Court has recognized that at some point a punitive damage award may be so excessive that it violates a defendant's right to due process. Likewise, the Court has recognized that due process requires minimum procedural safeguards to ensure that punitive damages awards do not result in arbitrary deprivations of property.

Model Case:

Terry Arnold worked for five years as a software design engineer for the High-tech Computer Company. The employment contract contained a non-competition clause which provided that Arnold could not work for any competitor of the company for a period of 18 months following termination of employment with High-tech.

Arnold received a lucrative offer of employment from the Newtech Computer Company and decided to accept the job despite the contractual restriction. High-tech could maintain a suit against Arnold for breach of contract and recover compensatory damages if the contractual noncompetition provision is valid. Moreover, the court might enjoin Arnold from working for any competitor for the term of the restriction.

High-tech might also seek punitive damages for this flagrant disregard of its rights, but it is unlikely to receive them. A contract breach does not generally support punitive damages unless the plaintiff establishes a tortious basis for them. For instance, if High-tech could demonstrate that Arnold fraudulently misappropriated trade secrets, then exemplary damages might be available. Only a few courts have interpreted such tortious basis to mean less than full proof of the elements of an independent tort. Because the elements of fraud are particularly difficult to prove, High-tech is unlikely to establish a basis for punitive damages in this case.

A. ENTITLEMENT AND PROCEEDINGS

Silverman v. King

247 N.J.Super. 534, 589 A.2d 1057 (1991).

■ LANDAU, J.A.D.

This is an appeal from dismissal of a claim for punitive damages made in conjunction with the complaint of plaintiff-appellant Jeffrey P. Silverman against defendant-respondent Roger King for damages arising out of a unique assault upon Silverman in an Atlantic City casino on April 15, 1987.

Silverman was the house dealer at a high stakes baccarat table. King had placed $22,500 in bets on the hand being played, and as the highest bettor was given "courtesy" to look at the "player" hand after it was dealt. When he exercised this right, Silverman "faced" the cards and "called" a "natural eight," a hand which made it very likely that King would win a $20,000 bet. King, a large man, jubilantly rose, went behind Silverman then still engaged in "facing" and "calling" the cards for the table, and threw his right arm around Silverman's neck and upper chest, lifting him off the floor. Silverman testified that King "lifted me off the ground by my throat and held me there with great force" for almost twenty seconds from initial contact to release. King's companion said, "Let him go" and pulled his arm from Silverman.

Silverman continued the deal, and despite discomfort, completed his shift. King told him he was only "joking around," inquired if he was "okay," and continued to play at Silverman's table.

Unfortunately, Silverman's body build and abnormal chest wall configuration rendered him particularly vulnerable to this strenuous physical embrace, well-intentioned or not. Not long after, Silverman developed symptoms of a condition diagnosed as thoracic outlet syndrome, which the jury in this case determined to have been proximately caused by the April 15 incident. That finding and the $66,000 compensatory damage award have not been challenged on appeal.

The sole issue before us is whether the essentially undisputed evidence, together with all legitimate inferences therefrom, could sustain a judgment arising from conduct which was malicious, wanton, willful or sufficiently egregious to warrant punitive damages. The trial judge granted King's motion for involuntary dismissal, reasoning that:

> There is none of the malice, wantonness, willful, malicious, aggregious [sic] conduct that is required when you have punitive damages to lift the case in the area of negligence to this higher level of willful, wanton, malicious, aggregious [sic] conduct.

> The man had just won $20,000 on the turn of two cards. He jumps up exuberant, as was described by the plaintiff's own witnesses, and runs over and grabs the dealer who had just dealt this $20,000 winning hand. That's all it was. There was no intention to do anything.

> There was no malice. There was no willful, wanton disregard of the rights of others. There was no aggregious [sic] conduct.

We affirm substantially for the reasons expressed by the trial judge. We add our recognition that all unintended consequences of intentional but non-malicious acts are not exempt from exposure to punitive damages. For example, no matter how good-natured its purpose, a pilot's congenial aerial buzzing of his neighbor's house clearly carries with it enough prospect of danger to warrant a trial judge to submit the question of outrageous and egregious conduct to a jury for possible assessment of punitive damages. There must be, in other words, foreseeability of unintended harmful consequences of a friendly, but intentional touching before it warrants the deterrent of punishment in addition to compensatory damages. [Citations.] We note that these authorities are consistent with the legislative standards for punitive damages established in the recently enacted New Jersey products liability statute. [Citation.]

Here, there was uncontradicted expert testimony that the kind of "hug" given by King would not be expected to cause injury to one not afflicted with a congenital predisposing skeletal condition such as Silverman's.

Every intentional tort carries with it a potential for the charge of conduct warranting punitive damages. The mere assertion of a request for punitive damages in an intentional tort case, however, does not create an absolute right to have that request placed before the jury. The trial court had a duty under *R.* 4:37–2(b) to scan the evidence to ascertain whether it presented a factual basis for a reasonable jury to conclude that the factors warranting punitive damages were present.

Here, while intentional conduct and even recklessness might have been demonstrated, the record did not show that King's conduct was such as would ordinarily be expected to present a danger beyond fleeting discomfort to a normal person. This was the kind of well-intentioned physical exuberance commonly seen at every athletic contest, both in the stands and on the field. While parties injured thereby should not suffer without recompense, punitive deterrents are not warranted where the conduct is neither mean-spirited nor so heedless of the likelihood of harm as to be deemed wanton. Here, the trial judge properly recognized that the extremely unlikely result of King's intentional but not predictably dangerous conduct could not as a matter of law render that conduct sufficiently outrageous or egregious to warrant punitive damages.

Affirmed.

---

1. Distinguish between conduct sufficient to support liability for compensatory damages and conduct sufficient to support discretionary punitive damages. In the principal case, the conduct can support a claim for battery because it was intentional contact in a manner that was not socially acceptable under the circumstances, or for negligence because the gambler took an unreasonable risk when he hugged the dealer so fiercely. It could not support punitive damages, however, because the conduct did not meet the minimum level of egregiousness necessary under the state's law. Therefore, the plaintiff recovered only compensatory damages.

Distinguish also punitive damages from the compensatory damages rule that a "thin-skulled plaintiff" may recover losses that stem from an unusual predisposition to injury. This is the rule that the tortfeasor takes the plaintiff "as he finds him" with predispositions that are rare. Thus, the plaintiff with a thin-skull can still recover from the tortfeasor for her serious head injuries even if another person would only have received minor injuries. The dealer in the principal case was such a plaintiff. Nonetheless, that fact alone will not support punitive damages. If the tortfeasor was aware of the unusual condition that caused the serious injury, then that additional fact might support a finding of malice, wilfulness, or wanton disregard of the safety of the plaintiff.

2. The concept of punitive damages has a longstanding meaning and heritage under the common law. In *Molzof v. United States*, 502 U.S. 301, 112 S.Ct. 711, 116 L.Ed.2d 731 (1992), the Court interpreted the meaning of the term "punitive damages" under the Federal Tort Claims Act, 28 U.S.C. 2674, in an action against the government for injuries sustained in a negligently performed surgical procedure at a Veteran's Administration hospital. The government conceded liability but claimed that the damages

requested for future medical expenses and loss of enjoyment of life were "punitive in effect" and consequently prohibited under the FTCA.

A unanimous Court rejected the government's contention that any damages that are not strictly compensatory are necessarily characterized as punitive. The Court stated that "punitive damages" is a "legal term of art" with a "long pedigree in the law." Thus, although some damages may fall in the "gray zone" for purposes of the FTCA, the Act only explicitly bars the recovery of those damages which are legally considered punitive damages by reference to traditional common-law principles.

3. *Standard of Conduct.* In the principal case, the court described the conduct giving rise to a claim for punitive damages as "malicious, wanton, willful, or sufficiently egregious conduct." Jurisdictions vary in their characterization of conduct rendering a defendant liable for punitive damages. For example, California Civil Code § 3294 provides:

§ 3294   When permitted.

(a) In an action for the breach of an obligation not arising from contract, where it is proven by clear and convincing evidence that the defendant has been guilty of oppression, fraud, or malice, the plaintiff, in addition to the actual damages, may recover damages for the sake of example and by way of punishing the defendant.

* * *

(c) As used in this section, the following definitions shall apply:

(1) "Malice" means conduct which is intended by the defendant to cause injury to the plaintiff or despicable conduct which is carried on by the defendant with a willful and conscious disregard of the rights or safety of others.

(2) "Oppression" means despicable conduct that subjects a person to cruel and unjust hardship in conscious disregard of that person's rights.

(3) "Fraud" means an intentional misrepresentation, deceit, or concealment of a material fact known to the defendant with the intention on the part of the defendant of thereby depriving a person of property or legal rights or otherwise causing injury.

See also Ga. Code Ann. § 51–12–5.1 (2000) ("Punitive damages may be awarded only in such tort actions in which it is proven ... that the defendant's action showed willful misconduct, malice, fraud, wantonness, oppression or that entire want of care which would raise the presumption of conscious indifference to consequences.")

Would the application of any of these standards change the result in the principal case? *See* Kanne v. Connecticut Gen. Life Ins., 607 F.Supp. 899 (C.D.Cal.1985), vacated on other grounds 859 F.2d 96 (9th Cir.1988) (punitive damages assessed against insurance company where the company failed to investigate, process and pay their medical claims promptly). *But see* Roberts v. Forte Hotels, Inc., 227 Ga.App. 471, 489 S.E.2d 540 (1997) (hotel's failure to provide dusk-to-dawn security did not evidence want of care sufficient to warrant award of punitive damages where manager hired security only for weekends because that was when a majority of problems occurred and hotel took other measures to improve security); Furek v. University of Delaware, 594 A.2d 506 (Del.1991) (student injured in hazing incident not entitled to punitive damages despite university's notice of previous hazing activities where university's ineffectual response was well-intentioned and not characterized by conscious disregard of a known risk).

4. *Procedures for Awarding Punitive Damages.* In most jurisdictions, the factfinder determines liability for and the amount of punitive damages. Thus, if either of the parties has demanded a jury trial, the jury will determine liability for punitive damages and the amount of punitive damages. Liability for punitive damages is never mandatory. Instead, the factfinder retains the discretion to decline to impose punitive damages even if the plaintiff demonstrates that the defendant's misconduct meets the requisite standard. In most jurisdictions, the factfinder is instructed to consider the purposes of punitive damages in deciding whether to impose punitive damages.

In determining the amount of punitive damages, the factfinder is instructed to consider several factors such as:

a. The nature and reprehensibility of defendant's conduct;

b. The seriousness of the harm resulting from the misconduct;

c. The defendant's awareness that such harm would result;

d. The duration of the misconduct, defendant's conduct upon discovery of the misconduct and any efforts to conceal the misconduct;

e. The profitability of defendant's misconduct;

f. The defendant's net wealth;

g. The relationship between the actual harm and the amount of punitive damages; and

h. The total deterrent effect of other damages and punishment imposed upon the defendant.

See, e.g., Kan. Stat. Ann. § 60–3702 (2000); Minn. Stat. Ann. § 549.20 (West 2000); Miss. Code Ann. § 11–1–65 (2001); Hodges v. S.C. Toof & Co., 833 S.W.2d 896 (Tenn.1992); Farmers Ins. Exchange v. Shirley, 958 P.2d 1040 (Wyo.1998).

5. *Judicial Review.* Punitive damage awards also are subject to judicial review in most jurisdictions. Indeed, the Supreme Court has indicated that judicial review of punitive damages may be constitutionally required. *See* Honda Motor Co. v. Oberg, 512 U.S. 415, 114 S.Ct. 2331, 129 L.Ed.2d 336 (1994). A court can set aside or remit an award of punitive damages if it is so excessive that it appears to be the product of passion or prejudice or shocks the judicial conscience. *See e.g.,* Paracelsus Health Care Corp. v. Willard, 754 So.2d 437 (Miss.1999) (a jury verdict awarding punitive damages may be altered or amended only when it is so excessive that it

evinces passion, bias, and prejudice on the part of the jury so as to shock the conscience).

In determining whether an award is excessive, courts are guided by many of the same factors that guide the trier of fact in determining the amount of the punitive damage award, including the reprehensibility of the defendant, the nature of the wrong; the profitability of the defendant's misconduct and the relationship between the amount of compensatory damages and the amount of punitive damages. *See, e.g.,* Moore v. Commissioner of Internal Revenue, 53 F.3d 712 (5th Cir.1995) (under Texas law, the nature of the wrong; the character of the conduct involved; the defendant's degree of culpability; the situation and sensibilities of the parties concerned; and the extent to which such conduct offends a public sense of justice); Alkire v. First Nat'l Bank of Parsons, 197 W.Va. 122, 475 S.E.2d 122 (1996) (the relationship between the harm from the defendant's conduct and the damages; the reprehensibility of the defendant's conduct; the defendant's profit from the conduct; the defendant's financial condition; litigation costs; any criminal sanctions imposed on the defendant; and the appropriateness of punitive damages to encourage fair and reasonable settlements).

Some states have altered the common law scheme of review as part of larger tort reform legislation. For example, New Jersey's Punitive Damage Act requires a trial judge to ascertain that a punitive damage award is "reasonable in amount" and "justified in the circumstances of the case, in light of the purpose to punish the defendant and to deter that defendant from repeating such conduct" before entering judgment on the verdict. Courts have interpreted this standard as permitting more judicial scrutiny of punitive awards than the common law "shocks the conscience" standard of review. *See* Inter Medical Supplies Ltd. v. EBI Medical Sys., 975 F.Supp. 681 (D.N.J.1997) *aff'd in part, rev'd on other grounds* 181 F.3d 446 (3d Cir.1999).

6. *State of Mind.* The Supreme Court has held that evidence of a defendant's state of mind is admissible with respect to an award of punitive damages. *See* Herbert v. Lando, 441 U.S. 153, 99 S.Ct. 1635, 60 L.Ed.2d 115 (1979). Thus, in *Palmetto State Medical Center v. Operation Lifeline,* 117 F.3d 142 (4th Cir.1997), the Fourth Circuit held that a lower court erred in excluding testimony by abortion protesters of their religious motives in an action for trespass filed by a clinic against the protesters. The Fourth Circuit explained that while the protesters' religious motives could not shield them from the consequences of their otherwise unlawful protest activity, testimony about their religious motives presented evidence of the protesters' state of mind. Therefore, the court concluded that the evidence was admissible in connection with the clinic's claim for punitive damages.

7. *Derivative Claim.* A claim for punitive damages is not considered an independent cause of action but is derivative in character. Therefore, although the elements of proof differ for punitive and compensatory damages, entitlement to an exemplary award is dependent upon the success of the underlying claim.

8. *Vicarious Liability.* Jurisdictions are split as to whether a principal can be held vicariously liable for punitive damages based on an agent's tortious conduct. A majority of jurisdictions follow the "complicity liability" rule. Under this theory, liability for punitive damages based on an agent's egregious conduct usually does not extend to a principal. The principal can be liable for punitive damages only if: (1) the principal authorized, participated in, consented to or ratified the egregious conduct; (2) the principal deliberately retained an unfit servant; or (3) if the agent engaging in the egregious conduct was employed in a managerial capacity and acted within the scope of her employment. *Compare* EEOC v. Wal–Mart Stores, 11 F.Supp.2d 1313 (D.N.M.1998) (Wal–Mart liable for punitive damages because employees engaged in discriminatory conduct were managerial employees and because Wal–Mart ratified discriminatory inquiry) *aff'd* 202 F.3d 281; Loughry v. Lincoln First Bank, 67 N.Y.2d 369, 502 N.Y.S.2d 965, 494 N.E.2d 70 (1986) (bank not liable for punitive damages based on the slanderous statements of one of its vice presidents where the vice president lacked any significant managerial responsibilities).

A minority of jurisdictions adopt a more liberal approach known as the "vicarious liability" rule. These jurisdictions permit the imposition of punitive damages against a principal any time its agent commits a wrongful act that would subject the actor to liability for punitive damages while acting within the scope of the actor's authority. *See, e.g.,* Magnum Foods v. Continental Cas. Co., 36 F.3d 1491 (10th Cir.1994) (under Oklahoma law principal could be held liable for punitive damages without a finding that it participated in or authorized the acts of its agent); Norcon v. Kotowski, 971 P.2d 158 (Alaska 1999) (punitive damages may be awarded against an employer for the acts of employees within the scope of their employment). These jurisdictions justify the award of punitive damages as a way to encourage principals to exercise closer control over their agents. *See* Stroud v. Denny's Rest., 271 Or. 430, 532 P.2d 790 (1975).

A few state legislatures have sought to restrict further a principal's liability for punitive damages based on the wrongful conduct of its agent. *See, e.g.,* Fla. Stat. Ann. § 768.72 (West 2001) (permitting an award of punitive damages only if the principal "actively and knowingly participated in" or "knowingly condoned, ratified or consented to" the conduct or if the principal "engaged in conduct that constituted gross negligence and that contributed to the loss."); Kan. Stat. Ann. § 60–3701 (2000).

9. *Actual Damages.* Jurisdictions are divided over what type of showing is necessary to satisfy the damage element of an underlying claim and, therefore, render a defendant liable for punitive damages. A few jurisdictions provide that a jury must award a plaintiff compensatory damages. *See, e.g.,* Bell v. McManus, 294 Ark. 275, 742 S.W.2d 559 (1988) ("[E]ven if nominal damages had been awarded, it still would not have supported an award of punitive damages."); N.J. Stat. Ann. § 2A:15–5.13 (West 2001) ("An award of nominal damages cannot support an award of punitive damages."). These jurisdictions hold that an award of nominal damages on

the plaintiff's underlying claim is insufficient to sustain an award of punitive damages.

Most jurisdictions allow punitive damages based on an award of either nominal damages or compensatory damages. *See, e.g.,* Ross–Simons of Warwick v. Baccarat, 182 F.R.D. 386 (D.R.I.1998); Bassett v. Toyota Motor Credit Corp., 818 F.Supp. 1462 (S.D.Ala.1993) ("Alabama allows for an award of punitive damages where the plaintiff proves at least nominal injury."). These jurisdictions reason that inherent in an award of nominal damages is a finding by the jury that the defendant has violated a plaintiff's legal right. Therefore, when a jury fails to award even nominal damages the jury has concluded, at least implicitly, that the defendant did not violate any legal right of the plaintiff. Awarding punitive damages under these circumstances would convert a defendant's otherwise lawful conduct into an actionable wrong merely because some malice attended the otherwise lawful conduct. *See* Whitaker, 734 A.2d at 253. Likewise, these jurisdictions hold that an award of compensatory or nominal damages is necessary to limit a plaintiff's standing to "bring suits expressing social condemnation and disapproval." In re Paris Air Crash v. Plaintiffs in MDL 172, 622 F.2d 1315 (9th Cir.1980).

No jurisdictions currently allow an award of punitive damages based on a showing of harm without an award of compensatory or nominal damages. *See, e.g.,* Life Ins. Co. of Ga. v. Smith, 719 So.2d 797 (Ala.1998) *overruling* Caterpillar, Inc. v. Hightower, 605 So.2d 1193 (Ala.1992) (award of at least nominal damages not a prerequisite to award of punitive damages); Garnes v. Fleming Landfill, 186 W.Va. 656, 413 S.E.2d 897 (1991) *overruling* Wells v. Smith, 171 W.Va. 97, 297 S.E.2d 872 (1982) (failure to return award for compensatory damages did not preclude award of punitive damages).

10. *Punitive Damages in Equity.* The traditional rule that punitive damages are not recoverable in equity derives from the historical limitations on powers of equity courts. The notion was that the equity court lacked the power to award exemplary damages, and was limited in granting compensatory damages as merely incidental to other relief. This limitation has lost its vitality following the merger of law and equity courts in most jurisdictions. Courts often draw upon the principle articulated by Judge Cardozo in *Susquehanna S.S. Co. v. Andersen & Co.*: "The whole body of principles, whether of law or of equity, bearing on the case, becomes the reservoir to be drawn upon by the court in enlightening its judgment." 239 N.Y. 285, 294, 146 N.E. 381, 384.

Courts have diverged in the interpretation of statutes that authorize "equitable relief" as to the permissibility of punitive damages. *Compare* Schoenholtz v. Doniger, 657 F.Supp. 899 (S.D.N.Y.1987) (punitive damages available against fiduciary under ERISA) *with* Whitaker v. Texaco, Inc., 566 F.Supp. 745 (N.D.Ga.1983) (ERISA does not authorize exemplary damages).

PROBLEM: THE INJURED ROOKIE

Palmer enrolled as a freshman at State University and was selected to be a member of the State University swimming team. As a new member of the swimming team, Palmer was considered a "rookie" by returning members who considered themselves "vets." Palmer resigned from the swimming team after one semester because Palmer was subjected to numerous incidents of hazing while a member of the team. For example, vets subjected Palmer and other rookies to a barrage of obscene, offensive and harassing language on a daily basis both during practice and outside of practice while rookies were in dorm common areas, dining rooms and classrooms.

Palmer and other rookies were required to participate in "Boot Camp"—an extended period of hazing during which rookies were physically and emotionally abused. During Boot Camp, Palmer was forced to participate in a strenuous calisthenic session even though Palmer was suffering from an injured shoulder at the time. Palmer initially refused to participate in the calisthenic session. However, when Palmer complained to a vet that the injury prevented Palmer from participating, the vet punched Palmer in the injured shoulder and threatened to continue punching Palmer until Palmer participated in the calisthenic session. The calisthenics aggravated Palmer's shoulder injury causing Palmer to suffer significant pain and suffering for a prolonged period and requiring Palmer to undergo a corrective surgery and several months of physical therapy.

The State University Student Handbook expressly prohibits hazing and provides that the University may deny registration to any student organization that is found to have engaged in hazing of its members. All students receive a copy of the State University Student Handbook upon enrollment in State University. Additionally, new students must attend a mandatory lecture discussing the hazards of hazing and the university's policies prohibiting hazing. Despite these measures, hazing has occurred at State University in the past. Two years before Palmer's injury, the Director of the University Student Health Services reported to the University Vice President for Student Affairs that two students had been treated for serious physical injuries resulting from hazing. In response to these incidents, the Vice President for Student Affairs sent a letter to all student organizations condemning these incidents and hazing generally and required all student organizations to conduct a review of their activities and certify to the University that the organizations did not engage in hazing. The University also conducted an investigation of these incidents, but because no knowledgeable students were willing to cooperate with the investigation, the University did not institute formal disciplinary proceedings against any students. One year later, the Director of University Health Services again reported to the Vice President for Student Affairs that several students had been treated for physical injuries as a result of a hazing incident. In response, the Vice President for Student Affairs sent a letter to all students condemning the incident and re-iterating the University's policies prohibiting hazing. The University again conducted an investigation of the incident, but again was unable to persuade knowledgeable students to cooperate with the investigation.

If Palmer files suit against the vet involved in the calisthenic session and State University, should either party be liable for punitive damages? If so, what evidence should the jury consider in determining the amount of punitive damages?

Wangen v. Ford Motor Co.

97 Wis.2d 260, 294 N.W.2d 437 (1980).

■ ABRAHAMSON, JUSTICE.

[Products liability suits for compensatory and punitive damages were commenced against Ford Motor Company based upon an automobile accident which involved a collision between a 1967 Ford Mustang and another car. The Mustang's fuel tank ruptured, a fire ensued, and all the occupants of the Mustang died or sustained severe injuries.

The circuit court denied Ford's motion to dismiss the complaints for failure to state a cause of action. It held that punitive damages may be awarded in products liability cases upon a sufficient evidentiary basis. The court of appeals divided the complaint for punitive damages into various categories of actions and concluded that they were recoverable in a products liability suit for compensatory damages predicated on strict liability in tort but not for negligence. The Wisconsin Supreme Court granted an appeal to address whether punitive damages are recoverable in a products liability suit based on negligence or strict liability. The portion of the supreme court's opinion discussing the availability of punitive damages in wrongful death and survival actions and for a parent's loss of society and companionship of a child have been omitted.] * * *

Ford Motor Company asserts that punitive damages are recoverable only in actions based on intentional, personal torts, and are not recoverable in product liability actions which are grounded in negligence or strict liability. Ford argues that the concept of punitive damages is antithetical to the theories of negligence and strict liability because punitive damages are based on the defendant's intentional conduct. Ford's argument is premised on two assumptions: that intentional conduct is the only conduct justifying punitive damages and that the same facts which justify compensatory damages must be sufficient to justify punitive damages. This court has never adopted this view of punitive damages.

* * *

This court has rested its analysis of punitive damages not on the classification of the underlying tort justifying compensatory damages but on the nature of the wrongdoer's conduct. Although the usual aggravating circumstances required for the recovery of punitive damages are often found as substantive elements of the tort itself, this court has said a claim for punitive damages may be supported by proof of aggravating circumstances beyond those supporting compensatory damages.

Punitive damages rest on allegations which, if proved, demonstrate a particular kind of conduct on the part of the wrongdoer, which has variously been characterized in our cases as malicious conduct or willful or wanton conduct in reckless disregard of rights or interests.

This court has not required proof of an intentional desire to injure, vex or annoy, or proof of malice, in order to sustain an award for punitive damages. "[M]alice or vindictiveness are not the *sine qua non* of punitive damages." [Citation.] It is sufficient if the injured party shows a reckless indifference to or disregard of the rights of others on the part of the wrongdoer. "Reckless indifference to the rights of others and conscious action in deliberate disregard of them ... may provide the necessary state of mind to justify punitive damages." 4 Restatement (Second) of Torts sec. 908, comment b, p. 465 (1977). Some commentators speak of the behavior justifying punitive damages as "flagrant indifference to the public safety." [Citations.] "A governing principle of these cases in allowing punitive damages has been the presence of 'circumstances of aggravation' in the tortious injury." [Citation.] We shall sometimes use the term "outrageous" in this opinion as an abbreviation for the type of conduct which justifies the imposition of punitive damages.

* * *

In Entzminger v. Ford Motor Co., 47 Wis.2d 751, 757 758, 177 N.W.2d 899, 903 (1970) this court made clear that the award of punitive damages depends on the character of the particular conduct in question, not on the mere fact that the defendant's conduct constituted a tort or a crime:

"Punitive damages are not allowed for a mere breach of contract ... or for all torts or for crimes but generally for those personal torts, which are malicious, outrageous or a wanton disregard of personal rights which require the added sanction of a punitive damage to deter others from committing acts against human dignity...."

* * *

If there is tortious conduct supporting a claim for compensatory damages, we can find no logical or conceptual difficulty in allowing a claim for punitive damages in a negligence or strict liability action if the plaintiff is able to establish the elements of "outrageous" conduct justifying punitive damages. * * *

This court rejects Ford's argument that as a matter of law, punitive damages cannot be recovered in any product liability case based on strict liability or negligence. We hold that punitive damages are recoverable in a product liability suit if there is proof that the defendant's conduct was "outrageous." Awarding punitive damages in a product liability case is a natural, direct outgrowth of basic common law concepts of tort law and punitive damages.

* * *

Although controversy continues to surround the doctrine of punitive damages in the twentieth century, and although some have questioned whether tort law which is designed to compensate an injured plaintiff should also serve the function of the criminal law, *i.e.,* to punish a defendant for the purpose of deterring him and others from further offenses, this court has consistently and frequently said that punishment and deterrence are important considerations in the law of torts in Wisconsin. * * *

In light of this court's repeated reaffirmation of the concept of punitive damages as a civil deterrent to "outrageous" behavior, and because apparently some businesses have found it in their interests to operate with reckless disregard to consumer safety, this court cannot, in good conscience, prohibit punitive damages in all product liability cases unless there is a strong showing that such prohibition is in the public interest.

* * *

Ford asserts that in product liability cases compensatory damages operate as a substantial punishment and deterrence against the manufacture and distribution of unreasonably unsafe products and that punitive damages are not necessary. Ford contends that product liability cases differ in nature from the traditional punitive damage tort case in which generally only one plaintiff is involved and in which compensatory damages are relatively small. In product liability cases there are potentially many plaintiffs who will recover compensatory damages. Ford maintains that there has been a substantial increase in the number of product liability cases brought and the amount of damages awarded; that Ford is exposed to multiple, substantial compensatory damage awards; and that the cost of paying products liability claims and buying products liability insurance has become a significant cost of doing business.

The counterargument, which is frequently made to Ford's argument and which we find persuasive, is that the need for punitive damages may be particularly appropriate in a product liability case because mere compensatory damages might be insufficient to deter the defendant from further wrongdoing. Some may think it cheaper to pay damages or a forfeiture than to change a business practice. In Funk v. H. S. Kerbaugh, 222 Pa. 18, 70 A. 953, 954 (1908), the defendant willfully carried out blasting in such a way as to damage buildings belonging to the plaintiff "because it was cheaper to pay damages ... than to do work in a different way." The possibility of the manufacturer paying out more than compensatory damages might very well deter those who would consciously engage in wrongful practices and who would set aside a certain amount of money to compensate the injured consumer. Punishment of manufacturers guilty of intentional or reckless breaches of their obligation by imposing punitive damages might diminish the profitability of misconduct and any unfair competitive advantages such manufacturers might otherwise have.

* * *

Ford also argues that punitive damages in a product liability case, unlike in the traditional punitive damage tort case, would not serve the purposes of punishment and deterrence because the public, not the manufacturer, would pay the damages through higher prices for goods. We recognize, as did the court of appeals, an inconsistency between the concept of punitive damages as a deterrent and the possibility that punitive damages can be passed on to consumers as a cost of production. This court adopted strict liability in tort in product liability cases partly because "the seller is in the paramount position to distribute the costs of the risks created by the defective product he is selling. He may pass the cost on to the consumer via increased prices." [Citation.] Manufacturers are, however, not always able to pass on to their customers all costs, including multiple punitive damage awards. * * *

Ford observes that a frequently given justification for punitive damages in the traditional punitive damage tort case is that they encourage redress of wrongs that might otherwise go unpunished; punitive damages provide an incentive to the injured party to sue. Ford argued that punitive damages are wholly unnecessary to encourage the bringing of claims in product liability cases, because compensatory damages provide sufficient incentive to the victim of a product accident to proceed with his claim for compensatory damages. Ford may be right for those instances where injuries are very severe, but is probably wrong for the many product liability cases where injuries are moderate or minor. But even if the injury to each individual is not severe, there is a public need to deter the production of unreasonably safe products, and the availability of punitive damages increases the likelihood that the injured customer will sue for recovery.

In summary, we are not persuaded by Ford's argument that punitive damages are unnecessary in product liability cases to effect punishment or deterrence, the objectives of imposing punitive damages in the traditional tort action.

Ford further argues that it is in the public interest for this court to outlaw punitive damages in all product liability cases because allowing the recovery of punitive damages would cause undesirable economic and social consequences.

* * *

Ford argues that if the punitive damages are not passed on to the consumer the innocent shareholder bears the burden. But the loss of investment and the decline in value of investments are risks which investors knowingly undertake, and investors should not enjoy ill-gotten gains. There is a public interest in encouraging shareholders and corporate management to exercise closer control over the operations of the entity, and the imposition of punitive damages may serve this interest.

Ford argues that as a practical matter there will be a limit to the amount of punitive damages a manufacturer can pay and to the number of times a manufacturer will be or should be punished for the same product.

Thus the injured parties who win the race to the courthouse reap "the bonanza of punitive damages." The later plaintiffs may receive little or no punitive damages. Ford further asserts that punitive damages are a windfall to the injured party and, if they are to be awarded, they should be awarded to the public. Although Ford's arguments have a certain equitable ring to them, we should not be sidetracked by them. Ford would solve the inequity of awarding punitive damages to some plaintiffs by having this court eliminate all punitive damages and by having us allow the wrongdoer to go unpunished. The supposed unfairness Ford attributes to punitive damages ignores the effort and money required of the early plaintiffs to uncover and prove the misconduct. Later plaintiffs will often be able to use the information gathered by the first plaintiffs and benefit from the early favorable verdicts and settlements. The "windfall criterion" overlooks that the payment of punitive damages to the injured party is justifiable as a practical matter, because such damages do serve to compensate the injured party for uncompensated expenses, *e.g.*, attorneys' fees and litigation expenses, and that the windfall motivates reluctant plaintiffs to go forward with their claims. If punitive damages were to be paid to the public treasury, fewer wrongdoers would be punished because the injured would have no inducement to spend the extra time and expense to prove a claim for punitive damages once an action had been brought. The basic question in determining whether punitive damages should be outlawed in product liability cases is not whether some injured party is going to make a profit but whether punitive damages will punish and deter, objectives which are in the public interest.

* * *

On the basis of the facts pleaded and reasonable inferences therefrom the complaint alleges that Ford knew of the defects in the design of the gas tank and filler neck and in the lack of barrier between the gas tank and passenger compartment in the 1967 Mustang and of the fire hazard associated with the design because of tests run by Ford as early as 1964; that for years before this accident Ford knew that these defects were causing serious burn injuries to occupants of these and similar cars; that years before the accident involved in the instant case Ford knew how to correct these defects in ways that would have prevented the plaintiffs' burns, but Ford intentionally concealed this knowledge from the government and the public; that despite this knowledge Ford deliberately chose not to recall its 1967 Mustangs and not to disclose the defects to the public by the issuance of warnings because Ford wanted to avoid paying the costs of recall and repair and wanted to avoid the accompanying bad publicity; and that Ford's conduct was intentional, reckless, willful, wanton, gross and fraudulent. These facts, if proved by the plaintiff, portray conduct which is willful and wanton and in reckless disregard of the plaintiff's rights. We conclude that the complaint alleges facts sufficient to state a claim for punitive damages in a product liability action predicated on negligence or strict liability. * * *

1. *Basis of Suit.* The requirements for recovery of punitive damages are distinct from those of the underlying claim. Punitive damages are never a matter of right, even if the underlying claim requires malicious or outrageous behavior. The plaintiff must convince the trier of fact that such additional damages are appropriate.

Conversely, may a plaintiff seek punitive damages when the underlying basis of the suit is strict liability, which requires no proof of the defendant's state of mind nor even any proof of fault? In addition to the principal case, *see also* Fischer v. Johns–Manville Corp., 103 N.J. 643, 512 A.2d 466 (1986) (punitive damages allowable in products liability case based upon strict liability). What advantage is it to the plaintiff to seek recovery under strict liability if there is also evidence sufficient to support a claim for punitive damages?

2. *Policy Implications.* The arguments usually advanced in opposition of punitive damages in products liability cases include:

(a) Punitive damages assessed against a corporation are simply passed along to the consumer through higher prices to reflect the greater cost of doing business;

(b) Even if competition makes it impossible to spread the cost of punitive damages through the price of the product, the burden then falls on the innocent shareholder;

(c) When a defective product injures several people and there are large claims for punitive damages in multiple cases, punitive damages cannot be administered fairly to avoid ruinous results to the defendant for a single defect appearing in many products;

(d) Only people can be deterred, not corporations with constantly changing personnel.

The arguments usually advanced in support of punitive damages in products liability cases include:

(a) Manufacturers of risky products will price themselves out of the market when they pass along all their costs, including punitive damages;

(b) If innocent shareholders ultimately bear the burden, that result is justifiable because the decline in value of investments is a risk investors knowingly undertake;

(c) Corporations, including their innocent shareholders, should not enjoy ill-gotten gains;

(d) There is a public interest in encouraging shareholders and corporate management to exercise closer control over a manufacturer's operations.

3. *Reckless Indifference.* To the extent that jurisdictions require a plaintiff to prove that a defendant acted with malice or ill will to recover punitive damages, proving entitlement to punitive damages may be problematic in products liability cases. It is unlikely that a manufacturer or supplier of a defective product would specifically intend to harm a particu-

lar consumer. Indeed, actual contact between the manufacturer or supplier and consumer is attenuated. *See* Owens–Corning Fiberglas v. Garrett, 343 Md. 500, 682 A.2d 1143 (1996). However, most jurisdictions also permit punitive damages when the defendant lacks an actual malicious desire to harm but acts with reckless indifference to the plaintiff's rights. *See* Smith v. Wade, 461 U.S. 30, 103 S.Ct. 1625, 75 L.Ed.2d 632 (1983) ("Most cases under state common law, although varying in their precise terminology, have adopted more or less the same rule, recognizing that punitive damages in tort cases may be awarded not only for actual intent to injure or evil motive, but also for recklessness, serious indifference to or disregard for the rights of others, or even gross negligence."); Restatement (Second) of Torts § 908 (2) (1979) ("Punitive damages may be awarded for conduct that is outrageous, because of the defendant's evil motive or his reckless indifference to the rights of others.").

Under what circumstances does a manufacturer or supplier of a defective product act with reckless indifference to the rights of consumers? At a minimum most jurisdictions require that a manufacturer or supplier have actual knowledge of the defect and knowledge of the potential for harm to consumers. A failure to detect a defect or appreciate the risk of a defect is insufficient. *See* Garrett, *supra* ("[A] plaintiff must show more than constructive knowledge: the plaintiff must show that the defendant actually knew of the defect and of the danger of the product at the time the product left the defendant's possession or control.")

Additionally, the manufacturer or supplier must be at fault in some way. For example, the manufacturer or supplier must act in bad faith in marketing the product, in failing to warn consumers of the defect or in failing to adequately test the product. *See* Garrett, *supra* ("Additionally, a products liability plaintiff must show that the defendant, having such actual knowledge, exhibited a conscious or deliberate disregard of the potential harm to consumers. * * * [T]he test requires a bad faith decision by the defendant to market a product, knowing of the defect and danger, in conscious or deliberate disregard of the threat to the safety of the consumer.)" Accordingly, in *Garrett*, the Maryland Court of Appeals vacated an award of punitive damages against an asbestos manufacturer because the plaintiff could not demonstrate that the manufacturer did not believe in good faith that its recommendations for exhaust ventilation, housekeeping and respirators were reasonable protections from the dangers of exposure to asbestos.

4. *Gross Negligence.* In some jurisdictions, punitive damages may be awarded based upon gross negligence. This standard differs significantly from maliciousness or reckless indifference because it is not premised upon conscious wrongdoing. It is a level of negligence greater than simple negligence but short of conscious indifference. It is frequently referred to as "entire want of care."

The lines among these standards are not bright ones. Jurisdictions sometimes provide their own definitions of these concepts in ways that blur the distinctions even further. Consider, for example, the definition of "gross negligence" articulated by the Texas Supreme Court in *Wal–Mart Stores, Inc. v. Alexander*, 868 S.W.2d 322 (Tex.1993):

> Gross negligence, to be the ground for exemplary damages, should be that entire want of care which would raise the belief that the act or omission complained of was the result of a conscious indifference to the right or welfare of the person or persons to be affected by it.

The court further explained:

> This definition, which is unique to Texas, combines the two recognized tests for gross negligence in American jurisprudence: "entire want of care" and "conscious indifference." The "entire want of care" test focuses on the objective nature of defendant's conduct, distinguishing gross negligence as being different in degree or quantity from ordinary negligence. The "conscious indifference" test focuses on the defendant's mental state, and thus "stresses a qualitative distinction from ordinary negligence." Under this approach, the actor, although not actually intending to cause harm, must have proceeded with knowledge that harm was a "highly probable" consequence.

Does the gross negligence standard alter the circumstances under which punitive damages may be awarded against a manufacturer or supplier of a defective product? Consider International Armament Corp. v. King, 674 S.W.2d 413 (Tex.App.Ct.1984) (a showing of actual knowledge of a defect is not necessary to prove gross negligence) *aff'd* 686 S.W.2d 595 (Tex.1985) (evidence demonstrated that manufacturer intentionally decided not to inspect product despite knowledge product could misfire if not fit together properly).

5. *Insurability of Punitive Damages.* Several jurisdictions have considered whether, as a matter of public policy, tortfeasors should be permitted to shift the punishment for their egregious acts to insurance companies. The threshold inquiry involves construction of the insurance contract to determine whether the policy provides indemnity coverage for exemplary damages. Some courts have liberally construed phrases such as "for all sums which the insured might become legally obligated to pay" to include potential liability coverage. *See, e.g.,* Dayton Hudson Corp. v. American Mut. Liability Ins. Co., 621 P.2d 1155 (Okl.1980).

Secondly, courts must consider whether the goals of punishment and deterrence would be undermined if a tortfeasor can be indemnified for punitive damages. The leading decision refusing to allow indemnification through insurance is *Northwestern National Casualty Co. v. McNulty*, 307 F.2d 432 (5th Cir.1962). In that case the Court of Appeals for the Fifth Circuit observed:

> Where a person is able to insure himself against punishment he gains a freedom of misconduct inconsistent with the establishment of sanctions against such misconduct. It is not disputed that insurance against criminal fines or penalties would be void as violative of public policy. The same public policy should invalidate any contract of insurance against the civil punishment that punitive damages represent.

The policy considerations in a state where * * * punitive damages are awarded for punishment and deterrence, would seem to require that the damages rest ultimately as well as nominally on the party actually responsible for the wrong. If that person were permitted to shift the burden to an insurance company, punitive damages would serve no useful purpose. Such damages do not compensate the plaintiff for his injury, since compensatory damages already have made the plaintiff whole. And there is no point in punishing the insurance company; it has done no wrong. In actual fact, of course, and considering the extent to which the public is insured, the burden would ultimately come to rest not on the insurance companies but on the public, since the added liability to the insurance companies would be passed along to the premium payers. Society would then be punishing itself for the wrong committed by the insured. 307 F.2d at 440.

Similarly, in *Public Service Mutual Ins. Co. v. Goldfarb*, 53 N.Y.2d 392, 425 N.E.2d 810, 442 N.Y.S.2d 422 (1981), the court refused to enforce an insurance contract specifically providing indemnity for punitive damages. The claim was for malpractice when a dentist sexually abused a patient. The court found that although the insurance company was in the awkward position of challenging the validity of one of its own contracts, there is an overriding public policy requiring meaningful punishment and deterrence.

Should the insurability of punitive damages turn on the nature of the defendant's conduct? In jurisdictions that allow punitive damages for reckless conduct as well as malicious behavior, would it make sense to distinguish the two for purposes of insurability? Some jurisdictions that otherwise refuse to enforce insurance contracts for punitive damages have allowed enforcement where the insured is only vicariously liable for the exemplary damages. *See, e.g.,* U.S. Concrete Pipe Co. v. Bould, 437 So.2d 1061 (Fla.1983).

6. *Successor Liability for Punitive Damages.* Generally, courts have found successor corporations liable for punitive damages based on the conduct of their predecessors. Courts finding successors liable have relied upon the successor's express or implicit assumption of the predecessor's liabilities. *See, e.g.,* City of Richmond v. Madison Mgmt. Group, 918 F.2d 438 (4th Cir.1990) (evidence supported an inference that successor implicitly assumed its predecessor's liabilities); Edwards v. Armstrong World Indus., 911 F.2d 1151 (5th Cir.1990) (successor to asbestos manufacturer liable for punitive damages because it assumed manufacturer's liabilities in merger agreement); Culbreath v. First Tennessee Bank Nat'l Association, 44 S.W.3d 518 (Tenn.2001) (successor bank liable for punitive damages where state and federal merger laws required successor corporation to assume predecessor's liabilities and merger agreement provided that successor assumed all of its predecessor's liabilities).

Some courts also have relied upon the successor corporation's knowledge of its predecessor's conduct and the successor's continuation of its predecessor's business. *See, e.g.,* Davis v. Celotex Corp., 187 W.Va. 566, 420 S.E.2d 557 (1992). A few courts have recognized a narrow exception precluding awards of punitive damages against an innocent successor. Under this exception, punitive damages may be inappropriate where the successor corporation is a new and different entity, its owners are wholly innocent of the alleged unlawful activities and the new owners improve production practices. *See* Sterling v. Velsicol Chem. Corp., 855 F.2d 1188 (6th Cir.1988).

7. *Punitive Damages for Statutory Claims.* Much like punitive damages are available in negligence and strict liability cases, punitive damages, generally, are available when a plaintiff recovers under a statutory claim if the plaintiff shows that the defendant acted with the level of ill will or malice prescribed by the common law. *See* Smith v. Wade, 461 U.S. 30, 103 S.Ct. 1625, 75 L.Ed.2d 632 (1983). No higher standard need be met even if the statute provides for compensatory liability on the same standard.

Recovery of punitive damages is precluded for some statutory rights. *See, e.g.,* Getty Petroleum Corp. v. Bartco Petroleum Corp., 858 F.2d 103 (2d Cir.1988) (Lanham Act, 15 U.S.C. § 1060, precludes recovery of punitive damages). For some statutory rights there are particularized requirements for recovery of punitive damages in order to harmonize them with the overall statutory scheme. For example, in *Kolstad v. American Dental Assoc.*, 527 U.S. 526, 119 S.Ct. 2118, 144 L.Ed.2d 494 (1999), the Supreme Court held that Title VII of the Civil Rights Act of 1964 permits punitive damages only when an employer intentionally discriminates against an employee with the knowledge that it may be acting in violation of federal law. The Court explained that the "egregious" behavior test is unnecessary and inappropriate in this context because egregiousness focuses upon external results whereas the Act focuses upon the mental state of the actor.

W.R. Grace & Co. v. Waters

638 So.2d 502 (Fla.1994).

■ Grimes, C.J.

Thomas Waters and his wife filed this action seeking compensatory and punitive damages against several manufacturers of asbestos-containing products, including W.R. Grace & Company (Grace). From the late 1950s until 1988, Waters worked as a tile setter. The complaint alleged that Waters had developed asbestosis as a result of exposure to Grace's products at various job sites.

Prior to trial, Grace filed a motion for summary judgment on the issue of punitive damages asserting that (1) Grace's conduct, as a matter of law, did not rise to the level required for the imposition of punitive damages in Florida; (2) since punitive damage judgments had been entered against it in other jurisdictions, a partial summary judgment should be entered in accordance with a prior "standard ruling" by the trial court;[1] and (3) the

---

1. The "standard ruling" was issued by Judge Harold Vann who administered the asbestos litigation docket in Dade County and elsewhere in Florida pursuant to administrative orders from this Court beginning in 1980. The ruling eliminated claims for punitive damages

punitive damages claim violated Grace's due process rights. The trial court granted Grace's motion and entered a partial summary judgment on the punitive damages issue based on the "standard ruling."

* * * [T]he district court of appeal affirmed the judgment for compensatory damages but held that the trial court erred in striking Waters' punitive damages claim. The court ruled that the fact that a defendant has already had punitive damages assessed against it does not preclude punitive damages in future litigation. The court reinstated Waters' punitive damages claim against Grace and remanded the case. However, the district court of appeal also certified to this Court the question concerning the propriety of imposing successive punitive damage awards against a single defendant for the same course of conduct.

Punitive damages are appropriate when a defendant engages in conduct which is fraudulent, malicious, deliberately violent or oppressive, or committed with such gross negligence as to indicate a wanton disregard for the rights of others. [Citations.] Punishment and deterrence are the policies underlying punitive damages. [Citation.]

Grace asks this Court to limit the imposition of punitive damage awards in mass tort litigation, or at least with respect to asbestos cases. The company warns of the likelihood of "overkill" brought about by multiple punitive damage awards against a single defendant for the same course of conduct. Grace argues that, in the context of asbestos litigation, the interests of punishment and deterrence are not advanced by the continued imposition of punitive damages. It contends that multiple awards of exemplary damages will lead to asset depletion threatening the solvency of corporations, and, ultimately, will result in the unavailability of even compensatory damages for future claimants. Grace further points out that it discontinued marketing asbestos-containing products over twenty years ago. Because the company has been assessed punitive damages in previous asbestos cases, Grace asserts that it "has been punished enough."

Roginsky v. Richardson Merrell, Inc., 378 F.2d 832 (2d Cir.1967), was one of the earliest cases to express concern over multiple punitive damage awards in mass tort litigation. In that case, the manufacturer of MER/29, a drug used to lower cholesterol levels, contested an award of punitive damages for personal injuries allegedly caused by MER/29. This was the first of seventy-five similar cases to be tried in the Southern District of New York. Several hundred other actions had been filed elsewhere, and the company had already sustained several large punitive damage awards in cases involving MER/29.

The court recognized the potentially devastating impact on the company if all plaintiffs in MER/29 cases were awarded punitive damages. However, the court stated:

We know of no principle whereby the first punitive award exhausts all claims for punitive damages and would thus preclude future judgments....

---

upon a showing that the defendant had already been subjected to a prior punitive damage award for the same conduct.

Neither does it seem either fair or practicable to limit punitive recoveries to an indeterminate number of first-comers, leaving it to some unascertained court to cry, "Hold, enough," in the hope that others would follow. Ultimately, the court declined to judicially limit successive punitive damage awards in products liability cases.

In the twenty-seven years following the Roginsky opinion, many courts have addressed the issue of multiple punitive damage awards against a single defendant for the same course of conduct. The courts of other jurisdictions have unanimously refused to limit the imposition of successive punitive damage awards in mass tort or products liability litigation. * * *

The solution to the problem which is most often suggested is the so-called "one bite" or "first comer" theory of punitive damages whereby, in successive litigation arising from a continuing episode, the award of exemplary damages to one plaintiff would preclude the recovery of punitive damages for all subsequent plaintiffs. This approach has been uniformly rejected. See State ex rel. Young v. Crookham, 290 Ore. 61, 618 P.2d 1268, 1272 (Or.1980) (This court cannot "endorse a system of awarding punitive damages which threatens to reduce civil justice to a race to the courthouse steps.").[2]

We acknowledge the potential for abuse when a defendant may be subjected to repeated punitive damage awards arising out of the same conduct. Yet, like the many other courts which have addressed the problem, we are unable to devise a fair and effective solution. Were we to adopt the position advocated by Grace, our holding would not be binding on other state courts or federal courts. This would place Floridians injured by asbestos on an unequal footing with the citizens of other states with regard to the right to recover damages from companies who engage in extreme misconduct. Any realistic solution to the problems caused by the asbestos litigation in the United States must be applicable to all fifty states. It is our belief that such a uniform solution can only be effected by federal legislation.

* * * [T]he district court of appeal suggested that Grace could use the fact that it had previously been assessed punitive damages as mitigation before the jury. However, Grace points out that advising the jury of previous punitive damage awards would actually hurt its cause. The introduction of such evidence would be extremely prejudicial to a defendant trying to convince a jury that its conduct is worthy of no punishment at all.

We agree with Grace's position on this point. We recognize that defendants in mass tort litigation who are forced to litigate the issue of liability and punitive damages in the same proceeding are at a severe disadvantage. We also recognize that even those defendants against whom

---

2. To limit recovery to the first punitive damage award would be particularly unfair in Florida which limits the amount of punitive damages to three times the award of compensatory damages. 768.73, Fla. Stat. (1993). If a slightly injured plaintiff were the first to recover punitive damages, the small award of compensatory damages would limit the amount of punitive damages. Under those circumstances, this amount would not be nearly enough to punish a defendant whose egregious conduct had caused injury to many persons.

no prior punitive damage awards have been assessed are prejudiced by the current procedure which permits evidence of a defendant's net worth to be introduced when liability for punitive damages has not yet been determined. * * *

We hold that henceforth trial courts, when presented with a timely motion, should bifurcate the determination of the amount of punitive damages from the remaining issues at trial. At the first stage of a trial in which punitive damages are an issue, the jury should hear evidence regarding liability for actual damages, the amount of actual damages, and liability for punitive damages, and should make determinations on those issues. If, at the first stage, the jury determines that punitive damages are warranted, the same jury should then hear evidence relevant to the amount of punitive damages and should determine the amount for which the defendant is liable. At this second stage, evidence of previous punitive awards may be introduced by the defendant in mitigation. In this manner, the defendant would also be able to build a record for a due process argument based on the cumulative effect of prior awards. This new procedure, of course, is meant only to supplement, not replace, the limitations on punitive damages set forth by the legislature in sections 768.71, 768.74, Florida Statutes (1993).

In conclusion, we hold that prior punitive damages assessed against a defendant do not preclude subsequent awards against the same defendant for injuries arising from the same conduct. We approve the decision below and remand for further proceedings consistent with this opinion.

––––––––

1. *On–Going Debate.* The assessment of multiple punitive damages awards against a responsible party arising out of the same incident has sparked considerable controversy. As the *Grace* court notes, *Roginsky v. Richardson–Merrell, Inc.*, 378 F.2d 832 (2d Cir.1967) was one of the first cases to raise concerns about awarding punitive damages in successive actions based on the same conduct and highlight the difficulty of trying to limit such awards. Courts and commentators today continue to raise the same concerns about multiple punitive damage awards against a single defendant arising from the same conduct. Nonetheless, while acknowledging these concerns, the majority of courts that have considered claims by defendants that multiple punitive damage awards were unfair or unconstitutional, including the *Grace* court, have refused to vacate the punitive damage awards before them. *See, e.g.,* Dunn v. HOVIC, 1 F.3d 1371 (3d Cir.1993). Why might courts be reluctant to vacate or reduce individual punitive damage awards based on concerns that the aggregate amount of multiple punitive damage awards is excessive or unfair?

The Supreme Court's recent punitive damage jurisprudence, discussed in the next section of this chapter, has added another layer to the debate over multiple punitive damage awards. In *State Farm v. Campbell*, 538 U.S. 408, 123 S.Ct. 1513, 155 L.E.2d 585 (2003) and Philip Morris v. Williams,

549 U.S. 346, 127 S.Ct. 1057, 166 L.Ed.2d 940 (2007), the Court held that punitive damages can be imposed solely to punish and deter the defendant for misconduct directed at the plaintiff and cannot be imposed to punish and deter even related misconduct that harmed third parties not before the court. The Court imposed these limitations specifically to protect the defendant from multiple punitive damage awards imposed to sanction the defendant for the same misconduct. In theory, if a punitive damage award in an individual case represents punishment solely for the harm to the plaintiff before the court, no two awards can be duplicative and a defendant will not be subject to repetitive sanctions. How effective is this limitation in practice? Consider that in *Campbell* and in *Williams*, the Court recognized that evidence of harm to third parties could be relevant to assess the reprehensibility of the conduct that harmed the plaintiff before the court.

2. *"One Bite" Approach.* In *Grace*, the court refuses to adopt a "one bite" approach to punitive damages which would permit only one plaintiff to recover a punitive damage award from a defendant for any act or omission if the plaintiff's cause of action is a product liability case. At least one state legislature has adopted this one bite approach to punitive damages. *See* Ga. Code Ann. § 51–12–5.1 (2000). Is there any justification for treating the first plaintiff to file a lawsuit differently from successive plaintiffs? Is a one bite approach likely to result in the race to the courthouse feared by the *Grace* court?

3. *Procedural Reform.* The court in *Grace* requires lower courts to bifurcate proceedings to determine the amount of punitive damages from the rest of the trial if a defendant so requests. The court adopts this procedural safeguard to protect the defendant from potentially prejudicial evidence relevant solely to a determination of the amount of punitive damages. Like the court in *Grace*, other states have imposed procedural safeguards intended to protect the defendant from arbitrary or excessive awards.

For example, several state legislatures have enacted measures providing for punitive damages to be awarded in bifurcated proceedings. Under most of these measures, the trier of fact determines whether the plaintiff is entitled to the compensatory damages, the amount of compensatory damages and whether the plaintiff is entitled to punitive damages in one proceeding. If the trier of fact determines that the plaintiff is entitled to punitive damages, the amount of those punitive damages is determined in a separate proceeding. *See, e.g.,* N.C. Gen. Stat. § 1D–25 (West 2000) (trier of fact determines amount of punitive damages separately from the amount of compensation for all other damages) Tex. Civ. Prac. & Rem. Code Ann. § 41.009 (West 2001) (on motion by the defendant, the court shall provide for bifurcated trial) *see also* N.J. Stat. Ann. § 2A:15–5.13 (West 2001) (upon request of defendant, trier of fact determines liability for and amount of compensatory damages in initial proceeding and liability for and amount of punitive damages in second proceeding). The New Jersey statute also excludes evidence solely relevant to punitive damages, such as evidence bearing on the defendant's financial condition, from the initial proceeding.

Another measure aimed directly at the problem of multiple or successive awards requires the trier of fact or a reviewing court to consider past awards in determining whether a punitive damage award is excessive. *See, e.g.,* Or. Rev. Stat. § 30.925 (1999) (amount of punitive damages must be based, in part, upon the total deterrent effect of punitive damage awards to persons in situations similar to the claimant's); Okla. Stat. Ann. § 9.1 (West 2000) (under limited circumstances, the trial court must reduce an award of punitive damages by the amount the defendant has previously paid as a result of all punitive damage verdicts entered in any court of the State of Oklahoma for the same conduct by the defendant).

Another common measure is to heighten the plaintiff's burden of proof above the traditional standard of preponderance of the evidence. *See, e.g.,* Calif. Civ. Code § 3294 (West 2001) (clear and convincing evidence); Or. Rev. Stat. § 18.537 (1999) (same); *see also* Colo. Rev. Stat. Ann. § 13–25–127 (West 2001) (beyond a reasonable doubt).

Yet another common reform places a cap or ceiling on the amount of punitive damage awards. Caps have been expressed in terms of absolute dollar amounts, by proportionate ratios to compensatory damages awarded and by a combination of the two. *See, e.g.,* Fla. Stat. Ann. § 768.73 (the greater of three times the amount of compensatory damages or $500,000); Va. Code. § 8.01–38.1 ($350,000 ceiling). Such statutes generally have withstood constitutional challenges. *See, e.g.,* Wackenhut Applied Tech. Ctr. v. Sygnetron Protection Sys., 979 F.2d 980 (4th Cir.1992) (upholding Virginia statute capping punitive damages); *Smith v. Department of Ins.,* 507 So.2d 1080 (Fla.1987) (cap on punitive damages does not violate separation of powers) *but see* State ex rel. Ohio Academy of Trial Lawyers v. Sheward, 86 Ohio St.3d 451, 715 N.E.2d 1062 (1999) (cap on punitive damages violated state right to jury trial).

A further variant is to require some portion of a punitive damage award to be paid to the state rather than the plaintiff. These so-called "extraction statutes" are essentially revenue-raising measures for states. Indeed, a governor of California proposed an extraction statute that would require 75% of a punitive damage award be paid to the state as a budget measure aimed at raising revenue. Governor Schwarzenegger estimated that the statute would raise almost half a billion dollars for the state. Adam Liptak, *Schwarzenegger Sees Money for State in Punitive Damages,* N.Y. TIMES (May 30, 2004). Such statutes are justified on the basis that punitive damages advance the public interest in punishing and deterring conduct that offends societal norms. Catherine M. Sharkey, *Punitive Damages as Societal Damages,* 113 YALE L.J. 347 (2003); *See, e.g.,* Ga. Code Ann. § 51–12–5.1 (2000) (75% of any punitive damage award paid into state treasury); Iowa Code Ann. § 668A.1 (West 2001) (allowing a plaintiff to receive no more than 25% of punitive damage award unless defendant's conduct was directed at the plaintiff specifically); Dardinger v. Anthem Blue Cross & Blue Shield, 98 Ohio St.3d 77, 781 N.E.2d 121 (2002). These statutes, likewise, generally have withstood constitutional scrutiny. *See, e.g.,* Shepherd Components, Inc. v. Brice Petrides–Donohue & Assoc., 473 N.W.2d

612 (Iowa 1991) (award of punitive damages to state rather than plaintiff was not an unconstitutional taking without compensation); Mack Trucks, Inc. v. Conkle, 263 Ga. 539, 436 S.E.2d 635 (1993) (state extraction statute did not violate equal protection clause).

Some courts have suggested that relief from multiple punitive damage awards is unnecessary because these procedural devices and the fact that punitive damages are never awarded as a matter of right but only as a matter of discretion are sufficient safeguards to protect a defendant from punitive damage overkill. *See, e.g.,* Maxey v. Freightliner Corp., 450 F.Supp. 955 (N.D.Tex.1978) ("Demanding strict proof will reduce the hazard of deterrence slipping into destruction to those cases of conduct so egregious as to have little equitable appeal."). Are these sufficient safeguards? Do better solutions exist?

4. *Federal Reforms.* The *Grace* court, like other courts and commentators, called for a national solution to the problems raised by multiple punitive damages. Congress has considered numerous proposals for federal legislation aimed at controlling punitive damages, including proposals to prohibit punitive damage awards in any civil action in which such damages are sought against a defendant based on the same conduct for which punitive damages have already been sought against that defendant. To date, none has been enacted.

5. *Net Wealth.* As *Grace* demonstrates, the relevance of a defendant's net wealth in determining the amount of punitive damages has been a troublesome issue for courts. In both *BMW v. Gore*, 517 U.S. 559, 116 S.Ct. 1589, 134 L.E.2d 809 (1996) and *Campbell*, discussed in the next section of this chapter, the Supreme Court expressed concern that evidence of a defendant's net wealth not be used to punish the defendant solely because it is wealthy. *See, e.g., Gore*, 517 U.S. at 585 ("The fact that BMW is a large corporation rather than an impecunious individual does not diminish its entitlement to fair notice of the demands that the several States impose on the conduct of its business."); *Campbell*, 538 U.S. at 427 ("The wealth of a defendant cannot justify an otherwise unconstitutional punitive damages award.").

Nonetheless, the prevailing view holds that wealth of the defendant is a relevant factor in determining the amount of punitive damages but that such proof is not necessary to sustain an award of punitive damages. *See, e.g.,* Kan. Stat. Ann. § 60–3701(b)(6) (2000) (court may consider financial condition of defendant in calculating the amount of punitive damages). On the other hand, some jurisdictions have concluded that evidence of a defendant's wealth is necessary to sustain an award for punitive damages. *See, e.g.,* Mont. Code Ann. § 27–1–221 (evidence of defendant's financial condition must be considered in separate proceeding to determine amount of punitive damages); Herman v. Sunshine Chem. Specialties, 133 N.J. 329, 627 A.2d 1081 (1993).

Consider the explanation given by one court for considering but not requiring proof of wealth:

The more wealth that the defendant has, the smaller is the relative bite that an award of punitive damages not actually geared to that wealth will take out of his pocketbook, while if he has very little wealth the award of punitive damages may exceed his ability to pay and drive him into bankruptcy. * * * What in economics is called the principle of diminishing marginal utility teaches, what is anyway obvious, that losing $1 is likely to cause less unhappiness (disutility) to a rich person than to a poor one. * * * But rich people are not famous for being indifferent to money, and if they are forced to pay not merely the cost of the harm to the victims of their torts but also some multiple of that cost they are likely to think twice before engaging in such expensive behavior again. Juries, rightly or wrongly, think differently, so plaintiffs who are seeking punitive damages often present evidence of the defendant's wealth. The question is whether they must present such evidence * * * The answer, obviously, is no. A plaintiff is not required to seek punitive damages in the first place, so he should not be denied an award of punitive damages merely because he does not present evidence that if believed would persuade the jury to award him even more than he is asking. Kemezy v. Peters, 79 F.3d 33, 35–36 (7th Cir.1996).

Compare the following explanation for requiring proof of wealth:

Because the quintessence of punitive damages is to deter future misconduct by the defendant, the key question before the reviewing court is whether the amount of damages "exceeds the level necessary to properly punish and deter." [Citation.] The question cannot be answered in the abstract. The reviewing court must consider the amount of the award *in light of the* relevant facts. The nature of the inquiry is a comparative one. Deciding in the abstract whether an award is "excessive" is like deciding whether it is "bigger," without asking "Bigger than what?" Adams v. Murakami, 813 P.2d 1348, 1350–51 (Calif. 1991) (emphasis in original).

Net worth, the value of a defendant's assets less the value of its liabilities, is the most common measure of wealth. *See, e.g.,* Rufo v. Simpson, 86 Cal.App.4th 573, 103 Cal.Rptr.2d 492 (2001). However, courts have recognized other factors may be relevant to determining the defendant's ability to pay punitive damages. *See, e.g.,* Bryant v. Waste Mgmt., 342 S.C. 159, 536 S.E.2d 380 (App.2000) (jury properly considered evidence of defendant's annual operating revenue, net income and net income per day in assessing defendant's financial condition).

While courts recognize evidence of financial information beyond a defendant's net worth, courts generally hold that evidence of wrongful profits standing alone is insufficient to assess a defendant's wealth. *See, e.g.,* Mason v. Texaco, Inc., 741 F.Supp. 1472 (D.Kan.1990) ("[T]he amount of profit received as a result of intentional wrongdoing is not the ceiling of punitive damage liability. * * * [T]he deterrent effect of punitive damages is served only by references to the net wealth of the wrongdoer."); Robert L. Cloud & Assoc. v. Mikesell, 69 Cal.App.4th 1141, 82 Cal.Rptr.2d 143

(1999) (income standing alone or wrongful profit standing alone are not sufficient evidence of defendant's ability to pay).

B. CONSTITUTIONAL LIMITS ON PUNITIVE DAMAGES

State Farm Mutual Automobile Insurance Company v. Campbell

538 U.S. 408, 123 S.Ct. 1513, 155 L.E.2d 585 (2003).

■ JUSTICE KENNEDY delivered the opinion of the Court.

We address once again the measure of punishment, by means of punitive damages, a State may impose upon a defendant in a civil case. The question is whether, in the circumstances we shall recount, an award of $145 million in punitive damages, where full compensatory damages are $1 million, is excessive and in violation of the Due Process Clause of the Fourteenth Amendment to the Constitution of the United States.

I

[The plaintiffs, a husband and wife (referred to collectively herein as the "Campbells"), were involved in a three-car accident in Utah. The driver of one of the other vehicles was killed, and the driver of the third vehicle was rendered permanently disabled. The Campbells "escaped unscathed."

Investigators and the witnesses to the accident concluded that the Campbells had caused the crash. Nonetheless, Campbell's insurance company, State Farm Mutual Automobile Insurance Company ("State Farm"), rejected the plaintiffs' offers to settle their claims for the policy limit of $50,000 ($25,000 per claimant) and took the case to trial, assuring the Campbells that "their assets were safe, that they had no liability for the accident, that [State Farm] would represent their interests, and that they did not need to procure separate counsel." At trial, a jury determined that Campbell was 100 percent at fault, and returned a verdict for $185,849, far more than the amount offered in settlement.

State Farm initially refused to cover the $135,849 in excess liability, informing the Campbells: " 'You may want to put for sale signs on your property to get things moving.' " However, State Farm ultimately paid the entire judgment, including the amounts in excess of the policy limits. The Campbells nonetheless filed a complaint against State Farm alleging bad faith refusal to settle, fraud, and intentional infliction of emotional distress.

At the trial of their bad faith claim, the Campbells argued that State Farm's decision to take the Campbells' case to trial was part of a national scheme to increase State Farm's profits by capping payouts on claims at below fair value. The Campbells referred to this scheme as State Farm's "Performance, Planning and Review" policy or the "PP & R" policy. To prove the existence of the PP & R policy, the Campbells introduced evidence of State Farm's claims adjustment practices for over 20 years involving claims arising in numerous States. Some of the evidence pertained to the handling of first-party rather than third-party automobile insurance claims like the claims at issue in the Campbells' case.

Before trial State Farm moved in limine to exclude evidence pertaining to conduct that occurred in unrelated cases outside of Utah and continued to object to the admission of this evidence during trial. However, the trial court denied State Farm's motion and objections, reasoning that such evidence was admissible to determine whether State Farm's conduct in the Campbell case was indeed intentional and sufficiently egregious to warrant punitive damages.

The jury awarded the Campbells $2.6 million in compensatory damages and $145 million in punitive damages. The trial court reduced to $1 million and $25 million respectively. On appeal, the Utah Supreme Court reinstated the $145 million punitive damages award. Relying in large part on the extensive evidence concerning the PP & R policy, the court concluded State Farm's conduct was reprehensible. The court also concluded that the ratio between punitive and compensatory damages was not unwarranted. State Farm appealed to the Supreme Court.]

II

We recognized in Cooper Industries, Inc. v. Leatherman Tool Group, Inc., 532 U.S. 424, 121 S.Ct. 1678, 149 L.Ed.2d 674 (2001), that in our judicial system compensatory and punitive damages, although usually awarded at the same time by the same decisionmaker, serve different purposes. [Citation.] Compensatory damages "are intended to redress the concrete loss that the plaintiff has suffered by reason of the defendant's wrongful conduct." [Citation.] By contrast, punitive damages serve a broader function; they are aimed at deterrence and retribution. [Citation.]

While States possess discretion over the imposition of punitive damages, it is well established that there are procedural and substantive constitutional limitations on these awards. [Citation.] The Due Process Clause of the Fourteenth Amendment prohibits the imposition of grossly excessive or arbitrary punishments on a tortfeasor. * * * To the extent an award is grossly excessive, it furthers no legitimate purpose and constitutes an arbitrary deprivation of property. [Citations.]

* * * We have admonished that "[p]unitive damages pose an acute danger of arbitrary deprivation of property. Jury instructions typically leave the jury with wide discretion in choosing amounts, and the presentation of evidence of a defendant's net worth creates the potential that juries will use their verdicts to express biases against big businesses, particularly those without strong local presences." [Citations] Our concerns are heightened when the decisionmaker is presented, as we shall discuss, with evidence that has little bearing as to the amount of punitive damages that should be awarded. Vague instructions, or those that merely inform the jury to avoid "passion or prejudice," [citation], do little to aid the decisionmaker in its task of assigning appropriate weight to evidence that is relevant and evidence that is tangential or only inflammatory.

In light of these concerns, in [BMW of North America v.] Gore, we instructed courts reviewing punitive damages to consider three guideposts: (1) the degree of reprehensibility of the defendant's misconduct; (2) the disparity between the actual or potential harm suffered by the plaintiff and the punitive damages award; and (3) the difference between the punitive damages awarded by the jury and the civil penalties authorized or imposed in comparable cases. [Citation.] We reiterated the importance of these three guideposts in Cooper Industries and mandated appellate courts to conduct de novo review of a trial court's application of them to the jury's award. [Citation.] Exacting appellate review ensures that an award of punitive damages is based upon an " 'application of law, rather than a decisionmaker's caprice.' " [Citation.]

III

Under the principles outlined in BMW of North America, Inc. v. Gore, this case is neither close nor difficult. It was error to reinstate the jury's $145 million punitive damages award. We address each guidepost of Gore in some detail.

A

"[T]he most important indicium of the reasonableness of a punitive damages award is the degree of reprehensibility of the defendant's conduct." Gore, 517 U.S., at 575, 116 S.Ct. 1589. We have instructed courts to determine the reprehensibility of a defendant by considering whether: the harm caused was physical as opposed to economic; the tortious conduct evinced an indifference to or a reckless disregard of the health or safety of others; the target of the conduct had financial vulnerability; the conduct involved repeated actions or was an isolated incident; and the harm was the result of intentional malice, trickery, or deceit, or mere accident. [Citation.] The existence of any one of these factors weighing in favor of a plaintiff may not be sufficient to sustain a punitive damages award; and the absence of all of them renders any award suspect. It should be presumed a plaintiff has been made whole for his injuries by compensatory damages, so punitive damages should only be awarded if the defendant's culpability, after having paid compensatory damages, is so reprehensible as to warrant the imposition of further sanctions to achieve punishment or deterrence. [Citation.]

Applying these factors in the instant case, we must acknowledge that State Farm's handling of the claims against the Campbells merits no praise. The trial court found that State Farm's employees altered the company's records to make Campbell appear less culpable. State Farm disregarded the overwhelming likelihood of liability and the near-certain probability that, by taking the case to trial, a judgment in excess of the policy limits would be awarded. State Farm amplified the harm by at first assuring the Campbells their assets would be safe from any verdict and by later telling them, postjudgment, to put a for-sale sign on their house. While we do not suggest there was error in awarding punitive damages based upon State Farm's conduct toward the Campbells, a more modest punishment for this reprehensible conduct could have satisfied the State's legitimate objectives, and the Utah courts should have gone no further. This case, instead, was used as a platform to expose, and punish, the perceived deficiencies of State Farm's operations throughout the country. The Utah Supreme Court's opinion makes explicit that State Farm was being condemned for its nationwide policies rather than for the conduct directed toward the Campbells. [Citation.] This was, as well, an explicit rationale of the trial court's decision in approving the award, though reduced from $145 million to $25 million. [Citation.]

* * * From their opening statements onward the Campbells framed this case as a chance to rebuke State Farm for its nationwide activities. [Citations.] * * *

A State cannot punish a defendant for conduct that may have been lawful where it occurred. Gore, supra, at 572, 116 S.Ct. 1589; [citations.] Nor, as a general rule, does a State have a legitimate concern in imposing punitive damages to punish a defendant for unlawful acts committed outside of the State's jurisdiction. Any proper adjudication of conduct that occurred outside Utah to other persons would require their inclusion, and, to those parties, the Utah courts, in the usual case, would need to apply the laws of their relevant jurisdiction. [Citation.]

Here, the Campbells do not dispute that much of the out-of-state conduct was lawful where it occurred. They argue, however, that such evidence was not the primary basis for the punitive damages award and was relevant to the extent it demonstrated, in a general sense, State Farm's motive against its insured. [Citation.] This argument misses the mark. Lawful out-of-state conduct may be probative when it demonstrates the deliberateness and culpability of the defendant's action in the State where it is tortious, but that conduct must have a nexus to the specific harm suffered by the plaintiff. A jury must be instructed, furthermore, that it may not use evidence of out-of-state conduct to punish a defendant for action that was lawful in the jurisdiction where it occurred. [Citation.] A basic principle of federalism is that each State may make its own reasoned judgment about what conduct is permitted or proscribed within its borders, and each State alone can determine what measure of punishment, if any, to impose on a defendant who acts within its jurisdiction. [Citation.]

For a more fundamental reason, however, the Utah courts erred in relying upon this and other evidence: The courts awarded punitive damages to punish and deter conduct that bore no relation to the Campbells' harm. A defendant's dissimilar acts, independent from the acts upon which liability was premised, may not serve as the basis for punitive damages. A defendant should be punished for the conduct that harmed the plaintiff, not for being an unsavory individual or business. Due process does not permit courts, in the calculation of punitive damages, to adjudicate the merits of other parties' hypothetical claims against a defendant under the guise of the reprehensibility analysis, but we have no doubt the Utah Supreme Court did that here. [Citation.] Punishment on these bases creates the possibility of multiple punitive damages awards for the same conduct; for in the usual case nonparties are not bound by the judgment some other plaintiff obtains. * * *

The Campbells have identified scant evidence of repeated misconduct of the sort that injured them. Nor does our review of the Utah courts' decisions convince us that State Farm was only punished for its actions toward the Campbells. Although evidence of other acts need not be identical to have relevance in the calculation of punitive damages, the Utah court erred here because evidence pertaining to claims that had nothing to do with a third-party lawsuit was introduced at length. * * * The reprehensibility guidepost does not permit courts to expand the scope of the case so that a defendant may be punished for any malfeasance, which in this case extended for a 20–year period. In this case, because the Campbells have shown no conduct by State Farm similar to that which harmed them, the conduct that harmed them is the only conduct relevant to the reprehensibility analysis.

B

Turning to the second Gore guidepost, we have been reluctant to identify concrete constitutional limits on the ratio between harm, or potential harm, to the plaintiff and the punitive damages award. [Citations.] We decline again to impose a bright-line ratio which a punitive damages award cannot exceed. Our jurisprudence and the principles it has now established demonstrate, however, that, in practice, few awards exceeding a single-digit ratio between punitive and compensatory damages, to a significant degree, will satisfy due process. In Haslip, in upholding a punitive damages award, we concluded that an award of more than four times the amount of compensatory damages might be close to the line of constitutional impropriety. [Citation.] We cited that 4–to–1 ratio again in Gore. [Citation.] The Court further referenced a long legislative history, dating back over 700 years and going forward to today, providing for sanctions of double, treble, or quadruple damages to deter and punish. [Citations.] While these ratios are not binding, they are instructive. They demonstrate what should be obvious: Single-digit multipliers are more likely to comport with due process, while still achieving the State's goals of deterrence and retribution, than awards with ratios in range of 500 to 1, [citation], or, in this case, of 145 to 1.

Nonetheless, because there are no rigid benchmarks that a punitive damages award may not surpass, ratios greater than those we have previously upheld may comport with due process where "a particularly egregious act has resulted in only a small amount of economic damages." [Citations.] The converse is also true, however. When compensatory damages are substantial, then a lesser ratio, perhaps only equal to compensatory damages, can reach the outermost limit of the due process guarantee. The precise award in any case, of course, must be based upon the facts and circumstances of the defendant's conduct and the harm to the plaintiff.

In sum, courts must ensure that the measure of punishment is both reasonable and proportionate to the amount of harm to the plaintiff and to the general damages recovered. In the context of this case, we have no doubt that there is a presumption against an award that has a 145–to–1 ratio. The compensatory award in this case was substantial; the Campbells were awarded $1 million for a year and a half of emotional distress. This was complete compensation. The harm arose from a transaction in the economic realm, not from some physical assault or trauma; there were no physical injuries; and State Farm paid the excess verdict before the complaint was filed, so the Campbells suffered only minor economic injuries for the 18–month period in which State Farm refused to resolve the claim against them. The compensatory damages for the injury suffered here, moreover, likely were based on a component which was duplicated in the punitive award. Much of the distress was caused by the outrage and humiliation the Campbells suffered at the actions of their insurer; and it is a major role of punitive damages to condemn such conduct. Compensatory damages, however, already contain this punitive element. See Restatement (Second) of Torts § 908, Comment c, p. 466 (1977) ("In many cases in which compensatory damages include an amount for emotional distress, such as humiliation or indignation aroused by the defendant's act, there is no clear line of demarcation between punishment and compensation and a verdict for a specified amount frequently includes elements of both").

* * *

The remaining premises for the Utah Supreme Court's decision bear no relation to the award's reasonableness or proportionality to the harm. They are, rather, arguments that seek to defend a departure from well-established constraints on punitive damages. While States enjoy considerable discretion in deducing when punitive damages are warranted, each award must comport with the principles set forth in Gore. Here the argument that State Farm will be punished in only the rare case, coupled with reference to its assets (which, of course, are what other insured parties in Utah and other States must rely upon for payment of claims) had little to do with the actual harm sustained by the Campbells. The wealth of a defendant cannot justify an otherwise unconstitutional punitive damages award. Gore, 517 U.S., at 585, 116 S.Ct. 1589 ("The fact that BMW is a large corporation rather than an impecunious individual does not diminish its entitlement to fair notice of the demands that the several States impose on the conduct of its business"); [citations.] The principles set forth in Gore must be implemented with care, to ensure both reasonableness and proportionality.

C

The third guidepost in Gore is the disparity between the punitive damages award and the "civil penalties authorized or imposed in comparable cases." [Citation.] * * *

Here, we need not dwell long on this guidepost. The most relevant civil sanction under Utah state law for the wrong done to the Campbells appears to be a $10,000 fine for an act of fraud, [citation], an amount dwarfed by the $145 million punitive damages award. The Supreme Court of Utah speculated about the loss of State Farm's business license, the disgorgement of profits, and possible imprisonment, but here again its references were to the broad fraudulent scheme drawn from evidence of out-of-state and dissimilar conduct. This analysis was insufficient to justify the award.

IV

An application of the Gore guideposts to the facts of this case, especially in light of the substantial compensatory damages awarded (a portion of which contained a punitive element), likely would justify a punitive damages award at or near the amount of compensatory damages. The punitive award of $145 million, therefore, was neither reasonable nor proportionate to the wrong committed, and it was an irrational and arbitrary deprivation of the property of the defendant. The proper calculation of punitive damages under the principles we have discussed should be resolved, in the first instance, by the Utah courts.

The judgment of the Utah Supreme Court is reversed, and the case is remanded for further proceedings not inconsistent with this opinion.

It is so ordered.

■ JUSTICE SCALIA, dissenting.

I adhere to the view expressed in my dissenting opinion in BMW of North America, Inc. v. Gore, 517 U.S. 559, 598–99, 116 S.Ct. 1589, 134 L.Ed.2d 809 (1996), that the Due Process Clause provides no substantive protections against "excessive" or " 'unreasonable' " awards of punitive damages. I am also of the view that the punitive damages jurisprudence which has sprung forth from BMW v. Gore is insusceptible of principled application; accordingly, I do not feel justified in giving the case stare decisis effect. [Citation.]

■ JUSTICE THOMAS, dissenting.

I would affirm the judgment below because "I continue to believe that the Constitution does not constrain the size of punitive damages awards." [Citations.] Accordingly, I respectfully dissent.

■ JUSTICE GINSBURG, dissenting.

Not long ago, this Court was hesitant to impose a federal check on state-court judgments awarding punitive damages.

* * *

It was not until 1996, in BMW of North America, Inc. v. Gore, 517 U.S. 559, 116 S.Ct. 1589, 134 L.Ed.2d 809, that the Court, for the first time, invalidated a state-court punitive damages assessment as unreasonably large. [Citations.] If our activity in this domain is now "well established," see ante, at 1519, 1525, it takes place on ground not long held.

In Gore, I stated why I resisted the Court's foray into punitive damages "territory traditionally within the States' domain." [Citation.] I adhere to those views, and note again that, unlike federal habeas corpus review of state-court convictions under 28 U.S.C. § 2254, the Court "work[s] at this business [of checking state courts] alone," unaided by the participation of federal district courts and courts of appeals. [Citation.] It was once recognized that "the laws of the particular State must suffice [to superintend punitive damages awards] until judges or legislators authorized to do so initiate system-wide change." Haslip, 499 U.S., at 42, 111 S.Ct. 1032 (KENNEDY, J., concurring in judgment). I would adhere to that traditional view.

I

The large size of the award upheld by the Utah Supreme Court in this case indicates why damages-capping legislation may be altogether fitting and proper. Neither the amount of the award nor the trial record, however, justifies this Court's substitution of its judgment for that of Utah's competent decisionmakers. * * *

III

When the Court first ventured to override state-court punitive damages awards, it did so moderately. * * * Today's decision exhibits no such respect and restraint. No longer content to accord state-court judgments "a strong presumption of validity," [citation], the Court announces that "few awards exceeding a single-digit ratio between punitive and compensatory damages, to a significant degree, will satisfy due process." [Citation.] Moreover, the Court adds, when compensatory damages are substantial, doubling those damages "can reach the outermost limit of the due process guarantee." [Citation.] In a legislative scheme or a state high court's design to cap punitive damages, the handiwork in setting single-digit and 1–to–1 benchmarks could hardly be questioned; in a judicial decree imposed on the States by this Court under the banner of substantive due process, the numerical controls today's decision installs seem to me boldly out of order.

* * *

I remain of the view that this Court has no warrant to reform state law governing awards of punitive damages. Gore, 517 U.S., at 607, 116 S.Ct. 1589 (GINSBURG, J., dissenting). Even if I were prepared to accept the flexible guides prescribed in Gore, I would not join the Court's swift conversion of those guides into instructions that begin to resemble marching orders. For the reasons stated, I would leave the judgment of the Utah Supreme Court undisturbed.

---

1. *Constitutional Challenges to Punitive Damages.* The Supreme Court considered several constitutional challenges to punitive damages in the years immediately preceding *Campbell*. The challenges proceeded along three lines: (1) Eighth Amendment challenges; (2) procedural due process challenges; and (3) substantive due process challenges. The Court was unreceptive to constitutional challenges to punitive damage awards at first, rejecting an Eighth Amendment challenge in *Browning–Ferris Industries v.*

Kelco Disposal, Inc., 492 U.S. 257, 109 S.Ct. 2909, 106 L.Ed.2d 219 (1989). Eventually, however, the Court recognized both procedural and substantive due process limits on such awards. Initially, the Court recognized these limitations in principle, but failed to provide any meaningful constraints. Ultimately, the Court's progression of decisions culminated in it striking down state punitive damages awards as unconstitutional under both procedural and substantive due process grounds.

2. *Substantive Due Process Limitations. Campbell* is the second case in which the Supreme Court struck down a state punitive damage award on substantive due process grounds as being unconstitutionally excessive. Prior to *Campbell*, the Supreme Court struck down a $2 million punitive damage award in a consumer fraud case. In BMW of North America v. Gore, 517 U.S. 559, 116 S.Ct. 1589, 134 L.E.2d 809 (1996), an Alabama jury awarded $4 million in punitive damages after BMW failed to disclose to the plaintiff that the plaintiff's new BMW had been repainted before sale. Evidence established that the repainting had diminished the value of the car by $4,000. On appeal, the Alabama Supreme Court reduced the punitive damage award to $2 million. Nonetheless, the Supreme Court concluded that the remitted award was unconstitutionally excessive.

In *Gore*, the Court adopted three "guideposts" to guide its excessiveness review. The Court considered: (1) the degree of reprehensibility of the defendant's misconduct; (2) the ratio of the actual and potential harm to the plaintiff to the punitive damage award; and (3) civil and criminal sanctions available for comparable misconduct. The Court ultimately concluded that all three guideposts indicated that the award in *Gore* was unconstitutionally excessive. First, the Court noted that "none of the aggravating factors associated with particularly reprehensible conduct [was] present" in *Gore* because BMW had inflicted purely economic harm on a plaintiff who was not financially vulnerable and because BMW had acted in good faith reliance on disclosure limitations in state consumer protection statutes in deciding not to disclose the repainting. Second, the Court observed that the $2 million punitive damage award was 500 times greater than the $4,000 in harm BMW's nondisclosure caused the plaintiff. Finally, the Court noted that the maximum civil penalties available for comparable nondisclosures ranged from only $5,000–$10,000.

3. *Third–Party Misconduct.* To what extent may a jury consider evidence of a defendant's conduct in other cases? For example, should a plaintiff in a products liability suit be permitted to introduce evidence of a defendant's sales of a defective product to other consumers? In both *Campbell* and *Gore*, the Court was troubled by the jury's apparent reliance on evidence of misconduct directed at parties other that the plaintiff. For example, in *Gore*, the plaintiff introduced evidence that BMW had sold 983 repainted cars as new to consumers in the United States. In *Campbell*, the Court noted that the Campbells introduced evidence of State Farm's claims adjustment practices in other third-party and first-party cases. The Court was concerned that evidence of misconduct directed at non-parties could lead a jury to impose punitive damages on the defendant to punish it for

the misconduct directed at the non-parties. The Court noted two potential problems with imposing sanctions to punish a defendant for misconduct directed at non-parties.

First, in *Gore*, the Supreme Court expressed concern that imposing punitive damages to sanction a defendant for conduct directed at non-parties who were residents of another State might impermissibly interfere with that State's ability to make its own policy choices about what conduct to sanction. The Court explained that a State may not impose punitive damages to deter or change a tortfeasor's lawful conduct in other states. Instead, a State's interest in protecting its *own* consumers and its *own* economy must support the size of a state punitive damage award. However, the Court expressly left open the question of whether a State properly may attempt to deter or change a tortfeasor's unlawful conduct in another state. Additionally, the Court acknowledged that even though lawful extraterritorial conduct could not support an award, evidence of extraterritorial conduct—even lawful conduct in other states—might be relevant to determine the degree of reprehensibility of the defendant's conduct.

In *Campbell*, the Court answered the question left open in *Gore*, concluding that a State could not attempt to deter or change a tortfeasor's conduct in another State even if that conduct was unlawful in the State where it occurred. The Court also recognized another potential problem with sanctions imposed to punish a defendant for misconduct directed at other parties, including other in-state parties. The Court noted that such sanctions would create the possibility of multiple punitive damages awards for the same conduct because nonparties would not be bound by the judgment in the case and could pursue their own claims for punitive damages. However, as it had in *Gore*, the Court continued to acknowledge that evidence of misconduct directed at non-parties could be relevant to determine the degree of reprehensibility of the defendant's misconduct.

Thus, the Court has drawn the following distinction: Evidence of misconduct directed at other parties cannot be used to impose punitive damages on a defendant for that misconduct directly. However, evidence of misconduct directed at non-parties can be used to show the increased reprehensibility of the misconduct directed at the plaintiff and, hence, to increase the punitive damage award for misconduct directed at the plaintiff. How meaningful is the distinction between punishing the defendant directly for misconduct directed at non-parties and punishing the defendant for the increased reprehensibility of its misconduct directed at the plaintiff? *Cf.* Thomas B. Colby, Beyond the Multiple Punishment Problem: Punitive Damages as Punishment for Individual, Private Wrongs, 87 MINN. L. REV. 583, 587 (2003) *with* Margaret Meriwether Cordray, The Limits of State Sovereignty and the Issue of Multiple Punitive Damage Awards, 78 ORE. L. REV. 275, 313 (1999) (noting that the distinction between punishing a defendant directly for other transactions and using evidence of other transactions to help evaluate the defendant's blameworthiness "is a fine one" and opining that juries may not be able to understand and apply it).

4. *Related Misconduct.* In *Campbell* the Court held that other misconduct evidence is relevant to reprehensibility only if it is evidence of misconduct that is "of the same sort" as the misconduct that injured the plaintiff or that is reasonably related to the misconduct that injured the plaintiff. Thus, the *Campbell* Court dismissed much of the evidence about State Farm's claims handling practices in other cases as being irrelevant. The Court distinguished these other cases from Campbell's case because these other cases were first-party cases rather than third-party cases or did not involve automobile insurance policies. How compelling is the Court's distinction? Why can't similar handling of these types of claims establish State Farm's reprehensibility? In her dissent, Justice Ginsburg criticized the majority's reasoning, describing in detail the nature of the evidence about these other cases:

> I count it significant that, on the key criterion "reprehensibility," there is a good deal more to the story than the Court's abbreviated account tells. Ample evidence allowed the jury to find that State Farm's treatment of the Campbells typified its "Performance, Planning and Review" (PP & R) program; implemented by top management in 1979, the program had "the explicit objective of using the claims-adjustment process as a profit center." [Citation.] "[T]he Campbells presented considerable evidence," the trial court noted, documenting "that the PP & R program ... has functioned, and continues to function, as an unlawful scheme ... to deny benefits owed consumers by paying out less than fair value in order to meet preset, arbitrary payout targets designed to enhance corporate profits." [Citation.] That policy, the trial court observed, was encompassing in scope; it "applied equally to the handling of both third-party and first-party claims." [Citations.] 123 S.Ct. at 1527–28.

Justice Ginsburg then described some of the evidence that the Campbells introduced to show that State Farm's handling of their claim was indicative of the PP & R policy. For example, Justice Ginsburg noted testimony that State Farm frequently attacked the character, reputation or credibility of a claimant in the claim file to create prejudice in the event the claim ever came before a jury and that a State Farm manager directed employees to falsely note in the Campbell file that the driver who was killed in the accident was speeding because he was on his way to see a pregnant girlfriend. State Farm employees testified that at the time of the Campbell case, the Utah manager was under pressure to reduce claim payouts to meet preset caps. Justice Ginsburg noted that the Campbells introduced State Farm's "Excess Liability Handbook" which instructed adjusters to pad files with "self-serving" documents, and to leave critical items such as evaluations of the insured's exposure out of claim files. Testimony indicated that a manager supervising the Campbell case ordered the claims adjuster to change the portions of his report indicating that Mr. Campbell was likely at fault and that the settlement cost was correspondingly high.

Finally, Justice Ginsburg noted the testimony of several former State Farm employees that they were trained to target "the weakest of the herd"—"the elderly, the poor, and other consumers who are least knowledgeable about their rights and thus most vulnerable to trickery or deceit, or who have little money and hence have no real alternative but to accept an inadequate offer to settle a claim at much less than fair value." Justice Ginsburg noted that the Campbells could be placed within the "weakest of the herd" category because the couple appeared economically vulnerable and because at the time of the case, Mr. Campbell had residuary effects from a stroke and Parkinson's disease. She concluded by observing:

> The Court dismisses the evidence describing and documenting State Farm's PP & R policy and practices as essentially irrelevant, bearing "no relation to the Campbells' harm." [Citation.] It is hardly apparent why that should be so. What is infirm about the Campbells' theory that their experience with State Farm exemplifies and reflects an overarching underpayment scheme, one that caused "repeated misconduct of the sort that injured them," [citation]? The Court's silence on that score is revealing: Once one recognizes that the Campbells did show "conduct by State Farm similar to that which harmed them," [citation], it becomes impossible to shrink the reprehensibility analysis to this sole case, or to maintain, at odds with the determination of the trial court, [citation], that "the adverse effect on the State's general population was in fact minor," [citation]. 123 S.Ct. at 1530.

5.   *Procedural Due Process Limits.* The Court has recognized only modest due process limits on the manner by which courts impose punitive damages. Thus, for example, in *Pacific Mutual Life Insurance Company v. Haslip*, 499 U.S. 1, 111 S.Ct. 1032, 113 L.Ed.2d 1 (1991), the Court rejected a challenge to Alabama's procedures for imposing punitive damages. Alabama, like most states, permitted juries to determine whether to impose punitive damages as well as the amount of punitive damages. The Alabama jury instructions informed juries that punitive damages were imposed to punish the defendant and deter the defendant and others from engaging in similar misconduct in the future and that they could chose not to impose punitive damages. *Id.* at 19. The instructions also told jurors to consider factors such as the character and the degree of the wrong in determining the amount of punitive damages. *Id.* Alabama also provided for judicial review of punitive damages. A reviewing court was to consider several factors, including the culpability of the defendant, the relationship between the size of the punitive damage award and the harm caused by the defendant's conduct and the profitability of the defendant's conduct, in deciding whether to reduce a punitive damage award. *Id.* at 21–22. The Court concluded that this process, and in particular, the factors guiding judicial review of punitive damage awards "imposes a sufficiently definite and meaningful constraint on the discretion of Alabama factfinders in awarding punitive damages." *Id.* at 22.

However, in *Honda Motor Co. v. Oberg*, 512 U.S. 415, 114 S.Ct. 2331, 129 L.Ed.2d 336 (1994), the Court did strike down an amendment to the

Oregon Constitution that prohibited judicial review of the size of a punitive damage award. The Court noted that judicial review of punitive damage awards was a well-established common law tradition that protected the defendant from arbitrary awards or awards based on bias. The Court concluded that the other safeguards Oregon provided to protect defendants from arbitrary or biased awards were insufficient to justify Oregon's departure from well-established common law practice. Most notably, the Court reasoned that Oregon's pattern jury instructions could not adequately protect the defendant because a jury might disregard the instructions.

Campbell seemingly imposes an additional due process limitation. Note that the Court observes: "A jury must be instructed, furthermore, that it may not use evidence of out-of-state conduct to punish a defendant for action that was lawful in the jurisdiction where it occurred."

The Court strengthened this procedural protection in *Philip Morris v. Williams*, 549 U.S. 346, 127 S.Ct. 1057, 166 L.E.2d 940 (2007). In *Williams*, an Oregon jury awarded $79.5 million in punitive damages to the wife of a heavy-smoker who died from smoking-related lung cancer. At trial, the plaintiff offered evidence about the number of smokers in Oregon who had likely purchased Philip Morris products and the number of those smokers who were likely to die from smoking-related illnesses. The plaintiff's attorney urged the jury to consider these other smokers in setting the punitive damage award. The Court struck down the award because this evidence and argument created an unreasonable risk that the jury would impose punitive damages to punish Philip Morris for the harm suffered by these other smokers. The Court held that due process required states to adopt procedures aimed at protecting the defendant from this type of unreasonable risk. Most notably, the Court observed that the trial court refused to accept Philip Morris' proposed jury instruction that would have specifically informed the jury that it could not impose punitive damages to punish Philip Morris for the harm to smokers other than the plaintiff.

6. *Punitive Damages in Contact Cases.* Generally, parties are not permitted to recover punitive damages for breach of contract. Courts have recognized an exception when the conduct constituting the breach of contract also constitutes an independent tort. However, breaches of the implied covenant of good faith and fair dealing are not considered a sufficiently independent tort. *See, e.g.,* Reid v. Key Bank of Southern Maine, 821 F.2d 9 (1st Cir.1987) (district court properly struck award of punitive damages based on a breach of the implied covenant of good faith because no recoverable torts existed to which damages could attach).

One exception to this rule arises is a claim based on an insurer's bad faith refusal to settle such as the Campbells' claim in the principal case. *See, e.g.,* Farmland Mutual Ins. Co. v. Johnson, 36 S.W.3d 368 (Ky.2000); Kapp v. Arbella Mut. Ins. Co., 426 Mass. 683, 689 N.E.2d 1347 (1998); Pierce v. International Ins. Co. of Illinois, 671 A.2d 1361 (Del.1996); Tadlock Painting Co. v. Maryland Cas. Co., 322 S.C. 498, 473 S.E.2d 52 (1996); Weiss v. United Fire and Cas. Co., 197 Wis.2d 365, 541 N.W.2d 753 (1995); Egan v. Mutual of Omaha Ins. Co., 24 Cal.3d 809, 169 Cal.Rptr.

691, 620 P.2d 141 (1979). Courts emphasize the unique nature of an insurance contract, the special, almost fiduciary, relationship between an insurer and insured, the unequal bargaining power between an insured and an insurer and the adhesive nature of the insurance contract as reasons for allowing punitive damages against insurers.

For example, in *Egan v. Mutual of Omaha Insurance*, 24 Cal.3d 809, 169 Cal.Rptr. 691, 620 P.2d 141 (1979), the California Supreme Court noted that "[t]he insured in a contract like the one before us does not seek to obtain a commercial advantage by purchasing the policy—rather, he seeks protection against calamity." Thus, the court reasoned:

> The special relationship between the insurer and the insured illustrates the public policy considerations that may support exemplary damages in cases such as this.

> As one commentator has noted, "The insurers' obligations are ... rooted in their status as purveyors of a vital service labeled quasi-public in nature. Suppliers of services affected with a public interest must take the public's interest seriously, where necessary placing it before their interest in maximizing gains and limiting disbursements ... [A]s a supplier of a public service rather than a manufactured product, the obligations of the insurer go beyond meeting reasonable expectations of coverage. The obligations of good faith and fair dealing encompass qualities of decency and humanity inherent in the responsibilities of a fiduciary. Insurers hold themselves out as fiduciaries, and with the public's trust must go private responsibility consonant with that trust." [Citation.] Furthermore, the relationship of insurer and insured is inherently unbalanced; the adhesive nature of insurance contracts places the insurer in a superior bargaining position. The availability of punitive damages is thus compatible with the recognition of insurers' underlying public obligations and reflects an attempt to restore balance in the contractual relationship. [Citation.] 620 P.2d at 145–46.

7. *Ratio.* In *Campbell* the Court refused to adopt a "bright-line" ratio which a punitive damage could not constitutionally exceed. However, the Court seemingly created a presumption that double-digit ratios were constitutionally unreasonable while acknowledging that greater ratios could be reasonable if the defendant committed "a particularly egregious act" that resulted in only a small measure of compensatory damages. The Court also intimated that smaller ratios of only 1–to–1 might be the limit when the plaintiff had recovered significant compensatory damages, noting "[w]hen compensatory damages are substantial, then a lesser ratio, perhaps only equal to compensatory damages, can reach the outermost limit of the due process guarantee."

On remand, the Utah Supreme Court felt unconstrained by the Supreme Court's suggestion that punitive damages could not exceed compensatory damages if the injured party had received significant punitive damages. Campbell v. State Farm Mut. Auto. Ins. Co., 98 P.3d 409 (Utah 2004). Further, the Utah Supreme Court expressly disagreed with the

Supreme Court's characterization of the reprehensibility of State Farm's conduct, noting "we find the blameworthiness of State Farm's behavior toward the Campbells to be several degrees more offensive than the Supreme Court's less than condemnatory view." *Id.* at ¶ 18. The Utah Supreme Court also took issue with the Supreme Court's characterization of the harm to the Campbells as economic harm. *Id.* at ¶ 30. Nonetheless, the Utah Supreme Court awarded the Campbells $9,018,780.75 in punitive damages—an amount which yielded a 9–to–1 ratio between compensatory and punitive damages. *Id.* at ¶ 41. The Utah Supreme Court concluded that the Supreme Court's decision permitted ratios exceeding the single digits only if a particularly egregious act resulted in only a small amount of economic damages or where the monetary value of noneconomic harm had been difficult to determine. *Id.* at ¶ 40. Because the Utah Supreme Court concluded that neither of those circumstances existed in the Campbells' case, the court concluded that it was limited to awarding punitive damages in the single-digit ratio range.

Subsequently, in *Exxon Shipping Company v. Baker*, 554 U.S. 471, 128 S.Ct. 2605, 171 L.Ed.2d 570 (2008), the Court struck down a $5 billion punitive damage judgment awarded to the plaintiffs in a case arising out of the grounding of the Exxon Valdez oil tanker in Prince William Sound, Alaska. Exercising its "federal maritime common law authority," the Court concluded that the award was excessive as a matter of common law. The Court capped all punitive damage awards in maritime cases at a ratio of 1–to–1 with compensatory damages. In reaching this holding, the Court differentiated its role in examining a judgment for conformity with maritime law from its role in due process review. However, in setting the 1–to–1 ratio cap, the Court reviewed empirical data on punitive damage awards in non-maritime civil cases. Perhaps more importantly, the Court remarked, "[a]nd our explanation of the constitutional upper limit confirms that the 1:1 ratio is not too low. In *State Farm*, we said that a single-digit maxim is appropriate in all but the most exceptional cases, and '[w]hen compensatory damages are substantial, then a lesser ratio, perhaps only equal to compensatory damages, can reach the outermost limit of the due process guarantee.' "

In light of *State Farm* and *Baker,* how likely is it that lower courts will deviate from this presumption? *See* Caprice L. Roberts, Ratios, (Ir)rationality & Civil Rights Punitive Awards, 39 Akron L. Rev. 1019 (2007) (noting that some courts have characterized the single-digit ratio as the constitutional limit). In what kind of cases would a double-digit ratio be reasonable? Consider the following case.

Mathias v. Accor Economy Lodging, Inc.

347 F.3d 672 (7th Cir.2003).

■ Posner, Circuit Judge.

The plaintiffs brought this diversity suit governed by Illinois law against affiliated entities (which the parties treat as a single entity, as shall we) that own and operate the "Motel 6" chain of hotels and motels. One of these hotels (now a "Red Roof Inn," though still owned by the defendant) is in downtown Chicago. The plaintiffs, a brother and sister, were guests there and were bitten by bedbugs, which are making a comeback in the U.S. as a consequence of more conservative use of pesticides. [Citations.] The plaintiffs claim that in allowing guests to be attacked by bedbugs in a motel that charges upwards of $100 a day for a room and would not like to be mistaken for a flophouse, the defendant was guilty of "willful and wanton conduct" and thus under Illinois law is liable for punitive as well as compensatory damages. [Citations.] The jury agreed and awarded each plaintiff $186,000 in punitive damages though only $5,000 in compensatory damages. The defendant appeals, complaining primarily about the punitive-damages award. * * *

The defendant argues that at worst it is guilty of simple negligence, and if this is right the plaintiffs were not entitled by Illinois law to any award of punitive damages. It also complains that the award was excessive—indeed that any award in excess of $20,000 to each plaintiff would deprive the defendant of its property without due process of law. The first complaint has no possible merit, as the evidence of gross negligence, indeed of recklessness in the strong sense of an unjustifiable failure to avoid a known risk, [citations], was amply shown. In 1998, EcoLab, the extermination service that the motel used, discovered bedbugs in several rooms in the motel and recommended that it be hired to spray every room, for which it would charge the motel only $500; the motel refused. The next year, bedbugs were again discovered in a room but EcoLab was asked to spray just that room. The motel tried to negotiate "a building sweep [by EcoLab] free of charge," but, not surprisingly, the negotiation failed. By the spring of 2000, the motel's manager "started noticing that there were refunds being given by my desk clerks and reports coming back from the guests that there were ticks in the rooms and bugs in the rooms that were biting." She looked in some of the rooms and discovered bedbugs. * * *

Further incidents of guests being bitten by insects and demanding and receiving refunds led the manager to recommend to her superior in the company that the motel be closed while every room was sprayed, but this was refused. This superior, a district manager, was a management-level employee of the defendant, and his knowledge of the risk and failure to take effective steps either to eliminate it or to warn the motel's guests are imputed to his employer for purposes of determining whether the employer should be liable for punitive damages. [Citations.] * * *.

The infestation continued and began to reach farcical proportions, as when a guest, after complaining of having been bitten repeatedly by insects while asleep in his room in the hotel, was moved to another room only to discover insects there; and within 18 minutes of being moved to a third room he discovered insects in that room as well and had to be moved still again. (Odd that at that point he didn't flee the motel.) By July, the motel's management was acknowledging to EcoLab that there was a "major problem with bed bugs" and that all that was being done about it was "chasing them from room to room." Desk clerks were instructed to call the "bedbugs" "ticks," apparently on the theory that customers would be less alarmed, though in fact ticks are more dangerous than bedbugs because they spread Lyme Disease and Rocky Mountain Spotted Fever. Rooms that the motel had placed on "Do not rent, bugs in room" status nevertheless were rented.

It was in November that the plaintiffs checked into the motel. They were given Room 504, even though the motel had classified the room as "DO NOT RENT UNTIL TREATED," and it had not been treated. Indeed, that night 190 of the hotel's 191 rooms were occupied, even though a number of them had been placed on the same don't-rent status as Room 504. * * *

* * * There was, in short, sufficient evidence of "willful and wanton conduct" within the meaning that the Illinois courts assign to the term to permit an award of punitive damages in this case.

But in what amount? In arguing that $20,000 was the maximum amount of punitive damages that a jury could constitutionally have awarded each plaintiff, the defendant points to the U.S. Supreme Court's recent statement that "few awards [of punitive damages] exceeding a single-digit ratio between punitive and compensatory damages, to a significant degree, will satisfy due process." State Farm Mutual Automobile Ins. Co. v. Campbell, 538 U.S. 408, 123 S.Ct. 1513, 1524, 155 L.Ed.2d 585 (2003). The Court went on to suggest that "four times the amount of compensatory damages might be close to the line of constitutional impropriety." [Citations]. Hence the defendant's proposed ceiling in this case of $20,000, four times the compensatory damages awarded to each plaintiff. The ratio of punitive to compensatory damages determined by the jury was, in contrast, 37.2 to 1.

The Supreme Court did not, however, lay down a 4-to-1 or single-digit-ratio rule-it said merely that "there is a presumption against an award that has a 145-to-1 ratio," State Farm Mutual Automobile Ins. Co. v. Campbell, supra, 123 S.Ct. at 1524—and it would be unreasonable to do so. We must consider why punitive damages are awarded and why the Court has decided that due process requires that such awards be limited. The second question is easier to answer than the first. The term "punitive damages" implies punishment, and a standard principle of penal theory is that "the punishment should fit the crime" in the sense of being proportional to the wrongfulness of the defendant's action, though the principle is modified when the probability of detection is very low (a familiar example is the heavy fines for littering) or the crime is potentially lucrative (as in the case of trafficking in illegal drugs). Hence, with these qualifications, which in fact will figure in our analysis of this case, punitive damages should be proportional to the wrongfulness of the defendant's actions.

Another penal precept is that a defendant should have reasonable notice of the sanction for unlawful acts, so that he can make a rational determination of how to act; and so there have to be reasonably clear standards for determining the amount of punitive damages for particular wrongs.

And a third precept, the core of the Aristotelian notion of corrective justice, and more broadly of the principle of the rule of law, is that sanctions should be based on the wrong done rather than on the status of the defendant; a person is punished for what he does, not for who he is, even if the who is a huge corporation.

What follows from these principles, however, is that punitive damages should be measured by standards or rules rather than in a completely ad hoc manner, and this does not tell us what the maximum ratio of punitive to compensatory damages should be in a particular case. To determine that, we have to consider why punitive damages are awarded in the first place. [Citation.]

* * * [S]till today one function of punitive-damages awards is to relieve the pressures on an overloaded system of criminal justice by providing a civil alternative to criminal prosecution of minor crimes. An example is deliberately spitting in a person's face, a criminal assault but because minor readily deterrable by the levying of what amounts to a civil fine through a suit for damages for the tort of battery. Compensatory damages would not do the trick in such a case, and this for three reasons: because they are difficult to determine in the case of acts that inflict largely dignitary harms; because in the spitting case they would be too slight to give the victim an incentive to sue, and he might decide instead to respond with violence—and an age-old purpose of the law of torts is to provide a substitute for violent retaliation against wrongful injury—and because to limit the plaintiff to compensatory damages would enable the defendant to commit the offensive act with impunity provided that he was willing to pay, and again there would be a danger that his act would incite a breach of the peace by his victim.

When punitive damages are sought for billion-dollar oil spills and other huge economic injuries, the considerations that we have just canvassed fade. As the Court emphasized in Campbell, the fact that the plaintiffs in that case had been awarded very substantial compensatory damages—$1 million for a dispute over insurance coverage-greatly reduced the need for giving them a huge award of punitive damages ($145 million) as well in order to provide an effective remedy. Our case is closer to the spitting case. The defendant's behavior was outrageous but the compensable harm done was slight and at the same time difficult to quantify because a large element of it was emotional. And the defendant may well have profited from its misconduct because by concealing the infestation it was able to keep renting rooms. Refunds were frequent but may have cost less than the cost of closing the hotel for a thorough fumigation. The hotel's attempt to pass off the bedbugs as ticks, which some guests might ignorantly have thought less unhealthful, may have postponed the instituting of litigation to rectify the hotel's misconduct. The award of punitive damages in this case thus serves the additional purpose of limiting the defendant's ability to profit from its fraud by escaping detection and (private) prosecution. If a tortfeasor is "caught" only half the time he commits torts, then when he is caught he should be punished twice as heavily in order to make up for the times he gets away.

Finally, if the total stakes in the case were capped at $50,000 (2 × [$5,000 + $20,000]), the plaintiffs might well have had difficulty financing this lawsuit. It is here that the defendant's aggregate net worth of $1.6 billion becomes relevant. A defendant's wealth is not a sufficient basis for awarding punitive damages. State Farm Mutual Automobile Ins. Co. v. Campbell, supra, 123 S.Ct. at 1525; BMW of North America, Inc. v. Gore, supra, 517 U.S. at 591, 116 S.Ct. 1589 (concurring opinion); Zazu Designs v. L'Oreal, S.A., 979 F.2d 499, 508–09 (7th Cir.1992). That would be discriminatory and would violate the rule of law, as we explained earlier, by making punishment depend on status rather than conduct. Where wealth in the sense of resources enters is in enabling the defendant to mount an extremely aggressive defense against suits such as this and by doing so to make litigating against it very costly, which in turn may make it difficult for the plaintiffs to find a lawyer willing to handle their case, involving as it does only modest stakes, for the usual 33–40 percent contingent fee.

In other words, the defendant is investing in developing a reputation intended to deter plaintiffs. It is difficult otherwise to explain the great stubborness with which it has defended this case, making a host of frivolous evidentiary arguments despite the very modest stakes even when the punitive damages awarded by the jury are included.

* * *

All things considered, we cannot say that the award of punitive damages was excessive, albeit the precise number chosen by the jury was arbitrary. It is probably not a coincidence that $5,000 + $186,000 = $191,000/191 = $1,000: i.e., $1,000 per room in the hotel. * * *

But it would have been helpful had the parties presented evidence concerning the regulatory or criminal penalties to which the defendant exposed itself by deliberately exposing its customers to a substantial risk of being bitten by bedbugs. That is an inquiry recommended by the Supreme Court. See State Farm Mutual Automobile Ins. Co. v. Campbell, supra, 123 S.Ct. at 1520, 1526; BMW of North America, Inc. v. Gore, supra, 517 U.S. at 583–85, 116 S.Ct. 1589. But we do not think its omission invalidates the award. We can take judicial notice that deliberate exposure of hotel guests to the health risks created by insect infestations exposes the hotel's owner to sanctions under Illinois and Chicago law that in the aggregate are comparable in severity to the punitive damage award in this case.

"A person who causes bodily harm to or endangers the bodily safety of an individual by any means, commits reckless conduct if he performs recklessly the acts which cause the harm or endanger safety, whether they otherwise are lawful or unlawful." 720 ILCS 5/12–5(a). This is a misdemeanor, punishable by up to a year's imprisonment or a fine of $2,500, or both. 720 ILCS 5/12–5(b); 730 ILCS 5/5–8–3(a)(1), 5/5–9–1(a)(2). * * * Of course a corporation cannot be sent to prison, and $2,500 is obviously much less than the $186,000 awarded to each plaintiff in this case as punitive damages. But this is just the beginning. Other guests of the hotel were endangered besides these two plaintiffs. And, what is much more important, a Chicago hotel that permits unsanitary conditions to exist is subject to revocation of its license, without which it cannot operate. Chi. Munic. Code §§ 4–4–280, 4–208–020, 050, 060, 110. We are sure that the defendant would prefer to pay the punitive damages assessed in this case than to lose its license.

------

1. Is Judge Posner's opinion consistent with the Supreme Court's opinion in *Campbell*? Does Judge Posner impermissibly allow the jury to impose punitive damages to punish the defendant for the harm that other guests suffered from being exposed to bedbugs? *See* Colleen P. Murphy, *The "Bedbug" Case and State Farm v. Campbell*, 9 Roger Williams U. L. Rev. 579 (2004).

2. New York courts have distinguished *Mathias* in a series of decisions denying punitive damages to hotel guests who were bitten by bed bugs during their stay in New York City. *See* Light v. Metropolitan Hotel Realty, 2011 WL 2175778 (S.D.N.Y. 2011); Grogan v. Gamber Corp., 19 Misc.3d 798, 858 N.Y.S.2d 519 (2008). In each case, the court distinguished *Mathias* because the hotel operator had hired a professional exterminator and followed the exterminator's recommendation. The courts also noted that a published recommendation of the New York City Department of Health and Mental Hygiene counseled "anyone with bed bugs to hire a pest control professional." Why would these circumstances preclude an award of punitive damages?

PART IV

RESTITUTIONARY REMEDIES

CHAPTER 16

UNJUST ENRICHMENT

A. THE UNJUST ENRICHMENT CONCEPT

Section Coverage:

Restitution is civil liability based upon unjust enrichment. A benefit is considered unjust enrichment when its retention without compensation would be wrongfully at the expense of another. The remedy may be a restoration of the benefit or its traceable product, or payment of money to eliminate the unjust enrichment.

An action in restitution is often just an additional remedial option for a plaintiff who has a claim in contract or tort, but sometimes it is the sole remedy available to a plaintiff. For example, when someone mistakenly confers a benefit on another, the sole basis of liability is unjust enrichment and the only remedy available is restitution.

Historically restitution developed separately both at law and in equity, although modern courts sometimes refer to all restitution as being in equity. The common law courts developed a restitutionary device called "quasi-contract" which was based upon the action of assumpsit. Assumpsit was the action plaintiffs used to recover for breaches of express contracts. The law courts adapted assumpsit for restitution by finding that an unjustly enriched defendant became party to a contract implied by law. The "contract" fashioned by the court was a fiction designed simply to oblige payment to the plaintiff of the amount of unjust enrichment.

One type of implied-in-law contract that developed at law was quantum meruit. This action allows recovery of the reasonable value of beneficial services rendered or materials furnished under circumstances not covered by express contract where retention of the benefit would constitute unjust enrichment. For example, if a contract is unenforceable for some reason such as impossibility, a plaintiff could use quantum meruit to recover the value of any work performed under the mistaken belief that the contract was enforceable. Without the restitutionary action, the defendant would be unjustly enriched at the plaintiff's expense.

The equity courts developed different restitutionary remedies, most notably constructive trusts and equitable liens. Substantive equity had already developed devices for enforcing express trusts, so the constructive trust became the method for disgorging unjust enrichment. Like the quasi-contract development at law, the constructive trust was based upon a fiction; the defendant became an involuntary trustee of the unjust enrichment for the benefit of the plaintiff. For example, if a fiduciary misappropriated money and used it to purchase land, the court of equity would impose a constructive trust to disgorge from the defendant the land and any profits traceable from it.

The common theme between restitutionary actions at law and in equity is that they are all based upon the idea of disgorging unjust enrichment. Sometimes the result may appear punitive in character, but the essence of the remedy is not to punish but to disgorge. For example, a constructive trust is used to disgorge property purchased with embezzled money even when that property has increased in value. It does not matter that the increase in value is attributable to the wise business judgment of the embezzler in making the investment with the misappropriated assets, because the wrongdoer must return all profit.

In other instances the defendant may have innocently acquired the unjust enrichment. Whether the defendant is a wrongdoer is not the key; the substantive questions are whether the defendant has been enriched and whether the retention of such enrichment would be unjust. The remedial aspect of restitution focuses on the measurement of the benefit in the hands of the defendant.

This section begins the study of restitution by examining the substantive concept of unjust enrichment. In each case the court first must find an enrichment in the sense that the defendant has received something of value. Then the court must find that the enrichment should be disgorged from the defendant to rectify an unjust result. As with any concept based upon the abstraction of justice, unjust enrichment is not capable of easy definition. The cases in this section struggle both with the concept of enrichment and with the injustice of the defendant's gain.

Model Case:

Owens leased a crane for purposes of performing a subcontract which involved lifting steel girders in the construction of a building. Owens left the crane at the construction site over the weekend, planning to resume operations the following Monday. Owens inadvertently forgot to lock it and left the keys in the ignition.

Joe Adler, owner of Joe's Truckstop and Cafe located adjacent to the construction area, received delivery of a large outdoor sign on Saturday. Joe saw the crane at the nearby site and attempted to inquire if the owner might help him out by lifting the sign into place. He found the construction site deserted, and noticing the keys in the crane he decided to "borrow" it for a few minutes to position the sign.

The next Monday Owens learned about the unauthorized use of the crane from a gas station attendant who had witnessed Joe putting up the sign. Owens sues Joe for unjust enrichment. The court may determine that the benefit enjoyed by Joe constitutes a "form of advantage" which would be unjust to retain without compensation. The restitutionary remedy would not depend upon the existence of a valid contract between Owens and Joe, nor would it be precluded by a showing that Owens in fact suffered no loss corresponding to Joe's gain. Rather, the focus in unjust enrichment is on the defendant's receipt or retention of a benefit rather than on providing compensation for losses incurred by the plaintiff. The court might measure the benefit which Joe received based upon the fair rental value of a crane to perform the job involved.

Matter of Estate of Zent

459 N.W.2d 795 (N.D. 1990).

■ Levine, Justice.

Ann Johnson appeals from a county court judgment disallowing her claim against the estate of John A. Zent. We reverse and remand.

Ann and John met in Mandan in late 1979 and developed a personal relationship which lasted until his death in 1988. Marriage was discussed but not accomplished. Throughout their close association, Ann and John maintained separate residences but spent considerable amounts of time together, six to ten hours a day almost every day.

As Ann characterizes the relationship, it had two stages. The first stage was social and involved going out to movies and dinners and vacationing together. In the second stage, Ann maintains that she was "a virtual houseservant and nursemaid" to John. During that period, John was gradually and progressively incapacitated by back surgery, a series of strokes and Alzheimer's disease. According to Ann, John began to deteriorate mentally in 1985, until her once-robust social companion was a confused old man in need of almost constant attention. In June 1988, John was admitted to a nursing home and died three weeks later.

On November 21, 1988, Ann filed a claim against John's estate seeking compensation in the amount of $31,025.00 for services rendered to him. She requested $9,125.00, or $5.00 per day for personal services rendered from 1980 to 1985, including "light housekeeping, assisting with the cooking, laundry, shopping, etc." She sought $21,900.00, or $20.00 a day, for services rendered from 1985–1988, including "taking him to clinic, hospital and surgical appointments; aftercare following surgeries; cooking and housecleaning; doing the laundry; taking care of pet dog; shopping for groceries and other items; and administering medication."

Howard A. Zent, John's son and personal representative, disallowed Ann's claim in its entirety. She then requested a hearing in county court. The county court affirmed the disallowance, determining that there was no express contract between Ann and John, no implied-in-fact contract, no implied-in-law contract, and that John was not unjustly enriched by services performed by Ann.

On appeal, Ann argues that the trial court erred in concluding that there was no contract implied in law and no unjust enrichment. We agree.

The concepts of contract implied in law and unjust enrichment are interrelated. A contract implied in law, or quasi-contract, is not a contract at all but rather an obligation imposed by law to do justice even though it is clear that no promise was ever made or intended. [Citations.] The essence of an implied-in-law contract is the receipt of a benefit by a decedent from the claimant, which it would be inequitable for the decedent to retain without paying for. [Citation.] If it would be inequitable for the decedent to retain the benefit, he is said to be unjustly enriched.[Citations.]. A person who is unjustly enriched at the expense of another is required to make restitution to the other. Restatement of Restitution § 1.

A determination of unjust enrichment is necessarily a conclusion of law because it holds that a certain state of facts is contrary to equity. [Citation.] The trial court's conclusions that unjust enrichment has not occurred and that there is no contract implied in law, are, therefore, fully reviewable. [Citation.] The trial court's findings of fact that support these legal conclusions are subject to the clearly erroneous standard of review[.] * * *

The conferral of any benefit which is commonly the subject of pecuniary compensation, including the rendition of personal services, is an adequate foundation for a legally implied promise to pay the benefit's reasonable value. [Citations.] Thus, the domestic and nursing services for which Ann seeks to recover may properly be the subject of restitution under an implied-in-law contract.

* * *

Ann testified both about the need for and the nature of her services to John. She testified that in the last three years of John's life, her relationship to John was that of a babysitter to her charge; that in his last three years he could not have lived alone without help because of his mental condition; that in his last year he was not able to dress or bathe himself and that she did these things for him; that she administered medication to him because he could not keep his pills straight. Ann testified that in May 1988, John's mental confusion was such that "he couldn't remember where the bathroom was at to try to get to the bathroom on time. By that time he was all messed up. So I had to get him cleaned up. That happened two, three times a day."

While the credibility and weight to be given Ann's testimony are matters for the fact-finder, we cannot overlook the fact that Ann's testimony on John's deteriorating condition and increasing need for attention was substantially corroborated by the testimony of John's treating physician who offered evidence that sometime after October of 1986, John's condition began to deteriorate and he would have been in need of someone to care for him.

* * *

The trier of fact is not required to accept expert opinions as conclusive. [Citations.] However, it is not free to arbitrarily disregard such testimony. [Citations.] Here, we can discern nothing in the record which discloses the reason for disregarding the medical diagnosis of Alzheimer's disease or the description of its symptoms and necessary treatment. Nor can we divine any such justification. Based upon the unrefuted medical evidence, we conclude that the trial court's finding that the services Ann rendered to John, at least during his deterioration from Alzheimer's, were neither required nor of an exceptional or peculiar nature is clearly erroneous. Rather, John, who required "skilled care," received it from Ann. Under the circumstances, we believe that Ann demonstrated that she conferred a valuable benefit upon John.

We also believe that the trial court clearly erred when it found that the services Ann provided were rendered gratuitously. If one confers a benefit gratuitously, the retention of that benefit without payment is not considered unjust. [Citations.] Whether the services were rendered gratuitously is a question of fact. [Citation.]

The burden rested upon the estate to show affirmatively that the services were performed gratuitously. [Citation.] The personal representative argues that the services rendered by Ann were presumptively gratuitous because she and John were like husband and wife. Whenever services are rendered by one family member to another, a presumption arises that the services are gratuitous and that compensation was not intended. [Citations.] However, the presumption does not apply to cases relying on implied-in-law contracts. [Citation.] Nor does it apply to non-family members unless the parties, although never married, lived together as husband and wife. [Citation.] Therefore, we are unpersuaded by the argument urging a presumption of gratuitousness.

* * *

* * * Justice is best served by permitting Ann to recover the reasonable value of those extraordinary services she rendered to John when he was unable to care for himself. Under the circumstances, the law should presume that those services were both given and received in the expectation of being paid for. [Citations.]

Although we hold that Ann is entitled to recover under a contract implied in law, we remand to the trial court for a determination of the duration and reasonable value of the variety of services rendered by Ann. The personal representative has raised certain defenses, including offsetting payments, which the trial court did not address, nor do we. On remand, the trial court may consider these matters and others it deems appropriate.

Reversed and remanded.

———

1.   Compare the facts of the principle case with those in *Henderson v. Fisher*, 236 Cal.App.2d 468, 46 Cal.Rptr. 173 (1965), reprinted *supra* in Chapter 4. In *Henderson*, there was an express contract between a young couple and an elderly friend with whom they had been close for many years. The friend's wife had just died at the time of the agreement and he could not live on his own. The couple contracted to move in with him and

to care for him, and the friend agreed to give the couple his house in exchange for their services. The case arose because the friend died very quickly, before he had executed his part of the agreement.

The couple sued for the house pursuant to the express contract because they had already fulfilled their part of the agreement—services until the friend's death. In the alternative, they sought quantum meruit for the value of the services rendered. The trial court gave the quantum meruit recovery, which was only a few hundred dollars because the friend did not receive care for many days before he died. On appeal, the appellate court granted specific performance because it found the contract enforceable. Notice that in that case the alternative remedy would have been restitutionary—the quantum meruit recovery for the value of the services—if the court had found the express contract to be unenforceable.

2. Compare the principal case with *In re Estate of Anderson*, 988 A.2d 977 (Me. 2010), in which an adult son brought a claim for unjust enrichment against the estate of his mother seeking restitution for benefits conferred by doing various household chores while living at home taking care of his mother. The court acknowledged that the mother did benefit from and was aware of the son's care during her final years but denied recovery, finding that such efforts did not require compensation and did not result in any injustice. *See also* Tkachik v. Mandeville, 487 Mich. 38, 790 N.W.2d 260 (2010) (husband who had abandoned cancer-stricken wife in the 18 months prior to her death was unjustly enriched by her payments on the house, taxes and other expenses when he subsequently received funds from her estate).

3. *Gifts.* A critical finding in the principle case is that the benefit conferred (the nursing services) were not a gift. Retention of a gift is not an unjust enrichment. The court in the principal case also noted that there is a presumption in the context of marriage that benefits given by one spouse to the other are gifts.

4. As indicated in the principal case, implied-in-fact contracts must be distinguished from contractual arrangements implied by law. The former is simply another species of express contract which has been inferred from the intentions and conduct of the parties in recognizing the existence of contractual rights and duties. In contrast, a quasi-contract is implied by law without regard to the intentions of the parties, and perhaps even against an expression of dissent. Therefore, it is a fiction created by the court to establish an enforceable obligation. The purpose of implying a contractual duty to pay restitution is to prevent someone from obtaining a benefit of money, services, or property without paying just compensation. In *In re Chateaugay Corp.*, 10 F.3d 944, 957 958 (2d Cir.1993), the court explained:

> A quasi-contract claim for unjust enrichment is based on "an obligation which the law creates, in the absence of any agreement, when and because the acts of the parties or others have placed in the possession of one person money, or its equivalent, under such circum-

stances that in equity and good conscience he ought not to retain it, and which ex aequo et bono belongs to another." 10 F.3d at 957.

5. There are several types of quasi-contract actions which provide restitution at law. An action in quantum meruit, which means in Latin "as much as he deserves," is a frequently employed remedy to compensate a plaintiff for the reasonable value of services rendered to a defendant. A second type of quasi-contract appears where the defendant has used or occupied realty belonging to another under circumstances constituting unjust enrichment.

Another group of quasi-contracts are derived from the common court actions for money had and received or for money paid. The use of the money counts to disgorge unjust enrichment dates back to the landmark decision of Moses v. Macferlan, 2 Burr. 1005 (K.B.1760), where Lord Mansfield used indebitatus assumpsit as a restitutionary tool.

6. A troublesome issue in quantum meruit has involved whether an expectation of payment by both parties is an essential element of the action. In *In re De Laurentiis Entertainment Group Inc.*, 963 F.2d 1269 (9th Cir.1992), a company arranged with an advertising agency to purchase television advertising from NBC on its behalf. When the company failed to pay, NBC sought to recover from the company in quantum meruit the reasonable value of the advertising it had provided. The court awarded recovery based on a quasi-contract, reasoning that the company had requested the advertising and benefitted from it and NBC had not intended to provide its services gratuitously. The court noted that, unlike an express contract, quasi-contracts are not based on intentions of parties to undertake performance or promises, but are created by law to prevent injustice. *See also* Bolen v. Paragon Plastics, Inc., 747 F.Supp. 103 (D.Mass.1990) (expectation of payment by holder of benefit determined by reference to objective standard, not subjective belief of party); In re Estate of Krueger, 235 Neb. 518, 455 N.W.2d 809, 814 (1990) (quantum meruit for labor and materials is grounded upon an implied promise to pay the reasonable value of the benefits received).

7. Although jurisdictions vary considerably in their precise formulation of the requirements for recovery under quantum meruit, some common elements include:

(1) the claimant furnished valuable services or materials;

(2) for the person sought to be charged;

(3) the services and materials were accepted, used and enjoyed by the person sought to be charged;

(4) the party who provided the services or materials did so with the reasonable expectation of receiving compensation;

(5) the party who accepted the services had reasonable notice that compensation for the benefits would be expected;

(6) and retention of the benefit without payment of reasonable compensation would constitute unjust enrichment.

See Vortt Exploration v. Chevron U.S.A., 787 S.W.2d 942 (Tex.1990); Midcoast Aviation, Inc. v. General Elec. Credit Corp., 907 F.2d 732 (7th Cir.1990).

8. For a useful overview of the Restatement (Third) of Restitution and Unjust Enrichment (2011) and analysis of the use of restitution in modern law, *see* Symposium, Restitution Rollout: The Restatement (Third) of Restitution & Unjust Enrichment, 68 Wash. & Lee L. Rev. No. 3 (2011).

Cross v. Berg Lumber Co.

7 P.3d 922 (Wyo. 2000).

■ LEHMAN, CHIEF JUSTICE.

This case concerns a disputed piece of heavy machinery, a road grader. Berg Lumber Company sued Richard Cross for the tortious conversion of this grader and for replevin. After a bench trial, the district court awarded Berg damages in the amount of $83,400 and ordered that the grader be returned to Berg. * * * Finding no error, we affirm.

* * *

In 1989, Berg Lumber Company purchased a Caterpillar 120 motor grader for $19,700. Berg used the grader to push dirt and snow and for road construction, grading, and maintenance. In 1991, Berg moved the grader to its Casper sawmill. At that time, Berg also contracted with Joe Crail to deliver logs to the Casper sawmill.

In October or November, 1991, without Berg's knowledge or permission, Crail took the grader from Casper to Richard Cross' ranch in Converse County, where Crail used the grader to grade access roads to facilitate logging. Crail damaged Cross' property by knocking down gates, burying irrigation ditches, and marring roads. * * *

Berg later learned that the grader was on the Cross ranch. He went there and saw it at Cross' shop, with the blade down and the wheels off. He spoke with Cross, who told him that he wanted to use the grader to repair the damage done by Crail. * * * Berg acquiesced and told Cross he would pick up the grader when the damage was repaired.

[There were several more contacts between Berg and Cross to recover the grader and further excuses made.] * * * In the summer of 1996, Berg's agent called Cross to reclaim the grader. Cross answered this demand by claiming that the grader was gone—that someone had come with a truck and hauled it away. On September 4, 1996, Berg's agent reported this alleged theft to the Converse County Sheriff's Office. Another Berg employee hired an airplane to fly him over the Cross ranch. From this aerial vantage, he located the grader concealed in an area that was not visible from the public road. By and through counsel, Berg formally demanded return of the grader on October 9, 1996. This lawsuit was filed on January 5, 1998.

At trial, both George Berg and Richard Cross testified. Among the other witnesses were several who established various elements of damage, including a heavy equipment expert from Wyoming Machinery Company who testified that the grader had a monthly rental value of $2,500. After hearing all the evidence, the district court entered judgment for the plaintiff in the sum of $83,400 and issued a Writ of Replevin directing Cross to return the motor grader to Berg Lumber. This appeal timely followed.

Cross argues that Berg admitted in the complaint that he authorized Crail to utilize the grader. Crail was authorized to use the grader, but not to take it. Berg never authorized Crail to take the grader to Cross' ranch.

* * *

Appellant contends the district court's damage calculation was erroneous because the court relied upon an improper legal standard. While damages are normally subject to clear error review, the underlying legal standards are pure issues of law subject to *de novo* review.

The district court awarded $83,400 in incidental damages as follows:

1. Return of the grader.
2. $10,000.00 to repair the engine.
3. $400.00 to replace the cutting edge and batteries.
4. $900.00 for tire replacement (50% depreciation).
5. $4,600.00 for costs of attempted recovery of the grader.
6. $67,500.00 for loss of use ($2,500.00 x 27 months since 10/96).

Each of these damage components was supported by competent nonspeculative evidence.

The proper remedy in a replevin action is return of the detained property plus incidental damages:

> Although the action of replevin is founded upon a tortious detention, it is not one to determine claims sounding in tort. It is analogous to an action of trespass, but is in part a proceeding in rem, to regain possession of the goods and chattels, and in part a proceeding in personam, to recover damages for the caption and detention, and is based not upon any act of the plaintiff, but upon the illegal acts of the defendant. It is a possessory action the gist of which is the right of possession in the plaintiff. The primary relief sought therein is the return of the property in specie; damages are merely incidental.

66 Am.Jur.2d *Replevin* § 3 (1973). * * *

The court awarded $67,500 for loss of use, based on $2,500 per month for 27 months between the date of conversion (October 1996) and the date of trial (January 1999). In effect, this is an award of restitution requiring the tortfeasor to disgorge the amount by which he was unjustly enriched by his wrongdoing. Appellant complains that this determination is legally erroneous, as this amount exceeds the quantum of Berg's injury.

* * * "For some types of tort actions and for certain kinds of breaches of contract, the injured party has an option of seeking restitutionary recovery. In these cases, damages are measured by the benefits received by the defendant rather than the losses sustained by the plaintiff." 22 Am. Jur.2d *Damages* § 34 (1988) (footnotes omitted). *See also* Restatement, *Restitution,* §§ 150–154. The plaintiff may "waive the tort and sue in assumpsit," meaning that the plaintiff can have a restitutionary recovery for the gains the defendant made by converting the chattel. For example, if the chattel was worth $10 when it was converted by the defendant, and he later sells it for $20, the plaintiff would choose this option. Dobbs, *The Law of Torts* § 67 (2000).

Historically, there has been much confusion about assumpsit and restitutionary remedies. At common law, assumpsit was a form of action whereby a legal obligation was implied at law. *See* Arthur L. Corbin, *Waiver of Tort and Suit in Assumpsit,* 19 Yale L.J. 221 (1910). One British jurist noted that "the whole history of this particular form of action has been what I may call a history of well-meaning sloppiness of thought." *Holt v. Markham,* 1 K.B. 504, 513 (1923).

"Restitution based upon unjust enrichment cuts across many branches of the law, including contract, tort, and fiduciary relationship, but it also occupies much territory that is its sole preserve." G. Palmer, *Law of Restitution* § 1.1 at 2 (1978). * * *. "One whose money or property is taken by fraud or embezzlement, or by conversion, is entitled to restitution measured by the defendant's gain if the victim prefers that remedy to the damages remedy." Dobbs, *Law of Remedies* § 4.1(1) p. 553 (1993).

* * * It is obvious that the owner of property, which has been wrongfully converted, should possess a right to institute such a suit for the injury as will afford him an ample indemnification. If the wrong doer hath sold, or used and then sold the property, the owner may waive the tort, and in assumpsit recover the net proceeds received both for the use and by the sale. * * * In an action *ex contractu,* nothing can be obtained from him except what has in fact been received for the use and by sale of the property: while in one *ex delicto,* he may be subjected vindictively to pay much more than the real value of the article converted. * * *

* * * The touchstone of the rule is the moral obligation arising out of unjust enrichment to the tortfeasor. The principle is of ancient origin. It has lost its early common law fictions and is firmly entrenched as a cause of action with only its "historical echoes" remaining. * * *

Thus, restitution is an appropriate remedy for some tortious conduct. [Citation.] Despite the historic limitation on the assertion of equity jurisdiction, the availability of the legal restitution remedy is not dependent upon inadequacy of alternative remedies. G. Palmer, *Law of Restitution* § 1.6 at 33–34 (1978).[2]

---

2. The distinction between legal and equitable restitution is a fine one which would not affect the outcome of this case. The primary difference is that with legal restitution, the

The phrase "unjust enrichment" is used in law to characterize the result or effect of a failure to make restitution of, or for, property or benefits received under such circumstances as to give rise to a legal or equitable obligation to account therefor. It is a general principle, underlying various legal doctrines and remedies, that one person should not be permitted unjustly to enrich himself at the expense of another, but should be required to make restitution of or for property or benefits received, retained, or appropriated, where it is just and equitable that such restitution be made, and where such action involves no violation or frustration of law or opposition to public policy, either directly or indirectly. [Citations.] Where wrongfully detained property has a value for use, the measure of damages is the value of such use during the detention period. 66 Am.Jur.2d *Replevin* § 120 (1973). * * *

The district court in this case found that Cross' conduct was "certainly egregious," but did not rise to "the level of misconduct necessary to support attorney's fees or punitive damages." Although there are some overlapping policies underlying the doctrines supporting punitive damages and the unjust enrichment remedy, they are not the same. One purpose of tort damages is to compensate the plaintiff for his loss, but the measurement of such loss is not always an exact science. Since restitution may exceed mere compensation to the plaintiff without exceeding the defendant's unjust gain, it is not punitive. Dobbs, *Law of Remedies* § 4.1(4). In the context of conversion, courts have recognized the legitimacy of restitutionary damages: However plausible, the appellant cannot be heard to say that his wrongful invasion of the respondent's property right to exclusive use is not a loss compensable in law. To hold otherwise would be subversive of all property rights since his use was admittedly wrongful and without claim of right. The theory of unjust enrichment is applicable in such a case. [Citations.] Thus, the unjust enrichment remedy is not punitive but is one method of compensating the plaintiff's loss. This remedy is particularly appropriate where the plaintiff's loss is more difficult to measure than the defendant's unjustly saved avoidance costs. *See* S. Levmore, *Unifying Remedies: Property Rules, Liability Rules, and Startling Rules,* 106 Yale L.J. 2149, 2157 (1997). * * * Beneath the cloak of restitution lies the dagger that compels the conscious wrongdoer to "disgorge" his gains. Disgorgement is designed to deprive the wrongdoer of *all gains flowing from the wrong rather than to compensate the victim of the fraud.* In modern legal usage the term has frequently been extended to include a dimension of deterrence. Disgorgement is said to occur when a "defendant is made to 'cough up' what he got, neither more nor less." * * * Where a wrongdoer is shown to have been a conscious, deliberate misappropriator of another's commercial values, gross profits are recoverable through a restitutionary remedy. [Citation.] Even Judge Posner, guru of the law and economics movement, has recognized that restitution has a rightful place in intentional tort cases: "to make the tort worthless to the tortfeasor and

---

parties have a right to a trial by jury. As this case was tried before a judge and neither party requested a jury trial, this issue is inapplicable.

thereby channel resource allocation through the market." R. Posner, *Economic Analysis of the Law* 194 (3rd ed.1986).[3]

In the case at bar, it would be difficult to calculate Berg's loss in terms of opportunity costs. Also, by converting and concealing the grader and then lying about its whereabouts, Cross engaged in willfully deceptive misconduct that should be discouraged. For these reasons, application of the unjust enrichment remedy is appropriate. The question remains, how does one measure the amount to be disgorged? There are five factors that assist in measuring restitution:

1.   the increased assets in the hands of the defendant from the receipt of property;

2.   the market value of services or intangibles provided to the defendant, without regard to whether the defendant's assets were actually increased; that is, the amount which it would cost to obtain similar services, whether those services prove to be useful or not;

3.   the use value of any benefits received, as measured by (i) market indicators such as rental value or interest or (ii) actual gains to the defendant from using the benefits, such as the gains identified in item (5) below;

4.   the gains realized by the defendant upon sale or transfer of an asset received from the plaintiff;

5.   collateral or secondary profits earned by the defendant by use of an asset received from the plaintiff, or, what is much the same thing, the savings effected by the use of the asset.

Dobbs, *Law of Remedies* § 4.5(1) (footnotes omitted).

The damages awarded in this case are supported by the second factor, the market or rental value of the grader (even if the grader did not prove to be useful); the third factor, the use value of the grader; and the fifth factor, the savings effected by using the grader.

This measure of damages can be termed negative unjust enrichment, *i.e.,* the defendant was unjustly enriched by not having to rent a road grader. A benefit is conferred upon the defendant where, by tortiously using the plaintiff's property, he saves expense or loss that might otherwise be incurred—benefit is any form of advantage. [Citation.] Thus, to measure negative unjust enrichment or recoverable profit, courts may consider saving of expense. [Citations.] "Unjust enrichment can occur when a defendant uses something belonging to the Plaintiff in such a way as to effectuate some kind of savings which results in or amounts to a business profit." [Citations.]

---

3.   Conversion (pure coercive transfer) is not an acceptable substitute for purchase on the free market. Restitutionary damages can thus be justified by applying Learned Hand's renowned negligence formula, where the tortfeasor is liable if the cost of reasonable precautions (B) is less than the product of the probability of injury (P) and the magnitude of potential loss (L). (B < PL). *See United States v. Carroll Towing Co.,* 159 F.2d 169, 173 (2d Cir.1947). Judge Hand's tort calculus can also be applied to intentional torts, where B has a negative value. *See* Posner at 193–95.

Historically, tort and contract have been the primary fonts of civil liability at common law; yet restitution based on unjust enrichment is also a vital legal theory. G. Palmer § 1.1 at 1–2. Not every circumstance demands application of the disgorgement principal; but in certain cases, where justice so requires, the law empowers judges and juries with this important tool to remedy wrongdoing. This is such a case.

* * * Affirmed.

---

1. The Restatement (Third) of Restitution and Unjust Enrichment (2011) begins with the following principle:

§ 1. Restitution And Unjust Enrichment

A person who is unjustly enriched at the expense of another is subject to liability in restitution.

Consider how this principle is different from punitive damages. As noted in the principal case, punitive damages may exceed the amount of the defendant's gain (restitution), which in turn may exceed the amount of the plaintiff's loss (compensatory damages). See Doug Rendleman, Measurement of Restitution: Coordinating Restitution with Compensatory Damages and Punitive Damages, 68 Wash. & Lee L. Rev. 973 (2011).

2. The plaintiff in the principal case could have brought a claim for conversion instead. That tort supports compensatory damages measured by the value of the item converted. Under the facts in the principal case, that measure would be less than the recovery in restitution for the fair rental value over the period in which the grader was withheld. In a conversion case, punitive damages are available only if the substantive requirements for them are met. See Chapter 15.

As in the principal case, restitution may provides an alternative basis for a claim that might otherwise be a tort or contract case. Although opinions often refer to restitution as merely an alternative remedy, it is best understood as an independent substantive basis of recovery that is allowed as necessary to avoid unjust enrichment.

3. Consider the following section of the Restatement (Third) of Restitution and Unjust Enrichment (2011) and compare it with the principles used in the principal case.

§ 40. Trespass, Conversion, And Comparable Wrongs

A person who obtains a benefit by an act of trespass or conversion, by comparable interference with other protected interests in tangible property, or in consequence of such an act by another, is liable in restitution to the victim of the wrong.

4. Courts have sometimes said that restitution is premised on natural justice. Lord Mansfield famously stated in *Moses v. Macferlan*, 2 Burr. 1005, 97 Eng. Rep. 676, 681 (K.B. 1760) that "the gist of this kind of action

is, that the defendant, upon the circumstances of the case, is obliged by the ties of natural justice and equity to refund the money."

Modern legal analysis usually finds an appeal to natural justice to be insufficiently precise to define what forms of enrichment are "unjust" in the sense of providing a legal basis for disgorgement. The Restatement notes: "Unless a definition of restitution can provide a more informative generalization about the nature of the transactions leading to liability, it is difficult to avoid the objection that sees in 'unjust enrichment,' at best, a name for a legal conclusion that remains to be explained; at worst, an open-ended and potentially unprincipled charter of liability." Restatement (Third) of Restitution & Unjust Enrichment § 1, comment b (2011).

5. In *Cablevision of Breckenridge v. Tannhauser*, 649 P.2d 1093 (Colo.1982), the court considered whether a cable company was entitled to restitution under quasi-contract for the value of its service from unauthorized users. The court explained the basic purpose and requirements of that doctrine:

> To recover under a theory of quasi-contract or unjust enrichment, a plaintiff must show (1) that a benefit was conferred on the defendant by the plaintiff, (2) that the benefit was appreciated by the defendant, and (3) that the benefit was accepted by the defendant under such circumstances that it would be inequitable for it to be retained without payment of its value. Application of the doctrine does not depend upon the existence of a contract, express or implied in fact, but on the need to avoid unjust enrichment of the defendant notwithstanding the absence of an actual agreement to pay for the benefit conferred. The scope of this remedy is broad, cutting across both contract and tort law, with its application guided by the underlying principle of avoiding the unjust enrichment of one party at the expense of another. * * *

> [T]he broad definition of benefit contained in the *Restatement of Restitution* 1 comment b (1937) [is instructive]:

> A person confers a benefit upon another if he gives to the other possession of or some other interest in money, land, chattels, or choses in action, performs services beneficial to or at the request of the other, satisfies a debt or a duty of the other, or in any way adds to the other's security or advantage. He confers a benefit not only where he adds to the property of another, but also where he saves the other from expense or loss. The word "benefit," therefore, denotes any form of advantage. 649 P.2d at 1096–97.

The court held that restitution was appropriate to prevent unjust enrichment of a condominium association in receiving unauthorized use of cable service without payment for its value.

Monarch Accounting Supplies, Inc. v. Prezioso

170 Conn. 659, 368 A.2d 6 (1976).

■ LOISELLE, ASSOCIATE JUSTICE.

[The plaintiff, Monarch Accounting Supplies, Inc. ("Monarch"), leased an office building from the defendant, Prezioso. Prezioso subsequently executed another lease with an outdoor advertising company for purposes of installing a large sign on the roof of the building. Monarch instituted suit against Prezioso for the unauthorized use of the premises, and the trial court awarded $245 for a fee Monarch paid to a structural engineer and $1360 for one-half of the rent already paid and to be paid by the advertising company to Prezioso. The defendant appealed.]

* * *

"A lease transfers an estate in real property to a tenant for a stated period, with a reversion in the owner after the expiration of the lease. Its distinguishing characteristic is the surrender of possession by the landlord to the tenant so that he may occupy the land or tenement leased to the exclusion of the landlord himself." [Citation.] The tenant acquires an interest in the real estate giving him the right to maintain ejectment or trespass against the landlord. [Citation.] And where the entire premises are leased, in the absence of any agreement, either expressed or implied or by covenant to the contrary, the tenant has the right of exclusive possession and control of the entire premises and the landlord or his agents or contractees have no right to enter upon the leased premises. [Citations.]

The instrument of lease demising the property to the plaintiff describes the premises as: "A certain parcel of land with a one story masonry building thereon ... with a second story addition." The instrument does not refer to the "roof." One provision gives the defendant "the right to enter into and upon said premises, or any part thereof, at all reasonable hours for the purpose of examining the same, or making such repairs or alterations therein as may be necessary for the safety and preservation thereof." A subsequent paragraph contains the language that "said premises shall be at all times open to the inspection of said Landlord and Landlord's agents ... for necessary repairs." A following paragraph, however, contains the language that "said Tenant shall also pay for all other utilities and repairs." The only evidence adduced at the trial on the issue of control was that the landlord made a minor repair of the roof in November, 1971, during the tenancy of the original lease.

In construing the instrument the court correctly determined both the leasehold's size and the parties' interests therein. [Citation.] The description of the demised premises, the provisions for repair and the limited nature of the defendant's right to enter only admit of a reversionary interest in the defendant. The fact of the minor repair to the roof does not contradict the implications growing out of the nature of the estate created by the lease. [Citations.] The court was not in error in concluding that, under the terms of the lease, the defendant did not reserve control of the roof of the premises leased and therefore did not have the right to lease the roof of the premises.

The court found that the plaintiff was entitled to receive, on an equitable basis by way of reimbursement, one-half of the total rent received by the defendant from Murphy, Inc. The court also awarded one-half of the rent to be expected from Murphy, Inc., for the remainder of the plaintiff's term. The plaintiff claims the award can be sustained under the doctrine of unjust enrichment. The inquiry then, is whether the plaintiff is entitled to damages for the unjust enrichment of the defendant. The inquiry goes not only to the type of recovery but also to whether recovery of any type was allowable.

The doctrine of unjust enrichment "is based upon the principle that one should not be permitted unjustly to enrich himself at the expense of another but should be required to make restitution of or for property received, retained or appropriated. . . . It is not necessary, in order to create an obligation to make restitution or to compensate, that the party unjustly enriched should have been guilty of any tortious or fraudulent act. The question is: Did he, to the detriment of someone else, obtain something of value to which he was not entitled?" [Citations.] "With no other test than what, under a given set of circumstances, is just or unjust, equitable or inequitable, conscionable or unconscionable, it becomes necessary in any case where the benefit of the doctrine is claimed to examine the circumstances and the conduct of the parties and apply this standard." [Citation.]

The defendant, under its agreement with Murphy, Inc., receives rental payments. That agreement overlooks the plaintiff's possessory interest in the roof, and, in that regard, it is to the detriment of the plaintiff. Although the plaintiff did not show any material physical damage to the premises it has a right either to sublet or assign the roof with the defendant's permission. * * * The facts of the case, therefore, show the defendant's receipt of a benefit, to which he was not entitled, to the detriment of the plaintiff. Furthermore, that showing entitles the plaintiff to an award of money damages. [Citations.]

The measure of recovery in this case focuses on the benefit to the defendant rather than on the loss to the plaintiff. The damages should be the benefit received. [Citation.] The benefit was the rent that was received by the defendant less his expenses, if any, in dealing with Murphy, Inc. The court, therefore, was in error in awarding only one-half of the accrued rent.

The court also erred by awarding a portion of the rent from the date of judgment until the end of the plaintiff's term. That rent has been neither received nor retained by the defendant even though he has the right, under the agreement with Murphy, Inc., to receive it. A prospective award is not properly includable within the concept of damages in this case since the focus of damages in unjust enrichment is not on the damage proximately caused by an injury, but on the benefit unjustly received and retained by the defendant. [Citations.] Whether the defendant will retain the rent from the sign for the period from February, 1975 to May, 1977, the unexpired term of the plaintiff's lease at the time of judgment, cannot be adjudged.

Further, the other item of damages awarded, one-half of the expense of the structural engineer, appears to have been part of an expenditure that was necessary for the proper support of the sign on the roof and as the defendant is not entitled to retain the benefit of the lease to Murphy, Inc., he would not be liable for such expenditures.

There is error in part, the judgment is affirmed except as to the amount of damages awarded and a new trial is ordered limited to that issue.

————————

1. Consider the following section of the Restatement (Third) of Restitution and Unjust Enrichment (2011) as it applies to the principal case.

§ 47.   Payment To Defendant In Respect Of Claimant's Property

If a third person makes a payment to the defendant in respect of an asset belonging to the claimant, the claimant is entitled to restitution from the defendant as necessary to prevent unjust enrichment.

2. In restitution, unlike compensatory damages, the focus is on the defendant's gains rather than on the plaintiff's losses. Note that in the principal case the plaintiff had not directly lost any tangible economic benefits nor incurred out-of-pocket expenses. Restitution was nonetheless appropriate to disgorge the extra rental payments received by the landlord.

In many situations the claimant has expended funds or rendered services equivalent to the value received by the defendant; if the enrichment was unjust, its measure is clear. Problems arise in cases where the plaintiff has incurred certain expenses yet the defendant received a lesser amount of benefit. Unless the defendant has acted improperly, such as by fraudulently inducing the plaintiff to build improvements on the defendant's land, restitution will be limited to the measure of the defendant's gains.

3. It is not necessary to prove tortious, illegal, or fraudulent conduct by the defendant to establish that the enrichment is unjust. In the principal case the landlord's conduct in re-leasing a portion of the premises without the tenant's consent may have been ill-advised, but it was not tortious. In some circumstances even an innocent party who holds a benefit may be ordered to restore the property to another in order to prevent unjust enrichment. *See Simonds v. Simonds,* reprinted *infra* in section D of this chapter.

4. For classical commentary on unjust enrichment, *see* Dawson, Restitution Without Enrichment, 61 B.U.L.Rev. 563 (1981); Sullivan, The Concept of Benefit in the Law of Quasi Contract, 64 Geo.L.J. 1 (1975); Dawson, Restitution or Damages?, 20 Ohio St.L.J. 175 (1959); Macaulay, Restitution in Context, 107 U.Pa.L.Rev. 1133 (1959); Patterson, The Scope of Restitution and Unjust Enrichment, 1 Mo.L.Rev. 223 (1936); Ames, The History of Assumpsit, 2 Harv.L.Rev. 53 (1888).

B.   Benefits Acquired by Agreement or Mistake

Section Coverage:

Restitution is premised upon the defendant's unjust enrichment without regard to how the benefit was received. Although the manner in which the defendant acquired the benefit is relevant to the justice of its retention, recovery in restitution does not require that the receipt be from wrongful conduct.

The circumstances under which the benefit was acquired originally may even have been by agreement. The parties may have attempted a contractual relationship which ultimately failed. If the plaintiff confers benefits upon the defendant pursuant to a contract that is not in force by the time of trial, the plaintiff can recover the specific benefit or its value in restitution. The failure of the contract can arise because it was unenforceable at its inception, or because it became unenforceable for a reason such as impossibility, or because the defendant materially breached and the plaintiff elected to treat the contract as ended.

Another circumstance in which a defendant may acquire a benefit without wrongful conduct is when the plaintiff confers it by mistake. The substantive question in restitution once again is whether retention of such enrichment would be unjust. The situations in which a mistake may serve as the basis for restitutionary relief are widely varied. Some examples are overpayment of a debt or accidental payment of someone else's debt, improvement of property under the mistaken belief of ownership, and mistakes about the formation or performance of a contract. The restitutionary device used to rectify the mistake varies; quasi-contract, subrogation, or specific restitution through constructive trust and equitable liens are available under appropriate circumstances.

Model Case:

Pat Denney wanted to acquire some gentle horses suitable for children's rides at carnivals. Mattson had several horses for sale of the type Denney wanted. The two parties negotiated an oral agreement for the sale, and Mattson gave Denney the horses in exchange for a check.

Denney then heard from a friend who was a first year law student that this contract violated the Statute of Frauds. Denney stopped payment on the check and took the horses out of town to a carnival to make money with them. After the carnival Denney concluded that this type of enterprise was not desirable and returned the horses to Mattson. In the meantime Mattson had received a better offer for the horses.

If the contract did violate the Statute of Frauds, Mattson could have rescinded it and received the horses in restitution. If the contract was valid, Mattson could have treated Denney's conduct as a breach of contract. Among the available remedies would be the restitution of the horses. Mattson might receive the profits Denney earned at the carnival under the rule that all profits are disgorged from conscious wrongdoers. The fact that Mattson lost nothing and may now be in a better position is not relevant.

Pyeatte v. Pyeatte

135 Ariz. 346, 661 P.2d 196 (1982).

■ Corcoran, Judge.

[A wife (plaintiff-appellee) and husband (defendant-appellant) entered into an oral agreement whereby each spouse agreed to provide in turn the sole support for the marriage while the other spouse was obtaining further education. The wife accordingly supported the husband for three years until his graduation from law school. Approximately one year following graduation, the parties obtained a dissolution of their marriage. Before the dissolution the wife had not yet received any support toward her contemplated continued education. The trial court awarded the wife $23,000 in damages for the husband's breach of express contract. On appeal, the court held that the terms of the spousal agreement were not sufficiently definite to constitute a binding, enforceable contract.] * * *

Appellee [contends] that the trial court's award should be affirmed as an equitable award of restitution on the basis of unjust enrichment. She argues that appellant's education, which she subsidized and which he obtained through the exhaustion of community assets constitutes a benefit for which he must, in equity, make restitution. This narrow equitable issue is one of first impression in this court. * * *

Restitution is available to a party to an agreement where he performs services for the other believing that there is a binding contract.

When Restitution for Services is Granted.

A person who has rendered services to another or services which have inured to the benefit of another . . . is entitled to restitution therefor if the services were rendered

* * *

(b) To obtain the performance of an agreement with the other therefor, not operative as a contract, or voidable as a contract and avoided by the other party after the services were rendered, the one performing the services erroneously believing because of a mistake of fact that the agreement was binding upon the other. . . .

Restatement of Restitution 40(b) at 155 (1937).

In order to be granted restitution, appellee must demonstrate that appellant received a benefit, that by receipt of that benefit he was unjustly enriched at her expense, and that the circumstances were such that in good conscience appellant should make compensation. John A. Artukovich & Sons v. Reliance Truck Co., 126 Ariz. 246, 614 P.2d 327 (1980); *Restatement of Restitution* 1 at 13 (1937). In *Artukovich,* the Supreme Court discussed unjust enrichment.

Contracts implied-in-law or quasi-contracts, also called constructive contracts, are inferred by the law as a matter of reason and justice from the acts and conduct of the parties and circumstances surrounding the transactions . . . and are imposed for the purpose of bringing about justice without reference to the intentions of the parties. . . .

Restatement of Restitution 1 provides, "A person who has been unjustly enriched at the expense of another is required to make restitution to the other." Comment (a) to that section notes that a person is enriched if he received a benefit and is unjustly enriched if retention of that benefit would be unjust. Comment (b) defines a benefit as being any form of advantage. . . .

Unjust enrichment does not depend upon the existence of a valid contract, . . . nor is it necessary that plaintiff suffer a loss corresponding to the defendant's gain for there to be valid claim for an unjust enrichment . . .

126 Ariz. at 248, 614 P.2d at 329.

A benefit may be any type of advantage, including that which saves the recipient from any loss or expense. Appellee's support of appellant during his period of schooling clearly constituted a benefit to appellant. Absent appellee's support, appellant may not have attended law school, may have been forced to prolong his education because of intermittent periods of gainful employment, or may have gone deeply into debt. Relieved of the necessity of supporting himself, he was able to devote full time and attention to his education.

The mere fact that one party confers a benefit on another, however, is not of itself sufficient to require the other to make restitution. Retention of the benefit must be unjust.

Historically, restitution for the value of services rendered has been available upon either an "implied-in-fact" contract or upon quasi-contractual grounds. [Citations.] An implied-in-fact contract is a true contract, differing from an express contract only insofar as it is proved by circumstantial evidence rather than by express written or oral terms. [Citations.] In contrast, a quasi-contract is not a contract at all, but a duty imposed in equity upon a party to repay another to prevent his own unjust enrichment. The intention of the parties to bind themselves contractually in such a case is irrelevant. [Citation.] To support her claim for restitution on the basis of an implied-in-fact contract, appellee must demonstrate the elements of a binding contract. For the reasons we have previously discussed, we cannot find the necessary mutual assent or certainty as to the critical terms of the agreement sufficient to establish such a contract. [Citation.]

Restitution is nevertheless available in quasi-contract absent any showing of mutual assent. While a quasi-contractual obligation may be imposed without regard to the intent of the parties, such an obligation will be imposed only if the circumstances are such that it would be unjust to allow retention of the benefit without compensating the one who conferred it. One circumstance under which a duty to compensate will be imposed is when there was an expectation of payment or compensation for services at the time they were rendered.

[A]n obligation to pay, ordinarily, will not be implied in fact or by law if it is clear that there was indeed no expectation of payment, that a gratuity was intended to be conferred, that the benefit was conferred officiously, or that the question of payment was left to the unfettered discretion of the recipient. [Citation.]

Although we found that the spousal agreement failed to meet the requirements of an enforceable contract, the agreement still has importance in considering appellee's claim for unjust enrichment because it both evidences appellee's expectation of compensation and the circumstances which make it unjust to allow appellant to retain the benefits of her extraordinary efforts.

We next address the question of whether restitution on the basis of unjust enrichment is appropriate in the context of the marital relationship. No authority is cited to the court in support of the proposition that restitution as a matter of law is inappropriate in a dissolution proceeding. In *Wisner* [Wisner v. Wisner, 129 Ariz. 333, 631 P.2d 115 (1981)], we observed that "[i]n our opinion, unjust enrichment, as a legal concept, is not properly applied in the setting of a marital relationship." Our observation was directed to the wife's claim in that case for restitution for the value of her *homemaking services* during the couple's 15 year marriage and for the couple's reduced income during the husband's lengthy training period. Where both spouses perform the usual and incidental activities of the marital relationship, upon dissolution there can be no restitution for performance of these activities. Where, however, the facts demonstrate an agreement between the spouses and an extraordinary or unilateral effort by one spouse which inures solely to the benefit of the other by the time of dissolution, the remedy of restitution is appropriate.

* * *

A number of jurisdictions have addressed the issue of restitution in the context of the marital relationship. The cases which have dealt with the issue involve two factual patterns: (1) The first group consists of those cases in which the couples had accumulated substantial marital assets over a period of time from which assets the wife received large awards of property, maintenance and child support. The courts have refused to apply the theory of restitution on the basis of unjust enrichment in each of these cases. (2) The second group consists of those cases in which the parties are divorced soon after the student spouse receives his degree or license and there is little or no marital property from which to order any award to the working spouse.

In the first group, the courts have consistently refused to find a property interest in the husband's education, degree, license or earning capacity or to order restitution in favor of the wife. Because restitution is a matter of equity, the circumstances of these cases preclude at the outset any basis for a finding of inequitable circumstances sufficient to support restitution inasmuch as the wife in each case had received substantial awards of the marital assets and was seeking, in addition to those assets, a property interest in the husband's education, degree, license or earning capacity. Because the property award itself is largely the product of the education, degree, license or earning capacity in which the wife sought a monetary interest, the courts hold that the wife realized her "investment" in the husband's education by having received the benefits of his increased earning capacity during marriage and by receipt of an award of property upon its dissolution. * * *

The second group presents the more difficult problem of the "working spouse" claiming entitlement to an equitable recovery where there is little or no marital property to divide and therefore the conventional remedies of property division or spousal maintenance are unavailable. The emerging consensus among those jurisdictions faced with the issue in this factual context is that restitution to the working spouse is appropriate to prevent the unjust enrichment of the student spouse. [Citations.]

Although in *Wisner* we dealt with the first group described above; *i.e.,* a marital community with substantial accumulated assets, we anticipated the second type of case in which (1) the community estate is consumed by the education of the husband which was obtained in substantial measure by the efforts and sacrifices of his wife; (2) the working wife is not entitled to spousal maintenance, having demonstrated an ability to support not only herself but her husband as well; and (3) the divorce follows closely upon the husband's completion of his education before the community realizes any benefit from that education and before the working spouse is able to further her own education and thus increase her own earning capacity. * * *

The Minnesota Supreme Court in *DeLa Rosa* [DeLa Rosa v. DeLa Rosa, 309 N.W.2d 755 (Minn.1981)] similarly affirmed an award of restitution to the wife for the financial support she provided her husband while he attended medical school, in a dissolution which occurred shortly after the husband's graduation.

The case at bar presents the common situation where one spouse has foregone the immediate enjoyment of earned income to enable the other to pursue an advanced education on a full-time basis. Typically, this sacrifice is made with the expectation that the parties will enjoy a higher standard of living in the future. Because the income of the working spouse is used for living expenses, there is usually little accumulated marital property to be divided when the dissolution occurs prior to the attainment of the financial rewards concomitant with the advanced degree or professional license. Furthermore, the working spouse is not entitled to maintenance . . . as there has been a demonstrated ability of self-support. The equities weigh heavily in favor of providing a remedy to the working spouse in such a situation.

The Kentucky Court of Appeals held in *Inman v. Inman* [578 S.W.2d 266 (Ky.App.1979)] that the wife was entitled to reimbursement for her monetary contribution to her husband's acquisition of his dentistry license. Although in *Inman* the parties had dissolved their marriage after 17 years and three children and had enjoyed the fruits of the husband's increased earning capacity for a number of years, by the time of the dissolution the couple's debts equalled or exceeded their assets, in large part due to the husband's mismanagement. * * * The Kentucky court relied on the reasoning of the dissent in *Graham* [In re Marriage of Graham, 194 Colo. 429, 574 P.2d 75 (1978)] in which the three dissenting justices stated:

As a matter of economic reality the most valuable asset acquired by either party during this six-year marriage was the husband's increased earning capacity....

The case presents the not-unfamiliar pattern of the wife who, willing to sacrifice for a more secure family financial future, works to educate her husband, only to be awarded a divorce decree shortly after he is awarded his degree. * * *

In cases such as this, equity demands that courts seek extraordinary remedies to prevent extraordinary injustice. [Citations.] * * *

The record shows that the appellee conferred benefits on appellant financial subsidization of appellant's legal education with the agreement and expectation that she would be compensated therefore by his reciprocal efforts after his graduation and admission to the Bar. Appellant has left the marriage with the only valuable asset acquired during the marriage his legal education and qualification to practice law. It would be inequitable to allow appellant to retain this benefit without making restitution to appellee. * * * By our decision herein, we reject the view that the economic element necessarily inherent in the marital institution (and particularly apparent in its dissolution) requires us to treat marriage as a strictly financial undertaking upon the dissolution of which each party will be fully compensated for the investment of his various contributions. When the parties have been married for a number of years, the courts cannot and will not strike a balance regarding the contributions of each to the marriage and then translate that into a monetary award. To do so would diminish the individual personalities of the husband and wife to economic entities and reduce the institution of marriage to that of a closely held corporation.

Generally, where claims are made by the working spouse against the student spouse, the trial court in each case must make specific findings as to whether the education, degree or license acquired by the student spouse during marriage involved an unjust enrichment of that spouse, the value of the benefit, and the amount that should be paid to the working spouse. A variety of methods of computing the unjust enrichment may be employed in ascertaining the working spouse's compensable interest in the attainment of the student spouse's education, degree or license.

The award to appellee should be limited to the financial contribution by appellee for appellant's living expenses and direct educational expenses. [Citation.]

Under the agreement between the parties, the anticipated benefit to appellee may involve a monetary benefit in a lesser amount than the benefit conferred by appellee on appellant. In that event, the award to appellee should be limited to the amount of the anticipated benefit to appellee. Appellee should not recover more than the benefit of her bargain. *Restatement of Restitution*, 107, Comment b, at 449 (1937).

Appellant further objects to the judgment of $23,000 against him on the ground that it directs the payment on terms over a period of time. The terms of payment were of benefit only to appellant. If he wanted to pay the judgment in a lump sum, he certainly could do so. In any event, the trial court, in entering an equitable judgment for money, has the authority to order that it be paid in periodic payments plus interest through the clerk of the court in a certain percentage of appellant's net income, and that appellee have the right to review his records to determine the accuracy of the net income calculations.

The relief granted to appellee is equitable in nature. The rule regarding equitable awards is set forth in Mason v. Ellison, 63 Ariz. 196, 160 P.2d 326 (1945), in which the Arizona supreme court stated:

> In an equity case the court "... adapts its relief and molds its decrees to satisfy the requirements of the case and to conserve the equities of the parties litigant. The court has such plenary power since its purpose is the accomplishment of justice amid all of the vicissitudes and intricacies of life...." [Citations.]

* * *

The nature of equity is individual justice. Since the benefit bestowed upon appellant by appellee was periodic in nature and dependent on her income, we find no abuse of the equity power of the court in awarding appellee periodic payments, especially where she can use them periodically to pursue her own education. By our affirmance of an installment method of payment in this case, we do not mean to promulgate a rule that will uniformly govern all awards in subsequent cases of that nature. Each will, by virtue of the equitable nature of the claim, require relief tailored to the facts and circumstances of the individuals. [Citation.]

The portion of the judgment in the amount of $23,000 is reversed and remanded for proceedings in accordance with this opinion.

---

1.   The American Law Institute published a Restatement (Third) of Restitution and Unjust Enrichment in 2011. Consider whether § 31 would change the result in the principal case.

§ 31.   Unenforceability

(1) A person who renders performance under an agreement that cannot be enforced against the recipient by reason of

(a) indefiniteness, or

(b) the failure to satisfy an extrinsic requirement of enforceability such as the Statute of Frauds,has a claim in restitution against the recipient as necessary to prevent unjust enrichment. There is no unjust enrichment if the claimant receives the counterperformance specified by the parties' unenforceable agreement.

(2) There is no claim under this section if enforcement of the agreement is barred by the applicable statute of limitations, nor in any other case in which the allowance of restitution would defeat the policy of

the law that makes the agreement unenforceable. Restitution is appropriate except to the extent that forfeiture is an intended or acceptable consequence of unenforceability.

2. Substantive entitlement to restitution depends upon whether the defendant has acquired a benefit which is unjust to retain. In *Pyeatte,* the disenfranchised wife had to show that the husband's retention of the educational benefits would be unjust. She had to demonstrate that the benefits conferred went beyond the ordinary services exchanged in the course of marriage and that the parties understood that no gift was intended. Often, courts employ a presumption that services rendered by one family member to another are gratuitous and therefore noncompensable in restitution.

3. Compare the principal case with *Matter of Estate of Zent,* 459 N.W.2d 795 (N.D.1990), reprinted *supra* in this chapter. The claimant in *Zent* was a woman who originally enjoyed a social relationship with a man who later developed Alzheimer's disease. As the disease progressively incapacitated him, the claimant provided various domestic and nursing care until he entered a nursing home and died several weeks later. The court awarded her restitution for the value of the services provided. How is the principal case different? Consider in particular how restitution was measured in each case.

Campbell v. Tennessee Valley Authority

421 F.2d 293 (5th Cir.1969).

■ Morgan, Circuit Judge.

This is an action in *quantum meruit* brought by Raymond Campbell against the Tennessee Valley Authority (hereafter TVA) to recover $30,240 for the microfilming of certain technical trade journals which were a part of TVA's technical library located at Muscle Shoals, Alabama. The District Court entered a judgment upon a verdict for Campbell in the amount of $30,240. We affirm.

Campbell entered into an oral agreement with Earl Daniel, Director of the TVA Technical Library, to reproduce 13 sets of technical trade journals on 16 mm. microfilm at a price of $90 per roll. Mr. Daniel had no authority to make such a purchase for TVA and entered into the agreement with Campbell without the knowledge of his superiors. Campbell photographed, developed and processed 336 rolls of 16 mm. film containing the journals in question, placed the film in cartridges and delivered them to the TVA Technical Library at Muscle Shoals. Under the terms of the oral agreement, the charge for this work was to have been $30,240. The cartridges were placed on the shelves of the library and were available to its patrons for approximately two months.[4] The microfilm cartridges were then returned to Campbell by registered mail along with a letter from Daniel

---

4. There is evidence in the record that in this two-month period three of the cartridges were each used once.

stating that there was no contract for their reproduction, that he had no authority to enter into such a contract, and that the price of the film was excessive. Campbell refused to accept the film and it was returned to the library, where it has since been stored. TVA has refused to pay for the film. The journals reproduced by Campbell were destroyed upon instruction by Daniel.

Campbell's original complaint relied on an express contract with TVA. TVA's motion for summary judgment on the ground that there could be no express contract since its employee Daniel had no authority to enter such a contract was granted. Campbell then amended his complaint to set out a claim for recovery based on *quantum meruit* or a contract implied in law. TVA then moved for and was granted the right to join librarian Daniel (whose employment had since been terminated) as a third-party defendant. Daniel's motion for summary judgment was granted on the ground that he could not be held liable to indemnify TVA in the event that it were held liable to Campbell since for Campbell to recover he had to prove that the microfilm benefited TVA in an economic sense and indemnity by an agent applies only to economic loss or detriment suffered by his principal.

The principal contention made by appellant TVA is that the District Court committed error in instructing the jury that the measure of damages in this case was "the fair market value of the microfilm that benefited TVA." It is TVA's contention that it "is obligated to pay not for the film itself, but only for the 'benefit', or unjust enrichment, if any, which it received by reason of the *use* it made of the film while it was in the library." The first question thus presented to this Court is whether a person who is entitled to recover from an agency of the federal government under a theory of *quantum meruit* is entitled to the reasonable, or fair market, value of the goods or services so provided, or to the reasonable value of the benefit so realized by the Government. In other words, is the measure of recovery to be determined by the amount of money that would be necessary to acquire on the open market the goods or services from which the benefit is derived, or is the measure of recovery how much the benefit has been worth to the person upon whom it was conferred?

* * *

In re Moyer, W.D. Virginia 1960, 190 F.Supp. 867, 873, held that "the measure of recovery * * * on the principle of *quantum meruit* * * * is the reasonable value of the work performed, less the amount of compensation, whether in money or otherwise, already received". Evans v. Mason, 82 Ariz. 40, 308 P.2d 245, 65 A.L.R.2d 936 (1957), an action in *quantum meruit* to recover for services rendered to decedent pursuant to a parol contract barred by the Statute of Frauds held that the measure of damages is the actual value of the services rendered to the decedent. On the other hand, Hill v. Waxberg (9 Cir.1956) 237 F.2d 936, 16 Alaska 477, an action by a contractor to recover for services and expenditures made in contemplation of a proposed building contract, held the "restitution is properly limited to the value of the benefit which was acquired". At 939.

This confusion in the cases is clarified by a statement made in a footnote of the Court's decision in Martin v. Campanaro (2 Cir.1946), 156 F.2d 127, 130 n. 5, *cert. den.,* 329 U.S. 759, 67 S.Ct. 112, 91 L.Ed. 654:

> The claimants are entitled to recover on a quantum meruit basis. But "quantum meruit" is ambiguous; it may mean (1) that there is a contract "implied in fact" to pay the reasonable value of the services, or (2) that, to prevent unjust enrichment, the claimant may recover on a quasi contract (an "as if" contract) for that reasonable value. It has been suggested that the latter is a rule-of-thumb measure of damages adopted in quasi contract cases where the actual unjust enrichment or benefit to the defendant is too difficult to prove; *see* Costigan, Implied-In-Fact Contracts, 33 Harv.Law Rev. (1920) 376, 387.

In the present situation the District Court was correct in using the "rule of thumb" measure of damages and in instructing the jury that the measure of damages was "the fair market value of the microfilm that benefited TVA," instead of instructing that the measure of damages was the reasonable value of the benefit realized by TVA from the microfilm, since the actual benefit to TVA would not have been susceptible of proof. The value realized by a library in having a particular reference work available to its patrons cannot be adequately expressed in dollars and cents. The real benefit is realized, not so much by the library itself, as by those who depend upon the library in their research activities, and the benefit is not so much that the books, technical journals and other research sources are actually *used,* on a regular basis, but that they are conveniently *available for use.* If use, rather than availability, were the only test of the benefit conferred by a book in a library, a good university library could be many times smaller than the present day standard and still retain its effectiveness as a center for research.

Furthermore, in view of the fact that the microfilmed technical journals furnished by Campbell had no readily marketable value to anyone except the TVA because of their unique character and the special circumstances[3] of this case, the District Court properly instructed the jury that the measure of recovery was the fair market value, even though the microfilm was available on the library's shelves for only two months.

* * * TVA argues that if the jury could find that the "fair market value of the microfilm that benefited TVA" could be the contract price between the parties, it could not exceed the lowest contract price that would have been obtainable had competitive bidding taken place on the microfilming under 16 U.S.C., Sec. 831h(b) (1964), and that the evidence is uncontradicted that University Microfilming, a division of Xerox Corporation, would have done the microfilming for $10,000. Thus, TVA contends that Campbell could recover no more than $10,000 and that his recovery of $30,240 was contrary to the law and the evidence.

---

3. The journals which had been reproduced had been destroyed, making the microfilm copies the only ones available. Moreover, there was evidence that the journals in question were a necessary part of a technical library. Likewise, it does not appear the microfilm copies had value to anyone other than to the library.

While there is authority for the proposition that the upper limit of recovery in an action of this nature is the amount agreed to by the parties in the unenforceable contract, the testimony of Holladay, the representative from the University Microfilm division of Xerox, that his company would have done the microfilming here in question for $10,000 did not constitute a bid under 16 U.S.C., Sec. 831h(b), and thus can in no way be considered an upper limit on Campbell's recovery. [Citation.] It is also hornbook law that the jury is in no way bound by the testimony of experts. * * *

The judgment of the District Court is Affirmed.

■ Rives, Circuit Judge (dissenting). * * *

Under the facts and circumstances of this case, I would hold that TVA is not liable to Campbell in any amount. If mistaken in that view, I would nonetheless hold that the extent of its liability is measured by the benefit it received from the limited use made of the film during the two months it remained in the TVA Technical Library.

This litigation began with the filing of a complaint which alleged that Earl Daniel, as agent of the TVA, acting within the line and scope of his authority, agreed with Campbell for him to produce and deliver microfilm of certain trade journals for which Campbell was to be paid $90.00 per roll; that TVA ordered 336 rolls, all of which were delivered; but that TVA refused to pay to Campbell the agreed amount of the contract, $30,240.00. The district court granted TVA's motion for summary judgment as to that claim.

Campbell then amended his complaint by filing counts in general assumpsit seeking to recover in quantum meruit.

While the amended complaint is broad enough to sustain recovery on a contract implied *in fact,* as well as on one implied *in law,* I repeat that the sole claim is on a contract implied *in law.* Judge Grooms correctly so charged the jury:

> "Members of the jury, this case began as a contract case, but it was determined at the outset that Mr. Earl Daniel had no authority to make a contract; the contract was void for that reason, and the contract aspect went out and then the complaint was amended to claim for work and labor and for goods and chattels, merchandise, goods and chattels sold to the defendant, T.V.A. on the theory of what we know as a quantum meruit. That is an old form of action, and it literally means as much as he deserves. Quantum means quantity, merit [sic], as much as he deserves. The case has proceeded since then on the theory of quantum meruit.

> * * *

> "As I stated to you the words quantum meruit, [literally] translated, means as much as he deserves. The basis of a recovery under a quantum meruit is that the defendant has received a benefit from the plaintiff which it is unjust for him to retain without paying for it.

Quantum meruit is a device to prevent unjust enrichment by requiring a recipient of work or services to pay the party furnishing such work and services as much as he reasonably deserves for this work."

I. TVA Is Not Liable to Campbell in Any Amount.

* * *

The jury verdict of $30,240.00 is in the exact amount the plaintiff Campbell claimed that Daniel promised for TVA to pay for the film (336 rolls at $90.00 per roll). A reading of the record makes obvious, I submit, that the unauthorized express contract has simply been enforced under the guise of a quasi contract or quantum meruit. * * *

The underlying principle is that of forbidding unjust enrichment. "A person who has been unjustly enriched at the expense of another is required to make restitution to the other." A.L.I. Restatement, Restitution § 1, p. 12.

Chapter 2 of that text "states the conditions under which there is a right to restitution because of a mistake in the conferring of a benefit." A.L.I. Restatement, Restitution Introductory Note, p. 26. Such a right may arise in the case of a person who has paid money (*Id.* § 16) or transferred property (*Id.* § 39), or rendered services (*Id.* § 40) to another which have inured to the latter's benefit, in the mistaken belief that he is performing a valid contract with the other, although the contract is later avoided. A right to restitution, however, does not arise in such cases unless the recipient of the property or services is *unjustly enriched*.

"Even where a person has received a benefit from another, he is liable to pay therefor only if the circumstances of its receipt or retention are such that, as between the two persons, it is unjust for him to retain it. The mere fact that a person benefits another is not of itself sufficient to require the other to make restitution therefor."

A.L.I. Restatement, Restitution p. 13.

Under the facts and circumstances of this case, it is doubtful whether TVA was *enriched* or *harmed* by Campbell's services when consideration is given to the fact that Campbell destroyed TVA's original journals. * * *

Assuming arguendo that TVA was benefited by Campbell's services, it was not unjustly enriched: It has been demonstrated that no authorized agent of TVA accepted delivery of the rolls of microfilm; that TVA has not wrongfully retained the microfilm, but has made every reasonable effort to return it to Campbell, and that upon Campbell's refusal to accept the film, TVA has stored it and forbidden its use. The only possible benefit retained by TVA is in the two-month period that the microfilm remained in its Technical Library. In that two months, three of the rolls were each used once. There was no evidence that the person making such limited use of the film knew or had reason to know that he was using film which did not belong to TVA or that he was in any way obligating TVA to pay for the film. Such knowledge is, I submit, necessary for this limited user to impose upon TVA a duty of restitution. *See* A.L.I. Restatement, Restitution §§ 40 and 41. Further, a precedent should not be laid for the public policy requirement of competitive bidding to be frustrated by the application of some principle of restitution or quasi contract. For all of the foregoing reasons, I am firmly of the opinion that TVA is not liable to Campbell in any amount.

II.   *If* Liable, What Is the Extent of TVA's Liability.

* * * It is incomprehensible to me that Campbell should be rewarded for *his* destruction of TVA's original trade journals. Perhaps the best precedent is the classic case of the son who murdered his father and mother, but was granted mercy because he was an orphan.

The majority holding measures the extent of TVA's liability by Campbell's loss. That overlooks the fundamental reason for granting restitution or quantum meruit relief, *viz.*, to avoid unjust enrichment. Ordinarily in such cases the benefit to the one and the loss to the other are co-extensive. However, when the benefit is less than the loss, the recovery is limited to the benefit. * * *

I respectfully dissent.

---

1.   *Purpose.* As the principal case demonstrates, awarding restitution in a "contract" setting has been a troublesome issue. One commentator has suggested that the difficulties in this area stem from the use of the term "restitution" to describe a variety of remedies awarded in a variety of circumstances. Andrew Kull, *Rescission and Restitution*, 61 Bus. Law. 569 (Feb. 2006). For example, restitution may provide an alternative remedy to expectancy damages for breach of contract when an express contract exists between the parties but the plaintiff is unable to prove its expectancy. See Chapter 10. Alternatively, restitution also may be awarded as in the principal case to prevent unjust enrichment when a party renders performance under the mistaken belief that a contract exists but lacks an enforceable contract claim.

The determination of the appropriate remedy requires an understanding of which type of restitution is at issue. When used as a remedy for breach of contract, the purpose of restitution is to place the non-breaching party in the position occupied before a contract was made. Thus, the focus is on expenditures the non-breaching party made in preparation for performance. When restitution is used as a remedy for unjust enrichment, the focus is on the benefit conferred on the defendant. Although the measurement of recovery may be identical in some instances, sometimes one remedy will produce a higher recovery for the claimant.

2.   *Rescission and Restitution.* A claim for rescission and restitution would return to both parties any benefits conferred in the transaction. Rescission and restitution are equitable remedies available for the breach of a contract or in other appropriate circumstance where benefits are ex-

changed pursuant to a failed agreement. The court will condition the availability of these remedies on the mutually equitable conduct of the plaintiff; the order that the defendant give restitution of benefits acquired under the rescinded agreement is conditioned upon the plaintiff's restitution of benefits received under the same agreement. The equitable maxim invoked for this principle is, "He who seeks equity must do equity."

Why was this remedy not available in the principal case?

3. *Restoring the Status Quo.* The different measures between damages and restitution were addressed in *Dravo Corporation v. L.W. Moses Co.*, 6 Wash.App. 74, 492 P.2d 1058 (1971). In that case a subcontractor partly performed a construction contract before termination by the general contractor. The subcontractor alleged wrongful termination of the contract and sought restitution for the value of the services rendered. The general contractor, Dravo, argued that the court should deduct from the subcontractor's recovery the cost of completing the work. The court disagreed, and held that restitution was properly measured by the reasonable value of the subcontractor's services, less any benefits which the subcontractor received. Accordingly, no deductions were made for the cost of completion nor, conversely, were the subcontractor's profits included. The objective was to return the parties to the *status quo ante.*

4. *Reasonable Value of Services.* How should the reasonable value of services be measured in an action for quantum meruit? In *Dravo*, the court suggested that the contract itself may provide evidence of the value of the benefits conferred. Also relevant were the actual expenditures by the subcontractor in performance. The services must be valuable, however, from the perspective of the defendant.

In *Campbell v. TVA*, did the defendant actually benefit from the microfilm of the trade journals or did the defendant suffer a detriment because the plaintiff destroyed the original journals?

PROBLEM: THE EQUIPMENT LOAN

Danzer is an employee of Carter, who owns a furniture store. Pennell, who operates an equipment rental business, has good personal and business relations with Carter. Carter's furniture store attracts as customers people who are moving or remodelling, and Carter frequently refers them to Pennell's rental business.

Danzer contacted Pennell during business hours and asked for the free use of carpet cleaning equipment for a few weeks. Pennell was under the erroneous impression that Carter wanted the equipment to clean carpets in the furniture store and had instructed Danzer to call. Pennell granted the request as a return favor to Carter.

In fact, Carter was not involved in the request. Danzer, acting independently, wanted the cleaning equipment to operate a personal business during the pre-holiday season. Danzer cleaned carpets for private homeowners during evening hours at a rate slightly less than that of professional cleaners. Pennell later discovered these facts and further learned that Danzer earned $500 cleaning carpets. The fair rental value of the equipment is $200. Is restitution appropriate? If so, how should it be measured?

Ward v. Taggart

51 Cal.2d 736, 336 P.2d 534 (1959).

■ TRAYNOR, JUSTICE.

At plaintiff William R. Ward's request in February, 1955, LeRoy Thomsen, a real estate broker, undertook to look for properties that might be of interest to Ward for purchase. During a conversation about unrelated matters, defendant Marshall W. Taggart, a real estate broker, told Thomsen that as exclusive agent for Sunset Oil Company he had several acres of land in Los Angeles County for sale. Thomsen said that he had a client who might be interested in acquiring this property. When Thomsen mentioned to Taggart that another broker named Dawson had a "For Sale" sign on the property, Taggart replied that Sunset had taken the listing away from Dawson. With Ward's authorization Thomsen submitted an offer on his behalf to Taggart of $4,000 an acre. Taggart promised to take the offer to Sunset. Taggart later told Thomsen that Sunset had refused the offer and would not take less for the property than $5,000 an acre, one-half in cash. Thomsen conveyed this information to Ward, who directed Thomsen to make an offer on those terms. Thomsen did so in writing. * * *

Plaintiffs did not learn until after they had purchased the property that Taggart had never been given a listing by Sunset and that he had never presented to Sunset and never intended to present plaintiffs' offers of $4,000 and $5,000 per acre. Instead, he presented his own offer of $4,000 per acre, which Sunset accepted. He falsely represented to plaintiffs that the least Sunset would take for the property was $5,000 per acre, because he intended to purchase the property from Sunset himself and resell it to plaintiffs at a profit of $1,000 per acre. All the reasons he gave for the unusual handling of the sale were fabrications. * * *

Plaintiffs brought an action in tort charging fraud on the part of Taggart and Jordan [a Taggart employee]. The case was tried without a jury, and the court entered judgment against both defendants for $72,049.20 compensatory damages, and against Taggart for $36,000 exemplary damages. The judgment also enjoined defendants from transferring notes and trust deeds received from plaintiffs and ordered them to discharge these and thereby reduce the amount of the judgment. Defendants appeal.

Defendants contend that the judgment must be reversed on the ground that there can be no recovery in a tort action for fraud without proof of the actual or "out-of-pocket" losses sustained by the plaintiff and that in the present case there was no evidence that the property was worth less than plaintiffs paid for it. * * * Although, as defendants admit, the evidence is clearly sufficient to support the finding of fraud, the only evidence submitted on the issue of damages was that the property was worth at least $5,000 per acre, the price plaintiffs paid for it. Since there was no proof that plaintiffs suffered "out-of-pocket" loss, there can be no recovery in tort for fraud. [Citation.] * * *

Even though Taggart was not plaintiff's agent, the public policy of this state does not permit one to "take advantage of his own wrong" (Civ.Code, 3517), and the law provides a quasi-contractual remedy to prevent one from being unjustly enriched at the expense of another. Section 2224 of the Civil Code provides that one "who gains a thing by fraud * * * or other wrongful act, is, unless he has some other and better right thereto, an involuntary trustee of the thing gained, for the benefit of the person who would otherwise have had it." As a real estate broker, Taggart had the duty to be honest and truthful in his dealings. [Citation.] The evidence is clearly sufficient to support a finding that Taggart violated this duty. Through fraudulent misrepresentations he received money that plaintiffs would otherwise have had. Thus, Taggart is an involuntary trustee for the benefit of plaintiffs on the secret profit of $1,000 per acre that he made from his dealings with them.

* * *

Accordingly, the judgment for $72,092.20, representing the $1,000 per acre secret profit, against defendant Taggart must be affirmed. The judgment against defendant Jordan, however, must be reversed. Although she permitted her name to be used in the dual escrows, she did not share in the illicit profit that Taggart obtained. One cannot be held to be a constructive trustee of something he has not acquired.

Taggart contends that if recovery is based on the theory of unjust enrichment, the judgment of exemplary damages must be reversed. * * *

Courts award exemplary damages to discourage oppression, fraud, or malice by punishing the wrongdoer. [Citations.] Such damages are appropriate in cases like the present one, where restitution would have little or no deterrent effect, for wrongdoers would run no risk of liability to their victims beyond that of returning what they wrongfully obtained. * * *

The judgment against Taggart is affirmed. The judgment against Jordan is reversed.

---

1. Benefits conferred by an agreement that was induced by fraud can be the subject of a claim in tort for misrepresentation or a claim for restitution. Compensatory damages for fraud can be measured in two ways, both of which properly focus upon the plaintiff's loss. The out of pocket loss measure allows the difference between the price paid and the value actually received. For example, if a seller of a house fraudulently represents that a leaky roof was recently repaired, the buyer can recover the difference between the price and the value of the defective house. The benefit of the bargain measure gives the difference between the value received and the

value if the representations were true. Under this measure the plaintiff could receive the difference between the value of the defective house and the value of the house if the roof were repaired. Jurisdictions vary on the permissibility of these measures for fraud or for negligent misrepresentation.

In the principal case, the defendant fraudulently induced the plaintiff to confer on him a benefit, specifically the additional $1000 per acre above the actual price. The tort action was successful substantively, but the remedy produced no recovery. Compensatory damages were not possible because the plaintiff had no actual loss; the value of the land received by the plaintiff was equal to the price paid. The secret profit of $1000 could only be disgorged by a restitutionary theory that the defendant made a "promise" by implication of law to return the secret profit.

2.   Compare *Ward* to the following facts: A buyer, Harper, made an offer to purchase a farm for $7000 to an agent for the owner. The agent fraudulently misrepresented that the seller would only convey a portion of it for $6000. In fact the seller was willing to sell it all for $6500, and the agent purchased the entire farm at that price. The agent then sold Harper a portion of it for $6000 and conveyed the rest to a close relative for $500.

Harper discovered these facts and sued. The original owner of the farm did not sue. How could compensatory damages in tort be measured? Is a restitutionary remedy appropriate under these facts? *See* Harper v. Adametz, 142 Conn. 218, 113 A.2d 136 (1955) (restitution by constructive trust). See Chapter 16 D, *infra*.

3.   If the theory of recovery is an implied-in-law contract, why should the court allow punitive damages as if it were a tort action rather than a contractual one? Is the use of the word "contract" so fictional that it has no meaning? Should it determine the statute of limitations?

QHG of Springdale, Inc. v. Archer

2009 Ark.App. 692, ___ S.W.3d ___ (2009).

■ D.P. MARSHALL JR., JUDGE.

This case illustrates the proverb: When a piece of paper blows into a law court, it may take a yoke of oxen to drag it out. The main piece of paper in this case is the 2002 employment contract between Dr. Ernest Archer, an OB/GYN, and his hospital-employer, QHG of Springdale.

Dr. Archer and QHG entered into their first employment contract in 2000. The parties operated under this agreement for two years. In October 2002, after much negotiation, the parties rescinded the first agreement and entered into a new one. The new agreement was a detailed five-year contract. This lawsuit turns on this second agreement.

Over time, Dr. Archer became dissatisfied with several aspects of his job. He claimed that QHG repeatedly denied his time-off requests for vacation and continuing medical education and failed to provide adequate personnel and equipment. Dr. Archer's chief complaint was QHG's failure to provide rotating call coverage. With the exception of a few weeks here and there, Dr. Archer was on call twenty-four hours a day, seven days a week for more than two years. In January 2004, exercising an option available to both parties under the contract, QHG terminated the employment relationship without cause upon 180–days' notice. The hospital sent Dr. Archer a letter, explaining that his termination would be effective in July 2004. Dr. Archer, however, resigned his medical staff privileges in May 2004 because he could no longer operate safely given problems with his hands. The next day, QHG terminated Dr. Archer for cause.

Dr. Archer then sued QHG. He alleged, among other things, that QHG broke the 2002 employment contract in several ways and that the hospital was unjustly enriched by him providing non-stop call coverage. These two claims were the core of the case at trial. The circuit court granted QHG's directed-verdict motion on the unjust-enrichment claim. Dr. Archer's breach-of-contract claim went to the jury, which found that QHG had violated the 2002 employment agreement and awarded Dr. Archer $387,500.00. QHG appeals the jury's award, and Dr. Archer cross-appeals the dismissal of his unjust-enrichment claim. * * *

[The court concluded that QHG lawfully terminated the contract pursuant to the without-cause termination clause but was obligated to pay Dr. Archer through July 2004 pursuant to the 180–day notice period provided in the clause. The court reversed the damage award and remanded for remittitur.]

What about QHG's failure to provide rotating call coverage and time off? Dr. Archer overperformed at QHG's demand. Damages for this overperformance, we conclude, must come as a *quantum meruit* award off the parties' contract. [Citation.] QHG's obligation to pay for these extra services is quasi-contractual, implied by law to prevent unjust enrichment. [Citations.]

"[W]hen an express contract does not fully address a subject, a court of equity may impose a remedy to further the ends of justice." [Citations.] The parties' 2002 agreement does not fully address rotating call. Under the agreement and QHG's policy, there had to be some rotation. Dr. Archer's providing round-the-clock call service was not the parties' bargain. Their contract, however, provides no yardstick for measuring the damages to Dr. Archer from QHG's breach. The parties made no express agreement about exactly how much rotation was required or the value of on-call services. Nor does the record demonstrate any tacit agreement that, if Dr. Archer provided on-call coverage beyond some point, then QHG was willing to be responsible for any resulting consequential damages to the doctor. [Citation.]

As QHG points out, in general Arkansas law allows no unjust-enrichment claim where the parties have a contract. [Citations.] "The mere fact that there is a contract between the parties does not prevent the grant of restitution in an appropriate case." Friends of Children, 46 Ark.App. at 61, 876 S.W.2d at 605.

The *Friends of Children* court gave an illustrative, though not exhaustive, list of these kinds of cases: "Appropriate cases include those ..." involving a rescission at law, the discharge of a contract by impossibility or frustration of purpose, or contracting parties who make a fundamental mistake about something important in their agreement. *Ibid.* The *Servewell* court recognized, but declined to apply on the facts there, other exceptions: where contracting parties make some agreement about a matter or "if the circumstances surrounding the parties' dealings can be found to have given rise to an obligation to pay." 362 Ark. at 612–13, 210 S.W.3d at 112.

The almost-completed [now published—eds.] Restatement (Third) of Restitution and Unjust Enrichment contains a section on overperformance that voices the unifying legal principles behind all these exceptions. This section also captures precisely why this record made a case for the jury—notwithstanding the parties' contract—on Dr. Archer's unjust-enrichment claim. The section is entitled "Performance of Disputed Obligation."

> If one party to a contract demands from the other a performance that is not in fact due by the terms of their agreement, the party on whom the demand is made may render such performance under protest or with reservation of rights, preserving a claim in restitution to recover the value of the benefit conferred in excess of the recipient's contractual entitlement.

Restatement (Third) of Restitution and Unjust Enrichment § 35(1) [2011—eds.]. All the exceptions reflect the limits of the reasons behind the general rule. Where the parties have an enforceable contract that fully addresses a subject, they must proceed on that contract in resolving their differences. But where the contract fails on some basis, or does not fully address a subject, or disputed performance is compelled under protest, then the parties' contract is no bar to an unjust-enrichment claim for restitution. [Citation.]

We turn, with this law in mind, to the facts here. In reviewing the directed verdict, we consider the record in the light most favorable to Dr. Archer's unjust-enrichment claim. [Citation.] The 2002 agreement required some call rotation. That requirement echoed QHG's policy that no doctor had to work 24/7. QHG demanded that Dr. Archer be on call all the time. He was. Early and often, however, Dr. Archer protested. He repeatedly asked QHG to relieve this burden. When the parties signed the 2002 agreement, another OB/GYN was working at QHG. This doctor's work was questionable; Dr. Archer was not comfortable rotating call with her, and QHG eventually terminated her. Both QHG and Dr. Archer expected the hospital to hire more OB/GYNs over time, more hands that could have helped cover call. As events played out, however, with the exception of a few weeks here and there, Dr. Archer was on call by himself for more than two years.

Why was rotating call coverage important? Because of the strong public policy requiring doctors to take care of their patients who need medical care. The Congress recognized this policy when it passed EMTALA, the

Emergency Medical Treatment and Active Labor Act. 42 U.S.C. § 1395dd (2006). Congress's purpose in enacting this statute is clear:

> Congress enacted EMTALA in response to its concern that hospitals were 'dumping' patients who were unable to pay, by either refusing to provide emergency medical treatment or transferring patients before their emergency conditions were stabilized. Through EMTALA, Congress sought to provide an adequate first response to a medical crisis for all patients.

In re Baby K, 16 F.3d 590, 593 (4th Cir.1994) (internal citations omitted).

QHG knew its EMTALA duties. The hospital made its own rules for doctors in Policy #201 to ensure statutory compliance. These rules required that "[o]n call physicians must respond within a reasonable period of time," which usually meant thirty minutes. Policy #201 established care guidelines for the services each emergency patient should receive and the on-call doctor's immediate and future duties to that patient. QHG's Policy also listed some of the potential penalties for an on-call physician's failure to comply with EMTALA: substantial personal fines, suspension of medical staff privileges, and investigation by peers and the Board of Medical Examiners.

Dr. Archer's obligations and potential penalties under EMTALA and QHG's policies hamstrung him into abiding by QHG's unrelenting call schedule. He overperformed for good reasons and under protest. Restatement (Third) of Restitution and Unjust Enrichment § 35(1) [2011]. The parties' 2002 agreement required him to be on call, but gave no particulars other than requiring some rotation. This indefiniteness created hurdles for a claim on the contract. Applied Pharmacy, 182 F.3d at 609. The precise terms of performance due from both parties on rotating call were disputed. Finally, while the legal risks and costs of nonperformance by Dr. Archer to him and QHG were substantial, his overperformance during their dispute insured that their patients received prompt medical care. See generally Restatement (Third) of Restitution and Unjust Enrichment § 35 cmt. a [2011].

This record, viewed in the light most favorable to Dr. Archer, shows that QHG has received something of value "under such circumstances that, in equity and good conscience, [the hospital] ought not to retain it." Friends of Children, 46 Ark.App. at 61, 876 S.W.2d at 606 (citation omitted). All the circumstances surrounding QHG's and Dr. Archer's dealings give rise to QHG's obligation to pay him something more. [Citation.] It was for the jury to say how much more. [Citation.] The circuit court therefore erred by directing a verdict on unjust enrichment. We reverse the court's judgment on that claim and remand for a trial on the merits.

Reversed and remanded on direct appeal and on cross-appeal.

1. Restitution is often invoked when the contractual relationship between the parties fails for some reason. However, as the principal case illustrates, restitution may be appropriate even if a valid contract exists between the parties. Generally, if one party to a contract demands from the other party performance that is not called for under the contract, the objecting party must refuse to perform the disputed obligations and seek legal redress. However, sometimes the objecting party faces the risk of incurring losses before its rights under the contract can be judicially determined. In those circumstances, the performing party may perform the disputed obligations "under protest" or "with a reservation of rights" and recover the value of the excess benefits in restitution. Both the Restatement (Third) of Restitution and Unjust Enrichment § 35 and the Uniform Commercial Code § 1–308 recognize a party's right to perform disputed obligations under protest and recover in restitution.

2. A party that performs disputed obligations under protest must act in good faith and in reasonable protection of its interests. Generally, that means the potential liability if the party fails to perform the disputed obligations would be greater than the cost of performing the disputed obligations and the party disputing the obligations will not have a meaningful opportunity to adjudicate the claim before the disputed performance is due. The potential liability or risk of loss to the disputing party must be something other than ordinary litigation costs involved in disputing a claim.

3. A party who disputes its obligations under the contract may reserve its right to seek restitution either before or while rendering performance without waiving its right to seek restitution. *See* Margason v. Roberts, 919 P.2d 818 (Colo. Ct. App. 1995).

Kansas Farm Bureau Life Ins. Co., Inc. v. Farmway Credit Union

256 Kan. 968, 889 P.2d 784 (1995).

■ ALLEGRUCCI, JUSTICE:

Kansas Farm Bureau Life Insurance Company, Inc., (KFB) sued Farmway Credit Union (Farmway) to recover policy proceeds it paid under a mistaken belief that the insured was dead. The district court entered summary judgment in KFB's favor on the grounds that KFB was entitled to repayment on an implied contract theory[.] * * *

In 1974, KFB issued a policy insuring the life of Keith J. Schreuder. That same year, Schreuder assigned the policy to Farmway as collateral. Around April 17, 1982, Schreuder disappeared. * * *

On April 18, 1989, when there had been a seven-year interval since Schreuder's disappearance, Farmway filed a petition in the District Court of Mitchell County, Kansas, seeking a court order which decreed that the insured was presumed dead. The district court's journal entry of May 17,

1989, decreed that Schreuder was declared to be dead and established the date of death as April 17, 1982.

Farmway submitted a claim to KFB for the policy proceeds. On May 26, 1989, KFB issued to Farmway a check for $86,221, which represented the face amount of the life insurance policy plus interest from the date of death. On June 5, 1989, KFB issued to Farmway a check for $11,721.71, which represented a refund of premiums plus interest paid on the policy after the date of death.

In April 1992, KFB learned that Schreuder was alive. On June 12, 1992, KFB demanded that Farmway return the money which had been paid to it. Farmway refused; KFB filed its petition in district court on August 21, 1992.

On cross-motions for summary judgment, the district court ruled in KFB's favor. It ordered Farmway to pay KFB $97,942.71 plus interest from June 12, 1992, when KFB first demanded return of the money.

We first determine if KFB was entitled to repayment based on a contract implied due to mutual mistake. Examination of KFB's petition in the district court shows that its original theories of recovery were unjust enrichment and mutual mistake of fact/implied contract. The district court's decision to grant KFB's motion for summary judgment was based on its theory of mutual mistake of fact and implied contract. The district court concluded that KFB's motion for summary judgment on the theory of unjust enrichment was moot. In the Court of Appeals, KFB argued that the district court's decision in its favor could be affirmed on the ground of unjust enrichment under the right-for-the-wrong-reason principle. The Court of Appeals stated that payment by mistake, implied contract, and unjust enrichment "are different names for what is essentially the same theory of recovery." This appears to be a correct statement. The Court of Appeals further stated:

An action to recover money paid to the defendant under a mistake of fact sounds in quasi contract, and the court will imply a promise to repay on the part of the defendant. [Citation.]. This court has explained:

> [I]t should be noted that a variety of similar terms are engaged by those dealing with the present subject, including the following: quasi-contracts, restitution, constructive contracts, and unjust enrichment. In this regard, the following statement found in 17 C.J.S., Contracts § 6, p. 571, is relevant:

> '[T]he terms "restitution" and "unjust enrichment" are modern designations for the older doctrine of quasi contracts, and the substance of an action for 'unjust enrichment' lies in a promise, implied by law, that one will restore to the person entitled thereto that which in equity and good conscience belongs to him.' [Citations.]

In the Court of Appeals, Farmway's main contention was "that there was no mistake of fact which would require repayment. It argue[d] the parties effected a compromise and settlement when KFB agreed to pay

Farmway's claim on the life insurance policy and that KFB is bound by the terms of the settlement." On this question the district court determined that Farmway had not come forward with evidence necessary to establish its claim, and the Court of Appeals agreed. Farmway contended, and the Court of Appeals rejected the claim, that compromise was shown by Schreuder's uncertain status, by the "in full settlement of all claims" boilerplate on KFB's checks, and by Farmway's unilateral belief that the policy might contain a double indemnity provision. There is no reason to revisit these conclusions. The Court of Appeals' rationale is sound, and, although Farmway does not entirely relinquish the argument, its primary focus has shifted in this appeal.

In its petition for review and in its supplemental brief in this court, Farmway layers the compromise-and-settlement argument with the contention that KFB is not entitled to recovery because, in relying on the court-ordered presumption of death, it assumed the risk that Schreuder was alive. * * *

The Restatement of Restitution § 11(1) (1936) provides: "A person is not entitled to rescind a transaction with another if, by way of compromise or otherwise, he agreed with the other to assume, or intended to assume, the risk of a mistake for which otherwise he would be entitled to rescission and consequent restitution." * * *

* * * KFB chose to pay the policy proceeds to Farmway based upon the presumption of death order and not on the mistaken fact that Schreuder was dead. Schreuder's death was not a fact. KFB was under no legal obligation to pay the proceeds to Farmway, and Schreuder's death remained in doubt after the presumption of death was entered by the district court[.] * * * KFB did not require Farmway to execute a restitution or indemnity agreement in the event Schreuder was not dead. We conclude that KFB assumed the risk that Schreuder was not dead and is not entitled to repayment from Farmway. Having so concluded, it follows that the district court erred in granting summary judgment to KFB and not to Farmway. In view of this holding, we need not consider Farmway's second issue that KFB's action is barred by the statute of limitations.

The judgment of the Court of Appeals affirming the district court is reversed. The judgment of the district court is reversed, and the case is remanded with directions to grant summary judgment to Farmway.

---

1. *Mistake.* Is the principal case consistent with section 6 of the Restatement (Third) of Restitution and Unjust Enrichment (2011) and comments?

> § 6.   Payment Of Money Not Due
>
> Payment by mistake gives the payor a claim in restitution against the recipient to the extent payment was not due.

Comment:

a.   General principles and scope; relation to other sections. Mistaken payment of money not due presents one of the core cases of restitution, whether liability is explained by reference to the transferee's unjustified enrichment or to the transferor's unintended dispossession. Such a payment gives rise to a *prima facie* claim in restitution, but the setting may be one in which opposing principles—representing fundamental limits to recovery in restitution—are simultaneously applicable. These counter-principles appear when a payment of money not due is made pursuant to a compromise, explicit or implicit; or when the payor will be held to have assumed the risk of uncertainty as to the fact or extent of an asserted liability. * * *

As in other cases of benefit conferred by mistake, the fact that the claimant may have acted negligently in making a mistaken payment is normally irrelevant to the analysis of the claim. * * * On the other hand, the recipient of a mistaken payment who is aware at the time of the payor's mistake is almost certain to be liable in restitution, because notice to the recipient will foreclose the most significant of the affirmative defenses.

2.   Consider the Monopoly game card that reads, "Bank error in your favor. Collect $200." Under the principle of the Restatement (Third) of Restitution and Unjust Enrichment (2011) § 6, could the bank get repayment even if it had been negligent in the error?

3.   Consider how the result in the principal case would be different if the missing person had colluded with the beneficiaries to disappear until after the life insurance payment. Fraud and concealment support restitution. Compare the result in *Ward v. Taggart, infra.*

C.   WAIVER OF TORT AND SUIT IN ASSUMPSIT

Section Coverage:

Waiver of tort and suit in assumpsit is a legal restitutionary remedy based on the implication of rights through quasi-contracts. Although the parties have no express or implied contract between them, the common law will imply a contract that requires a defendant to return unjust enrichment to a plaintiff who should more rightfully retain the benefit.

Historically this type of restitution was accomplished by allowing a plaintiff to use one of the old contract writs even in the absence of an express or implied contract. The writ of "money had and received" was thus used to recover under a quasi-contract any profit a wrongdoer received at the expense of the plaintiff. The fiction was that the defendant was acting as the plaintiff's agent. The writ of "goods sold and delivered" was used to recover the fair market value of converted goods on the fiction that the thief had promised to pay for them.

In many states the function of this basis of recovery is to recover profits from wrongdoers when the relationship between the parties does not support the imposition of a constructive trust. A plaintiff can bring an action in assumpsit against even a thief. Another function is to gain the typically longer contract statute of limitations by bringing an action in quasi-contract instead of tort. This result is important for plaintiffs who want to sue for conversion damages but are time-barred. The action in assumpsit based on "goods sold and delivered" allows the same measure of damages fair market value at time and place of conversion under a longer period of limitations. Some courts have found this result inappropriate, but most allow it.

Not all torts may be waived in favor of quasi-contract actions. Courts most commonly have permitted waiver of conversion. Waiver of trespass to chattel has been allowed. Jurisdictions have split on the permissibility of waiving trespass. Courts have rejected other torts, such as defamation, as suitable for the implication of a contract implied by law.

Model Case:

Jean Poindexter owns a coin shop in Metropolis. One night a thief defeated the security system and stole the coins that were in the vault. The thief erroneously believed that the most valuable coins would be in the vault. In fact Poindexter guarded the most valuable coins elsewhere and the coins in the vault were only moderately valuable.

The thief, Green, took the coins to an unsophisticated buyer who shared the misconception about their value. Green thus sold the coins for more than their fair market value. When these facts are discovered, Poindexter sues Green. Green has otherwise been a successful burglar and has assets to pay a judgment.

Poindexter has several choices. First, an action for tort would recover the fair market value of the coins at the time and place of conversion. If the conversion statute of limitations has run, the same measure is available with an assumpsit claim based upon the writ of "goods sold and delivered." The fictional contract is based upon an implied promise by the thief to pay for the goods at the moment of stealing them.

Alternatively, an assumpsit action based upon the writ of "money had and received" allows recovery of the resale price on the fiction that Green was acting as Poindexter's agent. Under the facts of this case, this recovery would be greater. The profit earned from the transaction with the unsophisticated buyer is taken from the wrongdoer and given to the plaintiff. Although the plaintiff thus recovers a windfall, the defendant cannot profit from the misdeed.

H. Russell Taylor's Fire Prevention Service, Inc. v. Coca Cola Bottling Corp.

99 Cal.App.3d 711, 160 Cal.Rptr. 411 (1979).

■ ZENOVICH, ASSOCIATE JUSTICE.

A complaint filed in Kern County Superior Court alleged that appellant Coca Cola Bottling Corporation (hereafter referred to as Coca Cola) was indebted to appellant H. Russell Taylor's Fire Prevention Service, Inc. (hereafter referred to as Taylor). * * *

By stipulation of the parties, Taylor amended its complaint in the indebitatus assumpsit count, and Coca Cola amended its answer to assert as a separate affirmative defense the bar of the statute of limitations set forth in Code of Civil Procedure section 338, subdivision 3.

Thereafter, the court entered findings of fact and conclusions of law rendering judgment for Taylor in the sum of $7,157. From this judgment Coca Cola appeals. * * *

In 1957, Coca Cola entered into an oral agreement with Taylor. Taylor was to periodically fill some of its own cylinders with carbon dioxide and supply them to Coca Cola's bottling plant in Bakersfield, California, for use as fire extinguishers. * * *

Pursuant to the oral agreement, Taylor made deliveries of cylinders to Coca Cola's plant until September 23, 1971. The trial court found that September 23, 1971, was the termination date for Taylor's services. Within 90 days, employees of Taylor demanded return of several hundred cylinders in Coca Cola's possession. Coca Cola began to return many of the cylinders, although 246 in number were still missing at the time of trial.

* * *

The trial court found that Coca Cola's failure to return the cylinders was a taking and detaining of goods and chattels. In addition, the court determined that Taylor waived the conversion claim and elected to treat the action as a purchase and sale of the cylinders. Having determined that an implied-in-law sale occurred once the tort was waived, the court applied the four-year statute of limitations of Commercial Code section 2725, subdivision (1), and held the suit timely filed. * * *

Procedurally, Taylor filed its complaint on June 4, 1975, more than three years after September 23, 1971, the date upon which demand was made for the outstanding cylinders. The trial court found that the suit was timely filed within the four-year statute of limitations set forth in Commercial Code section 2725, subdivision (1), since the indebitatus assumpsit theory legally transformed the tortious conversion of the cylinders into a *fictional* contract of sale. Coca Cola contends that the trial court erroneously applied the four-year limitations period even though the gravamen of Taylor's claim was for "taking, detaining, or injuring any goods, or chattels," a cause of action governed by the three-year limitations period provided in Code of Civil Procedure section 338, subdivision 3. Under Coca Cola's construction of the action brought by Taylor, the suit would be time barred if the limitations period of the Commercial Code is deemed inapplicable.

In ruling upon the applicability of a statute of limitations, it has been recognized that courts will look to the nature of the rights sued upon rather than to the form of action or to the relief demanded. Neither the caption, form, nor prayer of the complaint will conclusively determine the nature of the liability from which the cause of action flows. Instead, the true nature of the action will be ascertained from the basic facts *a posteriori*. [Citations.] Since the trial court found the four-year limitations period governing sales contracts applicable, it must be determined whether Taylor's indebitatus assumpsit cause of action is based on contract or tort. In order to pinpoint the proper nature of the rights sued upon, an examination of the theory underlying indebitatus assumpsit is appropriate.

The general contours of the assumpsit cause of action have been summarized by Professor Corbin as follows:

> The common counts in assumpsit are merely abbreviated and stereo-typed statements that the defendant is indebted to the plaintiff for a variety of commonly recurring reasons, such as . . . goods sold and delivered. They are allegations of indebtedness, and the action may be properly described as indebitatus assumpsit. . . . The common counts could be used for the enforcement of express promises if they were such as to create a money debt, *as well as for the enforcement of implied promises and quasi-contracts.* (1 Corbin, Contracts (1st ed. 1963) 20, p. 51, emphasis added.)

* * * [T]he California Supreme Court discussed the historical evolution of indebitatus assumpsit. The court stated:

> The action of *assumpsit,* in its development, had an interesting but stormy career at the common law. Although in existence for some years previous to that time, it came into prominence following the decision in Slade's Case in 1603 (Coke's Rep., vol. 2, p. 505; 2 Harvard Law Review, p. 16). It gradually gained prominence and widened in scope until 1760 when Lord Mansfield, in the case of *Moses v. Mcfarlan* (2 Burr, 1005, English Reports, Full Reprint, King's Bench Book 26, vol. 97, p. 676), described its function as follows: 'This kind of equitable action to recover back money, which ought not in justice to be kept, is very beneficial, and therefore much encouraged. It lies only for money which, *ex aequo et bono,* the defendant ought to refund; it does not lie for money paid by the plaintiff, which is claimed of him as payable in point of honor and honesty, although it could not have been recovered from him by any course of law; as in payment of a debt barred by the statute of limitations, or contracted during his infancy, or to the extent of principal and legal interest upon a usurious contract, or for money fairly lost at play: because in all these cases, the defendant may retain it with a safe conscience, though by positive law he was barred from recovering. But it lies for money paid by mistake; or upon a consideration which happens to fail; or for money got through imposition (express or implied); or extortion; or oppression; or an undue advantage taken of the plaintiff's situation, contrary to laws made for the protection of persons under those circumstances. In one word the gist of this kind of action is, that the defendant, upon the

circumstances of the case, is obliged by the ties of natural justice and equity to refund the money.'

Quoting the above, Mr. Holdsworth in his work on the History of English Law, volume 8, page 97, uses this language: 'It was thus in the action of *indebitatus assumpsit* that the larger part of our modern law of *quasi*-contract has originated.'

Authorities in support of the prevalent use of this form of action in the courts of the common law could be multiplied indefinitely, but we will close this branch of the discussion by a quotation from Professor Ames in volume 2 of the Harvard Law Review, page 69: 'The main outlines of the history of *assumpsit* have now been indicated. In its origin an action of tort, it was soon transformed into an action of contract, becoming afterwards a remedy where there was neither tort nor contract. Based at first only upon an express promise, it was afterwards supported upon an implied promise, and even upon a fictitious promise. Introduced as a special manifestation of the action on the case, it soon acquired the dignity of a distinct form of action, which superseded Debt, became concurrent with Account, with Case upon a bailment, a warranty, and bills of exchange, and competed with Equity in the case of essentially equitable *quasi*-contracts growing out of the principle of unjust enrichment. Surely it would be hard to find a better illustration of the flexibility and power of self-development of the Common Law.' (Philpott v. Superior Court, 1 Cal.2d at 518 519, 520 521, 36 P.2d at 638.)

Although recognizing that a tortious act frequently formed the basis for invoking assumpsit, the court determined that "its contractual quality was always its most distinct feature." (*Philpott, supra* at 526, 536 P.2d at 642, quoting 7 Holdsworth, History of English Law, p. 441.)

In the instant case, the trial court found that Coca Cola's failure to return the cylinders was conversion. Nonetheless, the court ruled that Taylor had waived the tort after making its demand for return of the chattels and *elected to treat the transaction as a sale of the cylinders.* This ruling appears to comport with California law, which allows a bailor in Taylor's position to treat the conversion as a *fictional or implied by law* contract of sale. [Citations.] Generally, where there is a waiver of tort and suit in assumpsit, the statute of limitations relating to actions of assumpsit rather than tort applies, although the determination of what limitation period is appropriate may depend on the substance of the action and the nature of the right violated rather than the form of action. [Citation.]

As *Philpott* and other authorities suggest, the nature of rights inherent in the indebitatus assumpsit cause of action appear to be based in *contract* principles. This reasoning is further bolstered by the realization that Taylor had to waive *tort* remedies in order to avail itself of the assumpsit theory. It has been recognized that when a party entitled to enforce two remedies either institutes an action upon one of such remedies or performs any act in pursuit of such remedy, he will be held to have made an election of such remedy and will not be entitled to pursue any other remedy for the enforcement of his right. [Citations.] Given the binding nature of the election made by proceeding under indebitatus assumpsit, we are of the opinion that the trial court correctly found that the gravamen of Taylor's claims was contractual in nature.

After determining that the nature of the rights was based in contract, the trial court applied the four-year statute of limitations governing *sales* contracts in Commercial Code section 2725, subdivision (1). Because Taylor's assumpsit claim created a fictional sale, the novel question presented in this case is whether the limitations period in the Commercial Code applies to sales contracts *implied by operation of law.* If this section is inapposite to implied-in-law contracts, Taylor's claim would be barred under the more restrictive time period of Code of Civil Procedure section 339, subdivision 1.[4] * * *

In order to determine whether *fictional* sales contracts are governed by the four-year period, it is pertinent to construe the language contained in the Commercial Code's limitation statute.

Commercial Code section 2725 deals with "contract[s] for sale" and, in definitional cross-references at the end of the section, makes reference to Commercial Code section 2106. Commercial Code section 2106 defines "contract for sale" as including "both a present sale of goods and a contract to sell goods at a future time." In addition, the section defines "present sale" as "a sale which is accomplished by the making of the contract." Since "contract" is a key word in Commercial Code section 2106, illumination is provided by consulting Commercial Code section 1201, subdivision (11). This latter provision states that " 'Contract' means the total legal obligation which results from the parties' agreement ..." Further clarity is provided by Commercial Code section 1201, subdivision (3), which defines "Agreement" as "the bargain of the parties in fact as found in their language or by implication from other circumstances including course of dealing or usage of trade or course of performance as provided in this code...."

Focusing upon Commercial Code section 1201, subdivision (3), it is important to note that the drafters of the Commercial Code defined agreement to mean *"the bargain of the parties ... by implication from other circumstances including...."* The deliberate insertion of the word "including" denotes that the drafters contemplated agreements which could be implied other than in fact. This is further supported by Commercial Code section 1102, which states that the code should be liberally construed. (Comm.Code, 1102.) Given the fact that indebitatus assumpsit is a well-established contractual theory, there is ample reason for allowing

---

4. Code of Civil Procedure section 339, subdivision 1, provides:

"[The periods prescribed for the commencement of actions other than for the recovery of real property, as follows:]

"Within two years: 1. An action upon a contract, obligation or liability not founded upon an instrument of writing, ..."

Taylor to employ the limitations period for sales contracts contained in Commercial Code section 2725.

* * *

We therefore find that the trial court did not commit error in determining that the four-year limitation period of Commercial Code section 2725 applied to Taylor's claim. Taylor was not barred from pursuing Coca Cola through the assumpsit cause of action.

* * * [Affirmed.]

1.   Some courts have refused to allow a waiver of tort and suit in assumpsit unless the defendant made a resale of the plaintiff's goods. This rule is identified with an old Massachusetts case, *Jones v. Hoar*, 22 Mass. 285 (1827), where the court refused to reconsider the resale requirement. Although this old rule is not followed in most jurisdictions today, some still adhere to it. *See* Janiszewski v. Behrmann, 345 Mich. 8, 75 N.W.2d 77 (1956).

2.   The advantage of a quasi-contract theory based upon the old writ of money had and received is that the plaintiff could recover the defendant's profits if the resale of plaintiff's goods was for a price greater than their fair market value. The legal fiction is that the defendant acts as the agent of the plaintiff during the resale.

When no resale occurs, the quasi-contract recovery is based upon the old writ of goods sold and delivered. The legal fiction is that the defendant personally purchased the goods from the plaintiff at the price of their fair market value. The measure of recovery under this theory is the same as the measure of damages for the tort of conversion which the plaintiff waives in favor of the recovery in quasi-contract. In such cases there is no advantage to the quasi-contract theory in terms of the amount of money recovered, but there is the advantage of the longer statute of limitations for contract than for tort.

3.   The position that no resale of the plaintiff's goods is necessary in order to waive the tort and sue in assumpsit derives from an old North Dakota case, *Braithwaite v. Aiken*, 3 N.D. 365, 56 N.W. 133 (1893). The court observed: "It is beneath the dignity of any tribunal to draw a distinction between the receipt of benefits in the shape of cash and the receipt of benefits in the form of property."

Is the *Braithwaite* position persuasive? If the defendant's resale of the plaintiff's goods takes the form of an exchange of the goods for property of value rather than an exchange of the goods for money, the court's position makes perfect sense. Is it equally sensible that restitution is needed to disgorge the benefit held by the defendant if there is no resale? The remedy of damages for conversion is available unless the statute of limitations has run. Should the legislative scheme of limitation be altered by legal fiction?

If California had taken the *Jones v. Hoar* position and required a resale, what would have been the result in the principal case?

4. On the limitations question, *see also* FDIC v. Bank One, Waukesha, 881 F.2d 390 (7th Cir. 1989) (limitations period for unjust enrichment should track the wrong; bringing claim as unjust enrichment rather than fraud justifies contract statute of limitations).

Felder v. Reeth

34 F.2d 744 (9th Cir.1929).

■ WILBUR, CIRCUIT JUDGE.

Appellants brought an action in the District Court for the territory of Alaska to recover $5,402.65 for goods, wares, and merchandise sold to the appellee and for appellee's checks cashed by appellant. The appellee admitted the obligations sued upon, and by second amended answer and counterclaim alleged that he was engaged in placer mining upon 1,200 acres of placer mining ground, and that to carry on said mining operations he purchased a certain hydraulic mining plant in San Francisco, and transported the same to a point 40 miles below his placer mining camp, for the reason that because of low water in the stream he could not transport the machinery to the mining camp; that it remained at that point during the seasons of 1919, 1920, and 1921 by reason of low water in the river; that the freight charge for transportation of this plant from San Francisco was $1,045; that during the summer of 1921 the appellants wrongfully took possession of the hydraulic plant, transported the same down the river to Bethel, and converted same to their own use and sold a part thereof. It is further alleged:

"That under the conditions then existing at said Golden Gate Falls and 'Supply Camp' the said mining machinery and equipment was reasonably worth to defendant and were of the value to him of $10,000.00."

"That defendant elects to waive the tort involved in the said unlawful taking and conversion of said property and to rely upon an implied contract upon the part of the plaintiffs, created by the law, to pay him the said sum of $10,000.00 for said machinery and equipment, the same being the reasonable value therefor by the time it reached the 'Supply Camp'; that the said plaintiffs, by reason of the premises, impliedly agreed, and in law did agree, to pay him the said sum of $10,000.00 for the said machinery and equipment."

Under the Alaska Code, a counterclaim to an action arising out of contract must be either one arising out of the transaction sued upon by the plaintiff, or, "In an action arising on contract, any other cause of action arising also on contract, and existing at the commencement of the action." Comp.Laws Alaska 1913, 896.

The purpose of the form of pleading adopted by the appellee waiving, or attempting to waive, the tort, and suing upon the implied obligation of the appellant, was to bring his counterclaim within the purview of the statute, authorizing the setting up of a counterclaim.

* * * Appellants admitted taking the property, and alleged that it was taken to avoid a total loss thereof by flood waters of the Riglugalic River, on whose banks it had been placed. Appellants alleged that the property was in an abandoned condition until the fall of 1921; that they took possession of the property, and transported it to Bethel, and notified the defendant; that appellee ignored the entire matter; that they retained possession of the hydraulic plant until 1923, when for the first time they had an opportunity to dispose of the same; and that they sold it for the sum of $550, and that that sum was all the property was worth in Kuskokwin Precinct.

* * * The court found that the appellee was indebted to the appellant in the sum of $8,690.21, and that the appellants were indebted to the appellees in the sum of $8,000, with 8 per cent interest from September 1, 1921, aggregating $12,480, and rendered judgment in favor of appellees for the difference, $3,789.79. With reference to the value of the hydraulic plant, the court found:

"That under the circumstances and conditions as they existed at that time and by reason of the fact that there was no market value for said machinery at that time and place, and by reason of the use that the defendant could have put it to, the said machinery was worth to him the sum of $8,000". * * *

There seems to be no doubt that appellees can assert their claim against the appellants in this action by a counterclaim in the event and because of the fact that they waived the tortious conversion and counted in assumpsit as for goods sold and delivered. [Citation.]

The most serious question in this case is the measure of damages for breach of the implied contract sued upon. At common law, under the older rule, the result of waiving the tort in a case of conversion and sale was a right to recover the amount received upon the sale, as for money had and received, but later cases hold that the action can be maintained as for goods sold and delivered without awaiting sale, or even after sale, and the measure of recovery is the market value of the property. [Citations.] In a case where the owner waives the tort if he accepts the tort-feasor as his agent both in the taking and in the sale, he would necessarily be limited in his recovery to the money received by the agent. There seems, however, to be no good reason why the owner cannot waive the tortious taking and ignore the subsequent sale and recover the reasonable value of the property taken as for goods sold and delivered. [Citations.] This was done by the appellee, who ignored the sale of his property made by the appellants, and sought to recover as upon an implied agreement to pay the value of the hydraulic plant. The complaint, construed more strongly against the pleader, does not allege the market value or reasonable value of the property taken by the appellants. The allegation is of the reasonable value "to him." This allegation is evidently based upon the case of *Swank v. Elwert,* 55 Or. 487, 105 P. 901, 902, par. 11, where it is said (page 906):

The general rule for the measure of damages for the destruction or conversion of personalty is the market value of the property at the time and place of the conversion, if it has such value. [Citations.] But if the property has no market value at the time and place of conversion, either because of its limited production, or because it is of such a nature that there can be no general demand for it, and it is more particularly valuable to the owner than any one else, then it may be estimated with reference to its value to him. [Citation.]

* * * Assuming that this is a proper measure of damages in a suit for conversion under the peculiar circumstances found by the court, it does not follow that the appellee is entitled to recover that amount upon his counterclaim in which he waived the tort. * * *

* * * In view of the fact that this case must be tried again, it should be stated that, as the appellee by his counterclaim seeks to recover the value of the property as upon an implied sale, he should be permitted to amend his counterclaim and allege that value.

If the wrong-doer has not sold the property, but still retains it, the plaintiff has the right to waive the tort, and proceed upon an implied contract of sale to the wrong-doer himself, and in such event he is not charged as for money had and received by him to the use of the plaintiff. The contract implied is one to pay the value of the property as if it had been sold to the wrong-doer by the owner. If the transaction is thus held by the plaintiff as a sale, of course the title to the property passes to the wrong-doer, when the plaintiff elects to so treat it. [Citations.]

If on the trial it appears that there is no market at the point of conversion or implied sale, as from the findings appears to be the case, the value must be determined at the nearest market less the costs of transportation thereto, [citation] for in case of a waiver of a tort in conversion the action ex contractu is sustained rather on the theory of benefit derived by the taker than of damage to the owner. [Citations.] * * *

Judgment reversed.

---

1. The miner in the principal case would have the best recovery under a conversion theory rather than under a quasi-contract theory. The reason that the contract theory was advanced instead of the tort one was procedural; under the old Field Code that governed the case the plaintiff could counterclaim only for the same type of claim. Thus, a contract counterclaim was permissible on a contract claim, but a counterclaim in tort was impermissible.

On remand in *Felder v. Reeth*, 62 F.2d 730 (9th Cir.1933), the miner tried to change his counterclaim to one for conversion. The court struck it as procedurally improper and dismissed it without prejudice to maintain a separate action. These difficulties do not trouble modern litigants under procedural rules based upon the Federal Rules of Civil Procedure.

2. The Restatement of Restitution and Unjust Enrichment (Third) provides:

§ 40.   Trespass, Conversion, And Comparable Wrongs

A person who obtains a benefit by an act of trespass or conversion, by comparable interference with other protected interests in tangible property, or in consequence of such an act by another, is liable in restitution to the victim of the wrong.

3. The waiver of tort and suit in quasi-contract theory does not apply to all torts. Conversion is the universally accepted tort that may be waived for these purposes. Trespass to chattel also has been waived successfully, as illustrated by the case of *Olwell v. Nye & Nissen, infra.*

The traditional rule allows no quasi-contract recovery for the wrongful use and occupation of land. The case most closely associated with this rule is *Phillips v. Homfray*, 24 Ch.D. 439 (1883), where no recovery was allowed for the use of a passageway on the plaintiff's land in order to remove coal. Recovery was allowed only for the value of the coal that was improperly taken. The plaintiff argued that the defendant had been saved expense and inconvenience by using the passageway for the operation, but the court held that this use of land did not deprive the plaintiff of anything nor did it enrich the defendant. Although a trespass action might ordinarily be maintained, the defendant in the case had died and the issue was which of the claims would survive against the estate. The court held that the defendant's estate was liable in quasi-contract only for the coal wrongfully taken because the estate had been enriched by the wrong.

A 1946 Virginia Supreme Court case, *Raven Red Ash Coal Co. v. Ball*, 185 Va. 534, 39 S.E.2d 231 (1946), rejected the rule that a quasi-contract cannot be used for the use and occupation of land. In this case, the defendant abused an easement for the removal of coal on the other side of the property. The court noted:

Where a naked trespass is committed, whether upon the person or property, assumpsit will not lie. If one commits an assault and battery upon another, it is absurd to imply a promise by the defendant to pay the victim a reasonable compensation. There is no basis for an implication of a contract where cattle inadvertently invade a neighbor's premises and trample down and destroy his crops. In each instance, a wrong and nothing more and nothing less has been committed. On the other hand, if a trespasser invades the premises of his neighbor, cuts and removes timber or severs minerals from the land and converts them to his own use, the owner may waive the tort and sue in assumpsit for the value of the materials converted. * * *

* * * To hold that a trespasser who benefits himself by cutting and removing trees from another's land is liable on an implied contract, and that another trespasser who benefits himself by the illegal use of another's land is not liable on an implied contract is illogical. The only distinction is that in one case the benefit he

received is the diminution in the other's property. In the other case, he still receives the benefit but does not thereby diminish the value of the owner's property. In both cases, he has received substantial benefit by his own wrong. As the gist of the action is to prevent the unjust enrichment of a wrongdoer from the illegal use of another's property, such wrongdoer should be held on an implied promise in both cases. 185 Va. at 542.

See also Edwards v. Lee's Adm'r, 265 Ky. 418, 96 S.W.2d 1028 (1936) (equitable accounting for profits derived from commercial exploitation of the Great Onyx Cave which extended partly under the plaintiff's property but to which the plaintiff had no access).

4. Recovery in quasi-contract was not allowed when the plaintiff wished to waive the tort of defamation in the 1949 New York case of *Hart v. E.P. Dutton & Co.,* 197 Misc. 274, 93 N.Y.S.2d 871 (1949). The statute of limitations barred the defamation claim against the publisher of a book about war spies. The plaintiff attempted to recover on the theory that profits from the book enriched the defendant at the expense of the plaintiff. The court observed:

> One who publishes a libel, especially if done maliciously, as charged in this complaint, is guilty of conduct which makes him liable for damages. An action for damages affords the plaintiff full compensation for any injuries which he has suffered. In addition to compensatory damages he may recover punitive damages if proper foundation is established by the proof. The law requires that a plaintiff must bring his action to recover such damages within one year. It would seem that it is not equitable and just to permit a person, who has been the subject of a libellous article published in a book, to acquiesce in or permit the sale and distribution of such book to continue for a period of nearly six years without taking any steps whatsoever to protest or stop the sale and distribution of the book and then to maintain an action for the profits derived from the sale and distribution of the book. 197 Misc. at 281.

PROBLEM: THE STOLEN MODEL ENGINE

Dalton owns a hobby shop that sells many items, including model railroad equipment for both child and adult enthusiasts. Tomkins is an adult hobbyist who belongs to a model railroad club.

Dalton has a display containing a few expensive brass engines. Tomkins purchased a small scale brass engine at a price of several hundred dollars in preparation for an upcoming public show sponsored by his club. Dalton had held that engine in inventory for several years. He acquired it when the limited production was made, and he priced it at his cost plus his standard mark-up. He had never reconsidered the price nor paid any attention to this engine as it sat in his display until Tomkins bought it.

The engine had appreciated in value considerably during the years it sat in Dalton's display. The production was limited and the item had become popular nationally among hobbyists. It often commanded a price double what Dalton had charged Tomkins.

Shortly after selling the engine to Tomkins, Dalton received a letter inquiring if he had such an engine in his inventory and, if so, offering to buy it at a price triple what Dalton had charged Tomkins. The letter explained that this model had sentimental value for the writer, who was seeking to replace one that had been stolen. Therefore, the offer was for an exceptionally high price.

Dalton, who was facing high bills at home from the recent hospitalization of a child, was eager for the extra cash. He attended the public show sponsored by Tomkin's club and he put the engine in his pocket at an opportune moment. He promptly sent it to the letter writer in exchange for the triple price offered.

The theft was not discovered until several days later, after the show was over. With the assistance of some friends who had noticed Dalton's strange behavior at the show, Tomkins successfully traced the theft to Dalton. Dalton now admits all these facts. What remedies does Tomkins have against Dalton?

Olwell v. Nye & Nissen Co.

26 Wash.2d 282, 173 P.2d 652 (1946).

■ MALLERY, JUSTICE.

On May 6, 1940, plaintiff, E.L. Olwell, sold and transferred to the defendant corporation his one-half interest in Puget Sound Egg Packers, a Washington corporation having its principal place of business in Tacoma. By the terms of the agreement, the plaintiff was to retain full ownership in an "Eggsact" egg-washing machine, formerly used by Puget Sound Egg Packers. The defendant promised to make it available for delivery to the plaintiff on or before June 15, 1940. It appears that the plaintiff arranged for and had the machine stored in a space adjacent to the premises occupied by the defendant but not covered by its lease. Due to the scarcity of labor immediately after the outbreak of the war, defendant's treasurer, without the knowledge or consent of the plaintiff, ordered the egg washer taken out of storage. The machine was put into operation by defendant on May 31, 1941, and thereafter, for a period of three years, was used approximately one day a week in the regular course of the defendant's business. Plaintiff first discovered this use in January or February of 1945, when he happened to be at the plant on business and heard the machine operating. Thereupon, plaintiff offered to sell the machine to defendant for $600 or half of its original cost in 1929. A counteroffer of $50 was refused, and, approximately one month later, this action was commenced to recover the reasonable value of defendant's use of the machine, and praying for $25 per month from the commencement of the unauthorized use until the time of trial. * * * The court entered judgment for plaintiff in the amount of $10 per week for the period of 156 weeks covered by the statute of limitations, or $1,560, and gave the plaintiff his costs.

Defendant has appealed to this court, assigning error upon the judgment, upon the trial of the cause on the theory of unjust enrichment, upon the amount of damages, and upon the court's refusal to make a finding as to the value of the machine, and in refusing to consider such value in measuring damages.

The theory of the respondent was that the tort of conversion could be "waived" and suit brought in quasi-contract, upon a contract implied in law, to recover, as restitution, the profits which inured to appellant as a result of its wrongful use of the machine. With this the trial court agreed and, in its findings of facts, found that the use of the machine "resulted in a benefit to the users, in that said use saves the users approximately $1.43 per hour of use as against the expense which would be incurred were eggs to be washed by hand; that said machine was used by Puget Sound Egg Packers and defendant, on an average of one day per week from May of 1941, until February of 1945 at an average saving of $10.00 per each day of use."

In substance, the argument presented by the assignments of error is that the principle of unjust enrichment, or quasi-contract, is not of universal application but is imposed only in exceptional cases because of special facts and circumstances and in favor of particular persons; that respondent had an adequate remedy in an action at law for replevin or claim and delivery; that any damages awarded to the plaintiff should be based upon the use or rental value of the machine and should bear some reasonable relation to its market value. Appellant therefore contends that the amount of the judgment is excessive.

It is uniformly held that in cases where the defendant *tortfeasor* has benefited by his wrong, the plaintiff may elect to "waive the tort" and bring an action in assumpsit for restitution. Such an action arises out of a duty imposed by law devolving upon the defendant to repay an unjust and unmerited enrichment. [Citations.]

It is clear that the saving in labor cost which appellant derived from its use of respondent's machine constituted a benefit.

According to the Restatement of Restitution 1(b), p. 12,

A person confers a benefit upon another if he gives to the other possession of or some other interest in money, land, chattels, or choses in action, performs services beneficial to or at the request of the other, satisfies a debt or a duty of the other, or in any way adds to the other's security or advantage. *He confers a benefit not only where he adds to the property of another, but also where he saves the other from expense or loss.* The word "benefit," therefore, denotes any form of advantage. (Italics ours)

It is also necessary to show that, while appellant benefitted from its use of the egg-washing machine, respondent thereby incurred a loss. It is argued by appellant that, since the machine was put into storage by respondent, who had no present use for it, and for a period of almost three years did not know that appellant was operating it and since it was not injured by its operation and the appellant never adversely claimed any title to it, nor contested respondent's right of repossession upon the latter's discovery of the wrongful operation, that the respondent was not damaged, because he is as well off as if the machine had not been used by appellant.

The very essence of the nature of property is the right to its exclusive use. Without it, no beneficial right remains. However plausible, the appellant cannot be heard to say that its wrongful invasion of the respondent's property right to exclusive use is not a loss compensable in law. To hold otherwise would be subversive of all property rights, since its use was admittedly wrongful and without claim of right. The theory of unjust enrichment is applicable in such a case.

We agree with appellant that respondent could have elected a "common garden variety of action," as he calls it, for the recovery of damages. It is also true that except where provided for by statute, punitive damages are not allowed, the basic measure for the recovery of damages in this state being compensation. If, then, respondent had been *limited* to redress *in tort* for damages, as appellant contends, the court below would be in error in refusing to make a finding as to the value of the machine. In such case the award of damages must bear a reasonable relation to the value of the property. [Citation.]

But respondent here had an election. He chose rather to waive his right of action *in tort* and to sue *in assumpsit* on the implied contract. Having so elected, he is entitled to the measure of restoration which accompanies the remedy.

Actions for restitution have for their primary purpose taking from the defendant and restoring to the plaintiff something to which the plaintiff is entitled, or if this is not done, causing the defendant to pay the plaintiff an amount which will restore the plaintiff to the position in which he was before the defendant received the benefit. If the value of what was received and what was lost were always equal, there would be no substantial problem as to the amount of recovery, since actions of restitution are not punitive. In fact, however, the plaintiff frequently has lost more than the defendant has gained, and sometimes the defendant has gained more than the plaintiff has lost.

In such cases the measure of restitution is determined with reference to the tortiousness of the defendant's conduct or the negligence or other fault of one or both of the parties in creating the situation giving rise to the right to restitution. If the defendant was tortious in his acquisition of the benefit he is required to pay for what the other has lost although that is more than the recipient benefited. *If he was consciously tortious in acquiring the benefit, he is also deprived of any profit derived from his subsequent dealing with it.* If he was no more at fault than the claimant, he is not required to pay for losses in excess of benefit received by him and he is permitted to retain gains which result from his dealing with the property. (Italics ours) Restatement of Restitution, pp. 595, 596.

Respondent may recover the profit derived by the appellant from the use of the machine.

Respondent has prayed "on his first cause of action for the sum of $25.00 per month from the time defendant first commenced to use said machine subsequent to May 1940 (1941) until present time."

In computing judgment, the court below computed recovery on the basis of $10 per week. This makes the judgment excessive, since it cannot exceed the amount prayed for.

* * *

We therefore direct the trial court to reduce the judgment, based upon the prayer of the complaint, to $25 per month for thirty-six months, or $900.

The judgment as modified is affirmed. Appellant will recover its costs.

D.   CONSTRUCTIVE TRUST

Section Coverage:

A constructive trust is a flexible restitutionary device that imposes an equitable duty on a defendant to convey property acquired under certain circumstances to the rightful owner. Those circumstances may include acquisition of title to property by fraud, various other wrongdoings, and mistake. Since the remedy of constructive trust is equitable in nature, the court must inquire into the adequacy of available legal remedies to provide redress for the claimant's injury.

The "trust" designation is merely a fictional relationship created by operation of law on the grounds that the constructive trustee would be unjustly enriched if allowed to retain the property. See Restatement (Third) of Restitution and Unjust Enrichment § 55. Justice Cardozo once colorfully described a constructive trust as "the remedial device through which preference of self is made subordinate to loyalty to others." Meinhard v. Salmon, 249 N.Y. 458, 164 N.E. 545 (1928).

Although early developments in England and in certain jurisdictions in the United States drew upon traditional doctrines of trust law with respect to constructive trusts, the remedy today bears little relationship to express trusts, which are created by the intention of the parties. See generally Powell, "Cardozo's Foot": The Chancellor's Conscience and Constructive Trusts, 56 Law & Contemp. Problems 7 (1993). The only similarity between them is that the trustee holds title to property subject to an equitable duty to hold it for or convey it to the holder of the beneficial interest. Their difference lies in the designation and relationship of the trustee. The trustee for an express trust is appointed pursuant to the intent of the parties and acts in a fiduciary role. The constructive trustee is designated by the court in order to recover the enrichment held by the wrongdoer.

A constructive trust must be distinguished from a resulting trust which may be implied from the facts surrounding a transfer of property. When a transferor of property does not intend the transferee to hold a beneficial interest in the property, the recipient may hold it in trust for the proper beneficiary even in the absence of an express trust. In contrast, a constructive trust is created without reference to the intention of the parties; it is created to meet the goal of preventing unjust enrichment.

Model Case:

A lawyer, Leslie Roberts, held an account on behalf of a client named Carter. One day Roberts hears a "hot tip" on a stock and wishes to purchase some immediately. Lacking any personal funds that were readily available for the transaction, Roberts embezzled $10,000 from the account with the intent of restoring the funds before Carter needed them. The embezzled money was used to purchase stock in Highflyer Corp., which increased in price to a current market value of $14,000. As a result of other poor investments, however, Roberts is now insolvent and the embezzlement is discovered before it could be covered up.

The court would impose a constructive trust on the stock for the benefit of Carter on the grounds that Roberts had abused the fiduciary relationship. Assuming that Carter could trace the misappropriated funds to the stock, a court would require Roberts to disgorge the profits made on the stock purchase in order to prevent unjust enrichment.

Roberts' insolvency affects the case in two ways. First, it makes a damages remedy at law inadequate, although the inadequacy rule has little force in restitution. Second, it means that Carter will have priority over Roberts' other creditors and will receive more than the loss to the account because the good asset is traceable to Carter's funds.

County of Cook v. Barrett

36 Ill.App.3d 623, 344 N.E.2d 540 (1975).

■ DEMPSEY, JUSTICE.

This is an appeal from the dismissal of the plaintiff's amended complaint for failure to state a cause of action.

The County of Cook filed a complaint and an amended complaint in chancery against former County Clerk, Edward J. Barrett, seeking the declaration of a constructive trust and an accounting for bribes allegedly received by him while he held office. * * *

The amended complaint was composed of three counts. The County represented that Barrett served as the elected Clerk of Cook County from 1956 through 1970, a position of trust imposing obligations to faithfully perform the duties of office in the interest of the people of Cook County and not for the incumbent's personal gain. His salary for the position was fixed by law and was to be his "only compensation for services rendered in the capacity of county clerk, or any other capacity." Ill.Rev.Stat., 1969, ch. 53, par. 49. Throughout the period of Barrett's tenure, the County Board of Commissioners at various times purchased and rented voting machines for use in elections. The board acted on the basis of contracts and proposals submitted and recommended by Barrett. By virtue of his office and influence with the board, his recommendations were "tantamount to the acceptance" of the proposals tendered by him. During this same time, he was also charged with the responsibility to care for voting machines in County custody which included the discretion to award contracts of insurance on the machines.

Count I charged that Barrett abused his position of trust by employing it to seek secret personal gains from the Shoup Voting Machine Corporation, in that he caused Shoup "... to secretly pay him money that constituted fees and/or allowances and/or bribes," as a consequence of which the County paid considerably more money for the voting machines purchased and rented from Shoup than it would have otherwise. It was alleged that these payments from Shoup to Barrett amounted to approximately $180,000 for the years 1967–1970 but were unknown for previous years and a detailed accounting was needed to determine the exact figure for the entire period covered by the complaint. The plaintiff prayed that Barrett be declared a constructive trustee for the citizens and taxpayers of the County for the amounts received by him from Shoup, and that he be required to account to the County for those sums.

* * *

Both in that motion [to dismiss] and in his brief on appeal, Barrett has suggested numerous reasons why the County cannot recover from him. He contends that the County is entitled only to fees and allowances which are legally collected, that to allow recovery by a public body of bribes or kickbacks paid to its officers would be against public policy; that the County alleged no damage and suffered none, that no money moved from the County to him, that if any money was paid it was paid by Shoup and Gallagher not by the County, and that since no money moved out of the County treasury it could not have been depleted; that the complaint did not allege that he had been unjustly enriched at the expense of the County or that in the absence of bribery the County would have paid less for voting machines or insurance. Attacking the equitable jurisdiction generally, he suggests that the facts alleged in the amended complaint did not warrant the grant of equitable relief and that there was an adequate remedy at law. Attacking the constructive trust doctrine specifically he contends that its application to one in his position would be unwarranted and unprecedented. * * *

A constructive trust arises not by any agreement or understanding of the parties but by operation of law and is imposed upon grounds of public policy, to prevent a person from holding for his own benefit that which he has gained by reason of a special trust or confidence reposed in him by an innocent party. Stated most succinctly, the purpose of the remedy is to prevent unjust enrichment.

The particular circumstances in which equity will impress a constructive trust are "... as numberless as the modes by which property may be obtained through bad faith and unconscientious acts." 4 Pomeroy's Equity Jurisprudence (5th Ed.) sec. 1045, p. 97. The barriers to its effective operation are few. The form of the property claim determines nothing, since a constructive trust will extend to reach real and personal property, choses in action and funds of money. To make out a case a plaintiff must allege facts which disclose either actual or constructive fraud or an abuse of a confidential relationship. It is the latter situation with which this case is concerned.

At all times and for all the transactions pertinent to the complaint Barrett was the fiduciary of the people of Cook County. As an elected public official he held a position of the highest public trust. In the transactions with Shoup and Gallagher, Barrett acted as the County's agent, negotiating terms of purchase and recommending County action. An agent is fiduciary to his principal and the relation is treated generally the same, and with virtually the same strictness, as that of trustee and beneficiary.

In deciding this appeal, it is not necessary to locate the perimeters of the fiduciary obligations due the public from their elected officials. It is sufficient to recognize that, when such an official acts as agent for the public body in business transactions, he owes to his principal duties of loyalty and good faith at least equal to those required of a private fiduciary in like circumstances. The obligations of a person who occupies the latter category are such that he must not place himself in a position which is adverse to that of his principal during the continuance of the agency.

... [A]n agent should not unite his personal and his representative characters in the same transaction; and equity will not permit him to be exposed to the temptation, or brought into a situation where his own personal interests conflict with the interests of his principal and with the duties which he owes to his principal. 3 Pomeroy's Equity Jurisprudence (5th Ed.) sec. 959, p. 819.

The remedy for breach of this duty is simple and salutary. Since a fiduciary is bound to act solely for the benefit of his principal, equity will intervene to prevent him from accruing any advantage however innocently from transactions conducted in behalf of the principal. So, when a fiduciary, who has acted for his beneficiary or principal, receives a gift, or bonus or commission from a party with whom he has transacted business, that benefit may be recovered from him by the beneficiary of the fiduciary relationship. In Janes v. First Fed. Sav. & Loan Ass'n [57 Ill.2d 398, 312 N.E.2d 605 (1974)], it was alleged that the defendant lending bank procured title insurance for its borrower on mortgaged property and charged the borrower the full price of that insurance, but subsequently received and retained a ten per cent rebate from the title insurance company. The reviewing court ruled that under such facts the bank held the rebate upon a constructive trust from the borrower as beneficiary in the absence of the borrower's express contrary authorization. * * *

In related contentions contained in both his pleadings and brief, Barrett assails the County's complaint for its failure to allege damage. He states that the averments that the County paid excess sums because of his misfeasance are speculative and that there was no averment that he was unjustly enriched at the County's expense. The absence of an allegation of damage is immaterial. A constructive trust is not an action for "recovery" or compensation under any theory of contract or tort. It is a strict equitable doctrine applied to cure a fiduciary's breach of his duty of loyalty by erasing the source of his conflict of interest, and transferring it to the innocent beneficiary. Bad faith is not an essential element of disloyalty and good faith is no defense to the charge. Courts are not interested in a fiduciary's particular motive for accepting a payment or gift, but rather with the general effect of such payments or gifts. Nor are courts concerned with the question of actual damage to the beneficiary. * * *

The defendant argues that since the County seeks only a money judgment and the accounts are not complicated and discovery is unnecessary, it would be improper for chancery to exercise jurisdiction over this controversy and thus deprive him of his constitutional right to a jury trial. This argument minimizes the underlying reason for equity jurisdiction the trust aspect of the controversy.

The County seeks, first and foremost, a declaration of the people's beneficial interest in and the right to possess the secret profits accrued by Barrett in breach of his fiduciary duty of loyalty. The recognition, execution and control of a trust or equitable interest is a matter exclusively within the jurisdiction of equity. As Barrett himself has argued, the County had no claim at law on money which came to him from third persons as bribes. Nor can Shoup and Gallagher claim these funds. The very conception of an equitable interest requires the simultaneous existence of two estates or ownerships in the same subject matter, the one legal, vested in one person, and recognized by a court of law, the second equitable, in another person, and recognized by a court of equity. Under the circumstances alleged in this case, only equity, applying this doctrine of the divisibility of legal and beneficial ownership, is capable of doing substantial justice between the parties.

When chancery exercises its exclusive jurisdiction to declare the County's equitable interest, it must then afford, as an incident, the complete remedy obtainable through an accounting. Where equity has jurisdiction for the purpose of granting equitable relief, the court may determine all issues of the case, whether legal or equitable. * * *

Reversed and remanded.

■ McGLOON, PRESIDING JUSTICE (specially concurring):

I concur with the decision of the court to reverse the order of the Circuit Court of Cook County and remand the cause, but would make the following observations.

The majority believes that defendant may be proven to have been a fiduciary of the people of Cook County from the allegations in the complaint that he was an elected public official and the County's agent in its dealings with Shoup and Gallagher. The fact that defendant may have been an elected official is, in my opinion, not crucial to our decision. The determinative factor is whether the particular facts alleged in the complaint could be proven to show that defendant was a fiduciary.

A fiduciary relationship may be created in many ways; an agency is but one relationship which creates fiduciary duties. The usual test for determining the existence of a fiduciary relationship is whether "confidence is reposed on one side and there is a resulting superiority and influence on the other side. It is not sufficient that confidence be reposed by one party, but the confidence must be actually accepted by the other party in order to constitute a fiduciary relationship." Whether such a relationship exists between the parties depends upon all the facts and circumstances of a particular case. * * *

In my opinion, the complaint contains allegations which may be proven to show that the County Board reposed its confidence in Barrett with regard to the voting machines and insurance contracts, and that Barrett accepted the confidence, thus creating a fiduciary relationship. It would not matter whether Barrett were an elected public official, a public employee, or a private person who had the confidence of the County Board in these matters. The relationship which if abused gives rise to an action for the declaration of a constructive trust involves a confidence reposed and accepted, as herein alleged. At trial upon remand, plaintiff would have to prove that Barrett had the confidence of the County Board, as opposed to being a person who merely made recommendations which may or may not have been followed as the Board saw fit.

The majority believes that every county official has a fiduciary relationship with the county, citing *People v. Bordeaux*, (1909) 242 Ill. 327, 89 N.E. 971. Such a conclusion is warranted, but with the caveat that the relationship exists only when the official performs his statutory duties. * * *

---

1. *Basis for Relief.* As recognized in the principal case, the substantive claims that may give rise to a constructive trust remedy are not limited to breach of fiduciary or confidential relationships. The circumstances which could support the conveyance of legal title to specific property to the rightful owner while avoiding unjust enrichment of the defendant are highly varied. Illustrations include acquisition of title to property by actual or constructive fraud, mistake, coercion, undue influence, duress, embezzlement, conversion, misuse or misappropriation of information, unconscionable conduct, infringement of copyright, and violation of duty imposed by confidential or fiduciary relationship. *See generally* 1 Dobbs, Law of Remedies § 4.3(2) (2d ed. 1993); 5 Scott, Law of Trusts § 462 (Fratcher 4th ed. 1989); 4 Pomeroy, Equity Jurisprudence §§ 1044–1058 (Symons 5th ed.

1941); Nelson v. Nelson, 288 Kan. 570, 205 P.3d 715, 729 (2009); Restatement (Third) of Restitution and Unjust Enrichment (2011) § 55 cmt. f.

2. *Priorities.* A primary advantage to the equitable remedy of a constructive trust over legal remedies, such as a money judgment, is that the rightful owner may compel conveyance of title to the subject property. Therefore, by obtaining specific enforcement of the trust, the beneficiary will effectively have a first priority position over other general unsecured creditors of the defendant. The equitable interest will prevail except against secured creditors who qualify as bona fide purchasers for value. *See* Restatement (Third) of Restitution and Unjust Enrichment § 55 cmt. D.

3. *Identification and Tracing.* A constructive trust requires the claimant to identify specific property which would form the res of the trust. *See* Burch & Cracchiolo, P.A. v. Pugliani, 144 Ariz. 281, 697 P.2d 674, 679 (1985) (General claim of damages will not give rise to a constructive trust); Baltimore & Ohio Railroad Co. v. Equitable Bank, 77 Md.App. 320, 550 A.2d 407, 412 (1988) (As a matter of law specific funds must be identified as traceable to the fraudulent or wrongful conduct to impose a constructive trust). Once property has been identified, the claimant may pursue specific restitution of the property directly from the holder or in the hands of a third party transferee who is not a bona fide purchaser.

Moreover, if the claimant-beneficiary can successfully trace the disposition or exchange of the titled property, the court may impose a constructive trust against the property's product in the hands of the defendant. The tracing requirement effects a type of compromise. It protects the equitable claimant by protecting their ability to reach and obtain title to specific property and to maintain rightful priority over unsecured creditors. On the other hand, the failure to trace title would preclude a constructive trust and prevent a claimant from choosing which assets they might prefer to satisfy liability. *See* Restatement (Third) of Restitution and Unjust Enrichment § 55 cmts. G, H.

4. *Measure of recovery.* Recovery in restitution may exceed the extent of a claimant's loss in some instances, such as a means to disgorge wrongful gains of a conscious wrongdoer. Restatement (Third) of Restitution and Unjust Enrichment (2011) § 55, cmt. I

Although a constructive trust may convey the appreciated value of the subject trust property, the principle is not absolute. In *Mattel, Inc. v. MGA Entertainment, Inc.*, 616 F.3d 904 (9th Cir. 2010) a company sought to impose a constructive trust on an extensive portfolio of intellectual property. The defendant misappropriated certain trademarked names while employed by the claimant and subsequently developed those ideas into entire product lines. Although the court agreed that certain aspects of the trademarks were proper subjects for a constructive trust, other products fell outside restitution and reasoned:

> In general, "[t]he beneficiary of the constructive trust is entitled to enhancement in value of the trust property." [Citation]. This is so "not because [the beneficiary] has a substantive right to [the

enhancement] but rather to prevent unjust enrichment of the wrongdoer-constructive trustee." Thus, a person who fraudulently acquired a house worth $100,000 in 2000 that appreciates to $200,000 by 2010 because of a strong real estate market can't complain when the rightful owner takes the benefit of the $100,000 increase. "[I]t is simple equity that a wrongdoer should disgorge his fraudulent enrichment." Janigan v. Taylor, 344 F.2d 781, 786 (1st Cir.1965).

This principle has the greatest force where the appreciation of the property is due to external factors rather than the efforts of the wrongful acquisitor. *Id*. at 787. "When the defendant profits from the wrong, it is necessary to identify the profits and to recapture them without capturing the fruits of the defendant's own labors or legitimate efforts." Dan B. Dobbs, *Dobbs Law of Remedies: Damages–Equity–Restitution* § 6.6(3) (2d ed. 1993). This is because "the aim of restitution has been to avoid taking the defendant's blood along with the pound of flesh." *Id*. § 6.6(3) n.4. A constructive trust is therefore "not appropriate to every case because it can overdo the job." *Id*. § 4.3(2).

When the value of the property held in trust increases significantly because of a defendant's efforts, a constructive trust that passes on the profit of the defendant's labor to the plaintiff usually goes too far. For example, "[i]f an artist acquired paints by fraud and used them in producing a valuable portrait we would not suggest that the defrauded party would be entitled to the portrait, or to the proceeds of its sale." [Citation.] 616 F.3d at 910–911.

5.   The prevailing view treats a constructive trust as a remedy, not an independent substantive cause of action. Tupper v. Roan, 349 Or. 211, 243 P.3d 50, 56 (2010); Zoeller v. East Chicago Second Century, Inc., 904 N.E.2d 213, 221 (Ind. 2009); Deutsche Bank National Trust Co. v. FDIC, 784 F.Supp.2d 1142, 1163 (C.D.Cal. 2011) (constructive trust is a remedy, not a freestanding substantive claim). The Restatement (Third) of Restitution and Unjust Enrichment explicitly recognizes this principle, providing: "Restitution . . . will sometimes yield a recovery where the claimant could not prove damages, but it does not create a cause of action where the claimant would otherwise have none." § 44, cmt. a; also see § 42, cmts. a & b. *But see* James Rogers, Restitution for Wrongs and the Restatement (Third) of the Law of Restitution and Unjust Enrichment, 42 Wake Forest L.Rev. 55 (2006) (arguing that the law of restitution does and should play an important substantive role, rather than being limited to remedial relief).

Stauffer v. Stauffer

465 Pa. 558, 351 A.2d 236 (1976).

■ Eagen, Justice.

On April 23, 1970, appellee Donald G. Stauffer joined with his wife, appellant Theresa E. Stauffer, in conveying to appellant alone for the stated consideration of one dollar the land and residence which both owned and had been occupying as tenants by the entireties. Subsequently, he brought this action in equity in the Court of Common Pleas of Chester County to compel a reconveyance. After a trial, the chancellor made his adjudication and entered a decree nisi in favor of Mr. Stauffer which granted the relief sought; on November 29, 1974, the court *en banc* dismissed the exceptions of Mrs. Stauffer and made the decree final. This direct appeal followed.

The record discloses that the parties were married on October 17, 1953, and that they became the owners of the land in question by means of a gift from Mrs. Stauffer's parents on August 3, 1956; their house was subsequently built and paid for primarily, if not entirely, out of the earnings of Mr. Stauffer. Toward the end of March, 1970, Mrs. Stauffer became suspicious that her husband had become involved with another woman, and on March 26 she consulted an attorney for advice about her domestic situation. Shortly thereafter, she confronted her husband with her suspicions, and he admitted to her not only that he had been engaged in an adulterous relationship, but that the "other woman" was Mrs. Stauffer's own sister, Victoria Gavin. Subsequently, Edward Gavin, the husband of Victoria, came to the Stauffer home, and in the presence of Mrs. Stauffer and Mr. Gavin, Mr. Stauffer wrote out a "confession" in which he detailed his involvement with Mrs. Gavin.

* * * [T]he chancellor concluded that appellant held what had been her husband's share in the property as constructive trustee for him because "the transfer of Plaintiff's interest in real property jointly held was fraudulently induced by threats and misrepresentations of the Defendant," and that "Plaintiff is entitled to a reconveyance of his interest in the real property." * * *

Although we have held that ordinarily, when a husband transfers property to his wife, a presumption arises that a gift was intended, such a presumption is, of course, rebuttable, and here the chancellor found that there was sufficient credible evidence to establish a constructive trust rather than a gift. The imposition of a constructive trust, unlike the finding of an express or a resulting trust, does not require that the parties specifically intended to create a trust; it is an equitable remedy designed to prevent unjust enrichment. There is thus no rigid standard for determining whether the facts of a particular case require a court of equity to impose a constructive trust; the test is whether or not unjust enrichment can thereby be avoided. This Court has repeatedly cited with approval the oft-quoted language of Justice (then Judge) Cardozo in Beatty v. Guggenheim Exploration Co., 225 N.Y. 380, 386, 122 N.E. 378, 380 81 (1919):

A constructive trust is the formula through which the conscience of equity finds expression. When property has been acquired in such circumstances that the holder of the legal title may not in good conscience retain the beneficial interest equity converts him into a trustee.... A court of equity in decreeing a constructive trust is bound by no unyielding formula. The equity of the transaction must shape the measure of relief.

Appellant strenuously argues that in this case no confidential relationship existed between the parties at the time of the transaction, and that therefore there can be no constructive trust; she cites Foster v. Schmitt, 429 Pa. 102, 107, 239 A.2d 471 (1968), for the proposition that a confidential relationship requires that the transferee occupy toward the transferor "such a position of advisor or counselor as reasonably to inspire confidence that he will act in good faith for the other's interest" and maintains that this was not the situation here. Appellant is mistaken, however, in assuming both that the chancellor found a confidential relationship in this case and that he needed to do so in order to impose a constructive trust.

The chancellor's determination was based not on the abuse of a confidential relationship, but on his conclusion that the transfer was "fraudulently induced by threats and misrepresentations of the Defendant." It is well-established that "[w]here the owner of property transfers it, being induced by fraud, duress or undue influence of the transferee, the transferee holds the property upon a constructive trust for the transferor," Restatement of Restitution 166 (1937), and that where the transfer is so induced, a constructive trust will be imposed without proof of a confidential relationship. Whether or not a confidential relationship exists in a given case is usually a question of fact to be determined by no inflexible rule but by a weighing of the particular factors present in that case. The mere finding of such a relationship does not in itself cause a constructive trust to be imposed; its effect is simply to impose a burden upon the party benefiting from the transaction of proving that he took no unfair advantage of his relationship with the other. By the same token, absent a finding of confidential relationship, the complaining party may still prove unjust enrichment.

But although the chancellor's conclusion in this case did not depend upon a finding of confidential relationship, we must still examine the actual relationship between the parties to determine whether or not the requisite unjust enrichment was present. In doing so, we must focus on the relationship between the parties at the time of the transaction in question. Therefore, although it is a pertinent factor, it is not necessarily a controlling one that the chancellor found "at all times during their marriage, the Plaintiff had made many important financial decisions, upon which the Defendant relied." Mr. Stauffer's decision to turn over to his wife, without meaningful consideration, his share of what the record indicates as by far his largest asset, was not an ordinary "important financial decision" and can only be interpreted in relation to the unique situation in which he found himself at that time. Furthermore, even if the relationship between the parties was not the sort in which our courts have traditionally found a confidential relationship sufficient to shift the burden of proof, we do not have to regard the transaction as merely an arm's-length one. Human relationships are frequently too complex to be classified simply as either "confidential" or "arm's-length," a relationship can have elements of confidentiality without being strictly a "confidential relationship," and less diligence is required of a plaintiff who relies to his detriment on the closeness of his relationship to the defendant than of one who deals on a genuinely arm's-length basis.

The record in this case indicates that when Mrs. Stauffer first became suspicious and later learned of her husband's adultery, her confidence in him was understandably severely undermined, and that her visits to a lawyer during this period were to obtain advice not only about the possibility of straightening out her marital difficulties, but also about securing her rights and those of her children in the event of a separation. We can also infer that she was particularly distressed that the woman her husband had become involved with was her own sister. Yet the chancellor, with sufficient basis in the record, found that up to the time of the conveyance the parties "continued to live together and carry on marital relations" and that at the time of the conveyance "the prevailing mood was that the Plaintiff and Defendant would continue to live together."

As for Mr. Stauffer, the record clearly suggests, whether or not he had formerly been the dominant party in the relationship, that after the discovery of his adultery he was not. His writing out a confession in the presence of his wife and Mr. Gavin suggests a sense of guilt, if not contrition. According to his testimony, his eventual decision to convey the property at his wife's urging came after she had repeatedly told him of her fears of the dire consequences of Mr. Gavin's purported lawsuit, and immediately after "a prolonged hysterical outburst" during which she first drove the family car so recklessly that he pulled the keys out of the ignition in fear and she later drove wildly away from her husband and her father after rejecting her husband's suggestion, agreed to by her father, that the property be conveyed not to her but to the children. He further testified that his only reason for yielding to his wife's urging about the property was the fear, induced by her, of the lawsuit, together with his impression that by agreeing to the transfer, he would "save the house for all of us, the family; not just for my wife and the children, for all of us as a family."

* * * Despite his own prior unfaithfulness, we cannot say that such faith was either implausible or unreasonable, given that his wife had always acted in good faith toward him in the past, he had confessed and terminated his adulterous affair, and according both to his testimony and the chancellor's finding the mood at the time of the conveyance was that husband and wife would continue to live together. * * * We cannot therefore find that the conveyance was an arm's-length transaction. * * *

It remains to be determined, nevertheless, whether or not the chancellor erred in his conclusion that Mrs. Stauffer took unfair advantage of Mr. Stauffer and fraudulently obtained his share of the property by means of threats and misrepresentations. * * * The chancellor based his ultimate conclusion of misrepresentation on the contract between the apparently ongoing marital relationship he found before the conveyance and the "total abatement" of the relationship on the part of Mrs. Stauffer that followed shortly after it:

Immediately after the transfer of April 23, 1970, the Defendant effected a total abatement of family atmosphere toward the Plaintiff in the household, ceased sexual relations with the Plaintiff and moved out of the bedroom. Admittedly, the Plaintiff and Defendant were in the midst of a domestic problem as evidenced by the confession of his adulterous relationship with the Defendant's sister, but this Court is swayed by the severe contrast in Defendant's behavior immediately after the transfer, the "hysterical outbursts" immediately prior to the transfer, and the constant conversation concerning the threat of a lawsuit by Mr. Gavin. These factors lead us to the belief that the Defendant sought to secure complete interest in the property for herself and the Chancellor is satisfied that the means employed to obtain such an interest amounted to such undue influence through misrepresentations and threats as to grant the Plaintiff a reconveyance of his interest in the real property.

It is clear that a fraudulent intention at the time of a transaction can be inferred from the totality of the circumstances surrounding the transaction, including subsequent conduct on the part of the defendant. We cannot, therefore, find that the evidence was insufficient to support the chancellor's conclusion in this case.

Appellant further contends that, regardless of whether the imposition of a constructive trust would ordinarily have been justified, appellee should have been barred from affirmative relief because, as a result both of his attempted fraudulent conveyance and of his adultery, he did not come into a court of equity with clean hands. The clean hands doctrine, however, does not require that a plaintiff be denied equitable relief merely because his conduct has been shown not to have been blameless. The bar of unclean hands is applicable in Pennsylvania only where the wrongdoing of the plaintiff directly affects the equitable relationship subsisting between the parties and is directly connected with the matter in controversy. [The court found that the chancellor had not abused his discretion in declining to apply the clean hands doctrine.]

As for Mr. Stauffer's adulterous relationship with Mrs. Gavin, it is clear that it directly affected the equitable relationship between the parties, but the question remains whether or not it was directly connected with the subject matter in controversy. Certainly there can be no doubt that the transaction in question would not have occurred had there been no adultery, and we therefore cannot say that it was merely collaterally or indirectly connected with it. Nevertheless, we cannot find on the facts of this case that the chancellor abused his discretion in declining to bar appellee from affirmative relief.

This Court has stated that "[e]quity will not stand aside a plaintiff whose rights have been transgressed and permit them to be appropriated because of previous bad conduct, and if the plaintiff offers reparation for what he has done, he may be granted relief, contingent upon repairing the injury he has inflicted." It may well be that the injury appellee has done to his wife and to his marriage is indeed irreparable, yet the record indicates that after the discovery of his adultery he has acted in good faith toward appellant. After confessing and terminating the adulterous relationship, he made the conveyance in question, according to appellant's own pleadings and testimony, for the purpose of securing his wife and children from the consequences of his prior conduct. The record also shows that after the conveyance he continued to make the mortgage payments due on the property. As for his wife, according to the chancellor's findings, after she learned of the adultery, she continued to live with him and maintain a marital relationship until the time of the transfer in issue. The chancellor here found that appellant fraudulently induced appellee to make the transfer after she learned of the adultery and while she continued to live with him as his wife. It would be inequitable to permit her to be unjustly enriched because of his previous adulterous conduct.

The decree is affirmed.

---

1. *Confidential and Fiduciary Relationships.* As discussed in the principal case, some courts have held that a constructive trust requires: (1) a confidential or fiduciary relation, (2) a promise, (3) a transfer of legal title to property in reliance on the promise, and (4) unjust enrichment of the transferee. *See, e.g.,* Sharp v. Kosmalski, 40 N.Y.2d 119, 351 N.E.2d 721, 386 N.Y.S.2d 72 (1976). Other courts have used the constructive trust in cases not involving a breach of fiduciary relations. In addition to the principal case, *see, e.g.,* American Nat'l Bank v. Federal Dep't Ins. Corp., 710 F.2d 1528 (11th Cir.1983).

Fiduciary relationships may be formal and informal, such as arising from moral, social, domestic or personal relationships. Smith v. Deneve, 285 S.W.3d 904, 911 (Tex. App. 2009). One court defined a confidential relationship as "any relationship of blood, business, friendship or association in which one of the parties reposes special trust and confidence in the other who is in a position to have an exercise influence over the first party". Estate of Draper v. Bank of America, 288 Kan. 510, 205 P.3d 698, 707 (2009).

2. Business dealings among family members may have the character of a confidential or fiduciary relationship and support imposition of a constructive trust if that trust is breached. In *Rawlings v. Rawlings*, 240 P.3d 754 (Utah 2010), a father deeded the family farm to his oldest child with the understanding that the property would continue to managed for the benefit of the entire family. The father subsequently died and over the course of many years, the siblings worked on the property and treated it as their "Mother's farm". When a dispute arose among the siblings, it was discovered that the son held legal title to the farm outright rather than in a family trust. The court found that the son stood in a confidential relationship to the family and ordered conveyance of title to the farm by constructive trust.

Similarly, in *Cassidy v. Cassidy*, 982 A.2d 326, 329 (Me. 2009), retired, ailing parents sold their family home and gave the proceeds to their son and spouse in exchange for a promise to occupy an apartment to be built on the son's property. The funds were transferred and the apartment was partially renovated when the son and spouse divorced. The court awarded the parents a constructive trust on a portion of the funds still held by the ex-daughter in law following the divorce decree, finding that an abuse of confidence and breach of the fiduciary relationship.

3.   The constructive trust is a useful device for effecting the transfer of property interests which would be unjust for the fictional trustee to retain. The remedy should not operate to deprive the defendant of property lawfully acquired. In *Ford v. Long,* 713 S.W.2d 798 (Tex.App.1986), for example, the husband killed his wife and was convicted of murder. The wife's will named her sister, Long, as the sole beneficiary of her estate. The sister sued for partition of certain property which had been jointly owned by the husband and wife. Ford defended by claiming homestead rights, as sole survivor of the community property, in a tract of land. The court imposed a constructive trust for Long as beneficiary on the portion of the property which Ford stood to gain by virtue of the state survivorship laws. The court did not, however, divest Ford of the portion of the tract he previously owned because that interest was neither acquired nor benefitted by the unlawful act.

4.   In *Snepp v. United States*, 444 U.S. 507, 100 S.Ct. 763, 62 L.Ed.2d 704 (1980), the Court examined whether to impose a constructive trust on profits of a book published by a former CIA agent. The agent, Snepp, based the book on his experiences with the CIA in South Vietnam. He had published the book without submitting the manuscript to the Agency for prepublication review, as required by the terms of employment with the Agency. The government brought suit to enforce Snepp's agreement, seeking among other remedies, to impose a constructive trust for the government's benefit on all profits that Snepp might earn from publishing the book in violation of his fiduciary obligations to the Agency. Although the government conceded that the book divulged no classified intelligence information, the Court observed that without the remedy of a constructive trust the government would have "no reliable deterrent against similar breaches of security." 444 U.S. at 514. Consequently, the Court reversed and remanded the case to reinstate the full judgment of the District Court which included imposition of a constructive trust. The Court stated:

> Snepp's employment with the CIA involved an extremely high degree of trust. * * * [H]e exposed the classified information with which he had been entrusted to the risk of disclosure.

> A constructive trust * * * protects both the Government and the former agent from unwarranted risks. This remedy is the natural and customary consequence of a breach of trust. It deals fairly with both parties by conforming relief to the dimensions of the wrong. If the agent secures prepublication clearance, he can publish with no fear of liability. If the agent publishes unreviewed

material in violation of his fiduciary and contractual obligation, the trust remedy simply requires him to disgorge the benefits of his faithlessness. Since the remedy is swift and sure, it is tailored to deter those who would place sensitive information at risk. And since the remedy reaches only funds attributable to the breach, it cannot saddle the former agent with exemplary damages out of all proportion to his gain. The decision of the Court of Appeals would deprive the Government of this equitable and effective means of protecting intelligence that may contribute to national security. 444 U.S. at 516.

Since the government conceded that the book contained no classified material, was the government's interest in confidentiality compromised by the agent's failure to obtain prepublication clearance? Assuming that Snepp breached a *contractual* duty, not a fiduciary obligation, was the majority correct in imposing a constructive trust? What advantages does a constructive trust hold for the government in contrast to damages for breach of contract?

Simonds v. Simonds

45 N.Y.2d 233, 380 N.E.2d 189, 408 N.Y.S.2d 359 (1978).

■ BREITEL, CHIEF JUDGE.

[In 1960 the plaintiff, Mary Simonds, entered into a separation agreement which required her husband, Frederick Simonds, to maintain in effect $7,000 of life insurance policies on his life with plaintiff as the named beneficiary. The agreement further required Frederick to obtain equivalent replacement insurance in the event that the existing policies lapsed or were cancelled. Frederick subsequently remarried, the life insurance policies lapsed, and he acquired several other policies totaling over $55,000 which designated either his second wife or his daughter as beneficiaries.

At the time of his death in 1971 he did not own any life insurance which designated plaintiff as beneficiary, and his estate was insolvent. Plaintiff brought an action against the second wife and daughter seeking to impose a constructive trust on the insurance proceeds to the extent of $7,000. The trial court granted partial summary judgment and imposed a constructive trust on $7,000 of the proceeds paid to the second wife. The appellate division affirmed.] * * *

There is no question that decedent breached his obligation to maintain life insurance with his first wife as beneficiary. Consequently, the first wife would of course be entitled to maintain an action for breach against the estate. The estate's insolvency, however, would make such an action fruitless. Thus, the controversy revolves around plaintiff's right, in equity, to recover $7,000 of the insurance proceeds.

Born out of the extreme rigidity of the early common law, equity in its origins drew heavily on Roman law, where equitable notions had long been accepted (*see* 1 Pomeroy, Equity Jurisprudence [5th ed.], 2 29). "Its great underlying principles, which are the constant sources, the neverfailing roots, of its particular rules, are unquestionably principles of right, justice, and morality, so far as the same can become the elements of a positive human jurisprudence." Law without principle is not law; law without justice is of limited value. Since adherence to principles of "law" does not invariably produce justice, equity is necessary. Equity arose to soften the impact of legal formalisms; to evolve formalisms narrowing the broad scope of equity is to defeat its essential purpose.

Whatever the legal rights between insurer and insured, the separation agreement vested in the first wife an equitable interest in the insurance policies then in force. An agreement for sufficient consideration, including a separation agreement, to maintain a claimant as a beneficiary of a life insurance policy vests in the claimant an equitable interest in the policies designated. This interest is superior to that of a named beneficiary who has given no consideration, notwithstanding policy provisions permitting the insured to change the designated beneficiary freely.

* * * [T]he policies now at issue are not the same policies in existence at the time of the separation agreement. But it has been held that mere substitution of policies, or even substitution of insurance companies, does not defeat the equitable interest of one who has given sufficient consideration for a promise to be maintained as beneficiary under an insurance policy. The persistence of the promisee's equitable interest is all the more evident where the agreement expressly provides for a change in policies, and in effect provides further that the promisee's right shall attach to the new policies.

For a certainty, the first wife's equitable interest would be easier to trace if the new policies were quid pro quo replacements for the original policies. The record does not reveal whether this was so. But inability to trace plaintiff's equitable rights precisely should not require that they not be recognized, much as in the instance of damages difficult to prove. The separation agreement provides nexus between plaintiff's rights and the later acquired policies. The later policies were expressly contemplated by the parties, and it was agreed that plaintiff would have an interest in them. No reason in equity appears for denying plaintiff that interest, so long as no one who has given value for the policies or otherwise suffered a detriment is involved. The second wife's innocence does not offset the wrong by the now deceased husband.

The conclusion is an application of the general rule that equity regards as done that which should have been done. Thus, if an insured, upon lapse or cancellation of insurance, followed by replacement with new insurance, has a contractual obligation to designate a particular person as beneficiary, equity will consider the obligee as a beneficiary.

In this case, then, the first wife's interest in the original policies extended as well to the later acquired policies. The husband, upon lapse or cancellation of the earlier policies, had by virtue of the separation agreement an obligation to name her as beneficiary on the later policies, an obligation enforceable in equity despite the husband's failure to comply with the terms of the separation agreement. Due to the husband's failure to do what he should have done, the first wife acquired not only a right at law to sue his estate for breach of contract, a right now worthless, but also an equitable right in the policies, a right which, upon the husband's death, attached to the proceeds.

And, since the first wife was entitled to $7,000 of the insurance proceeds at the time of the husband's death, she is no less entitled because the proceeds have already been converted by being paid, erroneously, to the named beneficiaries. Her remedy is imposition of a constructive trust.

In the words of Judge Cardozo, "[a] constructive trust is the formula through which the conscience of equity finds expression. When property has been acquired in such circumstances that the holder of the legal title may not in good conscience retain the beneficial interest, equity converts him into a trustee." Thus, a constructive trust is an equitable remedy. It is perhaps more different from an express trust than it is similar. As put so well by Scott and restated at the Appellate Division, "[the constructive trustee] is not compelled to convey the property because he is a constructive trustee; it is because he can be compelled to convey it that he is a constructive trustee".

More precise definitions of a constructive trust have been termed inadequate because of the failure to recognize the broad scope of constructive trust doctrine. As another leading scholar has said of constructive trusts, "[t]he Court does not restrict itself by describing all the specific forms of inequitable holding which will move it to grant relief, but rather reserves freedom to apply this remedy to whatever knavery human ingenuity can invent."

* * * [T]he purpose of the constructive trust is prevention of unjust enrichment. Unjust enrichment, however, does not require the performance of any wrongful act by the one enriched. Innocent parties may frequently be unjustly enriched. What is required, generally, is that a party hold property "under such circumstances that in equity and good conscience he ought not to retain it." A bona fide purchaser of property upon which a constructive trust would otherwise be imposed takes free of the constructive trust, but a gratuitous donee, however innocent, does not.

The unjust enrichment in this case is manifest. At a time when decedent was, certainly, anxious to remarry, he entered into a separation agreement with his wife of 14 years. As part of the agreement, he promised to maintain $7,000 in life insurance with the first wife as beneficiary. Later he broke his promise, and died with insurance policies naming only the second wife and daughter as beneficiaries. They have collected the proceeds, amounting to more than $55,000, while the first wife has collected nothing. Had the husband kept his promise, the beneficiaries would have collected $7,000 less in proceeds. To that extent, the beneficiaries have been unjustly enriched, and the proceeds should be subjected to a constructive trust.

[Affirmed].

1. *Inadequate Remedy at Law.* Since the constructive trust remedy is equitable, it remains discretionary with the court and may be denied if an adequate remedy at law exists. For example, in *Hughes Tool Co. v. Fawcett Publications, Inc.*, 297 A.2d 428 (Del.Ch.1972), *rev'd on other grounds*, 315 A.2d 577 (Del.1974), *aff'd* 350 A.2d 341 (Del.1975,) the plaintiff corporation brought suit against the author and publisher of a book, "Howard, The Amazing Mr. Hughes." The complaint sought an accounting for profits and a constructive trust. It alleged that the defendant's publication was an infringement on literary property in violation of a confidentiality agreement between the plaintiff's sole shareholder and the corporation. The court denied equitable relief by finding that the action was essentially a request for damages "camouflaged" by the prayer for an accounting and constructive trust. *See also* JP Morgan Chase Bank v. KB Home, 632 F.Supp.2d 1013, 1028 (D. Nev. 2009) (because money damages would make plaintiff whole, a constructive trust deemed not essential to the effectuation of justice).

Contrast *Joel v. Joel*, 43 So.3d 424 (Miss. 2010), where a son persuaded his elderly parents to purchase a house, but secretly included a provision in the deed that transferred title to himself upon the death of either of the parents. The parents later discovered that they merely held a life estate in the property, but the son died unexpectedly before the deed could be changed. The chancery court, observing that "equity must follow the law", determined that equitable restitution provided an appropriate remedy to convey fee simple title to the property because the parents had no contract with the son regarding the real estate so lacked an adequate remedy at law. The Mississippi Supreme court found that the son had abused his confidential relationship with the parents and affirmed imposition of a constructive trust.

2. The distinction between available legal and equitable remedies may have significant practical effects. In *Gilbert v. Meyer*, 362 F.Supp. 168 (S.D.N.Y.1973) the court held that a plaintiff requesting an accounting and the imposition of a constructive trust for violation of breach of fiduciary duties under the federal securities laws had an adequate remedy of money damages. Consequently, the claim was governed by a six year statute of limitation rather than a ten year limitations period governing equity actions. The court did not take equity jurisdiction and the legal claim was time-barred.

3. The principal case illustrates the usefulness of constructive trust in life insurance contexts. A constructive trust is also an appropriate remedy where an insurer pays the proceeds of a policy to a beneficiary having no insurable interest. *See* DeLeon v. Lloyd's London, 259 F.3d 344, 350 (5th Cir.2001).

4. An interesting use of the constructive trust remedy was demonstrated in *Brand v. Lipton,* 274 A.D.2d 534, 711 N.Y.S.2d 486 (N.Y.App.Div. 2000), which involved a dispute between life-long friends over the rights to prime season tickets to New York Jets professional football games. For many years, one of the parties purchased a block of tickets under a single account number and then shared them with three friends who paid the face value for the tickets. The account holder later became involved in a divorce and moved to Florida, so transferred the account to one of the remaining friends. Several years later, the new account holder decided to sell the extra tickets to third parties rather than continue the practice of sharing them with old friends. The court refused to dismiss a subsequent claim for imposition of a constructive trust upon the tickets, reasoning that a confidential relationship had been shown "so 'pregnant with opportunity for abuse and unfairness' as to require equity to intervene and scrutinize the transaction".

5. *Jury Trial.* In any case where equity takes jurisdiction, the parties' right to a jury trial is affected. *See* Kuhlman v. Cargile, 200 Neb. 150, 262 N.W.2d 454 (1978); *Dick v. Dick*, 167 Conn. 210, 355 A.2d 110 (1974). *See generally* Devlin, Jury Trial of Complex Cases, English Practice at the Time of the Seventh Amendment, 80 Colum.L.Rev. 43 (1980).

6. *Statute of Limitations.* A particularly vexing but often overlooked problem involves selecting the proper statute of limitations to claims seeking a constructive trust. Since state statutes often do not expressly cover constructive trusts, courts have tended to borrow the limitation period governing the underlying substantive claim of fraud, contract, or mistake. That limitation period then is incorporated into the doctrine of laches or is applied directly.

This approach has caused difficulties. In addition to problems with characterizing the substantive claim, complications develop when the defendant's conduct gives rise to multiple substantive claims with varying limitation periods. In that event, the court must choose which statute of limitations best effectuates the restitutionary goal of preventing unjust enrichment yet satisfies the fairness and evidentiary concerns of the defendant. *See generally* McSwain, Limitations Statutes and the Constructive Trust in Texas, 41 Baylor L.Rev. 429 (1989); Eichengrun, The Statute of Limitations For Constructive Trusts in North Carolina; Note, Developments in the Law Statutes of Limitations, 63 Harv.L.Rev. 1177 (1950); Dawson, Mistake and Statutes of Limitations, 31 Mich.L.Rev. 591 (1933). The statute of limitations on a constructive trust remedy begins when the wrongful withholding occurs and not necessarily the original date of transfer. *See* Goya Foods, Inc. v. Unanue, 233 F.3d 38, 46 (1st Cir.2000).

E.   EQUITABLE LIENS

Section Coverage:

Constructive trusts and equitable liens are both restitutionary remedies designed to prevent unjust enrichment. Although they share certain commonalities, significant differences exist in function and practical utility. A constructive trust provides an excellent vehicle to transfer legal title to traced assets, while an equitable lien merely imposes a security interest against property.

A claimant may prefer a constructive trust where property has increased in value, while an equitable lien would only give the aggrieved party a security interest to the extent of the benefits unjustly held by the defendant. Conversely, if the traced property has declined in value after being misappropriated or if the wrongdoer has dissipated some of the claimant's funds, an equitable lien typically is more advantageous than a constructive trust. In such instances, the equitable lien claimant has a charge or encumbrance on the identified property and is entitled to a deficiency judgment against the wrongdoer for the balance of the claim. See generally Restatement (Third) of Restitution and Unjust Enrichment § 56, cmt. B.

An equitable lien may also be the preferred remedy where the claimant cannot establish a severable interest in the defendant's property. Equity will not use restitution to effect a forfeiture of a defendant's property, so if title cannot be clearly conveyed by constructive trust then a lien will be placed on the property. Liens are intended to secure the obligation owed, so will be discharged if the defendant satisfies the debt which formed the basis for the judgment. A disadvantage of an equitable lien is that it necessitates a further order by the court for foreclosure of the subject property. Such orders are generally favored, yet may be declined in the court's discretion after balancing the respective equities of the parties.

For example, if a fiduciary embezzles a client's money to purchase a yacht, if the client can trace the misappropriated funds they may seek either an equitable lien or a constructive trust on the property. Although a constructive trust conveniently allows transfer of legal title to the yacht to prevent unjust enrichment, an equitable lien could be more advantageous if the market value of the yacht had declined. In that instance, the claimant could supplement the lien by obtaining a deficiency judgment for purposes of recovering the balance owed and could seek satisfaction of the claim from other assets of the defendant. If the defendant used the embezzled funds to make improvements to the yacht, though, then an equitable lien would be the sole restitutionary remedy available because the defendant held legal title to the yacht prior to the misconduct.

If the defendant is insolvent, a court could find that an action at law for money damages fraud would be inadequate and equitable restitution justified. In such cases, the equitable lien on the yacht would take priority over other general creditors. The plaintiff would be a general creditor for the claim on the differential amount. Although an equitable lien comes into existence at the time of the transaction giving rise to the claim, it does not become legally enforceable until judicially declared.

Model Case:

Chandler fraudulently induced Baxter to add an addition to Chandler's vacation house. Baxter, a building contractor, had been promised an important contract in connection with Chandler's business if the improvements were made, but the promise was fraudulent. The cost of the labor and materials for the addition was $5,000, but the addition actually enhanced the market value of the house by only $2,000.

If equitable relief is appropriate in this case, a court will allow Baxter to obtain an equitable lien on the property rather than a constructive trust because title to the land belonged to Chandler. The lien operates as an encumbrance against the property which could be satisfied by a foreclosure of the lien through sale of the house.

Baxter would not be entitled to foreclosure automatically. A court would consider the opportunity of Chandler to pay the charge out of other funds and any potential hardship to Chandler as a result of a forced sale. Other alternatives to immediate sale of the house to satisfy Baxter's lien would be to direct that it be mortgaged and Baxter reimbursed from the proceeds, or to appoint a receiver for receipt of any rentals produced from this vacation house.

Most jurisdictions would allow the amount of the lien to be $5,000 because the nature of Chandler's conduct was fraudulent. If Baxter had made the improvements simply by mistake under circumstances that makes retention of this enrichment unjust, then the lien should be limited to $2,000, the amount that the value of the property was actually enhanced.

Middlebrooks v. Lonas

246 Ga. 720, 272 S.E.2d 687 (1980).

■ JORDAN, PRESIDING JUSTICE.

Mary Middlebrooks filed a complaint against W.L. Lonas and Elvira Lonas, her parents, alleging that, in reliance on their promise to repay, she had loaned them $25,000 which they had since used to build a home on land which they owned, that they now refused to repay said loan and that, "[t]he above and foregoing transactions, promises, and delays constitute fraud and as such the defendants herein hold the said $25,000 through and by constructive and implied trust in favor of the plaintiff." The plaintiff further alleged that, "[t]he defendants herein have pledged, mortgaged and borrowed money upon the land . . . as well as all improvements thereon."

The defendants moved for summary judgment on the ground that the plaintiff's complaint failed to state a claim upon which equitable relief could be granted and on the ground that they had factually pierced the plaintiff's allegation that they had promised to repay the $25,000 without a present intent to do so. The trial court granted said motion and the plaintiff appeals. We reverse.

* * *

2.   Code Ann. § 108–106 states that "[t]rusts are implied . . . where, from any fraud, one person obtains the title to property which rightly belongs to another."

A promise made without a present intent to perform is a misrepresentation of a material fact and is sufficient to support a cause of action for fraud.

Thus, assuming that the remedies at law are inadequate, if a plaintiff proves that a defendant promised to repay a loan and did so without a present intent to perform, the plaintiff can "enforce either a constructive trust or an equitable lien on the fund," and, further, if a plaintiff proves that the fraudulently procured funds were used by the defendant to purchase other property, the plaintiff can reach the other property "by a proceeding in equity, and . . . can enforce a constructive trust or an equitable lien." [Citations.]

In the present case, it is undisputed that the defendants used the $25,000 to build a home on land which they already owned. Accordingly, assuming that the plaintiff's remedies at law are inadequate, if the plaintiff proves that the defendants promised to repay the $25,000 and did so without a present intent to perform, the plaintiff would be entitled to an equitable lien on the home and land.

A remedy at law, to exclude appropriate relief in equity, must be . . . the substantial equivalent of the equitable relief. It is not enough that there is a remedy at law. It must be plain and adequate, or, in other words, as practical and as efficient to the ends of justice and its prompt administration as the remedy in equity.

Regarding the inadequacy of her remedies at law, the plaintiff alleged that the defendants had mortgaged the home and lot. "A creditor of a mortgagor who obtains his judgment [at law] subsequently to the execution of a mortgage which has been duly registered takes it subject to the rights of the mortgagee . . ." [Citation.] In contrast, a plaintiff who similarly establishes entitlement to an equitable lien takes subject to the rights of a mortgagee only if the mortgagee is a bona fide purchaser. * * *

Judgment reversed.

––––––––––

1.   *Enforcement.* An equitable lien is imposed directly against particular property, such as a parcel of land, a fund of money, or a specific chattel, rather than on the defendant's general assets. The specific property must be identifiable with reasonable certainty and must be distinguishable from the general assets of the debtor. In re Carpenter, 252 B.R. 905 (E.D.Va. 2000). The lien is designed as security for a judicially decreed debt, enforceable through execution and sale after defendant has refused to pay the obligation. An equitable lien may be less expedient than a constructive trust because it requires foreclosure of the property in order to realize payment of the lien.

The defendant may discharge the lien and remove the encumbrance against the subject property by paying the claimant the amount of the underlying liability. Otherwise, the lienholder could seek a judicial sale of the property and apply the proceeds to satisfy the obligation owed. If the proceeds are insufficient, the claimant retains an unsecured claim against the defendant for the deficiency. *See* Restatement (Third) of Restitution and Unjust Enrichment § 56 cmt. C. The claimant does not need to wait indefinitely for the property to be sold to satisfy the debt, but the court will ordinarily authorize a sale of the property. *See* Disanza v. Gaglione, 126 Misc.2d 232, 482 N.Y.S.2d 413, 414 (Sup.Ct. 1984).

2. An equitable lien may be imposed as a remedial device to enforce a right to restitution where property can be reached as security for a claim to prevent unjust enrichment. Restatement (Third) of Restitution and Unjust Enrichment § 56 (2011); Crawford v. Silette, 608 F.3d 275, 282 (5th Cir. 2010) (where homeowner innocently used proceeds traced to fraudulently obtained funds to retire mortgage, court imposed equitable lien on the property to avoid unjust enrichment).

3. A second type of equitable lien may be recognized as a surrogate to replace a consensual lien that might otherwise have been obtained if a transaction had been carried out as originally contemplated, yet failed due to mistake or some kind of wrongful conduct. Sereboff v. Mid Atlantic Medical Services, Inc., 547 U.S. 356, 364–65, 126 S.Ct. 1869, 164 L.Ed.2d 612 (2006) (equitable lien sought in restitution and arising out of agreement are different species of relief); Onewest Bank v. Marshall, 18 A.3d 715, 722 (D. C. Ct. App. 2011) (assignee of mortgage properly alleged claim for equitable lien where intention to charge particular property as security for payment of debt was frustrated); M & B Joint Venture, Inc. v. Laurus Master Fund, Inc., 12 N.Y.3d 798, 907 N.E.2d 960, 879 N.Y.S.2d 812, 814 (2009) (equitable lien requires express or implied agreement of the parties that a lien be imposed on specific property); *see also* Restatement (Third) of Restitution and Unjust Enrichment § 56, cmt. E (2011).

In this group of cases courts commonly consider the following:

(1) a debt, duty or obligation between the parties arising out of an express or implied agreement of the parties;

(2) specific property or res to which the debt or obligation attaches;

(3) a clear intent, express or implied, that the property serve as security for the payment or obligation; and

(4) no adequate remedy at law.

See generally Amusement Ind., Inc. v. Stern, 693 F.Supp.2d 327, 358 (S.D.N.Y. 2010); Arena Resources, Inc. v. Obo, Inc., 148 N.M. 483, 238 P.3d 357, 361 (Ct. App. 2010); In re Varat Enterprises, Inc., 81 F.3d 1310, 1319 (4th Cir.1996); In re "RONFIN" Series C Bonds Sec. Interest Lit., 182 F.3d 366, 371 (5th Cir.1999).

4. *Priorities.* An important issue with respect to equitable liens involves its status in relation to the interests of other creditors with respect

to the property of the defendant. An equitable lien may be characterized as a "floating equity" which arises at the time of the conduct of the parties giving rise to its existence. *See* Regions Bank v. Wingard Properties, Inc., 394 S.C. 241, 715 S.E.2d 348 (S. C. App. 2011); Restatement (Third) of Restitution and Unjust Enrichment § 56, cmt. E. The lien is not enforceable, however, until a court renders judgment declaring its existence but the priority of the lienholder relates back to the time it was created by the conduct of the parties. The principle of relation back poses problems of sorting through priorities with respect to other lienholders. Secured creditors with the status of bona fide purchasers retain priority protection, while general unsecured creditors do not. *See* First Banc Real Estate, Inc. v. Johnson, 321 S.W.3d 322, 335 (Mo. Ct. App. 2010) (equitable lien did not survive foreclosure of prior secured claim and superior lien not waived).

5.   As reflected in the principal case, equitable liens merely grant a security interest in property, rather than specific relief. The Supreme Court, in *Department of the Army v. Blue Fox, Inc.*, 525 U.S. 255, 119 S.Ct. 687, 142 L.Ed.2d 718 (1999) made the following observation about the function of equitable liens:

> Liens, whether equitable or legal, are merely a means to the end of satisfying a claim for the recovery of money. Indeed, equitable liens by their nature constitute substitute or compensatory relief rather than specific relief. An equitable lien does not "give the plaintiff the very thing to which he was entitled"; instead, it merely grants a plaintiff "a security interest in the property, which [the plaintiff] can then use to satisfy a money claim," usually a claim for unjust enrichment, 1 D. Dobbs, Law of Remedies § 4.3(3), p. 601 (2d ed.1993); see also Laycock, The Scope and Significance of Restitution, 67 Texas L.Rev. 1277, 1290 (1989) ("The equitable lien is a hybrid, granting a money judgment and securing its collection with a lien on the specific thing"). Commentators have warned not to view equitable liens as anything more than substitute relief:

> "[T]he *form* of the remedy requires that [a] lien or charge should be established, and then enforced, and the amount due obtained by a sale total or partial of the fund, or by a sequestration of its rents, profits, and proceeds. These preliminary steps may, on a casual view, be misleading as to the nature of the remedy, and may cause it to appear to be something more than compensatory; but a closer view shows that all these steps are merely auxiliary, and that the *real* remedy, the final object of the proceeding, is the pecuniary recovery." 1 J. Pomeroy, Equity Jurisprudence § 112, p. 148 (5th ed.1941). 119 S.Ct. at 692.

PROBLEM: THE SHARED HOUSE

Walker, a single parent with two young children, lived in an apartment on Main Street. Walker, who is employed full time, arranged for a single friend, Shaw, to care for the children after school in Shaw's home located on nearby Burgandy Avenue. Shaw was a college student at the time. The house had been inherited, and it was mortgaged to pay tuition.

The apartment complex where Walker lived was purchased by a real estate developer who planned to tear it down and replace it with a commercial shopping center. When Walker received a notice from the landlord terminating the lease, Shaw offered to let the three Walkers temporarily move into Shaw's house until another apartment could be located.

The joint living arrangement proved satisfactory to everyone. Shaw was having financial difficulties with daily living expenses at the time. Since they got along well during the temporary stay, they decided to make it permanent. They orally agreed to continue sharing the home and the household expenses. Over a three year period Walker contributed one-half of the mortgage payments and paid $5,000 for adding a bath to the house. The improvement resulted in an increase of approximately $3,000 in the fair market value of the house.

Relations became strained after Shaw graduated. Shaw was employed and became engaged to be married. Walker agreed to move out, but they disputed whether Shaw should reimburse Walker for any of the prior contributions. Walker moved out and now seeks reimbursement for the improvement made to the Shaw home by requesting the court to impress an equitable lien on the property. What result?

Robinson v. Robinson

100 Ill.App.3d 437, 57 Ill.Dec. 532, 429 N.E.2d 183 (1981).

■ UNVERZAGT, JUSTICE:

This action was brought by the plaintiff, Ann M. Robinson, to obtain a dissolution of marriage from Wylie Robinson, and against his parents, Earl J. and Alice M. Robinson, to establish her rights in certain property owned by them, known as the Johnson Road property. * * *

The novel question presented by this appeal is whether one who improves real property which she knows to be owned by others, who neither request nor encourage the improvement but merely give their permission for the improvement, is entitled to restitution. * * *

Wylie and Ann began construction of the house in the spring of 1969 and occupied it in 1970. [The house was located on the Johnson Road property owned by Wylie's parents.] The construction work was done mainly by Wylie with substantial help from friends and family including Earl, Alice and Ann's father. Ann sanded and finished woodwork and cabinets. After the home was occupied, additional improvements in the amount of $5,000 were made. These included carpeting, drapes, kitchen cabinets, linoleum and paint.

All of the parties knew that the house was Wylie's and Ann's home and treated it as such. They did all of the landscaping and planted shrubbery.

They repaired it and maintained it. They made all of the loan payments and treated the interest thereon as a deduction on tax returns. They insured the house with a homeowner's policy. They had the only keys to the house and never paid or were asked for rent on it. The one connection Earl and Alice had with the house was that it was included on the farm tax bill since the lot was not subdivided. Earl and Alice paid the real estate tax bill. In exchange for that payment, Wylie worked additional time for his parents on their farm. * * *

There was no written agreement between the young and older Robinsons as to a transfer of title to the property. However, Wylie and his parents had many oral dealings over the years. They were very close. * * * The younger Robinsons and the older Robinsons exchanged services and assistance in the old fashioned country manner. Wylie worked for his parents on their farm each year and received a share of the farm income. Over the years he contributed a substantial amount of his time and knowledge to the construction of various farm improvements on his parents' farm.

Marital discord arose in 1977 and Wylie moved to his parents' home where he resided at the time of the hearing. From the relationship of the parties it can thus be seen that the younger Robinsons would have every expectation of eventual ownership of the home they constructed. However, the testimony was in strong disagreement on this point. * * *

The trial judge concluded that it would unjustly enrich Earl and Alice to gain the house without compensation to Ann.

A person who has been unjustly enriched at the expense of another is required to make restitution to the other. A person is enriched if he has received a benefit. A person is unjustly enriched if the retention of the benefit would be unjust. A person obtains restitution when he is restored to the position he formerly occupied either by the return of something he formerly had or by the receipt of its equivalent in money.

After hearing all of the evidence in this case, the trial court determined that Ann had an interest in the improvements made on the Johnson Road property. The court's rationale for the decision was that the evidence established that Earl and Alice had been unjustly enriched by the improvements made on the Johnson Road property. * * *

Earl and Alice argue that the evidence at trial did not establish recovery under a theory of unjust enrichment. They argue that as a general rule, improvements of a permanent character, made upon real estate, and attached thereto, without consent of the owner of the fee, by one having no title or interest, become a part of the realty and vest in the owner of the fee. * * *

In Olin v. Reinecke (1929), 336 Ill. 530, 534, 168 N.E. 676, the court said:

In equity, however, if the owner stands by and permits another to expend money in improving his land he may be compelled to surrender his rights to the land upon receiving compensation therefor, or he may be compelled to pay for the improvements. In such cases there is always some ingredient which would make it a fraud in the owner to insist upon his legal rights. Such an ingredient may consist in the owner encouraging the stranger to proceed with the improvement, or where one party acts ignorantly and without the means of better information and the other remains silent when it is in his power to prevent the expenditure of the money under a delusion. It has been held in such cases that to permit one to take advantage of the mistake of another would be revolting to every sentiment of justice. The exercise of such a judicial power, however, unless based upon some actual or implied culpability on the part of the party subjected to it, is a violation of constitutional rights.

In Pope v. Speiser (1955), 7 Ill.2d 231, 240, 130 N.E.2d 507, where the plaintiff placed valuable improvements on the defendant's farm with the knowledge and consent of the defendant and after repeated statements by the defendant that the farm would belong to the plaintiff upon the defendant's death, the court granted plaintiff an equitable lien in the land, after the defendant attempted to sell the farm to a third person.

These cases support the trial court's ruling granting Ann an interest in the Johnson Road property. The improvements were made with the knowledge, cooperation and approval of Earl and Alice. * * *

We determine that while he did not denominate it as such, the interest awarded to Ann in the Johnson Road property by the trial judge was an equitable lien. As this court stated in Calacurcio v. Levson (1966), 68 Ill.App.2d 260, 263, 215 N.E.2d 839:

> The trend of modern decisions is to hold that in the absence of an express contract, a lien based upon the fundamental maxims of equity may be implied and declared by a court of equity out of general considerations of right and justice as applied to the relationship of the parties and the circumstances of their dealing. An equitable lien is the right to have property subjected in a court of equity to payment of a claim. It is neither a debt nor a right of property, but a remedy for a debt.

The next question posed by this case is the extent or amount of the equitable lien. The trial court ruled that Ann was entitled to one-half of the appraised value of the improvements less the value of the land after making provision for payment of the construction loan.

Earl and Alice argue that if Ann is entitled to restitution her recovery should be measured by the subjective value to them or the value of the labor and materials that went into the house, and not the increased value of the land resulting from the addition of the house.

One scholar has suggested that when one builds a house on another's land, there are at least two feasible objective measures of restitution and one subjective measure. They are (1) the objective value of the labor and materials which went into the house; (2) the increased value of the land resulting from the addition of the house to it; and (3) the personal value to the defendant land-owner for his particular purposes. (*See* Dobbs, Remedies, 4.5 at 261 (1973).) We have been supplied no case which has adopted the latter approach perhaps because of the almost impossibility of determining the subjective approach.

The Illinois cases have variously given an equitable lien for (1) the cost of the improvements or (2) the enhanced value of the premises, or (3) a right to purchase the premises if the owner elects to sell. * * *

From the foregoing, we conclude there was an implied promise by Earl and Alice to deed the land in question to Wylie and Ann and that the trial court was correct in imposing an equitable lien on the premises amounting to the value of the improvements that Ann and Wylie constructed thereon, in order to prevent unjust enrichment to Earl and Alice. * * *

It is the opinion of this court that the trial court properly directed defendants Earl and Alice to perform their implied contract to pay the plaintiff one-half of the reasonable value of the permanent improvements placed on the premises by the plaintiff and her husband and on their failure or refusal so to do, the trial court correctly ordered the property sold to foreclose plaintiff's equitable lien. * * *

Earl and Alice next assert that the trial court erred in attaching a lien for Wylie's debts on the Johnson Road property. The trial court placed a lien on one-half of the property for Ann's attorney's fees, child support arrearage and one-half interest in the Teacher's Retirement Plan. We agree that this was erroneous because an equitable lien is a remedy and not a property right. As was said in Watson v. Hobson (1948), 401 Ill. 191, 201, 81 N.E.2d 885, in discussing the nature of an equitable lien:

> An equitable lien is the right to have property subjected, in a court of equity, to the payment of a claim. It is neither a debt nor a right of property but a remedy for a debt. It is simply a right of a special nature over the property which constitutes a charge or encumbrance thereon, so that the very property itself may be proceeded against in an equitable action and either sold or sequestered under a judicial decree, and its proceeds, in one case, or its rents and profits in the other, applied upon the demand of the creditor in whose favor the lien exists.

We have found no case in which a lien was imposed on an equitable lien under such circumstances, as if the latter were a piece of property. Wylie has disclaimed any interest in the Johnson Road property. No matter how obstinate or intractable the trial court may have felt his action was in disclaiming the interest, the trial court cannot create a lien upon an equitable lien where none is sought. That portion of the judgment is reversed. * * *

Affirmed in part; reversed in part and remanded.

———————

1. An equitable lien may be imposed on property to the extent necessary to secure a restitutionary claim for the value of labor or materials furnished toward making improvements on another's property. *See* Restatement (Third) Restitution and Unjust Enrichment § 56 (2011). The basis for granting an equitable lien rather than a constructive trust is that the claimant lacks title to the entire property and the improvements cannot be severed from the realty to effect specific restitution. Some courts have recognized that an action to establish a constructive trust in an interest in land is not barred by the statute of frauds. *See* Lathem v. Hestley, 270 Ga. 849, 514 S.E.2d 440 (Ga. 1999). *But see* Amusement Ind., Inc. v. Stern, 693 F.Supp.2d 327, 358 (S.D.N.Y. 2010) (Under Virginia law an equitable lien on real property must be in writing).

2. For classical commentary concerning equitable restitution, see the following references: Scott, The Trustee's Duty of Loyalty, 49 Harv.L.Rev. 521 (1936); Pound, The Progress of the Law, 1918 19 Equity, 33 Harv. L.Rev. 420 (1920); Huston, The Enforcement of Decrees in Equity (1915); Ames, Following Misappropriated Property into Its Product, 19 Harv. L.Rev. 511 (1906).

CHAPTER 17

LIMITATIONS ON RESTITUTIONARY REMEDIES

A. TRACING

Section Coverage:

Equity limits a person's ability to obtain a constructive trust, equitable lien, or right of subrogation against particular property by requiring the claimant to "trace" or follow the misappropriated property into its substituted form. Restitution of traced property may be asserted not only against the wrongdoer but also against a third party holding the exchanged property, provided the latter is not a bona fide purchaser.

Plaintiffs with equitable interests who can trace specific assets into their products enjoy two advantages. First, a claimant may obtain specific restitution of property which has subsequently increased in value through imposition of a constructive trust. The second, and perhaps even more important, advantage is that the holder of the equitable interest may receive a priority over the general creditors of insolvent or unavailable wrongdoers. If the person seeking an equitable restitutionary remedy cannot successfully identify the product of misappropriated money or property, the only remedy is a personal claim against the wrongdoer and the claimant will be forced to stand in line with other creditors.

Model Case:

An attorney named Blair embezzled $20,000 from a client's trust account. Half of the embezzled money went into a bank account that already contained some personal funds. Some but not all of the combined money in the account was spent on daily living expenses. Blair used the balance of the embezzled money to purchase a sailboat. Shortly thereafter Blair sold the sailboat and used the proceeds to pay a builder for some badly needed home repairs. With the cash left over after paying this bill, Blair purchased some jewelry for a family member's birthday. Thereafter the embezzlement was discovered, along with other misdeeds by Blair, who is now insolvent.

Whether the client will be able to assert an equitable lien against some or all of the money remaining in the bank account will depend upon the tracing presumptions followed in that jurisdiction. Jurisdictions follow a variety of approaches for tracing commingled funds in an account.

A constructive trust may be imposed on the jewelry provided the client can trace the various exchanges of property from the embezzled funds to the jewelry. An equitable lien may be placed on the house if the client similarly can demonstrate that the misappropriated assets were used to make the repairs. Because the client did not have title to the house originally, a court would not impose a constructive trust to effect specific restitution of the house to the client.

G & M Motor Company v. Thompson

567 P.2d 80 (Okl.1977).

■ BERRY, JUSTICE.

The question to be decided has not heretofore been decided in Oklahoma. Specifically, may a trial court impress a constructive trust upon proceeds of life insurance policies where a portion of the premiums were paid with wrongfully obtained funds? We hold sound reason and interest of justice require an affirmative answer.

The facts, for the purpose of deciding this question, are simple. A. Wayne Thompson was an accountant for G & M Motor Company [motor company] from January 1, 1968, until his death on August 2, 1970. During this period decedent embezzled $78,856.45 from motor company; a portion of which was used to pay premiums of various insurance policies insuring the life of decedent. The trial court impressed a constructive trust upon various items of real and personal property and a portion of the insurance proceeds in possession of decedent's surviving wife, Shirley Thompson, and child.

Court of Appeals, Division 1, upon wife's appeal, affirmed trial court's impressment of a constructive trust on the real and personal property, but modified the trust on insurance proceeds. The court, relying on American National Bank of Okmulgee v. King, 158 Okl. 278, 13 P.2d 164, said "only that part of the funds that the trial court found was used to pay for the payments of the policies while deceased was employed for appellee ... together with interest at the rate of 10% per annum from date of judgment ... until paid" are subject to a constructive trust in favor of motor company.

* * *

The proper basis for impressing a constructive trust is to prevent unjust enrichment. Restatement of Restitution § 160, Comment c [1937]. The Restatement of Restitution foresaw that a wrongdoer may exchange misappropriated property for other property; thus, § 202 provides:

> "Where a person wrongfully disposes of property of another knowing that the disposition is wrongful and acquires in exchange other property, the other is entitled ... to enforce ... a constructive trust of the property so acquired."

The drafters explained § 202 as follows:

"Where a person by the consciously wrongful disposition of the property of another acquires other property, the person whose property is so used is . . . entitled . . . to the property so acquired. If the property so acquired is or becomes more valuable than the property used in acquiring it, the profit thus made by the wrongdoer cannot be retained by him; the person whose property was used in making the profit is entitled to it. The result, it is true, is that the claimant obtains more than the amount of which he was deprived, more than restitution for his loss; he is put in a better position than that in which he would have been if no wrong had been done to him. Nevertheless, since the profit is made from his property, it is just that he should have the profit rather than that the wrongdoer should keep it. It is true that if there had been a loss instead of a profit, the wrongdoer would have had to bear the loss, since the wrongdoer would be personally liable to the claimant for the value of the claimant's property wrongfully used by the wrongdoer. If, however, the wrongdoer were permitted to keep the profit, there would be an incentive to wrongdoing, which is removed if he is compelled to surrender the profit. The rule which compels the wrongdoer to bear any losses and to surrender any profits operates as a deterrent upon the wrongful disposition of the property of others. Accordingly, the person whose property is wrongfully used in acquiring other property can by a proceeding in equity reach the other property and compel the wrongdoer to convey it to him. The wrongdoer holds the property so acquired upon a constructive trust for the claimant."

Thus, it is not necessary for a plaintiff to have suffered any loss or suffer a loss as great as the benefit of defendant. *See Id.* § 160, Comment d.

Where the wrongdoer mingles wrongfully and rightfully acquired funds, owner of wrongfully acquired funds is entitled to share proportionately in acquired property to the extent of his involuntary contribution. *Id.* § 210(2). This principle is specifically applicable to life insurance proceeds where a portion of the premiums were paid with wrongfully acquired money. *Id.* § 210, Comment a. The drafters said:

". . . Just as the claimant is entitled to enforce a constructive trust upon property which is wholly the product of his property, so he is entitled to enforce a constructive trust upon property which is the product in part of his own property and in part of the property of the wrongdoer. The difference is that where the property is the product of his property only in part, he is not entitled by enforcing a constructive trust to recover the whole of the property, but only a share in such proportion as the value of his property bore to the value of the mingled fund."

More particularly, § 210, Comment d, Illustration 5 addressed the instant matter. Illustration 5 provides:

"A insures his life for $10,000 and pays the premiums half with money wrongfully taken from B and half with money of his own. A dies. B is entitled to half of the proceeds of the policy. . . ."

The record indicates trial court determined extent of premiums paid with wrongfully acquired funds and impressed a constructive trust upon proceeds consistent with Illustration 5.

Having carefully considered the matter, we adopt the Restatement view. However, Motor Company has sought no more than the embezzled monies, interest and costs. Further, the surviving wife is an innocent beneficiary. Therefore, we cannot say trial court's judgment is against the clear weight of evidence. We hold Motor Company is entitled to a pro rata share of insurance proceeds, but not to exceed the total amount of embezzled monies, interest and costs.

* * * Court of Appeals opinion vacated in part. Judgment of trial court affirmed.

---

1.   The mechanics of tracing are simplest when the wrongdoer makes a single exchange of property or where embezzled money is deposited in an account which contains no other funds. The task of following property through numerous transactions vastly complicates the proof; however, equity rules permit tracing despite multiple exchanges either in form or number of transactions. The tracing rules provide an opportunity for a claimant to protect their property interest and may potentially allow disgorgement of property that has increased in value while in the hands of a conscious wrongdoer. Such a result is in accord with traditional principles of equitable restitution and permits the innocent party to receive the gains from a profitable investment. Such transactional gains are tempered by the principle of unjust enrichment, however, where excessive recovery in restitution by one claimant would detrimentally affect the ability of other creditors to recover against the wrongdoer. In those circumstances, the restitution claimant will not recover profits of the wrongdoing but may be limited to the losses sustained. *See generally* Restatement (Third) of Restitution and Unjust Enrichment (2011) § 58(3); cmt. i.

2.   *Commingled Funds.* Problems arise when the wrongdoer commingles the misappropriated funds with other funds which rightfully belong to the wrongdoer or to third parties. Although the misappropriated money has lost its separate identity in the commingled account, courts will impose an equitable lien on the account to allow restitution of the amount which rightfully belongs to the plaintiff. The claimant would be unjustly enriched if the court granted restitution of the entire fund; conversely, a wrongdoer should not be able to foreclose restitution simply by the act of commingling funds.

3.   *Withdrawals From Commingled Funds.* When a wrongdoer makes withdrawals from a commingled fund, tracing is still possible. The problem is how to identify whose money was removed and whose remains. Courts historically have created several fictional presumptions to meet the tracing requirement. The presumptions were devised to operate without regard to the actual intent of the wrongdoer except in the limited circumstance when

the wrongdoer replenishes a reduced commingled account with the intent of restoring the claimant's funds. Otherwise, the legal fictions for tracing commingled funds reflect sympathy for the claimant's task of satisfying the tracing requirement for restitutionary equitable remedies.

4. *First In, First Out Rule.* The original English solution to withdrawals from commingled accounts was formulated in *Devaynes v. Noble*, 1 Mer. 572 (1816), known as *Clayton's Case.* The court created the arbitrary rule that the first money put into the account would be presumed the first money withdrawn. For example, if the wrongdoer deposited $1,000 of the plaintiff's money in an account where there was already $800, then the law would presume that the first $800 withdrawn belonged to the wrongdoer. On the other hand, if the plaintiff's money was placed in the account first and the wrongdoer's own funds were deposited later, then withdrawals were deemed from the plaintiff's money up to the $1,000.

The plaintiff was either benefitted or hurt under this "first in, first out" rule depending entirely upon the fortuity of how the money was used. If the money that was arbitrarily determined to be the claimant's was dissipated, the equitable remedy was lost. If the money was used to invest in something of value that could still be traced, the plaintiff could follow it further to impress the constructive trust or equitable lien.

5. *"Jessel's Bag" Rule.* A different resolution of the problem of identifying withdrawals from a commingled fund appeared in a later English decision, *In re Hallett's Estate* (Knatchbull v. Hallett), 13 Ch. Div. 696 (1879). Under this approach, the first withdrawals from a commingled fund are presumed to belong to the wrongdoer and the remaining balance is subject to the equitable interest asserted by the claimant. This rule is known as the rule of Jessel's Bag, named after a member of the court, Sir George Jessel.

The rule of Jessel's Bag has the effect of benefitting the claimant in many cases because money withdrawn by a wrongdoer from a commingled fund is dissipated more typically than it is invested in traceable property. The money left in the account thus remains for the plaintiff's equitable claim.

The rule produces unsatisfactory results, however, when the first funds withdrawn by the wrongdoer are profitably invested but the remaining funds, which presumptively belong to the innocent claimant, are dissipated. A subsequent English decision, *In re Oatway* (Hertsler v. Oatway), 2 Ch. Div. 356 (1903), modified the rule of Jessel's Bag to give the claimant a choice between the assets traceable to the funds drawn out first or those withdrawn from the account at a later time.

6. Difficult tracing problems arise when a wrongdoer with a commingled account makes withdrawals which are dissipated, then later makes additional deposits of personal funds into the account. The Restatement (Third) of Restitution and Unjust Enrichment (2011) § 59(2)(a) rejects the tracing fictions and adopts a dual presumption which generally favors the claimant in such instances. First, those withdrawals that are either unt-

raceable or unprofitable are allocated to the wrongdoer. Second, the claimant retains the ability to elect tracing and obtaining restitution of the product of withdrawn funds where that may yield an advantageous result. This approach of marshaling assets in favor of the claimant reflects a departure from the previous Restatement position which limited recovery to the proportion that the claimant's property bore to the wrongdoer's in commingled accounts and traceable products of withdrawn funds. See Restatement of Restitution §§ 210–211 (1937).

For example, consider Illustration 6, Restatement (Third) of Restitution and Unjust Enrichment (2011) § 59:

> Grower delivers 500 turkeys to Processor, who commingles them with 500 turkeys of his own. Of the resulting mass of turkeys, Processor sells 500 to Buyer A and 500 to Buyer B. The proceeds from the sale to A are dissipated, but the proceeds from the sale to B are available for distribution when Processor makes an assignment for the benefit of creditors. The court holds that Grower's delivery to Processor was a bailment, not a sale, with the result that Processor's sale of Grower's turkeys constituted conversion. Grower is entitled to restitution (§ 40) and to a remedy via constructive trust or equitable lien from the traceable product of the converted turkeys. The rule of § 59(2)(a) permits Grower to identify as his the turkeys sold to B and to recover the proceeds in preference to Processor's general creditors.

7. A related issue involves whether replacement funds should be treated as a restoration of the claimant's money. On this point the revised Restatement (Third) follows the view that subsequent contributions into a commingled account are not deemed to restore the claimant's misappropriated property unless evidence shows an affirmative intention by the wrongdoer to effect that result. *See* Restatement (Third) of Restitution and Unjust Enrichment § 59(2)(b). If such intent is demonstrated, an equitable lien may be extended to cover the new deposits.

This presumption effectively tilts in favor of the account holder in that subsequent additions of funds are preserved for their benefit, and indirectly preserved for the benefit of other creditors. *See* Restatement (Third) of Restitution and Unjust Enrichment § 59, cmt. d. The general rule also holds that the claimant's equitable interest in the fund cannot exceed the lowest intermediate balance of the account.

PROBLEM: THE COMINGLED BANK ACCOUNT

Clark, a trusted employee of CRT Communications, embezzled $10,000 from the company. First Clark used $5,000 to purchase various building supplies to make home improvements. The improvements actually enhanced the fair market value of the home, however, by just $2,000.

Clark took the remaining $5,000 and placed it into a bank account which already contained $2,000 of personal funds. Consider the following sequence of transactions:

T1   Deposit of $5,000 added to original $2,000.

T2   Withdrawal of $2,000 to purchase 100 shares of stock in High-flier Corp. The stock has advanced to a current market value of $4,000.

T3   Withdrawal of $3,000 to pay for miscellaneous living expenses, leaving a balance of $2,000 in the account.

T4   Deposit of $1,000 for a final balance of $3,000.

(a) What would be the equitable interests that CRT could assert against the bank account and the stock according to the rules in *Clayton's Case, Hallett's Estate, Oatway,* and the Restatement? How much would the company recover altogether under each approach?

(b) What would be the appropriate equitable remedy that CRT could assert against the home? In what amount?

ProData Computer Services, Inc. v. Ponec

256 Neb. 228, 590 N.W.2d 176 (1999).

■ Miller-Lerman, J.

Ronald E. Ponec appeals an order of the district court for Douglas County imposing a constructive trust on certain assets owned by Ponec in favor of appellee ProData Computer Services, Inc. We affirm.

Appellees Marion R. Wamsat and Joseph Alan Hartley started ProData, a computer business, in 1981. When they created ProData, Wamsat and Hartley were its sole shareholders, a status they continued to hold at the time of trial. Wamsat and Ponec were married to each other during the years of ProData's early growth. They were married in 1962. Wamsat and Ponec separated in 1990 and divorced in 1991.

* * * Wamsat and Hartley detected several categories of financial transactions in which Ponec repeatedly converted ProData funds to his own use. The first category consisted of checks written by Ponec on ProData's DCBT money market account for large sums of cash. Ponec "buried" these checks in ProData's records as payments to fictitious vendors. The second category of questionable transactions included direct payments from ProData's DCBT account for personal luxuries Ponec afforded himself, including investments, jewelry, clothing, guns, and a country club membership. Wamsat and Hartley found that Ponec had funded monthly payments for his personally owned Mercedes Benz automobile from ProData's WSB operating account. Ponec had also taken customer checks made payable to ProData for professional services and deposited them directly into his own checking account.

ProData filed suit against Ponec on February 23, 1996, seeking a judgment of $754,523.06 against Ponec for alleged fraud, conversion, embezzlement, breach of fiduciary obligations, and breach of his employment contract with ProData.

After filing its petition and before trial, ProData obtained pretrial attachment of certain assets owned by Ponec, including the home in which Ponec and his present wife resided in Elkhorn, Nebraska, and investment accounts that Ponec maintained at Dain Bosworth, Inc., and Wallace Weitz & Co. Shortly before trial, with the court's permission, ProData added a cause of action seeking imposition of a constructive trust upon these assets and others owned by Ponec.

[The jury returned a verdict in favor of ProData for $579,507.30 and the trial court imposed a constructive trust on all property belonging to Ponec. Ponec appeals, claiming that the trial court erred in imposing a constructive trust on his house and several investment accounts.] * * *

General Principles

On appeal, Ponec does not dispute the amount or correctness of the jury's verdict in favor of ProData. Ponec's appeal is limited to his claims that the trial court should not have imposed a constructive trust upon the house in which Ponec resides with his wife or upon Ponec's investment accounts at Dain Bosworth, Inc., and Wallace Weitz & Co.

A constructive trust is a relationship, with respect to property, subjecting the person who holds title to the property to an equitable duty to convey it to another on the grounds that his or her acquisition or retention of the property would constitute unjust enrichment. An action to impose a constructive trust sounds in equity. [Citation]

A party seeking to impose a constructive trust has the burden to establish a constructive trust by clear and convincing evidence. Real property may be the subject of a constructive trust. Intangible property and liquid assets such as stocks, and bank and investment accounts may also be held subject to a constructive trust. Regardless of the nature of the property upon which the constructive trust is imposed, a plaintiff seeking to establish the trust must prove by clear and convincing evidence that the individual holding the property obtained title to it by fraud, misrepresentation, or an abuse of an influential or confidential relationship and that under the circumstances, such individual should not, according to the rules of equity and good conscience, hold and enjoy the property so obtained. [Citations] * * *

Mootness: Ponec's House

As his first assignment of error, Ponec claimed that for a variety of reasons the constructive trust imposed on his house in Elkhorn is improper. At oral argument of this case on January 8, 1999, counsel for both the parties stipulated that in view of the fact that the house had been disposed of, the appellate issue pertaining to the imposition of the constructive trust on the house is moot. We therefore treat the issue of the constructive trust on the house as moot. * * *

Ponec's Investment Accounts

Ponec claims that the trial court erred in imposing a constructive trust on his investment accounts at Dain Bosworth, Inc., and Wallace Weitz &

Co. Ponec admitted ownership of these accounts and he testified at trial that he deposited ProData funds into his investment accounts at Dain Bosworth, Inc., and Wallace Weitz & Co. Trial exhibits 57, 59, and 65 established, and Ponec admitted, that from October 1993 through December 1995, Ponec deposited a total of $67,931.99 of ProData's funds directly into his Dain Bosworth, Inc., accounts. Exhibits 71 and 83 established, and Ponec admitted, that in 1995, he used $20,000 in ProData funds to purchase investments for his Wallace Weitz & Co. account.

On appeal, Ponec nevertheless claims that a constructive trust cannot be imposed upon these investment accounts because he established them before the funds taken from ProData were discovered. Ponec also claims that a constructive trust is improper because part of the total investments in these accounts may have been purchased with funds other than those proved to have been wrongfully taken by Ponec from ProData. We find both of these arguments unpersuasive. Ponec admitted taking the funds at issue and forwarding them to Dain Bosworth, Inc., and Wallace Weitz & Co. for investment in his personal accounts. He admitted that neither ProData nor either of its shareholders received the benefit of the ProData funds or investments purchased therewith at Ponec's direction. Trial evidence supported ProData's claim that the corporation and its officers were unaware of Ponec's misdeeds for at least 4 years preceding their discovery of Ponec's unauthorized financial transactions.

We have previously stated:

Where money is the asset upon which the [constructive] trust is based, it is necessary that the specific amounts be identified and located, either by tracing the money to a specific and existing account, or where the funds have been converted into another type of asset such as by the purchase of real property, the money must be traced into the item of property. [Citation]

The fact that Ponec's investment accounts existed prior to the deposit of the funds he obtained from ProData is immaterial to our analysis of this case. Where money is the asset upon which a constructive trust is based, the amount of money subject to trust may be identified and located by, inter alia, tracing the money into a specific and existing account. In the instant case, the money from ProData has been clearly and convincingly traced into the two investment accounts.

Ponec suggests that the investment accounts should be excluded from imposition of a constructive trust, because the ProData funds as invested in Ponec's accounts may have appreciated in value. The law is clear that if the beneficiary of a constructive trust proves his or her entitlement to imposition of such a trust by clear and convincing evidence, the beneficiary's judgment interest may in appropriate cases be satisfied not only by the original value which constitutes the trust corpus, but also by the reasonable value of the appreciation of that asset.

Furthermore, we have recently observed: " 'An agent or other fiduciary who deals with the subject-matter of the agency so as to make a profit for himself will be held to account in equity as trustee for all profits and advantages acquired by him in such dealings. . . .' " *Mischke II*, 253 Neb. at 447, 571 N.W.2d at 255–56. In *Mischke II,* this court affirmed imposition of a constructive trust upon preexisting real and personal property and funds derived therefrom that were manipulated for personal gain by an estate's personal representative. We find no error in the trial court's finding that the fact that Ponec established the accounts before his misdeeds were discovered was not determinative as to imposition of a constructive trust upon the investment funds.

Ponec testified that during 1991 to 1995, he had no source of earned income other than his ProData salary and, in addition, some limited interest on investments. ProData introduced uncontroverted evidence that during that time period, at least $87,931.99 of its funds were deposited by Ponec directly into his personal investment accounts at Dain Bosworth, Inc., and Wallace Weitz & Co. ProData introduced further uncontroverted evidence that during that time, Ponec deposited more than $247,000 in checks made payable to ProData by its customers into Ponec's personal checking account for his own use. The trial evidence was also undisputed that from 1991 through 1995, Ponec issued drafts to himself for cash from ProData's accounts totaling more than $30,000, all for his personal use. * * * Upon our de novo review, we determine that the evidence clearly and convincingly establishes that the unauthorized ProData funds found their way into Ponec's investment accounts and that the imposition of a constructive trust on the accounts was proper.

Conclusion

The trial court's order provided generally that ProData was entitled to imposition of constructive trusts upon Ponec's assets, including but not limited to Ponec's house and Ponec's Dain Bosworth, Inc., and Wallace Weitz & Co. investment accounts. Issues surrounding the imposition of a constructive trust on the house are moot. The record on appeal demonstrates that ProData met its burden of proof by clear and convincing evidence as to the imposition of the constructive trust on the investment accounts. On this record, we find no error in the trial court's order imposing a constructive trust in favor of ProData on Ponec's Dain Bosworth, Inc., and Wallace Weitz & Co. investment accounts.

Affirmed

----

1. *Multiple Claimants.* The tracing rules do not artificially create priorities between multiple restitution claimants with respect to commingled assets, however. Cunningham v. Brown, 265 U.S. 1, 44 S.Ct. 424, 68 L.Ed. 873 (1924). Where multiple claimants are fraudulently deprived of property, some may be able to identify and trace the product of their separate property and obtain restitution through a constructive trust. Other victims may fail to receive equitable restitution, such as if their property was dissipated or otherwise became untraceable. Thus, although

various parties are similarly situated by virtue of innocently suffering property loss through fraud, the reality is that their relative recovery in equity may vary widely. See Restatement (Third) of Restitution and Unjust Enrichment § 59, cmt.g (law of restitution does not impose a rule of contribution or loss-sharing between innocent victims of wrongdoing). On the other hand, where such tracing of actual transactions cannot be accomplished, then courts may ratably allocate recovery from a commingled fund and its product in relative proportion to the claimant's losses. See Restatement (Third) of Restitution and Unjust Enrichment § 59(4).

2. In *Harris Trust and Savings Bank v. Salomon Smith Barney, Inc.*, 530 U.S. 238, 120 S.Ct. 2180, 147 L.Ed.2d 187 (2000), a trustee for a pension trust claimed that a brokerage company violated ERISA by participating in a prohibited transaction. ERISA allows civil actions for "appropriate equitable relief" in certain circumstances. The Court made the following observation regarding limitations in equity using an analogous situation where property was obtained by fraud:

"Whenever the legal title to property is obtained through means or under circumstances 'which render it unconscientious for the holder of the legal title to retain and enjoy the beneficial interest, equity impresses a constructive trust on the property thus acquired in favor of the one who is truly and equitably entitled to the same, although he may never, perhaps, have had any legal estate therein; and a court of equity has jurisdiction to reach the property either in the hands of the original wrongdoer, or in the hands of any subsequent holder, until a purchaser of it in good faith and without notice acquires a higher right and takes the property relieved from the trust.'" *Moore v. Crawford,* 130 U.S. 122, 128, 9 S.Ct. 447, 32 L.Ed. 878 (1889) (quoting 2 J. Pomeroy, Equity Jurisprudence § 1053, pp. 628–629 (1886)).

Importantly, that a transferee was not "the original wrongdoer" does not insulate him from liability for restitution. See also, *e.g.,* Restatement of Restitution ch. 7, Introductory Note, p. 522 (1937); 1 Dobbs, *supra,* § 4.3(2), p. 597 ("The constructive trust is based on property, not wrongs"). 120 S.Ct. at 2189.

3. In *Republic Supply Co. v. Richfield Oil Co.*, 79 F.2d 375 (9th Cir.1935), the issue was the best method for calculating the amount of an equitable lien upon a bank account which contains commingled funds. The court considered the argument that recovery should be limited to the lowest balance reached by the commingled account between the dates of misappropriations and the dates of acquisition of the specified pieces of property. It held that the appropriate method should be based upon the close of the banking day, when all transactions for that day are posted. The court also made the following observation about following misappropriated funds:

It is established beyond debate that no change of form can divest a trust fund of its trust character, and that the cestui may follow and reclaim his funds so long as he is able to trace and identify them, not as his original dollars or necessarily as any dollars, but through and into any form into which his dollars may have been converted. The underlying principle of this rule is that the cestui que trust has been wrongfully deprived of that which belongs to him; that his right to his funds has not been lost or destroyed by the misappropriation; and that if, and to the extent, the cestui is able to follow and identify the amount of the misappropriated funds as having been used in the acquisition of other property, he may recover. 79 F.2d at 377.

What would be the practical effect of a rule that a plaintiff's money is no longer traceable as soon as it is commingled with money not belonging to the plaintiff? Is this result defensible as a matter of public policy if some primary purposes of abolishing the commingled funds rules are to save judicial time and to reduce litigation costs?

4.   For classical commentary regarding the role of tracing in restitution, *see* Wade, The Literature of the Law of Restitution, 19 Hastings L.J. 1087 (1968); McConville, Tracing and the Rule in Clayton's Case, 79 L.Q.Rev. 388 (1963); Scott, Following the Res and Sharing the Product, 66 Harv.L.Rev. 872 (1953); Scott, The Right to Follow Money Wrongfully Mingled with Other Money, 27 Harv.L.Rev. 125 (1913); Ames, Following Misappropriated Property Into Its Product, 19 Harv.L.Rev. 511 (1906).

B.   BONA FIDE PURCHASER AND CHANGE IN POSITION

Section Coverage:

A person holding an equitable interest in property, such as through a constructive trust or an equitable lien, is precluded from enforcing that interest against a third person who has acquired legal title to the property for value and without notice of the equitable interest. There are two policies that result in the protection of the legal title obtained by a bona fide purchaser: (1) legal title is deemed superior and therefore will defeat equitable title, and (2) between two innocent parties, a court of equity will not impose the loss on the party who has innocently acquired title to the property for value. The bona fide purchaser defense applies with equal force to various property rights; the subject matter may involve realty, personalty, or negotiable instruments.

Consider a typical case where a trustee wrongfully conveys legal title to trust property to a third person who pays value and who has no notice that the transfer is in violation of the trust. The trust beneficiary possesses mere equitable title and therefore may not obtain specific restitution of the property in the hands of the bona fide purchaser who has legal title. The beneficiary's remedy will lie only against the wrongdoer.

Another defense to restitution is known as "change in position." A court may deny a restitutionary remedy if the defendant would be adversely affected by virtue of circumstances which have materially changed after receipt of the benefit. This defense is predicated upon the policy that a court retains discretion to withhold relief or to fashion an order to the extent desirable to achieve an equitable result. A court may appropriately determine that the defendant's change of circumstances should preclude restitution either entirely or only partially. Nonetheless, if the defendant has acted tortiously or was substantially more at fault than the claimant with respect to the subject matter involved, the court may order restitution despite the hardship from a change in position.

A common example of the change of position defense is where a person mistakenly delivers goods to another under circumstances which would constitute unjust enrichment. Ordinarily the recipient would be required to make restitution. If, however, the goods are subsequently destroyed by fire, not as a consequence of tortious conduct by the recipient and the recipient was no more at fault than the claimant for the loss, a court could properly decline to order restitution. One is not charged with a duty to care for the misdelivered goods until the recipient has knowledge of the mistake and had an opportunity to return the goods. The defense of changed circumstances is especially strong if the recipient has not beneficially used the goods and if an order to make restitution would effect an unreasonable hardship.

Model Case:

Cory Douglas was appointed by a court to serve as the guardian of the person and the estate of a minor named Rebecca. According to the terms of the court's order, Douglas had full fiduciary authority to manage Rebecca's assets on her behalf.

Douglas misappropriated several thousand dollars from the assets. Instead of paying the bill for tuition fees and boarding expenses to the private school which Rebecca attended, Douglas purchased a sports car for a favorite cousin. Douglas subsequently left the state and became insolvent.

A court may impose a constructive trust on the sports car, and order specific restitution to protect the equitable interest held by Rebecca as the beneficiary. The cousin, even if lacking knowledge of the breach of Douglas' fiduciary duties, would be characterized as a gratuitous donee. The cousin did not pay value for the sports car and therefore is not a protected bona fide purchaser.

City of Hastings v. Jerry Spady

212 Neb. 137, 322 N.W.2d 369 (1982).

■ Hamilton, District Judge.

This is an action brought by the appellee, City of Hastings, in equity to impress a constructive trust upon real property purchased by appellant, Jerry Spady Pontiac–Cadillac, Inc., from the Missouri Improvement Company, a subsidiary of Missouri Pacific Railroad Company. The District Court found generally for the City of Hastings and imposed a constructive trust.

During 1977 and part of 1978 Duane Stromer was city attorney for the City of Hastings, and during said period was also attorney for Jerry Spady Pontiac–Cadillac, Inc.

In 1976 the planning director for the City of Hastings began the development of the Hastings comprehensive plan. As part of this plan it was contemplated that F Street would be extended along property owned by the Missouri Pacific Railroad Company, but no longer used as railroad right-of-way. This extension of F Street was a material part of the comprehensive plan, since it would provide the city with its only major thoroughfare crossing the city from east to west in the south part of town.

The extension of F Street was clearly shown on the comprehensive plan that was submitted to the Hastings Planning Commission in March of 1977, which was attended by Duane Stromer in his capacity as city attorney. It became obvious at this point in time that the acquisition of the abandoned railroad right-of-way by the City of Hastings was an absolute necessity to accomplish the intent and purposes of the comprehensive plan insofar as it applied to the extension of F Street.

* * *

In August of 1977 Duane Stromer made a written offer to purchase the property for $6,890, which was rejected. In correspondence to the Missouri Pacific on September 6, 1977, Stromer advised the Missouri Pacific that the City of Hastings was not interested in purchasing the property because a decision had been made not to put a street through in that area. Stromer further advised that his offer was made personally without regard to the City of Hastings. The record reflects this to be a deliberate falsehood, for at the very same time the city planning director was, with city approval, obtaining appraisals so as to submit an offer of purchase to the Missouri Pacific.

On September 21, 1977, by letter, Stromer accepted an offer of the Missouri Pacific and agreed to pay $10,900 for the property. On September 22, 1977, the engineering committee of the city council held a meeting. The F Street property was on the agenda. Duane Stromer requested of the committee chairman that he be put on the agenda. At the meeting Stromer informed the committee that he had acquired the property and that he would be willing to transfer the property to the city for what he had in it, which was stated to be approximately $20,000.

It was at this point that the city council first learned of Stromer's conduct and an apparent conflict of interest. The mayor discussed the matter with Stromer and then advised the council that Stromer had agreed to get out of the transaction and to allow the city to proceed with its acquisition of the property.

On October 12, 1977, Stromer wrote to the Missouri Pacific and made the following statement: "Apparently, the City of Hastings, Nebraska is now interested in purchasing the said land which I did not know about at the time we began negotiations in April. To avoid any possible conflict, I must withdraw my offer to purchase the said land."

Before the letter arrived Mr. Henderson of the Missouri Pacific received a telephone call from Stromer advising him to disregard the letter when he received it. Stromer further advised Mr. Henderson that the deal was still on and he wanted the deed to be issued to the Bonnavilla Plaza Corporation. This corporation was wholly owned by Jerry Spady.

During November and December Stromer had advised the Missouri Pacific he was checking the title and that the money would be sent as soon as the title check had been completed. The City of Hastings, during this period, had completed appraisals on the property and had agreed to offer the Missouri Pacific the sum of $18,000. The matter was placed on the agenda for the city council meeting of January 9, 1978. The motion to offer the $18,000 was passed on said date. On that same date Stromer obtained a check from Jerry Spady Pontiac–Cadillac, Inc., in the amount of $10,900 and forwarded the check to the Missouri Pacific, requesting that the property be deeded to Jerry Spady Pontiac–Cadillac, Inc., which was done, and the deed was mailed to Stromer on February 8, 1978.

* * *

The record reflects that at no time had the City of Hastings ever authorized Duane Stromer to negotiate on its behalf, nor had the city any knowledge that Stromer was representing to others that he was negotiating on its behalf.

* * *

It is fundamental law that an attorney must not while representing a client do anything knowingly that is inconsistent with the terms of his employment or contrary to the best interests of his client. "An attorney is by virtue of his office disqualified from representing interests which are adverse in the sense that they are hostile, antagonistic, or in conflict with each other." [Citation.]

The facts in the record show that all negotiations with the Missouri Pacific for the purchase of the property in question were conducted by Duane Stromer representing to the sellers that he was representing the City of Hastings, himself, or the appellant. At all times during said negotiations Duane Stromer had actual knowledge that his employer, the City of Hastings, was interested in and intended to purchase the subject property. Duane Stromer, as city attorney, had a fiduciary duty to his employer not to act in a manner inconsistent with the employer's best interests. Clearly the action of Duane Stromer to actively participate in the acquisition of property either for himself personally or for a third-party client, when he had actual knowledge that his employer was not only interested in purchasing the property but considered it a necessity to accomplish the intent and purpose of the employer's comprehensive plan, was a breach of his fiduciary duty to his employer.

An attorney cannot purchase or negotiate for an interest in land in which his own client is interested. [Citations.]

The breach of fiduciary duty having been so clearly established, the City of Hastings was required to show only that Jerry Spady Pontiac–Cadillac, Inc., was not a bona fide purchaser for value. The trial court must have concluded that appellant had either actual or constructive knowledge of the City of Hastings' equitable claim to the property. The record before us requires such a finding. The letter of Duane Stromer to the Missouri Pacific on October 12, 1977, specifically refers to the City of Hastings' interest in the property, and although actual knowledge is not necessary, it is inconceivable that with the close personal association of Duane Stromer with Jerry Spady, as reflected in this record, appellant did not have actual knowledge of the equitable claim of the City of Hastings. Jerry Spady had actual knowledge that Duane Stromer was representing the City of Hastings and at the same time representing him.

It is clear that notice to, or knowledge of facts by, an attorney is notice to, or knowledge of, his client. [Citation.]

The actual knowledge of Duane Stromer of the city's interest in that property is imputed to his client, appellant herein, and that knowledge and notice of Stromer's breach of fiduciary duty negates any claim of being a bona fide purchaser for value by the appellant.

A bona fide purchaser exists where the purchaser takes without knowledge or notice of any suspicious circumstances which would put a prudent man upon inquiry. [Citations.]

Where, as here, the titleholder of real estate takes title to property with actual or constructive knowledge of the breach of a fiduciary duty by an attorney to his client amounting to fraud, the court will impose a constructive trust upon the title-holder and require that title be transferred to the defrauded party.

A constructive trust will be imposed against those who knowingly aid or participate in a breach of trust. [Citation.] To rule otherwise would permit wrongdoers to be unjustly enriched or otherwise benefit parties who have obtained property with actual or constructive knowledge of the fraudulent actions of their agent in acquiring the property.

The action and judgment of the trial court was correct and the judgment is affirmed.

----

1. *Notice.* A transferee must take property without notice of the facts that give rise to equitable restitutionary interests in order to receive protection as a bona fide purchaser. The notice requirement encompasses both actual knowledge as well as imputed knowledge where a party has reason to know facts that give rise to the claim in restitution. The constructive notice concept includes notice through statutes, recording of instruments, and a general duty of due diligence to inquire into the relevant facts regarding a transaction. *See* Restatement (Third) of Restitution and Unjust Enrichment § 69(2); cmts. a, f.

Commercial law may establish certain terms and requirements regarding the type of notice that bears upon whether a purchaser receives protection in a transaction. For example, a holder of negotiable instruments takes free of equitable claims if value was paid in good faith, even though the holder was negligent in failing to discover fraud. U.C.C. §§ 1–201(19)(25); 3–304; 8–304. The defense requires proof only that the transferee of a negotiable instrument is subjectively honest; there is no duty of due care imposing an objective standard of reasonable knowledge.

2.   In certain circumstances a principal will be charged with the knowledge of an agent acquired during the agency relationship. *See* Bronowski v. Magnus Enterprises, Inc., 61 A.D.2d 879, 402 N.Y.S.2d 868 (1978).

In a leading early case, *Newton v. Porter*, 69 N.Y. 133 (1877), thieves stole bearer bonds from the plaintiff, sold them, and used the proceeds to purchase other securities. The thieves subsequently were arrested and transferred the securities to the lawyers they had employed as payment for their services. The plaintiff sued the lawyers, seeking to impose a constructive trust on the securities which had been acquired with the proceeds of the stolen bonds. The court granted the constructive trust after determining that the lawyers had notice of the tainted history of the securities and thus were not bona fide purchasers. The decision is also noteworthy because the court imposed a constructive trust in a situation of simple theft.

3.   A person may be chargeable with constructive notice of an equitable restitutionary claim where a deed, will, mortgage, or other instrument has been recorded in a public office. *See* Restatement (Third) of Restitution and Unjust Enrichment § 69(3)(b). Conversely, a purchaser of real estate may be entitled to rely on recorded titles, and will not be subordinated to unrecorded equities of which the purchaser has no actual or constructive knowledge. *See, e.g.,* Matter of Phillips, 21 B.R. 565 (Bkrtcy.D.Conn.1982). On the other hand, notice may be imputed to a transferee in instances where a reasonably diligent investigation would have revealed the existence of the beneficiary's equitable interest.

4.   *Value.* What constitutes giving "value" for purposes of achieving bona fide purchaser status and consequently receiving protection from the interests of beneficiaries of constructive trusts and equitable liens? The Restatement (Third) of Restitution and Unjust Enrichment § 68 essentially tracks the rules regarding value pertaining to express trusts as stated in the Restatement (Second) of Trusts §§ 298–305.

Notably, satisfaction of an antecedent debt is not effective against the beneficiary of an express trust but the Restatement (Third) of Restitution and Unjust Enrichment § 68(2) refers the issue to local law to determine if it constitutes giving value sufficient to qualify as a bona fide purchaser. See Restatement (Second) of Trusts § 304.

Despite a division of authority, the modern trend shows some liberalization toward recognizing that a person receiving property as security for or in satisfaction of a pre-existing obligation is a purchaser for value. The rule that satisfaction of an antecedent debt does not constitute value has been changed by statute in commercial law. U.C.C. § 1–204(2); § 3–303(a)(3). The opposing view was followed in *Meier v. Meyer*, 153 Neb. 222, 43 N.W.2d 502 (1950). In that case the plaintiff made a loan induced by fraud to Owens. Owens deposited the money in a bank account and used part of the funds to discharge a pre-existing debt owed to a third party who had no notice of the fraud. The court allowed the plaintiff to impose a constructive trust on the funds traceable to the third party.

5. The requirement of giving value is not governed by the same principles as consideration for formation of a contract; the test for bona fide purchasers is a narrower one. Uniform Commercial Code § 1–201(44) defines value as "any consideration sufficient to support a simple contract," which would include the making of a promise. In contrast, an executory promise to make payment in the future for a transfer of property is not considered a transfer for value sufficient to cut off a beneficiary's equitable interest. The present payment of money or furnishing of goods or services may be made either by the transferee or by a third person, and may be made either prior or subsequent to the transfer of property, provided it occurs before notice of the equitable interest. See generally Restatement (Third) of Restitution and Unjust Enrichment § 68 cmt. e.

6. Will a transferee be accorded bona fide purchaser status if the value given in exchange for the property is significantly below the property's fair market value? In *Walters v. Calderon*, 25 Cal.App.3d 863, 102 Cal.Rptr. 89 (1972), the plaintiff sought to impose a constructive trust on a $60,000 note and deed of trust which had been assigned by the plaintiff's father, Walters, to a friend, Calderon, for $10 and the promise "to provide a home for and considerately care for W.S. Walters, including medical and burial expenses, for the remainder of W.S. Walters' life." The court held that the assignee had given sufficient value to satisfy the requirements of being a bona fide purchaser, and stated: "Generally, some value means any value whatever, even that of a peppercorn, a tomtit, or one dollar in hand."

Did the court confuse the adequacy of consideration necessary for contract formation with the requirement of value for purposes of characterizing a transferee as a bona fide purchaser? Compare Restatement (Third) of Restitution and Unjust Enrichment § 68, cmt. h, where it is suggested that evidence of below market value paid for property may suffice to put the transferee on notice of the existence of outstanding equitable claims.

7. A transferee, in addition to giving value and acquiring property without notice of equitable claims, must obtain legal title rather than equitable title in order to prevail as a bona fide purchaser over the competing equitable interests. In *Snuffin v. Mayo*, 6 Wash.App. 525, 494 P.2d 497 (1972), the court held that a vendee had acquired only an equitable title in an executory contract to purchase land, with legal title remaining in the vendor until the full purchase price had been paid. Consequently, the vendee was not considered a bona fide purchaser, and could not prevail in an unlawful detainer action.

Reisner v. Stoller

51 F.Supp.2d 430 (S.D.N.Y.1999).

[A widower, Ms. Reisner, sold her home and moved with her two sons to White Plains, New York. While living there she became involved in a romantic relationship with Mr. Augello, who was married to someone else. In 1977, she sought to purchase a home jointly with Augello. Although she assumed that she was the record owner, the deed and the mortgage were in his name only. She paid the down payment and moved into the home with her sons. For the next twenty years she paid all the mortgage payments to Augello in cash and he forwarded the payments to the bank using his personal checks. Ms. Reisner also paid for all utilities, taxes, expenses and maintenance of the premises, believing that she was the owner of the house. In 1992 she learned that her name was not on the deed. Augello maintained that she was merely renting the property from him and, when difficulties over ownership continued, he instituted eviction proceedings. The parties assert numerous claims regarding the property; the portion pertaining to the equitable interest asserted by Ms. Reisner is excerpted.]
* * *

Equitable Lien

An equitable lien is a right to charge specific property or its proceeds with the payment of a particular debt. With respect to real property, an equitable lien is created by implication when a party standing in a confidential relationship with the legal owner of the property makes payments from his or her own funds toward the purchase price, reduction of the mortgage or improvements to the real property under circumstances which would entitle that party to restitution. Restatement (First) of Restitution §§ 161–170 (1936). A court of equity imposes an equitable lien upon the property as a measure of restitution to prevent the owner of the property from being unjustly enriched by his abuse of the confidential relationship. Restatement (First) of Restitution § 161 cmt. a (1936).[29] The remedy is the embodiment of the maxim, "equity regards as done that which ought to be done."

The statute of frauds presents no bar to the recognition of an equitable lien upon real property because the lienor seeks to prevent unjust enrichment, not to enforce an oral conveyance of property. Further, with respect to mortgage payments, the equitable lien is merely a form of subrogation.[30]

Despite the under-current of fraudulent misrepresentation, actions seeking the imposition of a constructive trust or equitable lien are not

---

29. If the party claiming the lien had the benefit of the use and occupancy of the premises, he or she will not be credited for the amount paid for taxes, insurance, or ordinary maintenance and repairs to the extent that such payments are off-set by the value of such use and occupancy.

30. Restatement (First) of Restitution § 162 provides: ("where property of one person is used in discharging an obligation owed by another or a lien upon the property of another, under such circumstances that the other would be unjustly enriched by the retention of the benefit thus conferred, the former is entitled to be subrogated to the position of the obligee or lien-holder").

based on actual fraud—rather they seek to prevent unjust enrichment. *See* restatement (First) of Restitution § 161 cmt. a. Therefore, the statute of limitations for common-law fraud is not applicable. Claims for the creation of an equitable lien are subject to the six-year statute of limitations under N.Y.C.P.L.R. 213(1) pertaining to actions "for which no limitation is specifically prescribed by law." The six-year time period requires the party claiming the lien to file an action within six years from the date the cause of action accrues (*i.e.,* the date when the property is wrongfully withheld from the party asserting the lien)—it does not limit the amount of the lien to payments or improvements made within the six years prior to filing.

Once real property is found to be held subject to an equitable lien, if the owner of the property refuses to pay the amount of the lien, a court of equity may order the mortgage or sale of the property so that the lien may be paid out of the proceeds. *See* restatement (First) of Restitution § 161 cmt. b; *Disanza v. Gaglione,* 126 Misc.2d 232, 482 N.Y.S.2d 413, 415 (Sup.Ct.1984) (ex-wife's equitable lien could be enforced through execution and sale of former husband's property unless he paid amount of lien; execution and sale available only where lienor previously held title to property). If the property has been transferred to a bona fide purchaser,[FM 31: A bona fide purchaser is someone who purchases the property without notice and for value. *See* restatement (First) of Restitution § 161 cmt. d, § 172(1) and cmt. e, § 174. A properly filed lis pendens constitutes constructive notice to all potential purchasers and thus prevents the acquisition of the property by a bona fide purchaser capable of extinguishing an equitable interest in the property. *See* N.Y.C.P.L.R. § 6501. If property is transferred to someone who is not a bona fide purchaser, the purchaser acquires the property subject to the equitable lien. See restatement (First) of Restitution § 168(1) and cmt. b.] the court can trace the funds from the sale and impress a lien upon the property acquired with the proceeds. *See* restatement (First) of Restitution § 161 cmt. e. If the sale proceeds were not used to purchase new property, or are otherwise untraceable, a court of equity may enter a decree holding the defendant personally liable for the amount of the lien. *See* restatement (First) of Restitution §§ 4(d), 4(f), 161 cmt. e.

Here, the complaint alleges that Ms. Reisner, an elderly widow, became intimately involved with Augello, and trusted him to act in her best interests in connection with the purchase of her new home, obeying all of his legal instructions and financial demands. These allegations are clearly sufficient to support a finding that she and Augello stood in a confidential relationship. *See Williams v. Lynch,* 245 A.D.2d 715, 716, 666 N.Y.S.2d 749, 751–52 (3d Dep't 1997), *appeal dismissed,* 91 N.Y.2d 957, 694 N.E.2d 886, 671 N.Y.S.2d 717 (1998) (finding confidential relationship where parties' relationship was analogous to that of husband and wife, plaintiff reasonably trusted defendant, relied on him to protect her interests and "acceded to defendant's self-serving demands in certain financial matters because she trusted him"); *Sharp v. Kosmalski,* 40 N.Y.2d 119, 121, 351 N.E.2d 721, 386 N.Y.S.2d 72 (1976) (confidential relationship found to exist between 56–year–old widower whose education did not go beyond the eighth grade and school teacher 16 years his junior with whom plaintiff had established a very close relationship after the death of his wife).

The complaint further alleges that Ms. Reisner paid the downpayment on the Premises out of her own funds and made all subsequent mortgage payments in cash to Augello. The initial downpayment and all mortgage payments made between 1977 and 1992 were made under the mistaken belief that she had title to the Premises. Although she learned in June of 1992 that her name was not on the deed, Ms. Reisner continued to live on the Premises and make mortgage payments (and possibly other improvements to the property) for many years thereafter. The only conceivable explanation for such an arrangement is that, upon Ms. Reisner's discovery that title was held in Augello's name alone, Augello promised to transfer title to the Premises or grant Ms. Reisner a life estate in the Premises. Even in the absence of such an express (albeit oral) agreement, the complaint sufficiently states a claim for the creation of an equitable lien by implication. Assuming the truth of the allegations set forth in the complaint, Augello would be unjustly enriched if he were to enjoy the benefit of any improvements made to, or increased equity in, the Premises under these circumstances. Therefore, Ms. Reisner would be entitled to an equitable lien in the full amount of her expenditures as long as they amounted to less than the full purchase price of the property.

Further, Ms. Reisner's claim asserting an equitable lien on the Premises is not barred by the doctrine of res judicata. Since 1977, Augello has been under a continuing obligation to transfer title or some lesser interest in the Premises to Ms. Reisner. As long as Ms. Reisner continued to occupy the Premises, the implied trust relationship was not breached. Indeed, the cause of action did not accrue until the Premises were wrongfully withheld from Ms. Reisner, *i.e.,* the date that she was evicted from the Premises, which she alleges to have been April 13, 1998. Therefore, Ms. Reisner's claim for an equitable lien could not have been brought in the Supreme Court proceeding before Justice Sherwood. Having filed the within complaint on May 6, 1998, Ms. Reisner has asserted a timely claim for the imposition of an equitable lien against the Premises for payments she made toward the purchase price, reduction of the mortgage and improvements to Premises. The fact that damages are sought for the alleged RICO violations does not mean that Ms. Reisner's injuries are fully compensable at law. A cause of action for an equitable lien is adequately pled and the ad damnum provision requests "such other and further relief as may be just herein."
* * *

1. A bona fide purchaser's rights are superior to prior equitable interests. In contrast, a judgment creditor possessing a statutory lien on property is not accorded the same priority status over previous equitable claims even though the creditor had no notice of such equitable interest.

See Hunnicutt Construction, Inc. v. Stewart Title and Trust of Tucson Trust No. 3496, 187 Ariz. 301, 305, 928 P.2d 725, 729 (App.1996).

2. In *F.T.C. v. Network Services Depot, Inc.*, 617 F.3d 1127 (9th Cir. 2010), the FTC investigated a group of companies and their principals for an alleged Ponzi scheme. The companies subsequently retained a lawyer and paid a flat fee for representation. In an ensuing civil action, the government was awarded equitable monetary relief against the companies for various FTC violations. The court also imposed a constructive trust over a portion of the attorney's fees, reasoning that the lawyer's fees were paid from funds derived from the unlawful activities. The court rejected the attorney's argument that the fees should be exempted from equitable restitution on the basis of the bona fide purchaser for value rule, finding that the attorney had an obligation to make a good faith inquiry into the source of the fees.

See also Hale v. Finn, 388 S.C. 79, 694 S.E.2d 51, 59 (App. 2010) (constructive trust imposed to secure division of attorney's fees that would satisfy right to quantum meruit recovery from another attorney); Nichols v. Nichols, 222 P.3d 1049 (Ok. 2009) (when attorney's fee is paid directly to the prevailing party, a constructive trust attaches by operation of law to fee award for benefit of client's lawyer).

3. In *First Union Nat. Bank v. A.G. Edwards & Sons, Inc.*, 262 A.D.2d 106, 691 N.Y.S.2d 491 (1999), plaintiff banks sought to recover funds that were fraudulently obtained by a third party and were invested in various brokerage accounts. The plaintiffs alleged that an ordinarily prudent broker should have been on notice of facts and circumstances to investigate the source of the money. The court rejected the inquiry notice argument, reasoning that it would conflict with the "strong public interest in maintaining the finality of payments of money in business transactions to require frequent inquiries by firms into the sources of funds paid in the ordinary course of business."

Compare *In re Bell & Beckwith*, 838 F.2d 844, 849 (6th Cir.1988), where a bankruptcy trustee sought to recover assets of a debtor brokerage firm that were paid to an attorney for representing the firm's managing partner in a criminal case. The court held that the attorney was not a bona fide purchaser for value protected from a constructive trust on the funds because the circumstances surrounding the payment of the fees placed the attorney under a duty of inquiry to conduct a reasonable investigation to determine the source of the fee payment. The court quoted with approval the statement, "a person cannot shut his eyes or ears to avoid information and then say he had no notice or knowledge."

4. In *In re Marriage of Allen*, 724 P.2d 651 (Colo.1986), a husband misappropriated money from his employer, used the funds to improve his family residence and then subjected the property to division as marital property in a divorce settlement agreement. The employer sought a constructive trust against the traceable proceeds of property which the embezzler's wife held as part of the settlement arrangement. The court held that the wife could not claim bona fide purchaser status to defeat the construc-

tive trust claims even though she had acquired the property without knowledge of the embezzlement. Since she had not given "value" for the property, she was considered an innocent donee or a gratuitous transferee. The court reasoned that to give the ex-wife legal or equitable title to the products of the husband's wrongdoing by entering into the property settlement would constitute unjust enrichment.

5.   For classical commentary on the defense of bona fide purchaser, *see*: Ames, Following Misappropriated Property Into Its Product, 19 Harv. L.Rev. 511 (1906); Ames, Purchase for Value Without Notice, 1 Harv.L.Rev. 1 (1887); Gilmore, The Commercial Doctrine of Good Faith Purchase, 63 Yale L.J. 1057 (1954); Scott, Restitution from an Innocent Transferee Who is Not a Purchaser for Value, 62 Harv.L.Rev. 1002 (1949); Searey, Purchase for Value Without Notice, 23 Yale L.J. 447 (1914); Wade, The Literature of Restitution, 19 Hastings L.J. 1087 (1968).

Alexander Hamilton Life Ins. Co. v. Lewis

550 S.W.2d 558 (Ky.1977).

■ PALMORE, JUSTICE. * * *

The background [of this case] is that after their daughter had disappeared and her whereabouts had been unknown for over seven years the Lewises brought suit against the insurance company for the face amount of two insurance policies on her life, relying on KRS 422.130 (Presumption of Death). A judgment was entered in their favor and was paid by the insurance company. Then the daughter was discovered alive and the company filed its CR 60.02 motion to set the judgment aside. Following a denial of that relief this court held that the company was entitled to it under both CR 60.02(2) [newly discovered evidence] and CR 60.02(6) ["reason of an extraordinary nature justifying relief"].

After setting aside the order denying relief the trial court received evidence bearing on the disposition of the money by the Lewises and upon their present financial condition and entered a "judgment of restitution" directing them to repay $7218.40, being half of the money collected under the original judgment, without interest. The company appeals and the Lewises cross-appeal.

It is an accepted principle that money paid in obedience to a judgment that is later set aside must be repaid. [Citations.]

"A person who has conferred a benefit upon another in compliance with a judgment ... is entitled to restitution if the judgment is reversed or set aside, *unless restitution would be inequitable....*" (Emphasis added.) Restatement, *Restitution,* § 74.

The company insists that it is entitled to restitution in full. The Lewises rely on the portion of the Restatement, *Restitution,* § 74, that we have italicized, contending that in the name of "equity" restitution may be denied wholly or in part, as the circumstances warrant, and that in their situation it should be denied entirely. We see no just reason to deny any part of it.

The theory of restitution as a basis for recovery is about as old as the law itself. Though often assumed to be purely an equitable remedy, some of the earliest proceedings both at common law and in equity were founded upon it and were amplified in the course of time. The obvious justification for it is that one should not be unjustly enriched at the expense of another.

In Bridges v. McAlister, 106 Ky. 791, 51 S.W. 603, 21 KLR 428, 45 LRA 800, 90 Am.St.Rep. 267 (1899), the accountability of a party for actions taken under authority of a judgment later set aside was discussed at some length. Among other things the court concluded as follows: "When a judgment is reversed, restitution must be made of all that has been received under it, but no further liability should in any case be imposed." Our attention has not been directed to any precedent in this jurisdiction for relieving a party of the duty to restore all of the money paid to him under a judgment subsequently vacated. Understandably, of course, the receipt and disbursement of money by someone in a fiduciary capacity could very well present a different case, but when the party who received the money by authority of the judgment has spent some or all of it at his own volition and for his own ends, we find it difficult to accept the proposition that equity diminishes his accountability.

In this instance the Lewises spent $1935 to pay off a note, $1800 for improvements on their house, $3,000 for educating their son, $3155 for automobiles, and about $4800 for medical expenses and care of the returned daughter. They now have only about $6,000 in cash deposits, but their net worth substantially exceeds the amount received under the judgment against the insurance company.

According to § 142(1) of the Restatement, Restitution, "The right of a person to restitution from another because of a benefit received is terminated or diminished if, after the receipt of the benefit, circumstances have so changed that it would be inequitable to require the other to make full restitution." The *Comment* following that section explains that there is no such change in circumstances "where the money is used for the payment of living expenses, or even used to make gifts, unless such expenses were incurred or gifts made because of the receipt of the money and the amount of such payment was of such size that *considering the financial condition of the payee* it would be inequitable to require payment." [Emphasis added.]

The illustrations following that commentary do not reveal to our satisfaction a workable criterion for determining what is "inequitable." "Equity" is a broad term, allowing for as many different definitions as there are people who are familiar with it. Often overlooked, however, is the simple fact that both equity and equality are derived from the same word and have much more in common than a similar sound. We think of equity as an implement of sympathy and compassion, but its real meaning is more akin to equality. What is fair for one must be fair for the other. In this case, is it fair that the stockholders of the insurance company lose $7200 because the Lewises have spent the money? We do not think so. It was not the insurance company, but the Lewises, who claimed their daughter was dead, and it is not at all unjust to hold that when they took the money they had to do so at the risk of having to repay it if their claim proved to be unfounded, as it did. We perceive nothing in this record to raise an equitable defense in mitigation of the demand for restitution.

On the question of interest, there can be no doubt that the insurance company's claim for restitution, though quasi-contractual in nature, was "liquidated" and that interest ordinarily is recoverable as a matter of right on a liquidated claim. Interest may be allowed also on the basis of an implied contract, or quasi-contract, and probably should be if the money or property has been used for profit-making. * * *

When an innocent party uses the money or property of another in reliance upon a final unappealed judgment that says it is his, it can hardly be said that he is at fault unless and until he is put on notice of circumstances that justify or call for setting the judgment aside. In this case the Lewises learned on July 25, 1971, that their daughter was still alive. A private investigator employed by the insurance company discovered it on August 25, 1971. On the basis of these facts we are of the opinion that interest on the amount recoverable by the insurance company should run from July 25, 1971.

The judgment is reversed on the appeal and affirmed on the cross-appeal, with directions that a new judgment be entered in conformity with this opinion.

---

1. The newly revised Restatement (Third) of Restitution and Unjust Enrichment (2011) § 65 addresses the affirmative defense of change of position:

> If receipt of a benefit has led a recipient without notice to change position in such manner that an obligation to make restitution of the original benefit would be inequitable to the recipient, the recipient's liability in restitution is to that extent reduced.

2. The principal purposes, limitations and application of this equitable defense are explained in the comments to the Restatement (Third) of Restitution and Unjust Enrichment (2011):

> A transaction by which a claimant confers a benefit that is subject to restitution—the primary example in this context being a mistaken payment—will sometimes induce a detrimental change of position on the part of the recipient. If the recipient were thereafter required to restore the original benefit without deduction, the resulting liability in restitution would exceed the net enrichment of the recipient attributable to the transaction with the claimant. * * *

> The defense of change of position is available only to a recipient without notice (§ 69), and only to the extent that an obligation to make restitution would be inequitable to the recipient. The defense is

therefore unavailable to a conscious wrongdoer (§ 51(3)) or to a recipient who is primarily responsible for his own unjust enrichment (§ 52(3)).

* * * Much of the law of change of position is concerned with the distinction between transactions that result in economic loss and those that do not. A recipient who uses a mistaken payment to make a losing investment may have changed position, while one who merely repays a preexisting debt has not, because there is a loss in the first case but not in the second. See comment c. Notice on the part of the recipient precludes resort to the defense, because the recipient who acts with notice of the claimant's rights is in a better position than the claimant to avoid the loss that must later be allocated. See Comment f. Where the facts permit a direct comparison of the parties's responsibilities for the transaction giving rise to unjust enrichment, a recipient whose responsibility exceeds that of the claimant will not be allowed to assert the defense. (§ 52(3)). See Comments g and h. § 65, cmt. a.

3. In *CSX Transportation, Inc. v. Appalachian Railcar Services, Inc.*, 509 F.3d 384 (7th Cir. 2007), a train derailed and a number of railcars were damaged or destroyed. A company which owned a portion of track mistakenly believed that the derailment had occurred on its section of track so it paid the railroad for the damaged railcars.

A subsequent investigation revealed the mistake and the track owner brought an unjust enrichment claim against the railroad to recover the funds. The district court granted summary judgment to the defendant railroad on the basis that the funds had been paid voluntarily to discharge an uncertain obligation. Also, by the time the restitution claim was brought, the applicable statute of limitations had run. The defendant railroad therefore contended that restitution of the mistakenly paid funds should be denied on the basis of changed circumstances. The railroad asserted that because it reasonably believed the track owner was responsible for the derailment, it took no action to investigate the accident further and any possible claim against third parties would be barred by the statute of limitations.

The appellate court acknowledged that change of position could defeat the restitutionary claim if the railroad could not be returned to the status quo without being prejudiced. Conversely, the court observed that if the railroad had no potential claims against third parties, then the money paid by the claimant would constitute a windfall and must be repaid. Accordingly, the court reversed and remanded for a determination whether the railroad had reasonably relied on the payment of funds to their detriment.

4. A mistake of law may also influence whether change of position is considered an effective defense to a claim for equitable restitution. In *Island Federal Credit Union v. Smith*, 60 A.D.3d 730, 875 N.Y.S.2d 198 (2009) a son received funds from a joint bank account held as joint tenants with right of survivorship with his father. The father, however, had initially received the funds through a mistake of law when serving as executor of the estate of a third party. When the mistake was discovered,

the beneficiary of the estate sought restitution to recover the funds held by the son. Evidence showed that the son had dissipated the proceeds of the bank account. The court determined that issues of the son's detrimental reliance and the extent to which it would be unjust to require reimbursement of the funds presented questions of fact that should not be resolved on summary judgment.

5.   The defense of change of position is ineffective if the defendant's circumstances or actions take place after receiving notice of the facts giving rise to the restitutionary claim. In *Western Casualty & Surety Co. v. Kohm*, 638 S.W.2d 798 (Mo.App.1982), for example, the plaintiff insurance company paid the defendant insured the value, less the contractual deductible amount, of an automobile which had sustained significant damage in a collision. Several months later the insurance company discovered that the insurance policy did not provide for collision coverage. The court acknowledged that the mistake in coverage was attributable to the insurer and was not induced by the fraud or misrepresentations of the policyholder but still awarded restitution of the insurance proceeds. The court held that the fact that the insured had purchased a replacement automobile with the funds did not constitute a sufficient change of position to defeat restitution because the insured knew that he had no contractual right to receive the proceeds. *See also* Qatar National Bank v. Winmar, Inc., 650 F.Supp.2d 1, 10 (D.D.C. 2009) (company that received two consecutive payments of funds had constructive notice that the second payment must have been a mistake; therefore, the retention of the duplicate payment was unjust and the payor bank was entitled to restitution).

6.   The change of position defense has been asserted often in cases involving the mistaken payment of funds where the defendant or third parties in reliance on the payment take action materially affecting the defendant. For example, in Bank Saderat Iran v. Amin Beydoun, Inc., 555 F.Supp. 770 (S.D.N.Y.1983), the plaintiff bank mistakenly overpaid the defendant on behalf of one of its customers. The defendant shipped materials to the customer in exchange for the mistaken payment, and the customer subsequently went out of business. The bank sued for restitution and the court upheld the defendant's change of position defense on the basis that the defendant, if ordered to refund the money, would have no effective remedy against its former customer. *See also* Restatement (Third) of Restitution and Unjust Enrichment (2011) § 65 cmt. e; Alden Auto Parts Warehouse, Inc. v. Dolphin Equipment Leasing Corp., 682 F.2d 330 (2d Cir.1982) (plaintiff denied restitution where third party responsible for fraudulent inducement of equipment lease had gone out of business).

C.   VOLUNTEERS

Section Coverage:

The recipients of gifts are not obliged to pay the donors for them. Volunteers cannot force others to become their debtors by providing them with unrequested goods or services and then suing them for the value of the enrichment. The traditional rationale for denying restitution to an "officious intermeddler" is reinforced by the preference for contractual bargains for such transactions and that parties should not be forced to pay for benefits that could have been reasonably refused. The principle applies not only to gratuities but also to other benefits voluntarily bestowed even when a gift is not intended. If a benefit has been officiously conferred on an unwilling defendant who has no choice in its acceptance, a court will deny restitution. For example, an organization that decides to raise money by painting house numbers on curbs and then asking each homeowner for a payment for the service is not legally entitled to restitution. Even if uncooperative homeowners like the service, they had no choice of accepting it and thus are not bound to pay for it.

There are some exceptions to this broad rule that restitution is not available to volunteers. The most important one is that there may be restitution to a plaintiff who never intended a gift if the defendant does have a meaningful choice whether to accept the benefit. The principle is that a defendant should compensate an unofficious volunteer who is not acting gratuitously when the defendant could refuse the benefit but instead elects to retain it. For example, if someone takes a lost pet in need of immediate medical attention to a veterinarian when the owner cannot be located, the owner later has a choice whether to accept the return of the saved pet. Restitution is appropriate for the value of emergency treatment reasonably performed if the defendant elects to retain the benefit of the now healthy pet. If not, then the Good Samaritan can keep the abandoned animal.

Courts sometimes give restitution to a volunteer even when the defendant does not have a choice of acceptance. For example, a Good Samaritan who helps a lost child by paying for emergency treatment when the parents cannot be located is not officiously intermeddling; the parents must give restitution for benefit. Although the parent has no choice of acceptance, the fulfillment of the support obligation under circumstances of necessity is a saving to the parents that amounts to unjust enrichment.

Model Case:

Taylor operates an office building which was leased from its owner, Owens. Taylor in turn subleases office space to various businesses. Owens retained the ground floor office space for the Owens Realty offices, but leased the rest to Taylor.

During the first few months of this arrangement Taylor paid the heating bills for the entire building because the subleases provided that Taylor would supply heating and cooling. Taylor mistakenly believed that this obligation included the floor occupied by Owens, but in fact Owens was responsible for the heat in that portion of the building.

Taylor could recover from Owens the amount mistakenly paid because no gift was intended and the payment was not done officiously. Although some courts would be troubled that Owens had no choice in the substitution of creditors, most would not bar restitution with the volunteer defense under these circumstances. Taylor's innocence and the relative hardship of the parties would be relevant factors.

Everhart v. Miles

47 Md.App. 131, 422 A.2d 28 (1980).

■ WEANT, JUDGE.

[Miles (appellee) negotiated to purchase from Everhart (appellant) certain property: 101 acres of land which included barns, silos and a farmhouse, certain equipment and farm machinery, and 75 head of Holstein cattle. The total purchase price was $279,000. The parties' proposed agreement contemplated a $29,000 down payment, installment payments for the balance for most items, and a lease purchase option for the real property at the end of a ten year period.]

* * *

In May of 1978 Bruce Miles and his wife traveled from North Carolina to the Allegany Garrett Counties area for the purpose of taking over their proposed purchases. They moved onto the farm on or about 1 June 1978, at which time they made a down payment of Ten Thousand Dollars ($10,-000.00) in lieu of the originally agreed upon amount of Twenty-nine Thousand Dollars ($29,000.00). On this same date, a contract of sale was to have been executed; however, for various reasons this was never accomplished and negotiations continued. Nevertheless, the appellees lived on the farm, ran the dairy business, and made certain improvements; for example, they fixed the barn roof, renovated the farmhouse, installed a septic system, and replaced the house pump, despite the absence of a written agreement. Further, they made repairs to a tractor, a silo loader, and a field chopper. Also, through their efforts, approximately six hundred tons of silage were put into the silos; this silage remained behind when the appellees vacated the farm on 21 September 1978.

During the appellees' stay on the farm, efforts were made by the parties to have a written contract prepared that was agreeable to all parties but this never came about. Eventually, the appellees lowered their total offer for the purchase of the farm, equipment, and cattle to One Hundred and Eighty-nine Thousand Dollars ($189,000.00); this offer was flatly rejected by the appellant, thereby causing the appellees to depart forthwith.

[The trial court awarded restitution to the appellees in the amount of $33,794.02 on the ground that the appellant had been unjustly benefitted by the actions of the appellees.]

* * *

Unjust enrichment is defined as the unjust retention of a benefit to the loss of another, or the retention of money or property of another against the fundamental principles of justice or equity and good conscience. A person is enriched if he has received a benefit, and he is unjustly enriched if retention of the benefit would be unjust. Unjust enrichment of a person occurs when he has and retains money or benefits which in justice and equity belong to another. [Citation.]

Similarly, Williston on Contracts 1479 (3rd ed. 1970) sets forth the three elements that must be established to sustain a claim based on unjust enrichment; these are:

1.   A benefit conferred upon the defendant by the plaintiff;

2.   An appreciation or knowledge by the defendant of the benefit; and

3.   The acceptance for retention by the defendant of the benefit under such circumstances as to make it inequitable for the defendant to retain the benefit without the payment of its value.

Also, in speaking of unjust enrichment Restatement of Restitution 1 (1937) makes this comment, [a] person who has been unjustly enriched at the expense of another is required to make restitution to the other. However, these authorities maintain that unjust enrichment does not exist where the benefit has officiously been thrust upon the defendant. With this in mind, we turn to the facts of the instant case.

There is no doubt that the appellant knew and accepted that the appellees were expending substantial amounts of money for repairs and improvements of his real property. Further, the appellant benefited from the conditioning of his farm equipment, as well as from the retention of certain milk checks that monetized as a result of the appellees' labors.

The question then arises as to whether or not there was an officious conference of these benefits. Restatement of Restitution 2 (1937) indicates that officiousness is constituted by interference in the affairs of others not justified by the circumstances under which this interference takes place. In this regard the appellant argues that the appellees thrust the benefits in question upon him and thus that he should not be considered to be unjustly enriched. As support he relies on Gould v. American Water Works Service Co., 52 N.J. 226, 245 A.2d 14 (1968), *cert. denied,* 394 U.S. 943, 89 S.Ct. 1274, 22 L.Ed.2d 477 (1969). Specifically, he depends on the holding of the New Jersey court that the plaintiff therein was a volunteer. Accordingly the appellant would have us designate him similarly because in the present case there was no request for what was done and hence the fact that drawn out negotiations were unsuccessfully held was no basis for forcing liability on the appellant. *Gould,* however, is not directly on point. In that case the plaintiff dug a well on his own property without any request from the defendant American Water Works; rather, Mr. Gould did this on sheer speculation, hoping that he would be able to sell the well to the American Water Works at a later date. The negotiations spoken of in that case by the New Jersey court were negotiations carried on a long time after the drilling of the well and entailed the sale of same. Moreover, the unjust enrichment complained of was the alleged benefit that American Water Works Company obtained from Gould's experience in drilling for water across the road from some property later acquired by American Water Works. We can readily agree that in such a situation the plaintiff did occupy the position of a volunteer.

Be that as it may in our case the appellees were told to take over the farm and run it as they saw fit; in essence, they were told that it was theirs. In fact, although the appellant denies visiting the farm after July 1, he does admit that he did see that the appellees were making certain repairs and improvements thereon. Further, much of the work that was done appears to have been necessary in order to operate the farm. We cannot, therefore, hold that this constitutes officiousness, since it was neither thrust upon the appellant nor strictly voluntary on the part of the appellees.

Maryland has recognized the doctrine of unjust enrichment or restitution or melioration as it is sometimes called. * * * Certainly it would not be in equity and good conscience to allow the appellant herein to retain the fruits of the appellees' labors, which were performed without a contract but within the possessive blessing of the appellant and with his knowledge that improvements were being made.

Another case relied on by the appellant is the equity case of Welsh v. Welsh, 254 Md. 681, 255 A.2d 368 (1969). In *Welsh* the Court of Appeals reversed the trial court by finding that the occupiers of the land in question were not *bona fide* possessors when they built a service station notwithstanding the knowledge of the owner's claim to the property. Having so found, the Court held that the occupiers were not entitled to compensation for improvements made thereon. Of significance in the above-cited case is the fact that there was considerable dispute over the ownership of the land; in fact, an ejectment action had been instituted. In spite of knowledge of this, the claimants proceeded with the erection of an addition to the original service station building.

In the instant case, on the other hand, the appellees were in possession of the property in question with the wholehearted approbation of the appellant. In this regard, the lower court found that "[w]ith the consent of the [appellant], the [appellees] took possession of the farm and began to operate it. The parties assumed that a sale's contract would be executed." Furthermore, it is apparent that all of the improvements were made during the time that the negotiations concerning the terms of the contract to be executed were continuing.

One final note in reference to the *Welsh* case: there the Court of Appeals quoted with approval at pages 88 89, 255 A.2d at 372, the equitable doctrine of melioration or compensation for improvements as stated in 2 H. Tiffany, Real Property 625 (3rd ed. 1939):

> Since the rule that erections or additions made by one who has no rights to land are fixtures, and therefore not removable by him, even though he made them in the belief that he was the owner of the land, is calculated to cause hardships to an innocent occupant of another's land, by giving the benefit of his labor and expenditures to the landowner, the courts of this country, without either imputing fraud or

requiring proof of it, hold it inequitable to allow one to be enriched under such circumstances by the labor and expenditures of another who acted in good faith and in ignorance of any adverse claim or title. Applying this doctrine of 'unjust enrichment,' a court of equity will, on the principle that he who seeks equity must do equity, refuse its assistance to the rightful owner of the land as against an occupant thereof unless he makes compensation for permanent and beneficial improvements, made by the latter without notice of the defect in his title.

At no time during the appellees' stay on the farm did the appellant question their right to possession. In fact, according to the testimony, the appellant did not visit the farm subsequent to July 1 even though he knew of some of the appellees' labor and expenditures. Also, we find no assertion on the part of the appellant that he ever questioned the appellees' right to possession of the property in question or their right to make improvements thereon. * * *

Judgment affirmed.

————

1. Historically courts denied restitution in all cases involving real property improvements that could not be removed. Modern cases have tended to allow recovery if the improvements are not fixtures. The theory is that the defendant has a choice whether to accept the benefit if it is not affixed. For example, a coat of paint on a house cannot be refused even if it is conferred unofficiously. *See also* Restatement (Third) of Restitution and Unjust Enrichment § 2, cmt. e.(forced exchange, such as unrequested improvements to property, does not support restitution because recipient should not be obliged to pay for a benefit that could be rightfully refused).

The principal case allowed restitution for affixed improvements. Was the choice principle violated? Was the result a correct one? In contrast, a free-standing shed is capable of removal; if the landowner keeps it, restitution may be appropriate.

2. Judicial reception to volunteers has changed during the past century. Historically it was very difficult to get restitution for benefits that were conferred without agreement. For example, in *Glenn v. Savage*, 14 Or. 567, 13 P. 442 (1887), a large and valuable lot of defendant's lumber accidentally fell into the Columbia River and was about to be lost. The defendant was gone, so the plaintiff saved the lumber at his own expense. The defendant kept the salvaged lumber but refused to pay the plaintiff for the expense. The court denied restitution and said the defendant would only be liable if he had requested the service. The court observed:

The great and leading rule of law is to deem an act done for the benefit of another, without his request, as a voluntary act of courtesy, for which no action can be sustained. The world abounds with acts of this kind, done upon no request; but would more abound with ruinous litigation, and the overthrow of personal rights and civil freedom, if the law was otherwise. [Citation.] The law will never permit a friendly act, or such as was intended to be an act of kindness or benevolence, to be afterwards converted into a pecuniary demand. It would be doing violence to some of the kindest and best effusions of the heart to suffer them afterwards to be perverted by sordid avarice. Whatever differences may arise afterwards among men, let those meritorious and generous acts remain lasting monuments of the good offices, intended in the days of good neighborhood and friendship; and let no after-circumstances ever tarnish or obliterate them from the recollection of the parties. 14 Or. 567, 13 P. 442 (1887).

Under modern law the plaintiff in *Glenn v. Savage* would be likely to recover. Courts generally allow restitution to a plaintiff if (1) there was an initial intent to charge, (2) the actions were reasonably necessary for the preservation of the property, and (3) the defendant chose to accept the benefit later. *Also see* Restatement (Third) of Restitution and Unjust Enrichment § 2 (general rule of no liability for an unrequested benefit voluntarily conferred).

3. Mistaken improvement to property may justify restitution in certain instances, however, to the extent necessary to prevent unjust enrichment. *See* Restatement (Third) of Restitution and Unjust Enrichment § 10, cmt. a (unjust enrichment may be appropriate where the value of the improvements greatly exceeds the value of the unimproved property). Some states have enacted Betterment Acts which recognize the availability of restitution to prevent unjust enrichment for the good faith mistaken improvement of another person's property. *See* Ark. St. § 18–60–213; Kan. St. § 60–1004; V.T.C.A. § 22.021 (Texas).

Where the equities between the parties is relatively equivalent, the measure of restitution for improvements to realty is the amount of the increase in value of the property or the reasonable cost of the improvements, whichever is less. *But see* Kerr v. Miller, 159 Or.App. 613, 977 P.2d 438 (1999) (where mortgagee in good faith improved property in reliance on the mortgagor's representations that he would not exercise a right of redemption, court awarded the greater of reasonable costs or increased market value to make the improver whole and to disgorge profits).

4. The principle that restitution will not be available to a volunteer is captured in this colorful illustration from *Indiana Lumbermens Mut. Ins. Co. v. Reinsurance Results, Inc.*, 513 F.3d 652 (7th Cir. 2008):

One who voluntarily confers a benefit on another, which is to say in the absence of a contractual obligation to do so, ordinarily has no legal claim to be compensated. If while you are sitting on your porch sipping Margaritas a trio of itinerant musicians serenades you with mandolin, lute, and hautboy, you have no obligation, in the absence of a contract, to pay them for their performance no matter how much you enjoyed it; and likewise if they were gardeners whom you had hired and on a break from their gardening they took up musical instruments to serenade you. When voluntary transactions are feasible (in economic parlance, when transaction costs are low), it is better and cheaper to require the parties to make their own terms than for a court to try to fix them—better and cheaper that the musicians should negotiate a price with you in advance than for them to go running to court for a judicial determination of just price for their performance. 513 F.3d at 656.

5.   In *Teton Peaks Inv. Co., LLC. v. Ohme*, 146 Idaho 394, 195 P.3d 1207 (2008), a landowner brought an unjust enrichment claim against a neighboring landowner concerning a small amount of land that was on the wrong side of a fence. The court held that since the fence had encroached on the property for over sixty years, it constituted a de facto boundary agreement between predecessors in interest to the litigants. As a result, any "benefit", such as payment of property taxes or rezoning, had been conferred as an "officious intermeddler" and therefore barred unjust enrichment claims.

PROBLEM: THE POOR RICH NEIGHBORS

A farmer who owned a family farm was killed in a combine accident during the harvest season. The neighboring individual farmers attended the funeral and then undertook to harvest the crop for the bereaved family.

After this episode the deceased farmer's estate is discovered to be very large, even independent of the value of the farm land. Although the deceased had lived modestly, he was very wealthy. Can the kind neighbors charge the family for the value of the harvesting services provided after the funeral?

Jako v. Pilling Co.

848 F.2d 318 (1st Cir.1988).

■ TORRUELLA, CIRCUIT JUDGE.

Appellant Geza Jako is a physician and professor of otolaryngology. Beginning in 1963 Dr. Jako entered into an informal collaboration relationship with appellee Pilling Company, a manufacturer of specialized medical equipment. Dr. Jako made several recommendations regarding the design of equipment used in microsurgery of the larynx, mainly laryngoscopes. Pilling had manufactured laryngoscopes prior to 1963, but from 1963 to the mid-to-late 1970's, most of Pilling's laryngoscopes, as well as other instruments used in the course of larynx-microsurgery, were developed substantially according to the suggestions of Dr. Jako. Following industry practice, the instruments bore the name of the physician who suggested the modification, in this instance, *e.g.*, the "Jako laryngoscope."

Dr. Jako does not hold, nor has he ever held, a patent on any of the instruments developed as a result of his ideas. Dr. Jako never sought compensation for his services before 1984. Indeed, Pilling has never compensated persons for the use of their names or ideas in relation to product development unless the idea has been patented.

Dr. Jako has repeatedly stated that when he entered into the relationship with Pilling he believed it inappropriate for physicians to receive any money for their ideas. However, after several years with little or no contact between the parties, Dr. Jako sent Pilling a demand letter in December 1984. The letter demanded a one percent royalty payment for all products bearing his name sold within the prior fifteen years, and a three percent royalty payment on all future sales of similar products

* * *

Dr. Jako then filed a complaint alleging seven causes of action: count 1, breach of contract; count 2, restitution, unjust enrichment. * * *

The court found there was no evidence of an express contract between the parties prior to 1984. Furthermore, the court correctly held that there was no contract implied in fact. The conduct of the parties and the relationship between them showed no basis to find a contract implied in fact. * * *

As to count two, claiming unjust enrichment, the court similarly found the record silent on Dr. Jako's reasonable expectation that he would be paid. [Citation.] Examining the equities of this situation, we also agree that Dr. Jako is not entitled to any restitution. When Dr. Jako entered into this relationship, he sought only to benefit mankind by improving medical equipment. This he achieved. He also received the benefit of a very successful career promoted, in part, by the name recognition that resulted from the relationship. In effect, the relationship benefited both parties, so Pilling was not unfairly enriched.

* * * [W]e affirm the court's granting of summary judgment as to counts one and two. * * *

1. In a famous early case, *Bartholomew v. Jackson*, 20 Johns. 28 (N.Y.Sup.Ct.1822), it was observed: "The plaintiff performed the service without the privity or request of the defendant, and there was, in fact, no promise express or implied. If a man humanely bestows his labor, and even risks his life, in voluntarily aiding to preserve his neighbor's house from destruction by fire, the law considers the service rendered as gratuitous, and it therefore forms no ground of action."

2. In *Boring v. Google, Inc.*, 362 Fed. Appx. 273 (3d Cir. 2010), a homeowner brought suit for restitution against Google claiming that the company was unjustly enriched by using photographs of their home for Google Maps. The court denied the claim, finding that the plaintiffs were unable to prove that they conveyed any benefit to Google through having their home photographed for use in the program and they had no reasonable expectation of payment.

3. Distinguish gifts from mistakenly conferred benefits. A plaintiff can receive restitution for mistaken payments to a defendant if there are no circumstances making such restitution inequitable, such as changed circumstances. *See* Restatement (Third) of Restitution and Unjust Enrichment (2011) § 6.

4. Payments to one of the defendant's debtors poses different problems than payments to the defendant personally. When a volunteer discharges another's debt and sues for restitution, the effect is a substitution of the defendant's creditors. Because the defendant is deprived of the choice of creditors, the court may deny restitution, especially if the plaintiff was acting officiously. When plaintiffs act under the mistaken belief that they are personally liable for the debt, or when they are preserving their own interests as they unofficiously affect the debts of others, courts can balance the hardships and allow restitution even if the choice principle is violated. See Restatement (Third) of Restitution and Unjust Enrichment (2011) § 7.

In *Blue Cross v. Wheeler*, 93 A.D.2d 995, 461 N.Y.S.2d 624 (1983), the plaintiff insurance company paid the hospital bills of the defendant's wife in the mistaken belief that the health insurance policy was in effect at the time the debt was incurred. In fact the defendant had failed to pay the premiums for a long enough time that the policy had expired. The court allowed restitution because the defendant was unjustly enriched by the plaintiff's payment for necessaries furnished to the wife for which the husband was legally responsible.

Is the result in *Blue Cross* justifiable? The husband plaintiff was denied the choice of creditors, apparently without fraud and through no fault of his own. Does a change in creditors matter? Is the hospital more likely to forgive the debt or to arrange convenient terms than the insurance company?

Reconsider the longstanding rule that provision of necessaries to a defendant's legal dependents is not officious intermeddling. Is there a difference in a situation such as the one in *Blue Cross* between directly furnishing necessaries and indirectly doing so? The court thought not, but would the result have been different if the insurance company had sued the wife instead of the husband? She received the hospital treatment and apparently had no history of a relationship with the insurance company except that she was named as a covered dependent on the expired policy. Might the court then have balanced the hardships to produce a different result since the case would have involved the payment of her personal debt by a stranger?

Felton v. Finley

69 Idaho 381, 209 P.2d 899 (1949).

■ GIVENS, JUSTICE.

March 1944, Seigle Finley and W.E. or William Finley, two of the three surviving nephews of Seigle Coleman, who died testate December 4, 1943, employed respondent to contest the deceased Coleman's will, which was successfully done. [Citation.] At that time respondent told Seigle and William Finley that he would accept the employment only on condition that the other nephew and brother, Orval Finley, and the three sisters, Ida Davis, Nan Holder, and Rose Finley Nichles, likewise employ respondent as their attorney and that all six of the heirs participate in the contest.

Respondent requested Seigle and William Finley to contact their brother and sisters and secure signed contracts of employment similar to the ones which Seigle and William signed; namely, on a 50 per cent contingent basis. Respondent likewise wrote the other four heirs requesting their execution of such contracts. Such heirs never replied to respondent's initial letter or to subsequent letters written by him continuing to request their execution of such contracts of employment and advising them as to the course of the litigation.

Seigle and William Finley contacted two sisters, Nan Holder and Ida Davis in Pilot Rock, Oregon, with reference to their joining in the employment of respondent and related that:

> " * * * they said they would have nothing to do with it. My oldest sister, Ida Davis, is very religious and she said she didn't feel like protesting. She said, 'What you boys do is your business, but I will have nothing to do with it.' "

* * *

Testifying further that they (Seigle and William Finley) attempted to get the three sisters and the other brother to join with them that is, in the employment of respondent in the prosecution of the contest, stating further:

> A. I had quite a time contacting my brother (Orval). He was in Alaska part of the time and I called him in St. Paul, Minnesota, that's his home, and he said, "I am having nothing whatever to do with a dead man's money."

and that he (Orval),

> " * * * would have nothing to do one way or the other, what I did was my business, to forget about him."

and about the same as to Rose Finley Nichles:

> "She said she would have nothing to do with the estate. She said, 'If you and Bill sign, that's your business. I am not going to. There is no use sending the contract.' I read it to her over the phone and she said, 'No.' "

* * *

At the conclusion of the contest action, distributive checks were made out to each one of the six heirs jointly with respondent for their respective shares, which the three sisters and Orval refused to accept, taking the position they had never employed respondent and were not obligated to pay him any fee and subsequent conferences between respondent and Mrs. Holder were unavailing.

The present suit to establish the implied contract and to enforce the attorney's lien, resulted with findings, conclusions and decree there was an implied contract of employment, from which decree the present appeal was taken.

By stipulation, the appellants have been paid their distributive shares less the portion thereof claimed by respondent and decreed to him as his fee from them.

These facts are established by the record without dispute: that respondent wrote the appellants to the effect he had been employed by their two brothers and he desired their co-employment; that he wrote them of the progress of the litigation and that they refused to sign the contracts and did not answer his letters; that at least one of them had actual notice of the progress of the litigation and being a matter of public record, and they being parties to the probate proceedings, regardless of the contest because they were devisees under the will, they all had constructive notice of the proceedings; and that they did not repudiate respondent's appearing for them that though appellants did not affirmatively participate in the contest, they did not resist and immediately upon the contest being successfully concluded, claimed the additional shares in their Uncle's estate which had been made available to them by the prosecution of the suit and respondent's services in connection therewith, which resulted in benefits to the appellants, together with the two brothers who did actually employ him.

* * *

It is an elementary rule that, whenever services are rendered and received, a contract of hiring or an obligation to pay what they are reasonably worth will generally be presumed. * * *

The record herein affirmatively and positively shows the respondent was not undertaking the services herein for anyone gratuitously. It is also held the acceptance of benefits must be voluntary. The acceptance and receipt by appellants of their share of their enhanced inheritance were entirely voluntary, because there is no law which required them to accept the greater amount; they could have taken only the $500.00 which the will initially gave them and refused the additional sum. Whatever scruples or feelings they had about not signing contracts, taking a dead man's money or interfering with his will, had thus evidently disappeared when the money was made available to them, even though without their active participation. Nevertheless, it was solely through respondent's efforts and successful prosecution of the contest case which procured this additional money for them and which, when thus secured to them by respondent's services, they promptly demanded and have pocketed.

Such course of conduct on their part amounts to such ratification and recognition of respondent's actions as to create in law an implied contract of employment and fully justified the decree in respondent's favor. [Citation.]

The decree is, therefore, affirmed. Costs awarded to respondent.

■ HOLDEN, CHIEF JUSTICE (dissenting).

December 4, 1943, Seigle Coleman died testate. By will he bequeathed $5,000 to Wilbur Coleman and $500 each to certain nieces and nephews, and the remainder of his estate to certain charitable organizations. The will was later offered and admitted to probate. Thereafter, two of the three surviving nephews, Seigle Finley and William Finley, entered into a contract with respondent Felton by which they agreed to pay Felton one-half of all benefits which might be obtained by virtue of a contest of the will. One nephew, Orval Finley, and three nieces, Ida Davis, Nan Holder and Rose Finley Nichles, refused to sign identical contracts or to have anything to do with the contest or the employment of respondent. Then followed a contest of the will in the probate court. That court held the will to be validly executed, but held the clauses attempting to bequeath and devise part of the property to different institutions were void because the institutions were charitable and the will had been executed less than thirty days prior to the decease of Seigle Coleman. An appeal was taken to the district court. That court decreed the will was valid and properly executed; that the clauses attempting to devise the property to charitable organizations were void; that the will should be enforced as to the specific bequests other than those to the charitable institutions, and the balance of the property should be distributed to the heirs of Seigle Coleman; that inasmuch as Seigle Coleman had left no father, mother, wife, brothers or sisters, the property should be distributed in equal parts to the heirs of the deceased brothers and sisters, who are nephews and nieces of Seigle Coleman, deceased. Upon appeal the district court was affirmed.

* * *

It is urged in the case at bar that where one permits another to perform services for him, the law raises an implied promise to pay the reasonable value of the services. But respondent does not bring himself within the rule. Here, appellants, notwithstanding several efforts were made to induce them to employ respondent, refused to do so. It is true respondent performed services in contesting the will, but the services were performed for "S.P. Finley [Seigle]" and William Finley under the terms of a written contract. He was thus obligated to perform all the services he performed. He could not repudiate his solemn contract without committing a breach. Nor was respondent expected by those who thus employed him to perform such or any services gratuitously. The contract which respondent himself drew provided for the payment of the compensation which he thought his services were worth. The benefits which came to appellants were the result of the performance of the terms of the written contract entered into by respondent with Seigle and William Finley, not the result of any contract with appellants, because they refused to employ him. And, further, the services respondent performed in contesting the will were performed with knowledge appellants would not employ him. In fact, appellants were opposed to the contest and would not, and did not, have anything to do with it. No case has been cited and none can be found holding an implied promise or implied contract to pay for services under such facts and circumstances. * * *

But it is argued the acceptance of accruing benefits created an implied contract to pay respondent. In resolving that question the above stated facts of this case should be kept in mind. The courts are unanimous in holding an acceptance of benefits does not create an implied contract to pay.

* * *

The judgment should be reversed and the cause remanded with directions to dismiss the action.

ON REHEARING

■ HOLDEN, CHIEF JUSTICE.

* * * [T]he decree appealed from in the case at bar should be, and it is hereby, reversed and the cause remanded with directions to dismiss the action, in accordance with the views expressed in the fore-going dissenting opinion of Chief Justice Holden. Costs awarded to appellants.

————

1. In *Leibowitz v. Cornell University*, 584 F.3d 487 (2d Cir. 2009) a university employee's contract was not renewed; however, with permission of the University she continued to advise two graduate students in completing their theses. She sent the school a $25,000 bill which approximated $2,000 per day for her advising fees. Her claim for unjust enrichment was unsuccessful because the evidence indicated that her continued aid to the students was on a volunteer basis and the fees sought were grossly disproportionate to her former salary. *See also* Lindquist Ford, Inc. v. Middleton Motors, Inc., 557 F.3d 469 (7th Cir. 2009) (distinguishing between quantum meruit and unjust enrichment claims for labor performed absent express contract).

2. There is no recovery in restitution for benefits incidentally bestowed upon the defendant while the plaintiff pursues matters of personal benefit. See Restatement (Third) of Restitution and Unjust Enrichment § 2(1). For example, when a homeowner plants a hedge fence on the property line, the neighbor's property may increase in value. This enrichment is incidentally bestowed upon the neighbor by the homeowner's action and it is not unjust to retain it.

This principle applies even if the benefit was tangible. For example, if the neighbor had been saving money to plant a hedge along that line, the homeowner's action would produce a tangible savings. Moreover, the enrichment is not unjust even if the choice principle were not violated. For example, the homeowner might have asked the neighbor's opinion about having a hedge between them and offered to abandon the project upon objection. This friendly consultation would not make the enrichment unjust to retain unless the neighbor had promised to help with expenses if certain changes in the plans were made.

3.   In *Ashley County, Ark. v. Pfizer, Inc.*, 552 F.3d 659 (8th Cir. 2009), a county sued the manufacturers of cold and allergy medications that are used to produce methamphetamines for unjust enrichment, claiming that the companies were unjustly enriched by the services that the county provided in battling the methamphetamine epidemic. The court rejected the claim, finding the relationship too attenuated as the county did not perform the services with any expectation that the companies would compensate them, nor did the companies derive any benefit from the county's services, such as law enforcement and social services and treatment programs for drug dependents.

4.   In *Bashara v. Baptist Memorial Hospital System*, 685 S.W.2d 307 (Tex.1985), an attorney effected a settlement agreement with an insurance company on behalf of an injured client. While the suit was pending but before that settlement was achieved, a hospital filed a lien for charges incurred in treating the injured party. The insurance company subsequently paid the settlement amount and separately paid the hospital to discharge the lien. The attorney brought an action in quantum meruit against the hospital for services rendered. The court acknowledged that the attorney's actions benefitted the hospital by creating a "fund", but still disallowed the attorney's fees because quantum meruit requires that the efforts be undertaken "for the person sought to be charged."

5.   Should restitution be awarded if information developed in one proceeding is subsequently used in different litigation? When a plaintiff brings an individual action that has the effect of making litigation or settlement easier for subsequent claimants, has there been any unjust enrichment? The plaintiff's substantial litigation expense has effectively benefitted others who do not share in the original expenses. *But see* Eller Media Corp. v. National Union Fire Ins. Co., 355 Fed. Appx. 340 (11th Cir. 2009) (court denied unjust enrichment claim against insurance company which used work product produced by another company in connection with prior criminal proceeding for purposes of subsequent civil proceeding because some benefits had already been received).

PART V

CONCLUSION: COMPLETING THE REMEDIAL PICTURE

939

CHAPTER 18

JURY TRIALS

A. SUBSTANTIVE EQUITY AND EQUITABLE CLEAN-UP

Section Coverage:

The rule that limits equitable jurisdiction to cases in which the legal remedy is inadequate governs requests for injunctions and specific performance orders. (*See* Chapters 3 and 4) The historical independence of equity courts accounts for the inadequacy rule as well as for a separate basis of equity jurisdiction known as substantive equity. Cases involving trusts and mortgages, for example, were originally brought to the equity courts because the courts at law had no effective way of handling them fairly. Equity devised means of dealing with the special problems created in these areas, and thus any case concerning these substantive matters came under equitable jurisdiction. The inadequacy rule did not control in these limited instances.

The merger of law and equity brought procedural benefits, including that mixed claims of law and equity could be brought before one judge. The merger did not change the substantive differences between law and equity, however. One important difference that remains is that the federal Constitutional right to trial by jury in civil trials is reserved for actions at law; there is no jury right for equitable actions. This guarantee does not apply to the states, but many state constitutions have similar provisions.

When a plaintiff brings a purely legal claim to a merged court, such as an action for damages, there is a right to a jury trial. There is no such right when the claim is purely equitable, such as one for specific performance. Problems arise when the plaintiff brings a mixed claim that seeks both legal and equitable relief, or when a plaintiff brings one type of claim and the defendant counterclaims with a different type. The complex federal approach to these problems is studied in the next section. The most common state approach is the subject of this section.

Model Case:

Darby and Pendleton own adjoining businesses on Main Street in a summer tourist town. They have had a history of various disagreements, including perpetual arguments about political matters concerning the downtown businesses.

Another dispute began when Darby's employees had difficulty unloading merchandise through the regular service doors, which needed repairs. They began to use an entrance that required their vans to trespass on a portion of Pendleton's land. When Pendleton called to complain of the practice, Darby provided reassurance that the problem was temporary because the service doors were being repaired.

The practice became a regular one, however, because Darby's employees preferred the alternative entrance even after the service doors were repaired. Moreover, there were several instances when the Darby vans damaged some of Pendleton's landscaping. Pendleton's repeated calls to Darby brought only unfulfilled promises to correct the problem. The tourist season had begun and Darby was distracted by other matters. The increased business made Pendleton all the more eager to stop the annoying and damaging practice.

Pendleton sued Darby. The complaint sought an injunction against further trespasses and damages for the minor landscaping damage. The judge granted the order. In most states the judge would then "clean-up" the damages issue without benefit of a jury. The final judgment on damages for past losses would be entered by the judge who acted as trier of fact on both the legal and equitable claims.

Weltzin v. Nail

618 N.W.2d 293 (Iowa 2000).

■ SNELL, JUSTICE.

This is an interlocutory appeal from the Black Hawk County District Court. The appellant shareholders contend that their demand for a jury trial in their derivative suit was improperly stricken. We granted review and affirm the district court's ruling.

The plaintiffs/appellants in this case are shareholders of LaPorte City Cooperative Elevators. On behalf of the company, they brought a shareholder's derivative lawsuit against its directors and officers. A derivative lawsuit is unique in that the shareholders allege the company's directors have directly harmed it by their acts and omissions such that the company has suffered a loss. The shareholders indirectly assert their rights through the rights of the company.

In the present suit, the shareholders assert that the company's former directors and officers committed multiple breaches. Specifically, the shareholders allege former manager Michael Nail committed a negligent breach of his fiduciary duties and made fraudulent misrepresentations. They seek compensatory and punitive damages from Nail for his actions. The shareholders also contend that several former directors and the company's loan officer committed negligence in the performance of their duties. For these actions, the shareholders seek money damages. Although in equity, the shareholders filed a demand for jury trial with their petition.

* * * All defendants joined in a motion to strike the jury demand made by the shareholders. * * * Specifically, the issue is: Under Iowa law, do shareholders in a derivative lawsuit have the right to a jury, when several claims are legal in nature, all affirmative defenses are legal, and Iowa

recognizes the general inviolate right to a jury trial, but the overall nature of the action is equitable?

* * *

Whether the plaintiff in a shareholder's derivative suit is entitled to a jury is a fairly unsettled question across the country. [Citations.]

While never addressing the derivative suit issue, we have recognized that there is no right to a jury trial generally in cases brought in equity. [Citation.] "Generally, if the cause of action is equitable in character, even in part, and equity jurisdiction once attaches, full and complete adjustment of the rights of all parties will be properly made in the suit." [Citation.] Other legal sources have reached a similar conclusion specifically regarding shareholder's derivative suits. [Citation.] The shareholders here urge us to attach the right to a jury trial in equity because several of their claims and remedies are legal. They further argue that legal defenses raised should be heard by a jury.

* * * [In *Carstens v. Central Nat'l Bank & Trust Co.*, 461 N.W.2d 331 (Iowa 1990), the Iowa Supreme Court] stated: "We look at the *essential nature* of the cause of action, rather than solely at the remedy, to determine if a party is entitled to a jury trial." *Id.* at 333. (emphasis added); [citation]. This suggests that the remedy sought is of minimal importance—it is the nature of the cause of action, *i.e.,* where the case is properly docketed, that is the deciding factor.

* * * Here, it is clear that the nature of a shareholder's derivative suit is equitable only. [Citation.] This fact is admitted by the shareholders. Likewise, there is no common law counter-part to a derivative suit available to shareholders. The derivative suit exists only in equity. * * *

In their brief, the shareholders urge us to accept the proposition that "[t]he essential character of a cause of action to determine whether the right to jury trial exists is the *relief* it seeks." In support of this statement, the shareholders cite *Carstens.* This is a misstatement of the court's holding in that case. As noted earlier, the court explained that it was the *nature* of the case itself rather than solely the remedy that tips the balance in favor of or against providing a jury. *Id.* The court found that even though the trust beneficiaries were seeking money damages, a *legal* remedy, because the case could only be founded in equity, there was no right to a jury. *Id.* at 333–34 ("Generally, the remedies of a beneficiary against the trustee are exclusively equitable. . . . The district court correctly sustained the motion to strike the demand for jury.").

The shareholders also assert that a jury should hear legal defenses raised. Regarding legal defenses in equity, several Iowa cases have held:

We have recognized that a defendant has no right to a trial by jury of law issues raised in the answer to an action properly brought in equity. Once equity has obtained jurisdiction of a controversy the court will determine all questions material or necessary to accomplish full and complete justice between the parties, even though in doing so the court may be required to pass upon certain matters ordinarily cognizable at law.

[Citations.]

Similarly, if an action was brought at law, and an equitable defense raised, that would not invoke equity jurisdiction automatically. [Citation.] It should follow then that invoking a legal defense in a shareholder's derivative suit does not defeat equitable jurisdiction. * * *

The United States Supreme Court has oppositely ruled on this issue and held that a plaintiff in a shareholder's derivative suit, although in equity, is entitled to a jury under the Seventh Amendment. *Ross v. Bernhard,* 396 U.S. 531, 532–37, 542, 90 S.Ct. 733, 735–38, 740, 24 L.Ed.2d 729, 733–36, 738 (1970). However, the persuasion of this case is hindered by the fact that the Seventh Amendment has never been made applicable to the states. [Citations.] * * *

In *Ross,* the Court specifically disagreed with the proposition that "in no event does the right to a jury trial extend to derivative actions brought by the stockholders of a corporation." [Citation.] The Court declared that "legal claims are not magically converted into equitable issues by their presentation to a court of equity in a derivative suit." [Citation.]

Similar to our facts, in *Ross,* the shareholders of Lehman Corporation brought a derivative suit on behalf of the corporation alleging breach of fiduciary duties and negligence and requesting money damages. [Citation.] Generally, a fiduciary duty claim is one reserved for equity. However, tort claims such as negligence, breach of contract (asserted in *Ross*), and fraudulent misrepresentation (asserted in the present case) are direct wrongs against the corporation itself where the corporation could sue at law to obtain relief. The Supreme Court questioned why, when these legal claims were raised by shareholders instead, the " 'right to a jury trial should be taken away because the present plaintiff [could not] persuade the only party having a cause of action to sue . . .?' " [Citation.] Accordingly, it held that the legal claims must be heard by a jury under the Seventh Amendment. * * *

If we adopt the holding in *Ross,* it would then be necessary to determine which of the shareholders' claims in the present case are legal such that they should be heard by a jury. Fraudulent misrepresentation is a legal claim. [Citations.] Negligence is a legal claim. [Citation.] Breach of fiduciary duty is an equitable claim. [Citations.]

Confusion would be triggered when negligence or fraud were the actions that caused the alleged equitable breach. A breach of fiduciary duty claim is not an individual tort in its own right at common law. [Citation.] It is usually brought at law, bootstrapped by a tort like negligence or fraudulent misrepresentation. [Citation.] However, it is a recognized individual claim in equity under a derivative suit. [Citations.]

The question here becomes, if this court were to adopt the *Ross* reasoning, would the negligence and fraud claims be severable from the breach of duty claim such that a jury should hear them? Were we to adopt

Ross, this would create quite a quandary for the lower courts to distinguish between the claims. For this reason, as well as those stated throughout the opinion, we choose not to extend the Supreme Court's holding in relation to the Seventh Amendment to shareholder's derivative suits brought in Iowa.

The *Ross* minority similarly recognized this classification problem created by the majority. [Citation.] Justice Stewart stated:

> The fact is, of course, that there are, for the most part, no such things as inherently "legal issues" or inherently "equitable issues." There are only factual issues, and like chameleons [they] take their color from surrounding circumstances. Thus, the Court's "nature of the issue" approach is hardly meaningful.

[Citation.]

The issue of money damages makes it no clearer. "[A]n action seeking recovery of monetary damages will generally give rise to a right to trial by jury...." [Citations.] However, just because shareholders are seeking money damages in a derivative suit does not mean a jury is warranted because the derivative suit itself is founded in equity. [Citation.] * * * A request for reimbursement/restitution disguised as money damages is properly heard in equity. [Citation.]

In the present case, the shareholders seek money damages for the actions of the officers and directors that led to LaPorte City Cooperative Elevators losing a substantial amount of money by, *e.g.,* failing to collect on accounts receivable, failing to comply with the company's credit policy, and failing to maintain awareness about the company's financial situation. Through the defendant's actions, the shareholders are alleging the company lost money. Thus, they are actually seeking restitution, styled as money damages. Restitution is defined as an "[a]ct of ... restoration of anything to its rightful owner; the act of making good or giving equivalent for any loss, damage or injury...." Black's Law Dictionary 1477 (rev. 4th ed.1968). Restitution is an equitable remedy which creates no right to a jury. * * *

It should be noted there was a strong dissent in *Ross* claiming the majority opinion was ill-conceived and biased in favor of more juries. *Ross,* 396 U.S. at 543–51, 90 S.Ct. at 740–45, 24 L.Ed.2d at 739–43 (Stewart, J., dissenting). Specifically, the dissent argued the Seventh Amendment only preserved the right to a jury trial to suits cognizable at common law. [Citation.] A shareholder's derivative suit does not exist under common law and is solely a case in equity regardless that legal issues are raised.

> [W]hen the Court said ... "it is clear" that the remedy of a stockholder seeking to enforce the rights of a corporation—whatever their nature—is not in law but in equity, it was not because there were "procedural impediments" to a jury trial on "legal issues." Rather, it was because the suit itself was conceived of as a wholly equitable cause of action.

[Citation.]

Many states have taken the same approach and not afforded the right to a jury in derivative suits because of their equitable nature. [Citations.] * * *

The national trend appears to agree with the *Ross* dissent. Among the handful of states that allow a jury to hear legal issues stemming from equitable suits, many only provide advisory juries. [Citations.] Advisory juries are implicated where it is first recognized that the "issues are not triable by jury as a matter of right." [Citation.] The plaintiff is able to present his case to a jury, but the court is not bound by the jury's recommendation. We have never recognized the usefulness of this process, nor do we do so today.

Lastly, this court recognizes that in a shareholder's derivative suit a judge is simply better equipped to hear the complicated corporation and duty claims. [Citation.] The *Ross* dissent addressed the complexity problem: "[W]here the issues in the case are complex—as they are likely to be in a derivative suit—much can be said for allowing court discretion to try the case itself." [Citation.] For this reason, Justice Stewart boldly concluded that the majority's opinion had "a questionable basis in policy and no basis whatsoever in the Constitution." * * *

Certainly case complexity is present in almost every shareholder's derivative suit because the jury is asked to pass judgment on the intricate workings of a corporation. Often concepts like the business judgment rule and breach of fiduciary duty are difficult to understand. [Citation.] Similarly, derivative suits usually involve voluminous amounts of discovery and records to trace the actions of the corporation's officers and directors. With massive discovery comes increased length of trial. Moreover, there may be several plaintiffs and multiple defendants each being represented by different counsel. The present case is no exception. The shareholders are alleging negligence occurred over an extended period of time and was committed by multiple officers, directors, and contractors. Such a make-up is a recipe for complexity. Because juror competence would be challenged in almost every derivative suit, the court is further persuaded not to provide a jury. * * *

We deny the shareholders the right to a jury trial in this case because their right to bring a derivative suit exists only in equity where there is no general preference for a jury trial. To provide an avenue for shareholders to have a jury for their legal claims would prove inefficient and overly burdensome on the lower courts as well as untrained juries. To hold otherwise would further complicate already complex cases and force the court to determine which issues are legal and which are purely equitable prior to hearing an issue or submitting it to a jury.

---

1. *Substantive Equity.* Substantive equity historically developed as a response to deficiencies in the law. The inadequacy rule was not an issue because there simply was no remedy at law. The separate basis of equitable

jurisdiction has persisted despite the subsequent development of remedies at law and despite the merger of law and equity.

The problem confronting the Supreme Court in *Ross v. Bernhard*, 396 U.S. 531, 90 S.Ct. 733, 24 L.Ed.2d 729 (1970), was how to reconcile the historical development of substantive equity with the commands of the Seventh Amendment which provides for a right to jury trial in matters "at law." The Court decided to ignore the "historical accident" of the development of substantive equity and to focus instead upon the legal or equitable nature of the remedy sought in the underlying claim. As the principal case illustrates, the Court's decision in *Ross* applies only to federal jury trial rights because the Seventh Amendment does not apply to the states.

2. *Complex Litigation.* Why did the shareholders desire a jury trial? Why did the officers and directors want to avoid a jury trial? Is there any reason to believe that a group of jurors would decide such a case more sympathetically to the plaintiffs than a single judge? Consider the court's comments on the complexity of shareholder derivative actions. Is a group of jurors or one individual judge more likely to comprehend the extensive evidence involved? Is a group of jurors or one individual judge more likely to comprehend the "intricate workings of a corporation?" Does it matter that the judge is more experienced in hearing evidence than the nonprofessional jury? Does it matter that the various individuals on the jury have collectively among them more world experiences and knowledge about varied matters?

Colclasure v. Kansas City Life Insurance Company

290 Ark. 585, 720 S.W.2d 916 (1986).

■ DUDLEY, JUSTICE.

The appellee, Kansas City Life Insurance Company, loaned $450,000.00 to appellants. The installment promissory note evidencing the debt was secured by a mortgage on appellants' farm. When appellants defaulted on an annual installment payment, appellee accelerated the maturity date, made demand, and filed suit for foreclosure in chancery court. The appellants answered, and, in addition, filed a complaint in circuit court alleging that the appellee had indicated that a prospective buyer of the farm would be allowed to assume the debt, but then would not permit the assumption. Appellants filed motions to transfer the foreclosure suit to circuit court, to consolidate the cases, and to demand a jury trial. Appellee moved to dismiss the suit in circuit court, or, alternatively, to transfer and consolidate in chancery court. The trial court consolidated the cases in chancery court, with the circuit court complaint being treated as a counterclaim, and denied the demand for a jury trial. The day before the chancery case was set for trial, the appellants filed a motion for default judgment. Service of the motion was had on appellees' attorney the day of trial. The trial court denied the motion for default judgment, granted judgment for the debt, and, if not paid within 20 days, ordered the security sold at public auction. We affirm.

The appellants' first point of appeal is that this is a suit on a debt and the chancellor erred in denying them a jury trial. They contend that there is a distinction between a decree for a money judgment and a decree of foreclosure, and since the decree in this case grants a money judgment they were entitled to a jury trial. They cite cases from other jurisdictions which, they contend, entitle them to a jury trial. [Citations.]

In the cases cited by appellants there is a statute or rule of civil procedure which alters the common law and grants a right of jury trial when a money judgment is sought in a mortgage foreclosure proceeding. We do not have such a statute or rule but, instead, continue to follow the common law that a mortgage foreclosure proceeding is an equitable proceeding.

Appellants next contend that Article 2, Section 7 of the Constitution of Arkansas and the Arkansas Rules of Civil Procedure guarantee them the right to a trial by jury. The argument is without merit. The constitutional right to a jury trial is limited to those cases which were so triable at common law. [Citation.] A defendant in a mortgage foreclosure proceeding did not have a right to a jury trial at common law. The Rules of Civil Procedure simply set out the procedure by which a party may demand a jury when he has a right to one. ARCP Rule 38.

Foreclosure proceedings are equitable proceedings even though the chancellor may render an in personam judgment in addition to granting foreclosure. [Citation.] This is in line with our continued application of the clean-up doctrine, which allows the equity court, once it has properly acquired jurisdiction, to decide law issues incidental to or essential to the determination of the equitable issues. [Citation.] Appellants do not question that the law issue was incidental to the equitable issue in this case.

Appellants next argue that the clean-up doctrine violates Article 2, Section 7 of the Constitution of Arkansas. The argument is without merit. Our current constitution was ratified in 1874, and, by that time, our common law was replete with decisions upholding the clean-up doctrine. [Citations.] The constitution was obviously drafted with full knowledge of the clean-up doctrine, and the two are fully compatible.

The appellants next contend that the Seventh Amendment to the Constitution of the United States and *Beacon Theatres, Inc. v. Westover,* 359 U.S. 500, 79 S.Ct. 948, 3 L.Ed.2d 988 (1959), prevent the application of the clean-up doctrine. This argument also is without merit. * * * [T]he Seventh Amendment would not afford appellants the relief they seek since the Supreme Court of the United States has long recognized that the Seventh Amendment has not been, and should not be, extended to the states through the Fourteenth Amendment. [Citation.] * * *

Affirmed.

Ziebarth v. Kalenze

238 N.W.2d 261 (N.D.1976).

■ VOGEL, JUSTICE.

This case originated in the district court, Ward County, North Dakota, on a claim for equitable relief based upon contract. The plaintiff-appellee,

Silver Ziebarth, a cattle buyer, sought specific performance of a contract for the sale of cattle from the defendant-appellant, LeRoy Kalenze, a rancher in the business of selling cattle.

The district court, without a jury, found for Ziebarth. The court awarded damages in the sum of $4,589 plus costs in lieu of specific performance. Kalenze moved under Rule 41(b), N.D.R.Civ.P., at the end of the plaintiff's case, for dismissal of the action on the ground that the pleadings asked for specific performance of the contract, whereas the subject matter of the contract, the cattle, was no longer available, making specific performance impossible. The district court denied the motion.

Kalenze appeals to this court from the judgment entered on October 23, 1974. He demands a new trial at law on the issues of liability and damages. He also appeals from the order of the district court denying his 41(b) motion to dismiss, and asserts that he was deprived of a jury trial on the issue of damages because of the denial of the motion. He never filed a demand for a jury in the trial court.

* * *

The plaintiff Ziebarth brought this case in equity, demanding specific performance of the contract at the agreed price pursuant to the remedies available to a buyer under the Uniform Commercial Code, Section 41–02–95, N.D.C.C. (UCC 2–716). This section provides, in part:

1. Specific performance may be decreed where the goods are unique or in other proper circumstances.

2. The decree for specific performance may include such terms and conditions as to payment of the price, damages, or other relief as the court may deem just. [Emphasis supplied.]

The Code clearly allows the court to grant damages in an action by a buyer for specific performance, *in the court's decree* for specific performance. It is not clear, however, whether the Code allows damages to be awarded *in lieu of a decree* in equity. This case presents the unusual circumstance of a case brought in equity in which specific performance was not possible. The subject matter of the contract had been sold to a third party prior to commencement of the suit. It is not apparent from the pleadings or the testimony whether the plaintiff in this case knew that specific performance was impossible at the time he pled his case in equity.[1]

Of course, the defendant knew when he was served with process that specific performance was impossible, but he did not mention that fact in his answer. If the plaintiff had known that damages, and not specific performance, was the proper remedy in fact, the only remedy available in this case and had made the appropriate motion to amend, then the trial court should

---

1. The cattle were sold on December 23, 1972; the complaint was filed on January 22, 1973.

have allowed the plaintiff to amend his pleadings to conform to his remedy at law or dismissed the suit in equity. * * *

The case law on the issue of the court's jurisdiction to grant damages in lieu of the equitable relief prayed for is conflicting. Some courts recognize the doctrine of substituted legal relief in equity. Historically, where the ground for equitable relief failed, the bill in equity was dismissed and the parties were left to seek in the common-law courts whatever legal remedies remained. But in 1786, an equity court did not dismiss the bill, but retained jurisdiction for granting legal relief where specific performance failed only because of the defendant's wrongful conduct after the suit was begun. This became the basis for granting substituted legal relief in equity. James, Right to Jury Trial in Civil Actions, 72 Yale L.J. 655, 659 (1962). In order for the doctrine to be applied in a particular case, however, the plaintiff must first establish his right to equitable relief, to which damages might then be incidental or subsidiary. [Citation.] In Raasch v. Goulet, 57 N.D. 674, 223 N.W. 808 (1928), this court held that the right to recover damages under the doctrine of substituted legal relief (or equity's "clean up" jurisdiction, as it is sometimes referred to) depends on the right to specific performance and is not available until the latter is established.

It is thus the rule in some jurisdictions, and the traditional view, that the court cannot give judgment for damages in an action brought in equity unless the plaintiff first proves his right to equitable relief. * * * In our view, the fusion of law and equity, which has been the law of North Dakota since Statehood, and the law of the Territory of Dakota from the time of its adoption of the Field Code of Civil Procedure at the first legislative session in 1862, puts the authority to grant equitable or legal relief in courts of general jurisdiction, regardless of technicalities such as the rule of "substituted legal relief." Early judges, trained in common-law pleading, were perhaps unwilling to accept the fusion of law and equity at face value. [Citation.] More recently, however, we have at least followed the "clean up jurisdiction" theory [citation], and we have held that the existence of a remedy at law does not preclude equitable relief if the equitable remedy is better adapted to render more perfect and complete justice than the remedy at law. We believe that a legal remedy should be granted where equity fails. It would involve needless waste of time and money to send the case back for repleading and retrial to accomplish the same result we have now before us. We prefer to follow the rule stated in Livingston v. Krown Chemical Manufacturing, Inc., 50 Mich.App. 153, 212 N.W.2d 775 (1973), and allow damages even though specific performance is denied.

The holding of the two preceding paragraphs, of course, is limited to cases where the rules stated in them do not operate to deprive a litigant of a right to a jury trial. The distinction between law and equity is still of primary importance in determining the right to a jury trial. But a jury trial can be waived by failing to demand it. [Citations.]

In the present case, it is apparent that the defendant knew that specific performance was impossible when the complaint was served on him. He therefore must have known that the only possible remedy, if the plaintiff prevailed, would be damages. If so, he knew he had a right to a jury trial. The right to a jury trial, if demanded under the facts of this case, would be absolute. [Citations.] The defendant could have demanded a jury trial, even though the complaint on its face showed grounds for equitable relief only. * * * But in the absence of a demand, there was no error. * * * We hold today that the right to a jury trial is likewise waived if not demanded in a case where the complaint demands equitable relief but the defendant is aware that only legal relief could be granted if the plaintiff should prevail. * * *

[Reversed and remanded on other grounds.]

Ex parte Thorn

788 So.2d 140 (Ala.2000).

■ SEE, JUSTICE.

These petitions for the writ of mandamus seek an order directing the Montgomery Circuit Court to strike, as to the theory of piercing the corporate veil, plaintiff Raymond Victor Bethel's jury demand and to separate or sever that aspect of the case for trial before the judge. We grant the petitions.

In April 1998, Bethel sued Diesel "Repower", Inc. ("Diesel"), and its president, Rex Thorn, alleging breach of contract, fraud, fraudulent suppression, and negligence. Bethel's allegations arose out of two contracts between him and Diesel. The first contract was for Bethel's purchase of a marine engine and transmission; the second was for Bethel's purchase of three generators. Bethel claimed that he never received from Diesel the engine, the transmission, or any of the generators that he says he purchased and paid for in full. The original complaint requested a jury trial.

Thorn and Diesel each moved, pursuant to Rule 12(b)(6), Ala.R.Civ.P., to dismiss Bethel's complaint for failure to state a claim upon which relief can be granted. The trial court granted Thorn's motion to dismiss, but denied Diesel's. The trial court entered a final judgment in favor of Thorn and against Bethel, pursuant to Rule 54(b), Ala.R.Civ.P. Bethel appealed from the trial court's judgment, as it related to the fraud and fraudulent-suppression claims. This Court held that Bethel had stated claims against Thorn for promissory fraud, fraudulent misrepresentation, and fraudulent suppression. [Citation.]

After this Court had issued its opinion, Bethel filed an amended complaint, seeking to add Martha Thorn and Thorn's Diesel Service, Inc. ("Service"), as parties to the case, and to pierce Diesel's corporate veil. Bethel alleged that Diesel and its successor corporation, Service, were alter egos of Rex and Martha Thorn. Bethel also requested a jury trial on all counts asserted in the amended, or in the original, complaint.

The Thorns and Service moved to sever the claims seeking to pierce the corporate veil and impose individual liability on Rex and Martha Thorn, and to strike the jury demand as to those claims. The trial court denied the

Thorns and Service's motions, and they now petition this Court for writs of mandamus. The Thorns and Service contend that a party seeking to pierce the corporate veil has no right to a jury trial because, they argue, that theory is equitable in nature. They further argue that to include the piercing-the-corporate-veil issue in the jury trial would allow irrelevant and prejudicial evidence to be presented to the jury. We agree.

* * *

In determining whether a party has a right to a jury trial, this Court has looked to Article 1, § 11, of the Constitution of Alabama of 1901. This Court has stated:

"Article 1, § 11 of the Alabama Constitution of 1901 is a source of the right to jury trial in this state. That section provides: 'That the right of trial by jury shall remain inviolate.'

* * *

"Section 11, supra, however, in no way enlarges the right of jury trial. It does not extend to cases where jury trial was not available as of right prior to the Constitution. Nor does it extend to causes totally unknown to the common law or to the statutory law as it existed at the time of the adoption of the Constitution."

W & H Mach. & Tool Co. v. National Distillers & Chem. Corp., 291 Ala. 517, 520, 283 So.2d 173, 175–76 (1973). [Citations omitted]. At common law, purely legal claims were guaranteed the right to a jury trial. [Citations.] On the other hand, equitable claims carried no constitutional right to a jury trial. [Citations.]

The doctrine of "piercing the corporate veil" is equitable in nature. [Citations.] In *W & H Mach. & Tool Co. v. National Distillers & Chem. Corp.,* supra, this Court held that a claim to pierce the corporate veil on an alter ego theory was an equitable claim and, therefore, provided no right to a jury trial. * * *

National Distillers was decided before the July 3, 1973, effective date of the Alabama Rules of Civil Procedure, which merged legal and equitable actions into one "civil action." Rule 2, Ala.R.Civ.P. Although the Rules "supply one uniform procedure by which a litigant may present his claim in an orderly manner to a court empowered to give him whatever relief is appropriate and just," they leave intact one procedural difference between equity and law—the right to a jury trial. Under Rule 38(a), Ala.R.Civ.P., "[t]he right of trial by jury as declared by the Constitution of Alabama or as given by a statute of this State shall be preserved to the parties inviolate"; however, the fact that law and equity have been merged necessarily means that courts will be presented "cases in which issues to be tried to the jury are combined with issues to be tried to the court." Committee Comments to Rule 38, Ala.R.Civ.P. The test for determining when there is a right to trial by jury is: "[I]f an issue is of a sort which heretofore would have been tried to a jury, then the party has a constitutional right ... to have it tried to a jury under the merged procedure." Committee Comments to Rule 38, Ala.R.Civ.P.

In *Finance, Investment & Rediscount Co. v. Wells,* supra, decided in the context of a shareholder's derivative action, this Court revisited the question of when parties have a right to a jury trial. In that case, minority shareholders alleged mismanagement, breach of fiduciary duty, misappropriation of corporate funds, and diversion of corporate opportunities. * * * On rehearing, in order to harmonize *Wells* with *Ross v. Bernhard,* 396 U.S. 531, 90 S.Ct. 733, 24 L.Ed.2d 729 (1970), this Court reconsidered its original holding and announced that the right of trial by jury extended to a stockholder's derivative action, even though such an action was historically equitable. [Citations.]

Ross v. Bernhard, 396 U.S. 531, 542, 90 S.Ct. 733, 24 L.Ed.2d 729 (1970), held that "the Seventh Amendment preserves to the parties in a stockholder's suit the same right to a jury trial that historically belonged to the corporation and to those against whom the corporation pressed its legal claims." *Bernhard* explained that the preliminary question whether the derivative shareholder action may proceed is a question in equity to be decided by the trial court. 396 U.S. at 538. Once that question is answered, the corporation becomes the real party in interest and the jury may decide the legal issues:

> The heart of the action is the corporate claim. If it presents a legal issue, one entitling the corporation to a jury trial under the Seventh Amendment, the right to a jury is not forfeited merely because the stockholder's right to sue must first be adjudicated as an equitable issue triable to the court.

Bernhard, 396 U.S. at 538–39. Thus, under *Bernhard,* equitable issues are still to be determined by the trial court. Once the equitable issues are determined, the legal claims are submitted to the jury for its determination. 396 U.S. at 539–40. That a particular claim has equitable issues does not automatically take that claim away from the jury; instead, under postmerger law, in a civil action involving both equitable and legal issues, the trial court must decide the equitable issues without the assistance of a jury and, if a jury is requested, try the legal issues with a jury. [Citation.]

Accordingly, when both legal and equitable claims are joined in one action, then, the trial judge must arrange the order of trial so that the judge's decision on the equitable issues does not operate to deny a trial by the jury of the legal issues. [Citations.] A jury first must decide any factual issues that are purely legal in nature, along with any factual issues common to the legal and equitable claims. [Citations.] Once those factual findings are made, the trial judge must determine the remaining equitable issues. [Citation.]

As discussed above, the piercing-the-corporate-veil doctrine is an equitable doctrine. See *National Distillers,* supra. However, that doctrine is not a claim; "[i]t merely furnishes a means for a complainant to reach a second corporation or individual upon a cause of action that otherwise would have existed only against the first corporation." [Citation.] Therefore, to the extent that Bethel's claims raise equitable issues, the trial court must dispose of those issues without a jury, and to the extent Bethel's underlying claims of promissory fraud, fraudulent misrepresentation, and fraudulent suppression sound in law, those claims must be decided by a jury. In addition, those factual questions that are purely legal in nature, as well as those common to the legal and equitable issues, must first be decided by the jury. [Citation.] * * *

We grant in part the petitions of the Thorns and Service for the writ of mandamus. We direct the trial court to vacate its order denying the Thorns and Service's motions to strike the jury demand. The legal issues first must be tried to the jury, and then the equitable issues must be tried to the court. The trial court did not abuse its discretion in denying the Thorns and Service's motions to the extent they requested a severance of the piercing-the-corporate-veil issues, because those issues are not a claim; therefore, the petitions are denied to the extent they sought severance. However, we direct the trial court to separate the equitable issues for purposes of trial.

■ JOHNSTONE, JUSTICE (concurring specially).

There are good reasons why those aspects of Bethel's claims seeking to pierce the corporate veil are equitable. First, in some, Bethel seeks for the Court to relieve him of his original agreement and acknowledgment that the other party to the contract was a corporate entity and seeks for the Court to reform the contract into one binding the principals of the corporate entity, instead of the corporate entity itself. Second, in others, Bethel seeks to impose tort liability on Mrs. Thorn for the torts of what Bethel originally agreed and acknowledged was a corporate entity, as though, in essence, Mrs. Thorn were in partnership with Mr. Thorn.

A different case entirely would be presented if Bethel had always dealt with the Thorns as individuals or as business partners and had originally sued them in those capacities. In such an event, their interposing as a defense that they were really merely the principals of a corporate entity would not necessarily avoid Bethel's right to a jury trial on that aspect of the case; in that case, Bethel, not asking the Court for reformation or other equitable dispensation, could maintain, if true, that this particular defense by the Thorns was a mere sham. Because such a position would not be seeking an equitable remedy, it would be triable by a jury.

---

1. *Equitable Clean Up.* When a case raises both equitable and legal claims, most state courts continue to adhere to the equitable clean up doctrine employed by the courts in *Conclasure* and *Ziebarth*. Courts employ equitable clean up regardless of whether the equitable claim arises as a matter of substantive equity or arises in equity because it seeks equitable relief such as an injunction or specific performance. Equitable clean up can have harsh results when applied to deny a party the right to a jury trial on

a compulsory counterclaim. Thus, many courts accord the parties the right to a jury trial on a compulsory counterclaim raising legal claims even if the original action raises only equitable claims. *See* Johnson v. South Carolina Nat'l Bank, 292 S.C. 51, 354 S.E.2d 895 (1987); Hightower v. Bigoney, 156 So.2d 501 (Fla.1963). *But see* Lyn–Anna Properties, Ltd. v. Harborview Development Corp., 145 N.J. 313, 678 A.2d 683 (1996) (no right to a jury trial on compulsory legal counterclaim that was so interrelated to the original equitable complaint that it was deemed ancillary).

2. *Federal Approach.* As *Thorn* illustrates, under the federal approach, the court still resolves equitable issues by itself without the aid of the jury. Some preliminary equitable issues are resolved before submitting the case to the jury. For example, a court determines whether to award a preliminary injunction before any issues are submitted to the jury. Likewise, a court may need to decide preliminary equitable issues like whether a derivative suit may proceed before submitting the case to the jury. Aside from these preliminary issues, however, a court must submit all legal issues and any factual issues common to the plaintiff's legal and equitable issues to the jury first. The court then must accept the jury's findings on these common issues and resolve any remaining equitable claims consistent with those findings.

B.   RIGHT TO JURY TRIAL: FEDERAL APPROACH

Section Coverage:

The Seventh Amendment to the Constitution provides that in "[s]uits at common law, where the value in controversy shall exceed twenty dollars, the right of trial by jury shall be preserved." The Supreme Court has interpreted this Amendment to provide the right to a jury trial in suits in which legal rights, as opposed to solely equitable rights, are to be ascertained and determined.

The Supreme Court uses a historical analog test to characterize a claim as legal or equitable. The Supreme Court has explained that the right to a jury trial attaches to a cause of action if that claim ordinarily would have been tried to a jury in the English common law courts of the late 18th century. Likewise, the right to a jury trial attaches to new statutory actions that are analogous to such common law causes of action. In determining whether a statutory claim is more analogous to a common law or equitable action, courts look to the nature of the statutory action and the remedy sought. Thus, generally, if an action resembles a cause of action that historically arose at law and if the plaintiff seeks money damages, the claim is legal and a right to a jury trial attaches; if the claim seeks an injunction or specific performance, it is equitable. The Court has recognized, however, that not all claims for money are automatically legal claims. Indeed, many lower courts have held that claims for reinstatement and backpay against an employer are entirely equitable, without a right to a jury trial. The Supreme Court has never addressed the issue. Although it has cited lower court opinions with approval in the past, the Court recently expressly left open the issue of whether a claim for backpay was an equitable rather than a legal claim.

Even if a claim can be characterized as a legal action, a plaintiff is not entitled to have every determination in the case submitted to the jury. Rather the court must determine whether a particular trial decision or issue must be submitted to the jury to preserve the substance of the common law right to a jury trial. Thus, the Supreme Court has held that while a party has a right to have a jury determine liability, a party has no right to have a jury assess civil penalties in an action under the Clean Water Act. Likewise, the Court has held that while a plaintiff is entitled to a jury trial of its patent infringement claim, the plaintiff has no right to have the jury construe disputed claim terms.

When a case presents mixed questions of law and equity, the Supreme Court has held that the Seventh Amendment prohibits a court from resolving the legal issues or from resolving the equitable issues in a manner which precludes a jury from determining the legal issues or is inconsistent with the jury's resolution of the legal issues. In a series of opinions in the past thirty years, the Court has found a Constitutional guarantee to have all legal matters tried to a jury first. The judge may then resolve the equitable matters in a manner not inconsistent with the jury verdict. Because the Seventh Amendment does not apply to the states, these decisions do not affect state law. In fact, in contrast to the federal approach, many states apply the "equitable clean-up" doctrine which permits a judge sitting in equity to resolve any legal issues that are incidental to a claim that raises substantial equitable issues.

Model Case:

Sarah Martin's supervisor, Steve Durvil, made a sexual proposition to her at work one day. When Martin indicated that she was not interested in any personal relationship, Durvil told her to think about it longer. He hinted that her rating on her job performance might suffer if she remained uninterested in sexual relations.

Martin immediately reported the incident to the management, but no action was taken. Durvil repeated his comments a week later and this time he forcibly kissed her. She pushed away from him and left work. She was fired the next day.

Martin's suit in federal district court contains both legal and equitable claims against the employer. She seeks reinstatement, backpay, and distress damages under various sources of federal and state law. The parties have a right to a jury trial on the legal claim for damages first. Afterwards the judge will decide the equitable issues of backpay and reinstatement in a manner not inconsistent with the jury's findings of fact on the legal issues.

If the complaint had sought only the equitable relief of reinstatement and backpay under Title VII of the Civil Rights Act of 1964, neither party would be entitled to demand a jury trial. If the plaintiff prevailed she would be entitled to reasonable attorneys' fees under the Act as well. This award would not create a jury trial right because the fees are awarded as "costs" rather than as legal damages.

Feltner v. Columbia Pictures Television

523 U.S. 340, 118 S.Ct. 1279, 140 L.Ed.2d 438 (1998).

■ JUSTICE THOMAS delivered the opinion of the Court.

Section 504(c) of the Copyright Act of 1976 permits a copyright owner "to recover, instead of actual damages and profits, an award of statutory damages ..., in a sum of not less than $500 or more than $20,000 as the court considers just." 90 Stat. 2585, as amended, 17 U.S.C. § 504(c)(1). In this case, we consider whether § 504(c) or the Seventh Amendment grants a right to a jury trial when a copyright owner elects to recover statutory damages. We hold that although the statute is silent on the point, the Seventh Amendment provides a right to a jury trial, which includes a right to a jury determination of the amount of statutory damages. We therefore reverse.

I

Petitioner C. Elvin Feltner owns Krypton International Corporation, which in 1990 acquired three television stations in the southeastern United States. Respondent Columbia Pictures Television, Inc., had licensed several television series to these stations, including "Who's the Boss," "Silver Spoons," "Hart to Hart," and "T.J. Hooker." After the stations became delinquent in making their royalty payments to Columbia, Krypton and Columbia entered into negotiations to restructure the stations' debt. These discussions were unavailing, and Columbia terminated the stations' license agreements in October 1991. Despite Columbia's termination, the stations continued broadcasting the programs.

Columbia sued Feltner, Krypton, the stations, various Krypton subsidiaries, and certain Krypton officers in Federal District Court alleging, *inter alia,* copyright infringement arising from the stations' unauthorized broadcasting of the programs. Columbia sought various forms of relief under the Copyright Act of 1976 (Copyright Act), 17 U.S.C. § 101 *et seq.,* including a permanent injunction, § 502; impoundment of all copies of the programs, § 503; actual damages or, in the alternative, statutory damages, § 504; and costs and attorney's fees, § 505. On Columbia's motion, the District Court entered partial summary judgment as to liability for Columbia on its copyright infringement claims.[1]

Columbia exercised the option afforded by § 504(c) of the Copyright Act to recover "Statutory Damages" in lieu of actual damages. * * *

The District Court denied Feltner's request for a jury trial on statutory damages, ruling instead that such issues would be determined at a bench

---

1. During the course of the litigation, Columbia dropped all claims against all parties except its copyright claims against Feltner.

trial. After two days of trial, the trial judge held that each episode of each series constituted a separate work and that the airing of the same episode by different stations controlled by Feltner constituted separate violations; accordingly, the trial judge determined that there had been a total of 440 acts of infringement. The trial judge further found that Feltner's infringement was willful and fixed statutory damages at $20,000 per act of infringement. Applying that amount to the number of acts of infringement, the trial judge determined that Columbia was entitled to $8,800,000 in statutory damages, plus costs and attorney's fees.

The Court of Appeals for the Ninth Circuit affirmed in all relevant respects. [Citation]. Most importantly for present purposes, the court rejected Feltner's argument that he was entitled to have a jury determine statutory damages. * * * We granted certiorari. [Citation.]

II

Before inquiring into the applicability of the Seventh Amendment, we must " 'first ascertain whether a construction of the statute is fairly possible by which the [constitutional] question may be avoided.' " [Citations.] Such a construction is not possible here, for we cannot discern "any congressional intent to grant ... the right to a jury trial," [citation] on an award of statutory damages.

The language of § 504(c) does not grant a right to have a jury assess statutory damages. Statutory damages are to be assessed in an amount that "the court considers just." § 504(c)(1). Further, in the event that "the court finds" the infringement was willful or innocent, "the court in its discretion" may, within limits, increase or decrease the amount of statutory damages. § 504(c)(2). These phrases, like the entire statutory provision, make no mention of a right to a jury trial or, for that matter, to juries at all.

The word "court" in this context appears to mean judge, not jury. [Citation.] In fact, the other remedies provisions of the Copyright Act use the term "court" in contexts generally thought to confer authority on a judge, rather than a jury. [Citations.] In contrast, the Copyright Act does not use the term "court" in the subsection addressing awards of actual damages and profits, [citation], which generally are thought to constitute legal relief. * * *

We thus discern no statutory right to a jury trial when a copyright owner elects to recover statutory damages. Accordingly, we must reach the constitutional question.

III

The Seventh Amendment provides that "[i]n Suits at common law, where the value in controversy shall exceed twenty dollars, the right of trial by jury shall be preserved...." U.S. Const., Amdt. 7. Since Justice Story's time, the Court has understood "Suits at common law" to refer "not merely [to] suits, which the *common* law recognized among its old and settled proceedings, but [to] suits in which *legal* rights were to be ascertained and determined, in contradistinction to those where equitable rights alone were recognized, and equitable remedies were administered." [Citation.] The Seventh Amendment thus applies not only to common-law causes of action, but also to "actions brought to enforce statutory rights that are analogous to common-law causes of action ordinarily decided in English law courts in the late 18th century, as opposed to those customarily heard by courts of equity or admiralty." [Citations.] To determine whether a statutory action is more analogous to cases tried in courts of law than to suits tried in courts of equity or admiralty, we examine both the nature of the statutory action and the remedy sought. [Citation.]

Unlike many of our recent Seventh Amendment cases, which have involved modern statutory rights unknown to 18th-century England, [citations], in this case there are close analogues to actions seeking statutory damages under § 504(c). Before the adoption of the Seventh Amendment, the common law and statutes in England and this country granted copyright owners causes of action for infringement. More importantly, copyright suits for monetary damages were tried in courts of law, and thus before juries.

By the middle of the 17th century, the common law recognized an author's right to prevent the unauthorized publication of his manuscript. [Citation.] * * * Actions seeking damages for infringement of common-law copyright, like actions seeking damages for invasions of other property rights, were tried in courts of law in actions on the case. [Citation.] Actions on the case, like other actions at law, were tried before juries. [Citations.]

In 1710, the first English copyright statute, the Statute of Anne, was enacted to protect published books. [Citation.] Under the Statute of Anne, damages for infringement were set at "one Penny for every Sheet which shall be found in [the infringer's] custody, either printed or printing, published, or exposed to Sale," half ("one Moiety") to go to the Crown and half to the copyright owner, and were "to be recovered . . . by Action of Debt, Bill, Plaint, or Information." [Citation.] Like the earlier practice with regard to common-law copyright claims for damages, actions seeking damages under the Statute of Anne were tried in courts of law. [Citations.]

The practice of trying copyright damages actions at law before juries was followed in this country, where statutory copyright protections were enacted even before adoption of the Constitution. * * *

In 1790, Congress passed the first federal copyright statute, the Copyright Act of 1790, which similarly authorized the awarding of damages for copyright infringements. [Citation.] The Copyright Act of 1790 provided that damages for copyright infringement of published works would be "the sum of fifty cents for every sheet which shall be found in [the infringer's] possession, . . . to be recovered by action of debt in any court of record in the United States, wherein the same is cognizable." * * *

There is no evidence that the Copyright Act of 1790 changed the practice of trying copyright actions for damages in courts of law before juries. As we have noted, actions on the case and actions of debt were actions at law for which a jury was required. [Citation.] Moreover, actions to recover damages under the Copyright Act of 1831—which differed from the Copyright Act of 1790 only in the amount (increased to $1 from 50 cents) authorized to be recovered for certain infringing sheets—were consistently tried to juries. [Citations.]

Columbia does not dispute this historical evidence. In fact, Columbia makes no attempt to draw an analogy between an action for statutory damages under § 504(c) and *any* historical cause of action—including those actions for monetary relief that we have characterized as equitable, such as actions for disgorgement of improper profits. [Citations.] Rather, Columbia merely contends that statutory damages are clearly equitable in nature.

We are not persuaded. We have recognized the "general rule" that monetary relief is legal, [citation], and an award of statutory damages may serve purposes traditionally associated with legal relief, such as compensation and punishment. [Citations.] Nor, as we have previously stated, is a monetary remedy rendered equitable simply because it is "not fixed or readily calculable from a fixed formula." [Citation.] And there is historical evidence that cases involving discretionary monetary relief were tried before juries. [Citation.] Accordingly, we must conclude that the Seventh Amendment provides a right to a jury trial where the copyright owner elects to recover statutory damages.

The right to a jury trial includes the right to have a jury determine the *amount* of statutory damages, if any, awarded to the copyright owner. It has long been recognized that "by the law the jury are judges of the damages." [Citation.] Thus in *Dimick v. Schiedt*, 293 U.S. 474, 55 S.Ct. 296, 79 L.Ed. 603 (1935), the Court stated that "the common law rule as it existed at the time of the adoption of the Constitution" was that "in cases where the amount of damages was uncertain[,] their assessment was a matter so peculiarly within the province of the jury that the Court should not alter it." [Citation.] And there is overwhelming evidence that the consistent practice at common law was for juries to award damages. [Citations.]

More specifically, this was the consistent practice in copyright cases. * * * [J]uries assessed the amount of damages under the Copyright Act of 1831, even though that statute, like the Copyright Act of 1790, fixed damages at a set amount per infringing sheet. [Citations.]

Relying on *Tull v. United States, supra,* Columbia contends that the Seventh Amendment does not provide a right to a jury determination of the amount of the award. In *Tull,* we held that the Seventh Amendment grants a right to a jury trial on all issues relating to liability for civil penalties under the Clean Water Act, [citations], but then went on to decide that Congress could constitutionally authorize trial judges to assess the amount of the civil penalties, [citation]. According to Columbia, *Tull* demonstrates that a jury determination of the amount of statutory damages is not necessary "to preserve 'the substance of the common-law right of trial by jury.' " [Citation].

In *Tull,* however, we were presented with no evidence that juries historically had determined the amount of civil penalties to be paid to the Government.[9] Moreover, the awarding of civil penalties to the Government could be viewed as analogous to sentencing in a criminal proceeding. [Citation.] Here, of course, there is no similar analogy, and there is clear and direct historical evidence that juries, both as a general matter and in copyright cases, set the amount of damages awarded to a successful plaintiff. *Tull* is thus inapposite. As a result, if a party so demands, a jury must determine the actual amount of statutory damages under § 504(c) in order "to preserve 'the substance of the common-law right of trial by jury.'" * * *

For the foregoing reasons, we hold that the Seventh Amendment provides a right to a jury trial on all issues pertinent to an award of statutory damages under § 504(c) of the Copyright Act, including the amount itself. The judgment below is reversed, and we remand the case for proceedings consistent with this opinion.

It is so ordered.

■ JUSTICE SCALIA, concurring in the judgment.

It is often enough that we must hold an enactment of Congress to be unconstitutional. I see no reason to do so here—not because I believe that jury trial is not constitutionally required (I do not reach that issue), but because the statute can and therefore should be read to provide jury trial.

"[W]here a statute is susceptible of two constructions, by one of which grave and doubtful constitutional questions arise and by the other of which such questions are avoided, our duty is to adopt the latter." [Citation.] The Copyright Act of 1976 authorizes statutory damages for copyright infringement "in a sum of not less than $500 or more than $20,000 as the court considers just." 17 U.S.C. § 504(c). The Court concludes that it is not "fairly possible," [citation], to read § 504(c) as authorizing jury determination of the amount of those damages. I disagree.

In common legal parlance, the word "court" can mean "[t]he judge or judges, as distinguished from the counsel or jury." [Citation.] But it also has a broader meaning, which includes both judge and jury. [Citations.] * * *

* * * Section 504(c) is the direct descendant of a remedy created for unauthorized performance of dramatic compositions in an 1856 copyright statute. That statute provided for damages "not less than one hundred dollars for the first, and fifty dollars for every subsequent performance, as to the court having cognizance thereof shall appear to be just," enforced through an "action on the case or other equivalent remedy." [Citation.]

---

9. It should be noted that *Tull* is at least in tension with *Bank of Hamilton v. Lessee of Dudley,* 2 Pet. 492, 7 L.Ed. 496 (1829), in which the Court held in light of the Seventh Amendment that a jury must determine the amount of compensation for improvements to real estate, and with *Dimick v. Schiedt,* 293 U.S. 474, 55 S.Ct. 296, 79 L.Ed. 603 (1935), in which the Court held that the Seventh Amendment bars the use of additur.

Because actions on the case were historically tried at law, it seems clear that this original statute permitted juries to assess such damages. * * *

If a right to jury trial was consistent with the meaning of the phrase "as to the court . . . shall appear to be just" in the 1856 statutory damages provision, I see no reason to insist that the phrase "as the court considers just" has a different meaning in that provision's latest reenactment. * * *

As the majority's discussion amply demonstrates, there would be considerable doubt about the constitutionality of § 504(c) if it did not permit jury determination of the amount of statutory damages. Because an interpretation of § 504(c) that avoids the Seventh Amendment question is at least "fairly possible," I would adopt that interpretation, prevent the invalidation of this statute, and reserve the constitutional issue for another day.

––––––––––

1. *Characterization.* The Supreme Court applies a historical analog test in seeking to characterize a claim as legal or equitable for the purpose of determining whether the Seventh Amendment right to a jury trial attaches. Under this test, the Seventh Amendment right attaches to all causes of action that would have been tried to a jury in common law courts prior to the merger of law and equity. The right to a jury trial, however, is not frozen in time. The Seventh Amendment right to a jury trial also can attach to new statutorily created causes of action if those statutory causes of action are analogous to claims that would have been tried to a jury in the old common law courts.

In determining whether a new statutory claim is more analogous to a common law claim or an equitable claim, the Court examines both the nature of the claim and the nature of the relief sought. The Court generally has placed more emphasis on the remedy prong. *See, e.g.,* Chauffeurs, Teamsters & Helpers, Local No. 391 v. Terry, 494 U.S. 558, 110 S.Ct. 1339, 108 L.Ed.2d 519 (1990) (plurality opinion) (noting that examination of the remedy sought is "more important in our analysis"); Tull v. United States, 481 U.S. 412, 107 S.Ct. 1831, 95 L.Ed.2d 365 (1987) ("characterizing the relief sought is '[m]ore important' than finding a precisely analogous common-law cause of action in determining whether the Seventh Amendment guarantees a jury trial") (citations omitted) (alteration in the original). However, some members of the Court have downplayed the significance of a separate inquiry into the nature of the relief sought. *See, e.g.,* Terry, 494 U.S. at 592 (O'Connor, Scalia and Kennedy, JJ., dissenting) ("a single historical analog [can take] into consideration the nature of the cause of action and the remedy").

2. *Statutory Claims.* As the principal case illustrates, once the Seventh Amendment attaches to a statutory claim, Congress cannot deprive a litigant of his or her right to a jury trial by providing otherwise in the statute. However, Congress may provide statutorily for a jury trial even if the Seventh Amendment would not compel one.

3. *Backpay.* Characterizing a claim for backpay as legal or equitable has been particularly problematic for the federal courts. In *Lorillard v. Pons*, 434 U.S. 575, 98 S.Ct. 866, 55 L.Ed.2d 40 (1978), the Supreme Court held that a plaintiff was entitled to a jury trial on claims for backpay under the Age Discrimination in Employment Act (ADEA). In reaching this holding, the Court noted that the ADEA expressly authorized courts to grant "such legal or equitable relief as may be appropriate" and explicitly incorporated the powers, remedies and procedures of the Fair Labor Standards Act (FLSA). The Court further noted that courts consistently had recognized a right to a jury trial under the FLSA.

Lower courts have found a right to a jury trial on claims for backpay under a variety of different circumstances. For example, applying reasoning similar to the Supreme Court in *Lorillard*, at least one court has found a right to a jury trial under the Family Medical Leave Act (FMLA) based on legislative history indicating that Congress intended the remedial provisions to mirror those under the FLSA. *See* Frizzell v. Southwest Motor Freight, 154 F.3d 641 (6th Cir.1998). Other courts have recognized the right to a jury trial on claims for backpay under the Airline Deregulation Act and the Rehabilitation Act. *See, e.g.,* Crocker v. Piedmont Aviation, Inc., 49 F.3d 735 (D.C.Cir.1995); Waldrop v. Southern Co. Svcs., 24 F.3d 152 (11th Cir.1994).

In contrast, at least prior to 1991, most lower courts refused to recognize a right to a jury trial for claims for backpay under Title VII of the Civil Rights Act of 1964 (Title VII). *See, e.g.,* Ramos v. Roche Prod., Inc., 936 F.2d 43 (1st Cir.1991); Snider v. Circle K Corp., 923 F.2d 1404 (10th Cir.1991); Lincoln v. Board of Regents of Univ. System of Georgia, 697 F.2d 928 (11th Cir.1983). These courts characterized backpay as an equitable remedy, reasoning that backpay is merely an integral part of reinstatement. Although backpay is a form of monetary relief, these courts likened backpay to a claim for restitution rather than a claim for damages. However, prior to 1991 Title VII, unlike the FMLA and the ADEA, authorized equitable relief only. Compensatory and punitive damages were not available to a Title VII claimant. *See* 42 U.S.C. § 2000e–5(g) (1970) ("The court may * * * order such affirmative action as may be appropriate, which may include * * * reinstatement or hiring of employees, with or without back pay * * * or other equitable relief as the court deems appropriate.") *amended by* 42 U.S.C. § 1981a (1991).

Prior to 1991, the Supreme Court had not addressed the issue directly. Nonetheless, the Court had cited lower court opinions refusing to find a right to a jury trial with approval. Most notably, in finding a right to a jury trial on a claim for backpay under the Labor Management Relations Act (LMRA), a majority of the Court distinguished claims for backpay under Title VII from the claim for backpay under the LMRA. *See* Chauffeurs, Teamsters & Helpers, Local No. 391 v. Terry, 494 U.S. 558, 110 S.Ct. 1339, 108 L.Ed.2d 519 (1990). In *Terry*, the plaintiff, a union member, brought an action against his union alleging breach of its duty of fair representation. The plaintiff sought backpay for time lost as a result of the union's failure to file a grievance against his employer. A majority of the Court agreed that the plaintiff was entitled to a jury trial, finding backpay to be legal relief. In reaching its holding, the Court rejected the Union's argument that backpay under the LMRA should be deemed equitable relief because it was analogous to the backpay relief available under Title VII. The Court noted that "Congress specifically characterized backpay under Title VII as a form of 'equitable relief.' " Likewise, the Court characterized backpay under Title VII as restitutionary because sought from the employer, while noting that the backpay sought under the LMRA would be paid by the Union rather than the employer.

In 1991, Congress amended Title VII to expressly provide for the recovery of compensatory and punitive damages in addition to equitable relief for certain types of claims. Additionally, Congress expressly provided for a jury trial on those claims. In addressing the retroactivity of these amendments, the Supreme Court expressly left open the question of whether backpay was an issue for the court rather than a jury under either version of Title VII. *See* Landgraf v. USI Film Prod., Inc., 511 U.S. 244, 252 n. 4, 114 S.Ct. 1483, 128 L.Ed.2d 229 (1994) ("We have not decided whether a plaintiff seeking backpay under Title VII is entitled to a jury trial. [Citations.] Because petitioner does not argue that she had a right to jury trial even under pre–1991 law, again we need not address this question."). Should a litigant have the right to a jury trial of a claim for backpay under Title VII? S*ee* Allison v. Citgo Petroleum Corp., 151 F.3d 402, 423 n. 19 (5th Cir.1998) (right to a jury trial does not attach to claims for front pay or backpay because they are equitable remedies); Hennessy v. Penril Datacomm Networks, 69 F.3d 1344 (7th Cir.1995) (statute prohibits consideration of backpay by the jury as an element of compensatory damages). If not, how should a court resolve a claim for backpay under Title VII when the plaintiff also states claims for backpay under the FMLA or state employment laws? If so, what distinguishes backpay under Title VII from the other claims for backpay that courts have recognized as legal relief?

Markman v. Westview Instruments, Inc.

517 U.S. 370, 116 S.Ct. 1384, 134 L.Ed.2d 577 (1996).

■ JUSTICE SOUTER delivered the opinion of the Court.

The question here is whether the interpretation of a so-called patent claim, the portion of the patent document that defines the scope of the patentee's rights, is a matter of law reserved entirely for the court, or subject to a Seventh Amendment guarantee that a jury will determine the meaning of any disputed term of art about which expert testimony is offered. We hold that the construction of a patent, including terms of art within its claim, is exclusively within the province of the court.

I

* * * It has long been understood that a patent must describe the exact scope of an invention and its manufacture to "secure to [the paten-

tee] all to which he is entitled, [and] to apprise the public of what is still open to them." [Citation.] Under the modern American system, these objectives are served by two distinct elements of a patent document. First, it contains a specification describing the invention "in such full, clear, concise, and exact terms as to enable any person skilled in the art . . . to make and use the same." [Citation.] Second, a patent includes one or more "claims," which "particularly poin[t] out and distinctly clai[m] the subject matter which the applicant regards as his invention." [Citation.] "A claim covers and secures a process, a machine, a manufacture, a composition of matter, or a design, but never the function or result of either, nor the scientific explanation of their operation." [Citation.] * * *

Characteristically, patent lawsuits charge what is known as infringement, [citation], and rest on allegations that the defendant "without authority ma[de], use[d] or [sold the] patented invention, within the United States during the term of the patent therefor. . . ." [Citation.] Victory in an infringement suit requires a finding that the patent claim "covers the alleged infringer's product or process," which in turn necessitates a determination of "what the words in the claim mean." [Citations.]

Petitioner in this infringement suit, Markman, owns United States Reissue Patent No. 33,054 for his "Inventory Control and Reporting System for Drycleaning Stores." The patent describes a system that can monitor and report the status, location, and movement of clothing in a dry-cleaning establishment. The Markman system consists of a keyboard and data processor to generate written records for each transaction, including a bar code readable by optical detectors operated by employees, who log the progress of clothing through the dry-cleaning process. Respondent Westview's product also includes a keyboard and processor, and it lists charges for the dry-cleaning services on bar-coded tickets that can be read by portable optical detectors.

Markman brought an infringement suit against Westview and Althon Enterprises, an operator of dry-cleaning establishments using Westview's products (collectively, Westview). Westview responded that Markman's patent is not infringed by its system because the latter functions merely to record an inventory of receivables by tracking invoices and transaction totals, rather than to record and track an inventory of articles of clothing. Part of the dispute hinged upon the meaning of the word "inventory," a term found in Markman's independent claim 1, which states that Markman's product can "maintain an inventory total" and "detect and localize spurious additions to inventory." The case was tried before a jury, which heard, among others, a witness produced by Markman who testified about the meaning of the claim language.

After the jury compared the patent to Westview's device, it found an infringement of Markman's independent claim 1 and dependent claim 10. The District Court nevertheless granted Westview's deferred motion for judgment as a matter of law, one of its reasons being that the term "inventory" in Markman's patent encompasses "both cash inventory and the actual physical inventory of articles of clothing." [Citation.] Under the trial court's construction of the patent, the production, sale, or use of a tracking system for dry cleaners would not infringe Markman's patent unless the product was capable of tracking articles of clothing throughout the cleaning process and generating reports about their status and location. Since Westview's system cannot do these things, the District Court directed a verdict on the ground that Westview's device does not have the "means to maintain an inventory total" and thus cannot " 'detect and localize spurious additions to inventory as well as spurious deletions therefrom,' " as required by claim 1. [Citation.]

Markman appealed, arguing it was error for the District Court to substitute its construction of the disputed claim term "inventory" for the construction the jury had presumably given it. The United States Court of Appeals for the Federal Circuit affirmed, holding the interpretation of claim terms to be the exclusive province of the court and the Seventh Amendment to be consistent with that conclusion. [Citation.] Markman sought our review on each point, and we granted certiorari. [Citation.] We now affirm.

II

The Seventh Amendment provides that "[i]n Suits at common law, where the value in controversy shall exceed twenty dollars, the right of trial by jury shall be preserved...." U.S. Const., Amdt. 7. Since Justice Story's day, [citation], we have understood that "[t]he right of trial by jury thus preserved is the right which existed under the English common law when the Amendment was adopted." [Citation.] In keeping with our longstanding adherence to this "historical test," [citation], we ask, first, whether we are dealing with a cause of action that either was tried at law at the time of the founding or is at least analogous to one that was, [citation]. If the action in question belongs in the law category, we then ask whether the particular trial decision must fall to the jury in order to preserve the substance of the common-law right as it existed in 1791. [Citation].

A.

As to the first issue, going to the character of the cause of action, "[t]he form of our analysis is familiar. 'First we compare the statutory action to 18th-century actions brought in the courts of England prior to the merger of the courts of law and equity.' " *Granfinanciera, S.A. v. Nordberg,* 492 U.S. 33, 42, 109 S.Ct. 2782, 2790, 106 L.Ed.2d 26 (1989) (citation omitted). Equally familiar is the descent of today's patent infringement action from the infringement actions tried at law in the 18th century, and there is no dispute that infringement cases today must be tried to a jury, as their predecessors were more than two centuries ago. [Citation.]

B.

This conclusion raises the second question, whether a particular issue occurring within a jury trial (here the construction of a patent claim) is itself necessarily a jury issue, the guarantee being essential to preserve the right to a jury's resolution of the ultimate dispute. In some instances the answer to this second question may be easy because of clear historical evidence that the very subsidiary question was so regarded under the English practice of leaving the issue for a jury. But when, as here, the old practice provides no clear answer, [citation], we are forced to make a judgment about the scope of the Seventh Amendment guarantee without the benefit of any foolproof test.

The Court has repeatedly said that the answer to the second question "must depend on whether the jury must shoulder this responsibility *as necessary to preserve the 'substance of the common-law right of trial by jury.'*" [Citations.] " 'Only those incidents which are regarded as fundamental, as inherent in and of the essence of the system of trial by jury, are placed beyond the reach of the legislature.' " [Citations.]

The "substance of the common-law right" is, however, a pretty blunt instrument for drawing distinctions. We have tried to sharpen it, to be sure, by reference to the distinction between substance and procedure. [Citations.] We have also spoken of the line as one between issues of fact and law. [Citations.]

But the sounder course, when available, is to classify a mongrel practice (like construing a term of art following receipt of evidence) by using the historical method, much as we do in characterizing the suits and actions within which they arise. Where there is no exact antecedent, the best hope lies in comparing the modern practice to earlier ones whose allocation to court or jury we do know, [citations.]

C.

"Prior to 1790 nothing in the nature of a claim had appeared either in British patent practice or in that of the American states," [citation], and we have accordingly found no direct antecedent of modern claim construction in the historical sources. * * *

The closest 18th-century analogue of modern claim construction seems, then, to have been the construction of specifications, and as to that function the mere smattering of patent cases that we have from this period shows no established jury practice sufficient to support an argument by analogy that today's construction of a claim should be a guaranteed jury issue. Few of the case reports even touch upon the proper interpretation of disputed terms in the specifications at issue, [citations], and none demonstrates that the definition of such a term was determined by the jury. * * *

III

Since evidence of common-law practice at the time of the framing does not entail application of the Seventh Amendment's jury guarantee to the construction of the claim document, we must look elsewhere to characterize this determination of meaning in order to allocate it as between court or jury. We accordingly consult existing precedent and consider both the relative interpretive skills of judges and juries and the statutory policies that ought to be furthered by the allocation.

A.

The two elements of a simple patent case, construing the patent and determining whether infringement occurred, were characterized by the former patent practitioner, Justice Curtis. "The first is a question of law, to be determined by the court, construing the letters-patent, and the description of the invention and specification of claim annexed to them. The second is a question of fact, to be submitted to a jury." [Citations.]

In arguing for a different allocation of responsibility for the first question, Markman relies primarily on two cases, *Bischoff v. Wethered,* 9 Wall. 812, 19 L.Ed. 829 (1870), and *Tucker v. Spalding,* 13 Wall. 453, 20 L.Ed. 515 (1872). These are said to show that evidence of the meaning of patent terms was offered to 19th-century juries, and thus to imply that the meaning of a documentary term was a jury issue whenever it was subject to evidentiary proof. That is not what Markman's cases show, however. * * * In sum, neither *Bischoff* nor *Tucker* indicates that juries resolved the meaning of terms of art in construing a patent, and neither case undercuts Justice Curtis's authority.

B.

Where history and precedent provide no clear answers, functional considerations also play their part in the choice between judge and jury to define terms of art. We said in *Miller v. Fenton,* 474 U.S. 104, 114, 106 S.Ct. 445, 451, 88 L.Ed.2d 405 (1985), that when an issue "falls somewhere between a pristine legal standard and a simple historical fact, the fact/law distinction at times has turned on a determination that, as a matter of the sound administration of justice, one judicial actor is better positioned than another to decide the issue in question." So it turns out here, for judges, not juries, are the better suited to find the acquired meaning of patent terms.

The construction of written instruments is one of those things that judges often do and are likely to do better than jurors unburdened by training in exegesis. Patent construction in particular "is a special occupation, requiring, like all others, special training and practice. The judge, from his training and discipline, is more likely to give a proper interpretation to such instruments than a jury; and he is, therefore, more likely to be right, in performing such a duty, than a jury can be expected to be." [Citation.] Such was the understanding nearly a century and a half ago, and there is no reason to weigh the respective strengths of judge and jury differently in relation to the modern claim; quite the contrary, for "the claims of patents have become highly technical in many respects as the result of special doctrines relating to the proper form and scope of claims that have been developed by the courts and the Patent Office." [Citation.]

Markman would trump these considerations with his argument that a jury should decide a question of meaning peculiar to a trade or profession simply because the question is a subject of testimony requiring credibility determinations, which are the jury's forte. It is, of course, true that credibility judgments have to be made about the experts who testify in patent cases, and in theory there could be a case in which a simple credibility judgment would suffice to choose between experts whose testimony was equally consistent with a patent's internal logic. But our own experience with document construction leaves us doubtful that trial courts will run into many cases like that. In the main, we expect, any credibility determinations will be subsumed within the necessarily sophisticated analysis of the whole document, required by the standard construction rule that a term can be defined only in a way that comports with the instrument as a whole. [Citations.] Thus, in these cases a jury's capabilities to evaluate demeanor, [citation], to sense the "mainsprings of human conduct," [citation], or to reflect community standards, [citation], are much less significant than a trained ability to evaluate the testimony in relation to the overall structure of the patent. The decisionmaker vested with the task of construing the patent is in the better position to ascertain whether an expert's proposed definition fully comports with the specification and claims and so will preserve the patent's internal coherence. We accordingly think there is sufficient reason to treat construction of terms of art like many other responsibilities that we cede to a judge in the normal course of trial, notwithstanding its evidentiary underpinnings.

C.

Finally, we see the importance of uniformity in the treatment of a given patent as an independent reason to allocate all issues of construction to the court. As we noted in *General Elec. Co. v. Wabash Appliance Corp.*, 304 U.S. 364, 369, 58 S.Ct. 899, 902, 82 L.Ed. 1402 (1938), "[t]he limits of a patent must be known for the protection of the patentee, the encouragement of the inventive genius of others and the assurance that the subject of the patent will be dedicated ultimately to the public." Otherwise, a "zone of uncertainty which enterprise and experimentation may enter only at the risk of infringement claims would discourage invention only a little less than unequivocal foreclosure of the field," [citation], and "[t]he public [would] be deprived of rights supposed to belong to it, without being clearly told what it is that limits these rights." [Citation.] It was just for the sake of such desirable uniformity that Congress created the Court of Appeals for the Federal Circuit as an exclusive appellate court for patent cases, H.R.Rep. No. 97–312, pp. 20–23 (1981), observing that increased uniformity would "strengthen the United States patent system in such a way as to foster technological growth and industrial innovation." *Id.*, at 20.

Uniformity would, however, be ill served by submitting issues of document construction to juries. Making them jury issues would not, to be sure, necessarily leave evidentiary questions of meaning wide open in every new court in which a patent might be litigated, for principles of issue preclusion would ordinarily foster uniformity. [Citation.] But whereas issue preclusion could not be asserted against new and independent infringement defendants even within a given jurisdiction, treating interpretive issues as purely legal will promote (though it will not guarantee) intrajurisdictional certainty through the application of *stare decisis* on those questions not yet subject to interjurisdictional uniformity under the authority of the single appeals court. * * *

Accordingly, we hold that the interpretation of the word "inventory" in this case is an issue for the judge, not the jury, and affirm the decision of the Court of Appeals for the Federal Circuit.

It is so ordered.

_____

1. *Substance of the Right.* While the Court has employed a historical test to determine whether or not the Seventh Amendment right to a jury trial attaches to a claim, the Court generally has eschewed such a historical test when determining the scope of the right. Indeed, the use of a historical test to define the substance of the right to a jury trial could produce odd results. As Justice Ginsburg noted in *Gasperini v. Center for Humanities,* 518 U.S. 415, 116 S.Ct. 2211, 135 L.Ed.2d 659 (1996), "[i]f the meaning of the Seventh Amendment were fixed in 1791, our civil juries would remain, as they unquestionably were at common law, 'twelve good men and true.'" Instead, the Court has focused on whether a particular procedure is necessary to preserve the substance of the common law right. Thus, the Court has upheld the use of six person juries even though 12 person juries were required at common law. *See* Colgrove v. Battin, 413 U.S. 149, 93 S.Ct. 2448, 37 L.Ed.2d 522 (1973). However, the Supreme Court and lower federal courts have maintained that unanimous verdicts are necessary to preserve the substance of the right to a jury trial. *See* Murray v. Laborers Union Local No. 324, 55 F.3d 1445 (9th Cir.1995) (citing cases).

2. *Complexity Exception.* As the principal case illustrates, determining which issues or decisions need to be submitted to the jury also turns on a determination of what is necessary to preserve the substance of the right. However, in determining whether an issue must be submitted to the jury the Court has looked to history, examining whether the issue ordinarily was submitted to the jury at common law. Historical analogs have not been dispositive. In determining that claim construction is an issue for the court in the principal case, the Court also considered post–18th century precedent, policy issues and "functional considerations." In particular, the Court seemed persuaded that a court would be better equipped to determine the meaning of patent claims, in part, because of the "sophisticated analysis" that would be required. Should the complexity a decision be a factor in determining whether to allocate the decision to the court or the jury? Should the court rather than the jury resolve an otherwise clear issue of fact when determination of the disputed fact issue requires the synthesis of complex, sophisticated or highly technical evidence? Should the complexity of the entire claim be a factor courts consider in determining whether the Seventh Amendment right to a jury trial attaches in the first place?

For further discussion of a complexity exception to the Seventh Amendment, *see* Lisa S. Meyer, Taking the "Complexity" Out of Complex Litigation: Preserving the Constitutional Right to a Civil Jury Trial, 28 Val.

U. L. Rev. 337, 372 (1993); Morris S. Arnold, A Historical Inquiry into the Right to Trial by Jury in Complex Civil Litigation, 128 U. Pa. L. Rev. 829 (1980); Maxwell M. Blecher & Howard F. Daniels, In Defense of Juries in Complex Antitrust Litigation, 1 Rev. Litig. 47 (1980).

Dairy Queen, Inc. v. Wood

369 U.S. 469, 82 S.Ct. 894, 8 L.Ed.2d 44 (1962).

■ MR. JUSTICE BLACK delivered the opinion of the Court.

The United States District Court for the Eastern District of Pennsylvania granted a motion to strike petitioner's demand for a trial by jury in an action now pending before it on the alternative grounds that either the action was "purely equitable" or, if not purely equitable, whatever legal issues that were raised were "incidental" to equitable issues, and, in either case, no right to trial by jury existed. * * *

At the outset, we may dispose of one of the grounds upon which the trial court acted in striking the demand for trial by jury that based upon the view that the right to trial by jury may be lost as to legal issues where those issues are characterized as incidental to equitable issues for our previous decisions make it plain that no such rule may be applied in the federal courts. * * *

* * * Rule 38(a) expressly reaffirms that constitutional principle, declaring: "The right of trial by jury as declared by the Seventh Amendment to the Constitution or as given by a statute of the United States shall be preserved to the parties inviolate." Nonetheless, after the adoption of the Federal Rules, attempts were made indirectly to undercut that right by having federal courts in which cases involving both legal and equitable claims were filed decide the equitable claim first. The result of this procedure in those cases in which it was followed was that any issue common to both the legal and equitable claims was finally determined by the court and the party seeking trial by jury on the legal claim was deprived of that right as to these common issues. This procedure finally came before us in Beacon Theatres, Inc. v. Westover, [359 U.S. 500, 79 S.Ct. 948 (1959)] a case which, like this one, arose from the denial of a petition for mandamus to compel a district judge to vacate his order striking a demand for trial by jury.

Our decision reversing that case not only emphasizes the responsibility of the Federal Courts of Appeals to grant mandamus where necessary to protect the constitutional right to trial by jury but also limits the issues open for determination here by defining the protection to which that right is entitled in cases involving both legal and equitable claims. The holding in *Beacon Theatres* was that where both legal and equitable issues are presented in a single case, "only under the most imperative circumstances, circumstances which in view of the flexible procedures of the Federal Rules we cannot now anticipate, can the right to a jury trial of legal issues be lost through prior determination of equitable claims." That holding, of course, applies whether the trial judge chooses to characterize the legal issues presented as "incidental" to equitable issues or not. Consequently, in a case such as this where there cannot even be a contention of such "imperative circumstances," *Beacon Theatres* requires that any legal issues for which a trial by jury is timely and properly demanded be submitted to a jury. There being no question of the timeliness or correctness of the demand involved here, the sole question which we must decide is whether the action now pending before the District Court contains legal issues.

The District Court proceeding arises out of a controversy between petitioner and the respondent owners of the trademark "DAIRY QUEEN" with regard to a written licensing contract made by them in December 1949, under which petitioner agreed to pay some $150,000 for the exclusive right to use that trademark in certain portions of Pennsylvania. The terms of the contract provided for a small initial payment with the remaining payments to be made at the rate of 50% of all amounts received by petitioner on sales and franchises to deal with the trademark and, in order to make certain that the $150,000 payment would be completed within a specified period of time, further provided for minimum annual payments regardless of petitioner's receipts. In August 1960, the respondents wrote petitioner a letter in which they claimed that petitioner had committed "a material breach of that contract" by defaulting on the contract's payment provisions and notified petitioner of the termination of the contract and the cancellation of petitioner's right to use the trademark unless this claimed default was remedied immediately. When petitioner continued to deal with the trademark despite the notice of termination, the respondents brought an action based upon their view that a material breach of contract had occurred.

* * * The complaint then prayed for both temporary and permanent relief, including: (1) temporary and permanent injunctions to restrain petitioner from any future use of or dealing in the franchise and the trademark; (2) an accounting to determine the exact amount of money owing by petitioner and a judgment for that amount; and (3) an injunction pending accounting to prevent petitioner from collecting any money from "Dairy Queen" stores in the territory.

* * *

Petitioner's contention, as set forth in its petition for mandamus to the Court of Appeals and reiterated in its briefs before this Court, is that insofar as the complaint requests a money judgment it presents a claim which is unquestionably legal. We agree with that contention. * * *

We conclude therefore that the district judge erred in refusing to grant petitioner's demand for a trial by jury on the factual issues related to the question of whether there has been a breach of contract. Since these issues are common with those upon which respondents' claim to equitable relief is based, the legal claims involved in the action must be determined prior to any final court determination of respondents' equitable claims.* The Court of Appeals should have corrected the error of the district judge by granting the petition for mandamus. The judgment is therefore reversed and the cause remanded for further proceedings consistent with this opinion.

Reversed and remanded.

■ MR. JUSTICE HARLAN, whom MR. JUSTICE DOUGLAS joins, concurring.

I am disposed to accept the view, strongly pressed at the bar, that this complaint seeks an accounting for alleged trademark infringement, rather than contract damages. Even though this leaves the complaint as formally asking only for equitable relief,[10] this does not end the inquiry. The fact that an "accounting" is sought is not of itself dispositive of the jury trial issue. To render this aspect of the complaint truly "equitable" it must appear that the substantive claim is one cognizable only in equity or that the "accounts between the parties" are of such a "complicated nature" that they can be satisfactorily unraveled only by a court of equity. [Citations.] It is manifest from the face of the complaint that the "accounting" sought in this instance is not of either variety. A jury, under proper instruction from the court, could readily calculate the damages flowing from this alleged trademark infringement, just as courts of law often do in copyright and patent cases. [Citations.]

Consequently what is involved in this case is nothing more than a joinder in one complaint of prayers for both legal and equitable relief. In such circumstances, under principles long since established, [citation], the petitioner cannot be deprived of his constitutional right to a jury trial on the "legal" claim contained in the complaint.

On this basis I concur in the judgment of the Court.

---

1. *Early Seventh Amendment Jurisprudence*. The first in the line of cases where the Supreme Court reconsidered the application of the Seventh Amendment was *Beacon Theatres, Inc. v. Westover*, 359 U.S. 500, 79 S.Ct. 948, 3 L.Ed.2d 988 (1959). The plaintiff in that case sought declaratory relief and the defendant counterclaimed for damages for past violations of the antitrust laws. The trier of fact would confront the same questions under both claims. The Court held that the right to a jury trial must not depend on a race to the courthouse. It held that where equitable and legal claims are joined in the same action, there is a right to jury trial on the legal claims. A court cannot infringe upon this right by having an equitable trial of common issues in the claims or by trying the legal issues as

---

* This does not of course, interfere with the District Court's power to grant temporary relief pending a final adjudication on the merits. Such temporary relief has already been granted in this case (*see* McCullough v. Dairy Queen, Inc., 290 F.2d 871) and is no part of the issues before this Court.

10. Except as to the damage claim there is no dispute but that the complaint seeks only equitable relief.

incidental to the equitable ones. The principle was that the Seventh Amendment question depends on the nature of the issue tried.

2. *Historical Background.* For the historical background surrounding the adoption of the Seventh Amendment, *see* Krauss, The Original Understanding of the Seventh Amendment Right to Jury Trial, 33 U. Rich. L. Rev. 407 (1999); Amar, The Bill of Rights: Creation and Reconstruction 81–92 (1998); Wolfram, The Constitutional History of the Seventh Amendment, 57 Minn. L. Rev. 639 (1973); Henderson, The Background of the Seventh Amendment, 80 Harv. L. Rev. 289 (1966).

CHAPTER 19

ATTORNEY FEES

Section Coverage:

In the United States the prevailing party in a law suit is not ordinarily entitled to recover its litigation expenses, including attorney fees, from the losing party. Although some costs of suit, such as filing fees, are awarded to the prevailing party under Federal Rule 54(d) and similar state rules, "costs of suit" do not include other litigation expenses, such as attorney fees. This "American Rule" that expenses shall be borne by each party independently is in contrast to the British Rule which provides that the prevailing party is entitled to receive their litigation expenses as a matter of course. The principal justification in support of the American Rule is that a party should not be "penalized" for instituting or defending meritorious claims. Also, the imposition of attorney fees against the losing party may discourage the willingness of parties to legitimately resort to the judicial process for dispute resolution. The Rule has been sharply criticized, however, based on the rationale that the failure to reimburse a successful party their litigation expenses results prevents them from being "made whole" even if entirely successful on the merits.

A number of exceptions to the American Rule have developed through contract, common law, and statutes. The contractual exception is simply that parties to a contract are free to agree in advance of breach that reasonable attorney fees can be collected by the non-breaching party as necessary to enforce contract rights. Such fee arrangements are common in business, bank loans, and leases. As long as such provisions are not grounded in unconscionability, they are enforceable.

The common law has also recognized several exceptions to the American Rule based upon the inherent equitable power of courts to redress abuses of the litigation process or where special circumstances exist to warrant compensating or shifting litigation costs. For example, courts may impose reasonable costs of litigation against a party acting "vexatiously" or in bad faith. The standard for awarding fees under the bad faith exception requires more than a showing that the claim, defense, or appeal was weakly supported; the American Rule theory is that even weak cases deserve a day in court without fear of fee obligations upon loss. Rather, attorney fees awards for bad faith litigation are grounded in deterrence of unjustified or frivolous litigation. The line between weak claims and frivolous ones is rarely bright, but that distinction is essential for this exception.

Additionally, courts have recognized equitable exceptions based upon facilitating creation of a common fund, conferring a substantial benefit, and where the successful litigant served in the capacity of a private attorney general. These theories are all common law exceptions, although they often have statutory counterparts. The major exceptions to the American Rule of litigation expenses are found as specific statutory authorizations in areas such as civil rights, consumer protection, privacy, and environmental statutes.

Another common law exception is that the plaintiff who acts as a "private attorney general" sometimes receives attorney fees from the defendant. Under this theory, courts may award attorney fees to a private party who pursues a matter benefitting the public good, such as a determination of civil rights or effectuating environmental protection. Courts find the source of power to award fees in this circumstance, and numerous related ones, in their inherent equitable powers to carry out the interests of justice. In *Alyeska Pipeline Service Co. v. Wilderness Society*, 421 U.S. 240, 95 S.Ct. 1612, 44 L.Ed.2d 141 (1975), which introduces this Chapter, the Supreme Court specifically rejected as a matter of federal law the private attorney general basis for attorney fees except as expressly authorized by Congress. In *Alyeska* the federal Court of Appeals had awarded attorney fees to environmental organizations which had successfully challenged the issuance of permits necessary for the construction of the trans-Alaska oil pipeline. In response to *Alyeska*, Congress quickly authorized the recovery of attorney fees to prevailing parties under numerous civil rights, environmental, and other statutes involving matters of public interest.

The provision for attorney fees is particularly significant in public interest litigation because often the nature of the remedy sought is an injunction rather than damages. Therefore, no fund would be created to pay the plaintiff's attorney fees absent the statutory grant. The statutory language of these fee-shifting authorizations typically authorizes the federal court to award reasonable fees to the "prevailing party."

A court retains inherent power to regulate attorney fees in a supervisory role. Contractual provisions and settlement arrangements are all subject to judicial scrutiny. Although this power is invoked sparingly, judges staunchly preserve it and exercise it as needed in cases where the integrity of the court system and legal profession are in question.

Assuming that a party has established entitlement to an award of attorney fees, the next question involves determining what constitutes a "reasonable" fee. Many courts have calculated the reasonableness of the statutory fee according to the "lodestar" method which takes into account the number of hours spent on the successful issues in litigation multiplied times a reasonable hourly rate. The following materials will explore issues involving both the entitlement and the measurement of attorney fees to parties under both common law principles and statutory provisions.

Model Case:

Chris Taylor is a doctor who is the director of a division in a university hospital. Dr. Taylor is a strong believer in the desirability of voluntary affirmative action for groups historically excluded from the medical profession.

The Governing Board of the hospital determined that Dr. Taylor's division should have an assistant director. The Board took applications from doctors for this new position and consulted Dr. Taylor on the merits of each candidate. The applicants were narrowed to two final choices for the single position. One doctor was a member of a group historically excluded by the profession; the other was not. The Board chose the latter. Dr. Taylor made a major protest at a stormy Board meeting and, as a result, was fired.

Dr. Taylor's suit for unlawful employment discrimination under federal law is uncertain of success. On the one hand, if the discharge was retaliation for protesting unlawful discrimination, Dr. Taylor's activity may be protected under federal law. If so, a successful civil rights claim will include recovery of attorney fees in addition to any other available remedies. On the other hand, if the board did not engage in unlawful discrimination, then Dr. Taylor's advocacy of voluntary conduct would not be federally protected. At best Dr. Taylor would have a state claim of wrongful or retaliatory discharge. Such a claim would lie in tort or contract and would not include recovery of attorney fees. As a matter of common law there would be no basis for an exception to the American Rule that each party must bear litigation costs.

Alyeska Pipeline Service Co. v. Wilderness Society

421 U.S. 240, 95 S.Ct. 1612, 44 L.Ed.2d 141 (1975).

■ MR. JUSTICE WHITE delivered the opinion of the Court.

This litigation was initiated by respondents Wilderness Society, Environmental Defense Fund, Inc., and Friends of the Earth in an attempt to prevent the issuance of permits by the Secretary of the Interior which were required for the construction of the trans-Alaska oil pipeline. The Court of Appeals awarded attorneys' fees to respondents against petitioner Alyeska Pipeline Service Co. based upon the court's equitable powers and the theory that respondents were entitled to fees because they were performing the services of a "private attorney general." Certiorari was granted, 419 U.S. 823, 95 S.Ct. 39, 42 L.Ed.2d 47 (1974), to determine whether this award of attorneys' fees was appropriate. We reverse.

I

A major oil field was discovered in the North Slope of Alaska in 1968. In June 1969, the oil companies constituting the consortium owning Alyeska submitted an application to the Department of the Interior for rights-of-way for a pipeline that would transport oil from the North Slope across land in Alaska owned by the United States, a major part of the transport system which would carry the oil to its ultimate markets in the lower 48 States. A special interdepartmental task force studied the proposal and reported to the President. An amended application was submitted in December 1969, which requested a 54–foot right-of-way, along with applications for "special land use permits" asking for additional space alongside the right-of-way and for the construction of a road along one segment of the pipeline.

Respondents brought this suit in March 1970, and sought declaratory and injunctive relief against the Secretary of the Interior on the grounds that he intended to issue the right-of-way and special land-use permits in violation of § 28 of the Mineral Leasing Act of 1920, 41 Stat. 449, as amended, 30 U.S.C. § 185, and without compliance with the National Environmental Policy Act of 1969 (NEPA), 83 Stat. 852, 42 U.S.C. § 4321 et seq. On the basis of both the Mineral Leasing Act and the NEPA, the District Court granted a preliminary injunction against issuance of the right-of-way and permits.

Subsequently the State of Alaska and petitioner Alyeska were allowed to intervene. On March 20, 1972, the Interior Department released a six-volume Environmental Impact Statement and a three-volume Economic and Security Analysis. After a period of time set aside for public comment, the Secretary announced that the requested permits would be granted to Alyeska. Both the Mineral Leasing Act and the NEPA issues were at that point fully briefed and argued before the District Court. That court then decided to dissolve the preliminary injunction, to deny the permanent injunction, and to dismiss the complaint.

Upon appeal, the Court of Appeals for the District of Columbia Circuit reversed, basing its decision solely on the Mineral Leasing Act. Finding that the NEPA issues were very complex and important, that deciding them was not necessary at that time since pipeline construction would be enjoined as a result of the violation of the Mineral Leasing Act, that they involved issues of fact still in dispute, and that it was desirable to expedite its decision as much as possible, the Court of Appeals declined to decide the merits of respondents' NEPA contentions which had been rejected by the District Court. Certiorari was denied here.

Congress then enacted legislation which amended the Mineral Leasing Act to allow the granting of the permits sought by Alyeska and declared that no further action under the NEPA was necessary before construction of the pipeline could proceed.

With the merits of the litigation effectively terminated by this legislation, the Court of Appeals turned to the questions involved in respondents' request for an award of attorneys' fees.[13] Since there was no applicable statutory authorization for such an award, the court proceeded to consider whether the requested fee award fell within any of the exceptions to the general "American rule" that the prevailing party may not recover attorneys' fees as costs or otherwise. The exception for an award against a party who had acted in bad faith was inapposite, since the position taken by the

---

13. Respondents' bill of costs includes a total of 4,455 hours of attorneys' time spent on the litigation.

federal and state parties and Alyeska "was manifestly reasonable and assumed in good faith...." Application of the "common benefit" exception which spreads the cost of litigation to those persons benefitting from it would "stretch it totally outside its basic rationale...." The Court of Appeals nevertheless held that respondents had acted to vindicate "important statutory rights of all citizens ...," ensured that the governmental system functioned properly; and were entitled to attorneys' fees lest the great cost of litigation of this kind, particularly against well-financed defendants such as Alyeska, deter private parties desiring to see the laws protecting the environment properly enforced. Title 28 U.S.C. § 2412 was thought to bar taxing any attorneys' fees against the United States, and it was also deemed inappropriate to burden the State of Alaska with any part of the award. But Alyeska, the Court of Appeals held, could fairly be required to pay one-half of the full award to which respondents were entitled for having performed the functions of a private attorney general. Observing that "(t)he fee should represent the reasonable value of the services rendered, taking into account all the surrounding circumstances, including, but not limited to, the time and labor required on the case, the benefit to the public, the skill demanded by the novelty or complexity of the issues, and the incentive factor," the Court of Appeals remanded the case to the District Court for assessment of the dollar amount of the award.

II

In the United States, the prevailing litigant is ordinarily not entitled to collect a reasonable attorneys' fee from the loser. We are asked to fashion a far-reaching exception to this "American Rule"; but having considered its origin and development, we are convinced that it would be inappropriate for the Judiciary, without legislative guidance, to reallocate the burdens of litigation in the manner and to the extent urged by respondents and approved by the Court of Appeals.

At common law, costs were not allowed; but for centuries in England there has been statutory authorization to award costs, including attorneys' fees. Although the matter is in the discretion of the court, counsel fees are regularly allowed to the prevailing party.[18]

In 1796, this Court appears to have ruled that the Judiciary itself would not create a general rule, independent of any statute, allowing awards of attorneys' fees in federal courts. In Arcambel v. Wiseman, 3 U.S. (3 Dall.) 306, 1 L.Ed. 613, the inclusion of attorneys' fees as damages was overturned on the ground that "(t)he general practice of the United States

---

18. As early as 1278, the courts of England were authorized to award counsel fees to successful plaintiffs in litigation. Similarly, since 1607 English courts have been empowered to award counsel fees to defendants in all actions where such awards might be made to plaintiffs. Rules governing administration of these and related provisions have developed over the years. It is now customary in England, after litigation of substantive claims has terminated, to conduct separate hearings before special "taxing Masters" in order to determine the appropriateness and the size of an award of counsel fees. To prevent the ancillary proceedings from becoming unduly protracted and burdensome, fees which may be included in an award are usually prescribed, even including the amounts that may be recovered for letters drafted on behalf of a client.

is in opposition to it; and even if that practice were not strictly correct in principle, it is entitled to the respect of the court, till it is changed, or modified, by statute." This Court has consistently adhered to that early holding. * * *

To be sure, the fee statutes have been construed to allow, in limited circumstances, a reasonable attorneys' fee to the prevailing party in excess of the small sums permitted by § 1923. In Trustees v. Greenough, 105 U.S. 527, 26 L.Ed. 1157 (1882), the 1853 Act was read as not interfering with the historic power of equity to permit the trustee of a fund or property, or a party preserving or recovering a fund for the benefit of others in addition to himself, to recover his costs, including his attorneys' fees, from the fund or property itself or directly from the other parties enjoying the benefit. That rule has been consistently followed. Also, a court may assess attorneys' fees for the "willful disobedience of a court order . . . as part of the fine to be levied on the defendant(,)"; or when the losing party has "acted in bad faith, vexatiously, wantonly, or for oppressive reasons." These exceptions are unquestionably assertions of inherent power in the courts to allow attorneys' fees in particular situations, unless forbidden by Congress, but none of the exceptions is involved here. The Court of Appeals expressly disclaimed reliance on any of them.

Congress has not repudiated the judicially fashioned exceptions to the general rule against allowing substantial attorneys' fees; but neither has it retracted, repealed, or modified the limitations on taxable fees contained in the 1853 statute and its successors. Nor has it extended any roving authority to the Judiciary to allow counsel fees as costs or otherwise whenever the courts might deem them warranted. What Congress has done, however, while fully recognizing and accepting the general rule, is to make specific and explicit provisions for the allowance of attorneys' fees under selected statutes granting or protecting various federal rights. These statutory allowances are now available in a variety of circumstances, but they also differ considerably among themselves. Under the antitrust laws, for instance, allowance of attorneys' fees to a plaintiff awarded treble damages is mandatory. In patent litigation, in contrast, "(t)he court in exceptional cases may award reasonable attorney fees to the prevailing party." 35 U.S.C. § 285 (emphasis added). Under Title II of the Civil Rights Act of 1964, 42 U.S.C. § 2000a–3(b), the prevailing party is entitled to attorneys' fees, at the discretion of the court, but we have held that Congress intended that the award should be made to the successful plaintiff absent exceptional circumstances. Newman v. Piggie Park Enterprises, Inc., 390 U.S. 400, 402, 88 S.Ct. 964, 966, 19 L.Ed.2d 1263 (1968). Under this scheme of things it is apparent that the circumstances under which attorneys' fees are to be awarded and the range of discretion of the courts in making those awards are matters for Congress to determine. * * *

It is true that under some, if not most, of the statutes providing for the allowance of reasonable fees, Congress has opted to rely heavily on private enforcement to implement public policy and to allow counsel fees so as to encourage private litigation. Fee shifting in connection with treble-damages awards under the antitrust laws is a prime example; and we have noted that Title II of the Civil Rights Act of 1964 was intended "not simply to penalize litigants who deliberately advance arguments they know to be untenable but, more broadly, to encourage individuals injured by racial discrimination to seek judicial relief under Title II." But congressional utilization of the private-attorney-general concept can in no sense be construed as a grant of authority to the Judiciary to jettison the traditional rule against nonstatutory allowances to the prevailing party and to award attorneys' fees whenever the courts deem the public policy furthered by a particular statute important enough to warrant the award.

Congress itself presumably has the power and judgment to pick and choose among its statutes and to allow attorneys' fees under some, but not others. But it would be difficult, indeed, for the courts, without legislative guidance, to consider some statutes important and others unimportant and to allow attorneys' fees only in connection with the former. If the statutory limitation of right-of-way widths involved in this case is a matter of the gravest importance, it would appear that a wide range of statutes would arguably satisfy the criterion of public importance and justify an award of attorneys' fees to the private litigant. And, if any statutory policy is deemed so important that its enforcement must be encouraged by awards of attorneys' fees, how could a court deny attorneys' fees to private litigants in actions under 42 U.S.C. § 1983 seeking to vindicate constitutional rights? Moreover, should courts, if they were to embark on the course urged by respondents, opt for awards to the prevailing party, whether plaintiff or defendant, or only to the prevailing plaintiff? Should awards be discretionary or mandatory? Would there be a presumption operating for or against them in the ordinary case?

As exemplified by this case itself, it is also evident that the rational application of the private-attorney-general rule would immediately collide with the express provision 28 U.S.C. § 2412. Except as otherwise provided by statute, that section permits costs to be taxed against the United States, "but not including the fees and expenses of attorneys," in any civil action brought by or against the United States or any agency or official of the United States acting in an official capacity. If, as respondents argue, one of the main functions of a private attorney general is to call public officials to account and to insist that they enforce the law, it would follow in such cases that attorneys' fees should be awarded against the Government or the officials themselves. Indeed, that very claim was asserted in this case. But § 2412 on its face, and in light of its legislative history, generally bars such awards, which, if allowable at all, must be expressly provided for by statute, as, for example, under Title II of the Civil Rights Act of 1964, 42 U.S.C. § 2000a–3(b).

We need labor the matter no further. It appears to us that the rule suggested here and adopted by the Court of Appeals would make major inroads on a policy matter that Congress has reserved for itself. Since the approach taken by Congress to this issue has been to carve out specific exceptions to a general rule that federal courts cannot award attorneys' fees beyond the limits of 28 U.S.C. § 1923, those courts are not free to fashion drastic new rules with respect to the allowance of attorneys' fees to the prevailing party in federal litigation or to pick and choose among plaintiffs and the statutes under which they sue and to award fees in some cases but not in others, depending upon the courts' assessment of the importance of the public policies involved in particular cases. Nor should the federal courts purport to adopt on their own initiative a rule awarding attorneys' fees based on the private-attorney-general approach when such judicial rule will operate only against private parties and not against the Government.

We do not purport to assess the merits or demerits of the "American Rule" with respect to the allowance of attorneys' fees. It has been criticized in recent years, and courts have been urged to find exceptions to it. It is also apparent from our national experience that the encouragement of private action to implement public policy has been viewed as desirable in a variety of circumstances. But the rule followed in our courts with respect to attorneys' fees has survived. It is deeply rooted in our history and in congressional policy; and it is not for us to invade the legislature's province by redistributing litigation costs in the manner suggested by respondents and followed by the Court of Appeals.

The decision below must therefore be reversed.

■ Mr. Justice Marshall, dissenting.

In reversing the award of attorneys' fees to the respondent environmentalist groups, the Court today disavows the well-established power of federal equity courts to award attorneys' fees when the interests of justice so require. While under the traditional American Rule the courts ordinarily refrain from allowing attorneys' fees, we have recognized several judicial exceptions to that rule for classes of cases in which equity seemed to favor fee shifting. By imposing an absolute bar on the use of the "private attorney general" rationale as a basis for awarding attorneys' fees, the Court today takes an extremely narrow view of the independent power of the courts in this area—a view that flies squarely in the face of our prior cases.

* * * [W]hile as a general rule attorneys' fees are not to be awarded to the successful litigant, the courts as well as the Legislature may create exceptions to that rule. Under the judge-made exceptions, attorneys' fees have been assessed, without statutory authorization, for willful violation of a court order, for bad faith or oppressive litigation practices; and where the successful litigants have created a common fund for recovery or extended a substantial benefit to a class. While the Court today acknowledges the continued vitality of these exceptions, it turns its back on the theory underlying them, and on the generous construction given to the common-benefit exception in our recent cases.

* * * The cases plainly establish an independent basis for equity courts to grant attorneys' fees under several rather generous rubrics. The Court acknowledges as much when it says that we have independent

authority to award fees in cases of bad faith or as a means of taxing costs to special beneficiaries. But I am at a loss to understand how it can also say that this independent judicial power succumbs to Procrustean statutory restrictions—indeed, to statutory silence—as soon as the far from bright line between common benefit and public benefit is crossed. I can only conclude that the Court is willing to tolerate the "equitable" exceptions to its analysis, not because they can be squared with it, but because they are by now too well established to be casually dispensed with.

* * * [I]t is possible to discern with some confidence the factors that should guide an equity court in determining whether an award of attorneys' fees is appropriate. The reasonable cost of the plaintiff's representation should be placed upon the defendant if (1) the important right being protected is one actually or necessarily protected is one actually or necessarily shared by the general public or some class thereof; (2) the plaintiff's pecuniary interest in the outcome, if any, would not normally justify incurring the cost of counsel; and (3) shifting that cost to the defendant would effectively place it on a class that benefits from the litigation.

There is hardly room for doubt that the first of these criteria is met in the present case. Significant public benefits are derived from citizen litigation to vindicate expressions of congressional or constitutional policy. As a result of this litigation, respondents forced Congress to revise the Mineral Leasing Act of 1920 rather than permit its continued evasion. The 1973 amendments impose more stringent safety and liability standards, and they require Alyeska to pay fair market value for the right-of-way and to bear the costs of applying for the permit and monitoring the right-of-way. Although the NEPA issues were not actually decided, the lawsuit served as a catalyst to ensure a thorough analysis of the pipeline's environmental impact. Requiring the Interior Department to comply with the NEPA and draft an impact statement satisfied the public's statutory right to have information about the environmental consequences of the project, and also forced delay in the construction until safeguards could be included as conditions to the new right-of-way grants. * * *

The second criterion is equally well satisfied in this case. Respondents' willingness to undertake this litigation was largely altruistic. While they did, of course, stand to benefit from the additional protections they sought for the area potentially affected by the pipeline, the direct benefit to these citizen organizations is truly dwarfed by the demands of litigation of this proportion. Extensive factual discovery, expert scientific analysis, and legal research on a broad range of environmental, technological, and land-use issues were required. The disparity between respondents' direct stake in the outcome and the resources required to pursue the case is exceeded only by the disparity between their resources and those of their opponents—the Federal Government and a consortium of giant oil companies.

Respondents' claim also fulfills the third criterion, for Alyeska is the proper party to bear and spread the cost of this litigation undertaken in the interest of the general public. The Department of the Interior, of course, bears legal responsibility for adopting a position later determined to be unlawful. And, since the class of beneficiaries from the outcome of this litigation is probably coextensive with the class of United States citizens, the Government should in fairness bear the costs of respondents' representation. But, the Court of Appeals concluded that it could not impose attorneys' fees on the United States, because in its view the statute providing for assessment of costs against the Government, 28 U.S.C. § 2412, permits the award of ordinary court costs, "but (does) not included(e) the fees and expenses of attorneys." Since the respondents did not cross-petition on that point, we have no occasion to rule on the correctness of the court's construction of that statute.

Before the Department and the courts, Alyeska advocated adoption of the position taken by Interior, playing a major role in all aspects of the case. This litigation conferred direct and concrete economic benefits on Alyeska and its principals in affording protection of the physical integrity of the pipeline. If a court could be reasonably confident that the ultimate incidence of costs imposed upon an applicant for a public permit would indeed be on the general public, it would be equitable to shift those costs to the applicant. In this connection, Alyeska, as a consortium of oil companies that do business in 49 States and account for some 20% of the national oil market, would indeed be able to redistribute the additional cost to the general public. In my view the ability to pass the cost forward to the consuming public warrants an award here. * * *

---

1. The "American Rule" that parties pay their own litigation expenses is distinguished from the English rule. The English practice, followed in various forms in other countries tracing legal heritage to England, is that the winning party recovers litigation expenses as a matter of course from the losing party. Such litigation expenses include attorney fees, and the rule applies equally to prevailing plaintiffs and defendants. *See* McCormick, Damages § 60 (1935).

2. In response to *Alyeska*, Congress amended a number of federal environmental protection statutes to provide for an award of attorney's fees to prevailing parties, although the language for eligibility varies. Under the citizen suit provision of the Clean Air Act, for example, a court may award attorneys' fees whenever the court determines such award is "appropriate". *Compare* Ruckelshaus v. Sierra Club, 463 U.S. 680, 103 S.Ct. 3274, 77 L.Ed.2d 938 (1983) (fees denied to unsuccessful private attorney general which had challenged certain standards promulgated by EPA pursuant to citizen suit provision of Clean Air Act), *with* Southern Alliance for Clean Energy v. Duke Energy Carolinas, LLC., 650 F.3d 401 (4th Cir. 2011) (fees awarded under Clean Air Act where plaintiff succeeded in forcing defendant to comply with administrative evaluations by state regulators).

In several other environmental statutes Congress adopted the "prevailing or substantially prevailing" standard rather than the "whenever appropriate" language for fee awards. *See* Resurrection Bay Conservation Alliance v. City of Seward, Alaska, 640 F.3d 1087 (9th Cir. 2011) (applying award of attorney's fees to prevailing party under Clean Water Act citizen suit provision); Franklin County Convention Facilities Authority v. American Premier Underwriters, 240 F.3d 534 (6th Cir.2001) (attorney fees associated with identifying responsible party were essential part of clean-up action and thus recoverable under CERCLA).

3. In *Alyeska,* the Supreme Court held that the awarding of attorney fees on a "private attorney general" theory did not lie within the equitable jurisdiction of the federal courts in the absence of express statutory authorization. Such awards, the court held, "would make major inroads on a policy matter that Congress has reserved for itself." 421 U.S. 240, 269, 95 S.Ct. 1612, 44 L.Ed.2d 141 (1975). Examples of such authorization include the RICO statutes, *see* Rotella v. Wood, 528 U.S. 549, 120 S.Ct. 1075, 145 L.Ed.2d 1047 (2000), and Title II of the Civil Rights Act of 1964, *see* Newman v. Piggie Park Enterprises, Inc., 390 U.S. 400, 88 S.Ct. 964, 19 L.Ed.2d 1263 (1968), below.

4. The private attorney general theory may be available under state common law. See *Serrano v. Priest,* 20 Cal.3d 25, 141 Cal.Rptr. 315, 325, 569 P.2d 1303 (1977) where the California Supreme Court held that attorney fees could properly be awarded under a state common law theory of private attorney general to a plaintiff who had successfully challenged the California public school financing system as being in violation of state constitutional provisions guaranteeing equal protection of the laws. The California legislature subsequently codified the private attorney general doctrine. *See* § 1021.5 Calif. Code of Civ. Proc.; Olson v. Automobile Club of Southern Calif., 42 Cal.4th 1142, 74 Cal.Rptr.3d 81, 179 P.3d 882 (2008) (plain language of section 1021.5 authorizes an award of attorneys' fees to prevailing party which enforces important right affecting public interest).

5. *Common Fund*. Attorneys's fees may also be awarded in equity where litigation produces a common fund for the benefit of several claimants, such as produced in a successful class action. *See* Sprague v. Ticonic Nat'l Bank, 307 U.S. 161, 164, 59 S.Ct. 777, 778, 83 L.Ed. 1184 (1939) (fee award from fund generated is within "the historic equity jurisdiction of the federal courts"). The doctrine allows a party who creates, preserves, or increases the value of a fund in which others have a beneficial interest to obtain reimbursement from the fund for their litigation expenses. Under the "common fund" or "equitable fund" approach the defendant pays a specified sum of damages to the court in exchange for a release of liability. The attorney fees are then taken directly out of the damages fund prior to distribution to the plaintiffs. As such, this method is not technically an exception to the American Rule because the fees are not imposed directly against the losing party but rather are drawn from the fund itself. The plaintiff class thus shares its recovery with the attorneys, then, in a manner similar to contingency fee arrangements. The common fund doctrine is based on the rationale that the beneficiaries of litigation should share in its costs. *See* Boeing Co. v. Van Gemert, 444 U.S. 472, 478, 100 S.Ct. 745, 62 L.Ed.2d 676 (1980) (The doctrine "rests on the perception

that the persons who obtain the benefit of a lawsuit without contributing to its cost are unjustly enriched at the successful litigant's expense.") *Also see* In re Vioxx Products Liability Litigation, 802 F.Supp.2d 740 (E.D. La.2011) (court relied upon its inherent managerial authority and imposed common benefit attorney's fees in multidistrict litigation); Humphrey v. United Way of the Texas Gulf Coast, 802 F.Supp.2d 847 (S.D. Tex. 2011) (court declined to award attorney's fees under common fund doctrine and ERISA to avoid a windfall).

6. *Substantial Benefit Theory.* When litigation produces a "substantial benefit" either pecuniary or nonpecuniary in nature, the common law sometimes allows attorneys' fees. For example, in *Card v. Community Redevelopment Agency* a plaintiff obtained a declaratory judgment that a city ordinance amending a redevelopment plan was invalid. The amendment added new areas to the development; the invalidation resulted in increased taxes available to various city and county taxing agencies. The court awarded as attorney fees a portion of the incremental funds that would now go to the taxing agencies and divided the amount proportionally among them. 61 Cal.App.3d 570, 131 Cal.Rptr. 153 (1976).

The same theory was used in a case invalidating on Constitutional grounds a state government's practice of giving paid release time to workers on Good Friday. Attorney fees were awarded against the state on the theory that there was a future savings of funds formerly paid for work not performed. Mandel v. Hodges, 54 Cal.App.3d 596, 127 Cal.Rptr. 244 (1976). *Also see* Alyeska Pipeline Service Co. v. Wilderness Society, 421 U.S. 240, 95 S.Ct. 1612, 44 L.Ed.2d 141 (1975) (characterizing the substantial benefit theory as part of the common fund exception).

7. *Rule 11.* An increasingly significant tool available to courts to police abusive litigation practices is Fed.R.Civ.P.11. The rule allows the court to impose sanctions where pleadings or motions lack sufficient factual or legal basis or are filed for an improper purpose. *See* Cooter & Gell v. Hartmarx Corp., 496 U.S. 384, 110 S.Ct. 2447, 110 L.Ed.2d 359 (1990) (Central purpose of Rule 11 is to deter baseless filings and streamline the administration and procedure of federal courts; therefore attorney fees incurred on appeal were outside scope of the rule.); Willy v. Coastal Corp., 503 U.S. 131, 138, 112 S.Ct. 1076, 117 L.Ed.2d 280 (1992) (even where a federal court lacked subject matter jurisdiction it retains authority to impose Rule 11 sanctions for abuse of the judicial process); Jenkins v. Methodist Hospitals of Dallas, Inc., 478 F.3d 255, 264 (5th Cir.2007) (standard for evaluating attorney misconduct is objective standard of reasonableness).

8. In addition to Rule 11, several other statutory and procedural provisions are available to a court to deter litigation abuse. 28 U.S.C. § 1927 permits a court to assess litigation costs against an attorney who "multiplies the proceedings" in a case "unreasonably and vexatiously." The dollar amount of the sanction must bear a financial nexus to the excess proceedings. Courts have interpreted § 1927 to encompass conduct that objectively constitutes bad faith; a showing of malice or subjective ill will is

not required. Amlong & Amlong, P.A. v. Denny's, Inc., 457 F.3d 1180, 1190–91 (11th Cir.2006); Red Carpet Studios Div. of Source Advan. v. Sater, 465 F.3d 642, 646 (6th Cir.2006) (attorney is sanctionable under § 1927 where actions intentionally abuse the judicial process or knowingly disregards the risk that conduct will needlessly multiply the proceedings). Fed.R.Civ.P. 37 permits sanctions against parties or persons unjustifiably resisting discovery. Fed.R.App.P. 38 allows appellate courts to impose cost sanctions against an appellant for bringing a frivolous appeal.

Newman v. Piggie Park Enterprises, Inc.

390 U.S. 400, 88 S.Ct. 964, 19 L.Ed.2d 1263 (1968).

■ PER CURIAM.

The petitioners instituted this class action under Title II of the Civil Rights Act of 1964, § 204(a), 78 Stat. 244, 42 U.S.C. § 2000a–3(a), to enjoin racial discrimination at five drive-in restaurants and a sandwich shop owned and operated by the respondents in South Carolina. The District Court * * * found, on undisputed evidence, that Negroes had been discriminated against at all six of the restaurants. But the District Court erroneously concluded that Title II does not cover drive-in restaurants of the sort involved in this case. Thus the court enjoined racial discrimination only at the respondents' sandwich shop.

The Court of Appeals reversed the District Court's refusal to enjoin discrimination at the drive-in establishments, and then directed its attention to that section of Title II which provides that "the prevailing party" is entitled to "a reasonable attorney's fee" in the court's "discretion." § 204(b), 78 Stat. 244, 42 U.S.C. § 2000a–3(b).[40] In remanding the case, the Court of Appeals instructed the District Court to award counsel fees only to the extent that the respondents' defenses had been advanced "for purposes of delay and not in good faith." We granted certiorari to decide whether this subjective standard properly effectuates the purposes of the counsel-fee provision of Title II of the Civil Rights Act of 1964. We hold that it does not.

When the Civil Rights Act of 1964 was passed, it was evident that enforcement would prove difficult and that the Nation would have to rely in part upon private litigation as a means of securing broad compliance with the law.[41] A Title II suit is thus private in form only. When a plaintiff

---

40. "In any action commenced pursuant to this subchapter, the court, in its discretion, may allow the prevailing party, other than the United States, a reasonable attorney's fee as part of the costs, and the United States shall be liable for costs the same as a private person." 42 U.S.C. § 2000a–3(b).

41. In this connection, it is noteworthy that 42 U.S.C. § 2000a–3(a) permits intervention by the Attorney General in privately initiated Title II suits "of general public importance" and provides that, "in such circumstances as the court may deem just," a district court may "appoint an attorney for [the] complainant and may authorize the commencement of the civil action without the payment of fees, costs, or security." Only where a "pattern or practice" of discrimination is reasonably believed to exist may the Attorney General himself institute a civil action for injunctive relief. 42 U.S.C. § 2000a–5.

brings an action under that Title, he cannot recover damages. If he obtains an injunction, he does so not for himself alone but also as a "private attorney general," vindicating a policy that Congress considered of the highest priority. If successful plaintiffs were routinely forced to bear their own attorneys' fees, few aggrieved parties would be in a position to advance the public interest by invoking the injunctive powers of the federal courts. Congress therefore enacted the provision for counsel fees—not simply to penalize litigants who deliberately advance arguments they know to be untenable but, more broadly, to encourage individuals injured by racial discrimination to seek judicial relief under Title II.

It follows that one who succeeds in obtaining an injunction under that Title should ordinarily recover an attorney's fee unless special circumstances would render such an award unjust. Because no such circumstances are present here, the District Court on remand should include reasonable counsel fees as part of the costs to be assessed against the respondents. As so modified, the judgment of the Court of Appeals is *Affirmed.*

----

1.   Numerous civil rights, environmental, consumer, and privacy statutes passed by Congress in the past two decades provide for attorney fees. One of the most important statutory provisions for attorney fees is the Civil Rights Attorney's Fees Awards Act of 1976, codified in 42 U.S.C. § 1988. The Act declares:

> (b) In any action or proceeding to enforce a provision of [42 U.S.C. §§ 1981–1983, 1985, 1986], title IX of Public Law 92–318 [20 U.S.C. §§ 1681 *et seq.*], the Religious Freedom Restoration Act of 1993 [42 U.S.C. § 2000bb *et seq.*], the Religious Land Use and Institutionalized Persons Act of 2000 [42 U.S.C. § 2000cc, et. seq.], title VI of the Civil Rights Act of 1964 [42 U.S.C. §§ 2000d *et seq.*], or section 13981 of this title, the court, in its discretion, may allow the prevailing party, other than the United States, a reasonable attorney's fee as part of the costs.
> * * *

> (c) In awarding an attorney's fee under subsection (b) of this section in any action or proceeding to enforce a provision of 1981 or 1981a of this title, the court, in its discretion, may include expert fees as part of the attorney's fee.

2.   The enactment of federal fee-shifting statutes reflects a Congressional policy favoring such awards to litigants who have advanced some important public interest objective, such as protecting civil rights or the environment. Accordingly, the strong presumption favors such awards to prevailing parties, and judicial discretion with respect to authorizing fees is considerably limited. In *Piggie Park*, the Court observed that the prevailing party in a civil rights case should ordinarily recover attorney's fees unless special circumstances would render an award unjust. Courts have interpreted the "special circumstances" standard very strictly, generally holding that fee awards should be the rule rather than the exception. *See* Resurrec-

tion Bay Conservation Alliance v. City of Seward, Alaska, 640 F.3d 1087 (9th Cir. 2011) (district court abused its discretion in failing to award attorney's fees to prevailing party under Clean Water Act citizen suit provision); Tyler v. Corner Constr. Corp., Inc., 167 F.3d 1202, 1206(8th Cir. 1999) (special circumstance for denial of fees where settlement achieved merely to avoid nuisance suit).

3. In *Martin v. Franklin Capital Corp.*, 546 U.S. 132, 126 S.Ct. 704, 163 L.Ed.2d 547 (2005), the Court considered the proper standard for awarding fees under 28 U.S.C. § 1447(c), which provides that a federal district court *may* require payment of fees and costs when remanding a removed case to state court. The Supreme Court held that a district court should not award attorney's fees, absent unusual circumstances, when a removing party has an objectively reasonable basis for the removal. The Court distinguished *Piggie Park*, where the public policy of promoting civil rights enforcement influenced a strong presumption in favor of a fee award, yet was absent under the removal statute. *Also see* Houston Chronicle Publishing Co. v. City of League City, Tex., 488 F.3d 613, 623–24 (5th Cir.2007) (extremely strong showing of special circumstances required to justify denial of fees to a prevailing party under federal fee-shifting statute).

4. The *Piggie Park* Court distinguished entitlement to a fee award from the issue of measurement. Should the defendant's ability to pay fees be a relevant factor in calculating the amount of fees ultimately awarded? The courts of appeals which have considered the question have held that a party's financial condition is not a proper factor in the deciding whether to award fees but may be considered in fixing the amount given. *See* Wolfe v. Perry, 412 F.3d 707 (6th Cir.2005); Roth v. Green, 466 F.3d 1179 (10th Cir.2006).

5. Federal statutory provisions authorizing an award of attorney fees take many forms. Many federal fee-shifting statutes expressly limit recovery of fees to a "prevailing party" or "prevailing plaintiff." What result regarding fee eligibility where the statutory language is couched in terms of judicial discretion? *See* Hardt v. Reliance Standard Life Ins. Co., ___ U.S. ___, 130 S.Ct. 2149, 176 L.Ed.2d 998 (2010) (fee claimant need not be a prevailing party to be eligible for attorney fees under ERISA's fee-shifting statute; courts may exercise discretion to award fees and costs to either party provided they achieved some substantial degree of success on the merits); Molski v. M.J. Cable, Inc., 481 F.3d 724, 730 (9th Cir.2007) (monetary damages are not available in private suits brought under Title III of the ADA, 42 U.S.C. § 12188, but courts have discretion to award attorney's fees to prevailing parties).

6. Congressional legislation is not always expanding the exceptions to the American Rule. The Prison Litigation Reform Act of 1995, 42 U.S.C. § 1997e, limits recovery of attorney fees under § 1988 by prevailing inmates in Title VII civil rights actions. In *Boivin v. Black*, 225 F.3d 36 (1st Cir.2000), the appeals court reversed the lower court: the statutory cap (150% of recovery) included nominal damages, thus the maximum award of

attorney fees was $1.50. Conversely, the court in *Johnson v. Daley*, 117 F.Supp.2d 889 (W.D.Wis.2000), found that such limitations were unconstitutional, limiting representation without sufficient justification.

7. Under the antitrust laws allowance of attorney fees to a plaintiff awarded treble damages is mandatory, whereas in patent law the statute provides for attorney fees in "exceptional cases" to the prevailing party. 35 U.S.C. § 285. Other statutes including the Uniform Relocation Act, 42 U.S.C. § 4654, successful challenges of tax-related actions, 26 U.S.C. § 7430(c)(1)(B)(iii), awards for improper removal, 28 U.S.C. § 1447(c), expressly limit attorney fees to actual expenses incurred. *See* Quick v. NLRB, 245 F.3d 231 (3d Cir.2001) (most generously construed, the Act can only be interpreted to allow recovery of actual expenses); Wisconsin v. Hotline Industries, Inc., 236 F.3d 363 (7th Cir.2000) (discussion of "actual expenses" statutes).

8. *Equal Access to Justice Act*. Attorney fees also may be recoverable under the EAJA in limited circumstances where a party prevails in a civil suit against the United States. 28 U.S.C. § 2412. *See* Resolution Trust Corp. v. Eason, 17 F.3d 1126, 1134 (8th Cir.1994) (Act is limited waiver of sovereign immunity and is strictly construed.) The Act eliminates the financial disincentive and disadvantage otherwise faced by private parties in challenging unreasonable government actions. Sullivan v. Hudson, 490 U.S. 877, 883, 109 S.Ct. 2248, 2253, 104 L.Ed.2d 941 (1989).

The statutory framework contains two distinct provisions for awarding attorneys' fees to plaintiffs that prevail in civil suits against the United States. *See generally*, Maritime Management, Inc. v. United States, 242 F.3d 1326 (11th Cir.2001). The first provision waives sovereign immunity by making the United States liable for fees "to the same extent that any other party would be liable under the common law or under the terms of any statute which specifically provides for such an award." 28 U.S.C. § 2412(b). Such awards, which encompass the equitable exceptions to the American Rule such as involving bad faith litigation, are discretionary at a rate determined by the district court. *See also* Richlin Security Service Co. v. Chertoff, 553 U.S. 571, 128 S.Ct. 2007, 170 L.Ed.2d 960 (2008) (EAJA authorization for attorney fees includes awards for paralegal services at prevailing market rates).

In contrast, the second provision provides for a mandatory assessment of fees to plaintiffs who have (1) prevailed in a non-tort suit against the federal government, (2) the position of the United States was not "substantially justified", and (3) there are no special circumstances that make the award unjust. *See* 28 U.S.C. § 2412(d)(1)(A); Hackett v. Barnhart, 469 F.3d 937, 942 (10th Cir.2006). Parties must also qualify under statutorily prescribed net worth maximums. *See* 28 U.S.C. § 2412(d)(1)(C)(2)(B) (defining "party" for purposes of subsection (d) by net worth).

9. In *Scarborough v. Principi*, 541 U.S. 401, 124 S.Ct. 1856, 158 L.Ed.2d 674 (2004) the Supreme Court held that a provision in the EAJA that the plaintiff's application for fees must allege that the government's position was not substantially justified was merely a pleading requirement

and that a timely filed petition could be subsequently amended. The government retains the ultimate burden to prove that its position was substantially justified in order to defeat a fee award. *See* Pierce v. Underwood, 487 U.S. 552, 566, 108 S.Ct. 2541, 2550, 101 L.Ed.2d 490 (1988) ("Substantially justified" means being justified in substance or in the main, supported to a degree that could satisfy a reasonable person.) The Act creates a presumption in favor of awarding fees to prevailing parties, thereby shifting the burden to the government to demonstrate that its actions were reasonable. Thomas v. Peterson, 841 F.2d 332, 335 (9th Cir.1988); see *also* Martin v. Secretary of the Army, 463 F.Supp.2d 287, 291–292 (N.D.N.Y.2006) (conscientious objector was "prevailing party" in habeas proceeding and entitled to fees under EAJA where position of Army regarding his deployment was not substantially justified).

Fox v. Vice

___ U.S. ___, 131 S.Ct. 2205, 180 L.Ed.2d 45 (2011).

■ JUSTICE KAGAN delivered the opinion of the Court.

Federal law authorizes a court to award a reasonable attorney's fee to the prevailing party in certain civil rights cases. See 42 U.S.C. § 1988. We have held that a defendant may receive such an award if the plaintiff's suit is frivolous. In this case, the plaintiff asserted both frivolous and non-frivolous claims. * * *

This case arises out of an election for chief of police in the town of Vinton, Louisiana. The candidates were petitioner Ricky Fox (the challenger) and respondent Billy Ray Vice (the incumbent). By Fox's account, Vice resorted to an assortment of dirty tricks to try to force Fox out of the race. In particular, Vice sent an anonymous letter to Fox threatening to publish damaging charges against him if he remained a candidate. Vice also arranged for a third party to publicly accuse Fox of using racial slurs and then to file a criminal complaint against Fox repeating those allegations. And when prosecutors ignored that faux complaint, Vice leaked it to the press. Yet all of these machinations failed; Fox won the election. And Vice got an even greater comeuppance: He was subsequently convicted of criminal extortion for his election-related conduct.

Fox, however, chose not to let the matter rest; he filed this suit in Louisiana state court against Vice and the town of Vinton, also a respondent here. Fox's complaint asserted both state-law claims, including defamation, and federal civil rights claims under 42 U.S.C. § 1983, including interference with his right to seek public office. Vice and the town (Vice, for short) removed the case to federal court on the basis of the § 1983 claims.

At the end of discovery in the suit, Vice moved for summary judgment on Fox's federal claims. Fox conceded that the claims were "no[t] valid," and the District Court accordingly dismissed them with prejudice. In the same ruling, the court declined to exercise supplemental jurisdiction over the remaining state-law claims. The court instead remanded the now slimmed-down case to state court for adjudication. * * *

Vice then asked the federal court for an award of attorney's fees under § 1988, arguing that Fox's federal claims were "baseless and without merit." Vice stated that his lawyers had had to participate in five lengthy depositions and review numerous records to defend against Fox's charges. In support of his fee request, Vice submitted attorney billing records estimating the time spent on the whole suit, without differentiating between the federal and state-law claims.

The District Court granted the motion for attorney's fees on the ground that Fox's federal claims were frivolous. Although the state-law allegations had not been found frivolous (and indeed remained live), the court did not require Vice to separate out the work his attorneys had done on the two sets of claims. * * *

A divided Court of Appeals affirmed. 594 F.3d 423 (CA5 2010). The majority first rejected Fox's contention that all claims in a suit must be frivolous for the defendant to recover any fees. * * *

The Fifth Circuit's decision deepened a Circuit split about whether and to what extent a court may award fees to a defendant under § 1988 when a plaintiff asserts both frivolous and non-frivolous claims. * * * We granted certiorari[.] * * *

The statute involved here, 42 U.S.C. § 1988, allows the award of "a reasonable attorney's fee" to "the prevailing party" in various kinds of civil rights cases, including suits brought under § 1983. Most of our decisions addressing this provision have concerned the grant of fees to prevailing plaintiffs. When a plaintiff succeeds in remedying a civil rights violation, we have stated, he serves "as a 'private attorney general,' vindicating a policy that Congress considered of the highest priority." *Newman* v. *Piggie Park Enterprises, Inc.*, 390 U.S. 400, 402, 88 S. Ct. 964, 19 L. Ed. 2d 1263 (1968) *(per curiam)*. He therefore "should ordinarily recover an attorney's fee" from the defendant—the party whose misconduct created the need for legal action. *Christiansburg Garment Co.* v. *EEOC*, 434 U.S. 412, 416, 98 S. Ct. 694, 54 L. Ed. 2d 648 (1978). * * *

In *Christiansburg*, we held that § 1988 also authorizes a fee award to a prevailing defendant, but under a different standard reflecting the "quite different equitable considerations" at stake. *Id.*, at 419, 98 S. Ct. 694, 54 L. Ed. 2d 648. In enacting § 1988, we stated, Congress sought "to protect defendants from burdensome litigation having no legal or factual basis." Accordingly, § 1988 authorizes a district court to award attorney's fees to a defendant "upon a finding that the plaintiff's action was frivolous, unreasonable, or without foundation." [Citations]

These standards would be easy to apply if life were like the movies, but that is usually not the case. In Hollywood, litigation most often concludes with a dramatic verdict that leaves one party fully triumphant and the other utterly prostrate. The court in such a case would know exactly how to award fees (even if that anti-climactic scene is generally left on the cutting-room floor). But in the real world, litigation is more complex, involving multiple claims for relief that implicate a mix of legal theories and have different merits. Some claims succeed; others fail. Some charges are frivolous; others (even if not ultimately successful) have a reasonable basis. In short, litigation is messy, and courts must deal with this untidiness in awarding fees.

Given this reality, we have made clear that plaintiffs may receive fees under § 1988 even if they are not victorious on every claim. A civil rights plaintiff who obtains meaningful relief has corrected a violation of federal law and, in so doing, has vindicated Congress's statutory purposes. That "result is what matters," we explained in *Hensley* v. *Eckerhart*, 461 U.S. 424, 435, 103 S. Ct. 1933, 76 L. Ed. 2d 40 (1983): A court should compensate the plaintiff for the time his attorney reasonably spent in achieving the favorable outcome, even if "the plaintiff failed to prevail on every contention." The fee award, of course, should not reimburse the plaintiff for work performed on claims that bore no relation to the grant of relief: Such work "cannot be deemed to have been expended in pursuit of the ultimate result achieved." But the presence of these unsuccessful claims does not immunize a defendant against paying for the attorney's fees that the plaintiff reasonably incurred in remedying a breach of his civil rights.

Analogous principles indicate that a defendant may deserve fees even if not all the plaintiff's claims were frivolous. In this context, § 1988 serves to relieve a defendant of expenses attributable to frivolous charges. The plaintiff acted wrongly in leveling such allegations, and the court may shift to him the reasonable costs that those claims imposed on his adversary. That remains true when the plaintiff's suit also includes non-frivolous claims. The defendant, of course, is not entitled to any fees arising from these non-frivolous charges. * * *

The question then becomes one of allocation: In a lawsuit involving a mix of frivolous and non-frivolous claims, what work may the defendant receive fees for? Vice concedes, as he must, that a defendant may not obtain compensation for work unrelated to a frivolous claim. Similarly, we think Fox would have to concede (once he has lost the argument that the presence of any non-frivolous claim precludes a fee award) that the defendant may receive reasonable fees for work related exclusively to a frivolous claim. The question in dispute concerns work that helps defend against non-frivolous and frivolous claims alike—for example, a deposition eliciting facts relevant to both allegations.

Vice proposes authorizing the trial court to award fees for work that is "fairly attributable" to the frivolous portion of the lawsuit. But that standard is in truth no standard at all. * * *

That congressional policy points to a different and more meaningful standard: Section 1988 allows a defendant to recover reasonable attorney's fees incurred because of, but only because of, a frivolous claim. Or what is the same thing stated as a but-for test: Section 1988 permits the defendant to receive only the portion of his fees that he would not have paid but for the frivolous claim. * * * In short, the defendant has never shouldered the burden that Congress, in enacting § 1988, wanted to relieve. The basic American Rule thus continues to operate.[3]

A standard allowing more expansive fee-shifting would furnish windfalls to some defendants, making them better off because they were subject to a suit including frivolous claims. For under any more permissive test, the simple presence of a frivolous claim would allow the court to shift to the plaintiff some of the costs of defending against regular, non-frivolous charges. * * *

At the same time, the "but-for" standard we require may in some cases allow compensation to a defendant for attorney work relating to both frivolous and non-frivolous claims. Suppose, for example, that a plaintiff asserts one frivolous and one non-frivolous claim, but that only the frivolous allegation can legally result in a damages award. If an attorney performs work useful to defending against both, but did so only because of the defendant's monetary exposure on the frivolous charge, a court may decide to shift fees. Or similarly, imagine that the frivolous claim enables removal of the case to federal court, which in turn drives up litigation expenses. Here too, our standard would permit awarding fees for work relevant to both claims in order to reflect the increased costs (if any) of the federal forum. And frivolous claims may increase the cost of defending a suit in ways that are not reflected in the number of hours billed. If a defendant could prove, for example, that a frivolous claim involved a specialized area that reasonably caused him to hire more expensive counsel for the entire case, then the court may reimburse the defendant for the increased marginal cost. As all these examples show, the dispositive question is not whether attorney costs at all relate to a non-frivolous claim, but whether the costs would have been incurred in the absence of the frivolous allegation. * * *

The task remains of applying these principles to the fee award Vice received. The District Court's analysis suggests that Vice's attorneys would have done much the same work even if Fox had not brought his frivolous claims. As noted earlier, the court acknowledged that Fox's federal and state-law claims were "interrelated". The charges "arose out of the same transaction"—Vice's conduct in the campaign—and their "defense entailed proof or denial of essentially the same facts." [Citation] It therefore seems likely that Vice's attorneys would at least have conducted similar fact-

---

3. The test set out here differs from the one we adopted in *Hensley* v. *Eckerhart*, 461 U.S. 424, 435, 103 S. Ct. 1933, 76 L. Ed. 2d 40 (1983), to govern fee awards to plaintiffs in cases involving both successful and unsuccessful claims. That difference reflects the disparate legislative purposes we have recognized in the two settings. See *Christiansburg Garment Co.* v. *EEOC*, 434 U.S. 412, 419–420, 98 S. Ct. 694, 54 L. Ed. 2d 648 (1978). Congress authorized fees to plaintiffs to compensate them for the costs of redressing civil rights violations; accordingly, a plaintiff may receive fees for all work relating to the accomplishment of that result, even if "the plaintiff failed to prevail on every contention raised." *Hensley*, 461 U.S., at 435, 103 S. Ct. 1933, 76 L. Ed. 2d 40. By contrast, Congress authorized fees to defendants to remove the burden associated with fending off frivolous claims; accordingly, a defendant may recover for fees that those claims caused him to incur. In each context, the standard for allocating fees in "mixed" cases matches the relevant congressional purpose.

gathering activities—taken many of the same depositions, produced and reviewed many of the same documents, and so forth. * * *

The District Court's decision to award full attorney's fees to Vice failed to take proper account of this overlap between the frivolous and non-frivolous claims. Rather than apply the but-for standard we have set out, the court indicated that the paramount factor was the parties' "focus" in the litigation. * * *.

On this record, we must return the case to the lower courts. [Citations] In a suit of this kind, involving both frivolous and non-frivolous claims, a defendant may recover the reasonable attorney's fees he expended solely because of the frivolous allegations. And that is all. Consistent with the policy underlying § 1988, the defendant may not receive compensation for any fees that he would have paid in the absence of the frivolous claims. We therefore vacate the judgment of the Court of Appeals and remand the case for further proceedings consistent with this opinion.

---

1. *Prevailing Party.* The Court has consistently found that a claimant for attorney's fees under federal fee-shifting statutes must achieve "some degree of success on the merits." *See generally* Hensley v. Eckerhart, 461 U.S. 424, 103 S.Ct. 1933, 76 L.Ed.2d 40 (1983) (statutory threshold for prevailing party status for entitlement to attorney's fees depends upon whether party succeeds on any significant issue in litigation which achieves some of the benefit the parties sought in bringing suit); Farrar v. Hobby, 506 U.S. 103, 113 S.Ct. 566, 121 L.Ed.2d 494 (1992) (a nominal damages award held sufficient to support fee eligibility under 42 U.S.C. § 1988 to prevailing civil rights plaintiff).

Qualification for fees under federal fee-shifting statutes generally requires a prevailing party to: (1) obtain actual relief, such as an enforceable judgment or a consent decree; (2) that materially alters the legal relationship between the parties; and (3) modifies the defendant's behavior in a way that directly benefits the plaintiff at the time of the judgment or settlement. Energy Management Corp. v. City of Shreveport, 467 F.3d 471, 482 (5th Cir.2006); Buckhannon Board and Care Home, Inc. v. West Virginia Dept. of Health and Human Resources, 532 U.S. 598, 121 S.Ct. 1835, 149 L.Ed.2d 855 (2001) (party that failed to secure a judgment on the merits or a court-ordered consent decree but which achieved desired result through lawsuit held not entitled to attorney's fees as prevailing party). *But see* Hutchinson v. Patrick, 636 F.3d 1 (1st Cir. 2011) (court approved settlement had sufficient judicial imprimatur to qualify plaintiffs as prevailing parties for fee award eligibility).

2. In *Texas State Teachers Association v. Garland Independent School District*, 489 U.S. 782, 109 S.Ct. 1486, 103 L.Ed.2d 866 (1989), the Court refined the *Hensley* test of the appropriate standard for determining "prevailing part" status for attorney fee awards under the civil rights fee-shifting statute, 42 U.S.C. § 1988, where the plaintiff has achieved only

partial success on the merits. In *Garland*, several teachers' unions brought constitutional challenges concerning various school board policies limiting union activities and communications.

The Court resolved a debate in the lower courts and held that fee eligibility was predicated on demonstrating success on a "significant" issue in litigation, but did not require prevailing on the "central" issue in dispute. Justice O'Connor, writing for a unanimous Court, stated that administration of the so-called central issue test would be as difficult as searching for the "Golden Fleece." The Court explained that the principal consideration in establishing entitlement to any fee award is whether the legal relationship of the parties was "materially altered" in a manner consistent with the intentions of Congress in the fee-shifting statute. Beyond that showing, the degree of overall success relates to the *measure* of the fee; therefore, no fees would be given where the plaintiff achieved only technical or *de minimis* success. *See also* Villano v. Boynton Beach, 254 F.3d 1302 (11th Cir.2001) (overturned the district court's reduction of attorney fee award because it failed to consider public benefit as a distinct measure of success).

3. The focus on the degree of success obtained has remained as the touchstone for assessing eligibility as well as the measure of fees. The parameters of defining "success", though, are not always clear. *Sole v. Wyner*, 551 U.S. 74, 127 S.Ct. 2188, 167 L.Ed.2d 1069 (2007), is the most recent Supreme Court decision considering the issue of what constitutes a "prevailing party" for purposes of fee eligibility under federal fee-shifting statutes. In that case, the plaintiff obtained a preliminary injunction in District Court restraining the Florida Department of Environmental Protection from interfering, on First Amendment grounds, with her planned antiwar peace sign display comprised of nude performers on a public beach on Valentine's Day. The participants, however, ignored a designated screen erected by the State and set up their display outside the barrier which was designed to shield the public who did not want to see the play from observing the nude performers.

A subsequent request for permanent injunctive relief was denied and plaintiff sought recovery of attorney's fees under 42 U.S.C. § 1988. The plaintiff contended that she had "prevailed" within the meaning of the statute because she received permission to create the nude peace symbol without state interference, and that was her objective in commencing litigation. The state disagreed, claiming that fees should be denied because the permanent injunction was denied. The Supreme Court reversed the fee award, observing that petitioner only had "fleeting" success at the preliminary injunction stage. Characterizing her initial victory as "ephemeral", the Court held that the situation was like winning a battle but losing the war and therefore did not qualify her for an award of fees when the merits were ultimately decided against her.

See also DiLaura v. Township of Ann Arbor, 471 F.3d 666, 671 (6th Cir.2006) (money judgment, enforceable declaratory judgment or an injunction will alter the legal relationship between parties to support award of fees); Northern Cheyenne Tribe v. Jackson, 433 F.3d 1083 (8th Cir.2006) (preliminary injunction that grants only temporary relief and preserves the status quo does not constitute a judicially sanctioned material alteration of the legal relationship to confer prevailing party status).

4. In *Kay v. Ehrler*, 499 U.S. 432, 111 S.Ct. 1435, 113 L.Ed.2d 486 (1991), the Supreme Court held that an attorney, acting *pro se* in a successful civil rights suit, was not entitled to an award of a reasonable attorneys fee under 42 U.S.C. § 1988. The Court acknowledged that Congress had created the fee-shifting statutory model as a means to encourage litigation to protect civil rights, yet the principal consideration was to enable parties to attract independent counsel. The Court also observed that the concept of "attorney" implicitly contemplated an agency relationship. Additionally, the Court expressed reservations about the potential ethical and strategic disadvantages where a lawyer represents their own interests. Justice Stevens, writing for a unanimous Court, concluded: "The adage that a 'lawyer who represents himself has a fool for a client' is the product of years of experience by seasoned litigators."

See also Garcia v. Tansy, 216 F.3d 1087 (10th Cir.2000) (inmate also paralegal is not entitled to attorney fee award); Doe v. Board of Educ. of Baltimore County, 165 F.3d 260 (4th Cir.1998) (extending logic of *pro se* decision, attorney-parent cannot receive fee award for successful representation of own child). *But see* Colby v. Gunson, 349 Or. 1, 238 P.3d 374 (Or. 2010) (attorney acting *pro se* awarded fees under state statute which grants reasonable fees to any person who prevails in a suit seeking disclosure of a public record); Strange v. Monogram Credit Card Bank of Georgia, 129 F.3d 943 (7th Cir.1997) (attorney from lawyer's own firm can represent and recovery fees).

5. *Prevailing Defendant*. Although many federal fee-shifting statutes provide for the recovery of attorney fees to the "prevailing party," many courts have applied a dual standard whereby prevailing plaintiffs are awarded attorney fees as a matter of course, while successful defendants are held to a stricter standard for recovering fees. Redwood v. Dobson, 476 F.3d 462, 470 (7th Cir.2007) (defendant who seeks fees under 42 U.S.C. § 1988 for cost of defense in district court has a "tough row to hoe" because statute is "asymmetric" in plaintiff's favor and appellate review of the district court's decision is deferential); Thomas v. City of Tacoma, 410 F.3d 644 (9th Cir.2005) (although fee-shifting statute does not differentiate between a prevailing plaintiff and defendant, case law has filled the gap to favor successful plaintiff).

6. In *Christiansburg Garment Co. v. Equal Employment Opportunity Commission*, 434 U.S. 412, 98 S.Ct. 694, 54 L.Ed.2d 648 (1978), the Supreme Court recognized that a prevailing plaintiff in a Title VII discrimination case under the Civil Rights Act of 1964 ordinarily will receive a fee award absent special circumstances, yet a prevailing defendant could recover fees only by showing that the plaintiff's claim was "frivolous, unreasonable, or without foundation, even though not brought in subjective bad faith." The Court reasoned that a differing standard was justified in order

to encourage private attorney general actions to protect civil rights and, correspondingly, to shield such claimants from potential fee liability when the suit was meritorious yet unsuccessful. *See also* Independent Federation of Flight Attendants v. Zipes, 488 U.S. 1029, 109 S.Ct. 835, 102 L.Ed.2d 968 (1989), (Attorney fees could not be awarded against losing intervenors in a Title VII action absent showing that intervenor's action was frivolous, unreasonable or without foundation).

7. In *Fogerty v. Fantasy, Inc.*, 510 U.S. 517, 114 S.Ct. 1023, 127 L.Ed.2d 455 (1994), the Court departed from its traditional practice and held that a prevailing defendant in a copyright infringement action would be awarded fees on the same basis as a prevailing plaintiff. The Court distinguished *Christiansburg Garment* by observing that the public interest concerns in advancing civil rights were not equally present in the goals and objectives of the Copyright Act. The Court did not follow the "British Rule," however, which awards attorney fees as a matter of course to the prevailing party but stated that entitlement still remains within the equitable discretion of the court.

8. *Bad Faith Litigation.* A court has inherent power to award reasonable attorney fees to the prevailing party when the losing party has acted in bad faith in the conduct of the litigation. In *Chambers v. NASCO, Inc.*, 501 U.S. 32, 111 S.Ct. 2123, 115 L.Ed.2d 27 (1991), a buyer of a television station brought an action to compel completion of the transaction. The seller engaged in a series of delay and obstruction tactics designed to defraud the court and prevent enforcement of the court's orders. The Supreme Court upheld the district court's imposition of sanctions against the seller's sole shareholder under the purview of the bad faith exception to the American Rule. The Court explained that federal courts can invoke their inherent powers to impose attorney fees for bad faith actions:

> [A] court may assess attorney's fees when a party has " 'acted in bad faith, vexatiously, wantonly, or for oppressive reasons.' " In this regard, if a court finds "that fraud has been practiced upon it, or that the very temple of justice has been defiled," it may assess attorney's fees against the responsible party, as it may when a party "shows bad faith by delaying or disrupting the litigation or by hampering enforcement of a court order." The imposition of sanctions transcends a court's equitable power concerning relationships between the parties and reaches a court's inherent power to police itself, thus serving the dual purpose of "vindicat[ing] judicial authority without resort to the more drastic sanctions available for contempt of court and mak[ing] the prevailing party whole for expenses caused by the opponent's obstinacy." (Citations omitted.) 111 S.Ct. at 2133.

Further, the scope of inherent powers exercisable by federal courts sitting in diversity extends to permit sanctions even if the applicable state law did not recognize the bad-faith exception to the American Rule. *See also* Rodriguez v. United States, 542 F.3d 704 (9th Cir. 2008) (fees imposed against government for asserting reckless and frivolous defense of privilege); United States v. McCall, 235 F.3d 1211 (10th Cir.2000) (repeated attempts by government to foreclose on property after binding settlement agreement had been issued constituted bad faith). *But see* Griffin Ind., Inc. v. EPA, 640 F.3d 682 (6th Cir. 2011) (district court abused its discretion in granting attorney's fees under bad faith exception without making actual finding of subjective bad faith or improper purpose associated with mishandling release of confidential business documents).

Perdue v. Kenny

___ U.S. ___, 130 S.Ct. 1662, 176 L.Ed.2d 494 (2010).

■ JUSTICE ALITO delivered the opinion of the Court.

This case presents the question whether the calculation of an attorney's fee, under federal fee-shifting statutes, based on the "lodestar," *i.e.,* the number of hours worked multiplied by the prevailing hourly rates, may be increased due to superior performance and results. We have stated in previous cases that such an increase is permitted in extraordinary circumstances, and we reaffirm that rule. But as we have also said in prior cases, there is a strong presumption that the lodestar is sufficient; factors subsumed in the lodestar calculation cannot be used as a ground for increasing an award above the lodestar; and a party seeking fees has the burden of identifying a factor that the lodestar does not adequately take into account and proving with specificity that an enhanced fee is justified. Because the District Court did not apply these standards, we reverse the decision below and remand for further proceedings consistent with this opinion.

Respondents (plaintiffs below) are children in the Georgia foster-care system and their next friends. They filed this class action on behalf of 3,000 children in foster care and named as defendants the Governor of Georgia and various state officials (petitioners in this case). Claiming that deficiencies in the foster-care system in two counties near Atlanta violated their federal and state constitutional and statutory rights, respondents sought injunctive and declaratory relief, as well as attorney's fees and expenses.

The United States District Court for the Northern District of Georgia eventually referred the case to mediation, where the parties entered into a consent decree, which the District Court approved. The consent decree resolved all pending issues other than the fees that respondents' attorneys were entitled to receive under 42 U.S.C. § 1988.[2]

Respondents submitted a request for more than $14 million in attorney's fees. Half of that amount was based on their calculation of the lodestar-roughly 30,000 hours multiplied by hourly rates of $200 to $495

---

2. Title 42 U.S.C. § 1988(b) provides:

"In any action or proceeding to enforce a provision of sections 1981, 1981a, 1982, 1983, 1985, and 1986 of this title, title IX of Public Law 92–318, the Religious Freedom Restoration Act of 1993, the Religious Land Use and Institutionalized Persons Act of 2000, title VI of the Civil Rights Act of 1964, or section 13981 of this title, the court, in its discretion, may allow the prevailing party, other than the United States, a reasonable attorney's fee as part of the costs...." (Citations omitted.)

for attorneys and $75 to $150 for non-attorneys. [The remaining amount sought by respondents represented a fee enhancement for superior work and results.] * * *

The District Court awarded fees of approximately $10.5 million. See 454 F. Supp.2d 1260, 1296 (N.D.Ga.2006). [The court reduced certain hours and then calculated a lodestar sum of approximately $6 million.] * * *

The court then enhanced this award by 75%, concluding that the lodestar calculation did not take into account "(1) the fact that class counsel were required to advance case expenses of $1.7 million over a three-year period with no on[-]going reimbursement, (2) the fact that class counsel were not paid on an on-going basis as the work was being performed, and (3) the fact that class counsel's ability to recover a fee and expense reimbursement were completely contingent on the outcome of the case." * * * [The Eleventh Circuit affirmed. 532 F.3d 1209 (2008) and the Supreme Court granted certiorari. 556 U.S. 1165 (2009)].

The general rule in our legal system is that each party must pay its own attorney's fees and expenses, see *Hensley v. Eckerhart,* 461 U.S. 424, 429, 103 S.Ct. 1933, 76 L.Ed.2d 40 (1983), but Congress enacted 42 U.S.C. § 1988 in order to ensure that federal rights are adequately enforced. Section 1988 provides that a prevailing party in certain civil rights actions may recover "a reasonable attorney's fee as part of the costs." Unfortunately, the statute does not explain what Congress meant by a "reasonable" fee, and therefore the task of identifying an appropriate methodology for determining a "reasonable" fee was left for the courts.

One possible method was set out in *Johnson* v. *Georgia Highway Express, Inc.,* 488 F.2d 714, 717–719 (C.A.5 1974), which listed 12 factors that a court should consider in determining a reasonable fee.[4] This method, however, "gave very little actual guidance to district courts. Setting attorney's fees by reference to a series of sometimes subjective factors placed unlimited discretion in trial judges and produced disparate results."

An alternative, the lodestar approach, was pioneered by the Third Circuit in *Lindy Bros. Builders, Inc. of Philadelphia v. American Radiator & Standard Sanitary Corp.,* 487 F.2d 161 (1973), appeal after remand, 540 F.2d 102 (1976), and "achieved dominance in the federal courts" after our decision in *Hensley. Gisbrecht v. Barnhart,* 535 U.S. 789, 801, 122 S.Ct. 1817, 152 L.Ed.2d 996 (2002). "Since that time, '[t]he "lodestar" figure has, as its name suggests, become the guiding light of our fee-shifting jurisprudence.'"

---

4. These factors were: "(1) the time and labor required; (2) the novelty and difficulty of the questions; (3) the skill requisite to perform the legal service properly; (4) the preclusion of employment by the attorney due to the acceptance of the case; (5) the customary fee; (6) whether the fee is fixed or contingent; (7) time limitations imposed by the client or the circumstances; (8) the amount involved and the results obtained; (9) the experience, reputation, and ability of the attorneys; (10) the 'undesirability' of the case; (11) the nature and length of the professional relationship with the client; and (12) awards in similar cases." *Hensley v. Eckerhart,* 461 U.S. 424, 430, n. 3, 103 S.Ct. 1933, 76 L.Ed.2d 40 (1983).

Although the lodestar method is not perfect, it has several important virtues. First, in accordance with our understanding of the aim of fee-shifting statutes, the lodestar looks to "the prevailing market rates in the relevant community." *Blum v. Stenson,* 465 U.S. 886, 895, 104 S.Ct. 1541, 79 L.Ed.2d 891 (1984). Developed after the practice of hourly billing had become widespread, the lodestar method produces an award that *roughly* approximates the fee that the prevailing attorney would have received if he or she had been representing a paying client who was billed by the hour in a comparable case. Second, the lodestar method is readily administrable, and unlike the *Johnson* approach, the lodestar calculation is "objective," and thus cabins the discretion of trial judges, permits meaningful judicial review, and produces reasonably predictable results. [Citations]

Our prior decisions concerning the federal fee-shifting statutes have established six important rules that lead to our decision in this case.

First, a "reasonable" fee is a fee that is sufficient to induce a capable attorney to undertake the representation of a meritorious civil rights case. Section 1988's aim is to enforce the covered civil rights statutes, not to provide "a form of economic relief to improve the financial lot of attorneys." [Citations]

Second, the lodestar method yields a fee that is presumptively sufficient to achieve this objective. Indeed, we have said that the presumption is a "strong" one. [Citations]

Third, although we have never sustained an enhancement of a lodestar amount for performance, we have repeatedly said that enhancements may be awarded in " 'rare' " and " 'exceptional' " circumstances.

Fourth, we have noted that "the lodestar figure includes most, if not all, of the relevant factors constituting a 'reasonable' attorney's fee," and have held that an enhancement may not be awarded based on a factor that is subsumed in the lodestar calculation. We have thus held that the novelty and complexity of a case generally may not be used as a ground for an enhancement because these factors "presumably [are] fully reflected in the number of billable hours recorded by counsel." We have also held that the quality of an attorney's performance generally should not be used to adjust the lodestar "[b]ecause considerations concerning the quality of a prevailing party's counsel's representation normally are reflected in the reasonable hourly rate." [Citations]

Fifth, the burden of proving that an enhancement is necessary must be borne by the fee applicant.

Finally, a fee applicant seeking an enhancement must produce "specific evidence" that supports the award. This requirement is essential if the lodestar method is to realize one of its chief virtues, *i.e.,* providing a calculation that is objective and capable of being reviewed on appeal.

In light of what we have said in prior cases, we reject any contention that a fee determined by the lodestar method may not be enhanced in any situation. The lodestar method was never intended to be conclusive in all circumstances. Instead, there is a "strong presumption" that the lodestar figure is reasonable, but that presumption may be overcome in those rare circumstances in which the lodestar does not adequately take into account a factor that may properly be considered in determining a reasonable fee.

In this case, we are asked to decide whether either the quality of an attorney's performance or the results obtained are factors that may properly provide a basis for an enhancement. We treat these two factors as one. When a plaintiff's attorney achieves results that are more favorable than would have been predicted based on the governing law and the available evidence, the outcome may be attributable to superior performance and commitment of resources by plaintiff's counsel. Or the outcome may result from inferior performance by defense counsel, unanticipated defense concessions, unexpectedly favorable rulings by the court, an unexpectedly sympathetic jury, or simple luck. Since none of these latter causes can justify an enhanced award, superior results are relevant only to the extent it can be shown that they are the result of superior attorney performance. Thus, we need only consider whether superior attorney performance can justify an enhancement. And in light of the principles derived from our prior cases, we inquire whether there are circumstances in which superior attorney performance is not adequately taken into account in the lodestar calculation. We conclude that there are a few such circumstances but that these circumstances are indeed "rare" and "exceptional," and require specific evidence that the lodestar fee would not have been "adequate to attract competent counsel." [Citation]

First, an enhancement may be appropriate where the method used in determining the hourly rate employed in the lodestar calculation does not adequately measure the attorney's true market value, as demonstrated in part during the litigation. This may occur if the hourly rate is determined by a formula that takes into account only a single factor (such as years since admission to the bar) or perhaps only a few similar factors. In such a case, an enhancement may be appropriate so that an attorney is compensated at the rate that the attorney would receive in cases not governed by the federal fee-shifting statutes. But in order to provide a calculation that is objective and reviewable, the trial judge should adjust the attorney's hourly rate in accordance with specific proof linking the attorney's ability to a prevailing market rate.

Second, an enhancement may be appropriate if the attorney's performance includes an extraordinary outlay of expenses and the litigation is exceptionally protracted. * * * [W]hen an attorney agrees to represent a civil rights plaintiff who cannot afford to pay the attorney, the attorney presumably understands that no reimbursement is likely to be received until the successful resolution of the case, and therefore enhancements to compensate for delay in reimbursement for expenses must be reserved for unusual cases. In such exceptional cases, however, an enhancement may be allowed, but the amount of the enhancement must be calculated using a method that is reasonable, objective, and capable of being reviewed on appeal, such as by applying a standard rate of interest to the qualifying outlays of expenses.

Third, there may be extraordinary circumstances in which an attorney's performance involves exceptional delay in the payment of fees. An attorney who expects to be compensated under § 1988 presumably understands that payment of fees will generally not come until the end of the case, if at all. Compensation for this delay is generally made "either by basing the award on current rates or by adjusting the fee based on historical rates to reflect its present value." But we do not rule out the possibility that an enhancement may be appropriate where an attorney assumes these costs in the face of unanticipated delay, particularly where the delay is unjustifiably caused by the defense. In such a case, however, the enhancement should be calculated by applying a method similar to that described above in connection with exceptional delay in obtaining reimbursement for expenses.

We reject the suggestion that it is appropriate to grant performance enhancements on the ground that departures from hourly billing are becoming more common. As we have noted, the lodestar was adopted in part because it provides a rough approximation of general billing practices, and accordingly, if hourly billing becomes unusual, an alternative to the lodestar method may have to be found. However, neither respondents nor their *amici* contend that that day has arrived. Nor have they shown that permitting the award of enhancements on top of the lodestar figure corresponds to prevailing practice in the general run of cases.

We are told that, under an increasingly popular arrangement, attorneys are paid at a reduced hourly rate but receive a bonus if certain specified results are obtained, and this practice is analogized to the award of an enhancement such as the one in this case. The analogy, however, is flawed. An attorney who agrees, at the outset of the representation, to a *reduced hourly rate* in exchange for the opportunity to earn a performance bonus is in a position far different from an attorney in a § 1988 case who is compensated at the *full prevailing rate* and then seeks a performance enhancement in addition to the lodestar amount after the litigation has concluded. Reliance on these comparisons for the purposes of administering enhancements, therefore, is not appropriate.

In the present case, the District Court did not provide proper justification for the large enhancement that it awarded. The court increased the lodestar award by 75% but, as far as the court's opinion reveals, this figure appears to have been essentially arbitrary. Why, for example, did the court grant a 75% enhancement instead of the 100% increase that respondents sought? And why 75% rather than 50% or 25% or 10%?

The District Court commented that the enhancement was the "minimum enhancement of the lodestar necessary to reasonably compensate [respondents'] counsel." But the effect of the enhancement was to increase the top rate for the attorneys to more than $866 per hour, and the District Court did not point to anything in the record that shows that this is an appropriate figure for the relevant market.

The District Court pointed to the fact that respondents' counsel had to make extraordinary outlays for expenses and had to wait for reimbursement, but the court did not calculate the amount of the enhancement that is attributable to this factor. Similarly, the District Court noted that respondents' counsel did not receive fees on an ongoing basis while the case was pending, but the court did not sufficiently link this factor to proof in the record that the delay here was outside the normal range expected by attorneys who rely on § 1988 for the payment of their fees or quantify the disparity. Nor did the court provide a calculation of the cost to counsel of any extraordinary and unwarranted delay. And the court's reliance on the contingency of the outcome contravenes our holding in *Dague*. See 505 U.S., at 565.

Finally, insofar as the District Court relied on a comparison of the performance of counsel in this case with the performance of counsel in unnamed prior cases, the District Court did not employ a methodology that permitted meaningful appellate review. Needless to say, we do not question the sincerity of the District Court's observations, and we are in no position to assess their accuracy. But when a trial judge awards an enhancement on an impressionistic basis, a major purpose of the lodestar method-providing an objective and reviewable basis for fees, is undermined.

Determining a "reasonable attorney's fee" is a matter that is committed to the sound discretion of a trial judge, see 42 U.S.C. § 1988 (permitting court, "in its discretion," to award fees), but the judge's discretion is not unlimited. It is essential that the judge provide a reasonably specific explanation for all aspects of a fee determination, including any award of an enhancement. Unless such an explanation is given, adequate appellate review is not feasible, and without such review, widely disparate awards may be made, and awards may be influenced (or at least, may appear to be influenced) by a judge's subjective opinion regarding particular attorneys or the importance of the case. In addition, in future cases, defendants contemplating the possibility of settlement will have no way to estimate the likelihood of having to pay a potentially huge enhancement. [Citation]

Section 1988 serves an important public purpose by making it possible for persons without means to bring suit to vindicate their rights. But unjustified enhancements that serve only to enrich attorneys are not consistent with the statute's aim. In many cases, attorney's fees awarded under § 1988 are not paid by the individuals responsible for the constitutional or statutory violations on which the judgment is based. Instead, the fees are paid in effect by state and local taxpayers, and because state and local governments have limited budgets, money that is used to pay attorney's fees is money that cannot be used for programs that provide vital public services. [Citation]

For all these reasons, the judgment of the Court of Appeals is reversed, and the case is remanded for proceedings consistent with this opinion.

———————

1. *Lodestar Method.* As the principal case reflects, the standard method for determining fees is the "lodestar" method of multiplying a reason-

able hourly rate for each attorney times the number of hours reasonably spent on the litigation. The most critical factor in measuring an award of attorneys' fees is the "degree of success obtained." Hensley v. Eckerhart, 461 U.S. 424, 436, 103 S.Ct. 1933, 1941, 76 L.Ed.2d 40 (1983). The Supreme Court has treated the lodestar figure as presumptively reasonable, subject to adjustment only in rare or exceptional circumstances. Thus, the degree of success in the litigation ordinarily will be subsumed within other factors used to calculate a reasonable fee rather than seen as an independent basis for modifying the fee award. The overarching consideration with respect to fee measurement is "reasonableness" based on all the circumstances of the case. *See* Blanchard v. Bergeron, 489 U.S. 87, 109 S.Ct. 939, 103 L.Ed.2d 67 (1989); City of Riverside v. Rivera, 477 U.S. 561, 106 S.Ct. 2686, 91 L.Ed.2d 466 (1986) (attorneys fees not *per se* unreasonable under federal fee-shifting statute where exceeded the amount of damages recoverable by the plaintiff in the underlying civil rights action). Any adjustments to the lodestar based on the results obtained must be supported by evidence in the record; inadequate documentation will justify a downward reduction of the fee. *Also see* City of Burlington v. Dague, 505 U.S. 557, 505 U.S. 557, 112 S.Ct. 2638, 120 L.Ed.2d 449 (1992) (an enhancement for the risk of non-recovery because of the contingency arrangement of representation was not permitted under federal fee-shifting statutes).

2. What types of costs of litigation may be properly assigned to the losing party pursuant to fee-shifting statutes? In *West Virginia University Hospitals, Inc. v. Casey*, 499 U.S. 83, 111 S.Ct. 1138, 113 L.Ed.2d 68 (1991), the Court held that Section 1988 did not grant authority to shift expert witness fees to the losing party in civil rights case. Congress later amended section 1988 to provide for expert fees as part of the litigation costs awarded to a prevailing party. Many other statutes also expressly provide for shifting expert witness fees as a separate cost of litigation item distinct from attorney fees. *See* Toxic Substances Control Act, 15 U.S.C. §§ 2618(d), 2619(c)(2); Resource Conservation and Recovery Act, 42 U.S.C. § 6972(e); Administrative Procedure Act, 5 U.S.C. § 504(b)(1)(A); Equal Access to Justice Act, 28 U.S.C. § 2412(d)(2)(A).

In *Pazik v. Gateway Regional School Dist.*, 130 F.Supp.2d 217, 220 (D.Mass.2001), the court found that expert witness fees, along with the enumerated attorney fees, were among the "costs" that it might award in its discretion under the Individuals with Disabilities Education Act. Such a holding was consistent with the purpose of the statute to ensure a free appropriate public education. Id. at 221. Conversely, the court in *Padro v. Puerto Rico*, 100 F.Supp.2d 99, 110 (D.P.R.2000) refused to award expert witness fees under a Title VII general "costs" provision because such fees were expressly addressed and capped in another section of the statute. *See also* Neal v. Honeywell, Inc., 191 F.3d 827 (7th Cir.1999) (expert fees included as part of litigation costs under FCA); Hall v. Claussen, 6 Fed. Appx. 655 (10th Cir.2001) (statutory cap of expert fees awarded under ADA).

3. Courts generally calculate fees based upon the customary market rates for attorneys of like competence and experience in the same community doing similar work during the relevant period. *See* Bogan v. City of Boston, 432 F.Supp.2d 222, 229 (D.Mass.2006) (plaintiff had burden of establishing attorney's skill and experience and providing information regarding the prevailing market rate in Boston for similarly experienced lawyers). Should courts distinguish between commercial for-profit law firms and non-profit public interest law firms in measuring fees? *See* Blum v. Stenson, 465 U.S. 886, 104 S.Ct. 1541, 79 L.Ed.2d 891 (1984) (§ 1988 fee calculations do not vary depending on whether the plaintiff was represented by private counsel or a non-profit legal services organization.)

What should the measure of fees be if a private practicing attorney charges a plaintiff a lower rate than their other clients in a public interest case? *See* Save Our Cumberland Mountains, Inc. v. Hodel, 857 F.2d 1516 (D.C.Cir.1988) (prevailing market rate awarded to successful environmental interest group under the Surface Mining Control and Reclamation Act even though the attorney had charged the plaintiff a reduced rate.) *See also* Missouri v. Jenkins, 491 U.S. 274, 109 S.Ct. 2463, 105 L.Ed.2d 229 (1989) (market rates for paralegals and law clerks were the proper measure of costs under 42 U.S.C. § 1988 rather than the cost of their services to the attorney.) *See also* Hardrick v. Airway Freight Sys., Inc., 140 Lab.Cas. (CCH) P 34,023, 6 Wage & Hour Cas. 2d (BNA) 1307 (N.D.Ill.2000) (measure by cost of opportunity lost); Central States v. Central Cartage Co., 76 F.3d 114 (7th Cir.1996) (no question of fee-splitting because award is to party rather than attorney).

4. A number of jurisdictions will allow the plaintiff's attorney fees to be considered in calculating the amount of punitive damages. Brewer v. Home–Stake Production Co., 200 Kan. 96, 434 P.2d 828 (1967); Keller v. Davis, 694 S.W.2d 355 (Tex.App.1985) (punitive damages may include damages for inconvenience, reasonable attorneys' fees, and losses considered too remote for actual damages); *contra* Cordeco Development Corp. v. Santiago Vasquez, 539 F.2d 256 (1st Cir.1976). Fitting attorney fees under the umbrella of punitive damages is not viewed as an "exception" to the American Rule, but is justified as part of the punishment for the defendant's wrongful conduct. Those courts have further held, however, that attorney fees may not be recoverable as a separate item apart from punitive damages. Fitz v. Toungate, 419 S.W.2d 708 (Tex.Civ.App.1967). Does such a distinction seem justifiable? *See also* Neal–Pettit v. Lahman, 125 Ohio St.3d 327, 928 N.E.2d 421 (Ohio 2010) (although public policy of Ohio prohibits insurance coverage of punitive damages, it does not extend to preclude payment of attorney's fees on behalf of its insured even where the fees were based solely on an exemplary damages award).

Krause v. Rhodes

640 F.2d 214 (6th Cir.1981).

■ EDWARDS, CHIEF JUDGE.

[During the height of public protest over the Vietnam War there were numerous campus protests when President Nixon appeared to be expanding the war with an incursion into neighboring Cambodia. During such protests at Kent State University the Governor of Ohio called the National Guard to campus. The event that led to this lawsuit—and numerous other inquiries and investigations—was on May 4, 1970, when some Guard members shot into a crowd. This suit was the consolidated cases of nine persons injured and the personal representatives of four persons who were killed in that episode. The defendants were the Governor of Ohio, the president of the university and various officers and enlisted members of the Ohio National Guard. The complaint alleged that they "intentionally, recklessly, willfully and wantonly" caused an unnecessary deployment of the Ohio National Guard on the Kent State campus. It further alleged that the defendants ordered the Guard members to perform illegal actions which resulted in this historic tragedy.]

Steven Sindell, the original counsel for 12 of the plaintiffs in the 1970 Kent State shooting cases, appeals from orders entered by Judge William K. Thomas approving a settlement of this lengthy and bitterly fought litigation.

Sindell contends that his 33 1/3% contingency fee contracts for representation of these plaintiffs invalidate the limitation and allocation of attorneys' fees occasioned by the District Court's approval of a $675,000 "settlement" between the State of Ohio and the litigants. * * *

The record in this case is a long and tortuous one. The complaints, originally filed in 1970, were dismissed by the District Court on the theory that essentially the action was against the State of Ohio and barred by the Eleventh Amendment. On appeal, this court affirmed these dismissals by a divided panel. *See* Krause v. Rhodes, 471 F.2d 430 (6th Cir.1972). The United States Supreme Court, however, unanimously reversed the judgments below and remanded for trial. Scheuer v. Rhodes, 416 U.S. 232, 94 S.Ct. 1683, 40 L.Ed.2d 90 (1974). After the first trial, the jury returned a verdict for defendants of no cause for action.

Subsequent to this adverse jury verdict, all plaintiffs and their counsel (including Steven Sindell) signed an agreement naming the American Civil Liberties Union (ACLU) as lead counsel "for purposes of all appellate proceedings in this litigation." Sanford Jay Rosen headed a team of ACLU lawyers in prosecuting the successful appeal to this court, which reversed for new trial. Krause v. Rhodes, 570 F.2d 563 (6th Cir.1977), *cert. denied,* 435 U.S. 924, 98 S.Ct. 1488, 55 L.Ed.2d 517 (1978). Rosen and his team also represented plaintiffs in the first four days of the second trial of this case and in the discussions which led to settlement.

This case was settled by an agreement entered into by all parties and lawyers except Sindell. The State of Ohio (not a party to this litigation) voluntarily offered to pay $675,000 in full settlement, provided that $600,000 of this sum be paid directly to plaintiffs undiluted by legal fees or expenses. Judge Thomas entered a settlement and dismissal order providing for payment of $600,000 to plaintiffs, $50,000 as payment in full to the attorneys, and $25,000 to cover out-of-pocket expenses. The ACLU and most of the other attorneys, including lead counsel Rosen, agreed with the settlement and subsequently agreed to Judge Thomas' distribution of the $50,000 attorneys' fees fund. Judge Thomas limited distribution of the $50,000 to contingent fee contract holders and apparently based the fund's allocation upon work performed prior to the first adverse jury verdict, disregarding for this purpose any of the services rendered by counsel in the successful effort to reverse that verdict and the subsequent retrial which produced the settlement agreement. Thus, law firms associated with appellant Sindell received $33,740 of the $50,000 fund, while the ACLU and the lawyers associated therewith received nothing for their services.

Appellant Sindell's argument before this court is a simple contention that a contingent fee agreement is beyond the power of a federal judge to invalidate or modify on any grounds whatsoever. Judge Thomas, however, based his decision to limit attorneys' fees in these cases in part upon the trial court's traditional power to resolve fee disputes between litigants and their counsel. * * *

Certainly, this case is unique in the annals of litigation in the United States Courts. Judge Thomas found no exact controlling precedent for the actions which he felt required to take, nor do we. Nonetheless, we feel that his approval of the "settlement" offered by the State of Ohio, conditioned specifically upon $600,000 going to the individual plaintiffs without reduction by attorneys' fees, was within his judicial discretion.

A federal district judge has broad equity power to supervise the collection of attorneys' fees under contingent fee contracts. * * *

Indeed, the Code of Professional Responsibility (CPR) of the American Bar Association imposes considerable limitations upon the ability of lawyers to contract for contingent fees. *See* DR 2–106 and EC 2–20.[6] As

---

6. DR 2–106 Fees for Legal Services

(A) A lawyer shall not enter into an agreement for charge, or collect an illegal or clearly excessive fee.

(B) A fee is clearly excessive when, after a review of the facts, a lawyer of ordinary prudence would be left with a definite and firm conviction that the fee is in excess of a reasonable fee. Factors to be considered as guides in determining the reasonableness of a fee include the following:

    (1) The time and labor required, the novelty and difficulty of the questions involved and the skill requisite to perform the legal service properly.

    (2) The likelihood, if apparent to the client, that the acceptance of the particular employment will preclude other employment by the lawyer.

    (3) The fee customarily charged in the locality for similar legal services.

    (4) The amount involved and the results obtained.

    (5) The time limitations imposed by the client or by the circumstances.

    (6) The nature and length of the professional relationship with the client.

    (7) The experience, reputation, and ability of the lawyer or lawyers performing the services.

    (8) Whether the fee is fixed or contingent.

(C) A lawyer shall not enter into an arrangement for, charge, or collect a contingent fee for representing a defendant in a criminal case.

indicated by the drafters' footnotes, the cited CPR provisions are based largely upon Canon 13 of the old ABA Canons of Professional Ethics, adopted in 1908. Canon 13 provided:

Contingent Fees.

A contract for a contingent fee, where sanctioned by law, should be reasonable under all the circumstances of the case, including the risk and uncertainty of the compensation, *but should always be subject to the supervision of a court, as to its reasonableness.* (Emphasis added.)

Under the facts of this case, to allow Sindell to enforce his contingent fees to the letter would be, as the District Judge obviously agreed, totally unreasonable.[7] At the outset, had the court accepted Sindell's position, it would have been unable to approve the settlement and there would have been no funds to disburse in any manner. The State of Ohio had conditioned its settlement offer upon the plaintiffs' "netting" $600,000. The State cannot have been motivated by the same reasoning which ordinarily prompts litigants to settle cases; Ohio had a stake not just in disposing of litigation but in calming the bitter conflict over this case which had raged within its borders—as well as throughout the nation. Thus, the limitations imposed on fee recoveries were absolutely essential to a just settlement of this unique case. * * *

In closing, we note that Steven Sindell failed to produce any monetary benefit for these plaintiffs. We also observe that the ACLU lawyers who obtained this settlement are receiving nothing for their services. Under these facts, the award of $33,740 to Sindell and his present or former law firms is at least fair compensation.

It is appropriate that we now ring down the curtain on this tragic drama which so bitterly divided our nation in the decade of the '70's.

The judgment of the District Court is affirmed.

———————

EC 2–20 Contingent fee arrangements in civil cases have long been commonly accepted in the United States in proceedings to enforce claims. The historical bases of their acceptance are that (1) they often, and in a variety of circumstances, provide the only practical means by which one having a claim against another can economically afford, finance, and obtain the services of a competent lawyer to prosecute his claim, and (2) a successful prosecution of the claim produces a *res* out of which the fee can be paid. Although a lawyer generally should decline to accept employment on a contingent fee basis by one who is able to pay a reasonable fixed fee, it is not necessarily improper for a lawyer, where justified by the particular circumstances of a case, to enter into a contingent fee contract in a civil case with any client who, after being fully informed of all relevant factors, desires that arrangement. Because of the human relationships involved and the unique character of the proceedings, contingent fee arrangements in domestic relation cases are rarely justified. In administrative agency proceedings contingent fee contracts should be governed by the same consideration as in other civil cases. Public policy properly condemns contingent fee arrangements in criminal cases, largely on the ground that legal services in criminal cases do not produce a *res* with which to pay the fee.

7. Particularly since Sindell's firm took the "lion's share" of the $50,000 fund, despite his failure to produce any monetary benefit for plaintiffs.

1. Since the focus of the fee-shifting statutes is on the prevailing party, does that justify allowing the client to waive or otherwise negotiate fees in the settlement process? Should eligibility for statutory attorney fees be a "bargaining chip" in the settlement process? *Evans v. Jeff D.*, 475 U.S. 717, 106 S.Ct. 1531, 89 L.Ed.2d 747 (1986), involved a class action which alleged civil rights violations of emotionally and mentally handicapped children in health care and educational programs administered by the State of Idaho. The court appointed a legal aid attorney to represent the interests of the class. The parties negotiated a settlement which contained virtually all of the substantive relief sought, yet which was conditioned upon a waiver of attorney fees by the class.

The plaintiff's attorney contended that the conditional fee waiver effectively constituted "coercion" by exploiting his ethical obligation to recommend settlement in order to avoid the defendant's potential statutory liability for fees. The Supreme Court held that the approval of the class action settlement which included a waiver of statutorily authorized fees was within the district court's discretionary power. The Court found no "ethical dilemma", reasoning that a lawyer is always ethically bound to act in the client's best interests. Therefore, the client had the prerogative to waive fees in order to obtain the relief sought, and thus vindicate civil rights.

Justice Brennan, joined by Justices Marshall and Blackmun, strongly dissented, reasoning that fee awards differ from other remedies. The dissenters asserted that it did "not require a sociological study to see that permitting fee waivers will make it more difficult for civil rights plaintiffs to obtain legal assistance." Does the practice of allowing a fee waiver undermine the ability of plaintiffs in civil rights cases to attract competent counsel? Which is the better view? *See* Pinto v. Spectrum Chemicals and Laboratory Products, 200 N.J. 580, 985 A.2d 1239 (2010) (defendants barred from demanding waiver of attorneys fees as a condition of settlement in state law fee-shifting cases involving public interest law firms).

2. In *F.T.C. v. Network Services Depot, Inc.*, 617 F.3d 1127 (9th Cir. 2010) the FTC investigated a group of companies and their principals for an alleged Ponzi scheme. The companies subsequently retained a lawyer and paid a flat fee for representation. In an ensuing civil action, the government was awarded equitable monetary relief against the companies for various FTC violations. The court also imposed a constructive trust over a portion of the attorney's fees, reasoning that the lawyer's fees were paid from funds derived from the unlawful activities. The court rejected the attorney's argument that the fees should be exempted from equitable restitution on the basis of the bona fide purchaser for value rule, finding that the attorney had an obligation to make a good faith inquiry into the source of the fees.

See also Hale v. Finn, 388 S.C. 79, 694 S.E.2d 51, 59 (App. 2010) (constructive trust imposed to secure division of attorney's fees that would satisfy right to quantum meruit recovery from another attorney); Nichols v. Nichols, 222 P.3d 1049 (Ok. 2009) (when attorney's fee is paid directly to the prevailing party, a constructive trust attaches by operation of law to fee award for benefit of client's lawyer).

3.   What should be the relevance of a pre-existing contractual fee arrangement to determining a fee award pursuant to a fee-shifting statute? In *Blanchard v. Bergeron*, 489 U.S. 87, 94–95, 109 S.Ct. 939, 944, 103 L.Ed.2d 67 (1989), the Court held that the fees awarded under the fee-shifting statute were not automatically governed by or limited to the amount provided in a contingent fee arrangement. Although the terms of a contingency fee contract were relevant, it was not dispositive in determining what constituted a "reasonable fee" under § 1988. The Court noted that if contingent fee terms served as a strict limitation on an award of attorney fees, it might place an undesirable, artificial emphasis on recovery of damages in lieu of potentially valuable injunctive or declaratory relief in civil rights litigation.

4.   In a related vein, in *Venegas v. Mitchell*, 495 U.S. 82, 110 S.Ct. 1679, 109 L.Ed.2d 74 (1990), an attorney who had successfully represented a client in a civil rights action sought to recover his fee pursuant to a contingency fee contract which significantly exceeded the amount awarded under 42 U.S.C. § 1988. The Court upheld the validity of the contractual arrangement, finding that a "reasonable fee" under the fee-shifting statute will not override or replace otherwise valid contractual terms. The Court reasoned that Congress established fee-shifting statutes to benefit the party rather than the lawyer, yet clients remain free to contract on whatever terms they choose to obtain counsel of their choice. *See also* Astrue v. Ratliff, __ U.S. __, 130 S.Ct. 2521, 177 L.Ed.2d 91 (2010) (fee award is payable to litigant rather than the attorney; therefore, the funds were subject to a government offset to satisfy a pre-existing debt that was owed to the United States); Blum v. Stenson, 465 U.S. 886, 894–895, 104 S.Ct. 1541, 1547, 79 L.Ed.2d 891 (1984) (attorney fees awarded to prevailing parties even though they were represented without cost by a non-profit legal aid organization).

5.   In *Democratic Central Committee of D.C. v. WMATC*, 38 F.3d 603 (D.C.Cir.1994), the court held that the interest that attorneys had in being paid fees from a common fund never achieved the status of "private property" within the meaning of the takings clause of the Fifth Amendment. Therefore, modification of the fee agreement by the lower court did not amount to a compensable taking. The court observed that an award of fees from a common fund is discretionary and derived from the exercise of the court's inherent equitable power, not as a matter of right. The court reserved power to amend the fee arrangement contained in a compromise agreement consistent with changed circumstances.

CHAPTER 20

DECLARATORY RELIEF

A. NOMINAL DAMAGES

Section Coverage:

The relationship between substantive rights and remedies has been a theme throughout the preceding nineteen chapters. In the context of nominal damages, the identity of right and remedy takes particular meaning. The materials in this section concern cases in which there is a clearly established substantive right, but no available remedy except a declaration of that right.

In some of the areas previously studied, the absence of a compensable loss eliminated the substantive right such that the case could be dismissed. For example, if a plaintiff's only prayer is for distress damages or economic losses under circumstances in which the substantive law will not compensate those losses, then the lack of cognizable injury eliminates the claim. The reason is that in negligence cases a particular type of injury is an element of the claim.

In areas of the law where the injury is not an element of the action, proof of the substantive elements of the claim is sufficient to survive dismissal. If the plaintiff cannot establish compensable injury, the court awards nominal damages to vindicate the principle of the claim.

Model Case:

An author and university professor entered into a written contract which gave a publisher the exclusive rights to publish a novel. The publisher promised in exchange to pay the author a nonreturnable sum of $2,000 and royalties based upon a designated percentage of future sales of the book. The contract also provided that the publisher had the right to terminate the contract by giving the author 60 days written notice.

The author performed by delivering the completed manuscript, and the publisher tendered the $2,000 in return. However, the publisher subsequently breached the contract by refusing to publish the novel without giving the required written notice of termination. The author sued for damages resulting from delayed academic promotion and loss of prospective royalties. The court would deny compensatory damages and award nominals instead if the evidence failed to establish lost anticipated royalties with reasonable certainty or that the breach actually caused any delay in the author's promotion.

Spence v. Hilliard

181 Ga.App. 767, 353 S.E.2d 634 (1987).

■ McMURRAY, PRESIDING JUDGE.

This is a legal malpractice action in which plaintiff was represented by defendants in a previous lawsuit. Plaintiff, a landlord, was sued by his tenant. He engaged defendants to defend the tenant's suit and to pursue a counterclaim against the tenant. The counterclaim was compulsory in nature.

Defendants answered the tenant's lawsuit and they successfully defended it. Defendants did not, however, assert a counterclaim against the tenant. (Instead, defendants filed a claim against the tenant in a separate action. Of course, that claim failed because it should have been raised via counterclaim. OCGA 9–11–13(a).)

In this malpractice action, plaintiff contends that as a result of defendants' negligence he was damaged to the tune of $59,273.68. The trial court took issue with plaintiff's contention. In the court's view, plaintiff failed to prove that he suffered damages. It took the position that plaintiff failed to demonstrate the amount of damages he was entitled to recover against the tenant and that, moreover, plaintiff failed to demonstrate that a judgment against the tenant was collectible. Accordingly, the trial court directed a verdict in favor of defendants and plaintiff appeals. *Held:*

Assuming, arguendo, there was a fatal failure of proof with regard to actual damages, we must nevertheless reverse the judgment of the trial court. Nominal damages are recoverable in a legal malpractice action provided plaintiff carries the burden of proving that he was wronged. [Citations.] Thus, plaintiff was entitled to submit the issue of nominal damages to the jury whether or not actual damages were proven. [Citations.] It follows that it was error for the trial court to direct a verdict against plaintiff. [Citations.]

Judgment reversed.

---

1. Nominal damages reflect legal recognition that a litigant's rights have been violated even though no compensable harm has resulted. For example, a plaintiff may establish a claim for an intentional tort or breach of contract but not be entitled to compensatory damages because the harm is not to a legally protected interest, or it is insignificant, or the losses cannot be proven with reasonable certainty.

These awards are damages "in name only" and consequently they are a trivial sum. Common awards are one dollar or six cents.

2. Nominal damages function as the common law counterpart to declaratory judgment statutes because they declare rights, status, or legal relations. Historically they were given only in cases involving trespass to land where the trespasser did no harm. The plaintiff sued to establish

entitlement to exclusive possession to prevent an easement by prescription or adverse possession.

3.   Some jurisdictions will not allow an award of punitive damages without proof of actual damages. An award of nominal damages therefore precludes such recovery.

In the case of *Alcorn County v. U.S. Interstate Supplies, Inc.*, 731 F.2d 1160 (5th Cir.1984), the rule requiring actual damages to support punitive damages was extended to equity. The court held in that case that when a case is in equity for relief such as cancellation or rescission of a contract, there are produced no compensatory damages. Therefore there can be no exemplary damages.

Is it correct that relief such as cancellation or rescission of a contract are also forms of declaratory remedies? Would any similarity justify treating them like nominal damages for purposes such as the rule against punitive damages without actual damages?

Carey v. Piphus

435 U.S. 247, 98 S.Ct. 1042, 55 L.Ed.2d 252 (1978).

■ Mr. Justice Powell delivered the opinion of the Court.

In this case, brought under 42 U.S.C. § 1983, we consider the elements and prerequisites for recovery of damages by students who were suspended from public elementary and secondary schools without procedural due process. The Court of Appeals for the Seventh Circuit held that the students are entitled to recover substantial nonpunitive damages even if their suspensions were justified, and even if they do not prove that any other actual injury was caused by the denial of procedural due process. We disagree, and hold that in the absence of proof of actual injury, the students are entitled to recover only nominal damages.

Respondent Jarius Piphus was a freshman at Chicago Vocational High school during the 1973 1974 school year. On January 23, 1974, during school hours, the school principal saw Piphus and another student standing outdoors on school property passing back and forth what the principal described as an irregularly shaped cigarette. The principal approached the students unnoticed and smelled what he believed was the strong odor of burning marihuana. He also saw Piphus try to pass a packet of cigarette papers to the other student. When the students became aware of the principal's presence, they threw the cigarette into a nearby hedge.

The principal took the students to the school's disciplinary office and directed the assistant principal to impose the "usual" 20 day suspension for violation of the school rule against the use of drugs. The students protested that they had not been smoking marihuana, but to no avail. Piphus was allowed to remain at school, although not in class, for the remainder of the school day while the assistant principal tried, without success, to reach his mother.

A suspension notice was sent to Piphus' mother, and a few days later two meetings were arranged among Piphus, his mother, his sister, school officials, and representatives from a legal aid clinic. The purpose of the meetings was not to determine whether Piphus had been smoking marihuana, but rather to explain the reasons for the suspension. Following an unfruitful exchange of views, Piphus and his mother, as guardian *ad litem,* filed suit against petitioners in Federal District Court under 42 U.S.C. § 1983 and its jurisdictional counterpart, 28 U.S.C. 1343, charging that Piphus had been suspended without due process of law in violation of the Fourteenth Amendment. The complaint sought declaratory and injunctive relief, together with actual and punitive damages in the amount of $3,000. Piphus was readmitted to school under a temporary restraining order after eight days of his suspension.

* * *

Title 42 U.S.C. § 1983, Rev.Stat. 1979, derived from 1 of the Civil Rights Act of 1871, 17 Stat. 13, provides:

"Every person who, under color of any statute, ordinance, regulation, custom, or usage, of any State or Territory, subjects, or causes to be subjected, any citizen of the United States or other person within the jurisdiction thereof to the deprivation of any rights, privileges, or immunities secured by the Constitution and laws, shall be liable to the party injured in an action at law, suit in equity, or other proper proceeding for redress."

The legislative history of § 1983 * * * demonstrates that it was intended to "[create] a species of tort liability" in favor of persons who are deprived of "rights, privileges, or immunities secured" to them by the Constitution. Imbler v. Pachtman, 424 U.S. 409, 417 (1976).

Petitioners contend that the elements and prerequisites for recovery of damages under this "species of tort liability" should parallel those for recovery of damages under the common law of torts. In particular, they urge that the purpose of an award of damages under § 1983 should be to compensate persons for injuries that are caused by the deprivation of constitutional rights; and, further, that plaintiffs should be required to prove not only that their rights were violated, but also that injury was caused by the violation, in order to recover substantial damages. Unless respondents prove that they actually were injured by the deprivation of procedural due process, petitioners argue, they are entitled at most to nominal damages.

Respondents seem to make two different arguments in support of the holding below. First, they contend that substantial damages should be awarded under § 1983 for the deprivation of a constitutional right *whether or not* any injury was caused by the deprivation. This, they say, is appropriate both because constitutional rights are valuable in and of themselves, and because of the need to deter violations of constitutional rights. Respondents believe that this view reflects accurately that of the Congress that enacted § 1983. Second, respondents argue that even if the purpose of a § 1983 damages award is, as petitioners contend, primarily to compensate persons for injuries that are caused by the deprivation of constitutional rights, every deprivation of procedural due process may be *presumed* to cause some injury. This presumption, they say, should relieve them from the necessity of proving that injury actually was caused.

Insofar as petitioners contend that the basic purpose of a § 1983 damages award should be to compensate persons for injuries caused by the deprivation of constitutional rights, they have the better of the argument. Rights, constitutional and otherwise, do not exist in a vacuum. Their purpose is to protect persons from injuries to particular interests, and their contours are shaped by the interests they protect.

* * *

It is less difficult to conclude that damages awards under § 1983 should be governed by the principle of compensation than it is to apply this principle to concrete cases. But over the centuries the common law of torts has developed a set of rules to implement the principle that a person should be compensated fairly for injuries caused by the violation of his legal rights. These rules, defining the elements of damages and the prerequisites for their recovery, provide the appropriate starting point for the inquiry under § 1983 as well.

It is not clear, however, that common-law tort rules of damages will provide a complete solution to the damages issue in every § 1983 case. In some cases, the interests protected by a particular branch of the common law of torts may parallel closely the interests protected by a particular constitutional right. In such cases, it may be appropriate to apply the tort rules of damages directly to the § 1983 action. [Citation.] In other cases, the interests protected by a particular constitutional right may not also be protected by an analogous branch of the common law torts. [Citations.] In those cases, the task will be the more difficult one of adapting common-law rules of damages to provide fair compensation for injuries caused by the deprivation of a constitutional right.

* * *

In this case, the Court of Appeals held that if petitioners can prove on remand that "[respondents] would have been suspended even if a proper hearing had been held," 545 F.2d, at 32, then respondents will not be entitled to recover damages to compensate them for injuries caused by the suspensions. The court thought that in such a case, the failure to accord procedural due process could not properly be viewed as the cause of the suspensions. [Citations.] The court suggested that in such circumstances, an award of damages for injuries caused by the suspensions would constitute a windfall, rather than compensation, to respondents. [Citations.] We do not understand the parties to disagree with this conclusion. Nor do we.

The parties do disagree as to the further holding of the Court of Appeals that respondents are entitled to recover substantial although unspecified damages to compensate them for "the injury which is 'inherent in the nature of the wrong,'" 545 F.2d, at 31, even if their suspensions were justified and even if they fail to prove that the denial of procedural due process actually caused them some real, if intangible, injury. Respondents, elaborating on this theme, submit that the holding is correct because injury fairly may be "presumed" to flow from every denial of procedural due process. Their argument is that in addition to protecting against unjustified deprivations, the Due Process Clause also guarantees the "feeling of just treatment" by the government. * * *

Petitioners do not deny that a purpose of procedural due process is to convey to the individual a feeling that the government has dealt with him fairly, as well as to minimize the risk of mistaken deprivations of protected interests. They go so far as to concede that, in a proper case, persons in respondents' position might well recover damages for mental and emotional distress caused by the denial of procedural due process. Petitioners' argument is the more limited one that such injury cannot be presumed to occur, and that plaintiffs at least should be put to their proof on the issue, as plaintiffs are in most tort actions.

We agree with petitioners in this respect. * * * Even if respondents' suspensions were justified, and even if they did not suffer any other actual injury, the fact remains that they were deprived of their right to procedural due process. * * *

Common-law courts traditionally have vindicated deprivations of certain "absolute" rights that are not shown to have caused actual injury through the award of a nominal sum of money. By making the deprivation of such rights actionable for nominal damages without proof of actual injury, the law recognizes the importance to organized society that those rights be scrupulously observed; but at the same time, it remains true to the principle that substantial damages should be awarded only to compensate actual injury or, in the case of exemplary or punitive damages, to deter or punish malicious deprivations of rights.

Because the right to procedural due process is "absolute" in the sense that it does not depend upon the merits of a claimant's substantive assertions, and because of the importance to organized society that procedural due process be observed, [citations] we believe that the denial of procedural due process should be actionable for nominal damages without proof of actual injury. We therefore hold that if, upon remand, the District Court determines that respondents' suspensions were justified, respondents nevertheless will be entitled to recover nominal damages not to exceed one dollar from petitioners.

The judgment of the Court of Appeals is reversed, and the case is remanded for further proceedings consistent with this opinion.

It is so ordered.

———————

1.   In *Farrar v. Hobby*, 506 U.S. 103, 113 S.Ct. 566, 121 L.Ed.2d 494 (1992) the Court held that a civil rights plaintiff who receives a nominal damages award was a "prevailing party" eligible to receive attorney's fees under 42 U.S.C. § 1988, a federal fee-shifting statute. The technical nature of such an award, though, also necessarily affects the propriety of obtaining any fees. The Court reasoned:

> When a court awards nominal damages, it neither enters judgment for defendant on the merits nor declares the defendant's legal immunity to suit. * * * Of itself, "the moral satisfaction [that] results from any favorable statement of law" cannot bestow prevailing party status. No material alteration of the legal relationship between the parties occurs until the plaintiff becomes entitled to enforce a judgment, consent decree, or settlement against the defendant. A plaintiff may demand payment for nominal damages no less than he may demand payment for millions of dollars in compensatory damages. A judgment for damages in any amount, whether compensatory or nominal, modifies the defendant's behavior for the plaintiff's benefit by forcing the defendant to pay an amount of money he would otherwise not pay.

* * *

> [A] nominal damages award does render a plaintiff a prevailing party by allowing him to vindicate his "absolute" right to procedural due process through enforcement of a judgment against the defendant. In a civil rights suit for damages, however, the awarding of nominal damages also highlights the plaintiff's failure to prove actual compensable injury. 113 S.Ct. at 573–575.

What practical effect is likely to result from the increased uncertainty of recovering attorney fees when the recovery is only nominal? Do attorneys ever take cases that they expect will not produce actual damages?

2.   In *County of Dallas v. Wiland*, 216 S.W.3d 344 (Tex.2007), several deputy constables brought § 1983 claims against the county, alleging that the termination of their civil service employment violated both procedural and substantive due process rights. The Texas Supreme Court held that the deputies had procedural due process property interests in continued employment except for just cause, and remanded for determination of damages. The court, following *Carey*, reasoned that the right to procedural due process is "absolute" in the sense that it does not depend on the merits of the plaintiff's substantive claims. Therefore, because of the societal importance of protecting such rights, the denial of procedural due process would be actionable for nominal damages without proof of actual injury.

3.   In *Brandt v. Board of Education of City of Chicago*, 480 F.3d 460 (7th Cir.2007) a group of eighth grade students brought a class action suit claiming § 1983 violations by the school district for punishing them for conducting a protest by wearing prohibited T-shirts to school. The school disciplined the students by confining them to their home-room and, as a result, missing gym, science lab, computer lab, and various after-school activities. The court found no First Amendment infirmity, but also com-

mented on the relevance of nominal damages for constitutional violations. The court stated:

> [We now] consider the plaintiffs' damages claim. Even multiplied by 24 (the number of members of the plaintiff class), the damages sustained by an eighth grader as a consequence of missing phys ed and labs on nine days out of an entire school year are minuscule to the point of nonexistent; and *de minimis non curat lex* (the law doesn't concern itself with trifles) is a doctrine applicable to constitutional as to other cases. It is true that nominal damages can be awarded for a constitutional violation, *Carey v. Piphus*, 435 U.S. 247, 266–67, 98 S.Ct. 1042, 55 L.Ed.2d 252 (1978); as is sometimes true for other intentionally tortious conduct as well. But such an award presupposes a violation of sufficient gravity to merit a judgment, even if significant damages cannot be proved; and this is not such a case. In any event there has been no constitutional violation. 480 F.3d at 465.

4. In *Memphis Community School Dist. v. Stachura*, 477 U.S. 299, 106 S.Ct. 2537, 91 L.Ed.2d 249 (1986), the Court clarified the damages issues introduced in *Carey v. Piphus*. The issue in this case was whether 42 U.S.C. § 1983 authorizes an award of compensatory damages based upon the value or importance of a substantive constitutional right.

The plaintiff, Edward Stachura, was a tenured public school teacher in Memphis, Michigan. He taught seventh-grade life sciences with an approved textbook that included a chapter on human reproduction. During this part of the course he showed the class pictures of his wife during her pregnancy. He also showed the students two approved films concerning human growth and sexuality. A number of parents complained at an open school board meeting and he was suspended with pay. After he filed a lawsuit, he was reinstated the next fall.

The complaint alleged that Stachura's suspension deprived him of both liberty and property without due process of law and violated his First Amendment right to academic freedom. He sought compensatory and punitive damages under 42 U.S.C. § 1983 for these constitutional violations.

The jury found for the plaintiff and awarded compensatory and punitive damages. The Supreme Court granted certiorari limited to the question whether the trial court correctly instructed on damages for the deprivation of "any constitutional right." The Court held:

> We have repeatedly noted that 42 U.S.C. § 1983 creates " 'a species of tort liability' in favor of persons who are deprived of 'rights, privileges, or immunities secured' to them by the Constitution." [Citations.] Accordingly, when § 1983 plaintiffs seek damages for violations of constitutional rights, the level of damages is ordinarily determined according to principles derived from the common law of torts. [Citations.]
>
> Punitive damages aside, damages in tort cases are designed to provide "*compensation* for the injury caused to plaintiff by defendant's breach

of duty." 2 F. Harper & F. James, Law of Torts 25.1, p. 1299 (1956) (emphasis in original), quoted in *Carey v. Piphus, supra* * * *

The instructions at issue here cannot be squared with *Carey,* or with the principles of tort damages on which *Carey* and § 1983 are grounded. The jurors in this case were told that, in determining how much was necessary to "compensate [respondent] for the deprivation" of his constitutional rights, they should place a money value on the "rights" themselves by considering such factors as the particular right's "importance ... in our system of government," its role in American history, and its "significance ... in the context of the activities" in which respondent was engaged. These factors focus, not on compensation for provable injury, but on the jury's subjective perception of the importance of constitutional rights as an abstract matter. *Carey* establishes that such an approach is impermissible. The constitutional right transgressed in *Carey* the right to due process of law is central to our system of ordered liberty. [Citation.] We nevertheless held that *no* compensatory damages could be awarded for violation of that right absent proof of actual injury. *Carey* thus makes clear that the abstract value of a constitutional right may not form the basis for § 1983 damages.

Respondent nevertheless argues that *Carey* does not control here, because in this case a *substantive* constitutional right respondent's First Amendment right to academic freedom was infringed. The argument misperceives our analysis in *Carey.* That case does not establish a two-tiered system of constitutional rights, with substantive rights afforded greater protection than "mere" procedural safeguards. We did acknowledge in *Carey* that "the elements and prerequisites for recovery of damages" might vary depending on the interests protected by the constitutional right at issue. But we emphasized that, whatever the constitutional basis for § 1983 liability, such damages must always be designed "to *compensate injuries* caused by the [constitutional] deprivation." [Citations.] That conclusion simply leaves no room for noncompensatory damages measured by the jury's perception of the abstract "importance" of a constitutional right.

Nor do we find such damages necessary to vindicate the constitutional rights that § 1983 protects. Section 1983 presupposes that damages that compensate for actual harm ordinarily suffice to deter constitutional violations. *Carey, supra,* 435 U.S., at 257, 98 S.Ct., at 1043 ("To the extent that Congress intended that awards under § 1983 should deter the deprivation of constitutional rights, there is no evidence that it meant to establish a deterrent more formidable than that inherent in the award of compensatory damages"). Moreover, damages based on the "value" of constitutional rights are an unwieldy tool for ensuring compliance with the Constitution. History and tradition do not afford any sound guidance concerning the precise value that juries should place on constitutional protections. Accordingly, were such damages available, juries would be free to award arbitrary amounts without any evidentiary basis, or to use their unbounded discretion to punish unpopular defendants. [Citation.] Such damages would be too uncertain to be of any great value to plaintiffs, and would inject caprice into determinations of damages in § 1983 cases. We therefore hold that damages based on the abstract "value" or "importance" of constitutional rights are not a permissible element of compensatory damages in such cases. 106 S.Ct. at 2544–45.

5.   The reasoning of *Carey v. Piphus* was applied to mandate an award of nominal damages for a denial of First Amendment speech rights in *Risdal v. Halford*, 209 F.3d 1071 (8th Cir.2000). In contract, a failure to give nominal damages instructions to the jury in a case involving an illegal entry in violation of claimant's Fourth Amendment rights was not an error in *Miller v. Albright*, 657 F.3d 733 (8th Cir. 2011).

B.   DECLARATORY JUDGMENTS

Section Coverage:

The declaratory judgment is a federal and state statutory remedy that declares the rights or legal relations of parties. The statutory authorization for declaratory relief does not create any new rights nor expand the subject matter jurisdiction of courts; rather it enlarges the range of remedies available to litigants. Declaratory judgments are reviewable as final judgments and they have *res judicata* effect. The declaratory judgment is a discretionary remedy which is liberally construed by courts. The declaratory remedy is neither legal nor equitable but sui generis. It does not require that any other remedy be inadequate.

The Federal Declaratory Judgment Act, codified at 28 U.S.C. §§ 2201, 2202, embraces both constitutional and prudential considerations. A federal court's power to grant a declaratory judgment is limited by the requirement that the dispute present an actual "case or controversy" within the confines of Article III of the Constitution. The statute does not replace the traditional requirement of a justiciable controversy. The parties must have genuinely conflicting claims capable of judicial resolution rather than hypothetical concerns. Courts may not give advisory opinions. The difference between an abstract question and a "controversy" contemplated by the Declaratory Judgment Act is a matter of degree, determined by focusing on whether a substantial and immediate controversy exists between parties having adverse legal interests. In exercising its discretion whether to render declaratory relief. a court also considers various prudential factors, including whether the declaration will serve a useful purpose and will effectively settle the controversy. Other considerations may include whether the plaintiff has engaged in "procedural fencing" by seeking a declaratory judgment in federal court in anticipation of a state court action, whether parallel proceedings are pending in a state court action, and whether an alternative remedy may be better or more effective.

There are several advantages to a declaratory judgment over injunctions, damages, or restitution. The principal benefit of seeking declaratory relief is to determine the legal relationships of the parties at an early stage of a dispute before serious harm is done. A declaratory judgment is considered a "milder" remedy than an injunction because it does not command that specific actions be taken and does not bind parties in personam. Although a declaratory judgment is not coercive in the same sense as an injunction, the effect of a determination of rights or legal relations often will strongly influence parties to take steps to avert incurring liability or prosecution. In that regard, a declaratory judgment is a valuable tool for clarifying legal rights and is advantageous in saving the time and expense of protracted litigation. Declaratory judgments can be used in tandem with other remedies, including injunctive relief, to provide complete relief to a party when it would serve a useful purpose and terminate uncertainty.

Model Case:

Howell works as regional vice-president for the XYZ Chemical Company which specializes in direct sales of heavy duty cleaning supplies to large industrial plants. XYZ employed Howell pursuant to a written contract which contained a provision prohibiting "competition with the business of the company in any respect for a period of five years following dismissal or termination of employment."

Howell has an aggressive marketing attitude for the company's products. At a business development meeting with key company officers Howell suggested catalogue sales to out-of-state potential customers. The president rebutted the suggestion by responding, "We've always sold XYZ products just one way—direct customer contact. Catalogues are too impersonal."

Howell is dissatisfied with the company's stodgy marketing techniques and is thinking about leaving the job to pursue the idea of catalogue sales. Howell is concerned that the contract would preclude starting such a business.

A court would probably decline to give a declaratory judgment in such a case. Howell's contemplated business venture is not yet a demonstrable intention to compete. A justiciable controversy would arise if Howell resigns from XYZ and announces plans to start the catalogue business. Howell would benefit by obtaining a declaration of rights and obligations under the contract at that preliminary juncture before incurring substantial expenses in developing the new business. If the court determined that Howell's catalogue company in fact would be competing with XYZ within the language of the contract, then Howell could avoid future litigation with XYZ.

The Federal Declaratory Judgment statutes provide:

28 U.S.C. § 2201. (a) In a case of actual controversy within its jurisdiction, except with respect to Federal taxes * * *, a proceeding under section 505 or 1146 of title 11, or in any civil action involving an antidumping or countervailing duty proceeding regarding a class or kind of merchandise of a free trade area country (as defined in section 516A(f)(10) of the Tariff Act of 1930), as determined by the administering authority, any court of the United States, upon the filing of an appropriate pleading, may declare the rights and other legal relations of any interested party seeking such declaration, whether or not further relief is or could be sought. Any such declaration shall have the force and effect of a final judgment or decree and shall be reviewable as such.

28 U.S.C. § 2202. Further necessary or proper relief based on a declaratory judgment or decree may be granted, after reasonable notice and hearing, against any adverse party whose rights have been determined by such judgment.

F.R.C.P. Rule 57. These rules govern the procedure for obtaining a declaratory judgment under 28 U.S.C. § 2201. Rules 38 and 39 govern a demand for a jury trial. The existence of another adequate remedy does not preclude a declaratory judgment that is otherwise appropriate. The court may order a speedy hearing of a declaratory-judgment action.

The Uniform Declaratory Judgment Act has been adopted, with some variations, in a large majority of states. The following are selected provisions of the Uniform Act:

§ 1.   **Scope**. Courts of record within their respective jurisdictions shall have power to declare rights, status, and other legal relations whether or not further relief is or could be claimed. No action or proceeding shall be open to objection on the ground that a declaratory judgment or decree is prayed for. The declaration may be either affirmative or negative in form and effect; and [it] shall have the force and effect of a final judgment or decree.

§ 2.   **Power to Construe**. Any person interested under a deed, will, written contract or other writings constituting a contract, or whose rights, status or other legal relations are affected by a statute, municipal ordinance, contract or franchise, may have determined any question of construction or validity arising under the instrument, statute, ordinance, contract, or franchise and obtain a declaration of rights, status or other legal relations thereunder.

§ 3.   **Before Breach**. A contract may be construed either before or after there has been a breach thereof.

§ 4.   **Executor**. Any person interested as or through an executor, administrator, trustee, guardian or other fiduciary, creditor, devisee, legatee, heir, next of kin, or *cestui que trust*, in the administration of a trust, or the estate of a decedent, an infant, lunatic, or insolvent, may have a declaration of rights or legal relations in respect thereto: (a) To ascertain any class of creditors, devisees, legatees, heirs, next of kin or others; or (b) To direct the executors, administrators, or trustees to do or abstain from doing any particular act in their fiduciary capacity; or (c) To determine any question arising in the administration of the estate or trust, including questions of construction of wills and other writings.

§ 5.   **Enumeration not exclusive**. The enumeration in sections 2, 3, and 4 does not limit or restrict the exercise of the general powers conferred in section 1, in any proceeding where declaratory relief is sought, in which a judgment or decree will terminate the controversy or remove an uncertainty.

§ 6.   **Discretionary**. The court may refuse to render or enter a declaratory judgment or decree where such judgment or decree, if rendered or entered, would not terminate the uncertainty or controversy giving rise to the proceeding.

§ 7.   **Review**. All orders, judgments and decrees under this Act may be reviewed as other orders, judgments and decrees.

§ 8.   **Supplemental Relief**. Further relief based on a declaratory judgment or decree may be granted whenever necessary or proper. The application therefor shall be by petition to a court having jurisdiction to grant the relief. If the application be deemed sufficient, the court shall, on reasonable notice, require any adverse party whose rights have been adjudicated by the declaratory judgment or decree, to show cause why further relief should not be granted forthwith.

§ 9.   **Jury Trial**. When a proceeding under this Act involves the determination of an issue of fact, such issue may be tried and determined in the same manner as issues of fact are tried and determined in other civil actions in the court in which the proceeding is pending.

§ 10.   **Costs**. In any proceeding under this Act the court may make such award of costs as may seem equitable and just.

§ 11.   **Parties**. When declaratory relief is sought, all persons shall be made parties who have or claim any interest which would be affected by the declaration, and no declaration shall prejudice the rights of persons not parties to the proceeding. In any proceeding which involves the validity of a municipal ordinance or franchise, such municipality shall be made a party, and shall be entitled to be heard, and if the statute, ordinance or franchise is alleged to be unconstitutional, the Attorney–General of the State shall also be served with a copy of the proceeding and be entitled to be heard.

§ 12.   **Construction**. This Act is declared to be remedial; its purpose is to settle and to afford relief from uncertainty and insecurity with respect to rights, status and other legal relations; and is to be liberally construed and administered.

Public Service Commission of Utah v. Wycoff Company

344 U.S. 237, 73 S.Ct. 236, 97 L.Ed. 291 (1952).

■ MR. JUSTICE JACKSON delivered the opinion of the Court.

[The Public Service Commission of Utah filed suit in state court seeking to prevent the respondent company from transporting motion picture film and newsreels within the State of Utah without first obtaining authorization from the Commission. Respondent then instituted a proceeding in federal court requesting (1) a declaratory judgment that its activities constituted interstate commerce and therefore it would be free to operate without further permission from the Utah Commission and (2) an injunction preventing the Commission from interfering with its transportation over routes authorized by the Interstate Commerce Commission. The District Court sustained the contention of the Commission that the corporation's activities constituted intrastate commerce, and dismissed the complaint. The Court of Appeals reversed and the Supreme Court granted certiorari.]

* * * [I]t is clear that this proceeding cannot result in an injunction on constitutional grounds. In addition to defects that will appear in our discussion of declaratory relief, it is wanting in equity because there is no proof of any threatened or probable act of the defendants which might cause the irreparable injury essential to equitable relief by injunction.

The respondent appears to have abandoned the suit as one for injunction but seeks to support it as one for declaratory judgment, hoping thereby to avoid both the three-judge court requirement and the necessity for proof of threatened injury. Whether declaratory relief is appropriate under the circumstances of this case apparently was not considered by either of the courts below. But that inquiry is one which every grant of this remedy must survive.

The Declaratory Judgment Act of 1934, now 28 U.S.C. § 2201, styled "creation of remedy," provides that in a case of actual controversy a competent court may "declare the rights and other legal relations" of a party "whether or not further relief is or could be sought." This is an enabling Act, which confers a discretion on the courts rather than an absolute right upon the litigant.

Previous to its enactment there were responsible expressions of doubt that constitutional limitations on federal judicial power would permit any federal declaratory judgment procedure. Finally, as the practice extended in the states, we reviewed a declaratory judgment rendered by a state court and held that a controversy which would be justiciable in this Court if presented in a suit for injunction is not the less so because the relief was declaratory. Encouraged by this and guided by the experience of the thirty-four states that had enacted such laws, the Senate Judiciary Committee recommended an adaptation of the principle to federal practice. Its enabling clause was narrower than that of the Uniform Act adopted in 1921 by the Commissioners on Uniform State Laws, which gave comprehensive power to declare rights, status and other legal relations. The Federal Act omits status and limits the declaration to cases of actual controversy.

This Act was adjudged constitutional only by interpreting it to confine the declaratory remedy within conventional "case or controversy" limits. * * *

* * * [T]he propriety of declaratory relief in a particular case will depend upon a circumspect sense of its fitness informed by the teachings and experience concerning the functions and extent of federal judicial power. While the courts should not be reluctant in granting this relief in the cases for which it was designed, they must be alert to avoid imposition upon their jurisdiction through obtaining futile or premature interventions, especially in the field of public law. A maximum of caution is necessary in the type of litigation that we have here, where a ruling is sought that would reach far beyond the particular case. Such differences of opinion or conflicts of interest must be "ripe for determination" as controversies over legal rights. The disagreement must not be nebulous or contingent but must have taken on fixed and final shape so that a court can see what legal issues it is deciding, what effect its decision will have on the adversaries, and some useful purpose to be achieved in deciding them.

The complainant in this case does not request an adjudication that it has a right to do, or to have, anything in particular. It does not ask a judgment that the Commission is without power to enter any specific order or take any concrete regulatory step. It seeks simply to establish that, as presently conducted, respondent's carriage of goods between points within as well as without Utah is all interstate commerce. One naturally asks, "So what?" To that ultimate question no answer is sought.

A multitude of rights and immunities may be predicated upon the premise that a business consists of interstate commerce. What are the specific ones in controversy? The record is silent and counsel little more articulate. * * *

* * * We may conjecture that respondent fears some form of administrative or judicial action to prohibit its service on routes wholly within the State without the Commission's leave. What respondent asks is that it win any such case before it is commenced. Even if respondent is engaged solely in interstate commerce, we cannot say that there is nothing whatever that the State may require.

A declaratory judgment may be the basis of further relief necessary or proper against the adverse party (28 U.S.C. § 2202). The carrier's idea seems to be that it can now establish the major premise of an exemption, not as an incident of any present declaration of any specific right or immunity, but to hold in readiness for use should the Commission at any future time attempt to apply any part of a complicated regulatory statute to it. If there is any more definite or contemporaneous purpose to this case, neither this record nor the briefs make it clear to us. We think this for several reasons exceeds any permissible discretionary use of the Federal Declaratory Judgment Act.

In the first place, this dispute has not matured to a point where we can see what, if any, concrete controversy will develop. It is much like asking a declaration that the State has no power to enact legislation that may be under consideration but has not yet shaped up into an enactment. If there is any risk of suffering penalty, liability or prosecution, which a declaration would avoid, it is not pointed out to us. If and when the State Commission takes some action that raises an issue of its power, some further declaration would be necessary to any complete relief. The proposed decree cannot end the controversy.

Nor is it apparent that the present proceeding would serve a useful purpose if at some future date the State undertakes regulation of respondent. After a sifting of evidence and a finding of facts as they are today, there is no assurance that changes of significance may not take place before the State decides to move. Of course, the remedy is not to be withheld because it necessitates weighing conflicting evidence or deciding issues of fact as well as law. That is the province of courts. But when the request is not for ultimate determination of rights but for preliminary findings and conclusions intended to fortify the litigant against future regulation, it would be a rare case in which the relief should be granted.

Even when there is no incipient federal-state conflict, the declaratory judgment procedure will not be used to pre-empt and prejudge issues that are committed for initial decision to an administrative body or special tribunal any more than it will be used as a substitute for statutory methods of review. It would not be tolerable, for example, that declaratory judgments establish that an enterprise is not in interstate commerce in order to forestall proceedings by the National Labor Relations Board, the Interstate Commerce Commission or many agencies that are authorized to try and decide such an issue in the first instance. Responsibility for effective functioning of the administrative process cannot be thus transferred from the bodies in which Congress has placed it to the courts.

But, as the declaratory proceeding is here invoked, it is even less appropriate because, in addition to foreclosing an administrative body, it is incompatible with a proper federal-state relationship. The carrier, being in some disagreement with the State Commission, rushed into federal court to get a declaration which either is intended in ways not disclosed to tie the Commission's hands before it can act or it has no purpose at all.

Declaratory proceedings in the federal courts against state officials must be decided with regard for the implications of our federal system. State administrative bodies have the initial right to reduce the general policies of state regulatory statutes into concrete orders and the primary right to take evidence and make findings of fact. It is the state courts which have the first and the last word as to the meaning of state statutes and whether a particular order is within the legislative terms of reference so as to make it the action of the State. We have disapproved anticipatory declarations as to state regulatory statutes, even where the case originated in and was entertained by courts of the State affected. Anticipatory judgment by a federal court to frustrate action by a state agency is even less tolerable to our federalism. Is the declaration contemplated here to be *res judicata*, so that the Commission cannot hear evidence and decide any matter for itself? If so, the federal court has virtually lifted the case out of the State Commission before it could be heard. If not, the federal judgment serves no useful purpose as a final determination of rights. * * *

In this case, as in many actions for declaratory judgment, the realistic position of the parties is reversed. The plaintiff is seeking to establish a defense against a cause of action which the declaratory defendant may assert in the Utah courts. Respondent here has sought to ward off possible action of the petitioners by seeking a declaratory judgment to the effect that he will have a good defense when and if that cause of action is asserted. Where the complaint in an action for declaratory judgment seeks in essence to assert a defense to an impending or threatened state court action, it is the character of the threatened action, and not of the defense, which will determine whether there is federal-question jurisdiction in the District Court. If the cause of action, which the declaratory defendant threatens to assert, does not itself involve a claim under federal law, it is doubtful if a federal court may entertain an action for a declaratory judgment establishing a defense to that claim. This is dubious even though the declaratory complaint sets forth a claim of federal right, if that right is in reality in the nature of a defense to a threatened cause of action. Federal courts will not seize litigations from state courts merely because one, normally a defendant, goes to federal court to begin his federal-law defense before the state court begins the case under state law.

Since this case should be dismissed in any event, it is not necessary to determine whether, on this record, the alleged controversy over an action that may be begun in state court would be maintainable under the head of federal-question jurisdiction. But we advert to doubts upon that subject to indicate the injury that would be necessary if the case clearly rested merely on threatened suit in state court, as, for all we can learn, it may.

We conclude that this suit cannot be entertained as one for injunction and should not be continued as one for a declaratory judgment. The judgment below should be reversed and modified to direct that the action be dismissed.

Reversed and so ordered.

■ MR. JUSTICE REED, concurring.

* * * [The Declaratory Judgment] Act was intended by Congress as a means for parties in such controversies as that between this interstate carrier and the Utah Commission to settle their legal responsibilities and powers without the necessity and risk of violation of the rights of one by the other. The controversy here is clear and definite. A decision would settle the issue that creates the uncertainty as to the parties' rights. The Act intended operations to be conducted in the light of knowledge rather than the darkness of ignorance.

However, it was recognized that the Declaratory Judgment Act introduced a new method for determining rights into the body of existing law.

Therefore the language of the Act was deliberately cast in terms of permissive, rather than mandatory, authority to the courts to take cognizance of petitions seeking this new relief. This enables federal courts to appraise the threatened injuries to complainant, the necessity and danger of his acting at his peril though incurring heavy damages, the adequacy of state or other remedies, particularly in controversies with administrative bodies. But even in respect to controversies with administrative bodies, the Declaratory Judgment Act exists as an instrument to protect the citizen against the dangers and damages that may result from his erroneous belief as to his rights under state or federal law. [Citation.] It is a matter of discretion with federal courts.

* * * Here, the record does not show any unusual danger of loss or damage to respondent, a suit had already been filed and the record shows no reason why its result would not settle this controversy. Because of these circumstances, I concur with the reversal of the judgment.

----

1. As noted in *Wycoff*, a party may seek declaratory relief in federal court as a strategic measure to anticipate a defense to the defendant's threatened suit in state court. The party may gain a tactical advantage in selecting the forum and in shaping the issues for judicial declaration. In such circumstances, courts will not necessarily decline to render declaratory relief, but will generally consider such tactical maneuvers as one factor in exercising their discretion. *See* Nashoba Communications v. Town of Danvers, 893 F.2d 435 (1st Cir.1990) (declaratory judgment denied where viewed as an attempt to engage in a "preemptive strike" aimed at undermining the state suit).

In *Severe Records, LLC v. Rich*, 658 F.3d 571 (6th Cir. 2011), a company sought a declaratory judgment in anticipation of litigation because it had received multiple cease and desist orders from the defendant regarding the rights to use sounds recordings and musical compositions. The court held that federal question jurisdiction existed for the declaratory judgment claim because the plaintiff alleged facts in a well pleaded complaint that demonstrated the defendant could have filed a coercive action arising under federal law concerning declaration of authorship of the subject music.

2. One of the principal advantages of a declaratory judgment is determination of rights or legal relations at an early stage, prior to the incurrence of harm. *See* Texas Employers' Ins. Ass'n v. Jackson, 862 F.2d 491 (5th Cir.1988) (with the enactment of the Declaratory Judgment Act courts no longer would have to tell "the prospective victim that the only way to determine whether the suspect is a mushroom or a toadstool, is to eat it"). The range of issues potentially suitable for declaratory relief is quite broad, including the scope or constitutionality of a statute, ascertaining property rights under deeds or wills, determining the validity of

intellectual property rights, or declaring whether an employee is restricted by the terms of a covenant not to compete.

3. The strategic and practical benefit of clarifying legal rights at an early juncture intersects with the foundational requirements for standing that parties must demonstrate an actual, justiciable controversy capable of judicial resolution. The phrase in the Declaratory Judgment Act referencing deciding cases of "actual controversy", then, requires allegiance to the types of cases and controversies that are justiciable under Article III of the Constitution. *See* Aetna Life Insurance Co. v. Haworth, 300 U.S. 227, 57 S.Ct. 461, 81 L.Ed. 617 (1937). No bright line exists for whether a declaratory judgment action meets the case or controversy requirement, but the Supreme Court has observed that the dispute must be "real and substantial" and "definite and concrete, touching the legal relations of parties having adverse legal interests". MedImmune, Inc. v. Genentech, Inc., 549 U.S. 118, 127 S.Ct. 764, 166 L.Ed.2d 604 (2007); Native Village of Noatak v. Blatchford, 38 F.3d 1505, 1514 (9th Cir.1994) (no declaratory judgment where constitutional challenge to statute and regulatory programs mooted by repeal of laws in issue).

4. The Declaratory Judgment Act is an enabling act which provides a procedural mechanism for federal courts to determine rights and legal relations of parties with respect to matters within the court's jurisdiction. The Act does not confer subject matter jurisdiction; therefore, a litigant must show an independent basis for the court's power to act. *See* Skelly Oil Co. v. Phillips Petroleum Co., 339 U.S. 667, 70 S.Ct. 876, 94 L.Ed. 1194 (1950) (Congress enlarged the range of remedies available in federal courts but did not extend their jurisdiction with the Declaratory Judgment Act); Brockstedt v. Sussex County Council, 794 F.Supp.2d 489 (D.Del. 2011) (Declaratory Judgment Act creates a remedy where federal courts may declare the rights and legal relations of any interested party seeking a declaration with respect to cases of actual controversy); English v. District of Columbia, 815 F.Supp.2d 254, (D.D.C. 2011) (an involuntarily committed psychiatric patient failed to state a claim with respect to asserted due process violations by hospital, so not entitled to declaratory relief); Gritchen v. Collier, 254 F.3d 807 (9th Cir.2001) (declaratory judgment suit lacked jurisdictional basis where claim brought under civil rights statute; 42 U.S.C. § 1983 deemed inapplicable because police officer was not acting under color of state law when he threatened to bring defamation suit against motorist).

5. A declaratory judgment requires a sufficiently concrete controversy that the court's decree would not constitute an advisory opinion. Resolution of the issue of ripeness is particularly difficult when a party seeks a declaration of non-liability with respect to a future claim.

In *Levin Metals Corp. v. Parr–Richmond Terminal Co.*, 799 F.2d 1312 (9th Cir.1986), for example, Levin purchased a parcel of land from Parr–Richmond and discovered that it was contaminated with hazardous wastes. The parties subsequently filed claims against each other on various grounds, including a request by Parr–Richmond for a declaration of non-liability under CERCLA, a federal environmental protection statute, for clean-up costs or damages which might be incurred by Levin. The court observed that a declaratory judgment in the nature of a defense to a threatened or pending action would be ripe for adjudication if Levin could have brought a coercive action to enforce its rights. Since the statute authorized recovery of cleanup costs from responsible parties and Levin had already sought reimbursement, the declaratory judgment concerning the issue of non-liability presented a real and immediate controversy. *Also see* United States v. Davis, 261 F.3d 1 (1st Cir.2001) (declaratory judgment action was an appropriate remedy to resolve allocation of proportional liability among responsible parties for future costs associated with a soil remediation plan despite uncertainty of amounts); *But see* Hendrix v. Poonai, 662 F.2d 719 (11th Cir.1981) (hospital's request for declaratory relief of non-liability was an abstract question and premature to satisfy case or controversy requirement).

6. The declaratory judgment remedy often plays a particularly significant role in disputes involving intellectual property rights. In *Cardinal Chem. Co. v. Morton Int'l, Inc.*, 508 U.S. 83, 113 S.Ct. 1967, 124 L.Ed.2d 1 (1993), the Supreme Court examined whether a declaratory judgment regarding the validity of a patent should be vacated following a determination of non-infringement. The Court first determined that federal courts retained jurisdiction to consider the declaratory judgment issue even after a finding of non-infringement. The Court noted that the passage of the Declaratory Judgment Act served a useful purpose by allowing competitors to "clear the air" over patent rights even if a patentee had not yet filed an infringement action. The Court rejected prior federal court practice of vacating declarations of patent rights on the basis of mootness, observing the strong public interest in the finality of judgments in patent litigation. Otherwise, reasoned the Court, vacation of judgments could encourage unnecessary re-litigation, may unfairly deprive the patentee of appellate review, and it may prolong the life of invalid patents.

In *iMedImmune, Inc. v. Genentech, Inc.*, 549 U.S. 118, 127 S.Ct. 764, 166 L.Ed.2d 604 (2007), the Court held that a patent licensee could seek a declaratory judgment in federal court to establish that it had no duty to pay royalties under its license agreement even prior to terminating or breaching the agreement. Rather than basing jurisdiction on whether the licensee had a "reasonable apprehension of litigation", the Court adopted a more liberal "totality of the circumstances" approach in deciding whether an actual controversy existed. The Court observed: "The rule that a plaintiff must destroy a large building, bet the farm, or (as here) risk treble damages and the loss of 80 percent of its business, before seeking a declaration of its actively contested legal rights finds no support in Article III." 127 S.Ct. at 775.

In *Ass'n for Molecular Pathology v. U.S. Patent and Trademark Office*, 653 F.3d 1329 (Fed. Cir. 2011), the court found that the affirmative acts by the patent holder demanding royalty payments from a doctor running a university research laboratory, coupled with the doctor's preparation to undertake related clinical research activities, sufficed for declaratory judgment jurisdiction regarding the validity of the patents. *Also see* Hewlett–Packard Co. v. Acceleron LLC, 587 F.3d 1358 (Fed. Cir. 2009) (declaratory judgment jurisdiction appropriate where company took affirmative steps to contact non-competitor patent holder directly and made implied assertion of rights under patents); Surefoot LC v. Sure Foot Corp., 531 F.3d 1236 (10th Cir. 2008) (substantial controversy of sufficient immediacy warranted declaratory judgment jurisdiction to resolve trademark dispute).

7. The presence of a covenant not to sue may deprive a federal court of jurisdiction to decide a declaratory judgment claim. *See* Nike, Inc. v. Already LLC, 663 F.3d 89 (2d Cir. 2011) (covenant not to sue eliminated justiciable case or controversy necessary for subject matter jurisdiction in declaratory judgment action for non-infringement and cancellation of trademark registration); Technology Licensing Corp. v. Technicolor USA, Inc., 800 F.Supp.2d 1116 (E.D.Cal. 2011) (covenant not to sue for patent infringement divests the court of subject matter jurisdiction with respect to claims regarding patent validity because the covenant eliminates any case or controversy between the parties); Arris Group, Inc. v. British Telecommunications PLC, 639 F.3d 1368 (Fed. Cir. 2011) (refusal to grant covenant not to sue supported actual controversy regarding contributory infringement).

PROBLEM: THE CABLE SIGNAL DISPUTE

ABC Enterprises and Video Marketing Cable Co. (collectively, the "Cable Group") have franchise agreements with a national video programming service, Top Box Entertainment ("TBE") authorizing them to distribute TBE's services to individual subscribers in the Boston area. The video programming is transmitted by means of microwave signal which is received through specially tuned antennae and converter equipment. Subscribers pay a monthly fee for the service. However, persons who have a special antenna and converter system can receive the programming directly without paying a subscription fee.

On January 10, the Cable Group undertook a campaign to prevent "signal piracy" in their service area. They published in Boston area newspapers various advertisements which showed a picture of a police van and stated: "If you are illegally receiving TBE, soon this will be the only free ride for TBE thieves." The publications also stated that illegal reception of TBE signals carries a penalty of up to a $50,000 fine and two years in prison, and stated in boldface type: "To Avoid Prosecution, Call Before March 15th" The Cable Group also hired Brown and Walker, Inc. ("B & W") to conduct an anti-theft campaign in the Boston area.

The Cable Group and B & W sought to identify unauthorized users of the TBE signal. The effort involved visual inspection of the exterior of homes in the Boston area and the collection of photographs of homes to which were affixed "unauthorized" antennae apparently capable of receiving the TBE signal. In some instances, electronic devices were employed to determine whether these antennae were being used to receive the signal at the time of observation. They compiled a list of approximately 5,000 names and addresses of persons suspected of receiving TBE programming without a subscription.

The following January, approximately 5,000 people, including Jo Abrams, received a letter from B & W. On or through the envelope were visible the following statements: "Open Immediately—Pending Legal Action," and "Violation of Federal Law." The letter read as follows:

In recent weeks, areas of Boston have been subjected to a photographic and electronic survey in a search for violators of Section 705 of the Federal Communications Act of 1984. Your property is listed as maintaining an unauthorized microwave antenna which is tuned to and receiving the private, home entertainment programming of Top Box Entertainment ("TBE"). This illegal reception can no longer be tolerated. In order to avoid incurring legal liability, we demand that you take the following steps immediately:

1.   Remove the unauthorized equipment.

2.   Sign the enclosed subscription agreement to stop your illegal reception of the TBE signal.

3.   Return this agreement with payment of $300 to The Cable Group. This amount is considered to be an out of court settlement of all prior and present claims against you. THIS SETTLEMENT OFFER IS NOT NEGOTIABLE.

Abrams wishes to file a declaratory judgment in federal district court seeking a declaration that The Cable Group had improperly construed the Federal Communications Act, 47 U.S.C. § 605 ("FCA"), to make mere possession of a particular type of antenna a violation of the Act for which Abrams and members of the class might be held criminally or civilly liable. What result?

Steffel v. Thompson

415 U.S. 452, 94 S.Ct. 1209, 39 L.E.2d 505 (1974).

■ MR. JUSTICE BRENNAN delivered the opinion of the Court.

* * * This case presents the important question * * * whether declaratory relief is precluded when a state prosecution has been threatened, but is not pending, and a showing of bad-faith enforcement or other special circumstances has not been made. * * *

The parties stipulated to the relevant facts: On October 8, 1970, while petitioner [Steffel] and other individuals were distributing handbills protesting American involvement in Vietnam on an exterior sidewalk of the North DeKalb Shopping Center, shopping center employees asked them to stop handbilling and leave. They declined to do so, and police officers were summoned. The officers told them that they would be arrested if they did not stop handbilling. The group then left to avoid arrest. Two days later petitioner and a companion returned to the shopping center and again began handbilling. The manager of the center called the police, and petitioner and his companion were once again told that failure to stop their handbilling would result in their arrests. Petitioner left to avoid arrest. His companion [Becker] stayed, however, continued handbilling, and was arrested and subsequently arraigned on a charge of criminal trespass in violation of § 26–1503. Petitioner alleged in his complaint that, although he desired to return to the shopping center to distribute handbills, he had not done so because of his concern that he, too, would be arrested for violation of § 26–1503; the parties stipulated that, if petitioner returned and refused upon request to stop handbilling, a warrant would be sworn out and he might be arrested and charged with a violation of the Georgia statute.

[Petitioner brought a class action in federal court requesting an injunction against enforcement and a declaratory judgment that Georgia's criminal trespass statute[1] was being applied in violation of his first and fourteenth amendment rights. The state court stayed its proceedings against Becker pending resolution of the federal action. Following denial of relief in federal court, Steffel petitioned for certiorari with respect to the declaratory judgment suit.]

I

At the threshold we must consider whether petitioner presents an "actual controversy," a requirement imposed by Art. III of the Constitution and the express terms of the Federal Declaratory Judgment Act, 28 U.S.C. § 2201.

* * * [P]etitioner has alleged threats of prosecution that cannot be characterized as "imaginary or speculative." He has been twice warned to stop handbilling that he claims is constitutionally protected and has been told by the police that if he again handbills at the shopping center and disobeys a warning to stop he will likely be prosecuted. The prosecution of petitioner's handbilling companion is ample demonstration that petitioner's concern with arrest has not been "chimerical." In these circumstances, it is not necessary that petitioner first expose himself to actual arrest or prosecution to be entitled to challenge a statute that he claims deters the exercise of his constitutional rights. * * *

Nonetheless, there remains a question as to the *continuing* existence of a live and acute controversy that must be resolved on the remand we order today. * * * Here, petitioner's complaint indicates that his handbilling activities were directed "against the War in Vietnam and the United

---

1. This statute [Ga. Code Ann. § 26–1503 (1972)] provides:

"(a) A person commits criminal trespass when he intentionally damages any property of another without his consent and the damage there to is $100 or less, or knowingly and maliciously interferes with the possession or use of the property of another person without his consent. * * *

"(3) Remains upon the land or premises of another person, or within the vehicle, railroad car, aircraft, or watercraft of another person, after receiving notice from the owner or rightful occupant to depart.

"(c) A person convicted of criminal trespass shall be punished as for a misdemeanor."

States' foreign policy in Southeast Asia." Since we cannot ignore the recent developments reducing the Nation's involvement in that part of the world, it will be for the District Court on remand to determine if subsequent events have so altered petitioner's desire to engage in handbilling at the shopping center that it can no longer be said that this case presents "a substantial controversy, between parties having adverse legal interests, of sufficient immediacy and reality to warrant the issuance of a declaratory judgment."

II

* * * Sensitive to principles of equity, comity, and federalism, we recognized in *Younger v. Harris*, 401 U.S. 37 (1971), that federal courts should ordinarily refrain from enjoining ongoing state criminal prosecutions. We were cognizant that a pending state proceeding, in all but unusual cases, would provide the federal plaintiff with the necessary vehicle for vindicating his constitutional rights, and, in that circumstance, the restraining of an ongoing prosecution would entail an unseemly failure to give effect to the principle that state courts have the solemn responsibility, equally with the federal courts, "to guard, enforce, and protect every right granted or secured by the Constitution of the United States...."
* * *

* * * When no state criminal proceeding is pending at the time the federal complaint is filed, federal intervention does not result in duplicative legal proceedings or disruption of the state criminal justice system; nor can federal intervention, in that circumstance, be interpreted as reflecting negatively upon the state court's ability to enforce constitutional principles. In addition, while a pending state prosecution provides the federal plaintiff with a concrete opportunity to vindicate his constitutional rights, a refusal on the part of the federal courts to intervene when no state proceeding is pending may place the hapless plaintiff between the Scylla of intentionally flouting state law and the Charybdis of foregoing what he believes to be constitutionally protected activity in order to avoid becoming enmeshed in a criminal proceeding.

When no state proceeding is pending and thus considerations of equity, comity, and federalism have little vitality, the propriety of granting federal declaratory relief may properly be considered independently of a request for injunctive relief. Here, the Court of Appeals held that, because injunctive relief would not be appropriate since petitioner failed to demonstrate irreparable injury—a traditional prerequisite to injunctive relief—it followed that declaratory relief was also inappropriate. Even if the Court of Appeals correctly viewed injunctive relief as inappropriate—a question we need not reach today since petitioner has abandoned his request for that remedy[12]—the court erred in treating the requests for injunctive and declaratory relief as a single issue. * * *

---

12. We note that, in those cases where injunctive relief has been sought to restrain an imminent, but not yet pending, prosecution for past conduct, sufficient injury has not been found to warrant injunctive relief. [Citations.] There is some question, however, whether a

* * * Congress in 1934 enacted the Declaratory Judgment Act, 28 U.S.C. §§ 2201–2202. That Congress plainly intended declaratory relief to act as an alternative to the strong medicine of the injunction and to be utilized to test the constitutionality of state criminal statutes in cases where injunctive relief would be unavailable is amply evidenced by the legislative history of the Act. * * *

The "different considerations" entering into a decision whether to grant declaratory relief have their origins in [history]. First, as Congress recognized in 1934, a declaratory judgment will have a less intrusive effect on the administration of state criminal laws. As was observed in Perez v. Ledesma, 401 U.S. at 124–126 (separate opinion of BRENNAN, J.):

> Of course, a favorable declaratory judgment may nevertheless be valuable to the plaintiff though it cannot make even an unconstitutional statute disappear. A state statute may be declared unconstitutional *in toto*—that is, incapable of having constitutional applications; or it may be declared unconstitutionally vague or overbroad—that is, incapable of being constitutionally applied to the full extent of its purport. In either case, a federal declaration of unconstitutionality reflects the opinion of the federal court that the statute cannot be fully enforced. If a declaration of total unconstitutionality is affirmed by this Court, it follows that this Court stands ready to reverse any conviction under the statute. If a declaration of partial unconstitutionality is affirmed by this Court, the implication is that this Court will overturn particular applications of the statute, but that if the statute is narrowly construed by the state courts it will not be incapable of constitutional applications. Accordingly, the declaration does not necessarily bar prosecutions under the statute, as a broad injunction would. Thus, where the highest court of a State has had an opportunity to give a statute regulating expression a narrowing or clarifying construction but has failed to do so, and later a federal court declares the statute unconstitutionally vague or overbroad, it may well be open to a state prosecutor, after the federal court decision, to bring a prosecution under the statute if he reasonably believes that the defendant's conduct is not constitutionally protected and that the state courts may give the statute a construction so as to yield a constitutionally valid conviction. Even where a declaration of unconstitutionality is not reviewed by this Court, the declaration may still be able to cut down the deterrent effect of an unconstitutional state statute. The persuasive force of the court's opinion and judgment may lead state prosecutors, courts, and legislators to reconsider their respective responsibilities toward the statute. Enforcement policies or judicial construction may be changed, or the legislature may repeal the statute and start anew. Finally, the federal court judgment may have some *res judicata* effect, though this point is not free from difficulty and the governing rules remain to be developed

showing of irreparable injury might be made in a case where, although no prosecution is pending or impending, an individual demonstrates that he will be required to forego constitutionally protected activity in order to avoid arrest. [Citations.]

with a view to the proper workings of a federal system. What is clear, however, is that even though a declaratory judgment has "the force and effect of a final judgment," 28 U.S.C. § 2201, it is a much milder form of relief than an injunction. Though it may be persuasive, it is not ultimately coercive; noncompliance with it may be inappropriate, but is not contempt. (Footnote omitted.)

Second, engrafting upon the Declaratory Judgment Act a requirement that all of the traditional equitable prerequisites to the issuance of an injunction be satisfied before the issuance of a declaratory judgment is considered would defy Congress' intent to make declaratory relief available in cases where an injunction would be inappropriate. * * *

The only occasions where this Court has disregarded these "different considerations" and found that a preclusion of injunctive relief inevitably led to a denial of declaratory relief have been cases in which principles of federalism militated altogether against federal intervention in a class of adjudications. In the instant case, principles of federalism not only do not preclude federal intervention, they compel it. Requiring the federal courts totally to step aside when no state criminal prosecution is pending against the federal plaintiff would turn federalism on its head. * * *

III

* * * [T]he State's concern with potential interference in the administration of its criminal laws is of lesser dimension when an attack is made upon the constitutionality of a state statute as applied. A declaratory judgment of a lower federal court that a state statute is invalid *in toto*—and therefore incapable of any valid application—or is overbroad or vague—and therefore no person can properly be convicted under the statute until it is given a narrowing or clarifying construction—will likely have a more significant potential for disruption of state enforcement policies than a declaration specifying a limited number of impermissible applications of the statute. * * *

We therefore hold that, regardless of whether injunctive relief may be appropriate, federal declaratory relief is not precluded when no state prosecution is pending and a federal plaintiff demonstrates a genuine threat of enforcement of a disputed state criminal statute, whether an attack is made on the constitutionality of the statute on its face or as applied. The judgment of the Court of Appeals is reversed, and the case is remanded for further proceedings consistent with this opinion.

Reversed and remanded.

■ MR. JUSTICE STEWART, with whom THE CHIEF JUSTICE joins, concurring.

* * * Our decision today must not be understood as authorizing the invocation of federal declaratory judgment jurisdiction by a person who thinks a state criminal law is unconstitutional, even if he genuinely feels "chilled" in his freedom of action by the law's existence, and even if he honestly entertains the subjective belief that he may now or in the future be prosecuted under it.

* * * The petitioner in this case has succeeded in objectively showing that the threat of imminent arrest, corroborated by the actual arrest of his companion, has created an actual concrete controversy between himself and the agents of the State. He has, therefore, demonstrated "a genuine threat of enforcement of a disputed state criminal statute...." * * * Cases where such a "genuine threat" can be demonstrated will, I think, be exceedingly rare.

■ Mr. Justice Rehnquist, with whom The Chief Justice joins, concurring.

I concur in the opinion of the Court. Although my reading of the legislative history of the Declaratory Judgment Act of 1934 suggests that its primary purpose was to enable persons to obtain a definition of their rights before an actual injury had occurred, rather than to palliate any controversy arising from *Ex parte Young*, 209 U.S. 123, 28 S.Ct. 441, 52 L.Ed. 714 (1908), Congress apparently was aware at the time it passed the Act that persons threatened with state criminal prosecutions might choose to forego the offending conduct and instead seek a federal declaration of their rights. Use of the declaratory judgment procedure in the circumstances presented by this case seems consistent with that congressional expectation.

* * * [T]he Court's decision today deals only with declaratory relief and with threatened prosecutions. The case provides no authority for the granting of any injunctive relief nor does it provide authority for the granting of any relief at all when prosecutions are pending. The Court quite properly leaves for another day whether the granting of a declaratory judgment by a federal court will have any subsequent *res judicata* effect or will perhaps support the issuance of a later federal injunction. But since possible resolutions of those issues would substantially undercut the principles of federalism reaffirmed in *Younger v. Harris*, 401 U.S. 37 (1971), and preserved by the decision today, I feel it appropriate to add a few remarks.

First, the legislative history of the Declaratory Judgment Act and the Court's opinion in this case both recognize that the declaratory judgment procedure is an alternative to pursuit of the arguably illegal activity. There is nothing in the Act's history to suggest that Congress intended to provide persons wishing to violate state laws with a federal shield behind which they could carry on their contemplated conduct. * * * The plaintiff who continues to violate a state statute after the filing of his federal complaint does so both at the risk of state prosecution and at the risk of dismissal of his federal lawsuit. * * *

Second, I do not believe that today's decision can properly be raised to support the issuance of a federal injunction based upon a favorable declaratory judgment. The Court's description of declaratory relief as "a milder alternative to the injunction remedy," having a "less intrusive effect on the administration of state criminal laws" than an injunction, indicates to me critical distinctions which make declaratory relief appropriate where injunctive relief would not be. It would all but totally obscure these important distinctions if a successful application for declaratory relief came to be regarded, not as the conclusion of a lawsuit, but as a giant step toward obtaining an injunction against a subsequent criminal prosecution. * * *

A declaratory judgment is simply a statement of rights, not a binding order supplemented by continuing sanctions. State authorities may choose to be guided by the judgment of a lower federal court, but they are not compelled to follow the decision by threat of contempt or other penalties. If the federal plaintiff pursues the conduct for which he was previously threatened with arrest and is in fact arrested, he may not return the controversy to federal court, although he may, of course, raise the federal declaratory judgment in the state court for whatever value it may prove to have. In any event, the defendant at that point is able to present his case for full consideration by a state court charged, as are the federal courts, to preserve the defendant's constitutional rights. * * *

Third, attempts to circumvent *Younger* by claiming that enforcement of a statute declared unconstitutional by a federal court is *per se* evidence of bad faith should not find support in the Court's decision in this case. * * *

If the declaratory judgment remains, as I think the Declaratory Judgment Act intended, a simple declaration of rights without more, it will not be used merely as a dramatic tactical maneuver on the part of any state defendant seeking extended delays. Nor will it force state officials to try cases time after time, first in the federal courts and then in the state courts. I do not believe Congress desired such unnecessary results, and I do not think that today's decision should be read to sanction them. Rather the Act, and the decision, stand for the sensible proposition that both a potential state defendant, threatened with prosecution but not charged, and the State itself, confronted by a possible violation of its criminal laws, may benefit from a procedure which provides for a declaration of rights without activation of the criminal process. If the federal court finds that the threatened prosecution would depend upon a statute it judges unconstitutional, the State may decide to forego prosecution of similar conduct in the future, believing the judgment persuasive. Should the state prosecutors not find the decision persuasive enough to justify forbearance, the successful federal plaintiff will at least be able to bolster his allegations of unconstitutionality in the state trial with a decision of the federal district court in the immediate locality. The state courts may find the reasoning convincing even though the prosecutors did not. Finally, of course, the state legislature may decide, on the basis of the federal decision, that the statute would be better amended or repealed. All these possible avenues of relief would be reached voluntarily by the States and would be completely consistent with the concepts of federalism discussed above. * * *

------

1. An individual citizen may want to know the coverage of a penal statute in order to avoid criminal prosecution or to allow compliance with the statutory directive. Someone who fears the adverse application of a

statute typically wants rights to be adjudicated as early as possible and thus resorts to declaratory relief. If the declaratory action is brought prematurely, however, the court may determine that the prospective application of the criminal statute to the plaintiff does not present a justiciable controversy.

Conversely, a party may wait too long in requesting declaratory relief. Once criminal proceedings are commenced, a court will ordinarily decline to grant a declaratory judgment concerning application of the penal statute because it would promote needless proliferation of litigation. Although a declaratory judgment action is considered an optional rather than an extraordinary remedy, a court in its discretion may determine that the plaintiff's remedy should be defending the criminal charges. *See* Norcisa v. Board of Selectmen of Provincetown, 368 Mass. 161, 330 N.E.2d 830 (1975), reprinted *supra* in Chapter 9. The court in *Norcisa* further noted:

> The fundamental jurisprudential considerations underlying the general prohibition against enjoining a pending criminal prosecution apply with full force to support a prohibition against issuing declaratory decrees concerning a pending criminal prosecution. To conclude otherwise would encourage fragmentation and proliferation of litigation and disrupt the orderly administration of the criminal law.

The rule we adopt today in regard to the issuance of declaratory judgments when criminal litigation is pending is merely a logical extension of our rules which generally proscribe the issuance of such a judgment when an appropriate administrative proceeding is in progress, or when a civil proceeding in which the same issue is or can be raised is already pending between the parties.

2.   In *Calderon v. Ashmus*, 523 U.S. 740, 118 S.Ct. 1694, 140 L.Ed.2d 970 (1998), a state death-row inmate filed a class action and sought a declaratory judgment that California state officials were not entitled to assert Chapter 154 of the Antiterrorism and Effective Death Penalty Act of 1996, 28 U.S.C. s2261 ("AEDPA") in defending habeas claims. The AEDPA provides some procedural advantages to qualifying states in federal habeas proceedings in capital cases. State officials had publicly announced that they believed California qualified under Chapter 154 and they intended to invoke its protections. Since no actual federal habeas proceeding had been filed, however, the Court found that the respondent's request to determine the applicability of the AEDPA to California failed to raise a justiciable question under Article III as required for jurisdiction under the Declaratory Judgment Act. The Court observed that an advance ruling on a potential affirmative defense would inappropriately allow the respondent to gain a litigation advantage on a collateral issue. The Court noted that it met the "case or controversy" requirement by virtue of the continuing and imminent threat of arrest in violation of First Amendment protections. Moreover, the declaratory judgment action would not completely resolve potential future habeas claims under the AEDPA.

3.   In *Marine Equip. Mgmt. Co. v. United States*, 4 F.3d 643 (8th Cir.1993), owners of a sunken river barge sought a declaratory judgment

that they had successfully "abandoned" the barge within the meaning of the Rivers and Harbors Act and therefore could not be held liable for any future damage attributed to the sunken barge. Although the owners had filed a notice of abandonment with the Corps of Engineers, there were no pending administrative enforcement actions nor private claims asserted with respect to the barge. The court declined declaratory relief, finding no justiciable dispute sufficient to satisfy the case or controversy requirement of Article III. The court noted that the actual controversy prerequisite to the exercise of jurisdiction contemplates that the threat of enforcement must have some immediate coercive consequences, not the hypothetical situation of potential claims by unknown third parties.

4. The nonjoinder of an interested party in a declaratory judgment action also may have *res judicata* implications. In *Harris v. Quinones*, 507 F.2d 533 (10th Cir.1974), an insurance company obtained a declaratory judgment in state court that an automobile insurance policy it had issued was not in force on the date of an accident involving the daughter of the insured. The daughter and the other motorist involved in the accident were not named as parties to the state court action, but subsequently requested a declaratory judgment in federal court against the insurance company regarding the issue of coverage.

The federal court determined that the prior state court decision did not have *res judicata* effect with respect to the nonparties. The court, finding that the policy had been in force, stated that the daughter was not bound by the state court decision where her rights were not solely derivative from the policyholder. *Also see* Harborside Refrigerated Serv., Inc. v. Vogel, 959 F.2d 368 (2d Cir.1992) (preclusive effect of the declaratory judgment is limited to the subject matter of the declaratory relief sought); Andrew Robinson Intl, Inc. v. Hartford Fire Ins. Co., 547 F.3d 48 (1st Cir. 2008) (party receive final judgment for declaratory relief without res judicata precluding a later action for damages arising out of the same nucleus of operative facts).

5. A declaratory judgment may be one of several possible avenues for a party seeking resolution of a controversy. In circumstances where a claim for declaratory relief could have been resolved through another form of action that has a specific time limitation, that time period will also govern the declaratory judgment suit. Orangetown v. Gorsuch, 718 F.2d 29, 42 (2d Cir.1983). Thus, a litigant cannot evade the operative statute of limitations governing a damages claim simply by labeling the suit as one for declaratory relief. Gilbert v. City of Cambridge, 932 F.2d 51 (1st Cir.1991) (owners of apartment buildings seeking declaration of unconstitutionality of municipal ordinance were time-barred by running of limitations period governing coexisting damages claim).

PROBLEM: THE PROPERTY LINE

Green, Baker, and Jones owned parcels of land which adjoined each other at the intersection of the boundary lines of three states. Green decided to erect a fence along the boundary line of his property and began staking off the projected location of the fence. Baker believes that Green's stakes incorrectly identify the boundary line. Therefore Baker brings a suit requesting a declaratory judgment to establish the correct property line and a temporary injunction to restrain construction pending resolution of the dispute.

The tract belonging to Jones would be only partially affected by the court's decision, so Baker decided not to join Jones in the suit. Green claims that (a) the declaratory judgment action is not a justiciable controversy because no construction has actually commenced, (b) a remedy at law for damages would be more appropriate in the event that Baker is correct about the property line, and (c) the claim should be dismissed for failure to join Jones as an indispensable party. What result?

New York Times Co. v. Gonzales

459 F.3d 160 (2d Cir.2006).

■ WINTER, CIRCUIT JUDGE:

After the attacks on the World Trade Center and the Pentagon on September 11, 2001, the federal government launched or intensified investigations into the funding of terrorist activities by organizations raising money in the United States. In the course of those investigations, the government developed a plan to freeze the assets and/or search the premises of two foundations. Two *New York Times* reporters learned of these plans, and, on the eve of each of the government's actions, called each foundation for comment on the upcoming government freeze and/or searches.

The government, believing that the reporters' calls endangered the agents executing the searches and alerted the targets, allowing them to take steps mitigating the effect of the freeze and searches, began a grand jury investigation into the disclosure of its plans regarding the foundations. It sought the cooperation of the *Times* and its reporters, including access to the *Times'* phone records. Cooperation was refused, and the government threatened to obtain the phone records from third party providers of phone services. The *Times* then brought the present action seeking a declaratory judgment that phone records of its reporters in the hands of third party telephone providers are shielded from a grand jury subpoena by reporter's privileges protecting the identity of confidential sources arising out of both the common law and the First Amendment.

Although dismissing two of the *Times'* claims, Judge Sweet granted the *Times'* motion for summary judgment on its claims that disclosure of the records was barred by both a common law and a First Amendment reporter's privilege. He further held that, although the privileges were qualified, the government had not offered evidence sufficient to overcome them.

We vacate and remand. We hold first that whatever rights a newspaper or reporter has to refuse disclosure in response to a subpoena extends to the newspaper's or reporter's telephone records in the possession of a third party provider. We next hold that we need not decide whether a common law privilege exists because any such privilege would be overcome as a matter of law on the present facts. Given that holding, we also hold that no First Amendment protection is available to the *Times* on these facts in light of the Supreme Court's decision in *Branzburg v. Hayes*, 408 U.S. 665, 92 S. Ct. 2646, 33 L. Ed. 2d 626 (1972).

Background

A federal grand jury in Chicago is investigating how two *Times* reporters obtained information about the government's imminent plans to freeze the assets and/or search the offices of Holy Land Foundation ("HLF") and Global Relief Foundation ("GRF") on December 4 and 14, 2001, respectively, and why the reporters conveyed that information to HLF and GRF by seeking comment from them ahead of the search. Both entities were suspected of raising funds for terrorist activities. The government alleges that, "[i]n both cases, the investigations—as well as the safety of FBI agents participating in the actions—were compromised when representatives of HLF and GRF were contacted prior to the searches by *New York Times* reporters Philip Shenon and Judith Miller, respectively, who advised of imminent adverse action by the government." The government maintains that none of its agents were authorized to disclose information regarding plans to block assets or to search the premises of HLF or GRF prior to the execution of those actions. The unauthorized disclosures of such impending law enforcement actions by a government agent can constitute a violation of federal criminal law, *e.g.*, 18 U.S.C. § 793(d) (prohibiting communication of national defense information to persons not entitled to receive it), including the felony of obstruction of justice, 18 U.S.C. § 1503(a).

On October 1, 2001, the *Times* published a story by Miller and another reporter that the government was considering adding GRF to a list of organizations with suspected ties to terrorism. Miller has acknowledged that this information was given to her by "confidential sources." On December 3, 2001, Miller "telephoned an HLF representative seeking comment on the government's intent to block HLF's assets." The following day, the government searched the HLF offices. The government contends that Miller's call alerted HLF to the impending search and led to actions reducing the effectiveness of the search. The *Times* also put an article by Miller about the search on the *Times'* website and in late-edition papers on December 3, 2001, the day before the search. The article claimed to be based in part on information from confidential sources. The *Times* also published a post-search article by Miller in the December 4 print edition.

In a similar occurrence, on December 13, 2001, Shenon "contact[ed] GRF for the purposes of seeking comment on the government's apparent intent to freeze its assets." The following day, the government searched

GRF offices. The government has since stated that "GRF reacted with alarm to the tip from [Shenon], and took certain action in advance of the FBI search." It has claimed that "when federal agents entered the premises to conduct the search, the persons present at Global Relief Foundation were expecting them and already had a significant opportunity to remove items." Shenon reported the search of the GRF offices in an article published on December 15, 2001, the day after the government's search.

After learning that the government's plans to take action against GRF had been leaked, Patrick J. Fitzgerald, the United States Attorney for the Northern District of Illinois, opened an investigation to identify the government employee(s) who disclosed the information to the reporter(s) about the asset freeze/search. On August 7, 2002, Fitzgerald wrote to the *Times* and requested a voluntary interview with Shenon and voluntary production of his telephone records from September 24 to October 2, 2001, and December 7 to 15, 2001. Fitzgerald's letter stated that "[i]t has been conclusively established that Global Relief Foundation learned of the search from reporter Philip Shenon of the *New York Times*"; the requested interview and records were therefore essential to investigating "leaks which may strongly compromise national security and thwart investigations into terrorist fundraising." Anticipating the *Times*' response, the letter argued in strong language that the First Amendment did not protect the "potentially criminal conduct" of Shenon's source or Shenon's "decision ... to provide a tip to the subject of a terrorist fundraising inquiry." The *Times* refused the request for cooperation on the ground that the First Amendment provides protection against a newspaper "having to divulge confidential source information to the Government."

On July 12, 2004, Fitzgerald wrote again to the *Times* and renewed the request for an interview with Shenon and the production of his telephone records. He enlarged the request to include an interview with Miller and the production of her telephone records from September 24 to October 2, 2001, November 30 to December 4, 2001, and December 7 to 15, 2001. Fitzgerald stated that the investigation involved "extraordinary circumstances" and that any refusal by the *Times* to provide the pertinent information would force him to seek the telephone records from third parties, i.e., the *Times*' telephone service providers. The *Times* again refused the request and questioned whether the government had exhausted all alternative sources. The *Times* argued that turning over the reporters' telephone records would give the government access to all the reporters' sources during the time periods indicated, not just those relating to the government's investigation. The *Times* believed that such a request "would be a fishing expedition well beyond any permissible bounds."

* * * [T]he *Times* filed the present action in the Southern District of New York. The counts of the complaint pertinent to this appeal sought a declaratory judgment that reporters' privileges against compelled disclosure of confidential sources prevented enforcement of a subpoena for the reporters' telephone records in the possession of third parties. The claimed

privileges were derived from the federal common law and the First Amendment.

On October 27, 2004, the government moved to dismiss the complaint on the ground that plaintiffs have an adequate remedy under Federal Rule of Criminal Procedure 17. The *Times* opposed the government's motion to dismiss and moved for summary judgment. The government then filed a cross motion for summary judgment.

Judge Sweet denied the government's motion to dismiss. *New York Times Co. v. Gonzales*, 382 F. Supp. 2d 457 (S.D.N.Y. 2005). He concluded that he had discretion to entertain the action for declaratory judgment and had no reason to decline to exercise that discretion, especially because a motion to quash would not provide the *Times* the same relief provided by a declaratory judgment. *Id.* at 475–79. Judge Sweet granted the *Times'* motion for summary judgment on its claims that Shenon's and Miller's telephone records were protected against compelled disclosure of confidential sources by two qualified privileges. *Id.* at 492, 508. One privilege was derived from the federal common law pursuant to Federal Rule of Evidence 501; the other source was the First Amendment. *Id.* at 490–92, 501–08, 510–13. The government appealed.

Discussion

a) *The Declaratory Judgment Act*

Under the Declaratory Judgment Act, a district court "may declare the rights and other legal relations of any interested party seeking such declaration, whether or not further relief is or could be sought." 28 U.S.C. § 2201(a). A district court may issue a declaratory judgment only in "a case of actual controversy within its jurisdiction." *Id.* The Act does not require the courts to issue a declaratory judgment. Rather, it " 'confers a discretion on the courts rather than an absolute right upon the litigant.' " *Wilton v. Seven Falls Co.*, 515 U.S. 277, 287, 115 S. Ct. 2137, 132 L. Ed. 2d 214 (1995) (citing *Public Serv. Comm'n of Utah v. Wycoff Co.*, 344 U.S. 237, 241, 73 S. Ct. 236, 97 L. Ed. 291 (1952)).

The government argues that the district court should not have exercised jurisdiction over this action for two reasons: (i) because there is a "special statutory proceeding" for the Times' claim under Federal Rule of Criminal Procedure 17(c)'s provisions for quashing a subpoena, a declaratory judgment is unnecessary, and, (ii) because the district judge improperly balanced the factors guiding the exercise of discretion.

We review the underlying legal determination that Rule 17(c) is not a special statutory proceeding precluding a declaratory judgment action *de novo*, and we review the decision to entertain such an action for abuse of discretion. [Citation]

1.   Special Statutory Proceeding

Federal Rule of Civil Procedure 57 states that "[t]he existence of another adequate remedy does not preclude a judgment for declaratory relief in cases where it is appropriate." However, the Advisory Committee's Note purports to qualify this Rule by stating that a "declaration may not be rendered if a special statutory proceeding has been provided for the adjudication of some special type of case, but general ordinary or extraordinary legal remedies, whether regulated by statute or not, are not deemed special statutory proceedings." Fed. R. Civ. P. 57 advisory committee's note.

Rule 17(c)(2) permits a court to quash or modify a subpoena that orders a witness to produce documents and other potential evidence, when "compliance would be unreasonable or oppressive." Fed. R. Crim. P. 17(c)(2). Although Rule 17 itself is not a statute, it is referenced by 18 U.S.C. § 3484. The government contends that Rule 17(c) is a special statutory proceeding within the meaning of the Advisory Committee's Note and that its existence therefore renders declaratory relief inappropriate. It further notes that there is only one decision in which a plaintiff attempted to challenge federal grand jury subpoenas through a declaratory judgment action, *Doe v. Harris*, 225 U.S. App. D.C. 27, 696 F.2d 109 (D.C. Cir. 1982), and that did not entail a ruling on whether the complaint stated a valid claim for relief. *Id.* at 112.

However, since the enactment of the Declaratory Judgment Act, only a handful of categories of cases have been recognized as "special statutory proceedings" for purposes of the Advisory Committee's Note. These include: (i) petitions for habeas corpus and motions to vacate criminal sentences, *e.g.*, *Clausell v. Turner*, 295 F. Supp. 533, 536 (S.D.N.Y. 1969); (ii) proceedings under the Civil Rights Act of 1964, *e.g.*, *Katzenbach v. McClung*, 379 U.S. 294, 296, 85 S. Ct. 377, 13 L. Ed. 2d 290 (1964); and (iii) certain administrative proceedings, *e.g.*, *Deere & Co. v. Van Natta*, 660 F. Supp. 433, 436 (M.D.N.C. 1986) (involving a decision on patent validity before U.S. patent examiners). Each of these categories involved procedures and remedies specifically tailored to a limited subset of cases, usually one brought under a particular statute. Rule 17(c) is not of such limited applicability. Rather, it applies to all federal criminal cases. Were we to adopt the government's theory and treat a motion to quash under Rule 17(c) as a "special statutory proceeding," we would establish a precedent potentially qualifying a substantial number of federal rules of criminal and civil procedure as special statutory proceedings and thereby severely limit the availability of declaratory relief. Therefore, we hold that the existence of Rule 17(c) does not preclude *per se* a declaratory judgment.

2.   Application of the *Dow Jones* Factors

In *Dow Jones & Co., Inc. v. Harrods Ltd.*, 346 F.3d 357, 359–60 (2d Cir. 2003), we outlined five factors to be considered before a court entertains a declaratory judgment action: (i) "whether the judgment will serve a useful purpose in clarifying or settling the legal issues involved"; (ii) "whether a judgment would finalize the controversy and offer relief from uncertainty"; (iii) "whether the proposed remedy is being used merely for 'procedural fencing' or a 'race to res judicata' "; (iv) "whether the use of a declaratory judgment would increase friction between sovereign legal systems or improperly encroach on the domain of a state or foreign court"; and (v) "whether there is a better or more effective remedy." *Id.* (citations omitted).

We review a district court's application of the *Dow Jones* factors only for abuse of discretion. *Duane Reade*, 411 F.3d at 388. The district court did not abuse its discretion in entertaining the present action. Factors (i) and (ii) favor a decision on the merits. There is a substantial chance that the phone records, although they will not reveal the content of conversations or the existence of other contacts, will provide reasons to focus on some individuals as being the source(s). If so, the *Times* may have no chance to assert its claim of privileges as to the source(s)' identity. It would therefore be "useful" to clarify the existence of the asserted privileges now. *Dow Jones*, 346 F.3d at 359. Moreover, a declaratory judgment will "finalize the controversy" over the existence of any privilege on the present facts and provide "relief from uncertainty" in that regard. *Id.* For similar reasons, factor (iii) also calls for a decision on the merits. Seeking a final resolution of the privilege issue is surely more than "procedural fencing" on the facts of this case. *Id.* at 359–60. Factor (iv) is inapplicable on its face. As for factor (v), a motion to quash under Rule 17(c) would not offer the *Times* the same relief as a declaratory action under the circumstances of this case. First, a motion to quash is not available if the subpoena has not been issued. 2 Charles Alan Wright, Federal Practice and Procedure § 275 (3d ed. 2000) (citing *In re Grand Jury Investigation (General Motors Corp.)*, 31 F.R.D. 1 (S.D.N.Y. 1962)). Second, it is unknown whether subpoenas have been issued to telephone carriers or not, and if so, whether the carriers have already complied. It is also unclear whether, when a subpoena has been issued to a third party and the third party has complied, a motion to quash is still a viable path to a remedy. *See* Fed. R. Crim. P. 17(c) (not addressing whether a subpoena may be quashed after it is complied with).

The district court, therefore, did not abuse its discretion in concluding that it should exercise jurisdiction over this action. * * *

Conclusion

Accordingly, the judgment of the district court is vacated, and the case is remanded to enter a declaratory judgment in accordance with the terms of this opinion and without prejudice to the district court's redaction of materials irrelevant to the investigation upon an offer of appropriate cooperation.

---

1. As discussed in the principal case, in certain instances federal courts will decline jurisdiction over a declaratory judgment action either because another statutory remedy is more efficacious or provides the exclusive basis for redressing the dispute. *See* Schilling v. Rogers, 363 U.S. 666, 677, 80 S.Ct. 1288, 4 L.Ed.2d 1478 (1960) (federal courts may not issue a declaratory judgment under a federal statute that Congress intended to

be enforced exclusively through a judicially unreviewable administrative hearing). In *Telecare Corp. v. Leavitt*, 409 F.3d 1345 (Fed.Cir.2005), for example, the court held that the federal district court lacked jurisdiction to consider declaratory judgment action brought by employer under Administrative Procedure Act regarding claimed overpayment of Medicare benefits because an adequate remedy for recoupment of payments existed under Little Tucker Act. *Also see* Jilin Pharmaceutical USA, Inc. v. Chertoff, 447 F.3d 196 (3d Cir.2006) (declaratory action brought by alien regarding revocation by Immigration and Naturalization Service of alien's work visa was properly dismissed for lack of subject matter jurisdiction); Rooney v. Secretary of the Army, 405 F.3d 1029 (D.C.Cir.2005) (serviceman could not seek declaratory relief because petition for writ of habeas corpus was exclusive remedy from Army's revocation of prior discharge).

In *C & E Services, Inc. v. District of Columbia Water and Sewer Authority*, 310 F.3d 197 (D.C.Cir.2002), the court held that an unsuccessful bidder for a government contract lacked a recognizable property interest to support subject matter jurisdiction for a declaratory action. The court observed that the Declaratory Judgment Act was not an independent source of federal subject matter jurisdiction but rather presupposes the existence of a judicially recognizable remedial right. Otherwise, a judicial declaration telling an agency how to interpret a statute would constitute an "end run around Congress's clear intent" that the Department of Labor interpret and enforce the Service Contract Act. 310 F.3d at 201.

2. Assuming that an actual case or controversy exists over a matter within the federal court's jurisdiction, the court retains discretion as to the propriety of whether to exercise its jurisdiction. *See* AmSouth Bank v. Dale, 386 F.3d 763, 784–91 (6th Cir.2004) (jurisdiction declined where declaratory judgment would not serve useful purpose and claimants used action for purpose of procedural fencing); Adobe Systems, Inc. v. Kornrumpf, 780 F.Supp.2d 988 (N.D.Cal. 2011) (request for declaratory relief for copyright misuse dismissed because claim would give rise to duplicative litigation); Jensen v. Quality Loan Service Corp., 702 F.Supp.2d 1183 (E.D.Cal. 2010) (court exercised discretion to decline ruling on declaratory judgment claim sought in quiet title action because it would have been duplicative of other claims).

Although a federal district court has substantial discretion to exercise declaratory judgment jurisdiction, there must be well-founded reasons for declining to do so. Federal courts must act in accordance with the purposes of the Declaratory Judgment Act and the "principles of sound judicial administration when declining jurisdiction in declaratory suits." Electronics for Imaging, Inc. v. Coyle, 394 F.3d 1341, 1345 (Fed.Cir.2005).

3. An important factor affecting the court's discretion whether to grant declaratory relief is whether the decree will clarify and settle the controversy in a useful manner. For example, the absence of an interested party may preclude relief because that party is not bound by the order. Consequently, all persons with an interest in the determination of questions raised in a declaratory judgment suit should be parties before the

court. Diamond Shamrock Corp. v. Lumbermens Mut. Casualty Co., 416 F.2d 707 (7th Cir.1969).

In *Delpro Co. v. National Mediation Board of U.S.A.*, 509 F.Supp. 468 (D.Del.1981), a union filed an application with the National Mediation Board requesting it to investigate a representation dispute among the employees of Delpro. The company subsequently sought a declaratory judgment that it was not a carrier within the meaning of the Railway Labor Act and therefore was outside the statutory jurisdiction of the Board. The court denied the request for declaratory relief because the union had not been joined in the suit and would not be bound by the decree; therefore, the order would not finally resolve the controversy. The court stated that the non-joinder of an interested party prevented the declaratory judgment from serving a useful purpose, regardless of whether the absent party was indispensable within the meaning of FRCP 19(b).

4. *Abstention.* Special considerations of federalism, comity, and equity affect the exercise of discretion by a federal court to issue declaratory relief in situations where a pending state court proceeding involves matters related to the federal controversy. Under the abstention doctrine, a federal court which otherwise would possess the requisite jurisdiction over a dispute may choose to decline to exercise that jurisdiction in favor of the state forum.

The Supreme Court has visited the abstention doctrine in a wide variety of contexts. An early application of the abstention doctrine was raised in *Railroad Comm'n of Texas v. Pullman*, 312 U.S. 496, 61 S.Ct. 643, 85 L.Ed. 971 (1941). In *Pullman*, the Court held that a federal court should exercise discretion by "staying its hand" to permit a state court to decide important unsettled matters of state law. Further, in *Burford v. Sun Oil Co.*, 319 U.S. 315, 334, 63 S.Ct. 1098, 1107, 87 L.Ed. 1424 (1943), the Court applied abstention such that a federal court sitting in equity should not interfere with complex matters involving state administrative processes where the federal decision would be disruptive of important state policy. In *Younger v. Harris*, 401 U.S. 37, 91 S.Ct. 746, 27 L.Ed.2d 669 (1971), the Court, relying on principles of comity and federalism, held that a federal court should ordinarily refrain from enjoining ongoing state criminal proceedings, even where federal constitutional rights were implicated.

Finally, courts may rely upon the abstention doctrine to decline jurisdiction based upon considerations of judicial economy or "wise judicial administration." Colorado River Water Conservation Dist. v. United States, 424 U.S. 800, 817, 96 S.Ct. 1236, 1246, 47 L.Ed.2d 483 (1976). Under the *Colorado River* abstention analysis, the Court recognized that despite the "virtually unflagging obligation" of federal courts to exercise jurisdiction, if "exceptional circumstances" existed, the court may abstain based upon concurrent state court proceedings.

The Court in *Colorado River* identified four factors that a district court should consider when determining whether "exceptional circumstances" were present: (1) whether another court had assumed jurisdiction over property, (2) if the federal forum is inconvenient, (3) the desirability of avoiding piecemeal litigation, and (4) the order in which jurisdiction was obtained by the concurrent forums. The *Colorado River* factors were later supplemented in *Moses H. Cone Memorial Hosp. v. Mercury Constr. Corp.*, 460 U.S. 1, 103 S.Ct. 927, 74 L.Ed.2d 765 (1983), to include whether the federal law provides the rule of decision on the merits and whether the state court proceedings were inadequate to protect the federal court plaintiff's rights. In *Moses Cone*, the Court emphasized the limited and exceptional nature of the abstention doctrine, observing that dismissal of the federal suit did "not rest on a mechanical checklist, but on a careful balancing of the important factors as they apply in a given case, with the balance heavily weighted in favor of the exercise of jurisdiction." 460 U.S. at 16.

5.   Although the abstention doctrine and discretion under the Declaratory Judgment Act have areas of overlap, there are also significant differences in scope. *See* United States v. Commonwealth of Pennsylvania, Dept. of Envir. Resources, 923 F.2d 1071, 1073 (3d Cir.1991). *See also* St. Paul Ins. Co. v. Trejo, 39 F.3d 585 (5th Cir.1994) (dismissal of a declaratory judgment suit does not have to satisfy the more stringent *Colorado River* abstention test). The Declaratory Judgment Act presents a set of factors that are related to, but not co-extensive with, those articulated by the Supreme Court for the abstention doctrine where concurrent state proceedings are pending. In *Brillhart v. Excess Ins. Co.*, 316 U.S. 491, 62 S.Ct. 1173, 86 L.Ed. 1620 (1942), the Supreme Court provided guidance for the exercise of discretion regarding abstention from a declaratory judgment. Justice Frankfurter, writing for the majority, noted:

> Ordinarily it would be uneconomical as well as vexatious for a federal court to proceed in a declaratory judgment suit where another suit is pending in state court presenting the same issues, not governed by federal law, between the same parties. Gratuitous interference with the orderly and comprehensive disposition of a state court litigation should be avoided.

The Court identified several non-exclusive factors for federal courts to consider in deciding whether to entertain declaratory judgment actions:

> [A district court] should ascertain whether the questions in controversy between the parties to the federal suit, and which are not foreclosed under the applicable substantive law, can better be settled in the proceeding pending in the state court. This may entail inquiry into the scope of the pending state court proceeding and the nature of the defenses open there. The federal court may have to consider whether the claims of all parties in interest can satisfactorily be adjudicated in that proceeding, whether necessary parties have been joined, whether such parties are amenable to process in that proceeding, etc.

62 S.Ct. at 1176.

6.   In *Wilton v. Seven Falls Co.*, 515 U.S. 277, 115 S.Ct. 2137, 132 L.Ed.2d 214 (1995), the Court reaffirmed the *Brillhart* view that a federal district court has broad discretion in determining whether to exercise

jurisdiction in a declaratory judgment action during the pendency of parallel state court proceedings. The Court observed:

> By the Declaratory Judgment Act, Congress sought to place a remedial arrow in the district court's quiver; it created an opportunity, rather than a duty, to grant a new form of relief to qualifying litigants. Consistent with the nonobligatory nature of the remedy, a district court is authorized, in the sound exercise of its discretion, to stay or to dismiss an action seeking a declaratory judgment before trial or after all arguments have drawn to a close.

115 S.Ct. at 2143.

In sum, the mere existence of a related state court proceeding does not automatically trigger federal court abstention; instead the court should inquire into the adequacy and scope of the state forum to decide the claims.

7. In exercising discretion regarding whether to issue a declaratory judgment, courts have considered a variety of prudential factors beyond those enumerated in *Brillhart* and *Wilton*, including:

(1). Whether declaratory relief would settle the controversy;

(2). Whether the declaratory action would serve a useful purpose in clarifying the legal relations in dispute;

(3). Whether the declaratory remedy is being used merely for the purpose of "procedural fencing" or "to provide an arena for a race for *res judicata*";

(4). Whether the use of a declaratory action would increase friction between federal and state courts and improperly encroach upon state jurisdiction;

(5). Whether novel or complex state law issues better resolved by state court

(6). Whether there is an alternative remedy which is better or more effective;

(7). The convenience of the parties and witnesses;

(8). Principles of comity and restraint where the same issues are pending in a state court;

(9). Judicial economy in avoiding duplicative or piecemeal litigation;

(10). Discouraging forum shopping; and

(11). Potential inequities in permitting the plaintiff to gain precedence in time and forum.

See Stone Street Asset Trust v. Blue, 821 F.Supp.2d 672, 2011 WL 3290314 (D.Del. 2011) (quiet title action to property which was otherwise cognizable under Declaratory Judgment Act was dismissed under *Brillhart* abstention because parallel proceeding were pending in Louisiana state court and issues could better be settled under state law). *Also see* Surefoot LC v. Sure Foot Corp., 531 F.3d 1236 (10th Cir. 2008) (five factors); Adrian Energy Associates v. Michigan Public Serv., 481 F.3d 414 (6th Cir.2007) (five-fact test); Principal Life Ins. Co. v. Robinson, 394 F.3d 665 (9th Cir.2004) (three part test); Ameritas Variable Life Ins. Co. v. Roach, 411 F.3d 1328 (11th Cir. 2005) (nine factors); Sherwin–Williams Co. v. Holmes County, 343 F.3d 383 (5th Cir. 2003) (seven factors).

8. *Alsager v. District Court*, 518 F.2d 1160 (8th Cir.1975), illustrates some of the prudential considerations that may influence the exercise of discretion of federal courts to issue declaratory relief. In *Alsager*, parents sought a declaratory judgment that their constitutional rights were violated by state court proceedings which resulted in termination of their parental relationship with their six children. The district court had denied declaratory relief without reaching the constitutional issues on the basis that the relief requested would be ineffective—reasoning that it could not order a permanent disposition of all the children since they were in varying situations with respect to foster and institutional care. The Eighth Circuit Court of Appeals reversed, holding that the district court had abused its discretion in declining to issue declaratory relief. Even though some of the details regarding the disposition of each child remained, the court found that a declaratory judgment would be a useful permanent solution because it would "clear the air" and allow the parties to deal with the children in a manner consistent with their legal relationship.

9. *Political Question.* When a suit raises a political question, federal courts will decline to issue declaratory relief for lack of a justiciable case or controversy. In *Smith v. Reagan*, 844 F.2d 195 (4th Cir.1988), the plaintiff class sought a declaration that American prisoners of the Vietnam War continued to be held in captivity by the governments of Vietnam, Laos, and Cambodia, and that those prisoners were covered by the protections of the Hostage Act (22 U.S.C. § 1732 (1982)). They also sought a writ of mandamus compelling the President to comply with the terms of the Hostage Act, including certain investigatory and possible affirmative actions to secure the release of prisoners. The court dismissed the suit for lack of subject matter jurisdiction, finding that the claims directly raised the political question doctrine. The court observed that the Act prescribed no remedy for presidential noncompliance, so any declaratory relief would be merely advisory. More importantly, a judicial declaration of responsibilities under the Hostage Act would effectively seek to dictate foreign policy, a province constitutionally committed to the executive branch.

INDEX

References are to Pages

EMPLOYMENT
Age discrimination, jury trial, 962
Back pay claims, 39–40, 312, 962–963
Bribes received, 870–874
Constructive trust, 882–883
Contract jumping, 122–123
Damages, statutory cap, 37–39
Damages, duty to mitigate, 399–400, 680–683
Discrimination, 20, 34
Estoppel, withdrawing offer of employment, 168
Front pay, 39–42
Injunctions against competition, 73–75
Jury trials, 37–39, 962–963
Liquidated damages, 455–459
Negative injunction, 116–124
Noncompetition agreement, 73–75
Personal service, 116–124
Present value of contract, 608–609
Punitive damages, 772
Quantum meruit, 847–851
Sexual harassment, 310–314, 680–684
Specific performance, 110–111, 116–124, 683–684
Unclean hands, 174–177
Wrongful discharge, 37–39

ENVIRONMENTAL INJURY
Attorneys' fees, 975–984, 987, 995, 1005
Clean Water Act, 544
Diagnostic study, 36–37
Endangered Species Act, 89, 330–335
Environmental Protection Agency, 82
Injunction, statutorily mandated, 329–337
National Environmental Policy Act, injunction, 227–229
Nuisance damages, generally, 358–361
Nuisance, injunction against, 54–57, 75–76, 77–83, 357–363, 371–380
Oil spill, damages, 538–544
Restoration of land, 9–10, 538–544
Warning class of medical risks, injunction, 36–37
Water pollution, 35–36

EQUITABLE LIENS
See also Constructive Trusts; Restitution
Generally, 887–888
Adequacy of remedy at law, 889–890
Constructive trust compared, 887–888
Enforcement, 890–891
Improvements on property, 893–896
Fraud, 889–890
Priority over other creditors, 891–892
Property right distinguished, 889–892
Security interest, 890–892
Tracing, generally, 898

EQUITY
See also Equity Jurisdiction; Jury Trials
Accounting, legal and equitable, 970–972
Clean hands, generally, 168–169
Cleanup jurisdiction, 946–947, 947–950, 953–954

EQUITY—Cont'd
Constructive trust, see that topic
Damages contrasted, 3–4, 814–815
Derivative actions, shareholders, 941–946
Equitable lien, see that topic
Estoppel, 142–143
Jurisdiction, see Equity Jurisdiction
Jury trial avoided, 887, 941–950
Laches, generally, 142–143
Law courts, relation, 5–6, 27
Legal relief in equity, cleanup, 946–947, 947–950, 953–954
Merger of law and equity, 940, 950–953
Mortgages, 946–947
Mutuality of remedy, 106–111
Property interests, equity originally limited to, 27
Punitive damages, 773, 1013
Rescission, 843–844
Restitution, see that topic
Substantive, 940, 945–946
Tracing, 898
Unclean hands, generally, 168–169
Unconscionability, generally, 168–169,

EQUITY JURISDICTION
See also Equity; Jury Trials
Generally, 53
Adequacy of legal remedy, 44–45
History, 5, 940
Multiplicity of suits, 47
Substantive equity, 940, 945–946

ESTOPPEL
Generally, 142–143
Election of remedies, 201
Equitable tolling compared, 166
Misrepresentation, 165
Sovereign, against, 167–168
Statute of limitations, estopped to assert, 167

EXEMPLARY DAMAGES
See Punitive Damages

EXPECTANCY
See Contracts

FEDERAL RULES OF CIVIL PROCEDURE
Rule 8(c), 150
Rule 52(a), 240
Rule 57, p. 1022
Rule 65, p. 203, 232, 235–236, 243–244

FEDERAL RULES OF CRIMINAL PROCEDURE
Rule 42(a), 277–278
Rule 42(b), 267

FORESEEABILITY
See also Hadley v. Baxendale
Generally, 414–418, 419–429, 647–664
Proximate cause, 663
Tort and contract rules compared, 657–663

†